Do you remember . . . .

Battlestar Galactica

The Champions

Quark

War of the Worlds

Space: 1999

TekWar

Thunderbirds

The Time Tunnel

V

Nowhere Man

American Gothic

Phoenix Five

Manimal

Space: Above and Beyond

The Starlost

Relive all these shows and hundreds more, in

THE SCI-FI CHANNEL ENCYCLOPEDIA OF TV SCIENCE FICTION

THE
SCI-FI CHANNEL
ENCYCLOPEDIA
OF
TV
SCIENCE
FICTION

ROGER FULTON & JOHN BETANCOURT

ASPECT®

WARNER BOOKS

Grateful acknowledgment is given for permission to use the following images:
Lost in Space, Jonathan Harris © 1965 20th Century Fox/MPTV
Battlestar Galactica, Richard Hatch, Dirk Benedict © 1980 NBC/MPTV
Babylon 5 © 1992 Warner Bros./MPTV
Thunderbirds © 1966 BBC/MPTV
Highlander: The Series © 1994 by Gaumont Television and © Davis Panzer Productions, Inc. 1985

This Warner Books edition is published by arrangement with Boxtree Limited, an imprint of Macmillan Publishers, Ltd., London.

Aspect® is a registered trademark of Warner Books, Inc.
Warner Books, Inc., 1271 Avenue of the Americas, New York, NY 10020

Visit our Web site at http://warnerbooks.com

 A Time Warner Company

Printed in the United States of America

First Warner Books Printing: December 1998

10 9 8 7 6 5 4 3 2 1

Library of Congress Cataloging-in-Publication Data

Fulton, Roger.
    The sci-fi channel encyclopedia of TV science fiction / Roger Fulton and John Betancourt.
       p.   cm.
    ISBN 0-446-67478-8
    1. Science fiction television programs—Encyclopedias.   2. Fantastic television programs—Encyclopedias.   3. Horror television programs—Encyclopedias.   I. Betancourt, John.   II. Title.
PN1992.8.S35F82   1998
791.45'656—dc21
                                                                                                98-33572
                                                                                                CIP

The authors wish to thank the TV Times Picture Library for all their help.

CONTENTS

PREFACE

Welcome to the golden age of science fiction television. Never before have so many, and so many truly excellent, shows of the fantastic appeared on the airwaves.

As this book is assembled, U.S. science fiction fans can watch *Star Trek: Voyager, Star Trek: Deep Space Nine, Babylon 5* (soon to lead into *Crusade*), *Stargate SG-1, The Outer Limits, Sliders,* and *Gene Roddenberry's Earth: Final Conflict.* Fantasy fans have *Xena, Hercules, The Adventures of Sinbad* and *Conan the Adventurer.* And horror fans get *The X-Files, Buffy the Vampire Slayer, Poltergeist: The Legacy,* and *Profiler.* Do you like comedy? Try *Sabrina the Teenage Witch* or *3rd Rock from the Sun.* Superheroes? *Nightman.* Kids' shows? *Honey, I Shrunk the Kids.*

And that's just in the U.S. Abroad, we have *Red Dwarf, Lexx* (U.S. title: *Tales from a Parallel Universe*), *Neverwhere,* and so many more, most of which will eventually make their way here. With the continued growth of mini-dish satellite TV, and the increasing efficiency of cable television, we have more channels than ever before.

In fact, it was this explosion of a genre that gave birth to a whole new television outlet: Sci-Fi Channel. Now seen in 50 million homes around the globe, the channel is the world's leader in the realm of imaginative television.

This book incorporates and expands on Roger Fulton's excellent *The Encyclopedia of TV Science Fiction,* which appeared in England to great acclaim. Hopefully we can continue to update this encyclopedia as the flood of new science fiction programming continues. The astute reader will note that this book covers through roughly the first half of 1998—as far into each series as we were able to complete as of press time.

—Roger Fulton and John Betancourt
June 1998

ENTRY FORMAT

With so many diverse productions to include, there are bound to be exceptions, but this is the general rule . . .

Each entry covers one program in its entirety and consists, more or less, of the following:

Series name, e.g., BLAKE'S 7
and background, followed by regular cast, e.g.,
Blake Gareth Thomas *Avon* Paul Darrow

Production credits, e.g., *Creator:* Terry Nation
Production company, e.g., *A BBC Production*
Number and duration of episodes and whether color or black and white, e.g.

52 color 50-minute episodes

Season One
2 January–27 March 1978

This is followed, where relevant, or possible, by a guide to every episode transmitted (and in some cases ones that weren't), in chronological order of transmission, reading downward through left- and then right-hand entries. (In the case of most American series, this is the original U.S. running order.)

Episodes are treated as follows:
Title and author, e.g.

Redemption

---

w Terry Nation

followed by synopsis and appropriate supporting cast, plus director and, in some instances, designer credits, e.g.

Alta One Sheila Ruskin

Director: Vere Lorrimer
Designer: Sally Hulke

(Some entries include episode titles only, others consist solely of numbers of episodes.)

A FOR ANDROMEDA/
THE ANDROMEDA BREAKTHROUGH

A for Andromeda and its sequel, *The Andromeda Breakthrough*, screened in England in 1961–62, were British television's first attempts to create adult science fiction since the *Quatermass* sagas of the fifties.

Scripted by BBC producer John Elliot, from an original storyline by renowned astronomer and novelist Fred Hoyle, they dealt with the impact of an alien intelligence upon life on Earth and with the ruthless pursuit by rival factions of the scientific secrets that could prove the breakthrough of the century. The machinations of governments and big business were Elliot's territory (he went on to produce the power games of *Mogul* and *The Troubleshooters*) but the astronomical and scientific concepts were Hoyle's. In his novels such as *The Black Cloud*, Hoyle, professor of astronomy and philosophy at Cambridge, contended that man's first contact with an alien civilization would come through radio-astronomy and this idea forms the basis for the series, which begins with signals from space being received by a new radio telescope.

In the first series the signals are found to contain the "assembly and operating" instructions for a highly advanced computer, which then enables the research team literally to create life, first a misshapen blob, then a human embryo that grows rapidly into a beautiful young woman—Andromeda. *The Andromeda Breakthrough* dramatically upped the tempo of the power politics, set the intrigue against a worldwide environmental disaster, and revealed the purpose behind the original message—that of steering mankind down a less destructive path than the one it has taken. John Elliot's influence was greater in the second series—as well as scripting it he also produced and directed.

The hero of both series is Dr. John Fleming, an outspoken, idealistic young scientist. It is he who first decodes the signals from outer space—"It's a do-it-yourself kit, and it isn't human!"—and it is he who first recognizes the dangers of extending the frontiers of human knowledge too far, too fast.

No one-dimensional cipher, Fleming is a scientist with a conscience, in the grand *Quatermass* tradition, who ends up saving the world from a chain of events he himself set in motion. (The character of Fleming has been seen as being based on the maverick qualities of Hoyle himself.)

Throughout, Fleming finds himself in conflict with most people around him, including his own and foreign governments; a shady, Swiss-based business cartel called Intel (headed by the villainous Kaufman); and an amoral biologist, Prof. Madeleine Dawnay, who sees the Andromeda project as one great research opportunity.

A for Andromeda also marked the TV debut of a glamorous young actress called Julie Christie (plucked from a drama school by producer Michael Hayes), initially as the lab assistant, Christine, whose death provides the "blueprint" for Dawnay's embryo, and then as Andromeda herself, whose ambivalent relationship with Fleming blossoms in the sequel. In this, the part was taken over by another relative newcomer, Susan Hampshire. Frank Windsor, stalwart of *Z-Cars* and *Softly, Softly*, appeared in the first series as Fleming's self-seeking colleague Dennis Bridger.

Both *A for Andromeda* and *The Andromeda Breakthrough* are now hailed as early classics of British science fiction.

(Author's note: Although there is some overlapping of cast and production details, for ease of reference the story guides to each series are treated separately, beginning with the main cast, followed by synopsis, supporting cast and production details.)

A FOR ANDROMEDA

w Fred Hoyle and John Elliot *(a 7-part serial)*

Main Cast

The Scientists:

John Fleming Peter Halliday   *Prof. Reinhart* Esmond Knight
Prof. Madeleine Dawnay Mary Morris   *Dr. Geers* Geoffrey Lewis
Christine (Eps. 2–4)/*Andromeda* (Eps. 5–7) Julie Christie
Dennis Bridger Frank Windsor   *Harvey* John Murray-Scott
Dr. Hunter Peter Ducrow

Security:

Judy Adamson Patricia Kneale   *Maj. Quadring* Jack May
Harries John Nettleton

Whitehall:

J.M. Osborne Noel Johnson   *Gen. Vandenberg* Donald Stewart
Minister of Science Ernest Hare   *The Prime Minister* Maurice Hedley
Minister of Defense David King

Intel:

Kaufman John Hollis   *Egon* Peter Henchie

The year is 1970. While conducting routine checks at a new radio-telescope high in the Yorkshire Dales, Prof. Reinhart's staff picks up unexpected signals from the direction of the constellation Andromeda. These are taped and decoded by brilliant scientist John Fleming who reveals them to be a series of arithmetical instructions for building a highly advanced computer.

Once the implications sink in, Whitehall gives the go-ahead for the machine to be built at Thorness, a remote island rocket base off the Scottish coast. "Project Andromeda" is classified top secret but scientists, the military and the shady cartel Intel all begin to compete for the information and Fleming's friend Bridger is found to be selling secrets to Kaufman. While trying to evade arrest he falls to his death.

Meanwhile, the completed computer has begun to show its power and Fleming, increasingly wary, finds himself at loggerheads with biologist Madeleine Dawnay when the machine provides information that enables her to manufacture a living organism.

Later, the computer, in an attempt to extend its knowledge of humanity, compels lab assistant Christine to seize two exposed terminals—electrocuting her. Despite the incident, Dawnay continues her experiments. The result is a human embryo that matures rapidly, showing a startling resemblance to the dead Christine. Christened Andromeda, the girl learns at a phenomenal rate and also establishes a mental link with the computer, getting it to design a new missile system for the government, which has grown worried at the deteriorating political situation.

More than ever, Fleming sees the liaison as a menace and tries to sabotage the computer, which retaliates by "creating" a toxic enzyme that leaves Dawnay fighting for her life (though the full significance of the substance only becomes clear in the series' sequel). When Andromeda tries to kill him,

Fleming convinces her that if the computer were destroyed she would be free of its control. After wrecking the machine and burning the plans, they escape into the night . . .

Whelan Bernard Kilby
Osborne's secretary Brenda Peters
Interviewer Kenneth Kendall
Jenkins Terry Lodge
Oldroyd John Barrett
Capt. Lovell Frederick Treves
Mrs. Tate-Allan Margaret Denyer
Air Cmdr. Watling Jack Gwillim
Corporal Anthony Valentine
Lieut. de Felice Hugh Lund

Producers: Michael Hayes, Norman Jones
Designer: Norman James
Film cameraman: Peter Sargent
Film editor: Agnes Evan

A BBC Production
7 black and white 45-minute episodes
The Message
The Machine
The Miracle
The Monster
The Murderer
The Face of the Tiger
The Last Mystery

3 October–14 November 1961

THE ANDROMEDA BREAKTHROUGH

w Fred Hoyle and John Elliot *(A 6-part story)*

MAIN CAST

THE SCIENTISTS:

John Fleming Peter Halliday *Andromeda* Susan Hampshire
Prof. Madeleine Dawnay Mary Morris *Prof. Neilson* Walter Gotell
Dr. Geers Geoffrey Lewis

AZARAN:

Col. Salim Barry Linehan *Dr. Abu Zeki* David Saire
Abu Zeki's assistant Assad Obeid *The President* Arnold Yarrow
Nurse Heather Emmanuel *Lemka (Abu Zeki's wife)* Jean Robinson
Lemka's mother Miki Iveria

INTEL:

Kaufman John Hollis *Mlle. Gamboule* Claude Farell

WHITEHALL:

J.M. Osborne Noel Johnson *Burdett (Defense Minister)* David King
The Prime Minister Maurice Hedley *Osborne's PA* Philip Latham

---

Having destroyed the Thorness super-computer, Fleming is picked up by the security forces but manages to escape and, reunited with Andromeda, takes refuge on a small island. A recovered Dawnay is lured to the Middle East country of Azaran where Intel is developing a new computer from information supplied by Bridger (Series One). Fleming and Andromeda are recaptured by the British government but are then kidnapped by Intel, joining Dawnay in Azaran.

Already there are signs that something strange is happening to the world's weather—as a result of the toxic enzyme (Series One) finding its way into the sea, where it has multiplied and spread, absorbing nitrogen and lowering the air pressure. The outcome: tidal waves, hurricanes and tornadoes, as well as a drop in the atmosphere's oxygen level. In short, the world is slowly suffocating.

Fleming and Dawnay work to develop an antidote, although for Fleming the most pressing problem is the failing health of Andromeda who, though dying, is determined to work out the purpose of the message from space.

In Azaran, Col. Salim launches a military coup, backed by Intel. In turn, Gamboule, obsessed by ideas of world domination, seizes power by killing Salim. She, in *her* turn, is killed when a hurricane devastates Azaran, and Kaufman assumes (temporary) control before the President is ultimately reinstated. Andromeda is too weak to help as Fleming and Dawnay attempt to smuggle the antidote formula to Britain through a Canadian, Prof. Nielson, but she does convince Fleming that the "message" was meant for him all along and that he should try to realize his dream of helping mankind.

Preen Geoffrey Dunn
RAF officer Frederick Treves
Gunman James Urquhart
Jan Neilson Roy Wilson
Burdett's PA Jeffrey Gardiner
Ratclife Norman Scace
Intel man Michael Jacques
Yusel (Abu Zeki's brother) Earl Cameron
Sharpling David Chivers

Producer: John Elliot
Directors: John Elliot (*Eps. 1,3,5*) John Knight (*Eps. 2,4,6*)
Designer: Norman James
Film cameraman: Ken Westbury
Film editor: James Colina

A BBC Production
6 black and white 45-minute episodes
Cold Front
Gale Warning
Azaran Forecast
Storm Centres
Hurricane
The Roman Peace (50 mins.)

28 June–2 August 1962

ACE OF WANDS

This highly successful British children's adventure series of the early 1970s conjured up one of television's most dashing fantasy heroes—Tarot. A master magician, illusionist, escapologist and telepathic super-sleuth, Tarot was hailed at the start as "a 20th-century Robin Hood, with a pinch of Merlin and a dash of Houdini."

With his companions, Tarot tackled and despatched a collection of outrageous villains who wouldn't have felt out of place in *Batman*—adversaries such as Madame Midnight, the evil magician Mr. Stabs, art thief Tun-Ju, mad chessmaster Ceribraun and the bizarre Mama Doc.

Created by Trevor Preston, the series wove magic, the supernatural and science fiction into a set of fantasy adventures that weren't afraid to send out a shiver or two. Several tales had especially sinister storylines: In *The Beautiful People*, domestic machines turned on their owners; the unnerving *Mama Doc* turned people into life-sized dolls; and *Nightmare Gas* induced horrific dreams that could literally scare victims to death.

Sharing Tarot's adventures were, in the first two seasons, his stage assistant Lulli Palmer, who had a telepathic link with Tarot, his enterprising, ex-convict, stage manager Sam Maxted, and the eccentric Mr. Sweet, an antiquarian bookseller with a computer-like mind.

By Season Three, Mr. Sweet was still around, now working at a university, but Lulli and Sam had given way to Mikki Diamond, a young journalist, and her photographer brother, Chas. Mikki, too, had a telepathic link with Tarot. Completing the regulars was an inscrutable owl, Ozymandias.

REGULAR CAST
Tarot Michael Mackenzie *Sam* Tony Selby *(Seasons One and Two)*
Lulli Judy Loe *(Seasons One and Two)* *Mr. Sweet* Donald Layne-Smith
Mikki Petra Markham *(Season Three)* *Chas* Roy Holder *(Season Three)*
Ozymandias Fred the Owl

Created by: Trevor Preston
Producer: Pamela Lonsdale *(Seasons One &*
  Two), John Russell *(Season Three)*
Music: Andrew Brown
Magical adviser: Ali Bongo

A Thames Television Production

46 color 30-minute episodes
Season One: 13 episodes
29 July–21 October 1970
Season Two: 13 episodes
21 July–13 October 1971
Season Three: 20 episodes
19 July–29 November 1972

Season One
13 episodes

One and One and One are Four

w Trevor Preston *(a 3-part story)*
Tracking down a professor's stolen brainchild leads Tarot and his friends to arch-criminal Madame Midnight and her wicked henchman Teddy Talk, whose lair is guarded by a battery of scientific traps.
Madam Midnight Hildegard Neil
Teddy Talk Michael Standing
Professor Ekdorf Frederick Peisley
Kal Dave Prowse
Six Tony Caunter
Eight Chris Webb
Ma Epps Daphne Heard
Dr. Caulder Kenneth Watson
Mr. America Bruce Boa
Mr. Russia Jan Conrad
Reporter Carla Challoner
Boutique girl Nita Lorraine

Director: John Russell
Designer: Tony Borer

The Mind Robbers

w William Emms *(a 4-part story)*
Tarot investigates the mysterious disappearance of two government ministers and clashes with an old adversary, Señor Zandar and his cohort, Fat Boy. Lured into a trap when Zandar hypnotizes Lulli, Tarot must face a poisonous snake that hates people . . .
Señor Zandar Vernon Dobtcheff
Fat Boy Michael Wynne
Sir William Rowlands Geoffrey Lumsden
Miss Jellicoe Sheelah Wilcocks
Mr. Hardy John Golightly
John Copney Roger Kemp
General Craig Gerald Case
Castor Terry Walsh
Pollux Alan Chuntz
Guard Matthew Robertson

Director: Michael Currer-Briggs
Designer: Bernard Spencer

Now You See It, Now You Don't

w Don Houghton *(a 2-part story)*
A daring bank robbery leads Tarot, Lulli and Sam to an encounter with Falk, a power-mad Nazi-style villain whose base is a houseboat packed with computers.
Falk Christopher Benjamin
Macreedy Ray Barron
Gaston Alan Tucker
Cashier Tim Curry
Guard Billy Cornelius
Bank manager Kevin Stoney

Director: John Russell
Designer: Colin Andrews

The Smile

w Trevor Preston *(a 4-part story)*
Tun-Ju, "The Emperor of the Art Thieves," and his accomplice Mrs. Kite plot to steal the Mona Lisa. Sam loses his memory, and Tarot's head-on clash with the villain results in a deadly double-cross.
Tun-Ju Willoughby Goddard
Mrs. Kite Dorothy Reynolds
Bartlett Bonnington John Barron
Digger farmer Reg Lye
Japanese bodyguard Tom Gan
Sir Patrick Landau Patrick McAlinney
Lady Landau Diana King

Director: Michael Currer-Briggs
Designer: Frank Gillman

Season Two

Seven Serpents, Sulphur and Salt

w Trevor Preston *(a 3-part story)*
Tarot and company face the formidable Mr. Stabs, an evil magician who, aided by the beautiful Polandi and his wicked servant Luko, will stop at nothing to retrieve from Tarot the key to the secret of the Seven Serpents—not even murder.
Mr. Stabs Russell Hunter
Polandi Harriet Harper
Luko Ian Trigger
Charlie Postle Jack Woolgar
Mr. Christopher Llewellyn Rees
Mr. Thwaites Jonathan Cecil

Director: Pamela Lonsdale
Designer: Tony Borer

Joker

w P.J. Hammond *(a 3-part story)*
Why should well-behaved children suddenly go berserk and wreck their classrooms? Tarot shuffles a pack of surprises dealt by Uncle Harry and his troupe of traveling entertainers, forms "Spells on Wheels" and rescues Lulli from the hands of the joker.
Uncle Harry Dermot Tuohy

Jack Roy Holder
Queen Carmen Munroe
King Walter Sparrow
Miss Pascoe Lorna Heilbron
Headmaster George Waring
Headmistress Sheila Raynor

Director: John Russell
Designer: Bernard Spencer

Nightmare Gas

w Don Houghton *(a 3-part story)*
The beautiful but deadly Thalia and her monosyllabic brother Dalbiac steal a top-secret new gas, H23, which induces deep sleep and nightmares so vivid that the victim dies from shock.
Thalia Isobel Black
Dalbiac Jonathan Newth
Dr. Richard Winthrop Laurence Carter
Sergeant Lewis Wilson
Trooper Alan Chuntz

Director: Ronald Marriott
Designer: Harry Clark

The Eye of Ra

w Michael Winder *(a 4-part story)*
Ceribraun, an eccentric, wheelchair-bound chessmaster, plots to steal the Eye of Ra, a priceless diamond said to have the power to turn people into chalk statues. Tarot finds himself the prisoner of Ceribraun's talking computer and is menaced by giant chesspieces.
Ceribraun Oscar Quitak
Sir John Packham Howard Goorney
Fredericks Nicholas Smith
Mr. Quince Edward Jewesbury
Computer Charles Morgan
Sir Henry Carstairs Peter Williams

Director: John Russell
Designer: Bernard Spencer

Season Three

The Meddlers

w P.J. Hammond *(a 3-part story)*
Tarot acquires his new companions Chas and Mikki and investigates a supposed curse hanging over the London street market where they live.
Spoon Michael Standing
Mockers Barry Linehan
Dove Paul Dawkins
Drum Stefan Kalipha
Madge Honora Bruce
Accordion player Neil Linden
Chauffeuse Norma West

Director: John Russell
Designer: Bill Palmer

The Power of Atep

w Victor Pemberton *(a 4-part story)*
A strange dream about Egypt, shared by Tarot and Mikki, and a powerful voice at a seance, lead Tarot and friends to the tomb of Atep in Egypt's Valley of the Kings. There Tarot confronts his former stage partner and double, Quabal.
John Pentacle Sebastian Graham-Jones
High Priest Michael Mulcaster
Tramp Michael Rose
Fergus Wilson Joe Dunlop
Arab boy Lynval May

Director: Nicholas Ferguson
Designer: Harry Clark

Peacock Pie

w P.J. Hammond *(a 3-part story)*
Tarot and his friends clash with the bizarre Mr. Peacock, whose astonishing power of suggestion causes a bank robbery with no robber, traps Chas in a room without a door and strands Tarot at the top of a high building with no way down.
Mr. Peacock Brian Wilde
Mrs. MacFadyean Dorothy Frere
Young Mrs. MacFadyean Jean McCracken
Manageress Valerie Ost

Director: John Russell
Designer: Gordon Toms

Mama Doc

w Maggie Allen *(a 3-part story)*
One of Mr. Sweet's university colleagues disappears and the trail leads Tarot and his friends to a dolls' hospital run by the eccentric Mama Doc, who, with her accomplice Bobby, turns people into dolls.
Mama Doc Pat Nye
Posy Peagram Wendy Hamilton
Bobby Michael Mundell
Prof. Darian Robert Grange
Dr. Macdonald Ivor Roberts
Macdonald Children Bobby Collins, Claire McLellan

Mrs. Darian Angela Rooks
Lorry driver David Parsons

Director: Nicholas Ferguson
Designer: Philip Blowers

Sisters Deadly

w Victor Pemberton *(a 3-part story)*
Chas returns from a photo assignment at an old lady's 100th birthday party unable to recall what happened, including that while under hypnosis he robbed a village post office. Tarot uncovers a bizarre plot by "old ladies" to kidnap the Commander in Chief of the British Land Forces.
Letty Edginton Sylvia Coleridge
Mathilda Edginton Henrietta Rudkin*
Postmaster Bartlett Mullins
Major James Bree
General Frank Duncan
Old ladies Lucy Griffiths, Mysie Montie, Kathleen St. John, May Warden
General's driver Ronald Tye

Director: Darrol Blake
Designer: Andrew Drummond

* Henrietta Rudkin was a pseudonym for James Bree to prevent giving away the plot surprise.

The Beautiful People

w P.J. Hammond *(a 4-part story)*
Mikki is suspicious when she is barred from a village fete by two strange but beautiful girls and a handsome young man. Tarot discovers that very valuable prizes are on offer but are part of a bizarre alien plot.
Jay Edward Hammond
Emm Vivien Heilbron
Dee Susan Glanville
Elderly woman Kathleen Sainsbury
Old man Harry Hutchinson
Old lady Hilda Barry
Vicar Alex McDonald

Director: Vic Hughes
Designer: Eric Shedden

ADAM ADAMANT LIVES!

Adam Llewellyn De Vere Adamant was a man out of his time, an Edwardian adventurer frozen in 1902 and revived 64 years later to bring his towering intellect, deadly fighting skills and implacable integrity to a world whose values are no longer those he had defended.

Adamant's references—as detailed in *Radio Times* at the start of this BBC series in 1966—were impeccable. He was the ideal gentleman—elegant, courteous, honorable, charming and chivalrous, a friend of kings and statesmen. An *athlete*, boxer and swordsman, he moved like lightning and could handle any weapon with a deadly skill. A brilliant *scholar*, he was learned in every field of human knowledge. An *adventurer*, he was dedicated to fighting evil and undertook delicate and dangerous missions on behalf of his sovereign and country, in defense of the weak—especially women.

In 1902, Adam is lured by the beautiful Louise to a house where his archenemy, The Face—a megalomaniac hiding his identity behind a leather mask—injects him with an eternal life drug and freezes him in a block of ice.

In 1966, workmen on a building site discover the ice block and the stage is set for Adam Adamant's return—but in the strange new world of the Swinging Sixties, shown as a bewildering collage of sights and sounds.

As Adam finds his feet he discovers two companions. The first, Georgina Jones, is a fan, whose grandfather regaled her with tales of Adamant's heroic exploits. And in Episode 2, Adam meets former music hall artist and jack-of-all-trades William E. Simms, who becomes his loyal factotum.

For two seasons the trio foiled a succession of oddball villains and bizarre plots in an enjoyable series whose resemblance to *The Avengers* was hardly surprising—its script editor Tony Williamson had written several *Avengers* episodes and both series shared some of the same writers—including Brian Clemens!

The second series also added spice to Adam Adamant's role as caped crusader by regularly pitting him against his old nemesis The Face—alive, well and plotting in the present as he had been in the past.

Suave actor Gerald Harper was cast as Adam, who despite his many talents was given to smugness and a naive trust of women.

REGULAR CAST
Adam Adamant Gerald Harper   *Georgina Jones* Juliet Harmer
William E. Simms Jack May   *The Face* Peter Ducrow

Script consultant: Tony Williamson
Producer: Verity Lambert
Music: David Lee
Theme sung by Kathy Kirby

A BBC Production
29 black and white 50-minute episodes
Season One:
23 June–13 October 1966
Season Two:
31 December 1966–25 March 1967
(BBC1)

Season One
16 episodes

A Vintage Year for Scoundrels

w Tony Williamson, *additional material by* Donald Cotton & Richard Harris
In 1902, gentleman adventurer Adam Adamant is lured into a trap where his archenemy, The Face, condemns him to "die forever," entombed in a block of ice . . . In 1966, workmen discover Adam, still perfectly preserved. Reviving in hospital, he is plunged into modern London—an alien world of mini-skirts, cars, strip clubs, neon signs, blaring music and escalators. He is "rescued" by Georgina Jones, who helps him to come to terms with his new situation. In turn, Adam helps her against villainess Margo Kane and her henchmen Hicks and Hoggett.
Sir James Kenneth Benda
The Face Peter Ducrow
Gramps Bartlett Mullins
Hoggett Ivor Slater
Hicks Frank Jarvis
Detective Joby Blanshard
Margo Kane Freda Jackson

Directors: David Proudfoot, William Slater
Designer: Darrol Blake

Death Has a Thousand Faces

w Tony Williamson
A man is stabbed to death, a stick of Blackpool rock is the only clue, and a £50 million crime is in the making as Adam and Georgina face the "perils" of Blackpool's Golden Mile.
Parky Geoffrey Hinsliff
Jeffreys Michael Robbins
Susie Sheila Fearn
Danny Patrick O'Connell
William E. Simms Jack May (intro)
Madam Delvario Stephanie Bidmead
Kelvin John Rolfe

Director: Philip Dudley
Designer: Evan Hercules

More Deadly Than the Sword

w Terence Frisby
Adam helps a government minister who is being blackmailed into handing over defense secrets at a Japanese geisha house.
Sir Ernest Hampton Maurice Hedley
McLennon Barry Linehan
Suzu Lucille Soong
Hitomi Mona Chong
Madame Nagata Mary Webster
Ikezawa Andy Ho
Kodama Yuri Borienko
Hiram Geoffrey Alexander

Director: Leonard Lewis
Designer: Gwen Evans

The Sweet Smell of Success

w Robert Banks Stewart
A blue carnation, the emblem of success for a high-pressure sales campaign, is also the symbol for something rather more sinister.
Badenoch John Gatrell
Kinthly Charles Tingwell
Sales manager Bryan Kendrick
Advertising manager David Lander
Shani Mathieson Adrienne Corri
McLintock William Hurndell
Spalding Jack Howlett

Director: Philip Dudley
Designer: Gwen Evans

Allah Is Not Always with You

w Tony Williamson
A dying girl's last words lead Adam into the world of nightclubs, gambling . . . and murder.
Vargos Kevin Brennan
Lukas Nosher Powell
Ahmed David Spenser
Helen Jennifer Jayne
Fluffy Valerie Stanton
Calvert John Hollis
Sheik John Woodnutt

Director: Paul Ciappessoni
Designer: Evan Hercules

The Terribly Happy Embalmers

w Brian Clemens
The mystery of financiers who always seem to die twice leads Adam into a world of embalmers—and an appointment with death.
Sir George Marston John Scott
Wilson Jeremy Young
Mr. Percy Arthur Brough

Grantham Deryck Guyler
Velmer John Le Mesurier
George Hamilton Dyce
Susan Ilona Rodgers

Director: Paul Ciappessoni
Designer: Darrol Blake

To Set a Deadly Fashion

w Tony Williamson
The frantic world of high fashion and eccentric designers is a confusing one for Adam—until he finds it is also the setting for espionage and murder.
Oretta Dorvetti Nancy Nevinson
Maj. Fitzgibbon Bryan Coleman
Leo Dorvetti Alan Foss
Janine Gwendolyn Watts
Roger Clair Colin Jeavons
Mrs. Smythe Audrey Noble
Mylene Ruth Trouncer
Howarth Alister Williamson

Director: Leonard Lewis
Designer: Evan Hercules

The Last Sacrifice

w Richard Harris
A pleasant weekend party becomes a nightmare for a man who finds himself involved in black magic and human sacrifice.
Huge man Kenneth Ives
Esta Canfield Jennifer Daniel
Statton Glyn Dearman
Lord Rufus Pearmain William Dexter
James Denton Hugh Dickson
Minister John Dawson
Barber Ian Fairbairn

Director: Philip Dudley
Designer: Darrol Blake

Sing a Song of Murder

w John Pennington
Georgina is arrested for attempting to rob a bank; she and Adam find themselves in the world of pop music—and a sinister plot unfolds.
Kinkead Michael Standing
Sgt. Denis Cleary
Inspector Michael Beint
Melville Jerome Willis
Chauffeur James Blake
Carson Alex Scott
Felina Anne Kristen

Director: Moira Armstrong
Designer: Austin Ruddy

The Doomsday Plan

w Richard Harris
An outbreak of mysterious crimes, including the kidnapping of a BBC newsreader, leads Adam into the fanatical realm of Dr. Mort—prophet of doom!
BBC newsreader Kenneth Kendall
Dr. Mort Peter Vaughan
Streek Roy Hanlon
Maddox Andrew Robertson
Hinchcombe Geoffrey Lumsden
Man with parcel Talfryn Thomas
Samantha Isobel Black

Director: Paul Ciappessoni
Designer: Mary Rea

Death by Appointment Only

w Tony Williamson
Big business and high-priced escorts involve Adam in a wave of murders that shake the financial capitals of the world.
Sandra Webb Patricia Haines
Philippe Jervais Colin Vancao
Sir Nigel Dee David Garth
Daniels John Walker
Pamela Wentworth-Howe Christine Finn
Charles Fellows James Cairncross
Von Reison Edward Palmer

Director: Moira Armstrong
Designer: Ray London

Beauty Is an Ugly Word

w Vince Powell & Harry Driver
The world of beauty contestants and physical culture experts is the strange setting for a plot to destroy the human race.
Dr. Ryan Esmond Webb
Petherbridge John Baddeley
Paula Carter Annette Andreü
Max Eddie Stacey
Sinoda Peter Jeffrey
Victor Barry Jackson
PC Mullins John McKelvey

Director: Philip Dudley
Designer: Ken Jones

The League of Uncharitable Ladies

w John Pennington
The murder of a man in St James' Park leads Adam to a strange women's club in Pall Mall, and a committee of three old ladies called Faith, Hope and Charity, who are not what their names imply.
Prudence Geraldine Moffatt
Abstinence Eve Gross
Jarrot Gerald Sim
Charity Amelia Bayntun

Hope Sheila Grant
Faith Lucy Griffiths
Randolph John Carson

Director: Ridley Scott
Designer: Mary Rea

Ticket to Terror

w Dick Sharples
Four hundred commuters—including Simms—disappear without trace on an underground line, in one of the most sinister conspiracies in British criminal history.
Miss Caldwell Ann Lynn
Dr. Klein Max Adrian
Susan Denby Jan Quy
Harold Reg Lye
Engineer Jack Bligh
George Tommy Eytle
Armitage Michael Barrington

Director: Tina Wakerell
Designer: Evan Hercules

The Village of Evil

w Vince Powell & Harry Driver
A dead mouse, a young boy and a lonely mill lead Adam into a sinister web of evil that interrupts a quiet fishing holiday.
Joe Christopher Coll
Dr. Craigshaw John Bailey
Mr. Burke Trevor Baxter
Myra Bamford Colette O'Neil
Daniel Dinny Powell
Jerry Fletcher Len Jones
Mr. Corbett John Law

Director: Anthea Browne-Wilkinson
Designer: Sally Hulke

D for Destruction

w Tony Williamson
A series of deadly accidents in Adamant's old regiment draws him back into uniform and an encounter with the fanatical Col. Mannering who is infuriated by plans to phase out the Territorial Army.
Sgt. Major Jeffers Michael Ripper
Corp. Grey Walter Sparrow
Bailey Bryan Mosley
General Mongerson Patrick Troughton
Corp. Jenkins Anthony Blackshaw
Col. Mannering Iain Cuthbertson
Major Michael Sheard

Director: Moira Armstrong
Designer: Ken Jones

Season Two
13 episodes

A Slight Case of Reincarnation

w Tony Williamson, *story by* Brian Clemens
Adam Adamant is asked to protect an African leader from assassination—and recalls an old enemy.
Hinkaya Horace James
Hammond Patrick Kavanagh
Charlesworth Norman Pitt
Simpson John Cazabon
Logan William Hurndell
Dr. Sanderson Peter Madden
Dr. Heindrick Martin Miller
Sir Charles Thetford John Frawley
Lady Thetford Peggy Ann Wood
Louise Mary Yeomans

Director: Roger Jenkins
Designer: Ken Jones

Black Echo

w Donald & Derek Ford
An oil tanker delivers its load to a country house and the driver gets a shock that turns his hair white. And Adam Adamant again faces The Face.
Oil delivery man Kenneth Ives
Sir Henry Donald Eccles
Sir George Peter Bathurst
Beardsley Trevor Baxter
Sergei Brian Gilmar
Ireyna Judy Parfitt
Grand Duchess Vorokhov Gladys Cooper

Director: Moira Armstrong
Designer: Peter Kindred

Conspiracy of Death

w Vince Powell & Harry Driver
Jankers Johnson, an old wartime buddy of Simms, is mysteriously murdered at their former RAF aerodrome—but manages to get a message to Adam before he dies.
Johnson John Scott Martin
Davison Harold Goodwin
Onslow Derek Farr
Penrose George Woodbridge
Monique Annette Carell
Connelly David Blake Kelly
Dolly Fanny Carby

Director: Roger Jenkins
Designer: Michael Young

The Basardi Affair

w Ian Stuart Black
Adam gets involved in the world of international exploitation after the ruler of an oil-rich country is the victim of fierce intimidation.

Eileen Smith Suzanne Mockler
Sonia Fawzi Kate O'Mara
Chauffeur Joe Cornelius
Sheikh Abdul Zia Mohyeddin
Guard Roy Stewart
Prince Mahmud Salmaan Peer
Sir Robert William Kendall

Director: Henri Safran
Designer: Peter Kindred

The Survivors

w Vince Powell & Harry Driver
When inventions start appearing on the market after the death of their inventors, Adam is drawn into a sinister plot.
Minister Anthony Dawes
Singleton Edwin Richfield
Mrs. Granger Elizabeth Benson
Critchley Erik Chitty
Marty Roy Evans
Mrs. Clasp Hilda Fenemore
Blundell Edward Evans

Director: Moira Armstrong
Designer: Michael Young

Face in a Mirror

w John Pennington
The Face devises a plan to rid the world of Adamant by first discrediting and then destroying him. The scheme is so cunning it may just succeed.
Farnley Gerald Harper
Gladwin Edward Brayshaw
Lady Lydia Jean Marsh
Livingstone Fred McNaughton
Hudson Billy John
Roach Bob Godfrey
Baker Basil Dignam

Director: Henri Safran
Designer: Michael Young

Another Little Drink

w Ian Stuart Black
Georgina goes to a party organized by the manufacturer of a new soft drink, but finds it is not as innocuous as it appears.
Supervisor Norman Wynne
Carol Shelley Sally Bazely
Dr. Loton Meredith Edwards
Yorke Fredric Abbott
Addison Robert McBain
D.K. Davies Peter Bowles
Guard Michael Golden

Director: Laurence Bourne
Designer: Malcolm Middleton

Death Begins at Seventy

w Dick Sharples
When Simms gets a message from an old theater friend, he and Adam find themselves mixed up in strange goings-on at an old folks' home.
Timothy Henshaw George Benson
Charlie Pearson Windsor Davies
Matron Sheila Burrell
Mary Smith Cyd Hayman
Dr. Henry Heason Kenneth J. Warren
Harry Newley John Glyn-Jones
Young man Bill MacLean

Director: Ridley Scott
Designer: Peter Kindred

Tunnel of Death

w Richard Waring
When Georgina is nearly arrested, Adam becomes involved in uncovering the latest plot by The Face, who is busy organizing his biggest coup yet.
Sewerman Tex Fuller
Commissioner Hobson Geoffrey Chater
Scarlatti Arnold Diamond
Bruno Kenneth Ives
Constance Geraldine Newman
Brooke Walter Sparrow
Barker Jerold Wells

Director: Moira Armstrong
Designer: Michael Young

The Deadly Bullet

w Vince Powell & Harry Driver
After illusionist The Great Manton is killed while performing the bullet-catching trick, Adam uses his deductive skills to help a reluctant policeman find the murderer.
George Manton Henry Gilbert
Wanda Manton Sheila Brennan
Juanita Jill Curzon
Carlos Graham Corry
Oliver Meadows Nigel Stock
Insp. Foster Bill Kerr
Pop Williams Harold Bennett

Director: Henri Safran
Designer: Peter Kindred

The Resurrectionists

w Derek & Donald Ford
When a scientist destroys his invention for calming wild animals and then vanishes, Adam is drawn into a sinister encounter with agents of The Face.
Dr. Morris Vaine Bernard Kay
Sara Linden Wendy Gifford
Mr. Byers-Thompson Frank Williams
The Minister Peter Stephens
Miss Coburn Sheila Grant
Susan Tracey Crisp
Mrs. Withenshaw Cicely Paget-Bowman

Director: Ridley Scott
Designer: Malcolm Middleton

Wish You Were Here

w James MacTaggart
Simms's mother is charged with disturbing the peace, and when Simms goes to her aid he stumbles on a sordid plot.
Saville Peter Birrel
Mrs. Simms Hilda Barry
Sonia Marion Mathie
Lord Hawksmoor Michael Gwynn
Old lady Kitty Attwood
Hercules Skip Martin
Matron Terry Richards

Director: Moira Armstrong
Designer: Peter Kindred

A Sinister Sort of Service

w Tony Williamson
A number of carefully planned robberies take place throughout the country, and it's clear that only one man can be behind them—The Face.
Sir Nigel Dee David Garth
Jason Lang T.P. McKenna
Thomas Mark Moss
Miklo Josef Zaranoff
Sandra Verrel Frances Cuka
SS girl Clare Jenkins
Furrier David Kelly

Director: Laurence Bourne
Designer: Michael Young

THE ADDAMS FAMILY

Based (rather loosely) on the cartoons of Charles Addams, *The Addams Family* presented a classically screwball yet endearing family of weirdos, from millionaire train-wrecker Gomez Addams to his carnivorous-plant-raising wife, Morticia, from electrically powered Uncle Fester to torture-loving Grandmama, from kids Pugsley (pet: octopus) to Wednesday (pet: spider). And we can't forget harpsichordist/butler Lurch, helping hand Thing, or hairy Cousin Itt!

For two seasons, the Addams family entertained America before being consigned to syndication, where it continues. Several cartoon series have involved the Addams Family, and there was also a disappointing made-for-TV reunion movie, *Halloween with the New Addams Family*.

REGULAR CAST

Gomez Addams John Astin *Morticia Addams* Carolyn Jones
Lurch Ted Cassidy *Uncle Fester* Jackie Coogan
Grandmama Blossom Rock *Wednesday Addams* Lisa Loring
Pugsley Addams Ken Weatherwax *Cousin Itt* Felix Silla/Roger Arroyo (Tony Magro, *Voice*)
Thing hand of Ted Cassidy

Based on characters created by Charles Addams	64 black and white 30-minute episodes; 1 color 90-
Developed for television by David Levy	minute movie
Executive producer: David Levy	18 September 1964–8 April 1966
Producer: Nat Perrin	Reunion movie: 30 October 1977
Music: Vic Mizzy	

Season One

The Addams Family Goes to School

w Ed James & Seaman Jacobs
When the children hear fairy tales at school, a horrified Morticia decides to keep them at home.
Guest stars: Allyn Joslyn, Madge Blake, Rolfe Sedan, Nydia Westman
Director: Arthur Hiller

Morticia and the Psychiatrist

w Hannibal Coons & Harry Winkler
Gomez and Morticia seek help from a psychiatrist when Pugsley takes up with the Boy Scouts and abandons his pet octopus.
Guest star: George Petrie
Director: Jean Yarbrough

Fester's Punctured Romance

w Jameson Brewer
Fester decides to find a wife through a newspaper ad.
Guest stars: Merry Anders, Robert Nunn
Director: Sidney Lanfield

Gomez, the Politician

w Hannibal Coons & Harry Winkler
Gomez plays politics, backing a man for city council who promises to drain the bogs—to Morticia's horror.
Guest stars: Allyn Joslyn, Eddie Quillan, Bill Baldwin, Bob Le Mond
Director: Jerry Hopper

The Addams Family Tree

w Hannibal Coons, Harry Winkler & Lou Huston
When the snobs next door accuse the Addams Family of having no history, Gomez and Morticia trace their family genealogy.
Guest stars: Frank Nelson, Jonathan Hole, Kim Tyler, Rolfe Sedan
Director: Jerry Hopper

Morticia Joins the Ladies League

w Phil Leslie & Keith Fowler
Gorgo the circus gorilla befriends Pugsley and joins the family, proving a better butler than Lurch.
Guest stars: George Barrows, Dorothy Neumann, Peter Leeds, Pearl Shear
Director: Jean Yarbrough

Halloween with the Addams Family

w Keith Fowler & Phil Leslie
Gomez and Morticia mistake two bank robbers on the lam for trick-or-treaters.
Guest stars: Skip Homeier, Don Rickles, Goerge Barrows
Director: Sidney Lanfield

Green-Eyed Gomez

w Phil Leslie & Keith Fowler
An old suitor of Morticia's arrives for a visit, arousing Gomez's jealousy.
Guest stars: Del Moore, Pattee Chapman, Jimmy Ames
Director: Jerry Hopper

The New Neighbors Meet the Addams Family

w Hannibal Coons & Harry Winkler
A newlywed couple find the helpful meddling of Gomez and Morticia less than welcome.
Guest stars: Peter Brooks, Cynthia Petter, Eddie Mar
Director: Jean Yarbrough

Wednesday Leaves Home

w Harry Winkler & Hannibal Coons
When Wednesday gets scolded for using Uncle Fester's dynamite instead of her own, she packs up her spider and runs away.
Guest stars: Jessie White, Ray Kellogg
Director: Sidney Lanfield

The Addams Family Meet the VIPs

w Keith Fowler & Phil Leslie
Visiting dignitaries from the Soviet Union study a typical American Family—the Addamses.
Guest stars: Stanley Adams, Vito Scotti, Frank Wilcox
Director: Sidney Lanfield

Morticia, the Matchmaker

w Hannibal Coons & Harry Winkler
Cousin Melancholia (Carolyn Jones in a dual role) seeks a new man after the last one runs off to join the Foreign Legion.
Guest stars: Hazel Shermet, Lee Goodman, Barry Kelley, Hal Baylor, Lennie Bremen
Director: Jerry Hopper

Lurch Learns to Dance

w Jay Dratler, Jery Seelen & Charles Marion
Lurch doesn't want to attend the annual Butlers' Ball, so Gomez and Morticia teach him to dance.
Guest stars: Jimmy Cross, Penny Parker
Director: Sidney Lanfield

Art and the Addams Family

w Harry Winkler & Hannibal Coons
Grandmama needs painting lessons, so Gomez sends to Spain for Picasso—*Sam* Picasso.
Guest stars: Vito Scotti, Hugh Sanders
Director: Sidney Lanfield

The Addams Family Meets a Beatnik

w Jack Raymond
A beatnik crashes his motorcycle in front of the Addamses' house and ends up staying for a visit.
Guest stars: Tom Lowell, Barry Kelley, Barry Brooks
Director: Sidney Lanfield

The Addams Family Meets the Undercover Man

w Harry Winkler & Hannibal Coons
A government agent uses the mailman to investigate coded messages being transmitted from the Addamses' house.
Guest stars: Norman Leavitt, Rolfe Sedan, George Neise
Director: Arthur Lubin

Mother Lurch Visits the Addams Family

w Jameson Brewer
Lurch hasn't told his tiny mother he's the Addams Family butler; when she visits, Gomez and Morticia pretend to be his servants—only to be sacked.
Guest star: Ellen Corby
Director: Sidney Lanfield

The Addams Family Splurges

w George Haight & Lou Huston
Gomez uses a computer to calculate the cost of vacationing on the moon.
Guest stars: Roland Winters, Oman Soule, Bill Baldwin
Director: Sidney Lanfield

Cousin Itt Visits the Addams Family

w Henry Sharp, *story by* Tony Wilson
Gomez gets Cousin Itt a job at the zoo; the zoo commissioner assumes Itt's an exhibit.
Guest stars: Alan Reed, Bill Baldwin
Director: Sidney Lanfield

The Addams Family in Court

w Harry Winkler & Hannibal Coons
Grandmama gets arrested for fortune telling.
Guest stars: Hal Smith, James Flavin, Lela Bliss, Gail Bonney, Ray Walker
Director: Nat Perrin

Amnesia in the Addams Family

w Phil Leslie & Keith Fowler
After Gomez is hit on the head and comes down with amnesia, the rest of the family tries to cure him.
Director: Sidney Lanfield

Thing Is Missing

w Bill Lutz, *story by* Lorraine Edwards
When Thing disappears, Gomez hires a private investigator.
Guest stars: Tommy Farrell, Charles Wagenheim, Ray Kellogg
Director: Sidney Lanfield

Crisis in the Addams Family

w Sloan Nibley & Preston Wood, *story by* Preston Wood
Uncle Fester applies for a job with the family's insurance company.
Guest stars: Eddie Quillan, Parley Baer, Bebe Kelly
Director: Sidney Lanfield

Lurch and His Harpsichord

w Harry Winler & Hannibal Coons
When Lurch's favorite harpsichord is donated to a museum, everyone tries to interest him in new musical instruments.
Guest stars: Byron Foulger, Lennie Bremen, Ray Galvin
Director: Sidney Lanfield

Morticia, the Breadwinner

w Phil Leslie
Morticia tries to raise money when she thinks Gomez is broke.
Guest stars: Milton Frome, Maxine Semon, John "Red" Fox, Ceil Cabot
Director: Sidney Lanfield

The Addams Family and the Spacemen

w Harry Winkler & Hannibal Coons
The family is mistaken for aliens during a moonlight picnic and snail hunt.
Guest stars: Vito Scotti, Tim Herbert, Jimmy Cross, Bob LeMond
Director: Sidney Lanfield

My Son, the Chimp

w Henry Sharp, *story by* Don Quinn
Uncle Fester thinks his magic turned Pugsley into a chimp.
Guest star: Robert Nunn
Director: Sidney Lanfield

Morticia's Favorite Charity

w Elroy Schwartz & Jameson Brewer, *story by* Elroy Schwartz
Morticia rounds up prized possessions for a charity auction.
Guest stars: Parley Baer, Maida Severn, Donald Foster, John Lawrence
Director: Sidney Lanfield

Progress and the Addams Family

w Bill Freedman & Ben Gershman, *story by* Cecil Beard & Clark Haas
The Addams Family learns that their house has been condemned to make way for a new freeway.
Guest stars: Parley Baer, Natalie Masters, John Hart, Dick Reaves
Director: Sidney Lanfield

Uncle Fester's Toupee

w Harry Winkler & Hannibal Coons
When Uncle Fester's pen pal comes to visit, he dons a toupee to try to live up to his description in his letters.
Guest stars: Elizabeth Fraser, Frederic Downs
Director: Sidney Lanfield

Cousin Itt and the Vocational Counselor

w Hannibal Coons & Harry Winkler
Gomez and Morticia decide Cousin Itt should be a marriage counselor.
Guest star: Richard Deacon
Director: Sidney Lanfield

Lurch, the Teenage Idol

w Carol Henning, Mitch Persons & Ed Ring
Lurch records a song on the harpsichord and becomes a singing sensation.
Guest stars: Herkie Styles, Laurie Mitchell, Noanna Dix, Pam McMyler, Jacque Palmer, Patrick Moore
Director: Sidney Lanfield

Season Two

My Fair Cousin Itt

w Phil Leslie
Itt stars in a family production, and being a star goes to his head.
Guest stars: Sig Ruman, Jimmy Cross, Douglas Evans
Director: Sidney Lanfield

Morticia's Romance, Part 1

w Harry Winkler & Hannibal Coons
On her wedding anniversary, Morticia tells Pugsley and Wednesday how she and Gomez met.
Guest star: Margaret Hamilton
Director: Sidney Lanfield

Morticia's Romance, Part 2

w Harry Winkler & Hannibal Coons
Pugsley and Wednesday won't go to sleep until Morticia finishes the tale of how she and Gomez met.
Guest stars: Margaret Hamilton, Edward Schaal
Director: Sidney Lanfield

Morticia Meets Royalty

w Leo Rifkin
Thing falls for the lovely Lady Fingers when Gomez's aunt comes to visit.
Guest star: Elvia Allman
Director: Sidney Lanfield

Gomez, the People's Choice

w Joseph Vogel & Marvin Kaplan
Gomez runs for mayor.
Guest stars: Parley Baer, Eddie Quillan, Jack Barry, Lennie Breman, Bart "Buzz" Greene
Director: Sidney Lanfield

Cousin Itt's Problem

w Carol Henning, Ed Ring & Mitch Persons
Cousin Itt may be losing his hair, so it's up to Uncle Fester to concoct a hair-growth tonic.
Guest stars: Meg Wyllie, Frankie Darro
Director: Sidney Lanfield

Halloween—Addams Style

w Hannibal Coons & Harry Winkler
Morticia and Gomez try to summon a witch through a séance to prove to their children that witches exist.
Guest stars: Yvonne Peattie, Bob Jellison, Don McArt
Director: Sidney Lanfield

Morticia, the Writer

w Hannibal Coons & Harry Winkler
Morticia takes up writing, leaving Gomez feeling neglected.
Guest star: Peter Bonerz
Director: Sidney Lanfield

Morticia, the Sculptress

w Harry Winkler & Hannibal Coons
To keep up Morticia's spirits after a critic pans her work, Gomez pays Sam Picasso to buy her creations for his gallery.
Guest stars: Vito Scotti, Hugh Sanders
Director: Sidney Lanfield

Gomez, the Reluctant Lover

w Charles Marion & Leo Rifkin
When a smitten Pugsley sends his teacher one of Gomez's love letters, she visits the house in search of Gomez.
Guest stars: Jill Andre, Tom Browne Henry
Director: Sidney Lanfield

Feud in the Addams Family

w Rick Richard
Upper-class snobs visit, hoping to meet a member of the social set who turns out to be an in-law by marriage.
Guest stars: Fred Clark, Virginia Gregg, Kevin Tate
Director: Sidney Lanfield

Gomez, the Cat Burglar

w Phil Leslie
Gomez sleepwalks his way into a new career—cat burglar.
Guest stars: Ken Mayer, Bill White
Director: Sidney Lanfield

Portrait of Gomez

w Leo Salkin, Bill Lutz & Henry Sharp, *story by* Leo Salkin & Bill Lutz
When Cleopatra eats Morticia's favorite photo of Gomez, his search for the same photographer to have another one taken leads to the Department of Motor Vehicles.
Guest stars: Tom D'Andrea, Ralph Montgomery
Director: Sidney Salkow

Morticia's Dilemma

w Jerry Gottler & John Bradford
The Spanish woman betrothed to Gomez since childhood arrives to claim him as her own.
Guest stars: Anthony Caruso, Carlos Rivas, Bella Bruck
Director: Sidney Miller

Christmas with the Addams Family

w Hannibal Coons & Harry Winkler
Uncle Fester gets stuck in the chimney on Christmas Eve while trying to prove Santa really exists, leaving everyone else to dress up as Old Saint Nick.
Guest star: Gregg Martell
Director: Sidney Lanfield

Uncle Fester, Tycoon

w Sloan Nibley & Preston Wood
Uncle Fester falls for a bearded lady in a carnival.
Guest stars: Roy Roberts, Harold Peary
Director: Sidney Salkow

Morticia and Gomez vs. Fester and Grandmama

w Sloan Nibley & Preston Wood
Morticia hires a governess because Fester and Grandmama are spoiling the children.
Guest stars: Irene Tedrow, Loyal "Doc" Lucas
Director: Sidney Salkow

Fester Goes on a Diet

w Hannibal Coons & Harry Winkler
Fester must get in shape when another female pen pal plans to visit.
Guest stars: Jack La Lanne, William Keene, Peggy Mondo, Rolfe Sedan
Director: Sidney Lanfield

The Great Treasure Hunt

w Hannibal Coons & Harry Winkler
A treasure map turns up, so the Addamses charter a boat for the hunt.
Guest stars: Nestor Paiva, Richard Reeves
Director: Sidney Lanfield

Ophelia Finds Romance

w Hannibal Coons & Harry Winkler
Morticia tries to rekindle Cousin Itt's former romance with Ophelia.
Guest star: Robert Nichols
Director: Sidney Lanfield

Pugsley's Allowance

w Harry Winkler & Hannibal Coons
Pugsley decides to find a job when his allowance isn't enough.
Guest stars: Parley Baer, Jack Collins, Natalie Masters, Robert S. Carson, Tim Herbert
Director: Sidney Lanfield

Happy Birthday, Grandma Frump

w Elroy Schwartz
Gomez and Morticia plan to send Grandma Frump to a beauty farm for her birthday, but she thinks she's going to an old folks' home.
Guest star: Margaret Hamilton
Director: Sidney Lanfield

Morticia, the Decorator

w Gene Thompson
To sell Morticia a policy, an insurance salesman lets her decorate his home.
Guest stars: Eddie Quillan, Jeff Donnell
Director: Sidney Salkow

Ophelia Visits Morticia

w Art Weingarten
Ophelia drives Uncle Fester to join the Peace Corps.
Guest star: George Cisar
Director: Sidney Lanfield

Addams Cum Laude

w Sloan Nibley & Bill Lutz
School trouble for Pugsley and Wednesday—so Gomez buys the school.
Guest stars: Allyn Joslyn, Carol Byron, Pat Brown
Director: Sidney Lanfield

Cat Addams

w Paul Tuckahoe
Kitty Kat, the Addamses' pet lion, is sick, so a doctor is called.
Guest stars: Marty Ingles, Loyal "Doc" Lucas
Director: Stanley Z. Cherry

Lurch's Little Helper

w Phil Leslie
Gomez builds a robot to help Lurch with the housework; the robot's better at it.
Guest star: Robby the Robot
Director: Sidney Lanfield

The Addams Policy

w Harry Winkler & Hannibal Coons
Fester has an accident with his flame thrower, so Morticia files a claim with the insurance company.
Guest stars: Eddie Quillan, Parley Baer
Director: Sidney Lanfield

Lurch's Grand Romance

w Gene Thompson & Art Weingarten
Lurch falls in love with a diminutive friend of Morticia's.
Guest star: Diane Jurgens
Director: Sidney Lanfield

Ophelia's Career

w Harry Winkler *&* Hannibal Coons
Ophelia chooses opera singing as her new career, with voice help from Cousin Itt.
Guest stars: Ralph Rose, Ben Wright
Director: Sidney Lanfield

Reunion Movie:

Halloween with the New Addams Family

w George Tibbles
Crooks want to rob the Addams Family house on Halloween.
Guest stars: Henry Darrow, Patrick Campbell, Vito Scotti, Parley Baer, Felix Silla, Dean Sothern, Lisa Loring, Suzanne Krazna, Jennifer Surprenant, Kenneth Marquis, Elvia Allman, Jane Rose, David Johns, Clinton Beyerle, Terry Miller
Director: Dennis Steinmetz

THE ADVENTURES OF BRISCO COUNTY, JR.

Remember *The Wild Wild West*? These guys do. This clever nineties series is tinged with the same quirky streak of fantasy.

Ostensibly, it's an action-adventure, set in California's Old West in the 1890s, that follows the exploits of the eponymous adventurer Brisco County, Jr. But while it's a familiar Wild West scene of stagecoaches, shoot-outs and saloon singers, it's also a time when an eccentric professor can build a rocket in his barn and Chinese Tong warriors train in exotic initiation chambers beneath a curio shop. It's a world where outlaws hide out in a lavish gothic lair, and where an uncanny, telepathic horse called Comet is perfectly in tune with his master.

But, most bizarre of all, it's a world graced by the Orb, a mysterious metallic sphere (later revealed to be one of three found in a crater) that can selectively grant awesome powers to those who possess it. And *everyone* wants to possess it.

A Harvard Law graduate and son of the greatest sharp-shooting marshall in the land, Brisco is hired by a group of wealthy businessmen known as the robber barons to hunt down a group of 12 notorious outlaws led by the sinister John Bly. For Brisco, it's a personal matter too, as the Bly gang was also behind the cold-blooded murder of his father.

But Brisco is more than just a lawman, he's a dreamer and a romantic, a visionary constantly searching for "the coming thing." That brings him into contact with oddball inventor Prof. Wickwire (played by *The Addams Family*'s John Astin). Wickwire has his mind set on traveling to the stars and is fascinated by the thoughts of new technologies.

Brisco's regular companions in his adventures, however, are his faithful horse, Comet, bookish attorney Socrates Poole, who is his liaison with his employers, and bounty hunter/tracker Lord Bowler. Other recurring characters include Brisco's erstwhile girlfriend, Dixie Cousins, nutty outlaw Peter Hutter, Sheriff Aaron Viva, an energetic lawman who looks and sounds like Elvis Presley, and playboy/gambler Whip Morgan.

As for the Orb, it is first unearthed by Chinese coolies working on a railroad chain gang. Four workmen touch its glowing rods and suddenly acquire the strength to break their chains. The Orb later gets dubbed an "Unearthed Foreign Object" by a worker packing it up for transport on a train. "That's kind of a mouthful," says another who proceeds to scribble UFO on the side of the crate.

It's little moments like that that make this series such a delight. It's witty and playful, affectionately spoofing Western clichés and lacing the action with deft touches of fantasy.

In one wonderful sequence, Brisco hitches Prof. Wickwire's experimental rocket to the top of a railway wagon and rides it along the track to intercept a gold train robbery.

Some inspired casting also has a bunch of old Western stars in cameo roles including Paul Brinegar (*Rawhide*), James Drury (*The Virginian*) and Robert Fuller (*Laramie*). Stuart Whitman plays the leader of the robber barons, but his role is short-lived. Granted the strength of 12 men by the Orb, he pays the price for abusing his power and suddenly ages rapidly, turning into a skeleton before dissolving totally into dust.

Another episode had the ghost of Brisco's father appearing to offer him advice like Obi Wan Kenobi, telling him to feel the force. Brisco eventually discovers the secret of the orbs—that they were sent from a future time to benefit mankind—and has a final showdown with Bly, who turns out to be a fanatic from the future out to use the orbs' power to enslave his own time.

Alas, *The Adventures of Brisco County, Jr.* proved a touch too eccentric for U.S. audiences, lasting only one season on Fox.

REGULAR CAST

Brisco County, Jr. Bruce Campbell *Socrates Poole* Christian Clemenson
Lord Bowler Julius Carry   *John Bly* Billy Drago   *Dixie Cousins* Kelly Rutherford
Peter Hutter John Pyper-Ferguson   *Sheriff Aaron Viva* Gary Hudson
Whip Morgan Jeff Phillips

Creators/Executive producers: Jeffrey Boam, Carlton Cuse
Co-producers: David Simpkins, Paul Marks
Writers: Various, including David Simkins, Tom Chehak, Jeffrey Boam, Carlton Cuse, John McNamara, Brad Kern, John Wirth
Directors: Various, including Kim Manners, Joe Napolitano, Rob Bowman
Music: Randy Edelman
Special Effects: M. Kam Cooney

Boam/Cuse Productions, in association with Warner Bros. Television
27 color 60-minute episodes (pilot two hours)
U.S. premiere: 27 August 1993
U.K. premiere: 15 July 1994
(Sky One)

THE ADVENTURES OF
DON QUICK

Science fiction satire based on the character of Don Quixote, with its astronaut anti-hero, Don Quick, tilting at planets instead of windmills.

As a member of the Inter Galactic Maintenance Squad, Quick should only be concerned with nuts and bolts. But he's not satisfied with that role. Each time he and his trusty companion Sgt. Sam Czopanser (Sancho Panza, get it?) land on a new planet, he sees himself as the roving ambassador of Earth, and sets about trying to right imaginary wrongs. This penchant for interference invariably ends with him upsetting the balance of whatever society he encounters.

Impressively designed, the six-part series boasted some elaborate sets, rich costumes and clever technical effects—such as Quick being shrunk to a six-inch dwarf by the queen of a matriarchal planet. Alas, it was short on laughs.

REGULAR CAST

Captain Don Quick Ian Hendry   *Sgt. Sam Czopanser* Ronald Lacey

Executive producer: Peter Wildeblood

London Weekend Television Production
6 color 60-minute episodes
30 October–4 December 1970

The Benefits of Earth

w Peter Wildeblood
The Intrepid Don Quick lands on a planet inhabited by two alien races—one technically advanced but addicted to warfare and human sacrifice, the other living in a dream world of peace and sensitivity.
Babachuk Kevin Stoney

Goolmarg John Woodnutt
Dulcie Margaret Nolan
Grippik Patrick Durkin
Marvana Anouska Hempel
Gezool Donald Sumpter
Chief dreamer Thorley Walters

Director: Mike Newell
Designer: Bryan Bagge

People Isn't Everything

w Kenneth Hill
Astronauts Don and Sam trustingly leave their spaceship in charge of the first friendly face they find on the planet Ophiuchus. But that face belongs to Skip, a robot castaway who likes a drink . . .
Voice of Skip Tony Bateman
Dovax Jonathan Elsom
Broul Michael Sheard
Peleen Kate O'Mara
Skander Damien Thomas
Maloin Arne Gordon
Ziggs Glenn Williams
Clerk of the court Bryan Mosley
TV announcer John Carlin
Judge Lockwood West
Public prosecutor Dennis Edwards
Physiological expert Victor Platt
Mam Dovax Nan Munro
Bank clerks David Gooderson, James Ware
Rebel Colin Baker

Director: Quentin Lawrence
Designer: Bryan Bagge

The Higher the Fewer

w Peter Wildeblood
When Don and Sam land on the planet Melkior 5, they find themselves in the middle of a huge rubbish dump. The inhabitants have all taken refuge in 2000-story skyscrapers, with the top people living at the top, and the lower classes at the bottom. Then Don starts turning everything upside down.
Hendenno James Hayter
Guards James Appleby, John Lawrence
Mrs. Arborel Hildegard Neil
Arborel Derek Francis
Magdis Maggie Don
Beltane Oliver Cotton
Section leader Neil Wilson
Afghar Kenny Rodway

Director: Cliff Owen
Designer: Rodney Cammish

The Love Reflector

w Keith Miles
The population of the planet Herekos seems to consist wholly of beautiful girls. But there is danger in succumbing to their charms for the Queen Bee has the power to reduce men to six-inch dwarfs. Lieutenant Vasco, the only Spaniard ever to get into orbit, succumbed a generation ago. How will Quick fare?
Angeline Liz Bamber
Oriel Gay Soper
Juno Vicki Woolf
Magda Susan Porrett
Queen Bee Faith Brook
Lt. Vasco Michael Aldridge
Iris Anna Brett
Leonie Madeline Smith

Director: Cyril Coke
Designer: John Emery

The Quick and the Dead

w Keith Miles
When the astronauts inadvertently land in the crater of a live volcano, Sgt. Sam is convinced that he is dead. He's not much reassured by finding that the volcano houses a strange assortment of ancient gods.
Doris Jacqueline Clarke
Billy, a satyr Louis Mansi
Aphrodite Patricia Haines
Hera Pauline Jameson
Zeus Graham Crowden
Hephaestus Reg Lye
Frigg Gaye Browne
Odin Arthur Brough
Krimhilda Madeleine Mills
Flosshilda Yutte Stensgaard

Director: Bob Hird
Designer: Rodney Camish

Paradise Destruct

w Charlotte & Dennis Plimmer
To anyone but Don Quick, the planet Amity would seem a paradise. The girls are beautiful, the vegetation is lush and both night and winter have mysteriously been abolished. But Quick, as usual, cannot let well alone.
Jonquil Kara Wilson
Willow Lorna Heilbron
Sycamore Roy Marsden
Butternut Brian Oulton
Delphinium Madeleine Newbury
Oleander Leigh Lawson

Director: Bill Turner
Designer: John Emery

THE ADVENTURES OF SINBAD

The success of *Hercules* and *Xena* has opened the door for more fantasy series, including the syndicated *The Adventures of Sinbad,* which owes more to 1940s Hollywood's vision of *The Arabian Nights* than Sir Richard Burton's: There are few Arabs in sight (let alone veils for the women), but certainly that goes well with the tradition. All you really need is a swashbuckling hero (here Sinbad, played aptly by Zen Gesner) coming up against various sorcerers, monsters and other evil-doers each week. Add a few sword fights, some scantily clad maidens, and the formula is complete.

Filmed in South Africa, the show has a wonderfully lush look. Computer-generated monsters, a fast pace and a light tone go far to carry the stories along.

REGULAR CAST

Sinbad Zen Gesner *Doubar* George Buza
Maeve Jacqueline Collen (*Season One*) *Bryn* Mariah Shirley
Firouz Tim Progosh *Rongar* Oris Erhuero
Rumina Julianne Morris

Creator: Ed Naha
Executive producers: Peter Sussman, David Gerber, Ed Naha
Producers: Jonathan Hackett, Gavin Mitchell
Creative consultant: Robert Engels

An Atlantis Films Production in association with All American Television Productions

Season One

Premiere (Part 1)

w Ed Naha
Returning to Bagdad, Sinbad discovers his homeland in turmoil. He is arrested and sentenced to death, but escapes with the help of his older brother, Doubar. Meanwhile, the evil sorcerer Turok and his spiteful daughter Rumina have made off with the Prince's bride-to-be. At the urging of his father, Prince Casib reluctantly pardons Sinbad and hires him to rescue the kidnapped Princess.
Guest stars: Robin Dunne, Lawrence Bayne, Juan Chioran, Ian Tracey, Gary Reineke, Wayne Robson

Premiere (Part 2)

w Ed Naha
Sinbad and crew next reach the Isle of Dawn, where Sinbad is reunited with his tutor, the master magician Dim-Dim. Dim-Dim's apprentice, Maeve, joins the crew. When Rongar exposes the Grand Vizier as Turok's sinister accomplice, the Grand Vizier transforms himself into a monster and attacks.
Guest stars: Robin Dunne, Lawrence Bayne, Juan Chioran, Tim Progosh, Ian Tracey, Gary Reineke, Wayne Robson

The Beast Within

w Ed Naha
Sinbad is captured by Rumina, who plans to marry him. But when he refuses to cooperate, she matches him against her champion, Goz, a previous love interest whom she has transformed into a half-man, half-beast.
Guest star: David Johansson

Still Life

w John Lafia
Sinbad and crew land on a dark and mysterious island ruled by Vincenzo, an artist who creates incredibly lifelike statues. And now Vincenzo has designs on Maeve . . .
Guest star: Rob Stewart

King Firouz

w John Shirley
Firouz invents the Ruby-Beamer, a communications device that Admiral Azul covets as a weapon of war . . . and will kill to possess for his people.
Guest stars: Gesa Kozacs, Lisa Melman, Graham Clarke, Ronald France

The Ronin

w Ed Naha
Sinbad sails to Baronia, only to discover he's been chosen to act as champion for his old friend Kalel, the island's governor, in a duel to the death. The prize is control of all the local islands. Unfortunately, his opponent is going to be Tetsu, an unbeaten samurai with a magical sword.
Guest stars: Von Flores, Ron Smerczak, Dan Pawlick

Little Miss Magic

w Michael Cassutt

While sailing in a violent storm, Sinbad's ship is damaged and he is forced to stop at a deserted dock. Wandering into the strange town, he enters a tavern and soon wins "The Jewel of the City" in a card game—the Jewel being Serendib, a fifteen-year-old girl with magical powers. Unfortunately, there is no escape from the magically ensorcelled city . . . and Rumina is waiting to take advantage of their plight.
Guest stars: Emmanuelle Chriqui, Jeroen Kranenburg, Robyn Scott

The Ties That Bind

w Craig Volk

Maeve is captured by Norsemen who believe Thor has sent her as a tribute for a demon. Sinbad and crew set out to save her, battling carnivorous plants, giant spiders and ultimately the Gilling Demon.
Guest stars: Brett Hart, Robin Smith

Double Trouble

w Jule Selbo

The Caliph of Baghdad sends Sinbad and his crew to visit Omar of Basra, "The Savage Sultan," to retrieve a magical Egyptian obelisk that gives unlimited power to whomever owns it. Unfortunately, the evil sorceress Rumina has plans to steal the magical relic, as well as to make another attempt at winning Sinbad's heart.
Guest stars: Brian O'Shaughnessy, Adrienne Pearce

Conundrum

w Ed Naha

To free a beautiful woman, Sinbad and his crew must find three missing skulls and return them to their resting places. The catch: They will have to travel through portals that twist through time and space to lands no mortals have returned from alive.
Guest stars: Ashley Hayden, Danny Keogh, Farouk Valley-Omar, Toni Caprari

The Prince Who Wasn't

w Ardwright Chamberlain

In the land of Arborea, a usurper named Drax sits on the throne. Sinbad and his crew come to the aid of Prince Xander, whose father, the king, has been murdered and whose mother, the queen, has been captured by Drax. But things aren't really as they seem, especially when the dead walk by day and seek revenge . . .
Guest stars: Christopher Duncan, Jack Langedyk, Graham Weir, John Springett

The Village Vanishes

w James L. Novak

A mysterious note asking for help leads Sinbad and his crew to a village where people are turning gray and vanishing. It's the Vorgon, a creature that drains the life essence from humans. If the Vorgon defeats Sinbad and inhabits his body, it will have unlimited access to any portal in the world.
Guest stars: Gavin Van Den Berg, Dennis O'Connor, Bianca Amato, Anthony Bishop

The Masked Marauders of Mirhago

w Bob Engels

A message from the wizard Dim-Dim propels Sinbad's crew to the Kingdom of Mirhago, where they find that the good-natured government of a boy king and his wizard has been usurped by a greedy tax collector. With the help of some enchanted carpets, Sinbad takes to the air to put authority back in the right hands.

The Ghoul's Tale

w Craig Volk

Sinbad arrives at the Lake Isle of Leopold to help save Princess Gaia from the evil Ghoul Vatek, who controls the island's water supply.
Guest stars: Andrew Scorer, Tessa Jubber, Natasha Sutherland, Andre Roothman

The Isle of Bliss

w Victoria Wozniak

Sinbad and his crew are hired to retrieve the "Singing Sword," which grants one wish every 50 years, from the Isle of Bliss.
Guest stars: Monika Schnarre, Anton Stoltz, Sivuyile Ngesi

The Rescue

w Bob Engels

Sinbad and his crew defeat the giant monster Colossus while rescuing the beautiful Jial and returning her to her true love.
Guest stars: Mark Dymond, David Mellur, Talia Rogers

The Eye of Kratos

w A. Chamberlain

The pirate queen Talia persuades Sinbad and his crew to join her in stealing and destroying the "Eye of Kratos," a huge diamond worhiped by a sect of fanatic (and corrupt) priests.
Guest stars: Lisa Howard, Greg Latter, Marius Weyers, Lisa Higgs

The Bully

w Ed Naha
Sinbad helps Omar, the Sultan of Basra, slay a 40-foot Cyclops that has eaten his men and is threatening to eat an entire village of settlers from Basra . . . and catch up with the bully who killed his first girlfriend.
Guest stars: Brian O'Shaughnessy, Christo Loots, Peter Butler, Andrew Mackenzie, Ricky Rudolph

Monument

w George Lowell
A beautiful young lady with a bag of gold enlists Sinbad to help her find her missing father, a demented giant who is threatening the inhabitants of Mylagia.
Guest stars: Sabrina Grdevich, Jeroen Kranenburg, Gordon van Rooyen

The Trickster

w Ed Naha
Sinbad's evil nemesis Rumina schemes to kill Sinbad and his crew but, instead, is forced to join them in a life or death struggle against an unknown power. He introduces himself as Reynard, the mortal slave of the "Old Ones," the ancient gods who ruled the Earth before man arrived. Reynard explains that these gods waged a war against each other that nearly consumed them. Their power to hate is so great that it ties them to this small portion of Earth. When mortals trespass, their hatred emerges once again. Now that Sinbad and the others have defied their warning, the gods will whittle away at the group and eventually tear them apart. Each sets out to find weapons to defend themselves against the gods. In their search, they come across their deepest fears.
Guest stars: Ronald France, Alex Duncan

Siren's Song

w Craig Volk
Sinbad and his crew are drawn into a struggle between the great sea god Poseidon and the greedy Captain Fontassel, who has attempted to steal Poseidon's powerful golden trident.
Guest stars: Don Pawlick, David Thomas, Gamiet Pietersen, Richard Dennison, Walter Kyle

Vengeance of Rumina

w Ed Naha
The evil sorceress Rumina and the devil Scratch join forces to defeat Sinbad and his friends, steal their souls and bring Rumina's father, Turok, back to life.
Guest stars: Michael Copley, Toni Caprari, Juan Chioran, Gina Borthwick

The Sacrifice

w Ed Naha
Maeve is lost in a sea storm and Sinbad becomes separated from the crew as he searches for her. On a small island he meets Bryn, a woman with no memory of her past who is wearing a rainbow bracelet identical to his own. But he may not have time to question her, if the locals have their way and sacrifice her to a monster.
Guest stars: Jonathan Pienaar, Kevin Smith

The Return of the Ronin

w Ed Naha
Sinbad and Tetsu join forces to defeat seven mystical demons that are kidnapping women from an isolated village.
Guest stars: Von Flores, David Thomas, Nicola Hanekom, Nicola Hanekom

Heart and Soul

w Ed Naha
Sinbad and his crew are imprisoned by a beautiful vampire, who promises to spare them if Sinbad retrieves her heart from her vampire husband, Baron Orlock.
Guest stars: Gerard Rudolf, Michelle Bergers, Peryse Allen, Morne Visser, Neil Johnson, Mike Mcdonald, Rowan Dickinson, Bianca Reznikov

The Voyage to Hell

w Craig Volk
Sinbad and crew must journey to hell to save Young Timur from possession by his father's spirit.
Guest stars: Matthew Holdenby, Sean Michael, Dick Reineke, Terry Norton

Ali Rashid and the Thieves

w Craig Volk
Rongar returns to his homeland for revenge and ends up arrested.
Guest stars: Hakim Kalkazim, Bianca Amato, Nomuula Meth, Matthew Holdenby, Benjamin Ajori

The Gift

w Ed Naha
Sinbad and crew meet up with old friends at a wedding feast—only to encounter an army of killer dolls.
Guest stars: Dan Pawlick, Patrick Lyster, Julie Hartley, Catriona Andrews, Debbie Rivett, Graham Clarke, Glen Fisher, Peter Grummeck

Curse of the Gorgons

w Ed Naha
Sinbad and crew come to the aid of villagers who are being terrorized and enslaved by the three gorgon sisters: Eurayle, Stheno and Medusa.
Guest stars: Bonita Wolmarans, Tandi Buchan, Lloyd Kandlin, Robert Delport, Nigel Sweet, Lynita Crofford, Rick Rogers, Tony Hawes, Grant Preston, Lean Liebenberg, John Springett

The Beast of Basra

When a werewolf stalks Basra, Doubar is bitten and Sinbad must find a cure or risk losing his brother forever.

The Monster

w Steven Baum
The evil wizard Kumar uses a gentle giant named Uruk to carry out robberies. Sinbad and company help him break free, thwarting assassins and greedy merchants in the process.

Passengers

w Craig Volk
The wizard Kundalini books passage on the *Nomad,* transporting a mysterious trunk containing the body of his daughter.

As Firouz fights with the killer, Ria turns into the sword-wielding green goddess Mara. The crew does its best to stop their invincible opponent. Kundalini grabs the figure that was once his daughter and dives off the side of the *Nomad* into the churning waters.

Invaders

w Sandy Gunter
A spaceship crash-lands and Sinbad and crew are mistaken for demons.

The Book of Before

w Adam Armus & Nora Kay Foster
Dim-Dim sends Sinbad and his crew to protect the *Book of Before*—a mystical volume created before time began—from marauding Druids.
Guest stars: David Sherwood, Janey Strant, Michelle Myer

Survival Run

w Ed Naha
Sinbad is contracted by Prince Veedon to escort a dangerous prisoner to trial—but the prisoner turns out to be a beautiful young woman who is innocent of the murder she is accused of committing.

Complete as of press time.

THE ADVENTURES OF SUPERBOY

A syndicated show aimed at younger viewers, *The Adventures of Superboy* was surprisingly good. It capitalized on the acting talents of its stars, brought in recognizable villains from the comics, and put its special effects budget to good use, creating convincing-looking aliens and monsters. The durability of the show is evidenced by how well it survived the loss of its original Superboy—it went on, gathering momentum, and lasted a full four years (and 99 episodes).

REGULAR CAST
Superboy/Clark Kent Johnny Haymes Newton (*Season One*),
Gerard Christopher (*from Season Two*)
Lana Lang Stacy Haiduk

Syndicated
99 color 25-minute episodes
8 October 1988–11 May 1992

(For more information, see *Superboy*.)

Season One
The Jewel of Techal
A Kind of Princess
Back to Oblivion
The Russian Exchange Student
Countdown to Nowhere

Bringing Down the House
The Beast and the Beauty
The Fixer
The Alien Solution
Troubled Waters
The Invisible People

Kryptonite Kills
Revenge of the Alien (Parts 1 & 2)
Stand Up and Get Knocked Down
Meet Mr. Mxyzptlk
Birdwoman of the Swamps
Terror from the Blue
War of the Species
Little Hercules
Mutant
The Phantom of the Third Dimension
Black Flamingo
Hollywood
Succubus
Luthor Unleashed

Season Two
With This Ring I Thee Kill (Part 1)
Lex Luthor, Sentenced to Death (Part 2)
Metallo
Young Dracula
Nightmare Island
Bizarro, the Thing of Steel (Part 1)
Battle with Bizarro (Part 2)
Mr. & Mrs. Superboy
Programmed for Death
Superboy's Deadly Touch
The Power of Evil
Super Menace
Superboy . . . Rest in Peace
Yellow Peril's Spell of Doom
Microboy
Run, Dracula, Run
Brimstone
Abandon Earth (Part 1)
Escape to Earth (Part 2)
Superstar
A Woman Called Tiger Eye
Revenge from the Deep
The Haunting of Andy McAlister
Nick Knack
The Secrets of Superboy
Johnny Cassanova and the Case of the Secret
   Serum

Season Three
The Bride of Bizarro (Part 1)
The Bride of Bizarro (Part 2)
The Lair

Neila
Roads Not Taken (Part 1)
Roads Not Taken (Part 2)
The Son of Icarus
Carnival
Test of Time
Mindscape
Superboy . . . Lost
Special Effects
Neila and the Beast
Golem
A Day in the Double LIfe
Body Swap
Rebirth (Part 1)
Rebirth (Part 2)
Werewolf
People vs. Metallo
Jackson & Hyde
Mind Games
Wish for Armageddon
Standoff
The Road to Hell (Part 1)
The Road to Hell (Part 2)

Season Four
A Change of Heart (Part 1)
A Change of Heart (Part 2)
The Kryptonite Kid
The Basement
Darla Goes Ballistic
Paranoia
Know Thine Enemy (Part 1)
Know Thine Enemy (Part 2)
Hell Breaks Loose
Into the Mystery
To Be Human (Part 1)
To Be Human (Part 2)
West of Alpha Centauri
Threesome (Part 1)
Threesome (Part 2)
Out of Luck
Who Is Superboy?
Cat and Mouse
Obituary for a Superhero
Metamorphosis
Rites of Passage (Part 1)
Rites of Passage (Part 2)

THE ADVENTURES OF SUPERMAN

Youngsters reared on the spectacular big-screen image of Christopher Reeve as the Man of Steel might need some persuading, but to generations of British and American fans Superman will always be George Reeves and yes, they believed *this* man could fly. Week after week they had the message drummed home, as indelibly as the ink on a *Daily Planet* headline: "Faster than a speeding bullet, more powerful than a locomotive, able to leap tall buildings at a single bound. Look . . . up in the sky . . . it's a bird . . . it's a plane . . . it's Superman!"

Reeves, a 6 ft. 2½ in., 195 lb. bachelor who'd succeeded where 200 previous job applicants had failed, was a former light-heavyweight boxer who'd studied acting alongside Victor Mature and Robert Preston. He'd been in love with Vivien Leigh in *Gone with the Wind* and appeared in other movie classics such as *Blood and Sand* and *From Here to Eternity*, and he'd actually first donned the superhero tights and underpants for a 1951 cinema feature *Superman and the Mole Men* (re-edited for the TV series as a two-part story *The Unknown People*).

Superman may have fought tirelessly for "truth, justice and the American way," but he was, of course, an alien, a survivor of the doomed planet Krypton. He'd been launched into space as an infant by his scientist father, Jor El, just before the planet exploded and crash-landed on Earth in a field near Smallville, USA, where he was discovered by a childless farm couple, Jonathan and Martha Kent, who adopted him and named him Clark.

Because the boy was from a larger world with a red sun, Earth's yellow sun endowed him with super powers of flight, strength, X-ray vision, hearing and invulnerability, his only weakness being Kryptonite—fragments of his old home planet—which invariably fell into the wrong hands. As a man, Clark moved to Metropolis, working as a reporter on the *Daily Planet*. As Clark, he was bespectacled, meek and mild-mannered, but at the drop of his snap-brimmed hat he became Superman, scourge of the underworld.

Other regulars in the series were naive cub reporter Jimmy Olsen, gruff *Planet* editor Perry White, Metropolis police chief Insp. Henderson, and Lois Lane, the *Planet*'s impulsive star reporter, enamored of Supie but contemptuous of Clark. Lois was played abrasively (in the first 26-week American season) by Phyllis Coates and toned down for the rest by Noel Neill.

Though Superman's origins were pure science fiction, the shows were basically crime melodramas, shot on a low budget of $15,000 each, at the rate of roughly two a week, and frequently called for the Man of Steel to rescue Lois, Jimmy or both from mortal danger and clutches of crazed scientists, gangsters, madmen and pirates. Occasionally there was a sci-fi theme to the story, such as "Superman in Exile," when contamination from gamma rays leads Superman into a self-imposed exile; "Panic in the Sky," when exposure to Kryptonite in a meteor induces amnesia; "Through the Time Barrier," in which a scientist's time machine sends him, a crook, Lois, Jimmy, Perry and Clark back to the Stone Age; and "Mr. Zero," in which a small man from outer space who can paralyze people by pointing his finger at them falls among thieves.

Special effects were unsophisticated but effective. Reeves took off via wires, hydraulics and springboards, landed by jumping off a ladder and flew by being filmed lying on a glass table, with the Metropolis skyline (actually Hollywood) matted in later. Imagination did the rest.

When Superman first flew across British screens in 1956, ATV in the Midlands managed a prolonged 18-month run of some 78 episodes. These were culled from the first five U.S. seasons but shown at random, only vaguely following the original seasonal flow. In fact, Noel Neill's Lois Lane was the first to be seen over there, while Phyllis Coates's acid-tongued version occasionally elbowed her milder counterpart out of the schedules for the odd week later in the run.

The last adventure of Superman was made in 1957. Two years later George Reeves, who had been so synonymous with the role that other acting parts were almost impossible to come by, shot himself. His shows, though, have run and run.

REGULAR CAST

Superman/Clark Kent George Reeves
Lois Lane Phyllis Coates *(U.S. Season One)*, Noel Neill *(from Season Two)*
Jimmy Olsen Jack Larsen *Perry White* John Hamilton
Insp. Henderson Robert Shayne

Producers: Robert Maxwell, Bernard Luber *(Season One)* Whitney Ellsworth *(the rest)*
Directors: Thomas Carr *(33)*, Lee Sholem *(11)*, George Blair *(26)*, Harry Gerstad *(20)*, Phil Ford *(8)*, Howard Bretherton *(1)*, Lew Landers *(2)*, George Reeves *(3)*
Principal writers: David Chantler, Jackson Gillis, Whitney Ellsworth

ABC Production
104 black and white 30-minute episodes (Seasons 1 and 2), color (3–6)
U.S. premiere: Autumn 1952
U.K. premiere (all b/w): 23 February 1956–63 September 1957 (ATV Midlands)

ALF

ALF was the latest in a line of American comedy series that set an alien in a typical Earth household so that we can look at our world through his eyes and see how dumb we really are.

It's 1980s insult comedy laced with traditional U.S. morality, a sophisticated line in wisecracking satire, and a lineage that can be traced back through *Mork and Mindy* as far as *My Favorite Martian*.

ALF is a 230-year-old "alien life form" called Gordon Shumway. He was born on the "lower east side" of the planet Melmac and he looks like a cross between an aardvark and a dwarf orangutan. His arrival on Earth is dramatic. His spaceship (a classic sports model called a Phlegm 220) crash-lands through the garage roof of a typical American suburban home. ALF takes up residence with the Tanner family and quickly disrupts their lives with his unusual habits (he likes to eat cats!) and assertive personality. ALF doesn't understand simple things like manners. He just blurts out statements and opinions with scant regard for the consequences. Children love him because he's irreverent and clued up on pop culture (all he knows about Earth is what he sees on TV). Naturally there are plenty of conflicts, but the family—even grumpy old dad, Willie Tanner—are protective, loyal and loving.

ALF is the puppet creation of a former comic magician called Paul Fusco and has become a worldwide star. Britain is one of more than 60 countries to have shown *ALF*. There's also an *ALF* cartoon series as well as *ALF: The Movie*.

REGULAR CAST
Willie Tanner Max Wright *Kate Tanner* Anne Schedeen
Lynn Tanner Andrea Elson *Brian Tanner* Benji Gregory
ALF Himself! (Paul Fusco, *Voice*)
Trevor Ochmonek John La Motta *Raquel Ochmonek* Liz Sheridan
Jake Ochmonek Josh Blake *(Seasons Two and Three)*
Neal Tanner J.M.J. Bulloch *(Season Four)*

Creator: Paul Fusco
Producer: Tom Patchett
Writers: Various, including Paul Fusco, Tom Patchett, Bob & Howard Bendetson
Directors: Various, including Peter Bonerz, Nancy Heydorn, Tom Patchett, Paul Fusco

102 color 30-minute episodes
U.S. premiere: 22 September 1986
U.K. premiere: 25 April 1987
(ITV)

ALIEN NATION

For this 1989 U.S. series *V* creator, Kenneth Johnson, returned to his theme of alien landings—only this time the extra-terrestrial presence was largely benign.

A spin-off from the 1988 movie, which had starred James Caan and Mandy Patinkin, *Alien Nation*—the series—was both a cop show and a thinly veiled but effective commentary on racial intolerance.

Set in 1995 Los Angeles, it teamed Matt Sikes and George Francisco as a detective duo whose backgrounds are literally worlds apart. Sikes is a divorced, streetwise LAPD cop—impulsive and aggressive. The more intellectual and thoughtful George is a Newcomer—one of 250,000 inhabitants from the planet Tencton, whose slave ship had crash-landed in the Mojave Desert three years before.

Humanoid in appearance, apart from their bald, mottled heads, vestigial ears and enlarged craniums, the Tenctonese have tried to assimilate into human culture, but being smarter than the average Earthman has not endeared them to all their hosts and they are often derisively referred to as "Slags." As with any dispossessed group, some resent their lot while others strive to break through that resentment.

George is the first Newcomer police officer to reach the rank of detective. He moves his family into a better neighborhood; they are also the first Newcomers on the block. His wife, Susan, who can tolerate the occasional prejudice, worries about her daughter, Emily, who must attend a new school where she is the only Newcomer, while son, Buck, is a rebel, refusing to adapt to his new planet, defying his parents by speaking his native language and joining a Newcomer gang.

While most of the integration problems are seen through his family's eyes, George must also overcome Sikes's initial hostility toward his new partner before they inevitably become buddies. Sikes also becomes involved with Cathy, a Newcomer biochemist who moves into his apartment block.

The cop element of the series is pretty straightforward—a variation on the "chalk and cheese combo" formula of more conventional police dramas. It is in Johnson's detailed depiction of an alien culture—complete with its own "subtitled" language, rituals and biology—that *Alien Nation* acquires a real edge.

The Tenctonese get drunk on soured milk, while salt water can kill them. The small of the back is a major erogenous zone and their reproductive methods are novel. It takes two males to impregnate a female, and males and females then share the pregnancy. In one episode Susan is "prepared" by a Binnaum, a member of a revered religious sect. In a later story she gives birth to their "pod," and George incubates it, going through the same mood swings and emotions experienced by pregnant women, before he finally gives birth to their baby (an emergency delivery by Sikes!).

The racial commentary is obvious but rarely gets preachy. One scene in which Emily is greeted by a hostile anti-alien mob on her first day at school is highly effective with a protective Sikes mocking and shaming their intolerance by actually inviting them to kill the young girl.

The slave origins of the Tenctonese are carefully inked in as details emerge of their submissive existence at the hands of sadistic and abusive Overseers on the slave ship. When the vessel crashed, many of the Overseers escaped by disguising themselves as slaves, and continue to cause trouble for the Newcomers on Earth.

One lighter aspect of the series is the way many Newcomers have adopted the names of famous Earth figures, real and fictional. Watch out for Albert Einstein, Isaac Newton and Thomas Edison, Edgar and Rita Allan Poe, Dorian Grey, Silas Marner and Charlotte Brontë, Buster Keaton and Wyatt Earp, Paul Revere and John-Paul Sartre—even Peter Rabbit!

To the disappointment of its many fans *Alien Nation* only lasted one season, ending in a cliffhanger—a "will they live or die" crisis for the Franciscos—which was finally resolved in a 1994 "reunion" TV movie *Alien Nation: Dark Horizon*, which saw the Newcomers facing annihilation, then enslavement, in an Overseer plot. Another three TV movies followed—1995's *Body and Soul, Millennium* (not to be confused with the Chris Carter series) in January 1996 and *The Enemy Within* in October 1996. One other movie, *The Udara Legacy*, aired in July 1997.

MAIN CAST

Detective Matthew Sikes Gary Graham   *George Francisco* Eric Pierpoint
Susan Francisco Michele Scarabelli   *Emily Francisco* Lauren Woodland
Buck Francisco Sean Six   *Cathy Frankel* Terri Treas
Albert Einstein Jeff Marcus
Semi-regulars: Capt. Grazer Ron Fassler   *Burns* Jeff Doucette
Sgt. Dobbs Lawrence Hilton-Jacobs   *Jill* Molly Morgan

Characters created by Rockne S. O'Bannon
Developed for television by Kenneth Johnson
Executive producer: Kenneth Johnson
Producers: Arthur Seidel, Tom Chehak, Diane Frolov
Music: Joe Harnell *(pilot)*, Steve Dorff, David Kurtz, Larry Herbstritt

22 color 60-minute episodes
U.S. premiere: 18 September 1989
U.K. premiere: 1990
(Sky One)
(The series finally made it to terrestrial TV on ITV from January 1995.)

Pilot

w Kenneth Johnson

Los Angeles, the future: Three years after an alien slave ship crash-landed in the Mojave Desert, the Newcomers have been assimilated into Earth culture. George Francisco, the first Newcomer police officer to make detective, is teamed with streetwise LA cop Matthew Sikes. Still bitter over the death of his former partner, Tuggs, Sikes is less than welcoming. Their first assignment, to investigate an apparent vagrant suicide, uncovers a plot to discredit the Newcomers by suggesting they will turn into deadly insect-like monsters. George also helps discover that Tuggs was killed by a fellow cop after uncovering her involvement in an Overseer plot to manufacture a gas to make the Tenctonese slaves submissive.

Puente Loyda Ramos
Jill Molly Morgan
Jill's mother Diane Civita
Dr. Lee Evan Kim
Lyddie L. Scott Campbell
Dr. Ramna John Patrick Reger
Ketnes Tim Russ
Dr. Hurwitz Richard Mehana
Marcos Tony Acierto
Bernardo Bert Rosario
Blentu Trevor Edmund

Director: Kenneth Johnson

Fountain of Youth

w Diane Frolov

George and Sikes uncover a doctor's scheme to prolong the lives of humans by killing his Newcomer patients and removing a gland that gives them a longer life span.

Uncle Moodri James Greene
Henry James Steve Rankin
Harriet Beecher Susan Gibney
Sofia James Bonnie Urseth
Dr. James Trenner Jason Beghe
Dr. Edward Windsor Joel Polis
Lisa Bankcroft Gretchen German
Beth Meadows Wendy Kaplan

Director: John McPherson

Little Lost Lamb

w Diane Frolov

Sikes and George track down the killer of a young Newcomer prostitute. Meanwhile, Uncle Moodri helps Buck come to terms with his guilt over killing a gang member and face up to his responsibilities.

Uncle Moodri James Greene
Blentu Trevor Edmond
Svabo Noon Orsatti
Mary Heather McAdam
Charlotte Brontë Shannon Wilcox

Dallas Kimberly Kates
Dorian Grey Will Bledsoe

Director: Kevin Hooks

Fifteen with Wanda

w Steven Long Mitchell & Craig W. Van Sickle

Sikes and George are assigned to protect a Newcomer key witness, Buster Keaton. But taken into hiding on his wedding night, Buster has not had time to consummate his marriage and is being driven crazy with desire. Meanwhile, George and Sikes both try to deal with problems involving their children.

Buster Keaton David Bowe
Wanda Sachi Parker
Sal Lori Petty
Victoria Fletcher Joan McMurtrey
Kirby Sikes Cheryl Pollak
Blentu Trevor Edmond
Svabo Noon Orsatti
Thor Wayne Pere

Director: Rob Bowman

Takeover

w Tom Chehak

Susan is taken hostage after getting caught up in a hoodlum raid on the police station, and George and Sikes go to her rescue.

Kenny Dunstan Charley Lane
Andrew Craig Ji-Tu Cumbuka
Diane Elrea Gwynyth Walsh
Capt. McKnight Michael Fairman
Letitia Rosario Camila Griggs
Harry Dundee Will Egan
Tom Mulden Tracey Walter

Director: Steven Dubin

The First Cigar

w Andrew Schneider & Diane Frolov

When he's landed with a huge tax bill, George seeks a personal loan from a Newcomer entrepreneur, but is later shocked to learn she is a kingpin in the Slagtown drugs trade.

Betsy Ross Diana Bellamy
Uncle Moodri James Greene
Vahan Steve Susskind
Ramna John Patrick Reger
Svabo Noon Orsatti
Nina Jennifer Banko
Ruth Steelman Carolyn Mignini

Director: John McPherson

The Night of the Screams

w Tom Chehak
As Halloween approaches, a serial killer is stalking Newcomers with an MO that is eerily similar to that of the hero of one of their most grisly legends, Tagdot, a rebellious slave who killed the Overseers by chopping off their hands.
Uncle Moodri James Greene
Teddy Roosevelt Wayne Powers
Coroner Barkley Meagen Ray
John Macy Bradford English
Paul Revere David Opatoshu
John-Paul Sartre Mitch Pileggi
Mrs. Sartre Anya Liffey

Director: Gwen Arner

Contact

w Joe Menosky
While investigating the murder of a famous astronomer, George and Sikes uncover a scheme to contact a space probe that is trying to locate the missing Newcomer slave ship.
Professor Charles Tower Donald Hotton
Carl Peterson Joel Polis
Marissa Myers Annabelle Gurwitch
Sergius Jeffrey Josephson
Mr. Kim Michael Paul Chan
Concierge Curt Lowens
Dr. Morales Vincent Leahr
Jerry Bielack John Apicella
John Barrymore Alexis Arquette

Director: John McPherson

Three to Tango

w Diane Frolov & Andrew Schneider
George and Sikes must track down a radical Purist killer who has been murdering a rare breed of Newcomer called Binnaums—members of a revered order who act as catalysts in Tenctonese birth rituals.
May O'Naize Dana Andersen
Goran Charles Hayward
Drevni Alan Scarfe
Isaac Newton Patrick Johnston

Director: Stan Lathan

The Game

w Steven Long Mitchell & Craig W. Van Sickle
When Newcomers start showing up dead, killed by a blast of sea water that has bored a hole through their chest, George discovers an Overseer is playing the same sadistic game of Newcomer Roulette he played aboard the slave ship.

Joe Comet Joel Swetow
Dean Flack Billy Ray Sharkey
Tom Edison Sam Anderson
Alva Edison Isabel Wolfe
Ruthra Bill Allen
Coolock Andreas Katsulas
Mrs. Comet Maggie Egan

Director: David Carson

Chains of Love

w Andrew Schneider & Diane Frolov
George trails a Newcomer woman who is apparently mating and then killing her lovers.
Ralph Emerson Bennett Liss
Leonard Darren Dalton
Dr. Roscoe Brennan Teddy Wilson
Johnny Appleseed Theodore Raimi
Jenny Moffat Caitlin O'Heaney
Daniel Thom Zimmerle
Lance Lott John Mese

Director: Harry S. Longstreet

The Red Room

w Steven Long Mitchell & Craig W. Van Sickle
George is haunted by a bad dream in which he is asked to kill people—and soon he and Sikes find themselves in the middle of a federal investigation tracking down a deranged Newcomer who was programmed to kill while in the quarantine camps.
Jeffries John P. Connolly
Dr. Marcie Wright Katherine Justice
Marcus Byer Chuck Bennett
Dr. Chris Pettit Ray Reinhardt
Lois Allen Michele Lamar Richards
Silas Marner Tom Dugan
Amanda Russle Patricia Heaton

Director: Chuck Bowman

Spirit of '95

w Tom Chehak
George and his family find themselves caught up in the fervor surrounding the drive to give Newcomers the vote, when an ardent campaigner is kidnapped.
The Senator Bryan Clark
Jack Pearlman Clarence Felder
Carol Wilmington Marla Fries
Max Klay Mark Joy
Wyatt Earp Mark Thomas Miller
Mike Wilmington Mark L. Taylor
Mr. Hopper Harvey Jason

Director: Harry S. Longstreet

Generation to Generation

w Andrew Schneider & Diane Frolov
Sikes and George follow the trail of a mysterious Tenctonese box that is deadly to those who do not understand its powers.
Uncle Moodri James Greene
Lowell Bratigan Timothy Scott
Henryk Glass Scott Jaeck
Phillip Dunaway Ryan Cutrona
Lucille Peggy Doyle
Sydney Foley Michael Faustino
Howard Thayer Francis Guinan
Ruiz Tony Major
Lois Allen Michele Lamar Richards

Director: John McPherson

Eyewitness News

w Charles S. Kaufman & Larry B. William, Steven Long Mitchell & Craig W. Van Sickle
While George basks in the media spotlight as a "model Newcomer," Sikes tries to track down a human obsessed with a Tenctonese woman he was involved with on a dial-a-porn service.
Laura Lane Angela Bassett
Louis Denton Rob King
Virginia Hamm Deborah Goodrich
Bailey Joseph Graham
Ernie Hugh Maguire
Mrs. Denton Kelly Jean Peters
Arvin Kaufman Gene Butler
Joe David Hoskins

Director: Lyndon Chubbuck

Partners

w David Garber & Bruce Kalish
Before Susan transfers the pod to George, Sikes sets out to prove his partner's innocence in a drug case.
Theo Miles Gilbert Lewis
Sgt. Baxley Terry Beaver
Ken Jester Bill Kalmenson
Bud Anderson Tom Byrd
Chester Charles Croften Hardester

Director: Stan Lathan

Real Men

w Diane Frolov & Andrew Schneider
After Susan gives birth to the pod, it's George's turn to incubate it in his pouch and he goes through the same mood swings as pregnant women. Ridiculed over his pregnancy, George becomes determined to prove his masculinity and helps Sikes on the case of human body builders using Tenctonese steroids. But after a confrontation with a drugged-up suspect, George gives birth prematurely . . .

Karina Debbie Barker
Nick Coletta William Shockley
Victor Wendkos A.D. Muyich
Dan Zimmer Robert Neary
Marty Penn Hank Garrett
Carl Oscar Dillon
Andrey Neil Nash
Sol Birnbaum Martin Garner

Director: John McPherson

Crossing the Line

w Steven Long Mitchell & Craig W. Van Sickle
When Sikes recognizes the handiwork of a serial murderer called The Doctor, who eluded him once before, he vows not to lose him a second time.
Doctor of Death Tobin Bell
Beatrice Zepeda Jenny Gago
Cyndy Heather McComb
Lois Allen Michele Lamar Richards
Dutchman Ivory Ocean

Director: Gwen Arner

Rebirth

w Tom Chehak
After he nearly dies in a hold-up, Sikes becomes obsessed with finding the Newcomer who he believes brought him back to life with a strange crystal.
Young Sikes Ryan Cash
Billy Boardman Raffi Diblasio
Sikes's Dad John Sudol
Peter Rabbit Brian Thompson
Yokno Ellen Wheeler

Director: Tom Chehak

Gimme, Gimme

w Andrew Schneider & Diane Frolov
George goes looking for the murderer of a Newcomer corporate executive who invented a durable synthetic fabric.
Marilyn Houston Kim Braden
Lee Smith Joseph Cali
Sleepy Phil Alan Fudge
Rita Allan Poe Beverly Leech
Edgar Allan Poe David Selburg
Lois Allen Michele Lamar Richards
Cyril Roman Armin Shimerman
Mr. Elias Michael Zand

Director: David Carson

The Touch

w Steven Long Mitchell & Craig W. Van Sickle
Sikes's friend Cathy finds her life in danger after she grows concerned that a young Newcomer boy is being groomed to be an Overseer by being prevented from receiving "the touch" by which Newcomers learn to love and care for people.
Andy Day Mitchell Allen
Mr. Eugene Doug Ballard
Andy, aged 13 Jonathan Brandis
Lorraine Welch Barbara Bush
Ella Day Dorothy Fielding
Helen Yvette Freeman
Beatrice Zepeda Jenny Gago
Rigac Mike Preston
Troy Martin La Platney

Director: Harry S. Longstreet

Green Eyes

w Diane Frolov & Andrew Schneider
George wins a promotion, and his relationship with Sikes is strained as they investigate the deaths of two prominent Newcomers infected by a lethal virus that kills within 36 hours. Then flowers arrive anonymously at George's home, where Susan and Emily smell them, unaware they have been laced with the deadly bacteria. Finding out his partner's family has been exposed to the virus, Sikes hurries to the hospital. Meanwhile, the perpetrator readies a batch that will be sprayed over the city, effectively wiping out the entire Newcomer population.
Marilyn Houston Kim Braden
Michael Bukowski Geoffrey Blake
Darlene Bryant Lee Bryant
Lorraine Welch Barbara Bush
Rick Parris John Calvin
Martha Edith Fields
Beatrice Zepeda Jenny Gago
Noah Ramsey Andras Jones
Judge Kaiser Thomas Knickerbocker
Lois Allen Michele Lamar Richards

Director: Tom Chehak

The TV Movies:

Dark Horizon

w Andrew Schneider & Diane Frolov
Sequel to the last episode of the series. Susan and Emily are both on life support after being poisoned by the Purists who are mass-producing a new bacteriological poison to wipe out the entire Tenctonese race on Earth. Meanwhile, in deep space, an elite Overseer is despatched as the vanguard of a mission to find and recapture the escaped Tenctonese and enslave the human race.
DC Beatrice Zepeda Jenny Gago
Lorraine Clark Susanna Thompson
Dr. Lois Allen Michele Lamar Richards
May O'Naize Dana Anderson

Phyllis Bryant Lee Bryant
Ahpossno Scott Petterson
Commander Burak Nina Foch
Celinite Priestess Susan Appling

Director: Kenneth Johnson

U.S. premiere: 25 October 1994
U.K. premiere: 27 June 1996

Body and Soul

w Diane Frolov & Andrew Schneider, Renee & Harry Longstreet
The appearance of a strange abandoned baby fuels reports of the first half-human, half-Tenctonese birth, and a strange Newcomer giant is stalking the streets. Meanwhile, Matt tries to pursue a more physical relationship with Cathy but has to take an evening class in "alien sex" first!
DC Beatrice Zepeda Jenny Gago
Giant Tiny Ron
Child Aimee & Danielle Warren
Dr. Adrian Tivoli Pamela Gordon
Benson Leon Russom
Karina Tivoli Kristin Davis

Director: Kenneth Johnson

U.S. premiere: 10 October 1995

Millennium

w Kenneth Johnson
Sikes and Francisco go after an unscrupulous cult leader who's using a mind-expanding Tenctonese artifact to lure followers, including Buck. Meanwhile, Emily gets a human boyfriend.
DC Beatrice Zepeda Jenny Gago
Jennifer Kerrie Keane
Alana Herta Ware
Calaban Steve Flynn
Marina del Rey Susan Diol
Jason Webster Brian Markinson
Felix David Faustino

Director: Kenneth Johnson

U.S. premiere: 2 January 1996

The Enemy Within

w Diane Frolov & Andrew Schneider
Matt investigates a mysterious group called the Eenos—lowlife aliens living in the sewers of Los Angeles who eat the city's rubbish. Albert and May ask George to help them have a child, but Susan is not amused, and Cathy moves in with Matt.
DC Beatrice Zepeda Jenny Gago
Queen Mother Tiny Ron
May O'Naize Dana Anderson

Director: Kenneth Johnson
U.S. premiere: 12 November 1996

ALIENS IN THE FAMILY

Six-part children's serial about a young alien who comes to Earth on a mission and gets involved with an ordinary British family.

Adapted from the novel by Margaret Mahy, it was a mixture of science fiction and domestic drama for although Bond, the student from the planet Galgonqua, is the obvious alien, there is another alien of sorts *inside* the family—12-year-old Jacqueline (Jake). She is feeling like an outsider in her new family unit, now that her father, David, is remarried to Pip, who already has a 12-year-old daughter, Dora, and a younger son, Lewis.

Jake and Dora are not getting on at all well when they first meet Bond, but agree to help him. Bond's mission involves reaching a particular stone circle before his pursuing enemies, the awesome Wirdegens, catch him. The dangerous chase takes the group cross-country until they finally reach the circle where the Wirdegens show up and congratulate Bond on passing what he suddenly remembers was a test all along.

Special effects in the series were devised by the award-winning team from the 1986 fantasy *The Box of Delights*.

REGULAR CAST
Bond Grant Thatcher   *Jake* Sophie Bold   *Dora* Clare Wilkie
Lewis Sebastian Knapp   *David* Rob Edwards   *Philippa* Clare Clifford
Solita Elizabeth Watkins   *Wirdegen leader* Granville Saxton
Wirdegens Sue Soames, Tony Birch, James Woodward

Dramatized by Allan Barker, *story by* Margaret Mahy
Executive producer: Paul Stone
Director: Christine Secombe
Video effects: Robin Lobb
Music: Roger Limb, BBC Radiophonic Workshop
Designer: Paul Montague

A BBC Production
6 color 25-minute episodes
18 November–23 December 1987
(BBC1)

THE AMAZING SPIDERMAN

Marvel's comic strip came to life in this American series starring Nicholas Hammond as the superhuman, skyscraper-scaling, web-hurling hero.

Spiderman kicked off with a pilot film that showed how Peter Parker, a student scientist and aspiring news photographer, is bitten by a spider contaminated with highly radioactive material, and acquires the power to climb sheer walls and an arachnid's sixth sense.

Using his scientific know-how, Parker invents a special adhesive fluid that can be shot from a special holder, solidifying on contact with the air to form a strong rope. Hiding his true identity behind the distinctive "Spidey" costume, Parker uses his powers against the forces of crime and evil.

And that was about it. Week after week Spiderman foiled the designs of various crooks, kidnappers or terrorists, but the series never really took off, only occasionally venturing beyond the routine crime format.

REGULAR CAST
Spiderman/Peter Parker Nicholas Hammond   *Rita* Chip Fields
J. Jonah Jameson Robert F. Simon   *Capt. Barbera* Michael Pataki
Aunt May Irene Tedrow

Executive producers: Charles Fries, Daniel R. Goodman
Producers: Robert Janes, Ron Satlof, Lionel E. Siegel
Writers: Various

Directors: Various

A Charles Fries and Daniel R. Goodman Production
12 color episodes (plus one pilot film), 60 mins., unless stated

Season One
Spiderman (pilot)
Deadly Dust (a 2-part story)
The Curse of Rava
Night of the Clones
Escort to Danger

Season Two
Captive Tower
Photo Finish

Wolfpack
The Con Caper
A Matter of State
The Kirkwood Haunting
The Chinese Web (90 mins.)

U.S. premiere: 5 April 1978
U.K. premiere: 4 September–27 November 1981
(ITV, London)

AMERICAN GOTHIC

Creepy horror show focusing on the devilish doings of a small town Southern sheriff as he forces his will and vision of the future on those around him. Nifty and effective. Created by Shaun Cassidy.

REGULAR CAST
Sheriff Lucas Buck Gary Cole   Caleb Temple Lucas Black
Selena Coombs Brenda Bakke   Dr. Portis Fields Michael Genevie
Dr. Billy Peale John Mese   Merlyn Temple Sarah Paulson
Deputy Ben Healy Nick Searcy   Gail Emory Paige Turco
Dr. Matt Crower Jake Weber

Episodes
Pilot
A Tree Grows in Trinity
Eye of the Beholder
Damned If You Don't
Dead to the World
Potato Boy (Originally unaired)
Meet the Beetles
Strong Arm of the Law
To Hell and Back
The Beast Within
Rebirth

Ring of Fire (Originally unaired)
Resurrector
Inhumanitas
The Plague Sower
Doctor Death Takes a Holiday
Learning to Crawl
Echo of Your Last Goodbye (Originally unaired)
Triangle
Strangler (Originally unaired)
The Buck Stops Here
Requiem

ARE YOU AFRAID OF THE DARK?

Are You Afraid of the Dark? premiered on Nickelodeon in September 1992. It is an anthology series with several different kids in it. Every show starts with a meeting of The Midnight Society, a group that gets together to trade scary stories around a campfire. As soon as someone starts telling a scary story we get to see what is happening in that story. This show was a spooky and scary show for kids before it was popular to be scary for kids, which makes it very hip.

CAST
Frank Jason Alisharan   Gary Ross Hall
Betty Ann Raine Pare-Coulls   Kiki Jodie Resther

Season One (1992–93)
The Tale of the Phantom Cab
The Tale of the Laughing in the Dark
The Tale of the Lonely Ghost
The Tale of the Twisted Claw
The Tale of the Hungry Hounds
The Tale of the Super Specs

The Tale of the Captured Souls
The Tale of the Nightly Neighbors
The Tale of the Dark Music
The Tale of the Jake and the Leprechaun
The Tale of the Sorcerer's Apprentice
The Tale of the Prom Queen
The Tale of the Pinball Wizard

Season Two (1993–94)
The Tale of the Final Wish
The Tale of the Midnight Madness
The Tale of Locker 22
The Tale of the Thirteenth Floor
The Tale of the Dream Machine
The Tale of the Dark Dragon
The Tale of the Whispering Walls
The Tale of the Frozen Ghost
The Tale of the Full Moon
The Tale of the Shiny Red Bicycle
The Tale of the Magician's Assistant
The Tale of the Hatching
The Tale of Old Man Corcoran

Season Three (1994–95)
The Tale of the Midnight Ride
The Tale of Apartment 214
The Tale of Watcher's Woods
The Tale of the Phone Police
The Tale of the Dollmaker
The Tale of the Bookish Baby-sitter
The Tale of the Carved Stone
The Tale of the Guardian's Curse
The Tale of the Curious Camera
The Tale of the Dream Girl
The Tale of the Quicksilver
The Tale of the Dangerous Soup
The Tale of the Crimson Clown

Season Four (1995–96)
The Tale of the Renegade Virus
The Tale of the Long Ago Locket
The Tale of the Water Demons
The Tale of Cutter's Treasure (1-hour episode)
The Tale of the Quiet Librarian
The Tale of the Silent Servant
The Tale of the Room for Rent
The Tale of the Ghastly Grinner
The Tale of the Fire Ghost
The Tale of the Closet Keepers
The Tale of the Unfinished Painting
The Tale of Train Magic

Season Five (1996–97)
The Tale of the Dead Man's Float
The Tale of the Jagged Sign
The Tale of Station 109.1
The Tale of the Mystical Mirror
The Tale of the Chameleons
The Tale of Prisoners Past
The Tale of C7
The Tale of Badge
The Tale of the Unexpected Visitor
The Tale of the Vacant Lot
The Tale of the Door Unlocked
The Tale of the Night Shift
The Tale of the Manaha

ARK II

After an environmental disaster has devastated the world, a group of technologically advanced do-gooders (and their talking monkey) travel the ravaged land, helping small colonies of survivors in a souped-up motor home. *Ark II* was a short-lived live-action children's show that appeared in the U.S. on Saturday mornings in 1976.

REGULAR CAST
Samuel José Flores *Ruth* Jean Marie Hon
Jonah Terry Lester

Episodes
The Flies
The Slaves
Wild Boy
The Robot
Omega
The Tank
The Cryogenic Man

The Rule
Robin Hood
The Drought
The Lottery
The Mind Group
The Balloon
Don Quixote
Orkus

ASTRONAUTS

Two-thirds of the British comedy team The Goodies, Bill Oddie and Graeme Garden, wrote this four-handed 1980s ITV sitcom about the first British space mission—a claustrophic affair consisting of two men, one woman and Bimbo the dog.

The astronauts—all temperamentally incompatible—were locked together in a two-roomed skylab for several months. Constantly under surveillance, their only contact with the ground was an abrasive, unsympathetic American mission controller.

Given such a situation, there was no opportunity to, as Bill Oddie put it, "bring in the funny plumber when things got dull." *Astronauts* relied on the interaction between the Skylab trio—commander Malcolm Mattocks, an ex-RAF type who was lousy at handling people, posh woman doctor Gentian Foster and truculent technical officer David Ackroyd—and the controller, Col. Beadle. There were gags about the jargon (Skylab was "Pooh," mission control "Piglet"), the tedious routine, going to the toilet, homesickness, mysterious messages and space madness with Mattocks assuring the rest of the crew that "God is my co-pilot."

Astronauts was not a giant leap for TV comedy, and despite a networked peak-time run on Monday nights, its success was only moderate.

MAIN CAST
Cmdr. *Malcolm Mattocks* Christopher Godwin
Dr. *Gentian Foster* Carmen Du Sautoy   *David Ackroyd* Barrie Rutter
Col. *Beadle* Bruce Boa

Writers: Graeme Garden, Bill Oddie
Director: Douglas Argent
Producers: Tony Charles, Douglas Argent
Executive producer: Allen McKeown
Designer: John Hickson

Developed for television by Witzend Productions/ATV Network Production
6 color 13-minute episodes
26 October–7 December 1981

AUTOMAN

The title character of this American crime adventure is a hologram—a three-dimensional computer-generated picture that becomes a super sleuth.

Automan starts life as a character in a computer, created by Los Angeles policeman Walter Nebicher. Walter, who'd rather be out on the streets chasing crooks, is stuck with a job on the police computer at headquarters. His boss doesn't think much of Walter—or his computer—until Automan comes along to walk through walls and reach the crimes other cops can't.

The result: The pair becomes Los Angeles Police Department's brightest crime-fighting duo.

REGULAR CAST
Automan Chuck Wagner   *Walter Nebicher* Desi Arnaz Jr.
Lt. *Jack Curtis* Robert Lansing   *Roxanne Caldwell* Heather McNair
Capt. *E.G. Boyd* Gerald S. O'Loughlin

Creator: Glen A. Larson
Producers: Glen A. Larson, Donald Kushner, Peter Locke
Writers: Various, including Glen A. Larson, Doug Hayes Jr.
Directors: Various, including Lee Katzin, Winrich Kolbe, Kim Manners

A Glen A. Larson Production
13 color episodes
(one × 70 mins., 12 × 50 mins.)
Automan (Pilot)
The Biggest Game in Town
Staying Alive While Running a High Flash Dance Fever

The Great Pretender
Ships in the Night
Unreasonable Facsimile
Flashes and Ashes
Renegade Run
Murder MTC
Murder, Take One
Death by Design
Club Ten
Zippers

U.S. premiere: 15 December 1983
U.K. premiere: 12 May–28 August 1984
(BBC1)

THE AVENGERS

Taking a literal definition, *The Avengers* was not a "science fiction show," but then neither was it a show to be taken literally . . .

One of the most potent cocktails of fantasy and adventure that television has seen, *The Avengers* began as a straight crime thriller, evolved into a stylish secret agent romp and hit its peak in the mid-1960s as a tongue-in-cheek extravaganza that pitted its hero and heroine against some of the most outlandish villains the underworld—or any world—could muster.

Like few other long-running series, *The Avengers* moved with the times—more than that, it helped shape them. From the high boots and black leather of Honor Blackman to the catsuits of Diana Rigg, the show quickly became an innovative frontrunner in 1960s style culture. It was adored in America for its cultivated "Britishness," and adored in Britain for its creation of a sophisticated fantasy world. Brian Clemens, a co-producer on the series, once said, "We admitted to only one class—and that was the upper. Because we were a fantasy, we have not shown policemen or colored men. And you have not seen anything as common as blood. We have no social conscience at all."

Running through the series, from the first episode in 1961 to the 161st in 1969, was the debonair figure of old Etonian adventurer John Steed, played to the hilt of urbane charm by Patrick Macnee. Originally he was the sidekick, a foil for Ian Hendry as the main star, Dr. David Keel. When Hendry departed, Macnee moved to center stage where he was joined by a succession of lovely, liberated ladies—Cathy Gale (Honor Blackman), Emma Peel (Diana Rigg), Tara King (Linda Thorson) and then, in *The New Avengers*, Purdey (Joanna Lumley).

(Author's note: As this *is* a science fiction guide, it would be inappropriate to include a full episode rundown since the sf streak didn't really emerge until the Emma Peel era when almost every week, it seemed, a mad scientist or some such evil genius with a chip on his shoulder would unleash a bizarre bid for power or fortune. So I've covered, in brief, the early years featuring Ian Hendry and Honor Blackman and lingered over the later ones. Anyone seeking further information should check out Dave Rogers's books on the series, such as *The Avengers Anew* or *The Complete Avengers*. Meanwhile . . .)

Season One
AVENGING TIME!

REGULAR CAST
Dr. David Keel Ian Hendry   *John Steed* Patrick Macnee
Carol Wilson (Keel's receptionist) Ingrid Hafner
One-Ten Douglas Muir *(semi-regular)*

Young doctor David Keel teams up with a mysterious undercover agent, John Steed, to avenge the death of his fiancée when she is shot by a drugs gang. Steed then recruits Keel for his crusade against crime and they tackle an assortment of villains from diamond thieves, protection racketeers and arsonists to industrial spies and political assassins. However, they also hunt a killer who uses a radioactive isotope as a murder weapon ("The Radioactive Man"), foil a doctor who is deep-freezing patients as part of his suspended animation experiments ("Dead of Winter") and run down saboteurs at an atomic research station working on a radiation shield for astronauts ("Dragonsfield").
Format: Sydney Newman, Leonard White
Producer: Leonard White
Principal directors: Don Leaver, Peter Hammond

Writers: 23 used, including Brian Clemens, Richard Harris, Terence Feely, Dennis Spooner, John Lucarotti, Eric Paice

An ABC Weekend Network Production
26 black and white 60-minute episodes
Hot Snow
Brought to Book
Square Root of Evil
Nightmare
Crescent Moon
Girl on the Trapeze
Diamond Cut Diamond
The Radioactive Man
Ashes of Roses
Hunt the Man Down
Please Don't Feed the Animals

Dance with Death
One for the Mortuary
The Springers
The Frighteners
The Yellow Needle
Death on the Slipway
Double Danger
Toy Trap
The Tunnel of Fear

The Far Distant Dead
Kill the King
Dead of Winter
The Deadly Air
A Change of Bait
Dragonsfield

7 January–30 December 1961
(ABC—Northern)

Season Two
FOUR PLAY . . .

REGULAR CAST
John Steed Patrick Macnee *Cathy Gale* Honor Blackman

Exit Dr. Keel, enter Cathy Gale . . . and others. The second season saw Steed enlist three new companions for his war on crime—nightclub singer Venus Smith, idealistic doctor Martin King and Cathy Gale, anthropologist and judo expert. Venus featured in six episodes, King in just three. It was Cathy Gale who helped redefine *The Avengers* and set the trend for the years to come.

Plotwise, the setup was much the same. Fast-paced crime thrillers, laced with humor but with a growing rapport between the principals. Mostly, adversaries were assassins, smugglers, spies or saboteurs, but one story ("The White Dwarf") had Earth apparently threatened by a rogue star, while another ("The Golden Eggs") featured a deadly virus, sealed inside two gold-plated eggs.
Venus Smith Julie Stevens
Dr. Martin King John Rollason

Producers: Leonard White *(1–14, 18 uncredited)*, John Bryce *(15–17, 19–26)*
Principal directors: Richmond Harding, Jonathan Alwyn, Don Leaver, Peter Hammond, Kim Mills
Writers: *19 used, including* Martin Woodhouse, Eric Paice, Malcolm Hulke, Terrance Dicks, Roger Marshall
An ABC Television Network Production
26 black and white 60-minute episodes

Mr. Teddy Bear
Propellant 23
The Decapod
Bullseye
Mission to Montreal
The Removal Men
The Mauritius Penny
Death of a Great Dane
The Sell-Out
Death on the Rocks
Traitor in Zebra
The Big Thinker
Death Dispatch
Dead on Course
Intercrime
Immortal Clay
Box of Tricks
Warlock
The Golden Eggs
School for Traitors
The White Dwarf
Man in the Mirror
Conspiracy of Silence
A Chorus of Frogs
Six Hands Across a Table
Killerwhale

29 September 1962–23 March 1963
(ABC—Northern)

Season Three
GALE FORCE . . .

REGULAR CAST
Patrick Macnee, Honor Blackman

In which Steed acquires a past ("Brief for Murder") and Cathy gets a trendy new wardrobe . . .

Season Three saw *The Avengers* production team crystallize the series' sophisticated appeal, with increasingly offbeat situations and dialogue that swung effortlessly between suspense and humor. Among the regular battalions of crooks, spies and killers, the odd fanatic was popping up. In "November Five," a politician threatens to blow up the

House of Commons with a stolen nuclear warhead; in "The Grandeur That Was Rome," a Caesar-fixated nutter tries to take over the world by spreading bubonic plague in food grain. A New Year episode was the most fantasy-filled yet, with Steed trying to winkle out a killer at a fancy dress party ("Dressed to Kill"). This was also the first season to be sold abroad.

Producer: John Bryce
Story editor: Richard Bates
Principal directors: Peter Hammond, Bill Bain, Kim Mills
Writers: 13 used, including Brian Clemens, Malcolm Hulke, Roger Marshall, Eric Paice
An ABC Television Network Production
26 black and white 60-minute episodes
Brief for Murder
The Undertakers
The Man with Two Shadows
The Nutshell
Death of a Batman
November Five

The Gilded Cage
Second Sight
The Medicine Men
The Grandeur That Was Rome
The Golden Fleece
Don't Look Behind You
Death à la Carte
Dressed to Kill
The White Elephant
The Little Wonders
The Wringer
Mandrake
The Secrets Broker
The Trojan Horse
Build a Better Mousetrap
The Outside-in Man
The Charmers
Concerto
Esprit De Corps
Lobster Quadrille
28 September 1963–21 March 1964
(ATV)

Season Four
M-APPEAL
REGULAR CAST
John Steed Patrick Macnee   *Emma Peel* Diana Rigg

Honor Blackman had dropped out after two seasons. With the arrival of the new female lead, *The Avengers* reached new heights of fantasy, with a string of science fiction–oriented plots. Among the most bizarre were the killer robots, the Cybernauts, a man-eating plant from outer space and a machine that created torrential downpours out of thin air. Invariably, these fantastic situations arose out of ordinary, innocent-seeming locations, heightening the feeling of surrealism. This also became the first season to be sold to America, where it secured a prime-time network slot. *The Avengers* had hit the big time. (U.S. premiere: 28 March 1966)

Producer: Julian Wintle
Associate producer: Brian Clemens
Music: Laurie Johnson

An ABC Television Network Production
26 black and white 1-hour episodes
28 September 1965–25 March 1966
(Rediffusion, London)

(With the series now centered firmly in a fantasy world of exaggerated Englishness, I've included a brief rundown of all the Emma Peel episodes.)

The Town of No Return

w Brian Clemens
Steed and Emma find that a remote Norfolk village has been overrun by subversives training a pocket army to take over the country.
Brandon Alan MacNaughtan
Smallwood Patrick Newell
Piggy Warren Terence Alexander
Vicar Jeremy Burnham

Director: Peter Graham Scott

The Grave-Diggers

w Malcolm Hulke
Steed digs up a bizarre plot to jam the nation's early-warning radar system.
Sir Horace Winslip Ronald Fraser
Johnson Paul Massie
Miss Thirlwell Caroline Blakiston
Nurse Spray Wanda Ventham
Dr. Marlow Lloyd Lamble

Director: Quentin Lawrence

The Cybernauts

w Philip Levene
The Avengers' best-remembered adversaries—unstoppable killer robots, controlled by a power-mad crippled scientist.
Dr. Armstrong Michael Gough
Benson Frederick Jaeger
Jephcott Bernard Horsfall
Tusamo Bert Kwouk

Director: Sidney Hayers

Death at Bargain Prices

w Brian Clemens
A tycoon known as King Kane plots to hold Britain to ransom by converting an entire department store into a giant atomic bomb.
Horatio Kane André Morell
Wentworth T.P. McKenna
Farthingale Allan Cuthbertson
Professor Popple Peter Howell
Massey George Selway
Marco Harvey Ashby
Jarvis John Cater

Director: Charles Crichton

Castle De'ath

w John Lucarotti
Beneath a Scottish castle, the laird and his gillie plan to corner the fish market by driving them into their underground base with three midget submarines.
Ian Gordon Jackson
Angus Robert Urquhart
McNab Jack Lambert
Robertson James Copeland

Director: James Hill

The Master Minds

w Robert Banks Stewart
A club for intellectuals is the cover for a fiendish plan to hypnotize top people.
Sir Clive Todd Laurence Hardy
Holly Trent Patricia Haines
Desmond Leeming Bernard Archard
Dr. Fergus Campbell Ian McNaughton
Davinia Todd Georgina Ward

Director: Peter Graham Scott

The Murder Market

w Tony Williamson
A marriage bureau runs a murder racket on the side.
Mr. Lovejoy Patrick Cargill

Dinsford Peter Bayliss
Barbara Wakefield Suzanne Lloyd
Robert Stone John Woodvine

Director: Peter Graham Scott

A Surfeit of H$_2$O

w Colin Finbow
A scientist develops a rain-making device, which he plans to sell as a weapon.
Jonah Noel Purcell
Dr. Sturm Albert Lieven
Joyce Jason Sue Lloyd
Eli Barker Talfryn Thomas

Director: Sidney Hayers

The Hour That Never Was

w Roger Marshall
Steed attends a squadron reunion at his old RAF camp—but arrives to find the place deserted.
Ridsdale Gerald Harper
Philip Leas Dudley Foster
Hickey Roy Kinnear
Porky Purser Roger Booth

Director: Gerry O'Hara

Dial a Deadly Number

w Roger Marshall
A hi-tech murder device is accounting for a series of deaths in the financial world.
Henry Boardman Clifford Evans
Ruth Boardman Jan Holden
Fitch John Carson
John Harvey Peter Bowles
Frederick Yuill Gerald Sim

Director: Don Leaver

Man-Eater of Surrey Green

w Philip Levene
Steed and Emma trace several missing scientists to a research establishment where a man-eating plant from outer space is growing to dangerous size.
Sir Lyle Peterson Derek Farr
Dr. Sheldon Athene Seyler
Laura Burford Gillian Lewis

Director: Sidney Hayers

Two's a Crowd

w Philip Levene
Battling a quartet of spies, Steed finds himself facing some lethal toys—from a midget sub to model aircraft.
Brodny Warren Mitchell
Pudeshkin Wolfe Morris
Vogel Julian Glover
Ivenko John Bluthal

Director: Roy Baker

Too Many Christmas Trees

w Tony Williamson
A Dickensian party is a cover for the hosts' mind-bending attempts to unlock secret information in Steed's head.
Brandon Story Mervyn Johns
Dr. Felix Teasel Edwin Richfield
Janice Crane Jeanette Sterke

Director: Roy Baker

Silent Dust

w Roger Marshall
Steed and Emma investigate how whole areas of the countryside are being laid to waste—and uncover another bizarre plot to take over the country.
Omrod William Franklyn
Mellors Conrad Phillips
Croft Norman Bird
Clare Prendergast Isobel Black

Director: Roy Baker

Room without a View

w Roger Marshall
A fanatical hotelier tries to use kidnapped scientists to realize his plans for a chain of luxury hotels around the world.
Chessman Paul Whitsun-Jones
Varnals Peter Jeffrey
Carter Philip Latham
Pushkin Vernon Dobtcheff

Director: Roy Baker

Small Game for Big Hunters

w Philip Levene
Another dastardly plot—this time to use a new species of tsetse fly to take over a tropical country.
Col. Rawlings Bill Fraser
Simon Trent James Villiers
Swain Liam Redmond
Fleming Peter Burton

Director: Gerry O'Hara

The Girl from Auntie

w Roger Marshall
Emma gets held captive in a cage and Steed has to bid at auction to release her.
Georgie Price-Jones Liz Fraser
Gregorio Auntie Alfred Burke
Arkwright Bernard Cribbins
Ivanov David Bauer

Director: Roy Baker

The Thirteenth Hole

w Tony Williamson
Steed and Emma uncover a satellite spy ring—in a secret chamber beneath the 13th green of a golf course.
Reed Patrick Allen
Col. Watson Hugh Manning
Dr. Adams Peter Jones
Collins Francis Matthews

Director: Roy Baker

Quick-Quick Slow Death

w Robert Banks Stewart
A dance school is being used to infiltrate foreign spies into the country.
Lucille Banks Eunice Gayson
Ivor Bracewell Maurice Kaufmann
Nicki Carole Gray
Chester Read Larry Cross

Director: James Hill

The Danger Makers

w Roger Marshall
Trying to infiltrate a secret society whose members crave mortal danger, Emma has to negotiate a metal ring along a tortuous course of live electrical poles where one touch would mean instant death by electrocution.
Maj. Robertson Nigel Davenport
Dr. Lang Douglas Wilmer
Col. Adams Fabia Drake
Peters Moray Watson

Director: Charles Crichton

A Touch of Brimstone

w Brian Clemens
Steed and Emma unmask the notorious Hellfire Club—a replica of an 18th-century organization dedicated to overthrowing the government.
John Cartney Peter Wyngarde
Lord Darcy Colin Jeavons
Sara Carol Cleveland
Horace Robert Cawdron

Director: James Hill

What the Butler Saw

w Brian Clemens
Steed poses as a butler to expose an association that is selling vital defense plans.
Hemming Thorley Walters
Benson John Le Mesurier
Group Capt. Miles Denis Quilley
Maj. Gen. Goddard Kynaston Reeves

Director: Bill Bain

The House That Jack Built

w Brian Clemens
Emma is imprisoned in a house that is a huge machine—the posthumous revenge of a crazed, embittered scientist who once worked for her father.
Prof. Keller Michael Goodliffe
Burton Griffith Davies
Withers Michael Wynne
Pennington Keith Pyott

Director: Don Leaver

A Sense of History

w Martin Woodhouse
A fascist group tries to eliminate the last surviving founder of a plan to eradicate world poverty—at a Robin Hood–theme rag ball.
Richard Carlyon Nigel Stock
Dr. Henge John Barron
Grindley John Glyn-Jones
Duboys Patrick Mower
Marianne Jacqueline Pearce

Director: Peter Graham Scott

How to Succeed . . . at Murder

w Brian Clemens
A keep-fit school is the cover for a group of modern-day suffragettes intent on the elimination of all men.
Mary Merryweather Sarah Lawson
Sara Penny Angela Browne
Gladys Murkle Anne Cunningham
Henry Throgbottom Artro Morris
Joshua Rudge Jerome Willis

Director: Don Leaver

Honey for the Prince

w Brian Clemens
Steed and Emma foil an organization called Quite Quite Fantastic Ltd., which helps create people's fantasies—including assassination.
Ponsonby-Hopkirk Ron Moody
Prince Ali Zia Mohyeddin
Arkadi George Pastell
B. Bumble Ken Parry

Director: James Hill

Seasons Five/Six
Regular cast as for Season Four

With the American market now open, the next Emma Peel seasons were *The Avengers'* first to be filmed in color—a vital clause in the U.S. deal. The humor was as offbeat as ever, but the hazards and plots became even more way-out, reflecting the audience's growing fascination with the fantasy aspects of the series.
Executive producer: Julian Wintle
Producers: Albert Fennell, Brian Clemens

An ABC Television Network Production

Season Five
16 color 60-minute episodes

13 January–5 May 1967
(Rediffusion, London)

From Venus with Love

w Philip Levene
Steed and Emma tangle with the British Venusian Society, whose members are being fried by laser beams.
Venus Browne Barbara Shelley
Primble Philip Locke
Brigadier Whitehead Jon Pertwee
Crawford Derek Newark
Bertram Smith Jeremy Lloyd

Director: Robert Day

The Fear Merchants

w Philip Levene
Rival industrialists are being eliminated by a strange organization that exposes its victims to their greatest fear until they are driven out of their minds.
Pemberton Patrick Cargill
Raven Brian Wilde
Gilbert Garfield Morgan
Dr. Voss Annette Carell
Crawley Andrew Keir

Director: Gordon Flemyng

Escape in Time

w Philip Levene
A time machine, which apparently enables criminals to escape into the past, turns out to be a series of perfectly furnished rooms in a large mansion.
Thyssen Peter Bowles
Clapham Geoffrey Bayldon
Vesta Judy Parfitt
Anjali Imogen Hassall

Director: John Krish

The See-Through Man

w Philip Levene
Steed and Emma expose an invisible enemy agent as
an elaborately staged series of tricks.
Elena Moira Lister
Brodny Warren Mitchell
Quilby Roy Kinnear
Ackroyd Jonathan Elsom

Director: Robert Asher

The Bird Who Knew Too Much

w Brian Clemens, *story by* Alan Pattillo
Top secret information about a new missile base is
being smuggled east—in the mind of a trained par-
rot!
Jordan Ron Moody
Samantha Slade Ilona Rodgers
Tom Savage Kenneth Cope
Cunliffe Anthony Valentine

Director: Roy Rossotti

The Winged Avenger

w Richard Harris
A deranged cartoonist believes he is the hero of his
own cartoon strip, *The Winged Avenger,* and has
been killing evil, ruthless men.
Sir Lexius Cray Nigel Green
Prof. Poole Jack MacGowran
Arnie Packer Neil Hallett
Stanton Colin Jeavons

Directors: Gordon Flemyng, Peter Duffell

The Living Dead

w Brian Clemens, *story by* Anthony Marriott
Steed and Emma go ghost hunting and unearth a
vast underground city built to house 20,000 people
after a nuclear bomb has been dropped on Britain.
Masgard Julian Glover
Mandy Pamela Ann Davy
Geoffrey Howard Marion Crawford
Rupert Edward Underdown

Director: John Krish

The Hidden Tiger

w Philip Levene
PURRR, an organization of cat lovers, is plotting to
overthrow the entire country by using an electronic
device that will make cats attack at a given signal.

Cheshire Ronnie Barker
Dr. Manx Lyndon Brook
Angora Gabrielle Drake
Nesbitt John Phillips

Director: Sidney Hayers

The Correct Way to Kill

w Brian Clemens
Steed and Emma join forces with a pair of enemy
agents to trap a murderer. (Remake of Season Three
episode "The Charmers.")
Olga Anna Quayle
Nutski Michael Gough
Ivan Philip Madoc
Ponsonby Terence Alexander
Percy Peter Barkworth

Director: Charles Crichton

Never, Never Say Die

w Philip Levene
A scientist has created computerized duplicates that
he wants to use to keep great minds alive.
Prof. Stone Christopher Lee
Dr. Penrose Jeremy Young
Dr. James Patricia English
Eccles David Kernan

Director: Robert Day

Epic

w Brian Clemens
A crazed Hollywood veteran film director wants
Emma to star in his latest epic—*The Destruction of
Mrs. Emma Peel.*
Stewart Kirby Peter Wyngarde
Damita Syn Isa Miranda
ZZ Von Schnerk Kenneth J. Warren

Director: James Hill

The Superlative Seven

w Brian Clemens
Steed joins a group of invited specialists who are
taken to a deserted island and told only one of them
will leave . . .
Hana Wilde Charlotte Rampling
Mark Dayton Brian Blessed
Jason Wade James Maxwell
Max Hardy Hugh Manning
Jessel Donald Sutherland

Director: Sidney Hayers

A Funny Thing Happened on the Way to the Station

w Bryan Sherriff (*alias* Brian Clemens *&* Roger Marshall)
Steed and Emma foil a plot to blow up the Prime Minister's train.
Crewe John Laurie
Groom Drewe Henley
Bride Isla Blair
Salt Tim Barrett
Admiral Richard Caldicott
Ticket collector James Hayter

Director: John Krish

Something Nasty in the Nursery

w Philip Levene
The Guild of Noble Nannies are nobbling noblemen and stealing vital secrets.
Mr. Goat Dudley Foster
Miss Lister Yootha Joyce
Beaumont Paul Eddington
Sir George Collins Patrick Newell
Gordon Trevor Bannister
Martin Clive Dunn
Nanny Brown Penelope Keith

Director: James Hill

The Joker

w Brian Clemens
Prendergast, a deranged vicious criminal, stages an elaborate plot to kill Emma. (Remake of Season Three's "Don't Look Behind You.")
Prendergast Peter Jeffrey
Ola Sally Nesbitt
Strange young man Ronald Lacey

Director: Sidney Hayers

Who's Who???

w Philip Levene
An enemy agent uses his latest invention to transfer the minds of two assassins into the bodies of Steed and Emma.
Lola Patricia Haines
Basil Freddie Jones
Major B. Campbell Singer
Krelmar Arnold Diamond

Director: John Moxey

Season Six
8 color 60-minute episodes

28 September–17 November 1967
(Rediffusion, London)

Return of the Cybernauts

w Philip Levene
Back come the killer robots controlled by a rich art collector who wants to dispose of Steed and Emma by the most gruesome means possible.
Paul Beresford Peter Cushing
Benson Frederick Jaeger
Dr. Neville Charles Tingwell
Prof. Chadwick Fulton Mackay
Rosie Aimi MacDonald

Director: Robert Day

Death's Door

w Philip Levene
Enemy agents try to sabotage a conference by manipulating the participants' dreams.
Boyd Clifford Evans
Stapley William Lucas
Lord Melford Allan Cuthbertson
Becker Marne Maitland

Director: Sidney Hayers

The £50,000 Breakfast

w Roger Marshall, *story by* Roger Marshall *&* Jeremy Scott
Plotters try to benefit by concealing a financier's death. (Remake of Season Two's "Death of a Great Dane.")
Glover Cecil Parker
Miss Pegrum Yolande Turner
Sir James Arnall David Langton
Judy Anneke Wills
Minister Cardew Robinson

Director: Robert Day

Dead Man's Treasure

w Michael Winder
Emma is wired to a racing car simulator that goes faster and faster to force her to offer a clue to lost treasure.
Mike Norman Bowler
Penny Valerie Van Ost
Alex Edwin Richfield
Carl Neil McCarthy
Benstead Arthur Lowe

Director: Sidney Hayers

You Have Just Been Murdered

w Philip Levene
A blackmailer makes "mock" attempts on the lives of millionaires to force them to pay—and kills them for real if they don't.
Unwin Barrie Ingham
Lord Maxted Robert Flemyng
Needle George Murcell
Rathbone Leslie French
Jarvis Geoffrey Chater

Director: Robert Asher

The Positive Negative Man

w Tony Williamson
The head of a shelved research project takes his revenge—using phenomenal electrical charges as his weapon.
Cresswell Ray McAnally
Haworth Michael Latimer
Cynthia Wentworth-Howe Caroline Blakiston
Mankin Peter Blythe
Maurice Jubert Sandor Elès

Director: Robert Day

Murdersville

w Brian Clemens
Steed and Emma discover that the townsfolk of a small, sleepy village operate a discreet service—murder!
Mickle Colin Blakeley
Hubert John Ronane
Dr. Haynes Ronald Hines
Prewitt John Sharp
Jenny Sheila Fearn

Director: Robert Asher

Mission . . . Highly Improbable

w Philip Levene
Steed and Emma are among several people cut down to size by a scientist's reducing ray.
Shaffer Ronald Radd
Susan Jane Merrow
Prof. Rushton Noel Howlett
Chivers Francis Matthews
Gifford Nicholas Courtney

Director: Robert Day

Season Seven
TARA, MRS. PEEL

REGULAR CAST
John Steed Patrick Macnee Tara King Linda Thorson
Mother Patrick Newell Rhonda Rhonda Parker

And so to Tara King . . . the least distinctive *Avengers* girl, who entered the scene in the opening handover episode that also featured the departure of Emma Peel (Diana Rigg, who had left the show, had agreed to do one last episode). Linda Thorson was a controversial choice as her replacement—she came to the series fresh out of drama school. And there was to be no special fighting technique for Tara—she'd simply use whatever came to hand. The seventh season also introduced two other new characters with the American market in mind—Steed's outsize boss, Mother, and his Amazonian secretary, Rhonda. A running gag had Mother's "office" turning up in the most unexpected places—the top deck of a London bus, the middle of a field, even a swimming pool.

The plots shifted their stance now, with more emphasis on far-fetched secret agent–style plots.
Executive producer: Gordon L.T. Scott
Producers: Albert Fennell, Brian Clemens
Music: Laurie Johnson, Howard Blake

Story consultant: Philip Levene
Story editor: Terry Nation

An ABC Television Production
33 color 60-minute episodes
25 September 1968–21 May 1969
(Thames, London)

The Forget-Me-Knot

w Brian Clemens
Emma is kidnapped . . . there's a traitor in Mother's section . . . and Steed winds up with a new partner—Agent 69, Tara King.
Emma Peel Diana Rigg
Sean Mortimer Patrick Kavanagh
George Burton Jeremy Young
Karl Alan Lake

Director: James Hill

Game

w Richard Harris
A vengeful games king, Bristow, forces Steed to play a bizarre game, "Super Secret Agent," to save the life of Tara, who is trapped in a giant hourglass.
Bristow Peter Jeffrey
Manservant Garfield Morgan
Prof. Witney Aubrey Richards
Brig. Wishforth-Browne Anthony Newlands

Director: Robert Fuest

Super-Secret Cypher Snatch

w Tony Williamson
A window-cleaning firm, Classy Glass Cleaning, is the front for a group of hypnotic thieves.
Peters John Carlisle
Maskin Simon Oates
Lather Nicholas Smith
Webster Allan Cuthbertson

Director: John Hough

You'll Catch Your Death

w Jeremy Burnham
Steed sniffs out a plot to gain power using a deadly concentrated cold virus that makes its victims sneeze to death.
Col. Timothy Roland Culver
Butler Valentine Dyall
Glover Fulton Mackay
Matron Sylvia Kay
Dexter Dudley Sutton

Director: Paul Dickson

Split!

w Brian Clemens *(and* Dennis Spooner—*uncredited)*
An enemy mastermind tries to transfer a killer's personality to Tara's mind.
Lord Barnes Nigel Davenport
Peter Rooke Julian Glover
Dr. Constantine Bernard Archard
Harry Mercer Maurice Good

Director: Roy Baker

Whoever Shot Poor George Oblique Stroke XR40

w Tony Williamson
A computer is given a "brain transplant" by a cybernetic surgeon to discover the identity of a traitor.
Jason Dennis Price
Pelley Clifford Evans
Loris Judy Parfitt
Tobin Frank Windsor

Director: Cyril Frankel

False Witness

w Jeremy Burnham
Steed and Tara face a problem—how to unmask a traitor when it seems everyone is lying. It must be something in the milk.
Land Rio Fanning
Melville Barry Warren
Lord Edgefield William Job
Sloman Dan Meaden
Sykes John Bennett
Sir Joseph Tony Steedman

Director: Charles Crichton

All Done with Mirrors

w Leigh Vance
Steed is under house arrest at Mother's swimming pool and Tara is sent to unravel a mystery centered on a lighthouse.
Watney Dinsdale Landen
Sparshott Peter Copley
Barlow Edwin Richfield
Col. Withers Michael Trubshawe
Pandora Joanna Jones

Director: Ray Austin

Legacy of Death

w Terry Nation
An ornate dagger is the key to a secret treasure, and elderly Henry Farrer will go to great lengths to hang on to it.
Farrer Richard Hurndall
Sidney Stratford Johns
Humbert Ronald Lacey
Baron Von Orlak Ferdy Mayne
Dickens Kynaston Reeves
Oppenheimer Peter Swanwick

Director: Don Chaffey

Noon Doomsday

w Terry Nation
Gerald Kafka, head of Murder International, is out of jail and bent on revenge against the man who put him there—John Steed.
Farrington Ray Brooks
Grant T.P. McKenna
Kafka Peter Bromilow
Sunley Anthony Ainley
Perrier Peter Halliday

Director: Peter Sykes

Look (Stop Me If You've Heard This One), but There Were These Two Fellers . . .

w Dennis Spooner
Steed and Tara pose as a pantomime horse to deliver the knockout blow to Mr. Punch and his vaudevillian killers.
Maxie Martin Jimmy Jewel
Jennings Julian Chagrin
Bradley Marler Bernard Cribbins
Marcus Rugman John Cleese
Seagrave John Woodvine
Fiery Frederick Talfryn Thomas

Director: James Hill

Have Guns . . . Will Haggle

w Donald James
Steed and Tara double in ballistics in their duel with some gun-runners (part of an aborted Tara King pilot called "Invitation to a Killing").
Col. Nsonga Johnny Sekka
Adriana Nicola Pagett
Conrad Jonathan Burn
Spencer Timothy Bateson

Director: Ray Austin

They Keep Killing Steed

w Brian Clemens
A group of villains hatch a plot to provide one of their agents with a replica of Steed's face so he can plant a bomb at a peace conference.
Baron Von Curt Ian Ogilvy
Arcos Ray McAnally
Zerson Norman Jones
Capt. Smythe Bernard Horsfall

Director: Robert Fuest

The Interrogators

w Richard Harris & Brian Clemens
Col. Mannering sets up a brilliant plan to extract information from secret agents—in a dentist's waiting room.
Col. Mannering Christopher Lee
Minnow David Sumner
Caspar Philip Bond
Blackie Glynn Edwards

Director: Charles Crichton

The Rotters

w Dave Freeman
A madman threatens to unleash a highly contagious dry-rot virus on Europe.

Kenneth Gerald Sim
George Jerome Willis
Pym Eric Barker
Palmer John Nettleton

Director: Robert Fuest

Invasion of the Earthmen

w Terry Nation
The fanatical head of the strange Alpha Academy is training his students for the conquest of outer space.
Brett William Lucas
Huxton Christian Roberts
Emily Lucy Fleming
Bassin Christopher Chittell

Director: Don Sharp

Killer

w Tony Williamson
Steed and his fellow agents are threatened by a deadly assassin called REMAK (Remote Electro-Matic Agent Killer), a computer programmed for murder.
Lady Diana Forbes-Blakeney Jennifer Croxton
Merridon Grant Taylor
Brinstead William Franklyn
Clarke Richard Wattis

Director: Cliff Owen

The Morning After

w Brian Clemens
With the help of quadruple agent Merlin, Steed and Tara foil a brigadier's plot to hold the government to ransom with a nuclear bomb.
Merlin Peter Barkworth
Jenny Penelope Horner
Brig. Hansing Joss Ackland
Sgt. Hearn Brian Blessed

Director: John Hough

The Curious Case of the Countless Clues

w Philip Levene
Countless clues suggest that the murder in Dawson's flat was committed by press tycoon William Burgess—but Steed isn't so sure.
Earle Anthony Bate
Gardiner Kenneth Cope
Stanley Tony Selby
Doyle Peter Jones
Burgess George A. Cooper
Flanders Edward de Souza

Director: Don Sharp

Wish You Were Here

w Tony Williamson
A holiday hotel proves an unusual prison for Tara and her uncle, while their captors take over his vast business empire.
Charles Merrydale Liam Redmond
Maxwell Robert Urquhart
Basil Brook Williams
Parker Dudley Foster
Mellor Richard Caldicott

Director: Don Chaffey

Love All

w Jeremy Burnham
Civil servants are leaking secrets after reading a book that's hypnotizing them to fall in love with the next person they see.
Martha Veronica Strong
Bromfield Terence Alexander
Sir Rodney Robert Harris
Thelma Patsy Rowlands

Director: Peter Sykes

Stay Tuned

w Tony Williamson
Steed is hypnotized and conditioned to kill Mother.
Proctor Gary Bond
Lisa Kate O'Mara
Father Iris Russell
Kreer Roger Delgado

Director: Don Chaffey

Take Me to Your Leader

w Terry Nation
Mother is suspected of defecting to the enemy, and to clear his name, Steed and Tara have to track the destination of an unusual talking briefcase.
Stonehouse Patrick Barr
Capt. Tim John Ronane
Cavell Michael Robbins
Audrey Long Penelope Keith

Director: Robert Fuest

Fog

w Jeremy Burnham
Steed and Tara are on the trail of the Gaslight Ghoul, a murderer who is killing off delegates to a peace conference with the Victorian style of Jack the Ripper.
President Nigel Green
Travers Guy Rolfe

Carstairs Terence Brady
Sanders Paul Whitsun-Jones

Director: John Hough

Who Was That Man I Saw You With?

w Jeremy Burnham
Tara is accused of being a double agent and Steed has just 24 hours to clear her name.
Fairfax William Marlowe
Gen. Hesketh Ralph Michael
Zaroff Alan Browning
Gilpin Alan MacNaughtan
Dangerfield Alan Wheatley
Phillipson Bryan Marshall

Director: Don Chaffey

Homicide and Old Lace

w Malcolm Hulke & Terrance Dicks
Mother tells a story . . . of how Steed and Tara thwarted the Great Great Britain Crime—the theft of every art treasure in the country.
Harriet Joyce Carey
Georgina Mary Merrall
Col. Corf Gerald Harper
Dunbar Keith Baxter
Fuller Edward Brayshaw

Director: John Hough

Thingumajig

w Terry Nation
Steed and Tara do battle with a killer black box that feeds on electricity.
Teddy Jeremy Lloyd
Kruger Iain Cuthbertson
Truman Willoughby Goddard
Major Star Hugh Manning

Director: Leslie Norman

My Wildest Dream

w Philip Levene
A psychiatrist is conditioning patients to kill their enemies, and Steed is in danger from a jealous rejected suitor of Tara's.
Jaeger Peter Vaughan
Tobias Derek Godfrey
Chilcott Edward Fox
Slater Philip Madoc
Nurse Owen Susan Travers

Director: Robert Fuest

Requiem

w Brian Clemens
Steed is assigned to protect Miranda Loxton, key witness in a case against Murder International.
Miranda Angela Douglas
Firth John Cairney
Wells John Paul
Murray Denis Shaw
Rista Terence Sewards

Director: Don Chaffey

Take-Over

w Terry Nation
A gang of crooks takes over a country house intending to train a long-range weapon on a nearby conference.
Grenville Tom Adams
Laura Elisabeth Sellars
Bill Michael Gwynn
Circe Hilary Pritchard
Sexton Garfield Morgan

Director: Robert Fuest

Pandora

w Brian Clemens
Tara is brainwashed into believing she is a senile man's old flame by two brothers out to steal his hidden fortune.
Rupert Lasindall Julian Glover

Henry Lasindall James Cossins
Juniper John Laurie
Miss Faversham Kathleen Byron
Uncle Gregory Peter Madden

Director: Robert Fuest

Get-a-Way!

w Philip Levene
A "chameleon" liquid enables three Russian agents to escape from an impregnable monastery and carry out their mission to kill three British agents—including Steed.
Col. James Andrew Keir
Rostov Vincent Harding
Neville Terence Langdon
Lubin Robert Russell
Ezdorf Peter Bowles

Director: Don Sharp

Bizarre

w Brian Clemens
Steed and Tara try to get to the bottom of the mystery of the disappearing bodies at Happy Meadows Cemetery.
Capt. Cordell James Kerry
Jonathan Jupp John Sharp
Happychap Roy Kinnear
The Master Fulton Mackay

Director: Leslie Norman

THE NEW AVENGERS

REGULAR CAST
John Steed Patrick Macnee *Purdey* Joanna Lumley
Mike Gambit Gareth Hunt

1976 saw the return of John Steed with two "New Avengers"—Joanna Lumley as the long-legged, high-kicking Purdey and Gareth *Upstairs Downstairs* Hunt as the dour, kung-fu champ and weapons expert Mike Gambit.

The plots were similar to the Tara King *Avengers* era, with plenty of spy-type mysteries and less sf, but still stamped with the familiar fantasy style. The Cybernauts returned for one more crack at Steed and Co. in "The Last of the Cybernauts . . . ??," a disease-carrying man whose touch spelled instant death stalked Purdey in "The Midas Touch," and a man with the power to control birds was intent on taking over the world with his feathered army in "Cat Amongst the Pigeons."

Despite massive press hype (much of it centering on Joanna Lumley's stockings), *The New Avengers* never achieved the renown of their 1960s predecessors, though the series did good business around the world.

Producers: Albert Fennell, Brian Clemens
Writers: Brian Clemens, Dennis Spooner, Terence Feely, John Goldsmith
Directors: 12 used, principally Ray Austin, Sidney Hayers

Music: Laurie Johnson

An Avengers (Film and TV) Enterprises Ltd. Production and IDTV TV Production, Paris
26 color 60-minute episodes

Season One

The Eagle's Nest
House of Cards
The Last of the Cybernauts . . . ??
The Midas Touch
Cat Amongst the Pigeons
Target!
To Catch a Rat
The Tale of the Big Why
Faces
Gnaws
Dirtier by the Dozen
Sleeper
Three Handed Game

19 October 1976–19 January 1977
(Thames)

Season Two

Dead Men Are Dangerous
Angels of Death

Medium Rare
The Lion and the Unicorn
Obsession
Trap
Hostage
K Is for Kill (a 2-part story)
    Part 1: The Tiger Awakes
    Part 2: Tiger by the Tail
Complex
Forward Base
The Gladiators
Emily

8 September–1 December 1977
(Thames)

Author's note: The last four episodes are also known collectively as *The New Avengers in Canada*. Another company involved in these episodes was Nielsen-Ferns Inc., Toronto.

BABYLON 5

"Humans and aliens wrapped in 2,500,000 tons of spinning metal, all alone in the night. It can be a dangerous place but it's our last, best hope for peace. This is the story of the last of the Babylon stations. The year is 2258. The name of the place is *Babylon 5*."

It takes a brave show to try to crack the stranglehold the *Star Trek* dynasty has on TV sci-fi. Many have tried, few have measured up. *Babylon 5* is one of the better challengers.

Babylon 5 is a five-mile-long space station located deep in neutral space and serves as an intergalactic version of the UN. It's called Babylon 5 because it's the fifth and last of the Babylon stations. The first three were destroyed by sabotage and the fourth just disappeared off the map. "So why build a fifth?" its commander is asked. "Just plain old human stubbornness," is the reply.

The station's primary function is to host critical talks aimed at establishing lasting peace in a galaxy that has seen many years of conflict between the five major solar systems: Earth Alliance, Minbari Federation, Narn Regime, Centauri Republic and Vorlon Empire.

Ambassadors and diplomats from each government are present, including Earth's representative Jeffrey Sinclair, who also acts as Babylon 5's reluctant commander.

And while there may be no stranger breed of creature than politicians, the presence of some 250,000 inhabitants means their squabbles are just the tip of an iceberg. The station is a port of call for refugees, smugglers, businessmen and travelers from a hundred worlds. Here, alien cultures clash in a dark domain of suspicion and betrayal—clearly defined in the pilot story, in which the delicate new peace is threatened by a shape-shifting hit man who tries to assassinate the newly arrived Vorlon ambassador and pin the blame on Sinclair.

Sinclair is a former fighter pilot, haunted by his experiences in the Earth-Minbari war ten years previously. He's happy to leave most of the day-to-day running of the station to his ambitious and hot-headed second in command, Susan Ivanova. Michael Garibaldi is the station's sardonic security chief, and the human contingent of stars is completed by the dedicated medical officer, Dr. Stephen Franklin, and a telepath, Talia Winters.

The principal alien ambassadors are Delenn, a bald but elegant Minbari (whose secret mission is to guard against Sinclair remembering the truth about 24 "lost" hours of his war experience against the Minbari); Londo Mollari, a drinking, gambling, womanizing Centauran in a silly suit and a clown-like haircut; G'Kar, a calculating, reptilian Narn with the morals of a snake; and the mysterious Vorlon, Kosh, who remains hidden inside a bizarre costume that acts as a mobile life-support system called an exoskeleton. Also along for the ride is sixties sci-fi "veteran" Bill Mumy, aka Will Robinson of *Lost in Space*, as a Minbari attaché, while his *Lost in Space* mom, June Lockhart, also makes a guest appearance. Andreas Katsulas, who plays G'Kar, had earlier played Romulan commander Tomalak in *Star Trek: The Next Generation*.

The aliens look impressive—and so do the special effects, even if it does seem at times as if you're watching two different series. For exterior sequences are realized not by models, but in a super-slick computer-generated spacescape, including a dramatic Star Gate, a portal in space where ships emerge from hyperspace. It's the nearest thing to a wormhole this side of *Deep Space Nine*.

In the beginning, it was easy to get hung up on the similarities between *B5* and its *Trek* rival. But Straczynski has always maintained that his project dates back to 1988, and as the series has progressed, it's clear that his vision of the future is much darker.

In many ways, *Babylon 5* is *still* SFTV's best-kept secret. While *The X-Files* has exploded the *Star Trek* dynasty's grip on the hearts and minds of the media, *B5* has quietly turned itself into a proper epic, with a structured beginning, middle and end. Its dark corners, troubled minds and sinister plots have brought the scale of a novel to television. Indeed, Straczynski has admitted being inspired by Tolkien's *Lord of the Rings* in his theme of good vs. evil and light vs. dark. Straczynski's story arc is scheduled to run for five years, and the series' survival beyond the ratings-sensitive first season has allowed him the freedom to explore that arc to the full. Characters come and go—principally Sinclair, who was replaced as commander of Babylon 5 by Captain John Sheridan, played by Bruce Boxleitner, previously best-known for his role in *The Scarecrow and Mrs. King*. But Sinclair remained in the background, on Minbar, returning in Season Three as an important figure in the battle against the Shadows.

And while the *Trek* characters generally remain constant, *B5*'s regulars grow and change— literally in the case of Delenn, whose transformation into a human/Minbari hybrid advanced that whole plot cycle. And as the Narn-Centauri conflict escalated, the calculating G'Kar became a real figure of pathos, a tragic hero, while the clownish Londo became a scheming villain. And Vir quietly gained in stature, becoming a Centauri at odds with his people's aggressive streak.

And though the dialogue is frequently corny (sample: "General Hague is coming and *Hell* is coming with him!"), *Babylon 5* is rarely boring, which is more than can be said for *Star Trek: Voyager* in its early seasons.

REGULAR CAST
Commander Jeffrey Sinclair Michael O'Hare (*Season One only*)
Security Chief Michael Garibaldi Jerry Doyle
Lt. Commander Susan Ivanova Claudia Christian
Dr. Stephen Franklin Richard Biggs *Delenn* Mira Furlan
Londo Mollari Peter Jurasik *G'Kar* Andreas Katsulas
Psi Corps Telepath Talia Winters Andrea Thompson
Lennier Bill Mumy *Na'Toth* Caitlin Brown (*Season One*),
Mary Kay Adams (*Season Two*) *Vir Cotto* Stephen Furst
Ambassador Kosh Ardwright Chamberlain
Capt. John Sheridan Bruce Boxleitner (*from Season Two*)
Warren Keffer Robert Rusler (*Season Two only*)
Zack Allan Jeff Conaway (*regular from Season Three*)
Ranger Marcus Cole Jason Carter (*from Season Three*)

Creator: J. Michael Straczynski
Executive producers: Douglas Netter, J. Michael Straczynski
Producers: Robert Latham Brown (*pilot*), John Copeland, Richard Compton
Music: Stewart Copeland (*pilot*), Christopher Franke
Conceptual consultant: Harlan Ellison
Visual effects designer: Ron Thornton

Babylonian Productions Inc.
Pilot: Rattlesnake Productions Inc.

U.S. premiere: February 1993
(syndicated)
U.K. premiere: 16 May 1994
(Channel Four)

The Gathering (pilot)
(90 mins.)

w J. Michael Straczynski
An assassination attempt threatens the fragile peace on the new Babylon 5 space station. Its commander, Jeffrey Sinclair, finds himself accused of the murder bid, unless he can track down the real culprit and prove his innocence. (Screened at the end of first season run on Channel Four.)
Lt. Laurel Takashima Tamlyn Tomita
Dr. Benjamin Kyle Johnny Sekka
Telepath Lyta Alexander Patricia Tallman
Carolyn Sykes Blaire Baron
Del Varner John Fleck
Senator Paul Hampton
Eric Steven R. Bennett
Traveler William Hayes

Director: Richard Compton

Season One
Signs and Portents

22 color 60-minute episodes

Midnight on the Firing Line

w J. Michael Straczynski
Sinclair must maintain peace between the alien ambassadors aboard Babylon 5 when the Narn invade a peaceful Centauri agricultural colony on a distant planet, Raghesh 3. At the same time the presence of new Psi Corps telepath Talia Winters has a strange effect on Ivanova.
Carn Mollari Peter Trencher
Senator Paul Hampton

Director: Richard Compton

Soul Hunter

w J. Michael Straczynski
When Commander Sinclair rescues an injured alien and brings him aboard the space station, Ambassador Delenn recognizes him as a feared Soul Hunter, who collects the dying souls of aliens before they can go to their eternal rest.
Soul Hunter W. Morgan Sheppard
Second Soul Hunter John Snyder

Director: Jim Johnston

Born to the Purple

w Lawrence G. Ditillio
Londo's political career is in jeopardy when he falls for an exotic dancer who steals his secret files in order to gain her freedom from her sadistic slave owner.

Ko'Dath Mary Woronov
Adira Tyree Fabiana Udenio
Trakis Clive Revill

Director: Bruce Seth Green

Infection

w J. Michael Straczynski
An archaeologist smuggles some mysterious artifacts aboard Babylon 5 that transform his assistant into a cybernetic killing machine that threatens to destroy the entire space station.
Dr. Vance Hendricks David McCallum
Nelson Drake Marshall Teague
Patricia Healy Mary Ann Cramer
Aria Danica McKeller
Kiron Rodney Eastman
Roberts Michael Paul Chan

Director: Richard Compton

Parliament of Dreams

w J. Michael Straczynski
Sinclair is shaken by the arrival of his old lover Catherine Sakai, and G'Kar is terrified by a death threat from an old political enemy during a week-long festival when humans and aliens alike demonstrate their religious beliefs and customs.
Na'Toth Caitlin Brown *(intro)*
Catherine Sakai Julia Nickson
Lennier Bill Mumy *(intro)*
Tu'Pari Thomas Kopache
Du'Rog Mark Hendrickson

Director: Jim Johnston

Mind War

w J. Michael Straczynski
A genetically altered telepathic fugitive hides aboard Babylon 5 and seeks Talia's help in escaping from his pursuers before he mutates into a destructive superbeing. Meanwhile, Catherine experiences an incredible encounter with an immense alien spacecraft. (*Star Trek*'s Walter Koenig makes a guest appearance as a Psi Corps cop.)
Jason Ironheart William Allen Young
Kelsey Felicity Waterman
Bester Walter Koenig
Catherine Sakai Julia Nickson

Director: Bruce Seth Green

The War Prayer

w D.C. Fontana
When a group of racial fanatics called the Home
Guard infiltrates the station and attacks innocent
aliens, Ivanova is shocked to find her former lover is
their leader.
Malcolm Biggs Tristan Rogers
Kiron Maray Rodney Eastman
Aria Tensus Danica McKeller
Shaal Mayan Nancy Lee Grahn
Roberts Michael Paul Chan

Director: Richard Compton

And the Sky Full of Stars

w J. Michael Straczynski
Sinclair is abducted by two mysterious beings
known as the Knights, who probe his subconscious
to try to learn what happened ten years ago during
the space battle with the Minbari in which he lost his
memory for 24 hours.
Knight One Judson Scott
Knight Two Christopher Neame
Benson Jim Youngs
Mitchell Justin Williams

Director: Janet Greek

DeathWalker

w Lawrence G. Ditillio
When Jha'dur, an infamous scientist, arrives on
Babylon 5, Sinclair must decide whether to allow
her to perfect her experimental youth serum or pros-
ecute her for her biological war crimes against the
minority alien races throughout the galaxy.
Jha'dur Sarah Douglas
Ambassador Kalika Robin Curtis
Abbut Cosie Costa
Senator Hidoshi Aki Aleong

Director: Bruce Seth Green

Believers

w David Gerrold
Dr. Franklin provokes a moral dilemma that threat-
ens the stability of *Babylon 5* when he tries to save
the life of a dying alien child whose parents refuse a
simple, life-saving operation that conflicts with
their religious beliefs.
M'ola Tricia O'Neil
Tharg Stephen Lee
Shon Jonathan Charles Kaplan
Maya Hernandez Silvana Gallardo

Director: Richard Compton

Survivors

w Mark Scott Zicree
As the Earthforce president travels to dedicate the
opening of a new docking bay, a huge explosion de-
stroys part of the construction site and Garibaldi
finds himself accused of sabotage.
Major Lianna Kemmer Elaine Thomas
Agent Cutter Tom Donaldson
Nolan Jose Rosario
Lou Welch David Crowley

Director: Jim Johnston

Signs and Portents

w J. Michael Straczynski
Babylon 5's fighter pilots battle a fleet of space
raiders who abduct a Centauri nobleman and a valu-
able historical relic. Meanwhile, Garibaldi helps
Sinclair learn more about his mysterious amnesia,
unaware that the Minbari Grey Council has ordered
Delenn to kill Sinclair if he should ever learn the
complete truth.
Lord Kiro Gerrit Graham
Lady Ladira Fredi Olster
Raider Whip Hubley

Director: Janet Greek

By Any Means Necessary

w Kathryn M. Drennan
Babylon 5 is thrown into violent turmoil when the
Senate insists on repressive measures to break a
strike by loading-dock workers demanding im-
provements in their wages and working conditions.
Sinclair clashes with his political masters and jeop-
ardizes his career in a bid to end the dispute.
Neeoma Connally Katy Boyer
Orin Zento John Snyder
Eduardo Delvientos Jose Rey
Senator Hidoshi Aki Aleong

Director: Jim Johnston

The Quality of Mercy

w J. Michael Straczynski
Dr. Franklin helps a former physician, dying from a
painful neurological disease, in her experiments with
an alien healing machine. Meanwhile, Talia is traumatized after once again scanning the mind of a psychopathic serial killer. And the hedonistic Londo escorts
the virginal Minbari attaché Lennier on a night of wild
adventure in one of the station nightspots.
Karl Mueller Mark Rolston
Dr. Laura Rosen June Lockhart
Janice Rosen Kate McNeil
Centauri senator Damian London
Ombuds Wellington Jim Norton

Director: Lorraine Senna Ferrara

Grail

w Christy Marx

Aldous Gajic, a spiritual crusader on an intergalactic quest for the Holy Grail, visits Babylon 5 and is befriended by Jinxo, a petty thief. Together, they help Sinclair and Garibaldi combat a mind-eating creature called The Feeder, which is being used by a crime boss to enforce his criminal rule in "Downbelow," the station's underworld.

Aldous Gajic David Warner
Deuce William Sanderson
Jinxo Tom Booker
Ombuds Wellington Jim Norton

Director: Richard Compton

Eyes

w Lawrence G. Ditillio

Two high-ranking Earthforce security officers—undercover investigator Colonel Ari Ben Zayn, nicknamed "Eyes," and Psi Corps specialist Harriman Gray—arrive on Babylon 5 to evaluate the loyalty of Sinclair and his commanding officers via a telepathic survey. But Garibaldi helps to expose Ben Zayn's personal vendetta against Sinclair—who unexpectedly beat him for command of the space station because of Minbari influence.

Colonel Ari Ben Zayn Gregory Martin
Harriman Gray Jeffrey Combs

Director: Jim Johnston

TKO

w Lawrence G. Ditillio

Garibaldi helps a wrongfully disgraced prizefighter to regain his honor as a professional athlete by coaching him to compete in a violent alien sporting event known as the Mutai. Meanwhile, a rabbi arrives on Babylon 5 to console Ivanova on the death of her father. (Shown in a late-night slot in the U.K.)

Walker Smith Greg McKinney
The Muta-Do Soon-Teck Oh
Caliban Don Stroud
Sho-Rin Gyor James Jude Courtney
Rabbi Yossel Koslov Theodore Bikel
Andrei Ivanov Robert Phalen

Director: John C. Flinn III

A Voice in the Wilderness, Part 1

w J. Michael Straczynski

While investigating seismic activity on a supposedly uninhabited planet, Epsilon 3, Sinclair and Ivanova discover the remnants of a technologically advanced ancient civilization, guarded by a cybernetic 500-year-old dying alien called Varn.

Draal Louis Turenne
Varn Curt Lowens
Dr. Tasaki Jim Ishida

Director: Janet Greek

A Voice in the Wilderness, Part 2

w J. Michael Straczynski

Sinclair, Londo and Delenn all become embroiled in a struggle for control of Epsilon 3's super-technology between Earth Alliance and a group of alien outcasts, which turns into a race against time to stop the planet's automatic defenses from triggering a massive explosion that would destroy Babylon 5.

Draal Louis Turenne
Varn Curt Lowens
Captain Ellis Pierce Ron Canada
Takarn Michelan Sisti
Senator Hidoshi Aki Aleong
Lise Hampton Denise Gentile

Director: Janet Greek

Babylon Squared

w J. Michael Straczynski

When Babylon 4 mysteriously reappears from a violent time warp, Sinclair and Garibaldi lead a rescue team to help evacuate the crew before the space station disappears again. Meanwhile, Delenn learns that she has been elected the new leader of the Minbari but insists on fulfilling her spiritual mission aboard Babylon 5 involving Sinclair and an ancient Minbari prophecy. Back on Babylon 4, Sinclair and Garibaldi learn of a mysterious spiritual leader known as The One, whose identity comes as a real surprise . . .

Major Krantz Kent Broadhurst
Zathras Tim Choate
Lise Hampton Denise Gentile

Director: Jim Johnston

Legacies

w D.C. Fontana

Minbari warriors threaten to start a new war with the Earth Alliance when the corpse of a great military hero they bring to Babylon 5 for a memorial display is stolen. Meanwhile, Talia and Ivanova clash over the welfare of a 14-year-old orphan telepath.

Shai Alit Neroon John Vickery
Alisa Beldon Grace Una

Director: Bruce Seth Green

Chrysalis

w J. Michael Straczynski

Londo becomes obligated to a powerful mercenary agent. Sinclair and Catherine announce their wedding date. Garibaldi is critically wounded while trying to prevent the assassination of the Earth Alliance president. And after a rather solemn consultation with the enigmatic Vorlon ambassador, Delenn begins a bizarre transformation.

Catherine Sakai Julia Nickson
Morden Ed Wasser
Edgar Devereaux Edward Conery
Morgan Clark Gary McGurk

Director: Janet Greek

Season Two
The Coming of Shadows

22 color 50-minute episodes

Points of Departure

w J. Michael Straczynski

Commander Sinclair has been reassigned (as the first human ambassador to the Minbari homeworld). Babylon 5's controversial new commander is Captain John Sheridan—who was nicknamed "Starkiller" during the Earth-Minbari war. Meanwhile, Garibaldi is still critical after being shot in the back (see "Chrysalis"), Delenn's transformation is continuing and a rogue Minbari warship tries to provoke Sheridan into starting a war. And Lennier explains that the Minbari surrendered at the Battle of Line after it was discovered Minbari souls were reborn in humans. Lennier also reminds us that "the great Enemy is returning" and that "both races must join to stop the darkness."

Captain John Sheridan Bruce Boxleitner (intro)
Kalain Richard Grove
Hedronn Robin Sachs
General William Hague Robert Foxworth
Deeran Jennifer Anglin
Ambassadors Jonathan Chapman, Mark Hendrickson, Kristopher Logan
Techs Joshua Cox, Debra Sharkey, Kim Delgado
Merchants Russ Fega, Bennet Guillory
Young woman Catherine Hader
Vastor Michael McKenzie
Other pilot Brian Starcher
Ensign Kim Strauss

Director: Janet Greek

Revelations

w J. Michael Straczynski

Londo becomes more indebted to the sinister Morden, agent of the powerful mercenaries the Shadowmen. G'Kar warns of a coming threat from an ancient race out on the Rim. Dr. Franklin uses an experimental alien procedure to bring Garibaldi out of his coma and Talia helps him recall who shot him. Sheridan's younger sister Elizabeth visits and helps him confront his sadness and guilt over the death of his wife. And Delenn finally emerges from her cocoon.

Elizabeth Sheridan Beverly Leech
Garibaldi's aide Macauley Bruton
Anna Sheridan Beth Toussaint
Lou Welch David L. Crowley
Narn captain Mark Hendrickson
Med tech James Kiriyama-Lem
President Clark Gary McGurk
Narn navigator Michael McKenzie
Morden Ed Wasser
Guard Warren Tabata

Director: Jim Johnston

The Geometry of Shadows

w J. Michael Straczynski

Londo hears a bizarre prophecy about his own rise to power from the leader of the Technomages—human-looking wizards who also warn of "a storm coming." Ivanova is promoted to commander and asssigned to resolve a cultural dispute between two warring Drazi factions. And Garibaldi considers quitting . . .

Elric Michael Ansara
Refa William Forward
Lou Welch David L. Crowley
Green Drazi Kim Strauss, Jonathan Chapman
Purple Drazi Neil Bradley
Tech Joshua Cox
Devereaux Edward Conery
Guard Warren Tabata

Director: Michael Laurence Vejar

A Distant Star

w D.C. Fontana

Maynard, an explorer friend of Sheridan's, stops off with disturbing news of dark activities out on the Rim. When Maynard's vessel becomes trapped in hyperspace, Sheridan tries to find it using his fighters, but they are threatened by a mysterious Shadow craft. And Delenn's loyalty to her people is questioned.

Capt. Jack Maynard Russ Tamblyn
Patrick Daniel Beer
Ray Galus Art Kimro
Orwell Miguel A. Nunez Jr.
Ogilvie Patty Toy
Tech Joshua Cox
Comm tech Kim Delgado
Teronn Sandey Brown

Director: Jim Johnston

The Long Dark

w Scott Frost
A 100-year-old Earth ship arrives with two people aboard—one dead, one frozen in a deep sleep. But when the cryonic woman is revived, a mysterious evil is unleashed aboard Babylon 5.
Mariah Cirrus Anne-Marie Johnson
Amis Dwight Schultz
Aliens Jennifer Anglin, Neil Bradley
Medlab tech James Kiriyama-Lem
Markab ambassador Kim Strauss
Guard Warren Tabata

Director: Mario Di Leo

Spider in the Web

w Lawrence G. Ditillio
Talia witnesses the murder of an old friend, Taro Isogi, by "Free Mars" fanatic Abel Horn—and becomes the killer's next target. While protecting her, Garibaldi and Talia develop a mutual attraction. When Horn is finally caught Talia realizes something was controlling his mind. A greater conspiracy is behind the deaths . . .
Abel Horn Michael Beck
Amanda Carter Adrienne Barbeau
Taro Isogi James Shigeta
Zack Allan Jeff Conaway
Senator Elise Voudreau Jessica Walter
Thirteen/Psi Cop Annie Grindby
Tech Joshua Cox

Director: Kevin G. Cremin

A Race Through Dark Places

w J. Michael Straczynski
Talia is approached by Psi Corps Cop Bester to investigate an underground railway set up to help renegade telepaths elude the Psi Corps. But when she learns of the widespread corruption within the Corps she teams up with Sheridan and Dr. Franklin to thwart Bester and help the telepaths escape. And Delenn learns what it's like to be human. (In the U.S., this episode aired after "Soul Mates," as it was not ready for transmission in time, but the U.K. running order is the correct one.)
Bester Walter Koenig
Lurker Gianin Loffler
Telepaths Apesanahkwat, Diane DiLascio
Rick Brian Cousins
Man Eddie Allen
Bartender Kathryn Cressida
Psi cop Judy Levitt
Shooter Christopher Michael
Jason Ironheart William Allen Young

Director: Jim Johnston

Soul Mates

w Peter David
Londo is granted permission to divorce two of his three wives and surprises everyone by staying with the most ill-humored! And Garibaldi helps Talia thwart her ex-husband's scheme to turn her into an empath.
Matthew Stoner Keith Szarabajka
Timov Jane Carr
Daggair Lois Nettleton
Mariel Blair Walk
Lou Welch David L. Crowley
Trader Carel Struycken
Man Brian Michael McGuire

Director: John C. Flinn III

The Coming of Shadows

w J. Michael Straczynski
The "Introduction" is over and Straczynski's "Rising Action" stage begins as he starts to really crank up the arc story. The elderly Centauri emperor visits Babylon 5, with a surprising message for the Narn. But his intentions are undermined by Londo and Refa whose plot to expand their power ignites a new Centauri-Narn war. Meanwhile, Garibaldi receives a strange message from an old friend.
Ranger Fredric Lehne
Centauri prime minister Malachi Throne
Lord Refa William Forward
Centauri emperor Turhan Bey
Zack Allan Jeff Conaway
Ambassador Sinclair Michael O'Hare
Kha'Mak Neil Bradley
Kosh Ardwright Chamberlain
Narn pilots Jonathan Chapman, Kim Strauss
Customs guard Bryan Michael McGuire

Director: Janet Greek

Gropos

w Lawrence G. Ditillio
Dr. Franklin's father arrives as the general in command of 25,000 "ground pounding" soldiers, generating fear aboard Babylon 5 that the station will be turned into an armed camp. For Dr. Franklin, however, his father's presence is the opportunity to resolve some old family conflicts.
General Richard Franklin Paul Winfield
Lou Welch David L. Crowley
Sgt. Major Plug Ryan Cutrona
PFC Large Ken Foree
Pvt. Kleist Morgan Hunter
PFC Dodger Marie Marshall
Pvt. Yang Art Chudabala
Techs Joshua Cox, Elisa Beth Garver
ISN reporter Maggie Egan
Tonia Wallace Mowava Pryer

Director: Jim Johnston

All Alone in the Night

w J. Michael Straczynski
Leading a search to investigate "unusual sightings," Sheridan is kidnapped and held aboard a mysterious alien craft. Delenn learns that she has been expelled from the Grey Council. General Hague makes an unofficial visit to Babylon 5 and Sheridan's real mission to Babylon 5 is revealed.
Lt. Ramirez Nick Corri
Narn Marshall Teague
Hedronn Robin Sachs
Neroon John Vickery
General William Hague Robert Foxworth
Kosh Ardwright Chamberlain
Tech Joshua Cox

Director: Mario Di Leo

Acts of Sacrifice

w J. Michael Straczynski
As the Narn-Centauri war escalates, an increasingly desperate and isolated G'Kar asks both Delenn and Sheridan to come to the aid of his people. Ivanova has to be at her most creative when she tries to set up an ambassadorship with a visiting alien who wants the deal sealed with sex!
Taq Paul Williams
Narn Christopher Darga
Franke Glenn Morshower
Zack Allan Jeff Conaway
Correlilmurzon Ian Abercrombie
Centauri Paul Ainsley
Narn second Jennifer Anglin
Tech Joshua Cox
Bartender Kathryn Cressida
Narn captain Sandey Grinn
Centauri merchant David Sage

Director: Jim Johnston

Hunter, Prey

w J. Michael Straczynski
A fugitive with sensitive information about the Earth government tries to find refuge on Babylon 5. And Sheridan determines to try to find out more about the Vorlons.
Derek Cranston Bernie Casey
Dr. Everett Jacobs Tony Steedman
Zack Allan Jeff Conaway
Sarah Wanda De Jesus
Max Richard Moll
Tech Joshua Cox
Kosh Ardwright Chamberlain
Guard Bryan Michael McGuire
Lurker Damon C. Reiser
Aide Debby Shively
Merchant Robert Silver

Director: Menachem Binetski

There All the Honor Lies

w Peter David
Sheridan fights to clear his name after killing a Minbari warrior in self-defense and gets another lesson in understanding from Kosh. Meanwhile, Ivanova is furious when she's put in charge of overseeing the merchandising of Babylon 5 (souvenir teddy bears and baseball caps). "We're not some deep space franchise," she rails. "This station is about something."
Guinevere Corey Julie Caitlin Brown
Zack Allan Jeff Conaway
Ashan Sean Gregory Sullivan
Minbari Neil Bradley, Jonathan Chapman
Kosh Ardwright Chamberlain
Centauri envoy Vincent Duvall
Store owner Ossie Mair

Director: Mike Laurence Vejar

And Now for a Word

w J. Michael Straczynski
Babylon 5 becomes caught up in a sudden, deadly conflict when a Narn cruiser destroys a Centauri ship near the station. An ISN reporter is on hand to cover the story for the folks back home. (In a highly unusual episode, presented like a special TV news report, viewers—new and old—learn a lot about the station's personnel and background on the political situation.)
Cynthia Torqueman Kim Zimmer
Ronald Quantrell Christopher Curry
Psi cop Granville Ames
Johnny John Christian Graas
Mother Leslie Wing
Tech Joshua Cox
Dock worker Jose Rey

Director: Mario DiLeo

In the Shadow of Z'ha'dum

w J. Michael Straczynski
When a chance discovery links Morden with the death of his wife, Sheridan embarks on a dangerous interrogation. His persistence draws Delenn and Kosh to tell Sheridan about the Shadows and the Vorlons—"There are beings in the universe billions of years older than either of our races . . ." And he learns a darker secret, that the Shadows have been reawakened. Meanwhile, a new Earth peace agency begins to recruit Babylon 5 personnel to its Nightwatch program designed to root out troublemakers.
Zack Allan Jeff Conaway
Pierce Macabee Alex Hyde-White
Morden Ed Wasser

Director: David J. Eagle

Knives

w Lawrence G. Ditillio
An old acquaintance arrives on Babylon 5, requesting Londo's help in restoring his family's name. Sheridan is plagued by visions nobody else can see—including one of his wife's ship exploding. (This episode was originally intended to be aired before "In the Shadow of Z'ha'dum.")
Urza Jaddo Carmen Argenziano
Lord Refa William Forward
Techs Joshua Cox, Elisa Beth Garver
Centauri noble William Dennis Hunt

Director: Stephen L. Posey

Confessions and Lamentations

w J. Michael Straczynski
Dr. Franklin races against time to find a cure for a fatal epidemic spreading through the Markab population and causing panic on the station. When the Markab are quarantined, Delenn and Lennier insist on joining them to nurse the sick.
Dr. Lazarenn Jim Norton
Markab mother Diane Adair
Human Andrew Craig
ISN reporter Maggie Egan
Guard Mike Manzoni
Markab victim Michael McKenzie
Markab girl Bluejean Ashley Secrist
Markab ambassador Kim Strauss
Bartender Dan Woren
Doctor Rosie Malek-Yonan

Director: Kevin G. Cremin

Divided Loyalties

w J. Michael Straczynski
Babylon 5's first telepath, Lyta Alexander, returns with a shock warning that one of the station's leading officers is a "sleeper" spy for a top-secret government organization. In the ensuing investigation someone else's long-held secret is also revealed.
Lyta Alexander Patricia Tallman
Zack Allan Jeff Conaway
First man Douglas Bennett
Kosh Ardwright Chamberlain
Tech Joshua Cox
Running man Danny De La Paz
Med tech Jani Neuman
Security guard George Simms

Director: Jesus Trevino

The Long Twilight Struggle

w J. Michael Straczynski
A pivotal episode. Londo realizes he has been a pawn in a larger game and watches helplessly as the Narn-Centauri war reaches a turning point with a terrifying assault on the Narn homeworld. Sheridan is contacted by a powerful ally, Draal, custodian of Epsilon 3, who offers to put the planet's technology at his disposal. G'Kar is granted sanctuary on Babylon 5. And Sheridan is finally introduced to the Rangers.
Draal John Schuck
ISN reporter Rif Hutton
Lord Refa William Forward
Warmaster G'Sten W. Morgan Sheppard
Narns Neil Bradley, Jonathan Chapman
Techs Joshua Cox, Elisa Beth Garver

Director: John Flinn

Comes the Inquisitor

w J. Michael Straczynski
G'Kar tries to rally the Narn on Babylon 5. And Delenn submits to a voluntary interrogation to satisfy Kosh's worries that she is doing the right thing for the right reasons and is up to the task ahead. However, her chilling inquisitor, Sebastian, turns out to have been Jack the Ripper, abducted from Earth by the Vorlons!
Sebastian Wayne Alexander
Mr. Chase Jack Kehler
Narn mother Diane Adair
Kosh Ardwright Chamberlain
Centauri Jim Chiros
Tech Joshua Cox
Narns Mark Hendrickson, Kim Strauss
Guard Michael Francis Kelly
Human Craig Thomas

Director: Michael Vejar

The Fall of Night

w J. Michael Straczynski
As the Centauri war escalates—with the invasion of Drazi and Pak'ma'ra territories—a Narn war cruiser seeks help from Babylon 5. A Nightwatch official arrives on the station to gee up his members, and Earth signs a non-aggression treaty with the Centauri—much to Sheridan's dismay as he finds himself defying the pact to save the Narn vessel. Keffer goes in search of the Shadow ship. And Kosh takes a drastic step to save Sheridan's life when Centauri terrorists plant a bomb.
Frederick Lantz Roy Dotrice
Zack Allan Jeff Conaway
Pilot Juli Donald
Mitch Rick Hamilton
Na'Kal Robin Sachs
Mr. Welles John Vickery
Pak'ma'ra ambassador Donovan Brown
Techs Joshua Cox, Elisa Beth Garver
Narn Mark Hendrickson
Human/Minbari Kosh Joshua Patton
Drazi ambassador Kim Strauss

Director: Janet Greek

Season Three
Point of No Return

(*All episodes written by J. Michael Straczynski, the first time one person had written an entire season of a drama series since Terry Nation wrote all Season One of* Blake's 7.)

Matters of Honor

The Narn war is over. An Earth official arrives to investigate the mystery ship encountered by Lt. Keffer in hyperspace but receives little real co-operation. Londo attempts to sever his ties with Morden and Sheridan receives a new ship, the *White Star*, equipped with Minbari and Vorlon technology to use in the fight against the Shadows.
David Endawi Tucker Smallwood
Morden Ed Wasser
Large man Nils Allen Stewart
Kosh Ardwright Chamberlain
Drazi pilot Jonathan Chapman
Senator Kitty Swink
Psi cop Andrew Walker

Director: Kevin G. Cremin

Convictions

When a series of bombings strikes the station, Ivanova calls on a visiting group of monks to help solve the mystery. Lennier puts his own life on the line to save Londo, who later finds himself trapped in a crippled elevator with G'Kar.
Robert Carlson Patrick Kilpatrick
Brother Theo Louis Turenne
Morishi Cary-Hiroyuki Tagawa
Obnoxious man John Flinn
Security guards Rick Johnson, Tom Simmons
Lurker Jason Larimore
Med tech Gwen McGee
Drazi Mike McKenzie

Director: Michael Laurence Vejar

A Day in the Strife

Sheridan and Ivanova try to deal with an association of cargo pilots angered by the new ship screening policy. G'Kar's position among the Narn on Babylon 5 is threatened by the arrival of a Centauri-appointed liaison. An alien probe makes first contact with the station. Vir leaves to become the Centauri attaché to Minbar. And Franklin is becoming more addicted to stims.
Nar'Far Stephen Macht
Ta'Lon Marshall Teague
Dr. Gonzales Anne Betancourt
Narns Neil Bradley, Mark Hendrickson
Corwin Joshua Cox
Med tech Larita Shelby

Troublemaker John St Ryan
G'Dok Michael Bailey Smith

Director: David J. Eagle

Passing Through Gethsemane

Telepath Lyta Alexander returns to Babylon 5 as an aide to Kosh. And one of the monks, Brother Edward, begins to have terrifying visions—and discovers that he has a secret past, as a murderer who was punished by "death of personality."
Brother Edward Brad Dourif
Brother Theo Louis Turenne
Lyta Alexander Patricia Tallman
Malcolm Robert Keith
Kosh Ardwright Chamberlain
News anchors Lynn Blades, Steven Gonzalez
Businessperson Natalie Brunt
Centauri Mark Folger

Director: Adam Nimoy

Voices of Authority

Draal agrees to help the crew attempt to contact more of the First Ones—"it'll be fun." And as a political officer arrives to "advise" him, Sheridan works to hide his conspiracy of light from an increasingly powerful and suspicious Nightwatch.
Draal John Schuck
Julie Musante Shari Shattuck
Security guard James Black
Corwin Joshua Cox
ISN anchor Vimi Mani
Vice President Clark Gary McGurk

Director: Menachem Binetski

Dust to Dust

In the face of a highly distrustful Sheridan, the Psi Cop Bester returns to Babylon 5 to investigate a powerful illegal drug that enables the user to invade someone else's mind. It's a drug that G'Kar samples, using it to make some startling discoveries about Londo—and himself.
Bester Walter Koenig
Lindstrom Julian Neil
Narn image Jim Norton
Kosh Ardwright Chamberlain
Security guard Harry Hutchinson
Centauri diplomat John-Frederick Jones
Shop owner S. Marc Jordan
PSI cop Judy Levitt
Med tech Gwen McGee
Ashi Philip Moon
Crazed man Walter O'Neil
Vizak Kim Strauss
Ombuds Dani Thompson

Director: David J. Eagle

Exogenesis

Marcus and Franklin investigate a series of deaths caused by a mysterious alien parasite. Sheridan asks Ivanova to see if the newly promoted Lt. Corwin would be loyal to their secret council—but he misinterprets her invitation as a romantic advance. Marcus confesses his own fondness for Ivanova, and Shadow vessels are gathering on the edge of Centauri space . . .

Matthew Duffin James Warwick
Jacque Lee Waylie Small
Duncan Aubrey Morris
Corwin Joshua Cox
Vendor Ross Gottstein
Samuel Eric Steinberg
Trader Donald Willis
Man Michael McKenzie
Dr. Harrison Carrie Dobro
Kat Kat Cressida
Lurker Roger Rook
Woman Leslie Pratt

Director: Kevin G. Cremin

Messages from Earth

An archaeologist, Dr. Mary Kirkish, brings Sheridan news of a frightening alliance between Earth, Psi Corps and the Shadows that forces him to move against his government—an act of treason.

Dr. Mary Kirkish Nancy Stafford
Security guards Vaughn Armstrong, Merrin Dungey
ISN anchor Vimi Mani
Cook Lorraine Shields

Director: Michael Vejar

Point of No Return

Civil war looms as Earthforce President Clark imposes martial law throughout all Earth territories—including Babylon 5. Zack finds his loyalties put to the test when Nightwatch is ordered to take control of station security. And a Centauri prophet (played by *Star Trek*'s "first lady" Majel Barrett) gives Londo—and Vir—a surprising glimpse of their destiny.

Lady Morella Majel Barrett
Ta'Lon Marshall Teague
Security guard Vaughn Armstrong
General Smits Lewis Arquette
Lt. Gen. O'Reilly Ed Trotta
Passing Minbari Jonathan Chapman
Lt. Corwin Joshua Cox
ISN reporter Maggie Egan
Centauri official Milton James
Nightwatch guard Gunther Jensen

Director: Jim Johnston

Severed Dreams

Earthforce sends destroyers to seize control of Babylon 5, but Sheridan rallies the crew to fight back. A forceful Delenn persuades five of the Minbari Grey Council to join the alliance against Earth. As a battle rages inside and outside the station, Delenn arrives with reinforcements in the nick of time. Sheridan declares B5's independence.

Captain Sandra Hiroshi Kim Miyori
David Sheridan Rance Howard
Bill Trainor Phil Morris
Major Ed Ryan Bruce McGill
Drakhen James Parks
Religious Minbari Jonathan Chapman
Lt. Corwin Joshua Cox
ISN reporters Maggie Egan, Matt Gottlieb
Narn Kim Strauss

Director: David J. Eagle

Ceremonies of Light and Dark

In the aftermath of Babylon 5's declared independence, Nightwatch terrorists abduct Delenn. Londo acts against Lord Refa to curb the Centauri expansionist aggression. At a rebirth ceremony B5's leaders each confess a secret to Delenn—and she in turn gives them new uniforms symbolizing their freedom.

Lord Refa William Forward
Boggs Don Stroud
Sniper Paul Perri
Lennan Kim Strauss
Maintenance man Vincent Bilanco
Lt. Corwin Joshua Cox
Sparky the computer Harlan Ellison
Guard Doug McCoy
Morden Ed Wasser
Thug Jim Cody Williams

Director: John C. Flinn III

Sic Transit Vir

Vir meets his fiancée—and finds they have little in common. He also causes controversy when his unauthorized Schindleresque ruse to save the lives of more than 2000 Narn is discovered. Sheridan shares a romantic dinner with Delenn. (This episode features a *tour de force* performance from Stephen Furst, who comes over like Woody Allen as he contemplates the prospect of marriage.)

Lyndisty Carmen Thomas
Centauri official Damian London
Narn James Jude Courtney

Director: Jesus Trevino

A Late Delivery from Avalon

Sheridan unveils the Babylon Treaty, allowing the station to be used as neutral territory for peace negotiations, and many members of the League of Non-Aligned Worlds agree to contribute to B5's defense. And a mysterious traveler arrives on the station claiming to be the legendary King Arthur.
Arthur Michael York
Emmett Farquaha Michael Kagan
Merchant Roger Hampton
Old woman Dona Hardy
Security guards Michael Francis Kelly, Jerry O'Donnell
Med tech James Kiriyama-Lem
Lurker Robert Schuch

Director: Michael Vejar

Ship of Tears

Sheridan agrees to a strange request—to help Psi Cop Bester intercept a Shadow warship that is found to contain a cargo of telepaths in cryonic suspension—including the love of his life, Carolyn. Meanwhile, G'Kar presses for admission to the conspiracy of light, prompting a confession from Delenn.
Bester Walter Koenig
Carolyn Joan McMurtrey
Alison Diana Morgan
Med tech Debra Sharkey

Director: Michael Vejar

Interludes and Examinations

Sheridan's riling of Kosh to bring the Vorlons into the attack against the Shadows has unexpected and tragic consequences. Morden exacts his revenge against Londo, and Franklin's stim abuse comes to a head.
Dr. Lilian Hobbs Jennifer Balgobin
David Sheridan Rance Howard
Morden Ed Wasser
Vendor Jan Rabson
Brakiri Jonathan Chapman
Tech Maggie Ciglar
Ranger Glenn Martin
Med tech Doug Tompos

Director: Jesus Trevino

War without End, Part 1

The opening of two 900-year-old letters brings Ambassador Sinclair back to Babylon 5 to instigate a mission with Sheridan, Delenn, Marcus and Ivanova to pull Babylon 4 1000 years back through time to help the Minbari and their allies defeat the Shadows.
Zathras Tim Choate
Rathenn Time Winters

Ambassador Jeffrey Sinclair Michael O'Hare
Lt. Corwin Joshua Cox
Centauri guard Kevin Fry
Spragg Eric Zivot

Director: Michael Vejar

War without End, Part 2

Sheridan is still being tugged back and forward in time, glimpsing possible futures. Sinclair and the others complete their mission, and the identity of The One is fully explained. Finally, Sinclair travels back into the past with Babylon 4, using a cocoon like Delenn's, in Season One's "Chrysalis," to transform himself into a Minbari, so they would "accept" the station as a "gift." (This momentous two-parter solves numerous mysteries from previous episodes, most notably Season One's bewildering "Babylon Squared.")
Zathras Tim Choate
Major Krantz Kent Broadhurst
B4 first officer Bruce Morrow
Ambassador Jeffrey Sinclair Michael O'Hare
Centauri guard Kevin Fry
B4 tech Eddie Mui

Director: Michael Vejar

Walkabout

Franklin goes on a journey of self-discovery and gets involved with a singer who is hiding her own tragic secret. Kosh's enigmatic replacement, also to be known as Kosh—"We are all Kosh"—arrives, and Lyta joins Sheridan on a mission to see whether telepaths can jam Shadow vessels.
Cailyn Erica Gimpel
Lyta Alexander Patricia Tallman
Dr. Lilian Hobbs Jennifer Balgobin
Na'Kal Robin Sachs
Minbari captain Michael McKenzie

Director: Kevin G. Cremin

Grey 17 Is Missing

Marcus must fight to protect Delenn when a hostile member of the Warrior caste challenges her right to lead the Rangers. Garibaldi investigates the mysterious disappearance of a whole floor of the station and encounters an odd cult and a dangerous alien.
Jeremiah Robert Englund
Neroon John Vickery
Rathenn Time Winters
Supervisor Katherine Moffat
Maintenance worker Thom Barry

Director: John Flinn III

And the Rock Cried Out, No Hiding Place

Londo manipulates Vir and G'Kar in a scheme to gain power in the Centauri Royal Court by ridding himself of his deadly rival Lord Refa. Sheridan gets news of an active Resistance on Earth via Brother Theo's clerical contacts. And Delenn has a surprise for him, too—a massive fleet of White Star ships assembled for a counterattack against the Shadows.
Rabbi Leo Meyers Erick Avari
Lord Refa William Forward
Brother Theo Louis Turenne
Reverend Will Dexter Mel Winkler
Virini Francois Giroday
Origo Paul Keith
G'Dan Wayne Alexander
Singer Marva Hicks

Director: David J. Eagle

Shadow Dancing

Franklin, still on his walkabout, tries to stop a beating and is stabbed. As he lies dying, he has a spiritual experience—he literally "meets himself"—which drives him to survive. And after Sheridan's forces repel a massive Shadow assault, an unexpected visitor leaves a Shadow vessel and arrives on Babylon 5.
Barbara Shirley Prestia
Anna Sheridan Melissa Gilbert
Thugs John Grantham, Nicholas Ross Oleson
Brakiri Jonathan Chapman
Lt. Corwin Joshua Cox
Drazi ambassador Mark Hendrickson

Director: Kim Friedman

Z'ha'dum

The riddle of what happened to the *Icarus* is solved as Sheridan's wife, Anna, reappears and urges him to return with her to the Shadows' homeworld, Z'ha'dum, "to hear their side of the story." A stunned Sheridan agrees but, suspecting a trap, prepares to deliver a surprise of his own . . . (Anna is played by Bruce Boxleitner's real-life wife, Melissa Gilbert, formerly a star of *The Little House on the Prairie*.)
Anna Sheridan Melissa Gilbert
Justin Jeff Corey
Messenger Ron Campbell
Morden Ed Wasser
Kosh Ardwright Chamberlain
Lt. Corwin Joshua Cox

Director: Adam Nimoy

Season Four
No Surrender, No Retreat

(All episodes written by J. Michael Straczynski)

The Hour of the Wolf

Sheridan and Garibaldi are missing; Londo returns to Centauri Prime only to find the Emperor is mad and has made a deal with the Shadows to insure his godhood.
Morden Ed Wasser
Emperor Cartagia Wortham Krimmer
Director: David Eagle

What Ever Happened to Mr. Garibaldi?

Londo plots against Emperor Cartagia; Sheridan turns up alive on Z'ha'dum; and G'Kar begins his search for Garibaldi.
Lorien Wayne Alexander
Minister Damian London
Isaac Lenny Citrano
Harry Anthony DeLongis
Director: Kevin Dobson

The Summoning

The new Vorlon ambassador arrives; G'Kar is captured by Emperor Cartagia's forces.
Director: John McPherson

Falling Toward Apotheosis

Sheridan discovers the Vorlons hidden agenda and takes action against them.
Director: David Eagle

The Long Night

Londo and G'Kar work together to kill Emperor Cartagia; Sheridan has a plan to end the Shadow War.
Ericsson Bryan Cranston
Director: John LaFia

Into the Fire

Sheridan and Delenn confront the Shadows with their armada.
Durano Julian Barnes
Director: Kevin Dobson

Epiphanies

The Shadow War is over, but the fight with President Clark on Earth is just getting started. Bester shows up on B5, looking for a way to Z'ha'dum.
Director: John Flinn

The Illusion of Truth

ISN visits B5 and broadcasts an exposé of Sheridan, aided by a very disgruntled Garibaldi.
Director: Stephen Furst

Atonement

Sheridan sends Marcus and Dr. Franklin to Mars to help the Martian resistance movement.
Callenn Brian Carpenter
Dukhat Reiner Schone
Director: Tony Dow

Racing Mars

Marcus and Dr. Franklin contact the rebels, who have a traitor in their midst.
Dan Randall Jeff Griggs
Number One Marjorie Monaghan
Number Two Clayton Landey
Wade Mark Schneider
Captain Jack Donovan Scott
Director: Jesus Trevino

Lines of Communication

Sheridan launches the Voice of the Resistance; Delenn investigates alien ships preying on weak races along the edge of Minbari space.
Phillipe Pado Seganti
Forell G.W. Stevens
Director: John Flinn

Conflicts of Interests

Garibaldi finds work as a private detective and secret courier.
Zathras Tim Choate
Ben Charles Walker
Director: David Eagle

Rumors, Bargains and Lies

Delenn returns to Minbar only to discover the Warrior Castle has declared war and is trying to take over.
Drazi Ambassador Ron Campbell
Religious #1 Gary Siner
Religious #2 Chard Haywood
Neroon John Vickery
Director: Michael Vejar

Moments of Transition

Bester recruits Lyta Alexander back into Psi Corps; Delenn demands the surrender of the Warrior Caste on Minbar.
Shakiri Bart McCarthy
Director: Tony Dow

No Surrender, No Retreat

Sheridan leads a fleet against Proxima III to liberate the colony.
Cmdr. Sandra Levitt Marcia Miteman Gaven
Capt. Edward MacDougan Richard Gant
Capt. Trevor Hall Ken Jenkins
Director: Michael Vejar

The Exercise of Vital Powers

On Mars, a billionaire works against telepaths with the aid of Garibaldi.
William Edgars Efrem Zimbalist Jr.
Director: John LaFia

The Face of the Enemy

Garibaldi betrays Sheridan on Mars.
Alison Higgins Diana Morgan
Capt. James David Purdham
Capt. Frank Ricco Ross
Director: Michael Vejar

Intersections in Real Time

Sheridan is brutally interrogated on Mars.
William Raye Birk
Drazi Wayne Alexander
Interrogator Bruce Gray
Director: John LaFia

Between the Darkness and the Light

Alliances begin to unravel as Sheridan appears to be doomed.
Eisensen Marc Gomes
Felicia Musetta Vander
Director: David Eagle

End Game

Sheridan leads his forces against Earth.
Earthforce NCO Ungela Brockman
Gen. Lefcourt J. Patrick McCormack
Sen. Crosby Darolyn Seymour
Capt. Mitchell Julian Stone
Director: John Copeland

Rising Star

In the aftermath of victory, Sheridan is forced to resign his commission.
Luko Joey Dente
Lise Denise Gentile
Gen. Foote Michael Potter
Pres. Susanna Luckenko Beata Pozniak
Director: Tony Dow

The Deconstruction of Falling Stars

People from the future look back on Sherlidan and Delenn's accomplishments. Shot in the fifth season, this episode became the season finale, replacing Episode 422, "Sleeping in Light," the series conclusion, which aired at the end of Season Five.
Brother Alwyn Macomber Ray Brocksmith
Latimere Alastair Duncan
Daniel Eric Pierpoint
Brother Michael Neil Roberts
Director: Stephen Furst

Season Five
The Wheel of Fire

(Author's note: As all of these episodes had not been completed as of press time, titles and running order are tentative. Tracy Scoggins joins the cast as Captain Elizabeth Lochley and Claudia Christian departs.)

Episodes
No Compromises
The Very Long Night of Londo Mollari
The Paragon of Animals
A View from the Gallery
Learning Curve
Strange Relations
Secrets of the Soul
In the Kingdom of the Blind
Cat and Mouse

Phoenix Rising
A Tragedy of Telepaths
Day of the Dead
The Ragged Edge
The Corps Is Mother, the Corps Is Father
Meditations on the Abyss
Darkness Ascending
And All My Dreams, Torn Asunder
Movements of Fire and Shadow
The Fall of Centauri Prime
Objects in Motion
Objects at Rest
Wheel of Fire
Sleeping in Light

Television Movies
In the Beginning
Thirdspace
The River of Souls

BATMAN

"I make absolutely no excuses for *Batman*. It's not
meant to be a contribution to the culture of the world.
It's not meant to contain deep messages . . ."
—William Dozier, executive producer

Any show that includes the immortal refrain "Holy Priceless Collection of Etruscan Snoods" can't be all lowbrow, but there have been few greater champions of comic book culture than the caped crusader.

Here was a superhero who didn't fly, climbed buildings the hard way rather than leap them at a single bound, and clunk-clicked every trip in his Batmobile. A hero who faced death with as much dignity as anyone could muster in a fancy dress costume, but who always won in the end.

It was a carefully contrived camp formula that gave the kids a serious hero and presented knowing adults with a send-up of all the old radio serials and Saturday morning picture shows they'd ever known and loved. Nearly all the stories were two-parters, with the first episode ending in a cliffhanger. As Batman and his trusty sidekick, Robin the Boy Wonder, seemed doomed to a diabolical death at the hands of some nefarious villain, the alarmed voice of a narrator urged viewers to tune in for the conclusion "same bat-time, same bat-channel." In part two, a stroke of ingenuity—or sometimes luck—enabled the dynamic duo to escape, defeat their foe in a glorious fistfight and make Gotham City a safer place . . . until the next week, at least.

Behind the masks and capes, Batman and Robin were, of course, millionaire philanthropist Bruce Wayne and his youthful ward Dick Grayson, but while the bad guys did *their* best to put two and two together, the top guys on the side of the law, Commissioner Gordon and Chief O'Hara, never looked like coming up with the right answer.

Week after week, they'd get on the batphone to stately Wayne Manor where Bruce and Dick, aided by loyal butler Alfred, would slide down the batpoles behind the drawing room bookcase, emerging at the bottom in their crimebusting clothes, leap into the Batmobile and roar off to fight some of the most eccentric crooks ever invented.

Among Batman's regular nemeses were the Joker (the Clown Prince of Crime), the Riddler (the Prince of Puzzles), the Penguin (that Pompous Perpetrator of Foul Play) and Catwoman (the Felonious Feline). And the high-powered stars of Hollywood queued up to play the low-life of *Batman*. Vincent Price, Cesar Romero, Burgess Meredith, Otto Preminger, Roddy McDowall, Van Johnson, Ethel Merman, Tallulah Bankhead, Liberace, Zsa Zsa Gabor, Eartha Kitt, Shelley Winters and even Joan Collins all wore outlandish costumes and roguish grins as they consigned Batman to another fiendish fate.

And what fates. In their ceaseless campaign against crime, the dynamic duo have been frozen into ice pops, tied above a vat of bubbling wax, roasted on a spit, sealed in a sand-filled hourglass, trapped in a giant coffee cup beneath a percolator filled with acid, served up to carnivorous plants and corrugated into slabs of cardboard. But apart from the ghoulish voyeurism of watching them face more perils than Pauline, there was little actual violence. The fight scenes were carefully choreographed with comic book–style effects—*BIFF! ... ZAP! ... BAM!*—superimposed over the action.

Although production stopped in 1969 after 120 episodes and one feature film, as recently as 1988 the shows were still playing in 106 countries with a worldwide audience of 400 million.

BAT-CAST

Batman/Bruce Wayne Adam West *Robin/Dick Grayson* Burt Ward
Alfred Alan Napier *Aunt Harriet* Madge Blake
Commissioner Gordon Neil Hamilton *Chief O'Hara* Stafford Repp
Batgirl Yvonne Craig *(Season Three)* *Narrator* William Dozier

Executive producer: William Dozier
Producer: Howie Horowitz
Story consultant: Lorenzo Semple Jr.
Makeup: Ben Nye
Music: Neal Hefti *(theme)*, Nelson Riddle

A Greenaway Production for 20th Century Fox Television
120 color 30-minute episodes
U.S. premiere: 12 January 1966
U.K. premiere: 21 May 1966

Season One
34 half-hour episodes

21 May–11 September 1966
(Northern: ABC Television)

Hi Diddle Riddle/Smack in the Middle

w Lorenzo Semple Jr.
The twisted trail of the Riddler leads Batman to break the law and dance the Batusi with Molly, the Molehill Mob moll.
The Riddler Frank Gorshin
Molly Jill St. John
Harry Allen Jaffe
Insp. Basch Michael Fox

Director: Robert Butler

Fine Feathered Finks/The Penguin's a Jinx

w Lorenzo Semple Jr.
Bruce Wayne is caught trying to plant a bug in the Penguin's umbrella factory and is sentenced to die in the feathered felon's furnace.
The Penguin Burgess Meredith
Dawn Robbins Leslie Parrish
Sparrow Walter Burke
Hawkeye Lewis Charles

Director: Robert Butler

The Joker is Wild/Batman Gets Riled

w Robert Dozier
Batman and Robin are nearly unmasked by the Joker when he fashions his own devilish utility belt.
The Joker Cesar Romero
Queenie Nancy Kovack
Museum attendant Jonathan Hole
Asst. warden Merritt Bohn

Director: Don Weis

Instant Freeze/Rats Like Cheese

w Max Hodge
The notorious Mr. Freeze tries to turn the dynamic duo into ice pops with his deadly ice-gun.
Mr. Freeze George Sanders
Princess Sandra Shelby Grant
Chill Troy Melton
Nippy Guy Way

Director: Robert Butler

Zelda the Great/A Death Worse Than Fate

w Lorenzo Semple Jr.
Supersexy escape artiste Zelda kidnaps Aunt Harriet and holds her for ransom, then locks Batman and Robin in her inescapable doom-trap.
Zelda the Great Anne Baxter
Eivol Ekdal Jack Kruschen
Hilary Stonewin Barbara Heller

Director: Robert Butler

A Riddle a Day Keeps the Riddler Away/ When the Rat's Away, the Mice Will Play

w Fred De Gorter
The Prince of Puzzles tries to finish off the caped crusaders by shackling them to giant generator wheels.
Riddler Frank Gorshin
Mousey Susan Silo
Fangs Marc Cavell
Whiskers Tim Herbert
Ambassador Tris Coffin

Director: Tom Gries

The Thirteenth Hat/Batman Stands Pat

w Charles Hoffman
The Mad Hatter plots to uncowl Batman and kidnap the jury that once convicted him.
The Mad Hatter David Wayne
Cappy Roland La Starza
Dicer Gil Perkins
Babette Sandra Wells

Director: Norman Foster

The Joker Goes to School/He Meets His Match, the Grisly Ghoul

w Lorenzo Semple Jr.
The Joker plots to recruit high school dropouts and tries to electrocute our heroes.
The Joker Cesar Romero
Susie Donna Loren
Nick Kip King
Two-Bits Greg Benedict

Director: Murray Golden

True or False-Face/Super Rat Race

w Stephen Kandel
The devil of disguise, False-Face, glues the dynamic duo to the subway tracks, but is finally out-phonied by Batman.
False-Face Malachi Throne
Blaze Myrna Fahey
Midget Billy Curtis

Director: William A Graham

The Purr-Fect Crime/Better Luck Next Time

w Stanley Ralph Ross & Lee Orgel
The Catwoman nearly feeds Batman and Robin to her feline friends before the dynamic duo deducts one of her nine lives.
Catwoman Julie Newmar
Leo Jock Mahoney
Felix Ralph Manza

Director: James Sheldon

The Penguin Goes Straight/Not Yet, He Ain't

w Lorenzo Semple Jr. & John Cardwell
The mocking mountebank sets up his own Penguin Protective Agency and strings up the dynamic duo in a shooting gallery.
The Penguin Burgess Meredith
Sophia Starr Kathleen Crowley
Eagle-Eye Harvey Lembeck

Director: Leslie H. Martison

The Ring of Wax/Give 'Em the Axe

w Jack Paritz & Bob Rodgers
Batman and Robin nearly meet a waxy fate as they stop the Riddler from stealing an ancient Incan treasure.
Riddler Frank Gorshin
Moth Linda Gaye Scott
Matches Michael Greene
Tallow Joey Tata

Director: James B. Clark

The Joker Trumps an Ace/Batman Sets the Pace

w Francis & Marian Cockrell
In their efforts to save a visiting Maharajah from the Joker's clutches, the peerless pair are locked into a high chimney that begins to fill with lethal gas.
The Joker Cesar Romero
Jill Jane Wald
Maharajah Dan Seymour

Director: Richard C. Sarafian

The Curse of Tut/The Pharaoh's in a Rut

w Robert C. Dennis & Earl Barret
A latter-day King of the Nile claims Gotham City as his kingdom and inflicts an ancient pebble torture on Batman.
King Tut Victor Buono
Nefertiti Ziva Rodann
Grand Vizier Don Barry

Director: Charles R. Rondeau

The Bookworm Turns/While Gotham City Burns

w Rik Vollaerts
Holy Batstew! The dynamic duo are trapped inside a giant cookbook.
The Bookworm Roddy McDowall
Lydia Francine York
Mayor Linseed (semi-regular) Byron Keith

Director: Larry Peerce

Death in Slow Motion/The Riddler's False Notion

w Dick Carr
The Riddler makes a silent film comedy of Batman and Robin, and the Boy Wonder nearly gets sawn in half.
Riddler Frank Gorshin
Pauline Sherry Jackson
Van Jones Francis X. Bushman
Von Bloheim Theo Marcuse

Director: Charles R. Rondeau

Fine Finny Fiends/Batman Makes the Scenes

w Sheldon Stark
Are Batman and Robin doomed to be vanquished by a vacuum as the Penguin lets the air out of their lungs?
Penguin Burgess Meredith
Finella Julie Gregg
Octopuss Victor Lundin
Shark Dal Jenkins
Swordfish Louie Elias

Director: Tom Gries

Season Two
60 half-hour episodes

17 September 1966–2 April 1967
(Northern: ABC Television)

Shoot a Crooked Arrow/Walk the Straight and Narrow

w Stanley Ralph Ross
A latter-day Robin Hood who robs from the rich but doesn't always give to the poor strings up Batman and Robin for some jousting practice.
The Archer Art Carney
Maid Marilyn Barbara Nichols
Crier Tuck Doodles Weaver
Big John Loren Ewing
Everett Bannister Archie Moore
Alan A Dale Robert Cornthwaite

Director: Sherman Marks

Hot off the Griddle/The Cat and the Fiddle

w Stanley Ralph Ross
Catwoman leaves Batman and Robin out to fry in the midday sun—but a timely eclipse enables them to escape and overcome the feline fiend who's trying to steal two priceless violins.
Catwoman Julie Newmar
Jack O'Shea Jack Kelly
Driver James Brolin
John Buck Kartalian
Hostess Edy Williams

Director: Don Weis

The Minstrel's Shakedown/Barbecued Batman

w Francis & Marian Cockrell
A lute-strumming melodic fiend has the peerless pair hoisted on a spit to be roasted until well done.
The Minstrel Van Johnson
Amanda Leslie Perkins
Treble Norman Grabowski
Bass Remo Pisani
Courtland John Gallaudet
Scrubwoman Phyllis Diller

Director: Murray Golden

The Spell of Tut/Tut's Case Is Shut

w Robert C. Dennis & Earl Barret
Abu raubu simbu tu . . . King Tut plots to take over Gotham City with an ancient paralyzing potion. Batman foils him by drinking buttermilk to coat his stomach.
King Tut Victor Buono
Cleo Marianna Hill
Lapidary Peter Mamakos
Amenophis Tewfik Michael Pataki

Director: Larry Peerce

The Greatest Mother of Them All/Ma Parker

w Henry Slesar
Infamous Ma Parker and her children try to blow up the dynamic duo by rigging the Batmobile to explode at 60 mph—but naturally Batman sticks to the speed limit.
Ma Parker Shelley Winters
Legs Tisha Sterling
Mad Dog Michael Vandever
Pretty Boy Robert Biheller
Machine Gun Peter Brooks
Warden Crichton David Lewis

Director: Oscar Rudolph

The Clock King's Crazy Crimes/The King Gets Crowned

w Bill Finger & Charles Sinclair
Batman and Robin are captured by Clock King and his Second Hands and imprisoned in a giant hourglass. They escape by toppling the glass and running like hamsters inside so that it rolls into a truck!
The Clock King Walter Slezak
Car Hop Linda Lorimer
Millie Second Eileen O'Neill
Parkhurst Ivan Triesault

Director: James Neilson

An Egg Grows in Gotham/The Yegg Foes in Gotham

w Stanley Ralph Ross, *story by* Ed Self
Egghead gains legal control of Gotham City and attaches a truth machine to Bruce Wayne, suspecting him to be Batman. But the tables are turned in an eggstraordinary battle.
Egghead Vincent Price
Chicken Edward Everett Horton
Miss Bacon Gail Hire
Foo Yung Ben Welden
Benedict Gene Dynarski

Director: George Waggner

The Devil's Fingers/The Dead Ringers

w Lorenzo Semple Jr.
A crooked pianist named Chandell (Fingers) woos Aunt Harriet, while Batman and Robin are nearly perforated on a music roll cutter for a player piano.
Fingers Liberace
Doe Marilyn Hanold
Rae Edy Williams
Mimi Sivi Aberg

Director: Larry Peerce

Hizzoner the Penguin/Dizzoner the Penguin

w Stanford Sherman
The Penguin runs for Mayor against Batman—and nearly wins.
The Penguin Burgess Meredith
Mayor Linseed Byron Keith
Rooper Woodrow Parfrey
Themselves Paul Revere and The Raiders
Gallus George Furth
Klondike Don Wilson

Director: Oscar Rudolph

Green Ice/Deep Freeze

w Max Hodge
Mr. Freeze embarks on a campaign to discredit the dynamic duo and tries to turn them into human Popsicles in his Frosty Freezie Factory.
Mr. Freeze Otto Preminger
Miss Iceland Dee Hartford
Shivers Nicky Blair
Chill Ken Dibbs
Mayor Linseed Byron Keith

Director: George Waggner

The Impractical Joker/The Joker's Provokers

w Jay Thompson & Charles Hoffman
The Joker's new time device causes havoc in Gotham City; the Boy Wonder is sprayed with wax and Batman is trussed up on a giant duplicator.
The Joker Cesar Romero
Cornelia Kathy Kersh
Latch Luis Quinn

Director: James B. Clark

Marsha, Queen of Diamonds/Marsha's Scheme with Diamonds

w Stanford Sherman
Holy Matrimony! Marsha schemes to steal the Batjewels that power the Batcomputer by becoming Mrs. Batman!
Marsha Carolyn Jones
Grand Mogul Woody Strode
Sgt. O'Leary James O'Hara
Aunt Hilda Estelle Winwood

Director: James B. Clark

Come Back, Shame/It's the Way You Play the Game

w Stanley Ralph Ross
A crooked car-rustling cowboy unleashes a herd of stampeding cattle at the dynamic duo, but Batman draws them away by waving his cape like a matador.
Shame Cliff Robertson
Okie Annie Joan Staley
Messy James Timothy Scott

Director: Oscar Rudolph

The Penguin's Nest/The Bird's Last Jest

w Lorenzo Semple Jr.
Penguin tries every trick he knows to get sent to prison so that he can collaborate with jailed forger Ballpoint Baxter.
The Penguin Burgess Meredith
Chickadee Grace Gaynor
Cordy Blue Lane Bradford
Maty Dee Vito Scotti

Director: Murray Golden

The Cat's Meow/The Bats Kow Tow

w Stanley Ralph Ross
Using a voice-eraser, Catwoman steals the singing voices of Chad and Jeremy and demands a ransom after locking Batman and Robin in a giant echo chamber.
Catwoman Julie Newmar
Chad Chad Stuart
Jeremy Jeremy Clyde
Moe Ric Roman
Meanie Tom Castronova
Eenie Sharyn Wynters
Miney Chuck Henderson

Director: James B. Clark

Puzzles Are Coming/The Duo Is Slumming

w Fred De Gorter
The Puzzler casts the duo adrift in a balloon rigged to drop at 20,000 feet—but Robin jams the altimeter with a piece of chewing gum.
The Puzzler Maurice Evans
Rocket Barbara Stuart
Artie Knab Paul Smith
Blimpy Robert Miller Driscoll

Director: Jeffrey Hayden

The Sandman Cometh/The Catwoman Goeth

w Ellis St. Joseph
A European crook, Sandman, double-crosses Catwoman to steal all of a noodle queen's fortune for himself.
Sandman Michael Rennie
Catwoman Julie Newmar
J. Pauline Spaghetti Spring Byington
Cameo Don Ho
Female Newscaster Gypsy Rose Lee

Director: George Waggner

The Contaminated Cowl/The Mad Hatter Runs a Foul

w Charles Hoffman
The Mad Hatter sprays Batman's cowl with radioactive fumes in an effort to add it to his chapeau collection.
Mad Hatter (Jervis Tetch) David Wayne
Polly Jean Hale
Hattie Hatfield Barbara Morrison

Director: Oscar Rudolph

The Zodiac Crimes/The Joker's Hard Time/The Penguin Declines

w Stanford Sherman, *story by* Stephen Kandel
Batman and Robin are nearly devoured by a giant clam in this three-part tale in which the Penguin and the Joker join forces in a series of astrological capers.
The Joker Cesar Romero
The Penguin Burgess Meredith
Venus Terry Moore

Director: Oscar Rudolph

That Darn Catwoman/Scat, Darn Catwoman

w Stanley Ralph Ross
Catwoman's hypnotic drug turns Robin into a criminal.
Catwoman Julie Newmar
Pussycat Leslie Gore
Pat Pending J. Pat O'Malley

Director: Oscar Rudolph

Penguin Is a Girl's Best Friend/Penguin Sets a Trend/Penguin's Disastrous End

w Stanford Sherman
Pengy and Marsha, Queen of Diamonds, team up in a caper to turn gold bullion into guns, while the other dynamic double-act gets tied to a huge catapult.
Penguin Burgess Meredith
Marsha Carolyn Jones
Aunt Hilda Estelle Winwood
Beasley Bob Hastings
Gen. MacGruder Alan Reed Jr.

Director: James B. Clark

Batman's Anniversary/A Riddling Controversy

w William P. D'Angelo
It's Batman's anniversary as a crime-fighter, but the Riddler prepares a giant cake with quicksand icing.
The Riddler John Astin
Anna Gram Deanna Lund

Director: James B. Clark

The Joker's Last Laugh/The Joker's Epitaph

w Lorenzo Semple Jr., *story by* Peter Rabe
Batman is ordered to arrest Bruce Wayne for collaborating with the Joker's latest scheme.
The Joker Cesar Romero
Josie Phyllis Douglas

Director: Oscar Rudolph

Catwoman Goes to College/Batman Displays His Knowledge

w Stanley Ralph Ross
Catwoman takes a course in criminology and nearly cooks Batman and Robin in a cup of sulfuric acid.
Catwoman Julie Newmar
Cornell Paul Mantee
Cameo Art Linkletter

Director: Robert Sparr

A Piece of the Action/Batman's Satisfaction

w Charles Hoffman
Batman and Robin combine with Green Hornet and Kato to foil the rare stamp forging of Colonel Gumm.
Col. Gumm Roger C. Carmel
The Green Hornet Van Williams
Kato Bruce Lee
Pinky Pinkston Diane McBain

Director: Oscar Rudolph

King Tut's Coup/Batman's Waterloo

w Stanley Ralph Ross, *story by* Leo & Pauline Townsend
Tut seals Batman into a jeweled casket and drops it into a vat of water.
King Tut Victor Buono
Lisa Lee Meriwether
Neila Grace Lee Whitney

Director: James B. Clark

Black Widow Strikes Again/Caught in the Spider's Den

w Robert Mintz
Batman and Robin are caught in a giant web with two black widow spiders.
The Black Widow Tallulah Bankhead
Cameo George Raft
Tarantula Don Barry

Director: Oscar Rudolph

Pop Goes the Joker/Flop Goes the Joker

w Stanford Sherman
Robin is turned into a "Bat-mobile" as he is strung up in a moving display of giant palette knives. (First shown: 16/17 May 1967)
The Joker Cesar Romero
Baby Jane Towser Diana Ivarson
Bernie Park Reginald Gardiner

Director: George Waggner

Ice Spy/The Duo Defy

w Charles Hoffman
Batman tries to track down the notorious Mr. Freeze, who threatens to return the country to the ice age. (This story was absent from the original first U.K. run and was first shown: 8/9 June 1968.)
Mr. Freeze Eli Wallach
Glacia Glaze Leslie Parrish
Prof. Isaacson Elisha Cook

Director: Oscar Rudolph

Season Three
26 half-hour episodes

14 September 1974–8 March 1975
(London Weekend Television)

(For this season, the format changed, with more complete stories and fewer cliffhangers.)

Enter Batgirl, Exit Penguin

w Stanford Sherman
Penguin schemes to marry Barbara Gordon, the Commissioner's daughter, but she turns out to be a third secret crime-fighter, called Batgirl—and only Alfred knows . . .
The Penguin Burgess Meredith
Drusilla Elizabeth Harrower
Rev. Hazlitt Jonathan Troy

Director: Oscar Rudolph

Ring Around the Riddler

w Charles Hoffman
The Riddler schemes to take over the fight game in Gotham City—and calls in The Siren to help.
The Riddler Frank Gorshin
The Siren Joan Collins
Betsey Boldface Peggy Ann Garner
Kid Gulliver James Brolin

Director: Sam Strangis

The Wail of the Siren

w Stanley Ralph Ross
Commissioner Gordon and Bruce Wayne both fall under the spell of Lorelei Circe, the world-famous chanteuse who's determined to discover Batman's and Robin's true identities.
The Siren Joan Collins
Allegro Mike Mazurki
Andante Cliff Osmond

Director: George Waggner

The Sport of Penguins/A Horse of Another Color

w Charles Hoffman
Penguin and racehorse owner Lola Lasagne plot to win the Bruce Wayne Handicap—but Batgirl and Robin are riding in the same race.
Penguin Burgess Meredith
Lola Lasagne Ethel Merman
Glu Gluten Horace McMahon

Director: Sam Strangis

The Unkindest Tut of All

w Stanley Ralph Ross
Villainous King Tut nearly unmasks Batman in his brazen efforts to become master of the universe.
King Tut Victor Buono
Osiris James Gammon
Shirley Patti Gilbert

Director: Sam Strangis

Louie the Lilac

w Dwight Taylor
Louie plots to control the flower-children of Gotham City and tries to feed the caped crusaders to a man-eating lilac!
Louie the Lilac Milton Berle
Lila Lisa Seagram
Arbutus Richard Bakalyan
Primrose Schuyler Aubrey

Director: George Waggner

The Ogg and I/How to Hatch a Dinosaur

w Stanford Sherman
Egghead kidnaps the Commissioner, then he and Olga baffle Batman and Co. with onion-gas before scheming to hatch a 40-million-year-old dinosaur egg.
Egghead Vincent Price
Olga Anne Baxter
Mike Alan Hale Jr.
Omar Orloff Alfred Dennis

Director: Oscar Rudolph

Surf's Up! Joker's Under!

w Charles Hoffman
Batman, Robin and Batgirl foil the Joker's plot to become surfing champion of the world by draining the knowledge of a top young surfer.
The Joker Cesar Romero
Skip Parker Ronnie Knox
Hog Dog John Mitchum

Director: Oscar Rudolph

The Londoninium Larcenies/The Foggiest Notion/The Bloody Tower

w Elkan Allan
Batman, Robin and Batgirl answer "Ireland" Yard's call for help in solving a baffling series of fog-bound thefts.
Lord Ffogg Rudy Vallee
Lady Penelope Peasoup Glynis Johns
Prudence Lyn Peters
Supt. Watson Maurice Dallimore

Director: Oscar Rudolph

Catwoman's Dressed to Kill

w Stanley Ralph Ross
Catwoman sets a pattern-cutting machine to bisect Batgirl and tries to steal a cloth-of-gold coat.
Catwoman Eartha Kitt
Angora Dirk Evans
Manx James Griffith

Director: Sam Strangis

The Ogg Couple

w Stanford Sherman
Egghead, with Olga and her Cossacks, begins a series of well-planned raids leading up to a plot to steal 500 lbs. of caviar.
Egghead Vincent Price
Olga Anne Baxter
Old lady Violet Carlson

Director: Oscar Rudolph

The Funny Feline Felonies/The Joke's on Catwoman

w Stanley Ralph Ross
The Joker and Catwoman team up to steal a huge haul of dynamite.
The Joker Cesar Romero
Catwoman Eartha Kitt
Lucky Pierre Pierre Salinger

Director: Oscar Rudolph

Louie's Lethal Lilac Time

w Charles Hoffman
The terrific trio spoil Louie's smelly scheme to corner the lilac perfume market.
Louie Milton Berle
Sassafras Ronald Knight
Saffron John Dennis

Director: Sam Strangis

Nora Clavicle and the Ladies' Crime Club

w Stanford Sherman
A suffragette bent on destroying Gotham City ties the terrific trio into a terrific Siamese human knot.
Nora Clavicle Barbara Rush
Mayor Linseed Byron Keith
Mrs. Linseed Jean Byron

Director: Oscar Rudolph

Penguin's Clean Sweep

w Stanford Sherman
Penguin contaminates Gotham City's money with germs of a rare disease to make everyone throw it away.
Penguin Burgess Meredith
Miss Clean Monique Van Vooren
Doctor John Beradino

Director: Oscar Rudolph

The Great Escape/The Great Train Robbery

w Stanley Ralph Ross
Cowboy crook Shame sprays the Bat-gang with fear gas, turning them into sniveling cowards.
Shame Cliff Robertson
Calamity Jan Dina Merrill
Frontier Fanny Hermione Baddeley

Director: Oscar Rudolph

I'll Be a Mummy's Uncle

w Stanley Ralph Ross
King Tut discovers the secret of the Batcave while digging for a rare metal near Wayne Manor.
King Tut Victor Buono
Suleiman Joey Tata
Florence of Arabia Angela Dorian

Director: Sam Strangis

The Joker's Flying Saucer

w Charles Hoffman
The Joker builds a flying saucer, hoping to conquer the world by seeming to have come from outer space.
The Joker Cesar Romero
Emerald Corinne Calvert
Mayor Linseed Byron Keith
Prof. Greenleaf Fritz Feld
Mrs. Green Ellen Corby

Director: Sam Strangis

The Entrancing Dr. Cassandra

w Stanley Ralph Ross
The Bat-brigade are baffled by the "non-appearance" of two invisible adversaries who plan to release Gotham City's archfiends and reduce Batman and his pals to one-dimensional beings.
Dr. Cassandra Ida Lupino
Cabala Howard Duff
Warden Crichton David Lewis

Director: Sam Strangis

Minerva, Mayhem and Millionaires

w Charles Hoffman
The Bat-bunch matches wits with glamorous thief Minerva, who tries to cook the caped crusaders in a giant pressure cooker.
Minerva Zsa Zsa Gabor
Adonis William Smith
Monroe William Dozier
Customer Howie Horowitz

Director: Oscar Rudolph

BATTLESTAR GALACTICA

Billed as TV's most expensive series ever, *Battlestar Galactica* was derided by the critics and fought over by the lawyers, but still became a phenomenon.

Forgoing the big finish, the series *began* with the virtual destruction of the human race. In a distant galaxy, the 12 colonial tribes of Man come together to end a 1000-year war with a robot race called Cylons. But the Cylons spring a trap, devastating the humans' home planets and attacking their vast battlestar spaceships.

The remnants of mankind reassemble under the leadership of the final remaining battlestar, the *Galactica*, commanded by Adama, last member of the shattered colonial government. Forming a cumbersome caravan of some 220 assorted spacecraft, from shuttles to freighters, taxis to tankers, the survivors head off into deep space in search of the "lost" 13th colony—Earth. Naturally, the Cylons don't let it go at that and relentlessly pursue them through the galaxy.

Aside from the paternalistic Adama, the series' other main characters were his son, Apollo, who led the *Galactica*'s elite squadron of one-man Viper fighters; his handsome but impetuous buddy Starbuck; Adama's beautiful daughter, Athena, who was in charge of the ship's communications equipment; Starbuck's fancy, Cassiopea; Adama's second in command, Col. Tigh; Lt. Boomer, fighter pilot pal of Apollo and Starbuck; Apollo's adopted son, Boxey; and the villain of the piece, Count Baltar, a human traitor now in league with the Cylons.

Battlestar Galactica was the subject of eager lawsuits from 20th Century Fox who complained that it was a steal from *Star Wars*; for Apollo and Starbuck read Solo and Skywalker, for the Cylons read Stormtroopers, for the Imperious Leader read Darth Vader, etc. *Galactica* creator Glen A. Larson claimed his script was in the pipeline before *Star Wars* came out, and that if anything it was a lift from the Bible, with Adama as Moses leading the lost tribes to the Promised Land, pursued by the Egyptians—sorry, Cylons. Others have called it *Wagon Train* in space, with the Cylons replacing the marauding Indians and Lorne Greene reprising his famous father figure role of *Bonanza*'s Ben Cartwright.

The ace up *Galactica*'s sleeve was its dazzling special effects, masterminded by John Dykstra, who also did the tricks for *Star Wars*. But impressive though these were, they were diminished by the small screen and ultimately proved an expensive substitute for convincing characters and imaginative plotting.

MAIN CAST

Commander Adama Lorne Greene   *Capt. Apollo* Richard Hatch
Lt. Starbuck Dirk Benedict   *Col. Tigh* Terry Carter
Lt. Boomer Herb Jefferson Jr.   *Athena* Maren Jensen
Boxey Noah Hathaway   *Cassiopea* Laurette Spang
Flight Sgt. Jolly Tony Swartz   *Count Baltar* John Colicos
with:
Flight Corp. Rigel Sarah Rush   *Flight Officer Omega* David Greenan
Sheba Anne Lockhart   *Voice of Imperious Leader* Patrick Macnee
Imperious Leader Dick Durock   *Voice of Lucifer* Jonathan Harris

Creator/Executive producer: Glen A. Larson
Producers: Don Bellisario, John Dykstra, Paul Playdon, David O'Connell
Special effects co-ordinator: John Dykstra
Music: Stu Phillips

A Glen Larson Production in association with Universal Television
24 color 60-minute episodes
U.S. premiere: 17 September 1978
U.K.: 4 September 1980–30 April 1981
(Thames Television)

Saga of a Star World

(U.S.: One 3-hour episode, U.K.: three 60 mins.)
w Glen A. Larson
When their peace mission to end a 1000-year war with the robot Cylon race is all but wiped out by the treacherous enemy, the remnants of the 12 colonies of man gather under the protection of their last surviving battlestar, the *Galactica*. Led by Commander Adama, the rag-tag "wagon train" of 220 assorted spacecraft sets off in search of the lost 13th colony—Earth. Needing to refuel, the *Galactica* heads for the ore planet Carillon, where it finds a vast resort complex populated by humans and faces another mass Cylon attack.
Serina Jane Seymour
Uri Ray Milland
Adar Lew Ayres
Anton Wilfrid Hyde-White
Sandell David Tress

Director: Richard Colla

Lost Planet of the Gods

w Glen A. Larson, Don Bellisario *(a 2-part story)*
Striving to escape the relentless Cylon pursuit, the *Galactica* heads for a magnetic void that will scramble all navigational signals. Emerging, they are led by a mysterious pulsating star to Kobol, the lost planet of the Gods, where human life began. But the traitor Baltar is lying in wait and in the resulting Cylon attack Apollo's new bride, Serina, is killed.
Giles Larry Manetti
Sorell Janet Lynn Curtis
Brie Janet Louise Johnson
Sgt. Greenbean Ed Begley Jr.

Director: Christian Nyby

The Lost Warrior

w Don Bellisario
Crash-landing on a remote Western-style planet, Apollo helps a beautiful young widow and her fellow homesteaders in their fight against a ruthless land baron whose Cylon gunslinger Red-Eye confronts Apollo in a deadly laser shootout.
Vella Kathy Cannon
Puppis Johnny Timko
Bootes Lance LeGault
La Certa Claude Earl Jones
Marco Red West
Red-Eye Rex Cutter

Director: Rod Holcomb

The Long Patrol

w Don Bellisario
Starbuck, while testing a new ultrafast spaceship, loses the craft to a renegade convict and finds himself marooned on a mysterious planet where the prisoners serve terms for the crimes of their ancestors. Determined to escape, Starbuck incites a revolt.
Waiter John Holland
Robber James Whitmore Jr.
Croad Ted Gehring
Assault Sean McClory
Adultress Tasha Martell
Forger Ian Abercrombie

Director: Christian Nyby

The Gun on Ice Planet Zero

w Leslie Stevens, Michael Sloan & Don Bellisario *(a 2-part story)*
With the *Galactica* threatened by a giant, mountain-based laser on the ice planet Arcta, Apollo must lead a dangerous band of prisoners to the planet's surface to destroy the Cylon stronghold. The *Galactica* team discovers and joins forces with an enslaved clone society to defeat the Cylons.
Croft Roy Thinnes
Thane James Olson
Dr. Ravashol Dan O'Herlihy
Leda Christine Belford
Wolfe Richard Lynch
Tenna Britt Ekland
Ser Five Nine Danny Miller
Cadet Bow Alex Hyde-White
Killian Richard Milholland

Director: Alan Levi

The Magnificent Warriors

w Glen A. Larson
To save the fleet from starvation, Adama finds himself trapped into a compromising courtship of an old flame; and a fast-dealing card game leaves Starbuck the unwilling sheriff in a rugged farming community, which he is forced to defend against vicious pig-like creatures called Borays.
Belloby Brett Somers
Carmichael Olane Soule
Bogan Barry Nelson
Dipper Eric Server
Duggy Dennis Fimple

Director: Christian Nyby

The Young Lords

w Don Bellisario, Frank Lupo & Paul Playdon
After crash-landing on the planet Trillion, Starbuck is rescued by a band of children who decide to ransom the Galactican warrior to the Cylons in exchange for their imprisoned father.
Kyle Charles Bloom
Miri Audrey Landers
Ariadne Brigette Muller
Nilz Adam Mann
Megan Bruce Glover

Director: Don Bellisario

The Living Legend (aka Mission Galactica: The Cylon Attack)

w Glen A. Larson *(a 2-part story)*
Humanity is threatened with annihilation when Adama clashes with the hot-blooded, glory-hungry Cain, commander of the lost battlestar *Pegasus* who is obsessed with leading both ships in suicidal attacks on the Cylon forces. (This story was shown *last* by some ITV regions.)
Commander Cain Lloyd Bridges
Bojay Jack Stauffer
Tolen Rod Haase
Pegasus officer Junero Jennings

Director: Vince Edwards

Fire in Space

w Jim Carlson, Terrence McDonnell
Adama is critically injured when a Cylon kamikaze raid on the *Galactica* causes a fire to spread through the ship. Meanwhile, Boomer races against time to save Athena and Boxey from a fiery death.
Dr. Salik George Murdock
Fireleader William Bryant

Director: Christian Nyby

War of the Gods

w Glen A. Larson *(a 2-part story)*
The *Galactica* encounters the mysterious Count Iblis, who claims to be the last survivor of an alien culture. He is taken aboard the battlestar, where he charms the fleet with his omnipotent powers and grants the Council three wishes in return for blind allegiance and delivers them Baltar as their first! But then Adama discovers the stranger's true identity and a life-or-death struggle ensues between the mortals and . . . the Prince of Darkness.
Iblis Patrick Macnee
Dr. Salik George Murdock
Dr. Wilker John Dullaghan
Statesman John Williams
Brie Janet Louise Johnson

Director: Dan Haller

The Man with Nine Lives

w Don Bellisario
Starbuck must save an aging con man named Chameleon, whom he believes to be his father, from bloodthirsty Borellian henchmen.
Chameleon Fred Astaire
Siress Blassie Anne Jeffreys
Zed Frank Parker
Zara Patricia Stich
Maga Lance LeGault
Bora Robert Feero

Director: Rod Holcomb

Murder on the Rising Star

w Don Bellisario, James Carlson, Terrence McDonnell
Apollo uncovers a blackmail operation and finds his own life threatened as he works against time to clear Starbuck, who has been accused of murdering Ortega, a fellow Viper pilot.
Ortega Frank Ashmore
Pallon Lyman Ward
Elias Newell Alexander
Barton W.K. Stratton
Solon Brock Peters
Zara Patricia Stich

Director: Rod Holcomb

Greetings from Earth

(U.S.: Two-hour special, U.K.: Two 60 mins.)
w Glen A. Larson
Apollo and Starbuck intercept a primitive spaceship containing a family of six humans in suspended animation who are believed to be from Earth. When it is discovered that they cannot survive in the *Galactica*'s atmosphere, Adama gets Apollo, Starbuck and Cassiopea to accompany the travelers to their final destination, the planet Paradeen.

Geller Murray Matheson
Michael Randy Mantooth
Sarah Kelly Harmon
Hector Bobby Van
Vector Ray Bolger
Aggie Lesley Woods

Director: Ahmet Lateef

Baltar's Escape

w Don Bellisario
Baltar leads a prison revolt aboard the *Galactica*, taking many hostages including Adama and other council members. To rescue them, Apollo and Starbuck pose as Cylon robots and stage their own surprise attack.
Leiter Lloyd Bochner
Maga Lance LeGault
Bora Robert Feero
Taba Anthony DeLongis
Domra John Hoyt
Siress Tinia Ina Balin

Director: Winrich Kolbe

Experiment in Terra

w Glen A. Larson
Apollo is recruited by an angelic stranger to help rescue the inhabitants of the planet Terra from nuclear destruction at the hands of the evil Eastern Alliance, but is unable to prevent the start of a holocaust.
Brenda Melody Anderson
Dr. Horning Kenneth Lynch
President Peter D. MacLean
John Edward Mulhare
Supreme commandant Nehemiah Persoff
Max-Well Ken Swofford
Stone Sidney Clute

Director: Rod Holcomb

Take the Celestra

w Jim Carlson & Terrence McDonnell, *story by* David S. Arthur & David G. Phinney, Jim Carlson & Terrence McDonnell
When Starbuck enlists Apollo's aid in rekindling an old flame, their mission becomes embroiled in a struggle for control of a battlestar ruled by the iron-fisted Commander Kronus.
Kronus Paul Fix
Charka Nick Holt
Aurora Ana Alicia
Damon Randy Stumpf
Hermes Richard Styles

Director: Daniel Haller

The Hand of God

w Don Bellisario
Weary of evading their Cylon pursuers, the *Galactica* crew decides to take on a Cylon base star in a fight to the death. Starbuck and Apollo take off in a captured enemy craft to try to infiltrate the base star and give the *Galactica* a fighting chance. (No guest cast.)

Director: Don Bellisario

BEAUTY AND THE BEAST

After socialite attorney Catherine Chandler is rescued by a mysterious man-beast living beneath the city, one of the great romances of all times begins. Some viewers found it sappy; others loved Vincent and made him a cult figure. Unfortunately, just as the show was gathering momentum, star Linda Hamilton jumped ship. In the third season, her character was brutally murdered, and the shock to fans and viewers lost the series its formerly devoted audience.

REGULAR CAST

Catherine Chandler Linda Hamilton *Vincent* Ron Perlman
Father Roy Dotrice *Deputy District Attorney Joe Maxwell* Jay Acovone
Edie Ren Woods *Kipper* Cory Danziger
Mouse David Greenlee *Mary* Ellen Greer
Zach Zachary Rosencrantz *William* Ritch Brinkley
Diana Bennett Jo Anderson *Gabriel* Stephen McHattie
Elliot Burch Edward Albert *Mark* Lewis Smith

Creator: George R.R. Martin

56 color 60-minute episodes (one 2-hour episode was split for subsequent airings)
Aired in the U.S. 25 September 1987–3 August 1990

Season One

Once Upon a Time in the City of New York

w Ron Koslow
Following a brutal attack, New York socialite attorney Catherine Chandler is rescued by Vincent, a mysterious man-beast who lives beneath the subways of Manhattan.
Guest stars: John McMartin, Ray Wise, Ron O'Neal
Director: Richard Franklin

Terrible Savior

w George R.R. Martin
Catherine suspects Vincent of being the "man-beast" subway vigilante who fatally slashes criminals.
Guest stars: Delroy Lindo, Dorian Harewood
Director: Alan Cook

Siege

w David Peckinpah
Catherine and Vincent work to protect elderly tenants from a greedy land developer who wants to drive the old people from their rent-controlled apartments for a new land development project.
Guest stars: Albert Hague, Eda Reiss Merin, Louis Giambalvo
Director: Paul Lynch

No Way Down

w James Crocker
A street gang captures Vincent when he tries to protect Catherine.
Guest stars: Delroy Lindo, Chris Nash, Jeffrey Combs
Director: Tom Wright

Masques

w George R.R. Martin
A Halloween masquerade ball is the setting as Catherine and Vincent help an Irish peace activist.
Guest stars: John McMartin, Eric Pierpoint, Caitlin O'Heaney, Gerry Gibson
Director: Alan Cook

The Beast Within

w Andrew Laskos
As Catherine probes the murder of a New York longshoreman, she finds her life in danger . . . And, of course, only Vincent can help.
Guest stars: Asher Brauner, Michael Allredge, Michael Pniewski, Stan Kamber
Director: Paul Lynch

Nor Iron Bars a Cage

w Howard Gordon & Alex Gansa, story by Howard Gordon, Alex Gansa & Ron Perlman
When a Columbia University scientist captures Vincent, it's Catherine's turn to save him.
Guest stars: Michael Ensign, Christian Clemens, Darryl Hickman, Ellen Dow
Director: Tom Wright

Song of Orpheus

w Alex Gansa & Howard Gordon
When Father must return to the world above and face his former life, Vincent and Catherine try to unravel the mystery of his past.
Guest stars: Diana Douglas, Paul Gleason, Robert Symonds
Director: Peter Medak

Dark Spirit

w Robert Bernheim
An investigation into a wealthy businessman's death leads Catherine to voodoo.
Guest stars: Cliff DeYoung, Diana Barton, Obaka Adedunyo, Jessie Ferguson, Brett Hadley, Beah Richards
Director: Tom Wright

A Children's Story

w Ron Koslow
Catherine exposes corruption in a children's foster home, with help from Kipper, a boy from the world Below.
Guest stars: Richard Herd, Josh Williams, Joshua Rudoy
Director: Gabrielle Beaumont

An Impossible Silence

w Howard Gordon & Alex Gansa
When a deaf girl from the world Below witnesses a murder, she must give up everything she holds dear to convict the killer.
Guest stars: Terrylene Theriot, John M. Jackson, Chris Mulkey, Jason Bernard, Glenn Plummer
Director: Christopher Leitch

Shades of Gray

w George R.R. Martin & David Peckinpah
With Vincent and Father trapped underground, Catherine seeks help from a renegade in the world Below to save them.
Director: Tom Wright

China Moon

w Cynthia Benjamin
Vincent and Catherine help a Chinese girl escape an arranged marriage to a Tong leader.
Guest stars: Rosalind Chao, James Hong, Dennis Dun, Peter Kwong, Vincent Wong
Director: Christopher Leitch

The Alchemist

w Alex Gansa & Howard Gordon, story by Richard Setlowe
Catherine tries to find the source of a new recreational drug that's leaving people dead.
Guest stars: Tony Jay, Joey Aresco, Jeffrey Nordling
Director: Tom Wright

Temptation

w David Peckinpah
Catherine's boss finds himself in a conflict of interest when a beautiful attorney seduces him.
Guest stars: Isabella Hoffman, Milo O'Shea
Director: Gus Trikonis

Promises of Someday

w George R.R. Martin
Vincent's long-lost "brother" Devin arrives, visiting the world Below, posing as a new attorney in Catherine's office and dredging up painful memories.
Guest stars: Bruce Abbott, Andrew Held, John Franklin, Max Battimo
Director: Tom Wright

Down to a Sunless Sea

w Don Balluck
Catherine's old boyfriend from law school tries to win her back, and Catherine starts to fall for him again—against Vincent's good advice.
Guest stars: Jim Metzler, Marla Adams, Christine Jansen, Robert Cornthwaite, Eric Poppick
Director: Christopher Leitch

Fever

w Mark & Michael Cassutt
Greed comes to the world Below when Mouse discovers a sunken treasure ship.
Guest stars: David Clennon, Stan Ivar
Director: Tom Wright

Everything Is Everything

w Virginia Aldridge
Catherine and Vincent help a Gypsy clear his father's name and win his grandparents' trust.
Guest stars: Josh Blake, Robert Pastorelli, Will Kuluva
Director: Victor Lobl

To Reign in Hell

w Howard Gordon & Alex Gansa
Paracelcus kidnaps Catherine; Vincent prepares a battle to the death to win her back.
Guest stars: Tony Jay, Big John Studd, Beah Richards, Severn Darden
Director: Christopher Leitch

Ozymandias

w George R.R. Martin
Elliott Burch starts construction on a massive building that threatens the world Below, and only Catherine's promise of marriage can halt construction.
Guest stars: Julie Carmen, Bill Marcus, Linda Porter, Rutanya Alda, Sue Giosa, Carl Strano
Director: Frank Beascocchea

A Happy Life

w Ron Koslow
Catherine questions whether she and Vincent can ever have happy lives together, leading Vincent to break off their relationship in an attempt to make her happy.
Guest stars: Betsy Brantley, John McMartin, Sam Freed, Richard Young
Director: Victor Lobl

Season Two

Chamber Music

w Ron Koslow
Vincent and Catherine try to rescue a teenage musical prodigy who turned to drugs after a personal tragedy.
Guest stars: Terrance Ellis, Garland Spencer, Janet MacLachlan
Director: Victor Lobl

Remember Love

w Virginia Aldridge
It's a Wonderful Life comes to the tunnels as a guardian angel shows Vincent what the world would be like without him.
Guest stars: Tony Jay, Nicholas Hormann
Director: Victor Lobl

Ashes, Ashes

w Durrell Royce Crays, story by Roy Dotrice & Durrell Royce Crays
Vincent hides an escaped Russian seaman, unaware that he's carrying the plague.
Guest stars: Kamie Harper, Joshua Rudoy, Carolyn Finney, Tony Maggio, Adrian Paul, Joseph Campanella, Scott Hunter, Yevgeny Lanskoy
Director: Gus Trikonis

Dead of Winter

w George R.R. Martin
Parcelus attends the tunnel-dwellers' annual Winterfest in disguise, planning to kill the assembled guests.
Guest stars: Tony Jay, Beah Richards, Joseph Campanella, Marcie Leeds, Clive Rosengren
Director: Victor Lobl

God Bless the Child

w Alex Gansa & Howard Gordon
Catherine brings a pregnant former prostitute into the tunnels to give birth and build a new life.
Guest stars: Katy Boyer, Willard E. Pug, Marcie Leeds
Director: Gus Trikonis

Sticks and Stones

w Alex Gansa & Howard Gordon
A deaf girl who used to live Below joins a gang whose leader Catherine is trying to send to prison.
Guest stars: Terrylene, Ron Marquette, Ritch Brinkley, Kathryn Spitz, Ed Kelly, Warren Munson
Director: Bruce Malmuth

A Fair and Perfect Knight

w P.K. Simonds Jr.
Catherine tries to help a boy from the world Below when he pursues a college education.
Guest stars: Bill Calvert, Marcie Leeds, Zachary Rosencrantz, Phillip Waller
Director: Gus Trikonis

Labyrinths

w Virginia Aldridge, story by Howard Gordon & Alex Gansa
A teenage neighbor of Catherine's follows her Below, threatening the safety of the underground community.
Guest stars: Jonathan Ward, Daniel Banzali
Director: Daniel Attias

Brothers

w George R.R. Martin
A hideously deformed man flees a freak show and takes refuge in the tunnels.
Guest stars: Ritch Brinkley, Bruce Abbott, Kevin Scannell, Don Stark, Richard Camphuis
Director: Beth Hillshafer

A Gentle Rain

w M.M. Shelly Moore & Linda Campanelli
A woman recognizes a well-respected member of the world Below as the man who killed her son.
Guest stars: Scott Jack, Elayne Heilveil, Piper Laurie
Director: Gus Trikonis

The Outsiders

w Michael Berlin & Eric Estrin, *story by* P.K. Simonds, Alex Gansa, Howard Gordon
Violent outsiders invade the tunnels, bringing out Vincent's darker side.
Guest stars: Ritch Brinkley, Philip Walker, Anthony James
Director: Tom Wright

Orphans

w Alex Gansa & Howard Gordon
Following the death of her father, Catherine considers joining Vincent in the tunnels and forsaking life in the outside world.
Guest stars: John McMartin, Carolyn Finney, Philip Walker, Fredric Arnold, Douglas Roberts
Director: Victor Lobl

Arabesque

w Virginia Aldridge
A former tunnel dweller, now a ballerina, flees to the tunnels ahead of her ex-lover's henchmen.
Guest stars: Ken Brooks, Michelle Costello, Elyssa Davalos, Mark Neal, Kelli Williams
Director: Tom Wright

When the Blue Bird Sings

w Robert John Guttke & George R.R. Martin, *story by* Robert John Guttke
Catherine and Vincent are pursued by a young artist who is supposed to have died two years before.
Guest stars: Franc Luz, Beah Richards, Carolyn Finney, Terri Hanauer, Severn Darden
Director: Victor Lobl

The Watcher

w Linda Campanelli & M.M. Shelly Moore
Vincent almost loses Catherine forever when she is stalked by a man with deadly visions.

Guest stars: David Neidorf, Terri Hanauer, John Michael Bolger, Carolyn Finney, Joseph Carberry, Charlie Holliday
Director: Victor Lobl

A Distant Shore

w Marie Therese Squerciati
A tape piracy case takes Catherine to Los Angeles, far from Vincent.
Guest stars: Carolyn Finney, Debra Engle, Andy Bloch, Sal Jenco, Tina Andrews
Director: Michael Switzer

Trial

w P.K. Simonds Jr., *story by* Alex Gansa & Howard Gordon
Catherine prosecutes a fatal child abuse case.
Guest stars: Bill Marcus, Rosemary Dunsmore, Jayne Atkinson, Michael Holden, Scott Marlowe, Byron Morrow, Fritz Bronner, Amy Lynne
Director: Victor Lobl

A Kingdom by the Sea

w George R.R. Martin
After an assassination attempt, Elliott Burch asks Catherine for help.
Guest stars: R.G. Armstrong, Tom Ryan, Dean Norris, Ken Foree, Carl Crudup, Scott Wells, John Michael Bolger
Director: Gus Trikonis

The Hollow Men

w P.K. Simonds Jr., *story by* Andrew Laskos & P.K. Simonds Jr.
A pair of yuppie thrill-killers goes after Catherine when she fails to put them away.
Guest stars: Bill Marcus, John Michael Bolger, Willard E. Pugh, Brian Bloom, Tom Breznahan, John Deihl, Francois Giroday, Hal England, Apollo Dukakis
Director: Victor Lobl

What Rough Beast

w Alex Gansa & Howard Gordon, *story by* Alex Gansa, Howard Gordon & George R.R. Martin
An investigative reporter photographs Vincent and threatens to expose him, forcing Vincent to try to come to terms with his own inner beast.
Guest stars: Dan Shor, Sam Vlahos, Jim Metzler, Joseph Whipp, Tony Jay, Don Maxwell, Gary Hudson
Director: Michael Switzer

Ceremony of Innocence

w George R.R. Martin, *story by* Alex Gansa, Howard Gordon & George R.R. Martin
A tale of Vincent's birth brings out Vincent's dark side.
Guest stars: Tony Jay, Beah Richards, Ritch Brinkley, Richard Roundtree
Director: Gus Trikonis

The Rest Is Silence

w Ron Koslow, *story by* J. Larry Carroll & David Bennett Carren
Vincent loses his struggle to control his dark nature, threatening the safety and security of the other tunnel dwellers.
Guest stars: Joseph Campanella, Ritch Brinkely, Marcie Leeds
Director: Victor Lobl

Season Three

Though Lovers Be Lost (2 hours)

w Ron Koslow, Alex Gansa & Howard Gordon
Vincent tries to save Catherine from the leader of a vast criminal organization.
Guest stars: Stephen McHattie, Bill Marcus, Richard Roundtree, Marcie Leeds, Zachary Rosencrantz
Director: Victor Lobl

Walk Slowly

w M.M. Shelly Moore & Linda Campanelli
Official investigations into Catherine's death begin, while Vincent and friends mourn her loss.
Guest stars: Lewis Smith, Terri Hanauer
Director: Gus Trikonis

Nevermore

w P.K. Simonds Jr.
Vincent asks Elliott Burch to help track down Catherine's killer.
Guest stars: Stephen McHattie, Richard Roundtree, Bill Marcus, Stanley Kamel, M. Scott Wilkinson, Mike Jolly, Patrick St. Esprit
Director: Victor Lobl

Snow

w George R.R. Martin
Gabriel sends an assassin after Vincent; Diana (destined to be the new Catherine if only fans will accept her) learns of the tunnels.
Guest stars: Karen Elliot, Lance Henricksen, Randy Kaplan
Director: Gus Trikonis

Beggar's Comet

w George R.R. Martin
Vincent pursues revenge against Gabriel, who offers Elliott a chance to regain his wealth and power by betraying Vincent.
Guest stars: Mike Jolly, Stanley Kabel, John Lehne, Ben Piazza, Nick La Tour
Director: Victor Lobl

A Time to Heal

w Alex Gansa & Howard Gordon
Diana meets Vincent after he's injured.
Guest star: Daniel Farando
Director: Gus Trikonis

In the Forests of the Night

w P.K. Simonds Jr.
Rolley returns to the tunnels near death from a cocaine overdose, prompting Vincent to destroy one of Gabriel's drug labs.
Guest stars: Ed Morgan, Suzie Plakson, Tony Plana, Joseph Romeo, Miguel Sandoval
Director: Victor Lobl

The Chimes at Midnight

w M.M. Shelley Moore & Linda Campanelli
Gabriel captures Diana and orders her to tell Vincent his child is dying.
Guest stars: Steve Mittleman, Tom Donaldson, Lenny Gardner, Steven Gilborn
Director: Ron Perlman

Invictus

w George R.R. Martin
In the final episode, Gabriel imprisons Vincent, who alone has the power to save his dying son.
Guest stars: June Kyoko Lu, Tony Maggio, Alex Datcher
Director: Gus Trikonis

The Reckoning

w Alex Gansa & Howard Gordon
A woman Father once loved draws him from the tunnels while a psychopath is killing the helpers. (Unaired in the main network run.)
Guest stars: Marion Kodama Yu, Patrick Malone, Vachik Mangassarian, Patricia Place, John Pleshette, Terrylene Theriot, Jeff Corey, Fionnula Flanagan
Director: Kenneth R. Koch

Legacies

w Alex Gansa & Howard Gordon

A psychopathic killer buries Father alive, leaving Vincent precious minutes to save him. (Unaired in the main network run.)

Guest stars: David Graf, Matthew Kenemore, John Pleshette, Terrylene Theriot, Delane Vaughn, Teddy Wilson
Director: Gus Trikonis

BENJI, ZAX AND THE ALIEN PRINCE

American children's series about the adventures of 10-year-old alien Prince Yubi who arrives on Earth as a refugee. Pursued by enemies from his own planet, he tries to keep his identity secret, but comes to rely on two friends—a stray dog called Benji, and Zax, the guardian robot.

REGULAR CAST
Prince Yubi Chris Burton

Executive producers: Joseph Barbera, Margaret Loesch
Director: Joe Camp

13 color 20-minute episodes
5 October–28 December 1984
(BBC1)

BEWITCHED

One of the most successful comedies of all time, *Bewitched* starred the lovely Elizabeth Montgomery as Samantha, a witch who just happened to marry a mortal over her mother's objections. How Darin and Samantha made their marriage work, kept Darin's career afloat and survived the various pitfalls of magic, malicious in-laws and children made for a sometimes predictable but always watchable formula. The replacement of Dick York with look-alike Dick Sargent, due to York's health problems, provided a minor furor.

REGULAR CAST
Samantha Stephens Elizabeth Montgomery　*Darin Stephens* Dick York (*Seasons One–Five*), Dick Sargent (*Seasons Six–Eight*)
Tabitha Stephens Diane Murphy/Erin Murphy　*Adam Stephens* David Lawrence/ Greg Lawrence
Endora Agnes Moorehead　*Larry Tate* David White
Louise Tate Irene Vernon　*Gladys Kravitz* Alice Pearce (*Seasons One–Two*); Sandra Gould (*Seasons Three–Eight*)
Abner Kravitz George Tobias　*Esmeralda* Alice Ghostley
Aunt Clara Marion Lorne　*Uncle Arthur* Paul Lynde
Dr. Bombay Bernard Fox

Aired 1964–72 on ABC.
252 30-minute episodes (Seasons One–Two black and white; color thereafter)

Season One
I, Darin, Take This Witch, Samantha
Be It Ever So Mortgaged
Mother, Meet What's-His-Name
It Shouldn't Happen to a Dog
Help, Help Don't Save Me
Little Pitchers Have Big Ears
The Witches Are Out
The Girl Reporter

Witch or Wife
Just One Happy Family
It Takes One to Know One
. . . And Something Makes Three
Love Is Blind
Samantha Meets the Folks
A Vision of Sugar Plums
It's Magic
A Is for Aardvark

The Cat's Meow
A Nice Little Dinner Party
Your Witch Is Showing
Ling, Ling
Eye of the Beholder
Red Light, Green Light
Which Witch Is Which?
Pleasure O'Reilly
Driving Is the Only Way to Fly
There Is No Witch Like an Old Witch
Open the Door, Witchcraft
Abner Kadabra
George, the Warlock
That Was My Wife
Illegal Separation
Change of Face
Remember the Man
Eat at Mario's
Cousin Edgar

Season Two
Alias Darin Stephens
A Very Special Delivery
We're in for a Bad Spell
My Grandson, the Warlock
The Joker Is a Card
Take Two Aspirins and Half a Pint of Porpoise
  Milk
Trick or Treat
The Very Informal Dress
. . . And Then I Wrote
Junior Executive
Aunt Clara's Old Flame
A Strange Little Visitor
My Boss, the Teddy Bear
Speak the Truth
The Magic Cabin
Maid to Order
And Then There Were Three
My Baby, the Tycoon
Fastest Gun on Madison Avenue
The Dancing Bear
Double Tate
Samantha, the Dressmaker
The Horse's Mouth
Baby's First Paragraph
The Leprechaun
Double Split
Disappearing Samantha
Follow That Witch, Part 1
Follow That Witch, Part 2
A Bum Raps
Divided He Falls
Man's Best Friend
The Catnapper
What Every Young Man Should Know
The Girl with the Golden Nose
Prodigy

Season Three
Nobody's Perfect
The Moment of Truth
Witches and Warlocks Are My Favorite Things
Accidental Twins

A Most Unusual Wood Nymph
Endora Moves in for a Spell
Twitch or Treat
Dangerous Diaper Dan
The Short Happy Circuit of Aunt Clara
I'd Rather Twitch Than Fight
Oedipus Hex
Sam's Spooky Chair
My Friend Ben
Samantha for the Defense
Gazebo Never Forgets
Soapbox Derby
Sam in the Moon
Hoho, the Clown
Super Car
The Corn Is as High as a Guernsey's Eye
Trial and Error of Aunt Clara
Three Wishes
I Remember You . . . Sometimes
Art for Sam's Sake
Charlie Harper, Winner
Aunt Clara's Victoria Victory
The Crone of Cawdor
No More Mr. Nice Guy
It's Witchcraft
How to Fail in Business with All Kinds of Help
Toys in Babeland
Bewitched, Bothered and Infuriated
Nobody but a Frog Knows How to Live
Thre's Gold in Them Thar Pills

Season Four
Long Live the Queen
Business, Italian Style
Double, Double, Toil and Trouble
Cheap, Cheap!
No Zip in My Zap
Birdies, Bogies and Baxter
The Safe Sane Halloween
Out of Sync, Out of Mind
That Was No Chick, That Was My Wife
Allergic to Macedonian Dodo Birds
Samantha's Thanksgiving to Remember
Solid Gold Mother-in-Law
My, What Big Ears You Have
I Get Your Nanny, You Get My Goat
Humbug Not to Be Spoken Here
Samantha's Da Vinci Dilemma
Once in a Vial
Snob in the Grass
If They Never Meet
Hippie, Hippie, Hooray
A Prince for a Day
McTavish
How Green Was My Grass
To Twitch or Not to Twitch
Playmates
Tabitha's Cranky Spell
I Confess
A Majority of Two
Samantha's Secret Saucer
The No-Harm Charm
Man of the Year
Splitsville

Season Five

Samantha's Wedding Present
Samantha Goes South for a Spell
Samantha on the Keyboard
Darin Gone! And Forgotten?
It's So Nice to Have a Spouse Around the House
Mirror, Mirror on the Wall
Samantha's French Pastry
Is It Magic or Imagination?
Samantha Fights City Hall
Samantha Loses Her Voice
I Don't Want to Be a Toad
Weep No More, My Willow
Instant Courtesy
Samantha's Super Maid
Cousin Serena Strikes Again, Part 1
Cousin Serena Strikes Again, Part 2
One Touch of Midas
Samantha, the Bard
Samantha, the Sculptress
Mrs. Stephens, Where Are You?
Marriage, Witch's Style
Going Ape
Tabitha's Weekend
The Battle of Burning Oak
Samantha's Power Failure
Twitching for UNICEF
Daddy Does His Thing
Samantha's Good News
Samantha's Shopping Spree
Samantha and Darin in Mexico City

Season Six

Sam and the Beanstalk
Samantha's Yoo Hoo Maid
Samantha's Caesar Salad
Samantha's Curious Cravings
And Something Makes Four
Naming Samantha's New Baby
To Trick or Treat, or Not to Trick or Treat
A Bunny for Tabitha
Samantha's Secret Spell
Daddy Comes to Visit
Darin the Warlock
Sam's Double Mother Trouble
You're So Agreeable
Santa Comes to Visit and Stays and Stays
Samantha's Better Halves
Samantha's Lost Weekend
The Phrase Is Familiar
Samantha's Secret Is Discovered
Tabitha's Very Own Samantha
Super Arthur
What Makes Darin Run?
Serena Stops the Show
Just a Kid Again
The Generation Zap
Okay, Who's the Wise Witch?
A Chance of Love
If the Shoe Pinches
Mona Sammy
Turn on the Old Charm
Make Love Not Hate

Season Seven

To Go or Not to Go, That Is the Question
Salem, Here We Come
The Salem Saga
Samantha's Hot Bedwarmer
Darin on a Pedestal
Paul Revere Rides Again
Samantha's Bad Day in Salem
Samantha's Old Salem Trip
Samantha's Pet Warlock
Samantha's Old Man
The Corsican Cousins
Samantha's Magic Potion
Sisters at Heart
The Mother-in-Law of the Year
Mary, the Good Fairy
The Good Fairy Strikes Again
The Return of Darin the Bold
The House That Uncle Arthur Built
Samantha and the Troll
This Little Piggy
Mixed Doubles
Darin Goes Ape
Money Happy Returns
Out of the Mouth of Babes
Samantha's Psychic Pslip
Samantha's Magic Mirror
Laugh, Clown, Laugh
Samantha and the Antique Doll

Season Eight

How Not to Lose Your Head to Henry VIII, Part 1
How Not to Lose Your Head to Henry VIII, Part 2
Samantha and the Loch Ness Monster
Samantha's Not-So-Leaning Tower of Pisa
Bewitched, Bothered and Baldoni
Paris, Witch's Style
The Ghost Who Made a Specter of Himself
TV or Not TV
A Plague on Maurice and Samantha
Hansel and Gretel in Samanthaland
The Warlock in the Gray Flannel Suit
The Eight Year Itch Witch
Three Men and a Witch on a Horse
Adam, Warlock or Washout
Samantha's Magic Sitter
Samantha Is Earthbound
Serena's Richcraft
Samantha on Thin Ice
Serena's Youth Pill
Tabitha's First Day at School
George Washington Zapped Here, Part 1
George Washington Zapped Here, Part 2
School Days, School Daze
A Good Turn Never Goes Unpunished
Sam's Witchcraft Blows a Fuse
The Truth, Nothing but the Truth, So Help Me, Sam

Beyond Westworld

Westworld was an amusement park where superhuman androids helped visitors fulfil their Wild West fantasies. In *Beyond Westworld*, the powerful robots are sprung from the amusement park and sent out into the big wide world by their megalomaniac scientist creator, Simon Quaid, as the advance guard for his vision of a perfectly programmed society.

Ranged against them are John Moore and Pam Williams, the top agents of Delos, the giant corporation behind Westworld. They must expose and prevent the android threat whenever and wherever it occurs. Helping them out at Delos headquarters is computer genius Prof. Oppenheimer.

Beyond Westworld was the brainchild of writer-producer Lou Shaw (the man who created *Quincy!*).

REGULAR CAST
Simon Quaid James Wainwright *John Moore* Jim McMullan
Pamela Williams Connie Sellecca *Prof. Oppenheimer* William Jordan
Foley Stewart Moss *(pilot)*, Severn Darden *(series)*
Roberta Ann McCurry *Scotty S.* Newton Anderson

Creator/Executive producer: Lou Shaw
Based on a concept by: Michael Crichton
Writers: Various, including Lou Shaw, Martin Roth
Directors: Various, including Ted Post

5 color 60-minute episodes
Westworld Destroyed (pilot)

My Brother's Keeper
Sound of Terror
Takeover
The Lion
U.S. premiere: 5 March 1980
U.K. premiere: 31 August–21 September 1980, 1 January 1981
(Grampian/Granada)

The Bionic Woman

The Bionic Woman, alias Jaime Sommers, first appeared as Steve Austin's childhood sweetheart in a two-part story of *The Six Million Dollar Man* (U.S.: January 1975), in which she became his "jogging partner" after a terrible sky-diving accident.

When she was killed off at the end of the story, Americans howled in sorrow and protest and Jaime was brought back to life for another double dose with the explanation that she'd been deep-frozen until bionic surgery was possible. *The Bionic Woman*'s staying power was confirmed, and a second bionic series was born.

Jaime Sommers also had bionic legs and a bionic arm, but instead of a new eye she got a bionic ear, enabling her to hear conversations over a mile away—or talking at the back of the airbase classroom where she worked as a teacher when she wasn't gallivanting off on dangerous missions for Oscar Goldman's OSI agency. These involved such weighty tasks as flying down to South America to rescue an ambassador ("Angel of Mercy"), teaming up with Steve Austin to avert a missile threat to Los Angeles ("The Deadly Missiles"), saving a pet lion from angry farmers ("Claws"), or posing as a beauty queen to uncover a spy ring ("Bionic Beauty").

Alien plots weren't neglected either. Jaime was called on to tame the mysterious power of a living meteorite in "The Vega Influence"; in "The Pyramid," she was trapped within an underground structure with an alien who insisted that Earth was about to be destroyed; and in "Sanctuary Earth," she discovered a 14-year-old-girl from another planet inside a satellite that unexpectedly returned to Earth. And Jaime also faced an army of deadly female robots bent on capturing an energy ray weapon in "Fembots in Las Vegas."

Moreover, after we'd had the bionic man, the bionic woman and the bionic boy (see *The Six Million Dollar Man*), the nuclear family was completed by Max, *The Bionic Dog*—able to chew rifle barrels and outrun a motorbike.

Finally, Jaime bowed out of bionic duty with a splendid spoof of *The Prisoner* called "On the Run," in which she resigned and was sent to a special camp for ex-agents.

Bowing to the inevitable, Steve and Jaime eventually tied the knot in a 1994 TV movie, *Bionic Breakdown*, in which a computer virus also threatens Jaime's life.

REGULAR CAST
Jaime Sommers Lindsay Wagner Oscar Goldman Richard Anderson
Dr. Rudy Wells Martin E. Brooks
Jim Elgin Ford Rainey Helen Elgin (Steve Austin's mother) Martha Scott

Executive producer: Harve Bennett
Producer: Ken Johnson
Writers: Various
Directors: Various
Music supervisor: Hal Mooney

An MCA Television Production
57 color 60-minute episodes

U.S. premiere: 14 January 1976
U.K. premiere: 1 July 1976
(Author's note: ITV's regionalization meant that after the initial concerted launch, the series' fate was left to the whims of the individual companies, thus the length and composition of its various U.K. runs varied considerably around the nation. So, for ease of reference, I've listed the episodes in their original American seasons.)

Season One
Welcome Home, Jaime (Part 2)*
Angel of Mercy
Thing of the Past
Claws
The Deadly Missiles
Bionic Beauty
Jaime's Mother
Winning Is Everything
Canyon of Death
Fly Jaime
The Jailing of Jaime
Mirror Image
The Ghosthunter

Season Two
The Return of Bigfoot (Part 2)**
In This Corner, Jaime Sommers

Assault on the Princess
Road to Nashville
Kill Oscar (Parts 1 and 3)***
Black Magic
Sister Jaime
The Vega Influence
Jaime's Shield (a 2-parter)
Biofeedback
Doomsday Is Tomorrow (a 2-parter)

Deadly Ringer (a 2-parter)
Jaime and the King
Beyond the Call
The De Jon Caper
The Night Demon (aka The Daemon Creature)
Iron Ships and Dead Men
Once a Thief

Season Three
The Bionic Dog (a 2-parter)
Fembots in Las Vegas (a 2-parter)
Rodeo
African Connection
Motorcycle Boogie
Brain Wash
Escape to Love
Max
Over the Hill Spy
All for One
The Pyramid
The Antidote
The Martians Are Coming, The Martians Are Coming
Sanctuary Earth
Deadly Music
Which One Is Jaime?
Out of Body
Long Live the King
Rancho Outcasts
On the Run

* ITV's "premiere" episode of The Bionic Woman was actually a repackaged installment of The Six Million Dollar Man. Thus, the second half of the "two-part" opening story "Welcome Home, Jaime" was the true first episode of The Bionic Woman! (Confused? Try the next one!)
** In America this was the second half of a two-part story—the first half being an episode of The Six Million Dollar Man. Both parts were shown in Britain as The Six Million Dollar Man (December 1976—Thames).

*** This was actually a three-part story, but although all three episodes were screened over here as The Bionic Woman, in fact only Parts 1 and 3 were true Bionic Woman episodes. Part 2 was a Six Million Dollar Man and that's the way they played it in America.

BLAKE'S 7

*B*lake's 7 was an attempt to mount a serious space opera, to occupy the middle ground between the frolics of Doctor Who and the class of an Out of the Unknown. It might have been the beginning of a new creed of television science fiction—instead it became one of the last of a dying breed.

The series was created by Terry Nation, father of the Daleks and deviser of *Survivors*, who infused it with his own characteristically gloomy vision of the future.

Set in the "third century of the second calendar," it showed a near-omnipotent totalitarian government, the Federation, stifling freedom and creative endeavor, filling the air and water with tranquilizing drugs, and ruthlessly eliminating opponents either by killing them or shipping them out to a galactic penal colony.

Such is to be the fate of Roj Blake, former resistance leader, who is convicted on false charges and put aboard a prison ship. Escaping with some fellow prisoners in an abandoned alien spaceship, renamed *Liberator*, Blake becomes an intergalactic Robin Hood, leading his dogged band of raffish outlaws against a tyrannical empire with the same persistence that made his Sherwood counterpart a thorn in the Sheriff's side.

The original seven were Blake, cold computer genius Kerr Avon, cowardly thief Vila Restal, gentle giant Olag Gan, smuggler Jenna Stannis, Auron telepath Cally, and Zen—the *Liberator*'s almost-human computer.

As some of the heroes went, others came—the mercenary Del Tarrant, weapons expert Dayna Mellanby and blonde gunslinger Soolin. Plus, of course, the two other computer stars, the testy box of tricks, Orac, and the spaceship *Scorpio*'s obsequious Slave.

Leading the Federation pursuit of Blake and his crew were chief villainess Servalan and her hate-filled, obsessive huntsman, Travis.

The series rapidly built up a huge and devoted cult following and remains one of the most popular sci-fi series transmitted; its final episode was watched by more than 10 million viewers.

Nation himself wrote the entire first season of scripts and six subsequent stories, but his heroic ideals began to shift toward the end of Season Two. As Blake started to feel the pinch of revolutionary zeal, so the other characters began to emerge more forcefully, particularly Avon and Vila, whose sniping relationship was a pivotal feature of the series. And as Blake disappeared by the start of the third season, it was Avon who assumed control.

Blake's 7's greatest strength—and its enduring appeal—lay in its characterizations. These are not stereotype heroes who win every time. They frequently lose and show an alarming tendency to get killed off, a trend that reached its climax in the last episode, when most of the surviving outlaws were shot down with indulgent, slow-motion savagery. Also, there's little sanctimonious moralizing. The line between right and wrong is often shown as a thin one, and even the good guys are flawed—Blake becomes fanatical, Avon is paranoid and arrogant, Vila is spineless and Tarrant is conceited. In the face of such humanity, the fans happily overlooked the low-budget limitations of the series—the shaky sets and recycled props.

Blake's 7 started in Britain on the night *Star Wars* premiered in London. It was a good year for science fiction.

REGULAR CAST

Blake Gareth Thomas *(Seasons One–Two)*   Avon Paul Darrow
Vila Michael Keating   Cally Jan Chappell *(Seasons One–Three)*
Jenna Sally Knyvette *(Seasons One–Two only)*
Gan David Jackson *(Seasons One–Two)*   Zen Peter Tuddenham *(Seasons One–Three)*
Dayna Josette Simon *(Seasons Three–Four)*   Orac Peter Tuddenham *(Seasons Two–Four)**
Tarrant Steven Pacey *(Seasons Three–Four)*   Soolin Glynis Barber *(Season Four only)*
Servalan Jacqueline Pearce
Travis Stephen Grief *(Season One)*/Brian Croucher *(Season Two)*
Slave Peter Tuddenham *(Season Four)*

* In "Orac," the voice is by Derek Farr (uncredited)

Creator: Terry Nation
Script editor: Chris Boucher
Producers: David Maloney *(Seasons One–Three)*, Vere Lorrimer *(Season Four)*
Music: Dudley Simpson

A BBC Production
52 color 50-minute episodes

Season One
2 January–27 March 1978
Season Two
9 January–3 April 1979
Season Three
7 January–31 March 1980
Season Four
28 September–21 December 1981

Season One
(All stories written by Terry Nation.)

The Way Back

Roj Blake, a former resistance leader who has been "reprogrammed" by the Federation, is falsely convicted on a series of trumped-up charges and sentenced to transportation to the prison planet Cygnus Alpha. Waiting to board, he meets Jenna and Vila for the first time . . .
Bran Foster Robert Beatty
Glynd Robert James
Tarrant Jeremy Wilkin
Varon Michael Halsey
Maja Pippa Steel
Ravella Gillian Bailey
Richie Alan Butler
Arbiter Margaret John
Dr. Havant Peter Williams
Alta Morag Susan Field

Director: Michael E. Briant
Designer: Martin Collins

Space Fall

Aboard the prison ship bound for Cygnus Alpha, Blake attempts a mutiny. It fails, but when a mysterious unmanned space vessel appears alongside, Blake, Avon and Jenna are sent to investigate. After a struggle with a mind-blowing hallucinatory device, the rebels gain control of the ship and escape.
Avon Paul Darrow *(intro)*
Gan David Jackson *(intro)*
Leylan Glyn Owen
Raiker Leslie Schofield
Artix Norman Tipton
Teague David Hayward
Krell Brett Forrest
Nova Tom Kelly
Dainer Michael Mackenzie
Garton Bill Weston
Wallace Clinton Morris

Director: Pennant Roberts
Designer: Roger Murray-Leach

Cygnus Alpha

In the alien spaceship that they have named the *Liberator*, Blake, Jenna and Avon plan to free the prisoners on Cygnus Alpha. Blake teleports down but is captured by the planet's ruler, Vargas, who demands that he hand over the ship.
Vargas Brian Blessed
Leylan Glyn Owen
Artix Norman Tipton
Kara Pamela Salem
Laran Robert Russell
Arco Peter Childs

Selman David Ryall
Zen Peter Tuddenham *(intro)*

Director: Vere Lorrimer
Designer: Robert Berk

Time Squad

En route to attack a Federation communications complex, the *Liberator* crew takes on board a mysterious drifting projectile. While Blake, Avon and Vila proceed with the raid—ambushed then helped by Cally—the projectile's alien passengers cause problems back on the ship.
Cally Jan Chappell *(intro)*
Aliens Tony Smart, Mark McBride, Frank Henson

Director: Pennant Roberts
Designer: Roger Murray-Leach

The Web

Outlawed members of Cally's race use the telepathic powers to force her to sabotage the *Liberator* and lure it into a gossamer-like web surrounding an unknown planet, where they plan to use the ship's energy for their own ends.
Sayman Richard Beale
Geela Ania Marson
Novara Miles Fothergill
Decimas Deep Roy, Gilda Cohen, Ismet Hassam, Marcus Powell, Molly Tweedley, Willie Sheara

Director: Michael E. Briant
Designer: Martin Collins

Seek—Locate—Destroy

Stepping up his war against the Federation, Blake plans to steal a message decoder from a top security installation on the planet Centero. But things go badly wrong and Cally is taken prisoner by Travis and Servalan.
Travis Stephen Greif *(intro)*
Servalan Jacqueline Pearce *(intro)*
Rontane Peter Miles
Bercol John Bryans
Escon Ian Cullen
Prell Peter Craze
Rai Ian Oliver
Eldon Astley Jones

Director: Vere Lorrimer
Designer: Robert Berk

Mission to Destiny

Blake and his companions become involved in murder and intrigue surrounding a crippled spaceship that was on a mission to save its home planet, Destiny.
Kendall Barry Jackson
Sara Beth Morris
Mandrian Stephen Tate
Sonheim Nigel Humphreys
Levett Kate Coleridge
Grovane Carl Forgione
Rafford Brian Capron
Pasco John Leeson
Dortmunn Stuart Fell

Director: Pennant Roberts
Designer: Martin Collins

Duel

On an uncharted planet the last survivors of an ancient alien race force Blake and Travis to fight a duel so that they can learn about their kind.
Sinofar Isla Blair
Giroc Patsy Smart
Mutoid Carol Royle

Director: Douglas Camfield
Designer: Roger Murray-Leach

Project Avalon

Travis devises a plan to destroy Blake's crew and capture the *Liberator* using a plague-carrying android of Avalon, a captured resistance leader. But Avon's talents help Blake turn the tables—to Servalan's fury.
Avalon Julia Vidler
Chevner David Bailie
Mutoid Glynis Barber
Scientist John Baker
Terloc John Rolfe

Director: Michael E. Briant
Designer: Chris Pemsel

Breakdown

The limiter implant in Gan's brain malfunctions and he becomes unusually aggressive. The crew seeks help from a research station neurosurgeon, Professor Kayn. But Kayn alerts the Federation . . .
Kayn Julian Glover
Farren Ian Thompson
Renor Christian Roberts

Director: Vere Lorrimer
Designer: Peter Brachacki

Bounty

While Blake and Cally try to inspire a planet's rejected president to return to help his people, the *Liberator* is lured into a trap by a phony distress call from a group of bounty hunters.
Sarkoff T.P. McKenna
Tyce Carinthia West
Cheney Mark York
Tarvin Marc Zuber
Amagon guard Derrick Branche

Director: Pennant Roberts
Designer: Roger Murray-Leach

Deliverance

A spaceship crashes on the planet Cephlon. A *Liberator* search party finds one fatally injured survivor, Ensor, and Blake learns of Ensor's father's greatest creation—Orac.
Ensor Tony Caunter
Meegat Suzan Farmer
Maryatt James Lister

Director: Michael E. Briant *(and* David Maloney— uncredited)
Designer: Robert Berk

Orac

Despite competition from Travis and Servalan, Blake and his companions get to Orac first, and its dying creator, Ensor Sr., gives them the super-computer. Back on the ship, Orac makes its first prediction—the destruction of the *Liberator* . . .
Ensor Derek Farr
Phibians James Muir, Paul Kidd

Director: Vere Lorrimer
Designer: Martin Collins

Season Two

Redemption

w Terry Nation
The *Liberator* is attacked and boarded by aliens—the original owners of the ship come to reclaim their property. With Orac's help the crew are able to escape, pursued by an identical sister ship, which then blows up—thus confirming Orac's "prediction."
Alta One Sheila Ruskin
Alta Two Harriet Philpin
Slave Roy Evans

Director: Vere Lorrimer
Designer: Sally Hulke

Shadow

w Chris Boucher
Blake tries to enlist the help of the Terra Nostra, an interplanetary crime syndicate, in his fight against the Federation, but finds them more dangerous than he'd bargained for.
Largo Derek Smith
Bek Karl Howman
Hanna Adrienne Burgess
Chairman Vernon Dobtcheff
Enforcer Archie Tew

Director: Jonathan Wright Miller
Designer: Paul Allen

Weapon

w Chris Boucher
Blake and his crew set out to find a stolen secret weapon—a "delayed-effect" gun that can be triggered over great distances and many years after the victim has been shot. But Servalan is also after it in a plot involving a Blake clone.
Coser John Bennett
Rashel Candace Glendenning
Travis Brian Croucher *(intro)*
Fen Kathleen Byron
Carnell Scott Fredericks
Officer Graham Simpson

Director: George Spenton-Foster
Designer: Mike Porter

Horizon

w Allan Prior
Fleeing from pursuit ships, the exhausted *Liberator* crew heads out toward the edge of the galaxy. But they find the Federation has long arms—and on a planet called Horizon they are captured by the empire's puppet regime.
Kommissar William Squire
Ro Darien Angadi
Selma Souad Faress
Assistant kommissar Brian Miller
Chief guard Paul Haley

Director: Jonathan Wright Miller
Designer: Paul Allen

Pressure Point

w Terry Nation
Blake declares his intention of returning to Earth to attack Control—the computer complex that runs the entire Federation. But the raid ends in failure, and death for Gan after a clash with Travis deep underground.
Kasabi Jane Sherwin
Veron Yolande Palfrey
Arle Alan Halley

Berg Martin Connor
Mutoid Sue Bishop

Director: George Spenton-Foster
Designer: Mike Porter

Trial

w Chris Boucher
Travis stands trial at Space HQ, where Servalan is anxious to cover up her own failings. And a guilt-stricken Blake decides to desert his crew. But both men live to fight another day . . .
Zil Claire Lewis
Samor John Savident
Thania Victoria Fairbrother
Bercol John Bryans
Rontane Peter Miles
Par Kevin Lloyd
Lye Graham Sinclair
Guard commander Colin Dunn

Director: Derek Martinus
Designer: Gerry Scott

Killer

w Robert Holmes
On the planet Fosforon, Avon tries to persuade an old ally to help steal a vital component in the Federation cypher machine. On the *Liberator*, Blake and the others watch the salvage of a 700-year-old Earth ship and Cally senses great danger. Her fears are confirmed when a virulent plague breaks out.
Bellfriar Paul Daneman
Tynus Ronald Lacey
Gambrill Colin Farrell
Wiler Morris Barry
Tak Colin Higgins
Bax Michael Gaunt

Director: Vere Lorrimer
Designer: Sally Hulke

Hostage

w Allan Prior
Although he himself is now an outlaw, Travis is still determined to kill Blake and lures him into a trap, using the rebel's cousin Inga as a hostage.
Ushton John Abineri
Inga Judy Buxton
Joban Kevin Stoney
Space commander Andrew Robertson
Molok James Coyle
Mutoid Judith Porter

Director: Vere Lorrimer
Designers: Steve Brownsey & Gerry Scott

Countdown

w Terry Nation
Blake's crew arrives on the newly liberated planet Albian, to find the population facing destruction from a radiation device activated by the defeated garrison commander.
Grant Tom Chadbon
Cauder James Kerry
Provine Paul Shelley
Ralli Lindy Alexander
Tronos Geoffrey Snell
Selson Robert Arnold
Vetnor Sidney Kean
Arrian Nigel Gregory

Director: Vere Lorrimer
Designers: Steve Brownsey & Gerry Scott

Voice from the Past

w Roger Parkes
A mysterious telepathic signal forces Blake to reroute the *Liberator* to an isolated asteroid where a heavily disguised Travis is waiting to spring yet another trap.
Glynd Richard Bebb
Governor Le Grand Frieda Knorr
Nagu Martin Read

Director: George Spenton-Foster
Designer: Ken Ledsham

Gambit

w Robert Holmes
The search for Docholli, the man believed to know the secret location of Star One, the Federation's main control complex, brings the *Liberator* to Freedom City, a vast gambling town. But Travis and Servalan are on the same trail.
Krantor Aubrey Woods
Docholli Denis Carey
Chenie Nicolette Roeg
Croupier Sylvia Coleridge
Cevedic Paul Grist
Toise John Leeson
Jarrier Harry Jones
Zee Michael Halsey
Klute Deep Roy

Director: George Spenton-Foster
Designer: Ken Ledsham

The Keeper

w Allan Prior
One of the tribal chiefs on the planet Goth unknowingly holds the key to Star One. By the time he finds out which one, Blake discovers Travis has also learned the secret . . .
Gola Bruce Purchase
Tara Freda Jackson
Rod Shaun Curry

Fool Cengiz Saner
Old man Arthur Hewlett
Patrol leader Ron Tarr

Director: Derek Martinus
Designer: Eric Walmsley

Star One

w Chris Boucher
Blake finally reaches Star One and determines to destroy it. But aliens from Andromeda are gathering for a galactic invasion, and after a shootout in which Travis seriously wounds Blake before being killed by Avon, the *Liberator* is left standing alone against their battle fleet until the Federation ships can arrive.
Lurena Jenny Twigge
Stot David Webb
Parton Gareth Armstrong
Durkin John Brown
Marcol Paul Toothill
Leeth Michael Maynard

Director: David Maloney
Designers: Ray London & Ken Ledsham

Season Three

Aftermath

w Terry Nation
The war is won, but the *Liberator* is severely damaged. The crew escapes in one-man capsules, and Avon lands on a tribal planet where he is rescued by Dayna and her fugitive father. But Servalan arrives there too . . .
Dayna Josette Simon *(intro)*
Hal Mellanby Cy Grant
Chel Alan Lake
Lauren Sally Harrison
Tarrant Steven Pacey *(intro)*
Troopers Richard Franklin, Michael Melia

Director: Vere Lorrimer
Designers: Don Taylor & Gerry Scott

Powerplay

w Terry Nation
Back on the *Liberator*, Avon and Dayna find "Federation Space Captain" Tarrant is not all he seems to be. Meanwhile Vila and Cally fight their own battle for survival in a hospital that is not all *it* seems either.
Klegg Michael Sheard
Harman Doyne Byrd
Lom John Hollis
Mall Michael Crane
Zee Primi Townsend
Barr Julia Vidler
Nurse Catherine Chase
Receptionist Helen Batch

Director: David Maloney
Designer: Gerry Scott

Volcano

w Allan Prior
For the *Liberator*'s crew, the planet Obsidian offers the prospect of allies and a safe base from which to strike at the Federation. But it also holds a traitor, and a deadly secret of its own.
Hower Michael Gough
Bershar Malcolm Bullivant
Mori Ben Howard
Battle Fleet commander Alan Bowerman
Mutoid Judy Matheson
Milus Russell Denton

Director: Desmond McCarthy
Designer: Gerry Scott

Dawn of the Gods

w James Follett
The *Liberator* is mysteriously drawn off course, landing on an artificial planet where the crew falls into the clutches of the Thaarn, a creature from Cally's Auron legends.
Caliph Sam Dastor
Groff Terry Scully
Thaarn Marcus Powell

Director: Desmond McCarthy
Designers: Ray London & Gerry Scott

The Harvest of Kairos

w Ben Steed
A mysterious death awaits anyone who remains on the planet Kairos after the harvest week. And when Servalan finally captures the *Liberator*, it's on Kairos that she strands the crew.
Jarvik Andrew Burt
Dastor Frank Gatliff
Shad Anthony Gardner
Carlon Sam Davies
Guard Charles Jamieson

Director: Gerald Blake
Designer: Ken Ledsham

City at the Edge of the World

w Chris Boucher
Sent to open a strange vault in return for some crystals, Vila finds love and a temporary idyll on a bizarre odyssey that takes him 3000 light-years away.
Kerril Carol Hawkins
Bayban Colin Baker
Norl Valentine Dyall
Sherm John J. Carney

Director: Vere Lorrimer
Designers: Don Taylor & Gerry Scott

Children of Auron

w Roger Parkes
Servalan engineers a deadly virus that strikes the planet Auron. Cally is telepathically summoned home to help her people, but though Servalan is lying in wait, the *Liberator* crew succeeds in saving the planet's gene banks.
Deral Rio Fanning
Franton Sarah Atkinson
Ginka Ric Young
C A One Ronald Leigh-Hunt
C A Two Beth Harris
Patar Jack McKenzie
Pilot Four-Zero Michael Troughton

Director: Andrew Morgan
Designers: Ray London & Gerry Scott

Rumours of Death

w Chris Boucher
Avon returns to Earth to seek revenge on the Federation torturer who killed his girlfriend, Anna Grant, but finds the past was not what it seemed and the present holds only grief.
Sula (Anna Grant) Lorna Heilbron
Shrinker John Bryans
Chesku Peter Clay
Grenlee Donald Douglas
Forres David Haig
Balon Philip Bloomfield
Hob David Gillies

Director: Fiona Cumming
Designers: Paul Munting & Ken Ledsham

Sarcophagus

w Tanith Lee
After investigating an unmanned alien spaceship, Cally is taken over by a strange entity that assumes her form and begins to drain all energy from the *Liberator*. Only Avon is able to stand up to it and help Cally defeat the creature. (No guest cast.) "Dayna's Song" by Tanith Lee.

Director: Fiona Cumming
Designer: Ken Ledsham

Ultraworld

w Trevor Hoyle
The *Liberator* encounters the strange artificial planet of Ultraworld, which turns out to be a giant computer whose thirst for knowledge includes wiping clean the brains of new visiting species.
Relf Ronald Govey
Ultras Peter Richards, Stephen Jenn, Ian Barritt

Director: Vere Lorrimer
Designers: Jan Spoczynski & Ken Ledsham

Moloch

w Ben Steed
The *Liberator* crew trails Servalan to Sardos, where both are captured by Federation renegades who are aiming to harness the planet's advanced technology for their own ends. Then Sardos's supreme power shows itself as Moloch, a computer creature from the future.
Doran Davyd Harries
Grose John Hartley
Lector Mark Sheridan
Moloch Deep Roy
Chesil Sabina Franklyn
Poola Debbi Blythe

Director: Vere Lorrimer
Designers: Jan Spoczynski & Ken Ledsham

Death-Watch

w Chris Boucher
The ritual war fought by two professional champions seems like the ultimate spectator sport—until the crew of the *Liberator* discover that Tarrant's brother Deeta is one of the combatants and a scheming Servalan the "neutral" judge.
Deeta Steven Pacey
Vinni Mark Elliott
Max Stewart Bevan
Commentator David Sibley
Karla Katherine Iddon

Director: Gerald Blake
Designer: Ken Ledsham

Terminal

w Terry Nation
Responding to secret instructions he believes are from Blake, Avon heads for Terminal, an old artificial planet originally in orbit round Mars. But it's just an illusion created by Servalan to lure and capture the *Liberator*. With the crew stranded on Terminal, she departs in her prize only to be cheated when the ship—which had earlier passed through a strange particle field—begins to break up completely . . .
Blake Gareth Thomas
Kostos Gillian McCutcheon
Reeval Heather Wright
Toron Richard Clifford

Director: Mary Ridge
Designer: Jim Clay

Season Four

Rescue

w Chris Boucher
Cally dies in a series of explosions on Terminal. Avon and the rest are "rescued" by a stranger called Dorian, whose sinister purpose is revealed when they arrive on the planet Xenon, where they also meet his associate, Soolin.
Soolin Glynis Barber *(intro)*
Dorian Geoffrey Burridge
Creature Rob Middleton
Slave Peter Tuddenham *(intro)*

Director: Mary Ridge
Designer: Roger Cann

Power

w Ben Steed
Having killed Dorian, the outlaws try to get back to his spaceship, *Scorpio*—but first they become embroiled in a war between the planet's two tribes, the male-dominated Hommiks and the female Seska. When they finally make their escape they are joined by Soolin.
Gunn Sar Dicken Ashworth
Pella Juliet Hammond Hill
Kate Alison Glennie
Nina Jenny Oulton
Cato Paul Ridley
Luxia Linda Barr

Director: Mary Ridge
Designer: Roger Cann

Traitor

w Robert Holmes
Using Xenon as their new base, Avon needs to know why the Federation are suddenly making such easy territorial gains. They find the answer—a new pacifying drug—on the newly subdued planet Helotrix. And they also learn that Servalan did not die in the destruction of the *Liberator*.
Leitz Malcolm Stoddard
Colonel Quute Christopher Neame
Major Hunda Robert Morris
Practor John Quentin
Forbus Edgar Wreford
General Nick Brimble
The Tracer David Quilter
Avandir Neil Dickson
Igin George Lee
Sgt. Hask Cyril Appleton

Director: David Sullivan Proudfoot
Designers: Nigel Curzon, Roger Cann

Stardrive

w Jim Follett
Collision with an asteroid damages *Scorpio*'s main drives. The need to replace them is urgent enough to warrant a trip to the lair of the Space Rats—psychotic "Hell's Angels" of space.
Dr. Plaxton Barbara Shelley
Atlan Damien Thomas
Bomber Peter Sands
Napier Leonard Kavanagh

Director: David Sullivan Proudfoot
Designers: Nigel Curzon & Roger Cann

Animals

w Allan Prior
Dayna goes in search of her former tutor, Justin, a genetic engineer whose knowledge Avon now needs. She finds a horrifying genetic experiment—and is also captured by Servalan.
Justin Peter Byrne
Captain William Lindsay
Borr Max Harvey
Ardus Kevin Stoney
Og David Boyce

Director: Mary Ridge
Designers: Graham Lough, Roger Cann

Headhunter

w Roger Parkes
Avon sets out to recruit a cybernetics genius called Muller—but instead winds up with a homicidal android who plans to use Orac to dominate the galaxy.
Muller John Westbrook
Vena Lynda Bellingham
Technician Douglas Fielding
Android Nick Joseph
Voice Lesley Nunnerley

Director: Mary Ridge
Designers: Graham Lough, Roger Cann

Assassin

w Rod Beacham
Servalan hires a feared assassin, Cancer, to kill the *Scorpio* crew. Orac advises that they take the fight to Cancer, but no one knows what he—or she—looks like.
Verlis Betty Marsden
Nebrox Richard Hurndall
Cancer John Wyman
Piri Caroline Holdaway
Benos Peter Attard
Tok Adam Blackwood
Servalan's captain Mark Barratt

Director: David Sullivan Proudfoot *(and* Vere Lorrimer—*uncredited)*
Designer: Ken Ledsham

Games

w Bill Lyons
The planet Mecron is a vital source of Feldon, a rare and valuable energy crystal. The mining is controlled by Belkov, a renowned games player—and to reach his illicit private cache, the *Scorpio* crew must play a series of dangerous games.
Belkov Stratford Johns
Gambit Rosalind Bailey
Gerren David Neal
Guard James Harvey

Director: Vivienne Cozens
Designers: Eric Walmsley & Ken Ledsham

Sand

w Tanith Lee
Following up Federation concern over a lost expedition, Tarrant finds himself alone with Servalan on a planet where the sand is alive—and deadly.
Reeve Stephen Yardley
Chasgo Daniel Hill
Servalan's assistant Peter Craze
Keller Jonathan David
Computer Michael Gaunt

Director: Vivienne Cozens
Designers: Eric Walmsley & Ken Ledsham

Gold

w Colin Davis
Stealing a gold shipment from an undefended pleasure cruiser en route to Earth seems to be too good an opportunity to miss. But the *Scorpio* crew have been set up by Servalan, who for once has the Midas touch . . .
Keiller Roy Kinnear
Doctor Anthony Brown
Woman passenger Dinah May
Pilot Norman Hartley

Director: Brian Lighthill
Designer: Ken Ledsham

Orbit

w Robert Holmes
Egrorian, a renegade Federation scientist, offers Avon the ultimate weapon. But in return he wants Orac. Once again, Servalan is quietly manipulating the situation—but this time fails to get what she wants.
Egrorian John Savident
Pinder Larry Noble

Director: Brian Lighthill
Designer: Ken Ledsham

Warlord

w Simon Masters
Avon attempts to establish an anti-Federation alliance to spread the antidote to the empire's pacifying drug. He needs the cooperation of the most powerful warlord, Zukan—but he gets only treachery.
Zukan Roy Boyd
Zeeona Bobbie Brown
Finn Dean Harris
Boorva Simon Merrick
Chalsa Rick James
Lod Charles Augins
Mida Brian Spink

Director: Viktors Ritelis
Designer: Paul Allen

Blake

w Chris Boucher

Avon reveals that Orac has found Blake on the lawless planet Gauda Prime, where he has seemingly become a bounty hunter. *Scorpio* crash-lands on the planet, and when he meets Blake, Tarrant is convinced he has betrayed them. Avon is unsure of the truth but is forced to shoot Blake before Federation guards appear for the final shootout, in which Dayna, Tarrant, Vila and Soolin are all gunned down . . . and the guards move in for Avon.

Blake Gareth Thomas
Deva David Collings
Arlen Sasha Mitchell
Klyn Janet Lees Price

Director: Mary Ridge
Designer: Roger Cann

THE BOY FROM ANDROMEDA

Some of the best children's sci-fi drama in recent years has come out of Australia and New Zealand—and this six-part nineties adventure maintains that standard.

A joint New Zealand/Canadian production, it blends mystery and technology in an intriguing story of an alien artifact that awakens the sole survivor of a 100-year-old crashed spaceship.

On a holiday trip to the Tarawera volcano in New Zealand, teenager Jenny finds a strange metal fragment that acts like a video, playing back a story of a spacecraft plunging to Earth. With two other kids, hotelier's daughter Tessa and local lad Lloyd, who have similar fragments, she pieces them together to form something called a "fire key." The trio is attacked by the Guardian, a mysterious invisible creature, before the fire key leads them to a mysterious pod, hidden behind a waterfall. Inside is Drom, sole survivor of a crashed ship from the constellation of Andromeda, woken by the reassembling of the key.

Drom is on a quest to save the last of his people, an ancient race who left Earth millions of years ago, after an intergalactic war, and who are now seeking a new home as their world is dying. But they can't get past "the Gun"—the active Tarawera volcano—which, if triggered, would destroy Earth. The fire key could disarm the Gun, but the centuries-old Guardian (catchphrase "I will always be") is programmed to protect the Gun. Jenny and her friends must help Drom overcome the Guardian before the volcano erupts. In the traditions of children's drama they accomplish this while the adults, as usual, remain totally unaware of the extraterrestrial struggle.

Drom himself looked like a cut-down Edward Scissorhands, having three fingers with very long nails. But the best special effects were reserved for the confrontations with the Guardian, whose invisible menace was realized with *Predator*-like style.

Writer on the series was Ken Catran, author of earlier sci-fi adventures *Under the Mountain* and *Children of the Dog Star*.

MAIN CAST

Jenny Katrina Hobbs *Drom* Jane Cresswell *Tessa* Fiona Kay
Lloyd Anthony Samuels *Guardian* Brian Carbee *Drom's voice* John Watson
Guardian's voice Eugene Fraser
With: Heather Bolton, Paul Gittins, Andy Anderson, Brian McNeil, Alex Van Dam,
Dale Corlett, Grant McFarlane

Writer: Ken Catran
Creator: Jonathon Gunson
Producer: Caterina de Nave
Director: Wayne Tourell
Designer: Kirsten Shouler
Music: John Gibson

Special effects: Kevin Chisnell
South Pacific Pictures/Atlantis Films Production
6 color 30-minute episodes
6 October–10 November 1991
(BBC1)

BUCK ROGERS IN THE 25TH CENTURY

"Buck Rogers is a look at our world five centuries from
now, laced with a lot of fun, mischief and color."
—Glen A. Larson

Purists blanched, but *Buck Rogers in the 25th Century* was really a hero of the 1980s. Gone was the serious character of the original comic strip. This young Buck was a brash, fun-loving man who refused to take the computerized society of the future seriously.

The series too didn't take itself seriously—it aimed at escapist entertainment with a glossy, slick package packed with special effects. And Buck Rogers had one other weapon to fight the ratings war—sex, mainly in the slinky form of actress Erin Gray, who played Buck's sidekick, Wilma Deering, in alluring jumpsuits one size too small.

The premise behind the original 1929 comic strip (which ran for nearly 40 years) was that Buck Rogers, an ex-Air Force pilot, was overcome by a strange, noxious gas while surveying an abandoned mine shaft near Pittsburgh, and spent 500 years in a state of suspended animation.

In this series, however, Buck was an American astronaut who, in 1987, is launched on a deep space probe. His rocket is blown out of trajectory and Buck is frozen for 500 years, returning to Earth in the 25th century and becoming involved in a conflict between Earth and the Draconians, ruled by the evil (but beautiful) Princess Ardala.

Besides Buck and Wilma, other regulars were scientist Dr. Huer and Twiki, a vibrating-voiced little robot. Season Two saw the departure of Huer and the arrival of some new characters: Dr. Goodfellow (played with long-suffering dignity by Wilfrid Hyde-White), Admiral Asimov (presented as a descendant of author Isaac Asimov) and the tragic figure of Hawk, last survivor of a race of man-birds. The second season dumbed everything down enormously.

And there were plenty of guest stars, led by Buster Crabbe—who played Buck in the 1930s film serial—who came out of retirement, at age 71, to play an aging brigadier. Other notables were *My Favorite Martian* star Ray Walston, *Batman* villains Frank Gorshin, Cesar Romero and Julie Newmar, plus Woody Strode, Roddy McDowall, Jamie Lee Curtis and Jack Palance.

MAIN CAST

Capt. Buck Rogers Gil Gerard *Col. Wilma Deering* Erin Gray
Dr. Huer Tim O'Connor *(Season One only)* *Twiki* Felix Silla
Voice of Twiki Mel Blanc *Hawk* Thom Christopher
Dr. Goodfellow Wilfrid Hyde-White
Adm. Asimov Jay Garner
Princess Ardala Pamela Hensley
Kane Michael Ansara
Dr. Theopolis (computer) Eric Server *(Season One)*
Voice of Crichton Jeff David

Developed for TV by Glen A. Larson, Leslie Stevens
Executive producers: Glen A. Larson, John Mantley *(Season Two)*
Producers: Richard Caffey, Jock Gaynor *(both Season One)*, John Stephens *(Season Two)*
Supervising producers: Bruce Lansbury *(Season One)* Calvin Clements *(Season Two)*

A Glen A. Larson Production in association with Universal Television

34 color episodes (plus pilot), 60 mins., unless stated
U.S. premiere: 20 September 1979
U.K. premiere: 30 August 1980
(LWT)

Pilot episode

Awakening

(120 mins.)
w Glen A. Larson, Leslie Stevens
In the year 1987, astronaut Buck Rogers is launched on a deep space probe, but his rocket is blown off course and its lone passenger frozen for 500 years. When Buck awakens from his slumber, he is aboard the flagship of the Draconian fleet, en route to a peace conference on Earth. The lovely Princess Ardala is strongly attracted to him, but her earthly adviser Kane suspects he is a spy.
Kane Henry Silva
Draco Joseph Wiseman
Tigermen Duke Butler, H.B. Haggerty

Director: Daniel Haller
(This pilot episode was shown theatrically in the U.S. and Britain.)

Season One

Planet of the Slave Girls (aka Flight to Sorcerer's Mountain)

(105 mins.)
w Steve Greenberg, Aubrey Solomon, Cory Applebaum
When Dr. Huer suspects that poison in Earth's food supply is depleting the planet's fighting forces, he sends Buck and Wilma to Vistula, an agricultural planet that grows most of Earth's vegetables. There, Buck confronts a sorcerer named Kaleel and discovers a massive fleet poised to attack Earth.
Brigadier Gordon Buster Crabbe
Kaleel Jack Palance
Governor Saroyan Roddy McDowall
Duke Danton David Groh
Ryma Brianne Leary
Dr. Mallory Macdonald Carey

Director: Michael Caffey

Vegas in Space (aka Flight from Sinaloa)

w Anne Collins
Buck races against time to rescue a kidnapped girl from Sinaloa, an orbiting gambling paradise devoted to the pursuit of pleasure and vice.
Armat Cesar Romero
Falina Ana Alicia
Tangie Pamela Shoop
Velosi Richard Lynch
Marla Juanine Clay
Morphus Joseph Wiseman

Director: Sigmund Neufeld Jr.

The Plot to Kill a City (aka Death Squad 2500)

w Alan Brennert *(a 2-part story)*
Buck goes undercover to infiltrate the Legion of Death, a bizarre band of killers who plan to wipe out New Chicago, Buck's hometown and his last link with 20th-century Earth. But his true identity is discovered by the group's scientist leader, Kellogg. (Originally shown in the U.K. as a 105-minute episode.)
Sherese Nancy DeCarl
Argus Victor Argo
Quince John Quade
Kellogg Frank Gorshin
Varek Anthony James
Markos Robert Tessier
Barney James Sloyan
Joella Markie Post

Director: Dick Lowry

Return of the Fighting 69th

w David Bennett Carren
Noah Cooper, an aging starfighter pilot, is brought out of retirement to help Buck and Wilma blast through a treacherous asteroid belt to the stronghold of deadly Commander Corliss and his ally Roxanne.
Noah Cooper Peter Graves
Roxanne Trent Elizabeth Allen
Commander Corliss Robert Quarry
"Big Red" Murphy Woody Strode
Harriett Twain K.T. Stevens
Clayton Robert Hardy

Director: Phil Leacock

Unchained Woman (aka Escape from Zeta)

w Bill Taylor
Buck masquerades as a ruthless convict to help a beautiful female prisoner, Jen Burton, break out of jail. But they are pursued by Hugo, an indestructible android.
Jen Burton Jamie Lee Curtis
Malary Pantera Michael Delano
Sergio Sanwiler Bert Rosario
Ted Warwick Robert Cornthwaite
Majel Tara Buckman
Hugo Walter Hunter

Director: Dick Lowry

Planet of the Amazon Women

w D.C. Fontana, Richard Fontana
Legendary space hero Buck is put up for auction after being kidnapped by two conniving women and taken to Zantia—a planet ruled by women.
Nyree Liberty Godshall
Ariela Ann Dusenberry
Linea Teddi Siddell
Cassius Thorne Jay Robinson
Prime minister Anne Jeffreys
Flight controller Sean Garrison

Director: Phil Leacock

Cosmic Whiz Kid

w Alan Brennert & Anne Collins
Hieronymus Fox is a child genius, frozen in the 20th century and revived in the 25th to become president of the planet Genesia. When he is kidnapped by a ruthless criminal, Buck risks life and limb to rescue him.
Hieronymus Fox Gary Coleman
Roderick Zale Ray Walston
Lt. Dia Cyrton Melody Rogers
Koren Albert Popwell
Toman Lester Fletcher
Selmar Earl Boen

Director: Lesley Martinson

Escape from Wedded Bliss

w Cory Applebaum & Patrick Hoby Jr.
The beautiful but deadly Draconian Princess Ardala promises not to destroy Earth with her new ultimate weapon if granted one small request—to marry Buck Rogers
Princess Ardala Pamela Hensley *(re-intro)*
Kane Michael Ansara *(intro)*
Tigerman H.B. Haggerty

Director: David Moessinger

Cruise Ship to the Stars

w Anne Collins & Alan Brennert
Aboard a luxury space yacht, Buck is assigned to protect Miss Cosmos, a genetically perfect woman, from a mysterious kidnapper with strange powers.
Alison Kimberly Beck
Sabrina Trisha Noble
Jalor Leigh McCloskey
Miss Cosmos Dorothy Stratten
Captain Brett Halsey
Tina Patty Maloney

Director: Sigmund Neufeld Jr.

Space Vampire

w Kathleen Barnes & David Wise
The Vorvon, a galactic creature that steals souls and turns people into walking zombies, marks Wilma as his next victim.
The Vorvon Nicholas Hormann
Royko Christopher Stone
Dr. Ecbar Lincoln Kilpatrick
Nelson Phil Hoover
Twiki Patty Maloney *(this eps. only)*

Director: Larry Stewart

Happy Birthday, Buck

w Martin Pasko
A vengeful assassin capable of turning people into solid marble plans to eliminate Dr. Huer, who is planning his own surprise—a party to celebrate Buck's 534th birthday.
Col. Traeger Peter MacLean
Dr. Delora Batliss Tamara Dobson
Raylyn Derren Morgan Brittany
Carew Chip Johnson
Rorvik Bruce Wright
Niles Tom Gagen

Director: Sigmund Neufeld Jr.

A Blast for Buck

w John Gaynor, Dick Nelson, Alan Brennert
Buck submits himself to a mind probe to discover if a villain from his past is responsible for a sinister plot that threatens Earth. He summons up memories of his greatest adventures—and the beautiful women he has encountered in the 25th century.
Hieronymus Fox Gary Coleman
Kaleel Jack Palance
Noah Cooper Peter Graves
Kellogg Frank Gorshin
Ardala Pamela Hensley
Zale Ray Walston
Brig. Gordon Buster Crabbe
Ryma Brianne Leary
Tangie Pamela Susan Shoop
Jen Burton Jamie Lee Curtis

Director: David Phinney

Ardala Returns

w Chris Bunch & Allan Cole
Buck is forced into a dogfight in space—against himself—when he once again falls into the clutches of Princess Ardala, who has created four duplicates of him.
Tigerman H.B. Haggerty

Director: Larry Stewart

Twiki Is Missing

w Jaron Summers

Twiki the robot is seized by three treacherous women known as the Omni Guard, who become omnipotent when they join hands. Meanwhile, Wilma fights to prevent a giant spaceberg from igniting the Earth's atmosphere.
Kerk Belzak John P. Ryan
Stella Eddie Benton
Clare Janet Louie
Dawn Eugenia Wright
Pinchas David Darlow

Director: Sigmund Neufeld Jr.

Olympiad

w Craig Buck

Buck helps a defecting athlete during the 25th century's intergalactic Olympics—but the athlete has a powerful explosive implanted in his head. (Six top U.S. athletes appeared in this episode, including Olympic pole vault champion Bob Seagren and boxer Jerry Quarry.)
Jorex Leet Barney McFadden
Alaric Nicholas Coster
Lara Judith Chapman
Karl Paul Mantee
Rand Sorgon Bob Seagren
Quarod Jerry Quarry

Director: Larry Stewart

A Dream of Jennifer (aka Jennifer)

w Alan Brennert

Buck is startled by the mysterious appearance of his 20th-century girlfriend in 25th-century Chicago and tracks her down at a futuristic Mardi Gras. But before he can determine her true identity, he falls victim to a sinister alien plot.
Jennifer/Leila Anne Lockhart
Reeve Paul Koslo
Merlin Gino Conforti
Nola Mary Woronov
Lt. Rekoff Jessie Lawrence Ferguson
Toby Kaplin Cameron Young

Directors: Harvey Laidman & David Phinney

Space Rockers

w Chris Bunch & Allan Cole

Buck infiltrates the orbiting satellite *Musicworld* to stop sinister rock group manager Mangros from seizing power in the galaxy by exerting sonic mind-control over billions of youngsters listening to a galactic rock concert.
Lars Mangros Jerry Orbach
Joanna Judy Landers

Karana Nancy Frangione
Cirus Leonard Lightfoot
Rambeau Jesse Goina
Tarkas Paul LeClair

Director: Guy Magar

Buck's Duel to the Death

w Robert W. Gilmer

The people of the planet Katar turn to Buck to fulfil a prophecy that a 500-year-old man will defeat their cruel dictator, the Trebor.
Darius Keith Andes
The Trebor William Smith
Kelan Fred Sadoff
Dr. Doctor Robert Lussier
Vionne Elizabeth Stack
Neil Edward Power

Director: Bob Bender

Flight of the War Witch

w Robert W. Gilmer, William Mageean, *story by*
    David Chomsky *(a 2-part story)*

Buck makes a daring pioneer journey through a black hole into an alternate universe. There he is coerced into joining forces with his archenemy Ardala to save a peaceful planet from being destroyed by a deadly dictator called Zarina.
The Keeper Sam Jaffe
Tora Vera Miles
Zarina Julie Newmar
Chandar Kelly Miles
Pantherman Tony Carroll
Spirot Sid Haig
Kodus Donald Petrie

Director: Larry Stewart

Season Two

Time of the Hawk (aka Hawk)

w Norman Hudis *(a 2-part story)*

Buck Rogers battles a powerful foe, Hawk, a man-bird who has vowed vengeance on the human race after his people have been wiped out by marauding pirates. It's a duel that ends not in death, but in friendship.
Koori Barbara Luna
Simmons Susan McIver
Thordis Andre Harvey
Flagg Lance LeGault
Pratt Sid Haig
Voice of Twiki Bob Elyea (until "The Golden Man" inclusive)
Dr. Goodfellow Wilfrid Hyde-White *(intro)*
Hawk Thom Christopher *(intro)*
Adm. Asimov Jay Garner *(intro)*

Director: Vincent McEveety

Journey to the Oasis

w Robert & Esther Mitchell *(a 2-part story)*
Wilma falls in love with an alien ambassador. She is
unaware that he has a shocking secret that jeopardizes a vital peace conference.
Ambassador Duvoe Mark Lenard
Odee-X Felix Silla
Rolla Mike Stroka
Admiral Zite Len Birman
Zykarian Jr. Donn White

Director: Daniel Haller

The Guardians

w Paul & Margaret Schneider
A dying man entrusts Buck with a mysterious glowing jade box, which causes the *Searcher*'s crew to
have visions from the past and future. For Buck, it's
lunch with Mom on her front porch . . .
Lt. Devlin Paul Carr
Boy Shawn Stevens
Janovus Harry Townes
Buck's mum Rosemary DeCamp
Koori Barbara Luna
Mailman Howard Culver

Director: Jack Arnold

Mark of the Saurian (aka The Unseen)

w Francis Moss
Buck, feverish with flu, insists that a high-ranking
ambassador is really a terrifying lizard creature plotting to destroy the starship *Searcher*. But his friends
say he is just hallucinating.
Major Elif Barry Cahill
Ambassador Sorens Linden Chiles
Dr. Moray Vernon Weddle
Nurse Paulton Kim Hamilton
Crewman Andi Pike
Lt. Martin Alex Hyde-White

Director: Barry Crane

The Golden Man

w Calvin Clements & Stephen McPherson
When the *Searcher* is grounded on an asteroid, the
crew's only hope for survival rests with a strange
golden-skinned boy who has the power to alter molecular structure.
Alphie Bob Elyea
Velis David Hollander
Relcos Russell Wiggins
Hag Diane Chesney
Loran Bruce M. Fischer
Graf Anthony James

Director: Vincent McEveety

The Crystals

w Robert & Esther Mitchell
A young woman with no memory of her past has a
terrifying vision of her future, and a strange mummified creature threatens Buck, Wilma and Hawk.
Laura Amanda Wyss
Hall Sandy Alexander Champion
Kovick James R. Parkes
Johnson Gary Bolen
Petrie Leigh Kim
Lt. Martin Alex Hyde-White

Director: John Paterson

The Satyr

w Paul & Margaret Schneider
Buck is mysteriously transformed into a dangerous
goat-horned satyr-like creature when he tries to rescue a mother and her young son on an abandoned
planet.
Delph Bobby Lane
Syra Anne E. Curry
Pangor Dave Cass
Midshipman Dennis Freeman

Director: Victor French

Shgoratchx!* (aka The Derelict Equation)

w William Keys
The *Searcher* crew discovers a centuries-old
derelict spaceship with a peculiar crew aboard—
seven little men who call themselves the Zeerdonians. But their cargo consists of extremely volatile
solar bombs.
Ensign Moore Alex Hyde-White
General Xces Tommy Madden
General Zoman John Edward Allen
General Yoomak Billy Curtis
General Sothoz Harry Monty

Director: Vincent McEveety

*Pronounced Sagoratek

The Hand of the Goral

w Francis Moss
Buck, Hawk and Wilma return from a survey of a
bizarre planet and find the starship *Searcher* and its
human crew strangely altered.
Goral John Fujioka
Reardon Peter Kastner
Cowan William Bryant
Parsons Dennis Haysbert

Director: David Phinney

Testimony of a Traitor

w Stephen McPherson
Buck goes on trial for his life when he's accused of being responsible for the nuclear holocaust that devastated 20th-century Earth—and a probe of his own memory seems to prove his guilt.
Commissioner Bergstrom Ramon Bieri
U.S. president Walter Brooks
Gen. Arnheim David Hooks
Maj. Peterson John O'Connell
Gen. Myers William Sylvester
Col. Turner Bill Andes

Director: Bernard McEveety

The Dorian Secret

w Stephen McPherson
Buck rescues a beautiful stowaway called Asteria Eleefa, who is facing a death sentence. But the powerful warlord pursuing her suffocates the *Searcher* crew with deadly heat rays as he demands the woman's return.
Asteria Devon Ericson
Koldar Walker Edmiston
Saurus Denny Miller
Demeter William Kirby Cullen
Falgor Thomas Bellin
Chronos Eldon Quick

Director: Jack Arnold

BUFFY THE VAMPIRE SLAYER

Following events in the theatrical movie *Buffy the Vampire Slayer,* Buffy and her mom move to a new town to try to start over. Unfortunately, Sunnydale sits on a mystical convergence, which attracts the undead and the supernatural, so Buffy has more monster-slaying than ever. All is not doom and gloom: She has new friends and a new boyfriend . . . never mind that Angel is a 400-year-old vampire.

Lots of atmosphere, an appealing heroine in Sarah Michelle Gellar and plenty of teen angst have made *Buffy* a cult hit for the Warner Bros. network.

REGULAR CAST

Buffy Summers Sarah Michelle Gellar *Alexander "Xander" Harris* Nicholas Brendon
Rupert Giles Anthony Steward Head *Cordelia Chase* Charisma Carpenter
Willow Rosenburg Alyson Hannigan *Angel/Angelus* David Boreanaz
The Master Mark Metcalf (*Season One*) *Joyce Summers* Kristine Sutherland
Spike James Marsters (*Season Two*) *Drusilla* Juliet Landau (*Season Two*)
Principal Snyder Armin Shimerman (*Season Two*)

Creator: Josh Whedon
Co-producer: David Solomon
Consulting producer: Howard Gordon
Producer: Gareth Davies

Executive producers: Sandy Gallin, Gail Berman, Fran Rubel Kuzui, Kaz Kuzui
Co-executive producer: David Greenwalt
A Mutan Enemy Production

Season One

Welcome to the Hellmouth, Parts 1 & 2

w Joss Whedon
Vampire slayer Buffy Summers makes a fresh start in a new town, but soon finds her powers called upon: Her new hometown sits on top of a supernatural focal point and is home to a master vampire and his followers.
Guest stars: Ken Lerner, Julie Benz, J. Patrick Lawlor, Eric Balfour, Natalie Strauss, Amy Chance, Tupelo Jereme, Persia White, Deborah Brown, Mercedes McNab, Jeffrey Steven Smith, Teddy Lane Jr., Carmine D. Giovinazzo
Directors: Charles Martin Smith (Part 1), John Kretchmer (Part 2)

The Witch

w Dana Reston
Cheerleaders begin to suffer unexplainable accidents when an unpopular student's obsession with joining the squad gets out of hand.
Guest stars: Elizabeth Anne Allen, Robin Riker, Jim Doughan, Nicole Prescott, Amanda Wilmshurst, William Monaghan
Director: Stephen Cragg

Teacher's Pet

w David Greenwalt
A substitute teacher becomes infatuated with Xander, alarming Buffy.
Guest stars: Ken Lerner, Musetta Vander, Jackson Price, Jean Speegle, William Monaghan, Jack Knight, Michael Robb Verona, Karim Oliver
Director: Bruce Seth Green

Never Kill a Boy on the First Date

w Rob Des Hotel & Dean Batali
It's teen angst time when Buffy must choose between stopping the forces of darkness and dating the perfect boy.
Guest stars: Christopher Wiehl, Geoff Meed, Robert Mont, Andrew J. Ferchland
Director: David Semel

The Pack

w Matt Kiene & Joe Reinkmeyer
A class trip to the Sunnydale zoo transforms some of Buffy's classmates into a brutal pack of animal-like hunters.
Guest stars: Jeff Maynard, James Stephens, David Brisbin, Barbara K. Whinnery, Gregory White, Justin Jon Ross, Jeffrey Steven Smith, Patrese Borem, Eion Bailey, Michael McRaine, Brian Gross, Jennifer Sky
Director: Bruce Seth Green

Angel

w David Greenwalt
Buffy meets a mysterious and charismatic young man. The only catch: He's dead and a vampire.
Guest stars: Julie Benz, Andrew J. Ferchland, Charles Wesley
Director: Scott Brazil

I, Robot—You, Jane

w Ashley Gable & Thomas A. Swyden
A computer teacher tries to lure book-lover Giles into the world of technology as Willow begins a dangerous on-line romance.
Guest stars: Robia La Morte, Chad Lindberg, Jamison Ryan, Pierrino Mascarino, Edith Fields, Damon Sharp, Mark Deakins
Director: Stephen Posey

The Puppet Show

w Dean Batali & Rob Des Hotel
Giles is roped into coordinating the school talent show, which includes a ventriloquist whose dummy has a mind of its own.
Guest stars: Richard Werner, Burke Roberts, Armin Shimerman, Lenora May, Chasen Hampton, Natasha Pearce, Tom Wyner, Krissy Carlson, Michelle Miracle
Director: Ellen Pressman

Nightmares

w David Greenwalt, *story by* Joss Whedon
When a young boy suffers an accident that leaves him comatose, his unsettled spirit wreaks havoc on Sunnydale.
Guest stars: Jeremy Foley, Andrew J. Ferchland, Dean Butler, Justin Urich, J. Robin Miller, Terry Cain, Scott Harlan, Brian Pietro, Johnny Green, Patty Ross, Dom Magwili, Sean Moran
Director: Bruce Seth Green

Invisible Girl

w Ashley Gable & Thomas A. Swyden, *story by* Joss Whedon
An ignored student takes her revenge on those who tormented her.
Guest stars: Clea Duvall, Ryan Bittle, Denise Dowse, John Knight, Mercedes McNab, Mark Phelan, Skip Stellrecht, Julie Fulton
Director: Reza Badiyi

Prophecy Girl

w Joss Whedon
Giles's research predicts that Buffy is about to face the Master Vampire in a battle to the death—hers.
Guest stars: Robia La Morte, Andrew J. Ferchland, Scott Gurney
Director: Joss Whedon

Season Two

When She Was Bad

w Joss Whedon
Buffy must finally put the Master to rest for all time. Giles is the link to the Master's return from the dead, only no one realizes his importance until Buffy goes out on a wild goose chase.
Guest stars: Robia La Morte, Andrew J. Ferchland, Dean Butler, Brent Jennings, Armin Shimerman, Tamara Braun
Director: Joss Whedon

Some Assembly Required

w Ty King
Beautiful teenage girls turn up in the morgue, with missing body parts. A madman is building his dream women piece by piece and Buffy and Cordelia become his final objects of desire.
Guest stars: Robia La Morte, Jenny Calendar, Angelo Spizzirri, Michael Bacall, Ingo Neuhaus, Melanie MacQueen, Amanda Wilmshurst
Director: Bruce Seth Green

School Hard

w David Greenwalt
As Buffy organizes her school's parent-teacher conferences, she discovers she's scheduled for an even more important meeting: with Spike, the vampire even the Anointed One doesn't cross who has already killed two slayers and wouldn't mind making her the third.
Guest stars: Robia La Morte, Andrew J. Ferchland, Alexandra Johnes, Armin Shimerman, Keith Mackechnie, Alan Abelew, Joanie Pleasant
Director: John Kretchmer

Inca Mummy Girl

w Matt Kiene & Joe Reinkemeyer
Xander falls for a beautiful Peruvian exchange student, only to discover his love is an ancient mummy who needs to kill to stay alive.
Guest stars: Ara Celi, Seth Green, Jason Hall, Henrik Rosvall, Joey Crawford, Danny Strong, Kristen Winnicki, Gil Birmingham, Samuel Jacobs
Director: Ellen Pressman

Reptile Boy

w David Greenwalt
Buffy dates a college boy to make Angel jealous, but the plan backfires when he plots to sacrifice her to the fraternity's unholy patron, a giant repitilian monster.
Director: David Greenwalt

Halloween

w Carl Ellsworth
Halloween is supposed to be a quiet night for slayers, until a spell changes everyone into their costume . . . in Buffy's case, an 18th-century noblewoman romantically linked with Angel.
Guest stars: Seth Green, Robin Sachs
Director: Bruce Seth Green

Lie to Me

w Joss Whedon
A friend from Buffy's old school promises to deliver her to Spike in exchange for being changed into a vampire.
Director: Joss Whedon

The Dark Age

w Bruce Seth Green
As a youth, Giles rebelled against his destiny of being a Watcher. Unfortunately, that decision returns to haunt him now when friends who know his secret begin turning up dead.
Director: Bruce Seth Green

What's My Line?, Part 1

w Marti Noxon & Howard Gordan
It's career day at school, leaving Buffy depressed. Worse yet, Spike has a way to restore Drusilla to full health, and it requires Angel's unwilling help.
Director: David Solomon

What's My Line?, Part 2

w Marti Noxon & Howard Gordan
A second vampire slayer shows up to help Buffy thwart Spike's plans and rescue Angel.
Director: David Solomon

Ted

w David Greenwalt & Joss Whedon
Everyone loves Buffy's mother's new boyfriend, Ted, except Buffy, whose suspicious of his seeming perfection, violent temper, and almost mechanical efficiency.
Guest stars: John Ritter, Alyson Hannigan, David Boreanaz
Director: Bruce Seth Green

Bad Eggs

w Marti Noxon
A pair of Texan vampires comes to town just as the high school sex ed class gives out eggs for students to nurture as parents . . . never mind that the eggs contain the offspring of an evil creature.
Guest stars: Jeremy Ratchford, James Parks, Rick Zieff
Director: David Greenwalt

Surprise (Part 1 of a 2-part story)

w Marti Noxon
Spike and Drusilla gather the dismembered body parts of a demon called The Judge as their ultimate weapon to kill Buffy.
Guest stars: Seth Green, Robia La Morte, Brian Thompson, Eric Saiet
Director: Michael Lange

Innocence (Part 2 of a 2-part story)

w Joss Whedon
Angel reverts to his old persona of Angelus after Buffy inadvertently extinguishes his human soul in a moment of intimacy.
Guest stars: Seth Green, Robia LaMorte, Brian Thompson, Eric Saiet
Director: Joss Whedon

Phases

w Rob Des Hotel *&* Dean Batali
Buffy tries to protect a werewolf from a poacher as a new vampire victim turns up, claiming to have been attacked by Angel.
Guest stars: Jack Conley, Seth Green, Camila Griggs
Director: Bruce Seth Green

Bewitched, Bothered and Bewildered

w Marti Noxon
Xander strikes a deal with a student witch to help him win Cordelia's love.
Guest stars: Seth Green, Robia LaMorte, Elizabeth Anne Allen
Director: James A. Contner

Passion

w Ty King
Angel torments Buffy; Buffy seems a way to restore his human soul . . . and revoke her invitation for him to enter her house . . . but tragedy strikes first.
Guest stars: Robia LaMorte, Richard Assad, Danny Strong, Richard Hoyt Miller
Director: Michael E. Gershman

Killed by Death

w Rob Des Hotel *&* Dean Batali
While suffering from the flu, Buffy is unable to fight effectively; Angel puts her in the hospital. While there, she encounters a fiendish monster preying on the souls of children.
Guest stars: Richard Herd, Willie Garson, Andrew Ducote, Juanita Jennings
Director: Deran Sarafian

I Only Have Eyes for You

Not aired as of press time.

Go Fish

Not aired as of press time.

Becoming, Part 1

Not aired as of press time.

Becoming, Part 2

Not aired as of press time.

BUGS

Take three freelance troubleshooters—two male, one female—place them in the hi-tech world of the nearly possible, and put them up against an assortment of dastardly villains out to abuse technology for evil ends. Sound familiar?

It could be *The New Avengers* or even *The Champions*—but this is their nineties descendant, and it's no surprise to see *The Avengers* creator Brian Clemens credited as the guiding hand behind this new British action-adventure series.

BUGS was created to fill a perceived gap in the TV market for a simple, action-based series. No gritty social realism, no complex back story, in fact no complex characters—just goodies and baddies and lots of Bond or *Mission: Impossible*–style gadgets and adventure.

BUGS is timeless, set in a non-specific future and a non-specific location. It's filmed in London's Docklands deliberately to give it a slightly unreal urban backdrop that could just as easily be Turin or Frankfurt or some other European or even American city—a handy device when you're trying to stimulate foreign sales.

And the trio of heroes fit the pattern neatly—there's Ed, the daredevil pilot and acrobatic action man, equally at home scaling tall buildings or dangling from helicopters; Ros, the glamorous electronics wizard; and Beckett, the level-headed former military spook, always known by his surname . . .

Storylines have included holographics, computer hacking, a space shuttle mission, a gold-eating microbe, a wonder drug, artificial intelligence, remote-control implants, computer viruses that can affect people—and a recurring archvillain.

Most episodes start and end the same way: the hook, in which the villain makes his play, and a climax usually against the clock and frequently involving loud explosions. The cast—former soap stars Craig McLachlan and Jesse Birdsall and ex-*Bill* copper Jaye Griffiths—work hard. In fact, everyone works hard—from the stuntmen to the special effects teams—to create honest, escapist entertainment. And one other notable name in the credits is that of Stephen Gallagher, author of *Chimera*, as well as a couple of cerebral *Doctor Who* stories, *Warrior's Gate* and *Terminus*.

BUGS should work—and, on a superficial level, it does. But that's its trouble: It's too superficial. The characterization is flat, there's little chemistry, sexual or otherwise, and so there's no real involvement. The dramatic tension is curiously slack, the repartee by-the-numbers.

And what must have been intended as a strength—it's international, five-minutes-into-the-future flavor—is also a weakness, stranding the series in a dramatic no-man's-land as anonymous as its trademark locations. *BUGS* eschews the eccentric Englishness of *The Avengers*, but that was an essential, enduring part of that series' appeal.

Season Two is an improvement on the first—the adding of the *BUGS* team's nemesis, Jean Daniel helps—and the technology is clearly getting more, not less outlandish.

It's a reflection of the moribund state of British sci-fi that a mainstream action-adventure with sci-fi leanings is hailed in some quarters as a new dawn. It might yet break down a few barriers and kick-start a British sci-fi revival. Telefantasy's a funny old game. But this is not the stuff cults are made of.

REGULAR CAST
Ed Craig McLachlan *Ros* Jaye Griffiths *Beckett* Jesse Birdsall

Creators/Producers: Brian Eastman, Stuart Doughty
Production designers: Mark Raggett *(Season One)*, Marcus Rowland *(Season Two)*
Executive producer: Caroline Oulton
Series consultants: Brian Clemens *(Season One)*, Stephen Gallagher
Music: Gavin & Simon Greenaway

Carnival Films for the BBC
U.K. premiere:
Season One: 1 April–10 June 1995
Season Two: 6 April–22 June 1996
(BBC1)

Season One
(10 color 50-minute episodes)

Out of the Hive

w Duncan Gould, *story by* Brian Clemens
Edged out of a secret government project, Nick Beckett teams up with a gadgets whiz and an all-action daredevil to avenge the death of a friend and thwart an evil plan to steal a new piece of satellite technology and threaten world communications.
Cottrell William Chubb
Elena Brana Bajic
Moore Michael Attwell
Dent Richard Durden
Ballantyne Charlie Caine
Guard Jonathan McKenna
Storeman Robin Bowerman

Director: Brian Farnham

Assassins Inc.

w Stephen Gallagher
The trio come up against an evil genius who delights in inventing and marketing new and ingenious ways of killing. Her specialities include voice-activated bombs and miniaturized flying weapons that sniff out their targets' pheromones.

Irene Carmen Du Sautoy
Morasco Nick Reding
Roland Robert Morgan
Ralph Matt Patresi
Admiral Julian Curry
Embassy Man Togo Igawa
Regent Rex Wei
Nurses Ben Craze, Kia Miller

Director: Ken Grieve

All Under Control

w Duncan Gould, *story by* Brian Clemens
Ed, Ros and Beckett are called to an airport to investigate planes which seem to fly themselves, and become involved in a battle of wits with a blackmailer who thinks pilots are redundant.
Langford Susan Kyd
Wyman Tom Chadbon
Elverson Edward Jewesbury
Todd Philip Joseph
Kirkby Anthony Marsh
Security Michael Larkin
Controller Christopher Preston
Pilot Michael Sadler
Co-pilot Jan Shepherd

Director: Brian Farnham

Down Among the Dead Men

w Stephen Gallagher
Ed and Beckett take a submarine to hunt for a man who plans to steal £250 million from his old bank by hacking into undersea cables. Ed finds himself in an inferno of blazing oil, Beckett is shot and Ros has a gun put to her head.
Bryan Brian Deacon
Windette Tom Bradford
Juliet Pauline Moran
Hurry Matthew Marsh
McTiernan Ric Morgan
Dutch officer Ellis Van Maar
Vice chairman Paul Arlington
Chairman Tom Minnikin

Director: Andrew Grieve

Shotgun Wedding

w No on-screen credit, but script copyright by Amanda Coe
Ed poses as a professional assassin—and gets a contract to kill the female politician he, Ros and Beckett are supposed to be protecting.
Anna Katia Caballero
William James Coombes
Corelli George Jackos
Wence Jon Cartwright
Mackenzie Peter Guinness
Starkey Richard Rees
Spencer Andrew Tansey
Gina Maria Petrucci
Taylor Michael Carr

Director: Ken Grieve

Stealth

w Stephen Gallagher
The BUGS team are hired to thwart the activities of two beautiful and persistent women who are determined to get their hands on the secrets of revolutionary new cars. While one prototype is blown sky-high, Ros and Beckett find themselves aboard another, which has become a traveling nuclear bomb.
O'Neill Michael Feast
Sarita Julie Graham
Davina Rachel Fielding
Cray John Michie
Cardenas Chris Aberdein
Bob Rupert Bates

Director: Ken Grieve

Manna from Heaven

w Gregory Evans
A new, highly nutritious wonder food is about to be launched—and the BUGS team must protect it from a rival food manufacturer determined to keep it off the market.
Sally Lynsey Baxter
Zander Greg Hicks
Lennox Philip McGough
Glass Mark Fletcher
Harris John Leeson
Security man Bruce Barnden

Director: Brian Farnham

Hot Metal

w Alan Whiting, *story by* Brian Clemens
The BUGS team encounters a ruthless terrorist out to steal the volatile R6, a revolutionary new metal that can be made to explode by sound.
Charlesworth Nickolas Grace
Da Silva Raad Rawi
Kent Caroline Loncq
Vermeer Ian Gelder
Wallace Andrew Greenough

Director: Ken Grieve

A Sporting Chance

w Colin Brake
Ed's demonstration of tae kwon do leads the BUGS team into the world of supermen at a sporting academy where drugs are being used to produce outstanding athletes. But the research is being funded by a military man and it's power, not gold medals, that's on his mind.
Hunter Ian McNeice
Easterhaus Michael J. Jackson
De Freitas Susannah Morley
Hex Brett Fancy
Kane Adam Caine
Jason Nrinder Dhudwar

Director: Ken Grieve

Pulse

w Stephen Gallagher
When a friend of Ed's is threatened by villains who back up their demands with a bazooka, the trio discovers why a computer company is so keen to take over small firms with unrelated business interests. (This episode introduces the team's nemesis, Jean Daniel.)
Jean Daniel Gareth Marks
Patrick Marcel Anton Lesser
Clare Fiona Gillies
Lena Julie Peasgood
Neville David McAlister
Newsom Bill Leadbitter
Katie Abigail Ansell

Director: Brian Farnham

Season Two
(10 color 50-minute episodes)

What Goes Up . . .

w Colin Brake
First of a two-part story. Ed goes undercover as an astronaut as the team tries to find out who's behind threats to sabotage a satellite to be used to search for platinum deposits in the South China Sea—and finds himself facing disaster on a shuttle mission.
Zito Simon Dormandy
Vornholt Lesley Vickerage
Col. Stone Sean Arnold
Joy Su-Lin Looi
McNair Tom Lockyer
Mission control Rupert Baker
Guyana control Eric Carte
Kreshenski David Shelley

Director: Brian Farnham

. . . Must Come Down

w Colin Brake
Part 2 of a two-part story in which Beckett contacts an old girlfriend who provides a vital link to the other side of the world, Ed performs a space walk and Ros learns to use one of the most powerful weapons on Earth.
Zito Simon Dormandy
Vornholt Lesley Vickerage
Col. Stone Sean Arnold
Joy Su-Lin Looi
Amanda Emma Richler
Chuku David Yip
Haikudu Anthony Chinn
Mission control Rupert Baker
Jean Daniel Gareth Marks
Stokes Fintan McKeown

Director: Brian Farnham

Bugged Wheat

w Miles Millar & Alfred Gough
Government research into a strain of wheat resistant to all diseases is halted when their crop is devastated by a mystery virus. The villains attempt to see off the BUGS team using some particularly vicious insect allies.
Croll Richard Cordery
Pym Hugh Bonneville
Hawk Giles Thomas
Greenville Andrew Hawkins
Jean Daniel Gareth Marks
Prison governor Albert Welling
Lemon Hugh Lee

Director: Sandy Johnson

Whirling Dervish

w No on-screen credit
The BUGS team is called in when a plot is uncovered to put a successful independent airline out of business and discover that a cartel of major airlines is planning to sabotage a flight using radar-invisible Dervish fighter planes.
Selina Janet Amsbury
Jerome John Wheatley
Fisk Nick Frost
Bixon Peter Woodward
Strate Vincent Brimble
Jean Daniel Gareth Marks
Erhardt James Puddephatt
Captain John Melainey
Prison governor Albert Welling
Prison guard Linda Armstrong

Director: Andrew Grieve

Blackout

w Frank de Palma & Terry Borst
When armed raiders take control of a sophisticated new power station and start blacking out the city's financial district, Beckett, Ros and Ed struggle to avert a potential catastrophe.
Pascal Samantha Beckinsale
Travis Adrian Schiller
Alex Dugald Bruce-Lochart
Lacombe Martin McDougall
Kanin Dan Strauss
Kolvek Neil Boorman
Ekberg Ralf Beck
Max Alex Dower

Director: Andrew Grieve

Gold Rush

w Bruno Heller & Alison Leathart
A mysterious computer crash at the East European Monetary Commission brings the trio up against a speculator who is trying to engineer a collapse in East European currencies using a microbe that eats gold.
Kristo Sean Gilder
Vanguard Claire Oberman
Jean Daniel Gareth Marks
Pyke Miranda Pleasence
Dench Brian Gwaspari
Prison governor Albert Welling
Manager Jonathan Aris

Director: Brian Farnham

Schrodinger's Bomb

w Stephen Gallagher
Ed, Ros and Beckett discover that the man behind an illegal trade in antiques and "red mercury" is their old adversary Jean Daniel—even though he's still in jail.
Jean Daniel Gareth Marks
Roland Robert Morgan
Neumann Stephen Churchett
Cassandra Beth Goddard
General Maliq Ivan Kaye
Prisoner governor Albert Welling

Director: Andrew Grieve

Newton's Run

w Cal Clements Jr.
A deranged megalomaniac steals a cyborg dog from a research lab and plans to use it to get his hands on a secret stash of nuclear weapons.
Wence Jon Cartwright
Alkmaar George Rossi
Dr. Kim Clara Salaman
Tangsen Pete Lee-Wilson
Korvig Ralph Ineson
Dr. Siegel Alister Cameron

Director: Brian Farnham

The Bureau of Weapons

w Stephen Gallagher
First of a two-part story set in a strange East European city called Technopolis in which the trio tack-les its old foe Jean Daniel, who is behind a plot to use an artificial intelligence to take over the world. Not only can his computer virus infect the Internet, it can also affect the human brain, and when Ros stops an explosion, she unknowingly becomes infected.
Jean Daniel Gareth Marks
Cassandra Beth Goddard
Roland Robert Morgan
Briggs Simon Pearsall
Layla Julie Livesey
Rona Eve Barker
Governor Susan Franklyn
General Michael Jenn

Director: Andrew Grieve

A Cage for Satan

w Stephen Gallagher
Part 2 of a two-part story. Ros's brain has been infected by the deadly computer virus that is only triggered if she becomes aware she has it. But Ros knows something is wrong, and when Ed and Beckett's strange behavior makes her think they are trying to harm her, she seeks help from their great enemy, Jean Daniel.
Jean Daniel Gareth Marks
Cassandra Beth Goddard
Roland Robert Morgan
Talbot David Gant
Prison chief Otto Jarman
Doctor Todd Boyce

Director: Brian Farnham

THE BURNING ZONE

Much of what's wrong with American television was ably demonstrated in *The Burning Zone*, a show that went through so many transformations in its brief 19-episode run that no viewer who saw the first show would recognize the last. Only one original cast member remained . . . and nothing else was remotely the same.

It began as a nifty idea: What if the government had a secret team designed to spot and stop life-threatening outbreaks of diseases (such as Ebola and anthrax) before they got out of control? The team consisted of two doctors, a security expert, and the director in charge of the project.

But wait! *What if they fought shadowy government bad-guys, too?*

But wait! *What if they encountered the supernatural, à la* The X-Files?

But wait! *What if we replace the doctors with a much more handsome leading man and have a gang kidnap him to treat their leader?*

You get the idea. Viewers had the underlying premise yanked out from under them every few weeks. Despite some strong, engaging performances and memorable episodes early on, *The Burning Zone* never stuck with one premise long enough to develop an audience following.

REGULAR CAST
Dr. Edward Marcase Jeffrey Dean Morgan (*Episodes 1–13*)
Dr. Kimberly Shiroma Tamlyn Tomita (*Episodes 1–13*)
Michael Hailey James Black *Daniel Cassian* Michael Harris (*Episodes 2–19*)
Dr. Brian Taft Bradford Tatum (*Episodes 14–19*)

Creator: Coleman Luck
Executive producer: James Mcadams
Co-executive producer: Bob Carleton
Producer: Ed Ledding
Co-producer: Brian Chambers
Infectious disease consultant: Dr. Kimberly A.
  Shriner, M.D., F.A.C.P.
Director of photography: Bradford May
A Sandstar Production
19 color 60-minute episodes
Airdates: 3 September 1996–20 May 1997

Episodes
Pilot
The Silent Tower
St. Michael's Nightmare
Arms of Fire
Night Flight
Lethal Injection
Touch of the Dead
Hall of the Serpent
Blood Covenant
Faces in the Night
Midnight of the Carrier
Critical Mass
Death Song
The Last Endless Summer
The Last Five Pounds Are the Hardest
Elegy for a Dream
A Secret in the Neighborhood
Wild Fire
On Wings of Angels

CAPTAIN NICE

In this parody of superhero shows, timid chemist Carter Nash discovers a secret formula that turns him into Captain Nice, a reluctant crimefighter dominated by his mother (who makes him be a superhero!).

Carter Nash/Captain Nice William Daniels *Carter's Mother* Alice Ghostley
Sgt. Candy Kane Ann Prentiss *Mayor Finney* Liam Dunn
Chief Segal William Zuckert *Mr. Nash* Byron Foulger

15 color episodes
U.S. premiere: 9 January 1967

Episodes
The Man Who Flies Like a Pigeon
How Sheik Can You Get
That Thing
That Was the Bridge That Was
The Man with the Three Blue Eyes
Is Big Town Burning?
Don't Take Any Wooden Indians
That's What Mothers Are For
Whatever Lola Wants . . .
Who's Afraid of Amanda Woolf?
The Week They Stole Payday
It Tastes OK, but Something's Missing
May I Have the Last Dance?
One Rotten Apple
Beware of Hidden Prophets

CAPTAIN POWER AND THE SOLDIERS OF THE FUTURE

Before there was *Babylon 5,* Joseph Straczynski worked on this Mattel toy-line tie-in show. (It was designed solely to launch a line of toys; to his credit, Straczynski made it a palatable half-hour adventure show. Unfortunately, Mattel killed the show—and their MTS production company—after one season and 22 episodes.)

The premise: It is the year 2147. Following the seven-year Metal Wars, humanity has been enslaved by intelligent machines led by the evil Lord Dread. The few remaining freedom fighters, including Captain Jonathan Power, fight the BioDread Empire with the aid of specially designed powersuits, trying to save the human race.

REGULAR CAST
Captain Jonathan Power Tim Dunigan *Lord Dread* David Hemblen
Major Matthew "Hawk" Masterson Peter MacNeill
Corporal Jennifer "Pilot" Chase Jessica Steen
Lieutenant Michael "Tank" Ellis Sven-Ole Thorsen
Sgt. Robert "Scout" Baker Maurice Dean Wint
Overunit Wilson Helly Bricher *Colonel Cypher* Lorne Cossette
Blastarr John Rhys Davies (*voice*) *Mentor* Bruce Gary
Soaron Deryck Hazel (*voice*)

22 color 30-minute episodes
Syndicated in the U.S. in 1987

Episodes
Shattered
Wardogs
The Abyss
Final Stand
Pariah
A Fire in the Dark
The Mirror in Darkness
The Ferryman
And Study War No More
The Intruder
Flame Street
Gemini and Counting
And Madness Shall Reign
Judgement
A Summoning of Thunder (Part 1)
A Summoning of Thunder (Part 2)
The Eden Road
Freedom One
New Order (Part 1): The Sky Shall Swallow Them
New Order (Part 2): The Land Shall Burn
Retribution (Part 1)
Retribution (Part 2)

CAPTAIN SCARLET AND
THE MYSTERONS

Supermarionation reached twin peaks of sophistication and expense in Gerry Anderson's fifth sci-fi puppet series. With his company now flying the flag of Century 21, Anderson's latest show maintained his optimistic vision of a 21st century when nations are united under a benevolent world government.

It follows the efforts of a secret organization, Spectrum, to defend Earth against powerful Martian foes, the Mysterons, who have sworn vengeance on mankind after a Spectrum mission to Mars misinterpreted a peaceful gesture by the Mysterons and made an unprovoked attack on the Mysteron complex. Week by week the Mysterons' war of attrition continued, always with a taunting warning of where they would strike next. They were tough adversaries, too, possessing the power of retrometabolism, whereby they could kill, then reconstruct their victim as an agent under their control.

To lead the fight, Gerry and Sylvia Anderson created a new breed of TV hero—the indestructible Captain Scarlet. The man in red acquired his own mysterious regenerative power during his first close encounter with the Mysterons. It enabled him to take on the missions impossible, facing and surviving hazards from car and plane crashes to nuclear blasts.

A colorful supporting cast was assembled around the lead figure of Scarlet—a team of color-coded Spectrum agents and a quintet of glamorous pilots called Angels. All came complete with detailed "pasts," some of which preserved a continuity with earlier Supermarionation shows. The full line-up was:

Captain Scarlet: Spectrum's no. 1 agent; English, with a brilliant army career behind him.

Col. White: English ex-navy man, now Spectrum's commander-in-chief.

Captain Blue: American ex-test pilot and brilliant scholar who accompanies Scarlet on many of his missions.

Captain Grey: American ex-WASP who worked on the prototype Stingray.

Captain Ochre: American flyer and crack crimefighter.

Captain Magenta: Irishman who became New York's top gang boss. Recruited by Spectrum as its man inside the underworld.

Lt. Green: Col. White's Trinidadian right-hand man. Another ex-WASP.

Dr. Fawn: Aussie medic. The "Bones" of Spectrum.

The Angels—**Symphony, Melody, Rhapsody, Harmony** and **Destiny**—all combine courage and beauty. Rhapsody's "biography" described her as a Chelsea deb who once worked with Lady Penelope!

Principal villain was the elusive **Captain Black**, a Spectrum agent who becomes the Mysterons' Earth agent when they take him over. The Mysterons themselves are heard but never seen, save for two roving eyes that seek out their targets.

After the success of the *Thunderbirds*, there was again a heavy accent on hardware. Spectrum itself operated from a flying aircraft carrier, Cloudbase, and the ground agents relied on a range of hi-tech vehicles, including the ten-wheeled Spectrum Pursuit Vehicle (SPV), and the Maximum Security Vehicle (MSV).

Captain Scarlet and the Mysterons cost £1,500,000 to make, but significantly advanced the Supermarionation cause. The figures were perfectly proportioned, with the equipment that worked the eye, lip and hand movements housed in the body, so ending the "big-headed" marionette tradition. And if the eyes seemed uncannily real, that's because, in a sense, they were real. They were the eyes of Century 21 employees—production assistants, cameramen, continuity girls and secretaries—photographed, then superimposed onto plastic eyeballs.

The cast of voices was headed by Francis Matthews as Captain Scarlet, South African Donald Gray as Col. White, Captain Black and the menacing Mysterons, Ed Bishop as Captain Blue and *Emergency Ward 10* star Charles Tingwell as Dr. Fawn. Paul Maxwell, previously heard as Steve Zodiac in Fireball XL5, was Captain Grey, while Jeremy Wilkin (Virgil in the second series of *Thunderbirds*) voiced Captain Ochre and many of the guest characters.

The quirks of ITV regionalisation meant that Captain Scarlet was denied a nationwide launch. The series premiered in the Midlands area on 29 September 1967 and in London on 1 October (ironically in black and white), with the rest of the country soon after. Sporadic revivals followed 20 years later, but Captain Scarlet was properly introduced to a new generation with a BBC2 run in 1993.

VOICE CAST
Captain Scarlet Francis Matthews
Col. White/Mysteron voice/Captain Black Donald Gray
Captain Grey Paul Maxwell *Captain Blue* Ed Bishop
Captain Ochre Jeremy Wilkin *Captain Magenta* Gary Files
Lt. Green Cy Grant *Dr. Fawn* Charles Tingwell
Melody Angel Sylvia Anderson *Symphony Angel* Janna Hill
Harmony Angel Lian-Shin *Rhapsody Angel/Destiny Angel* Liz Morgan
Other voices: David Healy, Martin King, Shane Rimmer

Creator: Gerry and Sylvia Anderson
Executive producer: Gerry Anderson
Producer: Reg Hill
Script editor: Tony Barwick
Special effects: Derek Meddings
Characterization: Sylvia Anderson
Music: Barry Gray
Title song sung by The Spectrum

A Century 21 Production for ITC
32 color 30-minute episodes
29 September 1967–14 May 1968
(ATV, Midlands)

The Mysterons

w Gerry & Sylvia Anderson
The victims of an unprovoked Spectrum attack, the Mysterons begin their war of attrition by taking over the mind of Captain Black and vowing to assassinate the World President. Captain Scarlet meets with a car accident that has astonishing consequences.

Director: Desmond Saunders

Winged Assassin

w Tony Barwick
Col. White assigns Captains Scarlet and Blue to protect an Asian leader from another Mysteron death threat. When that threat emerges in the form of a Mysteron-controlled jet, Captain Scarlet finds he must put his invincibility to the test.

Director: David Lane

Big Ben Strikes Again

w Tony Barwick
The Mysterons threaten to destroy London by hijacking a nuclear device. Spectrum's only clue—to find the spot where the mugged driver heard Big Ben strike 13 times. With no time to defuse it, Captain Scarlet must take the bomb deep underground where only he can survive the blast.

Director: Brian Burgess

Manhunt

w Tony Barwick
Captain Black is detected while breaking into an atomic plant and only avoids capture by hiding in a radioactive room. Col. White has his first proof that the Mysterons control one of his men—and the net closes in on Black.

Director: Alan Perry

Avalanche

w Shane Rimmer
The Mysterons try to sabotage the Outer Space Defense System in northern Canada, but Captain Scarlet finds snow his best weapon—triggering a vast avalanche to bury the opposition

Director: Brian Burgess

White as Snow

w Peter Curran & David Williams
Singled out as the Mysterons' next target, Col. White seeks refuge in a submarine. But the Mysterons have a man on board. To protect his commander, Captain Scarlet must first attack him—laying himself open to a court martial where the sentence is death!

Director: Robert Lynn

The Trap

w Alan Pattillo
The Mysterons warn that they will "clip the wings of the world" and set a trap to wipe out the World Air Force Supreme Command. Trapped in a castle dungeon by Mysteron agents, Scarlet must escape in time to avert the plot.

Director: Alan Perry

Operation Time

w Richard Conway & Stephen J. Mattick
Spectrum is puzzled by the latest Mysteron threat: "to kill time," until a newspaper report reveals that a General Tiempo is to undergo a brain operation. The Mysterons have turned the surgeon into their agent, but Scarlet plays a substitution trick of his own.

Director: Ken Turner

Spectrum Strikes Back

w Tony Barwick
A seemingly innocent waiter is unexpectedly identified as a Mysteron reconstruction by a secret new detector device, and poses a pressing threat to a high-level Spectrum group.

Director: Ken Turner

Special Assignment

w Tony Barwick
Scarlet goes undercover when the Mysterons threaten to destroy North America. Forced to "resign" from Spectrum over heavy gambling debts, he is recruited by Captain Black who plans to use an SPV to carry a nuclear device into Nuclear City and start a deadly chain reaction. But first he orders Scarlet to shoot Captain Blue to prove his loyalty . . .

Director: Robert Lynn

The Heart of New York

w Tony Barwick
Thieves use a Mysteron threat to destroy the heart of New York as an opportunity to plan a multimillion-dollar bank raid.

Director: Alan Perry

Lunarville 7

w Tony Barwick
Moon settlement Lunarville 7 declares its neutrality in the war between Earth and the Mysterons. Sent to investigate, Scarlet discovers a strange Mysteron-style complex is being built on the far side of the moon.

Director: Robert Lynn

Point 783

w Peter Curran & David Williams
The Mysterons kill and then duplicate two Earth Forces officers, using them in a double plot to assassinate the Supreme Commander of Earth Forces. But each time Captain Scarlet is on hand to foil their attempts.

Director: Robert Lynn

Model Spy

w Bill Hedley
Angels Destiny and Symphony pose as models, with Captain Scarlet as PR man and Captain Blue as his photographer, when they are told to protect the famous French fashion designer André Verdain from the latest Mysteron death threat.

Director: Ken Turner

Seek and Destroy

w Peter Curran & David Williams
Three Mysteron-controlled Angel aircraft attack Destiny Angel as she is returning to Cloudbase with Captains Blue and Scarlet. Melody, Rhapsody and Harmony are immediately launched to combat the enemy and a fierce dogfight ensues.

Director: Alan Perry

Traitor

w Tony Barwick
Captain Scarlet is accused of being a traitor, when mystery explosions wreck several hovercraft, following a Mysteron warning that the Spectrum organization will be sabotaged from within.

Director: Robert Lynn

Renegade Rocket

w Ralph Hart
The Mysterons gain control of a Spectrum rocket. Col. White scrambles the Angels to intercept the enemy agent, while Captains Scarlet and Blue must stop the rocket hitting an unidentified target.

Director: Brian Burgess

Crater 101

w Tony Barwick
Captains Scarlet and Blue and Lt. Green embark on a hazardous mission to destroy a Mysteron moonbase unaware that the nuclear bomb they are carrying has been set to go off two hours earlier than they think.

Director: Ken Turner

Shadow of Fear

w Tony Barwick
Three astronomers are assigned to help in a Spectrum plan to discover the secrets of the Mysterons, using a satellite on Phobos, the Martian moon. But the Mysterons strike back and when the satellite starts transmitting, there is no equipment to receive its pictures.

Director: Robert Lynn

Dangerous Rendezvous

w Tony Barwick
Using a Mysteron diamond pulsator that Captain Scarlet has brought back from the moon, Col. White contacts the Mysterons and asks for an end to the war of nerves. But when Scarlet goes to keep the agreed rendezvous, he encounters only treachery.

Director: Brian Burgess

Fire at Rig 15

w Bryan Cooper
A Mysteron-reconstructed fire control expert sets out to destroy the refinery which supplies Spectrum, with Captain Scarlet in hot pursuit. In the breakneck chase Scarlet wrecks his SPV, but gets his man.

Director: Ken Turner

Treble Cross

w Tony Barwick
The Mysterons reconstruct a man they believe to have been drowned. But his life has been saved and Spectrum use him to set a trap for Captain Black.

Director: Alan Perry

Flight 104

w Tony Barwick
Captain Scarlet foils a Mysteron attempt to wreck a plane carrying a leading astrophysicist—but it means taking the full force of a crash-landing himself.

Director: Robert Lynn

Place of Angels

w Leo Eaton

A Mysteron-reconstructed research assistant steals a phial containing a deadly liquid and Scarlet faces a desperate race to reach her before she contaminates the Los Angeles water supply.

Director: Leo Eaton

Noose of Ice

w Tony Barwick

Captains Scarlet and Blue fly to the North Pole to try to prevent a Mysteron plot to destroy a unique Tritonium mine—source of an alloy vital to the world space program.

Director: Ken Turner

Expo 2068

w Shane Rimmer

A nuclear reactor is hijacked and the Mysterons threaten a disaster along the Eastern seaboard. Spectrum traces it to the site of Expo 2068 and discover a vital safety valve has been removed. With the reactor overheating, only Captain Scarlet can withstand the fierce temperatures. Can he deactivate it in time?

Director: Leo Eaton

The Launching

w Peter Curran & David Williams

A Mysteron-reconstructed newsman is used in a presidential assassination attempt at the launch of an atomic liner. The traditional champagne bottle has been laced with an extra kick—high explosive.

Director: Brian Burgess

Codename Europa

w David Lee

Captain Scarlet finds that a simple device is his best weapon when he uses a trip wire to overcome a Mysteron agent who has employed the full range of his electronic wizardry in a triple assassination plot.

Director: Alan Perry

Inferno

w Shane Rimmer & Tony Barwick

An irrigation plant in South America is targeted for destruction by the Mysterons. Spectrum teams are sent to guard the complex but discover too late that Captain Black has planted a homing device in an ancient Aztec statue that brings a Mysteron-controlled spacecraft on a crash course.

Director: Alan Perry

Flight to Atlantica

w Tony Barwick

Tampered champagne gives Spectrum personnel an unexpected kick—and results in the partial destruction of the World Navy Complex by Captains Blue and Ochre.

Director: Leo Eaton

Attack on Cloudbase

w Tony Barwick

An all-out attack on Cloudbase seems to bring victory to the Mysterons. Even Captain Scarlet has been killed for the last time. It all looks hopeless . . . until Symphony Angel wakes to realize it has all been a terrible dream!

Director: Ken Turner

The Inquisition

w Tony Barwick

Captain Blue drinks drugged coffee and revives to find himself facing an interrogation from a stranger who claims to be from Spectrum Intelligence. Blue is asked to reveal cipher codes to prove his identity but refuses and makes a desperate escape bid, only to find he has been held in a mock-up of Cloudbase. But help is on the way . . .

Director: Ken Turner

CAPTAIN VIDEO AND HIS VIDEO RANGERS

Earliest of the television space shows, *Captain Video* is one of the low-budget wonders of TV history, producing more than 1400 episodes—though many are lost.

The first of a trio of pioneering U.S. space operas (along with *Space Patrol* and *Tom Corbett, Space Cadet*), it began in 1949 and explored the galaxy on a props budget of just 25 dollars a week.

Captain Video—"Guardian of the Safety of the World"—was a scientific genius who set out to make the universe a safer place. From his secret mountain-top HQ, some time in the 21st century, he controlled a vast network of Video Rangers.

His exotic-sounding adversaries included Mook the Moon Man, Kul of Eos, Dr. Clysmok and Dr. Pauli, the evil head of the Astroidal Society whose scientific weaponry rivalled Captain Video's.

While Video had his Opticon Scillometer which allowed him to see through solid objects, and also his Cosmic Vibrator to shake up the opposition, Dr. Pauli was able to bend the path of bullets with his Trisonic Compensator and cover his tracks with his Cloaks of Silence and Invisibility.

The series aired in America from 1949 to 1955, running six nights a week at its peak.

MAIN CAST
Captain Video Richard Coogan (1949–50), Al Hodge (1951–55)
The Ranger Don Hastings *Dr. Pauli (1949)* Bran Mossen

DuMont Television Network Production
Made in black and white
U.S. premiere: 27 June 1949

CAPTAIN ZEP—SPACE DETECTIVE

Unusual BBC children's program that was a kind of "Doctor Whodunnit," involving viewers in solving various intergalactic crimes played out in different weekly dramas.

The series was set in the year 2095 at the SOLVE Academy for student space detectives. Each week, Captain Zep—"the most famous space detective of all time"—showed the students (young viewers) a video of a famous crime, featuring himself and his loyal crew.

He then asked questions and the students tried to guess whodunnit before the solution was revealed. Viewers at home were invited to answer a supplementary question about the action, with SOLVE badges as prizes.

Captain Zep ran for two series of six "cases" and was a novel, if lightweight, contribution to science fiction TV.

REGULAR CAST
Captain Zep Paul Greenwood *(Series One)*/Richard Morant *(Series Two)*
Jason Brown Ben Ellison *Prof. Spiro* Harriet Keevil *(Series One only)*
Prof. Vana Tracey Childs *(Series Two)*

Writers: Dick Hills *(Series One)*, Colin Bennett
  (Series Two)
Producer: Christopher Pilkington
Directors: Christopher Pilkington *(Series One)*,
  Michael Forte *(Series Two)*
Graphic designers: Ray Ogden, Dick Bailey

A BBC Production
12 color 30-minute episodes
Series One:
5 January–9 February 1983
Series Two:
9 March–13 April 1984

Series One

Case 1: Death on Delos

Captain Zep, in his spaceship *Zep One*, answers an urgent call to save the lives of the gentle plant people of the planet Delos.

Case 2: The Lodestone of Space

Zep is called upon to supervise the security arrangements on the planet Synope—seemingly a straightforward assignment.

Case 3: The Plague of Santos

Zep goes looking for a fellow SOLVE agent who has gone missing on the planet Santos.

Case 4: The G and R 147 Factor

Zep is called up to investigate the space hijacking of freight crafts carrying valuable supplies of the G and R 147 enzyme.

Case 5: The Tinmen of Coza

Captain Zep investigates a murder on the robot planet of Coza.

Case 6: The Warlords of Armageddia

While investigating the murder of Marshall Pax on the violent planet of Armageddia, Zep stumbles across a threat to Earth itself.

Series Two

Case 1: Death Under the Sea

The "new" Zep, Jason Brown and stunning new scientific adviser Vana, are sent to investigate the murder of the President of Aquabeta—a vast underwater city.

Case 2: The Missing Agent of Ceres

Captain Zep is sent to contact SOLVE's secret agent at the intergalactic fair on Ceres. But he's missing—either kidnapped or murdered!

Case 3: The Small Planet of Secrets

The people on Planet X are dying. They've run out of water. The old president knows the whereabouts of secret supplies but he is assassinated just as he's about to reveal the location.

Case 4: The Sands of Sauria

On the famous resort planet of Sauria, Zep gets caught up in a terrifying "meteor" attack, which kills hundreds of tourists.

Case 5: The Tree of Life

Zep is called up to find out why the Tree of Yath is dying. Without the fruit from this one tree the people will starve. Is it natural causes or is it sabotage?

Case 6: Death by Design

117 travelers die in space, all of whom were wearing new spacesuits checked and stamped by Zep. Can Zep clear his name?

CATWEAZLE

TV has seen some odd time travelers, but few as eccentric as the scrawny old 11th-century wizard who becomes trapped in the 20th century—twice!

This children's comic fantasy was created by actor/writer Richard Carpenter, later to script ITV's *Robin of Sherwood*, and ran for two seasons, giving its star Geoffrey Bayldon one of his most memorable roles, albeit clothed in rags and sporting a straggly goatee beard.

Trying to discover the secret of flight, using his powers of magic, Catweazle accidentally jumps through time into 20th-century England, where he is quickly bewildered by his new environment. He thinks the electric light is the sun in a bottle and puts everything from the TV to the telephone (or "telling bone") down to magic.

In the first series Catweazle is befriended by farmer's son Carrot and the two share a succession of chaotic misadventures before the wizard succeeds in returning to his own time.

Series Two repeated the formula but gave Catweazle a new young companion—Cedric, 12-year-old son of Lord and Lady Collingford—as he searched for the 13th sign of the zodiac that would help him get back to Norman times.

REGULAR CAST
Catweazle Geoffrey Bayldon
plus, Season One:
Carrot Robin Davies   *Mr. Bennett (his father)* Charles Tingwell
Sam (a farmhand) Neil McCarthy
Season Two:
Cedric Gary Warren   *Groome* Peter Butterworth
Lord Collingford Moray Watson   *Lady Collingford* Elspeth Gray

Creator: Richard Carpenter
Writer: Richard Carpenter
Directors: Quentin Lawrence *(Season One)*;
   David Reid, David Lane *(Season Two)*
Producers: Quentin Lawrence *(Season One)*,
   Carl Mannin *(Season Two)*

Executive producer (Season One): Joy Whitby
Associate producer (Season One): Carl Mannin

A *London Weekend International Production*
26 color 30-minute episodes

Season One
13 episodes
The Sun in a Bottle
Castle Saburac
The Curse of Rapkyn
The Witching Hour
The Eye of Time
The Magic Face
The Telling Bone
The Power of Adamcos
The Demi Devil
The House of the Sorcerer
The Flying Broomsticks
The Wisdom of Solomon
The Trickery Lantern

15 February–10 May 1970
(LWT)

Season Two
13 episodes
The Magic Riddle
Duck Halt
The Heavenly Twins
The Sign of the Crab
The Black Wheels
The Wogle Stone
The Enchanted King
The Familiar Spirit
The Ghost Hunters
The Walking Trees
The Battle of the Giants
The Magic Circle
The Thirteenth Sign

10 January–4 April 1971
(LWT)

THE CHAMPIONS

"Craig Stirling, Sharron Macready, and Richard Barrett
. . . *The Champions*. Endowed with the qualities and
skills of super humans . . . qualities and skills, both
physical and mental, to the peak of human performance.
Gifts given to them by the unknown race of people from
a lost city in Tibet. Gifts that are a secret to be closely
guarded . . . a secret that enables them to use their powers to their best advantage . . . as . . . *The Champions* of
Law, Order and Justice. Operators of the International
Agency of Nemesis!"

That opening narration said it all, really. *The Champions* were not superheroes in the comic strip
tradition, nor hi-tech heroes like *The Six Million Dollar Man* or *The Bionic Woman* (in 1968–69
who could afford the technology?). Rather they were three souped-up humans, whose physical
and mental senses were heightened in the series' opening episode *The Beginning*, giving them
phenomenal stamina, computer-like brainpower and dazzling insight, plus an ESP that bound
them together like triplets.

Their organization, Nemesis, was a small but powerful agency supported by all countries of the
world but answerable to none, dedicated to preserving the balance of power. Thus, the Champions'
missions were never trivial, dealing only with situations that might blossom into an international
incident—from major-league crime, assassinations, power politics, even the odd loopy scientist.

A cut above the regular adventure series of the day, *The Champions* also boasted three personable
stars in American Stuart Damon, William Gaunt (a sitcom star of the 1980s) and the lovely Alexandra
Bastedo. The fourth regular character was the trio's imperturbable boss, Tremayne.

The men behind the series were Monty Berman, a producer with series such as *The Saint*, *Gideon's
Way* and *The Baron* to his name; and Dennis Spooner, a prolific scriptwriter whose credits include
Gerry Anderson's *Fireball XL5*, *Stingray* and *Thunderbirds* as well as a year as story editor on *Doctor
Who*. He was also co-deviser of another contemporary thriller series, *Man in a Suitcase*.

The Champions ran for one 30-episode season.

REGULAR CAST
Craig Stirling Stuart Damon   Richard Barrett William Gaunt
Sharron Macready Alexandra Bastedo
Tremayne Anthony Nicholls

Creators: Monty Berman, Dennis Spooner
Producer: Monty Berman
Script supervisor: Dennis Spooner
Music: Edwin Astley, Robert Farnon, Albert Elms
Theme: Tony Hatch

An ITC Production
30 color 60-minute episodes
(originally shown in black and white)
U.K. premiere:
25 September 1968–30 April 1969
(ATV-Midlands)
U.S. premiere: 10 June 1968

The Beginning

w Dennis Spooner
A trio of Nemesis agents is sent to steal a lethal bacterium from the Chinese. Their mission is successful but while they try to escape, their plane is damaged and crashes in the remote peaks of Tibet. There, mysterious rescuers heal the agents and endow them with greatly increased mental and physical powers.
Old man Felix Aylmer
Whittaker Kenneth J. Warren
Chislenkan Joseph Furst
Ho Ling Eric Young
Chinese major Burt Kwouk

Director: Cyril Frankel

The Invisible Man

w Donald James
Nemesis is tipped off that the proceeds of a vast bank robbery are to be placed in a Swiss bank. They must find out from where the money is to be stolen.
Hallam Peter Wyngarde
Sumner James Culliford
Sir Frederick Basil Dignam
Van Velden Aubrey Morris
Boursin Steve Plytas

Director: Cyril Frankel

Reply Box No. 666

w Philip Broadley
The Nemesis trio jets to the Caribbean to solve a mystery involving a Greek-speaking parrot and the murder of a French businessman.
Jules Anton Rodgers
Nikko George Murcell
Bourges Brian Worth
Corinne Nike Arrighi
Clive Linbert Spencer
Semenkin George Roubicek
Cleo Imogen Hassall

Director: Cyril Frankel

The Experiment

w Tony Williamson
A power-mad scientist experimenting with his own methods of creating super-powered humans, takes a special interest in Craig, Sharron and Richard.
Dr. Glind David Bauer
Cranmore Allan Cuthbertson
Dr. Margaret Daniels Madalene Nicol
Marion Grant Caroline Blakiston
Officer Philip Bond
Barman Russell Waters
Dr. Farley Nicholas Courtney
Susan Nita Lorraine
Jean Jonathan Burn
Paul Peter J. Elliott

Director: Cyril Frankel

Happening

w Brian Clemens
An enemy organization plots to destroy vast tracts of Australia, including Sydney, by coupling a second atom bomb to one being tested.
Banner Jack MacGowran
Gen. Winters Grant Taylor
Joss Michael Gough
Aston Bill Cummings

Director: Cyril Frankel

Operation Deep-Freeze

w Gerald Kelsey
Sent to Antarctica to investigate an atomic blast, Craig and Richard are captured and left to die in an icy underground chamber by a tyrannical general who has set up a secret missile base.
Gen. Gomez Patrick Wymark
Hemmings Robert Urquhart
Jost Walter Gotell
Margoli Peter Arne
Ship's captain Dallas Cavell
Col. Santos George Pastell
Mendoza Michael Godfrey
Gregson Martin Boddey
Zerilli Derek Sydney
Hoffner Alan White

Director: Paul Dickson

The Survivors

w Donald James
The Nemesis agents have to solve the mystery of three murders in the Austrian Alps believed to be linked with buried Nazi treasure.
Emil Bernard Kay
Franz/Col. Reitz Clifford Evans
Richter Donald Houston
Schmeltz John Tate
Mine attendant Frederick Schiller
Hans John Porter Davison
Pieter Stephen Yardley
Heinz Hugo Panczak

Director: Cyril Frankel

To Trap a Rat

w Ralph Smart
The Champions follow a tricky trail to track down the suppliers of tainted drugs.
Walter Pelham Guy Rolfe
Sandra Edina Ronay
Edwards Michael Standing
Peanut vendor Toke Townley
Jane Purcell Kate O'Mara
Ambulance doctor John Lee
Ambulanceman Michael Guest

Director: Sam Wanamaker

The Iron Man

w Philip Broadley
Sharron becomes a secretary to a deposed dictator whose life is in jeopardy.
El Gaudillo George Murcell
Pedraza Patrick Magee
Callezon Robert Crewdson
Gen. Tornes Michael Mellinger
Carlos Stephen Berkoff
Cabello Norman Florence

Director: John Moxey

The Ghost Plane

w Donald James
A frustrated scientist's clash with officialdom leads to him selling his secrets to a foreign power—secrets that will provide supremacy in the air.
Dr. John Newman Andrew Keir
Vanessa Hilary Tindall
Coates Michael Wynne
Bridges Dennis Chinnery
Hardwick Tony Steedman
Admiral Derek Murcott
Pilot Paul Grist
Crolic John Bryans

Director: John Gilling

The Dark Island

w Tony Williamson
The Champions investigate a fiendish plan to sabotage the advance warning systems of the superpowers and launch missiles that threaten world peace.
Max Kellor Vladek Sheybal
Admiral Alan Gifford
Controller Bill Nagy
Perango Benito Carruthers
Kai Min Andy Ho
Radar operator Richard Bond
Withers Brandon Brady

Director: Cyril Frankel

The Fanatics

w Terry Nation
Richard Barrett infiltrates a band of dedicated assassins and learns that his boss, Tremayne, is one of their intended victims.
Croft Gerald Harper
Col. Banks Donald Pickering
Anderson Julian Glover
Roger Carson David Burke
Krasner David Morrell
Faber Barry Stanton
Collings John Robinson

Director: John Gilling

Twelve Hours

w Donald James
A visiting politician is the victim of a bomb explosion in a submarine—and with the oxygen running out, Sharron must operate to save his life.
Raven Mike Pratt
Adm. Cox Peter Howell
Lt. Cmdr. Street John Turner
Naval captain John Stone
Madame Drobnic Viola Keats
Drobnic Henry Gilbert
Jackson Laurie Asprey
Telegraphist Rio Fanning

Director: Paul Dickson

The Search

w Dennis Spooner
The Champions face the task of saving London from atomic destruction when a nuclear submarine is stolen.
Kruger Haller John Woodvine
Conrad Schultz Reginald Marsh
Dr. Rudolf Mueller Joseph Furst
Suzanne Taylor Patricia English
Allbrecht Ernst Walder
Innkeeper Gabor Baraker

Director: Leslie Norman

The Gilded Cage

w Philip Broadley
Richard Barrett is forced to break a code to save the life of a beautiful fellow prisoner.
Symons John Carson
Samantha Jennie Linden
Lovegrove Clinton Greyn
Orley Charles Houston
Brandon Tony Caunter
Haswell Sebastian Breaks
Manager Vernon Dobtcheff

Director: Cyril Frankel

Shadow of the Panther

w Tony Williamson
A voodoo mystery for the Champions in Haiti where a Nemesis scientist has died—apparently from fear.
Prengo Zia Mohyeddin
David Crayley Donald Sutherland
Riley Tony Wall
Charters Hedger Wallace
Doctor Christopher Carlos
Waiter Kenneth Gardiner

Director: Freddie Francis

A Case of Lemmings

w Philip Broadley
Nemesis investigates the apparent suicides of three Interpol agents.
Del Marco Edward Brayshaw
Umberto John Bailey
Claudine Jeanne Roland
Jacquet Michael Graham
Pillet Michael Slater
Madame Carnot Olive McFarland
Frenchman Jacques Cey
Frenchwoman Madge Brindley

Director: Paul Dickson

The Interrogation

w Dennis Spooner
Craig Stirling is caught up in a nightmare to which there seems no end. But is he dreaming or is it really happening?
Interrogator Colin Blakely

Director: Cyril Frankel

The Mission

w Donald James
A mission for tramps provides cover for a macabre organization running escape routes for war criminals.
Hogan Dermot Kelly
Pederson Anthony Bate
Sophia Patricia Haines
George Harry Towb
Maltman Robert Russell

Emil Boder Paul Hansard
Director: Robert Asher

The Silent Enemy

w Donald James
The Champions go to sea on a macabre mission to reconstruct the voyage of a nuclear sub that has been found with its entire crew dead.
Capt. Baxter Paul Maxwell
Adm. Parker Warren Stanhope
Stanton James Maxwell
Minoes Marne Maitland
Minister Esmond Knight
Lighthouse keepers David Blake Kelly, Rio Fanning

Director: Robert Asher

The Body Snatchers

w Terry Nation
The Champions encounter eerie drama in Wales and defeat a strange spy plot.
Squires Bernard Lee
Inge Kalmutt Ann Lynn
Yeats Philip Locke
Frank Nicholls J.G. Devlin
David Fenton Gregory Phillips
Lee Rogers Christina Taylor
White Frederic Abbott

Director: Paul Dickson

Get Me Out of Here!

w Ralph Smart
The Nemesis trio are called in to rescue a doctor being held against her will.
Anna Maria Martes Frances Cuka
Commandante Ronald Radd
Angel Martes Philip Madoc
Minister Eric Pohlmann
Cuevos Anthony Newlands
Josef Godfrey Quigley
Police captain Norman Florence
Detective Richard Montez

Director: Cyril Frankel

The Night People

w Donald James
The superhumans come up against the supernatural in a mystery with sinister implications.
Douglas Trennick Terence Alexander
Mrs. Trennick Adrienne Corri
Porth David Lodge
Jane Soames Anne Sharp
Dan Michael Bilton
George Whetlor Walter Sparrow
Hoad Jerold Wells
Clerk Frank Thornton

Director: Robert Asher

Project Zero

w Tony Williamson
Nemesis investigates when one scientist is murdered and many others disappear—becoming victims of a remarkable series of kidnappings.
Voss Rupert Davies
Antrobus Peter Copley
Forster Geoffrey Chater
Grayson Reginald Jessup
Miss Davies Jan Holden
Postmaster Nicholas Smith
Sloane Donald Morley
Travis John Moore
Wittering Maurice Browning
Chairman John Horsley
Hedges Eric Lander
Stewardess Jill Curzon
Pilot Bruce Beeby

Director: Don Sharp

Desert Journey

w Ian Stuart Black
Danger in the desert for the superhumans who try to restore a young Arab to his throne.
The Bey Jeremy Brett
Yusef Roger Delgado
Said Nik Zaran
Curtis Reg Lye
Branco Henry Soskin
Sheikh Peter Madden
Major Tuat Tony Cyrus
Sonia Yole Marinelli

Director: Paul Dickson

Full Circle

w Donald James
Craig poses as a prisoner and embarks on an escape plan with a fellow internee. But it leads to torture, not freedom.
Westerman Patrick Allen
Garcian Martin Benson
Booker John Nettleton
Sarah Gabrielle Drake
Carrington Jack Gwillim
Pickering James Donnelly
Sergeant Fairfax Lawrence James
Collins Victor Brooks

Director: John Gilling

Nutcracker

w Philip Broadley
The Champions are called in to test security at a vault—but the vault is programmed to kill.
Duncan William Squire

Lord Mauncey David Langton
Manager Michael Barrington
Warre John Franklyn-Robbins
Walcott John Brown
Travers David Kelsey
Guard Dervis Ward
Assistant Robert Mill

Director: Roy Ward Baker

The Final Countdown

w Gerald Kelsey
Nemesis is charged with finding a World War Two atom bomb that could launch another major war.
Von Splitz Alan MacNaughtan
Dr. Neimann Wolf Frees
Kruger Derek Newark
Wolf Eisen Basil Henson
Schultz Morris Perry
Anna Hannah Gordon
Heiden Norman Jones
Tom Brooks Michael Lees

Director: John Gilling

The Gun-Runners

w Dennis Spooner
Murder in the Burmese jungle takes the Champions into a gun-running mystery.
Hartington William Franklyn
Guido Selvameni Paul Stassino
Filmer David Lodge
Schroeder Guy Deghy
Police captain Eric Young
Nadkarni Wolfe Morris
Clerk Nicolas Chagrin

Director: Robert Asher

Autokill

w Brian Clemens
The top men in Nemesis get the killing bug—even Tremayne is affected—and Richard finds himself programmed to kill Craig.
Barka Eric Pohlmann
Klein Paul Eddington
Dr. Amis Harold Innocent
George Brading Richard Owens
Loretta Brading Rachel Herbert
Mechanic Conrad Monk
American colonel Bruce Boa

Director: Roy Ward Baker

THE CHARMINGS

The Charmings (as in Prince Charming, his wife Snow White Charming, and their two children) end up in 1980s California when Eric's mother-in-law, the Wicked Witch, casts a spell. They're stuck and must blend in until they can find a way back to the Enchanted Forest. A cute idea, if somewhat predictably—and sloppily—executed; continuity errors abound even in such basic matters as how the Charmings got to California.

REGULAR CAST

Prince Eric Charming Christopher Rich *Snow White Charming* Caitlin O'Heaney (*Season One*); Carol Huston (*Season Two*)
Thomas Charming Brandon Call *Cory Charming* Garette Ratliff
Lillian Judy Parfitt *The Mirror* Paul Winfield
Sally Miller Dori Brenner *Don Miller* Paul Eiding
Luther Cork Hubbert

Executive producers: Robert Sternin and Prudence Fraser
Supervising producer: Ellen Guylas
Producers: Al Lowenstein, Mark Fink, Danny Kallis, Roxie Wenk Evens (*pilot*)

20 color 30-minute episodes
U.S. premiere: 20 March 1987

Season One
The Charmings
The Mirror Cracked
Spring Fever
The Charmings Buy a Car
The Incredible Shrinking Prince
An '80s Kind of a Prince

Season Two
Lillian Loses the Kids
The Charmings Go Plastic
The Witch Is of Van Oaks

The Fish Story
Cindy's Back in Town
A Charming Halloween
Trading Places
Lillian Loses Her Powers
The Charmings and the Beanstalk
Yes, Lillian, There is a Santa Claus
The Charmings Get Robbed
Birth of a Salesman
The Man Who Came to Dinner
The Woman of His Dreams
Lillian's Protégé (Unaired in the U.S.)

CHOCKY

The *Chocky* stories were evidence that British-made television science fiction was alive and well, if somewhat hard to find in the 1980s.

Chocky is a highly intelligent alien who befriends Matthew, an ordinary English boy, existing, at first, as a voice inside his head. Chocky's presence unsettles Matthew and his family and leads eventually to a startling revelation.

The original story was written by John Wyndham and was the last work published before his death in 1969. Television writer Anthony Read updated the setting and gave Chocky a visual shape—a ball of glowing green energy. Following the success of the first series, which topped the children's ratings, Wyndham's family gave its approval for the character to be developed. That led to the second and third series, *Chocky's Children* and *Chocky's Challenge*, which established the existence of other "befriended" children around the world and then set about finding a solution to the world's energy problems.

REGULAR CAST
Matthew Gore Andrew Ellams *David Gore (his father)* James Hazeldine
Mary Gore (his mother) Carol Drinkwater *(Series 1 and 2)*
Polly Gore (his sister) Zoe Hart *(Series 1 and 2)*
Albertine Meyer Anabel Worrell *(Series 2 and 3)*
Arnold Meyer Prentis Hancock *(Series 2 and 3)*
Chocky's voice Glynis Brooks

Producers: Vic Hughes *(Series 1 and 2)*, Richard Bates *(Series 3)*
Executive producers: Pamela Lonsdale *(Series 1 and 2)*, Brian Walcroft *(Series 3)*

Thames Television Productions
18 color 30-minute episodes

Series One:
9 January–13 February 1984
Series Two:
7 January–11 February 1985
Series Three:
29 September–16 October 1986 (twice weekly)

Series One

Chocky

w Anthony Read, *from the novel by* John Wyndham *(a 6-part story)*
Twelve-year-old Matthew suddenly starts talking to himself and doing things he couldn't do before, such as binary code math. His parents think it's just a "passing phase" but Matthew tells them about Chocky "who lives inside his head." The family becomes increasingly unsettled—especially when a holiday incident brings unwelcome publicity and interest. Only after Matthew has been hypnotized, mysteriously kidnapped and interrogated, does Chocky reveal her "mission"—to bring a new form of unlimited cosmic power to Earth.
Mr. Trimble James Greene
Colin Devin Stanfield
Jane Kelita Groom
Mark Jonathan Jackson
Roger Peter John Bickford
Susan Catherine Elcombe
Miss Blayde Lynne Pearson
Landis Jeremy Bulloch
Alan Colin McCormack
Phyl Penny Brownjohn
Sir William John Grillo

Directors: Christopher Hodson & Vic Hughes
Designer: David Richens

Series Two

Chocky's Children

w Anthony Read *(a 6-part story)*
It's nearly a year since Chocky said goodbye to Matthew, and life appears to have returned to normal for the Gore family. But mysterious men are eavesdropping on their telephone conversations and further trouble lies ahead. Matthew goes on holiday to his Aunt Cissie's and while exploring a nearby windmill meets an unusual girl, Albertine. As their friendship grows, it becomes clear that Chocky is involved and is seeking their help. But the sinister Dr. Deacon is out to learn their secret and takes Albertine to his clinic. Matthew goes to find her and the scene is set for Chocky's Children from all over the world to "mentally" come to their rescue.
Deacon Ed Bishop
Luke Michael Crompton
Landis Jeremy Bulloch
Aunt Cissie Angela Galbraith
Doctor Brian de Salvo

Directors: Vic Hughes & Peter Duguid
Designer: David Richens

Series Three

Chocky's Challenge

w Anthony Read *(a 6-part story)*
Matthew and Albertine have continued their studies, Matthew in art and Albertine in math at Cambridge. Chocky now feels she can tell them about her secret plans to solve the planet's energy problems. Under her supervision, Albertine is to build the world's first cosmic energy collector—a source of unlimited power. But she will need help, so Chocky brings in other young children and they successfully complete a prototype. But other, more dangerous parties are interested, including the mysterious Mrs. Gibson who offers to finance the work. Her true motive becomes clear when she traps Chocky and Paul inside the cosmic power pack.
Prof. Ferris Richard Wordsworth
Dr. Liddle Illona Linthwaite
Prof. Draycott Roy Boyd
Prof. Wade Kristine Howarth
Mrs. Gibson Joan Blackham
Mike Freddie Brooks
Su Lin Karina Wilsher
Paul Paul Russell
Chocky's parent Norma Ronald
General Leon Eagles

Director: Bob Blagden
Designer: Peter Elliott

COLD LAZARUS

Playwright Dennis Potter's dying wish was that BBC1 and Channel 4 should join forces to produce and cross-schedule his two final dramas, *Karaoke* and *Cold Lazarus*. In an unprecedented spirit of co-operation, his wish was granted.

Karaoke starred Albert Finney, Julie Christie, Richard E. Grant, Hywel Bennett and Saffron Burrows in a multi-layered, four-part story about a writer, Daniel Feeld, who believes his own characters are ominously coming to life around him. When he learns that he's about to die, he arranges to have his body cryogenically frozen.

Cold Lazarus picks up the story 400 years in the future, in the London and Los Angeles of 2368, when Feeld's disembodied frozen head is revived in the laboratory of a group of cryobiologists who succeed in accessing his memory. The huge expense of their project incurs the wrath of Martina Matilda Masdon, the tycoon owner of the Science Center, who threatens to suspend the "Lazarus Operation." However, media mogul David Siltz sees entertainment potential in broadcasting Daniel's memories (Potter's metaphor for the artist's exploitation by the media) and he tops the ratings until the scientists, haunted by the morality of their actions, decide to pull the plug.

Cold Lazarus—also a four-parter—was Potter's first, and only, foray into science fiction, and though it failed to gather either great critical acclaim or big ratings, it did succeed in depicting an outrageous vision of the future, with over-the-top sets and costumes *Blake's 7* would have been proud of. Bizarre "inventions" included the auto-cube, a half-vegetable, half-machine steered by will-power, and hovering bubble cars.

The most ambitious effect was the Living Wall, a huge 3-D screen on which Feeld's memories are projected. The computer-generated wall took a year to complete and each shot comprised up to 30,000 separate 3-D computer images, which were wrapped in digitized film footage, giving the effect of Daniel's thoughts materializing and floating in space.

Albert Finney endured four-and-a-half-hour makeup sessions to achieve his disconcerting disembodied head look, and a strong cast included Frances de la Tour as the scientists' leader, Ciaran Hinds as her colleague and secret member of a subversive organization called RON (Reality Or Nothing), Diane Ladd as their tycoon employer and Henry Goodman as the media mogul David Siltz.

MAIN CAST

Daniel Feeld Albert Finney *Emma Porlock* Frances de la Tour *Martina Masdon*
Diane Ladd *Fyodor Glazunov* Ciaran Hinds *David Siltz* Henry Goodman
Luanda Partington Ganiat Kasumu *Tony Watson* Grant Masters *Blinda* Carmen Ejogo *Kaya*
Claudia Malkovich *Andrew Milton* David Foxe *Beth* Tara Woodward *Karl* Rob Brydon *From*
Karaoke: *Sandra Sollars* Saffron Burrows *Ben Baglin* Roy Hudd
Anna Griffiths Anna Chancellor *Nick Balmer* Richard E. Grant *Arthur "Pig"*
Mailion Hywel Bennett *Mrs. Haynes* Alison Steadman

Creator: Dennis Potter
Designer: Christopher Hobbs
Director: Renny Rye
Producers: Kenith Trodd, Rosemarie Whitman

A Whistling Gypsy Production
4 color 75-minute episodes

26 May–16 June 1996
(Channel 4)

Karaoke
4 color 70-minute episodes
28 April–19 May 1996
(BBC1)

CONAN THE ADVENTURER

The fantasy trend that brought Hercules, Xena and Sinbad to television so successfully also resurrected the character of Conan the Cimmerian, a Hyborian Age sword and sorcery adventurer created by Robert E. Howard for the pulp magazines in the 1930s. Taking its inspiration from the two Arnold Schwarzenegger movies, *Conan the Barbarian* and *Conan the*

Destroyer, Conan the Adventurer casts Ralph Moeller (who looks and sounds eerily like Schwarzenegger) as the hero.

After Conan's parents were slaughtered by barbaric Vanir raiders, he was enslaved and chained to a grist mill. Here he remained until he became an adult, when he was bought by a Hyrkanian pitmaster who traveled with a band of professional fighters staging contests for the amusement of the Vanir and their warlike neighbors, the Aesir.

Conan grew into a wild, fiercely proud young man possessing a Herculean physique acquired from years of toil at the grist mill. Escaping from the traveling gladiators, Conan fled to Arenjun, a notorious city of thieves and sorcerers. Uncivilized and untamed, wary of black magic, Conan gained a reputation as a bold and daring adventurer.

REGULAR CAST
Conan Ralf Moeller *Otli* Danny Woodburn
Vulkar Andrew Craig *Zzeben* Robert McRay
Karella Aly Dunne *Bayu* T.J. Storm

Supervising producer: Burton Armus   *A Keller Entertainment Group Production*
Producer: Peter Chesney

Season One
The Heart of the Elephant
Lair of the Beast-Man
Heir Apparent
The Siege of Ahl Sohn-Bar
A Friend in Need
The Ruby Fruit Forest
The Three Virgins
Ransom
The Curse of Afka
Impostor
Amazon Woman

Homecoming
The Taming
Red Sonja
Shadows of Death
The Child
The Crystal Arrow
Labyrinth
The Cavern
Antidote
Lethal Wizards
Heir Apparent

COUNTERSTRIKE

"A distant star. A dying planet. A race of desperate men
seeking another home, another world to take over. One
man is trying to stop them. A man not of this world . . ."

Low-budget 1969 BBC series that relied on psychological thrills rather than hi-tech frills for its *Invaders*-style story of an alien threat to take over Earth.

Centauran refugees from a doomed planet have come to Earth where, for about 15 years, they've been preparing to destroy the human race to make room for their own people. Their approach is covert and based on acts of subversion, rather than on outright open warfare (thus obviating the need for expensive spacecraft, elaborate costumes and lavish effects).

But they've reckoned without the Inter Galactic Council, a kind of United Nations of Space, which sends one of its agents to Earth in the guise of Simon King. King, who comes from the same Centauran star system, possesses acute physical and mental attributes to help him counter the Centauran plots. He's aided in his campaign by Mary, a doctor who discovers his secret when she treats him after he's been injured in the first episode. And King's reference points back to his base are the various faces of "Control," seen only on a triangular screen in his apartment.

The series was created by Tony Williamson, a well-known ITC contributor and previously script editor on *Adam Adamant Lives!*, and was one of the last of its kind to be recorded in black and white. The show was consistently rated in the top 20 but ended—with just nine of its ten episodes having been shown—one week before color came to BBC1.

REGULAR CAST

Simon King Jon Finch *Mary* Sarah Brackett

Creator: Tony Williamson
Producer: Patrick Alexander
Script editor: David Rolfe

A BBC Production
10 50-minute black and white episodes
8 September–10 November 1969
(BBC1)

King's Gambit

w Patrick Alexander
Two apparently respectable businessmen running an electronics factory are investigated by a journalist called Simon King. But the businessmen turn out to be far from respectable aliens plotting to take over the Earth by paralyzing the population. And King is an intergalactic agent sent to stop them.
Idris Evans Clive Merrison
Jill Angela Vincent
Sir Charles Cuttle Charles Durant
Jeffries Reg Whitehead
Armstrong Bernard Shine
Baldock Noel Johnson
Scaife Tom Kempinski
Dr. Webber Brian Badcoe
Control Katie Fitzroy

Director: Vere Lorrimer
Designer: John Hurst

Joker One

w Ray Jenkins
Every war has its flashpoint. The Centaurans think they've found one in a plane permanently stationed with a warhead on board, waiting for the attack command. They plan to send it off and so trigger an atomic war.
Paston Alexis Chesnakov
Pinot Robert Beatty
General Bruce Boa
Elaine Pinot Barbara Shelley
Flemyng Tim Seely
Control Katie Fitzroy

Director: Henri Safran
Designer: Ian Rawnsley

On Ice

w Max Marquis
Three scientists are mysteriously lost on a sledding party that sets out from a polar research station.
Garvin David Jackson
Dr. Richards Norman Claridge
Dr. Barker Donald Pelmear
Taffy Sadler David Jason

Dr. Cross Alexander John
Len Bryant Tom Watson

Director: Malcom Taylor
Designer: Ian Watson

Nocturne

w Anthony Skene
Simon King finds himself living in a nightmare between fantasy and reality when he is put to sleep and his dreams manipulated by the Centaurans who program him to kill a scientist. (This was a reworking of Skene's own script for *The Prisoner* episode "A, B & C.")
Inspector Neil Hallett
Chairman John Horsley
Mother Maria Aitken
Jacey Jenny McCracken
Plunkett Kevin Stoney
Beavis John Abineri
Control Fraser Kerr
President Jack Lambert
Policeman Keith James
Secretary April Walker

Director: Cyril Coke
Designer: Ian Watson

Monolith

w Anthony Skene
A Centauran plot to murder the richest man in the world is centered on the biggest tower block in the center of London, where the aliens run the dead man's business empire.
Outram John Baskcomb
Miss Roberts Daphne Newton
Mr. Bentley Colin Gordon
Control Anne Rutter
Charwoman Betty Woolfe
Shaughnessy Peter Bayliss
Boland Douglas Jones
Carole Carole Mowlam

Director: Henri Safran
Designer: Ian Rawnsley

Out of Mind

w David Cullen, *story by* Patricia Hooker
Mary, visiting a village where she stayed as a child, finds that the woman who used to look after her, Hannah Webley, is now regarded by the superstitious villagers as a witch. Mary is soon caught up in the ensuing witch-hunt.
Hannah Webley Hilary Mason
Harry Carter Michael Beint
Control Katie Fitzroy
John Rossiter Patrick Bedford
PC Brookfield Howard Goorney
Jerry Randall Freddie Earlle
Chief of Control Edward Brayshaw

Director: Henri Safran
Designer: Ian Rawnsley
(This episode was dropped by the BBC in a late program change but was not rescheduled. It remains unscreened—and the tape has since been erased.)

The Lemming Syndrome

w Cyril Abraham
A total of 143 people in one small seaside town commit suicide by drowning. Or were they under some strange and alien influence? Simon decides they were . . .
Control Katie Fitzroy
Sir George Halkyn Anthony Sharp
Everett Denis Cleary
Wyatt James Villiers
Pythian Robert James
Margo Deirdre Costello
Dr. Merrow Sonia Graham
Norman Bill Straiton

Director: Vere Lorrimer
Designer: Ian Watson

Backlash

w Paul Wheeler
During a period of student riots, strong calls for a return to "law and order" are made by General Falcon, a blood-and-guts Korean War veteran. As he starts to emerge as an important political figure capable of swaying public and government opinion, Simon King senses the sinister hand of the Centaurans at work.
Jonathan Fry Mark Edwards

Housing minister John Dawson
Gold James Beck
Evans Morris Perry
Student David Simeon
Lord Falcon Richard Hurndall
Johnson Roy Boyd
Control Katie Fitzroy

Director: Viktors Ritelis
Designer: David Spode

All That Glisters

w Adele Rose
Adults start acting childishly—a grown man plays hopscotch and another falls off a rocking horse. Is there any connection between this and the Centauran plan to take over Earth? It seems unlikely, but Centauran plans usually do—until they start to work . . .
Dr. Tate Lindsay Campbell
Mrs. Sengupta Nina Baden-Semper
Bessie Collier Mary Hignett
Gwen Gilbert Wendy Gifford
Control Fraser Kerr
Tom Gilbert Ian Dewar
Josh Tetley Frederick Arle
Bill Pearce Roy Pattison
Esmé Hooper Daphne Goddard
Observer Africa Oscar James

Director: Viktors Ritelis
Designer: John Hurst

The Mutant

w Dick Sharples
A deadly new germ gets loose at a biological warfare laboratory. Can an antidote be discovered before the germs spread into a killer plague?
Fenton Derrick Gilbert
Alice Cranshaw Marion Reed
Brixham Craig Hunter
Grant Arnold Diamond
MacAllister Sydney Conabere
Henley David Garth
Lawson Hedger Wallace
Charlesworth John Rapley
Dr. Leonard David Rowlands
Control Meriel Fairburn

Director: William Sterling
Designer: John Hurst

DARKROOM

This dark fantasy anthology series owed much to Rod Serling's *The Night Gallery:* The formats were almost identical, although *Darkroom* ran 60 minutes instead of half an hour. James Coburn introduced all 7 episodes, à la Rod Serling, from a photographer's darkroom.

Each show featured two to three different short teleplays. One memorable show starred a very young Helen Hunt battling a vampire.

REGULAR CAST
Host James Coburn

Episodes
Closed Circuit/Stay Tuned—We'll Be Right Back
The Bogeyman Will Get You/Uncle George
Needlepoint/Siege of 31 August

A Quiet Funeral/Makeup
The Partnership/Daisies/Catnip
Lost in Translation/Guillotine
Exit Line/Who's There?/The Rarest of Wines

DARK SHADOWS

The classic gothic soap opera, complete with ghosts, vampires and werewolves, *Dark Shadows* lasted for an astounding 1225 episodes (not a record for a genre show, however; *Captain Video* aired more than 1400!).

Of course, with such a long run, an episode guide would be the size of this whole book. Suffice to say, it's an enduring program despite terrible production values, with a dedicated and lasting following. If you're interested in more info, there are quite a few books on the subject. (And the series is available on videotape. Hundreds of volumes.)

REGULAR CAST
(most had multiple roles in addition to these)
Carolyn Stoddard Nancy Barrett   *Elizabeth Collins Stoddard* Joan Bennett
Mrs. Johnson Clarice Blackburn   *Cristopher Jennings* Don Briscoe
Josette Collins Mary Cooper   *Joe Haskell* Joel Crothers
Ben Stokes Thayer David   *Jeff Clarke* Roger Davis
Roger Collins Louis Edmunds   *Sam Evans* David Ford
Barnabas Collins Jonathon Frid   *Julia Hoffman* Grayson Hall
David Collins David Henesy   *Willie Loomis* John Karlen
Tony Peterson Jerry Lacy   *Victoria Winters* Alexandra Moltke
Sheriff Patterson Vince O'Brien   *Angelique Bouchard* Lara Parker
Jason McGuire Dennis Patrick   *Maggie Evans* Kathryn Leigh Scott
Grant Douglas David Selby   *Mrs. Sarah Johnson* Clarice Blackburn

Executive producer/Series creator: Dan Curtis   *Music:* Robert Cobert
Producers: Robert Costello, Peter Miner, & Lela
  Swift

DARK SHADOWS (1991)

A prime-time (and big-budget) attempt to remake the soap opera, which somehow lacked the soul of the original. After a four-hour premiere (two two-hour episodes), the show lasted an additional nine episodes.

REGULAR CAST
(as with the original series, many had multiple roles)
Barnabas Collins Ben Cross   *Victoria Winters* Joanna Going
Sheriff George Patterson Michael Cavanaugh   *Deputy Jonathan Harker* Steve Fletcher
Angelique Bouchard Lysette Anthony   *Carolyn Stoddard* Barbara Blackburn
Judge Isiah Braithwaite Brendon T. Dillon   *Willie Loomis* Jim Fyfe
Professor Michael Woodard Stefan Gierasch   *David Collins* Joseph Gordon-Levitt

Series creator: Dan Curtis
Executive producer: Dan Curtis
Line producer: Norman Henry
Associate producer: Bill Blunden, Armand Mastroianni
Co-producers: Jon Boorstin, William Gray

Supervising producer: Steve Feke
Producer: William Gray
Certain characters developed by Art Wallace
Music: Bob Cobert

Aired in the U.S. 13 January 1991–22 March 1991

DARK SKIES

"The truth is down here, third door on the right."

Suppose the Roswell Incident really was true. Suppose there had been a stealth-like alien invasion in 1947 and suppose the U.S. government had covered it up. Suppose all that and it doesn't take a giant leap to buy into the ultimate conspiracy theory that certain landmark historical events since could have been influenced by aliens.

Like a hybrid of *The Invaders* and *The X-Files*, this promising new U.S. thriller series offers an intriguing alternative slant on post-war American history.

Stepping into the scenario are a young couple, John Loengard, an idealistic young congressional aide, and his girlfriend Kimberly Sayers. Lured to Washington in 1961 by the Camelot-like aura of the Kennedy administration, they stumble across a rogue organization, Majestic-12, which is concealing evidence of alien invasion. Recruited by Majestic's leader, Captain Frank Bach, Loengard is shown the remains of one of the alien creatures recovered from the Roswell crash, and he joins Bach in searching out humans whose brains are the hosts for early-stage alien life-forms.

But Loengard becomes disillusioned with Majestic's obsessive secrecy and steals a piece of the alien craft to show President Kennedy. Regarded as outlaws by Bach and the organization, Loengard and Sayers disappear, until the news of Kennedy's assassination in Dallas in 1963 propels them on a *Fugitive*-style odyssey, pursued by devious agents and dangerous aliens. Thus the stage is set for what co-creator Bryce Zabel calls a "blend of fact, informed speculation and dramatic license" as the sixties are reinterpreted through the looking glass of UFOs and alien contact.

A series undoubtedly made possible by the success of *The X-Files*, *Dark Skies* had an interesting premise and an attractive pairing in Eric Close and *Party of Five* star Megan Ward.

MAIN CAST
John Loengard Eric Close *Kimberly Sayers* Megan Ward *Captain Frank Bach* J.T. Walsh

Creators: Bryce Zabel, Brent V. Friedman
Executive producers: Bryce Zabel, Brent V. Friedman, Joseph Stern
Directors: Various, including Tobe Hooper (pilot)
Music: Mark Snow

Bryce Zabel Productions Inc in association with BetaFilm and columbia Pictures Television
U.S. premiere: 21 September 1996
U.K. premiere: 20 January 1997 (Channel Four)
1 120-minute episode; 17 60-minute episodes
21 September 1996–31 May 1997

Episodes
The Awakening
Moving Targets
Mercury Rising
Dark Days Night
Dreamland
Inhuman Nature
Ancient Future
Hostile Convergence
We Shall Overcome
The Last Wave
The Enemy Within
The Warren Omission
White Rabbit
Shades of Gray
Burn Baby, Burn
Both Sides Now
To Prey in Darkness
Bloodlines

THE DAY OF THE TRIFFIDS

John Wyndham's deeply humanistic stories were a popular choice for television in the 1980s. ITV developed *Chocky* in 1984, and three years earlier the BBC turned in this successful six-part adaptation of *The Day of the Triffids*.

Wyndham's classic tale of evil plants taking over the world had been filmed before, as a melodramatic movie, in 1963. The TV version was more low-key, almost sober in its approach, bringing out the author's main theme of mankind's response to a holocaust.

The story is told through the eyes of ex-triffid farmer Bill Masen (played by John Duttine, a popular BBC star after his central role in *To Serve Them All My Days*). It begins with Masen in a hospital ward, his eyes bandaged after a near miss from a triffid sting, waiting to know if his sight has been saved. Meanwhile a dazzling cosmic phenomenon in the night sky blinds the watching millions. Masen wakes to find himself one of the few "seeing" people in a world of blindness and panic increasingly menaced by the triffids, which now start to roam the streets. He rescues a girl, Jo, from a street attack and they try to find others who are able to oppose the triffids.

A gang of blind scavengers led by Jack Coker provides an additional menace before Masen, Jo and their friends find refuge in a Sussex farmhouse where they prepare for their final confrontation with the triffids.

The monsters themselves were variously described as "scarily effective" and "a bunch of outsized plastic orchids left over from a Muppet show," but the series was generally well received.

MAIN CAST
Bill Masen John Duttine   *Jo* Emma Relph
Jack Coker Maurice Colbourne   *Dr. Soames* Jonathan Newth
John Stephen Yardley   *Beadley* David Swift
Miss Durrant Perlita Neilson   *Torrence* Gary Olsen
Mary Brent Jenny Lipman   *Dennis Brent* Desmond Adams
Susan Emily Dean/Lorna Charles

Writer: John Wyndham
Adapted by: Douglas Livingstone
Producer: David Maloney
Director: Ken Hannam
Designer: Victor Meredith
Visual effects: Steve Drewett
Music: Christopher Gunning

A BBC TV Production in association with RCTV Inc. and the Australian Broadcasting Corporation
6 color 30-minute episodes
10 September–15 October 1981

DEAD AT 21

MTV's first dramatic series just happened to be science fiction: Ed Bellamy, the young victim of a botched government experiment to create superintelligent humans, was implanted at birth with a computer chip that will kill him when he turns 21. He must find the chip's creator and get it removed while eluding the government assassin out to terminate the project (and him), aided only by his girlfriend. He can't go to the authorities for help, since he's been framed for murder.

REGULAR CAST
Edward Bellamy Jack Noseworth   *Maria Cavalos* Lisa Dean Ryan
Winston Whip Hubley

Based on a teleplay by Jon Sherman
9 June 1994–7 September 1994

Episodes

Pilot
Brain Salad
Love Minus Zero
Shock the Monkey
Gone Daddy Gone
Use Your Illusion

Live for Today
Tie Your Mother Down
Cry Baby Cry
Life During Wartime
Hotel California
In Through the Out Door (Part 1)
In Through the Out Door (Part 2)

THE DELTA WAVE

A ten-part children's drama about ESP and psychic powers, from the creators of *The Tomorrow People* (nineties-style) and *Mike & Angelo*.

Harebrained young Cambridge University scientist Dr. Ruby Munro discovers two children with phenomenal psychic abilities while running her Department for Experimentation into Linked Thought Activity (DELTA). The pair are Julia Stone, a 14-year-old orphan with wild visions of hidden mysteries, and Ed Curtis, a sports-mad ten-year-old with enough kinetic energy literally to turn his house upside down—usually when he's asleep, and blissfully unaware of the mayhem he's causing, much to his parents' consternation.

The kids' combined energies have explosive results and threaten to end Dr. Munro's project. Munro, a young woman who's still a boisterous kid at heart, tries to persuade her boss, Prof. Quealy, to give the project a second chance, but ends up packing her belongings into her hi-tech trailer, and the trio take to the road, homing in on perplexing phenomena and rooting out evil plots.

Broken down into five two-part adventures, the series stars Robin McCaffrey, from *Four Weddings and a Funeral*, as Dr. Munro, but its most notable factor is the large number of well-known guest stars in supporting roles—including Leslie Grantham, Graham Crowden, Dudley Sutton, Una Stubbs, Tom Georgeson, Daniel Peacock, Phyllida Law and *Drop the Dead Donkey*'s Victoria Wicks.

REGULAR CAST

Dr. Ruby Munro Robin McCaffrey *Julia Stone* Ania Sowinski *Ed Curtis* Jason Stracey

Producer: Alan Horrox

A Tetra Films Production

10 color 30-minute episodes
3 January–6 March 1996
(ITV)

A Twist of Lemming

w Lee Pressman *(a 2-part story)*
After they take to the road with Dr. Munro, Julia's and Ed's telepathic powers lead them to a weird lab full of terrified rabbits. Julia frees them, but the cruel Dr. Weevil traps Ed for his next experiment . . .
Prof Quealy Graham Crowden
Dr. Otto Weevil Dudley Sutton
Pete Curtis Ben Onwukwe
Sue Curtis Maria Douglas

Director: Roger Gartland

A Glitch in Time

w Lee Pressman *(a 2-part story)*
Julia stumbles through a hole in the fabric of time, winding up in the middle of a Victorian murder mystery that leads to a time-hopping adventure of swindle and double-cross.

Gill Pigeon Una Stubbs
Sheldon Hubble Mac McDonald
Olga Crick Victoria Wicks
Stump Nickolas Grace

Director: Niall Leonard

Dodgy Jammers

w Ken Allen Jones *(a 2-part story)*
A disastrous guitar lesson brings the DELTA team into a head-on collision with gangsters Rex and Roy Valentine.
Freddy Argyle Daniel Peacock
Rex Valentine Leslie Grantham
Roy Valentine Tom Georgeson
Winnie Horsefell Patsy Byrne
Mr. Seffel Brian Murphy

Director: A.J. Quinn

The Light Fantastic

w Grant Cathro & Alex Bartlette *(a 2-part story)*
Someone is after Julia and Ed . . . First it's a pair of men in dark suits and bowler hats who keep vanishing into thin air. Then it's a strange, haunting melody that puts Julia into a trance. The trail leads to Dottie Cruickshank's music academy and 1930s dancing wonder Dinsdale Draco.
Dottie Cruickshank Phyllida Law
Dinsdale Draco Peter Capaldi
Shelley Claire Russell
McKenzie Alex Bartlette
McClurg Grant Cathro

Director: Juliet May

Something Fishy

w Alex Shearer *(a 2-part story)*
Beneath a beautiful lake, fiendish Doctor Zeckler and his assistant Pickelet plot the transformation of the human race.
Doctor Zeckler Ian Hogg
Pickelet Paul Bigley
Fisherman Robert Blythe
PC Mead Stephen Bent
Miss Gower Elizabeth Estensen

Director: Rita Leena Lynn

THE DEMON HEADMASTER

This creepy series about a power-crazed headmaster continues the BBC tradition of well-made kids' drama.

And Terrence Hardiman exudes menace in the title role as the school head who plans to use his hypnotic powers to take over the world, by infiltrating Downing Street. Only the resistance of a courageous group of youngsters calling themselves SPLAT (The Society for Protection of our Lives Against Them) is able to stop him.

Undaunted, the Demon Headmaster returns for a second crack at the world title, this time experimenting with genetic engineering and transgenic implants at his new Biogenetic Research Center. Anonymously, he lures his old foe Dinah Hunter and her adopted family to the village where his center is located, and recruits his old ally, the erstwhile prefect, Rose Carter. Using his powers, the Demon Head takes control of the Center and the village. Only Dinah's new friend Simon escapes and together they must thwart their enemy yet again.

Both series are based on books by Gillian Cross.

MAIN CAST

Demon Headmaster Terrence Hardiman   *Mrs. Hunter* Tessa Peake-Jones   *Dinah Hunter*
Frances Amey   *Lloyd Hunter* Gunnar Cauthery   *Harvey Hunter* Thomas Szekeres
Rose Carter Katey Crawford Kastin
Season Two only: Simon James James Richard

Adapted by: Helen Cresswell, *from the books by* Gillian Cross
Director: Roger Singleton-Turner
Executive producer: Marilyn Fox

A BBC TV Production

Series One:
6 color 25-minute episodes
1–18 February 1996
Series Two:
7 color 25-minute episodes
25 September–6 November 1996
(BBC1)

DOCTOR WHO

"If you could touch the alien sand and hear the cries of strange birds, and watch them wheel in another sky—would that satisfy you?"

—The Doctor

When a grouchy Time Lord, tired of the discipline and order of his home planet, Gallifrey, first stole a clapped-out TARDIS and fled with his granddaughter, he started a myth that has become embedded in television history.

Doctor Who was the backbone of British TV science fiction for 26 years, an amazing legend of heroes and villains that has touched the dawn of time and peered over the edge of the universe.

It has been the mother ship for much of the creative talent to emerge in television fantasy over the past three decades—nearly everyone who's anyone has worked on the show.

Doctor Who was created in 1963 by the BBC's new Head of Drama, Sydney Newman. He had come to the Corporation from ABC Television where he had produced the successful *Armchair Theater*, activated *The Avengers* and launched the ITV Sunday space sagas *Target Luna* and *Pathfinders* (see separate entries).

As the new serial was to be for children, Newman wanted *Doctor Who* to have a high educational content in which the Doctor's travels would unroll the tapestry of history for his young audience. The space stories, too, had to be based on factual knowledge. And, quite definitely, no BEMs (Bug-Eyed Monsters). Almost immediately, producer Verity Lambert and script editor David Whitaker turned up with Terry Nation's Daleks and *another* legend was born, with as much carpet worn out behind the country's sofas as in front of them.

By turns frightening and cosy, bleak and humorous, innovative and traditional, silly and cerebral, *Doctor Who* evolved a format that allowed it to do anything, go anywhere, with only the mode of transport unchanged—the TARDIS (Time And Relative Dimension In Space), forever frozen as an old-fashioned police box.

The series' flexibility lay at the heart of its success and longevity, and crucial to that has been the changing face of the Doctor himself. When William Hartnell, the original Doctor, became too ill to play the part, the show faced a crisis—adapt or die. It adapted, by bringing in a new actor and explaining the change as a process of "regeneration." So far, with the advent of the latest movie, the Doctor is in his eighth incarnation and is allowed five more by the series' own Time Lord mythology. After that? Who knows.

Eight so far, though, and all different:

William Hartnell made him a man of mystery, a rather forbidding, tetchy Edwardian eccentric.

Patrick Troughton turned him into a Chaplinesque hobo in a funny hat and baggy check trousers, given to bursts of irrational behavior to confound all his foes.

Jon Pertwee brought a dash of the flamboyant dandy, all swirling cloaks and ruffled shirts as he raced to the rescue in his yellow roadster, Bessie.

Tom Baker took him back on the galactic road as a wide-eyed, curly-haired, grinning Gallifreyan rebel, an intellectual Bohemian in a floppy hat and flowing scarf.

Peter Davison was the most vulnerable—mild-mannered and sensitive, he wore his hearts on his Regency-coated sleeves and listened to his conscience.

Colin Baker's sixth Doctor was deliberately pitched to the other extreme—arrogant, brash and abrasive—in a self-conscious effort to be different.

Sylvester McCoy energetically steered the character out of the show's most troubled period since it was nearly axed by Michael Grade back in 1985. But with seasons lasting just 14 episodes, it became much harder to establish a presence than in the old days when *Doctor Who* ran for up to ten months of the year.

Paul McGann, with his long hair, Edwardian-style frock coat, glittery waistcoat and silk cravat, embodies the adventurer ideal—handsome, rugged but with a childlike zest for life.

But however often he appears, the Doctor has never really traveled alone. Right from the start he has shared his adventures with one or more companions, many of whom have become nearly as famous as the Time Lord himself.

At first there were the schoolteachers, Ian and Barbara, plus his granddaughter, Susan. Then the accent settled firmly on youth—mostly attractive and female. The Who Girls have included the orphaned Victoria, brainy Zoe, scientist Liz Shaw, leggy Jo Grant, liberated Nyssa, the Aussie "mouth on legs" Tegan, curvy Peri, strident Mel and the streetwise Ace. They've run the gamut of female stereotypes from the screamers and ankle sprainers to the stubborn, independent misses.

There have been far fewer male companions, but the best have been the young Scot Jamie, the artful dodger Adric and the ambivalent alien Turlough. Not forgetting, of course, the loyal men of UNIT, led by Brigadier Lethbridge-Stewart, and the canine robot, K9.

And the show spawned many memorable villains and monsters in its 26 years. Top of the list are the Daleks—"little green blobs in bonded polycarbite armor"—and their creator, Davros; others include the Cybermen, the Sontarans, the Ice Warriors, the Yeti, the Autons, the Sea Devils, the Terileptils, the Tractators, the slug-like Sil and the confectioner's nightmare, the Kandyman.

Then there are the humanoid villains, led by the Doctor's indestructible nemesis, the Master. He's one of several renegade Time Lords who have troubled the Doctor—others have been Omega, Borusa, the Rani and the Valeyard.

Danger has also come from without: in its time *Doctor Who* has been derided by critics, vilified by squeamish watchdogs and seen its audience ebb and flow. Its highest average viewing figure was 14.5 million for the 1979 story *City of Death* (peaking at 16.1 million for episode four), the lowest just 3.1 million for the first episode of the season 26 opener, *Battlefield*.

Since the 26th and last season ended in 1989, there were constant rumors of a comeback for the Time Lord, with Spielberg's Amblin Company in the frame at one time. Meanwhile, *Dimensions in Time*, a 3-D "adventure" set in *EastEnders'* Albert Square, was made for 1993's Children in Need appeal; two radio stories were aired starring Jon Pertwee—*The Paradise of Death* in September 1993, and *The Ghosts of N-Space* in 1996, and a 30th anniversary documentary, *30 Years in the Tardis*, materialized in November 1993.

The big breakthrough finally came in May 1996, with a BBCWorldwide/Universal Television TV movie, starring Paul McGann as the Eighth Doctor, Julia Roberts' brother Eric as The Master, and Sylvester McCoy, briefly reprising his role long enough to pass the baton to McGann.

If just getting the movie made was a triumph for executive producer and long-time fan Philip Segal (a veteran of *ER, seaQuest* and *Earth 2*), the *Doctor Who* for the nineties was always going to be controversial—unashamedly aimed at the U.S. market, as it inevitably had to be if the franchise was going to be revived. Much of the $3 million budget went on creating a spectacular TARDIS interior, elaborately designed with more than a hint of Jules Verne. However, to link the new to the old, props from the BBC series were scattered around as reminders.

Despite Segal's reverence for *Doctor Who*'s heritage, many British fans remained unimpressed by the international version with its slick American touches such as a motorbike chase through San Francisco and the Doctor's first screen kiss, and bemoaned the loss of the eccentric, low-budget British feel.

Its ultimate success—9 million viewers in the UK—can only be judged on whether the movie spawns a series. Fans held their breath. America's Fox network held an option. But ultimately they did not pick it up.

REGULAR CAST
(See episode guide)

Creators: Donald Wilson, C.E. Webber, Sydney Newman
Original theme: Ron Grainer

A BBC Production
695 episodes (25-minute unless stated)
black and white (Seasons 1–6)
color (from Season 7)

U.K. premiere: 23 November 1963
Last "proper" episode: 6 December 1989
(Author's note: Stories up to and including "The Gunfighters" in Season Three were originally identified by their separate episode titles, but for means of easy reference, have since become known collectively by the titles given here.)

The First Doctor: **WILLIAM HARTNELL**
(1963–1966)

Season One
(23 November 1963–12 September 1964)
REGULAR CAST
The Doctor William Hartnell *Susan Foreman* Carole Ann Ford
Ian Chesterton William Russell *Barbara Wright* Jacqueline Hill

---

Producer: Verity Lambert   *Story editor:* David Whitaker
Associate producer: Mervyn Pinfield

100,000 BC

w Anthony Coburn, C.E. Webber *(Ep. 1 only)*
(a 4-part story)
Curious about the knowledge displayed by one of their pupils, Susan Foreman, two of her teachers go to investigate her home—the TARDIS—and meet her grandfather. So begins an adventure in space and time that takes them back to the Stone Age and into a tribal power struggle over the secret of fire.
Za Derek Newark
Hur Alethea Charlton
Kal Jeremy Young
Horg Howard Lang
Old mother Eileen Way

Director: Waris Hussein
Designers: Peter Brachaki *(Ep. 1) and* Barry
   Newbery *(Eps. 2–4)*

An Unearthly Child
The Cave of Skulls
The Forest of Fear
The Firemaker
(23 November–14 December 1963)
NB: There also exists a pilot version of "An Unearthly Child."

The Daleks (aka The Mutants)

w Terry Nation *(a 7-part story)*
The TARDIS lands on the planet Skaro where the travelers become involved in the conflict between opposing survivors of centuries of neutronic war—the aryan Thals and the dreadfully mutated Daleks. (Filmed as *Doctor Who and the Daleks*, with Peter Cushing.)
Temmosus Alan Wheatley
Ganatus Philip Bond
Alydon John Lee
Antodus Marcus Hammond
Elyon Gerald Curtis
Dyoni Virginia Wetherell
Dalek voices David Graham, Peter Hawkins

Directors: Christopher Barry *(Eps. 1–2, 4–5) &*
   Richard Martin *(Eps. 3, 6, 7)*
Designers: Raymond Cusick *(Eps. 1–5, 7) &*
   Jeremy Davies *(Ep. 6)*

The Dead Planet
The Survivors
The Escape
The Ambush
The Expedition
The Ordeal
The Rescue
(21 December 1963–1 February 1964)

Inside the Spaceship

w David Whitaker *(a 2-part story)*
The Doctor juggles with the controls and the TARDIS is hurled back to the dawn of time. (Regular cast only.)

Directors: Richard Martin *(Ep. 1),* Frank Cox
   (Ep. 2)

The Edge of Destruction
The Brink of Disaster
(8–15 February 1964)

Marco Polo

w John Lucarotti *(a 7-part story)*
Landing in medieval China, the travelers join Marco Polo on his way to the court of Kublai Khan where the Doctor gambles away the TARDIS.
Marco Polo Mark Eden
Tegana Derren Nesbitt
Ping-Cho Zienia Merton
Kublai Khan Martin Miller
Ling-Tau Paul Carson
Chenchu Jimmy Gardner
Empress Claire Davenport

Directors: Waris Hussein *(Eps. 1–3, 5–7) &* John
   Crockett *(Ep. 4)*
Designer: Barry Newbery

The Roof of the World
The Singing Sands
Five Hundred Eyes
The Wall of Lies
Rider from Shang-tu
Mighty Kublai Khan
Assassin at Peking
(22 February–4 April 1964)

The Keys of Marinus

w Terry Nation *(a 6-part story)*
On the strange world of Marinus, the Doctor and his companions become involved in a quest for four lost keys to the Conscience of Marinus—which are also sought by the evil Voord.
Arbitan George Coulouris
Altos Robin Phillips
Sabetha Katharine Schofield
Voice of Morpho Heron Carvic
Darrius Edmund Warwick
Vasor Francis de Woolf
Yartek Stephen Dartnell

Director: John Gorrie
Designer: Raymond P. Cusick

The Sea of Death
The Velvet Web
The Screaming Jungle
The Snows of Terror
Sentence of Death
The Keys of Marinus
(11 April–16 May 1964)

The Aztecs

w John Lucarotti *(a 4-part story)*
The TARDIS lands in Mexico—at the height of the beautiful but bloodthirsty Aztec empire, and Barbara is mistaken for the reincarnation of a high priest.
Autloc Keith Pyott
Tlotoxl John Ringham
Ixta Ian Cullen
Cameca Margot van der Burgh
Tonila Walter Randall
Perfect victim André Boulay
Aztec captain David Anderson

Director: John Crockett
Designer: Barry Newbery

The Temple of Evil
The Warriors of Death
The Bride of Sacrifice
The Day of Darkness
(23 May–13 June 1964)

The Sensorites

w Peter R. Newman *(a 6-part story)*
After landing on the deck of a spaceship from Earth in the 28th century, the travelers help a telepathic race, the Sensorites, overcome an illness that is striking their planet.
John Stephen Dartnell
Carol Ilona Rodgers
Maitland Lorne Cossette
Sensorites: Ken Tyllsen, Joe Greig, Peter Glaze, Arthur Newall
First Elder Eric Francis
Second Elder Bartlett Mullins

Directors: Mervyn Pinfield *(Eps. 1–4)* & Frank Cox *(Eps. 5–6)*
Designer: Raymond P. Cusick

Strangers in Space
The Unwilling Warriors
Hidden Danger
A Race Against Death
Kidnap
A Desperate Venture
(20 June–1 August 1964)

The Reign of Terror

w Dennis Spooner *(a 6-part story)*
Spy story set in the time of the French Revolution in which the Doctor and his associates get involved in a "Pimpernel"-style plot to save people from the guillotine.
Lemaitre James Cairncross
Jean Roy Herrick
Jules Renan Donald Morley
Robespierre Keith Anderson
Physician Ronald Pickup
Jailer Jack Cunningham
Leon Colbert Edward Brayshaw
Rouvray Laidlaw Dalling
Judge Howard Charlton
Webster Jeffry Wickham
Danielle Caroline Hunt
Napoleon Tony Wall

Director: Henric Hirsch *(Ep. 3 directed, uncredited, by John Gorrie when Hirsch collapsed before recording)*
Designer: Roderick Laing

A Land of Fear
Guests of Madame Guillotine
A Change of Identity
The Tyrant of France
A Bargain of Necessity
Prisoners of Conciergerie
(8 August–12 September 1964)

Season Two
(31 October 1964–24 July 1965)
REGULAR CAST
As Season One, plus: Vicki Maureen O'Brien *(from Story 3)*

Producer: Verity Lambert
Associate producer: Mervyn Pinfield *(to Story 4)*

Story editors: David Whitaker *(Stories 1–2)*, Dennis Spooner *(Stories 3–8)*, Donald Tosh *(Story 9)*

Planet of Giants

w Louis Marks *(a 3-part story)*
The travelers find themselves miniaturized and thwart the crooked scheme of an insecticide manufacturer.
Forester Alan Tilvern
Farrow Frank Crawshaw
Smithers Reginald Barratt
Hilda Rowse Rosemary Johnson
Bert Rowse Fred Ferris

Directors: Mervyn Pinfield & Douglas Camfield *(Ep. 3)*
Designer: Raymond P. Cusick

Planet of Giants
Dangerous Journey
Crisis
(31 October–14 November 1964)

The Dalek Invasion of Earth

w Terry Nation *(a 6-part story)*
Landing on Earth in 2167, the Doctor and his companions confront the conquering Daleks who have turned Bedfordshire into a vast mine, from which they plan to extract the Earth's core. At the end, Susan elects to remain behind with the victorious freedom-fighters. (Filmed as *Daleks: Invasion Earth 2150 AD.)*
Carl Tyler Bernard Kay
David Campbell Peter Fraser
Dortmun Alan Judd
Jenny Ann Davies
Larry Maddison Graham Rigby
Wells Nicholas Smith
Robomen Martyn Huntley, Peter Badger

Director: Richard Martin
Designer: Spencer Chapman
World's End
The Daleks
Day of Reckoning
The End of Tomorrow
The Waking Ally
Flashpoint
(21 November–26 December 1964)

The Rescue

w David Whitaker *(a 2-part story)*
On the planet Dido, the Doctor encounters two survivors of a crashed spaceship and unmasks a murderer.
Vicki Maureen O'Brien *(intro)*
Bennett/Koquillion Ray Barrett *(alias* Sydney Wilson)
Space captain Tom Sheridan

Director: Christopher Barry
Designer: Raymond P. Cusick

The Powerful Enemy
Desperate Measures
(2–9 January 1965)

The Romans

w Dennis Spooner *(a 4-part story)*
The TARDIS trips back to ancient Rome where the Doctor's meeting with Nero results in the Great Fire of Rome.
Sevcheria Derek Sydney
Ascaris Barry Jackson
Delos Peter Diamond
Tavius Michael Peake
Nero Derek Francis
Poppaea Kay Patrick

Director: Christopher Barry
Designer: Raymond P. Cusick

The Slave Traders
All Roads Lead to Rome
Conspiracy
Inferno
(16 January–6 February 1965)

The Web Planet

w Bill Strutton *(a 6-part story)*
To the planet Vortis . . . and a war between the ant-like Zarbi and the butterfly creatures, the Menoptra.
Vrestin Roslyn de Winter
Hrostar Arne Gordon
Prapillus Jolyon Booth
Hlynia Jocelyn Birdsall
Hilio Martin Jarvis
Animus voice Catherine Fleming
Zarbi Robert Jewell, Jack Pitt, Gerald Taylor, Hugh Lund, Kevin Manser, John Scott Martin

Director: Richard Martin
Designer: John Wood

The Web Planet
The Zarbi
Escape to Danger
Crater of Needles
Invasion
The Center
(13 February–20 March 1965)

The Crusades

w David Whitaker *(a 4-part story)*
Into the past . . . to the 12th-century crusades and the conflict between Richard the Lionheart and the Saracens.
El Akir Walter Randall
Richard the Lionheart Julian Glover
Ben Daheer Reg Pritchard
William de Tornebu Bruce Wightman
Saphadin Roger Avon
Saladin Bernard Kay
Joanna Jean Marsh
Chamberlain Robert Lankesheer

Director: Douglas Camfield
Designer: Barry Newbery

The Lion
The Knight of Jaffa
The Wheel of Fortune
The Warlords
(27 March–17 April 1965)

The Space Museum

w Glyn Jones *(a 4-part story)*
The TARDIS lands on the planet Xeros, which has been turned into a space museum by the Moroks, and the travelers aid the rebelling Xerons.
Sita Peter Sanders
Dako Peter Craze
Lobos Richard Shaw
Tor Jeremy Bulloch
Morok commander Ivor Salter
Dalek voice Peter Hawkins

Director: Mervyn Pinfield
Designer: Spencer Chapman

The Space Museum
The Dimensions of Time
The Search
The Final Phase
(24 April–15 May 1965)

The Chase

w Terry Nation *(a 6-part story)*
Experimenting with a space-time visualizer taken from Xeros, the Doctor sees the Daleks in pursuit and a frantic chase through time ensues, ending with a battle on the planet of the Mechonoids, where the Doctor loses two companions (Ian and Barbara, who return to their own time) and gains a new one . . .
Dalek voices Peter Hawkins, David Graham
Rynian Hywel Bennett
Morton Dill Peter Purves
Capt. Briggs David Blake Kelly
Grey Lady Roslyn de Winter

Robot Dr. Who Edmund Warwick
Mechonoid voice David Graham
Steven Taylor Peter Purves *(intro)*

Director: Richard Martin
Designers: Raymond P. Cusick & John Wood

The Executioners
The Death of Time
Flight Through Eternity
Journey into Terror
The Death of Doctor Who
The Planet of Decision
(22 May–26 June 1965)

The Time Meddler

w Dennis Spooner *(a 4-part story)*
Materializing on the Northumbrian coast in 1066, the travelers come up against the Monk, another time traveler from the Doctor's planet, who is planning to change the outcome of the Battle of Hastings.
Steven Taylor Peter Purves
Monk Peter Butterworth
Edith Alethea Charlton
Eldred Peter Russell
Wulnoth Michael Miller
Ulf Norman Hartley
Sven David Anderson

Director: Douglas Camfield
Designer: Barry Newbery

The Watcher
The Meddling Monk
A Battle of Wits
Checkmate
(3–24 July 1965)

Season Three
(11 September 1965–16 July 1966)
REGULAR CAST
The Doctor William Hartnell   *Vicki* Maureen O'Brien *(exit Story 3)*
Steven Taylor Peter Purves   *Dodo Chaplet* Jackie Lane *(from Story 5)*

Producers: Verity Lambert *(Stories 1–2)*, John Wiles, *(Stories 3–6)*, Innes Lloyd *(from Story 7)*

Story editors: Donald Tosh *(to Story 5, Ep. 3)*, Gerry Davis *(from Story 5, Ep. 4)*

Galaxy 4

w William Emms *(a 4-part story)*
The Doctor, Steven and Vicki land on a doomed planet where they help the peace-loving Rills and their robots, the Chumblies, defeat the evil, women-dominated Drahvins.
Maaga Stephanie Bidmead
Drahvin One Marina Martin
Drahvin Two Susanna Carroll
Drahvin Three Lyn Ashley
Chumblies Jimmy Kaye, William Shearer, Angelo Muscat, Pepi Poupee, Tommy Reynolds

Rill voice Robert Cartland
Garvey Barry Jackson

Director: Derek Martinus
Designer: Richard Hunt

Four Hundred Dawns
Trap of Steel
Air Lock
The Exploding Planet
(11 September–2 October 1965)

Mission to the Unknown

w Terry Nation *(one episode)*
No regulars—this episode served as a one-act hint of things to come. On the planet Kembel, agent Marc Cory of the Space Special Security Service discovers that the Daleks are plotting a concerted alien attack on the Solar System. He is killed, but a tape of his findings survives . . .
Marc Cory Edward de Souza
Jeff Garvey Barry Jackson
Gordon Lowery Jeremy Young
Malpha Robert Cartland
Dalek voices David Graham, Peter Hawkins
Daleks Robert Jewell, Kevin Manser, John Scott-Martin, Gerald Taylor

Director: Derek Martinus
Designers: Richard Hunt & Raymond P. Cusick
(9 October 1965)

The Myth Makers

w Donald Cotton *(a 4-part story)*
Landing in the midst of the Trojan War, the Doctor helps Achilles defeat Hector, is taken for a god, and masterminds the fall of Troy. Vicki falls in love with Troilus and stays behind.
Achilles Cavan Kendall
Odysseus Ivor Salter
Agamemnon Francis de Woolf
Menelaus Jack Melford
Cyclops Tutte Lemkow
King Priam Max Adrian
Paris Barrie Ingham
Cassandra Frances White
Troilus James Lynn
Katarina Adrienne Hill *(intro)*

Director: Michael Leeston-Smith
Designer: John Wood

Temple of Secrets
Small Prophet, Quick Return
Death of a Spy
Horse of Destruction
(16 October–6 November 1965)

The Daleks' Master Plan

w Terry Nation & Dennis Spooner *(Eps. 6, 8–12)*
(a 12-part story)
The TARDIS lands in the jungles of Kembel in the year 4000. The doctor finds Cory's tape and meets another Earth agent, Bret Vyon. They discover that Mavic Chen, Guardian of the Solar System, has betrayed Earth to the Daleks, enabling them to build an awesome weapon, the Time Destructor. In a protracted struggle, the Doctor, aided by Vyon's sister, Sara Kingdom, is impeded by an old foe, the Meddling Monk. Fatalities: Katarina, Sara and Bret Vyon. (Nicholas Courtney, who played Bret Vyon, rejoined the series three years later as the Brigadier.)
Bret Vyon Nicholas Courtney
Mavic Chen Kevin Stoney
Sara Kingdom Jean Marsh
Katarina Adrienne Hill
Meddling Monk Peter Butterworth
Trantis Roy Evans
Malpha Bryan Mosley

Director: Douglas Camfield
Designers: Raymond P. Cusick *(Eps. 1–2, 5–7, 11)* Barry Newbery *(Eps. 3–4, 8–10, 12)*

The Nightmare Begins
Day of Armageddon
Devil's Planet
The Traitors
Counter Plot
Coronas of the Sun
The Feast of Steven*
Volcano
Golden Death
Escape Switch
The Abandoned Planet
Destruction of Time
(13 November 1965–29 January 1966)

* This episode was a Christmas story, set on Earth.

The Massacre of St. Bartholomew's Eve

w John Lucarotti *(Eps. 1–4)* & Donald Tosh *(Ep. 4)* *(a 4-part story)*
The travelers land right in the middle of the bitter 16th-century feud between the Catholics and Protestants in France—culminating in the bloody massacre of St. Bartholomew's Eve.
Nicholas David Weston
Anne Annette Robertson
Abbot of Amboise William Hartnell
Marshal Tavannes André Morell
Admiral de Coligny Leonard Sachs
Catherine de Medici Joan Young
Toligny Michael Bilton
Dodo Jackie Lane *(intro, Ep. 4)*

Director: Paddy Russell
Designer: Michael Young

War of God
The Sea Beggar
Priest of Death
Bell of Doom
(5–26 February 1966)

The Ark

w Paul Erickson & Lesley Scott *(a 4-part story)*
Having picked up Dodo on a brief stop in Wimbledon at the end of the previous story, the TARDIS now materializes in the far future, on a gigantic space ark, carrying the human population of a doomed Earth (the Guardians) and their slaves (the Monoids) to a new planet. In a tale of two halves, spanning 700 years, the Doctor teaches the two groups to live in peace together and finds a cure for the common cold.
Commander Eric Elliott
Zentos Inigo Jackson
Manyak Roy Spencer
Monoids Edmund Coulter, Frank George
Rhos Michael Sheard
Maharis Terence Woodfield
Dassuk Brian Wright

Director: Michael Imison
Designer: Barry Newbery

The Steel Sky
The Plague
The Return
The Bomb
(5–26 March 1966)

The Celestial Toymaker

w Brian Hayles *(uncredited additional material by Gerry Davis & Donald Tosh) (a 4-part story)*
The Doctor and his companions materialize in the domain of a malevolent mandarin, The Celestial Toymaker, who forces them to play some bizarre games for their freedom.
Toymaker Michael Gough
Clowns Campbell Singer, Carmen Silvera
Hearts Campbell Singer, Carmen Silvera, Peter Stephens, Reg Levers
Cyril Peter Stephens

Director: Bill Sellars
Designer: John Wood

The Celestial Toyroom
The Hall of Dolls
The Dancing Floor
The Final Test
(2–23 April 1966)

The Gunfighters

w Donald Cotton *(a 4-part story)*
Back in time again, to the Wild West and the gunfight at the OK Corral between the Earps and the Clantons.
Ike Clanton William Hurndell
Phineas Clanton Maurice Good

Billy Clanton David Cole
Seth Harper Shane Rimmer
Wyatt Earp John Alderson
Doc Holliday Anthony Jacobs
Bat Masterson Richard Beale
Pa Clanton Reed de Rouen
Johnny Ringo Laurence Payne

Director: Rex Tucker
Designer: Barry Newbery

A Holiday for the Doctor
Don't Shoot the Pianist
Johnny Ringo
The OK Corral
(30 April–21 May 1966)

The Savages

w Ian Stuart Black *(a 4-part story)*
Arriving on a distant planet, the travelers find an advanced civilization, the Elders, formed by transferring the life-force of the primitive, cave-dwelling Savages to their people. After helping to bring the two races together, Steven elects to stay on as their leader.
Chal Ewen Solon
Tor Patrick Godfrey
Capt. Edal Peter Thomas
Exorse Geoffrey Frederick
Jano Frederick Jaeger
Nanina Clare Jenkins
Senta Norman Henry
Wylda Edward Caddick

Director: Christopher Barry
Designer: Stuart Walker
(28 May–18 June 1966)

The War Machines

w Ian Stuart Black, *from an idea by* Kit Pedler *(a 4-part story)*
In London, the Doctor fights the menace of WOTAN, a highly sophisticated computer housed in the Post Office Tower, which plans to take over the world with mobile computers called War Machines. He loses Dodo, but gains two new companions—cockney seaman Ben and dolly secretary Polly. This was the first story set in the present day.
Prof. Brett John Harvey
Major Green Alan Curtis
Polly Anneke Wills *(intro)*
Ben Michael Craze *(intro)*
Sir Charles Summer William Mervyn
Prof. Krimpton John Cater
Kitty Sandra Bryant
Newsreader Kenneth Kendall

Director: Michael Ferguson
Designer: Raymond London
(25 June–16 July 1966)

Season Four
(10 September 1966–1 July 1967)

REGULAR CAST
The Doctor William Hartnell *(Stories 1–2)*/Patrick Troughton *(from Story 3)*
Polly Anneke Wills *(to Story 8)* *Ben* Michael Craze *(to Story 8)*
Jamie Frazer Hines *(from Story 4)*

Producer: Innes Lloyd
Associate producer: Peter Bryant *(Story 8, Eps. 1–3)*

Story editors: Gerry Davis *(to Story 9, Ep. 3)*, Peter Bryant *(Story 9, Eps. 4–7)*

The Smugglers

w Brian Hayles *(a 4-part story)*
Landing on a remote stretch of the Cornish coast in the 17th century, the Doctor and Co. find themselves in conflict with treasure-hunting pirates and local smugglers.
Cherub George A. Cooper
Squire Paul Whitsun-Jones
Capt. Pike Michael Godfrey
Blake John Ringham
Jacob Kewper David Blake Kelly
Tom Mike Lucas

Director: Julia Smith
Designer: Richard Hunt
(10 September–1 October 1966)

The Tenth Planet

w Kit Pedler, Gerry Davis *(Eps. 3–4) (a 4-part story)*
The TARDIS materializes at the South Pole in the late 1980s and the Doctor confronts a new enemy—the Cybermen, invaders from the tenth planet, Mondas, who want to destroy Earth and turn its people into Cybermen, too. The Cybermen are defeated, but the Doctor is worn out and begins to change . . .
General Cutler Robert Beatty
Dyson Dudley Jones
Barclay David Dodimead
Wigner Steve Plytas
Radar technician Christopher Matthews
Cybermen voices Roy Skelton, Peter Hawkins

Director: Derek Martinus
Designer: Peter Kindred
(8–29 October 1966)

The Second Doctor: **PATRICK TROUGHTON**
(1966–1969)

The Power of the Daleks

w David Whitaker *(plus uncredited additional material by* Dennis Spooner*) (a 6-part story)*
On the Earth colony of Vulcan in the distant future, the Doctor finds apparently servile Daleks, but the treacherous beings have set up a secret reproduction plant.
Quinn Nicholas Hawtrey
Bragen Bernard Archard
Lesterson Robert James
Janley Pamela Ann Davy
Hensell Peter Bathurst
Valmar Richard Kane
Kebble Steven Scott

Director: Christopher Barry
Designer: Derek Dodd
(5 November–10 December 1966)

The Highlanders

w Elwyn Jones, Gerry Davis *(a 4-part story)*
Landing at Culloden in 1746, The Doctor, Ben and Polly get caught up with a group of Highlanders fleeing from the Redcoats and avoid a one-way ticket on a prison ship to the West Indies. Piper Jamie McCrimmon turns the TARDIS trio into a quartet . . .
The Laird Donald Bisset
Jamie Frazer Hines *(intro)*
Kirsty Hannah Gordon
Lt. Algernon ffinch Michael Elwyn
Sergeant Peter Welch
Solicitor Grey David Garth
Perkins Sydney Arnold
Trask Dallas Cavell

Director: Hugh David
Designer: Geoff Kirkland
(17 December 1966–7 January 1967)

The Underwater Menace

w Geoffrey Orme *(a 4-part story)*
Materializing on an extinct volcano in the middle of
the ocean, the travelers are captured and taken far un-
derground to the lost city of Atlantis. There they meet
Prof. Zaroff, a scientist who is planning to drain the
Atlantic Ocean into the white-hot core of the Earth.
Ara Catherine Howe
Ramo Tom Watson
Lolem Peter Stephens
Damon Colin Jeavons
Zaroff Joseph Furst
Jacko Paul Anil
Sean P.G. Stephens

Director: Julia Smith
Designer: Jack Robinson
(14 January–4 February 1967)

The Moonbase

w Kit Pedler *(a 4-part story)*
On the Moon, in the year 2070, the Doctor discov-
ers that the Cybermen are determined to tamper with
the Gravitron—a machine that controls the weather
on Earth—to wreak climatic havoc on the planet.
Hobson Patrick Barr
Benoit André Maranne
Nils Michael Wolf
Sam John Rolfe
Dr. Evans Alan Rowe
Cybermen John Wills, Peter Greene, Keith
Goodman, Reg Whitehead, Sonnie Willis

Director: Morris Barry
Designer: Colin Shaw
(11 February–4 March 1967)

The Macra Terror

w Ian Stuart Black *(a 4-part story)*
On a planet run like a holiday camp, the Doctor and
his friends meet a man called Medok who tells them
the paradise is being infiltrated by a mysterious race
of giant crabs.
Pilot Peter Jeffrey
Sunnaa Jane Enshawe
Medok Terence Lodge
Ola Gertan Klauber
Controller Graham Leaman

Control voice Denis Goacher
Macra operator Robert Jewell

Director: John Davies
Designer: Kenneth Sharp
(11 March–1 April 1967)

The Faceless Ones

w David Ellis & Malcolm Hulke *(a 6-part story)*
The TARDIS lands at Gatwick Airport in 1966, and
the Doctor uncovers a plot by an alien race, the
Chameleons, to take over the identities of humans
using special charter flights to spirit away their vic-
tims. (Exit: Ben and Polly.)
Commandant Colin Gordon
Meadows George Selway
Jean Rock Wanda Ventham
Spencer Victor Winding
Blade Donald Pickering
Jenkins Christopher Tranchell
Crossland Bernard Kay
Samantha Briggs Pauline Collins
Ann Davidson Gilly Fraser

Director: Gerry Mill
Designer: Geoff Kirkland
(8 April–13 May 1967)

The Evil of the Daleks

w David Whitaker *(a 7-part story)*
An adventure that starts with the TARDIS being
stolen, sees the Doctor and Jamie whisked back to
Victorian Canterbury and thence to Skaro, where the
Daleks try to turn the Doctor into a Dalek. Instead he
makes some Daleks almost human. The result: civil
war—and a new passenger in the TARDIS.
Edward Waterfield John Bailey
Victoria Waterfield Deborah Watling *(intro)*
Mollie Dawson Jo Rowbottom
Theodore Maxtible Marius Goring
Ruth Maxtible Brigit Forsyth
Toby Windsor Davies
Kemel Sonny Caldinez

Director: Derek Martinus
Designer: Chris Thompson
(20 May–1 July 1967)
NB: Repeat of Episode 1 on 8 June 1968 contained
additional footage and voice-over.

Season Five
(2 September 1967–1 June 1968)
REGULAR CAST
The Doctor Patrick Troughton *Jamie* Frazer Hines
Victoria Waterfield Deborah Watling

Producers: Peter Bryant *(Stories 1, 5–7)*, Innes
Lloyd *(Stories 2–4)*
Story editors: Victor Pemberton *(Story 1)*

Peter Bryant *(Stories 2–4)*
Derrick Sherwin *(Stories 5–7)*

The Tomb of the Cybermen

w Kit Pedler & Gerry Davis *(a 4-part story)*
The TARDIS arrives on the planet Telos where an
Earth expedition is excavating the tomb of the last
Cybermen. The Doctor is soon up against his old
foes—plus the Cybermats, deadly little robot crea-
tures trained to attack by homing in on brain waves.
Toberman Roy Stewart
Prof. Parry Aubrey Richards
John Viner Cyril Shaps
Jim Callum Clive Merrison
Kaftan Shirley Cooklin
Eric Klieg George Pastell
Capt. Hopper George Roubicek
Cyberman controller Michael Kilgarriff

Director: Morris Barry
Designer: Martin Johnson
(2–23 September 1967)

The Abominable Snowman

w Mervyn Haisman & Henry Lincoln *(a 6-part
story)*
In Tibet, the Doctor and his friends meet an ex-
plorer, Travers, and discover the Yeti—fur-covered
robots controlled by a malevolent alien entity called
the Intelligence.
Travers Jack Watling
Khrisong Norman Jones
Thonmi David Spencer
Rinchen David Grey
Sapan Raymond Llewellyn
Songsten Charles Morgan
Padmasambhava Wolfe Morris
Ralpachan David Baron
Yeti Reg Whitehead

Director: Gerald Blake
Designer: Malcolm Middleton
(30 September–4 November 1967)

The Ice Warriors

w Brian Hayles *(a 6-part story)*
The far future: England is in the grip of a new, ever-
encroaching ice age. Arriving at a scientific base,
the Doctor and his companions are on hand when a
Martian ice warrior is found trapped in the ice. Once
revived, however, leader Varga has world conquest
on his mind.
Miss Garrett Wendy Gifford
Clent Peter Barkworth
Arden George Waring
Walters Malcolm Taylor
Storr Angus Lennie
Penley Peter Sallis
Varga Bernard Bresslaw

Director: Derek Martinus
Designer: Jeremy Davies
(11 November–16 December 1967)

The Enemy of the World

w David Whitaker *(a 6-part story)*
Double trouble for the Doctor when he tangles with
Salamander—a would-be world dictator who looks
exactly like him.
Astrid Mary Peach
Giles Kent Bill Kerr
Donald Bruce Colin Douglas
Benik Milton Johns
Salamander Patrick Troughton
Swann Christopher Burgess
Colin Adam Verney
Mary Margaret Hickey

Director: Barry Letts
Designer: Christopher Pemsel
(23 December 1967–27 January 1968)

The Web of Fear

w Mervyn Haisman & Henry Lincoln *(a 6-part
story)*
The Doctor again fights the Yeti and the Intelli-
gence—this time in the London Underground. His
ally: Col. Lethbridge-Stewart, later to form a special
anti-alien task force, UNIT.
Prof. Travers Jack Watling
Anne Travers Tina Packer
Corp. Lane Rod Beacham
Corp. Blake Richardson Morgan
Capt. Knight Ralph Watson
Harold Chorley Jon Rollason
Staff Sgt. Arnold Jack Woolgar
Col. Lethbridge-Stewart Nicholas Courtney

Director: Douglas Camfield
Designer: David Myerscough-Jones
(3 February–9 March 1968)
(NB: Inside one of the Yeti costumes was John Levene, later a cast regular as UNIT's Sgt. Benton.)

Fury From the Deep

w Victor Pemberton *(a 6-part story)*
At a gas refinery on the northeast coast of England,
the Doctor, Jamie and Victoria tangle with a para-
sitic seaweed that turns people into weed creatures.
Robson Victor Maddern
Harris Roy Spencer
Price Graham Leaman
Maggie Harris June Murphy
Chief engineer Hubert Rees
Van Lutyens John Abineri
Quill Bill Burridge
Oak John Gill

Director: Hugh David
Designer: Peter Kindred
(16 March–20 April 1968)

The Wheel in Space

w David Whitaker, *story by* Kit Pedler *(a 6-part story)*
Having left Victoria behind on Earth, the TARDIS now materializes in an abandoned rocket, in the orbit of a giant space station. There, they again fight off invading Cybermen—helped by a new companion, Zoe.
Zoe Wendy Padbury *(intro)*
Leo Ryan Eric Flynn

Dr. Gemma Corwyn Anne Ridler
Tanya Lernov Clare Jenkins
Jarvis Bennett Michael Turner
Enrico Casali Donald Sumpter
Armand Vallance Derrick Gilbert
Sean Flannigan James Mellor

Director: Tristan de Vere Cole
Designer: Derek Dodd
(27 April–1 June 1968)

Season Six
(10 August 1968–21 June 1969)
REGULAR CAST
The Doctor Patrick Troughton   *Jamie* Frazer Hines
Zoe Wendy Padbury

Producers: Peter Bryant *(Stories 1–6)*, Derrick Sherwin *(Story 7)*

Script editors: Derrick Sherwin *(Stories 1–2, 6)*, Terrance Dicks *(Stories 3–5, 7)*

The Dominators

w Norman Ashby *(alias Mervyn Haisman & Henry Lincoln) (a 5-part story)*
The Doctor hopes for a peaceful holiday on the planet Dulkis but finds the island he lands on has been taken over by the cruel Dominators and their deadly robots, the Quarks, with the aim of turning the world into a radioactive power source.
Rago Ronald Allen
Toba Kenneth Ives
Cully Arthur Cox
Kando Felicity Gibson
Teel Giles Block
Balan Johnson Bayly
Senex Walter Fitzgerald

Director: Morris Barry
Designer: Barry Newbery
(10 August–7 September 1968)

The Mind Robber

w Peter Ling, Derrick Sherwin *(Ep. 1 only— uncredited) (a 5-part story)*
The crew of the TARDIS find themselves in a bizarre white void, and then the Land of Fiction, populated by strange white robots, mythical monsters and fictional characters, and ruled by an aged Master who wants the Doctor to take his place.
Master Emrys Jones
Stranger/Gulliver Bernard Horsfall
Rapunzel Christine Pirie
Medusa Sue Pulford
Karkus Christopher Robbie
D'Artagnan/Sir Lancelot John Greenwood

Director: David Maloney
Designer: Evan Hercules
(14 September–12 October 1968)

The Invasion

w Derrick Sherwin, *from an idea by* Kit Pedler *(an 8-part story)*
With the help of Brigadier Lethbridge-Stewart's newly formed task force, UNIT, the Doctor foils the Cybermen's latest plot to invade Earth—after first paralyzing the population.
Isobel Watkins Sally Faulkner
Benton John Levene
Tobias Vaughn Kevin Stoney
Packer Peter Halliday
Brig. Lethbridge-Stewart Nicholas Courtney
Sgt. Walters James Thornhill
Capt. Turner Robert Sidaway
Prof. Watkins Edward Burnham

Director: Douglas Camfield
Designer: Richard Hunt
(2 November–21 December 1968)

The Krotons

w Robert Holmes *(a 4-part story)*
The Doctor and Zoe try out the Kroton Teaching Machine, and their combined brain power reawakens a dormant—and dangerous—crystalline race.
Selris James Copeland
Vana Madeleine Mills
Thara Gilbert Wynne
Elek Philip Madoc
Axus Richard Ireson
Beta James Cairncross
Kroton voices Roy Skelton, Patrick Tull

Director: David Maloney
Designer: Ray London
(28 December 1968–18 January 1969)

The Seeds of Death

w Brian Hayles *(a 6-part story)*
The Ice Warriors prepare for an attack on Earth by sending Martian seed pods containing a deadly fungus along the T-Mat, an instantaneous travel device linking the Moon with the Earth.
Gia Kelly Louise Pajo
Brent Ric Felgate
Radnor Ronald Leigh-Hunt
Fewsham Terry Scully
Phipps Christopher Coll
Eldred Philip Ray
Slaar Alan Bennion
Computer voice John Witty
Ice Warriors Tony Harwood, Sonny Caldinez

Director: Michael Ferguson
Designer: Paul Allen
(25 January–1 March 1969)

The Space Pirates

w Robert Holmes *(a 6-part story)*
Materializing on a space beacon, the TARDIS travelers are caught up in a raid by Space Pirates, and join forces with space miner Milo Clancey to end their thieving ways.
Dervish Brian Peck
Caven Dudley Foster
Gen. Hermack Jack May
Maj. Ian Warne Donald Gee
Technician Penn George Layton
Milo Clancey Gordon Gostelow
Madeleine Issigri Lisa Daniely
Dom Issigri Esmond Knight
Lt. Sorba Nik Zaran

Director: Michael Hart
Designer: Ian Watson
(8 March–12 April 1969)

The War Games

w Terrance Dicks & Malcolm Hulke *(a 10-part story)*
On an Earth-like planet, the Doctor and his companions become involved in the war games of aliens who have captured and brainwashed soldiers from different periods of Earth's history, to train an invincible army. With a handful of Resistance fighters, the Doctor opposes the War Lord and his assistant, the War Chief, but finally has to call on his own people, the Time Lords, to help. After ending the "games," the Time Lords bring the Doctor to trial for "intervening" and exile him to Earth—with a changed appearance. Jamie and Zoe are sent back to their own eras. (This story did more than end an era—it introduced the Time Lords and "filled in" the Doctor's own history.)
Lady Jennifer Buckingham Jane Sherwin
Lt. Carstairs David Savile
War Chief Edward Brayshaw
Gen. Smythe Noel Coleman
Von Weich David Garfield
War Lord Philip Madoc
Scientist Vernon Dobtcheff
Russell Graham Weston
Security chief James Bree
Time Lords Bernard Horsfall, Trevor Martin, Clyde Pollitt
Moor David Troughton

Director: David Maloney
Designer: Roger Cheveley
(19 April–21 June 1969)

The Third Doctor: **JON PERTWEE**
(1970–1974)

Season Seven
(3 January–20 June 1970)
REGULAR CAST
The Doctor Jon Pertwee *Liz Shaw* Caroline John
Brigadier Lethbridge-Stewart Nicholas Courtney
Sgt. Benton John Levene *(from Story 3)*

Producers: Derrick Sherwin *(Story 1),*
  Barry Letts *(Stories 2–4)*

Script editor: Terrance Dicks

Spearhead from Space

w Robert Holmes *(a 4-part story)*
Exiled to Earth, the Doctor agrees to help UNIT investigate strange meteorites that have landed. He comes up against the Nestene—an alien intelligence which is planning to use Autons, plastic replicas of human beings, to replace key figures in the government. (First color story.)

Seeley Neil Wilson
Capt. Munro John Breslin
Channing Hugh Burden
Hibbert John Woodnutt
Maj. Gen. Scobie Hamilton Dyce
Ransome Derek Smee

Director: Derek Martinus
Designer: Paul Allen
(3–24 January 1970)

Doctor Who and The Silurians

w Malcolm Hulke *(a 7-part story)*
The Silurians, an intelligent prehistoric race, are re-vived by work at an atomic research center and plan to recapture the world by unleashing a deadly disease and destroying the Van Allen belt.
Dr. Lawrence Peter Miles
Maj. Baker Norman Jones
Miss Dawson Thomasine Heiner
Capt. Hawkins Paul Darrow
Silurian scientist Pat Gorman
Masters Geoffrey Palmer
Young Silurian Nigel John
Dr. Quinn Fulton Mackay

Director: Timothy Combe
Designer: Barry Newbery
(31 January–14 March 1970)

The Ambassadors of Death

w David Whitaker, Malcolm Hulke *(uncredited rewrites) (a 7-part story)*
A manned space probe returns to Earth—but with an alien crew aboard. The Doctor flies into space in search of the *real* astronauts.
Taltalian Robert Cawdron
Van Lyden Ric Felgate
Ralph Cornish Ronald Allen
Gen. Carrington John Abineri

Quinlan Dallas Cavell
Reegan William Dysart
Corporal Benton John Levene *(intro—later Sgt. Benton)*
Astronauts Steve Peters, Neville Simons

Director: Michael Ferguson
Designer: David Myerscough-Jones
(21 March–2 May 1970)

Inferno

w Don Houghton *(a 7-part story)*
The Doctor clashes with Prof. Stahlman, head of a project to release a new energy source from the Earth's core. His own efforts to reactivate the TARDIS console hurl him into a parallel world where his friends are enemies and Stahlman's Inferno project has a terrifying outcome.
Prof. Stahlman Olaf Pooley
Bromley Ian Fairbairn
Sir Keith Gold Christopher Benjamin
Petra Williams Sheila Dunn
Greg Sutton Derek Newark
Primords Dave Carter, Peter Thompson, Pat Gorman, Walter Henry, Philip Ryan

Directors: Douglas Camfield & Barry Letts* *(uncredited)*
Designer: Jeremy Davies
(9 May–20 June 1970)

* Took over later episodes when Camfield fell ill.

Season Eight
(2 January–19 June 1971)

REGULAR CAST
The Doctor Jon Pertwee   Jo Grant Katy Manning
The Brigadier Nicholas Courtney
Capt. Mike Yates Richard Franklin *(except Story 4)* Sgt. Benton John Levene
(except Story 4)
The Master Roger Delgado

Producer: Barry Letts   *Script editor:* Terrance Dicks

Terror of the Autons

w Robert Holmes *(a 4-part story)*
With a new companion, Jo Grant, an over-keen, newly fledged UNIT agent, the Doctor faces his newest and trickiest foe . . . The Master, a villainous renegade Time Lord, who arrives on Earth to pave the way for a Nestene invasion with the Autons.
Rossini John Baskcomb
Prof. Philips Christopher Burgess
Rex Farrel Michael Wisher
Mrs. Farrel Barbara Leake
McDermott Harry Towb
Auton leader Pat Gorman
Auton policeman Terry Walsh

Director: Barry Letts
Designer: Ian Watson
(2–23 January 1971)

The Mind of Evil

w Don Houghton *(a 6-part story)*
The Doctor exposes the Master's deadly scheme to wreck a world peace conference using an alien mind parasite that feeds on criminal evil—and a stolen nerve-gas missile.
Prison governor Raymond Westwell
Dr. Summers Michael Sheard
Barnham Neil McCarthy
Corp. Bell Fernanda Marlowe
Capt. Chin Lee Pik-Sen Lim
Vosper Haydn Jones
Mailer William Marlowe

Director: Timothy Combe
Designer: Ray London
(30 January–6 March 1971)

The Claws of Axos

w Bob Baker & Dave Martin *(a 4-part story)*
The Doctor uses the TARDIS to save Earth from an alien parasite creature, Axos, by forcing it into a time-loop.
Chinn Peter Bathurst
Bill Filer Paul Grist
Sir George Hardiman Donald Hewlett
Axon man Bernard Holley
Winser David Savile
Minister Kenneth Benda
Capt. Harker Tim Pigott-Smith
Corp. Bell Fernanda Marlowe

Director: Michael Ferguson
Designer: Kenneth Sharp
(13 March–3 April 1971)

Colony in Space

w Malcolm Hulke *(a 6-part story)*
The Time Lords restore the TARDIS' ability to move through time and space, and send the Doctor (and Jo) to a bleak alien world where they help colonist farmers overcome an exploitive mining corporation, and prevent the Master from gaining control of the most deadly weapon in the galaxy.
Ashe John Ringham
Winton Nicholas Pennell

Mary Ashe Helen Worth
Norton Roy Skelton
Primitive Pat Gorman
Caldwell Bernard Kay
Dent Morris Perry
Morgan Tony Caunter
Guardian Norman Atkyns

Director: Michael Briant
Designer: Tim Gleeson
(10 April–15 May 1971)

The Daemons

w Guy Leopold *(alias Robert Sloman & Barry Letts) (a 5-part story)*
An archaeological dig near the village of Devil's End starts a series of terrifying events as the Master releases the power of Azal, last survivor of an ancient alien race called the Daemons.
Miss Hawthorne Damaris Hayman
Winstanley Rollo Gamble
Dr. Reeves Eric Hillyard
Bert Don McKillop
Tom Girton Jon Croft
Bok Stanley Mason
Azal Stephen Thorne

Director: Christopher Barry
Designer: Roger Ford
(22 May–19 June 1971)

Season Nine
(1 January–24 June 1972)
REGULAR CAST
As Season Eight, except:
The UNIT men (Stories 1 and 5 only), The Master (Stories 3 and 5 only)

Producer: Barry Letts

Script editor: Terrance Dicks

Day of the Daleks

w Louis Marks *(a 4-part story)*
The Doctor and Jo fight to prevent the death of diplomat Sir Reginald Styles and a war that will deliver Earth's future to the Daleks and their ferocious, gorilla-like slaves, the Ogrons.
Sir Reginald Styles Wilfrid Carter
Ogron Rick Lester
Chief Dalek John Scott Martin
Controller Aubrey Woods
Anat Anna Barry
Shura Jimmy Winston
Boaz Scott Fredericks
Monia Valentine Palmer

Director: Paul Bernard
Designer: David Myerscough-Jones
(1–22 January 1972)

The Curse of Peladon

w Brian Hayles *(a 4-part story)*
On the planet Peladon, the Doctor exposes a plot by High Priest Hepesh to sabotage his king's bid to join the Galactic Federation.
King Peladon David Troughton
Hepesh Geoffrey Toone
Grun Gordon St. Clair
Aggedor Nick Hobbs
Alpha Centauri Stuart Fell
Arcturus Murphy Grumbar
Ssorg Sonny Caldinez
Izlyr Alan Bennion
Voice of Alpha Centauri Ysanne Churchman
Voice of Arcturus Terry Bale

Director: Lennie Mayne
Designer: Gloria Clayton
(29 January–19 February 1972)

The Sea Devils

w Malcolm Hulke *(a 6-part story)*
The Master, supposedly held captive on a small island, plots to revive a machine with which he can control underwater lizard creatures called Sea Devils and conquer the world.
Capt. Hart Edwin Richfield
Trenchard Clive Morton
Third Officer Jane Blythe June Murphy
Sea Devil Pat Gorman
Cmdr. Ridgeway Donald Sumpter
Lt. Cmdr. Mitchell David Griffin
Chief Sea Devil Peter Forbes-Robertson
Ldg. Telegraphist Bowman Alec Wallis

Director: Michael Briant
Designer: Tony Snoaden
(26 February–1 April 1972)

The Mutants

w Bob Baker & David Martin *(a 6-part story)*
A summons from the Time Lords takes the Doctor and Jo to the planet Solos where they help its mutant inhabitants realize their destiny—against the wishes of the cruel Earth Marshal.
Marshal Paul Whitsun-Jones
Stubbs Christopher Coll
Cotton Rick James

Varan James Mellor
Ky Garrick Hagan
Jaeger George Pravda
Sonderguard John Hollis
Administrator Geoffrey Palmer
Mutt John Scott Martin

Director: Christopher Barry
Designer: Jeremy Bear
(8 April–13 May 1972)

The Time Monster

w Robert Sloman *(a 6-part story)*
In his unceasing quest for power, the Master unleashes Kronos, an entity that feeds on time, and causes the destruction of Atlantis.
Dr. Ruth Ingram Wanda Moore
Stuart Hyde Ian Collier
Krasis Donald Eccles
Hippias Aidan Murphy
Kronos Marc Boyle
Dalios George Cormack
Galleia Ingrid Pitt
Lakis Susan Penhaligon
Minotaur David Prowse

Director: Paul Bernard
Designer: Tim Gleeson
(20 May–24 June 1972)

Season Ten
(30 December 1972–23 June 1973)
REGULAR CAST
As Season Eight, except:
The Brigadier, Sgt. Benton (Stories 1 and 5 only)
Capt. Yates (Story 5 only), The Master (Story 3 only)

Producer: Barry Letts

Script editor: Terrance Dicks

The Three Doctors

w Bob Baker & Dave Martin *(a 4-part story)*
The Time Lords are under siege, their energy being drained through a black hole by Omega, an embittered Time Lord trapped in a world of anti-matter. The Doctor is joined by his two previous selves and together they succeed in defeating Omega. The grateful Time Lords lift their exile sentence.
Omega Stephen Thorne
Doctor Who William Hartnell
Doctor Who Patrick Troughton
President of the Council Roy Purcell
Time Lord Graham Leaman
Ollis Laurie Webb
Dr. Tyler Rex Robinson
Chancellor Clyde Pollitt

Director: Lennie Mayne
Designer: Roger Liminton
(30 December 1972–20 January 1973)

Carnival of Monsters

w Robert Holmes *(a 4-part story)*
Free to roam the cosmos again, the Doctor sets off for Metebelis 3, but winds up trapped in the Scope, an alien peepshow containing various galactic life-forms—including the Drashigs, ferocious swamp dragons.
Kalik Michael Wisher
Orum Terence Lodge
Shirna Cheryl Hall
Vorg Leslie Dwyer
Major Daly Tenniel Evans
Claire Daly Jenny McCracken
Andrews Ian Marter
Pletrac Peter Halliday

Director: Barry Letts
Designer: Roger Liminton
(27 January–17 February 1973)

Frontier in Space

w Malcolm Hulke *(a 6-part story)*
The Doctor and Jo are caught up in a power struggle between Earth and Draconia—with the Master manipulating both sides to provoke space war, and the Daleks standing by to cash in.
Draconian Prince Peter Birrel
President of Earth Vera Fusek
Gen. Williams Michael Hawkins
Gardiner Ray Lonnen
Prof. Dale Harold Goldblatt
Draconian captain Bill Wilde
Draconian emperor John Woodnutt
Chief Dalek John Scott Martin

Director: Paul Bernard
Designer: Cynthia Ključo
(24 February–31 March 1973)

Planet of the Daleks

w Terry Nation *(a 6-part story)*
On the planet Spiridon, the Doctor and Jo help a group of Thals prevent thousands of dormant Daleks from being revived to conquer the galaxy.
Taron Bernard Horsfall
Vaber Prentis Hancock

Codal Tim Preece
Wester Roy Skelton
Rebec Jane How
Latep Alan Tucker
Dalek voices Michael Wisher, Roy Skelton

Director: David Maloney
Designer: John Hurst
(7 April–12 May 1973)

The Green Death

w Robert Sloman *(a 6-part story)*
A mysterious death near the site of a new chemical refinery brings UNIT to Wales, and the Doctor faces a twin threat—a plague of giant green maggots caused by industrial pollution, and the BOSS, a maniac computer. Jo leaves to marry an ecologist.
Clifford Jones Stewart Bevan
Stevens Jerome Willis
Hinks Ben Howard
Elgin Tony Adams
Dave Talfryn Thomas
BOSS's voice John Dearth
Nancy Mitzi McKenzie

Director: Michael Briant
Designer: John Borrowes
(19 May–23 June 1973)

Season Eleven
(15 December 1973–8 June 1974)
REGULAR CAST
The Doctor Jon Pertwee *Sarah Jane Smith* Elisabeth Sladen
plus:
The Brigadier (Stories 1, 2 and 5), Sgt. Benton, Capt. Yates (Stories 2 and 5)

Producer: Barry Letts   *Script editor:* Terrance Dicks

The Time Warrior

w Robert Holmes *(a 4-part story)*
With stowaway journalist Sarah Jane Smith, the Doctor follows the trail of missing scientists back to the Middle Ages—and into the hands of an alien warrior, the Sontaran Linx.
Irongron David Daker
Bloodaxe John J. Carney
Meg Sheila Fay
Linx Kevin Lindsay
Prof. Rubeish Donald Pelmear
Eleanor June Brown
Edward of Wessex Alex Rowe
Hal Jeremy Bulloch

Director: Alan Bromly
Designer: Keith Cheetham
(15 December 1973–5 January 1974)

Invasion of the Dinosaurs*

w Malcolm Hulke *(a 6-part story)*
The Doctor battles Operation Golden Age—an MP and a scientist's bizarre plot to reverse time and return Earth to a pre-technological era.
Charles Grover, MP Noel Johnson
Butler Martin Jarvis
Prof. Whitaker Peter Miles
Gen. Finch John Bennett
Mark Terence Wilton
Adam Brian Badcoe

Director: Paddy Russell
Designer: Richard Morris
(12 January–16 February 1974)

* Part 1 titled "Invasion" only

Death to the Daleks

w Terry Nation *(a 4-part story)*
The time travelers are involved in a struggle between Daleks, Exxilons and humans for the antidote to a space plague.
Lt. Dan Galloway Duncan Lamont
Lt. Peter Hamilton Julian Fox
Jill Tarrant Joy Harrison
Bellal Arnold Yarrow
Dalek voices Michael Wisher
Capt. Richard Railton John Abineri

Director: Michael E. Briant
Designer: Colin Green
(23 February–16 March 1974)

The Monster of Peladon

w Brian Hayles *(a 6-part story)*
Returning to Peladon, the Doctor finds the planet torn by civil war, with the Ice Warriors imposing their own rule of terror, with a monster-making machine.
Ettis Ralph Watson
Eckersley Donald Gee
Thalira Nina Thomas
Ortron Frank Gatliff
Alpha Centauri Stuart Fell
Alpha Centauri's voice Ysanne Churchman
Gebek Rex Robinson

Aggedor Nick Hobbs
Sskel Sonny Caldinez
Azaxyr Alan Bennion

Director: Lennie Mayne
Designer: Gloria Clayton
(23 March–27 April 1974)

Planet of the Spiders

w Robert Sloman *(a 6-part story)*
An alien crystal is the key to a web of invasion and revolution as the Doctor clashes with the Spiders of Metebelis 3. Mortally wounded, his dying body goes through another regeneration . . .
Lupton John Dearth
Moss Terence Lodge
Keaver Andrew Staines
Barnes Christopher Burgess
Land Carl Forgione
Cho-je Kevin Lindsay
Tommy John Kane
Tuar Ralph Arliss
Arak Gareth Hunt
Queen Spider Kismet Delgado
Lupton's Spider Ysanne Churchman
The Great One Maureen Morris

Director: Barry Letts
Designer: Rochelle Selwyn
(4 May–8 June 1974)

The Fourth Doctor: TOM BAKER
(1974–1981)

Season Twelve
(28 December 1974–10 May 1975)
REGULAR CAST
The Doctor Tom Baker *Sarah Jane Smith* Elisabeth Sladen
Harry Sullivan Ian Marter

Producers: Barry Letts *(Story 1)* Philip Hinchcliffe *(Stories 2–4)*

Script editor: Robert Holmes

Robot

w Terrance Dicks *(a 4-part story)*
Still recovering from his latest change, the Doctor combats a group of unscrupulous scientists planning to start a Third World War, and a rampaging giant robot, and gains a second companion.
Harry Sullivan Ian Marter *(intro)*
Jellicoe Alec Linstead
Miss Winters Patricia Maynard
Prof. Kettlewell Edward Burnham
Robot Michael Kilgarriff
The Brigadier Nicholas Courtney
Sgt. Benton John Levene

Director: Christopher Barry
Designer: Ian Rawnsley
(28 December 1974–18 January 1975)

The Ark in Space

w Robert Holmes *(a 4-part story)*
Aboard a space station in the future, an insect race, the Wirrn, threaten to devour and absorb the human race as it lies in cryogenic suspension.
Vira Wendy Williams
Noah Kenton Moore
Rogan Richardson Morgan
Wirrn operators Stuart Fell, Nick Hobbs
Libri Christopher Masters
Voices Gladys Spencer, Peter Tuddenham

Director: Rodney Bennett
Designer: Roger Murray-Leach
(25 January–15 February 1975)

The Sontaran Experiment

w Bob Baker, Dave Martin *(a 2-part story)*
Leaving the ark, the Doctor goes to Earth where he finds and defeats a Sontaran officer, Styre, who is conducting cruel experiments on humans.
Styre/The Marshal Kevin Lindsay
Erak Peter Walshe
Krans Glyn Jones
Roth Peter Rutherford
Vural Donald Douglas

Director: Rodney Bennett
Designer: Roger Murray-Leach
(22 February–1 March 1975)

Genesis of the Daleks

w Terry Nation *(a 6-part story)*
The Time Lords send the Doctor to Skaro where the war between the Thals and the Kaleds is in its final stage. His mission: to prevent the birth of the Daleks, created by the crippled Kaled genius, Davros.
Davros Michael Wisher
Nyder Peter Miles
Gharman Dennis Chinnery
Sevrin Stephen Yardley

Ronson James Garbutt
Kavell Tom Georgeson
Bettan Harriet Philpin

Director: David Maloney
Designer: David Spode
(8 March–12 April 1975)

Revenge of the Cybermen

w Gerry Davis *(a 4-part story)*
Returning to the Ark to recover the TARDIS, the Doctor and his companions are plunged into a fight to the death between the Cybermen and the Vogans, inhabitants of a planet of gold—a substance deadly to the Cybermen.
Lester William Marlowe
Commander Stevenson Ronald Leigh-Hunt
Kellman Jeremy Wilkin
Vorus David Collings
Magrik Michael Wisher
Cyberleader Christopher Robbie
Tyrum Kevin Stoney
Sheprah Brian Grellis

Director: Michael E. Briant
Designer: Roger Murray-Leach
(19 April–10 May 1975)

Season Thirteen
(30 August 1975–6 March 1976)
REGULAR CAST
The Doctor Tom Baker *Sarah Jane Smith* Elisabeth Sladen
Harry Sullivan Ian Marter *(Stories 1 and 4 only)*
RSM Benton John Levene *(Stories 1 and 4 only)*

Producer: Philip Hinchcliffe   *Script editor:* Robert Holmes

---

Terror of the Zygons

w Robert Banks Stewart *(a 4-part story)*
The Doctor solves the riddle of the Loch Ness monster—it's a half-creature, half-machine called the Skarasen, created by an alien race, the Zygons, as part of their plan to take over the world.
Duke of Forgill/Broton John Woodnutt
The Caber Robert Russell
Sister Lamont Lillias Walker
Angus Angus Lennie
Zygons Keith Ashley, Ronald Gough
The Brigadier Nicholas Courtney

Director: Douglas Camfield
Designer: Nigel Curzon
(30 August–20 September 1975)

Planet of Evil

w Louis Marks *(a 4-part story)*
A mayday call brings the Doctor and Sarah to Zeta Minor, a planet on the edge of the known universe where he battles with a man who becomes an anti-matter monster.
Sorenson Frederick Jaeger
Vishinsky Ewen Solon
Salamar Prentis Hancock
Morelli Michael Wisher
De Haan Graham Weston
Reig Melvyn Bedford

Director: David Maloney
Designer: Roger Murray-Leach
(27 September–18 October 1975)

Pyramids of Mars

w Stephen Harris *(alias* Lewis Greifer & Robert Holmes) *(a 4-part story)*
An inexplicable force draws the TARDIS to an old priory in 1911, where the Doctor finds Egyptologist Marcus Scarman has been possessed by the spirit of Sutekh, a malevolent god-like being seeking to escape from his Egyptian tomb.
Marcus Scarman Bernard Archard
Namin Peter Mayock
Dr. Warlock Peter Copley
Laurence Scarman Michael Sheard
Sutekh Gabriel Woolf

Director: Paddy Russell
Designer: Christine Ruscoe
(25 October–15 November 1975)

The Android Invasion

w Terry Nation *(a 4-part story)*
The TARDIS lands in a replica of an English village on the planet of the Kraals, an alien race plotting to conquer Earth with android copies of humans.
Corporal Adams Max Faulkner
Morgan Peter Welch
Guy Crayford Milton Johns
Styggron Martin Friend
Kraal Stuart Fell
Col. Faraday Patrick Newell

Director: Barry Letts
Designer: Philip Lindley
(22 November–13 December 1975)

The Brain of Morbius

w Robin Bland *(alias* Terrance Dicks) *(a 4-part story)*
On the storm-lashed planet of Karn, the Doctor has a brush with the witch-like Sisterhood of the Flame, and grapples with the mind of an evil Time Lord, Morbius, whose brain has been installed in a monstrous new body by a disreputable surgeon, Solon.
Solon Philip Madoc
Condo Colin Fay
Chica Gilly Brown
Maren Cynthia Grenville
Voice of Morbius Michael Spice

Director: Christopher Barry
Designer: Barry Newbery
(3–24 January 1976)

The Seeds of Doom

w Robert Banks Stewart *(a 6-part story)*
In which the Doctor faces the "growing" menace of the Krynoid—an alien plant form that incites a vegetable revolution against the animal kingdom, aided by demented millionaire botanist Harrison Chase.
Richard Dunbar Kenneth Gilbert
Hargreaves Seymour Green
Harrison Chase Tony Beckley
Scorby John Challis
Sir Colin Thackeray Michael Barrington
Amelia Ducat Sylvia Coleridge
Arnold Keeler/Voice of the Krynoid Mark Jones

Director: Douglas Camfield
Designers: Roger Murray-Leach *(Eps. 1–6)*, Jeremy Bear *(Eps. 1–2 only)*
(31 January–6 March 1976)

Season Fourteen
(4 September–20 November 1976)
(1 January–2 April 1977)

REGULAR CAST
The Doctor Tom Baker   *Sarah Jane Smith* Elisabeth Sladen *(exit Story 2)*
Leela Louise Jameson *(from Story 4)*

Producer: Philip Hinchcliffe

Script editor: Robert Holmes

The Masque of Mandragora

w Louis Marks *(a 4-part story)*
In Renaissance Italy, the travelers get involved in family intrigue, a secret sect—the Brothers of Demnos—and an alien energy force, the Mandragora Helix, which seeks to plunge Earth back into the Dark Ages.
(Filmed in and around Portmeirion.)
Count Federico Jon Laurimore

Capt. Rossini Antony Carrick
Giuliano Gareth Armstrong
Marco Tim Pigott-Smith
Hieronymous Norman Jones
High priest Robert James
Brother Brian Ellis

Director: Rodney Bennett
Designer: Barry Newbery
(4–25 September 1976)

The Hand of Fear

w Bob Baker & Dave Martin *(a 4-part story)*
The Doctor and Sarah tangle with Eldrad, an alien criminal regenerated by the power of a nuclear explosion, before the companions have to part, when the Doctor is summoned back to Gallifrey.
Dr. Carter Rex Robinson
Prof. Watson Glyn Houston
Miss Jackson Frances Pidgeon
Driscoll Roy Boyd
Eldrad Judith Paris

Director: Lennie Mayne
Designer: Christine Ruscoe
(2–23 October 1976)

The Deadly Assassin

w Robert Holmes *(a 4-part story)*
Returning alone to Gallifrey, the Doctor witnesses the murder of the President and finds his old foe The Master plotting to use the power of a black hole to destroy the Time Lords. (The Doctor's only "solo" story.)
The President Llewellyn Rees
Cmdr. Hildred Derek Seaton
Castellan Spandrell George Pravda
Co-ordinator Engin Erik Chitty
Chancellor Goth Bernard Horsfall
Commentator Runcible Hugh Walters
Cardinal Borusa Angus Mackay
The Master Peter Pratt

Director: David Maloney
Designer: Roger Murray-Leach
(30 October–20 November 1976)

The Face of Evil

w Chris Boucher *(a 4-part story)*
The Doctor is captured by the primitive Sevateem tribe, befriended by a warrior girl, Leela, and threatened by a mad computer—the legacy of his own age-old mistake.
Leela Louise Jameson *(intro)*
Calib Leslie Schofield

Tomas Brendan Price
Neeva David Garfield
Jabel Leon Eagles
Gentek Mike Elles

Director: Pennant Roberts
Designer: Austin Ruddy
(1–22 January 1977)

The Robots of Death

w Chris Boucher *(a 4-part story)*
A warped scientist raised by robots incites a "robot rebellion" aboard a mobile mining factory, the Sandminer.
Dask David Bailie
Borg Brian Croucher
Toos Pamela Salem
Uvanov Russell Hunter
Poul David Collings
SV7 Miles Fothergill
D84 Gregory de Polney

Director: Michael E. Briant
Designer: Kenneth Sharp
(29 January–19 February 1977)

The Talons of Weng-Chiang

w Robert Holmes *(a 6-part story)*
The Doctor plans to take Leela to an authentic Music Hall—but they wind up fighting a war criminal from the future and his body-snatching Chinese Tong of the Black Scorpion in the sewers of Victorian London.
Weng-Chiang Michael Spice
Li H'sen Chang John Bennett
Mr. Sin (a homunculus) Deep Roy
Henry Jago Christopher Benjamin
Casey Chris Gannon
Prof. Litefoot Trevor Baxter
Lee Tony Then

Director: David Maloney
Designer: Roger Murray-Leach
(26 February–2 April 1977)

Season Fifteen
(3 September 1977–11 March 1978)
REGULAR CAST
The Doctor Tom Baker *Leela* Louise Jameson
Voice of K9 John Leeson *(from Story 2, except Story 3)*

Producer: Graham Williams

Script editors: Robert Holmes *(Stories 1–4)*,
Anthony Read *(Stories 5–6)*

Horror of Fang Rock

w Terrance Dicks (a 4-part story)
A deadly alien entity, the Rutan, stalks a turn-of-the-century lighthouse at Fang Rock where the survivors of a shipwreck have come ashore.
Vince John Abbott
Reuben Colin Douglas
Lord Palmerdale Sean Caffrey
Skinsale Alan Rowe
Adelaide Annette Woollett
Harker Rio Fanning

Director: Paddy Russell
Designer: Paul Allen
(3–24 September 1977)

The Invisible Enemy

w Bob Baker & Dave Martin (a 4-part story)
When the nucleus of a malignant virus lodges in the Doctor's brain, cloned microcopies of the Time Lord and Leela journey into his brain to confront it.
Safran Brian Grellis
Lowe Michael Sheard
Prof. Marius Frederick Jaeger
Voice of the Nucleus/Voice of K9 John Leeson
Ophthalmologist Jim McManus

Director: Derrick Goodwin
Designer: Barry Newbery
(1–22 October 1977)

Image of the Fendahl

w Chris Boucher (a 4-part story)
Dr. Fendelman's experiments on a skull eight million years older than man, revives the Fendahl, a powerful life-sapping force that materializes through his psychic assistant, Thea.
Adam Colby Edward Arthur
Thea Ransome Wanda Ventham
Maximillian Stael Scott Fredericks
Dr. Fendelman Denis Lill
Ted Moss Edward Evans
David Mitchell Derek Martin
Martha Tyler Daphne Heard
Jack Tyler Geoffrey Hinsliff

Director: George Spenton Foster
Designer: Anne Ridley
(29 October–19 November 1977)

The Sun Makers

w Robert Holmes (a 4-part story)
Landing on Pluto, the Doctor and Leela help a band of rebels overthrow the corrupt and oppressive rule of Gatherer Hade and the Collector.
Cordo Roy Macready
Hade Richard Leech
Marn Jonina Scott
Goudry Michael Keating
Mandrel William Simons
Veet Adrienne Burgess
Collector Henry Woolf
Bisham David Rowlands
Synge Derek Crewe

Director: Pennant Roberts
Designer: Tony Snoaden
(26 November–17 December 1977)

Underworld

w Bob Baker & Dave Martin (a 4-part story)
Materializing aboard a spaceship at the edge of the universe, the travelers become involved in its crew's quest to find the long-lost race banks of their home planet, Minyos.
Jackson James Maxwell
Tala Imogen Bickford-Smith
Orfe Jonathan Newth
Herrick Alan Lake
Idmon Jimmy Gardner
Idas Norman Tipton
Tarn Godfrey James
Rask James Marcus

Director: Norman Stewart
Designer: Dick Coles
(7–28 January 1978)

The Invasion of Time

w David Agnew (alias Anthony Read, Graham Williams from an idea by David Weir) (a 6-part story)
Returning to Gallifrey, the Doctor poses as a traitor to lure a powerful alien race, the Vardans, into a time loop, only to face an even greater threat from the Sontarans. He gains a victory, but loses his companion, Leela, who falls in love!
Andred Chris Tranchell
Castellan Kelner Milton Johns
Cardinal Borusa John Arnatt
Vardan leader Stan McGowan
Rodan Hilary Ryan
Nesbin Max Faulkner
Presta Gai Smith
Stor Derek Deadman

Director: Gerald Blake
Designer: Barbara Gosnold
(4 February–11 March 1978)

Season Sixteen
(2 September 1978–24 February 1979)
REGULAR CAST
The Doctor Tom Baker Romana Mary Tamm
Voice of K9 John Leeson
(except Story 5)

Producer: Graham Williams

Script editor: Anthony Read

The Ribos Operation

w Robert Holmes (a 4-part story)
With a new companion, graduate Time Lady Romanadvoratrelundar (Romana), and a new Mark II K9, the Doctor is assigned a new quest by the White Guardian—to gather the six scattered segments of the Key of Time. The first is hidden on the planet of Ribos, which a conman called Garron is trying to sell to warlord Graff Vynda-K.
The Guardian Cyril Luckham
Garron Iain Cuthbertson
Unstoffe Nigel Plaskitt
Graff Vynda-K Paul Seed
Sholakh Robert Keegan
Captain Prentis Hancock

Director: George Spenton Foster
Designer: Ken Ledsham
(2–23 September 1978)

The Pirate Planet

w Douglas Adams (a 4-part story)
Searching for the second segment to the Key of Time, the Time Lords land on a planet-draining hollow world manned by a half-man, half-machine called The Captain.
The Captain Bruce Purchase
Mr. Fibuli Andrew Robertson
Mentiad Bernard Finch
Pralix David Sibley
Mula Primi Townsend
Kimus David Warwick
Queen Xanxia Rosalind Lloyd

Director: Pennant Roberts
Designer: Jon Pusey
(30 September–21 October 1978)

The Stones of Blood

w David Fisher (a 4-part story)
The trail of the third key segment leads the Doctor and Romana to Earth and a struggle with a 3000-year-old pagan goddess and her bloodthirsty stone creatures, the Orgi. (This was the 100th Doctor Who story.)

Prof. Rumford Beatrix Lehmann
Vivien Fay (the Cailleach) Susan Engel
Dr. Vries Nicholas McArdle
Martha Elaine Ives-Cameron
Megara voices Gerald Cross, David McAlister

Director: Darrol Blake
Designer: John Stout
(28 October–18 November 1978)

The Androids of Tara

w David Fisher (a 4-part story)
Finding the fourth key segment is easy. Getting it gives the Doctor and Romana an identity crisis involving android doubles, the Crown Prince of Tara and a wicked nobleman.
Count Grendel Peter Jeffrey
Prince Reynart Neville Jason
Zadek Simon Lack
Farrah Paul Lavers
Lamia Lois Baxter
Till Declan Mulholland
Archimandrite Cyril Shaps
Kurster Martin Matthews

Director: Michael Hayes
Designer: Valerie Warrender
(25 November–16 December 1978)

The Power of Kroll

w Robert Holmes (a 4-part story)
The Time Lords are caught up in a feud between refinery technicians and green-skinned Swampies, and menaced by a giant squid-like monster, the Kroll, which has swallowed the fifth segment!
Fenner Philip Madoc
Thawn Neil McCarthy
Dugeen John Leeson
Rohm-Dutt Glyn Owen
Varlik Carl Rigg
Ranquin John Abineri
Skart Frank Jarvis

Director: Norman Stewart
Designer: Don Giles
(23 December 1978–13 January 1979)

The Armageddon Factor

w Bob Baker & Dave Martin *(a 6-part story)*
After narrowly averting Armageddon between two
warring planets, the Doctor completes the Key to
Time, but when confronted by the Black Guardian,
decides it's too dangerous to be allowed to remain
intact.
The Marshal John Woodvine
Princess Astra Lalla Ward

Merak Ian Saynor
Shapp Davyd Harries
The Shadow William Squire
Drax Barry Jackson
The Black Guardian Valentine Dyall

Director: Michael Hayes
Designer: Richard McManan-Smith
(20 January–24 February 1979)

Season Seventeen
(1 September 1979–12 January 1980)
REGULAR CAST
The Doctor Tom Baker *Romana* Lalla Ward
Voice of K9 David Brierley *(from Story Three)*

Producer: Graham Williams

Script editor: Douglas Adams

Destiny of the Daleks

w Terry Nation *(a 4-part story)*
With Romana now regenerated in the likeness of
Princess Astra, the travelers land on Skaro where
they find the Daleks searching for Davros to give
them an edge in their war with the ruthless Movel-
lans.
Tyssan Tim Barlow
Cmdr. Sharrel Peter Straker
Agella Suzanne Danielle
Lan Tony Osoba
Veldan David Yip
Jall Penny Casdagli
Davros David Gooderson
Dalek voice Roy Skelton

Director: Ken Grieve
Designer: Ken Ledsham
(1–22 September 1979)

The Creature from the Pit

w David Fisher *(a 4-part story)*
The travelers answer a distress call from the planet
Chloris and fall into the hands of its despotic ruler
Adrasta.
Adrasta Myra Frances
Karela Eileen Way
Torvin John Bryans
Edu Edward Kelsey
Organon Geoffrey Bayldon
Ainu Tim Munro

Director: Christopher Barry
Designer: Valerie Warrender
(27 October–17 November 1979)

City of Death

w David Agnew *(alias* David Fisher, Douglas
Adams & Graham Williams) *(a 4-part story)*
A plot to steal the *Mona Lisa* alerts the Doctor to an
alien creature's scheme to prevent the explosion that
scattered him throughout history—and created life
on Earth.
Count Julian Glover
Countess Catherine Schell
Kerensky David Graham
Duggan Tom Chadbon
Hermann Kevin Flood
Art gallery visitors John Cleese, Eleanor Bron

Director: Michael Hayes
Designer: Richard McManan-Smith
(29 September–20 October 1979)

Nightmare of Eden

w Bob Baker *(a 4-part story)*
A space liner is overrun with monsters released from
a naturalist's crystal "recordings" of the planet
Eden.
Tryst Lewis Flander
Rigg David Daker
Dymond Geoffrey Bateman
Della Jennifer Lonsdale
Stott Barry Andrews
Fisk Geoffrey Hinsliff
Costa Peter Craze

Director: Alan Bromly *(plus* Graham Williams
—*uncredited)*
Designer: Roger Cann
(24 November–15 December 1979)

The Horns of Nimon

w Anthony Read *(a 4-part story)*
The Doctor prevents a bull-like alien race from invading a planet via a black hole in space.
Teka Janet Ellis
Seth Simon Gipps-Kent
Sorak Michael Osborne
Soldeed Graham Crowden
Co-pilot Malcolm Terris
Voice of the Nimons Clifford Norgate

Director: Kenny McBain
Designer: Graeme Story
(22 December 1979–12 January 1980)

Shada

w Douglas Adams *(a 6-part story)**
The Doctor and Romana visit a Time Lord living "in retirement" as Cambridge don Professor Chronotis,
to retrieve a book, *The Ancient Law of Gallifrey.*
Also after the book is a power-crazy mind-thief, Skagra, who wants to use it to free a powerful Time Lord, Salyavin, from the prison planet Shada. But Chronotis is really Salyavin and a galactic chase ensues before the Doctor defeats Skagra and leaves Chronotis in peace on Earth.

* This story was never transmitted, as filming was interrupted by a strike, and the adventure was shelved by the BBC. However, it was released on video in 1992.
Chronotis Denis Carey
Skagra Christopher Neame
Clare Keightley Victoria Burgoyne
Chris Parsons Daniel Hill

Director: Pennant Roberts
Designer: Victor Meredith

Season Eighteen
(30 August 1980–21 March 1981)
Regular Cast
The Doctor Tom Baker
Romana Lalla Ward   *Voice of K9* John Leeson *(both exit Story 5)*
Adric Matthew Waterhouse *(from Story 3)*
Nyssa Sarah Sutton *(from Story 6)*

Producer: John Nathan-Turner
Executive producer: Barry Letts

Script editor: Christopher H. Bidmead

The Leisure Hive

w David Fisher *(a 4-part story)*
The Time Lords visit an artificial galactic entertainment center, the Leisure Hive, and become embroiled in a struggle for control between the native Argolians and their reptilian enemies, the Foamosi.
Mena Adrienne Corri
Pangol David Haig
Brock John Collin
Vargos Martin Fisk
Hardin Nigel Lambert
Klout Ian Talbot
Guide Roy Montague

Director: Lovett Bickford
Designer: Tom Yardley-Jones
(30 August–20 September 1980)

Meglos

w John Flanagan & Andrew McCulloch *(a 4-part story)*
A prickly, cactus-like character called Meglos impersonates the Doctor to steal the Dodecahedron, a crystal that powers the underground civilization of Tigella.
Caris Colette Gleeson
Deedrix Crawford Logan
Zastor Edward Underdown

Lexa Jacqueline Hill
Gen. Grugger Bill Fraser
Lt. Brotadac Frederick Treves
Earthling Christopher Owen

Director: Terence Dudley
Designer: Philip Lindley
(27 September–18 October 1980)

Full Circle

w Andrew Smith *(a 4-part story)*
The TARDIS enters E-Space where, on the planet Alzarius, the Doctor finds a divided human community, learns the secret of Mistfall and picks up a new young passenger, Adric, who stows away in the Time Lord's craft.
Adric Matthew Waterhouse *(intro)*
Varsh Richard Willis
Login George Baker
Tylos Bernard Padden
Keara June Page
Nefred James Bree
Garif Alan Rowe
Omril Andrew Forbes
Dexeter Tony Calvin

Director: Peter Grimwade
Designer: Janet Budden
(25 October–15 November 1980)

State of Decay

w Terrance Dicks *(a 4-part story)*
On a medieval planet, the Doctor helps a group of rebels oppressed by their tyrannical rulers, a trio of vampires living in a lost spaceship and, using a scout ship, he literally "drives" a stake through the stirring Great Vampire, last survivor of a race believed destroyed by the Time Lords.
Aukon Emrys James
Zargo William Lindsay
Camilla Rachel Davies
Kalmar Arthur Hewlett
Tarak Thane Bettany
Veros Stacy Davies
Ivo Clinton Greyn

Director: Peter Moffatt
Designer: Christine Ruscoe
(22 November–13 December 1980)

Warriors' Gate

w Steve Gallagher *(a 4-part story)*
The TARDIS is "hijacked" by Biroc, a time-sensitive Tharil who departs into a white void where E-Space and N-Space intersect. While the Doctor follows Biroc to a mirrored Gateway, his friends encounter a trader, Capt. Rorvik, who is trapped in the void with his cargo of Tharils and intends to blast his way out—a potentially catastrophic maneuver. After the Doctor foils him, Romana elects to remain with the Tharils while the TARDIS returns to N-Space.
Rorvik Clifford Rose
Packard Kenneth Cope
Sagan Vincent Pickering
Aldo Freddie Earlle
Royce Harry Waters
Lane David Kincaid
Lazlo Jeremy Gittins
Biroc David Weston

Director: Paul Joyce
Designer: Graeme Story
(3–24 January 1981)

The Keeper of Traken

w Johnny Byrne *(a 4-part story)*
Intrigue threatens the peaceful harmony of Traken—and the Doctor finds the evil influence of the Master is at work again, in the form of a statue-like creature called Melkur.
The Keeper Denis Carey
Consul Kassia Sheila Ruskin
Consul Tremas Anthony Ainley
Nyssa Sarah Sutton *(intro)*
Seron John Woodnutt
Katura Margot Van der Burgh
Luvic Robin Soans
Melkur Geoffrey Beevers
Neman Roland Oliver

Director: John Black
Designer: Tony Burrough
(31 January–21 February 1981)

Logopolis

w Christopher H. Bidmead *(a 4-part story)*
When the Master's meddling with the mathematical calculations of Logopolis threatens to unravel the Universe, it takes the combined power of the two Time Lords to avert catastrophe. But the Master's treachery prompts a fight in which the Doctor falls to his death—and a new regeneration.
The Master Anthony Ainley
Tegan Jovanka Janet Fielding *(intro)*
Aunt Vanessa Dolores Whiteman
The Monitor John Fraser
Detective Inspector Tom Georgeson
The Doctor Peter Davison *(intro)*

Director: Peter Grimwade
Designer: Malcolm Thornton
(28 February–21 March 1981)

The Fifth Doctor: PETER DAVISON
(1982–1984)

Season Nineteen
(4 January–30 March 1982)

REGULAR CAST
The Doctor Peter Davison *Tegan* Janet Fielding
Nyssa Sarah Sutton *Adric* Matthew Waterhouse

Producer: John Nathan-Turner

Script editors: Eric Saward *(Stories 1, 3, 5, 7),* Anthony Root *(Stories 2, 4, 6)*

Castrovalva

w Christopher H. Bidmead *(a 4-part story)*
The Doctor's latest regeneration is the least successful and he needs the recuperative powers of his TARDIS Zero Room. However, the Master, who has kidnapped Adric, causes the loss of the Zero Room and draws the Doctor to the apparently calm planet of Castrovalva.
The Master/Portreeve Anthony Ainley *(alias Neil Toynay!)*
Shardovan Derek Waring
Ruther Frank Wylie
Mergrave Michael Sheard
Head of Security Dallas Cavell

Director: Fiona Cumming
Designer: Janet Budden
(4–12 January 1981)

Four to Doomsday

w Terence Dudley *(a 4-part story)*
Aboard an alien starship, the TARDIS crew encounter the frog-like Urbankans who are traveling to Earth, apparently in peace. However, their leader, Monarch, believes he is God and is planning to travel faster than light to meet himself face-to-face.
Monarch Stratford Johns
Enlightenment Annie Lambert
Persuasion Paul Shelley
Bigon Philip Locke
Lin Fitu Burt Kwouk
Kurkutji Illario Bisi Pedro
Villagra Nadia Hamman

Director: John Black
Designer: Tony Burrough
(18–26 January 1982)

Kinda

w Christopher Bailey *(a 4-part story)*
Arriving on Deva Loka, the Doctor is caught up in the reappearance of the Mara. An Earth expedition to assess Deva Loka as a potential new home finds its numbers reducing as it confronts the mystical powers of an ancient evil.
Sanders Richard Todd
Hindle Simon Rouse
Todd Nerys Hughes
Panna Mary Morris
Karunna Sarah Prince
Anatta Anna Wing
Dukkha Jeffrey Stewart

Director: Peter Grimwade
Designer: Malcolm Thornton
(1–9 February 1982)

The Visitation

w Eric Saward *(a 4-part story)*
The Terileptils have come to Earth in the 17th century and are responsible for the spread of the Great Plague. Their explosive attempts to return home won't endear them to humanity either . . .
Richard Mace Michael Robbins
Terileptil leader Michael Melia
Squire John John Savident
Charles Anthony Calf
Ralph John Baker
Elizabeth Valerie Fyfer
Android Peter Van Dissel

Director: Peter Moffatt
Designer: Ken Starkey
(15–23 February 1982)

Black Orchid

w Terence Dudley *(a 2-part story)*
Heroic exploits on the cricket field and murderous events off it test the Doctor as the TARDIS team get involved with the Cranleigh family in 1925 England. The attic hides a dark family secret and Nyssa sees double. (This was the first purely historical story since "The Highlanders" in 1966.)
Lady Cranleigh Barbara Murray
Charles Cranleigh Michael Cochrane
Sir Robert Muir Moray Watson
George Cranleigh (The Unknown) Gareth Milne
Latoni Ahmed Khalil
Ann Talbot Sarah Sutton

Director: Ron Jones
Designer: Tony Burrough
(1–2 March 1982)

Earthshock

w Eric Saward *(a 4-part story)*
In the 25th century, the Cybermen once again attack Earth and the ensuing battle costs the Doctor dearly as a foolhardy Adric allows himself to be trapped on a doomed spaceship spiraling back through time on a collision course with an Earth populated by . . . dinosaurs.
Prof. Kyle Clare Clifford
Lt. Scott James Warwick
Briggs Beryl Reid
Berger June Bland
Cyber leader David Banks
Ringway Alec Sabin

Director: Peter Grimwade
Designer: Bernard Lloyd
(8–16 March 1982)

Time-Flight

w Peter Grimwade *(a 4-part story)*
The Master is trapped on a primordial Earth and is trying to rebuild his TARDIS engines using the alien powers of the feuding Xeraphin. He succeeds in dragging Concorde and the Doctor's TARDIS back along the time contour. While one Xeraphin aids the Doctor, his nemesis utilizes the metamorphic powers of the other.
The Master/Kalid Anthony Ainley *(alias Leon Ni Taiy)*

Capt. Stapley Richard Easton
First Officer Bilton Michael Cashman
Flight engineer Scobie Keith Drinkel
Prof. Hayter Nigel Stock
Angela Clifford Judith Byfield
Anithon Hugh Hayes

Director: Ron Jones
Designer: Richard McManan-Smith
(22–30 March 1982)

Season Twenty
(3 January–16 March 1983, 25 November 1983)
REGULAR CAST
The Doctor Peter Davison *Tegan* Janet Fielding
Nyssa Sarah Sutton *(to Story 4)* *Turlough* Mark Strickson *(from Story 3)*

Producer: John Nathan-Turner | *Script editor:* Eric Saward

Arc of Infinity

w Johnny Byrne *(a 4-part story)*
Hedin, a treacherous Time Lord on Gallifrey, is helping the renegade and long-believed dead Omega to re-enter this universe from his anti-matter prison by "bonding" him with the Doctor. But the process is incomplete and a bitter Omega determines to take the universe down with him.
Renegade/Omega Ian Collier
President Borusa Leonard Sachs
Councillor Hedin Michael Gough
Commander Maxil Colin Baker
Castellan Paul Jerricho
Chancellor Thalia Elspet Gray
Ergon Malcolm Harvey

Director: Ron Jones
Designer: Marjorie Pratt
(3–12 January 1983)

Snakedance

w Christopher Bailey *(a 4-part story)*
The Doctor takes Tegan, still affected by the influence of the snake-like creature, the Mara, to its home planet Manussa. There, local festivities draw the powerful evil back into the real world for another dangerous confrontation. (A sequel to "Kinda.")
Ambril John Carson
Tahna Colette O'Neil
Lon Martin Clunes
Chela Jonathan Morris
Dojjen Preston Lockwood
Dugdale Brian Miller

Director: Fiona Cumming
Designer: Jan Spoczynski
(18–26 January 1983)

Mawdryn Undead

w Peter Grimwade *(a 4-part story)*
The Black Guardian seeks revenge on the Doctor for cheating him out of the Key to Time in his previous incarnation. He uses Turlough, a young alien trapped on Earth, as his agent. By chance, one of Turlough's teachers is an old friend of the Doctor— but with an alarming memory loss.
Black Guardian Valentine Dyall
Brig. Lethbridge Stewart Nicholas Courtney
Mawdryn David Collings
Dr. Runciman Roger Hammond
Headmaster Angus MacKay
Matron Sheila Gill
Ibbotson Stephen Garlick

Director: Peter Moffatt
Designer: Stephen Scott
(1–9 February 1983)

Terminus

w Steven Gallagher *(a 4-part story)*
Arriving on an alien spaceship carrying plague victims, the Doctor and his friends are separated. While Turlough, prompted by the Black Guardian, tries to find more ways of killing the Doctor, Nyssa finds her destiny with the hapless Lazars and remains to sort out a cure.
Kari Liza Goddard
Valgard Andrew Burt
Eirak Martin Potter
Black Guardian Valentine Dyall
Olvir Dominic Guard
Sigurd Tim Munro
Bor Peter Benson
Garm R.J. Bell

Director: Mary Ridge
Designer: Dick Coles
(15–23 February 1983)

Enlightenment

w Barbara Clegg *(a 4-part story)*
The Doctor, Tegan and Turlough find themselves part of a race being run by the Eternals, beings who utilize the emotions and attributes of mortals to find pleasure in their incessant existence. Turlough finally discovers the good within himself, banishing both Guardians from the Doctor's life—for now.
White Guardian Cyril Luckham
Black Guardian Valentine Dyall
Wrack Lynda Baron
Striker Keith Barron
Jackson Tony Caunter
Marriner Christopher Brown

Director: Fiona Cumming
Designer: Colin Green
(1–9 March 1983)

The King's Demons

w Terence Dudley *(a 2-part story)*
While King Richard fights in the Crusades, the Doctor faces Kamelion, a shape-changing android posing as King John, controlled by the Master. After a fierce battle of wills, Kamelion sides with the Doctor.
Master/Sir Gilles Anthony Ainley *(alias James Stoker [Master's joke])*
King (Kamelion) Gerald Flood
Ranulf Frank Windsor
Isabella Isla Blair

Hugh Christopher Villiers
Sir Geoffrey Michael J. Jackson

Director: Tony Virgo
Designer: Ken Ledsham
(15–16 March 1983)

The Five Doctors

w Terrance Dicks *(90-minute special)*
Doctors and companions past and present are brought together by a renegade Time Lord to play the lethal Game of Rassilon in the Death Zone. President Borusa seeks immortality and will stop at nothing to achieve it—including treachery, murder and breaking more than one of the legendary Laws of Time. (This 20th-anniversary story featured footage from the "lost" tale "Shada.")
With Tom Baker, Jon Pertwee, Patrick Troughton, William Hartnell and . . . Richard Hurndall as *the First Doctor*
Borusa Philip Latham
Castellan Paul Jerricho
Rassilon Richard Matthews
Master Anthony Ainley
Chancellor Flavia Dinah Sheridan
Old Companions:
Nicholas Courtney, Elisabeth Sladen, Lalla Ward, Carole Ann Ford, Caroline John, Richard Franklin, Frazer Hines, Wendy Padbury

Director: Peter Moffatt
Designer: Malcolm Thornton
(25 November 1983)

Season Twenty-One
(5 January–30 March 1984)
REGULAR CAST
The Doctor Peter Davison   *Tegan* Janet Fielding *(exit Story 4)*
Turlough Mark Strickson *(exit Story 5)*
Perpugillian Brown (Peri) Nicola Bryant *(from Story 5)*
The Doctor Colin Baker *(intro Story 6)*

Producer: John Nathan-Turner

Script editor: Eric Saward

Warriors of the Deep

w Johnny Byrne *(a 4-part story)*
Earth, 2084. Two global powers rule the planet, an uneasy truce awaiting one slip that might spark Armageddon. On an underwater base, Sea Base Four, a group of spies might be that slip—or it could be the invasion force of the Doctor's old foes, the Silurians and the Sea Devils.
Vorshak Tom Adams
Solow Ingrid Pitt

Nilson Ian McCulloch
Bulic Nigel Humphreys
Karina Nitza Saul
Maddox Martin Neil
Preston Tara King(!)
Sauvix Christopher Farries
Icthar Norman Comer

Director: Pennant Roberts
Designer: Tony Burrough
(5–13 January 1984)

The Awakening

w Eric Pringle *(a 2-part story)*
Tegan's wish to visit her English uncle turns disastrously wrong during his village's annual re-enactment of the English Civil War. The Malus, an evil force that has lain in the church crypt, reawakes to exert its powers over time and people with lethal results.
Sir George Denis Lill
Jane Hampden Polly James
Joseph Willow Jack Galloway
Col. Wolsey Glyn Houston
Will Chandler Keith Jayne

Director: Michael Owen Morris
Designer: Barry Newbery
(19–20 January 1984)

Frontios

w Christopher H. Bidmead
(a 4-part story)
In the far future, on the newly colonized planet of Frontios, the human inhabitants find themselves repeatedly and illogically bombarded by asteroids brought down by the gravitational powers of the malicious Tractators.
Range William Lucas
Norna Lesley Dunlop
Brazen Peter Gilmore
Plantagenet Jeff Rawle
Gravis John Gillett
Cockerill Maurice O'Connell

Director: Ron Jones
Designer: David Buckingham
(26 January–3 February 1984)

Resurrection of the Daleks

w Eric Saward *(two 45-minute episodes)*
On a prison ship in deep space sits Davros, evil creator of the Daleks. After losing their war against the Movellans *(Destiny of the Daleks)*, the Daleks, using mercenaries led by the sadistic Lytton, come in search of their creator. But Davros does not trust his "children" and a terrible battle ensues. Sickened by the carnage, Tegan decides to leave.
Lytton Maurice Colbourne
Davros Terry Molloy
Stien Rodney Bewes
Styles Rula Lenska
Col. Archer Del Henney
Prof. Laird Chloe Ashcroft
Kiston Les Grantham

Director: Matthew Robinson
Designer: John Anderson
(8–15 February 1984)

Planet of Fire

w Peter Grimwade *(a 4-part story)*
Resting in Lanzarote, Turlough finds an alien artifact from his home planet in the possession of Peri, an American student he saves from drowning. As the Master repossesses Kamelion, the Doctor takes Turlough to meet his own people, and after Kamelion is destroyed and the Master defeated, Turlough leaves the Doctor in the care of Peri.
Master Anthony Ainley
Timanov Peter Wyngarde
Voice of Kamelion Gerald Flood
Malkon Edward Highmore
Sorasta Barbara Shelley
Prof. Howard Foster Dallas Adams
Amyand James Bate

Director: Fiona Cumming
Designer: Malcolm Thornton
(23 February–2 March 1984)

The Caves of Androzani

w Robert Holmes *(a 4-part story)*
The Doctor and Peri are caught up in the political battles being waged on the twin planets of Androzani. While Peri is captured by the disfigured Jek, the Doctor battles the gunrunner Stotz. But both travelers contract a lethal disease for which there is only enough cure for one. As Peri recovers, the Doctor changes before her eyes.
Sharaz Jek Christopher Gable
Stotz Maurice Roeves
Salateen Robert Glenister
Morgus John Normington
Krepler Roy Holder
Chellak Martin Cochrane
President David Neal

Director: Graeme Harper
Designer: John Hurst
(8–16 March 1984)

The Sixth Doctor: COLIN BAKER
(1984–1986)

The Twin Dilemma

w Anthony Steven *(&* Eric Saward—*uncredited) (a 4-part story)*
The new Doctor throws himself into the mystery of the missing Sylveste twins, which takes him and a frightened, distrustful Peri to the planet Jaconda where he confronts the evil, slug-like Gastropods and finally defeats them.

Edgeworth Maurice Denham
Mestor Edwin Richfield
Hugo Kevin McNally
Drak Oliver Smith
Romulus Gavin Conrad
Remus Andrew Conrad

Director: Peter Moffatt
Designer: Valerie Warrender
(22–30 March 1984)

Season Twenty-two
(45-minute episodes)
(5 January–30 March 1985)
REGULAR CAST
The Doctor Colin Baker   *Peri* Nicola Bryant

Producer: John Nathan-Turner

Script editor: Eric Saward

Attack of the Cybermen

w Paula Moore *(alias* Paul Wolsey & Eric Saward) *(a 2-part story)*
Earth, 1985: The Doctor and Peri become involved in a plot by the Cybermen to destroy the planet by diverting Halley's Comet. Traveling to the Cyberworld, Telos, with the mercenary Lytton, the Doctor discovers the Cybermen have another foe—the Cryons.
Lytton Maurice Colbourne
Griffiths Brian Glover
Russell Terry Molloy
Cyber leader David Banks
Cyber controller Michael Kilgarriff
Bates Michael Attwell
Stratton Jonathan David
Varne Sarah Greene
Flast Faith Brown

Director: Matthew Robinson
Designer: Marjorie Pratt
(5–12 January 1985)

Vengeance on Varos

w Philip Martin *(a 2-part story)*
On the planet Varos, entertainment is supplied by videos of torture and mutilation, and rulers are voted in by their ability to survive torturous elections! Into this scenario comes the repellent alien trader Sil, trying to gain a financial foothold—and enjoying the torture, too.

Governor Martin Jarvis
Sil Nabil Shaban
Jondar Jason Connery
Arak Stephen Yardley
Etta Sheila Reid
Quillam Nicholas Chagrin
Areta Geraldine Alexander
Chief Forbes Collins

Director: Ron Jones
Designer: Tony Snoaden
(19–26 January 1985)

The Mark of the Rani

w Pip & Jane Baker *(a 2-part story)*
At Lord Ravensworth's mine, the Doctor discovers his old academy foe the Rani is inspiring 19th-century Luddite attacks as she seeks chemicals needed to restore harmony on her chosen base planet Miasimia Goria. When the Master joins in, the havoc really starts.
Rani Kate O'Mara
Master Anthony Ainley
Lord Ravensworth Terence Alexander
George Stephenson Gawn Grainger
Jack Ward Peter Childs
Luke Ward Gary Cady
Tim Bass William Ilkley

Director: Sarah Hellings
Designer: Paul Trerise
(2–9 February 1985)

The Two Doctors

w Robert Holmes *(a 3-part story)*
The Doctor meets up with a former self when a Space Station is destroyed by the Sontarans. Trailing the aliens to Spain, the Two Doctors also find themselves menaced by the cannibalistic Androgum, Shockeye.
Doctor Patrick Troughton
Jamie Frazer Hines
Chessene Jacqueline Pearce
Shockeye o' the Quancing Grig John Stratton
Dastari Laurence Payne
Oscar Botcherby James Saxon
Stike Clinton Greyn
Varl Tim Raynham

Director: Peter Moffatt
Designer: Tony Burrough
(16 February–2 March 1985)

Timelash

w Glen McCoy *(a 2-part story)*
The Doctor and Peri arrive on the planet Karfel, where he was once an honored guest (in his third incarnation). Since the Borad took over, though, life there has changed, with dissenters hurled into the destructive Timelash.
Tekker Paul Darrow
Borad Robert Ashby
Mykros Eric Deacon

Android Dean Hollingsworth
Brunner Peter Robert Scott
Katz Tracy Louise Ward
Vena Jeananne Crowley
Sezon Dicken Ashworth

Director: Pennant Roberts
Designer: Bob Cove
(9–16 March 1985)

Revelation of the Daleks

w Eric Saward *(a 2-part story)*
On the planet Necros, Davros is hailed as The Great Healer, a galactic savior. However, the Doctor uncovers his real plan as one of universal carnage involving his creations, the Daleks. But not all Daleks are Davros fans . . .
Davros Terry Molloy
Kara Eleanor Bron
Orcini William Gaunt
Jobel Clive Swift
DJ Alexei Sayle
Vogel Hugh Walters
Takis Trevor Cooper
Tasambeker Jenny Tomasin
Lilt Colin Spaull

Director: Graeme Harper
Designer: Alan Spaulding
(23–30 March 1985)

Season Twenty-three
THE TRIAL OF A TIME LORD

(14 25-minute episodes)
(6 September–6 December 1986)

REGULAR CAST
The Doctor Colin Baker *Peri* Nicola Bryant *(exit Story 2)*
Mel Bonnie Langford *(from Story 3)*
The Valeyard Michael Jayston *The Inquisitor* Lynda Bellingham

Producer: John Nathan-Turner

Script editor: Eric Saward *(Eps. 1–8, 13)*

Parts 1–4

w Robert Holmes
The Doctor is on trial again. His crime: breaking the laws of time, and he sits condemned before his own people. He cannot recall how he got there, so the malicious prosecutor, the Valeyard, shows him a recent exploit involving the planet Ravlox and a pair of con men, Dibber and Glitz.
Katryca Joan Sims
Glitz Tony Selby
Dibber Glen Murphy

Merdeen Tom Chadbon
Broken Tooth David Rodigan
Humker Billy McColl
Tandrell Siôn Tudor Owen
Drathro Roger Brierley

Director: Nick Mallett
Designer: John Anderson
(6–27 September 1986)

Parts 5–8

w Philip Martin
Aware that Peri is not "in court" with him, the Doctor wonders where she is. The Valeyard then shows "recent" events in Thoros Beta involving the sluggish Sil and a series of brain transplants by the scientist Crozier. Peri becomes the final host for Sil's master, Kiv—and is "seemingly" destroyed by the Warrior King Yrcanos.
Yrcanos Brian Blessed
Sil Nabil Shaban
Kiv Christopher Ryan
Crozier Patrick Ryecart
Lukoser Thomas Branch
Matrona Kani Alibe Parsons
Frax Trevor Laird
Tuza Gordon Warnecke

Director: Ron Jones
Designer: Andrew Howe-Davies
(4–25 October 1985)

Parts 9–12

w Pip & Jane Baker
At last the Doctor is able to present evidence in his defense: an adventure from his future in which he and a new companion, Mel, save the passengers aboard the space-liner *Hyperion III* from the genetically engineered killer plant people, the Vervoids.

Prof. Lasky Honor Blackman
Janet Yolande Palfrey
Commodore Michael Craig
Rudge Denys Hawthorne
Grenville/Enzu Tony Scoggo
Bruchner David Allister
Doland Malcolm Tierney

Director: Chris Clough
Designer: Dinah Walker
(1–22 November 1986)

Parts 13–14

w Robert Holmes *(Part 13)*, Pip & Jane Baker *(Part 14)*
The trial is exposed as a charade by the Master who is within the Time Lords' Matrix. He brings Mel and Glitz out of time as witnesses in the Doctor's favour—and shows the Valeyard to be an evil future interim incarnation of the Doctor. The Doctor then battles and defeats his evil self within the Matrix.
Master Anthony Ainley
Keeper of the Matrix James Bree
Glitz Tony Selby
Mr. Popplewick Geoffrey Hughes

Director: Chris Clough
Designer: Michael Trevor
(29 November–6 December 1986)

The Seventh Doctor: SYLVESTER McCOY
(1987–1996)

Season Twenty-four
(7 September–7 December 1987)
REGULAR CAST
The Doctor Sylvester McCoy   *Mel* Bonnie Langford
Ace Sophie Aldred *(from Story 4)*

Producer: John Nathan-Turner   *Script editor:* Andrew Cartmel

Time and the Rani

w Pip & Jane Baker *(a 4-part story)*
The TARDIS is forced down on the planet Lakertya by the Rani who needs the Doctor's mental powers to control her latest creation. The crash transforms the Doctor into his new form and, though confused, he and Mel overcome the Rani, leaving her to the mercy of her slaves, the Tetraps.

The Rani Kate O'Mara
Beyus Donald Pickering
Faroon Wanda Ventham
Ikona Mark Greenstreet
Urak Richard Gauntlett

Director: Andrew Morgan
Designer: Geoff Powell
(7–28 September 1987)

Paradise Towers

w Stephen Wyatt *(a 4-part story)*
Arriving at the apparently palatial Paradise Towers, the Doctor and Mel find those that live there under threat. The Rezzies, Kangs and Caretakers have only one thing in common—something is killing them off.
Chief caretaker Richard Briers
Deputy chief caretaker Clive Merrison
Tabby Elizabeth Spriggs
Tilda Brenda Bruce
Maddy Judy Cornwell
Pex Howard Cooke
Bin Liner Annabel Yuresha
Fire escape Julie Brennon
Blue Kang leader Catherine Cusack

Director: Nicholas Mallett
Designer: Martin Collins
(5–26 October 1987)

Delta and the Bannermen

w Malcolm Kohll *(a 3-part story)*
The Doctor and Mel win a chance to join a party of aliens who are due to holiday in Disneyland, Earth. A stray satellite sends the group crashing to a Welsh holiday camp in the 1950s, where the evil Bannermen are pursuing the Chimeron queen, Delta.

Gavrok Don Henderson
Goronwy Hugh Lloyd
Delta Belinda Mayne
Burton Richard Davies
Weismuller Stubby Kaye
Tollmaster Ken Dodd
Billy David Kinder
Hawk Morgan Deare

Director: Chris Clough
Designer: John Asbridge
(2–16 November 1987)

Dragonfire

w Ian Briggs *(a 3-part story)*
On the planet Svartos, the Doctor and Mel go dragon hunting with Glitz and a young Earth girl, Ace. They discover that the dragon contains a key to a prison—a key that the evil Mr. Kane will stop at nothing to find.
Kane Edward Peel
Glitz Tony Selby
Belazs Patricia Quinn
Kracauer Tony Osoba
McLuhan Stephanie Fayerman
Bazin Stuart Organ

Director: Chris Clough
Designer: John Asbridge
(23 November–7 December 1987)

Season Twenty-five
(5 October 1988–4 January 1989)
REGULAR CAST
The Doctor Sylvester McCoy *Ace* Sophie Aldred

Producer: John Nathan-Turner

Script editor: Andrew Cartmell

Remembrance of the Daleks

w Ben Aaronovitch *(a 4-part story)*
The 25th-anniversary story takes the Doctor back to Earth, November 1963, to retrieve the Hand of Omega—a powerful Gallifreyan weapon he had left behind previously. But Davros and his Daleks are after it, too—and so is the Dalek Supreme and his faction. In the conflict, the Doctor goads Davros into using the device, which he has programmed to fly into Skaro's sun and turn it into a super nova.
Davros Terry Molloy
(alias Emperor Dalek Roy Tromelly)
Rachel Pamela Salem
Gilmore Simon Williams
Ratcliffe George Sewell
Mike Dursley McLinden
Harry Harry Fowler
Alison Karen Gledhill
Headmaster Michael Sheard

Director: Andrew Morgan
Designer: Martin Collins
(5–26 October 1988)

The Happiness Patrol

w Graeme Curry *(a 3-part story)*
On Terra Alpha, the Doctor and Ace find that to be a killjoy is fatal—the Happiness Patrol see to that. While Helen A rules the planet, the Kandyman rules the kitchen.
Helen A Sheila Hancock
Joseph C Ronald Fraser
Gilbert M Harold Innocent
Susan Q Lesley Dunlop
Daisy K Georgina Hale
Trevor Sigma John Normington
Earl Sigma Richard D. Sharp
Kandyman David John Pope

Director: Chris Clough
Designer: John Asbridge
(2-16 November 1988)

Silver Nemesis

w Kevin Clarke *(a 3-part story)*
The Doctor and Ace try to thwart the multiple threats of a mad 17th-century noblewoman, a group of Fourth Reich activists and the Cybermen over control of Nemesis, a statue made of living metal, which has returned to Earth 350 years after the Doctor himself launched it into space.
De Flores Anton Diffring
Lady Peinforte Fiona Walker
Richard Gerard Murphy
Karl Martin Yenal
Cyber leader David Banks

Director: Chris Clough
Designer: John Asbridge
(23 November–7 December 1988)

The Greatest Show in the Galaxy

w Stephen Wyatt *(a 4-part story)*
The Psychic Circus has a reputation throughout the galaxy. The Doctor persuades Ace to visit but the circus is a death-trap run by the vile Three Gods of Ragnarok.
Captain T.P. McKenna
Mags Jessica Martin
Ringmaster Ricco Ross
Stallslady Peggy Mount
Chief Clown Ian Reddington
Whizzkid Gian Sammarco
Nord Daniel Peacock
Deadbeat Chris Jury
Morgana Deborah Manship

Director: Alan Wareing
Designer: David Laskey
(14 December 1988–4 January 1989)

Season Twenty-six
(6 September–6 December 1989)
REGULAR CAST
The Doctor Sylvester McCoy *Ace* Sophie Aldred

Producer: John Nathan-Turner

Script editor: Andrew Cartmel

Battlefield

w Ben Aaronovitch *(a 4-part story)*
An Arthurian legend, a nuclear convoy and a re-union with an old friend, as Cornwall becomes the battlefield for warriors from another dimension.
Brigadier Nicholas Courtney
Morgaine Jean Marsh
Mordred Christopher Bowen
Peter Warmsley James Ellis
Doris Angela Douglas
Brigadier Bambera Angela Bruce

Director: Michael Kerrigan
Designer: Martin Collins
(6–27 September 1989)

The Curse of Fenric

w Ian Briggs *(a 4-part story)*
Vampires walk, and an ancient Viking curse comes to roost at an isolated World War Two research station.
Dr. Judson Dinsdale Landen
Commander Millington Alfred Lynch
Mr. Wainwright Nicholas Parsons
Jean Joann Kenny
Phyllis Joanne Bell
Kathleen Corey Pulman
Vershinin Marek Anton

Director: Nicholas Mallett
Designer: David Laskey
(25 October–15 November 1989)

Ghost Light

w Marc Platt *(a 3-part story)*
The Doctor takes Ace to Victorian Perivale and the scene of her greatest nightmare.
Josiah Samuel Smith Ian Hogg
Mrs. Pritchard Sylvia Syms
Nimrod Carl Forgione
Insp. MacKenzie Frank Windsor
Control Sharon Duce

Director: Alan Wareing
Designer: Nick Somerville
(4–18 October 1989)

Survival

w Rona Munro *(a 3-part story)*
A search for friends in Perivale turns up cats—and an old foe.
Master Anthony Ainley
Patterson Jilian Holloway
Karra Lisa Bowerman
Midge William Barton
Harvey Gareth Hale
Len Norman Pace

Director: Alan Wareing
Designer: Nick Somerville
(22 November–6 December 1989)

The Eighth Doctor:
PAUL MCGANN
(1996)

Doctor Who

(85-minute TV movie)
w Matthew Jacobs
While transporting the Master back to Gallifrey, the Doctor's TARDIS malfunctions, landing in San Francisco on 30 December 1999. Emerging from the time machine, the Doctor is wounded in a gangland fight and rushed to hospital. Mystified by the fact that this stranger apparently has two hearts, Dr. Grace Holloway struggles unsuccessfully to revive him. Meanwhile the Master has escaped and takes over the body of a paramedic. After the Doctor regenerates into his new body, he turns to Grace to help him discover his identity, find the Master and save the Universe—again.
Doctor Paul McGann
Old Doctor Sylvester McCoy
Master Eric Roberts
Dr. Grace Holloway Daphne Ashbrook
Chang Lee Yee Jee Tso

Salinger John Novak
Dr. Swift Michael David Simms
Old Master Gordon Tipple
Curtis Dolores Drake
Wheeler Catherine Lough
Miranda Eliza Roberts
Pete William Sasso
Ted Joel Wirkkunen
Professor Wagg Dave Hurtubise
Gareth Jeremy Radick

Designer: Richard Hudolin
Director: Geoffrey Sax
Producers: Peter Ware, Matthew Jacobs
Executive producers: Philip Segal, Alex Beaton; for the BBC, Jo Wright
A BBC Worldwide/Universal Television Production
U.S. Premiere: 14 May 1996
U.K. Premiere: 27 May 1996
(BBC1)

DOOMWATCH

*D*oomwatch was the first "green" television drama series. It caught the stirrings of ecological awareness in the early 1970s and hit the target with a string of prophetic bullseyes.

The advances of science and technology promised a bright future, but here was a show that pointed out clouds, not silver linings. As a word, *Doomwatch* quickly entered the national vocabulary; newspapers learning the new language of ecology saw in it a ready-made banner headline.

The program title stood—loosely—for the Department for the Observation and Measurement of Science, a fictional government department set up to watch and control advances in science. *Doomwatch* was headed by Dr. Spencer Quist, an abrasive but incorruptible scientist who didn't give a damn for the vested interests of politicians and businessmen. He ran a highly strung and independent team, including the dashing duo Dr. John Ridge and Tobias "Toby" Wren, who were constantly clashing with the authorities.

The series was devised by Gerry Davis and Dr. Kit Pedler and evolved out of their private obsession with the inherent dangers to mankind in scientific progress. The two had worked together on *Doctor Who* and, finding common cause, kept tabs on each new, devastating hazard, filling scrapbooks with examples on pesticides, defoliation, chemical and atomic waste, pollution, genetic experiments, noise and so on.

They called their new series "sci-fact" and, indeed, many of the issues it raised became mirrored in real headlines over the coming months and years.

It soon gained a huge following and its first series audience of 12 million was the record for a first run. There were other surprises, too. The death of Toby Wren, blown up while trying to defuse a bomb on a South Coast pier, astonished viewers who weren't used to seeing their TV heroes die.

But it couldn't last. New faces came and went—including Dr. Fay Chantry, brought in to give women a higher profile—but increasing emphasis on character conflicts was pushing the show away from its roots, and toward more conventional drama.

By the third season Pedler and Davis had left and were soon publicly disassociating themselves from the program. After the third series' opening episode in which Ridge held the world to ransom with phials of anthrax, Pedler said he was "absolutely horrified."

"When we started it," he commented, "the clear object of the series was to make serious comment about the dangerous facts of science which should be drawn to the public. They have made a total travesty of the program."

Producer Terence Dudley defended the show, insisting that the third series *was* confronting the issues, and it did cover such subjects as lead poisoning, the population explosion, pesticides and river pollution. But the end was nigh and *Doomwatch* didn't come up for a fourth time.

REGULAR CAST

Dr. Spencer Quist John Paul *Dr. John Ridge* Simon Oates*
Toby Wren Robert Powell *(Season One only)*
Colin Bradley Joby Blanshard *Pat Hunisett* Wendy Hall *(Season One only)*
Barbara Mason Vivien Sherrard *(Seasons Two and Three only)*
Geoff Hardcastle John Nolan *(Season Two only)*
Dr. Fay Chantry Jean Trend *(Season Two only)*
Dr. Anne Tarrant Elizabeth Weaver *(Season Three regular)*
Minister John Barron *(Season Three regular)*
Cmdr. Neil Stafford John Brown *(Season Three only)*

Series devised by Gerry Davis, Kit Pedler
Producer: Terence Dudley
Script editor (Seasons One and Two): Gerry Davis
Script consultant (Season Three): Anna Kaliski
Music: Max Harris

*NB: In Season Three, Ridge appears in just four episodes—1, 4, 7, 10.

A BBC Production
37 color 50-minute episodes
Season One:
9 February–11 March 1970
Season Two:
14 December 1970–22 March 1971
Season Three:
5 June–14 August 1972
(BBC1)

Season One

The Plastic Eaters

w Kit Pedler & Gerry Davis
A plane dissolves in mid-air, its plastic components eaten away . . . Doomwatch faces its first challenge—to halt the disastrous spread of a man-made virus with the power to melt all plastic.
Minister John Barron
Miss Wills Jennifer Wilson
Jim Bennett Michael Hawkins
Hal Symonds Kevin Stoney

Director: Paul Ciappessoni
Designers: Ian Watson & Barry Newbery

Friday's Child

w Harry Green
Doomwatch is unwillingly drawn into a controversy that confronts Quist with a fundamental ethical question, when a scientist breeds a human embryo that he plans to bring to life in a flask.
Dr. Patrick Alex Scott
Mrs. Patrick Mary Holland

Mrs. Norman Delia Paton
Det. Sgt. Bill Straiton
Gwilliam Richard Caldicott
Prosecuting solicitor John Graham
Defending solicitor Margaret John

Director: Paul Ciappessoni
Designer: Ian Watson

Burial at Sea

w Dennis Spooner
Deaths occur on a luxury yacht owned by a famous pop group that strays close to a secret dumping ground for surplus chemical weapons, including a defoliant.
Angela Connor Nova Sainte-Claire
Cobie Vale Julian Barnes
Peter Hazlewood Brian Spink
Tranton Peter Copley
Dr. Collinson Gerald Sim
Johnny Clive John Stone
Astley John Horsley
Minister John Savident

Director: Jonathan Alwyn
Designer: Moira Tait

Tomorrow, the Rat

w Terence Dudley

Geneticist Dr. Mary Bryant's experiment in rat-breeding gets out of hand, and London is plagued with a new mutant breed of intelligent killer with a taste for human flesh.

Dr. Mary Bryant Penelope Lee
Joyce Chambers Eileen Helsby
Dr. Hugh Preston Robert Sansom
Fred Chambers Ray Roberts
Reporter John Berryman
Minister Hamilton Dyce
Small boy Stephen Dudley

Director: Terence Dudley
Designer: John Hurst

Project Sahara

w Gerry Davis, *additional dialogue by* N.J. Crisp

A state computer programmed with highly personal information on its citizens—the electronic invasion of privacy becomes an issue for the Doomwatch team, which falls under the baleful eye of a newly established security section.

Commander Keeping Nigel Stock
Dr. Stella Robson Hildegard Neil
Barker Robert James
Computer technician Margaret Pilleau
Computer voice Peter Hawkins
Jack Foster Philip Brack
Old man Erik Chitty

Director: Jonathan Alwyn
Designer: Moira Tait

Re-Entry Forbidden

w Don Shaw

A new nuclear-powered rocket is being tested, with the first British astronaut aboard. The smallest error could turn it into a flying nuclear bomb, spreading radioactive fallout over a wide area of Europe. And an error occurs . . .

Bill Edwards Craig Hunter
Max Friedman Noel Sheldon
Dick Larch Michael McGovern
Charles Goldsworthy Joseph Furst
Carol Larch Veronica Strong
BBC man, London James Burke
BBC man, Houston Michael Aspel
Gus Clarke Kevin Scott
Col. Kramer Grant Taylor

Director: Paul Ciappessoni
Designer: Ian Watson

The Devil's Sweets

w Don Shaw

A new chocolate liqueur mix contains a drug that makes people susceptible to subliminal advertising. But it's also potentially lethal and when Doomwatch secretary Pat Hunnisett takes a give-away choc, the results involve the team in a desperate race to save her life.

Jack John Comer
Shipton Maurice Roëves
Scott William Fox
Mrs. Tyler Bay White
Pegg John Law
Benson John Young
Dr. Gray Mary Loughran
Dr. Green Patrick Connell

Director: David Proudfoot
Designer: John Hurst

The Red Sky

w Kit Pedler & Gerry Davis

The rising crescendo of everyday sounds becomes more than an irritant, when noise from a high-flying aircraft actually kills . . .

Capt. Gort Edward Kelsey
Dana Colley Jennifer Daniel
Bernard Colley Aubrey Richards
Dr. O'Brien Dudley Jones
Reynolds Paul Eddington
Mrs. Knott Sheila Raynor
Duncan Michael Elwyn

Director: Jonathan Alwyn
Designer: Moira Tait

Spectre at the Feast

w Terence Dudley

Quist convenes a conference of top scientists to make recommendations about pollution. Many of the delegates become victims of what is thought to be food poisoning. Are they being got at?

Fielding William Lucas
Whitehead Richard Hurndall
Bau Oscar Quitak
Egri George Pravda
Royston David Morrell
Mrs. Bonenti Karen Ford
Laura Lindsay Helen Downing

Director: Eric Hills
Designer: Moira Tait

Train and De-Train

w Don Shaw
Doomwatch investigates a mass extermination of wildlife in Somerset and finds the trail apparently leading to field trials of a new pesticide.
Branston Bill Wilde
Ellis David Markham
Mitchell George Baker
Miss Sephton Patricia Maynard
Miss Jones Rosemary Turner
Stephens Brian Badcoe
Ministry inspector Peter Whitaker

Director: Vere Lorrimer
Designer: Ian Watson

The Battery People

w Elwyn Jones
Tough ex-miners in South Wales drinking gin instead of beer and giving their wives the cold shoulder . . . A village's odd behavior puts Doomwatch on the trail of a new hormone that's making factory workers impotent.
Col. Smithson Emrys Jones
Vincent Llewellyn Jeremy Young
Dai Edward Evans
Bryn Michael Newport
Davies David Davies
Elizabeth Llewellyn Eliza Ward
Jones Ray Mort
Mrs. Adams Mary Hignett

Director: David Proudfoot
Designer: Stuart Walker

Hear No Evil

w Harry Green
One northern firm's answer to unofficial strikes is to use the latest scientific discoveries to manipulate the lives of its employees. Quist is forced to fight them with their own methods.
Falken Griffith Jones
Operator Derrick O'Connor
Cook Peter Miles
Owen Brian Cox
Reid Michael Ripper
Mrs. Reid Tessa Shaw

Director: Frank Cox
Designer: Tim Gleeson

Survival Code

w Kit Pedler & Gerry Davis
An object that falls into the sea near a south coast pier is identified as a nuclear device and must be defused. Toby Wren thinks he has succeeded—then finds another wire . . .

Air Commodore Parks Donald Morley
Wing Commander Colin Rix
Geoff Harker Ray Brooks
Toni Harker Stephanie Turner
Sam Billings Tommy Godfrey
Commander Sefton Robert Cartland
Minister Hamilton Dyce
Len White Edwin Brown
Chief Supt. Charles John Dawson

Director: Hugh David
Designer: Ian Watson

Season Two

You Killed Toby Wren

w Terence Dudley *(pre-title sequence by* Kit Pedler & Gerry Davis)
In the aftermath of the death of Toby Wren, Quist—already riddled with self-doubts—finds himself under attack on all fronts. Meanwhile, Ridge is out to stop some human/animal embryo experiments.
Air Commodore Parks Donald Morley
Len White Edwin Brown
Minister John Barron
Permanent secretary Macdonald Hobley
Dr. Anne Tarrant Elizabeth Weaver
Dr. Judith Lennox Shirley Dixon
Sam Billings Tommy Godfrey
Dr. Warren Robert Gillespie
Prof. Eric Hayland Graham Leaman
Tribunal chairman Edward Underdown

Director: Terence Dudley *(pre-title sequence:* Hugh David)
Designer: Graham Oakley

Invasion

w Martin Worth
Two boys go missing while exploring caves beneath a mansion that houses deadly chemical weapons, and Ridge is held for 24 hours by a mysterious army unit in a remote Yorkshire village.
Dave David Lincoln
Joe Bates Victor Platt
Sandy Larch Arthur Brough
Sgt. Harris Anthony Sagar
Tom Hedley Peter Welch
Mrs. Smith Sheila Raynor
Mrs. Hunter Joyce Windsor
Major Sims Geoffrey Palmer
Duncan Michael Elwyn

Director: Jonathan Alwyn
Designer: Jeremy Davies

The Islanders

w Louis Marks
The 200 inhabitants of the idyllic Pacific island of St. Simon are evacuated following earth tremors. A return to their island home is dangerous—but the islanders question the kind of future they have in an increasingly polluted Britain.
Thomas George A. Cooper
Isaac David Buck
Inspector Charles Rea
Joan Shelagh Fraser
Alice Geraldine Sherman
Mullery Geoffrey Chater
Miss Marshall Rachel Treadgold
Busby George Waring
Dr. Somerville Robert Sansom

Director: Jonathan Alwyn
Designer: Stanley Morris

No Room for Error

w Roger Parkes
Doomwatch investigates allegations that children have died after taking a new "wonder drug."
Senior house officer Anthony Ainley
Dr. Ian Phelps Anthony Sharp
Nigel Waring John Wood
Prof. Lewin Angus Mackay
Minister's PPS Michael Culver
Hilda Freda Dowie
Elliott Norman Scace
Gillian Blake Sheila Grant

Director: Darrol Blake
Designer: Graham Oakley

By the Pricking of My Thumbs . . .

w Robin Chapman
Sixteen-year-old Stephen Franklin is expelled from school because, his father says, he has an obscure genetic defect—an extra "Y" chromosome.
Stephen Franklin Barry Stokes
Oscar Franklin Bernard Hepton
Mary Franklin Patsy Byrne
Judy Franklin Sally Thomsett
MacPherson David Janson
Painton Robert Yetzes
Ensor Olaf Pooley
Botting Colin Jeavons
Avery David Jarrett
Jenkins Martin Howells

Director: Eric Hills
Designer: Tim Gleeson

The Iron Doctor

w Brian Hayles
An electronic watchdog that constantly monitors the health of the patients, diagnoses any change in their condition and prescribes treatment. "A great step forward" claim the hospital governors. But is it?
Dr. Carson Barry Foster
Dr. Whittaker James Maxwell
George Harold Bennett
Mr. Faber Frederick Schiller
Dr. Godfrey Keith Grenville
Sister Trewin Amanda Walker
Mr. Kemp Frank Littlewood
Mr. Tearson Raymond Young

Director: Joan Kemp-Welch
Designer: Ian Watson

Flight into Yesterday

w Martin Worth
The effects of jet-lag acquire a personal significance for Quist when he is ordered home by the Prime Minister on the eve of addressing a major ecological conference in Los Angeles.
Minister John Barron
Duncan Michael Elwyn
PM's secretary John Quarmby
Miss Wills Jennifer Wilson
Thompson Desmond Llewellyn
Ainslie Robert Urquhart

Director: Darrol Blake
Designer: Christine Ruscoe

The Web of Fear

w Gerry Davis
The Scilly Isles are sealed off following an outbreak of yellow fever and Doomwatch is drawn into a virus hunt involving spiders.
Minister John Savident
Duncan Michael Elwyn
Patterson Desmond Cullum-Jones
Dr. Seaton Walter Horsbrugh
Jenson John Lee
Griffiths Glyn Owen
Janine Stephanie Bidmead
Dr. George Anthony Newlands

Director: Eric Hills
Designer: Jeremy Davies

In the Dark

w John Gould
A man called McArthur is threatened by a crippling disease that will eventually turn him blind, mute and deaf. He's being kept alive by computers, but Quist convinces him that he should have the machines turned off.
Flora Seton Alethea Charlton
Andrew Seton Simon Lack
McArthur Patrick Troughton
Journalist David Purcell
Naval officers Michael Ellison
Dr. Jackson Joseph Greig

Director: Lennie Mayne
Designer: John Hurst

The Human Time Bomb

w Louis Marks
A new age demands a new architecture—and a study into urban neurosis caused by living in tower blocks imposes its own stresses on Fay Chantry.
Mrs. Hetherington Joan Phillips
Hetherington Talfryn Thomas
Cavendish John Quayle
Mrs. Frank Ursula Hirst
Donovan Ray Armstrong
Grant Patrick Godfrey
Scobie Roddy McMillan
Sir Billy Langley Kevin Brennan

Director: Joan Kemp-Welch
Designer: Colin Shaw

The Inquest

w Robert Holmes
Every dog within a five-mile radius of Silby must be destroyed"—the death of a ten-year-old schoolgirl from rabies brings a shock recommendation from Doomwatch scientist Colin Bradley.
Dr. Fane Frederick Treves
Philips David Spurling
Mary Lincoln Judith Furse
Pritchard Frederick Hall
Marge Jean Marlow
McAlister Robert Cawdron
Harry Garry Smith
Coroner Edward Evans

Director: Lennie Mayne
Designer: Graham Oakley

The Logicians

w Dennis Spooner
Industrial spies are blamed for a break-in at a chemical factory in which vital papers are stolen.
Malcolm Priestland Robin Davies
David Wagstaffe Stuart Knee

Colin Tredget Peter Duncan
Richard Whetlor Robert Barry Jr.
Withers John Kelland
Priestland Noel Johnson
Kelsey Michael Grover

Director: David Proudfoot
Designer: Graham Oakley

Public Enemy

w Patrick Alexander
A clash between ideals and economics as Doomwatch probes "revolting, dangerous and now deadly" pollution at a metals firm.
Arnold Payne Derek Benfield
Lewis Trevor Bannister
Gerald Marlowe Glyn Houston
Jimmy Brookes John Trayhorn
Dr. Barton Roy Purcell
Nicholls Bill Weston
Donovan Norman Florence
Duncan Michael Elwyn

Director: Lennie Mayne
Designer: Graham Oakley

Season Three

Fire and Brimstone

w Terence Dudley
Ridge, disillusioned by the world about him, holds mankind to ransom by planting phials of anthrax in Moscow, Paris, Rome, New York, Berlin and London, and demanding that the governments tell the truth about environmental dangers.
Dr. Richard Poole Henry Knowles
Julie Caroline Rogers
Duncan Michael Elwyn
Police sgt. John Drake
Prison Officer Clarke Eric Longworth
Warren Talfryn Thomas
PCs Jonathan Pryce/David Waterman

Director: Terence Dudley
Designer: Graham Oakley

High Mountain

w Martin Worth
In the wake of the Ridge affair, the government wants to close down Doomwatch. Quist's integrity is questioned when he is offered a private "Doomwatch" to lend respectability to a giant industrial combine.
Ian Drummond Ronald Hines
Cowley John Scott
Barman Kedd Senton
Manservant Ian Elliott
Drummond Moultrie Kelsall
Mrs. Bell Betty Cardno
Gillie David Grahame

Director: Lennie Mayne
Designer: Graham Oakley

Say Knife, Fat Man

w Martin Worth

Anarchist students steal plutonium and threaten to make an atomic bomb. Then a group of gangsters tries to muscle in on the action.

Lawson Alan Hockey
Eddie Peter King
David Adrian Wright
Sarah Elisabeth Sladen
Susan Maria O'Brien
Rafael Peter Halliday
Chief Supt. Mallory Geoffrey Palmer
Prof. Holman Hugh Cross
Williams Sean Lynch

Director: Eric Hills
Designer: Graham Oakley

Waiting for a Knighthood

w Terence Dudley

A vicar's mental breakdown is found to be due to lead poisoning, and industrialist Richard Massingham becomes drawn into the pollution debate.

Rev. Frank Simpson Anthony Oliver
Mrs. Simpson Margaret John
Richard Massingham Frederick Jaeger
Peggy Massingham Ann Firbank
Stephen Massingham Stephen Dudley
Josie Julie Neubert
Joan Sylvester Glen Walford
Det. Chief Insp. Logan Don McKillop
Norman Sylvester Bruce Purchase

Director: Pennant Roberts
Designer: Ray London

Without the Bomb

w Roger Parkes

A doctor invents a contraceptive that can be sold in the form of a lipstick. But it has a startling side effect—it's also an aphrodisiac.

Dr. James Fulton Brian Peck
Mrs. Joan Fulton Antonia Pemberton
Harry Brooke Charles Hodgson
Clive Hughes Kenneth Benda
Lady Holroyd Katherine Kath
Amanda Fulton Sally Anne Marlowe
Roger Halls John Gregg

Director: Darrol Blake
Designer: Jeremy Davies

Hair Trigger

w Brian Hayles

Anne Tarrant is horrified when she visits a research unit that is controlling psychopaths and epileptics by means of temporal lobotomies.

Beavis Michael Hawkins
Dr. McEwan Barry Jackson

Prof. Hetherington Morris Perry
Miss Abrahams Pamela Saire
Robbie Damon Sanders
Emily Gillian Lewis
Police inspector Victor Platt

Director: Quentin Lawrence
Designer: Oliver Bayldon

Deadly Dangerous Tomorrow

w Martin Worth

An Indian family living in a tent in St. James's Park—one of them suffering from malaria—draws Doomwatch into the problems of homeless immigrants, and Ridge into a protest against the horrors of widespread DDT use.

Duncan Michael Elwyn
Hanif Khan Madhav Sharma
Senator Connell Cec Linder
Miss Brandon Lorna Lewis
Susan Maria O'Brien
His Excellency Renu Setna
Indian family Ahmad Nagi, Farhat, Talib & Rahat Shamsi

Director: Darrol Blake
Designer: Jeremy Davies

Enquiry

w John Gould

Doomwatch discovers that a new aerosol nerve gas, designed to defeat an enemy army without inflicting any casualties on them or the civilian population, is not as safe as is claimed.

Mike Clark Jack Tweddle
Dr. Evans Michael Forrest
Dr. Margery Becker Margaret Ashcroft
Dr. O'Dell Eddie Doyle
Col. Jones Barrie Cookson
Susan Lewis Ann Curthoys
Stephen Grigg Michael Keating
Mr. Clark James Ottaway

Director: Pennant Roberts
Designer: Ray London

Flood

w Ian Curteis

"One more inch! A mere inch! And we would have had a full-scale disaster in the very heart of London." A freak tide threatens to flood the capital.

BBC reporter Tim Nicholls
Critchley Raymond Mason
Ericson Wensley Pithey
Dr. Ridley Derek Benfield
General Robert Raglan
GLC man Robert James
Ministry of Defense man Michael Lees
Lt. Cmdr. Morrison Patrick Jordan

Director: Quentin Lawrence
Designer: Oliver Bayldon

Cause of Death

w Louis Marks
Headlines allege euthanasia at a clinic run by Dr. Cordell. And Ridge's geriatric father is a patient there.
Dr. Cordell John Lee
Susan Maria O'Brien
Edna Jennifer Wilson
Phillip Nicholas Courtney
Wilfred Ridge Graham Leaman
Hospital sisters Margaret Ford, Patsy Trench

Director: Lennie Mayne
Designer: Graham Oakley

The Killer Dolphins

w Roy Russell
Quist hears about dolphins being trained by the Navy to attach explosives to the hulls of enemy ships.
Professore Fillippo Balbo Angelo Infanti
Susan Maria O'Brien
Giula Rita Giovannini
Paola Maria Totti Viviane Ventura
Bill Manzero Richardson Morgan

Commodore Aylward Frank Duncan
Cavalli Bruno Barnabe

Director: Darrol Blake
Designer: Jeremy Davies

Unbroadcast episode:

Sex and Violence

w Stuart Douglas
An extreme right-wing politician tries to win power under the cloak of a women's clean-up campaign that is fostering an atmosphere of outrage and intolerance. Quist's team are called in to probe a suspected conspiracy of corruption. (Though recorded for the third series, this episode was deemed unsuitable over its use of real footage of a military execution.)
Arthur Ballantyne Nicholas Selby
Mrs. Catchpole June Brown
Lord Purvis Donald Eccles
Steven Granger Bernard Horsfall
Mrs. Hastings Angela Crow
Mrs. Angela Cressy Noel Dyson
Prof. Fairbairn Brian Wilde

Director: Darrol Blake
Designer: Jeremy Davies

DRACULA: THE SERIES

Eileen Townsend arrives in Europe with her two sons, Max and Chris, and leaves them with their uncle Gustav Helsing while she is away on business. Little does she know that their neighbor, billionaire Alexander Lucard (A. Lucard = Dracula spelled backward) is really a vampire. The boys, Uncle Gustav, and Gustav's ward, Sophie, soon form a vampire-fighting team.

A cute, sometimes scary Canadian-produced syndicated series that could easily have lasted several more seasons.

REGULAR CAST
Eileen Townsend Lynne Cormack   *Christopher Townsend* Joe Roncetti
Max Townsend Jacob Tierney   *Alexander Lucard (Dracula)* Geordie Johnson
Gustav Helsing Bernard Behrens   *Klaus Helsing* Geraint Wyn Davies
Sophie Metternich Mia Kirshner

Episodes
Children of the Night
Double Cross
The Vampire Solution
The Boffin
Double Darkness
Black Sheep
What a Pleasant Surprise!
Damsel in Distress
Mind Over Matter
A Little Nightmare Music
Get a Job

The Great Tickler
Bad Blood
Sophie, Queen of the Night
My Girlfriend's Back, and There's Gonna Be Trouble
Bats in the Attic
My Fair Vampire
Decline of the Romanian Vampire
I Love Lucard
My Dinner with Lucard
Klaus Encounters of the Interred Kind

EARLY EDITION

Stockbroker Gary Hobson's life is in shambles. He has just been thrown out by his wife, his boss isn't happy with his work, and things have never looked worse. Then a cat shows up with a newspaper filled with tomorrow's news. At first he goes through the typical greed-related emotions, but ultimately he realizes he has a special gift and gets to work preventing tragedies.

REGULAR CAST
Gary Hobson Kyle Chandler Chuck Fisher Stevens

Creator: Patrick Q. Pace, Vik Rubenfeld, Ian Abrams
Developed by Bob Brush
Executive producers: Bob Brush, Michael Dinner, Lillah McCarthy, Deborah Joy LeVine
Co-executive producers: Ian Abrams, Richard Heus
Producer: Robert Rabinowitz
Consulting producer: John Romano
Co-producers: Patrick Q. Pace, Vik Rubenfeld

A Three Characters and Angelica Films/TriStar Television production in association with CBS Productions.
37 color 60-minute episodes
U.S. premiere: 28 September 1996

Season One
Pilot
The Choice
Baby
The Paper
Thief Swipes Mayor's Dog
Hoops
After Midnight
Gun
His Girl Thursday
The Wrong Man
Christmas
Frostbit
Mob Wife
The Wall (Part 1)
The Wall (Part 2)

Bat Masterson
The Jury
Psychic
The Cat
Phantom at the Opera
Faith
Dad
Love Is Blind

Season Two
Home
The Medal
The Wedding
Jenny Sloan
Downsized
Angels and Devils
Redfellas
March in Time
A Regular Joe
A Bris Is Just a Bris
A Minor Miracle
Romancing the Throne
Walk, Don't Run
The Return of Crumb
Mum's the Word
When or Where
The Fourth Carpathian
The Quality of Mercy
Show Me Monet
Don't Walk Away, Renee
Hot Time in the Old Town
Second Sight

EARTH 2

Star Trek may once have been dubbed a "Wagon Train to the stars," but this one-season drama deserves the tag far more.

It's set some 200 years in the future, when Earth's population is forced to live in sterile space stations as the mother planet is too polluted to be inhabitable. In a last-ditch effort to save her son and 200 other children slowly dying from a mysterious syndrome affecting those born on space stations, Devon Adair organizes a renegade expedition to colonize a new Earth-like planet.

As a result of near-lethal opposition by the governing Council, which intends to sabotage their dream, Devon and a small band of colonists crash-land on the planet. Virtually unarmed and low on supplies, the castaways face a struggle to survive as they begin a dangerous 3400-mile trek toward New Pacifica, the one place on the planet identified as being capable of sustaining a large-scale civilization and where the official colonizing expedition is due to land.

Along the way they encounter natural obstacles, bizarre new life-forms and mystical occurrences, as well as internal conflicts. Principal among those life-forms are the tall Terrians, an aboriginal-type race given to literally popping up out of the ground, and who seem to hold the clue to the improving health of Devon's physically impaired son Ulysses, communicating via dreams and visions. The other principal alien creatures are the Grendlers, a bunch of nomadic, slobbering scavengers.

The cast is fine—*NYPD Blue* cast-off Debrah Farentino as the mission leader, Devon; Sullivan Walker as a philosophical cyborg; Clancy Brown as a rugged single-parent handyman; and for added sex appeal, Jessica Steen as a fresh-faced doctor who is also a Council agent and Antonio Sabato Jr. as a pilot. Also lurking menacingly, for a while, is Tim Curry, guest starring as a dangerous schemer who somehow got to the planet before them.

Despite a highly impressive pilot—the pre-crash sequences are excellent—*Earth 2*'s problem is that it gets too repetitive too soon, and it's a hardy viewer who can complete the full season trek with them. Besides having predictable plots and clichéd characters, it's *dull*.

Its trio of creators, Michael Duggan, Carol Flint and Mark Levin, had virtually no previous sci-fi experience. Duggan was a writer on *St. Elsewhere*, Flint a writer/producer on *China Beach* and Levin the same on *The Wonder Years*. It shows.

REGULAR CAST
Devon Adair Debrah Farentino *Alonzo Solace* Antonio Sabato Jr.
John Danziger Clancy Brown *Yale* Sullivan Walker *Dr. Julia Heller* Jessica Steen
Morgan Martin John Gegenhuber *Bess Martin* Rebecca Gayheart
Ulysses Adair Joey Zimmerman *True Danziger* J. Madison Wright
with: *Zero* Tierre Turner *Walman* Walter Norman *Magus* Marcia Magus
Baines Rockmond Dunbar

Creators: Billy Ray, Michael Duggan, Carol Flint & Mark Levin
Executive producers: Michael Duggan, Carol Flint, Mark Levin
Music: David Bergeaud

An Amblin Television and Universal Television Co-Production
21 color 60-minute episodes (pilot 120 minutes)
U.S. premiere: 6 November 1994
U.K. premiere: 4 October 1995
(Sky One)

First Contact

w Michael Duggan, Carol Flint, Mark Levin, story by Billy Ray, Michael Duggan, Carol Flint, Mark Levin

It's 200 years in the future, when Earth's population is forced to live in huge space stations. A wealthy woman leads the Eden project, an expedition to colonize a distant planet she believes could offer a new beginning. But her dream is sabotaged by the government, and a small group crash-land on the planet, which is inhabited by strange alien creatures.
Commander O'Neill Richard Bradford
Newscaster Beth Colt
Controllers Hedy Thom, John Verea
Navigator Marcia Firesten
Terrians Brian Steele, Russell Werkman

Director: Scott Winant

The Man Who Fell to Earth (Two)

w Mark Levin
The colonists encounter Gaal, another human who claims to be a stranded astronaut. Commander O'Neill turns up but when he threatens to expose him, Gaal has the commander killed by Grendlers. Meanwhile, Ulysses' health improves, and Terrian dreams haunt Alonzo.
Commander O'Neill Richard Bradford
Gaal Tim Curry

Director: Felix Enriquez Alcala

Life Lessons

w Jennifer Flackett
Gaal starts to stir up conflict by playing on True's disenchantment with the planet. And Alonzo, now without a ship to fly, must come to terms with his new situation.
Gaal Tim Curry

Director: Daniel Sackheim

Promises, Promises

w P.K. Simmonds
Gaal enslaves Terrians using an electronic collar, and the last Terrian enlists the colonists' help to free his tribe and gain their revenge. And Uly takes a turn for the worse.
Gaal Tim Curry
Terrians Brian Steele, Russel Werkman

Director: Felix Enriquez Alcala

A Memory Play

w Mark Levin & Jennifer Flackett
The colonists start blaming each other for the crash. To settle them down Devon has Yale replay the incident via his robotic eye—but he finds that it *was* caused by sabotage. Meanwhile, a search party finds some new survivors who have been stricken by a highly infectious virus.
Les Firestein Julius Carry
Alex Wentworth LaTanya Richardson
Grendler Jeff Deist

Director: Deborah Reinisch

Natural Born Grendlers

w Jennifer Flackett & P.K. Simmonds, *story by*
Carl Cramer & David Solmonson
Bess barters with a Grendler and receives edible fruit plus equipment from the Eden Project's damaged cargo pods. And Alonzo suffers bizarre dreams as he comes to terms with his new life on the ground. (This episode was shown out of sequence in the U.S.)

Director: Michael Grossman

Water

w Carol Flint
Devon and Danziger encounter Terrians while searching for a reliable water supply. And Julia becomes uncomfortable about her feelings for Alonzo—and her covert allegiance to the Council to which she reports via virtual reality.
Reilly Terry O'Quinn
Terrians Brian Steele, Russel Werkman

Director: Joe Napolitano

The Church of Morgan

w Michael Duggan
Dr. Heller prepares to perform a risky procedure on Uly who is scared that he may be turning into a Terrian. And surprise admissions strain Bess and Morgan's relationship.
Reilly Terry O'Quinn

Director: Joe Napolitano

The Enemy Within

w Eric Estrin & Michael Berlin
Dr. Heller resists the Council's pressure on her to let them have Uly who has become a bridge between the humans and the Terrians. Instead she conducts an experiment by injecting herself with Uly's Terrian-tainted DNA. But when the group discovers her "treachery" they leave her behind, alone, as they continue their trek.
Reilly Terry O'Quinn
Terrian Brian Steele
Jesse James John David Garfield
Frank James Clifford Happy

Director: John Harrison

Redemption

w Arthur Sellers
Alonzo regrets leaving Julia behind and decides to go back for her. Reunited, though still distrustful of her, the group must face a terrifying new adversary, a genetically engineered killer, and Julia gets a second chance to prove her loyalty now lies with Devon's band.
Reilly Terry O'Quinn
Z.E.D. Jeff Kober

Director: Joe Ann Fogle

Moon Cross

w Carol Flint
With cold weather coming, Uly leads the colonists to a mysterious deserted biosphere. On a scouting trip Alonzo encounters a Terrian woman and learns something of their rituals, and returns with her to the biosphere. And the Terrians initiate Uly as the link between the two species.
Mary Kelli Williams
Terrians Brian Steele, Russell Werkman
Mary's parents Laurie Ciarametaro, Kevin Wiggins

Director: Sandy Smolan

Better Living through Morganite, Part 1

w P.K. Simmonds
First of a two-part story. When Yale starts having violent nightmares, the colonists fear he might revert to his former criminal self. Morgan stakes a claim to a newly discovered power source—mysterious sunstones that may be linked to the Terrians.
Terrians Brian Steele, Russell Werkman

Director: Jim Charleston

Better Living through Morganite, Part 2

w P.K. Simmonds
Mary reveals a Terrian plan to retaliate by "killing those who killed the Earth." As the colonists desperately try to set things straight, Yale learns the truth about his past.
Mary Kelli Williams
Terrians Brian Steele, Russell Werkman
Soldier David Elliot
Woman Leslie Cook
Newscaster Patrick Henry Finnegan

Director: Frank DePalma

Grendlers in the Mist

w Heather MacGillvrey & Linda Mathious
Several of the colonists report strange dreams about mothers. While wondering about their significance the group stumbles upon messages from a mysterious woman who apparently fears for the lives of herself and her son. And Bess helps True when she starts to inquire about the mother she's never met . . .
Whalen Tim Ransom
Dell Curry Francia Di Mase
Grendler Jeff Deist

Director: Janet Davidson

The Greatest Love Story Never Told

w Mark Levin & Jennifer Flackett
Danziger gets caught in a wind-storm and is given shelter by a group of cavern dwellers. Following a dream message, Alonzo tells Devon she must go alone to find him and she's surprised to find their leader says he already knows her.
Sheppard Patrick Bauchau
Katrina Lilyan Chauvin
Ragamuffin Andrew J. Ferchland
Elder Roy Dotrice
Terrians Brian Steele, Russel Werkman
Ivan Ivan Schwarz
Larken Dain Turner

Director: James Frawley

Brave New Pacifica

w Carol Flint
The colonists discover an intriguing form of transport that could speed up their journey to New Pacifica—a "space-fold" that acts as a kind of natural circulatory system within the planet. And the Grendlers discover a macabre delicacy—human blood.
Grendlers Jeff Deist, Lisa Ebeyer

Director: Joe Napolitano

After the Thaw

w Theo Coban
It's Day 109, and the colonists' 40th day stuck in the biodome, and their food supply is still dwindling. While searching for plant life, Julia stumbles on the preserved body of a Terrian—but the discovery has strange and violent consequences.
Elder Roy Dotrice
Ragamuffin Andrew J. Ferchland
Grendlers Jeff Deist, Lisa Ebeyer

Director: Michael Grossman

The Boy Who Would Be Terrian King

w Heather MacGillvray & Linda Mathious
Uly celebrates his ninth birthday. Adair dreams of her son as an adult, leading rebel Terrians. True tries to care for a sick Koba.
Future Uly Michael Reilly Burke
Max Nicholas Sadler
Future True Kathy Molter
Terrians Brian Steele, Russel Werkman
Guards Tierre Turner, Mike McCoy, Karen Whittle

Director: Jim Charleston

Survival of the Fittest

w John Harrison
Four of the colonists are tested to their physical and psychological limits while on an abortive mission to recover one of the Eden Project's lost cargo pods. And the group learns a valuable lesson about being human.
Grendler Jeff Deist

Director: John Harrison

Flower Child

w Carl Cramer
It's now 130 days into the colonists' stay on the planet. On another scouting mission, Bess and Danziger find a colorful flower that sprays them with a pollen-like substance. Later, when the pair starts to exhibit strange symptoms, they are found to be infected with a mysterious organism—which they subsequently realize holds the key to "jump-starting" spring.
Grendler Jeff Deist

Director: Jim Charleston

All About Eve

w Robert Crais

Plagued by a deadly illness that is slowly killing them, the colonists discover a stranded Earth starship, with the inhabitants in deep-sleep pods. After a strange virtual reality experience, Morgan attempts to revive the sleepers. Only two survive, scientists who tell them their illness is linked to a computer monitoring movement on the planet. While the other colonists recover, Devon worsens and is put into cold sleep by her friends.

Reilly Terry O'Quinn
Dr. Franklin Bennett Christopher Neame
Elizabeth Anson Margaret Gibson
Eve Heady Thom
Eben Synge Erin Murphy

Director: John Harrison

EERIE, INDIANA

If you head out of Cicely, Alaska, and take a left at *Twin Peaks*, you might find yourself in *Eerie, Indiana*. Tagged as a *Twilight Zone* for kids, *Eerie, Indiana* was a nineties venture into American small-town weirdness that deserved better than its brief run. This eccentric community—described in the opening credits as "the center of weirdness for the entire planet," was the home of teenager Marshall Teller who, with his friend Simon, encountered all manner of oddballs, aliens and paranormal freaks. Even Elvis seemed to have taken up residence here.

Gremlins director Joe Dante was creative consultant on the show and directed several episodes himself, including the pilot about a body-snatching cult of kitchenware fanatics. It's that kind of weird. Other episodes featured a dental brace that acted as an antenna, tuning in to the thoughts of dogs; a man who downloaded his brain onto an eight-track tape; veteran actor Ray Walston as an alien explorer who transports Simon to Pluto; a traveling museum of the parabelievable; a killer tornado with a personality—plus a tornado hunter (played by *Max Headroom*, Matt Frewer); a cash machine that develops a crush on Simon; and a vast warehouse under the town that stores everything that ever gets lost in the world.

Throughout, the tone of the show was light, sometimes even matter-of-fact in its weirdness, rather than scary. It was also wonderfully original, coming up with some very off-the-wall concepts. In *The Lost Hour*, for example, when Marshall forgets to put his watch back one hour in the autumn, he finds himself trapped in a time warp with several other citizens who also forgot.

Marshall was played by Omri Katz, formerly John Ross Ewing in *Dallas*, while Justin Shenkarow, who co-starred as his pal Simon, went on to become a resident in another offbeat town, Rome, Wisconsin, location for the Emmy Award–winning series *Picket Fences*.

REGULAR CAST
Marshall Teller Omri Katz *Simon Holmes* Justin Shenkarow
Marilyn Teller Mary-Margaret Humes *Edgar Teller* Francis Guinan
Syndi Teller Julie Condra

Creators: Karl Shaefer, José Rivera
Executive producer: Karl Schaefer
Co-executive producers: John Cosgrove, Terry Dunn-Meurer
Producers: José Rivera, Gary Markowitz, Walter Barnett, Michael Cassutt
Story editor: Matt Dearborn
Creative consultant: Joe Dante

An Unreality, Inc. and Cosgrove-Meurer Production in association with Hearst Entertainment
19 color 30-minute episodes
U.S. premiere: 15 September 1991
U.K. premiere: 23 March–27 July 1993
(Channel Four)

Foreverware

w Karl Schaffer *&* José Rivera

Marshall's family is taken by a cult of body-snatching kitchenware fanatics who seal their children in human-sized containers to preserve their youth.

Director: Joe Dante

The Retainer

w Karl Schaffer & José Rivera
When Marshall's friend gets an experimental retainer from the town's weird orthodontist, he discovers that it acts as an antenna allowing him to hear what dogs are thinking—and their minds are full of plans for a canine revolution.
Director: Joe Dante

The ATM with the Heart of Gold

w Matt Dearborn
Eerie's Savings and Loans get its first automatic teller machine, which promptly becomes obsessed with Simon and showers him with money—until Eerie goes bankrupt!
Director: Sam Pillsbury

The Losers

w Gary Markowitz & Michael R. Perry, *story by* Gary Markowitz
When Marshall sets out to find his father's lost briefcase, he and Simon discover a vast warehouse under the town where a two-man bureaucracy is responsible for all the lost items in the world.
Director: Joe Dante

America's Scariest Home Video

w Karl Schaffer
Simon's baby brother is zapped into the television—while a mummy from the horror movie that's being shown is zapped into his living room.
Director: Sam Pillsbury

No Fun

w Michael R. Perry
When Simon mysteriously turns into a humorless workaholic drone after undergoing a school eye test, Marshall determines that the school nurse is hypnotizing kids and removing their sense of humor.
Director: Bryan Spicer

Heart on a Chain

w José Rivera
Marshall and Devon both have a crush on Melanie, a beautiful new girl at school who is waiting for a heart transplant donor. When Devon is killed in a car accident, his heart is transplanted into her body. However, the jealous organ creates problems for Marshall and Melanie as they try to become sweethearts.
Director: Joe Dante

The Dead Letter

w James L. Crite
Marshall finds an undelivered letter and is haunted by a mischievous ghost-kid who needs him to deliver it to his 80-year-old sweetheart.
Director: Tim Hunter

Who's Who

w Julia Poll
A girl called Sarah has an unusual talent—everything she draws comes to life.
Director: Tim Hunter

The Lost Hour

w Vance De Generes
When he forgets to set his watch back for daylight saving time, Marshall finds himself trapped in a time warp with a strange collection of Eerie citizens who also failed to change their watches.
Director: Bob Balaban

Marshall's Theory of Believability

w Matt Dearborn
When Professor Zircon's Traveling Museum of the Parabelievable comes to town, Marshall and Simon discover there's more to life than Bigfoot and UFOs.
Director: Bob Balaban

Tornado Days

w Michael Cassutt
A killer tornado with a personality comes after Marshall and only Howard the Tornado Hunter can save him.
Howard Matt Frewer

Director: Ken Kwapis

The Hole in the Head Gang

w Karl Schaffer
Exploring Eerie's haunted mill, Marshall and Simon discover a gray-haired boy with no memory of his past and also unearth a real ghost, Grungy Bill—the worst bank robber east of the Mississippi.
Grungy Bill Claude Akins
Mr. Radford John Astin

Director: Joe Dante

Mr. Chaney

w José Rivera
Every 13 years Eerie elects a Harvest King to ensure the town another cycle of prosperity. Unfortunately, previous Harvest Kings have all mysteriously disappeared. When Marshall wins the new crown, he finds out why—Eerie's got a werewolf.
Mr. Radford John Astin

Director: Mark Goldblatt

No Brain, No Pain

w Matt Dearborn
Eerie's resident homeless hobo, Chappy Furnell, was the smartest man in the world until he downloaded his brain onto an eight-track tape. Now a zapper-packing redhead wants Chappy—for his greatest invention, the Brainalyzer.
Director: Greg Beeman

The Loyal Order of Corn

w Michael Cassutt
Simon finds himself transported to Pluto by an alien explorer and only Marshall can save him.
Ned Ray Walston
Mr. Radford John Astin

Director: Bryan Spicer

Zombies in P.J.S.

w Julia Poll
Eerie's residents are turned into sleepshopping zombies by a seductive salesman called the Donald. Only Marshall, Simon and Dash are immune to his siren song, and must find a cure for his consumer fever.
Mr. Radford John Astin

Director: Bob Balaban

Reality Takes a Holiday

w Vance De Generes
Marshall is bewildered to discover that everyone in Eerie has become an actor on a TV show and his town has turned into a Hollywood studio.
Mr. Radford John Astin

Director: Ken Kwapis

The Broken Record

w José Rivera
Marshall tries to save a friend with an abusive father who claims that subliminal messages in heavy metal records are ruining his son. But the tables are turned when he tries to play one backward for the police—only to hear his own voice verbally abusing his son.
Director: Todd Holland

ERASMUS MICROMAN

A cross between a mad professor and Doctor Who, *Erasmus Microman* first burst onto the screen when he dragged two bored children inside his TV lair and led them on an educational time trip to meet history's greatest scientists.

A second series saw the 1005-year-old Microman return from a sojourn as Inspector of Black Holes for the Universal Space Federation to chase through time the deranged Dr. Dark, an interloper from a parallel universe who sought to plunge the planet into a new dark age.

REGULAR CAST
Erasmus Microman Ken Campbell *Dr. Dark* Lee B. McPlank *(Series Two)*

Writers: Stephen Trombley *(Series One)*, Gary Hopkins *(Series Two)*
Producers: John Slater, Stephen Trombley
Director: David Richards
Designer: Rod Stratfold

A Mirageland Production for Granada Television
14 color 25-minute episodes
Series One:
3 March–14 April 1988
Series Two:
3 November–15 December 1989

ESCAPE FROM JUPITER

The fruit of this unusual Australian/Japanese collaboration is an adventure series that blends conventional drama with some impressive and elegant computer-generated graphics.

It's unfortunate, then, that you can see the join—this is a bit like watching two totally different series (a slightly disconcerting response shared with *Babylon 5*).

The 13-part series focuses on the adventures of five children who live on Io, the innermost of Jupiter's 16 moons—Michael, whose father is a mining engineer; computer whiz Kumiko; tough guy Gerard and his chocolate-loving kid sister Anna; and bespectacled tunnel-rat Kingston.

Despite being warned of the dangers by eccentric Professor Ingessol, the colony's administrator, Duffy, presses ahead with a risky deep drilling program. It has disastrous effects, sparking a volcanic eruption, causing the moon to crumble, and forcing the children and a small group of surviving adults to flee to a derelict space station, which they convert into a makeshift spacecraft for a perilous journey back to Earth.

Along the way they battle with unreliable computer and life-support systems, depleted food and fuel reserves, asteroids and, at the final hurdle, a rogue defense satellite that cripples their craft. As the adults battle to save the ship from falling into the sun, the children make a rescue dash to Earth in a shaky space tug.

A largely unknown cast featured Steve Bisley, who had appeared with Mel Gibson in *Mad Max*, and in a BBC thriller, *Call Me Mister*.

The series—which actually aired in the U.K. before Australia—marked a first venture into sci-fi for satellite station The Family Channel.

CAST
Michael Daniel Taylor   *Gerard* Justin Rosniak   *Kumiko* Anna Choy
Duffy Steve Bisley   *Professor Ingessol* Arthur Dignam
Kingston Abraham Forsythe   *Anna* Robyn Mackenzie   *Helen* Anne Tenney
Beth Linden Wilkinson   *Tatsuya* Kazuhiro Muroyama   *Akiko* Saemi Baba

Executive producer: Ron Saunders
Producer: Terry Jennings
Directors: Katherine Woods, Funitaka Tamura,
   Kagari Tajima
Writers: John Patterson, David Ogilvy, Martin
   Daley

An NHK/Film Australia Co-production in association with the ABC
13 color 30-minute episodes
10 April–3 July 1994
(Family Channel)

THE FANTASTIC JOURNEY

One of the more fanciful theories about the Bermuda Triangle has been that it contains a time-space warp that projects victims into some other dimension—and that was the basis for this fanciful American adventure series.

A small scientific expedition sets off across the Caribbean to study a natural phenomenon known as "red tide." On board a yacht run by Ben Wallace and his mate Carl Johanson are science professor Paul Jordan, his teenage son, Scott, Eve Costigan, Dr. Fred Walters, medical adviser Jill Sands and a pair of scientific assistants, Andy and George.

Soon after setting sail they are enveloped by a green cloud, to the accompaniment of clanging bells, and a sudden violent storm capsizes the boat. The two assistants are drowned and the others washed up on a strange island where they encounter Varian, a man from the 23rd century whose spaceship had crashed, marooning him here. They have a run-in with Sir James Camden and his band of Elizabethan privateers before the group splits up, with Varian, Scott and Dr. Fred going it alone into the ensuing series where, with the addition of two new regulars, a half-human, half-alien called Liana and a 1960s scientist, Willoway (from Episode 3), they cross various time zones in search of a way home.

REGULAR CAST
Varian Jared Martin *Dr. Fred Walters* Carl Franklin
Scott Jordan Ike Eisenmann *Liana* Katie Saylor
Dr. Jonathan Willoway Roddy McDowall *(from Ep. 3)*

Executive producer: Bruce Lansbury
Producer: Leonard Katzman
Story consultants: Dorothy (D.C.) Fontana, Calvin Clements Jr.
Music: Robert Prince

Bruce Lansbury Productions, in assoc. with Columbia Pictures Television
10 50-minute color episodes (pilot 70 minutes)
U.S. premiere: 3 February 1977
U.K. premiere: 5 March-6 May 1977 (BBC1)

Vortex (pilot)

w Michael Michaelian, Katharyn Michaelian Powers, Merwin Gerard, *story by* Merwin Gerard
A scientific team in the Bermuda Triangle stumbles on a time warp into a different dimension where they encounter Varian, a man from the 23rd century who opens their eyes to wonders beyond the dreams of science.
Ben Wallace Leif Erickson
Sir James Camden Ian McShane
Carl Johanson Scott Brady
Prof. Jordan Scott Thomas
Eve Susan Howard
Jill Karen Somerville

Director: Andrew V. McLaglen

Atlantium

w Katharyn Michaelian Powers
All seems well at the gleaming white city of the Atlantians, but the Source—a master brain that controls all around it—is in need of energy and Scott is singled out as the supply.
Dar-L Gary Collins
Rhea Mary Ann Mobley
Atar Jason Evers
Itar Albert Stratton

Director: Barry Crane

Beyond the Mountain

w Howard Livingstone
Separated from her friends, Liana finds herself in a village of beautiful men and women led by Jonathan Willoway. Meanwhile Varian, Fred and Scott are lost in a swamp and captured by green-skinned aliens who claim they are the rightful owner of Willoway's people—a race of androids.
Cyrus John David Carson
Rachel Marj Dusay
Aren Joseph Della Sorte
Willoway Roddy McDowall *(intro)*

Director: Irving Moore

The Children of the Gods

w Leonard Katzman
Resting amid the ruins of a Grecian temple, the travelers are captured by children with strange powers who hate the older generation.
Alpha Mark Lambert
Sigma Bobby Eilbacher
Delta Cosie Costa
Beta Stanley Clay

Director: Alf Kjellin

A Dream of Conquest

w Michael Michaelian
Varian and his companions cross another time zone and find would-be conqueror Consul Tarant plotting to invade the other time zones.
Tarant John Saxon
Argon Morgan Paull
Lara Lenore Stevens
Luther Robert Patten
Nikki Johnny Doran
Neffring Bobby Porter

Director: Vincent McEveety

An Act of Love

w Richard Fielder
Secretly injected with Cupid's arrow, Varian falls deeply in love with Gwenith, an alien whose people are living in a geologically unstable zone.
Gwenith Christina Hart
Maera Ellen Weston
Zaros Jonathan Goldsmith
Baras Vic Mohica
Arla Belinda Balaski

Director: Virgil Vogel

Funhouse

w Michael Michaelian
Varian and his companions come across a deserted carnival where Appolonius, a powerful sorcerer, offers to entertain them. (Unscreened in U.K. first run, after being scheduled, then withdrawn.)
Appolonius Mel Ferrer
Roxanne Mary Frann
Barker Richard Lawson

Director: Art Fisher

Turnabout

w D.C. Fontana & Ken Kolb
Liana is imprisoned in a society where men treat women as slaves. But Queen Halyana has plans for a revolution.
Halyana Joan Collins
Morgan Paul Mantee
Adrea Julie Cobb
Connell Beverly Todd

Director: Victor French

Riddles

w Katharyn Michaelian Powers
Varian and his fellow wanderers learn of a mysterious stone—the key to a doorway back to their own times.
Kedryn Dale Robinette
Krysta Carole Demas
Rider Dax Xanos
Simkin William O'Connell

Director: David Moessinger

The Innocent Prey

w Robert Hamilton
The travelers befriend two survivors from a crashed spacecraft. But the two men are criminals and their arrival has a disturbing effect on a group of people who cannot understand the concept of evil.
Tye Nicholas Hammond
York Richard Jaeckal
Rayat Lew Ayres
Natica Cheryl Ladd
Roland Jim Payner

Director: Vincent McEveety

FIREBALL XL5

With *Fireball XL5*, Gerry Anderson's Supermarionation took its giant leap into space fantasy. Set in the year 2063, the series charted the interplanetary adventures of a spacecraft and its crew: handsome blond pilot Steve Zodiac, glamorous blonde space doctor Venus, math genius Professor Mat Matic, and a transparent "auto pilot," Robert the Robot. There was also a pet—a strange creature called the Lazoon, who had a habit of imitating sounds and a hungry passion for Martian Delight.

XL5 was part of a World Space Fleet based at Space City, an island in the Pacific Ocean, run by Commander Zero and Lieutenant Ninety. Its mission: to patrol sector 25 of the universe, beyond the solar system. The biggest craft of its kind, the 300-foot long *XL5* had a detachable nose cone called Fireball Junior, used for landings while the mother ship stayed in orbit. Other equipment included hoverbikes called jetmobiles.

The Fireball shows contained an imaginative array of detailed space models and miniature sets, both terrestrial and alien—all given an extra atmospheric twist by the black and white photography. The special effects were again masterminded by Derek Meddings who later graduated from the Anderson studio floor to become an Oscar-winning creator of dazzling effects for such films as *Moonraker* and *Superman*.

The voice of Steve Zodiac was provided by Paul Maxwell; John Bluthal, a renowned character actor, was Commander Zero; while Sylvia Anderson played all the female characters, including Venus.

Fireball XL5's impact was tremendous. It is still the only Gerry Anderson production to have been fully networked on American television (NBC, 1963), and in its modest way stands as a role model for series such as *Star Trek*. It has always been fondly remembered by its contemporary audience.

CHARACTER VOICES
Steve Zodiac Paul Maxwell   *Venus* Sylvia Anderson
Prof. Mat Matic David Graham   *Cmdr. Zero* John Bluthal
Robert the Robot Gerry Anderson   *Lt. Ninety* David Graham

Creators: Gerry & Sylvia Anderson
Producer: Gerry Anderson
Associate producer: Reg Hill
Music: Barry Gray
Title song sung by Don Spencer
Special effects: Derek Meddings

An AP Films Production for ATV/ITC
39 black and white 30-minute episodes
28 October 1962–23 June 1963 *(Eps. 1–35)*
6–27 October 1963 *(Eps. 36–39)**
(ATV, London region)

* The last four episodes were immediately followed by repeats of earlier episodes.

Planet 46

w Gerry & Sylvia Anderson
Steve Zodiac and his crew intercept a planetomic
missile on a course to destroy Earth. Seeking out the
source of the attack, on Planet 46, Steve and Venus
are captured by a race of Subterrains who launch another missile—with Venus on board as a hostage.

Director: Gerry Anderson

The Doomed Planet

w Alan Fennell
A flying saucer leads to Steve Zodiac saving a planet
that is doomed to be destroyed because it is in the path
of another planet that has broken orbit.

Director: Alan Pattillo

Space Immigrants

w Anthony Marriott
A spaceship, the *Mayflower III*, piloted by Venus, is
carrying pioneers to a new planet. But they are unaware of the danger that awaits them from an evil
race of little people called the Lillispatians.

Director: Alan Pattillo

Plant Man from Space

w Anthony Marriott
The World Space Patrol foils a fiendish plan hatched
by Prof. Matic's old friend Dr. Rootes, to overcome
Earth by strangling it with a strange kind of plant
life.

Director: John Kelly

Spy in Space

w Alan Fennell
Refueling at a space station, Steve and the *Fireball*
crew walk into a trap laid by the notorious Mr. and
Mrs. Space Spy who plan to seize *Fireball*, holding

Venus as hostage. All seems lost until an ingenious
device of Mat Matic's sends Mr. Space Spy screaming into orbit.

Director: Alan Pattillo

The Sun Temple

w Anthony Marriott
On the planet Rejusca, Steve and Zoonie must save
Venus from a pair of sun worshippers who plan to
make her a sizzling sacrifice to their god.

Director: John Kelly

XL5 to H2O

w Alan Fennell
Fireball responds to an urgent distress call from the
last two survivors of a planet menaced by a weird
fish man armed with a poisonous smoke gun.

Director: John Kelly

Space Pirates

w Anthony Marriott
The *Fireball* crew gets involved in a complicated
game of bluff and double bluff to outwit a gang of
space pirates plundering freighters from the min-
eral-rich planet Minera. The final bluff is that this
whole saga is a bedtime story Venus is telling to
Cmdr. Zero's son, Jonathan.

Director: Bill Harris

Flying Zodiac

w Anthony Marriott
Steve nearly falls victim to sabotage at a Space City
circus as part of a scheme by Mr. and Mrs. Space
Spy to help alien nomads take over Earth. Then
Venus wakes up . . . it was only a dream. (Dreams
provided a recurring source of storylines for APF
scriptwriters!)

Director: Bill Harris

Space Pen

w Dennis Spooner
Posing as criminals, the *Fireball* crew head for the prison planet Conva in pursuit of two Space City raiders, and wind up facing death in Mr. and Mrs. Space Spy's lethal water chamber.

Director: John Kelly

Space Monster

w Gerry & Sylvia Anderson
Zoonie's talent for mimicry gets the *Fireball* folk out of a tight spot when they investigate the disappearance of the patrol ship *XL2* and find themselves menaced by a space monster.

Director: John Kelly

The Last of the Zanadus

w Anthony Marriott
Zoonie falls sick—victim of a plot by the evil Kudos, lone inhabitant of the planet Zanadu, to destroy all lazoons with a deadly virus. *Fireball* flies to Zanadu where Steve defeats Kudos and obtains the antidote.

Director: Alan Pattillo

Planet of Platonia

w Alan Fennell
Sent to bring the King of the Platinum Planet back to Earth for trade talks, the *Fireball* crew foils a bomb plot by the king's aide, Volvo, to kill his ruler and plunge the two planets into war.

Director: David Elliott

The Triads

w Alan Fennell
Steve, Venus and Mat encounter Graff and Snaff, a couple of friendly giants, on Triad—a planet three times the size of Earth—and help them in their efforts to explore space.

Director: Alan Pattillo

Wings of Danger

w Alan Fennell
Investigating strange signals coming from Planet 46—the home of the Subterrains—Steve Zodiac is unknowingly poisoned by a robot bird equipped with deadly radium capsules. Swift surgery by Venus saves his life, but the bird is waiting to "pounce" again . . .

Director: David Elliott

Convict in Space

w Alan Fennell
Mr. and Mrs. Space Spy pull the old "can you help, our spaceship has broken down" routine to trick Steve into releasing convicted space robber Grothan Deblis who is being taken to Planet Conva, the prison planet. They want Deblis to lead them to where he has hidden his stolen plans.

Director: Bill Harris

Space Vacation

w Dennis Spooner
A quiet, relaxing vacation on the rich and beautiful planet of Olympus turns into a race against time for Steve when he and the *Fireball* crew become caught up in an interplanetary feud.

Director: Alan Pattillo

Flight to Danger

w Alan Fennell
To win his astronaut's wings Lt. Ninety must complete a solo orbit of the moon. But disaster strikes when his rocket catches fire, and he is feared lost until Mat picks up a drifting object on his spacemanscope. Lt. Ninety's wings are well earned!

Director: David Elliott

Prisoner on the Lost Planet

w Anthony Marriott
Answering a distress call from uncharted space, Steve finds himself on a misty planet, dominated by a giant smoldering volcano, where he meets a beautiful Amazonian exile who threatens to activate the volcano if she is not helped to escape.

Director: Bill Harris

The Forbidden Planet

w Anthony Marriott
Prof. Matic's new invention, the ultrascope, picks out the planet Nutopia—never before seen by eyes from Earth, and reputed to be the perfect planet. But the Nutopians are watching *them*, and decide to kidnap the Earthlings using their travel transmitter.

Director: David Elliott

Robert to the Rescue

w Dennis Spooner
Steve, Mat and Venus are imprisoned on an Unknown Planet by two Domeheads, Magar and Proton, who propose to wipe their Earth memories and keep them there forever. Before his brainwashing begins Steve orders Robert to rescue them . . . Coming out of a trance later, the crew finds they are bound for home, but remember nothing.

Director: Bill Harris

Dangerous Cargo

w Dennis Spooner
On a mission to destroy an unstable ghost planet, Steve and Mat set the explosives, then find they've been trapped in a mineshaft by Subterrains. With the seconds ticking away, they struggle to escape before the planet blasts into a blazing inferno.

Director: John Kelly

Mystery of the TA2

w Dennis Spooner
When the *Fireball* team finds the wreck of a spaceship that disappeared 48 years before, their search for the lost pilot, Col. Denton, leads them to Arctan where they discover Denton is living happily as king of the planet's Ice People.

Director: John Kelly

Drama at Space City

w Anthony Marriott
Jonathan Zero's midnight exploration of *Fireball XL5* turns into a terrifying adventure when Zoonie orders Robert to take off. Racing in pursuit, Cmdr. Zero and Lt. Ninety are horrified to see *XL5* on fire. Boarding the ship they find Jonathan out cold and Zoonie, also unconscious, but holding a fire extinguisher. The brave little Lazoon has saved the day.

Director: Alan Pattillo

1875

w Anthony Marriott
Mat Matic's new time machine whisks Steve, Venus and Commander Zero back to the Wild West of 1875, where Steve becomes a sheriff and Venus and Zero bank robbers! (This episode utilized leftovers from Anderson's puppet western *Four Feather Falls*.)

Director: Bill Harris

The Granatoid Tanks

w Alan Fennell
Scientists on a glass-surfaced planet radio for help when they are menaced by six Granatoid tanks. *Fireball XL5* responds but is powerless to halt the assault until a surprise stowaway, Ma Doughty, turns out to be wearing Plyton pearls—the only substance that can repel the Granatoids.

Director: Alan Pattillo

The Robot Freighter Mystery

w Alan Fennell
Steve Zodiac resorts to subterfuge to prove that an unscrupulous pair of space salvage contractors, the Briggs Brothers, are sabotaging robot supply freighters so that they can pick up the pieces.

Director: David Elliott

Whistle for Danger

w Dennis Spooner
A plant disease has wiped out all vegetation on the jungle planet Floran. *Fireball* explodes an Ellvium bomb to kill the disease and restore the plant life—but the inhabitants are suspicious and imprison Steve, Mat and Venus in a 100 ft. high tower.

Director: John Kelly

Trial by Robot

w Alan Fennell
Robots have vanished from four planets—and the disappearances are linked to visits by a famous robot scientist, Prof. Himber. Then Robert also goes missing, but Steve and Mat are prepared and follow their robot on a three-month journey to Planet 82 where they are captured and put on trial by the mad professor—ruler of his own robot race.

Director: Alan Pattillo

A Day in the Life of a Space General

w Alan Fennell
Lt. Ninety is promoted to general and his erratic commands trigger confusion and finally disaster as *XL5* crashes into Space City, setting it ablaze. What a nightmare . . . and that's just what poor old Lt. Ninety is having!

Director: David Elliott

Invasion Earth

w Dennis Spooner
A strange cloud hangs in the space sky and two *Fireball* craft sent to investigate explode with a blinding flash. *XL5*, returning to Space City, discovers that the cloud hides an alien invasion fleet poised to take over.

Director: Alan Pattillo

Faster Than Light

w Anthony Marriott
An out-of-control *Fireball* breaks the light barrier and the crew finds they have emerged in a sea of air.

Director: Bill Harris

The Day the Earth Froze

w Alan Fennell
Icemen from the ice planet Zavia work to destroy Earth by deflecting the sun's rays using a giant disc, so lowering the temperature and causing even the sea to freeze solid. After escaping from an ice jail, *Fireball*'s crew manage to destroy the deflector and the thermometer begins to rise again.

Director: David Elliott

The Fire Fighters

w Alan Fennell
Real fireballs are plunging to Earth, from a mysterious gas cloud. Steve and his crew must contain the cloud before it reaches the atmosphere. Their plan goes smoothly until a technical fault means Steve must complete the work by hand.

Director: John Kelly

Space City Special

w Dennis Spooner
Astronaut of the Year Steve Zodiac needs all his skills to talk Venus down after she takes over the controls of a supersonic airliner whose pilot has been sent into a trance by Subterrains. And it's awards all around as Venus and Mat pick up plaudits for bravery, service and courage.

Director: Alan Pattillo

Ghosts of Space

w Alan Fennell
A seemingly deserted planet . . . electric rocks . . . weird, poltergeist-like happenings . . . all part of a mystery that unravels after Steve takes a geologist to the Planet Electon.

Director: John Kelly

Hypnotic Sphere

w Alan Fennell
Steve, Venus and Prof. Matic are thrown into a trance by a mysterious sphere that has already immobilized a series of space tankers. Luckily, Robert the Robot is unaffected and, after saving the ship from disaster, provides the videotape clue that helps the *Fireball* crew defeat their evil assailant.

Director: Alan Pattillo

Sabotage

w Anthony Marriott
A neutron bomb planted aboard *XL5* is detonated by remote control. As the craft pitches helplessly, a sinister Gamma spaceship moves in to stun the crew with its gamma rays and "beams" them aboard the vessel.

Director: John Kelly

Space Magnet

w Anthony Marriott
Fireball XL5 becomes trapped in the powerful gravitational pull of the planet Magneton and the crew discover that its invisible inhabitants, "the Solars," are plotting to bring the Moon into their orbit.

Director: Bill Harris

THE FLASH

Action adventure series built around the DC Comics superhero. Barry Allen is your average mild-mannered American guy, with a steady career as a police chemist. One night his lab is hit by lightning and as sparks fly and chemicals zip around, Barry is transformed into the fastest man on Earth.

Donning a special red suit designed to withstand his high speeds, Barry becomes *The Flash*, Central City's latest weapon in the war against crime, while trying to keep his identity secret. His only confidante is research scientist Tina McGee, played by English actress Amanda Pays. Even his lab assistant Julio never figures who his boss is.

Opponents include a gang of motorcycle hoodlums, an invisible man, a super-crook called The Ghost, and scientists who want to clone him.

Inevitably, all this costumed crusading had a campy feel, but the special effects sequences of The Flash running at super speed were highly effective.

MAIN CAST
Barry Allen/The Flash John Wesley Shipp *Tina McGee* Amanda Pays
Julio Mendez Alex Desert

Based on the character created by: Gardner Fox, Harry Lampert
Executive producers: Danny Bilson, Paul Le Meo
22 color 60-minute episodes (pilot 120 minutes)

U.S. premiere: 20 September 1990
U.K. premiere: 8 May 1992
(Sky One)

THE FLYING NUN

Sister Bertrille joins Convent San Tanco in Puerto Rico and discovers that her new cornette can help her to fly, perhaps due to her naturally buoyant personality. (Landings are more of a problem.) Besides the flying, there are no fantasy elements . . . But watch carefully for two episodes written by acclaimed writer Harlan Ellison (who has penned such works as "The City on the Edge of Forever" for *Star Trek.*)

REGULAR CAST
Sister Bertrille Sally Field *Sister Jacqueline* Marge Redmond
Mother Superior Madeleine Sherwood *Carlos Ramirez* Alejandro Rey
Sister Sixto Shelley Morrison *Sister Ana* Linda Dangcil
Captain Gaspar Formento Vito Scotti (*Season Two*)
Marcello Manuel Padilla Jr. (*Season Three*)

Produced by Screen Gems, Inc.   82 color 30-minute episodes

FOREVER KNIGHT

Nick Knight, a 13th-century vampire, seeks to regain his mortality and rid himself of the vampire curse by embracing the mortal world. He takes his first step by joining the police force (night shift, of course). Serving as a homicide detective, he starts cleaning up the crime-ridden city with the help of his partner, Tracey Vetter. Assisting his quest for a cure is Dr. Natalie Lambert, the only mortal who knows his secret.

Despite a low budget, this Canadian production rounded up its share of followers during a brief late-night run on CBS before moving on to syndication.

REGULAR CAST
Nick Knight Geraint Wyn Davies *Captain Joe Reese* Blu Mankuma
Detective Tracey Vetter Lisa Ryder *Javier Vachon* Ben Bass
Lacroix Nigel Bennett *Dr. Natalie Lambert* Catherine Disher

Co-creator: Barney Cohen
Co-creator/Executive producer: James D. Parriott
Producer: Richard Borchiver

Supervising producer: Lionel E. Siegel
Executive producer: Jon Slan
71 color episodes

Episodes
Nick Knight (1989 Pilot)

Season One
Dark Knight (1992 pilot)
Dark Knight: The Second Chapter
For I Have Sinned
Last Act
Dance by the Light of the Moon
Dying to Know You
False Witness
Cherry Blossoms
I Will Repay
Dead Air
Hunters
Dead Issue
Father Figure
Spin Doctor
Dying for Fame
Only the Lonely
Unreality TV
Feeding the Beast
To Die For/If Looks Could Kill
Fatal Mistake
1966
Love You to Death

Season Two
Killer Instinct
A Fate Worse Than Death
Stranger Than Fiction
Bad Blood
Forward into the Past
Capital Offense
Hunted
Faithful Followers
Undue Process
Father's Day
Can't Run, Can't Hide

Near Death
Crazy Love
Baby, Baby
Partners of the Month
The Fire Inside
Amateur Night
The Fix
Curiouser and Curiouser
Beyond the Law
Queen of Harps
Close Call
Be My Valentine
The Code
A More Permanent Hell
Blood Money

Season Three
Black Buddha (Part 1)
Black Buddha (Part 2)
Outside the Lines
Blackwing
Blind Faith
My Boyfriend Is a Vampire
Hearts of Darkness
Trophy Girl
Let No Man Tear Asunder
Night in Question
Sons of Belial
Strings
Fever
Dead of Night
Games Vampires Play
Human Factor
Avenging Angel
Fallen Idol
Jane Doe
Ashes to Ashes
Francesca
Last Knight

GALACTICA 1980

Hastily produced sequel to *Battlestar Galactica*, this series was voted third worst science fiction show of all time by American critics.

The premise was straightforward. Having fled from the robot Cylon race that destroyed their homeworlds at the start of the original series, the Battlestar fleet reaches Earth after a 30-year odyssey with the Cylons still dogging their trail. Joy at finding the home of their long-lost 13th tribe turns to dismay when they realize Earth is not sufficiently advanced to help them repel the Cylon hordes. Determined not to expose the planet to the robot warriors, the Galacticans decide to try to speed up Earth's technology. A sub-plot involved a group of Galactican children on Earth, with an air force colonel trying his darnedest to prove they were aliens, and there was a brief flurry of Cylon conflict before the series fizzled out.

Lorne Greene recreated his role as Adama, avuncular commander of the *Galactica*, and there were a couple of new space heroes in Kent McCord as the untempestuous Troy (Adama's grown-up grandson), and Barry Van Dyke as his impulsive pal Dillon. Also hanging around was TV reporter Jamie Hamilton (Robyn Douglass) who became the only Earthling to board the *Galactica*. Villainy was taken care of by Richard Lynch and then Jeremy (Sherlock Holmes) Brett as the renegade Xavier. Masterminding the new campaign was a mysterious boy wonder, Dr. Zee, a 14-year-old genius whose origins were belatedly revealed in the last episode.

In America, ABC had wanted *Galactica 1980* produced quickly to fill a gap in early evening schedules, so the shows were tailored to a "family" audience. Violence was toned down and morality/educational angles played up. But the critics were cruel and the audiences unreceptive. Battlestar fans deserted the ship, which sank in the ratings. Even a late re-entry by Dirk Benedict (later Face in *The A-Team*), to re-create his *Battlestar Galactica* role of Starbuck, failed to save the show, which was scuppered after just ten episodes.

MAIN CAST

Commander Adama Lorne Greene *Capt. Troy* Kent McCord
Lt. Dillon Barry Van Dyke *Jamie Hamilton* Robyn Douglass
Dr. Zee Robbie Rist *(Galactica Discovers Earth)* Patrick Stuart *(all other episodes)*
Col. Boomer Herb Jefferson Jr.   *Col. Sydell* Alan Miller
Brooks Fred Holliday *Xavier* Richard Lynch, Jeremy Brett *(Spaceball)*

Creator/Executive producer: Glen A. Larson
Theme: Stu Phillips, Glen Larson
Director of photography: Frank P. Beascoechea
Miniatures and special photography: Universal Hartland, *supervisors* David M. Garber, Wayne Smith

ABC TV Production in association with Glen A. Larson Productions and Universal MCA Ltd.
10 color 60-minute episodes
U.S. premiere: 27 January 1980
U.K. premiere: 1 September–20 October 1984 (Seven episodes*)
(Grampian)

Galactica Discovers Earth

w Glen A. Larson *(a 3-part story)***
Finding Earth ill equipped to meet the Cylon menace, the Galacticans dispatch teams to try to speed up its technological advance. Troy and Dillon become entangled with newsgirl Jamie Hamilton who tags along when they are recalled to the *Galactica* where renegade Xavier, impatient with the slow progress, has decided to use time travel to bestow Galactican secrets on an earlier Earth generation. Unwisely he plumps for Nazi Germany so Troy, Dillon and Jamie pursue him back in time.
Gen. Cushing Richard Eastham
Prof. Mortinson Robert Reed
Carlyle Pamela Susan Shoop
Willy Brion James
Sheriff Ted Gehring
German commander Curt Lowens
Stockwell Christopher Stone

Director: Sidney Hayers

The Super Scouts

w Glen A. Larson *(a 2-part story)*
A surprise Cylon attack forces Troy and Dillon to take a group of Galactican children to Earth where they pose as a scout troop on a camping trip. But three of the kids become critically ill after drinking polluted water and with Air Force Col. Sydell's net closing in, Adama and Dr. Zee must stage an emergency rescue mission.
Stockton Mike Kellin
Sheriff Ellsworth John Quade
Spencer George Deloy
Nurse Valerie Carlene Watkins
Moonstone Eric Larson
Starla Michelle Larson
Jason Eric Taslitz

Director: Vince Edwards

Spaceball

w Frank Lupo, Jeff Freilich, Glen A. Larson
Treacherous Xavier, now in disguise (as Jeremy Brett!) sends Troy and Dillon on a phony mission in a sabotaged Viper spacecraft, so that he can kidnap the earthbound Galactican children. However, they're taken by Jamie Hamilton to a baseball camp for underprivileged kids where, with both Xavier and Col. Sydell waiting to pounce, they play ball . . . Galactican style!
Hal Bert Rosario
Billy Paul Koslo
Tommy Wayne Morton
Stratton Trent Dolan
Red Bill Molloy

Director: Barry Crane

*Until the BBC's run in 1988, all ITV regional runs began with Episode 4, "The Super Scouts."
**First shown in the U.K. on 7 May 1984 as a TV movie, *Conquest on Earth*, which combined the first part of this story with footage from the later episodes, "The Night the Cylons Landed" and "So This Is New York." The three original first episodes were finally shown in their "proper" form in the BBC's run (17–31 March 1988).

The Night the Cylons Landed

w Glen A. Larson
A Cylon craft, damaged by a Galactican Viper, crashes on America's East Coast. Luckily for its survivors, lookalike humanoid Andromus and Centurion Andromidus, it's Halloween and they have *no* trouble blending in. While Troy and Dillon pursue them, the Cylon duo plots to take over a New York radio station and call up the Cylon fleet.
Andromus Roger Davis
Norman William Daniels
Col. Briggs Peter Mark Richman
Shirley Lara Parker
Andromidus Neil Zevnik

Director: Sig Neufeld

So This Is New York

w Glen A. Larson
Troy and Dillon don tuxedos for an onstage dance with a star, elude Central Park thugs and rescue a girl trapped in a blaze started by the Cylons who've been hanging out at a media costume party. But can they stop the Cylon pair broadcasting to their hostile space fleet?
Guest cast as previous episode plus:
Arnie Val Bisoglio
Mildred Marj Dusay
Star Heather Young
Himself Wolfman Jack

Director: Barry Crane

Space Croppers (aka Harvest Home)

w Robert L. McCullogh
Desperate to replenish the space fleet's food supplies after a Cylon attack destroys their farm ship, Troy and Dillon team up with a farmer who faces his own threat—from a powerful land baron. Dealing with that *and* getting the crop planted calls for a little help from their friends in space . . .
Hector Ned Romero
Steadman Dana Elcar
Trent Bill Cort
Louise Anna Navarro
Gloria Ana Alicia
Maze Andy Jarrell
Barrett Bill McKinney

Director: Daniel Haller

The Return of Starbuck

w Glen. A Larson
The fate of space warrior Lt. Starbuck is revealed in a vivid dream of teenage genius Dr. Zee in which Starbuck crashes on a desolate planet where he reassembles a Cylon robot for company and encounters a mysterious (and pregnant) woman. When his story is told, Dr. Zee finally learns the truth about the identity of the woman's baby.
Starbuck Dirk Benedict
Centurion Rex Cutter
Angela Judith Chapman

Director: Ron Satlof

GALLOPING GALAXIES!

Wacky space comedy from the team behind *Rentaghost*, Bob Block and Jeremy Swan. Set in the 25th century, it followed the interplanetary merchant ship *Voyager* as it boldly went through asteroid belts, time warps and black holes, supposedly under the control of SID (Space Investigation Detector), a bossy computer.

Manning the spaceship was a crew of three—Captain Pettifer, Second Officer Morton and Communications Officer Webster (replaced in Season Two by Mr. Elliott), who were joined by an assortment of odd aliens and by Miss Mabel Appleby who arrived by accident after a time-warp wobble. They were pursued by a notorious space pirate and his disintegrating robots.

REGULAR CAST
Voices of SID and Junior Kenneth Williams *Capt. Pettifer* Robert Swales
Second Officer Morton Paul Wilce
Communications Officer Webster Nigel Cooke *(Season One only)*
Mabel Appleby Priscilla Morgan *Elsie Appleby* Josie Kidd
Space Pirate Chief Murphy Sean Caffrey *(Season One)*,
Niall Buggy *(Season Two)*
Robot 7 Michael Deeks *Robot 20* Matthew Sim
Robot 35 Julie Dawn Cole *Dinwiddy Snurdle* James Bree
Mr. Elliott James Mansfield *(Season Two only)*

Creator and writer: Bob Block
Producer: Jeremy Swan
Designers: Alan Spalding, Nick Somerville
  (Season One), John Ashbridge, Jonathan
  Taylor *(Season Two)*
Music: Jonathan Cohen

A BBC Production
10 color 25-minute episodes
1–29 October 1985
20 November–18 December 1986
(BBC1)

GEMINI MAN

This 1976 pilot and subsequent one-season series were an attempt to turn an invisible flop into a visible success.

Ben Murphy (alias wisecracking outlaw Kid Curry from *Alias Smith & Jones*) starred as Sam Casey, an investigator for a government organization called Intersect. During an underwater salvage operation he is caught in a radiation explosion that alters his body's molecular structure. Casey can now disappear at will—a knack exploited by his no-nonsense boss Leonard Driscoll who turns him into his new secret agent, assigned to such tasks as guarding an Olympic swimmer, driving a truckload of chemicals and fighting a mad scientist's computerized robot.

But there is a catch. Casey can stay invisible for a total of just 15 minutes each day. If he miscalculates and allows his brief moments out of sight to add up to more than that in any 24-hour period, he will vanish for good.

Presumably someone, somewhere wasn't counting, because the *Gemini Man* did disappear after just one season.

It was produced by Harve Bennett, who was also responsible for *The Six Million Dollar Man* and *The Bionic Woman*.

REGULAR CAST
Sam Casey Ben Murphy *Dr. Abigail Lawrence* Katherine Crawford
Leonard Driscoll Richard Dysart *(in pilot)/*William Sylvester

Executive producer: Harve Bennett
Writer/Producer: Leslie Stevens *(pilot)*
Director: Alan J. Levi *(pilot)*

A Harve Bennett Production in association with Universal TV and NBC TV
11 color 50-minute episodes (pilot 95 minutes)
Codename: Minus One (pilot)
Smithereens
Minotaur
Sam Casey, Sam Casey
Night Train to Dallas

Run, Sam, Run
Targets
Buffalo Bill Rides Again
Escape Hatch
8, 9, 10—You're Dead
Return of the Lion
Suspect Your Local Police

U.S. premiere: 23 September 1976 (series)
U.K.: 12 October–28 December 1976
(BBC1)

GENE RODDENBERRY'S
EARTH: FINAL CONFLICT

Three years ago, Earth started picking up radio transmissions: "People of Earth, we are here to help. People of Earth, we are the Companions."

Seventy-one aliens calling themselves Taelons or "Companions" arrived and established diplomatic relations with every major world capital. They offered their vast knowledge of science and technology to help us solve our most oppressive problems. Famine became a thing of the past. Global divisions waned. They quickly became an invaluable resource.

However, a small group of individuals refuse to believe the Companions are as good as they claim and have organized an underground resistance. They managed to infiltrate the Companions' circle of human aides with one of their own, William Boone. As Head of Interspecies Relations, Boone is implanted with the Taelon technology and comes to play a pivotal role in the resistance.

Based on a number of completed scripts by Gene Roddenberry—who quit work on this project to concentrate on launching the syndicated *Star Trek: The Next Generation* and never took it up again—*Earth: Final Conflict* offers many of the same humanist themes found in *Star Trek*. Since it has become the highest-rated new syndicated science fiction program, expect it to be around for quite a few seasons to come.

REGULAR CAST

William Boone Kevin Kilner *Lili Marquette* Lisa Howard
Da'an Leni Parker *Ronald Sandoval* Von Flores
Augur Richard Chevolleau *Jonathan Doors* David Hemblen
Dr. Julianne Belman Majel Barrett Roddenberry

Creator: Gene Roddenberry
Executive producers: David Kirschner, Majel Barrett Roddenberry, Seaton Mclean, Rick Okie
Co-executive producer: Paul Gertz
Producer: John Calvert
Producer/Production designer: Stephen Roloff

An Atlantis Films Production in association with Tribune Entertainment and Roddenberry/Kirchner Productions
U.S. premiere: 6 October 1997

Season One

Decision

w Gene Roddenberry
After the death of his wife, police captain William Boone is recruited by the Companions to serve as Commander of Security and Interspecies Relations—then secretly drafted to join the human resistance movement.
Kwai-Ling Miranda Kwok
Kate Lisa Ryder
Corr Michael Filipowich
Ed Jordan Paul Boretski

Director: Allan Eastman

Truth

w Richard C. Okie *&* Raymond Hartung
Boone doggedly pursues his wife's murderer, determined to find out if Da'an or the underground resistance ordered her execution.
Kwai-Ling Miranda Kwok
Morovsky John Evans
Kate Lisa Ryder
Corr Michael Filipowich
Dee Dee Shari-Lee Guthrie
Dan Spicer Chad Mcfadden

Director: Allan Eastman

Miracle

w D.C. Fontana
When her hands are regenerated by Taelon technology, a young woman becomes a pawn in a power

play between the Companions and a charismatic religious leader.
Julie Emily Hampshire
Ne'eg Janet Zenik
Travis Murray Peter Krantz

Director: David Warry-Smith

Avatar

w Malcolm Macrury
A serial killer with a Taelon implant tries to kill Da'an while acting out an ancient Taelon myth about good conquering evil.
Clifton Samuel Marvin Kaye
James Pike Richard Mcmillan
Prison guard Patrick Gallagher
Warden Cole Peter Macneill
Dr. Kaplan Hrant Alianak

Director: Jeff Woolnough

Old Flame

w Paul Gertz
Boone's double-agent cover is put to the test when a long-lost love resurfaces in his life, claiming to be working against the Companions.
Elyse Colette Stevenson
Ramon Matt Birman
Ainsley Lloyd Adams
Peter Danny Lima

Director: Ken Girotti

Float Like a Butterfly

w Paul Gertz
Boone and Lili visit a small Amish town to investigate the mysterious deaths of several citizens.
Jedediah Trevor Blumas
Samuel Andrew Dinner
Rachel Good Haley Lochner
Elijah Good Brett Porter
Amos Richard Denison
Lucas Ed Fielding
Sarah Brenda Bazinet
Jacob Steven Bush
Abraham George Dawson

Director: Jeff Woolnough

Resurrection

w Paul Gertz
Jonathan Doors launches a media attack against the Taelons—and leaves Boone to deal with the ramifications.
Zo'or Anita La Selva
Pieter Bakker Robert Dodds
Bettor Matt Gordon
Bud Lanier Jeffrey Knight
Cynthia Clarkson Kristin Lehman
Anne Portnoy Laura Press
Agent Price J. Craig Sandy

Director: Milian Cheylov

Horizon Zero

w Richard C. Okie
When the Companions cancel a manned mission to Mars, astronauts steal a Taelon shuttle to get there on their own.
Paul Chandler Bobby Johnston
Philip Hart Andrew Lewarne
Frauke Manheim Angela Asher
General Kromer Neil Dainard
Newscaster Sandra Caldwell

Director: David Warry-Smith

Scorpion's Dream

w Harry Doc Kloor
When a deadly weapon bioengineered by the Taelons is stolen, Boone must find it before it's used against them.
Larry Clark Jonathan Potts
Janice Claudette Mink
Dr. Basi Sugith Varughese
Nickel Joe Roncetti
Security guard Ken Girotti

Director: Ken Girotti

Live Free or Die

w Malcolm Macrury
Da'an is kidnapped and held for ransom by a group of renegade soldiers who claim the Taelons used their unit for bioengineering experiments, then abandoned them.
Major Ray Mcintyre Nigel Bennett
Captain Lucas Johnson Maurice Dean Wint

Director: David Warry-Smith

The Scarecrow Returns

w Paul Gertz
The resistance tries to unlock the secrets of an alien probe that has been gathering information on Earth.
Sahjit Jinnah Damon D'oliveira
Rayna Armitraj Sonia Dhillon

Director: David Warry-Smith

Sandoval's Run

w Paul Aitken
When Sandoval's implant malfunctions, he is freed from Taelon mind control—but it's going to kill him if it isn't fixed.
Dee Dee Shary-Lee Guthrie
Dr. Sharpe Diana Belshaw
Nell Hagar T.I. Forsberg

Director: Milan Cheylov

The Secret of Strandhill

w George Carson
When an ancient grave in Ireland reveals surprising secrets, Boone and Sandoval are dispatched by Da'an to investigate.
Zo'or Anita La Selva
Siobhan Beckett Kari Matchett
O'Malley Chris Wiggins
Ma'el Leni Parker

Director: Gordon Langevin

Pandora's Box

w Malcolm Macrury
When an ancient alien evil is brought to Earth, a Taelon experiment ends in disaster.
Zo'or Leni Parker
Rho-Ha Anita La Selva
Maj. Ray Mcintyre Nigel Bennett
Capt. Lucas Johnson Maurice Dean Wint

Director: Tibor Takacs

If You Could Read My Mind

w Paul Gertz *&* Julie G. Beers
A human psychic intrudes on the Companions' mental plane. Da'an tries to find her; Boone falls in love with her; the underground wants to use her; and everyone else wants her dead.
Katya Petrenko Shauna Macdonald
Judson Corr Michael Filipowich
Zo'or Anita La Selva
Quo'on Leni Parker
Madam Marie Norma Clarke

Director: Milan Cheylov

The Wrath of Achilles

w Damian Kindler
Auger creates a computer virus that escapes and threatens the Taelons' existence on Earth.
Agent Lassiter Peter Kelly Gaudreault

Director: Stephen Williams

Not aired as of press time:
The Devil You Know
Law & Order
Through the Looking Glass
Infection
Destruction
The Joining

GET SMART

Spoofs don't come much funnier than this Emmy award–winning sixties series, which sent up the whole spy genre of its day.

Created by comic writers Mel Brooks and Buck Henry, *Get Smart* starred Don Adams as Agent 86, Maxwell Smart, a willing but inept secret agent working for Washington-based U.S. intelligence agency C.O.N.T.R.O.L., which was headed by The Chief, Thaddeus.

With the aid of his beautiful and brilliant partner, Agent 99, dog Fang, robot Hymie and fellow operative Agent 13, Max strove tirelessly to defeat the forces of K.A.O.S., an organization led by evil mastermind Siegfried and his assistant Starker, who, not surprisingly, wanted to rule the world. *Get Smart* abounded with witty gags and one-liners and gave the world the catchphrase "Would you believe . . .?" uttered by Max whenever his first excuse wasn't accepted.

But the series also featured a remarkable line in gadgetry, which more than warrants its inclusion in this collection. Radio transmitters turned up all over the place—Max had a phone in his shoe—and there was a sandwich phone, a short-wave table tennis bat, a coffee and doughnut transmitter and an ice-cream cone phone. Other oddities included a miniature torpedo hammer, an electronic mosquito anti-personnel device, a remote-control doorknob, a vase bazooka and bullet-proof pyjamas. And, of course, there was the Cone of Silence. When Max wanted to hold a private conversation with The Chief, two glass bell jars would descend over them, linked by a tube making their speech inaudible.

Get Smart ran for five seasons and 138 episodes (all but the very first were in color). Romance between Max and Agent 99 led to their marriage and the birth of twins, a boy and a girl.

The eighties saw a brace of TV movie revivals, *The Nude Bomb* (aka *The Return of Maxwell Smart*) in 1980, and *Get Smart Again!* (1988), the latter reuniting most of the series' main cast, with the notable exception of Edward Platt (The Chief) who had died.

Main Cast
Maxwell Smart, Agent 86 Don Adams *Agent 99* Barbara Feldon
Thaddeus, The Chief Edward Platt *Agent 13* Dave Ketchum
Hymie the Robot Dick Gautier *Agent 44* Victor French
Conrad Siegfried Bernie Kopell *Starker* King Moody
Larrabee Robert Karvelas
With: *Carlson* Stacy Keach *99's mother* Jane Dulo

Creators: Mel Brooks, Buck Henry
Executive producer: Leonard B. Stern
Producers: Arne Sultan, Mel Brooks, Jesse Oppenheimer
Writers: Various, including Mel Brooks, Buck Henry, Stan Burns, Mike Marmer, Gerald Gardner, Dee Caruso
Directors: Various, including Richard Donner, Don Richardson, Bruce Bilson, Jerry Hopper, Don Adams

Music composed and conducted by Irving Szathmany

TA/Norton Simon Inc. Production
138 30-minute episodes (all color, except the first)
U.S. premiere: 18 September 1965
U.K.: 1966–1970
(BBC1)

THE GIRL FROM TOMORROW

Australian adventure series about a curious teenager from the year 3000 who gets trapped in 1990.

The series opens in the far future, a calm and contemplative age. Like any other 13-year-old, Alana devotes her time and energies to such consciousness-raising exercises as honing her kinetic powers with the aid of a headband device called a transducer. Life's pretty good. Showers work without water and clothes can be cleaned in seconds.

Alana's mother is part of a time-travel team researching the ecologically ravaged 26th century. Alana sneaks into the lab to see her mother return from a trip into the past with a ruthless renegade called Silverthorn. He overpowers his captors and seizes Alana, escaping with her into the time machine, which is catapulted back to the 20th century.

Waking up on a Sydney rubbish dump, Alana is alone, frightened and bewildered by the noise and pollution. Luckily, she gets befriended by Jenny, a rebellious, purple-haired teenager, her mum, Irene, and sci-fi-obsessed kid brother, Petey, who immediately suspects Alana is an alien. There's plenty of culture shock humor as Alana goes to Jenny's school and tries to adjust to 20th-century customs, while facing a race against time to find Silverthorn and the time machine before it returns, automatically, to her own time.

In the last confrontation, Jenny is critically injured and Alana takes her back to the future to cure her, setting up a sequel series, *Tomorrow's End*. This sees Alana and Jenny going back to Silverthorn's time to try to stop him from causing a catastrophe that will destroy the future.

MAIN CAST
Alana Katherine Cullen   *Jenny* Melissa Marshall   *Petey* James Findlay
Irene Helen O'Connor   *James* Andrew Clarke   *Silverthorn* John Howard
Eddie Miles Buchanan   *Tulisa* Helen Jones   *Arva* Pauline Chan
Bruno Monroe Reimers
Series Two only: Lorien Catherine McClements   *Draco* Marshall Napier
Vance Paul Sonkkila   *Macro* Andrew Windsor
With: Jeremy Scrivener, Connie Gower, Martin Reefman, Anna Maria Monticelli

Writers: Mark Shirrefs, John Thomson (*Series One*), Mark Shirrefs, *story by* Mark Shirrefs, John Thomson (*Series Two*)
Executive producer: Ron Saunders
Producer: Noel Price
Director: Kathy Mueller (*Series One*), Noel Price (*Series Two*)
Music: Nicholas McCallum

Australian Film Foundation/Film Australia Production
Series One:
12 color 25-minute episodes
3 May–19 July 1991
Series Two:
12 color 25-minute episodes
13 July–20 August 1993
(BBC1)

GOODNIGHT SWEETHEART

A TV repair man of the nineties walks down a London alley and suddenly finds himself back in 1940. He's not wreathed in a blue light, or sucked into a swirling vortex. In fact, there's no tangible evidence of temporal distortion or a rip in the space-time continuum. He just walks down an alley and winds up back in wartime London. It's time travel, but not as we know it.

Only Fools and Horses star Nicholas Lyndhurst stars in this engaging sitcom from *Birds of a Feather* creators Laurence Marks and Maurice Gran, as TV engineer Gary Sparrow, married to a woman who's rapidly losing patience with his feeble attempts to better himself. His forties world becomes an escape from the modern world. Back there, Sparrow gets involved with Phoebe, a publican's married daughter, and he shuttles back and forth in time between his two loves.

Culture clash humor flows as Sparrow orders broccoli quiche in the 1940 pub and explains his modern manner by claiming he's from America, while singing Elton John songs and dropping knowing hints about the war. Mostly, though, it's a romantic comedy. And that's about it, really. A second series followed in spring 1995, and a third in winter/spring 1996.

MAIN CAST
Gary Sparrow Nicholas Lyndhurst   *Yvonne Sparrow* Michelle Holmes
Phoebe Dervla Kirwan   *Eric* David Ryall   *Ron* Victor McGuire
PC Deadman Christopher Ettridge   *Donald* Ben Lobb (Season One only)

Creators: Laurence Marks, Maurice Gran

Series One
6 color 30-minute episodes

Rites of Passage
Fools Rush In
Is Your Journey Really Necessary
The More I See You
I Get Along Without You Very Well
In the Mood

18 November–23 December 1993
(BBC1)

Series Two
10 color 30-minute episodes

Don't Get Around Much Anymore
I Got It Bad and That Ain't Good
Just One More Chance
Who's Taking You Home Tonight?
Wish Me Luck
As You Wave Me Goodbye
Would You Like To Swing on a Star?
Nice Work If You Can Get It

Let Yourself Go
Don't Fence Me In

20 February–1 May 1995
(BBC1)

Series Three:
11 color 30-minute episodes

Between the Devil and the Deep Blue Sea
It Ain't Necessarily So
One O'Clock Jump
It's a Sin to Tell a Lie
Change Partners
Goodnight Children, Everywhere
Turned Out Nice Again
There's Something About a Soldier
Someone to Watch Over Me
The Yanks Are Coming
Let's Get Away from It All

26 December 1995–4 March 1996
(BBC1)

THE GREATEST AMERICAN HERO

Curly-haired high school teacher Ralph Hinkley is on a desert field trip with his class of disobedient misfits, when their bus breaks down. Ralph goes for help and is nearly run over by FBI agent Bill Maxwell who is looking for his missing partner, unaware that he has been murdered by a group of bald-headed religious fanatics. As Ralph and Bill talk, a huge UFO appears and beams down a ghostly replica of the dead agent who presents them with a red flying suit that grants its special wearer (Ralph) the power to become invisible, and have X-ray vision and long-distance sight. Naturally, Ralph loses the instruction manual . . .

I Spy star Robert Culp co-starred as the neurotic FBI agent who convinces Ralph to use the suit and powers to fight crime—despite his fear of heights—and Connie Selleca played his attorney girlfriend. They later married. Other characters include Kevin, Ralph's son by a former marriage, and Tony and Rhonda, kids in Ralph's high school class.

The series ran from 1981–83 in America where, for some first-season episodes, Ralph's surname was changed to Hanley to avoid confusion with the Hinckley who tried to assassinate Reagan.

A pilot was also made in 1986, for a sequel series, *The Greatest American Heroine*, in which the aliens decide to give Ralph's suit to someone else and get Ralph to find his replacement—Holley Hathaway, a day school worker dedicated to making the world a better place. The series was never made.

REGULAR CAST
Ralph Hinkley William Katt   *Bill Maxwell* Robert Culp
Pam Davidson Connie Selleca
With: Tony Villicana Michael Pare   *Rhonda Blake* Faye Grant
Agent Carlisle William Bogert   *Kevin Hinkley* Brandon Williams
Mrs. Davidson June Lockhart

Creator: Stephen J. Cannell
Executive producers: Stephen J. Cannell, Juanita Bartlett, Jo Swerkling, Jr.
Theme: Mike Post, Stephen Geyer
Sung by: Joey Scarbury
Writers: Various, including Stephen J. Cannell, Juanita Bartlett, Patrick Burke Hasburgh, Frank Lupo, Robert Culp

Directors: Various, including Rod Holcomb, Gabrielle Beaumont, Arnold Laven, Ivan Dixon, Bruce Kessler, Chuck Bowman, Robert Culp

43 color 30-minute episodes (pilot two hours)
U.S. premiere: 18 March 1981

THE GUARDIANS

Television has frequently embraced the "what if?" strand of science fiction to offer ideas about the kind of society the future might hold. *The Guardians* was such a series.

A political thriller, it unraveled an uncomfortable scenario for a not-too-distant future. After a general strike, galloping inflation, massive unemployment and the failure of a coalition government, England is run by a committee of dedicated experts and their sinister paramilitary police, The Guardians.

Peace and order have been restored from the chaos. But the price exacted is a high one—individual freedom. The 13-part series followed the growing conflict between those representing order and those dedicated to its overthrow who adopted the name of their unseen leader Quarmby.

Among the leading characters were Tom Weston, a Guardian officer who becomes a pawn in the struggle between resistance and government; his wife, Clare; Dr. Benedict, a psychiatrist who emerges as one of the leading rebels; Sir Timothy Hobson, the prime minister, and his son, Christopher; and Norman, a sinister and powerful civil servant.

The Guardians was welcomed by most critics as entertaining and thought-provoking, raising questions about the nature of democracy and suggesting, in the end, the idea that self-government is better than "strong" government.

MAIN CAST
Tom Weston John Collin   *Clare Weston* Gwyneth Powell
Sir Timothy Hobson Cyril Luckham
Christopher Hobson Edward Petherbridge
Dr. Benedict David Burke   *Norman* Derek Smith
Eleanor Lynn Farleigh

Creators: Rex Firkin, Vincent Tilsley
Producer: Andrew Brown
Theme: Wilfred Josephs

London Weekend Television Production
13 color 60-minute episodes
10 July–2 October 1971

The State of England

w Vincent Tilsley
The Guardians have brought order to the land. But the people, oppressed by the new regime, begin to react. Dissenters appear.
First worker Windsor Davies
Peter Lee Robin Ellis
Receptionist Patricia Dermott
First minister Garth Watkins

Director: Robert Tronson
Designer: Colin Pigott

Pursuit

w Hugh Whitemore
As the Prime Minister, Sir Timothy Hobson, is leaving a Cabinet meeting, he narrowly avoids an assassin's bullet, and is rushed to safety by a squad of Guardians.
Assassin Peter Hutchins
Newscaster Michael Smee
Interrogator Richard Kane
Sir Francis Wainwright Richard Hurndall

Director: James Goddard
Designer: Colin Pigott

Head of State

w John Bowen
An embarrassing diplomatic situation develops when the French president, due in London for important defense talks, refuses to come unless he meets the true Head of State. But who is *really* in charge?
Geoff Hollis Peter Howell
Bullmore John Bryans
Felicien de Bastion André Maranne
Cockney Guardian Stephen Yardley
Birmingham Guardian Ray Lonnen
General Kenneth Benda

Director: Robert Tronson
Designer: John Emery

The Logical Approach

w John Bowen
Using his skill and acumen, Sir Timothy Hobson finally usurps power and becomes an effective rather than a nominal prime minister.
Gary Wilson Jimmy Ray
Paula Hollis Monica Grey
Steve Brian Deacon

Lady Sarah Mary Merrall
Sam Wilson Ken Jones
Quarmby William Simons

Director: Tony Wharmby
Designer: Bryan Bagge

Quarmby

w John Bowen
After the stabbing of Hollis, the Home Secretary, an immediate investigation is made by the PM and Norman to discover who shot the murderer, Sam Wilson. It reveals that the shot came from a hidden sniper. But who is the mastermind behind the killings?
Miss Quarmby Joan Heal
Detective David Cook
CID officer Geoffrey Morris
M15 officer Leon Eagles
Capt. Gerald Barclay Laurence Carter
Peter Petra Davies

Director: Robert Tronson
Designer: John Emery

Appearances

w Monty Poole
Having killed a detective in cold blood, Benedict now turns back to the routine business of causing chaos for the Guardians and the government.
Dr. Thorn Dinsdale Landen
Dr. Banks Richard Moore
Man in clock shop Derrick Gilbert
Jordan Martin Fisk
Miss Quarmby Joan Heal
Newscaster Michael Smee

Director: Mike Newell
Designer: Andrew Drummond

This Is Quarmby

w Arden Winch
Quarmby has struck many times against the regime with bomb attacks and assassinations. But now the resistors launch a new campaign to get their message across, reaching the man in the street and confusing Norman and the Guardians.
Dace Richard Vernon
Gibb Robert Russell
TV presenter Christine Shaw
First Guardian John Rhys-Davies

Director: Brian Parker
Designer: Bryan Bagge

The Dirtiest Man in the World

w John Bowen

Guardians officer Tom Weston is still "confined" to the rehabilitation center and making no effort to escape. Benedict sees his value as a pawn in the struggle against the government and the Guardians but must encourage him to break out.
Dirtiest man Graham Crowden
Quarmby Peter Barkworth
Male nurse Ian Stirling

Director: Derek Bailey
Designer: Frank Nerini

I Want You to Understand Me

w John Bowen

Hobson's government is stronger than ever, with the Guardians clamping down on personal freedom. But the more repressive their measures, the more ruthless the resistance becomes.
Det. Sgt. Arnold Robert Morris
Paul Michael Culver
Jenny Ann Curthoys
Andy Christopher Martin
Barbara Barbara Ewing
Bob John White
Henryson Norman Bird
Ernest Fred McNaughton
Major Raymond Adamson
Quarmby Artro Morris

Director: Robert Tronson
Designer: John Emery

The Nature of the Beast

w Jonathan Hales

Clare has problems. Her husband, Tom, now a drug addict, is still at large and being hunted by the Guardians. She turns to Benedict for help, but he plans to use Tom as a scapegoat for Quarmby.
Young Guardian lieutenant Nikolas Simmonds
Guardian private Richard Borthwick
Barry Anthony Bate
Carole Pamela Roland
First man Jonathan Hales
Barbara Hilda Kriseman

Director: Mike Newell
Designer: Andrew Drummond

The Roman Empire

w John Bowen

Dissatisfaction with Hobson's government is spreading—from sinister events in public to unrest and plotting in the Cabinet.
Ruth Elizabeth Adare
Patience Kathleen Michael
Hobbs James Grout
Industrialist Keneth Thornett
Steve John Rapley
Announcer Richard Grant
Major Eric McCaine
Insp. Arnold Robert Morris
Whittaker Brian Worth
Hawkins Brian Badcoe

Director: Moira Armstrong
Designer: Colin Pigott

The Killing Trade

w Jonathan Hales

Tom is still lying in a coma at Benedict's flat. Every hour he remains there means increased danger for the others if the Guardians discover him. So Quarmby must dispose of Tom. (No guest cast.)

Director: Derek Bailey
Designer: Bryan Bagge

End in Dust

w John Bowen

No one in England is safe anymore—not even the disillusioned PM. The Guardians have not been disbanded and Quarmby terrorists continue their attacks. As conflict grows inside and outside the Cabinet the stage is set for a showdown. But where does Norman stand? Who will Chris Hobson side with?
Sgt. Arnold Robert Morris

Director: Robert Tronson
Designer: John Emery

HALFWAY ACROSS THE GALAXY AND TURN LEFT

Any series that can come up with a title like that has to have something going for it, and this comedy adventure from Australia proved a summer hit with young fans in 1994.

Made by the producers of *The Flying Doctors*, it followed the fortunes of a family from the planet Zyrgon who are forced to flee after their father is found to have fiddled the state lottery for the 27th time. Escaping the evil clutches of the Law Enforcer, with a handsome space pilot, Lox, their only directions are to go "halfway across the galaxy and turn left."

That, of course, brings them neatly to our primitive planet where, as they try to fit in to their new community, things get chaotic, as the family can't help being conspicuous just by acting naturally.

Based on a novel by children's writer Robin Klein, the series explored several role reversals. The youngest daughter, X, is the leader and organizer, the children expect obedience from their parents, Dad does the cooking and Mum is the bread-winner.

MAIN CAST
X Lauren Hewett *Qwrk* Jeffrey Walker *Dovis* Silvia Seidel *Father* Bruce Myles
Mother Jan Friedl *Jenny* Kellie Smythe *Colin* Che Broadbent
Froggatt Denis Moore *Mrs. Froggatt* Ellen Cressey *Andrew* Brandon McLean
Shane Michael Walsh *Michelle* Tenley Gillmore *Dallas* Katrina Lambert
Lox Paul Kelman *Voice of Dovis* Amanda Douge

Executive producer: Terry Ohlsson
Producer: Jan Marnell
Director: Brendan Maher
Writers: Various, including Ray Boseley, Vince Moran

Crawfords Australia Production
28 color 25-minute episodes
31 May–6 September 1994
(ITV)

HARD TIME ON PLANET EARTH

"The penalty for rebellion against the council is termination, but because of your heroic services as a warrior, you are exiled to the primitive planet Earth, in human form, until you learn to restrain your hostility . . ."

Disney-backed comedy adventure series about a super-warrior from a distant solar system who rebels against his government and finds himself banished to Earth.

Here, his sentence will be determined by "Control," a small flying computer—which looks like a disembodied, floating eye—which keeps track of his efforts to help humanity and files regular reports to the folks back home. When Jesse, as the warrior is known, has totted up enough brownie points, he will be allowed to return to his own world.

So, while trying to adjust to the ways of California man, and hold down a job, Jesse manages to save a few lives, foil a few crooks and help the oppressed. It clearly wasn't enough, however, and Jesse's Hard Time ended after just 13 episodes with no parole in sight.

REGULAR CAST
Jesse Martin Kove *Voice of Control* Danny Mann

Creators: Jim Thomas, John Thomas
Executive producers: Jim & John Thomas, Richard Chapman, E. Jack Kaplan
Writers: Various, including Jim & John Thomas, Richard Chapman, E. Jack Kaplan, Daniel Freudenberger, Michael Piller, Bruce Cervi, Nick Corea
Directors: Robert Mandel, Roger Duchowny, James A. Contner, Timothy Bird, Michael Lange, Charles Correll, Bill Corcoran, Al Waxman, Ric Rondell

A Demos-Bard/Shanachie Production in association with Touchstone Television, Walt Disney Television
13 color 60-minute episodes
Hard Time on Planet Earth (pilot)

Something to Bank On
Losing Control
The Way Home
All That You Can Be
Battle of the Sexes
Death Us Do Part
The Hot Dog Man
Jesse's Fifteen Minutes
Rodeo
Not in Our Stars
The All American
Wally's Gang

U.S. premiere: 1 March 1989
U.K. premiere: 19 August 1990
(Yorkshire)

HELPING HENRY

Unusual series that uses the device of showing the world through alien eyes to inform and entertain pre-school children. Henry, though, is not your everyday run-of-the-mill space traveler—he's come to check out Earth disguised as a dining room chair. Guided by a young friend, Stephen, he makes hopelessly confused reports back to his superiors on the distant planet of Holgon, Cosmics 1 and 2—a clear case of upholstering the truth.

The 13 15-minute episodes covered aspects of Earth life such as pets and animals, shopping, transport, clothes and household appliances—"just because the fridge is cold doesn't mean it's not well." Deadpan comedian Jeremy Hardy co-wrote the shows and supplied the voice of Henry. Richard Vernon (Slartibartfast in *The Hitch-Hiker's Guide to the Galaxy*) played the ill-informed Cosmic 1.

CAST
Henry Jeremy Hardy *Cosmic 1* Richard Vernon
Cosmic 2 Martin Wimbush *Stephen* Ian Harris
Tricia Miranda Borman

Writers: "Chips" Hardy, John Henderson
Producer: Madeleine French
Director: Philip Casson
Puppeteer: Roman Stefanski
Puppet by Jim Hennequin, Peter Fluck

Chips Hardy and Co Production
13 color 15-minute episodes
28 February–19 May 1988
(Channel Four)

HERCULES:
THE LEGENDARY JOURNEYS

Hercules began in a series of five TV movies for the "Universal Action Pack" in 1994. When they proved popular, the series launched with 13 episodes and was quickly renewed for 24 more—and has been running ever since. Star Kevin Sorbo was an interesting choice for the lead role, and viewers more used to Steve Reeves and a Hercules bursting with muscles had to get used to Sorbo's leaner look. But Sorbo throws himself into the campy role with gusto, and his enthusiasm is catching.

As an interesting sidenote, Sorbo almost got Dean Cain's role as Superman in *Lois and Clark: The New Adventures of Superman*. It is interesting to wonder what both series would have been like if the two actors had actually landed each other's roles!

The series is shot on location in and around Auckland, New Zealand.

REGULAR CAST
Hercules Kevin Sorbo *Iolaus* Michael Hurst

Executive producers: Rob Tapert, Sam Raimi
Co-executive producer: John Schulian
Supervising producer: Robert Bielak
Producer: Eric Gruendemann
Co-producer: David Eick
Associate producer: Liz Friedman
Coordinating producer: Bernadette Joyce
Line producer: Chloe Smith
Music: Joseph LoDuca

Produced by Renaissance Pictures in association with MCA TV
U.S. series premiere: week of 23 January 1995

Movies

Hercules and the Amazon Women (1994)
Hercules and the Lost Kingdom (1994)
Hercules and the Circle of Fire (1994)
Hercules and the Underworld (1994)
Hercules in the Maze of the Minotaur (1994)
The Battle for Mt. Olympus (animated, 1998)

Season One

13 color 60-minute episodes

The Wrong Path
Eye of the Beholder
Road to Calydon
The Festival of Dionsyus
Ares
As Darkness Falls
Pride Comes before a Brawl
The March to Freedom
The Warrior Princess
The Gladiators
The Vanishing Dead
The Gauntlet
Unchained Heart

Season Two

24 color 60-minute episodes

The King of Thieves
All That Glitters
What's in a Name?
Siege at Naxos
The Outcast
Under the Broken Sky
The Mother of All Monsters
The Other Side
The Fire Down Below
Cast a Giant Shadow
Highway to Hades
The Sword of Veracity
The Enforcer
Once a Hero
Heedless Hearts
Let the Games Begin
The Apple
Promises
King for a Day
Protean Challenge
The Wedding of Alcmene
The Power
Centaur Mentor Journey
Cave of Echoes

Season Three

22 color 60-minute episodes

Mercenary
Doomsday
Love Takes a Holiday
Mummy Dearest
Not Fade Away
Monster Child in the Promised Land
The Green-Eyed Monster
Prince Hercules
A Star to Guide Them
The Lady & the Dragon
Long Live the King
Surprise
Encounter
When a Man Loves a Woman
Judgment Day
The Lost City
Les Contemptibles
Reign of Terror
End of the Beginning
War Bride
A Rock and a Hard Place
Atlantis

Season Four

22 color 60-minute episodes

Beanstalks & Bad Eggs
Hero's Heart
Regrets I've Had a Few
Web of Desire
Stranger in a Strange World
Two Men and a Baby
Prodigal Sister
. . . And Fancy Free
If I Had a Hammer
Hercules On Trial
Medea Culpa
Men in Pink
Armageddon Now (Part 1)
Armageddon Now (Part 2)
Yes Virginia, There Is a Hercules
Porkules
One Fowl Day
My Fair Cupcake
War Wounds
Twilight
Top God
Reunion

HIGHLANDER: THE SERIES

"I was born 400 years ago in the Highlands of Scotland. I am
Immortal, and I am not alone. Now is the time of the
Gathering. In the end there can be only one."

Fantasy adventure series based on the two *Highlander* movies starring Christopher Lambert and Sean Connery. It follows the fortunes of one Immortal, Duncan MacLeod of the clan MacLeod, known to his friends as Mac and to other immortals as The Highlander.

Immortals can be killed only by being beheaded. They remain hidden among everyday mortals but, when confronted by another Immortal, must do battle, with the winner beheading the loser to receive the Quickening, a transfer of power energy and knowledge from one Immortal to the other. This will continue until only one is left alive (or the ratings slide, whichever comes soonest).

Duncan has tried to turn his back on this tradition and live his life unnoticed, among mortals. But other Immortals keep seeking him out and putting his warrior skills to yet another ultimate test. He also has to contend with prying media and suspicious authorities.

Adrian Paul, who stars as MacLeod, studied Kung Fu and Kung Fu swordwork for five years—ideal qualifications for his role as the darkly brooding Immortal, and the regular duels are impressively staged in some spectacular locations, notably the roof of the Paris opera house. Christopher Lambert turned up as the mentor of Duncan MacLeod in the series' opening episode.

In the first season, MacLeod runs an antique shop and lives with his French girlfriend, sculptress Tessa Noel. The other series regular is Richie Ryan, a young kid from the wrong side of the tracks, befriended by MacLeod after breaking into his shop.

Early in Season Two, Tessa is killed in a random act of violence and her death inspires MacLeod to become more involved in mortal affairs and strive to improve the sorry state of the world. Richie, "killed" in the same shocking incident that claimed Tessa's life, becomes Immortal himself and briefly goes off on his own. MacLeod, meanwhile, sells his shop and moves into a loft above a martial arts studio run by black-belted, black Italian Charlie De Salvo.

Another new recurring character is Joe Dawson, head of an age-old organization known as The Watchers. Introduced at the end of Season One, the Watchers have observed and chronicled the Immortals through many generations. Joe is an admirer of MacLeod and, after an initial confrontation, the two become allies. Joe and MacLeod also have to confront the renegade Watchers who believe the only good Immortal is a dead one and periodically come after MacLeod's head.

The series has certainly attracted its share of big-name guests, including The Who's Roger Daltrey, in a recurring role as MacLeod's old compatriot, Hugh Fitzcairn, singer Sheena Easton and Adrian Paul's ex-wife, Meilani, known throughout the U.S. as the star of a Diet Pepsi ad.

Season Three introduced a powerful new nemesis for MacLeod, Kalas (played by British actor David Robb), an immortal former monk with the voice of an angel, whose swordsmanship and power forces Mac to flee to France. In a season-ending clash atop the Eiffel Tower, they fight a climactic duel to the death. Mac also loved and lost a trauma surgeon, Anne Lindsey, before finally admitting his love for Amanda, the immortal cat-burgler introduced in the first season and brought back as a recurring character.

Season Four brought things full circle, with Duncan returning to the land of his birth (albeit briefly). It also introduced some interesting new Immortals (Kanis, the master of hounds; Mikey, the giant idiot), brought back some friends (Andrew Cord, Kenny, the child Immortal) and villains (Kanwulf the Destroyer, who killed Duncan's father; Mark Roszca, who killed Tessa and Richie in the second season). Unfortunately, though, Big Things are happening behind the scenes, as Watchers are being murdered. The problem comes to the forefront in everyone's mind when Joe Dawson is put on trial by the Watchers for revealing their existence to Duncan MacLeod and a price is put on Duncan's head.

Season Five brings more tangles to the web that is Duncan's life: Methos persuades Richie to give up his sword, and Kronos, one of the Four Horsemen of the Apocalypse, turns out to be real . . . and an Immortal. Then people Duncan has killed over the years begin showing up alive and seemingly well. Is it the coming Millennium? An archaeologist warns Duncan that demons are awakening and that Duncan has been chosen to fight the coming evil—but he is tricked into killing Richie Ryan.

Season Six sees the demon destroyed and Duncan grieving; he has lost a lot of friends along the way. The healing process is slow, but complete by the final two episodes, in which he gets the *It's a Wonderful Life* treatment from his old (but now quite dead) friend Fitz.

Season Seven: There won't be one, but watch for a spin-off series tentatively titled *Chronicles of the Raven.*

(Note: A complete episode guide to the series is now available from Warner Books.)

REGULAR CAST

Duncan MacLeod Adrian Paul Tessa Noel Alexandra Vandernoot
Richie Ryan Stan Kirsch Randi Amanda Wyss
Amanda Elizabeth Gracen *(intro Season One, semi-regular Season Three)*
From Season Two: Charlie DeSalvo Philip Akin Joe Dawson Jim Byrnes
Season Three only: Anne Lindsay Lisa Howard

Based on the character created by Gregory Widen	Theme: *Princes of the Universe* by Queen
Executive producers: Bill Panzer, Peter Davis, Marla Ginsburg, Christian Charret	*Davis-Panzer/Gaumont Television, France Productions in association with Rysher Tpe and Reteitalia*
Supervising producers: David Abramowitz, Kevin Droney	109 color 60-minute episodes
	U.S. premiere: September 1992
	U.K. premiere: 3 April 1994

Season One

The Gathering
Innocent Man
Road Not Taken
Bad Day in Building A
Free Fall
Deadly Medicine
Mountain Men
Revenge Is Sweet
The Sea Witch
Eyewitness
Family Tree
See No Evil
Band of Brothers
For Evil's Sake
For Tomorrow We Die
The Beast Below
Saving Grace
The Lady and the Tiger
Avenging Angel
Eye of the Beholder
Nowhere to Run
The Hunters

Season Two

The Watchers
Studies in Light
Turnabout
The Darkness
Eye for an Eye
The Zone
The Return of Amanda
Revenge of the Sword
Run for Your Life
Epitaph for Tommy
Bless the Child
The Fighter
Under Color of Authority
Unholy Alliance, Part 1
Unholy Alliance, Part 2
The Vampire
Warmonger
Pharaoh's Daughter
Legacy
Prodigal Son
Counterfeit, Part 1
Counterfeit, Part 2

Season Three

The Samurai
Line of Fire
The Revolutionary
The Cross of St. Antoine
Rite of Passage
Courage
The Lamb
Obsession
Shadows
Blackmail
Vendetta
They Also Serve
Blind Faith
Song of the Executioner
Star-Crossed
Methos
Take Back the Night
Testimony
Mortal Sins
Reasonable Doubt
Finale, Part 1
Finale, Part 2

Season Four

Homeland
Brothers in Arms
The Innocent
Leader of the Pack
Double Eagle
Reunion
The Colonel
Reluctant Heroes
The Wrath of Kali
Chivalry
Timeless
The Blitz
Something Wicked
Deliverance
Promises
Methuselah's Gift
The Immortal Cimoli
Through a Glass, Darkly
Till Death
Judgement Day

Season Five

One Minute to Midnight
Prophecy
The End of Innocence
Manhunt
Glory Days
Dramatic License
Money No Object
Haunted
Little Tin God
The Messenger
The Valkyrie
Comes a Horseman
Revelations 6:8
The Ransom of Richard Redstone
Duende
The Stone of Scone
Double Jeopardy

Forgive Us Our Trespasses
The Modern Prometheus
Archangel

Season Six

Avatar
Armageddon
Sins of the Father
Diplomatic Immunity
Patient Number 7
Black Tower
Unusual Suspects
Justice
Deadly Exposure
Two of Hearts
Indiscretions
To Be
Not to Be

THE HITCH-HIKER'S GUIDE TO THE GALAXY

"The history of *The Hitch-Hiker's Guide to the Galaxy*
is one of idealism, despair, struggle, passion, success,
failure and enormously long lunch-breaks."
—Hurling Frootmig, 17th acting editor

*T*he Hitch-Hiker's Guide began life in the cultural ghetto of a Radio 4 serial, and by expressing ideas above its station rose through the ranks of repeats, a book and a record until it finally materialized before our square eyes in 1981, when it was hailed as the first inter-galactic multi-media epic.

Making a visual version of a cult radio show carried the huge risk that the result might not live up to listeners' preconceptions. But it did, and the series, created by Douglas Adams, is widely held to be the funniest science fiction TV show ever.

Neither did it squander the opportunities TV provided, stamping its own visual ID in the innovative use of computer graphics to accompany narrator Peter Jones' guide entries (a style adapted some seven or eight years later by *The Daily Telegraph* for its own TV ad campaign).

The Hitch-Hiker's Guide to the Galaxy is part satire, part fantasy, in which Arthur Dent, a typical, nonplussed Englishman still in his dressing gown, is swept up into galactic events of far-ranging magnitude, dealt with in a down-to-earth, prosaic manner that turns everyone and everything into a cosmic joke.

The basic plot—as if it really mattered—begins with Ford Prefect, a field researcher for the Guide (the standard reference for information on the universe), on Earth to update the entry on our world. With his human friend Arthur, he narrowly escapes the planet's destruction to make way for a hyperspace bypass.

They eventually find themselves aboard a stolen starship with two-headed con-man Zaphod Beeblebrox, his pilot girlfriend Trillian, and Marvin the Paranoid Android, a manic-depressive robot whose capacity for mental activity is as boundless as the infinite reaches of space, but whose capacity for happiness could be fitted into a matchbox, without even taking the matches out first . . .

Other stars of the shows are the Vogons, fat, ugly, green aliens who write the worst poetry in the Universe; Slartibartfast, designer of the Fjords; the Dish of the Day, a talking dinner; and a pair of pan-dimensional beings disguised as white mice who are searching for the Ultimate Question to Life, the Universe and Everything. They already have the answer—42.

REGULAR CAST

Arthur Dent Simon Jones *Ford Prefect* David Dixon
Voice of the Book Peter Jones
Zaphod Beeblebrox Mark Wing-Davey *(from Ep. 2)*
Trillian Sandra Dickinson *(from Ep. 2)*
Marvin David Learner *(Eps. 2–3, 5–6)*
Voice of Marvin Stephen Moore *(Eps. 2–3, 5–6)*

Writer/creator: Douglas Adams
Producer: Alan J.W. Bell
Associate producer: John Lloyd
Designers: Andrew Howe-Davies *(Eps. 1–6)*,
   Tom Yardley-Jones *(Eps. 4–6)*
Animated sequences: Rod Lord
Radiophonic music: Paddy Kingsland

A BBC Production
6 color 35-minute episodes
5 January–9 February 1981
(BBC2)
first rpt: 4 June–9 July 1981
(BBC1)

Episode One

Arthur Dent is not convinced when his best friend Ford Prefect tells him that the world is about to end in 12 minutes, particularly when Ford reveals that he is an alien from the planet Betelgeuse and not from Guildford after all . . .
Mr. Prosser Joe Melia
Barman Steve Conway
Vogon captain Martin Benson
Aliens Cleo Rocos, Andrew Mussell

Episode Two

Rescued from Earth, moments before its destruction to make way for a hyperspace bypass, Arthur and Ford are on board the actual demolition spacecraft of the Vogons. Should they face certain death by being flung into the cold vacuum of space? Or should they tell the Vogon captain how good they think his poetry is?
Vogon captain Martin Benson
Vogon guard Michael Cule
Newscaster Rayner Bourton
Gag Halfrunt Gil Morris
Voice of Eddie (the computer) David Tate

Episode Three

Zaphod Beeblebrox heads the stolen spaceship *Heart of Gold* for the legendary planet of Magrathea whose business is building other planets. Arthur continues his search for a good cup of tea.
Voice of Eddie David Tate
Slartibartfast Richard Vernon

Episode Four

Arthur is astonished to learn that Earth was not what it had seemed and neither were the mice—and he's quite put out to learn that they are after his brain.
Slartibartfast Richard Vernon
Lunkwill Antony Carrick
Fook Timothy Davies
Majikthise David Leland
Vroomfondel Charles McKeown
Shooty Matt Zimmerman
Bang Bang Marc Smith
Voice of Deep Thought Valentine Dyall

Episode Five

Having been blown to smithereens when a computer exploded on the planet Magrathea, the travelers find themselves in the restaurant at the end of the Universe.
Garkbit (head waiter) Jack May
Bodyguard Dave Prowse
Max Quordlepleen Colin Jeavons
Zarquon Colin Bennett
Dish of the Day Peter Davison

Episode Six

As a spectacular finale to his Disaster Area rock concert, megabig superstar Hotblack Desiato crashes an unmanned black spacecraft into the sun—unmanned, that is, apart from Arthur, Ford, Trillian and Zaphod . . .
Newscaster Rayner Bourton
Captain Aubrey Morris
No. 1 Matthew Scurfield
No. 2 David Neville
No. 3 Geoffrey Beevers
Marketing girl Beth Porter
Management consultant Jon Glover
Hairdresser David Rowlands

HOLMES AND YOYO

American comedy series about a bungling, accident-prone detective who is assigned a new partner—Yoyo, a six-foot electronic robot who's not much brighter than he is, despite a computer brain.

From Leonard Stern, executive producer on *Get Smart*, it starred Walter Matthau lookalike Richard B. Shull and John Schuck, best remembered as Rock Hudson's assistant in *MacMillan and Wife*.

REGULAR CAST
Alexander Holmes Richard B. Shull   *Gregory "Yoyo" Yoyonovitch* John Schuck
Captain Harry Sedford Bruce Kirby   *Officer Maxine Moon* Andrea Howard

Executive producer: Leonard Stern

A Universal Production
13 color 25-minute episodes
Holmes and Yoyo (pilot)
Funny Money
The Dental Dynamiter
The Last Phantom
Yoyo Takes a Bride
The Thornhill Affair
The K.9 Caper

The Hostages
Key Witness
Dead Duck
Connection, Connection II
The Cat Burglar
Bye, Bye Bennie

U.S. premiere: 25 September 1976
U.K. run: 29 October 1976–9 February 1977

HOMEBOYS IN OUTER SPACE

Comedy and science fiction seldom mix well, as *Homeboys* demonstrates: Ty and Morris, childhood friends, grow up to own a spaceship together, doing odd jobs to support themselves. They hang out in a bar, visit planets, and have a spaceship named the *Hoopty* with a wise-cracking computer. Think you've seen it all before on (non-sci-fi) comedies? Chances are you have.

There are a few bright moments, however, when guest stars appear. James Doohan is particularly amusing in a parody of his "Scotty" character from *Star Trek* in several episodes, as is Sherman Helmsley's appearance as "George," a crazed dry-cleaner.

REGULAR CAST
Tybedus "Ty" Walker Flex   *Morris Clay* Darryl M. Bell
Loquatia Rhona L. Bennett   *Vashti* Kevin Michael Richardson
Amma Paulette Braxton   *Pippen* James Doohan

Creator: Ehrich van Lowe
Producers: Jeffrey Lampert, Lore Kimbrough, Sten Foster, Miguel Nunez, Ted Schachter
Consulting producer: Cary H. Miller
Creative consultants: Stu Kreisman, Chris Cluess
Consulting producers: Mike Reiss, Al Jean

Executive producer: Ehrich van Lowe
Music: Kevin Guillaume

21 color 30-minute episodes
27 August 1996–13 May 1997

Episodes
There's No Space Like Home/Return of the Jed Eye
G Marks the Spot
Papa's Got a Brand New Old Bag
Behold a Pale Planet
Loquatia Unplugged
House Party
Dog Day Afternoon
Devil in Ms. Jones

Trading Places
Stepford Guys (aka A Man's Place Is in the Homey)
Hoopty Doopty
Super Bad Foxy Lady Killer
I Love Lucifer
El Voyage Fantastico
The Longest Yard
Full Metal Jackass
Happy Happy, Droid Droid

HONEY, I SHRUNK THE KIDS

Peter Scolari stars as scientist Wayne Szalinski, taking over Rick Moranis's role in the Disney movie of the same name (and its sequels). The Disney label says much: It's wholesome family fare, a bit on the silly and implausible side, but it's clearly aimed at younger viewers—the same audience that made the movie series a hit in theaters and in direct-to-video releases. Mostly harmless. Syndicated in 1997.

REGULAR CAST
Wayne Szalinski Peter Scolari   *Diane Szalinski* Barbara Alyn Woods
Amy Szalinski Hillary Tuck   *Nick Szalinski* Thomas Dekker
Quark (the dog) Matisse

Honey, We've Been Swallowed by Grandpa

Wayne, Diane, and Amy are accidentally shrunk to near-microscopic size while in their van, then swallowed by Grandpa Murdock. The Szalinskis must escape their "fantastic voyage" before the shrinking wears off in three hours.

Honey, We're Stuck in the '70s

Amy swipes her father's time machine, going back to 1976 to meet the then-teenage Mr. O'Donnell, her history teacher.

Honey, the House Is Trying to Kill Us

After their home is burglarized, Wayne invents a home security system: F.R.A.N., the Felon Repeller & Accident Neutralizer (pat. pending), who takes her duties very seriously—including protection from bad fashion choices and rich food.

Honey, I'm Haunted

Nick tests out the Szalinski Retina-Rotator, which enhances his vision and lets him see ghosts. A dead 1930s gangster decides he wants a body so much that he pops in on Wayne and decides to stay.

Honey, You've Got Nine Lives

It's brain-swap time, as Diane accidentally exchanges brains with a supercilious cat named Persephone, and Wayne switches brains with Quark.

Honey, I Shrunk the Science Dude

Wayne accidentally shrinks his younger brother, TV scientist Randy Rude the Science Dude, and himself, before Randy is to speak at the kids' school.

Honey, I Know What You're Thinking

Amy uses the Szalinski Brainiactivator gas to enhance her intelligence, which gives her the ability to read thoughts; when it leaks out at a sleepover, everyone in the house is affected with different results.

Honey, I Got Duped

Wayne clones himself accidentally, leaving him with an unstable molecular structure—the slightest physical contact results in another clone—so he sends his guileless clone out into the real world, where Bianca is waiting to take advantage of his inventions.

Honey, They're After Me Lucky Charms

Wayne and his boss find a pot of gold in an abandoned mine, but a visit from a leprechaun raises questions of science vs. magic.

Honey, They Call Me the Space Cowboy

Wayne uses the revamped Szalinski Time Hopper to take the family back to 1864 for a picnic, but the Szalinskis attract the attention of the Blacklung Gang, who steal the time machine.

Honey, You're Living in the Past

When Diane has trouble relating to her daughter and a young client, she uses the Szalinski Memory Lane Mobile to access suppressed memories and revisit her youth. Unfortunately, a power surge leaves her stranded in her 16-year-old brain.

Honey, I'm Streakin'

Wayne has too much to do and too little time, so he accelerates his molecules and becomes the fastest man on Earth.

Honey, Meet the Barbarians

Diane runs for the school board, but Wayne's inventions may cost her the election, especially when he brings back Vikings from A.D. 930.

Honey, You Drained My Brain

While trying her first civil case, Diane is overmatched by the brilliant defense attorney, so Wayne fashions a portable brain enhancer to give Diane a mental boost. Unfortunately, the device increases intelligence by leaching power from others' brains, as they discover in court the next day.

Honey, He's Not Abominable . . . He's Just Misunderstood

When Amy is injured in a snowboarding accident, she is rescued by a Yeti, who follows her home.

Honey, I'm in the Mood for Love

Wayne distills cocoa pheromones from chocolate and creates aphrodisiac bonbons, which Nick brings to the high school's Sweetheart's Dance. Unfortunately, everyone falls in love with the wrong person, making it a Midsummer's Nightmare.

Honey, the Bear Is Bad News

Wayne spruces up Jentech's first toy, a cloyingly cute stuffed bear named Fwuffy. Unfortunately, when Fwuffy is infected with a computer virus, he plans to rule the world.

From Honey, with Love

Wayne is secretly recruited to make spy inventions for the Canadian Ministry of Intelligence. When his superspy friend, Dalton Pearce, is incapacitated by one of his inventions, Wayne must step in to stop Canada's most notorious supervillain, disgruntled ex-Mountie Pierre LeBecque.

Honey, It's No Fun Being an Illegal Alien

Ar'nox, the Intergalactic Ranger, drops by Earth with a gift for his old friends; his star cruiser is hijacked by some Men in Dark Suits working for the Illuminati.

Honey, I'm Dreaming. But Am I?

When nightmares bother his family, Wayne uses one of his inventions to enter their dreams . . . annoying Morpheus, the master of the realm of dreams.

Honey, the Garbage Took Us Out

Wayne invents trash-eating Protozoa, which his boss wants to use to clean up Jentech before the EPA inspectors visit.

Honey, You're So Transparent

Amy, while interning at Jentech Labs, tests a new device on herself to help her father, only to be rendered invisible with chameleon DNA . . . Which may prove useful in finding the mole who's stealing Jentech inventions and sabotaging equipment.

I DREAM OF JEANNIE

Astronaut parachutes to Earth; finds genie in bottle on desert island. A simple premise that played itself out for five years (and will continue to play forever in syndication), with a naive Jeannie getting her master into various perilous (and always humorous) situations. At first only Tony Nelson knew about Jeannie, but as the series progressed, his best friend, Roger Healey, was let in on the secret. Dr. Bellows always suspected something odd was going on, but could never prove it.

Two reunion movies appeared, but without Larry Hagman much of the magic was gone.

REGULAR CAST
Jeannie Barbara Eden *Major Anthony Nelson* Larry Hagman
Major Roger Healey Bill Daily *Dr. Alfred Bellows* Hayden Rorke

Creator: Sidney Sheldon
30 black and white episodes; 109 color episodes
18 September 1965–26 May 1970

he power of the Adamcos! Geoffrey Bayldon
ed through time as the eccentric wizard
weazle.

Davros (Michael Wisher), creator of the Daleks, in
the **Doctor Who** story "Genesis of the Daleks."

third regeneration of Doctor Who, Jon Pertwee, with Elisabeth Sladen as Sarah Jane Smith, aboard
of the series' lesser-known craft, the Whomobile, in the 1974 story "The Planet of the Spiders."

Heroic astronaut Steve Zodiac, glamorous medic Venus and pet Zoonie joined the supermariona crew of Gerry Anderson's first space fantasy, **Fireball XL5**, in 1962's giant leap for puppetkind.

Speak no evil and Lennier no evil . . . two luminary "Invaders from the Fifth Dimension" spook Will Robinson (Billy Mumy) in **Lost in Space**.

The classic shot: David Vincent (Roy Thinnes) was forever on the run from **The Invaders**.

Above left: The Invisible Man, Peter Brady, and his niece Sally (Deborah Watling) go on a 1958 publicity walkabout at the Tower of London.

Above right: Lost in the **Land of the Giants** the hapless crew of the *Sprindrift* find life is a lot larger than the one they left behind.

Left: Ray Walston (top) and Bill Bixby teamed up as "Uncle" Martin and Tim O'Hara in the hugely popular 1960s sitcom **My Favorite Martian**.

Out of This World star Boris Karloff (center) on the set of the series' fourth play, "Imposter," wit
cast members (from left) Angela Browne, Patrick Allen, John Carson, June Shaw and Glyn Owe

Above: It may look like Del Boy's three-whee
but this mean machine was part of the elite
Earth Space Control Fleet in **Phoenix Five**.

Left: This well-dressed monster was one the
parents of Spider County, come to reclaim his
children in an episode of **The Outer Limits**.

een's Pawn Number Six (Patrick McGoohan) vs human chess in **The Prisoner** episode heckmate."

John Mills was the last of the fabled quartet of TV professors in Nigel Kneale's **Quatermass**.

amour and grit: ex-New Avenger Joanna Lumley d retired man from U.N.C.L.E., David McCallum ove) as time detectives Sapphire & Steel.

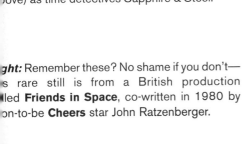

ght: Remember these? No shame if you don't— s rare still is from a British production lled **Friends in Space**, co-written in 1980 by on-to-be **Cheers** star John Ratzenberger.

Catherine Schell turned a lot of heads when she joined the cast of Gerry Anderson's galactic fanta
Space: 1999 as Maya, a beautiful alien with the power to transform herself into any animal.

The forgotten heroes of TV puppet fantasy—Husky the Martian, the Gabblerdictum bird, Slim
Venusian and Captain Larry Dart—together cruised the solar system in **Space Patrol**.

r Maidens Fulvia (Judy Geeson) and Andrea chi Mellin) in pursuit of their runaway men.

Dressed for the moon: little Jimmy Wedgwood (Michael Hammond) in 1960's **Target Luna**.

d-pressed scientists Tony Newman (James Darran) and Doug Phillips (Robert Colbert) found no t relief at the end of **The Time Tunnel**—they invariably emerged into an epic war or disaster.

Simon (Spencer Banks) and Liz (Cheryl Burfield) in the **Timeslip** story "The Year of the Burn-Up."

A youthful William Shatner with Patricia Bre: in **The Twilight Zone** tale "Nick of Time."

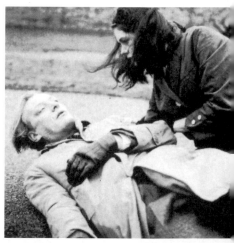

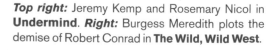

Above: Reflections in the water face Straker (Ed Bishop) and Foster (Michael Billington): **U.F.O.**

Top right: Jeremy Kemp and Rosemary Nicol in **Undermind**. ***Right:*** Burgess Meredith plots the demise of Robert Conrad in **The Wild, Wild West**.

Season One (*black and white*)

The Lady in the Bottle
My Hero
Guess What Happened on the Way to the Moon?
Jeannie and the Marriage Caper
G.I. Jeannie
Jeannie and the Murder Caper
Anybody Here Seen Jeannie?
Americanization of Jeannie
The Moving Finger
Djinn and Water
Whatever Became of Baby Custer?
Where'd You Go-Go?
Russian Roulette
What House Across the Street?
Too Many Tonys
Get Me to Mecca on Time
Richest Astronaut in the World
Is There an Extra Jeannie in the House?
Never Try to Outsmart a Jeannie
My Master, the Doctor
Jeannie and the Kidnap Caper
How Lucky Can You Get?
Watch the Birdie
Permanent House Guest
Bigger Than a Bread Box
My Master, the Great Rembrandt
My Master the Thief
This Is Murder
My Master the Magician
I'll Never Forget What's-Her-Name

Season Two (*color*)

Happy Anniversary
Always on Sunday
My Master the Rich Tycoon
My Master the Rainmaker
My Wild-Eyed Master
What's New, Poodle Dog?
Fastest Gun in the East
How to Be a Genie in Ten Easy Lessons
Who Needs a Green-Eyed Jeannie?
The Girl Who Never Had a Birthday, Part 1
The Girl Who Never Had a Birthday, Part 2
How Do You Beat Superman?
My Master the Great Caruso
The World's Greatest Lover
Jeannie Breaks the Bank
My Master the Author
The Greatest Invention in the World
My Master the Spy
You Can't Arrest Me . . .
One of Our Bottles Is Missing
My Master the Civilian
There Goes the Best Genie I Ever Had
The Greatest Entertainer in the World
My Incredible Shrinking Master
My Master the Pirate
A Secretary Is Not a Toy
There Goes the Bride

My Master, Napoleon's Buddy
The Birds and the Bees Bit
My Master the Swinging Bachelor
The Mod Party

Season Three

Fly Me to the Moon
Jeannie or the Tiger
Second Greatest Con Artist in the World
My Turned-on Master
My Master the Weakling
Jeannie, the Hip Hippie
Everybody's a Movie Star
Who Are You Calling a Genie?
Meet My Master's Mother
Here Comes Bootsie Nightingale
Tony's Wife
Jeannie and the Bank Robbery
My Son the Genie
Jeannie Goes to Honolulu
Battle of Waikiki
Genie, Genie, Who's Got the Genie?, Part 1
Genie, Genie, Who's Got the Genie?, Part 2
Genie, Genie, Who's Got the Genie?, Part 3
Genie, Genie, Who's Got the Genie?, Part 4
Please, Don't Eat the Astronauts
My Master, the Ghostbreaker
Divorce, Genie Style
My Double-Crossing Master
Have You Ever Had a Genie Hate You?
Operation: First Couple on the Moon
Haven't I Seen Me Somewhere Before?

Season Four

U-F-Oh Jeannie
Jeannie and the Wild Pipchicks
Tomorrow Is Not Another Day
Abdullah
The Used Car Salesman
Djinn, Djinn, Go Home
The Strongest Man in the World
Indispensable Jeannie
Jeannie and the Top Secret
How to Marry an Astronaut
Dr. Bellows Goes Sane
Jeannie, My Guru
The Case of My Vanishing Master, Part 1
The Case of My Vanishing Master, Part 2
Ride 'Em, Astronaut
Invisible House for Sale
Jeannie, the Governor's Wife
Is There a Doctor in the House?
The Biggest Star in Hollywood
Porcelain Puppy
Jeannie for the Defense
Nobody Loves a Fat Astronaut
Around the World in 80 Blinks
Jeannie-Go-Round
Jeannie and the Secret Weapon
Blackmail Order Bride

Season Five

Jeannie at the Piano
Djinn, Djinn, the Pied Piper
Guess Who's Going to Be a Bride?, Part 1
Guess Who's Going to Be a Bride?, Part 2
Jeannie's Beauty Cream
Jeannie and the Bachelor Party
The Blood of Jeannie
See You in C-U-B-A
The Mad Home Wrecker
Uncle a Go-Go
The Wedding
My Sister the Homewrecker
Jeannie the Matchmaker
Never Put a Genie on the Budget
Please Don't Give My Jeannie No More Wine

One of Our Hotels Is Growing
The Solid Gold Jeannie
Mrs. Djinn Djinn
Jeannie and the Curious Kid
Jeannie, the Recording Secretary
Help, Help, a Shark
Eternally Yours, Jeannie
An Astronaut in Sheep's Clothing
Hurricane Jeannie
One Jeannie Beats Four of a Kind
My Master the Chili King

TV Movies

I Dream of Jeannie—15 Years Later (Aired 20 October 1985)
I Still Dream of Jeannie (Aired 20 October 1991)

THE INCREDIBLE HULK

"Philosophically the show reaches out to an even broader point—how can man learn to control the demon within him."

—MCA TV press handout

"It did not seem possible that there could be a sillier series than *The Man From Atlantis* . . ."

—*The Sun*, June 1978

We'd had *The Six Million Dollar Man*, *The Bionic Woman* and *Man from Atlantis*, now there was Dr. David Banner, a sensitive, compassionate scientist whose search for a way to unleash man's secret source of strength had a bizarre result.

Banner's desire to find a way of tapping some kind of super-strength is triggered when he fails to rescue his wife from a blazing car. Experimenting with gamma rays, he accidentally receives an overdose, bringing about a Jekyll and Hyde personality he cannot control. Every time anger and frustration overpower his normally placid emotions, Banner is transformed into the Hulk—a 7 ft. tall, green-skinned man-beast with phenomenal strength. His shirt splits, his shoes vanish, but, as this was a family show, his trousers stay on.

After a couple of 90-minute pilot films, the series took on the familiar mantle of *The Fugitive*, a "lumbering man" show with Banner/Hulk searching for the scientific answers and antidote to his plight. Each week he encountered various strangers who tried to help, hinder or understand him. The usual format was: Banner meets good guy/girl. They get in trouble. Banner gets cross and turns into the Hulk who stomps the bad guys. His anger subsides and he becomes mild-mannered David Banner again.

The regular "villain" of the show was nosy, headline-hunting reporter Jack McGee who believes the Hulk is a killer and trails him round the country, desperate to expose Banner's secret.

Bill Bixby, familiar to TV fans as *The Magician*, starred as David Banner, and former Mr. World and Mr. Universe Lou Ferrigno was the Hulk. Ferrigno, whose first major acting role was in Arnold Schwarzenegger's film *Pumping Iron*, was anxious not to portray the Hulk as a simple beast, but as a man striving to control the beast within him. Whatever the motivation, this TV Hulk bore little resemblance to the Marvel Comics original.

One in-joke, partly lost on younger fans, was the guest appearance of Ray "Uncle Martin" Walston as an aging magician (with Bixby as his assistant) in an episode called . . . "My Favorite Magician."

REGULAR CAST
Dr. David Banner Bill Bixby *The Hulk* Lou Ferrigno
Jack McGee Jack Colvin

Executive producer: Ken Johnson
Producers: Chuck Bowman, Jim Parriott, Nicholas Corea, James G. Hirsch, Bob Steinhauer, Karen Harris, Jill Sherman
Directors: Various, including Ken Johnson, Sig Neufeld, Reza Badiyi, Jeff Hayden
Writers: Various, including Ken Johnson, Richard Matheson, Nick Corea, Jill Sherman, Karen Harris

An MCA Television Production

80 color episodes (55 minutes except where stated) plus two pilot films
U.S. premiere: 10 March 1978
U.K. premiere: 26 May 1978

(Author's note: As with most American series, the U.K. running order for *The Incredible Hulk* deviated from the U.S. original—and differed in the length and composition of various runs around the ITV regions. So for ease of reference I've listed the episodes in their original American order.)

Pilot films

The Incredible Hulk (120 mins.)*
Death in the Family (aka Return of the Incredible Hulk) (120 mins.)*

* U.K. running time: 90 minutes

Season One

The Final Round
The Beast Within
Of Guilt, Models and Murder
Terror in Time Square
747
The Hulk Breaks Las Vegas
Never Give a Trucker An Even Break
Life and Death
Earthquakes Happen
The Waterfront Story

Season Two

Married (aka Bride of the Incredible Hulk) (120 minutes)†
The Autowuk Horror
Ricky
Rainbow's End
A Child in Need
Another Path
Alice in Disco Land
Killer Instinct
Stop the Presses
Escape from Los Santos
Wildfire
A Solitary Place
Like a Brother
The Haunted
Mystery Man (a 2-part story)
The Disciple (sequel to Another Path)
No Escape
Kindred Spirits
The Confession
The Quiet Room
Vendetta Road (aka Vendetta)

† U.K. running time: 105 minutes

Season Three

Metamorphosis
Blind Rage
Brain Child (aka Odyssey)
The Slam
My Favorite Magician
Jake
Behind the Wheel
Homecoming
The Snare
Babalao
Captive Night (aka Hostage Night)
Broken Image
Proof Positive (aka Nightmare)
Sideshow
Long Run Home
Falling Angels
The Lottery
The Psychic
A Rock and a Hard Place
Death Mask
Equinox (aka Masquerade)
Nine Hours
On the Line

Season Four

Prometheus (a 2-part story)
Free Fall
Dark Side
Deep Shock
Bring Me the Head of the Hulk
Fast Lane
Goodbye, Eddie Cain
King of the Beach
Wax Museum
East Winds
The First (a 2-part story)
The Harder They Fall
Interview With the Hulk
Half Nelson
Danny
Patterns

Season Five

The Phenom
Two Godmothers
Veteran
Sanctuary
Triangle

Slaves
A Minor Problem

The Incredible Hulk made a comeback with two 120-minute TV movies:
1988 *The Incredible Hulk Returns*
1989 *Trial of the Incredible Hulk*

INTO THE LABYRINTH

Into the Labyrinth combined magic and time travel in three moderately successful series depicting a world of suspended time and a never-ending duel between good and evil.

At the heart of the story was the white sorcerer Rothgo (played by Ron Moody) who, down through time, has been constantly got at by the beautiful but evil witch Belor (Pamela Salem). Three teenagers get caught up in their struggle and a quest for the Nidus—a source of magical power that has protected Rothgo until it is stolen by Belor. The third series saw Rothgo "substituted" by a new magician, a bit of a bungler called Lazlo, but the battle went on, up and down the centuries. Each week, the protagonists would pop up as different characters from history or mythology.

Into the Labyrinth was devised by Bob Baker and Peter Graham Scott and utilized the scriptwriting talents of such writers as John Lucarotti, Christopher Priest, Robert Holmes, and Baker himself.

REGULAR CAST
Rothgo Ron Moody*   *Belor* Pamela Salem   *Phil* Simon Beal
Terry Simon Henderson*   *Helen* Lisa Turner*
Lazlo Chris Harris†   *Bram* Howard Goorney†

Devisors: Bob Baker, Peter Graham Scott
Producer: Peter Graham Scott
Executive producer: Patrick Dromgoole
Designer: John Reid
Music: Sidney Sagar

* Series One and Two only
† Series Three only

An HTV Production
21 30-minute episodes
Series One:
13 May–24 June 1981
Series Two:
3 August–21 September 1981
Series Three:
28 July–8 September 1982

Series One

w Bob Baker *(Ep. 1)* Andrew Payne *(Eps. 2, 4)*, Anthony Read *(Eps. 3, 7)*, Ray Jenkins *(Eps. 5–6) (a 7-part story)*
A sudden thunderstorm drives Terry and his sister, Helen, to seek shelter in a cave. There they meet another boy, Phil, and are led by mysterious voices to discover Rothgo, a magician from another age, trapped in the rock. After releasing him, the teenagers become involved in the search for the stolen Nidus. The quest spans thousands of years and they encounter Rothgo and Belor in the pagan times of the druids; in medieval England; old Baghdad; the fields of the Civil War; revolutionary France; and finally in ancient Greece.
Robin of Loxley Tony Wright
Marian Patricia Driscoll
Sheriff of Nottingham Conrad Phillips
Ali Derrick Branche

Colonel Ewen Solon

with:
Paul Lavers, Edwina Ford, Peewee Hunt, Suzanne Wright, Phillip Manikum, David Trevena, Adele Saleem, William Byers, June Barrie, Simeon Andrews, Tim Bannerman, John Abineri, Jeremy Arnold

Director: Peter Graham Scott

Seven episodes:
Rothgo
The Circle
Robin
Masrur
Conflict
Revolution
Minotaur

Series Two

w Bob Baker *(Ep. 1)*, Christopher Priest *(Ep. 2)*, John Lucarotti *(Eps. 3, 6)*, Ivan Benbrook *(Ep. 4)*, Robert Holmes *(Ep. 5)*, Martin Worth *(Ep. 7)* *(a 7-part story)*

Once again the powers of goodness and light are challenged by Belor. This time she holds the Albedo, an energy source strong enough to neutralize the Nidus and so destroy Rothgo. In a catastrophic collision between the Albedo and the Nidus, Rothgo's power source is split into five fragments, each pursuing its own course through time and space. Rothgo recalls Phil, Terry and Helen to help retrieve them and sends them to the Wagnerian world of the Nibelung; the dangerous days of the Gunpowder Plot; the Alamo; ancient India (where Belor appears as the goddess Kali); Victorian London; and the Great Siege of Malta. The final confrontation comes at the burial of Tutankhamen.

Loke Howard Goorney
King James I Patrick Malahide
Davey Crockett Jack Watson
Jim Bowie Norman Bowler
Kadru Cyril Shaps
La Valette Ewen Solon

with:
David Trevena, Peter Burroughs,
Stephen Lyons, Ian Mackenzie,
Laura Cairns, April Johnson,
Jon Glentoran, Paul Nicholson,
Rita McKerrow, Roger Snowden,
Dino Shafeek, Jacob Witkin,
Michael O'Hagan, Edwina Ford,
Brian Coburn, Ian Brimble,
Jo Anderson, Suzi Arden,
Mark Buffery, Simeon Andrews

Director: Peter Graham Scott

Seven episodes:
The Calling
Treason
Alamo
Cave of Diamonds
Shadrach
Siege
Succession

Series Three

w Bob Baker, Robert Holmes, Ian Benbrook, Jane McCloskey, Gary Hopkins, Moris Farhi, David Martin *(one episode each!)* *(a 7-part story)*

The unreliable magician Lazlo draws Phil into Delta Time where history is turned upside down. There they must seek and find the Scarabeus missing from the magician's ornate bracelet—or be devoured by a creeping green slime. They encounter Long John Silver; Dr. Jekyll and Mrs. Hyde (guess who's Mrs. Hyde); Incas and Conquistadores; treachery during the Great Fire of London; the Phantom of the Opera; Kubla Khan; and King Arthur's Knights of the Round Table. Their footsteps along the dangerous Delta timetrack are dogged by Belor and her odious "familiar" Bram. In the final battle with Belor, in the shape of Morgan Le Fay, Lazlo—as Merlin—recaptures the Scarabeus and fastens it to his bracelet. He and Phil are released from Delta Time (and the creeping green slime) and Phil returns to his own time possessing his own magical power source.

Long John Silver Godfrey James
Mayor Thomas Bloodworth Frank Windsor
Matacarpi/Phantom of the Opera Conrad Phillips
Kubla Khan Peter Copley
King Arthur Ewen Solon
D'Avray Norman Bowler

with:
Walter Sparrow, Sara Markland,
Geoff Serle, Hubert Tucker,
Nick Chilers, Tim Bannerman,
June Marlow, Mhairi Harkens,
John Abineri, Mark Buffery, Lily Kar,
Jason Lake, Jo Crawford,
Phillip Manikum, Gina Bellman,
Michael Feldman, Shireen Shah,
Pavel Douglas, Barry Jackson,
Paul Nicholson, Bobby Collins,
Paddy Joyce

Directors: Peter Graham Scott *(Eps. 1–3, 6–7)*, Ken Price *(Ep. 4)* Alex Kirby *(Ep. 5)*

Seven episodes:
Lazlo
Dr. Jekyll and Mrs. Hyde
Eye of the Sun
London's Burning
The Phantom of the Opera
Xanadu
Excalibur

THE INVADERS

> "How does a nightmare begin? For David Vincent, architect, returning home from a business trip, it began a few minutes past four on a lost Tuesday morning, looking for a short cut he never found. It began with a welcoming sign that gave hope of black coffee. It began with a closed, deserted diner, and a man too long without sleep to continue his journey. In the weeks to come, David Vincent would go back to how it all began many times."
>
> —Opening narration on *Beachhead*

The Invaders was pure paranoia and its hero, David Vincent, the TV embodiment of the graffiti cliché: "Just because you're paranoid, doesn't mean they're *not* out to get you."

The premise was simple. Alien beings from a dying planet have landed on Earth. Their ultimate goal is to take over our world. With their ability to assume human form, they have already begun to infiltrate all the strata of Earth society—government, police and media. Eventually, they will control the planet. One man, architect David Vincent, has seen them land, knows they are here. Somehow he must convince a skeptical world that he is not crazy, that they really are out to get us . . .

In the 1950s, film-makers had exploited McCarthyist America's fears of Communist subversion with allegorical tales of insidious alien takeover such as *Invasion of the Body Snatchers* (1956). But in 1967, *The Invaders* had no political implications. Its intention was simply to scare.

Vincent's nightmare begins when he stops to rest while driving along a remote road. He is awakened by a strange noise and sees a flying saucer land. Returning to the scene later, he finds only a honeymoon couple who claim to have seen nothing. Vincent notices that the little fingers of the newlyweds protrude at an odd angle. But no one believes him.

And that's the way the series goes. Vincent responds to any call, any sighting, repeating his story to anyone who will listen. And sometimes people do. But they invariably turn out to be other invaders, until Vincent no longer knows whom he can trust. The aliens themselves were amorphous beings who needed recharging every 10–12 days in special regeneration chambers to retain their disguises; otherwise they reverted to their natural form and died. But Vincent couldn't even show the authorities a dead alien—when they were killed they disintegrated, leaving behind nothing but ashes and a scorched outline.

Toward the end of the second season, Vincent's solo crusade did turn into a team effort of sorts, with the addition of a group called The Believers, led by businessman Edgar Scoville, who provided cash aid and connections. But by that time, the repetitive format of the series had begun to pall with American audiences and it ended after just 43 episodes—a short run by contemporary U.S. standards.

A Quinn Martin production, many critics dubbed *The Invaders* as just another "running man" show like Martin's other famous series *The Fugitive*. There were undoubtedly similarities—both men crossed and recrossed the country in pursuit of their quarry—but there was one vital difference. Richard Kimble got his man. David Vincent never did. No matter how many aliens he killed he couldn't get them all . . .

Some 27 years after the original series went off the air in America, someone finally got around to making a sequel. The four-hour mini-series, in November 1995, brought back Roy Thinnes for a brief reprise as David Vincent, but it was *Quantum Leap*'s Scott Bakula who became the main alien-chaser, as ex-con Nolan Wood. And that nice Richard Thomas from *The Waltons* co-starred as the chief alien villain, posing as a car mechanic.

The mini-series did at last show the aliens in their non-human form and revealed why they want our world—their planet is dying and they need carbon monoxide to survive. No wonder they choose Los Angeles as a base. They also need to consume lots of cigarettes and eat fatty foods. *And* they attract a lot of flies—so now you know what to look out for . . .

REGULAR CAST
David Vincent Roy Thinnes *Edgar Scoville* Kent Smith
(*from Season Two episode* "The Believers")

Creator: Larry Cohen
Executive producer: Quinn Martin
Producer: Alan Armer
Theme: Dominic Frontière

A Quinn Martin Production in association with ABC
43 color 60-minute episodes
U.S. premiere: 10 January 1967
U.K. premiere: 21 January 1967

(*The Invaders* debuted over here at the same time as it started in America, running simultaneously, for a few weeks at least, in ITV's London region, though the first coherent run was on Granada Television. Overall, though, the show's run round the ITV regions was typically sporadic: it achieved a U.K. network run only when the rights were taken up by the BBC in 1984.)

Season One
17 one-hour episodes
20 February–10 July 1967
(Granada Television)

Beachhead

w Anthony Wilson
David Vincent sights a flying saucer landing but when he returns to the scene with the police and his business partner Alan Landers the ship is gone and Vincent is considered a crackpot. So begins his quest to convince the world aliens have arrived.
Alan Landers James Daly
Ben Holman J.D. Cannon
Kathy Adams Diane Baker
Carver John Milford
Old lady Ellen Corby
Mr. Kemper Vaughn Taylor
Sergeant John Milbury

Director: Joseph Sargent

The Experiment

w Anthony Spinner
Famed astrophysicist Dr. Curtis Lindstrom also discovers proof of the presence of aliens. Vincent tries to keep him alive so that he can expose the invaders at an international conference.
Lloyd Lindstrom Roddy McDowall
Dr. Curtis Lindstrom Laurence Naismith
Dr. Paul Mailer Harold Gould
Minister Dabbs Greer
Lt. James Willard Sage

Director: Joseph Sargent

The Mutation

w David Chandler
Vincent investigates a landing in Mexico unaware he is being led into an alien trap.
Vikki Suzanne Pleshette
Mark Evans Edward Andrews
Fellows Lin McCarthy
Alien Roy Jenson
Miguel Rodolfo Hoyos

Director: Paul Wendkos

The Leeches

w Dan Ullman
Following the disappearance of several leading scientists, Vincent is contacted by an electronics expert who fears he is next in line to be abducted by the aliens.
Warren Doneghan Arthur Hill
Tom Wiley Mark Richman
Eve Doneghan Diana van der Vlis
Hastings Robert H. Harris
Noel Markham Theo Marcuse

Director: Paul Wendkos

Genesis

w John W. Bloch
Vincent's search leads him to a sea lab where life is being created in a secret project.
Greg Lucather John Larch
Selene Lowell Carol Rossen
Sgt. Hal Corman Phillip Pine
Joan Corman Louise Latham
Steve Gibbs Tim McIntire
Dr. Ken Harrison William Sargent
Dr. Grayson Frank Overton

Director: Richard Benedict

Vikor

w Don Brinkley
A dying telephone operator's incredible account of what he has seen draws David Vincent to a vast industrial plant owned by a famous war hero.
George Vikor Jack Lord
Nexus Alfred Ryder
Sherri Vikor Diana Hyland
Police sgt. Richard O'Brien
Hank Sam Edwards

Director: Paul Wendkos

Nightmare

w John Kneubuhl
David Vincent discovers terrifying evidence that the
aliens are turning insects into carnivores.
Ellen Woods Kathleen Widdoes
Oliver Ames Robert Emhardt
Miss Havergill Jeanette Nolan
Ed Gidney James Callahan
Constable Gabbard William Bramley

Director: Paul Wendkos

Doomsday Minus One

w Louis Vittes
Vincent's help is requested when a saucer is seen
near the site of an underground nuclear test.
Major Rick Graves William Windom
General Beaumont Andrew Duggan
Tomkins Wesley Addy
Carl Wyeth Robert Osterloh
Spence Tom Palmer

Director: Paul Wendkos

Quantity: Unknown

w Don Brinkley, *story by* Clyde Ware
While investigating a mysterious cylinder found in
a plane crash, Vincent himself is accused of being an
alien.
Harry Swain James Whitemore
Col. Griffith William Talman
Diane Oberly Susan Strasberg
A.J. Richards Milton Selzer
Walt Anson Barney Phillips

Director: Sutton Roley

The Innocents

w John W. Bloch, *story by* Norman Klenman,
Bernard Rothman & John W. Bloch
Vincent is kidnapped and taken aboard an alien fly-
ing saucer.
Nat Greely William Smithers
Magnus Michael Rennie
Sgt. Ruddell Robert Doyle
Edna Greely Patricia Smith
Helen Katherine Justice
Capt. Ross Dabney Coleman

Director: Sutton Roley

The Ivy Curtain

w Don Brinkley
Vincent uncovers an alien indoctrination center in
an Ivy League school.
Barney Cahill Jack Warden
Stacy Susan Oliver
Mr. Burns David Sheiner

Dr. Reynard Murray Matheson
Lt. Alvarado Barry Russo

Director: Joseph Sargent

The Betrayed

w John W. Bloch, *story by* Theodore Sturgeon
& John W. Bloch
Vincent finds computer controls and a mysterious
tape that could be proof of an invasion.
Simon Carver Ed Begley
Susan Carver Laura Devon
Evelyn Bowers Nancy Wickwire
Neal Taft Norman Fell
Joey Taft Victor Brandt

Director: John Meredyth Lucas

Storm

w John Kneubuhl
A meteorologist calls in Vincent after a bizarre hur-
ricane that has veered erratically to spare a fishing
village.
Father Joe Joseph Campanella
Lisa Barbara Luna
Dr. Malcolm Gantley Simon Scott
Luis Perez Carlos Romero
Danny Paul Comi

Director: Paul Wendkos

Panic

w Robert Sherman
In the woods of West Virginia, Vincent pursues Nick
Baxter, an ailing invader whose touch freezes hu-
mans to death.
Nick Baxter Robert Walker
Madeline Flagg Lynn Loring
Gus Flagg R.G. Armstrong
Deputy Wallace Len Wayland
George Grundy Ford Rainey

Director: Robert Butler

Moonshot

w John W. Bloch & Rita Lakin, *story by* Rita
Lakin
Vincent investigates the death of two lunar astro-
nauts in a strange red fog.
Gavin Lewis Peter Graves
Hardy Smith John Ericson
Angela Smith Joanne Linville
Stan Arthur Kent Smith
Tony LaCava Anthony Eisley
Charlie Coogan Strother Martin

Director: Paul Wendkos

Wall of Crystal

w Don Brinkley & Dan Ullman, *story by* Dan Ullman
The aliens kidnap Vincent's brother and pregnant wife to force him to keep quiet about his latest discoveries.
Theodore Booth Burgess Meredith
Dr. Bob Vincent Linden Chiles
Grace Vincent Julie Sommars
Taugus Edward Asner
Joe McMullen Lloyd Gough

Director: Joseph Sargent

The Condemned

w Robert Sherman
Vincent is framed by the aliens for the apparent death of Morgan Tate, an industrialist who had stolen a vital alien file.
Morgan Tate Ralph Bellamy
Carol Tate Marlyn Mason
Lewis Dunhill Murray Hamilton
Det. Carter Larry Ward
John Finney John Ragin

Director: Richard Benedict

Season Two
26 one-hour stories
7 November 1967–9 February 1968*
(Granada Television)

* See subsequent note, after "The Captive."

Condition: Red

w Laurence Heath
The alien infiltration of an Alien Defense Command unit poses a new problem for Vincent.
Laurie Keller Antoinette Bower
Dan Keller Jason Evers
Dr. Rogers Roy Engel
Mr. Arius Mort Mills
Gen. Winters Robert Brubaker
Capt. Connors Burt Douglas
Capt. Albertson Forrest Compton

Director: Don Medford

The Saucer

w Dan Ullman
Vincent manages to capture tangible proof of the alien invasion—a flying saucer.
Annie Rhodes Anne Francis
Robert Morrison Charles Drake
John Carter Dabney Coleman
Joe Bonning Robert Knapp
Sam Thorne Kelly Thorsden

Director: Jesse Hibbs

The Watchers

w Jerry Sohl, Earl Hamner Jr., *story by* Earl Hamner Jr. & Michael Adams
A blind girl helps Vincent find the link between an electronic wizard and the aliens. (This episode also features Kevin McCarthy, star of *Invasion of the Body Snatchers*.)
Margaret Cook Shirley Knight
Paul Cook Kevin McCarthy
Ramsey Leonard Stone
Danvers Walter Brooke
Simms Robert Yuro
General John Zaremba

Director: Jesse Hibbs

Valley of the Shadow

w Robert Sabaroff, *story by* Howard Merrill & Robert Sabaroff
Vincent tries to convince a small town community that the man they've locked up on a murder charge is really an alien.
Sheriff Clements Ron Hayes
Maria McKinley Nan Martin
Will Hale Harry Townes
Capt. Taft (alien) Joe Maross
Major Ted Knight
Capt. Taft (human) James B. Sikking

Director: Jesse Hibbs

The Enemy

w John W. Bloch
A nurse witnesses an alien's horrifying transformation into his natural state.
Gale Frazer Barbara Barrie
Blake Richard Anderson
Sheriff Russell Thorson
Vern Hammond Paul Mantee
Sawyer Gene Lyons

Director: Robert Butler

The Trial

w George Eckstein, David W. Rintels
A friend of Vincent's goes on trial for the "murder" of an alien.
Charlie Gilman Don Gordon
Janet Wilk Lynda Day
Allen Slater Harold Gould
Robert Bernard Russell Johnson
Judge Malcolm Atterbury
Fred Wilk John Rayner
Bert Wisnofsky Bill Zuckert

Director: Robert Butler

The Spores

w Ellis Kadison & Joel Kane, story by Al Ramius, John Shaner, Ellis Kadison, Joel Kane
Vincent searches for a suitcase full of experimental spores, each capable of producing a full-grown alien upon brief exposure to the Earth's atmosphere.
Tom Jessup Gene Hackman
Ernie Goldhaver John Randolph
Jack Palay Mark Miller
Sally Palay Patricia Smith
Hal James Gammon
Mavis Judee Morton
Roy Kevin Coughlin
Mattson Wayne Rogers

Director: William Hale

Dark Outpost

w Jerry Sohl
Investigating the aliens' vulnerability to minor human diseases, Vincent finds himself aboard a flying saucer.
Dr. John Devin William Sargent
Hal Tim McIntire
Steve Tom Lovell
Vern Andrew Prine
Eileen Dawn Wells
Col. Harris Whit Bissell

Director: George McCowan

Summit Meeting

w George Eckstein (a 2-part story)
Vincent is alerted to an alien plot to assassinate world leaders at the testing of an experimental rocket. But he must rely on an attractive alien informer to help him warn the authorities in time.
Michael Tressider William Windom
Ellie Markham Diana Hyland
Per Alquist Michael Rennie
Thor Halvorsen Eduard Franz
Jonathan Blaine Ford Rainey

Director: Don Medford

The Prophet

w Warren Duff, story by Jerry De Bono
An alien evangelist begins to glow as he prophesies the coming of a "host from the skies."
Brother Avery Pat Hingle
Sister Claire Zina Bethune
Bill Shay Roger Perry
Brother John Richard O'Brien
Brother James Byron Keith

Director: Robert Douglas

Labyrinth

w Art Wallace
Vincent takes chest X-rays of an alien to the head of a UFO research project as proof of their existence.
Dr. Samuel Crowell Ed Begley
Laura Crowell Sally Kellerman
Dr. Harry Mills James Callahan
Prof. Edward Harrison John Zaremba
Argyle Martin Blaine

Director: Murray Golden

The Captive

w Laurence Heath
An alien held captive by a communist UN delegation convinces his captors that David Vincent is a spy.
Dr. Katherine Serret Dana Wynter
Peter Borke Fritz Weaver
Sanders Don Dubbins
Josef Lawrence Dane
Leo Peter Coe

Director: William Hale

(The following remaining second-season episodes were originally treated as a "third" season in Britain.)
25 June–17 September 1970,
(Granada Television)

The Believers

w Barry Oringer
The series undergoes a format change as David Vincent organizes a small group of "Believers" to help in his battle against the aliens.
Edgar Scoville Kent Smith (intro)
Bob Torin Anthony Eisley
Elyse Reynolds Carol Lynley
Torberg Than Wyenn
Harland Donald Davis
Lt. Sally Harper Kathleen Larkin
Prof. Hellman Rhys Williams

Director: Paul Wendkos

The Ransom

w Robert Collins
Vincent captures an important alien leader but Earth is threatened with massive reprisals if he is not released.
Alien leader Alfred Ryder
Bob Torin Anthony Eisley
Cyrus Stone Laurence Naismith
Claudia Stone Karen Black
Garth Lawrence Montaigne
Kant John Ragin

Director: Lewis Allen

Task Force

w Warren Duff
The aliens plot to take over the nation's news media by exploiting the weakness of the heir to a powerful publishing empire.
William Mace Martin Wolfson
Jeremy Mace Linden Chiles
June Murray Nancy Kovack

Director: Gerald Mayer

The Possessed

w John W. Bloch
Following up a lead from an old friend, Vincent discovers the aliens are using radio implants to program human beings.
Ted Willard Michael Tolan
Martin Willard Michael Constantine
Janet Garner Katherine Justice
Adam Lane William Smithers
Burt Newcomb Charles Bateman

Director: William Hale

Counter-Attack

w Laurence Heath
The Believers plan to attack the aliens' spaceships using radio navigational beams. Meanwhile, Vincent is falsely accused of murder and ridiculed in the press.
Joan Surrat Anna Capri
Archie Harmon Lin McCarthy
Alien leader Donald Davis
Jim Bryce John Milford
Lt. Conners Ken Lynch
Earl Warren Vanders

Director: Robert Douglas

The Pit

w Jack Miller
A scientist belonging to Vincent's group who claims he has proof of alien infiltration is declared insane.
Prof. Julian Reed Charles Aidman
Pat Reed Joanne Linville
Jeff Brower Donald Harron

Director: Lewis Allen

The Organization

w Franklin Barton
Vincent learns that a crime syndicate is hunting aliens to recover stolen narcotics.
Peter Kalter J.D. Cannon
Mike Calvin Chris Robinson
Mr. Weller Larry Gates

Kurt Roy Poole

Director: William Hale

The Peacemaker

w David W. Rintels
A top military man asks Vincent to set up peace talks with the aliens.
Gen. Concannon James Daly
Sarah Concannon Phyllis Thaxter
Archie Harmon Lin McCarthy
Alien leader Alfred Ryder

Director: Robert Day

The Vise

w William Blinn, *story by* Robert Sabaroff & William Blinn
Vincent tries to stop the appointment of a black alien to a vital post in the space program by turning to other blacks for help.
James Baxter Raymond St. Jacques
Arnold Warren Roscoe Lee Browne
Celia Baxter Janet MacLachlan

Director: William Hale

The Miracle

w Robert Collins, *story by* Robert Collins & Norman Herman
A young girl witnesses the fiery death of an alien near a religious shrine and believes it was a vision.
Beth Ferguson Barbara Hershey
Ferguson Edward Asner

Director: Robert Day

The Life Seekers

w Laurence Heath
Two aliens contact Vincent saying they wish to stop the invasion of Earth. (Missing from first U.K. run.)
Keith Barry Morse
Capt. Battersey R.G. Armstrong
Capt. Trent Arthur Franz
Claire Diana Muldaur

Director: Paul Wendkos

The Pursued

w Don Brinkley
An attractive alien loses control of her synthetic emotions and turns to David Vincent for help.
Anne Gibbs Suzanne Pleshette
Hank Will Geer

Director: William Hale

Inquisition

w Barry Oringer

A zealous government official tries to pin the explosive death of a senator on Vincent and his "group of fanatics."

Andrew Hatcher Mark Richman
Joan Seeley Susan Oliver
Jim John Milford

Director: Robert Glatzer

(NB: BBC2's reruns ran from 7 September 1984 to 22 August 1985, but excluded the two-part story "Summit Meeting" and the episodes "The Prophet" and "The Captive." A second run of all episodes went out in the nineties.)

The Invaders (mini-series)

(2 color 2-hour episodes)
w James Dott
Sequel to the 1960s series. Nolan Wood is an ex-pilot who lost his family and landed in jail for manslaughter after he saw *something* seven years earlier. Upon his release, he looks for his wife, Amanda, and son, but she happens to have married a mechanic. Now someone wants him out of the way. Nolan is framed for murdering a doctor who has evidence the extra-terrestrials exist, and the dead man's fiancée, Dr. Ellen Garza, teams up with Nolan to uncover the truth.

Nolan Wood Scott Bakula
David Vincent Roy Thinnes
Ellen Garza Elizabeth Pena
Jerry Thayer Richard Thomas
Amanda Thayer DeLane Matthews
Kyle Thayer Mario Yedidia
Coyle Terence Knox

with: Richard Belzer, Jon Polito, Jon Cypher, Elinor Donahue

Director: Paul Shapiro
Fox Television Production

U.S. premiere: 12, 14 November 1995

THE INVISIBLE MAN (1958–59)

H.G. Wells's famous creation has inspired three television series and this underrated 1958–59 British version, more properly known as *H.G. Wells' Invisible Man*, was the first.

It owes nothing to Wells but its name, being set in fifties Britain with a hero, Peter Brady, who remains a "good guy" throughout.

While successfully testing his theory of optical density—a principle that every form of matter could be reduced to invisibility through total refraction—promising young scientist Brady turns unexpectedly invisible when an experiment misfires. Unable to reverse the process, Brady becomes stuck as *The Invisible Man*. At first pursued and imprisoned by the men from the ministry, he proves his loyalty, allowing subsequent episodes to follow his adventures as he takes on an assortment of villains for both friends and country. Underlying the series, however, is Brady's search for an antidote, a way to restore his 6 ft. 2 in. frame to full visibility.

The series' star was kept anonymous. The most viewers ever saw was a suit of clothes and a bandaged head. On the whole, Brady remained completely invisible—even down to his goosepimples! His presence, however, was conveyed through his actions and mannerisms. While sitting at a desk, for example, he would pick up a paper-knife, twirling it in unseen fingers or tapping it on the desk. He sipped wine and puffed cigarettes through invisible lips, drove cars and motorbikes and even enjoyed an invisible kiss with actress Zena Marshall.

All sorts of special effects contributed to the Invisible Man's presence, with many of the delicate tricks still hailed as some of the best effects seen on television. Jack Whitehead, who once pulled the strings for Muffin the Mule, used his skills to raise a glass, suspended on two fine wires, to an invisible mouth, to jerk down the springs on a chair to simulate sitting, and to lift a hat from an invisible head. There were several ways, too, of making the Invisible Man appear to be driving a car. A stuntman lay flat on the floor with the nearside door slightly open so that he could see where he was going, steering with one hand at the bottom of the wheel and using the other hand to operate the foot pedals. Another way was to have the driver "built into" the upholstery. A false seat was dropped over him with small holes cut out for him to see through. On one occasion, during filming in London's Lincoln's Inn Fields, two pedestrians attempted to wrest control of a "riderless" motorcycle combination, unaware that a stuntman, concealed in the sidecar, was steering the bike.

The second series also featured more "subjective" camera work, so that viewers saw the world through the eyes of the Invisible Man.

Because so many people, including stuntmen and technicians, made *The Invisible Man* what he wasn't, producer Ralph Smart (*Danger Man*, *William Tell*) decided not to name the actors who played him and none was ever credited. But his voice was revealed as that of actor Tim Turner, while the man in the overcoat, playing the headless body, was short-built Johnny Scripps who "saw" through a button in the coat.

The female lead in the series was Lisa Daniely, as Brady's sister, Diane (Dee), and making her ITV debut was Deborah Watling, as his young niece Sally.

MAIN CAST

Voice of Peter Brady Tim Turner   *Diane* Lisa Daniely
Sally Deborah Watling

Producer: Ralph Smart
Music: Sidney John Key *(Season One)*
Production supervisor: Aida Young
An Official Films/ITP (Incorporated Television Program) Ltd Production for ATV
26 black and white 30-minute episodes

Season One:
14 September–14 December 1958
Season Two:
12 April–5 July 1959
(ITV, London region)
U.S. premiere: 4 November 1958

Season One

Secret Experiment

w Michael Connor & Michael Cramoy
Scientist Peter Brady becomes invisible following a laboratory accident. He is at first detained as a security risk but escapes and then outwits a fellow scientist, Crompton, who is out to steal his notes.
Dr. Hanning Lloyd Lamble
Kemp Bruce Seton
Sir Charles Anderson Ernest Clark
Crompton Michael Goodliffe

Director: Pennington Richards

Crisis in the Desert

w Ralph Smart
Colonel Warren, of British Military Intelligence, asks Brady's help in rescuing one of his agents, Jack Howard, from the secret police of a Middle East state. There, Brady meets rebel leader, Yolanda.
Yolanda Adrienne Corri
Hassan Erich Pohlmann
Omar Martin Benson
Nesib Peter Sallis
Jack Howard Howard Pays
Col. Warren Douglas Wilmer
Corporal Derren Nesbitt
Surgeon Derek Sydney

Director: Pennington Richards

Behind the Mask

w Stanley Mann & Leslie Arliss, *story by* Stanley Mann
Brady is quite willing to help when horribly disfigured Raphael Constantine asks to be made invisible—until he realizes Constantine is planning an invisible assassination.
Constantine Dennis Price
Max Edwin Richfield
Marcia Barbara Chilcott
Josef David Ritch
Juan Michael Jacques
President Domecq Arthur Gomez
Official John Wynn Jones

Director: Pennington Richards

The Locked Room

w Lindsay Galloway, *story by* Ralph Smart
A beautiful scientist from behind the Iron Curtain criticizes her government while she is in London and efforts are made to "recall" her. Brady, believing she can help him regain his visibility, attempts to rescue her.
Tania Zena Marshall
Dr. Hanning Lloyd Lamble
Dushkin Rupert Davies
Clerk Emrys Leyshon
Phillips Noel Coleman
Porter Alexande Doré

Director: Pennington Richards

Picnic with Death

w Leonard Fincham & Leslie Arliss, *story by* Leonard Fincham

Through his niece Sally, Brady becomes involved with a woman whose husband and sister-in-law are planning to murder her.

John Norton Derek Bond
Carol Norton Faith Brook
Lindy Norton Margaret McCourt
Janet Norton Maureen Pryor
Sir Charles Ernest Clark
Stableman Michael Ripper

Director: Pennington Richards

Play to Kill

w Leslie Arliss, *story by* Robert Westerby

Celebrated actress Barbara Crane is being blackmailed. Was she really to blame for a fatal accident on a lonely clifftop road? Brady sets out to clear her name.

Barbara Crane Helen Cherry
Colonel Colin Gordon
Tom Hugh Latimer
Simon Garry Thorne
Manton Ballard Berkeley
Arthurson Vincent Holman

Director: Peter Maxwell

Shadow on the Screen

w Ian Stuart Black, *story by* Ralph Smart & Philip Levene

Sonia Vasa, a communist spy, tries to trap the Invisible Man into revealing his secret by posing as a refugee seeking his help in getting her scientist husband into the West.

Stephan Vasa Edward Judd
Sonia Vasa Greta Gynt
Bratski Redmond Phillips
Captain Andre Mikhelson
Commissar Anthony Newlands
Sir Charles Ernest Clark
Woman in lift Irene Handl

Director: Pennington Richards

The Mink Coat

w Ian Stuart Black, *story by* Leonore Coffee

When Penny Page flies to France, she is unaware that vital stolen atomic secrets are hidden in the lining of her mink coat, making her the target for the thieves. Luckily, Brady and his sister are among her fellow passengers.

Penny Page Hazel Court
Walker Derek Godfrey
Bunny Harold Berens
Marcel Murray Kash
Customs officer Keith Rawlings

Madame Dupont Joan Hickson
Photographer John Ruddock

Director: Pennington Richards

Blind Justice

w Ralph Smart

Peter Brady becomes a blind woman's "eyes" as she tries to trap the drug-smuggling gang responsible for framing and murdering her husband.

Katherine Holt Honor Blackman
Arthur Holt Philip Friend
Sandy Mason Jack Watling
Simmons Julian Somers
Sparrow Leslie Phillips
Det. insp. Heath Robert Raglan
Det. sgt. Desmond Llewellyn

Director: Pennington Richards

Jailbreak

w Ian Stuart Black

Joe Green, jailed for robbery with violence, protests his innocence and makes repeated escape attempts. Believing his story, Brady helps him prove his alibi.

Joe Green Dermot Walsh
Doris Denny Dayvis
Brenner Michael Brennan
Governor Ralph Michael
Sharp Ronald Fraser
Taylor Charles Farrell
Robson Maurice Kaufman

Director: Pennington Richards

Bank Raid

w Doreen Montgomery & Ralph Smart

Brady's niece Sally is kidnapped and held hostage by a gang of crooks who force him to rob a bank to save her life.

Crowther Willoughby Goddard
Williams Brian Rawlinson
Headmistress Patricia Marmont

Director: Ralph Smart

Odds against Death

w Ian Stuart Black, *story by* Stanley Mann

Brady uses his invisibility to manipulate the casino tables in Italy as he tries to help a brilliant scientist who is gambling his daughter's life away.

Prof. Owens Walter Fitzgerald
Suzy Owens Julia Lockwood
Lucia Colette Wilde
Caletta Alan Tilvern
Bruno Peter Taylor
Croupier Peter Elliott
Manager Olaf Pooley

Director: Pennington Richards

Strange Partners

w Michael Cramoy

Brady discovers that being The Invisible Man is a defense against detection by humans—but not by a dog, when he is tricked into the visiting the home of Lucian Currie who wants him to murder his ailing partner, Vickers.

Insp. Quillan Victor Platt
Collins Jack Melford
Vickers Patrick Troughton
Ryan Robert Cawdron
Doctor Reginald Hearne
Lucian Currie Griffith Jones

Director: Pennington Richards

Season Two

Point of Destruction

w Ian Stuart Black

When four test pilots are killed in plane crashes while experimenting with a new fuel diffuser, Brady steps in to investigate and finds one of the team is in league with an enemy agent.

Scott Duncan Lamont
Dr. Court John Rudling
Katrina Patricia Jessel
Stephan Derren Nesbitt
Jenny Jane Barrett
Control officer Barry Letts

Director: Quentin Lawrence

Death Cell

w Michael Connors

A beautiful but frightened young woman escapes from a mental home to seek The Invisible Man's help, claiming she has been held there as she is the only person who can prove the innocence of her fiancé, George Wilson, who's awaiting execution for murder.

Ellen Summers Lana Morris
Dr. Trevor Ian Wallace
George Wilson William Lucas
Sir Charles Bruce Seton
Prison governor Jack Lambert
Miss Beck Bettina Dickson
Mrs. Willis Patricia Burke

Director: Peter Maxwell

The Vanishing Evidence

w Ian Stuart Black

Peter Thal, an international spy, murders Prof. Harper and steals vital papers. MI5 sends Brady to Amsterdam to track him down.

Prof. Harper James Raglan

Thal Charles Grey
Col. Ward Ernest Clark
Jenny Reyden Sarah Lawson
Porter Michael Ripper
Insp. Strang Peter Illing
Superintendent Ewen Solon

Director: Peter Maxwell

The Prize

w Ian Stuart Black

Arriving in Scandinavia to collect a prize for his contribution to science, Brady finds the guest of honor, Russian writer Tania Roskoff, has been arrested at the border.

Tania Mai Zetterling
Gunzi Anton Diffring
Prof. Kenig Tony Church
General Desmond Roberts
Sentry Clive Baxter
Capt. Bera Richard Clarke
Agasha Ruth Lodge

Director: Quentin Lawrence

Flight Into Darkness

w Ian Stuart Black, *story by* William H. Altman

Talked into believing that his remarkable new antigravity discovery will endanger mankind, Dr. Stephens destroys his papers and disappears. Brady promises Pat Stephens he will try to find her father.

Dr. Stephens Geoffrey Keen
Wilson Esmond Knight
Wade John Harvey
Sir Jasper Michael Shepley
Pat Stephens Joanna Dunham
Sewell Colin Douglas
Fisher Alex Scott

Director: Peter Maxwell

The Decoy

w Brenda Blackmore

Identical twins Terry and Toni Trent, an American stage musical act, are on tour in Britain when one of them disappears. The Invisible Man volunteers to solve the mystery.

Toni and Terry Trent Betta St. John
Capt. Rubens Robert Gallico
Stavros Philip Leaver
Andreas Wolf Morris
Giorgio Barry Shawzin
General Lionel Murton
First secretary Bruno Barnabe

Director: Quentin Lawrence

The Gun Runners

w Ian Stuart Black
Brady is sent to investigate gun-running in the Mediterranean state of Bay Akim, accompanied by government agent Zena Fleming.
Col. Grahame Bruce Seton
Zena Fleming Louise Allbritton
Sardi Paul Stassino
Arosa Charles Hill
Hotel manager Josef Attard
Malia Laurence Taylor
Ali James Booth
Airport clerk Morris Sweden
Receptionist Ann Dimitri

Director: Peter Maxwell

The White Rabbit

w Ian Stuart Black
After a terrified rabbit materializes before a young French doctor's eyes, French Security call in Brady to investigate a château where Monsieur Rocher is plotting to gain world power by creating an invisible army.
Suzanne Dumasse Marla Landi
Hugo Austin Trevor
Rocher Paul Daneman
Valois Arnold Marle
Prof. Blaire Arnold Diamond
Max Reed de Rouen
Louise Myrtle Reed
Dr. Dumasse Keith Pyott
Colette Isobel Black
Brun André Cherisse
Chauffeur Andrée Muller

Director: Quentin Lawrence

Man in Disguise

w Brenda Blackmore, *story by* Leslie Arliss
Brady is tricked by a beautiful girl in Paris and loses his passport. When the girl's accomplice, Nick, uses it to impersonate him on a drug run, Brady finds himself involved in an international drug-smuggling racket.
Nick Tim Turner
Madeleine Leigh Madison
Matt Lee Montague
Det. insp. Robert Raglan
Sgt. Day Howard Pays
Sgt. Winter Jeanette Sterke
Victor Robert Rietty
Club manager Denis Shaw
Aylmer Felix Felton

Directors: Quentin Lawrence, Peter Maxwell

Man in Power

w Ian Stuart Black
A Middle East king is murdered by his power-crazy Army chief and Brady becomes involved in thwarting a dangerous plot to install a dictatorship.

General Shafari André Morell
King Rashid Vivian Matalon
Princess Taima Nadia Regin
Prince Jonetta Gary Raymond
Hassan Andrew Keir
Col. Fayid Derek Sydney
Ambassador Ivan Craig

Director: Peter Maxwell

The Rocket

w Michael Pertwee
Brady's ingenuity is tested when gambling losses prompt one of his aides, Smith, to sell rocket secrets to a foreign power.
Smith Glyn Owen
Reitter Russell Waters
Prof. Howard Robert Brown
Det. insp. Robert Raglan
Mrs. Smith Jennifer Wright
Driver Evans Harold Goodwin
Sgt. Maurice Durant
Bill Colin Croft

Director: Quentin Lawrence

Shadow Bomb

w Tony O'Grady (*alias* Brian Clemens) & Ian Stuart Black, *story by* Tony O'Grady
Brady risks his life trying to save his friend Barry Finch from being blown up by a new type of bomb detonator that will be triggered the moment even a shadow falls on it.
Capt. Barry Finch Conrad Phillips
Betty Jennifer Jayne
Lloyd Walter Gotell
Lt. Daniels Ian Hendry
General Martin Anthony Bushell

Director: Quentin Lawrence

The Big Plot

w Ian Stuart Black, *story by* Tony O'Grady (*alias* Brian Clemens) & Robert Smart
When a plane crash reveals that a canister of Uranium 235, used to make atomic bombs, was being smuggled into England, Brady must break a plot to start World War Three, involving atomic bombs hidden in every major world capital.
Waring William Squire
Helen Barbara Shelley
Lord Peversham John Arnatt
Officers Richard Warner, Derrick Sherwin
MacBane Edward Hardwicke
Minister Basil Dignam
Sir Charles Ewen MacDuff
Hanstra Terence Cooper

Director: Peter Maxwell

Unbroadcast first pilot: (Title Unknown)

w Doreen Montgomery & Ralph Smart

Peter Brady becomes invisible in a laboratory accident. He goes home to his sister, Jane, and niece Sally. When Sally is kidnapped, Brady must break into a bank to buy her freedom. (This version had different music and inferior effects, but elements of the story emerged in "Secret Experiment," "Bank Raid" and "Picnic with Death.")

Brady's voice Robert Beatty
Jane Lisa Daniely
Sally Deborah Watling
Crowther Willoughby Goddard
Williams Brian Rawlinson

Director: Ralph Smart

THE INVISIBLE MAN (1975)

The 1975 American version of *The Invisible Man* was a short-lived action-adventure series starring ex-UNCLE hero David McCallum as invisible scientist Dr. Daniel Weston.

In the pilot TV film, Weston discovers how to make himself invisible and must then try to keep the secret from unscrupulous agents who want to use it as a means of achieving world power. He has a friend Nick Maggio (Henry Darrow) who makes a lookalike mask for him to wear so that he can appear in public (and we can get to see the star once in a while).

In the series, Weston and his visible wife, Kate, take on various assignments for the government such as testing out a security system ("The Fine Art of Diplomacy"), unmasking a fake spiritualist ("Man of Influence"), helping a scientist defector to return home ("Barnard Wants Out"), rescuing the kidnapped daughter of a vital mob trial witness ("Sight Unseen") and secretly returning stolen money ("Pin Money").

Melinda Fee played Kate (some viewers were wryly concerned that she spent so much time with a naked—if invisible—man!), and their boss Carlson was played by Jackie Cooper in the pilot and Craig Stevens in the series.

Despite its personable stars and some good special effects, *The Invisible Man* never caught on in America and ended after its first-season run of just 13 episodes.

REGULAR CAST
Dr. Daniel Weston David McCallum   *Kate Weston* Melinda Fee
Walter Carlson Craig Stevens (Jackie Cooper *in the pilot*)

Pilot credits:
Teleplay: Steven Bochco
Director: Robert Michael Lewis
Producer: Steven Bochco
Executive producer: Harve Bennett
Music: Richard Clements
A Harve Bennett Production in association with Universal/NBC

Series credits:
Producer: Leslie Stevens
Executive producer: Harve Bennett
Story editor: Seeleg Lester
Theme: Henry Mancini
13 color 50-minute episodes (pilot 80 minutes)
(one × 80 mins, 12 × 50 mins.)
The Invisible Man (pilot)

The Klae Resource
The Fine Art of Diplomacy
Man of Influence
Eyes Only
Barnard Wants Out
Go Directly to Jail
Pin Money
Stop When the Red Lights Flash
Sight Unseen
The Klae Dynasty
Attempt to Save Face
Power Play

Silverton Productions Inc/Universal
U.S. premiere: 8 September 1975
U.K.: 26 September–22 December 1975
(BBC1)

THE INVISIBLE MAN (1984)

The third of television's *Invisible Man* series was, in effect, the first—a stylishly staged six-part BBC adaptation of H.G. Wells' original 1897 novel.

Pip Donaghy starred as the heavily bandaged "mad scientist" Dr. Griffin who turns his scientific brilliance to bad ends, for power and destruction. Embarking on a personal reign of terror, he becomes a homicidal maniac, invisible morally as well as physically. He is a fugitive, a lonely and pathetic outcast; his acts lead ultimately to his own self-destruction.

Frank Middlemass co-starred as Griffin's unwilling and untrustworthy helper, the tramp Thomas Marvel, and David Gwillim appeared as the Invisible Man's old colleague Dr. Samuel Kemp who is forced to shelter Griffin and listens, horrified and fascinated, to the story of how he discovered the secret of invisibility.

Originally intended as a Sunday teatime serial, *The Invisible Man* was upgraded from the family classics slot to a weekday mid-evening one, where it became a solid success for the former *Doctor Who* combo of producer Barry Letts and script editor Terrance Dicks.

MAIN CAST

Griffin, The Invisible Man Pip Donaghy   *Reverend Bunting* Michael Sheard
Thomas Marvel Frank Middlemass   *Dr. Samuel Kemp* David Gwillim
Dr. Cuss Gerald James   *Mr. Hall* Ron Pember   *Mrs. Hall* Lila Kaye
Teddy Henfrey Jonathan Adams   *Sandy Wadgers* Roy Holder
Mrs. Roberts Anna Wing   *Constable Jaffers* John Quarmby
Lucy Merelina Kendall   *Colonel Adye* Frederick Treves

Dramatized by James Andrew Hall, *from the novel by* H.G. Wells
Producer: Barry Letts
Director: Brian Lighthill
Script editor: Terrance Dicks
Visual effects designer: John Brace
Video effects supervisor: Dave Jervis
Designer: Don Giles
Music: Stephen Deutsch
A BBC Production

Six color 30-minute episodes
The Strange Man's Arrival
The Unveiling of the Stranger
Mr. Marvel's Visit to Iping
Dr. Kemp's Visitor
Certain First Principles
The Hunting of the Invisible Man

4 September–9 October 1984
(BBC1)

JAMIE

Jamie was a 13-year-old boy who traveled through time on a magic carpet, meeting such notable historical characters as Guy Fawkes, Nelson, Samuel Pepys, Robert the Bruce and William the Conquerer.

Jamie discovers his carpet in a junk shop and learns its secret from the mysterious Mr. Zed who prompts him to make his journeys back into the past. Jamie would sit on his carpet, which would rise, then whirl round faster and faster, flipping back through time.

Mr. Zed remained an enigma. Nobody could say what age he was—sometimes he was young, sometimes he was incredibly old. But he was certainly "not of this world" . . .

In the course of the 13-part series (which filled a corner of ITV's Sunday teatime schedules), Jamie tries to warn the Gunpowder plotters of impending treachery, joins Nelson's crew at the Battle of Trafalgar, meets his father as a young boy, travels to old Baghdad and 19th-century London, fights the Great Fire of London, learns the legend of Robert the Bruce and the spider and, finally, goes back to 1066. On some of his sorties he was joined by his best friend, Tink.

REGULAR CAST

Jamie Dodger Garry Miller *Molly Dodger (his mum)* Jo Kendall
David Dodger (his dad) Ben Aris *Mr. Zed* Aubrey Morris
Tink Bellow Nigel Chivers

Writer: Denis Butler
Producer: Antony Kearey
Executive producer: Francis Coleman
Directors: Antony Kearey, Geoffrey Nethercott,
    Bryan Izzard, John Reardon, David Coulter

London Weekend Television Production
13 color 30-minute episodes
The Carpet
Remember, Remember
The Sugar Islands
England Expects

Summer Holiday
Prince of Fire
The Climbing Boy
The Devil's Rookery
London Bridge Is Falling Down
New Lamps for Old
Buttercap
The Last Adventure
Dragon's Wake

6 June–5 September 1971
(LWT)

JASON OF STAR COMMAND

Half-baked live-action kids' series about the exploits of ace space pilot Jason and his comrades in Star Command as they fight the never-ending fight against the villainous galactic gangster, Dragos.

Notable mainly for the presence in some episodes of James "Scotty" Doohan as Jason's commander, the series' general format was three-part stories with a cliffhanger ending to each episode.

REGULAR CAST

Jason Craig Littler *Dragos* Sid Haig

A Filmation Production
U.K.: 28 color 30-minute episodes

U.K. premiere:
1979 (BBC Wales) as part of *Yr Awr Fawr* (The Big Hour), a Sunday morning children's program

---

JET JACKSON, THE FLYING COMMANDO

Early American foray into science fiction that followed the daredevil exploits of Jet Jackson, hero of his nation's "Secret Squadron" of top agents who fought to thwart the evil designs of foreign powers and other nefarious influences.

Jet had two regular companions—a mechanic pal called Ikky, and an inventive scientist friend, Tut. Their adventures were played out against a cold war–type background with threats of radiation, nuclear weapons and missile warfare never far away.

The series ran originally in the U.S. in 1952, as *Captain Midnight,* becoming *Jet Jackson* upon syndication two years later. It was seen in the U.K. by ITV viewers in Wales and the West of England, where it was the first sf-based show to emerge on the new channel run by TWW, collaring a regular early Monday evening slot until it ran out of steam toward the end of a 39-episode run, skipping weeks and changing days.

REGULAR CAST

Jet Jackson Richard Webb *Ikky* Sid Melton
Tut Olan Soule

Producer: George Bilson
Director: D. Ross Lederman

39 black and white 30-minute episodes
U.K.: 20 April 1959–23 February 1960
(TWW)

JOE 90

Gerry Anderson's ninth TV puppet show—and the sixth of the Supermarionation series—*Joe 90* marked a conscious change of style and pace.

Gone were the hi-tech hardware and jut-jawed heroes of *Thunderbirds* and *Captain Scarlet*. In their place . . . a bespectacled nine-year-old boy.

A normal, adventure-loving schoolboy, Joe was the adopted son of a brilliant electronics engineer, Professor Ian McClaine, creator of BIG RAT (Brain Impulse Galvanoscope Record And Transfer), a sophisticated device which recorded the brain patterns of one person and transferred them to another. At the behest of Shane Weston, Deputy Head of the World Intelligence Network (an organization dedicated to maintaining the balance of power throughout the world), Prof. McClaine used his brainchild on Joe, giving him the specialist attributes of an appropriate highly skilled adult, and making him WIN's Most Special Agent, on the assumption that Joe could boldly go where no man could venture—and get away with it.

At the outset of each mission, Joe sat in a special chair that rose up into a circular cage that revolved as the BIG RAT tape was run, amid electronic noises and a psychedelic light show. Once the transfer was complete, Joe donned a pair of "electrode glasses" to trigger the knowledge. In the course of the series he became an astronaut, test pilot, racing driver, aquanaut, computer boffin and a brain surgeon, among others.

Joe carried with him an ordinary-looking schoolboy's case that appeared to contain the usual scholarly paraphernalia. But when he flipped the case over and pressed two small studs, secret lids opened revealing compartments containing his electrode glasses, his WIN badge, pistol, pocket transmitter, ammo and secret reports. What more could a boy wish for?

CHARACTER VOICES
Joe 90 Len Jones   *Prof. McClaine* Rupert Davies
Shane Weston David Healy   *Sam Loover (his deputy)* Keith Alexander
Mrs. Ada Harris (the professor's housekeeper) Sylvia Anderson
Other voices: Gary Files, Martin King, Shane Rimmer, Jeremy Wilkin

Format: Gerry & Sylvia Anderson
Executive producer: Reg Hill
Producer: David Lane
Script editor: Tony Barwick
Music: Barry Gray

A Century 21 Production for ITC
(Presented by ATV)
30 color 30-minute episodes
29 September 1968–20 April 1969
(ATV—Midlands)

The Most Special Agent

w Gerry & Sylvia Anderson
Professor McClaine gives his adopted son, Joe, amazing powers via a pair of special glasses, enabling him to become an invaluable agent of the World Intelligence Network. Joe's first mission: to steal a new Russian prototype plane.

Director: Des Saunders

Most Special Astronaut

w Tony Barwick
Joe acquires the brain pattern of a top astronaut to

save two men in a space station who are without an air supply.

Director: Peter Anderson

Project 90

w Tony Barwick
Prof. McClaine is kidnapped by spies anxious to learn more about Big Rat. Joe saves his father using the brain pattern of a balloonist.

Director: Peter Anderson

Hi-jacked

w Tony Barwick
Joe has himself nailed into a crate so he can catch a dangerous gun-runner and smuggler red-handed.

Director: Alan Perry

Colonel McClaine

w Tony Barwick
Joe delves into the brain patterns of an explosives expert and a top driver to transport a dangerous cargo across Africa.

Director: Ken Turner

The Fortress

w Shane Rimmer
A microfilm hidden in a remote jungle could blow the cover of every WIN agent in the area if it falls into the wrong hands. Joe has to find it first.

Director: Leo Eaton

King for a Day

w Shane Rimmer
Joe impersonates the heir to a Middle East throne who has been kidnapped to prevent his enthronement. Then Joe is kidnapped himself.

Director: Leo Eaton

International Concerto

w Tony Barwick
Wonder-boy Joe 90 receives the brain patterns of a top pianist who is also a secret agent.

Director: Alan Perry

Splashdown

w Shane Rimmer
Joe acquires the skills of a top test pilot to investigate the disappearance of two electronics experts.

Director: Leo Eaton

Big Fish

w Shane Rimmer
Joe becomes one of the world's leading aquanauts and prevents an international incident when a sub breaks down in enemy waters.

Director: Leo Eaton

Relative Danger

w Shane Rimmer
Joe is given the brain pattern of a leading underground explorer in an effort to save the lives of three men trapped in an old silver mine.

Director: Peter Anderson

Operation McClaine

w Gerry Anderson & David Lane
Joe becomes a brilliant brain surgeon and performs a life-or-death operation on a famous writer.

Director: Ken Turner

The Unorthodox Shepherd

w Tony Barwick
Joe is given the persona of a World Bank president to investigate a flood of forged notes—an investigation that leads him to a supposedly haunted church. (This episode featured location work that sowed the seeds for *The Secret Service*—see separate entry.)

Director: Ken Turner

Business Holiday

w Tony Barwick
Joe becomes a "colonel" to ensure that a former World Army base is destroyed to prevent it becoming a threat to world peace.

Director: Alan Perry

Arctic Adventure

w Tony Barwick
A secret nuclear bomb is buried in the icy waters of the Arctic Sea. Joe is sent to retrieve it.

Director: Alan Perry

Double Agent

w Tony Barwick
Joe's life is in danger when he is given the brain patterns of a double agent.

Director: Ken Turner

Three's a Crowd

w Tony Barwick
Joe receives the brain patterns of a lovely girl who has attracted his father's attention but who is suspected of being a spy.

Director: Peter Anderson

The Professional

w Donald James

Joe receives the skills of a burglar to help him break into a castle to recover some stolen gold.

Director: Leo Eaton

The Race

w Tony Barwick

The brain patterns of a Monte Carlo rally winner help Joe take up a challenge WIN must win to ensure its own future.

Director: Alan Perry

Talkdown

w Tony Barwick

Joe becomes a test pilot to find out why a hypersonic fighter plane crashed.

Director: Alan Perry

Breakout

w Shane Rimmer

Two Canadian convicts escape from jail and threaten the life of their prime minister. Joe, on holiday, and using the brain patterns of a bobsled champion, goes to the rescue.

Director: Leo Eaton

Child of the Sun God

w John Lucarotti

Joe discovers a lost jungle tribe and has to prove that he is a god, to save his life.

Director: Alan Perry

See You Down There

w Tony Barwick

Joe uses a variety of brain patterns to make a ruthless businessman, who operates by fraud, believe he is going mad.

Director: Leo Eaton

Lone-Handed 90

w Desmond Saunders & Keith Wilson

Joe dreams of becoming a sheriff and taking part in a rip-roaring Western adventure.

Director: Ken Turner

Attack of the Tiger

w Tony Barwick

Joe is sent on a hazardous mission, against an Eastern Alliance rocket base that is threatening to hold the world to ransom by launching a nuclear weapon into orbit.

Director: Peter Anderson

Viva Cordova

w Tony Barwick

Joe becomes a Mexican president's bodyguard—without the president knowing.

Director: Peter Anderson

Mission X-41

w Pat Dunlop

Joe parachutes into an enemy research station in a daring search for a new formula.

Director: Ken Turner

Test Flight

w Donald James

The brain pattern of a computer specialist and an explosives expert (again) helps Joe avert a sabotage threat.

Director: Peter Anderson

Trial at Sea

w Donald James

Joe races against time to prevent a new hoverliner from being blown up.

Director: Leo Eaton

The Birthday

w Tony Barwick

At a special celebration to mark his tenth birthday, Joe and his friends look back over some of the exciting moments of his young life.

Director: Leo Eaton

JOURNEY TO THE UNKNOWN

This 1968 Anglo-American hybrid can only marginally be counted as science fiction—even though it has been lumped into the sf category in America.

Produced by Joan Harrison, a former associate of Alfred Hitchcock, it was more a collection of psychological suspense dramas—encompassing devil worship, reincarnation, the supernatural, murder and revenge.

But it did touch on science fiction—in "Stranger in the Family," a remake of an *Out of the Unknown* episode; in "The Madison Equation," where a jealous husband programs a computer to kill his errant wife; and in "Jane Brown's Body," in which a suicide victim is brought back to life by a new experimental drug.

The anthology of 17 stories was made in Britain by Hammer Films and marked that company's first TV venture. It has since notched up two more series—*Hammer House of Horror* in 1980 and *Hammer House of Mystery and Suspense* in 1984. However, the series' £12 million budget (£70,000 an episode) was all-American, the cash coming from ABC-TV and 20th Century Fox. And *Journey to the Unknown* premiered in America in September 1968, several weeks prior to its British debut.

REGULAR CAST
None

Executive producers: Joan Harrison, Norman Lloyd
Executive consultant: Jack Fleischmann
Producer: Anthony Hinds
Theme: Harry Robinson

Hammer Film Productions Ltd/20th Century Fox Television
17 color 60-minute episodes
U.S. premiere: 26 September 1968
U.K. premiere: 16 November 1968
(LWT)

The New People

w Oscar Millard & John Gould, *story by* Charles Beaumont
Luther Ames, rich, charming and bored, plays Mephistopheles in his small circle and condemns to death any who break his unwritten laws.
Hank Prentiss Robert Reed
Anne Prentiss Jennifer Hilary
Luther Ames Patrick Allen
Helen Ames Melissa Stribling
Matt Dystal Milo O'Shea
Terry Lawrence Adrienne Corri
David Redford Damian Thomas
Susan Redford Suzanne Mokler
Ben Anthony Colby
Rhoda Beryl Richardson
Manservant Robert Webber

Director: Peter Sasdy

Somewhere in a Crowd

w Michael J. Bird
TV commentator William Searle is disturbed by the appearance of five strangely familiar faces at a series of tragic happenings, and discovers that the five were killed in a train crash two years earlier, which he survived.
William Searle David Hedison
Ruth Searle Ann Bell
Max Newby Jeremy Longhurst
Marielle Jane Asher
Douglas Bishop Ewen Solon
Hugh Baillie Tenniel Evans
Watchers George McGrath, Frank Cousins, Kaplan Kaye, Ann King, Elizabeth Robillard

Director: Alan Gibson

Matakitas Is Coming

w Robert Heverley
A young researcher, June Wiley, is trapped in a closed library where she discovers that she has been pledged to the devil.
June Wiley Vera Miles
Ken Talbot Dermot Walsh
Sylvia Ann Gay Hamilton
Matakitas Leon Lissek

Director: Michael Lindsay-Hogg

Jane Brown's Body

w Anthony Skene, *story by* Cornell Woolrich
A young girl is brought back to life by Dr. Ian Denholt's experimental serum, but has no memory of the past. However, she learns, remembers—and then follows the path that led to her death.
Jane Brown Stefanie Powers
Paul Amory David Buck
Dr. Ian Denholt Alan McNaughtan
Pamela Denholt Sarah Lawson
Receptionist Arthur Pentelow
Robert Clive Graham
Mrs. Brown Yvonne Gilan
Butler Lewis Fiander

Director: Alan Gibson

Do Me a Favor and Kill Me

w Stanley Miller, *story by* Frederick Rawlings
Fading actor Jeff Wheeler asks a friend to kill him to spare his obscurity, telling him to ignore any requests to call it off. Then he changes his mind.
Jeff Wheeler Joseph Cotten
Faith Wheeler Judy Parfitt
Harry Vantese Douglas Wilmer
Dirk Brogan Kenneth Haigh
Betty Joyce Blair
Chris David Warbeck
Asst. director David Baxter
Wardrobe dresser Hugh Futcher
Lisa Carol Cleveland
Golfer Tom Gill

Director: Gerry O'Hara

Poor Butterfly

w Jeremy Paul, *story by* William Abney
Commercial artist Steven Miller receives a costume party invitation that takes him back 40 years, into a tragic past.
Steven Miller Chad Everett
Rose Beacham Susan Brodrick
Robert Sawyer Edward Fox
Ben Loker Bernard Lee
Mrs. Loker Susan Richards
Friar Tuck Norman Chappell
Nelson Antony Webb
Queen Victoria Fay Compton
Lady Hamilton Linda Cole
Guest Martin Lyder
Diana Marty Cruikshank

Director: Alan Gibson

The Madison Equation

w Michael J. Bird
A jealous husband programs a highly sophisticated computer to electrocute his unfaithful wife. But instead, it kills him . . .

Inga Madison Barbara Bel Geddes
Ralph Madison Allan Cuthbertson
Stuart Crosbie Paul Daneman
Barbara Rossiter Sue Lloyd
Adam Frost Jack Hedley
Sir Gerald Walters Richard Vernon
Gen. Wannamaker Lionel Murton
Frederick Shea Aubrey Morris
Insp. Bridges Lloyd Lamble

Director: Rex Firkin

Girl of My Dreams

w Robert Bloch & Michael J. Bird, *story by* Richard Matheson
Opportunist Greg Richards tries to exploit the psychic dreams of a shy young cashier, Carrie, who is able to predict people's deaths.
Carrie Clark Zena Walker
Greg Richards Michael Callan
Sue Tarleton Justine Lord
Mrs. Wheeler Jan Holden
Mr. Thwaite David Langton

Director: Peter Sasdy

The Last Visitor

w Alfred Shaughnessy
Barbara King, a young girl in need of rest, is terrorized by a mysterious prowler at a seaside hotel.
Barbara King Patty Duke
Mrs. Walker Kay Walsh
Mr. Plimmer Geoffrey Bayldon
Mrs. Plimmer Joan Newell
Butler Blake Butler
Mitchell John Bailey
Fred Michael Craze

Director: Don Chaffey

Eve

w Paul Wheeler & Michael Ashe, *story by* John Collier
A lonely misfit, Albert Baker falls in love with a wax window-display mannequin, and steals her to make her his own.
Eve Carol Lynley
Albert Baker Dennis Waterman
Mrs. Kass Hermione Baddeley
George Esmond Errol John
Jennifer Angela Lovell
Royal Michael Gough
Mr. Miller Peter Howell
Loverly-Smith Nicholas Phipps
Girl in cinema Elna Pearl
Night watchman Frank Forsyth
Detective Barry Linehan
Kim Barry Fantoni
Youths John Nightingale, Marcus Hammond

Director: Robert Stevens

The Indian Spirit Guide

w Robert Bloch
Jerry Crown, an unscrupulous private detective, tries to set himself up for life with a wealthy widow, Leona Gillings, who wants to contact her late husband in the spirit world. But he fails to reckon with the powers of the world beyond.
Leona Gillings Julie Harris
Jerry Crown Tom Adams
Chardur Marne Maitland
Joyce Tracy Reed
Miss Sarah Prinn Catherine Lacey
Mrs. Hubbard Dennis Ramsden
Bright Arrow Julian Sherrier

Director: Roy Ward Baker

The Killing Bottle

w Julian Bond, *story by* L.P. Hartley
Jimmy Rintoul, a young man hopeful of becoming a composer, is caught in a trap of madness and murder when he tries to have his agent's brother, Randolph, committed to an asylum so that he can claim the family fortune.
Rollo Verdew Roddy McDowall
Vera Verdew Ingrid Brett
Jimmy Rintoul Barry Evans
Randolph Verdew William Marlowe
Policeman Eddie Byrne
Hodgson John Rudling

Director: John Gibson

Stranger in the Family

w David Campton
Charles Wilson and his family are hounded from place to place because his son, Boy, is a mutant with dangerous powers to command the minds of others. (Remake of an episode of *Out of the Unknown*.)
Boy Anthony Corlan
Paula Janice Rule
Sonny Maurice Kaufmann
Charles Wilson Phil Brown
Margaret Wilson Jane Hylton
Dr. Evans Gerald Sim
Wally Gold Ronald Radd
Brown Glynn Edwards
Miss Payne Ann Wrigg
Drunk James Donelly

Director: Peter Duffell

The Beckoning Fair One

w William Woods & John Gould, *story by* Oliver Onions
A young artist recovering from a mental breakdown falls under the spell of a long-dead coquette whose portrait exerts a hold over him.
Jon Holden Robert Lansing
Kit Beaumont Gabrielle Drake
Derek Wilson John Fraser
Mr. Barrett Larry Noble
Mrs. Barrett Gretchen Franklin
Crichton Clive Francis

Director: Don Chaffey

One on an Island

w Oscar Millard, *story by* Donald E. Westlake
Alec Worthing, a young man dominated by his mother, buys a boat to sail round the world when she dies. He is shipwrecked on a desert island where a young woman walks out of the sea . . .
Alec Worthing Brandon de Wilde
Uncle George David Bauer
Vicki Suzanna Leigh
Joe Hallum Robert Sessions
Preston John Ronane
Baker Victor Maddern

Director: Noel Howard

Paper Dolls

w Oscar Millard, *story by* L.P. Davies
American exchange teacher Craig Miller tries to solve the mystery of a group of psychically linked quadruplets, in which the most powerful, Steven, directs his three brothers in evil deeds.
Craig Miller Michael Tolan
Jill Collins Nanette Newman
Boys Roderick Shaw, Barnaby Shaw
Bart Brereton John Welsh
Mrs. Latham Dorothy Alison
Joe Blake Kenneth J. Warren
Dr. Yarrow Edward Hardwicke
Albert Cole Michael Ripper
Vicar George Benson
Emily Blake June Jago

Director: James Hill

Miss Belle

w Sarett Rudley, *story by* Charles Beaumont
A rejected spinster takes her bitterness out on her small nephew by dressing him as a girl. Then a roguish American comes to the house and asks Miss Belle for work . . .
Drake George Maharis
Miss Belle Weston Barbara Jefford
Robert Kim Burfield
Girl Adrienne Posta

Director: Robert Stevens

JUPITER MOON

This space-age soap opera has the dubious distinction of being the only sci-fi series to have been killed off by a real space war!

Launched in 1990 as one of the fresh new shows commissioned by satellite channel British Satellite Broadcasting, *Jupiter Moon* beamed down to a handful of "squarials" for 115 episodes before falling victim to the satellite rivalry between BSB and Rupert Murdoch's Sky. When the two organizations merged into BSkyB, *Jupiter Moon* became permanently lost in space. It remained a real curio—a series seen by few and forgotten by most of those, until it found a new home on the Sci-Fi Channel with its U.K. launch on 1 November 1995.

Jupiter Moon was created by veteran soap producer William Smethurst and was quickly dubbed "*Crossroads* in space," after one of his previous series. It followed the lives and loves (now there's a familiar phrase) of the pupils and crew of an outer-space college in the year 2050. The school was part of the space platform Ilea orbiting one of Jupiter's moons, where liquid hydrogen was being manufactured to support 21st-century industry. In the launch episode, set on New Year's Eve 2049, midnight strikes and so does a deadly space virus. That set the tone for a series that made no pretence of being anything other than a drama-packed soap.

Regular characters in those early days included Eliot Creasy, Ilea's captain, a 40-something-year-old seafarer who was rather fond of moonshine gin; Chantal de Grecay, a brilliant young French physicist; Finbow Lewis, a gauche, rather obsessive Australian first officer; Cats Kitebrook, a daredevil space pilot who earned his nickname "Cat's Eyes" by dodging space debris; and Piers Gilpin, a good-natured 25-year-old ship's doctor given to melodramatics.

The trappings were poly-tech rather than hi-tech, though sci-fi concessions included an automatic café, and geodesic greenhouse—but no little green men. Over its short life, characters came and went, but the essential mix remained the same.

CAST INCLUDES
Eliot Creasy Andy Rashleigh *Chantal de Grecay* Caroline Evans
Finbow Lewis Phil Willmott *Victoria Frobisher* Nicola Wright
Cats Kitebrook Toby Rolt (*later* Nick Hutchison) *Sara Robbins* Karen Murden
Piers Gilpin Dominic Arnold *Rosie Greenwood* Carolyn Backhouse (*Eps. 1–38*)
Daniel Wetherby Daniel Beales *Fiona McBride* Lisa Benjamin
Henry Carson Ian Brooker (*from Ep. 44*) *Herlinde Gothard* Nikki Brooks
Mercedes Page Anna Chancellor *Prof. Charles Brelan* Richard Derrington
Pegleg Johnson Terry Molloy *Melody Shaw* Suzy Cooper
Voice of PETRA Charlotte Martin *Jorge Amado* Peter Polycarpou

---

Creator/producer: William Smethurst
Primetime Television/Andromeda Television Production

115 color 30-minute episodes
U.K. run: April–November 1990
(Galaxy Channel)

KAPPATOO

Off-beat nineties children's sci-fi comedy about a cool kid from the year 2270 who does a time-swap with his 20th-century double.

The series sets out to amuse while offering some trenchant observations on what we're doing to the planet and on what life might be like in the 23rd century.

Kappatoo's is a world with a language of its very own, of "ambience optimizers," "anthro-kinetic platforms" and "master-class domestic computers." Like the eighties series *Luna*, it's packed with examples of futurespeak, such as "in the ecofluge" (in big trouble), "wazz off" (get lost) and "I'm quaized to little toff chuffs" (absolutely delighted).

Teenager Simon Nash stars in the dual role of Kappatoo and his 20th-century twin Simon Cashmere, while comedian and game-show host Andrew O'Connor plays a computer. In the sequel, *Kappatoo II*, Rula Lenska plays scheming 23rd-century villainess Zeta, who is always out to get the time-twins, and Nicholas Parsons appears as an over-the-top quiz show host of the future. Some things never change . . .

MAIN CAST

Kappatoo/Simon Cashmere Simon Nash *Computer* Andrew O'Connor
Steve Williams Graeme Hawley *Sigmasix* Felipe Izquierdo
Lucy Cashmere Nina Muschallik *Derek Cashmere* John Abbot
Carol Cashmere Gillian Eaton *Donut* Lou Hirsch
Series One only: Tracey Cotton Denise Outen *Martin Midgeley* David Dexter
Belinda Blunt Tika Viker-Bloss *Mufour* Vanessa Hadaway
Kappatoo's father Prentis Hancock *Mr. Coppitt* Anthony Pedley
Miss Davies Liz Edmonds *Delta Four* Perrin Sledge
Series Two only: Psycho Peter Kelly *The Presenter* Nicholas Parsons
Zeta Rula Lenska *Hazel* Janet Dale *Brian* Nicholas Day *Sharon* Joanna Hall
Melanie Sarah Alexander

Adapted by: Ben Steed, *from his own novel*
Producer: Roy Marshall
Directors: Tony Kysh (*Series One*), Alistair Clark
  (*Series Two*)

Tyne Tees/World Wide International Television Production

Series One:
7 color 30-minute episodes
A Stitch in Time
Ravages of Time
Time-Slime and the Tiswas
Tracey Times Two
Time-Fuse
Mean-Time

Out of Time
23 May–4 July 1990
(ITV)

Series Two:
7 color 30-minute episodes
Time After Time
It's About Time
Bad Timing
Bang on Time
Wrong Time, Wrong Place
Dangerous Times
Home Time

9 April–21 May 1992
(ITV)

KINDRED: THE EMBRACED

*K*indred: The Embraced, a vampire series based on the book *Vampire: The Masquerade* by Mark Rein-Hagen, developed a cult following from its brief appearance on Fox. It has even earned a three-volume video release, which includes all broadcast episodes plus an unaired episode.

The plot: A detective discovers vampire clans clashing in modern-day San Francisco and falls in love with a beautiful vampire woman. It's a complex soap opera, involving murder, "Mafia wars, forbidden liaisons and inhuman hunger in a spellbinding saga of erotic danger and unworldly suspense!"

REGULAR CAST

Detective Frank Kohanek C. Thomas Howell *Prince Julian Luna* Mark Frankel
Caitlin Bryne Kelly Rutherford *Lillie Langtry* Stacey Haiduk
Sonny Erik King *Archon* Patrick Bauchau
Cash Channon Roe *Sasha* Brigid Conley Walsh
Daedalus Jeff Kober

Episodes
Pilot—The Embraced
Prince of the City
Romeo and Juliet
Live Hard, Die Young, and Leave a Good Looking Corpse

The Rise and Fall of Eddie Fiori
Bad Moon Rising
Cabin in the Woods
Nightstalker (Unaired in U.S.)

KNIGHTS OF GOD

Ambitious 1987 adventure serial set in a future Britain devastated by Civil War.

It is the year 2020. The country is split between North and South; London has been destroyed and replaced by Winchester as the capital. The Royal Family has been deposed and no one knows whether the King of England is still alive.

Out of the carnage has arisen a new ruling order—a brutal military and religious governing elite called the Knights of God, led by Prior Mordrin, a ruthless dictator who sends rebels to be brainwashed at special re-education camps.

Meeting at one of these camps are teenagers Gervase Edwards, who has been through the Knights' mind-altering program, and Julia, who has not. They fall in love and escape, joining the growing resistance to the evil regime as they set out to find the rightful King of England and help restore him to the throne.

The quest element helped foster the semi-medieval style of *Knights of God*, with the grim, rundown future offset by some high-tech elements such as the Knights' crow-like black helicopters. But the 13-part series—which carried a £1 million price tag—caused jitters among ITV network bosses, worried that the serial might prove too gritty for family viewing in its Sunday teatime slot.

An impressive cast of nearly 50 included John Woodvine as Mordrin, Julian Fellowes as his scheming henchman Hugo, and Patrick Troughton, Gareth Thomas, Ann Stallybrass and Don Henderson as rebels.

MAIN CAST
Gervase George Winter *Julia* Claire Parker *Mordrin* John Woodvine
Owen Gareth Thomas *Arthur* Patrick Troughton
Hugo Julian Fellowes *Beth* Shirley Stelfox *Colley* Don Henderson
Simon Nigel Stock *Brigadier Clarke* Barrie Cookson
Williams John Vine *Tyrell* Peter Childs *Nell* Ann Stallybrass
Dai Owen Teale *Dafydd* Tenniel Evans *Father Gregory* Frank Middlemass
Helicopter pilot Christopher Brown

Writer: Richard Cooper
Directors: Andrew Morgan, Michael Kerrigan
Producer: John Dale
Executive producer: Anna Home
Designer: Christine Ruscoe

TVS Production
13 color 30-minute episodes
6 September–6 December 1987

KOLCHAK: THE NIGHT STALKER

"Ancient, fabled monsters stalk 20th-century America. They lurk in the dark corners of cities, alleyways, abandoned buildings, scientific research centers, within sewers, sports stadia, high-rise flats and hospitals . . . all set to pounce on their next unsuspecting victim."
—Central TV press handout

Where monsters tread, only Carl Kolchak dares to follow. A walking pastiche of newshound clichés, Kolchak is an unorthodox, down-at-the-heels reporter with a gift for snappy patter and a nose for the supernatural.

Barely tolerated by his ulcer-ridden editor, and despised by the cops and politicians, Kolchak works a lonely beat, his only companions a camera and a tape recorder into which he narrates his findings. And though he always gets his monster he never gets his scoop as the lid is slammed down on his story.

Kolchak, played by Darren McGavin, first appeared in a brace of U.S. TV movies, *The Night Stalker* and *The Night Strangler* (both seen on British TV). The first, about a vampire on the loose in Las Vegas, broke all ratings records. The second explored the strange underground world of old Seattle, lair for an alchemist who is murdering women to retain his youthful looks.

Convinced that his character was a winner, McGavin himself co-produced the series, retaining the movies' narrative style, but adding more character humor and toning down the violence.

Each story featured a new monster—from Jack the Ripper, a bloodthirsty werewolf and a succubus (female demon) to a rampaging robot, a legendary swamp monster and an invisible space force. But in the best horror tradition, McGavin kept his monsters in the shadows, favouring the power of suggestion over grisly and explicit shocks.

REGULAR CAST

Carl Kolchak Darren McGavin *Tony Vincenzo* Simon Oakland
Ron Updyke Jack Grinnage *Edith Cowles* Ruth McDevitt

Creator: Jeff Rice
Executive producer: Darren McGavin
Producers: Paul Playdon *(Eps. 1, 2)*, Cy Chermak *(Eps. 3–20)*
Theme: Gil Mellé
Story consultant: David Chase

Francy Productions Inc. for Universal TV
20 color 60-minute episodes
U.K.: 15 October–10 December 1983
14 November 1984–4 March 1985
(Central)
U.S. premiere: 13 September 1974

The Ripper

w Rudolph Borchert
The shocking murders of several young women leave Chicago stunned and lead crime reporter Carl Kolchak to a man he believes is the original Jack the Ripper.
Jane Plumm Beatrice Colen

Director: Allen Baron

The Zombie

w Zekial Marko & David Chase, *story by* Zekial Marko
Kolchak covers a gangland war and finds himself face to face with an avenging killer—a zombie.
Capt. Winwood Charles Airdman
Benjamin Sposato Joseph Sirola
Victor Friese Val Bisoglio

Director: Alex Grasshoff

U.F.O. (aka They Have Been, They Are, They Will Be . . .)

w Rudolph Borchert, *story by* Dennis Clark
Kolchak unravels a series of mysterious murders to discover an invisible alien force is draining the bone marrow from animals and humans.
Capt. Quill James Gregory
Dr. Winestock Mary Wickes
Woman speaker Maureen Arthur
Alfred Brindle Dick Van Patten
Gordy John Fiedler
Monique Carol Anne Susi

Director: Allen Baron

The Vampire

w David Chase, *story by* Bill Stratton
A trail of bloodless bodies sets Kolchak on the track of a female vampire stalking the city of Los Angeles.
Faye Kruger Kathleen Nolan
Catherine Rawlins Suzanne Clarney
Lt. Matteo Williams Daniels
Gingrich Milt Kamen
Deputy John Doucette
Ichabod Crane Jan Murray
Swede Larry Storch

Director: Don Weis

The Werewolf

w David Chase & Paul Playdon
The last cruise of an old luxury liner turns into a voyage of horrors when the full moon brings out a bloodcurdling werewolf.
Capt. Wells Henry Jones
Paula Griffin Nita Talbot
Bernhardt Stiegliz Eric Braeden

Director: Don Weis

Firefall (aka The Doppelganger)

w Bill S. Ballinger
Kolchak fights fatigue as he challenges the satanic powers that threaten the life of a famous Chicago pianist.
Ryder Bond Fred Beir
Sgt. Mayer Philip Carey
Cardindale David Doyle
Maria Madlyn Rhue

Director: Don Weis

The Devil's Platform

w Donn Mullally, *story by* Tim Maschler
A scheming politician in league with the Devil transforms himself into a "hound from hell" to kill off his rivals.
Robert Palmer Tom Skerritt
Susan Driscoll Julie Gregg
Lorraine Palmer Ellen Weston

Director: Allen Baron

Bad Medicine

w L. Ford Neale *&* John Huff
Kolchak discovers a creature stalking Chicago that takes eerie animal form and uses its hypnotic eyes to transfix and kill wealthy matrons for their jewels.
Capt. Joe Baker Ramon Biere
Charles Rolling Thunder Victor Jory
Indian Richard Kiel
Dr. Agnes Temple Alice Ghostley

Director: Alex Grasshoff

The Spanish Moss Murders

w Al Friedman *&* David Chase, *story by* Al Friedman
Kolchak is earmarked for death by a legendary Bayou swamp monster that shrouds its victims in slimy moss.
Capt. Siska Keenan Wynn
Dr. Aaron Pollack Severn Darden
Fiddler Randy Boone
Pepe La Rue Johnny Silver
Henry Villon Maurice Marsac

Director: Gordon Hessler

The Energy Eater (aka Matchemonedo)

w Arthur Rowe *&* Rudolph Borchert, *story by* Arthur Rowe
A new hospital becomes a monument to horror when a bizarre invisible creature begins creating destruction within its walls.
Jim Elkhorn William Smith
Janice Elson Elaine Giftos
Don Kibbey Tom Drake
Walter Green Michael Strong
Capt. Webster Robert Yuro
Diana Jayne Jillson

Director: Alex Grasshoff

Horror in the Heights (aka The Rakshasah)

w Jimmy Sangster
Elderly ghetto-dwellers are gnawed to death by an alien monster that appears to each of its victims as a figure of trust.

Harry Starman Phil Silvers
Lane Marriot Murray Matheson
Elderly Hindu Abraham Sofaer
Julius Freeman Benny Rubin
Officer York Shelly Novack
Barry Barry Gordon

Director: Michael T. Caffey

Mr. R.I.N.G.

w L. Ford Neale *&* John Huff
A rampaging robot breaks out of a scientific institute and terrorizes the community.
Mrs. Walker Julie Adams
Leslie Dwyer Corrine Michaels
Capt. Atkins Bert Freed
Guard Donald Barry

Director: Gene Levitt

Primal Scream (aka The Humanoids)

w Bill S. Ballinger *&* David Chase
Prehistoric oil cells from the Arctic grow into a primitive, ape-like creature.
Capt. Molnar John Morley
Kitzmiller Pat Harrington
Dr. Lynch Katherine Woodville
Dr. Fisk Lindsay Workman
Jack Burton Jamie Farr

Director: Robert Scheerer

The Trevi Collection

w Rudolph Borchert
Kolchak stalks a beautiful witch who brings to life some wooden mannequins.
Madame Trevi Nina Foch
Lecturer Marvin Miller
Doctor Bernard Kopell
Madeleine Lara Parker

Director: Don Weis

Chopper

w Steve Fisher *&* David Chase, *story by* Robert Zemeckis *&* Bob Gale
A headless corpse on a motorbike is slaying members of a gang of hoodlums.
Captain Jonas Larry Linville
Studs Spake Arthur Metrano
Lila Morton Sharon Farrell
Norman Kahill Frank Alletter
Prof. Eli Stig Jay Robinson
Watchman Jesse White
Herb Bresson Jim Backus

Director: Bruce Kessler

Demon in Lace

w Stephen Lord, Michael Kozoll & David Chase, *story by* Stephen Lord

Kolchak uncovers a succubus, a female demon that takes over attractive young women and lures men into an embrace with death.

Prof. C. Evan Spate Andrew Prine
Capt. Joe Soka Keenan Wynn
Coach Toomey Jackie Vernon
Registrar Carolyn Jones

Director: Don Weis

Legacy of Terror

w Arthur Rowe

Aztec sun-worshippers set about acquiring fresh human hearts to revive a centuries-old mummy.

Captain Webster Ramon Bieri
Tillie Jones Pippa Scott
Mr. Eddy Sorrell Booke
Prof. Rodriguez Victor Campos

Director: Don McDougall

The Knightly Murders

w Michael Kozoll & David Chase, *story by* Paul Magistretti

Chicago is menaced by a 12th-century knight.

Captain Vernon Rausch John Dehner
Mendel Biggs Hans Conreid
Ralph Robert Emhart

Director: Vincent McEveety

The Youth Killer

w Rudolph Borchert

Kolchak tries to solve the mystery of why perfectly fit young men die from old age.

Helen Cathy Lee Crosby
Sgt. Orkin Dwayne Hickman
Bella Sarkof Kathleen Freeman
Cab driver Demosthenes

Director: Don McDougall

The Sentry

w L. Ford Neale & John Huff

A reptilian creature threatens an underground establishment when scientists there take away its eggs.

Lt. Irene Lamont Kathie Brown
Dr. Verhyden Albert Paulsen
Dr. Beckwith John Hoyt
Col. Brody Frank Marth
Jack Flaherty Tom Bosley

Director: Seymour Robbien

KUNG FU: THE LEGEND CONTINUES

Grandson of the original Kwai Chang Caine from *Kung Fu*, this Kwai Chang Caine is also a Shaolin priest. He sometimes assists with—one might say meddles in—his own son's work (he's a policeman).

Unlike the original series, this update goes beyond emphasizing the metaphysical. Caine actually possesses supernatural powers. He can enter other dimensions, vanish from locked rooms, etc. The supernatural elements became more and more pronounced as the series progressed. If its syndicated package—it was part of the Prime Time Entertainment Network, along with *Babylon 5*—hadn't collapsed with the advent of UPN and the WB networks, it might well have continued. There are continuing rumors of a reunion movie.

REGULAR CAST
Kwai Chang Caine Keith Carradine   *Peter Caine* Chris Potter
Lo Si (The Ancient) Kim Chan   *Captain Paul Blaisdell* Robert Lansing
Captain Karen Simms Kate Trotter   *Chief Frank Strenlich* William Dunlop
Detective Kermit Griffin Scott Wentworth

Executive producer: Michael Sloan
Supervising producer: Maurice Hurley
Executive in charge of production: Nigel Watts
Producer: Susan Murdoch
Co-producers: David Carradine, Larry Lalonde, Phil Bedard

Associate producer: Bernie Joyce

87 color 60-minute episodes (color 120-minute pilot)
Syndicated 1993–1997

Season One

Initiation
Shadow Assassin
Sunday at the Hotel with George
Sacred Trust
Force of Habit
Pai Gow
Disciple
Challenge
Rain's Only Friend
Secret Place
Dragon's Eye
Blind Eye
The Lacquered Box
Illusion
Straitjacket
Reunion
Dragonswing
Shaman
I Never Promised You a Rose Garden
Redemption, Part 1
Redemption, Part 2

Season Two

Return of the Shadow Assassin
May I Ride with You?
Dragon's Daughter
An Ancient Lottery
Laurie's Friend
Temple
Only the Strong Survive
Out of the Woods
Tournament
The Bardo
The Possessed
Warlord
The Innocent
Magic Trick
Aspects of the Soul
Kundela
The Gang of Three
Sunday Afternoon in the Museum with George
Dragonswing II
Sing Wah
Enter the Tiger
Retribution

Season Three

Rite of Passage
Plague
May I Walk with You?
The Return of Sing Ling
Manhunt
Gunfighters
The Chinatown Murder Mystery: The Case of
    the Poisoned Hand
Target
Citizen Caine
Quake!
Goodbye Mr. Caine
The Sacred Chalice of I-Ching
Eye Witness
Demons
Deadly Fashion
Cruise Missiles
The Promise
Flying Fists of Fury II
Banker's Hours
Kung Fu Blues
Brotherhood of the Bell
Destiny

Season Four

Dark Vision
The First Temple
Circle of Light
Prism
Manhunt
Black Widow
Shaolin Shot
Phoenix
Special Forces
Dragon's Lair
Veil of Tears
Chill Ride
Escape
Who Is Kwai Chang Caine?
Storm Warning
A Shaolin Treasure
Dark Side of the Chi
Ancient Love
Blackout
Time Prisoners
Requiem
A Shaolin Christmas
May I Talk with You?

LAND OF THE GIANTS

The fourth and final chapter of Irwin Allen's television science fiction quartet was a mix of *Lost in Space* and *Gulliver's Travels.*

In the year 1983, the spaceship *Spindrift*, with its roll call of seven passengers and crew, is on a routine sub-orbital flight from California to London when it passes through a mysterious white cloud, emerging over a world where everything is 12 times larger. In this *Land of the Giants* they find a society that exactly mirrors theirs, complete with political and social upheavals and a highly advanced scientific community. Indeed, it appears the giants are aware of Earth and had been probing our atmosphere, which is what caused the *Spindrift* to drift into their world in the first place.

The space travelers find friends and make enemies—notably a giant detective, Inspector Kobick—and encounter a range of menaces from the expected (giant cats and insects) to the sinister (sadistic children and inquisitive scientists) and the totally bizarre (*Lost in Space* star Jonathan Harris as a "pied piper" figure).

At the time, the show was Allen's most expensive so far, costing more than 250,000 dollars per episode, most of the cost being swallowed up by the elaborate props, and optical and photographic effects. Allen's stable of regular writers and directors brought their final total over his four shows to some 274 episodes in six years.

REGULAR CAST
THE "LITTLE PEOPLE"
Steve Burton Gary Conway *Dan Erickson* Don Marshall
Betty Hamilton Heather Young *Mark Wilson* Don Matheson
Alexander Fitzhugh Kurt Kasznar *Valerie Scott* Deanna Lund
Barry Lockridge Stefan Arngrim
GIANT
Insp. Kobick Kevin Hagen *(semi-regular)*

Creator/Executive producer: Irwin Allen
Director of Photography: Howard Schwartz
Special effects: L.B. Abbott, Art Cruickshank, Emil Kosa Jr.
Music: Johnny Williams

An Irwin Allen Production for 20th Century Fox Television

51 color 60-minute episodes
U.S. premiere: 22 September 1968
U.K. premieres:
Season One (26 episodes)
7 December 1968–31 May 1969
(London Weekend Television)
Season Two (25 episodes)
24 January–12 October 1972
(Thames Television—run included repeats from first season.)

Season One
26 episodes

The Crash

w Anthony Wilson
1983: Passengers and crew on a London-bound spaceship crash-land after passing through a mysterious cloud and find themselves in a land of giants—a society similar to Earth, but 12 times bigger!
Female assistant Anne Dore
Entomologist Don Watters
Boy Pat Michenaud

Director: Irwin Allen

Ghost Town

w Gil Ralston & William Welch
Marooned in the land of the giants, the space travelers find that even the giant children can be dangerous.
Akman Percy Helton
Granddaughter Amber Flower
Tramp Raymond Guth

Director: Nathan Juran

Framed

w Mann Rubin
The "little people" clear a giant tramp of the murder of a photographer's model.
Photographer Paul Carr
Hobo Doodles Weaver
Model Linda Peck
Policeman Dennis Cross

Director: Harry Harris

Underground

w Ellis St. Joseph
The travelers help an underground leader to destroy papers that could cost the lives of his associates.
Gorak John Abott
Policeman Lance Le Gault
Sentry Jerry Catron
Guard Paul Trinka

Director: Sobey Martin

Terror-Go-Round

w Charles Bennett
A Gypsy giant captures the travelers and plans to sell them to a circus as performing midgets.
Carlos Joseph Ruskin
Luigi Arthur Batanides
Pepi Gerald Michenaud
Policeman Arch Whiting

Director: Sobey Martin

Flight Plan

w Peter Packer
A miniaturized giant and his two friends try to use the space travelers to glean powerful knowledge from Earth.
Joe Linden Charles
First giant William Bramley
Second giant Myron Healey
Guard John Pickard

Director: Harry Harris

Manhunt

w J. Selby & Stanley Silverman
The travelers risk their lives to save a giant convict who becomes bogged down in quicksand as he attempts to flee pursuing guards.
Convict John Napier

Director: Sobey Martin

The Trap

w Jack Turley
When a giant scientist imprisons Betty and Valerie in a specimen jar, the travelers must sacrifice some of their precious fuel to save them.
Assistant Morgan Jones
Scientist Stewart Bradley

Director: Sobey Martin

The Creed

w Bob & Esther Mitchell
When young Barry gets appendicitis, unexpected aid is offered by a giant doctor.
Dr. Brulle Pal Fix
Janitor Henry Corden
Cop Harry Lauter
Cop Grant Sullivan

Director: Sobey Martin

Double-Cross

w Bob & Esther Mitchell
The travelers become involved with two giant thieves who plan to steal a valuable ruby.
Hook Willard Sage
Lobo Lane Bradford
Curator Howard Culver
Policeman Ted Jordan

Director: Harry Harris

The Weird World

w Ellis St. Joseph
The *Spindrift* group encounter the nearly-mad survivor of an earlier space flight.
Kagan Glenn Corbett
Watchman Don Gazzaniga

Director: Harry Harris

The Golden Cage

w Jack Turley
Mark is nearly tricked into betraying his friends when the giants send out a beautiful girl as bait.
Marna Celeste Yarnall
Scientist Douglas Bank
Giants Dawson Palmer, Page Slattery

Director: Sobey Martin

The Lost Ones

w Bob & Esther Mitchell
The travelers meet up with four teenage boys, victims of a space-wreck two years earlier.
Dolf Tommy Webb
Joey Jack Chaplain
Hopper Lee Jay Lambert
Nick Zalman King
Trapper Dave Dunlop

Director: Harry Harris

Brainwash

w William Welch
Steve is brainwashed and nearly destroys a new-found means of contacting Earth.
Ashim Warren Stevens
Dr. Kraal Leonard Stone
Prisoner Len Lesser
Policeman Robert Dowdell

Director: Harry Harris

The Bounty Hunter

w Dan Ullman
A reward is offered for the capture of the *Spindrift* folk.
Girl Kimberley Beck
Camper Paul Sorenson

Director: Harry Harris

On a Clear Night You Can See Earth

w Sheldon Stark *&* Anthony Wilson
Two of the titchy group are captured by Murtrah, a mad giant scientist.
Murtrah Michael Ansara

Director: Sobey Martin

Deadly Lodestone

w William L. Stuart
Hiding in a storm drain, two of the travelers hear a giant detective outline a new method of finding them.
Kobick Kevin Hagen
Dr. Brulle Paul Fix
Sgt. Karf Bill Fletcher
Mr. Secretary Robert Emhardt
Nurse Helg Sheila Mathews
Warden Gene Dynarski

Director: Harry Harris

The Night of Thrombeldinar

w Bob *&* Esther Mitchell
While searching for food, Fitzhugh is captured by two giant orphans who think he is a magic elf who brings gifts to children.
Garna Teddy Quinn
Tobek Michael A. Freeman
Okun Jay Novello
Housewife Miriam Schiller
Parleg Alfred Ryder

Director: Sobey Martin

Seven Little Indians

w Bob *&* Wanda Duncan
When four of the spacefolk are captured, the others effect a courageous rescue from the zoo.
Kobick Kevin Hagen
Grotius Cliff Osmond
Sgt. Arnak Chris Alcald

Director: Harry Harris

Target Earth

w Arthur Weiss
Mark's knowledge is needed to help the giants perfect a guidance system. In return, the travelers will be returned to Earth.
Altha Dee Hartford
Franzen Arthur Franz
Kobick Kevin Hagen
Logar Peter Mamakos

Director: Sobey Martin

Genius at Work

w Bob *&* Esther Mitchell
A scientific formula which enables Fitzhugh to become giant-sized creates problems for the others.
Jodar Ronny Howard
Zurpin Jacques Aubuchon
Kobick Kevin Hagen
Small giant Vic Perrin

Director: Sobey Martin

Return of Inidu

w Bob *&* Esther Mitchell
The Earthlings must prove that a giant magician is innocent of a murder.
Inidu Jack Albertson
Grot Tony Benson
Enog Peter Haskell

Director: Sobey Martin

Rescue

w Bob *&* Esther Mitchell
Two giant children are trapped in an abandoned drain shaft after chasing the travelers. With other giants unable to reach the youngsters, Steve devises an ingenious but hazardous plan to rescue them.
Kobick Kevin Hagen
Mother Lee Meriwether
Father Don Collier
Tedor Buddy Foster
Leeda Blair Ashley
Lt. Emar Michael J. Quinn
Sgt. Gedo Tom Reese
Newscaster Roy Rowan

Director: Harry Harris

Sabotage

w Bob & Esther Mitchell
The *Spindrift* crew becomes involved in a struggle between a sympathetic giant senator and the power-mad chief of the Police Bureau.
Bolgar Robert Colbert
Zarkin John Marley
Secretary Elizabeth Rogers
Obek Parley Baer
Newsboy Keith Taylor
Policeman Douglas Bank

Director: Harry Harris

The Shell Game

w William Welch, Bob & Esther Mitchell
The travelers build a hearing aid for a giant deaf boy.
Osla Gary Dubin
Talf Larry Ward
Mr. Derg Tol Avery
with Jan Shepard

Director: Harry Harris

The Chase

w Arthur Weiss & William Welch
Insp. Kobick forces the little people to help him trap some underground freedom fighters—but the Earthlings turn the tables on him.
Kobick Kevin Hagen
SID Man Erik Nelson
Naylor Robert F. Lyons
Golan Patrick Sullivan Burke
Sergeant Norman Burton

Director: Sobey Martin

Season Two
25 episodes

The Mechanical Man

w William L. Stuart
A giant scientist enlists Mark's help in solving a problem with a super-robot he has built.
Prof. Gorn Broderick Crawford
Zoral Stuart Margolin
Robot James Daris

Director: Harry Harris

Six Hours to Live

w Dan Ullman
The Earth group risk their safety to prove the innocence of a young giant awaiting execution for murder.
Harry Cass George Mitchell
Martha Cass Anne Seymour
Joe Simmons Richard Anderson
Sloan Bill Quinn

Guear Larry Pennell
Gateman Michael J. Quinn

Director: Sobey Martin

The Inside Rail

w Richard Shapiro
Fitzhugh leads his friends into danger at a racetrack because of his love of a flutter.
Chief Ribers Arch Johnson
Moley Ben Blue
Sergeant Joe Turkel
Hood Vic Tayback

Director: Harry Harris

Deadly Pawn

w Arthur Weiss
Fitzhugh, Valerie and Barry become pawns on a giant's chessboard.
Kronig Alex Dreier
Dr. Lalor John Zaremba
Guard Charlie Briggs

Director: Nathan Juran

The Unsuspected

w Bob & Esther Mitchell
Steve becomes a dangerous madman when he accidentally swallows poison and tries to turn his friends over to Inspector Kobick.
Kobick Kevin Hagen
Sgt. Eson Leonard Stone

Director: Harry Harris

Giants and All That Jazz

w Richard Shapiro
Dan, a talented jazz trumpeter, uses his skill to save his friends and help a kindly giant.
Biff Sugar Ray Robinson
Hanley William Bramley
Loach Mike Mazurki
Nell Diana Chesney

Director: Harry Harris

Collector's Item

w Sidney Marshall, Bob & Wanda Duncan
A penniless giant kidnaps Valerie and puts her in a fancy costume, in a music box.
Garak Guy Stockwell
Tojar Robert H. Harris
Mrs. Garak Susan Howard
Goldsmith George Sperdakos

Director: Sobey Martin

Every Boy Needs a Dog

w Jerry Thomas
Barry takes his dog Chipper to a giant vet and endangers the lives of all his fellow travelers.
Ben Michael Anderson Jr.
Dr. Howard Oliver McGowan
Mr. Clinton Bob Shayne

Director: Harry Harris

Chamber of Fear

w Arthur Weiss
While trying to rescue Fitzhugh, the travelers become involved with jewel thieves who operate a wax museum.
Jolo Cliff Osmond
Deenar Christopher Cary
Mara Joan Feeman
Monk Robert Tiedeman

Director: Sobey Martin

The Clones

w Oliver Crawford, Bob & Esther Mitchell
An evil scientist makes exact copies of Valerie and Barry.
Dr. Arno William Schallert
Dr. Greta Le Gault Sandra Giles

Director: Nathan Juran

Comeback

w Richard Shapiro
The travelers meet a kindly but ugly giant who was once a famous star of the monster movies, and try to help him to make a comeback.
Egor John Carradine
Gorilla Janos Prohaska
Manfred Jesse White
Quigg Fritz Feld

Director: Harry Harris

A Place Called Earth

w William Welch
The adventurers encounter Earth people from the future who prove more of a threat than the giants.
Olds Warren Stevens
Fielder Jerry Douglas
Bron Jerry Quarry *(the U.S. heavyweight boxer)*

Director: Harmon Jones

Land of the Lost

w William Welch
When four of the Earth group are accidentally carried away by a giant's balloon, they discover a new land, ruled by a despot.
Titus Nehemiah Persoff
Andros Clint Ritchie
Slave Peter Canon
Boy Brian Nash

Director: Sobey Martin

Home, Sweet Home

w William Welch
After finding a space capsule, Steve and Fitzhugh return briefly to Earth but are forced to go back to the giants' planet.
Ranger Jack William H. Bassett
Deabody William Benedict
Sloacum Robert Adler
Guard Pete Kellett

Director: Harry Harris

Our Man O'Reilly

w Jackson Gillis
The Earth people get unexpected help from a superstitious giant who thinks they are leprechauns.
O'Reilly Alan Hale Jr.
Krenko Alan Bergmann
Harry Billy Halop
Jake Michael J. Quinn

Director: Sobey Martin

Nightmare

w William Welch
When the space travelers are accidentally exposed to radiation from a new power device, they become invisible to the giants.
Berger Torin Thatcher
Ardre Yale Summers
Kobick Kevin Hagen

Director: Nathan Juran

Pay the Piper

w Richard Shapiro
The travelers are lured away by a giant Pied Piper.
Piper Jonathan Harris
Senator Peter Leeds
Timmy Michael-James Wixted

Director: Harry Harris

The Secret City of Limbo

w Bob *&* Esther Mitchell
The Earth people help prevent a war between the surface-dwelling giants and a race from below the ground.
Taru Malachi Throne
General Aza Joseph Ruskin
Mylo Peter Jason
Dr. Krane Whit Bissell

Director: Sobey Martin

Panic

w Bob *&* Wanda Duncan
Kirmus, a giant scientist, promises to return the travelers to Earth.
Kirmus Jack Albertson
Marad Mark Richman
Mrs. Evers Diane McBain

Director: Sobey Martin

The Deadly Dart

w William L. Stuart
Mark is accused of murdering a giant policeman.
Sgt. Barker Christopher Dark
Doc Jelko Kent Taylor
Bertha Fry Madlyn Rhue
Lt. Grayson John Dehner
Zoral Donald Barry
Insp. Swain Willard Sage

Director: Harry Harris

Doomsday

w Dan Ullman
The Earth travelers uncover a bomb plot and help to trap a saboteur.
Dr. North Francine York
Workin Ed Peck
Kobick Kevin Hagen

Director: Harry Harris

A Small War

w Shirl Hendryx
The Earth people are unwillingly drawn into a war with a giant boy and his toy soldiers.
Alek Sean Kelly
Mr. Erdap Charles Drake

Director: Harry Harris

The Marionettes

w William Welch
The travelers are able to help improve the act of a giant puppeteer who has aided them.
Goalby Frank Ferguson
Brady Bob Hogan
Lisa Victoria Vetri
Harem dancer Sandra Giles
Knife thrower Carl Carlsson

Director: Sobey Martin

Wild Journey

w William Welch
Steve and Dan are given the chance to relive the hours before their space flight.
Thorg Bruce Dern
Berna Yvonne Craig
Security guard Martin Liverman
SID man Erik Nelson

Director: Harry Harris

Graveyard of Fools

w Sidney Marshall
To aid their ambitions, three power-mad giants transport four of the little people to a strange, distant land inhabited by giant insects.
Melzac/Bryk Albert Salmi
Tagor John Crawford
Janitor Michael Stewart

Director: Sobey Martin

LAND OF THE LOST

Seventies adventure series about a family marooned in a prehistoric world after slipping through a time warp.

While exploring the Colorado River, forest ranger Rick Marshall and his kids, Will and Holly, are inexplicably catapulted through a time doorway and spend the first season searching for a way back to their own time.

Season Two introduced Enik, a tall, lizard-like creature who had also fallen through a time warp, only for him this was the future. The travelers discover that the Land of the Lost is a closed universe built by Enik's ancestors and that the only way to escape is via a time portal contained in a mysterious device called the Pylon.

For Season Three, dad Rick succeeds in activating the doorway and is swept back to his own time—only to be replaced in the *Land of the Lost* by his brother Jack—another short-lived role for Ron Harper who had previously survived one season on the *Planet of the Apes*.

Star Trek writers D.C. Fontana and David Gerrold contributed scripts and special dinosaur effects were achieved using stop-motion animation. Richard Kiel, best known as James Bond's metal-mouthed adversary, Jaws, had a recurring role as the Marshalls' enemy Malak.

The early nineties saw the creators of the original series, Sid and Marty Krofft, conjure up a revival that ran for at least two seasons, with a new lost family, the Porters.

ORIGINAL SERIES, MAIN CAST

Rick Marshall Spencer Milligan *Holly* Kathy Coleman *Will* Wesley Eure
Jack Marshall Ron Harper *(Season Three only)* *Enik* Walker Edmiston
Chaka (monkey boy member of a prehistoric tribe) Philip Poley
Malak Richard Kiel

Creators: Sid & Marty Krofft
Executive producers: Albert J. Tenzer *(Seasons One, Two)* Sid & Marty Krofft *(Season Three)*
Writers: Various, including David Gerrold, Margaret Armen, Larry Niven, Walter Koenig, Dick Morgan, Ben Bova, D.C. Fontana, Theodore Sturgeon, Greg Strangis, Jon Kubichan
Directors: Dennis Steinmetz, Bob Lally, Gordon Wiles, Joe Scanlan, Rick Bennewitz
Animation director: Gene Warren Jr.

43 color 30-minute episodes
U.S. premiere: 7 September 1974

Land of the Lost (Revival)
Cast:
Tom Porter Timothy Bottoms
Annie Porter Jennifer Drugan
Kevin Porter Robert Gavin

U.S. premiere: 7 September 1991

LEGEND

Following his years as *MacGyver,* Richard Dean Anderson returned to series television in *Legend,* a lighthearted Western adventure series set in the 1890s. Anderson starred as Ernest Pratt, a gambling, womanizing, hard-drinking writer who created a dashing literary hero, Nicodemus Legend, the main character in a wildly imaginative series of dime novels set in the Wild West.

In the premiere episode, Pratt learns that someone has been impersonating Legend. A warrant has been issued in Sheridan, Colorado, for Legend's arrest on charges of "malicious mischief, theft of water rights, and disturbing livestock." Of course, Pratt travels to Sheridan to clear his hero's name.

There he meets the eccentric scientist and inventor Janos Bartok (John de Lancie—better known as Q from *Star Trek*). Bartok, a great admirer of Pratt's tales, and has taken the liberty of "borrowing" the Legend persona in order to help the townspeople of Sheridan. Pratt reluctantly agrees to help by assuming the persona of Nicodemus Legend. After that, he's stuck—everyone thinks he's Nicodemus Legend. Aided by Bartok's futuristic inventions, he becomes a reluctant hero.

REGULAR CAST

Ernest Pratt Richard Dean Anderson *Janos Bartok* John de Lancie
Ramos Mark Adair Rios *Skeeter* Jarrad Paul

Creator: Michael Piller

12 color 60-minute episodes
18 April 1995–8 August 1995

Birth of a Legend

w Michael Piller & Bill Dial
When Pratt learns that a warrant has been issued for the arrest of his dime-novel character, he travels to Sheridan, Colorado, as a publicity stunt and ends up assuming the identity of Legend to stop a land takeover.
Vera Slaughter Stephanie Beacham
Katherine Sullivan Katherine Moffat
Silas Slaughter John Pennell
Sheriff Sam Moats Douglas Rowe
Skeeter Jarrad Paul
John Wesley Coe Tim Thomerson
Aidar Brull Pete Schrum
Mrs. Brull Betsy Beard
Victoria Stephanie Copperman
Geezer Dick Bellerue
Jesse James Forrie J. Smith
Frank James Monty Stuart
Mom Karen Veau
Girl Savannah Morgan
Antonio Nicholas Glaesser
Mr. Fat Jack Ong
Son Eddie Mui
Man with knife Jerry Woods
Miss Freeman Jennifer Wilson
Autograph boy Merik Woodmansee
Barman Bob Sorenson
Governor Denehy John Furlong

Director: Charles Correll

Mr. Pratt Goes to Sheridan

w Michael Piller & Bill Dial
A bank robber is willing to surrender—but only to the great Nicodemus Legend.
Jim Siringo Stephen Baldwin
Mayor Brown Robert Donner
Lamar John Chappel
Barnes Michael Moss
G.H. Winslow Randy Oglesby
Mrs. Yancie Lily Nielsen
Amos White Rusty Ferracane
Marshall Billy Joe Patton
Shotgun rider Bob Lester
Lady #1 Marian Wald
Lady #2 Mona Tadych
Dealer Claude File

Director: William Gereghty

Legend on His President's Secret Service

w Robert Wilcox
Pratt kidnaps President Grant to thwart an assassination attempt designed to start a second Civil War.
Ethan Catridge Steele Ken Jenkins
Julia Grant Fionnula Flanagan
Abigail Steele Leah Lail
Potter Alan Brooks
Ulysses S. Grant G.W. Bailey
Grady Robert Shelton
Rubin Aaron Chadwick
Lynch Patrick Moord
Henrietta Ana Auther
Redneck #1 Maro Miles
Redneck #2 Stephen Foster

Director: Michael Vejar

Custer's Next to Last Stand

w Bill Dial
Pratt's longtime friend Libbie Custer—wife of Major General George Armstrong Custer—asks Pratt to help win back her husband's command.
George Armstrong Custer Alex Hyde-White
Mayor Brown Robert Donner
Cainer Richard Cox
Libbie Custer Ashley Laurence
Standing Beaver Pato Hoffman
Miles McKinney Fritz Sperberg
Whipple Ted Parks

Director: William Gereghty

The Life, Death and Life of Wild Bill Hickok

w Peter Allen Fields
To help the aging Wild Bill Hickok (who has lost his nerve and most of his eyesight), Pratt and Bartok capture a band of dangerous train robbers and give credit to Hickok.
Wild Bill Hickok William Russ
Jack McCall John Pyper-Ferguson
Marjorie Debbie James
Chamberlain Brown Robert Donner
Grady Robert Shelton
Henry Clark Ray
Henchman Ed Adams
Tommy Squirrel Mike Faherty
Boy Adam Beech

Director: Michael Caffey

Knee-High Noon

w Steve Stoliar & Fredrick Rappaport, *story by* Steve Stoliar
Pratt is manipulated by a stage mother who wants her son to be "Nicodemus Legend Jr."
Faber Andrew Hill Newman
Laura Davenport Mary-Margaret Humes
Ben Davenport Michael Patrick Carter
Lyle Ray McKinnon
Vine Don Collier
Smoky Dick Bellerue
Druggist Harlan Kudson

Director: James L. Conway

Gospel According to Legend

w Jim Considine
A charlatan evangelist visits Sheridan and bilks the townsfolk out of their money and land by predicting the end of the world.
Mordechai/Willy Miles Robert Englund
Edgar Taggert Tim Considine
Daniel the guard Brendan Kinkade
Brother Jude Phillip Connery
Driver Hamilton Mitchell
Heron Twin #1 Tina Peeler
Heron Twin #2 Tessa Harper
Operator Rick Taylor

Director: Michael Vejar

Bone of Contention

w George Geiger
Competing paleontologists feud when they think they've made the find of the century in Sheridan.
Rudolph Kendall Bruce Gray
Beth McMillian Beth Toussaint
Miles McMillan Robert Toeves
Dave Larson Patrick Kilpatrick
Henrietta Anna Auther
Sheriff Motes Douglas Rowe

Director: Charles Correll

Revenge of the Herd

w Tim Burns
To help sell his new book to German publishers, Pratt serves as their buffalo hunting guide—and tries to scare them off the hunt with a mechanical monster.
Lamar John Chappel
Harry Parver Bob Balaban
Ludwig Hauptman Reiner Schoene
Rolf Hauptman Christian Arin
Chamberlain Brown Robert Donner
Towashie Rodney A. Grant
Smoky Dick Bellerue
Helmut John Dahlstrand
Lone Eagle George Salazar
Indian Frank Soto
Little girl Kaitlin Williams
Mother Beth Wilkerson
Young Arapaho Deryle Lujan
Gizzard-Eating Williams Mike Casper

Director: Bob Balaban

Fall of a Legend

w Ron Friedman, *story by* Bob Shayne
After Pratt is falsely accused of murder, he learns that his fame makes it impossible for him to hide.

Sheriff Motes Douglas Rowe
Chamberlain Brown Robert Donner
Milton Faber Andrew Hill Newman
Drusilla Lisa Akey
Dr. Costa Hamilton Mitchell
Smoky Dick Bellerue
Luis Halewa Peter Cirino
Henchman James Reeves
Seth Gary Kirk
Bonnie Blue Linda Dearmond
Elijah Michael Wayne
Harold Jerome Zelle
Louise Kim Breckon
Dan Rusch John Dennis Johnston
Amos Michael Ruud

Director: Bob Balaban

Clueless in San Francisco

w Carol Caldwell & Marianne Clarkson, *story by* Carol Caldwell
Pratt visits San Francisco as Nicodemus Legend, trying to help a white woman who has spent her entire life among the Indians find her real parents.
Paytents Molly Hagan
Delilah Pratt Janis Paige
Chai James Hong
Zorelda Patty Maloney
Quelle Heure Dennis Burkley
Tattoo man Charles Young
Melissa Walsh Debbie Bartlett
Mrs. O'Hara Catherine Gilman
Grandmother Walsh Grace Etchen
Reporter #1 Gary Clarke
Reporter #2 Bazzel Baz

Director: Charles Correll

Skeletons in the Closet

w David Rich
Pratt makes a film for the newly invented Zoetrope, but gets distracted by an ancient mystery.
Sheriff Stapleton Robert Keith
Seamus Calhoun John Verson
Mashburn Kevin Fry
Maria Marisol Padilla Sanchez
Theresa Dunleavy Lara Flynn Boyle
Father Jaime Ramon Chavez
Mrs. Ruiz Gina Carrzoza
Large Man Joseph H. Redondo

Director: Steve Shaw

LEXX
(TALES FROM A PARALLEL UNIVERSE)

The producers of this 1997 series created a novel pilot: no less than four movies, detailing the adventures of a spaceship, the *Lexx*, and its oddball crew of four as they fulfilled an ancient prophecy and ended the rule of His Shadow, an oppressive dictator. Word is in that Canada's Space: The Imagination Station will produce 20 one-hour episodes of *LEXX: The Dark Zone*. According to their press release, the series "continues the darkly weird, edgy and sexy intergalactic voyage of the *Lexx*, a dragonfly-shaped bug about the size of Manhattan that has been genetically altered to be used both as a spaceship and as the most destructive weapon in two universes."

The series is being written and directed by Paul Donovan for a fall 1998 premiere on Space. In addition to its original cast, *Lexx* will get two new characters in its hour-long format, a shape changer named Wist (Doreen Jacobi) and a machine inhabited by the mind of the evil but brilliant Mantrid.

REGULAR CAST
Stanley Tweedle Brian Downey   *Kai* Michael McManus
Zev Eva Haberman   *790* Jeffrey Hirschfield

Episodes
I Worship His Shadow
Super Nova

Eating Pattern
Giga Shadow

LOGAN'S RUN

A futuristic version of *The Fugitive*, Logan ran for just 14 episodes (including the obligatory movie-length pilot) with his companions Jessica and Rem the android.

Set in the 23rd century, some 200 years after a nuclear holocaust, the series depicted a world of pocket civilizations—each an isolated law unto itself, with its inhabitants largely unaware of the alternatives. One of these closed societies is the City of Domes, a precisely programmed world where population control is achieved by people voluntarily submitting to a youthful euthanasia. On their 30th birthday—known as Lastday—all inhabitants undergo the spectacular extermination ceremony of Carousel. Those who refuse and opt to run from the city are hunted and killed by Sandmen, the Domed City's elite police.

Logan is a Sandman who is persuaded by Jessica, a member of the underground, to run with her in search of a mythical place in the Outside World, known as Sanctuary, where people can grow old gracefully. On the run (in a dinky little hovercraft) they encounter other groups and societies—some friendly, some threatening. But always their goal remains Sanctuary where they hope to find other runners and, ultimately, return to the Domed City to disprove the institution of Carousel. Early on, they stumble upon a Mountain City where they meet Rem, an android who becomes their trusted companion.

The trio are relentlessly pursued by Sandmen, led by Logan's onetime partner and best friend Francis who has been promised a life beyond 30 as a city elder if he can bring back the fugitives.

The series, based on the novel and 1976 feature film of the same name, was brought to television by Ivan Goff and Ben Roberts (whose track record included *Charlie's Angels*), and described as human dramas projected into the future. "Psychologically," said Goff, "Logan and Jessica face the same concerns that baffled Adam and Eve."

In the end, despite some enjoyable sequences, *Logan's Run* was a fairly antiseptic series, aimed firmly at the family audience. The relationship between Logan and Jessica was more like brother and sister than Adam and Eve, despite the wispy little mini-dress Jessica *always* wore (and which never looked dirty or crumpled), and the whimsical Rem was the only character with a sense of humor.

REGULAR CAST
Logan Gregory Harrison *Jessica* Heather Menzies
Rem Donald Moffat *Francis* Randy Powell

Based on the novel by William F. Nolan &
George Clayton Johnson
Executive producers: Ivan Goff & Ben Roberts
Producer: Leonard Katzman
Story editor: D.C. Fontana

An MGM Television Production
13 color 60-minute episodes (pilot 80 minutes)
U.S. premiere: 16 September 1977
U.K. premiere: 7 January–2 April 1978
(Central)

Logan's Run (pilot)

w William F. Nolan & Saul David
Logan and Jessica flee the "utopian" world of the Domed City, pursued by Francis and his Sandmen. In a mountain city they are "captured" by two robots, Draco and Siri, who need someone to serve, and rescued by Rem who joins their search for Sanctuary.
Siri Lina Raymond
Draco Kenne Curtis
Riles Ron Hajek
Akers Gary Dontzig
Ketcham Anthony De Longis

Director: Robert Day

The Collectors

w James Schmerer
Jessica and Logan are captured by alien invaders who manipulate their minds into believing they have found Sanctuary. Rem finds other captives from yet another planet and devises a plan that could free them all.
John Linden Chiles
Joanna Leslie Parrish
Karen Angela Cartwright
Martin Lawrence Casey

Director: Alexander Singer

Capture

w Michael Edwards
After Francis captures Logan, Jessica and Rem, they in turn are seized by James Borden, a collector of antique weapons who also makes a sport of hunting men. He selects Logan and Francis as his next quarry—but the Sandmen unite to turn the tables.
Borden Horst Bucholz
Irene Mary Woronov
Benjamin Stan Stratton

Director: Irving J. Moore

The Innocent

w Ray Brenner & D.C. Fontana
The fugitives meet a beautiful young woman who was left by her parents to live alone in a clinical, computerized atmosphere with only two robots for company. When the girl, Lisa, develops a crush on Logan she schemes to eliminate her rival—Jessica.
Lisa Lisa Eilbacher
Strong Lou Richards
Jeremy Barney McFadden
Patrick Brian Kerwin
Friend Gene Tyburn

Director: Michael Preece

Man Out of Time

w Noah Ward
Logan and his companions meet up with a scientist from 200 years in the past who has traveled into the future to find a way of preventing the holocaust.
David Eakins Paul Shenar
Analog Mel Ferrer
Lab Tech One Woodrow Chambliss
Comp Tech Four Gene Tyburn
Gold Hank Brandt

Director: Nicholas Colastino

Half Life

w Shimon Wincelberg
Logan, Jessica and Rem encounter a society able to divide its people physically into two halves—the Positives (goodies) and the Castouts (baddies). When Jessica herself is processed, Logan and Rem must try to reunite the two halves.
Patron/Modok William Smith
Positive 14/Brawn Leon Birman
Rama II Kim Cattrall
Rama I Jeanne Sorel
Woman positive Betty Jinette

Director: Steven Stern

Crypt

w Al Hayes & Harlan Ellison
The runners discover the frozen bodies of six people in a ruined city and a serum to bring them back to life permanently. But after they've revived initially, one vial of serum accidentally breaks, leaving only enough to keep three alive . . .
David Pera Christopher Stone
Rachel Greenhill Ellen Weston
Dexter Kim Soon-Teck Oh
Victoria Mackie Neva Patterson
Frederick Lyman Liam Sullivan
Sylvia Reyna Adrienne Larussa

Director: Michael Caffey

Judas Goat

w John Meredyth Lucas
The fugitives meet Hal 14 who claims to be a runner but is really a Sandman sent to lure Logan's heroes back to the Domed City.
Hal 14 Nicholas Hammond
Matthew Lance Le Gault
Jonathan Wright King
Garth Spencer Milligan
Morgan Morgan Woodward

Director: Paul Krasny

Fear Factor

w John Sherlock
Logan, Jessica and Rem are trapped by strange scientists experimenting to produce a master race by removing the ability to experience emotion from the minds of their "patients."
Dr. Rowan Ed Nelson
Dr. Paulson Jared Martin
Psychiatrists William Wellman Jr., Peter Brandon, Carl Byrd

Director: Gerald Mayer

Futurepast

w Katharyn Michaelian Powers
Logan and Jessica find their lives in peril when a beautiful woman tries dream analysis on them.
Ariana Mariette Hartley
Clay Michael Sullivan
Sandmen Ed Couppee, Joey Fontana
Woman Janis Jamison

Director: Michael O'Herlihy

Carousel

w D.C. Fontana & Richard L. Breen Jr.
When Logan is shot with a dart that erases his memory, he is captured by Francis and taken back to the Domed City. Rem and Jessica must rescue him before he is sent to Carousel.
Diane Rosanne Katon
Michael Ross Bikell
Jonathan Wright King
Morgan Morgan Woodward
Sheila Melody Anderson
Darrel Regis J. Cordic

Director: Irving J. Moore

Night Visitors

w Leonard Katzman
The three fugitives are welcomed into a strange house that Rem, searching his memory bank, decides is haunted and their hosts are ghosts from the spirit world.
Gavin George Maharis
Marianne Barbara Babcock
Barton Paul Mantee

Director: Paul Krasny

Turnabout

w Michael Michaelian & Al Hayes
When Logan, Jessica, Rem *and* Francis are all captured by desert horsemen and sentenced to death, Logan finds himself trying to save his archenemy.
Gera Gerald McRaney
Asa Nehemiah Persoff
Samuel Harry Rhodes
Mia Victoria Racimo
Phillip John Furey

Director: Paul Krasny

Stargate

w Dennis O'Neill
When they encounter strange people from a planet much hotter than Earth, Logan and Jessica have to fight to save Rem who's being dismantled to provide spare parts for the aliens' spaceship.
Timon Eddie Firestone
Xorah Paul Carr
Pata Darrell Fetty
Arcana Ian Tanza

Director: Curtis Harrington

LOIS & CLARK: THE NEW ADVENTURES OF SUPERMAN

"I wanted it to be a romantic comedy with family values, rather than action-packed like the movies."
—Deborah Joy LeVine (series creator)

Anyone who thought the Superman legend was just about played out in films and TV had a pleasant surprise when this new version breezed in.

These *New Adventures* had looked for a new angle—and found one with a fresh combination of wit, fun, sophisticated banter and a lightness of touch that mostly eluded its predecessors.

Superman can still bend steel with his bare hands and fly around the world in seconds, but he's become a superhero for the nineties. And his alter ego, Clark Kent, is a New Man, too, less of a klutz and more a simple, upright guy.

You still have to strain credibility to wonder how a pair of glasses can blind a bright girl like Lois Lane to the obvious similarities between Clark and Superman—but then that's an accepted part of the myth, so why worry now.

Lois and Clark are still writing for the *Daily Planet* in Metropolis and gruff Perry White is still editor. Jimmy Olsen is still seeking a chance to prove himself, but here come the twists: Also on staff is a man-eating, tart-with-a-heart gossip writer, Cat Grant, who actually finds *Clark* attractive, and in this series' version of Lex Luthor we've got a villain who's as charming as he is wicked—and he's got hair. Plus, with Superman reluctant to "commit" to Lois, this Lex nearly gets the girl.

This is a very modest Superman—in the pilot he doesn't assume his heroic guise in an arctic fortress; he has his adopted mom, Martha Kent, run up a natty red, blue and yellow number on the family sewing machine, fussing over the colors and emblem, as he tries it on in front of the mirror.

Production values are high—though not in the movies' league—and the flying sequences are excellently realized. Actor Dean Cain still has to look the part in a wire harness, but many of the effects are computer-generated. Cain and Teri Hatcher, who plays Lois, also make a presentable pair. Cain had already won teen fans as Shannen Doherty's fleeting love interest in *Beverly Hills 90210*, while Teri Hatcher had had several minor roles, most notably in the film *Soapdish*. And John Shea, who'd played Bobby Kennedy in *Kennedy*, gave Lex Luthor something he's never had before—sex appeal.

Season Two introduced some cast changes—John Shea was seen only occasionally as Luthor, Jimmy Olsen got a new face, and Tracy Scoggins left—and it turned up the heat on Lois and Clark's romance to the point where in the last episode Clark proposed. Viewers had to wait until the start of Season Three for Lois' answer—and then we had the wedding that never was, with a clone storyline that left fans wondering whether they'd have to go through it all over again, plus a cliffhanger that had Superman zipping off to New Krypton! Season Four promised finally to get the lovers to the altar, and there were hints of a season-ending pregnancy.

REGULAR CAST

Clark Kent/Superman Dean Cain *Lois Lane* Teri Hatcher
Lex Luthor John Shea *Perry White* Lane Smith
Jimmy Olsen Michael Landes *(Season One)* Justin Whalin *(Season Two)*
Catherine "Cat" Grant Tracy Scoggins *Martha Kent* K. Callan
Jonathan Kent Eddie Jones

Developed for television by Deborah Joy LeVine
Based on the DC Comics characters created by Jerry Siegel *and* Joe Shuster
Producers: Chris Long, Grant Rosenberg, Jim Michaels, Philip J. Sgriccia, Jimmy Simone
Supervising producers: Chris Ruppenthal, John McNamara
Executive producers: Deborah Joy LeVine, Robert Butler, David Jacobs, Robert Singer,

Jim Crocker, Randall Zisk (both Season Two), Eugenie Ross-Leming, Brad Buckner
Visual effects supervisor: John Sheele
Music: Jay Gruska

A Roundelay/December 3rd Production in association with Warner Bros. Television
U.S. premiere: May 1993 (pilot)
U.K. premiere: 8 January–4 June 1994 (BBC1)

Season One
21 color episodes, 45 minutes except where stated

Pilot

(U.S.: 2 hours, U.K.: 75 minutes)
w Deborah Joy LeVine
Clark Kent, a human-like alien with superpowers, works with fellow *Daily Planet* reporters Lois Lane and Jimmy Olsen to prevent reclusive billionaire Lex Luthor and scientist Dr. Antoinette Baines from sabotaging Earth's first orbiting space station. The world is astonished by its new superhero, and Lois aptly dubs him "Superman."
Lucy Lane Elizabeth Barondes
Dr. Samuel Platt Kenneth Tigar
Henderson Mel Winkler
Dr. Antoinette Baines Kim Johnston Ulrich

Director: Robert Butler

Strange Visitor

w Bryce Zabel
A ruthless government investigator arrives at the *Daily Planet* demanding that its reporters reveal the whereabouts of Superman—and insists they submit to a lie detector test. Lois and Clark discover a warehouse containing the wreckage of many spacecraft and Clark learns more about his own origins.
Jason Trask Terence Knox
George Thompson Joseph Campanella
Burton Newcomb George Murdock
Lucy Lane Elizabeth Barondes

Director: Randall Zisk

Neverending Battle

w Dan Levine
Luthor threatens to cause an endless succession of disasters in Metropolis to prove that Superman can't be everywhere at once to save everyone. To protect innocent lives, Clark vows never to turn into Superman again.
Asabi Shaun Toub
Mr. Cleveland Larry Linville
Floyd Roy Brocksmith
Jules Miguel A. Nunez Jr.
Albert Tony Jay
Insp. Henderson Brent Jennings
Monique Mary Crosby

Director: Gene Reynolds

I'm Looking Through You

w Deborah Joy LeVine
An invisible man terrorizes Metropolis, staging violent robberies and helping vicious criminals escape. Superman must make the invisible visible.

Alan Morris Leslie Jordan
Helene Morris Patrika Darbo
Henry Barnes Jim Beaver
Detective Burke Thomas Ryan
Murray Brown Jack Carter

Director: Mark Sobel

Requiem for a Superhero

w Robert Killebrew
Lois discovers that her father, Dr. Sam Lane, is inadvertently helping a corrupt boxing promoter create an army of cybernetic athletes and so Superman steps into the ring to defeat the killer robots.
Dr. Sam Lane Denis Arndt
Max Menken Matt Roe
Tommy Garrison Joe Sabatino

Director: Randall Zisk

I've Got a Crush on You

w Thania St. John
Lois poses as a nightclub performer and Clark as a barman to infiltrate a criminal gang they suspect of setting destructive fires around Metropolis.
Toni Taylor Jessica Tuck
Johnny Michael Milhoan
Lou Johnny Williams

Director: Gene Reynolds

Smart Kids

w Dan Levine
Lois and Clark save Metropolis from the rule of several children, victims of a secret experiment to boost their intelligence.
Phillip Scott McAfee
Dudley Jonathan Hernandez
Karen Sheila Rosenthal
Aymee Courtney Peldon
Dr. Alfred Carlton Michael Cavanaugh
Inez Emily Ann Lloyd

Director: Robert Singer

The Green, Green Glow of Home

w Bryce Zabel
Lois and Clark come up against anti-UFO government agent Jason Trask again as they investigate a strange green crystal in Clark's hometown that saps Superman of his powers. After overcoming the threat, they name the green crystal Kryptonite in honor of Superman's new home world.
Jason Trask Terence Knox
Wayne Irig Jerry Hardin
Sheriff Rachel Harris Joleen Lutz
Carol Sherman L. Scott Caldwell

Director: Les Landau

Man of Steel Bars

w Paris Qualles
Superman is banished when the citizens of Metropolis blame him for causing abnormally hot temperatures, after Lex Luthor has schemed to undermine his good deeds.
Mayor Berkowitz Sonny Bono
Dr. Katherine Goodman Elaine Kagen
Dr. Edward Saxon Richard Fancy
Judge Diggs Rosalind Cash
Patricia Cheng Haunani Minn
Nigel Tony Jay
Murray Mindlin Tom La Grua

Director: Robert Butler

Pheromone, My Lovely

w Deborah Joy LeVine
When Luthor rejects the advances of his former lover, the beautiful chemist Miranda, she threatens to spray Metropolis with a new perfume that will permanently free romantic inhibitions.
Miranda Morgan Fairchild
Nigel Tony Jay

Director: Bill D'Elia

Honeymoon in Metropolis

w Dan Levine
Lois and Clark pose as newlyweds in a luxurious hotel suite in order to spy on a corrupt congressman who is selling defense secrets to a greedy weapons manufacturer.
Congressman Harrington Charles R. Frank
Thaddeus Roarke Charles Cyphers
"Sore Throat" Richard Libertini

Director: James A. Contner

All Shook Up

w Bryce Zabel
After trying to deflect a gigantic meteor from its collision course with Earth, Superman falls back to the planet in a state of complete amnesia. Meanwhile, a three-mile-wide fragment is still hurtling toward Earth . . .
General Zeitlin J.A. Preston
Insp. Henderson Richard Belzer
Prof. Stephen Daitch Richard Roat
Secretary John Cosgrove David Sage
Homeless man Matt Clark
Mystique Jenifer Lewis
Dr. Jerri McCorkle Suanne Spoke

Director: Felix Enrique Alcala

Witness

w Bradley Moore
Lois witnesses the murder of reclusive scientist Vincent Winninger who was about to reveal a powerful industrialist's scheme to destroy the Amazon rain forest.
Vincent Winninger Elliott Gould
Dr. Hubert Charlie Dell
Lt. Henderson Richard Belzer
Barbara Trevino Claudette Nevins
Mr. Tracewski Brian George
Sebastian Finn/Aide William Mesnik
Golf pro Phil Mickelson

Director: Mel Damski

Illusions of Grandeur

w Thania St. John
Lois and Clark investigate a world-famous magician whom they suspect of kidnapping the children of Metropolis' wealthiest families. (Special guest is magician Penn Jillette of the double act Penn and Teller.)
Dr. Novak Ben Vereen
Constance Marietta Deprima
Rose Collins Eve Plumb
Nick Collins Jarrett Lennon
Mark Moskal Stephen Burleigh
Darren Romick Penn Jillette

Director: Michael Watkins

Ides of Metropolis

w Deborah Joy LeVine
Lois and Clark help a computer programmer, falsely convicted of murder, combat a software virus that is destroying the nation's computer networks.
Eugene Laderman Todd Susman
Detective Betty Reed Melanie Mayron
Henry Harrison Paul Gleason
Lena Harrison Jennifer Savidge
Nigel Tony Jay
Judge Richard Gant

Director: Philip J. Sgriccia

The Foundling

w Dan Levine
An "origins" episode. Superman learns that the small globe retrieved from his spacecraft many years ago contains a hologram message from his father, Jor-El, that reveals all the secrets of his alien origin. Then a teenage burglar steals it and sells it to Lex Luthor.
Jor-El David Warner
Jack Miner Chris Demetral
Nigel Tony Jay
Louie Robert Costanzo
Denny Brandon Bluhm
Lara Eliza Roberts

Director: Bill D'Elia

The Rival

w Tony Blake & Paul Jackson
Lois and Clark investigate a rival newspaper publisher they suspect of causing tragic accidents so his reporters can be first to write the stories.
Preston Carpenter Dean Stockwell
Linda King Nancy Everhard
Himself Bo Jackson

Director: Michael Watkins

Vatman

w H.B. Cobb & Deborah Joy LeVine, *story by* H.B. Cobb
Luthor creates a Superman clone and orders him to destroy the real Superman. But the cloning process is defective and Luthor's creation turns against him.
Dr. Fabian Leek Michael McKean

Director: Randall Zisk

Fly Hard

w Thania St. John
Five terrorists invade the *Daily Planet* building and hold the staff hostage while they search for the secret vault of an infamous thirties gangster.
Fuentes Robert Beltran
Willie Macon McCalman
Jack Miner Chris Demetral
Flashback sequence:
Dragonetti John Shea
Billy Dean Cain

Director: Philip J. Sgriccia

Barbarians at the Planet

w Dan Levine & Deborah Joy LeVine
When the *Daily Planet* goes bust, Luthor buys the newspaper and destroys the building. And, when Superman is unable to declare his love for Lois, she accepts Luthor's proposal of marriage, unaware of his involvement in many of the criminal activities that plague Metropolis. Meanwhile, Luthor puts into operation a plan to finally destroy Superman.
Jack Miner Chris Demetral
Devane Patrick Kilkpatrick
Mrs. Cox Beverly Johnson
Steven Sanchez Castulo Guerra

Director: James R. Bagdonas

The House of Luthor

w Deborah Joy LeVine & Dan Levine
The *Daily Planet* staff tries to prove Luthor guilty of the newspaper arson and strives to prevent his marriage to Lois who now has doubts of her own. Mean-

while Luthor lures Superman to his headquarters, imprisons him inside a cage coated with stolen Kryptonite and leaves him to die . . .
Jack Miner Chris Demetral
Lt. Henderson Richard Belzer
Mrs. Cox Beverly Johnson
Franklin Stern James Earl Jones
Ellen Lane Phyllis Coates

Director: Alan J. Levi

Season Two
22 color 45-minute episodes

Madame Ex

w Tony Blake & Paul Jackson
Lex Luthor's ex-wife, Arianna Carlin, hires a Lois Lane lookalike to discredit the reporter's image and uses subliminal messages to incite the citizens of Metropolis against Superman.
Arianna Carlin Emma Samms
Det. Ryder Thomas Ryan
Gretchen Kelly Denise Crosby
Dr. Heller Earl Boen
Capt. Keene Jack Kruschen
Sheldon Bender Barry Livingston

Director: Randall Zisk

Wall of Sound

w John McNamara
A new criminal, dubbed the Soundman, uses sound waves in a scheme to blackmail Metropolis into handing over half its money. And Lois, jealous of Clark winning a prestigious award, decides they should work separately on their stories.
Lenny Stoke Michael Des Barres
Derek Camden Scott Colomby
Amazon women Cory Everson, Erika Andersch
Dr. Green Richard Balin
Mayor Sharpe Pamela Roberts

Director: Alan J. Levi

The Source

w Tony Blake & Paul Jackson
Lois must prove her innocence when she is implicated in a scandal involving an employee of an electronics firm who is accusing his bosses of deliberate negligence.
Stuart Hofferman Peter Scolari
Eric Thorp Tim Grimm
Sheldon Bender Barry Livingston
Oliver Jeffrey Joseph
Daniel Hansen Patrick Pankhurst
Diane Marla Frees

Director: John T. Kretchmer

The Prankster

w Grant Rosenberg

The Prankster, Kyle Griffin, seeks revenge on Lois, whose investigative article led to his imprisonment five years ago. He aims to build a new super weapon and use it to destroy the *Daily Planet* building.

Kyle Griffin Bronson Pinchot
Victor Rick Overton
Edwin Griffin Harold Gould
Pete Leonard Termo
Mick Barrows John Fleck
Randall Loomis J.D. Cullum
Diane Marla Frees

Director: James Hayman

Church of Metropolis

w John McNamara

Lois and Clark try to bring down a worldwide criminal network called Intergang that is using violent crimes to ruin flourishing business areas. And a beautiful district attorney, Mayson Drake, becomes attracted to Clark.

Bill Church Peter Boyle
Martin Snell Bruce Weitz
Mayson Drake Farrah Forke
Uncle Mike Dick Miller
Silhouette cop Steven Gilborn
Judge Michael Holden
Baby Rage Dwayne L. Barnes

Director: Robert Singer

Operation Blackout

w Kate Boutilier

Ryan Wiley, the ex-fiancé of Lois' old college friend, causes an electrical blackout in Metropolis as he and a rogue colonel plot to hijack a military defense satellite.

Ryan Wiley Charles Rocket
Charles Fane J.T. Walsh
Molly Flynn Melora Hardin
Andy Tucker Bill Erwin

Director: Michael Watkins

That Old Gang of Mine

w Gene Miller & Karen Kavner

A scientist revives infamous crime boss Al Capone and other notorious criminals to test a new theory about eliminating anti-social behavior. But when Capone decides to take over Metropolis, Clark is "fatally injured" during a shootout and Lois realizes that she cares more for him than she had admitted.

Dr. Emil Hamilton John Pleshette
Al Capone William Devane
Clyde Barrow Joseph Gian

Bonnie Parker Amy Hathaway
John Dillinger Robert Clohessy
Detective Wolfe Ray Abruzzo
Bobby Bigmouth Sal Viscuso

Director: Lorraine Senna Ferrara

A Bolt from the Blue

w Kathy McCormick

A lightning bolt miraculously transfers Superman's powers to a young man who calls himself Resplendent Man and tries to charge people for his services. But the transfer has been witnessed by Gretchen Kelly who sees in it a way to bring her beloved Lex Luthor back to life . . .

Little Will Waldecker Leslie Jordan
Wandamae Waldecker Cindy Williams
Gretchen Kelly Denise Crosby
Distraught woman Jean Sincere

Director: Philip J. Sgriccia

Season's Greedings

w Dean Cain

The Christmas episode. A dejected toymaker, fired because his products were not popular enough, seeks revenge on the children of the city and invents a new toy that fires a yellow mist causing everyone to act like greedy children.

The Toyman (aka Mr. Schott) Sherman Hemsley
Ms. Duffy Isabel Sanford
Orphanage worker Dick Van Patten
Angela Denise Richards
Harry Dom Irrera

Director: Randall Zisk

Metallo

w Tony Blake & Paul Jackson, *story by* James Crocker

Two evil scientist brothers create a half-human robot, powered by green Kryptonite, to use as the ultimate super criminal—but need a human brain to complete their work. They find it in a hoodlum who is dating Lois' kid sister, Lucy.

Rollie Vale Christian Clemenson
Emmet Vale John Rubenstein
Johnny Corben Scott Valentine
Lucy Lane Roxana Zal
Det. Tuzzolino Louis Mustillo
Mrs. Vale Dee Rescher
Postal inspector Mary Pat Gleason

Director: James R. Bagdonas

Chi of Steel

w Hilary Bader
Lois and Clark combat an evil martial arts master who works for a company exploiting illegal Chinese immigrants.
Harlan Black Brian Doyle-Murray
Chen Chow Yuji Okumoto
Grandfather Chow James Hong
Lin Chow Leila Hee Olsen
Doorman Steve Eastin
Tong gang leader Dana Lee

Director: James Hayman

The Eyes Have It

w Kathy McCormick, *story by* Kathy McCormick & Grant Rosenberg
Superman is blinded by an ultraviolet ray gun while attempting to rescue Lois from a pair of kidnappers convinced she knows the location of a secret device for transferring knowledge on beams of light.
Dr. Neal Faraday Harvey J. Alperin
Dr. Harry Leit David Bowe
Munch Gerrit Graham
Mayson Drake Farrah Forke

Director: Bill D'Elia

The Phoenix

w Tony Blake & Paul Jackson
Gretchen Kelly finally succeeds in bringing Lex Luthor back to life—though he's horrified to find he's now bald! He vows to win back his fortune (squandered by his lawyer, Sheldon Bender) and the love of Lois Lane.
Lex Luthor John Shea
Gretchen Kelly Denise Crosby
Nigel St. John Tony Jay
Sheldon Bender Barry Livingston
Bobby Bigmouth Sal Viscuso
Rollie Vale Christian Clemenson
Bomb squad leader Randy Crowder

Director: Philip J. Sgriccia

Top Copy

w John McNamara
Diana Stride, ace television reporter and former Intergang assassin, sets out to expose Superman's true identity, but is forced to try to kill him when he guards an informant who could reveal *her* true identity.
Diana Stride Raquel Welch
Mr. Darryl Robert Culp
Rolf Wayne Péré
Doctor Tom Virtue
Mayson Drake Farrah Forke

Director: Randall Zisk

Return of the Prankster

w Grant Rosenberg
Lois Lane is left standing in her underwear in the middle of her office when The Prankster returns to Metropolis with a special freezing device that temporarily paralyzes people. It's just the prelude to a plot to kidnap the President.
Kyle Griffin "The Prankster" Bronson Pinchot
Victor Rick Overton
Dr. Emil Hamilton John Pleshette
Carrigan Cliff DeYoung
Edwin Griffin Harold Gould
Bobby Bigmouth Sal Viscuso

Director: Philip J. Sgriccia

Lucky Leon

w Chris Ruppenthal
Jimmy is arrested for murder and Superman is duped into stealing nuclear warheads. On the romance front, Lois and Clark have such a wonderful time on their first date that Lois slams the door in Clark's face and asks Perry for a new partner! And in a shock conclusion Mayson Drake is killed by a car bomb.
Mayson Drake Farrah Forke
Mr. Darryl Robert Culp
Lucky Leon John Kapelos
Gregor Mark Rolston
Paul Borges Sam Vlahos
Police detective Michael Leopard
Gen. Jason Jackson David Jean-Thomas

Director: Jim Pohl

Resurrection

w Gene Miller & Karen Kavner
Lois and Clark investigate Mayson's death and uncover a plot to free prisoners from jail using a pill that induces a death-like sleep, and a larger plan to steal a deadly virus and release it on Metropolis. Meanwhile Lois is attracted to Dan Scardino, a government agent working on the same case.
Stanley Gables Dennis Lipscomb
Dan Scardino Jim Pirri
Albie Swinson Curtis Armstrong
Sean Macarthy Peter McDonald
Diego Martinez Eddie Frias
Big Buster Danny Woodburn
Craven Don Pugsley

Director: Joseph L. Scanlan

Tempus Fugitive

w Jack Weinstein & Lee Hutson
Lois and Clark learn of a future Utopia created by their descendants when they are visited by H.G. Wells in his time machine. But Wells' fellow traveler, Tempus, is taken with the violent 20th century and decides to change the "boring" future by going back into the past to kill Superman as a baby.
H.G Wells Terry Kiser
Tempus Lane Davies
Frank James Joshua Devane
Jesse James Don Swayze
with Robert Costanzo

Director: James Bagdonas

Target: Jimmy Olsen!

w Tony Blake & Paul Jackson
Jimmy and two other unsuspecting youngsters are brainwashed into acting as assassins by an unscrupulous mother and daughter. While Lois and Clark try to help him, they find themselves drifting apart as Dan Scardino continues to make a play for Lois.
Dan Scardino Jim Pirri
Claudette Wilder Michelle Phillips
with Claire Yarlett, Meredith Scott Lynn, Charles Napier, Erick Avari, David Sage, Alaina Reed Hall

Director: David S. Jackson

Individual Responsibility

w Chris Ruppenthal
Intergang's new boss is out to gain control of the *Daily Planet* and possesses a chunk of red Kryptonite that makes Superman less than enthusiastic about stopping him.
Bill Church Jr. Bruce Campbell
Dr. Friskin Barbara Bosson
with O'Neal Compton, David Graf, Kelly Mullis

Director: Alan J. Levi

Whine, Whine, Whine

w Kathy McCormick & John McNamara
Superman is sued by an obnoxious young musician for injuring him during a rescue. Meanwhile Clark must decide who's more important to the world—Clark Kent or Superman—and Lois must choose between Clark and Dan Scardino.
Dan Scardino Jim Pirri
Bill Church Jr. Bruce Campbell
Dr. Friskin Barbara Bosson
Calvin Dregg Jason Carter
Elise Michele Abrams
Bobby Bigmouth Sal Viscuso

Constance Hunter Kay Lenz
Martin Pfinch-Lupus Martin Mull
with Cliff Bemis, Richard Portnow
Special appearances by Frank Gorshin, Adam West

Director: Michael Watkins

And the Answer Is...

w Tony Blake & Paul Jackson
Clark is blackmailed into robbing a jewelry store and is then ordered to kill Lois. When his plan to put her in suspended animation nearly backfires, he decides that the time has come to propose. He proposes, Lois answers: "Clark . . ." and the credits roll.
Jace Mazik Maurice Godin
Nigel Tony Jay

Director: Alan J. Levi

Season Three
22 color 45-minute episodes

We Have a Lot to Talk About

w John McNamara
"Who's asking? Clark or Superman?" Lois reveals that she had guessed Clark was Superman but, confused and upset at him keeping the truth from her, she rejects his marriage proposal. Meanwhile, Intergang boss Bill Church marries his beautiful nurse, Mindy, and plans to give up his life of crime. But his son conspires with Mindy to take control of the organization.
Bill Church Peter Boyle
Bill Church Jr. Bruce Campbell
Mindy Jessica Collins
Bobby Bigmouth Sal Viscuso
Grant Burton Mark Goodman
Man in black David Sederholm
Timid man David Weisenberg

Director: Philip J. Sgriccia

Odinary People

w Eugenie Ross-Leming & Brad Buckner
Lois and Clark vacation on the isolated island of a freakishly deformed criminal, Spencer Spencer, who schemes to kidnap Superman and insert his own mind into the man of steel's perfect body.
Spencer Spencer David Leisure
Dr. Pescado Carlos Lacamara
Belzer Vincent Guastaferro
Klavel Peter Kent
Heidi Greta Blackburn

Director: Michael Watkins

Contact

w Chris Ruppenthal
A vengeful computer genius abducts Lois and implants her with hypnotic commands to distract Superman so he can take over the world's computer software market. Superman foils his plot, but also calls off his relationship with Lois.
Star Olivia Brown
Bob Fences Patrick Labyorteaux
Dr. Martin Solsvig Larry Hankin
Simone Rochelle Swanson

Director: Daniel Attias

When Irish Eyes Are Killing

w Grant Rosenberg
Lois' former lover Patrick Sullivan arrives in Metropolis to claim an ancient Irish crown with mystical powers but must sacrifice Lois to obtain it. And a jealous Clark admits he still loves Lois and wants to start dating again.
Patrick Sullivan Julian Stone
Veronica Kipling Ilana Levine
Colleen Sheelagh Cullen
Star Olivia Brown
Shamus/Robber Tom Todoroff
Mr. McCarthy Patrick McCormack

Director: Winrich Kolbe

Just Say Noah

w Brad Buckner & Eugenie Ross-Leming
When happily married couples start vanishing after attending a celebrated therapist's retreat, Lois and Clark pose as lovers to investigate and uncover a fanatical scheme to flood the Earth and form a new society. (Dean Cain's mother, Sharon Thomas, has a cameo as a nun.)
Larry Smiley Mac Davis
Star Olivia Brown
Jeremy Brian R. Richardson
Michelle Sitkowitz Nancy Cassaro
Arnold Sitkowitz Rob LaBelle
Brian Michael C. Mahon
Betty Erin Donovan
Kathy Jennifer Hooper
Nun Sharon Thomas
Cassandra Smiley Marte Boyle Slout

Director: David S. Jackson

Don't Tug on Superman's Cape

w David Simkins
Star Trek: The Next Generation star Jonathan Frakes and his real-life wife Genie Francis guest star as a wealthy, evil couple with a passion for rare objects, who want to add Superman to their collection.
Tim Lake Jonathan Frakes
Amber Lake Genie Francis
Bad Brain Johnson Michael Harris
Dr. Peterson Klein Kenneth Kimmins

Director: Steven Dubin

Ultra Woman

w Gene O'Neill & Noreen Tobin
"Who's asking—Lois or Ultra Woman?" Scheming sisters Lucille and Nell Newtrich try to use red Kryptonite to render Superman mortal while transferring his powers to themselves. But they accidentally pass them on to Lois who gets a chance to learn the responsibility of being a superhero. It makes her realize how much she loves Clark and this time it's *her* turn to do the proposing . . .
Lucille Newtrich Shelley Long
Nell Newtrich Mary Gross
Dr. Peterson Klein Kenneth Kimmins
Husband Lawrence A. Mandley
Woman Evie Peck
Thug Thomas Rosales

Director: Mike Vejar

Chip off the Old Clark

w Michael Jamin & Sivert Glarum
Did Superman father an illegitimate "super" child? Lois *really* wants to know. And a villainous master of disguise wants to kidnap the boy and use his superpowers to launch a nuclear missile.
Leigh-Anne Stepanovic Susan Batten
Donald Rafferty/Anonymous Joel Brooks
Dr. Peterson Klein Kenneth Kimmins
Jesse Alex D. Linz
President Michael Kagan
Grandpa/Anonymous Zale Kessler
Elderly woman/Anonymous Ernestine Mercer
Real Anonymous Dave Coulier
Themselves Michael Burger, Maty Monfort, Dave Nemeth
Hacker Eric Saiet
Rebel leader Kristof Konrad
Secret Service agent Big Daddy Wayne

Director: Michael Watkins

Super Mann

w Chris Ruppenthal
Three young Nazi soldiers, placed in hibernation by scientists during World War Two, awake to lead a large group of followers in America.
Steve Law Sean Kanan
Hank West Paul Kersey
Lisa Sandra Hess
Dr. Peterson Klein Kenneth Kimmins
Senator Truman Black Linden Chiles
Skip Sean Whalen
Voss Jack Stauffer
Karen Mary Jacobsen
Ned Tom Hines
TV anchorman Jack Owen
William Stockdale Douglas Stark

Director: James R. Bagdonas

Virtually Destroyed

w Dean Cain, *story by* Dean Cain *&* Sean Brennan
A madman traps Lois in his computer-generated virtual world and Superman relies on Jimmy's computer wizardry to rescue her. (Romance note: Clark also reveals that he's a virgin—"I've never really crossed the intimacy threshold.")
Jaxon Xavier Andrew Mark Berman
Kombat Andrew Bryniarski
Computer voice Paula Poundstone

Director: Jim Charleston

Home Is Where the Hurt Is

w Eugenie Ross-Leming *&* Brad Buckner, *story by* William A. Akers
Christmas episode. New Intergang leader Mindy Church coerces the world's crime leaders to join her in destroying Superman and hires an ingenious assassin, Joey Bermuda, to expose Superman to a rare Kryptonian virus. Meanwhile Lois' dysfunctional parents visit for the holidays.
Mindy Church Jessica Collins
Joey Bermuda Robert Carradine
Ellen Lane Beverly Garland
Sam Lane Harve Presnell
Henchman Joel Swetow
Baby Gunderson Kathy Trageser
Crime boss Anthony Powers
Snitch E.J. Callahan
Mugger Barney Burman

Director: Geoffrey Nottage

Never on Sunday

w Grant Rosenberg
A ruthless illusionist arrives in Metropolis looking for revenge and Clark finds himself at the mercy of the man's supernatural voodoo powers, experiencing strange, frightening visions. And Lois' mom hires a wedding consultant!

Baron Sunday Cress Williams
Ellen Lane Beverly Garland
Beverly Lipman Carol Lawrence
Ziggy Gary Dourdan
Matt Young Ben Reed
Rod Clemons Les Lannom
Star Olivia Brown

Director: Michael Lange

The Dad Who Came In from the Cold

w David Simkins
When Lois and Clark obtain a mysterious computer with the power to destroy the world, Jimmy's estranged secret agent father wants it back—at any cost.
Jack Olsen James Read
Trevanian Ben Slack
Sweet Tart Una Damon
Bud Collins James F. Dean

Director: Alan J. Levi

Tempus, Anyone?

w John McNamara
Time-traveling villain Tempus returns, kidnapping Lois and transporting her to a parallel version of Metropolis. There, Lois teams up with H.G. Wells to persuade the more cynical version of Clark to use Superman's powers to stop Tempus from ruling the city.
Tempus Lane Davies
H.G. Wells Hamilton Camp
Lana Lang Emily Procter
Major domo Lee Arenberg
Rookie cop Eric Stuart
Spy Chuck Butto
Bank guard Lee Spencer

Director: Winrich Kolbe

I Now Pronounce You . . .

w Chris Ruppenthal
With her wedding day imminent, Lois accidentally becomes involved in a plot by Dr. Mamba, a mad biologist funded by Lex Luthor, to kill the President and replace him with a clone. Unknown to Clark, Lois is kidnapped and her place at the altar taken by a clone . . .
Dr. Mamba Tony Curtis
President Fred Willard
Ellen Lane Beverly Garland
Sam Lane Harve Presnell
Reverend Bob Brad Garrett
Manager Oliver Muirhead
Church deacon Paul Linke
Cindy Ria Pavia
Agent Roberts Joshua Devane
Delivery driver Charles Gunning
Maid Natalie Strauss

Director: Jim Pohl

Double Jeopardy

w Brad Buckner & Eugenie Ross-Leming
With Lois held prisoner in his underground bunker, Luthor schemes to regain her love. Lois escapes but is knocked down and loses her memory, taking on the identity of a character in a novel she had been writing. Meanwhile the Lois clone decides she loves Clark and wants to kill the real Lois.
Lex Luthor John Shea
Red Dixon Billy Dean
Bibbo Bibowski Troy Evans
Church deacon Paul Linke
Passenger Ron Porterfield

Director: Chris Long

Seconds

w John McNamara, *story by* Corey Miller & Philip W. Chung
Luthor takes Lois, still suffering from amnesia, back to his underground lair, and his final plan to gain Lois' love could mean death for Superman.
Lex Luthor John Shea
Dr. Peterson Klein Kenneth Kimmins
Asabi Shaun Toub
Leonard, the lab assistant Andrew Shaifer
Bank v.p. Joseph Chapman
Doctor Mark Daniel Cade

Director: Alan J. Levi

Forget Me Not

w Grant Rosenberg
Clark investigates a string of murders that lead him to one of the doctors treating Lois' amnesia. The trauma of Lois' recent experiences causes some of her memory to return—but now she thinks she's in love with her psychiatrist!
Dr. Maxwell Deter Larry Poindexter
Dr. Elias Mendenhall Charles Cioffi
Nurse Reilly Audrie Neenan
Sally Reynolds Julie Cobb
Homer Blackstock Patrick Cranshaw
Agnes Moskowitz Lillian Adams
Detective McCloskey Vasili Bogazianos

Director: James Bagdonas

Oedipus Wrecks

w David Simkins
Lois resumes working with Clark, but still thinks she's in love with Deter. Meanwhile a devious inventor's electromagnetic wave wreaks havoc in Me-tropolis, but also causes Lois to regain her memory totally. The engagement is back on!
Dr. Maxwell Deter Larry Poindexter
Herkimer Johnson Daniel Roebuck
Mrs. Johnson Renee Taylor
Dr. Klein Kenneth Kimmins
Worker Bill Dearth
Paramedic Reggie Jordan

Director: Kenn Michael Fuller

It's a Small World After All

w Teri Hatcher & Pat Hazell, *story by* Teri Hatcher
Lois discovers that a former shy classmate, cosmetics boss Annette Westman, is getting revenge on her old "friends" by shrinking them with a special shampoo and imprisoning them in a doll's house.
Annette Westman Elizabeth Anne Smith
Joe Malloy Steve Young
Dr. Peterson Klein Kenneth Kimmins
Hans Don Brunner
Julie Charlton Rainer Grant
Dick Charlton Tim Bohn
Les Barrish Jim Hanks
Debbie Malloy Leslie Sachs
Fortune teller Ellen Gerstein

Director: Philip J. Sgriccia

Through a Glass, Darkly

w Chris Ruppenthal
First of a two-part story. Ching and Sarah, two mysterious strangers from Superman's past, test the man of steel.
Ching Jon Tenney (Teri Hatcher's real-life husband)
Sarah Justine Bateman

Director: Chris Long

Big Girls Don't Fly

w Eugenie Ross-Leming & Brad Buckner
Confronting his mysterious past and his imperiled future, in the face of a hideous and powerful Assassin, Superman must make the most harrowing decision of his life. And Lois must help him determine the fate of thousands of people, as well as his own.
Ching Jon Tenney
Sarah Justine Bateman
Assassin Roger Daltrey

Director: Philip J. Sgriccia

Season Four
22 episodes

Lord of the Flys

w Brad Buckner & Eugenie Ross-Leming
With Clark trying to save his fellow Kryptonians, Lord Nor and his henchman come to Earth and plot to take over, starting with Smallville.
Zara Justine Bateman
Lord Nor Simon Templeman
Ching Mark Kiely
Jen Mai Mark Lindsay Chapman
Trey J.G. Hertzler
Colonel Cash Richard Grove
Drull Eric Allen Kramer
Ran Dan Hildebrand
Ralph James Dumont
Lieutenant Small Mark Kretzmann

Director: Philip J. Sgriccia

Battleground Earth

w Eugenie Ross-Leming & Brad Buckner
Lord Nor uses Kryptonian law to sentence Superman to death, and he has captured Clark's adoptive parents to make sure Superman submits.
Zara Justine Bateman
Lord Nor Simon Templeman
Ching Mark Kiely
Jen Mai Mark Lindsay Chapman
Trey J.G. Hertzler
Colonel Cash Richard Grove
Drull Eric Allen Kramer
Ran Dan Hildebrand
Messenger Julian Barnes

Director: Philip J. Sgriccia

Swear to God, This Time We're Not Kidding

w John McNamara
Not even the "Wedding Destroyer" can stop the super-wedding of the century.
Myrtle Beech Delta Burke
Dr. Voyle Grumman Charles Fleischer
Ellen Lane Beverly Garland
Sam Lane Harve Presnell
Leo Nunk Ray Buktenica
Mike David Doyle
Emily Channing Leann Hunley
Lamont Billy "Sly" Williams
Head paramedic Jerry Giles
Messenger David Lewman

Director: Michael Lange

Soul Mates

w Brad Kern
Before Lois and Clark can consummate their marriage, H.G. Wells shows up with a warning: Go back in time and stop a curse or suffer dire consequences.
Tempus Lane Davies
H.G. Wells Terry Kiser
The Sorcerer Clive Revill
Soldier #1 Nick Meaney
Soldier #2 Tim O'Hare

Director: Richard Friedman

Brutal Youth

w Tim Minear
Lois and Clark investigate the rapid aging and death of one of Jimmy's friends . . . and discover it's happening to Jimmy too.
Veda Doodsen Caroline McWilliams
Dr. Klein Kenneth Kimmins
Young Connor Schenk John D'Aquino
Old Jimmy Olsen Jack Larson
Old Connor Schenk Sandy Ward
Old Benny Rockland Don Keefer
Mister Larry Randl Ask
Bank teller Lynn Tufeld
Guard Steven Rodriguez
Ancient Lois Barbara Pilavin

Director: David Grossman

The People v. Lois Lane

w Grant Rosenberg
When Lois is framed for murdering an informant, the evidence piles up against her.
Angela Winters Jasmine Guy
Professor Jefferson Cole Alan Rachins
D.A. Clemmons Granville Van Dusen
Veronica Stewart Maryedith Burrell
Wolcott David Kriegel
Sheila Danko Kim Tavares
Wanda Julie Payne
Judge Samuelson Jim Jansen
Matron Marianne Muellerleile
Elroy Sikes Peter Spellos
Detective Norman Large
Bailiff Eric Fleeks
Reporter Brad Heller
Bobby Anthony Embeck

Director: Robert Ginty

Dead Lois Walking

w Brad Buckner & Eugenie Ross-Leming

Clark breaks Lois out of prison when she is sentenced to death, and together they try to prove her innocence.

Professor Jefferson Cole Alan Rachins
D.A. Clemmons Granville Van Dusen
Wolcott David Kriegel
Sheila Danko Kim Tavares
Dr. Klein Kenneth Kimmins
Dr. Bains Michael Krawic
State trooper Christopher Titus
Lou Ken Thorley

Director: Chris Long

Bob and Carol and Lois and Clark

w Brian Nelson

Lois and Clark's new neighbors are perfect, except for one small detail: Bob is a super-assassin called Deathstroke.

Bob Stanford Antonio Sabato Jr.
Grant Gendell Kenneth Mars
Dr. Klein Kenneth Kimmins
Carol Stanford Sydney Walsh
Denzler Steve Hytner
Agent Rawlins Rif Hutton
Aurora Betsy Lynn George
Dr. Kobiyashi Darrell Kunitomi

Director: Oz Scott

Ghosts

w Michael Gleason

A con man uses fake ghosts to scare people into selling their homes, and when he accidentally summons a real ghost, he incorporates her into his scheme.

Herbie Saxe Drew Carey
Katie Banks Kathy Kinney
Mink Mahoney Richard Zavaglia
Lilah Monroe Lee Benton
Bertha Avery Jean Speegle Howard

Director: Robert Ginty

Stop The Presses

w Brad Kern

When Perry is promoted, Lois is tapped to fill his shoes as editor of the *Planet*. All is well until she kills one of Clark's stories, which not only results in the couple's first major fight, but also prevents them from uncovering a sinister plot to assassinate the Man of Steel!

Ethan Press Charles Esten
Eric Press Jeff Juday

Colonel Raymond O'Keefe
Ralph James Dumont
Carly Bahni Turpin
Technician Nicholas Shaffer
Researcher Tanika Ray
Reporter #1 Nicole Robinson
Reporter #2 James Martin Jr.
Darlene Krisinda Cain

Director: Peter Ellis

'Twas the Night before Mxymas

w Tim Minear

Mister Mxyzptlk puts the Earth into a time loop, and each time events repeat themselves, people turn more and more bitter and hopeless. Only Superman seems immune . . .

Mister Mxyzptlk Howie Mandel
Ellen Lane Beverly Garland
Sam Lane Harve Presnell
William B. Caldwell Keene Curtis
Ralph James Dumont
Bartender Monty Hoffman
Bank robber Michael Monks
Newscaster Ben McCain
Cop Pancho Demmings
Brenda Brandi Andres

Director: Michael Vejar

Lethal Weapon

w Grant Rosenberg

Perry's son is out of prison and out to destroy Superman with red Kryptonite.

Hank Landry John Spencer
Jerry White Andre Nemec
Dr. Klein Kenneth Kimmins
Carter Landry Tom Wilson
Mayor Nancy Dussault
Thug Stephen Pocock

Director: Jim Charleston

Sex, Lies, and Videotape

w Dan Wilcox

A snooping tabloid journalist snaps an intimate picture of Lois Lane and Superman, leading the world to believe they are having an affair. Will this ruin Superman's reputation and stop him from preventing a war?

Randy Goode Jack Wagner
Samantha Julie Brown

Director: Philip J. Sgriccia

Meet John Doe

w Tim Minear
Tempus runs for President, using future technology to plant subliminal messages into the minds of voters.
Tempus Lane Davies
President Garner Fred Willard
Andrus William Christopher
Doctor Dussel Victor Raider-Wexler
Barrett Robert Arce
Randolph Richard Cody
Homeless man Dennis Fimple
Anchor Ben McCain
Cop Shirley Jordan
Suit #1 Scott A. Smith
Suit #2 Cynthia Kania
Suit #3 Mary Amadeo Ingersoll

Director: Jim Pohl

Lois and Clarks

w Eugenie Ross-Leming & Brad Buckner
With Superman trapped in the time stream, Lois searches for a way to rescue him and stop Tempus's mind control scheme. H.G. Wells may provide the key.
Tempus Lane Davies
President Garner Fred Willard
H.G. Wells Hamilton Camp
Dragon Rick Dean
Anchor Ben McCain
Rustic John Kendall

Director: Chris Long

AKA Superman

w Jeffrey Vlaming
Jimmy lets a woman think he's secretly Superman, which may mean death for all involved.
Garret Grady Dwight Schultz
Penny Barnes Kristanna Loken
Peters Vito D'Ambrosio
Chester Paladin Michael Paul Chan
Doris Michole White
Steve McBride Granville Ames

Director: Robert Ginty

Faster Than a Speeding Vixen

w Brad Kern
Superman has to deal with super-vigilante Vixen, the *Daily Planet*'s mysterious new owner, and a plot to resurrect Lex Luthor's empire.

Leslie Luckabee Patrick Cassidy
Troll/Mr. Smith Keith Brunsmann
Vixen Lori Fetrick
Bank chairman Peter Vogt
Hit man Michael Eugene Stone
Detective Michael Holden
Cop Barry Wiggins
Announcer Ben McCain

Director: Neal Ahern

Shadow of a Doubt

w Grant Rosenberg
The *Daily Planet*'s new owner turns ot be Lex Luthor's scheming son—and he has romantic designs on Lois and plans to kill Superman.
Leslie Luckabee Patrick Cassidy
Lex Luthor (voice) John Shea
Troll/Mr. Smith Keith Brunsmann
Dr. Klein Kenneth Kimmins
Edward Hanson Matt Roe
Dr. Angelo Martinelli Pierrino Mascarino
Detective Leonard Kelly-Young
Lawrence Rankin Michael Keenan

Director: Philip J. Sgriccia

Voice from the Past

w John McNamara
Lois is kidnapped: Lex Luthor's son as Superman tries to find out if he can have children.
Leslie Luckabee Patrick Cassidy
Troll/Mr. Smith Keith Brunsmann
Dr. Klein Kenneth Kimmins
Carolyn Stacy Rukeyser
Cop Terence Mathews

Director: David Grossman

I've Got You Under My Skin

w Tim Minear
A man pursued by the mob swaps bodies with Clark Kent, leaving Clark on the lam—and him with Superman's powers.
Woody Samms Tim Thomerson
Becky Samms Stacy Keanan
Asabi Shaun Toub
Little Tony Howard George
Mug Joe Maruzzo
Beat cop Frank Novak
S.W.A.T. Commander Dorian Gregory

Director: Eugenie Ross-Leming

Toy Story

w Brad Kern
The Toyman kidnaps children from orphanages and gives them better lives, but his intentions go wrong when he takes revenge on his former employers by stealing their children as well.
The Toyman Grant Shaud
Dr. Klein Kenneth Kimmins
Wendy Stacey Travis
Alice Mary Frann
Alex Turner Jeffrey Byron
Ms. Beckett Irene Olga Lopez
Nanny Susan Isaacs
Brittany Turner Jillian Berard
Ryan Myles Jeffrey
Anchorman Ben McCain
Joey Brian McLaughlin
Woman Laurie Stevens

Director: Jim Pohl

The Family Hour

w Brad Buckner & Eugenie Ross-Leming
Final episode. Lois and Clark seek a way to have children; complicating things is Dr. Mensa, criminal genius with super mental powers.
Dr. Fat Head Mensa Harry Anderson
Ellen Lane Beverly Garland
Sam Lane Harve Presnell
Misha Brian George
Constance Bailey Jane Morris
Carter Clavens Rick Lawless
Guard Michael E. Bauer
Lieutenant Eric Fleeks
Cop Denise Ryan-Sherman

Director: Robert Ginty

LOST IN SPACE

After launching the Poseidon adventures of *Voyage to the Bottom of the Sea* in 1964, producer Irwin Allen looked for further fortunes in the stars and found himself *Lost in Space*.

Set in 1997, *Lost in Space* charted the adventures of the Space Family Robinson, selected from more than two million volunteers to embark on a 5½-year voyage to colonize a distant planet in the Alpha Centauri system. Enemy agent Dr. Zachary Smith sneaks aboard the *Jupiter 2* spaceship and reprograms their robot to destroy it. But his sabotage backfires when he becomes trapped aboard and by the time they regain control the ship is far off course.

Astrophysicist John Robinson (played by Walt Disney's ex-*Zorro* star, Guy Williams), his down-to-earth biochemist wife, Maureen, and children, Judy, Penny and Will, are the pioneering family. Aided by handsome geologist/pilot Major Don West, they set about trying first to survive and then to escape from their galactic desert island, hindered by the self-centered desires of the idle, whining scoundrel, Dr. Smith. Despite the wholesome nature of the family, it was Smith who became the star of the show, along with the robot, a 7 ft. "bubble-headed booby" who was forever warning of imminent danger.

Young actor Billy Mumy already had a list of more than 50 film and TV credits by the time he was cast as Will, including pivotal roles in three *Twilight Zone* stories ("Long Distance Call," 1960; "It's a Good Life," 1961; and "In Praise of Pip," 1963). Angela Cartwright, who played Penny, had the dubious credential of being one of the Von Trapp children in *The Sound of Music*, while Jonathan Harris (Dr. Smith) had enjoyed a three-year run with Michael Rennie in *The Third Man*.

Although the series degenerated into increasingly camp comic fantasy—in which a carrot monster was the final straw!—the early black and white shows had a hard edge of serious science fiction, occasionally sustaining a decent level of suspense. This was mildly heightened by the use of cliffhanger endings to each episode—though these were always the first moves in a *new* story, that week's adventure having been safely resolved. The early shows in particular also took a high moral tone, stressing the virtues of family unity and handing out lessons in prejudice, social behavior, loyalty, responsibility and manners. In one episode Will is even told to take his elbows off the table!

REGULAR CAST

Prof. John Robinson Guy Williams *Maureen Robinson* June Lockhart
Judy Marta Kristen *Penny* Angela Cartwright *Will* Billy Mumy
Don West Mark Goddard *Dr. Zachary Smith* Jonathan Harris
Robot Bob May

Creator/Producer: Irwin Allen
Story editor: Anthony Wilson
Music: Johnny Williams, others
Director of photography: Gene Polito (Season One), Frank Carson
Special effects: L.B. Abbott, Hal Lydecker (Season One)

CBS/An Irwin Allen Production in association with Jodi Production Inc, Van Bernard Productions Inc for 20th Century Fox Television
83 60-minute episodes (1965–68)
black and white (Season One)
color (from Season Two)
U.S. premiere: 15 September 1965
U.K. premiere: 2 October 1965
(Incomplete run in Northern region by ABC Weekend Television)

Season One
29 episodes

The Reluctant Stowaway

w Shimon Wincelberg
The Robinson family blasts off in their *Jupiter 2* spaceship bound for Alpha Centauri. The unexpected presence on board of a saboteur, Dr. Smith, sends the ship off course, becoming "lost in space."
TV commentator Don Forbes
General Hal Torey

Director: Tony Leader

The Derelict

w Peter Packer, *story by* Shimon Wincelberg
Searching for a clue as to their whereabouts, the *Jupiter 2* crew is drawn into a cavernous spaceship where they discover the wonders of an advanced alien civilization.
TV commentator Don Forbes
Giant Dawson Palmer

Director: Alex Singer

Island in the Sky

w Norman Lessing, *story by* Shimon Wincelberg
After John has plummeted to the unknown planet's surface, Smith tampers with the *Jupiter 2*'s rockets and the ship crash-lands. The party begins the search for John in the space chariot.

Director: Tony Leader

There Were Giants in the Earth

w Carey Wilbur, *story by* Shimon Wincelberg
Alarmed by the prospect of a 150 degree drop in temperature, the Robinsons head south and encounter cyclopean giants.
Giant Dawson Palmer

Director: Leo Penn

The Hungry Sea

w William Welch, *story by* Shimon Wincelberg
Data from the robot warns that the planet's elliptical orbit will bring it perilously close to the sun. Barely escaping a fiery death, the Robinsons decide to head back to their spaceship—but the elements haven't finished with them yet!

Director: Sobey Martin

Welcome Stranger

w Peter Packer
A long-lost astronaut lands on the Robinsons' planet and after helping to repair his ship, both the family and Smith see him as a ticket back to Earth—John and Maureen for the children, Smith for himself!
Jimmy Hapgood Warren Oates

Director: Alvin Ganzer

My Friend, Mr. Nobody

w Jackson Gillis
Penny befriends a cosmic force that she encounters in a secret cave.
Voice William Bramley

Director: Paul Stanley

Invaders from the Fifth Dimension

w Shimon Wincelberg
Luminous aliens invade the Robinson space colony and capture Smith, planning to use his brain to replace their burned-out computer. But sly old Smith talks them into letting him bring them Will instead.
Alien Ted Lehmann
Luminary Joe Ryan

Director: Leonard Horn

The Oasis

w Peter Packer
Dr. Smith samples some untested alien fruit and grows into a giant.

Director: Sutton Roley

The Sky Is Falling

w Barney Slater & Herman Groves
Unable to understand each other, mutual mistrust grows between the Robinsons and a visiting alien family until Will and the aliens' son find a way to achieve friendship.
Rethso Don Matheson
Moela Francoise Ruggieri
Lunon Eddie Rosson

Director: Sobey Martin

Wish Upon a Star

w Barney Slater
A typical *Lost in Space* morality tale. Will finds a thought machine that can turn wishes into reality, but it begins to arouse selfish emotions in the family. When Smith's greed gets too great, a strange creature comes to reclaim the device.
Rubberoid Dawson Palmer

Director: Sutton Roley

The Raft

w Peter Packer
The Robinsons build a small space craft from parts of the *Jupiter*, planning to send Don back to Earth for help. But Dr. Smith plots to hijack it.
Bush creature Dawson Palmer

Director: Sobey Martin

One of Our Dogs Is Missing

w William Welch
A 20-year-old space dog lands on the planet and helps rescue Judy from the clutches of a great hairy mutant (another addition to the Dawson Palmer monster club!).

Director: Sutton Roley

Attack of the Monster Plants

w William Read Woodfield & Allan Balter
Giant cyclamen plants that can duplicate anything fed into them create a replica of Judy and devour a vital fuel supply.

Director: Justus Addis

Return from Outer Space

w Peter Packer
Will uses a discarded matter transfer unit to make a Christmas trip back to Earth. But no one there will believe his story.

Aunt Clara Reta Shaw
Sheriff Baxendale Walter Sande
Davey Sims Donald Losby
Ruth Templeton Sheila Mathews

Director: Nathan Juran

The Keeper, Part 1

w Barney Slater
An alien beast-collector threatens to add Will and Penny to his bizarre menagerie. (This story reunited the *Third Man* partnership of Jonathan Harris and Michael Rennie.)
The Keeper Michael Rennie
Lighted head Wilbur Evans

Director: Sobey Martin

The Keeper, Part 2

While trying to steal the alien's spaceship Smith accidentally releases the Keeper's animals. The Keeper threatens to let his beasts overrun the planet unless Will and Penny are turned over to him.
(Guest cast as Part 1)

Director: Harry Harris

The Sky Pirate

w Carey Wilbur
Tucker, a grizzled old space pirate, kidnaps and then befriends Will, raising everybody's hopes of rescue.
Tucker Albert Salmi

Director: Sobey Martin

Ghost in Space

w Peter Packer
A turbulent "ghost" threatens the castaways' camp and Dr. Smith, convinced it's the troubled spirit of his uncle Thaddeus, sets out to exorcise it.
Presence Dawson Palmer

Director: Sobey Martin

The War of the Robots

w Barney Slater
Will repairs a highly advanced robotoid that pretends to help the Robinsons while secretly plotting to capture them for its alien master. (The "guest villain" is none other than Robby the Robot—mechanical star of sci-fi film classic *Forbidden Planet*.)

Director: Sobey Martin

The Magic Mirror

w Jackson Gillis
Penny and her pet bloop fall through a magic mirror into a strange dark world inhabited by a lonely alien boy.
Boy Michael J. Pollard

Director: Nathan Juran

The Challenge

w Barney Slater
A ruler from another planet and his son try to prove their superiority by challenging Will and his father to a test of strength and courage. (Guest role here for a young Kurt Russell, while Guy Williams gets to relive his *Zorro* days in a swordfight.)
Ruler Michael Ansara
Quano Kurt Russell

Director: Don Richardson

The Space Trader

w Barney Slater
Smith sells the robot to a dodgy space trader for a 12-day food supply, then tries to buy it back by offering himself in exchange believing that the trader won't "collect" for 200 years.
Trader Torin Thatcher

Director: Nathan Juran

His Majesty Smith

w Carey Wilbur
Dr. Smith schemes his way into becoming king of a mysterious alien civilization—but is horrified when he discovers he has been chosen for his uselessness and is due to be skinned and stuffed in a primitive ritual.
Nexus Liam Sullivan
Alien Kevin Hagen

Director: Harry Harris

The Space Croppers

w Peter Packer
Once again sensing a chance to get back to Earth, Smith decides to marry the matriarchal head of a space clan whose strange crop threatens to devour all life on the Robinsons' planet.
Sybilla Mercedes McCambridge
Effra Sherry Jackson
Keel Dawson Palmer

Director: Sobey Martin

All That Glitters

w Barney Slater
Using a space thief's magic key, Dr. Smith finds a strange neck-ring that turns everything he touches into platinum—including Penny!
Bolix Werner Klemperer
Ohan Larry Ward

Director: Harry Harris

Lost Civilization

w William Welch
Exploring an underground world, Will awakens a sleeping princess and triggers an alien civilization's plans to conquer the universe with its "frozen" army.
Princess Kym Karath
Major domo Royal Dano

Director: Don Richardson

A Change of Space

w Peter Packer
Will climbs aboard an alien spacecraft and shoots off into the sixth dimension, returning as an intellectual giant. When Smith tries it he returns as a decrepit old man.
Alien Frank Graham

Director: Sobey Martin

Follow the Leader

w Barney Slater
Trapped in a cave by a rock fall, John Robinson is possessed by the unseen spirit of an alien warrior. But Will's love for his father overcomes the spirit and drives it away.
Alien voice Gregory Norton

Director: Don Richardson

Season Two
30 episodes

Blast Off into Space

w Peter Packer
Despite Smith's rascally dealings with intergalactic prospector Nerim, the Robinsons manage to get *Jupiter 2* into space before the mining blasts cause the planet to disintegrate.
Nerim Strother Martin

Director: Nathan Juran

Wild Adventure

w William Read Woodfield & Allan Balter
Jupiter 2 almost returns to Earth, but Smith is lured out into space by a seductive Lorelei, Athena the green girl, and the ship must change course to rescue him.
Athena Vitina Marcus

Director: Don Richardson

The Ghost Planet

w Peter Packer
Fooled into thinking it's Earth, Smith causes the ship to land on an alien planet run by Cyborgs who try to enslave the travelers.
Automaton voice Sue England
Summit voice Michael Fox

Director: Nathan Juran

The Forbidden World

w Barney Slater
The *Jupiter 2* is forced down on another alien planet where Smith drinks some unusual nectar that turns him into a human bomb.
Tiabo Wally Cox
Monster Janos Prohaska

Director: Don Richardson

Space Circus

w Bob & Wanda Duncan
Will nearly joins Dr. Marvello's intergalactic circus to save his family from the troupe's monster. Smith also tries to join, singing "Tiptoe through the Tulips."
Dr. Marvello James Westerfield
Fenestra Melinda Fee
Bisho Harry Vartresian
Nubu Michael Greene
Monster Dawson Palmer

Director: Harry Harris

The Prisoners of Space

w Barney Slater
The Robinsons are tried by a mysterious tribunal for committing space crimes. All are vindicated except Smith who is found guilty but insane and released into the custody of the robot.
Monster Dawson Palmer

Director: Nathan Juran

The Android Machine

w Bob & Wanda Duncan
The Robinsons help a simple android develop into a higher-grade model by teaching her the meaning of love.
Verda Dee Hartford
Mr. Zumdish Fritz Feld

Director: Don Richardson

The Deadly Games of Gamma 6

w Barney Slater
Smith and the Robinsons become embroiled in an alien's intergalactic gladiatorial fights—with the losers incurring invasion of their home planets.
Myko Mike Kellin
Geoo Harry Monty
Gromack Ronald Weber
Alien leader Peter Brocco
Alien giant Chuck Robertson

Director: Harry Harris

The Thief of Outer Space

w Jackson Gillis
Will helps a futuristic Arab chieftain to find his long-lost princess.
Thief Malachi Throne
Slave Ted Cassidy
Fat princess Maxine Gates

Director: Don Richardson

The Curse of Cousin Smith

w Barney Smith
A low plausibility reading even by *Lost in Space* standards . . . Smith's equally rascally cousin arrives on the Robinsons' planet and tries to do Zachary out of his inheritance.
Jeremiah Smith Henry Jones

Director: Justus Addiss

West of Mars

w Michael Fessier
Smith is mistaken for his double—a notorious intergalactic gunslinger.
Enforcer Allan Melvin
Dee Mickey Manners
Pleiades Pete Ken Mayer
Bartender Eddie Quillan

Director: Nathan Juran

A Visit to Hades

w Carey Wilbur
Smith's greed lands him in a Hell-like place, a prison for a devilish political revolutionary called Morbus.
Morbus Gerald Mohr

Director: Don Richardson

The Wreck of the Robot

w Barney Slater
The robot becomes the blueprint for an alien machine that could threaten the entire universe.
Alien Jim Mills

Director: Nathan Juran

The Dream Monster

w Peter Packer
Sesmar, a white-haired space scientist, tries to drain the Robinsons' human emotions to bolster his android creation.
Sesmar John Abbott
Raddion Dawson Palmer
Midgets Harry Monty, Frank Delfino

Director: Don Richardson

The Golden Man

w Barney Slater
A galactic morality tale . . . Penny and the family become involved in a war between the leaders of two alien civilizations—one a handsome Golden Man called Keema, the other a big ugly frog. Guess which one turns out to be a prince of a guy?
Keema Dennis Patrick
Frog alien Ronald Gans
Handsome alien Bill Troy

Director: Don Richardson

The Girl from the Green Dimension

w Peter Packer
Smith gets involved again with Athena the green-skinned girl.
Athena Vitina Marcus
Ursuk Harry Raybould

Director: Nathan Juran

The Questing Beast

w Carey Wilbur
Penny and Will become embroiled in a bumbling futuristic knight's lifelong quest for a fire-breathing female beast.

Sagramonte Hans Conried
Que Track voice Sue England
Gundemar Jeff County

Director: Don Richardson

The Toymaker

w Bob & Wanda Duncan
Will and Dr. Smith are imprisoned in a fourth-dimensional toyland and meet up again with Zumdish of the Celestial Department Store.
Zumdish Fritz Feld
O M Walter Burke
Security guard Tiger Joe Marsh
Monster Dawson Palmer
Wooden soldier Larry Dean

Director: Robert Douglas

Mutiny in Space

w Peter Packer
Will, Smith and the Robot are shanghaied by a renegade spaceship admiral.
Admiral Zahrk Ronald Long

Director: Don Richardson

The Space Viking

w Margaret Brookman Hill
It's off to Valhalla as Dr. Smith finds himself pitted against the mighty Thor.
Brynhilde Sheila Mathews
Thor Bern Hoffman

Director: Ezra Stone

Rocket to Earth

w Barney Slater
Smith nearly makes it back to Earth in a rocket he steals from a bungling space magician.
Zalto Al Lewis

Director: Don Richardson

The Cave of the Wizards

w Peter Packer
A chance to get to Alpha Centauri is blown when Smith is seduced by the luxurious powers of a computer—the relic of a lost civilization. (No guest cast.)

Director: Don Richardson

Treasure of the Lost Planet

w Carey Wilbur

Smith and Will are reunited with space pirate Tucker—first seen in Season One—and get involved in his bizarre treasure hunt.

Tucker Albert Salmi
Deek Craig Duncan
Smeek Jim Boles

Director: Harry Harris

Revolt of the Androids

w Bob & Wanda Duncan

Smith dreams of transforming a rundown android into an all-powerful machine—but reckons without the tender loving care of female 'droid Verda.

Verda Dee Hartford
Idak Don Matheson
Monster Dawson Palmer

Director: Don Richardson

The Colonists

w Peter Packer

With the Robinsons enslaved by a real Amazon, Will and the Robot must find a way to defeat her.

Niolani Francine York

Director: Ezra Stone

Trip through the Robot

w Barney Slater

When the Robot, with a failing powerpack, stumbles into a misty valley, an ionic reversal enlarges him to the size of a house, and Will and Smith have to crawl inside—à la *Fantastic Voyage*—to fix him. (No guest cast.)

Director: Don Richardson

The Phantom Family

w Peter Packer

An alien scientist makes android copies of Smith, Don and the girls, then forces Will and the Robot to teach them to act like their human counterparts.

Lemnoc Alan Hewitt

Director: Ezra Stone

The Mechanical Man

w Barney Slater

When tiny mechanical men want the Robot as their leader, they improve him by trading the voice and personality of Smith for his. (No guest cast.)

Director: Seymour Robbie

The Astral Traveler

w Carey Wilbur

Will stumbles through a space warp and finds himself in a haunted Scottish castle with a monster in the loch . . .

Hamish Sean McClory
Angus Dawson Palmer

Director: Don Richardson

The Galaxy Gift

w Barney Slater

Penny is given a magic amulet but aliens enlist Smith's help to make her give it up, promising to return him to Earth.

Arcon John Carradine
Saticon Jim Mills

Director: Ezra Stone

Season Three
24 episodes

The Condemned of Space

w Peter Packer
The *Jupiter 2* stops at a space station to refuel and finds it's a computerized space prison.
Phanzig Marcel Hillaire

Director: Nathan Juran

Visit to a Hostile Planet

w Peter Packer
The Robinsons are taken for dangerous aliens when they land on Earth 50 years before their own time.
Grover Pitt Herbert
Cragmire Robert Foulk
Craig Robert Pine
Charlie Norman Leavitt
Stacy Clair Wilcox

Director: Sobey Martin

Kidnapped in Space

w Robert Hamner
The Robot turns surgeon when mechanical men kidnap the Robinson party to make him operate on their leader.
Aliens Grant Sullivan, Carol Williams
Young Smith Joey Russo

Director: Don Richardson

Hunter's Moon

w Jack Turley
Scouting out a strange planet, John is regarded as a prize quarry by a hunter.
Megazor Vincent Beck

Director: Don Richardson

The Space Primevals

w Peter Packer
The space family is menaced by a primitive race controlled by a mammoth computer.
Rangah Arthur Batanides

Director: Nathan Juran

The Space Destructors

w Robert Hamner
Smith discovers a Cyborg manufacturing machine and dreams of conquering the universe with his own army.
Cyborg Tommy Farrell

Director: Don Richardson

The Haunted Lighthouse

w Jackson Gillis
The *Jupiter 2*, with a strange young passenger, J-5, aboard takes off, but encounters an American lighthouse in space.
J-5 Lou Wagner
Col. Fogey Woodrow Parfrey
Zaybo Kenya Coburn

Director: Sobey Martin

Flight into the Future

w Peter Packer
Landing on an unknown green planet, Will, Dr. Smith and the Robot experience strange adventures of illusions in time.
Sgt. Smith Don Eitner
Cmdr. Fletcher Lew Gallo

Director: Sobey Martin

Collision of the Planets

w Peter Packer
Aliens, planning to destroy an erratic planet the Robinsons are on, refuse to give them time to prepare their ship for lift-off. (Early role for *Hill Street Blues* star Daniel J. Travanti.)
Ilan Dan Travanti
Aliens Linda Gaye Scott, Joey Tata

Director: Don Richardson

The Space Creature

w William Welch
After everyone vanishes from the *Jupiter 2*, Will faces a fearsome blue misty specter. (No guest cast.)

Director: Sobey Martin

Deadliest of the Species

w Robert Hamner
The Robot falls in love with an evil alien female super-robot and helps her in her quest to rule the universe.
Alien leader Ronald Gans
Female robot Sue England
Mechanical men Lyle Waggoner, Ralph Lee

Director: Sobey Martin

A Day at the Zoo

w Jackson Gillis
Penny is abducted and placed on display at a zoo by galactic showman Farnum B.
Farnum Leonard Stone
Oggo Gary Tigerman
Mort Ronald Weber

Director: Irving J. Moore

Two Weeks in Space

w Robert Hamner
A disguised quartet of monsters, on the run from the galactic cops, give Smith the idea to turn the *Jupiter 2* into a holiday hotel.
Zumdish Fritz Feld
MXR Richard Krisher
QZW Eric Matthews
Non Edy Williams
Tat Carroll Roebke

Director: Don Richardson

Castles in Space

w Peter Packer
When a ferocious bandit threatens to abduct an Ice Princess in the Robinsons' care, the Robot fights like a bull to save her.
Chavo Alberto Monte
Reyka Corinna Tsopei

Director: Sobey Martin

The Anti-Matter Man

w Barney Slater *&* Robert Hammer
John Robinson's evil counterpart from an anti-matter world tries to take the prof's place in the family circle.
Drun Mark Goddard

Director: Sutton Roley

Target: Earth

w Peter Packer
Will foils a plot by shapeless aliens to duplicate the Robinsons and use the Robot to help them conquer Earth.
Gilt Proto James Gosa
Mike officer Brent Davis
2nd officer Thant Brann

Director: Nathan Juran

Princess of Space

w Jackson Gillis
An old space captain thinks Penny is a lost princess of his planet and grooms her for a royal visit.
Kraspo Robert Foulk
Fedor Arte Johnson
Aunt Gamma Sheila Mathews

Director: Don Richardson

The Time Merchant

w Bob *&* Wanda Duncan
Smith tricks a time merchant, Dr. Chronos, into returning him to Earth just before Jupiter's flight, but in doing so risks changing the course of the past and imperiling the lives of the Robinsons.
Dr. Chronos John Crawford
General Byron Morrow
Sergeant Hoke Howell

Director: Ezra Stone

The Promised Planet

w Peter Packer
The *Jupiter 2* lands on a turned-on planet populated solely by hippie youngsters.
Bartholomew Gil Rogers
Edgar Keith Taylor

Director: Ezra Stone

Fugitives in Space

w Robert Hamner
Smith and Don are framed and jailed on a prison-planet. Will and the Robot go to the rescue.
Creech Michael Conrad
Warden Tol Avery
Guard Charles Horvath

Director: Ezra Stone

Space Beauty

w Jackson Gillis
Judy wins a galactic beauty contest and is nearly carted off to a planet of fire.
Farnum Leonard Stone
Nancy Dee Hartford
Miss Teutonium Miriam Schiller

Director: Irving J. Moore

The Flaming Planet

w Barney Slater
A plant-creature grows fond of Smith, then comes close to engulfing the ship until a home is found for it on a war-ravaged planet.
Sobram Abraham Sofaer

Director: Don Richardson

The Great Vegetable Rebellion

w Peter Packer
The travelers land on a lush planet and fall into the hands of a carrot monster who proposes to turn them all into plants.
Tybo Stanley Adams

Director: Don Richardson

The Junkyard of Space

w Barney Slater
The Robinsons encounter a mechanical junk man who acquires the Robot's memory banks and nearly makes off with the *Jupiter* but is stopped by Will's emotional appeal.
Junk Man Marcel Hillaire

Director: Ezra Stone

LUNA

"Tedium tocks in the viron prompt Jo-oy to program habitel limbs at the saline."

Futuristic ITV children's comedy series of the 1980s with a language all its own that emerged as a cross between Orwellian doublespeak and Stanley Unwin's gobbledygook.

Created by ex-Monkees drummer and *Metal Mickey*-taker Michael Dolenz, *Luna* was set 50 years in the future, when animals have been replaced by furry little robots and speech has evolved into "techno talk." This was a language designed for the computer age when words have to be abbreviated, linked or even lost in favor of numbers to allow more speedy electronic processing.

So, there are "dimi males" and "dimi females" (children) and families are divided into "habiviron groups," each person possessing an "egothenticity" card which they lose at their peril. Time is measured in "ticks," "tocks" and "tacks"; and for birthday, read "batch day." The episode titles alone reached sublime heights of techno talk.

Main characters in the series were Gramps, teenagers Brat and Luna (played in the first series by actress/pop star Patsy Kensit), Andy the robot and bureaucrat beings 80H and 40D.

Writer Colin Bennett, who also starred in the series, described *Luna* as a kind of morality play, conveying the idea that in future human ethics would still have to be observed—that the silicon chip would not be the answer to everything.

Luna lasted for two six-part series, in 1983 and 1984.

REGULAR CAST
Luna Patsy Kensit *(Series One)*, Joanna Wyatt *(Series Two)*
Brat Aaron Brown *Gramps* Frank Duncan
Andy Colin Bennett *80H* Roy Macready *40D* Natalie Forbes *(Series One only)*
32C Vanessa Knox-Mawer *(Series Two)* *Mother* Linda Polan
Jazzmine Hugh Spight *Mr. Efficiecity* Russell Wootton

Creator: Michael Dolenz
Producer: Michael Dolenz
Directors: Michael Dolenz, Chris Tookey *(Series Two)*
Executive producer: Lewis Rudd
Writers: Colin Bennett, Colin Prockter
Designer: Tony Ferris

Central Production
12 color 30-minute episodes

Series One:
Habiviron Sweet Habiviron
The Clunkman Cometh
All the World's a Teletalk Linkup
Happy Batch Day, Dear Luna

Environmental Ambience Stable, Wish You Were Here
When Did You Last See Your Pater Batch Mix Donor?
22 January–26 February 1983

Series Two:
You Can't Judge A Videotalker By Its Blurb
Go Forth and Quadruplicate
The Happiest Earth Revolves of Your Span
It Isn't How You Vict or Flunk But How You Co-Participate
A Bureaubureau in the Hand is Worth a Pension
You're Only as Multi-Tocked as You Perceive
11 February–17 March 1984

THE MAN FROM ATLANTIS

Soggy series that started well but ended up as just another TV also-swam. *The Man From Atlantis*, played by *Dallas* star Patrick Duffy in his first major TV series, had piercing green eyes, gills, webbed hands and feet and could outswim a dolphin. The last survivor of the lost city of Atlantis, he first appeared in a set of four TV movies.

Washed up on a California beach after a storm, this half-dead amphibian is rushed to a naval hospital where a beautiful doctor, Elizabeth Merrill, saves his life by popping him back in the water after X-rays have shown he has gills where his lungs should be. Dr. Merrill christens the submariner Mark Harris and recruits him for the Foundation for Oceanic Research. While helping Dr. Merrill and her colleagues in the supersub *Cetacean*, he hopes to find out if he is indeed the sole survivor of his race. The quartet of TV movie-episodes combined some exploration of the character with stories about a missing submarine, alien invasion, space spores and a crazy scientist, but once the "series proper" began, the quest for the Atlantean's origins ebbed away as the plots trod the same deep water as the tail-end of *Voyage to the Bottom of the Sea*, with silly villains, sea monsters, undersea races and time travel stories.

Victor Buono played the lead villain, Mr. Schubert, with the same tongue-in-cheek style he'd used as King Tut in *Batman*. The other main regulars were Brent, Shubert's incompetent accomplice, and C.W. Crawford, the director of the research foundation.

REGULAR CAST

Mark Harris Patrick Duffy   *Dr. Elizabeth Merrill* Belinda J. Montgomery
C.W. Crawford Alan Fudge   *Mr. Schubert* Victor Buono   *Brent* Robert Lussier

WITH

Dr. Miller Simon (Eps. 2–4) Kenneth Tigar
Cetacean *crew (from Ep. 5):*
Jomo Richard Williams   *Chuey* J. Victor Lopez
Jane Jean Marie Hon   *Alan* Anson Downes

Executive producer: Herbert F. Solow
Producer: Herman Miller
Music: Fred Karlin
Special effects: Tom Fisher

A Solow Production for NBC

17 color episodes
3×100 mins., 1×75 mins, 13×60 mins.
U.S. premiere: 4 March 1977
U.K. premiere:
24 September 1977–14 January 1978
(ITV)

The Man From Atlantis (pilot)

(100 mins.)
w Mayo Simon
After a storm, a young man is found washed up on a beach. Nearly dead after hours out of the life-sustaining ocean water, he is nursed back to health by Dr. Elizabeth Merrill and eventually agrees to undertake a hazardous mission to locate a missing sub. Several miles beneath the sea he finds an underwater habitat where he confronts loopy scientist Mr. Schubert for the first time.
Admiral Pierce Art Lund
Phil Roth Larry Pressman
Lt. Cmdr. Johnson Allen Case
Dr. Doug Berkely Joshua Bryant
Ernie Smith Dean Santoro

Director: Lee H. Katzin

The Death Scouts

(100 mins.)
w Robert Lewin
Now working for the Foundation for Oceanic Research, Dr. Merrill and Mark try to discover clues to his origins. Called in by the coast guard to investigate the disappearance of three scuba divers, they encounter two water-breathing humanoids who Mark thinks could be his people, but who turn out to be scouts from an alien civilization intent on colonizing Earth.

Lioa/Dilly Tiffany Bolling
Xos/Chazz Burr DeBenning
Ginny Mendoza Annette Cardona
Grant Stockwood Alan Mandell
Herb Wayland Vincent Deadrick

Director: Marc Daniels

Killer Spores

(100 mins.)
w John D.F. Black
A NASA space probe returns to Earth contaminated with ectoplasmic matter that is capable of invading humans, placing them in a catatonic stupor or forcing them to do things against their will. The spores, visible only to Harris because of the unique structure of his eyes, communicate with him and demand that he help them return to space or see mankind destroyed.
Edwin Shirley Ivan Bonar
Sub captain Fred Beir
Col. Manzone James B. Sikking

Director: Reza Badiyi

The Disappearances

(75 mins.)
w Jerry Sohl & Luther Murdoch
When Dr. Merrill is kidnapped, Mark Harris and Miller Simon must locate a remote island off the coast of South America and penetrate the carefully guarded complex of mad scientist Dr. Mary Smith.
Dr. Smith Darleen Carr
Jane Smith Pamela Peters Solow
Dick Redstone Dennis Redfield
Dr. Medlow Ivor Francis
Sub captain Fred Beir

Director: Charles Dubin

Melt Down

w Tom Greene
Villainous Mr. Schubert causes the world's sea level to rise alarmingly by melting the polar ice caps, and won't stop unless Mark submits himself to his genetic study.
Trubshawe James E. Brodhead

Director: Virgil Vogel

Mudworm

w Alan Caillou
Mr. Schubert loses control of his latest invention—a robot-like machine designed to gather a radioactive mineral from the sea bed. Discovering that the "Mudworm" has taken on "human" characteristics, Mark tries to reason with it.

Director: Virgil Vogel

The Hawk of Mu

w David Balkan, Luther Murdoch
After Mark rescues an ancient stone hawk from its watery crypt, evil Mr. Schubert steals it for his own malevolent purposes, unaware that the statue has the power to come to life and cause worldwide electrical blackouts.
Juliette Schubert Vicky Huxtable
Vicki Carole Mallory
Smith Sydney Lassick

Director: Harry Harris

Giant

w Michael Wagner
Investigating a "leak" in the ocean, Mark is swept into the inner world where he meets Thark, a nine-foot-tall gold prospector whose sluice mining is draining the world of its water. Realising the threat, he and Mark join forces to close off the sluice gate. Complicating matters is a gold-seeking con man called Muldoon.

Thark Kareem Abdul-Jabbar
Muldoon Ted Neeley

Director: Richard Benedict

Man O' War

w Larry Alexander
It's the Man from Atlantis v. the world's biggest jellyfish when Mr. Schubert plots to extort money by sabotaging an international swimming gala.
Dashki Harvey Jason
Announcer Gary Owens

Director: Michael O'Herlihy

Shoot-out at Land's End

w Luther Murdoch
A time warp in the ocean throws Mark back to the old West, where he encounters his twin—desperado Billy Jones—who is identical in every way, except that he has scars where the webbing on his hands has been removed.
Billy Patrick Duffy
Clint Hollister Pernell Roberts
Bettina Washburn Jamie Smith Jackson
Artemus Washburn Noble Willingham
Virgil Bill Zuckert

Director: Barry Crane

Crystal Water, Sudden Death

w Larry Alexander
Investigating a disturbance in the Pacific, Mark finds Mr. Schubert trying to get his hands on some precious crystals located within a forcefield. Penetrating it, Mark encounters a mysterious white-skinned, white-suited race called the Deepspeople, who talk in a strange clicking language.
Havergal Rene Auberjonois
Conrad Rozelle Gayle
Click One Tina Lennert
Click Two Flip Reade
Click Three Whitney Rydbeck

Director: David Moessinger

The Naked Montague

w Stephen Kandel
Mark travels back in time to 14th-century Italy where he gets involved with Romeo and Juliet, "rewriting" the story to give it a happy ending!
Romeo John Shea
Juliet Lisa Eilbacher
Mercutio Scott Porter

Director: Robert Douglas

C.W. Hyde

w Stephen Kandel
C.W. Crawford accidentally swallows a deep-sea enzyme that alters his appearance and mind, resulting in Jekyll and Hyde personalities.
Lew Calendar Val Avery
Belle Michele Carey
Sarah Pamela Peters Solow

Director: Dann Cahn

Scavenger Hunt

w Peter Allan Fields
Investigating a loss of five poisonous gas canisters, Mark Harris re-encounters conman Jake Muldoon and his tame, two-legged, two-headed giant sea monster, called Oscar.
Jack Muldoon Ted Neeley
Oscar Tony Urbano
Canja Ted Cassidy
Toba Yabo O'Brien
Trivi Eugenia Wright

Director: David Moessinger

Imp

w Shimon Wincelberg
Mark and his friends tangle with Moby, a water-breathing imp whose magic touch makes his victims revert to their childhood—with sometimes fatal results.
Moby Pat Morita

Director: Paul Krasny

The Siren

w Michael Wagner
Mark tangles with a mermaid who can "capture" humans with her nerve-penetrating wail. She has been kidnapped by a modern-day pirate, Stringer, who is using her to lure mariners to his lair.
Hugh Trevanian Michael Strong
Amanda Laurette Spang
Stringer Neville Brand
Caine Timothy Scott
Jenny Lisa Blake Richards
Siren Carol Miyaoka

Director: Ed Abroms

Deadly Carnival

w Larry Alexander
Mark infiltrates an oceanside carnival where a government agent was working before he was found mysteriously drowned, and foils a plot to steal a priceless Egyptian artifact from a museum.
Moxie Bill Barty
Summersday Anthony James
Charlene Baker Sharon Farrell

Director: Dennis Donnelly

THE MAN FROM U.N.C.L.E.

"It all began with the idea of a never-never world in which an international group where everybody is good works together to beat the hell out of whoever is bad. I picked UNCLE simply as a bunch of letters I could make a name out of."

—Sam Rolfe, producer

The Man From U.N.C.L.E. was a 1960s escapist fantasy about the far-fetched exploits of a pair of super-spies, Napoleon Solo and Illya Kuryakin, role models for every young boy with a ballpoint pen to talk to . . .

UNCLE stood for United Network Command for Law and Enforcement, and existed to protect the world from all forms of disruption, terror and exploitation. Its never-never world was entered via a hidden door in a New York tailor's shop (Del Floria's), unlocked by a steamy squeeze on the trouser press.

It was the cue for a series of all-action, tongue-in-cheek spy adventures involving futuristic hardware, glamorous girls, complex plots, exotic locations and cliffhanging climaxes. Science fiction? Well . . . there was always THRUSH.

THRUSH were the bad guys, forever plotting to rule the world by foul means rather than fair. Modelled on the SPECTRE organization of the Bond movies, they were prompted by a diabolical computer into inflicting a variety of space-age perils such as a death ray ("The Maze Affair"), a human vaporizer ("The Arabian Affair"), invisible killer bees ("The Birds and the Bees Affair"), a radiation projector ("The Moonglow Affair"), even a volcano-activating device ("The Cherry Blossom Affair").

Other weeks Napoleon and Illya found themselves up against lone madmen, from the crazy sea captain hijacking the world's brightest brains as a hedge against the holocaust, to an industrial tycoon hoping to further his ambitions with a willpower-sapping gas.

The coveted hardware included radios disguised as pens or cigarette packets, guns disguised as canes, nerve paralyzing bombs and the all-purpose UNCLE gun—a combination rifle, pistol and submachine gun that also fired sleep darts. A distinctive touch about the THRUSH gun was its infra-red sight, which "branded" its target with a thrush a second before the gun was fired.

As for the main characters, the head of UNCLE was Mr. Alexander Waverly, an amiable Englishman played by Leo G. Carroll, but the series really made stars out of Robert Vaughn as Napoleon Solo (the sophisticated, extrovert bachelor who nearly always got the girl) and David McCallum as Illya Kuryakin (the enigmatic, introspective Slav who never let personal relationships get in the way of his work).

A spin-off series, *The Girl From U.N.C.L.E.*, ran for just one year. Stefanie Powers starred as feisty April Dancer, with Noel Harrison (son of Rex) as English agent Mark Slate.

REGULAR CAST
Napoleon Solo Robert Vaughn *Illya Kuryakin* David McCallum
Mr. Waverly Leo G. Carroll

Creator/Producer (Season One): Sam Rolfe
Producer (Season Two): David Victor
Executive producer: Norman Felton
Writers: Various, including Alan Caillou, Peter Allan Field, Dean Hargrove
Directors: Various, including Richard Donner, Joseph Sargent, Alvin Ganzer

An Arena Production for MGM Television
U.S. premiere: 22 September 1964
U.K.: 90 (out of 105) color 50-minute episodes (first shown in black and white)
24 June 1965–22 March 1968 (BBC1)
(Author's note: the BBC stuck devotedly to the UNCLE cause, screening 90 episodes in two bumper runs between 24 June 1965 and 19 May 1966, and 20 October 1966 to 22 March 1968. The second run also included the 29 episodes of *The Girl From U.N.C.L.E.*, which alternated with *The Man* until November 1967.

The episode guide below lists *both* series in their original U.S. order, with details of the episodes not transmitted in Britain in their original format.)

Season One
29 black and white 50-minute episodes

The Vulcan Affair
(not transmitted in U.K. Theater release with additional material as *To Trap a Spy*)
The Iowa Scuba Affair
The Quadripartite Affair
The Shark Affair
The Deadly Games Affair
The Green Opal Affair
The Giuoco Piano Affair (sequel to "The Quadripartite Affair")
The Double Affair
(not transmitted in U.K. Theater release with additional material as *The Spy with My Face*)

The Project Strigas Affair
The Finny Foot Affair
The Neptune Affair
The Dove Affair
The King of Knaves Affair
The Terbuf Affair
The Deadly Decoy Affair
The Fiddlesticks Affair
The Yellow Scarf Affair
The Mad, *Mad* Tea Party Affair
The Secret Sceptre Affair
The Bow-Wow Affair
The Four Steps Affair
(not transmitted in U.K. Compiled from additional material made for cinema features *To Trap a Spy* and *The Spy with My Face*)
The See Paris and Die Affair
The Brain Killer Affair
The Hong Kong Shilling Affair
The Never Never Affair
The Love Affair
The Gazebo in the Maze Affair
The Girls from Nazarone Affair
The Odd Man Affair

Season Two
30 color 50-minute episodes

The Alexander the Greater Affair
(a 2-part story, not transmitted in U.K. Released theatrically as *One Spy Too Many*)
The Ultimate Computer Affair
The Foxes and Hounds Affair
The Discotheque Affair
The Recollectors Affair
The Arabian Affair
The Tigers Are Coming Affair
The Deadly Toys Affair
The Cherry Blossom Affair
The Virtue Affair

The Children's Day Affair
The Adriatic Express Affair
The Yukon Affair (sequel to "The Gazebo in the Maze Affair")
The Very Important Zombie Affair
The Dippy Blonde Affair
The Deadly Goddess Affair
The Birds and the Bees Affair
The Waverly Ring Affair
The Bridge of Lions Affair
(a 2-part story, not transmitted in U.K. Released theatrically as *One of Our Spies Is Missing*)
The Foreign Legion Affair
The Moonglow Affair
(pilot for *The Girl From U.N.C.L.E.*)
The Nowhere Affair
The King of Diamonds Affair
The Project Peephole Affair
The Round Table Affair
The Bat-Cave Affair
The Minus X Affair
The Indian Affairs Affair

Season Three
30 color 50-minute episodes

The Her Master's Voice Affair
The Sort of Do-It-Yourself Dreadful Affair
The Galatea Affair
(with Noel Harrison as Mark Slate)
The Super Colossal Affair
The Monks of St. Thomas Affair
The Pop Art Affair
The Thor Affair
The Candidate's Wife Affair
The Come with Me to the Casbah Affair
The Off-Broadway Affair
The Concrete Overcoat Affair
(a 2-part story, not transmitted in U.K. Released theatrically as *The Spy in the Green Hat*)
The Abominable Snowman Affair
The My Friend the Gorilla Affair
The Jingle Bells Affair
The Take Me to Your Leader Affair
The Suburbia Affair
The Deadly Smorgasbord Affair
The Yo-Ho-Ho and a Bottle of Rum Affair
The Napoleon's Tomb Affair
The It's All Greek to Me Affair
The Hula Doll Affair
The Pieces of Fate Affair
The Matterhorn Affair
The Hot Number Affair
The When in Roma Affair
The Apple-a-Day Affair
The Five Daughters Affair
(a 2-part story, not transmitted in U.K. Released theatrically as *The Karate Killers*)
The Cap and Gown Affair

Season Four
16 color 50-minute episodes

The Summit-5 Affair

The Test Tube Killer Affair
The J for Judas Affair
The Prince of Darkness Affair
(a 2-part story, not transmitted in U.K. Released theatrically as *The Helicopter Spies*)
The Master's Touch Affair
The Thrush Roulette Affair
The Deadly Quest Affair
The Fiery Angel Affair
The Survival School Affair
The Gurnius Affair
The Man from THRUSH Affair
The Maze Affair
The Deep Six Affair
The Seven Wonders of the World Affair
(a 2-part story, not transmitted in U.K. Released theatrically as *How to Steal the World*)

NB: The Men from UNCLE also came out of retirement for a 1983 TV movie, *The Fifteen Years Later Affair*, shown in the U.K. on 21 April 1984 as *Return of the Man from U.N.C.L.E.* This also starred Patrick Macnee as the organization's "new" director.

(An unbroadcast UNCLE pilot called "Solo" also exists. This is identical to "The Vulcan Affair" but features Will Kuluva as Mr. Allison instead of Leo G. Carroll as Mr. Waverly.)

The Girl From U.N.C.L.E.
---

29 color 50-minute episodes (shown in U.K. in black and white)
U.S. premiere: 13 September 1966
The Dog-Gone Affair
The Prisoner of Zalimar Affair
The Mother Muffin Affair
(with Robert Vaughn as Napoleon Solo)
The Mata Hari Affair
The Montori Device Affair
The Horns-of-the-Dilemma Affair
The Danish Blue Affair
The Garden of Evil Affair
The Atlantis Affair
The Paradise Lost Affair
The Lethal Eagle Affair
The Romany Lie Affair
The Little John Doe Affair
The Jewels of Topango Affair
The Faustus Affair
The UFO Affair
The Moulin Ruse Affair
The Catacomb and Dogma Affair
The Drublegratz Affair
The Fountain of Youth Affair
The Carpathian Caper Affair
The Furnace Flats Affair
The Low Blue C Affair
The Petit Prix Affair
The Phi Beta Killer Affair
The Double-O-Nothing Affair
The UNCLE Samurai Affair
The High and Deadly Affair
The Kooky Spook Affair

MANIAC MANSION

Based on the computer game of the same name, *Maniac Mansion* was a show that seemed to have everything going for it: name recognition value, an excellent creative team (most of the cast and crew came from Canada's *SCTV*), and little real competition: the science fiction programming boom hadn't yet hit, so the airwaves certainly had room for more fantastic television.

Unfortunately, it just wasn't very funny. From the start it felt tired, which may explain why it ended up as an original series on the religious and wholesomely programmed Family Channel.

REGULAR CAST
Dr. Frederick Sergio Edison Joe Flaherty *Casey Edison* Deborah Theaker
Tina Edison Kathleen Robertson *Ike Edison* Avi Phillips
Turner Edison George Buza *Idella Muckle-Orca* Mary Charlotte Wilcox
Harry Orca (the Fly) John Hemphill

Creators: Eugene Levy, Michael Short, John Hemphill, and Paul Flaherty
Developed for television by Cliff Ruby, Elana Lesser, Bob Carrau
Supervising producers: Seaton McLean, Michael Short
Producer: Jamie Paul Rock

Executive producers: Peter Sussman, Eugene Levy, Barry Jossen
Co-producers: David Flaherty, John Hemphill

66 color 30-minute episodes
U.S. airdates: 1990–93

Season One

The 10th Anniversary Special
Flystruck
Trapped Like Rats
Love Thy Neighbor
Fred's a-Courtin'
The Sandman Cometh
Good On Ya
Bring Me Harry Orca
Dad's Bummed Out
Webs, the Really Tangled Kind
National Security Risk
A Little Old Time Jazz
Hawaii Blues
Good Cheer On Ya
Brainiac Mansion
Little Big Fly
Money Dearest
Turner: The Boss
The Case of the Broken Record
The Live Show
Tina's Excellent Adventure
The Cliffhanger

Season Two

Luck Be a Lady This Season
The New Look
Late Night Harry
Turner: The Rebellious Years
Man and Machine
Driving Ms. Idella
The Celebrity Visitor

The Attack of Killer Keifer
Lenny . . . One Amour Time (Part 1)
Lenny . . . One Amour Time (Part 2)
Ugle Like Me
A Hatfull of Brain
Buried by the Mob
Misery Loves Company
Down and Out in Cedar Springs
Ike's Got It Bad . . . Real Bad
Turnernator Too
Baby Heat
Streetcar Named Idella
Turner's Imaginary Friend
Idella's Breakdown
Sophisticated Lady

Season Three

Long Hot Mansion
Raging Lenny
College Days
The Prince's Broad
Ike's Black Eye
Science Is Only Skin Deep
Ike's New Buddy
As the Worm Turns
Cape Scary
Wrestling with the Truth
The Science Fair
Love: Turner Style
(untitled)
Water under the Bridge
Tina and the Teardrops
Ike for President
Freddie Had a Little Lamb

MANIMAL

Short-lived American adventure series about a professor of criminology with the inherited powers to transform himself at will into any animal he chooses.

It could have been the premise for an interesting, original fantasy—instead it was little more than *Magnum* in an animal suit, with the hero, Jonathan Chase, using his powers to solve crimes from an arms heist to smuggling, murder and espionage. His secret is shared by police detective Brooke McKenzie.

The transformation scenes were well done, though their credibility was spoiled by the fact that when Chase changed back he was always fully clothed on the spot. But the series, a product of the Glen A. Larson conveyor belt, stuck closely to the tried and trusted action formula.

REGULAR CAST
Jonathan Chase Simon MacCorkindale *Brooke McKenzie* Melody Anderson
Ty Michael D. Roberts *Lt. Rivera* Reni Santoni

Creator: Glen A. Larson
Producer: Glen A. Larson
Writers: Various, including Glen A. Larson, Michael Berk
Directors: Various, including Russ Mayberry, Dan Haller

A Glen A. Larson Production
7 color 50-minute episodes (pilot 70 minutes)
Manimal (pilot)

Illusions
Female of the Species
Night of the Beast
High Stakes
Night of the Scorpion
Scrimshaw
Breath of the Dragon

U.S. premiere: 30 September 1983
U.K. premiere: 4 June–23 July 1984
(BBC1)

M.A.N.T.I.S.

Brilliant scientist Dr. Miles Hawkins is crippled, so he invents a bodysuit that circumvents his damaged spine—a Mechanically Augmented Neuro Transmitter Interception System, or M.A.N.T.I.S.—and discovers he can not only walk, but has near super-powers. Of course, being rich and noble, he ends up using the suit to catch criminals who otherwise would not be caught.

An interesting idea, but one we've seen before. Run-of-the-mill plots made it a one-season wonder.

REGULAR CAST
Dr. Miles Hawkins Carl Lumly *John Stonebrake* Roger Rees
Taylor Savidge Christopher Russell Garten *Lt. Leora Maxwell* Galyn Gorg
Capt. Hetrick Gary Graham *Det. Paul Warren* Jerry Wasserman

Creators: Sam Raimi, Sam Hamm
Developed by Bryce Zabel
Theme: Christopher Franke
Music: Christopher Franke unless otherwise credited

22 60-minute episodes; 1 2-hour movie
U.S. premiere: 26 August 1994

Episodes

M.A.N.T.I.S. (pilot movie; cast changed when series began)

Season One

First Steps
Tango Blue
Days of Rage
Cease Fire
Soldier of Misfortune
Gloves Off
The Black Dragon

To Prey in Darkness
Fire in the Heart
Thou Shalt Not Kill (Part 1)
Revelation (Part 2)
Through the Dark Circle
The Eyes Beyond
Faces in the Mask
The Sea Wasp
Progenitor
Switches
The Delusionist
Fast Forward
Spider in the Tower

MAX HEADROOM

Max Headroom began as a stylish satire on television culture and became a phenomenon.

The world's first computer-generated TV presenter turned into one of the 1980s most charismatic media celebrities, moving from video linkman to chat-show host, Coca-Cola salesman and star of an American adventure series from the makers of *Dallas*. In the end, over-exploitation may have killed the video star, but the Max Headroom effect has been felt worldwide.

Max's genesis started in 1982, with a commitment by Chrysalis Records exective Peter Wagg and C4's commissioning editor Andy Park to find a new way of linking pop videos. The name and characterization came from advertising copywriter George Stone, and visualization from directors Rocky Morton and Annabel Jankel. The result was a £750,000 television film, *Max Headroom*, written by Steve Roberts, first screened on Channel Four in April 1985.

Set "20 minutes into the future," it depicts a decaying urban environment where television is the only growth industry. A fierce ratings battle is raging and Network 23 is winning, thanks to its use of "blipverts"—a form of subliminal selling where 30 seconds of commercials are condensed into a three-second burst, giving viewers no time to change channels. But the blipverts, created by the station's teenage computer whiz-kid Bryce Lynch, have a lethal side-effect—they cause some viewers literally to explode. Anxious to preserve profits and ratings, Network 23 president Grossman is determined to keep the lid on the story. But when the station's own star investigative reporter, Edison Carter, uncovers disturbing evidence, Grossman and Bryce unleash two disreputable body-snatchers to bring him in. After a remarkable pursuit in which Carter's "guide" Theora Jones and Bryce vie for control of the building's computer-operated systems, Carter strikes his head on a parking garage gate. Bryce proposes to keep Carter's disappearance quiet by translating his memory and physical appearance into data, and the computer generates him onto a TV screen. Thus Max Headroom is born, taking his name from the last words Carter saw in the garage: a warning about the height of the ceiling . . . the Max. Headroom.

Ultimately, Carter gets his man and Max winds up in the hands of a hard-up pirate TV channel called Big-Time Television where his scratch-style stammer and razor wit make him a megastar.

Once the Max Headroom character was established, the media machine took over. The film was followed by the video and chat-show series, *The Max Headroom Show*, lucrative ad campaigns, records, books, computer games and even cosmetics. In America, Lorimar produced a multi-million-dollar adventure series for the ABC network, beginning with a reworking of the original film story. Some 14 episodes were made, spanning two seasons from March 1987, but failed to secure high enough ratings to justify any more.

Canadian actor Matt Fewer reprised the role, which had called for a four-and-a-half-hour make-up job to transform him into his alter ego (and an equally uncomfortable one and a half hours to take it all off again), while Amanda Pays was also back as Theora Jones. Among new faces in the series were Chris Young as Bryce Lynch—now more of a good guy—and Jeffrey Tambor as Carter's producer, Murray.

Steve Roberts remained with the show—as executive story editor, a regular writer, and co-producer of the second season.

MAX HEADROOM—THE MOVIE
CAST
Edison Carter/Max Headroom Matt Frewer *Grossman* Nickolas Grace
Dominique Hilary Tindall *Blank Reg* Morgan Shepherd
Theora Jones Amanda Pays *Bryce Lynch* Paul Spurrier
Breugal Hilton McRae *Mahler* George Rossi *Murray* Roger Sloman
Gorrister Anthony Dutton *Ben Cheviot* Constantine Gregory
Edwards Lloyd McGuire *Ms Formby* Elizabeth Richardson
Ashwell Gary Hope *Body bank receptionist* Joane Hall
ENG reporter Howard Samuels *Helipad reporter* Roger Tebb
Eyewitness Val McLane *Exploding man* Michael Cule

Screenplay: Steve Roberts, *from an original idea by* George Stone, Rocky Morton, Annabel Jankel
Directors: Rocky Morton, Annabel Jankel
Producer: Peter Wagg
Executive producer: Terry Ellis
Designer: Maurice Gain
Director of photography: Phil Meheux
Music: Midge Ure, Chris Cross

Max dialogue: Paul Owen, David Hansen
Special makeup: Coast to Coast

Chrysalis Visual Programming Ltd for Channel Four
70 minutes, color
4 April 1985
(Channel Four)

MAX HEADROOM—THE SERIES
REGULAR CAST
Edison Carter/Max Headroom Matt Frewer *Theora Jones* Amanda Pays
Ben Cheviot George Coe *Bryce Lynch* Chris Young
Murray Jeffrey Tambor *Ms. Formby* Virginia Kiser *(Season One only)*
Ashwell Hank Garrett *(except Eps. 4, 10, 12)*
Edwards Lee Wilkof *(except Eps. 4, 8, 10, 12)*
Blank Reg William Morgan Sheppard *(except Eps. 1–2, 5, 8–9, 13)*
Dominique Concetta Tomei *(Eps. 3–4, 6–7, 10, 12 and 14 only)*

Executive producers: Philip De Guere *(Ep. 1)*, Peter Wagg *(Eps. 2–14)*
Producers: Peter Wagg, Brian Frankish, Steve Roberts *(Season Two only)*
Executive story editors: Steve Roberts *(Season One)*, Michael Cassutt *(Season Two)*
Music: Cory Lerios *(Season One)* Michael Hoenig, Chuck Wild *(Season Two, main theme)*

Designer: Richard B. Lewis
Director of photography: Paul Goldsmith, Robert Stevens *(Eps. 1, 3 only)*

A Chrysalis/Lakeside Production in association with Lorimar Telepictures
14 color 60-minute episodes
U.S. premiere: 31 March 1987
U.K. first run: 2 March–14 June 1989
(Channel Four)

Season One (U.S.)

Blipverts

w Joe Gannon, Steve Roberts & Philip DeGuere, *based on the British screenplay by* Steve Roberts

Initially a reworking of the British film, with Edison Carter investigating blipverts, the episode deviates after Carter hits his head. It is Grossberg (Grossman in the original) who uses newly created Max Headroom as a Network 23 gimmick, before his chi-canery is exposed by Carter at a press conference Grossberg calls to announce Edison's "tragic death."

Breughel Jere Burns
Mahler Rick Ducommon
Grossberg Charles Rocket
Martinez Ricardo Gutierrez *(plus Eps. 2–5, 8)*
Gorrister Ken Swofford
Florence Billie Bird

Director: Farhad Mann

Rakers

w Steve Roberts & James Crocker, *story by* James Crocker

Theora is told that her young brother Shawn is involved in "raking," a high-speed gladiatorial contest between two youths on motorized skateboards who wear spiked gloves and try to score "rakes," or hits, on their opponent. Zik-Zak, Network 23's main sponsor, is keen to see raking televised—if the sport can be legalized. Can Carter expose the vicious truth—and save Shawn?

Shawn Peter Cohl
Jack Friday Wortham Krimmer
Rik J.W. Smith
Peller Howard Sherman
Promoter Joseph Ruskin
Ped Zing Arsenio "Sonny" Trinidad

Director: Thomas J. Wright

Body Banks

w Steve Roberts

Bodysnatchers Breughel and Mahler kidnap a Fringer girl, Rayna, for a corrupt Body Bank, and her friend Mel threatens Theora's life unless Edison helps him find her. While Edison seeks the help of Blank Reg at Big Time TV, a man called Plantaganet blackmails Ms. Formby into giving him Bryce and Max Headroom.

Breughel Jere Burns
Mahler Rich Ducommon
Rik J.W. Smith
Mel Scott Kraft
Plantaganet John Winston

Director: Francis De Lia

Security Systems

w Michael Cassutt

Edison probes a take-over of Security Systems Inc.—part of a bid to set up a worldwide security monopoly. But he finds himself branded a credit fraudster by a computer, A-7, and ends up a prisoner in a freezer.

Valerie Towne Carol Mayo Jenkins
Rik J.W. Smith
Voice of A-7 Sally Stevens

Director: Tommy Lee Wallace

War

w Michael Cassutt, Steve Roberts, Martin Pasko & Rebecca Parr

Network 23 is losing ratings when it is offered exclusive rights to film a guerrilla war as it happens in their own city. Cheviot declines, but when a rival network starts to notch up impressive figures, Edison investigates the sinister tie-up between TV and terrorists.

Janie Crane Lisa Niemi
Braddock Gary Swenson

Ped Zing Arsenio "Sonny" Trinidad
Croyd Hauser Robert O'Reilly
Lucian J. Michael Flynn
Hewett Richard Lineback

Director: Thomas J. Wright

The Blanks

w Steve Roberts

Network 23's politician, Peller, has the Blanks—those without computer records—rounded up by the Metrocops. Then computers start to go down and a Blank, Bruno, threatens to disable the city by sunset unless the captured Blanks are released.

Janie Crane Lisa Niemi
Peller Howard Sherman
Bruno Peter Crook

Director: Tommy Lee Wallace

Season Two (U.S.)

Academy

w David Brown

Blank Reg is arrested for "zipping"—hijacking network frequencies—and goes on a TV trial series called *You, the Jury*. But Theora and Edison trace the real culprits to Bryce's old school, the Academy of Computer Sciences.

Sidney Harding James Greene
Lauren Sharon Barr
Shelley Keeler Maureen Teefy

Director: Victor Lobl

Deities

w Michael Cassutt

Edison is reluctant to investigate the Church of Entropic Science, which is offering "immortality" to people having their personality stored on computer to await future resurrection, as he was once very close to its leader, Vanna Smith.

Vanna Smith Dayle Haddon

Director: Thomas J. Wright

Grossberg's Return

w Steve Roberts

Archvillain Grossberg resurfaces at Network 66, a rival station clocking up huge ratings with its new VuDoze system that allows people to sleep and view simultaneously. He is determined to take over Network 66 and bring down Network 23.

Grossberg Charles Rocket
Harriet Garth Caroline Kava
Lauren Sharon Barr
Thatcher Stephen Elliott

Director: Janet Greek

Dream Thieves

w Steve Roberts, *story by* Charles Grant Craig
The death of an old reporting rival, Paddy Ashton, and Network 66's new concept, Dream-Vu, which offers amazing, dreamlike shows, leads Carter to the Mind's Eye—a place where derelict Fringers are paid for their sleep in special cubicles.
Paddy Ashton Mark Lindsay Chapman
Breughel Jere Burns
Greig Ron Fassler
Bella Jenette Goldstein
Finn Vernon Weddle

Director: Todd Holland

Whacketts

w Arthur Sellers, *story by* Dennis Rolfe
Big Time TV has a hit on its hands with *Whacketts*—an old-style game show that is so addictive that people are stealing sets to watch it, causing a tower block literally to collapse under the weight of stolen sets. Naturally, the Networks want a piece of the action . . .
Grossberg Charles Rocket
Lauren Sharon Barr
Ziskin Bert Kramer
Haskel Bill Maher
Biller Richard Frank

Director: Victor Lobl

Baby Grobags

w Chris Ruppenthal
Carter investigates the Ovu-Vat Grobag center, which allows working women to have their babies grown in bags in front of TV monitors. He finds a distressed couple claiming their baby has been stolen. Meanwhile, the Network 66 airs its new show *Prodigies*—a debate between brilliant babies. (Not transmitted in the U.S.)
Grossberg Charles Rocket
Breughel Jere Burns
Lauren Sharon Barr
Helen Amanda Hillwood
Cornelia Firth Millicent Martin

Director: Janet Greek

Neurostim

w Arthur Sellars & Michael Cassutt
Zik-Zak's sales are up by 700 percent—thanks to a Neurostim bracelet that feeds ads directly into the consumer's mind by stimulating the brain. When Edison's investigations threaten to expose them, Zik-Zak prepare a special bracelet to make him a complete addict of their products.
Lauren Sharon Barr
Edison's dream girl Joan Severance

Director: Maurice Phillips

Lessons

w Adrian Hein & Steve Roberts, *story by* Colman Dekay & Howard Brookner
Carter and Theora witness a raid by Metrocops and the Network 23 censor on a secret school for Fringer children. Edison's overt sympaties bring him into direct conflict with the Network censor.
Lauren Sharon Barr
Frances Laura Carrington
Traker Mike Preston
Dragul John Durbin
Blank Bruno Peter Crook

Director: Victor Lobl

MEEGO

Meego features Bronson Pinchot as the title character, a cute 9000-year-old alien from the planet Marmazon IV, who crash lands on Earth and ends up as the nanny to three cute children while—à la *My Favorite Martian*—he repairs his ship. At first only the youngest and cutest of the children knows the truth about Meego; cute child #2 is suspicious and wants to find out the truth and turn him in—for *any*thing; and eldest cute child is TV-cool (as is obvious from his use of words like "dude" and "awesome").

Barclay, the dog, is the only actor under five feet tall worth saving from this cloying mush. Ed Begley Jr. and Bronson Pinchot are sorely wasted. CBS wisely saw fit to cancel this show after only six episodes, though the threat remains that some of the remaining unaired episodes will show up in the coming summer to fill holes in its schedules.

REGULAR CAST
Meego Bronson Pinchot *Dr. Edward Parker* Ed Begley Jr.
Maggie Parker Michelle Trachtenberg *Tripp Parker* Erik von Detten *(pilot)*, Will Estes *(series)*
Alex Parker Jonathan Lipnicki

Executive producers: Thomas L. Miller, Robert
L. Boyett, Michael Warren, Ross Brown

6 color 30-minute episodes
U.S. aired: 17 September 1997–24 October 1997

Episodes
Pilot
Love and Money
The Truth about Cars and Dogs
It's Good to Be King
Fatal Attraction
Halloween

MEN INTO SPACE

Semi-educational American series about the adventures of a space pioneer, Col. Edward
McCauley, and his crew in and around their small moon colony.

The series, made in 1959, prided itself on its authenticity and an absence of monsters or little
green men. Each script was said to have been submitted to the American Defense Department and
anything that couldn't possibly happen was then ruled out.

REGULAR CAST
Col. Edward MacCauley William Lundigan

SEMI-REGULARS
Mary McCauley Joyce Taylor (Angie Dickinson *in pilot*)
Lt. Johnny Baker Corey Allen
Capt. Harvey Sparkman Ken Dibbs
General Norgarth Tyler McVey

A United Artists Production for CBS
U.S.: 38 black and white 25-minute episodes
U.S. premiere: 30 September 1959

U.K. premiere: 9 July–1 October 1960
(BBC)

METAL MICKEY

Advance publicity called it a "children's science fiction comedy series," but really, *Metal Mickey*
was never more than a sitcom with a robot as its star.

Mickey (always billed as "playing himself") was a 5 ft. tall robot with magical powers and a
metallic catchphrase: "boogie, boogie." He was built by scientific whiz-kid Ken Wilberforce to
help around the house, but naturally brought more chaos than order. Various episodes had him
getting kidnapped, getting hiccups, becoming a pop star, communicating with aliens, traveling
into the future, teleporting people and shrinking. Everyday stuff.

The ITV series, which first appeared in 1980, also attracted attention for its other Mickey—
former Monkee Mickey Dolenz, who produced and directed.

REGULAR CAST
Father Michael Stainton   *Mother* Georgina Melville
Granny Irene Handl   *Ken* Ashley Knight
Haley Lucinda Bateson   *Janey* Lola Young
Steve Gary Shail . . . *and* Metal Mickey *as himself*

Writer: Colin Bostock-Smith
Producer: Michael Dolenz
Directors: Michael Dolenz, David Crossman,
Nic Phillips
Designers: Mike Oxley, Rae George, David Cat-
ley, James Dillon, Phil Coulter
Music: Phil Coulter

A London Weekend Television Production
39 color 30-minute episodes
Season One:
6 September–25 October 1980
Season Two:
4 April–9 May 1981

Season Three:
5 September–26 December 1981
(including Christmas episodes)
Season Four:
18 September 1982–15 January 1983

Season One
Metal Mickey Lives
School Master Mickey
Mickey Makes Money
Taking the Mickey
Hiccy Mickey
Top Secret Mickey
Mickey in Love
Music Man Mickey

Season Two
Caveman Mickey
Mickey the Demon Barber
Hard Man Mickey
Many a Mickey
Mickey Plays Cupid

Season Three
It Came from Outer Mickey
A Girlfriend for Mickey

Goodbye Mickey *(postponed from Season Two)*
Mickey and the Future
Football Crazy Mickey
Medical Mickey
Fairy Godmother Mickey
Marshal Mickey
Merry Christmas Mickey
Pantomickey

Season Four
Maturity Mickey
A Night Out with Mickey
Go Away Mickey
Video Mickey
His Worship the Mickey
Fancy Mickey
Mickey Meets Mumsie
Mickey Under Siege
The Incredible Shrinking Mickey
Mickey Pops the Question
Somebody Stop Mickey
Mickey Saves the World
Detective Mickey
Mickey to the Rescue
The Confessions of Mickey
Mickey and the Magic Wishbone

MIGHTY MORPHIN POWER RANGERS

The hottest kids' adventure serial since the Turtles, the *Mighty Morphin Power Rangers* combine the dynamics of the dinosaurs with martial arts skills, as they battle to save the world from evil intergalactic sorceress Rita Repulsa.

The Rangers are ordinary teenagers who "morph" into superheroes complete with power suits, weapons and Thunderzords, invincible robotic fighting machines. The original five were: Jason, a karate black belt whose color is red, weapon is the power sword and whose power comes from the T-Rex; Kimberley, a bright, strong-willed champion gymnast—pink is her color, a power bow is her weapon and the pterodactyl is her beast; Trini, a quiet, observant martial arts expert who studies Eastern philosophy. Her color is yellow, her animal is the saber-toothed tiger and her weapon a power dagger; Billy, super-intelligent but shy—he communicates in techno-speak and spends his time at the computer. Blue is his color, a power lance is his weapon and the triceratops his dinosaur; Zack, an energetic charmer who lives for his music and dancing. His color is black, his power comes from the mastodon and his weapon is the power axe; a sixth, Green Ranger, Tommy, subsequently joined the team and was "promoted" to White Ranger and endowed with unique powers and an enchanted white saber. Jason was later replaced by Rocky, Zack by Adam and Trini by Aisha.

The *Mighty Morphin Power Rangers'* juvenile mix of action, comedy and entertainment made them an instant success in America. In the U.K., their adventures have been seen on GMTV and on Sky One.

MAIN CAST
Jason Austin St. John *Trini* Thuy Trang *Zack* Walter Jones
Kimberly Amy Jo Johnson *Billy* David Yost *Tommy* Jason Frank
Bulk Paul Schrier *Skull* Jason Narvy *Alpha 5* Romy J. Sharf
Rita Barbara Goodson *Squatt* Michael J. Sorich *Goldar* Ryan O'Flannigan
Zordon Bob Manahan *Rocky* Steve Cardenas *Adam* Johnny Yong Bosch
Aisha Karan Ashley

Executive producers: Haim Saban, Shuki Levy

Saban International Productions
color 30-minute episodes

U.S. premiere: September 1993
U.K. premiere: October 1993
(Sky One)

MIKE & ANGELO

Long-running children's comedy drama series about a friendly and inventive, if over-eager, young alien living with an American family in England.

Angelo started out as a mystery house guest, found by Mike King lurking in his wardrobe in the new house he and his mother, Rita, move into, and although Angelo could do all kinds of amazing tricks, such as talk to plants and dance on the ceiling, writers Lee Pressman and Grant Cathro admitted that they didn't actually decide the character was an alien until the second series. "If anything he was an angel," they said.

First shown in 1989, it began its eighth series in early 1997. Angelo underwent a transformation at the start of the third series, with Tim Whitnall taking over the role from Tyler Butterworth.

MAIN CAST
Mike King Matt Wright *(Series 1–3)* Michael Benz *(Series 5–7)*
Rita King Shelley Thompson *(Series 1–6)*
Angelo Tyler Butterworth *(Series 1–3)* Tim Whitnall *(Series 3–7)*
Mr. Pinner John Levitt *Philippa* Alessia Gwyther

Created and written by: Lee Pressman, Grant Cathro

Thames Television Production
(Series 1–4)
A Tetra Films Production for Carlton Television
(Series 5–7)
73 color 25-minute episodes
Series One:
16 March–18 May 1989
Series Two:
14 September–16 November 1989

Series Three:
14 November 1990–20 February 1991
Series Four:
17 October–19 December 1991
Series Five:
7 January–11 March 1993
Series Six:
22 February–26 April 1994
Series Seven:
5 January–9 March 1995

MILLENNIUM

Former FBI agent Frank Black has the ability to step inside the minds of serial killers based on the flimsiest of evidence. When his immersion into these sick and twisted minds brings him too close to the edge—and a serial killer begins stalking his family—he leaves the FBI and moves his family to Seattle. However, his abilities are needed there, and he is recruited by the secret Millennium Group, which has been fighting evil for nearly 2000 years.

Millennium's chief claim to fame: its creator, Chris Carter of *The X-Files*. Although initially intriguing, the series hit the same doom-and-gloom notes over and over throughout the first season, leaving some viewers cold. The second season lightened the tone somewhat, and a few cross-ties to *The X-Files* (longtime viewers of both will pick them up immediately) helped revive interest in the show.

REGULAR CAST
Frank Black Lance Henriksen *Catherine Black* Megan Gallagher
Jordan Black Brittany Tiplady

Creator: Chris Carter
Executive producers: Chris Carter, James Wong, Glen Morgan
Co-executive producers: John P. Kousakis, Ken Horton

Consulting producer: Chip Johannessen
Co-producer: Robert Moresco
Supervising producer: Darin Morgan
U.S. premiere: 25 October 1996

Episodes

Season One

(21 episodes)
Pilot
Gehenna
Dead Letters
Kingdom Come
The Judge
522666
Blood Relatives
The Well Worn Lock
Wide Open
Weeds
Wild and Innocent
Loin Like a Hunting Flame
Force Majeure
The Thin White Line
Sacrament
Walkabout
Covenant
Lamentation
Powers, Principalities, Thrones and Dominions
Broken World
Maranatha
Paper Dove

Season Two

The Beginning and the End
Beware of the Dog
Sense and Antisense
Monster
A Single Blade of Grass
19:19
The Curse of Frank Black
The Hand of Saint Sebastian
Jose Chung's Doomsday Defense
Goodbye Charlie
Midnight of the Century
Luminary
The Mikado
Owls
The Pest House
Roosters
Siren
In Arcadia Ego
Anamnesis
A Room with No View
Somehow, Satan Got Behind Me
The Fourth Horseman
The Time Is Now

(Incomplete as of press time)

MISSION GENESIS

The Sci-Fi Channel's first original dramatic series, *Mission Genesis* tells the story of a crew of clones who are awakened prematurely when their spaceship is attacked by aliens. It seems they are carrying enough genetic material to repopulate Earth . . . which has been destroyed by a plague. A passably entertaining, if low-budget, science fiction series—certainly a cut above most network science fiction shows.

REGULAR CAST
Reb Gordon Michael Woolvett *Yuna* Nicole deBoer
Lise Sara Sahr *Gret* Kelli Taylor
Gen Julie Khaner *Bren* Jason Cadieux
Zak Craige Kirkwood

Executive producers: Wilf Copeland, Alex Nassar
Producers: Jeff Copeland, Barry Pearson
Directors: George Mendeluk, Don McCutcheon

13 color 30-minute episodes
U.S. air date: July 21, 1997–December 22, 1997

Episodes
Awakening
Lullaby
Legacy
Reflections
Plague
Cycles
Refugee
Hunt
Fugue
Siege
Prime
Aurora

MORK & MINDY

Mork from Ork first landed on Earth in an episode of *Happy Days* called "My Favorite Orkan." He made such an impact that he was given his own series and by the end of 1978 America's kids were twisting their ears, chirruping "Nanu, nanu," and offering each other split-fingered handshakes. The *Mork & Mindy* cult had taken hold.

There hadn't been a TV alien like Mork since Uncle Martin in *My Favorite Martian* (and, really, Mork was nothing like him) and there hasn't been a TV alien like him since until *ALF* (and Mork was nothing like him, either). Mork may be part of the same lineage but he was unique, the lunatic creation of stand-up comedian Robin Williams.

As Mork, Williams took the classic "stranger in a strange land" theme and literally stood it on its head. Totally unaccustomed to the ways of Earth, alien Mork sits on his head, drinks with his fingers, talks to eggs, wears suits backward, grows down not up and wears a watch on his ankle. Williams dominated the show. His lightning improvisation, funny voices, frenetic rubber-faced clowning and relentless stream of ad-libbed one-liners gave the one-gag variants their velocity and momentum. His co-star, Pam Dawber (Mindy) admitted: "He is the show, I'm lucky I got my name in the title."

A misfit in his own world because of his sense of humor, Mork was sent to observe Earth's primitive society whose customs were beyond Orkan understanding. Landing in his giant eggshell near Boulder, Colorado, he was befriended by Mindy McConnell, a clerk at her father's music store, and came to live with her family where he tried to adjust to Earth's ways while everyone else tried to get used to his.

Mork and Mindy's relationship started out platonic. But three seasons and 93 shows is a long time and eventually, after Mindy had graduated as a journalism student and become a TV reporter, they fell in love and married, honeymooning on Ork. Then Mork discovered *he* was pregnant, and laid an egg from which hatched their middle-aged son Mearth—who will grow younger each year.

The series introduced various regular characters over the three seasons, including Exidor, a crazy UFO prophet, grouchy neighbor Mr. Bickley, brother and sister Remo and Jean da Vinci from the Bronx, Mindy's ambitious cousin Nelson and her TV station boss Miles Sternhagen. And, of course, Mearth, played by Williams' childhood hero Jonathan Winters.

Williams himself found *Mork & Mindy* launched him into movies, with a succession of star roles including *Popeye* (1980), *The World According to Garp* (1982), and *Good Morning Vietnam* (1988).

Mork & Mindy was popular with parents as well as kids, for behind the off-the-wall insanity, it was one of the most moral shows on television—part of a long U.S. tradition of blending comedy and pathos to teach simple lessons about life. These were spelt out by Mork at the end of each episode when he would report back to the Orkan leader Orson what he had learned about Earthlings.

MAIN CAST

Mork Robin Williams *Mindy McConnell* Pam Dawber
Frederick McConnell Conrad Janis *Cora Hudson* Elizabeth Kerr
Eugene Jeffrey Jacquet *Voice of Orson* Ralph James
Exidor Robert Donner *Franklin Delano Bickley* Tom Poston
Remo da Vinci Jay Thomas *Jean da Vinci* Gina Hecht
Nelson Flavor Jim Staahl *Mearth* Jonathan Winters
Miles Sternhagen Foster Brooks

Creators: Gary K. Marshall, Dale McRaven, Joe Gauberg
Producers: Garry K. Marshall
Principal writers: Dale McRaven, April Kelly, Tom Tonowich, Ed Scharlach, Bruce Johnson
Principal directors: Howard Storm, Bob Claver

Miller-Milkis Productions Inc and Henderson Production Co Inc. in association with Paramount Television
93 color 30-minute episodes (pilot 60 minutes)
U.S. premiere: 14 September 1978
U.K. premiere: 10 March 1979
(London)

THE MUNSTERS

Perhaps it was something in the air, but 1964 saw the debut of both *The Addams Family* and *The Munsters*, a much more traditional family of monsters: father Herman, who looks like Frankenstein's Monster; wife Lily and Grandpa Dracula, both vampires; werewolf son Eddie; and Marilyn, the plain one. Dumber and sillier than *The Addams Family*, *The Munsters* actually proved more successful, perhaps because of its accessibility to younger viewers. Not only did the Munster family graduate to a theatrical movie, *Munster, Go Home,* they returned for a successful TV reunion in 1981 in *The Munsters' Revenge,* and launched a follow-up series in 1988, *The New Munsters* (with a new cast).

REGULAR CAST
Herman Munster Fred Gwynne *Lily Munster* Yvonne de Carlo
Grandpa Al Lewis *Eddie Wolfgang Munster* Butch Patrick
Marilyn Munster Beverly Owen *(1964),* Pat Priest *(1965–66)*
The Raven (voice) Mel Blanc/Bob Hastings

Creators: Norm Liebmann, Ed Haas, Al Burns, Chris Hayward
Executive producer: Irving Paley
Music: Jack Marshall

70 black and white 30-minute episodes
New episodes aired 24 September 1964–12 May 1966

Season One
Munster Masquerade
My Fair Monster
Walk on the Mild Side
Rock-a-Bye Munster
Pike's Pique
Low-Cal Munster
Tin Can Man
Herman the Great
Knock Wood, Here Comes Charley
Autumn Croakus
The Midnight Ride of Herman Munster
The Sleeping Cutie
Family Portrait
Grandpa Leaves Home
Herman's Rival
Grandpa's Call of the Wild
All-Star Munster
If a Martian Answers, Hang Up
Eddie's Nickname
Bats of a Father
Don't Bank on Herman
Dance with Me, Herman
Follow That Munster
Love Locked Out
Come Back Little Googie
Far Out Munsters
Munsters on the Move
Movie Star Munster
Herman the Rookie
Country Club Munsters
Love Comes to Mockingbird Heights
Mummy Munster
Lily Munster, Girl Model

Munster the Magnificent
Herman's Happy Valley
Hot Rod Herman
Herman's Raise
Yes, Galen, There Is a Herman

Season Two
Herman, the Master Spy
Herman's Child Psychology
Bronco Bustin' Munster
Herman Munster, Shutterbug
Herman, Coach of the Year
Happy 100th Anniversary
Operation Herman
Lily's Star Boarder
John Doe Munster
A Man for Marilyn
Herman's Driving Test
Will Success Spoil Munster?
Underground Munster
The Treasure of Mockingbird Heights
Herman's Peace Offensive
Herman Picks a Winner
Just Another Pretty Face
Heap Big Herman
The Most Beautiful Ghoul in the World
Grandpa's Lost Wife
The Fregosi Emerald
Zombo
Cyrano De Munster
The Musician
Prehistoric Munster
A Visit from Johann
Eddie's Brother

Herman, the Tire Kicker
A House Divided
Herman's Sorority Caper
Herman's Lawsuit
A Visit from the Teacher

Theatrical Movie
Munsters Go Home

TV Movies
The Munsters' Revenge
The New Munsters

MY FAVORITE MARTIAN

Forget H.G. Wells . . . forget Orson Welles, come to that. As far as TV is concerned, Martians are just regular people with not the slightest intention of waging war on any world.

My Favorite Martian was one of the 1960s' biggest hit comedies and a forerunner of *Mork & Mindy* and *ALF* in its premise of a lone alien visitor living among human beings.

The Martian, played totally straight by veteran actor Ray Walston, crash-lands on Earth during one of his regular reconnaissance trips. His arrival is witnessed by Tim O'Hara (Bill Bixby), a young reporter for the Los Angeles *Sun*. Rescued and befriended by O'Hara, the Martian goes to stay with him, as his "Uncle Martin," establishing a situation ripe for comic exploitation. And audiences quickly warmed to the extraterrestrial who combined folksy wisdom with alien magic—Martin sported a pair of retractable antennae, could become invisible at will, read minds and talk to animals.

TV's favorite Martian was created by John L. Greene, an American TV writer who first began toying with the idea of a stranded alien in 1955. Control of Uncle Martin's destiny eventually passed to producer Jack Chertok, with Greene one of a team of scriptwriters working on the project (though when one episode called for Martin to get "involved" with a striptease dancer called Peaches, Greene felt as lost as any parent might feel). Mostly, the humor was mischievous but comfortable, with Martin game to help Tim in his career and domestic life . . . but only up to a point. Special effects were gentle rather than spectacular; Uncle Martin's antennae were strapped to Walston's back and push-button controlled by the actor himself, and when Martin flew, it was courtesy of wires and harness.

The series' only other regular characters were O'Hara's landlady, Mrs. Brown and, occasionally, her teenage daughter, Angela, and O'Hara's editor, Harry Burns.

My Favorite Martian premiered in America in September 1963 and was on British screens within two months, becoming a regular—and repeated—visitor over the next few years. It spawned an animated version (16 episodes) in 1973, with *Lost in Space*'s Jonathan Harris as the voice of Uncle Martin and Edward Morris as the voice of Tim O'Hara.

REGULAR CAST
Uncle Martin (The Martian) Ray Walston
Tim O'Hara Bill Bixby   *Mrs. Brown* Pamela Britton
Angela Brown Ann Marshall
Harry Burns J. Pat O'Malley *(both Season One only)*
Detective Bill Brennan Alan Hewitt *(Seasons 2, 3)*

Creator: John L. Greene
Writers: Various (and numerous)
Directors: Various, including Sheldon Leonard,
   Sidney Miller, Alan Rafkin
Music: George Greeley
Producer: Jack Chertok

A Jack Chertok Production
107 30-minute episodes (75 black and white; 32 color)
U.S. premiere: 29 September 1963
U.K. premiere run:

7 November 1963–16 September 1964
(Rediffusion, London)
Note: Trying to ascertain exactly how many episodes of this series have been shown in the U.K. is a tricky business, given ITV's fragmented state at the time. I have definite transmission dates for 67 episodes (all b/w) between November 1963 and May 1968, based on several different regional schedules. It seems likely, though, that all 75 of the b/w episodes did find their way over here. I have no record of any color episodes transmitted in the U.K.

MY SECRET IDENTITY

When teenager Andrew Clement is accidentally zapped by gamma rays in next-door neighbor Dr. Benjamin Jeffcoate's lab, he discovers he has acquired super powers, just like the comic book heroes he admires. Taking on the guise of Ultraman, he sets out to help stop crime.

Such a simple premise has kept superheroes alive in comic books for decades, and it served *My Secret Identity* well, too—this syndicated Canadian production lasted three seasons (from 1988 to 1991) and 72 30-minute episodes. Jerry O'Connell (later to play Quinn Mallory on *Sliders*) made a sympathetic and appealing hero.

REGULAR CAST
Andrew Clement Jerry O'Connell *Dr. Benjamin Jeffcoate* Derek McGrath
Stephanie Clement Wanda Cannon *Erin Clement* Marsha Moreau
Kirk Stevens Christopher Bolton (*Seasons 2–3*) *Mrs. Shellenbach* Elizabeth Leslie

Season One
My Secret Identity
A Walk on the Wild Side
Only Trying to Help
The Track Star
Memories
You've Got a Friend
For Old Time's Sake
The Lost Weekend
Forbidden Ground
It Only Hurts for a Little While
Grounded
The Eyes of the Shadow
The Video Connection
Toxic Time Bomb
Two Faces Have I
One on One
Stranger in the House
Secret Code
Look Before You Leap
Breaking the Ice
Give the Guy a Chance
When the Sun Goes Down
Lookin' for Trouble
The Set Up

Season Two
Out of Control
Not So Fast
Nowhere to Hide
Photon Blues
Heading for Trouble
Long Shot
Along for the Ride
Collision Course
Troubled Waters
Don't Look Down
Caught in the Middle
Secrets for Sale

Running Home
Missing
Stolen Melodies
Toe to Toe
Reluctant Hero
Split Decision
Misfire
White Lies
Off the Record
Best Friends
More Than Meets the Eye
Seems Like Only Yesterday

Season Three
Ground Control
Trading Places
Drop Out
Sour Grapes
First Love
Novel Idea
David's Dream
Bump in Time
Calendar Boy
Moving Out
Teen Hot Line
Trial by Peers
A Life in the Day of Dr. Gentlemen
My Other Secret Identity
Pirate Radio
From the Trenches
The Invisible Dr. J
Three Men and a Skull
The Great Indoors
Dr. J's Brain Machine
Slave for a Day
Big Business
My Old Flame
A Bank, a Holdup, a Robber, and a Hero

MYSTERY SCIENCE THEATER 3000

If you get together with a couple of friends and a few beers to watch a cheesy old sf or horror movie, what do you end up doing? Unless you're really intense, the odds are you start making fun of the movie—and that's a fun enough way to pass a hour or two.

For the uninitiated, *Mystery Science Theater 3000* (aka *MST3K* or *MST3000*) is like watching you and your pals watch a hoary old film. The only difference here is that the watchers are an average guy and his robot buddies.

The average guy is Mike Nelson (replacing janitor Joel Robinson, played by creator Joel Hodgson, who escaped back to Earth), a hired temp blasted into space in the *Satellite of Love*, by his wicked bosses in Deep 13. As an ongoing experiment, they force him to watch lousy films and monitor his reactions. To remain cheerful—and sane—Mike heckles the screen from start to finish, with the help of Gypsy, Tom Servo and Crow, three robots constructed from parts of the satellite.

We see the show from behind their seats in the theater, seeing their silhouettes in the bottom of the screen and hearing their comments, drawn mostly from U.S. pop culture, but also science, philosophy, history and current affairs. Three times during the film Mike and the bots are given a break when they do host segments and more send-ups to annoy the scientists, headed by Dr. Clayton Forrester.

MST3K began in 1988, on an independent station, KTMA TV23, in Minneapolis, but reached true cult status on America's Comedy Central cable channel. There has also been a *MST3K* movie, based around *This Island Earth*. But seven seasons and 144 "episodes" later, declining ratings caused its cancellation. However, the Sci-Fi Channel stepped in to pick up the series for an eighth season, ordering 13 episodes for airing in 1997, in both the U.S. and, for the first time, in Britain.

REGULAR CAST
Mike Nelson Michael J. Nelson *Dr. Clayton Forrester* Trace Beaulieu
With the voices of:
Tom Servo Kevin Murphy *Crow T. Robot* Trace Beaulieu *Gypsy* Jim Mallon

Creator: Joel Hodgson
Head writer: Michael J. Nelson
Producer: Jim Mallon
A Best Brains Inc. Production

Seasons 1–7: 144 episodes
U.S. premiere: 1988
U.K. premiere: February 1997
(The Sci-Fi Channel)

NEVERWHERE

A British fantasy series is a rare event—and *Neverwhere*'s credentials make it worthy enough to be included here, even if it does stretch the sci-fi tag just a bit!

Neverwhere was billed as a witty, scary, urban fantasy. Almost five years in the making, it was written by Neil Gaiman, creator of *The Sandman* series of best-selling graphic novels, and based on an original idea by Gaiman and comedian Lenny Henry whose Crucial Films company made it.

It's a journey through an alternative London, a real and imagined world above and below the streets of the capital, and inhabited by a bizarre population of the dispossesed and outsiders as well as monsters, murderers, saints and sinners, pale Gothic girls in velvet and a real angel!

The hero is Richard Mayhew, a young Scot with a dull job in the city and a safe, secure future, mapped out by his safe, secure fiancée Jessica. Then Richard has a chance encounter with Door, a girl with the mysterious power to open doors where none exist, allowing her to slip from place to place. She's first seen trying to flee from two assassins, the Dickensian double-act of Croup and Vandemar— "Obstacles Obliterated, Nuisances Eradicated, Bothersome Limbs Removed and Tutelary Dentistry

Undertaken"—who've just massacred her family. Though wounded, she manages to "open a door," tumbling as if from nowhere onto the Strand in front of Richard and Jessica.

Ignoring his fiancée's protests, Richard plays Good Samaritan, but his act of kindness plunges him out of his safe, secure world and into a fantastical conspiracy revolving around a quest for a sacred key, and a fallen angel's evil plan to get back to heaven. Door's family were aristocratic "openers," all with the same power she possesses. Now the Angel—known as the Angel Islington—needs Door to use the special key to open a door to Heaven so he can take revenge on those who cast him down. However, Door is able to outwit the Angel and in a climax worthy of *Doctor Who*, consigns him and his assassins into a whirling vortex.

Richard is at last able to return to his old life, but finds it suddenly empty. His destiny, it seems, is Down Below . . .

Neverwhere is amazingly ambitious, both in its creation of a fantastical other-worldly London, and a striking array of characters, many, like the Angel, named after London places.

There's the Marquis de Carabas, a charismatic hustler with a heart, an eccentric Earl who holds Court in a traveling tube train, a fearsome female mercenary called Hunter whose own personal quest is to find and slay the legendary beast of London, and Door's iron worker friend Hammersmith. Above the streets is Old Bailey, a nomad of the rooftops, living on rook stew, with his own strange power over life and death. Then there are the tribes—the Black Friars, gun-toting keepers of the key (it turns out to be the key to reality!); the Velvets, strange Gothic girls who sleep in a huge hall hanging upside down from the rafters; the Rat Speakers, humans who speak fluent rat; and the Sewer Folk who wear green and brown and sell their sewer finds at a traveling bazaar called the Floating Market.

Maybe it all works better on paper, but unfortunately while always watchable, *Neverwhere* is never gripping TV. The plot lacks pace and too many of the characters make only a fleeting impression while the principals lack real charisma. It's not especially witty—unless you count Croup and Vandemar's banter—and certainly isn't scary, not even when Vandemar bites the head off rats or pigeons!

And some intriguing ideas are never seen through—Anasthesia's death on Knight's Bridge, for example: one minute she, Richard and Hunter are approaching the bridge, then Richard has his regular vision of a great beast, then he and Hunter are running down the other side alone. "The bridge has taken its toll," Hunter tells him. We've seen nothing—what a cop-out! And we learn that Door's family lived in "an associative house," every room of which is located somewhere else. What a great concept—but it's never explored.

MAIN CAST

Richard Mayhew Gary Bakewell *Door* Laura Fraser *Mr. Croup* Hywel Bennett
Mr. Vandemar Clive Russell *Marquis de Carabas* Paterson Joseph
Old Bailey Trevor Peacock *Hunter* Tanya Moodie *Angel Islington* Peter Capaldi
Earl's Court Freddie Jones *The Abbot* Earl Cameron *Serpentine* Julie T. Wallace
Lamia Tamsin Greig *Hammersmith* Tony Pritchard *Jessica* Elizabeth Marmur
Lord Rat Speaker Sean O'Callaghan *Varney* Nick Holder *Anasthesia* Amy Marston
With: Portico Michael Culver *Ruislip* Morgan Johnson *Lear* Philip Fowler
Mr. Stockton Stratford Johns *Iliaster* Richard Leaf *Tooley* Arthur Whybrow
Halvard Timothy Bateson *Clarence* Adrian Irvine

Devised by Neil Gaiman, Lenny Henry
Writer: Neil Gaiman
Director: Dewi Humphreys
Producer: Clive Brill
Title graphics: Dave McKean
Music: Brian Eno

A Crucial Films Production for BBC North

6 color 30-minute episodes
Door
Knightsbridge
Earl's Court to Islington
Blackfriars
Down Street
As Above, So Below

12 September–17 October 1996
(BBC2)

NIGHT GALLERY

"Night Gallery—like a huge diamond turning slowly in
the bony grasp of a skeleton—dazzles with the reflection of at least 100 stories which might—just might—
generate a nightmare or two . . ."

—publicity release

Night Gallery—or to give it its full title, *Rod Serling's Night Gallery*—only occasionally
ventured into the realm of science fiction. The main stamping ground of this American anthology
series from the creator of *The Twilight Zone* was the occult, the supernatural and sheer horror—
reflecting the dark side of Serling's imagination.

Each segment was introduced by Rod Serling in an art gallery where he invited us to view a
painting that depicted the coming tale as a moment of nightmare frozen on canvas.

Of the 100 or so stories, Serling himself wrote about a third, and the series utilized top
Hollywood talent behind and in front of the camera.

Tales that had an sf angle included "The Nature of the Enemy," in which a mission controller
(Joseph Campanella) monitors the efforts of an astronaut (Richard Van Vleet) to investigate the
strange disappearance of a team that landed on the Moon. In "The Little Black Bag," Burgess
Meredith played a discredited physician and skid row wino who discovers a medical bag and its
contents that have accidentally returned to the 20th century from the 21st, enabling him to effect
miraculous cures. "The Different Ones" starred Dana Andrews as a father who sends his misfit
son to another planet in accordance with the Federal Conformity Act of 1993; "Camera Obscura"
had a heartless moneylender hurled through time by a most unusual camera; "Class of '99"
featured Vincent Price as a futuristic instructor in bigotry addressing a strange graduating class;
"You Can Come Up Now, Mrs. Millikan" had an inventor's wife agreeing to be the subject of his
latest experiment.

Two of the Serling stories were nominated for Emmys: "They're Tearing Down Tim Riley's
Bar," in which a lonely widower saw the story of his life paralleled in the destruction of his
favorite bar; and "The Messiah of Mott Street," which starred Edward G. Robinson as a sick old
Jew waiting to see the coming of the Messiah before he dies.

In America, the first two seasons (1970–71) featured hour-long episodes, each with two or three
playlets. The third and final season was reduced to half hours.

Serling himself is said to have become increasingly disillusioned by the studio's heavy-handed
treatment of his idea and retired from television when the series ended, dying two years later in
1975, aged 50.

REGULAR CAST
Host-narrator Rod Serling

Creator: Rod Serling
Producer: Jack Laird
Directors: Various, including Steven Spielberg,
John Badham, Jeannot Szwarc, Leonard
Nimoy, Gene Kearney, Jeff Corey
Writers: Various, including Rod Serling, Jack
Laird, Gene Kearney

A Jack Laird Production for Universal
98 color episodes (durations vary)
U.S. premiere: 8 November 1969
U.K. premiere: 18 April 1973*
(Thames Television, London)

* The three-in-one TV movie premiere, showcasing three stories—
one directed by Steven Spielberg—was screened on 4 August 1970 on
BBC2.

NightMan

From Glen Larson, producer of *Magnum P.I., Knight Rider, Six Million Dollar Man,* and *The Fall Guy,* comes another action hour, this one based on a popular comic book of the same title. Enter the world of San Francisco at the turn of the 21st century. Johnny Domino is a hot jazz musician who shares his electrifying talents with the elite club crowd by night and teaches kids by day.

Johnny withstands a cosmic event that leaves him with incredible sensory powers that change his life forever. Thus is born NightMan, the superhero of the next millennium.

Routine plots and state-of-yesterday's-art special effects helped consign this show to the syndication market. Many fans of the comics have expressed disappointment.

REGULAR CAST
Johnny Domino/NightMan Matt Mccolm *Frank Dominus* Earl Holliman
Raleigh Jordon Derek Webster *Jessica Rodgers* Felecia M. Bell
Lt. Charlie Dann Michael Woods

Executive producers: Glen A. Larson, Stephen A. Miller
Syndicated (1997–   )
18 color 60-minute episodes

Episodes
Pilot (Part 1)
Pilot (Part 2)
Whole Lotta Shakin' . . .
I Left My Heart
Still of the Night
Face to Face
Chrome
Takin' It to the Streets
Lady in Red
That Ol' Gang of Mine
Bad Moon Rising
Constant Craving
You are Too Beautiful
Do You Believe in Magic?
The House of Soul
Nightwoman
Chrome 2
Bad to the Bone
Hitchhiker
Devil in Disguise
Double Vision
Amazing Grace

1990

This BBC drama series from 1977 looked just a few years into Britain's future and saw a population overwhelmed by bureaucracy, and the country practically a police state.

Parliament is just a cipher; the rights of the individual sublimated in a concept of the common good that is maintained by the Home Office's Public Control Department, using rationing, identity cards and electronic surveillance.

These tyrannical bureaucrats have turned the Channel and the North Sea into a watery equivalent of the Berlin Wall—and illegal immigration has given way to undercover emigration as doctors and scientists try to escape.

Devised by Wilfred Greatorex, creator of ITV's *The Power Game,* the series starred Edward Woodward as dissident journalist Jim Kyle, Home Affairs correspondent for one of the three remaining newspapers. He aids a growing resistance movement which smuggles people out of the country, runs an underground press and generally hinders the PCD at every turn. Ranged against him are Herbert Skardon, ruthless controller of the PCD, and his deputies Delly Lomas (Season One) and Lynn Blake (Season Two).

The series was born out of Greatorex's own "suffering" at the hands of zealous VATmen and his resentment at the growing power of the burgeoning bureaucracy of the 1970s—a sentiment shared by many for whom the memory of overkill VAT raids on small shopkeepers still rankled. Greatorex played on this paranoia to take the powers of the administrators a stage or two further.

Some critics carped, but *1990* was essentially a thriller series, not a solemn political statement, and retained the adventure motifs of car chases, tight spots and close shaves.

REGULAR CAST
Jim Kyle Edward Woodward   *Herbert Skardon* Robert Lang
Dave Brett Tony Doyle   *Faceless* Paul Hardwick

SEASON ONE ONLY
Delly Lomas Barbara Kellerman   *Dan Mellor* John Savident
Henry Tasker Clifton Jones   *Greaves* George Murcell
Jack Nichols Michael Napier Brown *(Eps. 1–3, 7–8)*
Tommy Pearce Mathias Kilroy *(Eps. 1–3)*
Marly Honor Shepherd *(Eps. 1, 5, 7)*

SEASON TWO ONLY
Lynn Blake Lisa Harrow *(Eps. 1–2, 4–8)*
Kate Smith Yvonne Mitchell *(Eps. 1–3, 5–8)*
PCD Insp. Macrae David McKail *(Eps. 1–2, 4–5, 7–8)*
Tony Doran Clive Swift *(Eps. 1–2, 4)*
Digger Radford Stanley Lebor *(Eps. 3–5)*

Devised by Wilfred Greatorex
Producer: Prudence Fitzgerald
Theme: John Cameron

A BBC Production
16 color 55-minute episodes

Season One:
18 September–31 October 1977
Season Two:
20 February–10 April 1978
(BBC2)

Season One

Creed of Slaves

w Wilfred Greatorex
Newspaperman Jim Kyle, a resolute opponent of the Public Control Department's repressive bureaucracy, tries to help a doctor who has been trying in vain to get his asthmatic daughter out of the country.
Dr. Vickers Donald Gee
Mrs. Vickers Eileen Davies
Tina Vickers Sophie Coghill
PCD inspector Stacy Davies
Randall Paul Chapman
Grey Luke Hanson
Mrs. Grey Lynn Dalby
Wilkie Robert Swales
Emigration officer Malcolm Rennie
Nolan Willie Johah
Harper Bruce Lidington
Burnley Desmond Jordan
Emigrant Bill Rourke

Director: Alan Gibson
Designer: Rochelle Selwyn

When Did You Last See Your Father?

w Wilfred Greatorex
Kyle learns that the Home Secretary is about to abolish all exit visa appeals and redoubles his efforts to help Dr. Vickers.
Dr. Vickers Donald Gee
Henry Duncan Reginald Jessup
Chairperson Gillian Raine
Norton John Hamill
Ian Cursley Peter Attard

Carol Harper Alix Kirsta
Randall Paul Chapman

Director: David Sullivan Proudfoot
Designer: Judy Steele

Health Farm

w Edmund Ward
Kyle is assigned to investigate an Adult Rehabilitation Center where murderers and political dissidents alike are treated with drugs that "reshape" their minds.
Dr. Gelbert Donald Douglas
Charles Wainwright Ray Smith
Halloran Howard Bell
Agnes Culmore Mitzi Rogers
Ivor Griffith John Rhys-Davies

Director: Kenneth Ives
Designer: Robert Berk

Decoy

w Edmund Ward
Dr. Sondeberg, the power behind many presidential desks, pays a state visit to Britain. Meanwhile Kyle plans to use a motorized caravan to help top brains flee the country.
Dr. Sondeberg Graham Crowden
Sammy Calhoun Victor Maddern
Kingston Antony Scott
Carr George Mallaby
Bowden Alan Tucker

Director: Alan Gibson
Designer: Rochelle Selwyn

Voice From the Past

w Arden Winch
"The age of the common man seems to be degenerating in the age of the common denominator."
Avery Richard Hurndall
Mitchell Esmond Knight
Brian Simon Chandler
Baker Michael Graham Cox
Luff Simon Lack
Sefton Raymond Mason
Bland John Quarmby
Williams Joby Blanshard

Director: David Sullivan Proudfoot
Designer: Judy Steele

Whatever Happened to Cardinal Wolsey?

w Wilfred Greatorex
An outraged attorney general orders the PCD to intimidate the pregnant wife of a judge who is upholding appeals and trying to dispense justice fairly.
Philip Carter John Castle
Attorney General Graham John Phillips
Susie Carter Anna Cropper
PCD inspector Jones Frank Mills
Lena Janie Booth
Ed Burbank Ed Bishop
PCD Supervisor Wade James Lister

Director: David Sullivan Proudfoot
Designer: Judy Steele

Witness

w Wilfred Greatorex
"We'll get Kyle . . . He's an enemy of the State . . . and of this Department." The PCD net begins to close in around Jim Kyle.
Dr. Vickers Donald Gee
Bingham Peter Myers
Paul Mark Heath
Technician Michael Cashman
Maggie Kyle Patricia Garwood
Bevan Jonathan Scott-Taylor
Prosecutor John Bennett
Defense counsel Yvonne Gillian

Director: Alan Gibson
Designer: Rochelle Selwyn

Non-Citizen

w Edmund Ward
Kyle is punished for his "misdeeds" by being stripped of his citizenship, but still succeeds in turning the tables on the PCD and the nation's Privilege Card holders.
Agnes Culmore Mitzi Rogers

Auckland Edward Judd
Woman non-citizen Julia Sutton
Prof. Cheever Vernon Dobtcheff
Sammy Calhoun Victor Maddern
"Nutter" Stonebridge Colin Edwynn
Frank Woodcock Tony Sympson

Director: Bob Hird
Designer: Robert Berk

Season Two

Pentagons

w Wilfred Greatorex
A pentagon, one of a growing army of dissent groups, prepares to take on the hated PCD.
Everton Oscar James
Tomson John Nolan
Green Paul Beech
Sewell Norman Mitchell
Frank Fenton Barry Lowe
Perez Edward de Souza

Director: Peter Sasdy
Designer: Paul Joel

The Market Price

w Wilfred Greatorex
The government of Kate Smith turns its attention to the black marketeers providing food when official supplies in the supermarkets begin to run low. Peter Greville from the Ministry of Food tries to keep Kyle informed of the PCD's movements but soon suspicion falls on him and his family.
Peter Greville Lyndon Brook
Rev. Newgate Max Harvey
Mrs. Greville Ann Curthoys
Jodie Greville Jane Foster
Alf Turner Michael Cassidy
Charles Graydon John Ronane
Miss Dalton Fiona Walker

Director: Roger Tucker
Designer: John Hurst

Trapline

w Edmund Ward
Kyle falls into the hands of Police Commissioner Hallam.
Richard Hallam John Paul
William Grainger John Carson
Tony Borden Norman Eshley
Harry Blaney Donald Burton
Barbara Fairlie Sandra Payne

Director: Peter Sasdy
Designer: Judy Steele

Ordeal by Small Brown Envelope

w Edmund Ward
When the comments in the press by Kyle and Doran again annoy Skardon, he decides to implement ASH—Automatic Systematic Harassment. Confronted by a stream of bailiffs, bills and official nightmares, "the noiseless steamroller of the State," Doran and his wife soon reach a crisis.
Jane Doran Hermione Gregory
Arthur Haynes Jim Norton
Harry Blaney Donald Burton
Carter John Saunders

Director: Kenneth Ives
Designer: Michael Young

Hire and Fire

w Edmund Ward
An extortionist network collecting money from repressed workers causes trouble for both Kyle and Skardon.
George Molloy David Buck
Johnny Rolfe Ken Kitson
Gerald Arnold James Greene
James Conrad John Bolt
Ernest Harrison Joseph Brady
Robert Jessup Simon Cadell
Mrs. Hutchinson Sally Travers
Joe Hutchinson Colin Douglas

Director: Alan Gibson
Designer: John Hurst

You'll Never Walk Alone

w Wilfred Greatorex
"The authorities have refused me an exit visa for the Chess Championship because they fear I might not come back."

Alan Adam Bareham
Philip Ross David Rintoul
Cyrus Asher Geoffrey Burridge
Nancy Skardon Joyce Carey
Abe James Murray
Annie Sue Woodley

Director: David Sullivan Proudfoot
Designer: Judy Steele

Young Sparks

w Jim Hawkins
Dissident groups are growing and sinking their differences in the battle against the PCD.
Alan Adam Bareham
Pallin George Pravda
Liz Julia Schofield
Riley William Wilde
Mayers Peter Clay
Sanders Martin Fisk

Director: Kenneth Ives
Designer: Michael Young

What Pleases the Prince

w Wilfred Greatorex
"We always said there'd be Peace Crimes Trials one day . . . We're winning now." The PCD begins to divide against itself.
John Brooks Michael Tarn
Robert Brooks Michael Osborne
Verna Wells Primi Townsend
Mrs. Brooks Jenny Laird
Barbara Fairlie Sandra Payne

Director: Alan Gibson
Designer: John Hurst

NOWHERE MAN

"My name is Thomas Veil, or at least it was. I'm a photographer. I had it all: a wife—Alyson—friends, a career. And in one moment it was all taken away, all because of a single photograph. I have it. They want it—and they will do anything to get the negative. I'm keeping this diary as proof that these events are real. I know they are . . . they *have* to be."

—Opening narration

America's *TV Guide* called it the 1995 season's coolest cult hit—and it was. Rooted in the running man tradition of *The Fugitive*, and with more, much more, than a passing nod to *The Prisoner*, *Nowhere Man* is the best paranoia trip TV has seen in years.

Photojournalist Tom Veil indeed has it all—a beautiful wife, Alyson, and a successful career, crowned by a prestigious exhibition of his award-winning photos. The couple heads off to their favorite restaurant for a quiet celebration and in the time it takes Tom to take a leak, his whole life and identity are suddenly stripped away. He comes out of the men's room to find his wife gone, another couple sitting at their table and a maître d' who doesn't recognize him. Worse follows. At home, his front door key won't work, his wife doesn't recognize him either and a strange man claiming to be her husband runs him off the property.

It's a conspiracy all right, and *everyone*'s in on it—his mother, the cops, little girls on bikes, even his dog. Suddenly people are after him and he doesn't know why, except that it has something to do with a photo called *Hidden Agenda* that he took of an execution in a Central American jungle that's now missing from his studio.

Forced to go on the run, Veil strives to find answers that might help him defeat "them" and get his identity back. Who can he trust? Practically no one . . .

Created for America's fledgling Paramount network by Lawrence Hertzog, a writing veteran of such churn-'em-out formula shows as *Hart to Hart* and *Hardcastle and McCormick*, *Nowhere Man* spins some wonderfully surreal and existential variations on the paranoia theme as, like Number 6 in *The Prisoner*, Tom Veil keeps trying to outwit the conspirators. There's even a version of The Village in the episode "Paradise on Your Doorstep" in which Veil is maneuvered into a haven for other disenfranchised people who have all lost their identities at the hands of the enemy. And like Patrick McGoohan's hero, Veil refuses to join in, even with people who claim to be on his side. He's not going to be a number either, though in another episode, "Heart of Darkness," in which he tags along with a group of right-wing survivalist recruits, he just happens to be sixth in line, and guess what he gets called?

Nowhere Man is a passionate defense of the individual in the face of overwhelming odds, and Tom Veil a dogged hero who clings tenaciously to his identity and the belief that he can, someday, win back his life.

On the Internet, fans of the show, dubbed Nowhere Maniacs, have delighted in scouring episodes for clues. Others have been frustrated at not being able to pick up any. Herzog is unrepentant, calling *Nowhere Man* "a show about being stymied, played with, manipulated and f***** over." Sound familiar?

In star Bruce Greenwood, the series also has another bankable asset. Wearing a permanent frown of suspicion under his shaggy mane of light brown hair, Greenwood makes a highly personable hero. TV junkies may recall him as the manipulative Dr. Seth Griffin in *St. Elsewhere* or, at a pinch, the sociopath Pierce Lawton on *Knots Landing*.

Unlike Richard Kimble in *The Fugitive*, Tom Veil didn't have to keep running for four years—the cancellation of the series meant that *Nowhere Man* needed to reach a conclusion in its first and only season.

REGULAR CAST
Thomas Veil Bruce Greenwood

Creator/Executive producer: Lawrence Hertzog
Producer: Peter Dunne
Supervising producer: Joel Surnow
Filmed on location in Portland, Oregon

Lawrence Hertzog Productions in association with Touchstone Television

25 color 60-minute episodes (premiere 90 minutes)

U.S. premiere: 28 August 1995
U.K. premiere: 3 October 1995
(Sky One)

Absolute Zero

(90-min. premiere)
w Lawrence Hertzog
After an exhibition of his photos, photojournalist Tom Veil and his wife Alyson go for a meal. Tom visits the washroom, but when he returns Alyson is gone, and the waiter claims not to recognize him. At his house his wife denies knowing him and a man claiming to be her husband runs him off at the point of a shotgun. Initially, Tom tries to believe Alyson is playing a joke on him, but comes to realize his identity is being stripped away, leaving him with nothing to distinguish himself, not even a bank card. His only clue lies at the gallery where one picture, *Hidden Agenda*, which depicts an execution by hanging in a Third World country, is missing. He again tries to talk to his wife and she at first seems to be trying to warn him, before telling a cop he's trying to accost her. Frustrated and angry, Tom hits the cop and is sent to the Calaway Psychiatric Hospital where his interrogator is the cigar-smoking Dr. Bellamy. Escaping with Bellamy as his hostage, Tom returns to his studio hoping to find more clues. A violent confrontation with white-coated killers ensues and Tom flees into the desert where his on-the-road quest for answers begins . . .
Alyson Veil Megan Gallagher
Dave "Eddie" Powers Ted Levine
Larry Levy Murray Rubenstein
Dr. Bellamy Michael Tucker
Father Thomas Bernie McInerney
Mrs. Veil Mary Gregory

Director: Tobe Hooper

Turnabout

w Lawrence Hertzog
After using one of Dr. Bellamy's credit cards, Tom is mistaken for Bellamy and taken to the enemy's headquarters, Clear Springs Sanitarium, where he's asked to help break a young woman whose identity is being similarly erased.
Ellen Combs Mimi Craven
Supervisor George Delhoyo
Dr. Hayne Phil Reeves
Peter Combs Ernie Garrett
Jessica Combs Jordyn Field
Adam Combs Chris Mastrandrea
Monk Tobias Anderson

Director: Tobe Hooper

The Incredible Derek

w Joel Surnow
With the help of Derek, a ten-year-old psychic blind boy, and a license plate detail from his *Hidden Agenda* photo, Tom hopes to find something that can lead him to the organization that's erasing his existence.
Derek Zachery McLemore
Bert Mike Starr

Harry Corners Tim DeZarn

Director: James Darren

Something About Her

w Lawrence Hertzog
Tom is apprehended at the scene of a fake accident involving a young girl. In a hi-tech lab he is injected with drugs, hooked up to a virtual reality machine and deluded that he's in a loving, trusting relationship—in an effort to get him to reveal the whereabouts of his negatives. (Strong overtones of *The Prisoner* episode "A, B and C.")
Karin Stolk Carrie Ann Moss
Dr. Moen Raphael Sbarge
Mr. Grey Kent Williams

Director: James Whitmore Jr.

Paradise on Your Doorstep

w Lawrence Hertzog
Tom is maneuvered into a haven for the "Disenfranchised." On the surface, everything looks idyllic, but Tom is ever suspicious and refuses to be assimilated into this community of lost souls. (What else could this episode be but a homage to The Village . . .)
Dierdre Coltrera Saxon Trainor
Paul Stephen Meadows
Master of Ceremonies Mark Vincent
Pilot Ted Roisum

Director: Tom Wright

The Spider Web

w Joel Surnow
While staying in a seedy motel, Tom is amazed to see his ordeal being re-enacted on a low-budget TV series, *The Lenny Little Show,* including dialogue and experiences from as recently as the previous day. He tracks down his tormentors—only to find even this act is being turned into a new plot twist.
Max Webb Richard Kind
Robert (Lenny Little) Michael Maguire
Angie (Nancy Little) Kate Hodge
Phil Nicholas Pryor

Director: Tom Wright

A Rough Whimper of Insanity

w Joel Surnow
Tom befriends a reclusive young computer genius, who, through virtual reality, helps him enjoy a brief interlude with Alyson, and then hack into Veil's deleted personal files.
Scott Jordan Sean Whalen
Alyson Veil Megan Gallagher
Pam Peters Karen Moncrief

Director: Guy Magar

The Alpha Spike

w Erica Byrne
While working as a groundsman at a prestigious boarding school, Tom uncovers an experiment, begun by Dr. Bellamy, which is now being used to brainwash the students.
Sheriff Norman Wade Bryan Cranston
Kyle Mencks Jackson Price
Headmaster Gordon James McDonnell
Vickie Jennifer Banko
Dr. Bellamy Michael Tucker *(voice-over)*

Director: Steven Robman

You Really Got a Hold on Me

w Jake & Mike Weinberger
Tom befriends Gus, a quirky drifter, who reveals that his own existence was erased 25 years before. Gus is near the end of his "road" and tries to persuade Tom to quit before he ends up like him, but instead Tom helps Gus rediscover a reason to keep on running.
Gus Shepard Dean Stockwell

Director: Michael Levine

Father (aka Validation)

w Art Monterastelli
Returning to his hometown in search of something that connects him to his past, Tom is unexpectedly reunited with his estranged father, but is tormented by doubts that he may be linked to the conspiracy.
Jonathan Crane Dean Jones
Beth Crane Donna Bullock
Marty Gary Rooney
Morris Joseph Carberry
Johnny Crane Cody Hill

Director: Guy Magar

The Enemy Within

w Peter Dunne
While camping in Pennsylvania farm country, Tom is accidently shot. Nursed back to health by a local woman, he realizes he has finally found a safe place and someone to trust. But after helping her and the townspeople take on a giant food conglomerate, Tom realizes his own fight is not yet over.
Emily Noonan Maria Bello
Tobe Alder Raye Birk
Ed Durrant James Lashly
Will Thomas Peter Kjenaas
Doc Wilson Scott Parker

Director: Ian Toynton

It's Not Such a Wonderful Life

w Lawrence Hertzog
At long last Tom's torment seems to be over. Federal agents make contact and inform him that they've been trying to find him for months to get him to testify in a hearing against his enemy. He's reunited with Alyson and his mother and is poised to celebrate Christmas at a "safe house." However, there's just one minor item the officials need . . . his negatives.
Alyson Veil Megan Gallagher
Mrs. Veil Mary Gregory
Sandra Wilson Carol Huston
Rick Willie C. Carpenter
Roy W. Earl Brown

Director: Tim Hunter

Contact (aka Deep Throat)

w Lawrence Hertzog
A dissident from the Organization makes contact with Tom and offers to help him get his life back if, first, he will kill the man primarily responsible for the decision to erase his identity.
Deep Throat Robin Sachs *(voice-over)*
Richard Grace Joseph Lambie

Director: Reza Badiyi

Heart of Darkness

w David Ehrman
Using information supplied by his new contact, Veil infiltrates the Organization's own private army—as recruit Number Six!—led by renowned fanatic Cyrus Quinn.
Gary Greer Scott Coffey
C.W. Knox Patrick Kilpatrick
Commander Quinn James Tolkan

Director: Stephen Stafford

Forever Jung

w Joel Surnow
While working at a nursing home, Tom stumbles upon a genetics laboratory and exposes a bizarre fountain of youth experiment in which the elderly residents are made young again—with deadly consequences.
Dr. Seymour Leon Russom
Old Pauline Edith Fields
Young Pauline Melanie Smith
Max Bob Palioca
Rudy Paul Marin
Nurse Ellman Freda Foh Shen

Director: Stephen Stafford

Shine a Light on You (aka Masons)

w Art Monterastelli
Tom goes to New Mexico in search of John Meyerson, a man he believes to be linked to the organization. But when he witnesses what a town is convinced is an alien landing, Tom uncovers a secret operation funded by his enemies.
Dr. John Meyerson Bill Geisslinger
Helen Meyerson Dorie Barton
Bud Atkins Roy Brocksmith
Sheriff Wilkes George Gerdes
Hank Bower Tom McCleister

Director: Stephen Stafford

Stay Tuned

w Lawrence Hertzog
Tom clashes with a political candidate backed by the Organization who is using subliminal mind control to brainwash a small town into voting for him as Governor.
Jim Hubbard Cliff DeYoung
Janet Cowen Karen Witter
Michael Billy O'Sullivan

Director: Mel Damski

Hidden Agenda

w David Ehrman
Tom agrees to meet Hale, the man who's been giving him clues to help him unravel the mystery surrounding the Organization, and tells him the story of how he came to take the *Hidden Agenda* photo. But he's unaware that his contact has been caught by the Organization, which is now using him to get Tom.
Alexander Hale Robin Sachs
Harrison Barton Dwight Schultz
Luis Borjes Anthony Guzman

Director: Michael Levine

Doppelganger

w Schuyler Kent
In search of a journalist, Clare Hillard, Tom visits an Ohio town where he discovers that a nearly identical man has adopted his name, profession and his photos—including *Hidden Agenda*. And when Clare is found dead, Tom becomes the prime suspect.
Clare Hillard Jamie Rose
Jane Butler Mia Korf
Det. Tanner Richard Penn
Lucy Laura Leigh Hughes

Director: Ian Toynton

Through a Lens Darkly (aka Shutterbug)

w Art Monterastelli
Tom is picked up by the Organization and taken on a chemically induced trip down memory lane and forced to relive a traumatic time with his childhood sweetheart, Laura, until he agrees to hand over the negatives.
Man Sam Anderson
Laura at 30 Sydney Walsh
Teen Tom Jason Waters
Young Tom Trevor O'Brien
Teen Laura Monica Creel
Young Laura Julia Whelan

Director: Ian Toynton

The Dark Side of the Moon (aka The Mugging)

w David Ehrman
When Tom is mugged and the negatives are stolen along with his other possessions, he finds himself the target of a vicious street gang as he searches for the thief.
Margo Juliet Tablak
Mackie Trevor Goddard
Father Ray Dan Martin
Bradley Maurice Chasse
Tiny Evan Matthews
Blaze Caton Lyles

Director: James Whitmore Jr.

Calaway

w Joel Surnow
Tom infiltrates the Illinois psychiatric hospital where his ordeal began and is caught by a familiar face—former patient Joe "J.C." Carter who has now joined the medical staff. And he witnesses another man, Michael Kramer, undergoing the first phase of conditioning—just as he did all those months ago.
Joe "J.C." Carter/Dr. Novik Jay Arlen Jones
Michael Kramer Robert Cicchini
Dr. Gilmore Bruce Gray

Director: Ian Toynton

Zero Minus Ten

w Jane Espenson
Tom awakes from a coma to learn that he was in a bad car crash and that his entire ordeal was just a terrible nightmare. At his bedside is his wife Alyson and his best friend, Larry Levy, a man Veil swears he saw dead and stuffed into a closet several months before.
Alyson Megan Gallagher
Larry Murray Rubenstein
Ben Dobbs Choppy Guillotte
Doctor David Bodin

Director: James Whitmore Jr.

Marathon

w Art Monterastelli

Veil is nearing the end of his tether when he enlarges a print of his *Hidden Agenda* photo and discovers new clues that lead him to a Washington research facility and the forbidding Project Marathon. However, he also makes a valuable new ally in the FBI who gives him the key to a safety deposit box containing a dossier on his case.

Stanley Robman Nicolas Surovy
Jenny Tsu Elsie Sniffen
Sparky Oz Tortora

Director: Stephen Stafford

Gemini

w Lawrence Hertzog & Art Monterastelli

Tom's nightmare journey reaches a climax as he discovers the identity of the four hanging victims in his *Hidden Agenda* photo. And he finally learns the shocking truth behind his own ordeal.

Senator Wallace Hal Linden
Robert Barton Francis X. McCarthy
Iverson Edward Edwards

Director: Stephen Stafford

OCEAN ODYSSEY
(A.K.A. OCEAN GIRL)

Australian children's fantasy-drama series set around an undersea research colony, about the adventures of Neri, a mysterious young girl who may just be the most amazing thing science has seen this century. She can swim to extraordinary depths, at extraordinary speeds, without breathing apparatus—and she can communicate with whales, especially Charley, a humpback whale. Ran for two series, in 1995 and 1996.

CAST INCLUDES:
Neri Marzena Godecki
With: Jeffrey Walker, David Hoflin, Alex Pinder, Kerry Armstrong

Creator/Producer: Jonathan M. Shiff
Writer: Jenny Sharp
Director: Brendan Maher

Produced in association with Network Ten Australia
26 color 25-minute episodes

Series One:
2 April–25 June 1995
Series Two:
11 June–3 September 1996
(BBC2)

OBJECT Z

A mystery object hurtling through space on a collision course with good old Earth. In the chaos that follows, traditional enemies combine to save mankind from annihilation. That was the theme of a pair of children's serials of the mid-sixties, *Object Z* and its sequel, the aptly named *Object Z Returns*. Central figures in the unfolding dramas were TV commentator/reporter Peter Barry, his assistant Diana Winters, a mysterious scientist, Professor Ramsay, and a supporting cast of world leaders and boffins.

The first serial was originally written by Christopher McMaster as an adult program, but adapted to meet Rediffusion's need for a children's drama.

REGULAR CAST

Peter Barry Trevor Bannister   *Professor Ramsay* Ralph Nossek
Diana Winters Celia Bannerman *(Series One only)*
June Challis Margaret Neale   *Robert Duncan* Denys Peek
Brian Barclay Brandon Brad00y   *Keeler* Arthur White
Ian Murray (Home Secretary) William Abney
Sir John Chandos (Prime Minister) Julian Somers
Terry Toni Gilpin *(Series Two only)*

Writer: Christopher McMaster

Director/Producer: Daphne Shadwell

Designer: Andrew Drummond

Rediffusion Network Production

Object Z

When a mystery object is detected hurtling toward Earth, anxious world leaders prepare to launch a rocket to destroy the unknown projectile. Are aliens coming? If so, what do they want? Or is it all a hoax perpetrated by scientist Professor Ramsay and his colleagues to frighten the world into peace? (You bet it is!)

Capt. Wade Terrence J. Donovan
President McCone Robert O'Neil
Dr. Baranov Jeffry Wickham
Dr. Rickover Lindsay Campbell
Premier Yeremenko Dmitri Makaroff
with: David Munro, Terence Woodfield, Penny Morrell, Roger Rowland, Hugh Munro, John Newman, Roy Herrick, Bernard Kay, Richard Bidlake, Milton Johns

6 black and white 30-minute episodes
The Meteor
The World in Fear
Flight from Danger
The Aliens
Too Late
The Solution

19 October–23 November 1965
(ITV)

Object Z Returns

Scientists spot three more objects on their screens, moving in formation toward Earth at tremendous speed. Are they out-of-control asteroids or space ships? Prof. Ramsay is freed from jail to work out the truth with his assistants, Robert Duncan and June Challis. This time it's no hoax, as the alien craft—from a water-covered world—land in Earth's oceans and the world begins to freeze.

Premier Petrov Paul Armstrong
Voice Terence Woodfield
Dr. O'Toole Barry Lowe
Dallier David Saire
Radio operator Roy Herrick

6 black and white 30-minute episodes
The Voice from Space
The Machine
The Monsters
The Menace from the Depths
The Big Freeze
The Eleventh Hour

22 February–29 March 1966
(ITV)

ONE STEP BEYOND

"What you are about to see is a matter of human record. Explain it? We cannot. Disprove it? We cannot. We simply invite you to explore with us the amazing world of the unknown, to take that *One Step Beyond.*"

Neither science nor, by its own assertion, fiction, *One Step Beyond* dealt with the realm of psychic phenomena. Technically that puts it one step beyond the province of this volume.

Yet this vintage anthology series, which did as much as any to blur the edges of reality, repeatedly crops up in genre guides and has long been accepted into the hearts of television fantasy fans.

Created in America, it ran there for two years (1959–61) and 94 episodes (as *Alcoa Presents . . .*). But what isn't widely known is that 13 of those episodes, all for the third and final season, were made in Britain.

The U.K. 13 were made at the now long-lost MGM film studios in Borehamwood by Lancer Films, and were hailed as the first time British Television production had gone into an association with an established American network show. Using mainly British scripts, they featured British casts, with Anton Rodgers, Peter Wyngarde, Donald Pleasence, Christopher Lee, Adrienne Corri, Roger Delgado and a young Michael Crawford among the stars.

Like the rest of the series, the stories dealt with various psychic phenomena—supernatural visitations, ESP, dreams that are portents of disaster, hallucinations of the future, reincarnations of the past. These episodes—and the series as a whole—were directed and hosted by American actor John Newland who took a sardonic delight in introducing what became renowned as a genuinely spooky glimpse of the paranormal.

(Author's note: a full episode guide would be space-consuming and probably inappropriate, given the series' general stamping ground, but here is a rundown of the British-made episodes, the U.K. 13.)

REGULAR CAST
Host John Newland

Series creator: Merwin Gerard
Series producer: Collier Young
Director: John Newland
Music: Harry Lubin

A *Collier Young* Production
96 black and white 30-minute episodes
U.S. premiere: 20 September 1959

The U.K. 13

Director: John Newland
Executive producer: Collier Young
Producer: Peter Marriott
Story supervisor: Martin Benson
A *Lancer Films Production*
13 black and white 30-minute episodes
29 November 1961–28 February 1962

Eye Witness

w Derry Quinn
Henry Soames, night news editor of the *Boston Globe*, experiences the 1883 Krakatoa earthquake in the quiet of his office and while unconscious writes an exclusive "eyewitness" account.
Henry John Meillon
Nora Rose Alba
Mark Anton Rodgers
Jake Robin Hughes
Frank John Phillips
Leo J.G. Devlin
Richards Robert Ayres
Danny Howard Knight
with Gordon Stern, Janet Blandes, Patricia English

Nightmare

w Martin Benson
Artist Paul Roland, haunted by the face of a girl he has never met, feels compelled to keep painting her portrait.
Paul Peter Wyngarde
Jill Mary Peach
Lady Diana Ambrosine Phillpotts
Heathcote Ferdy Mayne

Stapleton Richard Caldicott
Meg Jean Cadell
Doctor Patrick Holt

The Confession

w Larry Marcus
Harvey Laurence, an old man on a Hyde Park soapbox, constantly tells the story of his guilt in allowing a man to die for the murder of a woman he knew was still alive—but no one ever listens.
Laurence Donald Pleasence
Sarah Adrienne Corri
Policeman Robert Raglan
KC Raymond Rollett
Mrs. Evans Eileen Way
Martha Carmel McSharry
Locksmith Jack Newmark
with Douglas Ives, Gerald James, Julian Orchard, Brenda Dunrich

The Avenger

w Martin Benson
A general's replica of an old 18th-century tyrant's party stirs up spirits of the ancient gathering and the consequences are chillingly similar.
General André Morell
Marianne Lisa Gastoni
Priest Stanley van Beers
Doctor Carl Jaffe
Orderly Richard Leech
Gardener Steve Plytas
Sergeant Walter Gotell
Musicians Carl Duering, Jan Conrad, Charles Russell, Robert Crewdson

The Stranger

w Larry Marcus
The fingerprints of a man who helped keep three earthquake victims alive until their rescue 11 days later show he had "died" in prison some time ago.
Cole Bill Nagy
Hadley Peter Dyneley
Warden Patrick McAlliney
Peter Graham Stark
Teacher Harold Kasket
Guard Ken Wayne
Barber Mark Baker

Signal Received

w Derry Quinn
Three sailors on HMS *Hood* are given separate glimpses of the future—revealing their own fates and that of the ship. (One of the three, Robin Hughes, subsequently became an actor and appeared in the *One Step Beyond* story "Eye Witness.")
Watson Mark Eden
Breed Terry Palmer
Hughes Richard Gale
Mrs. Breed Viola Keats
with Patrick McLoughlin, Patrick Jordan, Anne Ridler, Sally Layng, Garrard Green, Jennifer Daniel, John Downing, Susan Richards, Mark Burns, Charles Lamb

The Prisoner

w Larry Marcus
Concentration camp survivor Ruth Goldman kills a German soldier in retribution for Nazi atrocities, but her doctor insists the man has been dead for six years.
German Anton Diffring
Ruth Catherine Feller
Nurse Faith Brook
Samuel Sandor Elés
Doctor Gerard Heinz
Woman Annette Carell

The Sorcerer

w Derry Quinn
A farmer's supernatural powers enable a German officer, anxious about his fiancée's faithfulness, to visit her flat 800 km away in Berlin.
Reitlinger Christopher Lee
Klaus Martin Benson
Elsa Gabrielli Licudi
Scholl Alfred Burke
Letterhaus George Pravda
Landlord Peter Swanwick
Johann Frederick Jaeger
with Edwin Richfield, Richard Shaw

That Room Upstairs

w Merwin Gerard *&* Larry Marcus
An American couple rents a large house in London. When the wife hears the voice of a child calling for help she goes to one of the upstairs rooms where she finds a wasted girl crying in pain. To her horror her surroundings suddenly change into an old nursery . . .
Esther Lois Maxwell
Will David Knight
Hudson Anthony Oliver
Child Gilda Emmanueli
Man David Markham
Woman Jane Hylton
Doctor Carl Bernard

The Tiger

w Ian Stuart Black
A neglected child "wishes" an unusual way to drive out her unwanted governess.
Pamela Pauline Challenor
Miss Plum Pamela Brown
Mrs. Murphy Elspeth March
Cleaning lady Patsy Smart
Solicitor Brian Parker
Inspector Michael Collins

The Villa

w Derry Quinn
Mary sees a beautiful villa while taking part in a hypnotic experiment. The next day she accompanies her husband to Milan . . . and to the beautiful villa.
Mary Elizabeth Sellars
Jim Geoffrey Toone
Stella Marla Landi
Mr. Hudson David Horne
Tony Michael Crawford
Lionel Kenneth Cope
Bertollini Robert Rietty
Porter Gertan Klauber

The Face

w Derry Quinn
Haunted since childhood by a seaman's face in a recurring dream of murder, Stephen Bolt hangs around the docks in the hope of recognizing the face. One day he gets drunk and wakes up on a Spanish ship where one of the seaman has *that* face.
Stephen Sean Kelly
Mark John Brown
Rosemary Penelope Horner
Isiah Victor Platt
Hogan Robert Cawdron
Sergeant John Scott
Tattooist Erik Chitty
Norriss Andrew Faulds
Second officer Roger Delgado
Spanish sailor Derek Sydney
with Michael Peake, Leon Cartez, Paula Byrne

Justice

w Guy Morgan
A respected bank manager in a little Welsh village confesses to a murder and supplies evidence of his guilt—but witnesses swear he was asleep in a church pew when the crime was committed.
PC Jones Clifford Evans

Mrs. Jones Barbara Mullen
Mr. Roberts Meredith Edwards
Mrs. Roberts Pauline Jameson
Insp. Pugh Edward Evans
Supt. Rees Ewan Roberts
Mr. Owen Jack Melford
Mrs. Owen Helen Sessions
Dr. Evans Martin Benson

OTHERWORLD

Land of the Lost meets *The Fantastic Journey* in a short-lived series about a family lost in another dimension.

The Sterlings, touted as "a typical Southern California family," slip into the parallel universe of Otherworld while on a sightseeing tour of the ancient Pyramids, when a strange alignment of the planets opens up a portal between the two universes.

They discover that the Great Pyramid was built, not as the mere tomb of a king, but as a barricade at the portal, and that thousands of years ago it was common for people to pass between the two dimensions.

Not so now, however, and Hal and June Sterling and their three children become fugitives in this alien environment as they strive to reach the Capital Province of Imar where the Supreme Governors have the power to return them to their own world. It's a perilous task, as they are pursued by the Zone Troopers of the Imperial Kommander Nuveen Kroll.

Otherworld's eight episodes ranged from the comic ("Rock and Roll Suicide") through the blatantly ludicrous ("Village of the Motorpigs"), to the excellent (a beauty and the beast–style story, "Mansion of the Beast"). But they never did make it home.

REGULAR CAST

Hal Sterling Sam Groom *June Sterling* Gretchen Corbett
Trace Tony O'Dell *Gina* Jonna Lee
Smith Brandon Crane (*pilot*), Chris Herbert (*series*)
Nuveen Kroll Jonathan Banks

Executive producers: Philip De Guerre (*pilot only*), Roderick Taylor
Producers: Roderick Taylor (*pilot only*), Lew Hunter
Created by: Roderick Taylor, Philip De Guerre

MCATV International
8 color 55-minute episodes
U.S. premiere: 25 January 1985
U.K. premiere: 7 September–2 November 1985 (HTV)
(U.K. running orders varied around the regions, so the following guide lists the episodes in their original U.S. order.)

Rules of Attraction (pilot)

w Roderick Taylor
The Sterling family is on holiday in Egypt when, while sightseeing at the ancient pyramids, they slip through a dimensional gateway into a parallel universe "just slightly different from our reality." There, they become fugitives from the authorities in their quest for Capital where lies their only hope of return to their own world.

Nova Amanda Wyss
Bureaucrat Ray Walston
Litten Conrad Bachmann
Prof. Kroyd James Costy

Director: William Graham

The Zone Troopers Build Men

w Coleman Luck, *story by* Roderick Taylor &
Bruce A. Taylor
The Sterlings are living quietly for a while in a
peaceful town, when Trace is suddenly snatched by
Zone Troopers because of low school grades and put
through strenuous training. To leave he must be-
come an officer, as only officers can resign.
Hilbird Racks Dominick Brascia
Sightings Mark Lenard

Director: Richard Compton

Paradise Lost

w Josef Anderson, *story by* Roderick Taylor &
Bruce A. Taylor
Following a powerful storm, the Sterlings are
washed up on the shores of a beautiful island, setting
for a paradise-lost resort. Their host is the equally
beautiful and mysterious Scarla who falls in love
with Hal.
Scarla Barbara Stock

Director: Tom Wright

Rock and Roll Suicide

w Roderick Taylor & Bruce A. Taylor
Gina and Trace introduce rock and roll to the other
kids in a Centrex City high school and become in-
stant celebrities but also risk exposing the whole
family to the attention of Kroll.
Host Joyce Little
Claxxon Warren Munson
Billy Sunshine Michael Callan

Director: Roderick Taylor

Village of the Motorpigs (aka Tribunal)

w Roderick Taylor & Bruce A. Taylor
While trying to put as much distance as possible between themselves and the Zone Troopers, the Sterlings fall into the hands of a tribe of neo-Barbarians
whose social set-up is opposed to the family entity.
(This was formerly the pilot, Part 2.)

Chalktrauma Marjoe Gortner
Rev Jeff East
Pango Vincent Schiavelli
Pigseye David Katims
Motorface Donald Gibb
Motorpig Jerry Potter

Director: Paul Michael Glaser

I Am Woman, Hear Me Roar (aka You've Come a Long Way, Baby)

w Bruce A. Taylor & Coleman Luck, *story by*
Roderick Taylor, Bruce A. Taylor, Coleman
Luck
The Sterlings wander into a province called Ador
where men are second-class citizens and women
rule.
Lieutenant Wayne Alexander
Belisama Elaine Giftos
Gretchen Askyou Susan Powell
Sam Askyou Dennis Howard

Director: Tom Wright

Mansion of the Beast

w Roderick Taylor, Coleman Luck, Bruce A. Taylor, *story by* Roderick Taylor, Coleman Luck
June is held prisoner by a creature—half-man, half-
beast—who falls in love with her and tells her she is
his only salvation from a terrible fate.
Vorago Alan Feinstein
Aiken John Astin

Director: Corey Allen

Princess Metra

w Douglas Lloyd McIntosh, *story by* Roderick
Taylor & Bruce A. Taylor
When the Sterlings arrive in Metraplex, Gina is mis-
taken for a long-lost princess and, seeing this as a
way to get closer to home, assumes her new identity.
Zal Philip Simone
Kort Drake Hogestyn
Vertleena Joan Foley

Director: Peter Medak

OUT OF THE UNKNOWN

"Without doubt the best adult science fiction series ever
to be written for the small screen."
—*Daily Express*

The cause of British adult science fiction was never better served than by this prestigious BBC
anthology series of single plays.

Drawn heavily from the written works of top-notch sf writers such as Isaac Asimov, John Wyndham, Ray Bradbury and Frederick Pohl, *Out of the Unknown* ran for four seasons on BBC2 between 1965 and 1971—two black and white, two color—and became a magnet for some of the brightest talent around at the time.

Inspiration came from producer Irene Shubik who already had an enviable track record in the field—as story editor for ABC Television, she had helmed the pioneering 1962 ITV science fiction anthology series *Out of This World*, and had also established a reputation for picking winners for ABC's renowned *Armchair Theater* series.

Among the dramatists working on the first season were Terry Nation, Leon Griffiths and Bruce Stewart (later to script the first, and best, *Timeslip* stories for ATV), all of whom had worked with Shubik on *Out of This World*. The directorial credits included Philip Saville (*Boys from the Blackstuff*), Alan Bridges and Peter Sasdy, and among the ranks of BBC designers were Barry Learoyd, Peter Seddon and Ridley Scott who, of course, found greater acclaim as director of *Alien* and *Blade Runner*. And the series regularly attracted high-caliber casts with David Hemmings, Milo O'Shea, Warren Mitchell, Donald Houston, Rachel Roberts, George Cole, Anton Rodgers, Ed Begley and Marius Goring among the stars.

Being an anthology, *Out of the Unknown* was never tied to one style of science fiction, though it eschewed membership of the "bug-eyed monster" club. Some stories were played for suspense ("The Counterfeit Man," "Time in Advance," "Lambda 1," "The World in Silence"), some played on fears ("Some Lapse of Time," "Frankenstein Mark II"), and others aimed for satire ("The Midas Plague"), black comedy ("Second Childhood") or whimsy ("Andover and the Android," "Satisfaction Guaranteed"). Nearly all had *something* to offer the starved intellect.

The third and fourth seasons, produced in color by Alan Bromly, saw a shift in style toward what Bromly called "plays of psychological suspense," with mostly supernatural thrills. Only gradual at first, the transition was almost total in the fourth and final season.

Explaining the decision to take the series away from pure science fiction, Bromly told *Radio Times*: "To do these things really successfully must involve you in spending an enormous amount of money on special effects . . . which is beyond the reach of television." He added: "When everybody has seen men walking on the moon and sat through a cliffhanger about getting them back alive, then just setting a story somewhere in space is not, you can see, the automatic thrill it was."

It wasn't a view shared by everyone and although Bromly's reign included plays by Michael J. Bird and the prolific Nigel Kneale, it was not a series for purists. The era of the science fiction anthology was over.

Producers: Irene Shubik (*Seasons One and Two*) Alan Bromly (*Seasons Three and Four*)
Script editors: Irene Shubik (*Seasons One and Two*) Roger Parkes (*Seasons Three and Four*)
Theme music: Norman Kay (*Seasons One and Two*)

A BBC Production
49 episodes—12 × 50 min. (Season One)
37 × 60 min. (Seasons Two–Four)
black and white (Seasons One and Two)
color (Seasons Three and Four)
Season One:
4 October–20 December 1965

Season Two:
6 October 1966–1 January 1967
Season Three:
7 January–1 April 1969
Season Four:
21 April–30 June 1971
(BBC2)

Season One

No Place Like Earth

w Stanley Miller, *story by* John Wyndham
Wandering on Mars is a lone, homesick Earthman, stranded when Earth exploded. One day he learns of a reborn Earth, and his hope is also rekindled.
Bert Terence Morgan
Zaylah Hannah Gordon
Annika Jessica Dunning
Blane Alan Tilvern

Harris Bill Treacher
Carter Vernon Joyner
Freeman Joseph O'Conor
Major Khan George Pastell
Spaceship captain Jerry Stovin
Chief officer Geoffrey Palmer
Security guard Roy Stewart

Director: Peter Potter
Designer: Peter Seddon

(4 October 1965)

The Counterfeit Man

w Philip Broadley, *story by* Alan Nourse
Aboard a spaceship bound for Earth are a crew of tired, edgy explorers returning from a fruitless mission to the barren planet Ganymede. Then a routine medical check reveals that one man, Westcott, has a blood sugar count of zero—which means he is not human. Some entity has taken over his mind and body.
Dr. Crawford Alex Davion
Westcott David Hemmings
Capt. Jaffe Charles Tingwell
Donnie Peter Fraser
Jensen Anthony Wager
Scotty Keith Buckley
Gerry David Savile
Dave Geoffrey Kenion
Frank Barry Ashton
Ken David Munro
Commander Hedger Wallace
Officer Lew Luton
Guard Derek Martin

Director: George Spenton-Foster
Designer: Trevor Williams

(11 October 1965)

Stranger in the Family

w David Campton
Boy is a child ahead of his time—a mutant born with amazing mental powers of perception and persuasion. His parents have tried to protect him but he is shadowed by a strange group of men who have their own plans for his future. To 18-year-old Boy, it seems only one person understands him—the lovely Paula. But their relationship is doomed to tragedy.
Boy Richard O'Callaghan
Hall Joby Blanshard
Paula Justine Lord
Sonny Eric Lander
Lorry driver Peter Thornton
Charles Wilson Peter Copley
Margaret Wilson Daphne Slater
Brown John Paul
Evans Jack May
Mrs. Pain Bay White
Director Maurice Podbray
Assistant Clive Graham
Swain Brian Vaughan

Director: Alan Bridges
Designer: Barry Learoyd

(18 October 1965)

The Dead Past

w Jeremy Paul, *story by* Isaac Asimov
In the 21st century, historian Arnold Potterley requests permission from the World Government to use its Chronoscope—a device able to recapture any event from the past on screen—to view a scene from ancient Carthage. It seems a harmless request, but Araman, the official in charge of the Chronoscope, not only forbids it but warns Potterley he risks "intellectual anarchy" if he pursues the matter. Determined not to be thwarted, Potterley persuades a young physicist, Foster, to build his own private Chronoscope. The result is unexpected and frightening.
Arnold Potterley George Benson
Jonas Foster James Maxwell
Thaddeus Araman David Langton
Caroline Potterley Sylvia Coleridge
Miss Clements Shirley Cain
Laurel Frances Alger
Ralph Nimmo Willoughby Goddard

Director: John Gorrie
Designer: Norman James

(25 October 1965)

Time in Advance

w Paul Erickson, *story by* William Tenn
The future: people with criminal tendencies can be licensed to commit a crime—provided they first serve an appropriate term of imprisonment. A convict spaceship is returning to Earth from a penal colony in outer space. Aboard are Crandall and Henck, the first men ever to survive the seven years of rigorous punishment, which earns them the right to commit a murder. As the ship lands, reporters press forward to ask the men who their victims will be.
Chief guard Oliver MacGreevy
Crandall Edward Judd
Henck Mike Pratt
Henson Dyson Lovell
The Examiner Peter Madden
Newsreader Michael Harding
Ryman Jerome Willis
Marie Judy Parfitt
Polly Wendy Gifford
Stephenson Peter Stephens
Captor Patrick Scanlan
Dan Danvers Walker
Police officer Phillip Voss
Ballaskia Ken Parry

Director: Peter Sasdy
Designer: Tony Abbott

(1 November 1965)

Come Buttercup, Come Daisy, Come . . . ?

w Mike Watts
A chilling comedy. Fishmonger Henry Wilkes cultivates carnivorous plants in his suburban garden, feeding them diced rabbit and massive doses of vitamins. He gives them pet names and talks to them.
Henry Wilkes Milo O'Shea
Danny Jack Wild
Monica Wilkes Christine Hargreaves
Anne Lovejoy Patsy Rowlands
Mrs. Bryant Ann Lancaster
Norman Eric Thompson
Dr. Chambers Desmond Jordan
Mrs. Dixon Julie May
Milkman Nigel Lambert
Det. Sgt. Crouch Bernard Kay
Det. Con. Fraser Alan Heywood
Mina-Mina trained by Barbara Woodhouse

Director: Paddy Russell
Designer: John Cooper

(8 November 1985)

Sucker Bait

w Meade Roberts, *story by* Isaac Asimov
Time: the far future. Mark Annuncio is a Mnemonic, one of a group of specially selected children rigorously trained to soak up facts and store them in the subconscious and to recall them in association with other facts in a human way no computer can match. Mark and his attendant psychologist, Dr. Sheffield, are viewed with mistrust by scientists aboard the spaceship *Triple G*, hurtling toward the planet Troan to discover why a colony died there within three years. But Mark's insatiable curiosity comes to threaten not only the expedition's purpose, but also the lives of its members.
Captain Bill Nagy
Mark Clive Endersby
Dr. Sheffield John Meillon
Cimon David Knight
Novee Burt Kwouk
Fawkes Roger Croucher
Rodriguez Tenniel Evans
Vernadsky David Sumner
Crewmen Peter Diamond, John McArdle

Director: Naomi Capon
Designer: William McCrow

(15 November 1965)

The Fox and the Forest

w Terry Nation, *story by* Ray Bradbury,
additional material by Meade Roberts
In the year 2165, time travel is a luxury that privileged government workers may use to take holidays in the past. David and Sarah Kirsten chose 1938 and liked it so much they decided to stay. But they are too important to be allowed to escape from the future, so "hunters" are sent to bring them back—remorseless pursuers, who blend in so well, that to the "hunted" everyone they meet becomes suspect.
David Frederick Bartman
Sarah Liane Aukin
Joe Warren Mitchell
Shaw Marne Maitland
Boy Aziz Resh
Mexican woman Serafina di Leo
Faber Eric Flynn
Dancer Delphine
Guitarist Domingo de Lezaria
American couple Robert MacLeod, Bettine Milne
Mexicans Guido Adorni, José Berlinka
Man in mask Dean Francis
Bellboy Steve Georgio
Singer/guitarist Patrick Scanlan
Beth Marcella Markham
Hotel manager George Roderick

Director: Robin Midgley
Designer: Peter Seddon

(22 November 1965)

Andover and the Android

w Bruce Stewart, *story by* Kate Wilhelm
Roger Andover's aunt Mathilde wants him to marry and take over the family electronics business. Determined to avoid complicated human relationships, Roger acquires one of the secret new super-androids that he can pass off as his wife—a beautiful "woman" called Lydia. Despite some anxious moments when she is introduced to the family, Lydia looks like being the perfect wife. She never argues and is always eager to please. Then her circuits get confused.
Sir Felix Ronald Ibbs
Cullen Fulton Mackay
Prof. Tzhilyantsi Robert Eddison
Purvis Robin Parkinson
Charlie David Coote
Phoebe Helen Lindsay
Andover Tom Criddle
French David Conville
Eleanor Lisa Daniely
Patrice John Malcolm
Mathilde Marda Vanne
Lydia Annette Robertson
Bernard Erik Chitty
Barnaby Peter Bathurst
Fred Fred Hugh

Director: Alan Cooke
Designer: Lionel Radford

(29 November 1965)
(repeated 29 December 1965, BBC1)

Some Lapse of Time

w Leon Griffiths, *story by* John Brunner
Dr. Max Harrow is awakened from a recurrent nightmare in which he is pursued by barbaric accusing figures, to find a tramp collapsed on his doorstep. The
tramp is suffering from a genetic radiation disorder
that should have killed him in infancy as it did Har-
row's baby son. The man is the living image of Har-
row's nightmare figures. Clutched in his hand is a
human finger bone and he speaks a strange, unknown
tongue. Why did he collapse outside Harrow's house?
What is his motive for tracing him?
Max Harrow Ronald Lewis
Diana Harrow Jane Downs
Policeman Peter Bowles
Smiffershon John Gabriel
Dr. Gordon Faulkner Richard Gate
Det. Sgt. Cloudby George Woodbridge
Prof. Leach Moultrie Kelsall
Dr. Laura Danville Delena Kidd
Radiologist Laidlaw Dalling
Anderson Blake Butler
Nurse Jane Bolton
Sister Bridget McConnel

Director: Roger Jenkins
Designer: Ridley Scott

(6 December 1965)

Thirteen to Centaurus

w Stanley Miller, *story by* J.G. Ballard
Thirteen people are living in a steel-encased, self-
sufficient world of their own, known as "the Station." All but one has been conditioned to accept it
as their only home, their Earth memories carefully
erased to ensure the Station functions efficiently.
The odd man out is psychologist Dr. Francis, re-
sponsible for maintaining the blocks. Then Abel, a
boy born in the strange community, starts asking
questions. Dr. Francis knows he should stop them,
but, curious, gives partial answers. But Abel is not
so docile as the others.
Capt. Peters Lionel Stevens
Dr. Francis Donald Houston
Zenna Peters Carla Challoner
Abel Granger James Hunter
Matthias Granger John Moore
Mrs. Granger Joyce Donaldson
Sarah Granger Janet Gallagher
Mrs. Peters Wendy Johnson
Matthew Peters Karl Lanchbury
Jeremiah Baker Peter Bennett
Mrs. Baker Christine Lander
Mark Baker Roy Hills
Ruth Baker Janet Fairhead
Sgt. Burke Robert Russell
Capt. Sanger John Line
Col. Chalmers John Abineri
Gen. Short Noel Johnson
Dr. Kersh Robert James

Director: Peter Potter
Designer: Trevor Williams

(13 December 1965)

The Midas Plague

w Troy Kennedy Martin, *story by* Frederick Pohl
The Robot Age has arrived, producing more than
enough of everything. Man has only to consume
and, in theory, enjoy himself. But superabundance
brings problems for Morrey, who is low on the so-
cial scale in a world where such values have been re-
versed and only the rich are privileged enough to
lead the simple life, while the "poor" are swamped
with more goods than they can possibly consume.
Morrey Graham Stark
Edward Julian Curry
Wainwright Victor Brooks
Henry Anthony Dawes
George Robert Sidaway
Edwina Anne Lawson
Gideon Graham Lines
Police robot Michael Earl
Counsel Geoffrey Alexander
Judge A.J. Brown
Prisoner Sydney Arnold
Analyst David Nettheim
Fred Sam Kydd
Rebel leader David Blake Kelly
Rebels Richard Davies, Arne Gordon
Sir John John Barron

Director: Peter Sasdy
Designer: William McCrow

(20 December 1965)

Season Two

The Machine Stops

w Clive Donner & Kenneth Cavander, *story by*
   E.M. Forster
An Edwardian vision of a future dominated by ma-
chines. A mother and her son struggle to maintain
their natural bond of love in a world in which human
beings have become tyrannized by machines.
Vashti Yvonne Mitchell
Kuno Michael Gothard
Airship attendant Nike Arrighi
Airship passenger Jonathan Hansen
Voice of friend Jane Jordan Rogers
Girl Lucy Hill

Director: Philip Saville
Designer: Norman James

(6 October 1966, BBC2)
(BBC1 rpt: 15 April 1967)*

* At the time of their original transmission, BBC2 was still
unavailable in parts of the country, so six of the Season Two
plays were also showcased on BBC1.

Frankenstein Mark II

w Hugh Whitemore
A stranger calls at the home of divorcee Anna Preston, asking to collect some of her ex-husband's belongings. Anna agrees, but is suspicious, and tries to contact her "ex" at the space-research establishment where he worked. But none of his colleagues can tell her where he is and the authorities block all her efforts to find out. Anna grows more convinced that he is in danger, but the truth is more horrifying than even she can imagine.
Dr. Morrison David Langton
Security man Michael Beint
Dr. Giddy Bernard Archard
Anna Preston Rachel Roberts
Smithers Wolfe Morris
Mrs. Burgoyne Annette Kerr
Insp. Gilliat Richard Carpenter
Nurse Dorothea Phillips
George Preston Basil Henson

Director: Peter Duguid
Designer: Tony Abbott

(13 October 1966)

Lambda 1

w Bruce Stewart, *story by* Colin Kapp
In a distant future, a new form of space travel has evolved—travel through the Earth by a system known as Tau whereby the displacement of atoms enables one solid body to pass through another. But it's still experimental, and when a spaceship gets lost, anxiety mounts, especially as the wife of the Senior Controller is on board. The controller and a friend set out on a rescue mission.
Bridie Mary Webster
Julie Kate Story
Ferris Michael Lees
Dantor Charles Tingwell
Alex Geoffrey Frederick
Birch Geoffrey Kenion
Harvey Anthony Wager
Mary Jessica Dunning
American Murray Kash
Brett Danvers Walker
Porter Sebastian Breaks
Benedict Ronald Lewis
Rorsch Jan Conrad
Oriental Andy Ho
Caradus Peter Fontaine

Director: George Spenton-Foster
Designer: Peter Seddon

(20 October 1966)

Level Seven

w J.B. Priestley, *story by* Mordecai Roshwald
After completing his final training on defense computers, "H" is entitled to three weeks' leave. But his colonel tells him he must first visit certain underground installations. "H" goes to Level 7, 4500 ft. below ground, unaware that he has been sent there for good . . .
X127 ("H") Keith Buckley
Colonel Michael Bird
General Anthony Bate
Doctor Tom Criddle
Woman commandant Jane Jordan Rogers
X117 David Collings
R747 Michele Dotrice
New man Sean Arnold
Air supply officer Anthony Sweeny
Radio Man One David Cargill
Radio Man Two Raymond Hardy
Man Glenn Williams
Woman Patricia Denys

Director: Rudolph Cartier
Designer: Norman James

(27 October 1966, BBC2)
(BBC1 rpt: 29 April 1967)

Second Childhood

w Hugh Leonard
Charles Dennistoun, a 60-year-old contestant on *You Bet a Million*—a quiz show for millionaires—wins the jackpot prize, a course in rejuvenation. But his friends and family have mixed feelings, and the repercussions have blackly comic effects on all concerned.
Charles Dennistoun Nigel Stock
Kenneth Dennistoun Donald Pickering
Joan Dennistoun Geraldine Newman
Betty Dennistoun Betty Cooper
Tom Dennistoun John Horsley
Ronnie Cash Roland Curram
Dr. Willi Herstein Robin Phillips
Dr. Gerhardt Keppler Hugo Schuster
Dr. Odile Keppler Caroline Blakiston
Maid Sybilla Kay

Director: John Gorrie
Designer: Tony Abbott

(10 November 1966, BBC2)
(BBC1 rpt: 6 May 1967)

The World in Silence

w Robert Gould, *story by* John Rankine
College student Sarah Richards is alone in fearing and disliking the new teaching machines but even she does not foresee the terrifying situation that arises when her supervisor, Stephen Kershaw, re-arranges the machines to conform with revised fire regulations.
Sarah Richards Deborah Watling
Eric Lonsbury John Baskcomb
George Kenneth Gardiner
Stephen Kershaw Mark Eden
Geoffrey Harrison John Allison
Florrie Nadine George
Harold Stephen Whittaker
Freda Sara Aimson
Mrs. Richards Susan Field
Davison Noel Davis
Chief Supt. Mailer Richard Hampton
Gen. Harboard Keith Pyott
Dr. Hammond Erik Chitty

Director: Naomi Capon
Designer: William McCrow

(17 November 1966)

The Eye

w Stanley Miller, *story by* Henry Kuttner
Julian Clay is accused of murdering Andrew Maddox—a charge he cannot deny because "The Eye," a device which records the past, saw him do it. However, the law affords one loophole.
Andrew Maddox Leslie Sands
Julian Clay Anton Rodgers
Stevens John Wentworth
Munder Eric Young
Bea Valerie Gearson
Judge Frank Singuineau
Josephine Wanda Ventham
Caller Peter Noel Cook

Director: Peter Sasdy
Designer: Norman James

(24 November 1966)

Tunnel under the World

w David Campton, *story by* Frederick Pohl
In a world where brain patterns run machinery, and powerful new advertising techniques appear daily, Guy and Mary Birkett live apparently humdrum lives—until one day Guy makes a discovery. (This tale was a satire on advertising and featured miniature "people" being studied on a table top by an advertising firm.)

Guy Birkett Ronald Hines
Mary Birkett Petra Davies
Swanson Timothy Bateson
Miss Mitkin Fanny Carby
Spelman Peter Madden
Salesman Bryan Hunt
April Dorn Gay Hamilton
Waiter Patrick Parnell

Director: Alan Cooke
Designer William McCrow

(1 December 1966)

The Fastest Draw

w Julian Bond, *story by* Larry Eisenberg
A science fiction western. Millionaire eccentric Amos Handworthy is determined to keep the Old West alive and has installed an original Pecos saloon as part of his fully automated electronics factory. When Peter Stenning flies in from England to work in this strange set-up, he becomes irresistibly drawn into conflict with his domineering boss.
Peter Stenning James Maxwell
The Pilot Jerry Stovin
Marie Crane Patricia English
Amos Handworthy Ed Begley
Emma Bowles Annette Carell

Director: Herbert Wise
Designer: Peter Seddon

(8 December 1966, BBC2)
(BBC1 rpt: 13 May 1967)

Too Many Cooks

w Hugh Whitemore, *story by* Larry Eisenberg
Dr. Andrew Cook, inventor of a process for making living replicas of human beings, has unwittingly duplicated himself and becomes a secret weapon in the Solar System's struggle for economic survival against a powerful alien culture, the Sentients.
Dr. Andrew Cook Paul Daneman
Wattari Marius Goring
Mrs. Emily Cook Jean Aubrey
Brenner John Wood
Dr. Duval Cyril Shaps
Easterbrook John Gabriel
Czesni John Hollis

Director: John Gibson
Designer: Raymond Cusick

(15 December 1966)

Walk's End

w William Trevor
Dr. Saint's offer of a free place in his comfortable old-folks' home appears entirely philanthropic to Miss Claythorpe. However, he is suspiciously vague about the treatment that goes with it.
Dr. Saint John Robinson
Mrs. Dakers Brenda de Banzie
Maid Sally Travers
Matron Elizabeth Begley
Miss Claythorpe Susan Richards
Miss Ormsby Mary Hinton
Maj. Gregory Sebastian Shaw
Mr. Bone Felix Aylmer
Mrs. Hope Ailsa Grahame
Mr. Wardle Henry Oscar
Mr. Quire Carleton Hobbs
Manservants Sylvester Morand, Christopher Owen

Director: Ian Curteis
Designer: William McCrow

(22 December 1966)

Satisfaction Guaranteed

w Hugh Leonard, *story by* Isaac Asimov
First of two Asimov comedies about robots. Larry Belmont, an ambitious executive working for U.S. Robots, embarks on a business trip, leaving his wife, Claire, to take charge of Tony—a robot that, though indistinguishable from a man, is programmed to do housework 24 hours a day, seven days a week.
Dr. Inge Jensen Ann Firbank
K.G. Bullen Bruce Boa
Larry Belmont Barry Warren
Claire Belmont Wendy Craig
Brenda Claffern Helen Horton
Miriam Swann Valerie Colgan
Deirdre Schwartz Patty Thorne
Tony Hal Hamilton
Assistant Rodney Archer

Director: John Gorrie
Designer: Norman James

(29 December 1966, BBC2)
(BBC1 rpt: 22 April 1967)

The Prophet

w Robert Muller, *from the story* The Reason *by* Isaac Asimov
Dr. Susan Calvin has seen some strange developments in her 60 years as a robot psychologist, but none stranger than robot QT-1. (The character of Dr. Calvin had also appeared in another Asimov story, "Little Lost Robot," in the 1962 ITV anthology series *Out of This World*, and appears again in a Season Three episode, "Liar!")
Dr. Susan Calvin Beatrix Lehmann
Interviewer James Cossins
QT-1 Tenniel Evans
Greg Powell David Healy
Mike Donovan Brian Davies
Martha Powell Julie Allan
Abigail Donovan Judy Keirn
Van Muller Michael Wolf
Robots Ron Eagleton, Robin Sherringham, Chris Blackwell, Jim Wyatt, Graham Lawson, George Rutland, Tony Barnes, Derek Davis
Robot voices David Graham, Haydn Jones, Roy Skelton

Director: Naomi Capon
Designer: Richard Henry

(1 January 1967, BBC2)
(BBC1 rpt: 20 May 1967)

Season Three

Immortality Inc.

w Jack Pulman, *story by* Robert Sheckley
An aging man of the future reaches back into the 20th century for a "young, active body" into which he can transfer his mind; and a young man from 1969 is suddenly transported into a strange and terrifying future.
Mark Blaine Charles Tingwell
Dr. Cole Robert MacLeod
Tom Clarke Derek Benfield
Marie Thorne Dallia Penn
Earth Blaine Peter Van Dissel
Reilly Peter Swanwick
Reject Donald Morley
Theologian Christopher Denham
Sammy Tom Rowman
Hull Peter Copley
Irma Henderson Nancie Jackson
Davis Tommy Eytle
Clerk Dee MacDonald
Technicians John Berwyn, Brian Cullingford, Edward Davies, John Gulliver, Tony Handy

Director: Philip Dudley
Designer: Peter Seddon

(7 January 1969)

Liar!

w David Campton, *story by* Isaac Asimov
Robot RB34 is to be demonstrated to the press to quieten public concern about possible dangers from the growing number of robots. But RB34 has a fault—it is telepathic. Somehow it has been programmed to read minds—secret schemes, desires and all. And who is without his secrets?
Herbie (RB34) Ian Ogilvy
Dr. Lanning Hamilton Dyce
Dr. Susan Calvin Wendy Gifford
Dr. Bogert Gerald Sim
Milton Ashe Paul Chapman
Hargraves Roy Hanlon
Kelvin Brooke Robert James
Cleaner Jumoke Debayo
Brooke's secretary Anna Perry
Jamieson Edwin Richfield
Mary Curl Jenny Russell
Receptionist Rita Davies

Director: Gerald Blake
Designer: Martin Johnson

(14 January 1969)

The Last Lonely Man

w Jeremy Paul, *story by* John Brunner
Time: the future. The government of the day has won many votes with the introduction of its new Contact Service just before the election. Contact banished the fear of death. A man's body may die, but his mind can now pass into someone still alive—a relative, friend or loved one. But what of the man who is friendless and unloved? He must make Contact with someone—whatever the cost.
James Hale George Cole
Rowena Hale June Barry
Patrick Wilson Peter Halliday
Man Norman Hartley
Girl Annabella Johnston
Ambulanceman Berry Fletcher
Police inspector Guy Standeven
Sir Barrimore Jones Gerald Young
Mary Lillias Walker
Sam Peter Welch
George Bryan Mosley
Young girl Gillian Shed
Young man Albert Lampert
Consultant Eve Ross
Goddard Anthony Woodruff
Jenkins Richard Wardale
Henry Stanley Meadows

Director: Douglas Camfield
Designer: Richard Wilmont

(21 January 1969)

Beach Head

w Robert Muller, *story by* Clifford Simak
Commandant Decker, disenchanted veteran of 36 faultless space missions, finds the cause and cure for his dissatisfaction when a new planet subtly defeats the "infallible" technology that has hitherto overcome all eventualities, however unknown.
Tom Decker Ed Bishop
Cassandra Jackson Helen Downing
Bertrand Le Maitre John Gabriel
Oliver MacDonald James Copeland
A.G. Tiosawa Robert Lee
N.B. Waldron Vernon Dobtcheff
Ensign Warner-Carr Barry Warren

Director: James Cellan Jones
Designer: Tony Abbott

(28 January 1969)

Something in the Cellar

w Donald Bull
Eccentric professor Monty Lafcado, haunted by the powerful memory of his dead mother, builds a monster computer in his cellar.
Monty Lafcado Milo O'Shea
Bettina June Ellis
Fred Murray Melvin
Dr. Pugh Clive Morton
Inspector Clifford Cox
Sergeant Brian Grellis
Waitress Nova Sainte-Claire
Taxi driver Lane Meddick
Blonde Priscilla Tanner
Monster John Lawrence

Director: Roger Jenkins
Designer: John Wood

(4 February 1969)

Random Quest

w Owen Holder, story by John Wyndham
Physicist Colin Trafford is blown up in a laboratory accident and finds himself in a parallel world where he has a ready-made life as a novelist, a new group of friends and business acquaintances, and is married to a beautiful girl who apparently hates him. How can Colin explain that he is not the man she thinks he is?
Colin Trafford Keith Barron
Taxi driver George Lee
Ottilie Tracy Reed
Mrs. Walters Beatrice Kane
Dr. Harshom Noel Howlett
Munnings Arnold Ridley
George Charles Lamb
Martin Bernard Brown
TV newsreader McDonald Hobley
Gerry Carole Boyer
Trevor Bernard Finch
Bates Reg Peters
Laura Anna Darlington
Nurse Maclean Molly Weir
Mrs. Gale Beryl Cook

Director: Christopher Barry
Designer: Roy Oxley

(11 February 1969)

The Naked Sun

w Robert Muller, story by Isaac Asimov
Baley, a detective from Earth, is assigned to investigate a murder on the planet Solaria, where all the inhabitants live in isolation attended by a large number of robots, and communicating by a form of three-dimensional viewer.
Baley Paul Maxwell
Minnim Sheila Burrell
Daneel David Collings
Gruer Neil Hallett
Thool Eric Chitty
Attlebish Ronald Leigh-Hunt
Quemot John Robinson
Leebig Frederick Jaeger
Gladia Trisha Noble
Rikaine Paul Stassino
Bik John Hicks
Robots David Cargill, Raymond Hardy, Roy Patrick, John Scott Martin, Gerald Taylor

Director: Rudolph Cartier
Designer: James Weatherup

(18 February 1969)

The Little Black Bag

w Julian Bond, story by C.M. Kornbluth
An electronic medical kit of the future is accidentally transported back in time to the present day when it falls into the hands of a drunken, disqualified doctor, Roger Full, who builds up a successful practice in cosmetic surgery, while being blackmailed by a vicious young woman, Angie. (Also filmed in America for *Rod Serling's Night Gallery*.)
Dr. Gillis Robert Dean
Mike James Chase
Dr. Hemingway Dennis Bowen
Al Harvey Hall
Dr. Roger Full Emrys Jones
Samuels Leon Cortez
Angie Geraldine Moffatt
First youth Bill Lyons
Second youth Peter King
Johnny Ian Frost
Edna Flannery Elizabeth Weaver
Mallinson Alan Downer
Mr. Collins John Dunbar
Kelland John Woodnutt
Receptionist Katherine Kessey
Mrs. Coleman Honora Blake

Director: Eric Hills
Designer: Barry Learoyd

(25 February 1969)

1 + 1 = 1.5

w Brian Hayles
Comedy set at the beginning of the next century. Britain is proud of its population control system, based on computer analysis and an anti-fertility factor. But national complacency is rudely shattered when Mary Beldon, the wife of a highly esteemed population officer, becomes pregnant for the second time, though she is licensed for only one child.
Mary Beldon Julia Lockwood
Henry Beldon Garfield Morgan
John Stewart Bernard Horsfall
TV announcer Bernard Holley
Miss Harvey Lynda Marchal
Mrs. Proctor Frances Bennett
Gosford Geoffrey Palmer
Minister Petra Davies
Secretary Clare Shenstone
First man Steve Peters
Second man Derek Chafer
Susanna Chloe Ashcroft
Reporter Juan Moreno
Yates Davyd Harries
Computer voice John Witty

Director: Michael Ferguson
Designer: Barry Learoyd

(4 March 1969)

The Fosters

w Michael Ashe
An old tramp is found dead with signs that someone had tried to operate on his head; a youth disappears; the wife of biochemist Harry Gerwyn falls into a coma that baffles the doctors. Then a caller, introducing himself as Mr. Foster, invites Gerwyn to visit him and his sister at a quiet suburban address. The Fosters appear a perfectly ordinary retired couple—but they possess scientific knowledge far in advance of Gerwyn.
Bob Alan Ross
Geoff Anton Darby
Anne Pauline Cunningham
Miss Foster Freda Bamford
Mr. Foster Richard Pearson
Sally Gerwyn Ann Penfold
Harry Gerwyn Bernard Hepton
Mary Gerwyn Yvonne Manners
Calton Kevin Stoney
Digby John Dawson
Geoff's mother Rose Hill
Japhet John Berwyn
Cazalet Richard Pescud

Director: Philip Dudley
Designer: Marilyn Taylor

(11 March 1969)

Target Generation

w Clive Exton, *story by* Clifford Simak
A puritan, superstitious, inward-looking community of the future is confined within The Ship. They have been there for generations and have long forgotten why. They know that one day they will feel a tremor in the ship, but only one man, Jon Hoff, has inherited the secret of what must be done when the tremor comes. (Remake of a version first scripted for ITV's *Out of This World* in 1962.)
Jon Hoff David Buck
Joe Manx Ronald Lacey
Joshua Owen Berry
Jon as a boy Gary Smith
Jon's father Godfrey Kenton
Mary Hoff Suzan Farmer
Martin Toke Townley
Mrs. Kane Ruth Kettlewell
George Michael McGovern

Director: Roger Jenkins
Designer: Tony Abbott

(18 March 1969)

The Yellow Pill

w Leon Griffiths, *story by* Rog Phillips
Well-known psychiatrist John Frame is asked by the police to examine a murderer. It seems a routine case, but the young man seems to possess startling powers and knows intimate details of the psychiatrist's private life. (This, too, was a remake of a version shown in *Out of This World*.)
John Frame Francis Matthews
Helen Carter Angela Browne
Insp. Slinn Glynn Edwards
Wilfrid Connor Stephen Bradley
Plain-clothes men Steve Peters, James Haswell
Radio voice Carl Conway

Director: Michael Ferguson
Designer: Roy Oxley

(25 March 1969)

Get off My Cloud

w David Climie, *story by* Peter Phillips
Science fiction writer Marsham Craswell has had a mental breakdown. Though lying inert on a hospital bed, in his mind he is living through one of his own fantasies. In an effort to bring him back to reality, a doctor uses a new device to link the writer's mind to that of the most level-headed man he knows, Pete, an Irish sports reporter. But when Pete finds himself in Craswell's bizarre world, he wonders if he was wise to take the job.
Young Pete Robert Duncan
Parnell Jon Croft
Pete Donal Donnelly
Stephen Peter Barkworth
Marsham Craswell Peter Jeffrey
Police Sgt. Alec Ross
Taxi driver Royston Tickner
Garer Vicki Woolf

Director: Peter Cregeen
Designer: Raymond P. Cusick

(1 April 1969)

Season Four

Taste of Evil

w John Wiles
Stephen Chambers, a new master of Warby Stones school for "ultra-intelligent boys," finds strange things happening to him. Reason tells him that they must be linked with the boys' Psychic Phenomena Club.
Chambers Maurice Roëves
Mackinley Peter Copley
Bellows Jack Lambert
Maurice Gerry Davis
Andrew John Moulder-Brown
Crabbe Sebastian Abineri
Sinclair Keith Skinner
Boston Martin Howells
Cull Ian Pigot
Matron Katherine Parr
Boys John Ash, Norman Bacon, Paul Frazer, Brent Oldfield, Shane Raggett, David Smith, Mark Wilding

Director: Michael Ferguson
Designer: Paul Allen

(21 April 1971)

To Lay a Ghost

w Michael J. Bird
Young photographer Eric Carver and his bride Diana—a girl with a traumatic past—move into an old house with which she feels a strong affinity. When a ghost appears in pictures he takes of her in their new home, Eric calls in a psychic researcher—and precipitates a crisis.
Eric Carver Iain Gregory
Diana Carver Lesley-Anne Down
Dr. Phillimore Peter Barkworth
Ewan Mackenzie Clifford Cox
Police inspector Geoffrey Russell
Thomas Hobbs Walter Randall

Director: Ken Hannam
Designer: Fanny Taylor

(28 April 1971)

This Body Is Mine

w John Tully
Research physicist Allen Meredith discovers a means of transferring his mind into another man's body—but the process is reciprocal.
Jack Gregory Jack Hedley
Allen Meredith John Carson
Ann Meredith Alethea Charlton
Elizabeth Gregory Sonia Graham
George Simpson Hector Ross
Tony Randall Darryl Kavann

Sheila Norma West
John Pinner Anne Kidd
Harvey Bruno Barnabee
Rawlinson John Rolfe

Director: Eric Hills
Designer: Sally Hulke

(5 May 1971)

Deathday

w Brian Hayles, *novel by* Angus Hall
Adam Crosse seems a normal, well-integrated member of society. But in reality, his marriage is a failure, he is a hypochondriac and a tranquilizer addict, needing only a final nudge to push him over the edge. One morning, his wife tells him she has a lover.
Adam Crosse Robert Lang
Lydia Crosse Lynn Farleigh
Quilter John Ronane
Postman Roy Evans
Stanley Hudson Lindsay Campbell
Dorothy Hudson Valerie Lush
Det. Chief Insp. Schofield Simon Merrick
Det. Sgt. Roberts Leslie Schofield
Joanne Susan Glanville
Arnold Douglas Wells
Telephone operator Gina Manicorn
Newsreader Tim Gudgin

Director: Raymond Menmuir
Designer: John Stout

(12 May 1971)

The Sons and Daughters of Tomorrow

w Edward Boyd
The small East Anglian village of Plampton has one distinction—a famous unsolved murder. A cynical journalist decides to go there to see what he can stir up. But Plampton is a community linked by telepathy and led by a witch . . .
Shawlor Gascoyne William Lucas
Simon Willows Malcolm Tierney
Rosa Cavendish Margery Withers
Hamilton White David Griffin
Jeanette Pamela Salem
Wilfrid Russell Arthur Pentelow
Isiah Christopher Reynolds
PC Wilkes Chris Tranchell
Tom Palfrey Edward Evans
Dr. Lesley Clifford Brenda Kaye
Coroner Les Shannon
Undertakers Brian Jacks, Peter Wilson-Holmes

Director: Gerald Blake
Designer: David Spode

(19 May 1971)

Welcome Home

w Moris Farhi

Psychiatrist Frank Bowers comes home after six months in hospital following an accident, to find another man in his place—a man who looks nothing like him, but who his wife and everyone else says is her husband.
Penny Bowers Jennifer Hilary
Bowers-One Anthony Ainley
Bowers-Two Bernard Brown
Det. Sgt. Greene Gerald Sim
Dr. Liam Moore Derek Benfield
Sam Sheppard David Morrell
Sheila Sherwood Margaret Anderson
John Sherwood Alan Downer
Miss Pringle Pamela Craig
PC Jones David Munro

Director: Eric Hills
Designer: Sally Hulke

(26 May 1971)

The Last Witness

w Martin Worth

A man, Harris, wakes up in a hotel on a small island after a shipwreck. He keeps recognizing flashes of what he sees, until he realizes his visions are of actions yet to come—culminating in murder. (Later remade as an episode of *Hammer House of Mystery and Suspense*.)
Harris Anthony Bate
Mrs. Kemble Sheila Brennan
Dr. Benson James Kerry
Sgt. Walker Lawrence James
David Michael McStay
Ann Denise Buckley
Businessman Brian Sullivan
Mrs. Fane Joyce Carey
Barbara Joanna Ross
Bus driver Milton Brehaut

Director: Michael Ferguson
Designer: Chris Pemsel

(2 June 1971)

The Man in My Head

w John Wiles

A small group of soldiers have been briefed for a dangerous mission. But the briefing has been imprinted on their subconscious minds and can only be released by a special signal.
Stock Martin Thurley
Sanders David Whitman
Fulman Robert Oates
Camber Robert Walker
Brinson Tom Chadbon
Ira Marianne Benet
Denman James Drake
Lydia Elizabeth Bell
Hine Kenneth Watson

Director: Peter Cregeen
Designer: Jeremy Davies

(9 June 1971)

The Chopper

w Nigel Kneale

The vengeful spirit of a dead motorcyclist is reluctant to leave his wrecked machine and manifests itself to a woman journalist as motorbike noise.
Jimmy Reed Patrick Troughton
Chaser George Sweeney
Sandie Margaret Brady
Rupert Molloy David Wood
Lorna Venn Ann Morrish

Director: Peter Cregeen
Designer: Tim Harvey

(16 June 1971)

The Uninvited

w Michael J. Bird

A middle-aged couple are disturbed during the night by a series of unwelcome visitations. (Later remade as an episode of *Hammer House of Mystery and Suspense*.)
George Pattison John Nettleton
Millicent Pattison June Ellis
Donald Ramsey Brian Wilde
Frances Mervyn Shirley Cain
Jack Mervyn Geoffrey Palmer
Jessica Ramsey Hilary Mason
Blonde woman Bobbie Oswald
PC Wheeler David Sinclair
Fuller David Allister

Director: Eric Mills
Designer: John Burrowes

(23 June 1971)

The Shattered Eye

w David T. Chantler

A chance meeting with an old tramp brings a violent force into a young painter's life.
Lester Freddie Jones
Alec Richard Warwick
Gwenn Tessa Wyatt
Gavin Peter Arne
Barton John Wentworth
Tony Sebastian Breaks
Randall James Copeland
Perris John Saunders
Jackson Lee Fox
Arcade manager Michael Lynch

Director: Peter Hammond
Designer: Chris Thompson

(30 June 1971)

OUT OF THIS WORLD

Considering ITV's timid approach to adult science fiction over the years, it seems somewhat remarkable to record that they can claim the honor of Britain's first series of science fiction plays. Yet there they were, straddling the summer of 1962, 13 one-hour dramas introduced by the master of the macabre, Boris Karloff.

And through the lineage of its creator, Irene Shubik, this pioneering anthology was also the ancestor of the BBC's prestigious *Out of the Unknown* (see previous entry). At the time, Shubik was ABC Television's story editor and had already established a strong track record in picking plays for *Armchair Theater*.

For *Out of This World* she tapped the talents of leading sf writers including genre giants Isaac Asimov, Philip K. Dick and Clifford Simak, enlisting notable British TV writers such as Clive Exton and Leon Griffiths to adapt their stories. The series also featured the work of another promising writer—Terry Nation, later to become the creator of the Daleks, *Survivors* and *Blake's 7*.

Being an anthology, *Out of This World* found time and space to explore different styles and moods of science fiction, from the grimmer suspense of "Impostor," "Botany Bay" and "The Dark Star," through tender intrigue in "Medicine Show" and the macabre comedy of "Vanishing Act," to broad satire in "The Tycoons."

(The principal British script in Shubik and White's original schedule, John Wyndham's "Dumb Martian," was "lifted" by ABC's drama boss Sydney Newman and shown in the preceding Sunday's *Armchair Theater* slot as a curtain raiser to the series proper, with Boris Karloff appearing at the play's end to announce the impending start of the series, six days later. It is listed here, in that context, for ease of reference.)

REGULAR CAST
Host Boris Karloff

Story editor: Irene Shubik
Producer: Leonard White

An ABC Television Network Production
13 black and white 60-minute plays
30 June–22 September 1962

Dumb Martian

story by John Wyndham
Too old to fly, 35-year-old boorish space pilot Duncan Weaver is drafted as keeper of a remote space station. To offset the loneliness, he buys Lellie, a Martian girl, as wife and housekeeper. Like all "Marts," Lellie has a totally expressionless face, and Weaver treats her as little better than a dumb animal. But when an intelligent young geologist, Dr. Alan Whint, joins them, Lellie becomes a point of conflict between the two men and proves to be not as dumb as her husband thought.
Reception clerk Garfield Morgan
Chief Charles Morgan
Duncan Weaver William Lucas
Harry Michael Bird
Mac Michael Pratt
Alastair Morris Perry
Lellie Hilda Schroder
Withers Raymond Adamson
Alan Whint Ray Barrett

Director: Charles Jarrott
Designer: James Goddard
Producer: Sydney Newman

An ABC Television Network Production
60 minutes, black and white, for *Armchair Theater*

(24 June 1962)

The Yellow Pill

dramatized by Leon Griffiths, *story by* Rog Phillips
An alleged murderer is brought by the police to psychiatrist Dr. Frame, claiming that he was born in 1962 and comes from another time. Though a complete stranger, he possesses an uncanny knowledge of the doctor's private life. (Remade for *Out of the Unknown*.)
John Frame Nigel Stock
Michael Connor Richard Pasco
Insp. Slinn Peter Dyneley
Helen Carter (receptionist) Pauline Yates
with Gerald Turner, Robert Pitt

Director: Jonathan Alwyn
Designer: Robert MacGowan

(30 June 1962)

Little Lost Robot

dramatized by Leo Lehman, *story by* Isaac Asimov

The time: 2039. The place: Hyper Base 7, near Saturn. Black, an engineer, working on a space project, angrily tells a robot to "get lost"—and the mechanical man takes him at his word, joining up with a group of 20 others who are in revolt against their masters. Base commander Maj. Gen. Kallner sends for robot psychologist Susan Calvin who is very fond of robots and treats them like children. She is horrified to hear that the "lost" robot has been modified.

Black Gerald Flood
Robot Roger Snowden
Peter Bogert Murray Hayne
Maj. Gen. Kallner Clifford Evans
Dr. Susan Calvin Maxine Audley
Walensky Haydn Jones

Director: Guy Verney
Settings: Douglas James

(7 July 1962)

Cold Equations

adapted by Clive Exton, *story by* Tom Godwin

Teenager Lee Cross stows away on a mercy rocket flight taking life-saving serum to six men on the planet Woden, hoping to see her brother who has been there for eight years. But her extra weight means the rocket doesn't have enough fuel to reach its destination, presenting the pilot, Capt. Barton, with a difficult equation that he and ground control strive desperately to solve.

Bill May William Marlowe
Capt. Barton Peter Wyngarde
Perry Godfrey James
Selfe Patrick Holt
Commander Delhart Peter Williams
Lee Cross Jane Asher
Gerry Cross Richard Gale
Ship's records clerk Piers Keelan

Director: Peter Hammond
Designer: Paul Bernard

(14 July 1962)

Impostor

dramatized by Terry Nation, *story by* Philip K. Dick

Earth is at war with the Outspacers. Security officer Maj. Peters believes that an Outspace robot bomb is masquerading as top scientist Roger Carter. Condemned to death, a horrified Carter tries desperately to prove his innocence . . . or is Peters right?

Frank Nelson Glyn Owen
Maj. Peters Patrick Allen
Roger Carter John Carson
Jean Baron (Carter's secretary) Angela Browne
Paul Kirby Keith Anderson
Alan Richards Philip Anthony
Control Colin Rix
Security chief Paul Bacon
Darvi Louida Vaughan
Landon Alec Ross
Mary Carter June Shaw
Mute-O Walter Randall

Director: Peter Hammond
Designer: Robert Fuest

(21 July 1962)

Botany Bay

w Terry Nation

Psychiatry student Bill Sheridan discovers that patients at an institution where he is working are being possessed by aliens. When he reveals his belief he is forced to kill a "possessed" orderly in self-defense. Convicted of murder, Sheridan is committed to the same clinic. His only hope of convincing the world that a covert invasion is taking place is to persuade his brother Dave and girlfriend Betty that he is not crazy . . .

Bill Sheridan William Gaunt
Pierce Storm Durr
Monroe Norman Johns
Adams Donald Douglas
Garfield Anthony Bate
Miss Hayes Virginia Stride
Dave Sheridan Julian Glover
Janitor Reginald Smith
Betty Madison Ann Lynn
Harding Richard Clarke
Wilson Peter Jesson
Tyler Aubrey Morris
Dr. Polk Jerry Stovin

Director: Guy Verney
Designer: Douglas James

(28 July 1962)

Medicine Show

dramatized by Julian Bond, story by Robert
Moore Williams
The close-knit community of a small American town
is thrown into hysteria by the arrival of two mysteri-
ous medicine men whose remarkable cures seem to
originate with a strange machine. Doctor's wife, Lil
Harmon, tries to find out its secret—and why the two
strangers ask only for seeds in payment.
Dr. Harmon Alan MacNaughtan
Lil Harmon Jacqueline Hill
Sam Barrett Vic Wise
Ellen Madeleine Burgess
Yanvro Carl Bernard
Pienster Peter Madden
Silas Washam Nigel Arkwright
Mrs. Washam Natalie Lynn
Donna Culver Elaine Millar
Jason Kemper Ken Wayne
Mrs. Culver Margo Cunningham
Culver Rory MacDermot
Dr. Lapham Martin Wyldeck
Sheriff Raymond Adamson

Director: Richmond Harding
Designer: Adrian Vaux

(4 August 1962)

Pictures Don't Lie

dramatized by Bruce Stewart, story by Kather-
ine Maclean
Radio research worker Nathen picks up signals com-
ing from a spaceship hovering near Earth and suc-
ceeds in communicating with his "opposite number"
aboard the ship. Speech and pictures are received
showing that the occupants are humanoid—and
friendly. But can they trust us?
Nathen Gary Watson
Major Race Roger Avon
Butch Judy Cornwell
Col. Ford Reginald Marsh
Parker Blake Butler
Jacob Luke Milo O'Shea
Dr. Trayne Madi Hedd
Bud Kenneth Watson
Journalists Richard Wilding, Gordon Sterne,
David Hemmings
Commander Frank Gatliff
Aliens Bill Mills, Gary Wyler
Man from the Ministry Norman Claridge

Director: John Knight
Set: Brian Currah

(11 August 1962)

Vanishing Act

w Richard Waring
Struggling, hen-pecked conjuror Edgar Brocklebank
buys a box that once belonged to a famous dead ma-
gician, the Great Vorg, and becomes an instant suc-
cess. But no one, least of all Edgar, can explain away
the complete disappearance of his attractive assistants
and countless objects and animals that have passed
through his box.
Edgar Brocklebank Maurice Denham
Harold William Job
John Philip Grout
Freda Hoggin Jennifer Wilson
Harriet Brocklebank Joan Heath
Maj. Bentley Edward Dentith
Shop assistant Barry Wilsher
Customer Ivor Bean
Mr. Hoggin Cameron Miller
Benjy Hoggin Terence Woodfield
Furrier John Frawley
Second furrier Evan Thomas
Reporter William Buck
Reg Herbert Richard Klee
Mr. Daventry Robert Lankesheer
Schreiber David Lander
Nancy Sheena Marshe
Youth Donald Webster
Insp. Wright Derek Newark
Vorg Godfrey Quigley

Director: Don Leaver
Designer: Robert Fuest

(18 August 1962)

Divided We Fall

dramatized by Leon Griffiths, story by Raymond F. Jones
2033: Eddy, the world's most powerful computer,
has accused synthetic beings, "the Syns," of work-
ing as fifth columnists for a hostile space power.
Syns can be identified by a variation in their brain
waves. Tests become compulsory and all detected
Syns are arrested. Scientist Arthur Bailey is called
on to help. But two years on the planet Cyprian,
without automation, have made him distrustful of
Eddy and sceptical of the Syns' existence.
Dr. Waldron Ronald Radd
Col. Tanner Gerald Harper
Dr. Arthur Bailey Bernard Horsfall
Jean Bailey (his wife) Ann Bell
Burrows John Barcroft
Sheen Ian Clark
Passenger Kenneth Keeling
Dr. Exner Norman Scace
"Eddy" Piers Keelan
Prison guard Bill Mills
Security guard Marc Ashlyn
Sir Gerald Christie Clive Morton

Director: John Knight
Designer: Ann Spavin

(25 August 1962)

The Dark Star

adapted by Denis Butler, *from the novel* Ape of London *by* Frank Crisp

A mysterious disease is sweeping through London, giving its victims superhuman strength in the early stages. Most alarmingly, however, it seems to be selecting targets, with each link in the chain leading a step higher in status. Where will it end and how did it start? Scotland Yard chiefs and scientist Dr. Howard must find out—fast.

Joan Thurgood Rosemary Miller
Jim Thurgood John Garvin
George Chalmers Michael Hawkins
Miss Guthrie Vanessa Thornton
Commander Delabo Bruce Beeby
John Irvine Jerome Willis
Det. Sgt. Grant Ronald Wilson
Supt Hartley William Dextor
Mrs. Chalmers Yvette Rees
Dr. Howard Barrie Cookson
Asst. Comm. Lucas Keith Pyott
Police Sgt. Charles Bird
Dr. Kendal John Moore

Director: Peter Hammond
Designer: Philip Harrison

(1 September 1962)

Immigrant

adapted by Terry Nation, *story by* Clifford Simak

What is the secret of Kimon—the strange El Dorado planet, rich in mineral wealth, which only allows the very brightest minds to become immigrants, and from where no one has ever returned to spend the vast fortunes they have sent back to relatives on Earth? A baffled World Government asks the latest "immigrant," Seldon Bishop, to solve the mystery.

Seldon Bishop Gary Raymond
Pat Penelope Lee
Maggie Christine Shaw
Johnston Walter Glennie
Roberts Gary Hope
Kate Bishop Ann Saker
Morley John Horsley
Kimonian man Ian Shand
Monty Archer Bruce Boa
Maxine Vivienne Drummond
For Frank Singuineau
Kimonian employment officer Jill Melford
David Peter Layton
Elaine Jo Rowbottom
Father Donald Eccles

Director: Jonathan Alwyn
Settings: Voytek

(8 September 1962)

Target Generation

adapted by Clive Exton, *story by* Clifford Simak

A belief handed down through the centuries that when the Tremor comes it signifies the beginning of the End; a community where reading is heresy; and a letter marked "to be opened only in an emergency." These elements come together for Jon Hoff who *can* read and must decide whether the beginning of the End is emergency enough! (Remade for *Out of the Unknown.*)

Jon's father Michael Golden
Jon (as a boy) Hugh Janes
Jon Hoff Dinsdale Landen
Joe Manx Paul Eddington
Mary Hoff Susan Maryott
Martin Edwin Finn
Mrs. Kane Ann Tirard
George Mathias Philip Madoc
Joshua Bert Palmer

Director: Alan Cooke
Designer: Douglas James

(15 September 1962)

The Tycoons

adapted by Bruce Stewart, *story by* Arthur Sellings

When zealous taxman Oscar Raebone calls unexpectedly on the Project Research Company, a firm making novelty dolls, and encounters the Tycoons, mysterious strangers led by Abel Jones, he turns up a situation that can only be described as out of this world . . .

Abel Jones Charles Gray
Mary Jones Geraldine McEwan
Fred Smith John Cater
Miss Cook Patricia Mort
Oscar Raebone Ronald Fraser
Mr. Starling Alastair Williamson
Mr. Crampsey Edwin Apps
Bubbles Jill Curzon
Girl Sheree Winton

Director: Charles Jarrott
Designer: Patrick Downing

(22 September 1962)

OUT OF THIS WORLD (U.S.)

U.S. sitcom about a girl called Evie who is your average teenager except for one thing—her father, Troy, is an alien.

On her 13th birthday Evie inherits special powers from her extra-terrestrial dad. These include freezing time, making things thinner and "gleeping"—using the power of her thoughts to turn objects, or people, into whatever she wants them to be. As the series progresses, and Evie gets older, she gains more powers—including clairvoyance.

Troy remains heard but never seen, communicating with Evie and her mother Donna via an energy cube.

Like so many juvenile U.S. sitcoms, the series was short on laughs and long on moralizing. Doug McClure, best known as Trampas in the sixties Western series *The Virginian*, provided loony interludes as the town's oddball mayor—and later police chief—Kyle Applegate, an ex ham actor whose most famous role was as a costumed crimefighter, Mosquito Man. His job as mayor was later taken by Donna.

Other recurring characters included Evie's Uncle Beano and boyfriend Chris and school pal Lindsay. The series ran for four seasons in America.

MAIN CAST

Evie Garland Maureen Flannigan　*Donna Garland* Donna Pescow
Beano Froelich Joe Alaskey　*Kyle Applegate* Doug McClure
Lindsay Selkirk Christine Nigra　*Voice of Troy* Burt Reynolds

Created by: John Boni, Bob Booker
Based on a format by: D.L. Wood
Executive Producer: Bob Booker
Writers: Various, including John Boni, Mike Scully, Bob Booker, Brian Scully, Laura Levine, Tommy Thompson, Frank Mula

Directors: Various, including Bob Claver, Jack Regas, Scott Baio

Bob Booker Productions
96 color 25-minute episodes
U.K. premiere: 9 April 1990
(ITV)

THE OUTER LIMITS

"There is nothing wrong with your television set. Do not attempt to adjust the picture. We are controlling transmission . . . we will control the horizontal. We will control the vertical . . . For the next hour, sit quietly and we will control all you see and hear . . . You are about to participate in a great adventure. You are about to experience the awe and mystery which reaches from the inner mind to *The Outer Limits*."

The Outer Limits was *the* bug-eyed monster show. Other series might explore the bizarre or the fantastic with the aim of exciting, amusing or merely arousing dormant gray cells, but this 1960s American anthology series was designed to scare the living daylights out of its audience.

Week after week, your television set was taken over by some of the creepiest aliens ever created for the small screen. These weren't cuddly ETs, these were full-blooded agents of terror, collectively dubbed "the Bears" by producer Joseph Stefano.

Stefano, writer of the screenplay for Hitchcock's classic *Psycho*, said of the grizzly creations: "The Bear is that one splendid, staggering, shuddering effect that induces awe or wonder or tolerable terror . . ." And among his more memorable "bears" were giant bugs with ugly humanoid faces for "The Zanti Misfits," living rocks for "Corpus Earthling," a shimmering mouthless Andromedan conjured up for "The Galaxy Being," a flat-faced cyclops in "O.B.I.T.," and "The Invisibles"—slug-like parasites that burrowed into their human hosts, attaching themselves to the spinal cord and dominating the subject's will.

But there was more to *The Outer Limits* than its monsters. Its brief was also to explore people and the nature of humanity through advancing and expanding diverse aspects of science such as time and space travel, other dimensions, strange experiments and alien psychologies.

The Outer Limits was created by television producer and playwright Leslie Stevens but it was Stefano who gave the show its discipline and its "bears." He encouraged the imaginative cinematography that won the series critical praise for its visual style—lots of low, wide-angled shots, deep shadows and dim lighting to heighten the tension and produce a "film noir" look and feel.

The only "regular" star apart from the disembodied voice of narrator Vic Perrin, was William O. Douglas Jr., who donned many of the outlandish monster costumes. But the show also gave big breaks to such "promising" young actors as David McCallum, Robert Culp and Martin Landau.

The Outer Limits played in America between 1963 and 1965.

REGULAR CAST
Narrator Vic Perrin

Creator/Executive producer: Leslie Stevens
Producers: Joseph Stefano *(Season One)* Ben Brady *(Season Two)*
Director of photography: Conrad Hall
Special effects: Projects Unlimited, John Nickolaus, Kenneth Peach, M.B. Paul, Larry Butler, Frank Van Der Veer
Music: Dominic Frontiere, Harry Lubin *(Season Two)*

A Daystar-Villa di Stefano Production for United Artists Television

49 black and white 60-minute episodes
U.S. premiere: 16 September 1963
U.K. premiere: 16 April–8 October 1964
(Granada Television)

(Author's note: as with many American series, the U.K. running order of *The Outer Limits* differed considerably from the original U.S. seasons—and even varied around those ITV regions that took it. For ease of reference, the episodes are listed in the original American sequence.)

Season One
32 episodes

The Galaxy Being

w Leslie Stevens
A radio station engineer experimenting with a 3-D TV receiver accidentally establishes contact with a friendly being from the galaxy Andromeda—and a surge of electrical power brings it to Earth where it causes unintentional terror.
Cast: Cliff Robertson, Jacqueline Scott, Lee Philips, William O. Douglas Jr., Mavis Neal, Allyson Ames

Director: Leslie Stevens

The Hundred Days of the Dragon

w Allan Balter & Robert Mintz
The new U.S. president is substituted with the agent of an Oriental despot who can alter skin structure and change his appearance.
Cast: Sidney Blackmer, Phil Pine, Mark Roberts, Nancy Rennick, Joan Camden, Clarence Lung, Richard Loo

Director: Byron Haskin

The Architects of Fear

w Meyer Dolinsky
A group of scientists create a fake alien to try to shock mankind from its course of self-destruction, but find that fear is not the answer . . .
Cast: Robert Culp, Geraldine Brooks, Leonard Stone, Martin Wolfson

Director: Byron Haskin

The Man with the Power

w Jerome Ross
A meek college professor acquires awesome and uncontrollable powers after a brain operation—powers to control inter-planetary electro-magnetic forces.
Cast: Donald Pleasence, Priscilla Morrill, Edward C. Platt, Fred Beir

Director: Laslo Benedek

The Sixth Finger

w Ellis St. Joseph (*additional material by* Joseph Stefano)
A scientist invests a machine that can speed up the process of evolution and tests it on a young, uneducated miner with immediate effect—the subject's forehead becomes higher, his fingers develop a third joint and the stub of a sixth finger begins to grow.
Cast: David McCallum, Edward Mulhare, Jill Haworth, Constance Cavendish, Nora Marlowe, Robert Doyle

Director: James Goldstone

The Man Who Was Never Born

w Anthony Lawrence
A spaceman passes through the time barrier into the future and finds Earth a barren desert—the result of Man's greed and selfishness. He brings back with him a battered, disfigured survivor from the 21st century—a man who can change the fatal course of history.
Cast: Martin Landau, Shirley Knight, John Considine, Karl Held, Maxine Stuart

Director: Leonard Horn

O.B.I.T.

w Meyer Dolinksy
A murder investigation reveals the existence of an alien via an electronic surveillance device.
Cast: Peter Breck, Jeff Corey, Harry Townes, Alan Baxter, Joanne Gilbert

Director: Gerd Oswald

The Human Factor

w David Duncan
The brains of two men are inadvertently switched during a secret experiment at a Greenland military base.
Cast: Gary Merrill, Harry Guardino, Sally Kellerman, Joe de Santis, Ivan Dixon

Director: Abe Biberman

Corpus Earthling

w Orin Borstein, *additional material by* Lou Morheim & Joseph Stefano
A doctor overhears a sinister conversation between two "rocks" planning to take over the Earth by possessing the bodies of humans. But is the plot real or all in his mind?
Cast: Robert Culp, Salome Jens, Barry Atwater

Director: Gerd Oswald

Nightmare

w Joseph Stefano
Creatures from the planet Ebon abduct some humans and subject their prisoners to an intensive interrogation.
Cast: Ed Nelson, James Shigeta, John Anderson, Martin Sheen, David Frankham, Bill Gunn

Director: John Erman

It Crawled Out of the Woodwork

w Joseph Stefano
A ball of dust sucked into a vacuum cleaner at the Energy Research Commission feeds on the motor's power and grows to an uncontrollable size.
Cast: Scott Marlowe, Kent Smith, Barbara Luna, Edward Asner, Michael Forrest, Joan Camden

Director: Gerd Oswald

The Borderland

w Leslie Stevens
Scientists and spiritualists open a door into the fourth dimension where they find everything is a mirror image of itself.
Cast: Nina Foch, Mark Richman, Gladys Cooper, Philip Abbott, Barry Jones, Gene Raymond, Alfred Ryder

Director: Leslie Stevens

Tourist Attraction

w Dean Riesner
A tycoon captures an enormous and supposedly extinct prehistoric fish while on a fishing cruise in South America.
Cast: Ralph Meeker, Henry Silva, Janet Blair, Jerry Douglas, Jay Novello

Director: Laslo Benedek

The Zanti Misfits

w Joseph Stefano
The dusty saloon of a Western ghost town—and a military garrison awaits the arrival of criminal exiles from the planet Zanti.
Cast: Bruce Dern, Michael Tolan, Robert F. Simon, Olive Deering, Claude Woolman

Director: Leonard Horn

The Mice

w Joseph Stefano & Bill S. Ballinger, *idea by* Lou Morheim

A cultural and scientific exchange has been arranged with the planet Chromo, and Earth awaits the arrival of the first Chromite.

Cast: Henry Silva, Diana Sands, Michael Higgins, Dabney Coleman, Ronald Foster, Hugh Langtry

Director: Alan Crosland Jr.

Controlled Experiment

w Leslie Stevens

Two Martians decide to make a thorough investigation of an Earth murder, so they record, play back and analyze the actual killing.

Cast: Barry Morse, Carroll O'Connor, Robert Fortier, Grace Lee Whitney

Director: Leslie Stevens

Don't Open Till Doomsday

w Joseph Stefano

Eloping teenagers spend their wedding night in a room that has been unoccupied since 1929. In it is a box containing a particularly malevolent alien.

Cast: Miriam Hopkins, Russell Collins, Buck Taylor, Nellie Burt, Melinda Plowman, David Frankham

Director: Gerd Oswald

Z-Z-Z-Z-Z

w Meyer Dolinsky (*additional material by* Joseph Stefano)

An entomologist's new assistant is really a queen bee in human form out to lure him into her world as a human drone.

Cast: Philip Abbott, Joanna Frank, Marsha Hunt, Booth Coleman

Director: John Brahm

The Invisibles

w Joseph Stefano

An undercover agent joins a secret society whose members have deliberately allowed their minds to be perverted by parasitic alien creatures.

Cast: Don Gordon, George Macready, Dee Hartford, Walter Burke, Tony Mordente, Neil Hamilton, Richard Dawson

Director: Gerd Oswald

The Bellero Shield

w Joseph Stefano & Lou Morheim

During an experiment with lasers, a scientist accidentally traps a space traveler from a remote light world. He is eager to learn the mysteries of the universe, but his wife tries to use the knowledge to her advantage.

Cast: Martin Landau, Sally Kellerman, Chita Rivera, Neil Hamilton, John Hoyt

Director: John Brahm

The Children of Spider County

w Anthony Lawrence

Five young geniuses vanish on the same day—and their father, an alien from a distant planet, arrives on Earth to claim his children.

Cast: Lee Kinsolving, Kent Smith, John Milford, Crahan Denton

Director: Leonard Horn

Specimen: Unknown

w Stephen Lord, *additional material by* Joseph Stefano

An officer in an experimental spacecraft finds a strange limpet-like growth on the outside of the ship.

Cast: Stephen McNally, Richard Jaeckel, Arthur Batanides, Gail Kobe, Russell Johnson

Directors: Gerd Oswald & Robert H. Justman

Second Chance

w Lou Morheim & Lin Dane (*alias* Sonya Roberts)

A group of people board a space ride at a funfair—only to find it's the real thing.

Cast: Simon Oakland, Janet DeGore, Don Gordon, John McLiam

Director: Paul Stanley

Moonstone

w William Bast

Lunar Expedition 1 has established a base on the moon, and finds a strange object that involves them in civil war on a distant planet.

Cast: Ruth Roman, Alex Nicol, Tim O'Connor, Curt Conway, Harri Rhodes

Director: Robert Flory

The Mutant

w Allan Balter & Robert Mintz, *story by* Joseph Stefano & Jerome Thomas
Earth's overflowing population has inhabited Annex One, a remote world with a climate similar to that of Earth. All goes well for the colonists until they meet . . . the "thing."
Cast: Larry Pennell, Warren Oates, Walter Burke, Betsy Jones-Moreland

Director: Alan Crosland Jr.

The Guests

w Donald S. Sanford, *based on a teleplay by* Charles Beaumont
A drifter arrives at a house where time stands still and where the residents are captives of a strange alien.
Cast: Geoffrey Horne, Nellie Burt, Vaughn Taylor, Gloria Grahame, Luana Anders

Director: Paul Stanley

Fun and Games

w Robert Specht & Joseph Stefano, *story by* Robert Specht
A man and a woman are mysteriously transported to a distant planet where they have been selected to fight beings from another world in a gladiatorial contest to the death, with the losers forfeiting the lives of their entire planet.
Cast: Nick Adams, Nancy Malone, Ray Kellogg, Bill Hart

Director: Gerd Oswald

The Special One

w Oliver Crawford, *additional material by* Joseph Stefano
A private tutor engaged to give scientific training to a young boy is an alien from the planet Xenon—and his lessons are in conquest.
Cast: Richard Ney, Macdonald Carey, Flip Mark, Marion Ross

Director: Gerd Oswald

A Feasibility Study

w Joseph Stefano
The Luminoids, grotesque inhabitants of a distant planet, select human beings for their slave labor.
Cast: Sam Wanamaker, Phyllis Love, Joyce Van Patten, David Opatoshu

Director: Byron Haskin

The Production and Decay of Strange Particles

w Leslie Stevens
A nuclear holocaust becomes imminent as a cluster of strange particles from another galaxy starts multiplying, unleashing incredible powers.
Cast: George Macready, Leonard Nimoy, Rody Solari, Joseph Ruskin, Allyson Ames, John Duke, Signe Hasso

Director: Leslie Stevens

The Chameleon

w Robert Towne, *story by* Robert Towne, Lou Morheim & Joseph Stefano
An intelligence agent disguises himself as an alien to infiltrate a group of space creatures who have landed on Earth.
Cast: Robert Duvall, Henry Brandon, Howard Caine, Douglas Henderson

Director: Gerd Oswald

The Forms of Things Unknown

w Joseph Stefano
A group of women with murder on their mind encounter a man from the past, a corpse that won't lie down and an eerie house containing a thousand clocks. (Unused pilot for an unsold series *The Unknown*.)
Cast: David McCallum, Vera Miles, Sir Cedric Hardwicke, Barbara Rush, Scott Marlowe

Director: Gerd Oswald

Season Two
17 episodes

Soldier

w Harlan Ellison, *additional material by* Seeleg Lester
A twist in time lands a soldier of the future in the present. He is the "ultimate soldier," trained to utterly destroy his enemy. But who is his enemy? (Hugo Award winner.)
Cast: Lloyd Nolan, Michael Ansara, Alan Jaffe, Tim O'Connor, Catherine McLeod, Jill Hill, Ralph Hart, Ted Stanhope

Director: Gerd Oswald

Cold Hands, Warm Heart

w Milton Krims, *story by* Dan Ullman
An astronaut returns in triumph from the first orbit of Venus. But his success is marred by strange dreams and inexplicable body temperature changes.
Cast: William Shatner, Geraldine Brooks, Malachi Throne, Lloyd Gough

Director: Charles Haas

Behold, Eck!

w John Mantley, *story by* William R. Cox, *based on a novel by* Edwin Abbott
An eye specialist finds his lab wrecked, patients dead or in shock and babbling of strange beings. The doctor puts on a pair of his own glasses and sees . . . the Invisible.
Cast: Peter Lind Hayes, Joan Freeman, Parley Baer, Jack Wilson

Director: Byron Haskin

Expanding Human

w Francis Cockrell
A university professor experiments with a drug that expands human consciousness—which not only increases his sensitivity, but also alters his appearance.
Cast: Skip Homeier, Keith Andes, James Doohan, Vaughn Taylor, Aki Aleong, Mary Gregory, Barbara Wayne, Robert Doyle

Director: Gerd Oswald

Demon with a Glass Hand

w Harlan Ellison
Alien soldiers from the distant future invade Earth. Their mission: to try to stop a war that is to happen in the future between Earth and themselves. They capture what seems to be the last survivor—a man with a strange hand. (Hugo Award winner.)
Cast: Robert Culp, Arline Martel, Steve Harris, Abraham Sofaer, Rex Holman, Robert Fortier

Director: Byron Haskin

Cry of Silence

w Robert C. Dennis, *based on a story by* Louis Charbonneau
Driving through a remote canyon, a couple are menaced by moving tumbleweeds.
Cast: Eddie Albert, June Havoc, Arthur Hunnicutt

Director: Charles Haas

The Invisible Enemy

w Jerry Sohl, *additional material by* Byron Haskin, Seeleg Lester, Ben Brady
Holy sand sharks! The noble-minded, steel-nerved leader of an expedition to Mars is menaced by a strange monster that "swims" in a sea of sand.
Cast: Adam West, Rudy Solari, Joe Maross, Chris Alcaide, Ted Knight, Bob Doqui, Peter Marko, Mike Mikler, Anthony Costello, James Tartan

Director: Byron Haskin

Wolf 359

w Seeleg Lester, *story by* Richard Landau
A scientist solves the secrets of creation by reproducing a miniature planet. But its development is so accelerated that it soon surpasses Earth and a potential nightmare is unleashed.
Cast: Patrick O'Neal, Sara Shane, Ben Wright, Peter Haskell

Director: Laslo Benedek

I, Robot

w Robert C. Dennis, *stories by* Otto Binder
A robot is accused of murder. The authorities insist on its destruction but its owner insists on the due process of law and hires an attorney to defend it.
Cast: Howard da Silva, Ford Rainey, Leonard Nimoy, Marianna Hill, John Joyt, Hugh Sanders, Read Morgan

Director: Leon Benson

The Inheritors

w Sam Newman & Seeleg Lester, *from an idea by* Ed Adamson *(a 2-part story)*
Four soldiers, struck by bullets handmade from the ore of a meteorite, develop a powerful alien intelligence that turns them into geniuses. They embark on a mysterious project involving a number of handicapped children.
Cast: Robert Duvall, Steve Ihnat, Ivan Dixon, Dee Pollack, James Frawley, Ted De Corsia

Director: James Goldstone

Keeper of the Purple Twilight

w Milton Krims, *based on a teleplay by* Stephen Lord
A sinister creature from outer space exchanges its advanced knowledge with a scientist's human emotions—but finds itself unable to understand such things as love and beauty.
Cast: Warren Stevens, Robert Webber, Gail Kobe, Curt Conway, Edward C. Platt

Director: Charles Haas

The Duplicate Man

w Robert C. Dennis, *story by* Clifford Simak
A 21st-century space anthropologist creates a duplicate of himself to recapture an escaped alien creature obsessed with a single emotion—hate.
Cast: Ron Randell, Sean McClory, Constance Towers, Mike Lane, Alan Gifford

Director: Gerd Oswald

Counterweight

w Milton Krims, *short story by* Jerry Sohl
Six carefully chosen passengers board a spaceship for a flight to a distant planet. But an alien force, fearing for its own security, creates terror and panic aboard the vessel.
Cast: Michael Constantine, Jacqueline Scott, Larry Ward, Charles Hradilac, Shary Marshall, Crahan Denton

Director: Paul Stanley

The Brain of Colonel Barham

w Robert C. Dennis, *story by* Sidney Ellis
Space explorer Alec Barham, suffering from an incurable disease, consents to have his brain transplanted into a robot man.
Cast: Grant Williams, Elizabeth Perry, Anthony Eisley *(Barham)*, Douglas Kennedy, Martin Kosleck, Peter Hansen, Wesley Addy, Paul Lukather, Robert Chadwick

Director: Charles Haas

The Premonition

w Sam Roeca & Ib Melchoir, *story by* Sam Roeca
A test pilot is about to crash when suddenly time stands still and the world around him freezes. As he struggles to return to the animate present, great danger threatens his family.
Cast: Dewey Martin, Mary Murphy, William Bramley, Emma Tyson, Dorothy Green, Kay Kuter

Director: Gerd Oswald

The Probe

w Seeleg Lester, *story by* Sam Neuman
A cargo plane flies into a hurricane and ditches into the sea. The crew scramble into a life-raft and run aground on a strange solid surface.
Cast: Mark Richman, Peggy Ann Garner, Ron Hayes, Janos Prohaska

Director: Felix Feist

THE OUTER LIMITS (1995)

Back in the sixties, aliens took over the airwaves as an unseen voice ominously announced: "There is nothing wrong with your TV set . . .for the next hour we will control all that you see and hear . . ." What followed was pretty scary stuff, but it *was* the sixties and sci-fi *was* comparatively new to TV.

Three decades later, there's little that audiences haven't seen and heard. A robot? Done that. Brave new world? Been there. Bug-eyed monster? Got the T-shirt. So on the face of it, *The Outer Limits*, nineties-style, can never hope to claim the same hallowed corner in our TV attic.

And in fairness, it doesn't try slavishly to emulate its pioneering predecessor. The control voice is still there (though the credit sequence is stunningly corny) and it's still an anthology series. But there's no monster of the week, *every* week—though those we do get are much more slickly realized than the old rubber costumes. And though the new *Outer Limits* is much sexier than its aged ancestor, complete with occasional nudity, this update has actually moved closer to that *other* big anthology series of the era—*The Twilight Zone*. Some stories are intended to scare, but all are meant to make us think—morality tales, wrapped up with a homespun "thought for the week."

That's the only flaw in what is otherwise a largely entertaining series. Indeed, the new *Outer Limits* launched with an impressive pilot, "Sandkings," starring three generations of the Bridges dynasty—Lloyd, son Beau and grandson Dylan. And the series' guest list has continued to be an interesting one. *Next Generation* favorite Michael Dorn appeared as an astronaut, *thirtysomething*'s Timothy Busfield played a detective, *The Waltons*' Richard Thomas was a scientist, David Warner a ruthless businessman, Rebecca De Mornay a beautiful alien, and Leonard Nimoy returned for the series' only remake of a sixties episode, *I Robot*. Then, he played the robot put on trial for murdering its creator. This time he's the defending attorney.

As in all anthologies, some installments work better than others, but the series is at its best when it doesn't labor the morality. The makers would do well to remember that they may think they control the transmission, but these days we viewers control the remote!

REGULAR CAST
Control Voice Kevin Conway

Executive producers: Pen Densham, Richard B. Lewis, John Watson
Co-executive producers: Michael Cassutt *(Season One)*, Jonathan Glassner, Scott Shepherd *(both Season Two)*
Producers: Justis Greene, Brent-Karl Clackson
Executive consultant: Joseph Stefano (Season One)
Theme: Mark Mancina, John Van Tongren

A Trilogy Entertainment Group and Atlantis Films Production
43 color 45-minute episodes (60 minutes on Sky) unless stated (Season One 21 episodes, Season Two 27 episodes)
U.S. premiere: 26 March 1995
U.K. premiere: 1 May 1995
(BBC2)

Season One:

Sandkings (90-minute premiere)

w Melinda Snodgrass, *novella by* George R.R. Martin
Research biologist Dr. Simon Kress has transformed inert eggs brought back from the Martian surface into living organisms. When one of these organisms almost escapes, the project is shut down. But Kress doesn't want to abandon the work so he steals a sample of the soil and begins raising the strange scorpion-like creatures in his barn. As the Sandkings begin to show some intelligence, building elaborate castles in the sand, Kress alienates his family as he gradually descends into dementia, until he finally loses control of the creatures.
Dr. Simon Kress Beau Bridges
Colonel Kress Lloyd Bridges
Cathy Kress Helen Shaver
Josh Kress Dylan Bridges
Dave Stockley Kim Coates

Director: Stuart Gillard

Valerie 23

w Jonathan Glassner
Lonely paraplegic Frank Hellner reluctantly agrees to allow an experimental "inorganic human" robot named Valerie to be his companion for a week. As the sensual Valerie becomes increasingly affectionate, Frank succumbs to her passion. But when he starts dating his physical therapist Rachel, Valerie turns jealously homicidal.
Frank Hellner Bill Sadler
Valerie Sofia Shinas
Rachel Rose Nancy Allen
Charlie Rogers Don Butler
Technician Bruce Harwood

Director: Timothy Bond

Blood Brothers

w Brad Wright
Two brothers, one noble, one greedy, wrestle for control of a million-dollar drug company—and a vaccine that could hold the secret to eternal life becomes the focus for their bitter, and deadly, struggle.
Michael Deighton Martin Kemp
Spencer Deighton Charles Martin-Smith
Carl Toman Thomas Cavanagh
Tricia Lange Kate Vernon
Darrow George Touliatos
Patricia Fowler Colleen Winton

Director: Tibor Takacs

The Second Soul

w Alan Brennert
An alien race, the N'Tal, have made contact with mankind. They don't seek to enslave or destroy us but they do want something—our dead! The aliens are wraith-like parasites who need to inhabit the bodies of other species to survive. Dr. Michael Alders is assigned to lead the N'Tal reinhabitation project and finds himself unable to decide whether the N'Tal's intentions really are benign. His dilemma grows when a friend is killed in a car crash and her body given to the N'Tal.
Dr. Michael Alders Mykelti Williamson
Jim Heatherton D.W. Moffett
Karen Heatherton/Llanar Rae Dawn Chong
Kadimas Richard Grove
Jeffrey Littman Kent Gallie
Nancy Madison Graie
David Aftergood Julian Christopher

Director: Paul Lynch

White Light Fever

w David Kemper
An experiment threatens nature's order of existence, when eccentric centenarian billionaire Harlan Hawkes pays a brilliant cardiologist to help him cheat death.
Dr. Mac McEnerney Bruce Davison
Harlan Hawkes William Hickey
Dr. Anne Crain Sonja Smits
Jesse Wells Michelle Beaudoin
Walker Benjamin Ratner

Director: Tibor Takacs

The Choice

w Ann Lewis Hamilton
A young girl with strange psychic powers is shunned by her friends but welcomed by a nanny with similar gifts, who tries to prevent her falling into the hands of a shadowy government agent.
Aggie Travers Thora Birch
Karen Ross Megan Porter Follows
Jean Anderson Frances Sternhagen
Terry Walsh Matthew Walker
Joe Travers Page Fletcher
Leslie Travers Sandra Nelson

Director: Mark Sobel

Virtual Future

w Shawn Alex Thompson
A brilliant young scientist finds a way to see the future, but gets caught up in a billionaire's ambitious political schemes and must change the future to save his own life.
Jack Profit Josh Brolin
Isabelle Profit Kelly Rowan
Bill Trenton David Warner
Wayne Fowler Bruce French

Director: Joseph L. Scanlan

Living Hell

w Pen Densham & Melinda Snodgrass
Construction worker Ben Kohler's life is saved by having an experimental chip implanted in his brain, but later he starts seeing and experiencing images of violent killings and hears a strange haunting voice calling out to him . . .
Ben Kohler Sam Robards
Dr. Jennifer Martinez Elizabeth Pena
Wayne Haas Stephen Shellen

Director: Graeme Campbell

Corner of the Eye

w David Schow
A disillusioned priest is given healing powers by demonic aliens who use him as they attempt to save their planet by destroying Earth.
Father Anton Jonascu Len Cariou
Dr. Pallas Chris Sarandon
Father John Royce Justin Louis
Officer Fletcher Bill Croft
Carlito Callum Keith Rennie
Victorine Tamsin Kelsey
Miranda Vanessa Morley

Director: Stuart Gillard

Under the Bed

w Lawrence Meyers
A young child is abducted from his bedroom and the only witness is his six-year-old sister. And under hypnosis, the traumatized girl says the boogeyman got him . . .
Dr. Jon Hoffman Timothy Busfield
Det. Caitlin Doyle Barbara Williams
Sharon Rosman Laura Bruneau
Jillian Rosman Colleen Rennison
Andrew Rosman Henry Beckman

Director: Rene Bonniere

Dark Matters

w Alan Brennert
Pilot Paul Stein's transport vessel is suddenly thrown out of hyperspace by a chunk of dark matter that warps time and space, trapping the ship in a black, starless void alongside another vessel which vanished ten years earlier—with Paul's brother Kevin aboard.
Paul Stein John Heard
Lydia Manning Annette O'Toole
Rob Anderson Michael Dolan
Erin Whitley Allison Hossack

Director: Paul Lynch

The Conversion

w Brad Wright, *story* "Two Strangers" *by* Richard B. Lewis
A greedy, vengeful ex-con's life changes when he encounters visitors from another world who instil in him a new sense of compassion for others.
Henry Marshall Frank Whaley
Lucas John Savage
Mary Kerry Sandomirsky
Woman Rebecca DeMornay
Bartender Roger R. Cross
Ed William B. Davis

Director: Rebecca DeMornay

Quality of Mercy

w Brad Wright
When one of Earth's best fighter pilots is taken as a prisoner in the intergalactic wars, he's thrown into a dank, dark cell, where his fellow inmate is a traumatized young cadet who is being painfully turned into an alien by their captors. But appearances can be deceptive . . . and a secret told in pity could prove fateful.
Major John Skokes Robert Patrick
Bree Tristan Nicole DeBoer

Director: Brad Turner

The New Breed

w Grant Rosenberg
A gifted scientist's nanotechnology has created microscopic robots that can repair damaged cells and render man impervious to disease. A desperate friend, who has just been told he has terminal cancer, injects the nanobots into his body and they cure him. But they go on to correct *every* defect, turning him into a superhuman who cannot even take his own life . . .
Dr. Stephen Ledbetter Richard Thomas
Andy Groening Peter Outerbridge
Judy Hudson Tammy Isbell
Dr. Merritt L. Harvey Gold
Dr. Katzman Veena Sood

Director: Mario Azzopardi

The Voyage Home

w Grant Rosenberg
When an astronaut returning from Mars discovers an alien aboard the ship, he must face the loss of his crewmates and sacrifice his own life to prevent the creature reaching Earth.
Ed Barkley Jay O. Sanders
Alan Wells Matt Craven
Pete Claridge Michael Dorn

Director: Tibor Takacs

Caught in the Act

w Rob Forsyth
A particularly raunchy episode. A chaste student is possessed by a strange alien force that gives her an insatiable sexual appetite, perpetuated by seducing willing men who are then "consumed" by her body. Can her boyfriend's "pure" love overcome her craving?
Hannah Valesic Alyssa Milano
Jay Jason London
Professor Hugaro Saul Rubinek
Det. Barnett Garry Chalk
Quarterback Kavan Smith
Karl Stephen Fanning

Director: Mark Sobel

The Message

w Brad Wright
A deaf woman with a hearing implant is plagued by nightmares and strange sounds in her head that turn out to be a cry for help from an alien planet.
Jennifer Winter Marlee Matlin
Robert Larry Drake

Director: Joseph L. Scanlan

I, Robot

w Alison Lea Bingeman, *story by* Otto Binder
Remake of an episode from the 1960s series. Adam, a powerful robot, is put on trial for murder after killing its creator.
Thurman Cutler Leonard Nimoy
Adam Jake McKinnon
Mina Link Cyndy Preston
Col. Birch Nathaniel Deveaux
Det. Barclay Ken Schneider
Judge Clancy Ken Kramer
Dr. Linstrop Robert Clothier
Dr. Link Don Mackay
Voice of Adam John Novak

Director: Adam Nimoy

If These Walls Could Talk

w Manny Coto
Physicist and skeptic Levi Mitchell is a man with a mission—to prove ghosts don't exist. Then he meets Lynda Tillman who tells him her son was "taken" by a haunted house. Investigating, he discovers that the house isn't haunted—it's alive and it's hungry!
Levi Mitchell Dwight Schultz
Lynda Tillman Alberta Watson

Director: Tibor Takacs

Birthright

w Michael Berlin & Eric Estrin
An environmentally friendly U.S. senator's life changes drastically after a freak accident, when he discovers he's actually an alien in disguise, with a mission to change surreptitiously the Earth's atmosphere making it poisonous to man but compatible for the aliens.
Richard Adams Perry King
Dr. Leslie McKenna Mimi Kuzyk

Director: William Fruet

Voice of Reason

w (not known)
A civilian with strong ties to the military desperately tries to convince a high level committee that aliens are trying to take over the human race.
Randal Strong Gordon Clapp
Thronwell Daniel J. Travanti
Waters Lochlyn Munro
Perry Kate Robbins
Callahan Don S. Davis
Fisk Gillian Barber

Director: (not known)

Season Two

A Stitch in Time

w Steven Barnes
FBI agent Jamie Pratt is investigating a puzzling series of murders committed over the last 30 years with the same gun—but it's a gun that hadn't even been made when the first murder was carried out.
Dr. Theresa Givens Amanda Plummer
Jamie Pratt Michelle Forbes
Corey Wulf Andrew Airlee
Jerome Horowitz Sam Khouth
Warren Adrian Hughes
Alison Kendall Cross
Young Theresa Corrie Clark

Director: Mario Azzopardi

Resurrection

w Chris Brancato
Life on Earth has been wiped out by biological warfare, leaving only androids. But two of those androids, Martin and Alicia, have a secret project— Cain, a human cloned from the DNA of a single hair. But they must keep his existence hidden from the military droids determined to stamp out any trace of the human race.
Alicia Heather Graham
Martin Nick Mancuso
Cain Dana Ashbrook
Moloch Ken Kirzinger
with: Patrick Keating

Director: Mario Azzopardi

Unnatural Selection

w Eric A. Morris
A couple decide to have a genetically enhanced baby—it's a process that should bring them perfection, but could bring them a monster. Then they learn the dark secret that their neighbours keep in the basement.
Howard Sharp Alan Ruck
Joanne Sharp Catherine Mary Stewart
Fran Blake Mary Elizabeth Rubens
Tony Blake Andrew Wheeler
Timmy Blake Ryan Slater
John Arkelian Harrison Robert Coe

Director: Joseph L. Scanlan

I Hear You Calling

w Scott Shepherd, *story by* Catherine Weber
A reporter picks up a suspicious conversation on her mobile phone. Investigating, she becomes involved in a deadly game of cat and mouse concerning a strange man with violet eyes, an ill-fated cruise and people who disappear leaving behind only a pile of purple ash.
Carter Jones Ally Sheedy
Strange man Michael Sarrazin
Herbert Jones Ken Pogue
Toby Collins John Tench
Harmon Jon Cuthbert
Taylor Jano Frandsen

Director: Mario Azzopardi

Mind Over Matter

w Jon Cooksey & Ali Marie Matheson
When an accident puts his colleague into a coma, a scientist decides to test the power of his new virtual reality system to tap into her brain and admit his true feelings. But he doesn't expect his invention to have feelings too . . .
Sam Stein Mark Hamill
Rachel Debrah Farentino
Dr. Sarrazin Scott Hylands

Director: Brad Turner

Beyond the Veil

w Chris Brancato
After flashbacks of an alien abduction drive him to the brink of suicide, Eddie Wexler is committed to an asylum where he and other "abductees" are treated with a controversial technique. But have their abductors infiltrated the institute? (Michael O'Keefe is better known as Fred in *Roseanne*, while Stephen McHattie played the assassin in *The X-Files* episode "Nisei.")
Eddie Wexler Michael O'Keefe
Courtney Finn Carter
Dr. Sherrick Stephen McHattie
with: Nathaniel Deveaux, Alex Diaklin

Director: Allan Eastman

First Anniversary

w Jon Cooksey & Ali Marie Matheson, *story by* Richard Matheson Sr.
As he celebrates his first wedding anniversary, Norman Glass thinks he's the luckiest man alive—until he experiences increasingly violent revulsion when he touches, smells or tastes his beautiful wife, Ady.
Norman Glass Matt Frewer
Ady Michelle Johnson
Barbara Jayne Heitmeyer
Dennis Clint Howard
Dr. Phillips Paul McLean
First Ady Kathrin Nicholson
with: Steve Bacic

Director: Brad Turner

Straight and Narrow

w Joel Metzger
When his mother decides to send him to an ultra-strict private school, rebellious teenager Rusty Dobson finds out that it doesn't just build the leaders of tomorrow—it controls them, using computer chips implanted in the students' brains.
Rusty Dobson Ryan Phillippe
Dr. Werner Tom Butler
Charlie Walters Jonathan Scarfe
Harrison Taylor Kavan Smith
Principal Kern Peter Donat
Marianne Dobson Jane McDougall
James Scardale Tygh Runyan

Director: Joseph L. Scanlan

Trial by Fire

w Brad Wright
On the day of his inauguration as U.S. President, a peace-loving liberal is faced with his first crisis—an armada of alien ships is approaching Earth. But are they invaders bent on conquest, or explorers reaching out to another civilization.
President Charles Halsey Robert Foxworth
Elizabeth Halsey Diana Scarwid
Tarkman Ian Tracey
General Covington Lawrence Dane
Janet Brevson Teryl Rothery
Dr. Norris Bruce Harwood
with: Dale Wilson

Director: Jonathan Glassner

Worlds Apart (aka Remittance Man)

w Chris Dickie
Space agency director Nancy MacDonald gets a lesson in the meaning of time and distance with an unexpected signal from astronaut Christopher Lindy who disappeared 20 years earlier, and is now stranded, alone, on an unknown and hostile planet.
Lt. Christopher Lindy Chad Willett
Nancy MacDonald Bonnie Bedelia
Greg Tilman Michael MacRae
Col. Raymond Chen Robert Ito
Senator O'Reilly Donnelly Rhodes

Director: Brad Turner

The Refuge

w Alan Brennert
Raymond Bava collapses during a blizzard and awakens in a private refuge run by Sanford Valle. But a sudden moment of violence leads him to a question: What is reality?
Raymond Bava James Wilder
Sanford Valle M. Emmet Walsh
Gina Beaumont Jessica Steen
Dr. Franklin Dreeden Paul Jarrett
Thomas Valle David McNally
Justine Valle Deb Podowski
Debi Lisa Melilli

Director: Ken Girotti

Inconstant Moon

w Brad Wright, *story by* Larry Niven
When lonely physics professor Stanley Hart realizes that the sun has gone nova, he knows that mankind has only a few hours to live. In that time he resolves to make up for lost years, by courting Leslie, a woman he has secretly loved for two years.
Stanley Hart Michael Gross
Leslie Joanne Gleason
Henry Walker Jeremy Hart
Crazed man Tom Heaton
Bartender William deVry

Director: Joseph L. Scanlan

From Within

w Jonathan Glassner
Madness overtakes a small town when workers in a salt mine unearth ancient parasitic worms that attack the brains of their hosts, causing a breakdown of inhibitions. As the townsfolk turn to lust and violence, their only hope of salvation lies with Howie, a mentally slow boy who remains unaffected.
Howie Morrison Neil Patrick Harris
Sheila Morrison Christine Hurt
Jake Hart Patrick Stevenson
Charlotte Nichols Gabrielle Miller
Evan Charles Andre
Clark Aaron Pearl
Sheriff Lewis David Fredericks

Director: Neill Fearnley

The Heist

w Steven Barnes
An embittered ex-soldier helps a radical militia leader hijack an army shipment. But instead of weapons, the container holds a deadly alien lifeform that begins a "chilling" series of attacks—literally freezing its victims.
Lee Taylor Costas Mandylor
Capt. Teri Washington Jasmine Guy
Major Mackie Colm Feore
Calvin Taylor Philip Granger
Tyson Ruddick Barry Pepper
Bethany Wallace Katya Gardner

Director: Brad Turner

Afterlife

w John Whelpley

Linden Stiles, a man convicted of murder, is given a grim choice—accept execution or become the subject of a secret military experiment. Opting for the experiment, he discovers he is to be injected with DNA from an alien life form.

Linden Stiles Clancy Brown
Maculhaney Alan Rachins
Dr. Ellen Kursaw Barbara Garrick
General Post Duncan Fraser
Priest Sean Allan
Alien Terry Howson

Director: Mario Azzopardi

The Deprogrammers

w James Crocker

With Earth under alien rule and millions dead, mankind has been programmed to slavery. A small band of rebels kidnaps Evan, the alien leader's personal slave, and deprograms him until he agrees to join them and assassinate his former master.

Evan Cooper Erich Anderson
Trent Davis Brent Spiner
Jill Cooper Nicole Oliver
Akira Matsumoto Sam Khouth
Koltok & Megwan Vince Hammond

Director: Joseph L. Scanlan

Paradise

w Jonathan Walker & Chris Dickie

When three apparently healthy young women age and die within hours, Dr. Christina Markham and her sheriff husband are baffled and frightened. Only after Christina's mother Helen and her long-time friend Gerry vanish is the answer to the puzzle finally revealed.

Dr. Christina Markham Mel Harris
Sheriff Grady Markham Geraint Wyn Davies
Gerry Harold Gould
Helen Maxine Miller
Young Helen Heather Hanson

Director: Mario Azzopardi

The Light Brigade

w Brad Wright

Sequel to the first season episode "Quality of Mercy." On a desperate mission, a young cadet learns the difference between heroic ideals and the bitter realities of war.

Cadet Wil Wheaton
Major John Skokes Robert Patrick

Chief Graham Greene
Boramir Adrian Hughes
Engineer Mike Kopsa
Soldier Adrian Holmes

Director: Michael Keusch

Falling Star

w Michael Bryant

Suicidal pop singer Melissa McCammon encounters an ardent fan from the future who persuades her to give life a second chance. But in the process she changes history and now authorities from the future want Melissa dead.

Melissa McCammon Sheena Easton
Brian Chason John Pyper-Ferguson
Terry McCammon Xander Berkeley
Janet Marshall Kristen Lehman
Rachel Conners Sarah Strange
Geoff Chancelor Peter Bryant

Director: Ken Girotti

Out of Body (aka Ethically Yours)

w James Crocker

Scientist Rebecca Warfield experiments on herself to find out what really happens during an out-of-body experience. But her assistant Amy, secretly a religious fanatic opposed to the work, tampers with the equipment, leaving Rebecca trapped in another dimension.

Rebecca Warfield Peri Gilpin
Ben McCormick Victor Garber
Amy Joely Fisher
John Wymer William B. Davis
Dr. Minkoff Alan Robertson
Carl Haven Richard Sargent

Director: Mario Azzopardi

Vanishing Act

w Chris Dickie, *story by* Jonathan Walker

Husband Trevor McPhee shows up ten years after he disappeared, insisting that he's only been gone a few hours. After reconciling with his wife he vanishes again—for another decade.

Trevor McPhee Jon Cryer
Theresa McPhee Jessica Lundy
Ray Carter Dean McDermott
Dr. Golden Eric Schneider
Young Mark McPhee Brennan Kotowich
Older Mark McPhee Richard Ian Cox

Director: Jonathan Glassner

The Sentence

w Melissa Rosenberg
An ambitious inventor creates a "virtual prison" with which convicts serve a life sentence in just a few hours. His demonstration seems to work, until they connect an innocent man to the apparatus . . .
Dr. Jack Henson David Hyde Pierce
Dana Elwin Andrea Roth
Senator Meade Garwin Sanford
Cory Izacks Doron Bell Jr.
Detective Robyn Driscoll
Convict P. Adrien Dorval

Director: Joseph L. Scanlan

Season Three

Second Thoughts

w Sam Egan
A dying scientist transfers his memories and experiences into a retarded man's brain.
Karl Durand Howie Mandel
Rose Ciotti Jennifer Rubin
Dr. Valerian John Gilbert

Director: Mario Azzopardi

Re-Generation

w Tom J. Astle
When a woman is impregnated with her dead son's cells to create a clone, she begins experiencing his memories, which may include his own murder.
Justin Liam Ranger
Rebecca Highfield Kim Cattrall
Graham Highfield Daniel Benzali
Dr. Lucy Cole Teryl Rothery

Director: Brenton Spencer

Last Supper

w Scott Shepherd
A young man brings home his date, only to discover his father saved her from a government experiment 20 years before . . . And she hasn't aged a day since then.
Frank Martin Peter Onorati
Jade Sandrine Holt
Carol Martin Dey Young
Dr. Lawrence Sinclair Michael Hogan
Danny Fred Savage

Director: Helen Shaver

Stream of Consciousness

w David Shore
When people can tap into a virtual Internet at will, the man who can't because of a brain injury is considered a cripple . . . until a virus threatens the "Stream" and he is the last person still functioning.
Ryan Unger George Newbern
Cheryl Suki Kaiser
Mark Shane Meier
Stanley Blu Mankuma

Director: Joe Nimziki

Dark Rain

w David Braff
When most of the world is rendered sterile after a chemical war, parents flee a government agency intent on using their healthy newborn to repopulate the world.
Tim Don Franklin
Sherry Rachael Crawford
Dr. Royce Alan Scarfe

Director: Mario Azzopardi

The Camp

w Brad Wright
A conquered humanity has lived in concentration camps for 12 generations, forced to work for alien masters, until one woman discovers the secret of the camp guards and leads a rebellion.
Woman Harley Jane Kozak
Commandant David Hemblen
Bearded man Bill Cobbs
Scarred man John Tench

Director: Jonathan Glassner

Heart's Desire

w Alan Brennert
An alien makes four outlaws virtually invincible in the Old West.
Jake Miller Caspar Van Dien
Ben Miller Gary Basaraba
J.D. Kelton Jed Rees
Preacher David Longworth
Miriam Turner Ocean Hellman
Tom Grant John Novak
Frank Kelton Esai Morales

Director: Mario Azzopardi

Tempests

w Hart Hanson
When a spaceship on a rescue mission crashes, its crew comes up against predatory alien spiders who have the power to cause powerful hallucinations.
John Virgil Eric McCormack
Dr. Vasquez Kenneth Welsh
Governor Mudry Marie Stillin
Corinne Virgil Charlene Fernetz
Captain Parker Burt Young

Director: Mario Azzopardi

The Awakening

w James Crocker
An emotionless woman is cured with a brain implant.
Beth Carter Lela Rochon
Dr. Steven Molstad Gordon Pinsent
Joan Garrison Michele Greene
Kevin Flynn Roger R. Cross
Dolly Kellerman Micki Maunsell

Director: George Bloomfield

New Lease

w Sam Egan
Two doctors discover the power to bring the dead back to life . . . but the resurrected dead return changed.
Dr. James Houghton Stephen Lang
Terence Kelly Oscar Reynolds
Page Houghton Nancy Sorel
Dr. Charles McCamber Michael Ontkean

Director: Jason Priestley

Double Helix

w Jonathan Glassner
A brilliant scientist trying to unlock the key to future human evolution goes too far when he uses himself as a test subject, increasing his intelligence—and mutating his body.
Dr. Martin Nodel Ron Rifkin
Paul Nodel Ryan Reynolds
Dean Hardwick Ken Pogue

Director: Mario Azzopardi

Dead Man's Switch

w Ben Richardson
Four loners man doomsday devices deep underground, mankind's last defense against an alien invasion . . . until something or someone begins picking them off one by one.
Ben Conklin James LeGros
Donnelly Rhodes General James Eiger

Director: Jeff Woolnough

Music of the Spheres

w Steven Barnes
Alien sounds beamed to Earth have an addictive—and mutating—effect on teenagers.
Dr. Emory Taylor Howard Hesseman
Devon Taylor Joshua Jackson
Dr. Evan Swift Larry Musser
Joyce Taylor Kirsten Dunst
Vic Ryan Taylor

Director: David Warry-Smith

The Revelations of Becka Paulson

w Brad Wright, *story by* Stephen King
When a trailor-park wife shoots herself in the head, her mind starts to work overtime, a picture starts talking to her, and she learns her town's—and husband's—deepest secrets.
Becka Paulson Catherine O'Hara
Joe Paulson John Diehl
Doc Fink Bill Dow
Handsome man Steven Weber

Director: Steven Weber

Bodies of Evidence

w Chris Dickie, *story by* Chris Dickie & Ryland Kelley
The crew of a space station is lured to their deaths by impossible visions, but when the captain reaches Earth, he's accused of murder.
Captain William Clark Mario Van Peebles
Dr. Helene Dufour Guylaine St. Onge
Robin Dysart Jennifer Beals

Director: Melvin Van Peebles

Feasibility Study

w Joseph Stefano
A suburb is abruptly transported to another world as part of a study to see if humanity would make a good slave race. (Remake of a story from the original series.)
Joshua Hayward David McCallum
Sarah Hayward Laura Harris
Mr. Tenzer Malcolm Stewart

Director: Ken Girotti

A Special Edition

w Naren Shankar, *story by* Naren Shankar & Jonathan Glassner
Using clips from previous episodes, a muckracking journalist tries to broadcast his proof that the government has been secretly cloning people.
Donald Rivers Alan Thicke
Dr. Avery Strong Bruce Harwood

Director: Mario Azzopardi

Hearts and Minds

w Naren Shankar
A squad of soldiers fights aliens on a distant planet to protect a mineral that's a source of energy for Earth.
Lieutenant Rosen Christine Elise
Captain Taverner Miguel Fernandes

Director: Brad Turner

In Another Life

w Naren Shankar, *story by* Naren Shankar,
Brad Wright & Chris Brancato
Mason Stark is pulled into a parallel world by a du-
plicate of himself and asked to kill yet another ver-
sion of himself—a psychotic killer.
Kristin Kelly Rowan
Mason Stark Mitchell Laurance
Mr. Stark Matthew Laurance

Director: Allan Eastman

In the Zone

w Naren Shankar, *story by* Jon Povill
An aging athlete undergoes experimental treatments
to speed up his reflexes and becomes unbeatable . . .
but the side effects may kill him.

Tanner Brooks Adrian Pasdar
Jessica Brooks Claudette Mink
Michael Chen Pat Morita

Director: David Warry-Smith

Rite of Passage

w Chris Dickie
The alien known as Mother takes away the baby be-
longing to two teenagers living in a sheltered com-
mune, so they decide to get the baby back at any cost.
Brav Jimmy Marsden
Shal Emmanuelle Vaugier
Mother Camille Mitchell

Director: Jimmy Kaufman

PATHFINDERS . . .

A generation of British sci-fi fans cut their teeth on adventures such as this trilogy of children's space serials, packaged as part of ITV's Sunday "Family Hour" in 1960–61.

The three stories, *Pathfinders in Space, Pathfinders to Mars* and *Pathfinders to Venus*, continued the interplanetary adventures of the space family Wedgwood, launched in the spring of 1960 with *Target Luna* (see separate entry).

Initially, the formula was much the same as *Target Luna*, with Prof. Wedgwood's daring young son, Jimmy, and his pet hamster, Hamlet, repeating their rocket ride to the Moon (though this time his brother, sister and dad made the trip, too, and they actually landed there).The later serials widened the field, introducing new characters, new destinations—and even new sets. Designer David Gillespie filled the Teddington studios with foam plastic to create a Martian landscape of lichen and quicksand; while on *Pathfinders in Space*, Canadian designer Tom Spaulding devised an alien spaceship made entirely of triangles—even down to the light fittings and seats.

Among the new faces were Gerald Flood as science reporter and all-around good guy Conway Henderson, Pamela Barney as Moon Buff Prof. Mary Meadows, George Coulouris as Harcourt Brown, a fanatic convinced that life exists on other worlds, and Graydon Gould (voice of Mike Mercury in *Supercar*) as American astronaut Capt. Wilson.

All three sagas were scripted by Malcolm Hulke and Eric Paice with an eye to the possible, if not the probable . . . (Hulke later joined the ranks of the *Doctor Who* writers, contributing several stories between 1967 and 1974, notably "The War Games" which first introduced the Time Lords and explained the Doctor's origins, and both men wrote regularly for *The Avengers*.)

(NB: These *Pathfinders* serials should not be confused with an ITV drama series of the seventies, called *Pathfinders*, which was about the exploits of a wartime RAF bomber squadron.)

REGULAR CAST
Prof. Wedgwood Peter Williams *(Story One regular only)*
Geoffrey Wedgwood Stewart Guidotti   *Conway Henderson* Gerald Flood
Prof. Mary Meadows Pamela Barney   *John Field* Astor Sklair
Harcourt Brown George Coulouris *(Stories 2 and 3)*
Margaret Henderson Hester Cameron *(Stories 2 and 3)*
Ian Murray Hugh Evans   *Jimmy Wedgwood* Richard Dean *(Story One only)*
Valerie Wedgwood Gillian Ferguson *(Story One only)*

Producer: Sydney Newman   *ABC Television Network Productions*
Program advisor: Mary Field

Story One

Pathfinders in Space

w Malcolm Hulke & Eric Paice

A sequel to *Target Luna*. Rocket man Prof. Wedgwood heads the first team of Moon explorers, successfully blasting off from his Scottish rocket station, Buchan Island, in MR1 (Moon Rocket One). When his back-up supply rocket fails due to the automatic pilot cracking up, science reporter Conway Henderson and the Wedgwood brood decide to pilot the ship manually, determined to save the mission. As both rockets fly on toward the Moon, a third craft appears from nowhere. The Wedgwood rockets duly land on the Moon—but they are 150 miles apart. While Prof. Wedgwood treks across the lunar desert, the others explore some caverns, discovering a calcified figure and an ancient alien spaceship—evidence that a previous civilization had been there before them. As the reunited explorers prepare to return to Earth, one of their rockets is destroyed by meteorites. It takes a daring scheme by Prof. Wedgwood to get them *all* home safely, using the alien craft.

Dr. O'Connoll Harold Goldblatt
Jean Cary Irene Sutcliffe
Michael Kennedy Michael Guest

Director: Guy Verney
Designers: Tom Spaulding *(Eps. 1, 3–7)*, David Gillespie *(Eps. 1–2)*

7 black and white 30-minute episodes

Convoy to the Moon
Spaceship from Nowhere
Luna Bridgehead
The Man in the Moon
The World of Lost Toys
Disaster on the Moon
Rescue in Space

11 September–23 October 1960

Story Two

Pathfinders to Mars

w Malcolm Hulke & Eric Paice

Hard on the heels of his last lunar expedition, Prof. Wedgwood plans another mission to the Moon. Unable to pilot his new rocket, MR4, due to a broken arm, Wedgwood entrusts the task to his friend Conway Henderson. With Wedgwood's eldest son, Geoffrey, Henderson's young niece Margaret, Prof. Meadows (and, of course, Hamlet, the pet hamster) the party awaits the arrival of the last crew member, Australian scientist Prof. Hawkins. However, unknown to them, they are joined instead by an impostor, Harcourt Brown, a fanatical sci-fi writer determined to prove that life exists on Mars—whatever the cost. Brown hijacks the rocket, holding Margaret hostage, and after six weeks' enforced journey the MR4 reaches the red planet only to find airless deserts and dust. Searching for precious water for the journey back to Earth, the crew encounters terrifying quick-growing lichens and dangerous quicksands. But with Earth moving away from Mars at 20 miles a second, the explorers must leave soon or face 16 months in the lifeless Martian desert. With not enough fuel to get home, Henderson risks using the Sun's pull to aid their efforts.

Prof. Wedgwood Peter Williams *(Ep. 1 only)*
Prof. Hawkins Bernard Horsfall *(Eps. 1–2 only)*

Director: Guy Verney
Designer: David Gillespie

6 black and white 30-minute episodes

The Impostor
Sabotage in Space
The Hostage
Lichens!
Zero Hour on the Red Planet
Falling into the Sun

11 December 1960–15 January 1961

Story Three

Pathfinders to Venus

w Malcolm Hulke & Eric Paice

While returning to Earth from their perilous journey to Mars, the MR4 intercepts a distress call being beamed from Venus by an American astronaut, Capt. Wilson. Responding to the SOS, they divert to Venus but all they find is the astronaut's ransacked spaceship—and evidence of alien life. Harcourt Brown wanders off, finds Capt. Wilson and persuades him to go with him in search of the Venusians. Pursuing them, the rest of the crew are threatened by carnivorous plants, cornered by primitive ape-men, trapped by roof-falls, menaced by molten lava and attacked by pterodactyls. Escaping all that, they head back to the MR4, only to find that the volcanic ash has turned the area into a raging inferno. Escape seems impossible but a little détente goes a long way, as a Russian ship is on the way with vital fuel supplies. Harcourt Brown, however, elects to remain on Venus to continue his quest for a higher intelligence.

Capt. Wilson Graydon Gould
Venusian Bob Bryan *(Eps. 4–5, 8)*
Venusian child Brigid Skemp *(Eps. 5–8)*
Col. Korolyov Robert James *(Ep. 8)*

Directors: Guy Verney *(Eps. 1–5, 7)*, Reginald Collin *(Eps. 6–8)*
Script associate: Ivan Roe
Designers: David Gillespie *(Eps. 1–8)*, Douglas James *(Eps. 6–8)*
Special effects: Derek Freeborn

8 black and white 30-minute episodes

SOS from Venus
Into the Poison Cloud
The Living Planet
The Creature
The Venus People
The City
The Valley of the Monsters
Planet on Fire

5 March–23 April 1961

PHOENIX FIVE

Low-budget Australian space series that cheaply went where *Star Trek* had boldly gone before.

It followed the adventures of the crew of the galactic patrol ship *Phoenix Five*, "the most sophisticated craft in the Earth Space Control Fleet."

This handpicked team—Captain Roke, a typical Kirk clone with a solution to every problem; Ensign Adam Hargraves, a young space cadet always ready to shoot first and skip the questions; compassionate Cadet Tina Culbrick; and their computeroid Carl—roamed the planets protecting galactic citizens and warding off the repeated plots and attacks of the evil humanoid Zodian and a rebel scientist Platonus. The latter, a chip off the Ming block, dreamed of ruling the galaxies. By means of his computer, he subverted an innocent victim whom he used in an attempt to capture or destroy the *Phoenix* and its crew.

The series' limitations were apparent in the lack of supporting players, few sets (Platonus was invariably seen threatening all and sundry from the same set each time), the standard quarries and scrubland doubling as alien worlds, and very little model work—mostly just the *Phoenix* craft flying through space.

Each tale had a happy ending and a strong moral message.

REGULAR CAST
Captain Roke Mike Dorsey   *Ensign Adam Hargraves* Damien Parker
Cadet Tina Culbrick Patsy Trench   *Carl* Stuart Leslie
Earth Space Controller Peter Collingwood
Zodian Redmond Phillips   *Platonus* Owen Weincott

Writer/script editor: John Warwick
Director: David Cahill
Producers: Peter Summerton *(Eps. 1–10),* John Walters *(Eps. 11–26)**
**Took over following death of Peter Summerton.*

An Artransa Park Production in association with the Australian Broadcasting Commission
26 color 25-minute episodes
10 January–3 July 1970
(STV)

Zone of Danger

Introducing the handpicked crew of *Phoenix Five*, assigned to patrol space and thwart the megalomaniacal designs of their archenemy Zodian.

Two Heads Are Better Than One

An emissary from the planet Tylantia begs for an audience with the controller. A large force field is closing in and threatens to destroy his planet. Roke and his crew are sent to investigate.

Human Relics

Aboard the *Phoenix Five*, the crew receives a strange signal from the asteroid Arcticus. Responding, they find a 20th-century space capsule and an astronaut in a coma.

The Stowaway

On rest leave, the crew is indulging in a 20th-century game of baseball when Adam is overcome by a strange chameleon.

The End Is to Begin

On a routine galactic patrol, Roke's crew sees the planet Lionicus explode and sights a cargo ship off-course. Roke and Adam investigate and find the crew all missing.

Six Guns of Space

On a routine patrol, the *Phoenix Five* runs into an old-fashioned naval-style bombardment coming from one of the moons of Corallus.

The Pirate Queen

The *Phoenix* is escorting a cargo ship carrying vital medical supplies to an Earth space colony when the vessels are attacked by an old space frigate.

Two into One Won't Go

Zodian devises a new plan to destroy Earth Control and rule the Federated Galaxies of Space. He bribes the pompous governor of Planetoid 93 into injecting a micro transistor into Capt. Roke's bloodstream.

Back to Childhood

Cadet Tina finds a rare Cannibalis plant that Capt. Roke decides to take back to Earth Control for examination.

A Sound in Space

Ensign Adam Hargraves "materializes" a copy of the Pipes of Pan. He and Tina are hit by an unseen force when he blows a "dead" note on the pipes. Carl the Computeroid absorbs the ultrasonic sound and sets out to discover the source.

A Gesture from Kronos

Capt. Roke is "reversed" when he falls victim to a Zodian time warp. He talks backward, his uniform colors are reversed. His reaction powers are severely tested as he flies the Astro Scout Ship to the one person who can help him—Kronos, the guardian of time in space

The Cat

Investigating the mysterious disappearance of the colonists of the planet Lynxonia, the *Phoenix* crew find just one clue—a tiny black kitten. Surely it could not be responsible for strange growling noises heard in the planet's dark rocky areas.

The Baiter Is Bitten

The *Phoenix Five* flies into a strange phenomenon—fog, followed by rain and then deep water, causing the reactors to seize up, trapping the crew.

The Hunter

Platonus bribes the hunter king of a deserted planet to track down and kill the crew of the *Phoenix Five*.

Slave Queen

Roke is ordered to find the missing heir to the throne of Celex—a girl called Estella who was captured as a child by a warlike and backward race from another world.

Space Quake

A doctor on a dying planet injects Adam with an aging serum but will only supply the antidote in return for safe passage to another planet.

The Planet of Fear

Exploring a strange planet, Roke and Adam meet an astronaut who was lost ten years earlier, and has acquired mysterious powers from the evil Platonus, turning him into a human booby trap.

Something Fishy

Phoenix Five is sent to find out why contact has been lost with the prison colony on the planet Zedden.

Toy Soldier

Tina shows Adam a tiny antique toy soldier she has bought while on leave.

The Bigger They Are

Platonus programs a young gentle giant to destroy the *Phoenix Five* and her crew.

Shadow Ship

Returning to Earth for a routine check, Tina is struck down by an agonizing virus.

Efficiency Minus

The crew is shocked when told they have failed their annual check-ups and will have to be separated.

Spark from a Dying Fire

Adam and Tina fall victim to the hypnotic powers of the strange sparks erupting from a fiercely destructive asteroid, and are set to fight a duel.

Dream City

Computeroid Carl picks a flower for Tina, unaware that Platonus has programmed him to pick a very special flower . . .

A Little Difficulty

Phoenix Five, pride of Earth Space Control's Galactic Fleet, disappears!

General Alarm

Roke and his crew are assigned to collect a reformed tyrant from a prison planet and return him to Earth.

PLANET OF THE APES

1974 adventure series based on the hugely successful film of the same name, with Ape star Roddy McDowall re-creating his sympathetic role as the young chimp Galen.

Thrust more than a thousand years into the future when their spacecraft passes through a time warp, astronauts Alan Virdon and Pete Burke find the world has been turned upside down—the apes are the rulers, men little more than menials, technology virtually non-existent.

The main narrative thrust of the series is of the apes pursuing the astronauts whose superior knowledge could destabilize the simian society and threaten the ascendancy of the apes. Virdon and Burke, meanwhile, cling to the hope of finding a way of getting back to their own time.

But though essentially aimed at providing action entertainment for a family audience, the series did retain some of the flavor of Pierre Boulle's original allegorical novel, making a few trenchant observations on man's morality, prejudices and fears through the creation of the ape society in which orangutans were the ruling class, gorillas the muscle-headed enforcers and chimpanzees the intellectuals. This aspect of the series was not lost on the British critics who gave it their blessing.

It is the thoughtful chimp Galen who befriends the astronauts and becomes their ally in the flight from the gorilla leader Urko. The other leading ape is the orangutan councilor Zaius who spends much of his time trying to moderate the excesses of Urko. Roddy McDowall and the other "ape" actors endured grueling three-and-a-half-hour makeup sessions to achieve the distinctive simian look.

Planet of the Apes premiered in Britain in October 1974, and the series was a great success, regularly pulling in audiences of up to 12 million. But in America it achieved a modest 27 percent rating—three below the required minimum—and paymaster CBS abruptly halted production after just 14 of the scheduled 24 episodes, leaving the story hanging (literally) in mid-air.

REGULAR CAST
Galen Roddy McDowall   *Virdon* Ron Harper   *Burke* James Naughton
Urko Mark Lenard   *Zaius* Booth Colman

Producer: Stan Hough
Executive producer: Herbert Hirschman
Makeup: Dan Striepeke
A 20th Century Fox Television Production for CBS

14 color 60-minute episodes
U.S. premiere: 13 September 1974
U.K. premiere: 13 October 1974–19 January 1975
(London Weekend Television)

Escape from Tomorrow

w Art Wallace
Passing through a time warp, astronauts Virdon and Burke land back on Earth in an unimaginable future. Captured by gorillas, they find an ally in the chimp Galen, who is fascinated by their origin. He helps them escape back to their spaceship where Virdon retrieves a magnetic memory disc that might help them return to the past, and the three become fugitives.
Farrow Royal Dano
Turvo Ron Stein
Veska Woodrow Parfrey
Ullman Biff Elliott
Proto Jerome Thor
Grundig William Beckley
Arno Bobby Porter

Director: Don Weiss

The Gladiators

w Art Wallace
The loss of the precious magnetic disc causes Burke and Virdon to become involved with gladiators, the burly Tolar and his reluctant son Dalton.
Jason Pat Renella
Tolar William Smith
Dalton Marc Singer
Barlow John Hoyt
Gorilla sergeant Eddie Fontaine

Director: Don McDougall

The Trap

w Edward J. Lakso
When Burke and Urko are trapped by an earthquake in an old San Francisco subway tunnel, Virdon and Galen get ape soldiers to cooperate in a rescue. Meanwhile, in the tunnel, Urko is enraged when he sees an old zoo poster showing caged apes being fed peanuts.
Zako Norm Alden
Mema Ron Stein
Olam Eldon Burke
Miller John Milford
Jick Mickey LeClair
Lisa Cindy Eilbacher

Director: Arnold Laven

The Good Seeds

w Robert W. Lenski
When Galen is wounded, the fugitives take refuge at a gorilla farm where they win over their hosts by teaching them some valuable lessons about farming and saving the hostile son's valuable cow, which goes into a difficult labor to give birth to twins.
Anto Geoffrey Deuel
Polar Lonny Chapman
Zantes Jacqueline Scott
Remus Bobby Porter
Jillia Eileen Ditz Elber
Gorilla officer Dennis Cross

Director: Don Weiss

The Legacy

w Robert Hamner
In the ruins of a one-time city Virdon and Burke hope to find a key that could unlock their past. Instead, they barely escape the pursuing gorillas—aided in part by a young woman, Arn, and an opportunist street urchin, Kraik.
Scientist Jon Lormer
Gorilla captain Robert Phillips
Gorilla sergeant Wayne Foster
Kraik Jackie Earle Haley
Arn Zina Bethune

Director: Bernard McEveety

Tomorrow's Tide

w Robert W. Lenski
Virdon and Burke are captured by the chimp head of a fishing colony and nearly find themselves enslaved.
Hurton Roscoe Lee Browne
Romar Jim Storm
Soma Kathleen Bracken
Gahto John McLiam
Bandor Jay Robinson

Director: Don McDougall

The Surgeon

w Barry Oringer
When Virdon is shot and seriously wounded, Galen and Burke work out an elaborate scheme to enlist the aid of Kira, a female ape who is a surgeon.
Kira Jacqueline Scott
Leander Martin Brooks
Haman Ron Stein
Travin Michael Strong
Girl Janie Smith Jackson
Jordan Phil Montgomery

Director: Arnold Laven

The Deception

w Anthony Lawrence, Ken Spears & Joe Ruby, story by Anthony Lawrence
Burke becomes the object of the affections of a blind female ape, Fauna.
Sestus John Milford
Fauna Jane Actman
Perdix Baynes Barron
Zon Pat Renella
Chilot Eldon Burke

Director: Don McDougall

The Horse Race

w David P. Lewis & L. Booker Bradshaw
Under Urko's very nose, Virdon manages to run a horse race, winning, as part of the stakes, the life of a blacksmith's young son.
Barlow John Hoyt
Prefect Henry Levin
Kagan Wesley Fuller
Zandar Richard Devon
Martin Morgan Woodward
Gregar Meegan King
Zilo Joseph Tornatore

Director: Jack Starrett

The Interrogation

w Richard Collins
Burke is captured and cruelly questioned, while Galen and Virdon work out a rescue plan with the help of Galen's parents, Ann and Yalu.
Wanda Beverly Garland
Ann Anne Seymour
Yalu Normann Burton
Susan Lynn Benesch
Dr. Malthus Harry Townes
Peasant gorilla Eldon Burke
Gorilla leader Ron Stein

Director: Alf Kjellin

The Tyrant

w Walter Black
The fugitive trio help remove Aboro, a corrupt tyrant, from office, even though they have to risk an encounter with Urko to do it.
Aboro Percy Rodrigues
Dako Joseph Ruskin
Augustus Tom Troupe
Janor Michael Conrad
Mikal James Daughton

Director: Ralph Senensky

The Cure

w Edward J. Lakso
The astronauts come across a village devastated by malaria and manage to help the local medical officer, Zoran, to discover quinine.
Zoran David Sheiner
Amy Sondra Locke
Talbert George Wallace
Mason Albert Cole
Kava Ron Soble
Inta Eldon Burke
Neesa Ron Stein

Director: Bernard McEveety

The Liberator

w Howard Dimsdale
Galen and the astronauts are captured by a tribe of humans who prey on other humans and turn them over to gorillas as slaves.
Brun John Ireland
Miro Ben Andrews
Clim Peter G. Skinner
Talia Jennifer Ashley
Gorilla guard Ron Stein
Villager Mark Bailey

Director: Arnold Laven

Up Above the World So High

w S. Bar-David (*alias* Shimon Wincelberg) & Arthur Browne Jr.
The astronauts help a human, Leuric, to make a workable hang glider, arousing the unwelcome interest of a lady chimp scientist, Carsia.
Leuric Frank Aletter
Konag Martin Brooks
Carsia Joanna Barnes
Gorilla guard Ron Stein
Trooper Eldon Burke

Director: John Meredyth Lucas

POLTERGEIST: THE LEGACY

The Legacy, a secret society dedicated to protecting the world from the supernatural, has vast resources at its disposal. Its members travel anywhere the dark forces break through into our world—facing ghosts, zombies, vampires, and all manner of unholy menaces.

Another made-for-cable series, *Poltergeist: The Legacy* premiered on Showtime for three seasons; latest news has it moving to the Sci-Fi Channel for a fourth season. In theory it is a spin-off from the *Poltergeist* movies, but except for dealing with the supernatural, the two have nothing in common.

REGULAR CAST
Dr. Derek Rayne Derek de Lint *Nick Boyle* Martin Cummins
Alex Moreau Robbi Chong *Dr. Rachel Corrigan* Helen Shaver
Kat Corrigan Alexandra Purvis *Father Philip Callaghan* Patrick Fitzgerald
William Sloan Daniel J. Travanti

Executive producer: Grant Rosenberg
Production designer: Sheila Haley

Season One
Pilot
Sins of the Father Past
Town without Pity
The Tenement
Twelfth Cave
Man in the Mist
Ghost in the Road
Doppelganger
The Substitute

Do Not Go Gently
Crystal Scarab
The Bell of Girardius
Fox Spirit
The Thirteenth Generation
Dark Priest
Revelations
The Bones of St. Anthony
Inheritance
The Signalman
The Reckoning
Traitor Among Us

Season Two

The New Guard
Black Widow
Lights Out
Spirit Thief
The Gift
Let Sleeping Demons Lie
Lives in the Balance
Transference
Ransom
Dark Angel
Rough Beast
Devil's Lighthouse

Finding Richter
Repentance
Lullaby
Silent Partner
Shadow Fall
Fear
Morning Light
Mind's Eye
Someone to Watch Over Me
The Choice
Trapped
Reunion

THE POWERS OF MATTHEW STAR

Adventure series about a young alien prince living on Earth who drops out of school to become a secret agent.

Matthew Star is the 17-year-old son of the rulers of a planet called Quadris. When their regime is overthrown by tyrants, they send their son to Earth in the care of a companion, Walt Shepherd, who is given the task of protecting young Matthew from alien assassins and helping him to develop his powers of telepathy and telekinesis so he can return to Quadris and lead a revolution.

Posing as guardian and ward, Walt and Matthew arrive in an American small town where Matt enrols in high school and Walt gets a job as a football coach/science teacher.

And that was where the problem began for U.S. critics. They couldn't take seriously a show where the lead looked way too old to be in school. As a comedy it might have worked, but as an adventure it misfired and ran for just one season from September 1982. *Star Trek*'s Leonard Nimoy directed one episode.

MAIN CAST
Matthew Star Peter Barton   *Walt Shepherd* Lou Gossett Jr.
Pam Elliott (Matthew's girlfriend) Amy Steel
Chip Frye (his best friend) Bob Alexander
Major Wymore (his government contact) James Karen

Creator/Producer: Harve Bennett
Writers: Various, including Steven E. deSouza
(*pilot*), Gregory S. Dinallo, Richard Matheson
Directors: Various, including Ivan Nagy (*pilot*),
Ron Satlof, Leonard Nimoy, Corey Allen, Lou
Gossett Jr.

21 color 60-minute episodes
U.S. premiere: 17 September 1982
(NBC)

THE PRETENDER

In many ways, *The Pretender* is cut from the same cloth as both *The Fugitive* and *Nowhere Man*: a brilliant man-on-the-run uses his superior intellect to elude capture. Here, Jarod is pursued by agents of The Center, where he has been held prisoner since childhood. The interesting twist is that Jarod has the ability to learn and perfectly emulate any job almost instantly. In effect, he can pretend to be almost anyone, from a surgeon to a lawyer, from an FBI agent to a U.S. marshal.

The shadowy Center remains an enigma. Who runs it? What is its real purpose? As Jarod stays one step ahead of the dogged Miss Parker and her henchmen, he uses his talent to help people in trouble. Kind of like Bill Bixby's character in *The Incredible Hulk,* or Logan and Jessica in *Logan's Run,* or—well, you get the idea: the man-on-the-run-doing-good is a familiar plot device in any genre.

REGULAR CAST
Jarod Michael T. Weiss *Miss Parker* Andrea Parker
Sydney Green Patrick Bauchau

Executive producers: Steven Long Mitchell, Craig Van Sickle
Co-executive producer: Tommy Thompson
Creators: Steven Long Mitchell, Craig Van Sickle
Supervising producer: Kimberly Costello

Producer: Tim Iacofano
Produced by MTM Entertainment in association with NBC Studios
U.S. premiere: 19 September 1996

Season One
Pilot
Every Picture Tells a Story
Flyer
Curious Jarod
The Paper Clock
To Serve and Protect
A Virus Among Us
Not Even a Mouse
Mirage
The Better Part of Valor

Potato Head Blues
Prison Story
Bazooka Jarod
Ranger Jarod
Jeraldo!
Under the Reds
Keys
Unhappy Landings
Jarod's Honor
Baby Love
The Dragon House (2-hour season finale)

PREY

"**F**orty thousand years ago, the most advanced species on Earth was wiped out by a powerful new life form. Us. Now another new species has evolved—stronger, smarter, and dedicated to our annihilation. Leading the fight against them is Dr. Sloan Parker, the bioanthropologist who uncovered their existence. Once again, it's survival of the fittest . . . and this time we are the prey."

Slick production values, storylines that continue from episode to episode, and bad guys as villainous as they come make *Prey* a strong new contender. If the producers can keep up the quality, and viewers catch on, it could be the next *X-Files* . . . If not, it could fizzle out into another *Burning Zone*.

REGULAR CAST
Dr. Walter Attwood Larry Drake *Dr. Sloan Parker* Debra Messing
Tom Daniels Adam Storke *Dr. Ed Tate* Vincent Ventresca
Detective Ray Peterson Frankie R. Faison

Creator: William Schmidt
Executive producers: Charlie Craig, William Schmidt

Producers: Donald Marcus, Phil Parslow
Supervising producer: Jeremy R. Littman

THE PRISONER

"The series was posing the question, 'Has one the right to tell a man what to think, how to behave, to coerce others? Has one the right to be an individual?'"
—Patrick McGoohan

One of the most enigmatic and talked-about series ever, *The Prisoner* overturned the conventions of television drama by challenging its unsuspecting audience to think on more than one simple level.

It was devised by Patrick McGoohan who was its star and its executive producer. He also shared in the writing and direction. It was his series. Before it began he said: "If people don't like it, there's only one person to blame—me!"

Faced with something that was part spy thriller, part fantasy, part allegory, many people found the effort too much and remained angry, frustrated and confused by the absence of quick, easy answers. But for daring to be different, *The Prisoner* won a passionate cult status that has remained unshakable for more than 20 years.

It began innocently enough. A government employee abruptly resigns from his top-secret job. He goes home and is seen packing, apparently for a holiday. Suddenly gas hisses through the keyhole and he loses consciousness. He awakes apparently in the same room, but when he looks out of the window he sees the strange, beautiful landscape of The Village. Abducted by persons unknown, he has become *The Prisoner*.

Immediately the questions are thrown up. Where is this Village? Who runs it and why? It's a self-contained community with its own shops, a café, a labor exchange, and an old folks' home. It has its own radio and television service and its own newspaper, *The Tally Ho*. But its telephones only allow local calls and its taxis won't leave the village limits.

The village is full of people who used to work for various governments and who had access to classified information. Some help run the place, others are prisoners like himself. But everyone has a number. The Prisoner is told *he* is Number Six. At the head of the visible hierarchy is Number Two, served by an ever-present mute dwarf butler. But Number Two is answerable to the unseen authority of Number One.

As to *why* he is there, that becomes chillingly clear from the outset. The authorities want "information," in particular, they want to know why he resigned. Successive Number Twos try every technique available, from drugs, brainwashing, torture, psychological warfare, even dream manipulation, to find out. Meanwhile, The Prisoner is seeking answers of his own—including the identity of Number One. Above all, though, he wants to escape—a task made hard by constant electronic surveillance, and harder still by "Rover," a bizarre large white balloon that hunts down and retrieves errant inmates.

The series becomes a cat-and-mouse battle with The Prisoner initially thwarted at each turn but refusing to submit and gradually gaining the upper hand until, in a riot of surreal chaos, he finally escapes . . . from his physical prison, at least.

What did it all mean? Certainly, the series could be viewed, on a limited level, as a story of an imprisoned secret agent, but it's the deeper issues raised and the wider meanings sought that have given it its enduring appeal. The series was a persuasive defense of a man's right to assert his individuality in the face of an increasingly conformist society, and the declaration "I am not a number, I am a free man!" its most passionate slogan. The series also explored themes of education, democracy, misuse of power, psychiatry, drugs and violence. And ultimately it posed the premise that everyone is a prisoner of his or her self, hemmed in by our own weaknesses. In the final episode, The Prisoner "unmasks" Number One who stands, fleetingly, revealed as himself, the enemy within.

The Prisoner was McGoohan's follow-up to the long-running *Danger Man*, and much speculation centered on whether Number Six was the same character, John Drake. *Prisoner* script editor George Markstein said it was, McGoohan said it wasn't. Others have suggested that *The Prisoner* was McGoohan's way of "resigning" from *his* previous job . . .

REGULAR CAST
Number Six Patrick McGoohan *Butler* Angelo Muscat
Supervisor (8 out of 17) Peter Swanwick
Voice of village announcer Fenella Fielding

Devised by Patrick McGoohan
Executive producer: Patrick McGoohan *(except Eps. 14–15, 17)*
Producer: David Tomblin
Script editor: George Markstein *(Eps. 1–12, 16)*
Director of photography: Brendan J. Stafford
Theme: Ron Grainer

Filmed at MGM Studios, Borehamwood and on location at Portmeirion, North Wales

An Everyman Films Production for ATV
17 color 60-minute episodes
29 September 1967–2 February 1968
(ATV Midlands)

(repeats continue into the 1990s, on Channel four and cult satellite channel Bravo)
U.S. premiere: 1 June 1968

For further information on *The Prisoner*, write to:
Six of One
PO Box 66, Ipswich
IP2 9TZ

Arrival

w George Markstein & David Tomblin

After abruptly resigning from his top secret job, a government employee is abducted to an idyllic-looking prison-camp called The Village. Stripped of all identity, he's known as Number Six and so begins his titanic struggle to defy his jailers who want to pick his brain to find out why he resigned.
Woman Virginia Maskell
Number Two Guy Doleman
Cobb Paul Eddington
New Number Two George Baker
Taxi driver Barbara Yu Ling
Maid Stephanie Randall
Doctor Jack Allen
Welfare worker Fabia Drake
Shopkeeper Denis Shaw
Gardener/Electrician Oliver MacGreevy
Ex-admiral Frederick Piper
Waitress Patsy Smart
Labor exchange manager Christopher Benjamin
Supervisor Peter Swanwick
Hospital attendant David Garfield
Croquet players Peter Brace, Keith Peacock

Director: Don Chaffey

The Chimes of Big Ben

w Vincent Tilsley

With the aid of an apparent ally, Nadia, Number Six effects an escape by sea, air and land, ending up in what appears to be his London office. He is about to reveal why he resigned when the chiming of Big Ben tips him off that he has been tricked.
Number Two Leo McKern
Nadia Nadia Gray
General Finlay Currie
Fotheringay Richard Wattis
Colonel J Kevin Stoney
Number Two's assistant Christopher Benjamin
Karel David Arlen
Supervisor Peter Swanwick
Number 39 Hilda Barry
Judges Jack Le-White, John Maxim, Lucy Griffiths

Director: Don Chaffey

A, B and C

w Anthony Skene

Number Two subjects Number Six to an experimental process by which dreams can be penetrated and manipulated, using a wonder drug that turns subconscious thoughts into pictures on a TV screen.
Engadine Katherine Kath
Number Fourteen Sheila Allen
Number Two Colin Gordon
"A" Peter Bowles
Blonde lady Georgina Cookson
"B" Annette Carol
Flower girl Lucille Soong
Maid at party Bettine Le Beau
Thugs Terry Yorke, Peter Brayham
Henchman Bill Cummings

Director: Pat Jackson

Free for All

w Paddy Fitz (*alias* Patrick McGoohan)

Number Six views the impending election of a new Number Two as just another trick but runs for office all the same—only to find, as anticipated, that his victory is a hollow one.
Number Two Eric Portman
Number 58 Rachel Herbert
Labor exchange manager George Benson
Reporter Harold Berens
Man in cave John Cazabon
Photographer Dene Cooper
Supervisor Kenneth Benda
Waitress Holly Doone
Mechanics Peter Brace, Alf Joint

Director: Patrick McGoohan

The Schizoid Man

w Terence Feely

The Prisoner's double is brought into the village to try to break Number Six by convincing him that he is someone else . . . Number Twelve.
Alison Jane Merrow
Number Two Anton Rodgers
Supervisor Earl Cameron
Number 36 Gay Cameron
Doctor David Nettheim
Nurse Pat Keen
Guardians Gerry Crampton, Dinny Powell

Director: Pat Jackson

The General

w Joshua Adam (*alias* Lewis Greifer)
Everyone in the Village is ordered to attend the sensational "Speedlearn" classes promising a university degree in three minutes. Number Six thwarts the scheme with his computer-blowing question: Why?
Number Two Colin Gordon
Number Twelve John Castle
Professor Peter Howell
Announcer Al Mancini
Professor's wife Betty McDowall
Supervisor Peter Swanwick
Doctor Conrad Phillips
Man in buggy Michael Miller
Waiter Keith Pyott
Man in café Ian Fleming
Mechanic Norman Mitchell
Projection operator Peter Bourne
Corridor guards George Leech, Jackie Cooper

Director: Peter Graham Scott

Many Happy Returns

w Anthony Skene
Number Six awakes in a deserted village. There is no one to stop him as he escapes back to London by raft—a journey of 25 days. From calculations of times and tides, the Village is deemed to be off the coast of Morocco. Number Six flies off to locate it—only to be ejected from his plane to land back where he started.
Colonel Donald Sinden
Thorpe Patrick Cargill
Mrs. Butterworth Georgina Cookson
Group captain Brian Worth
Commander Richard Caldicott
Gunther Dennis Chinnery
Ernst Jon Laurimore
Gypsy girl Nike Arrighi
Maid Grace Arnold
Gypsy man Larry Taylor

Director: Joseph Serf (*alias* Patrick McGoohan)

Dance of the Dead

w Anthony Skene
Death strikes amid the gaiety of a village carnival and Number Six is put on trial when he makes an audacious bid to smuggle out an SOS on the corpse.
Number Two Mary Morris
Doctor Duncan Macrae
Girl Bo-Peep Norman West
Town crier Aubrey Morris
Psychiatrist Bee Duffell
Day supervisor Camilla Hasse
Dutton Alan White
Night supervisor Michael Nightingale

Night maid Patsy Smart
Maid Denise Buckley
Postman George Merritt
Flowerman John Frawley
Lady in corridor Lucy Griffiths
Second doctor William Lyon Brown

Director: Don Chaffey

Checkmate

w Gerald Kelsey
Number Six participates in a bizarre game of chess in which the pieces are human beings. He is trying to discover who are the prisoners and who are the warders.
Rook Ronald Radd
First psychiatrist Patricia Jessel
Number Two Peter Wyngarde
Queen Rosalie Crutchley
Man with the stick George Coulouris
Second psychiatrist Bee Duffell
Supervisor Basil Dignam
Painter Danvers Walker
Shopkeeper Denis Shaw
Assistant supervisor Victor Platt
Nurse Shivaun O'Casey
Skipper Geoffrey Reed
Sailor Terence Donovan
Tower guards Joe Dunne, Romor Gorrara

Director: Don Chaffey

Hammer Into Anvil

w Roger Woddis
Seeking to avenge the death of a persecuted girl, Number Six plays cat-and-mouse with Number Two, making him think that *he* is the one being spied on.
Number Two Patrick Cargill
Bandmaster Victor Maddern
Number 14 Basil Hoskins
Psychiatric director Norman Scace
New supervisor Derek Aylward
Number 73 Hilary Dwyer
Control room operator Arthur Gross
Supervisor Peter Swanwick
Shop assistant Victor Woolf
Lab technician Michael Segal
Shop kiosk girl Margo Andrew
Female code expert Susan Sheers
Guardians Jackie Cooper, Fred Haggerty, Eddie Powell, George Leach

Director: Pat Jackson

It's Your Funeral

w Michael Cramoy
Number Six averts a planned assassination—despite being subjected to a ruthless campaign to discredit him so that even the intended victim will not believe his warnings.
New Number Two Derren Nesbitt
Watchmaker's daughter Annette Andre
Number 100 Mark Eden
Retiring Number Two Andre Van Gyseghem
Watchmaker Martin Miller
Computer attendant Wanda Ventham
Number Two's assistant Mark Burns
Supervisor Peter Swanwick
Artist Charles Lloyd Pack
Number 36 Grace Arnold
Stallholder Arthur White
MC councillor Michael Bilton
Koshu opponent Gerry Crampton

Director: Robert Asher

A Change of Mind

w Roger Parkes
Number Six is the subject of a sinister plan to transform his mental processes by sound waves and drugs, but turns the tables by getting Number Two declared "unmutual."
Number 86 Angela Browne
Number Two John Sharp
Doctor George Pravda
Number 42 Kathleen Breck
Supervisor Peter Swanwick
Lobo man Thomas Heathcote
Committee chairman Bartlett Mullins
Number 93 Michael Miller
Social group members Joseph Cuby, Michael Chow
Number 48 June Ellis
Woodland men Hohn Hamblin, Michael Billington

Director: Joseph Serf (*alias* Patrick McGoohan)

Do Not Forsake Me Oh My Darling

w Vincent Tilsley
Number Six's mind is imprisoned in the body of an army colonel via Professor Seltzman's "mind-swopping" machine.
Janet Zena Walker
Number Two Clifford Evans
Colonel Nigel Stock
Seltzman Hugo Schuster
Sir Charles John Wentworth
Villiers James Bree
Minister Kynaston Reeves
Stapleton Lloyd Lamble
Danvers Patrick Jordan
Camera shop manager Lockwood West
Potter Fredric Abbott

Café waiter Gertan Klauber
Old guest Henry Longhurst
First new man Danvers Walker
Young guest John Nolan

Director: Pat Jackson

Living in Harmony

w David Tomblin, *story by* David Tomblin & Ian L. Rakoff
The Prisoner finds himself in a Wild West township, tricked into becoming a sheriff. It's really just a drug-induced trip—but can he be forced to carry a gun and kill?
Kid (Number Eight) Alexis Kanner
Judge (Number Two) David Bauer
Kathy Valerie French
Town elder Gordon Tanner
Bystander Gordon Sterne
Will Michael Balfour
Mexican Sam Larry Taylor
Town dignitary Monti De Lyle
Horse dealer Douglas Jones
Gunmen Bill Nick, Les Crawford, Frank Maher
Horsemen Max Faulkner, Bill Cummings, Eddie Eddon

Director: David Tomblin

The Girl Who Was Death

w Terence Feely, *idea by* David Tomblin
The Prisoner's "bedtime story" for village children. Number Six meets a girl who believes they are made for each other; he is a born survivor, she is a born killer. (Note the name of the actor playing the bowler!)
Schnipps (Number Two) Kenneth Griffith
Sonja Justine Lord
Potter Christopher Benjamin
Killer Karminski Michael Brennan
Boxing MC Harold Berens
Barmaid Sheena Marsh
Scots Napoleon Max Faulkner
Welsh Napoleon John Rees
Yorkshire Napoleon Joe Gladwin
Bowler John Drake
Little girl Gaynor Steward
Little boys Graham Steward, Stephen Howe

Director: David Tomblin

Once Upon a Time

w Patrick McGoohan
It's make or break time as the Prisoner faces ruthless interrogation from Number Two in a process called "Degree Absolute," from which only one man will emerge the winner.
Number Two Leo McKern
Supervisor Peter Swanwick
Umbrella man John Cazabon
Number 86 John Maxim

Director: Patrick McGoohan

Fall Out

w Patrick McGoohan

Controversial final episode that infuriated those looking for pat answers. Having survived "Degree Absolute," the Prisoner finally wins the right to be an individual, and discovers the identity of Number One—himself. He escapes the Village—with the former Number Two and Number 48 (the "symbol" of youth revolt) plus the omnipresent Butler—but remains a prisoner of his own self.

Former Number Two Leo McKern
President Kenneth Griffith
Number 48 Alexis Kanner
Supervisor Peter Swanwick
Delegate Michael Miller

Director: Patrick McGoohan

PROFILER

Dr. Samantha Waters, a forensics agent, has the unique ability to see into the minds of serial killers. She uses this talent to aide the FBI as part of the Violent Crimes Task Force. Complicating her life is the ongoing search for the serial killer known as Jack of All Trades, who murdered Sam's husband.

A dark, moody program, part of NBC's Saturday Thrillogy lineup, *Profiler* has garnered a cult following and is already well into its second season.

REGULAR CAST
Dr. Samantha Waters Ally Walker   *Bailey Malone* Robert Davi
John Grant Julian McMahon   *Nick Cooper* A. Martinez
Grace Alvarez Roma Maffia   *George Fraley* Peter Frechette
Nathan Brubaker Michael Whaley

Season One
Pilot:
Ring of Fire
Unholy Alliance
I'll Be Watching You
Unsoiled Sovereignty
Modus Operandi
Night Dreams
Cruel and Unusual
The Sorcerer's Apprentice
Shattered Silence

Doppelganger
Learning from the Masters
The House That Jack Built
Shadow of Angels
Film at 11
Crisis:
Blue Highways
FTX: Field Training Exercises
Into the Abyss
Venom (Part 1)
Venom (Part 2)

PROJECT UFO

An early forerunner of pseudo-documentary series such as *Sightings*, and modern cult dramas such as *The X-Files*.

This series, described by U.S. critics as "National Enquirer television" and allegedly based on real events, followed the investigations of the American Air Force's Project Blue Book. Major Jake Gatlin and his sidekick Sgt. Harry Fitz were assigned to look into reported UFO sightings of "high strangeness" and "high credibility" across America.

Each episode was listed as an "incident" and ranged from a rancher and his family being assaulted by alien creatures ("The Howard Crossing Incident"), an airliner chased by a boomerang-shaped craft ("The Medicine Bow Incident") and a whole rash of high-flying careers jeopardized because sightings aroused disbelief. In one episode ("The Rock and Hard Place Incident") Gatlin and Fitz even have a sighting of their own.

In Season Two, a new investigator, Capt. Ben Ryan, joined the team, but the formula was the same, with the subjects telling their tales to the Blue Book boys.

Executive producer for the series was Jack Webb, laconic star of the vintage crime series *Dragnet*.

REGULAR CAST
Major Jake Gatlin William Jordan *(Season One only)*
Sgt. Harry Fitz Caskey Swaim   *Libby Virdon* Aldine King
Capt. Ben Ryan (Season Two) Edward Winter

Creator: Harold Jack Bloom
Executive producer: Jack Webb
Producer: Col. William T. Coleman
Music: Nelson Riddle

A Mark VIII Ltd Production in association with NBC TV

26 color 60-minute episodes
U.S. premiere: 12 February 1978
U.K.: Season One:
17 May–9 August 1979
Season Two:
3 January–10 April 1980
(Southern)

Season One

The Washington DC Incident

A U.S. Air Force pilot sights a UFO and gives chase until, over Washington, DC, he plummets to his death.
with: Anne Schebeen, Frances Reid

The Joshua Flats Incident

Several prominent citizens see a UFO and the air force is called in.
with: David Yanez, Barbara Luna, Jim Davis

The Fremont Incident

A police officer sees an alien craft land and strange figures emerging from it, but when he reports the incident he is ridiculed.
with: Rod Perry, Frank Aletter

The Howard Crossing Incident

A rancher and his family are assaulted by alien creatures after a glowing white ball crashes to Earth on their land.
with: Leif Erickson

The Medicine Bow Incident

A boomerang-shaped craft chases a commercial airliner and a would-be politician says he has been attacked by a UFO.
with: Kenneth Mars, Paul Picerni

The Nevada Desert Incident

An air force lieutenant sees four metallic flying objects and a huge mother ship. He reports it and so endangers his career and marriage.
with: Scott Hylands, Adrienne La Russa, Andrew Duggan, Donna Douglas

The Forest City Incident

Two schoolboys spot a UFO but their principal fears bad publicity will arise from an official investigation.
with: Stacy Keach Sr., Skip Homeier

The Desert Springs Incident

An immense UFO pursues two men as they ride a cable car from the top of a mountain.
with: Peggy Webber, Buckley Norris

The French Incident

The son of a presidential envoy is abducted by a flying saucer in the village of Brebeuf—and the White House orders Gatlin and Fitz to investigate.
with: Eric Braeden, Kip Niven, Maria Grimm, Morgan Woodward

The Waterford Incident

The boys at a military academy claim a saucer flew over the school, discharging a strand-like substance.
with: Craig Stevens, Dr. Joyce Brothers

The Doll House Incident

An elderly caretaker is confronted by two aliens who offer him a strange lotus-shaped loaf of bread in return for a jug of water.
with: Alf Kjellin, Marta Kristen

The Rock and Hard Place Incident

Gatlin and Fitz have their own UFO sighting as a flying saucer leaves a trail of exploding color over the restaurant where they are dining.
with: Elaine Joyce, Paul Brinegar, Robert Ginty

The St Hillary Incident

Two nuns see a UFO and after reporting the incident, are pressured by the church authorities to deny their claim.
with: Pamela Franklin

Season Two

The Underwater Incident

Gatlin is promoted and Captain Ryan takes over Project Blue Book. His first assignment is to investigate claims by fishermen that their boat was sunk by a UFO plunging into the sea.
with: Laurette Spang, Allen Case, Scott Thomas, Caroline McWilliams

The Devilish Davidson Lights Incident

Ryan and Fitz investigate reported sightings in Davidson, California.
with: Kim Hunter, Jared Martin, Jenny Sullivan, Isaac Ruiz

The Pipeline Incident

The three-man crew of an Alaskan cargo plane is crossing the Yukon border when they see a target closing in on them at incredible speed. The object performs bizarre maneuver and chases them.
with: Randolph Mantooth, Cameron Mitchell, Donald May

The Incident on the Cliffs

A woman with a history of mental illness sees four UFOs, but despite filmed evidence, her claims are refuted by her husband and psychiatrist.
with: Trish Stewart, William Reynolds

The Wild Blue Yonder Incident

A student pilot faces expulsion after sighting a supposed flying saucer during an air exercise and recklessly diving to chase it.
with: Rebecca York, W.K. Stratton

The Believe It or Not Incident

A student claims he has been warned by aliens that unless the world's pollution is cleared up they will take the Earth by force.
with: Mark Slade, Anne Lockhart

The Camouflage Incident

Three businessmen are attacked by a UFO. One of them manages to film the craft but refuses to reveal the results.
with: Gary Crosby

The Island Incident

A doctor and his party in the South Pacific see a small UFO fly out of a huge mother ship but the islanders later deny the sighting.
with: James Olson, Marlyn Mason

The Superstition Mountain Incident

A student finds two pieces of pure magnesium left behind by a UFO and is warned by a Gypsy to be careful in telling anyone about the Overlords' visit.
with: Josh Albee, Leslie Ackerman, Anna Karen

The I-Man Incident

A large but very delicate UFO hovers over a ten-year-old girl on a beach and plays her a startling message, echoing a signal sent from Earth 15 years before.

The Scoutmaster Incident

A scoutleader sees a strange light followed by a crash. He receives mysterious burns but then becomes reluctant to discuss the incident.
with: Russell Wiggins, Steve Patrick

The Atlantic Queen Incident

A ship's officer sights a UFO on a return crossing but his captain believes he has invented the story.
with: Peter Brown, John Anderson, Morey Amsterdam, Jayne Meadows

The Whitman Tower Incident

A mysterious blip appears on the radar screen at Los Angeles Airport. Then residents of a nearby apartment building are startled by a UFO outside their windows.
with: Fred Holliday, Linda Foster, Christopher Woods, Vic Perrin

Q.E.D.

Q.E.D.—which stands for Quentin E. Deverill, not *quod est demonstrandum* (gee, four years of Latin can come in handy!)—was a short-lived series clearly intended as a successor to *The Wild Wild West,* only set in England in 1912. Like *The Wild Wild West,* it involved scientific inventions far ahead of their time and an evil genius, Dr. Kilkiss, who wanted to conquer the world.

Deverill, an American inventor and amateur sleuth, was joined on his adventures by his chauffeur/butler, his secretary, and an American reporter. The series was produced in England by John Hawkesworth, better known for *Upstairs, Downstairs* and *The Duchess of Duke Street.* After an exciting premiere episode, the show became bogged down in darkly ponderous Message Stories and was quickly canceled.

R<small>EGULAR</small> C<small>AST</small>
Quentin E. Deverill Sam Waterston *Phipps* George Innes
Charlie Andrews A.C. Weary *Dr. Stefan Kilkiss* Julian Glover
Jenny Martin Caroline Langrishe

Aired in the U.S. from 23 March 1982–27 April 1982

Q<small>UANTUM</small> L<small>EAP</small>

"It all started when a time travel experiment I was conducting went a little ca-ca."
—Dr. Sam Beckett

While Sam put it bluntly, *Quantum Leap*'s opening narration was a little more elegant: "Theorizing that one could time travel within his own lifetime, Dr. Sam Beckett stepped into the Quantum Leap accelerator and vanished. He woke to find himself trapped in the past, facing mirror images that were not his own and driven by an unknown force to change history for the better."

Quantum Leap not only flouted the usual time-travel conventions of not changing history, it made a virtue out of it. "Every time-travel show worries about the ramifications of changing history," said creator Don Bellisario—the man behind *Magnum* and *Airwolf*—"But we don't."

If ever a series out-performed its format, this was it. Here was a show tailor-made for the nostalgic nineties, playing down the sci-fi to play up the feel-good factor, as quantum physicist Sam leaped around in time, playing cosmic Lone Ranger "to put right what once went wrong."

With his leaps (mostly) confined to his own lifetime—8 August 1953 onward—it was the perfect way for viewers to revisit their own lives and relive the highs and lows of the past four decades.

Nearly every episode ended the same way. Wreathed in blue light, Sam would dematerialize from one life to rematerialize in another body at a crisis point in its life. Taking it all in, he would sum up his predicament in the same two words: "Oh boy!"

It was an endearing catchphrase, perfectly pitched so fans would share in Sam's anticipation of another troublesome adventure next week.

His only companion on his leaps was Al Calavicci, an observer from the Quantum Leap project who appeared as a hologram, invisible to everyone except Sam, animals and children. A rumpled, cigar-smoking womanizer, forever rambling on about his ex-wives, Al acted as Sam's "Tonto," dispensing world-weary wisdom and statistical probabilities about the lastest leap, coughed up by the project computer Ziggy, via an unreliable hand-set that played up like a flashlight with fading batteries.

Viewers only ever saw Sam as himself (otherwise star Scott Bakula's role would have been a small one!). It was only when Sam saw himself in the mirror that we all got a chance to see what kind of face and body everyone around him was seeing. Initially, those faces were white and male, but with the format established, the writers grew bolder and Sam wound up playing women, blacks, children, a Down's Syndrome man and even a chimp!

The show's theory of time travel was explained in the pilot episode by Sam who compared life to a piece of string. "One end is birth, the other is death. Tie the ends together to make a loop. Ball the loop and all the days touch. Thus you can leap from one to another."

The initially sketchy details about project Quantum Leap were gradually filled in, as was Sam's memory, which had been "Swiss-cheesed" by his leaping. When Sam leaped into a new body, that bemused person materialized in the project's "waiting room." Normally they were heard of but never seen, though a couple of exceptions were sex psychologist Dr. Ruth, and a desperate killer who escaped onto the streets of the future.

Sam's adventures were often light and comic, sometimes creepy, sometimes thrilling. They especially confronted prejudice of all shapes, sizes, colors and creeds. And there were some very poignant scenes, such as Sam trying to warn his own family of impending tragedy in their lives and playing John Lennon's *Imagine* to his sister, two years before Lennon would write it. And a shameless homage to *Ghost* had hologram Al "dancing" with the wife who believed him dead— a wrong that was neatly righted in the series' final episode.

The series also had semi-religious undercurrents. Sam became convinced his leaps were being controlled by God, and the series even introduced an evil leaper, Alia, with her own hologram companion, Zoey (played by Carolyn Seymour, who starred as Abby Grant in Terry Nation's *Survivors*).

Quantum Leap rejuvenated the careers of both its stars. Bakula had appeared in a couple of TV flops—*Eisenhower and Lutz* and *Gung Ho*—and former child star Dean Stockwell had dropped out of acting before a string of comeback appearances in films such as *Blue Velvet, Married to the Mob* and *Paris, Texas*.

The series had a rough baptism in America when it was first shown in 1989, languishing at number 88 in the ratings. A switch to a late-night graveyard slot could have killed it off but half a million howls of protest from "Leapers," the show's loyal fans, saved it from the axe.

In the end, though, Sam never made it home—to be reunited with his wife, Donna, introduced in an earlier episode, and the daughter he fathered on another leap. An often baffling last episode (which reverted to using Mike Post's much-loved earlier version of the theme music) saw him materialize in a bar on the day of his birth, as himself, and discuss his destiny with an enigmatic bartender he thought was God! Sam didn't get easy answers and some ends were left loose, all of us having to make do with: "Sometimes, 'that's the way it is' is the best explanation."

REGULAR CAST
Dr. Sam Beckett Scott Bakula *Al Calavicci* Dean Stockwell
Gushie Dennis Wolfberg (*semi-regular*)

Creator: Donald P. Bellisario
Executive producer: Donald P. Bellisario
Co-executive producers: Deborah Pratt (*Seasons Two–Five*), Michael Zinberg (*Seasons Two–Four*), Charles Johnson (*Season Five*)
Producers: Various, including Deborah Pratt, John Hill, Harker Wade, Paul M. Belous, Robert Wolterstorff, Michael Zinberg, Paul Brown, Jeff Gourson, Chris Ruppenthal, Tommy Thompson, Robin Jill Bernheim
Theme: Mike Post

Bellisarius Productions in association with Universal Television/MCA
96 color episodes, 50 minutes except where stated
U.S. premiere: 26 March 1989
U.K. premiere: 13 February 1990
Last episode (U.K.): 21 June 1994
(BBC2)

Season One

Quantum Leap (pilot, aka Genesis)
(90 min.)

w Donald P. Bellisario
Mid-1990s: Dr. Sam Beckett is the head of a time-travel experiment that one day succeeds in working— almost. From a hi-tech lab, Sam wakes to find himself in a strange bed, with a strange wife and with an unfamiliar face staring back at him from the mirror. It's

1956, and Sam is Tom Stratton, test pilot—an interesting job for someone with no idea how to fly . . .
Peg Stratton Jennifer Runyon
Mikey Stratton Christian Van Dorn
Capt. "Bird Dog" Birdell John Allen Nelson
Dr. Ernst (Weird Ernie) Bruce McGill
Dr. Burger W.K. Stratton
Capt. Tony LaMott Larry Poindexter
John Beckett Newell Alexander

Director: David Hemmings

Star-Crossed

w Deborah Pratt
15 June 1972: Sam materializes in the body of an English professor struggling with an over-amorous student and succeeds in reuniting his own future girlfriend, Donna, with her estranged father—at Watergate.
Donna Teri Hatcher
Jamie Lee Leslie Sachs
Col. Wojohowitz Michael Gregory
Oscar Michael McGrady
Harry Ken Gibbel
Frank Charles Walker

Director: Mark Sobel

The Right Hand of God

w John Hill
24 October 1974: Sam bounces into the body of a boxer—and straight into a sucker punch. But, as Clarence "Kid" Cody, he finds he has to fight another day to help a nun build a chapel and defeat a group of mobsters.
Gomez Alex Cólon
Sister Angela Michelle Joyner
Sister Sarah Nancy Kulp
Jake Edwards Guy Stockwell
Dixie Teri Copley
Roscoe Jonathan Gries
Father Muldooney Lewis Arquette
Chalky James Cavan
Tiger Joe Jackson Roger Hewlett

Director: Gilbert Shilton

How the Tess Was Won

w Deborah Arakelian
5 August 1956: Sam lands in the middle of Texas as a mild-mannered vet and thinks his task is to outcowboy the headstrong daughter of a rancher. But a young man called Buddy is about to strum a familiar tune that needs the right name—"Peggy Sue."
Tess McGill Kari Lizer
Chance McGill Lance LeGault
Wayne Marshall R. Teague
Teenage boy (Buddy) Scott Fults
Orly Tommy Bush

Director: Ivan Dixon

Double Identity

w Donald P. Bellisario
8 November 1965: Quantum leaping doesn't seem so bad when Sam wakes in an attic to hear he's a terrific lover—but his enthusiasm wanes when he learns he's a Mafia hit man whose rival in love is a very jealous godfather.
Teresa Teri Garber
Don Geno Michael Genovese
Tony Joe Santos
Primo Nick Cassavettes

Segundo Tom Silardi
Adriano Mark Margolis
Frankie Page Moseley

Director: Aaron Lipstadt

The Color of Truth

w Deborah Pratt
8 August 1955: Materializing as an old black man in a redneck Alabama town, Sam finds himself driving Miz Melny and becoming a driving force in the birth of the civil rights movement.
Miz Melny Susan French
Nell Kimberly Bailey
Clayton Jim Ingersoll
Sheriff Blount Royce D. Applegate
Billy Joe Bob Michael Kruger
Toad Jeff Tyler
Miz Patty Jane Abbott
Willis Michael D. Roberts

Director: Michael Vejar

Camikazi Kid

w Paul Brown
6 June 1961: Sam is an acne-riddled 17-year-old who loves junk food and cars. He jokes that he's here to clear up his complexion, but he really needs to worry about an older sister who's about to enter a bad marriage. (In one delightful incidental scene typical of early leaps, Sam teaches little Michael Jackson the moonwalk, in a washroom. *Beverly Hills 90210*'s Jason Priestley also has a small role in this episode.)
Cheryl Romy Windsor
Bob Thompson Kevin Blair
Chuck Thompson Robert Costanzo
Jill Holly Fields
Pencil Jason Priestley
Dad Richard McGonagle
Janie Janet Carroll

Director: Alan J. Levi

Play It Again, Seymour

w Scott Shepherd & Donald P. Bellisario, *story by* Scott Shepherd, Donald P. Bellisario & Tom Blomquist
14 April 1953: Sam leaps into those mean streets down which a man must walk, especially if he happens to be a Bogey lookalike with a dead partner and cops breathing down his neck. It's like a scene from a pulp novel Sam once read. (Sam also encounters a young Bogey fan who looks a lot like a young Woody Allen . . .)
Allison Claudia Christian
Seymour Willie Garson
Lt. Lannon Richard Riehle
Lionel Paul Linke
Young boy Kevin Mockrin

Director: Aaron Lipstadt

Season Two

Honeymoon Express

w Donald P. Bellisario
27 April 1960: In order to convince a Senate committee to renew funding for the Quantum Leap project, Al needs Sam to prove his existence in the past by altering a historical event. Meanwhile Sam is a newlywed whose bride's homicidal ex-husband wants to kill him.
Diane Alice Adair
Roget Mathieu Carriere
Henri James Mastrantonio
Porter Hank Rolike
Committee chairman Warren Frost

Director: Aaron Lipstadt

Disco Inferno

w Paul Brown
1 April 1976: White polyester suits, platform heels, star signs and people getting down to that disco beat. It's the seventies, and Sam finds himself living the perilous life of a stuntman on a disaster movie who must also prevent a family tragedy. (This episode cleverly intercut footage from the film *Earthquake* to show Lorne Greene trying to rescue him.)
Ray Stone Michael Greene
Chris Stone Kris Kamm
Shannon Kelli Williams
Traci Duvore Arnetia Walker
Rick (director) Peter Onorati

Director: Gilbert Shilton

The Americanization of Machiko

w Charlie Coffey
4 August 1953: Sam goes back to small-town America as a Navy man returning home with a surprise— a Japanese wife. But now he must make his family and the townspeople accept her.
Machiko McKenzie Leila Hee Olsen
Lenore McKenzie K. Callan
Henry McKenzie Wayne Tippit
Naomi Elena Stiteler
Rusty Patrick Massett
Rev. Felcher Chuck Walling

Director: Gilbert Shilton

What Price Gloria?

w Deborah Pratt
16 October 1961: For the first time, Sam becomes a woman—beautiful secretary Samantha—and experiences sexual harassment as he helps save his roommate, Gloria, from committing suicide after being jilted by a two-timing lying married man.

Gloria Collins Jean Sagal
Buddy Wright John Calvin
Gail Wright Laurel Schaefer
Johnny Jack Armstrong
Parker Gregg Berger
Richard Matt Landers

Director: Alan J. Levi

Blind Faith

w Scott Shepherd
6 February 1964: The Beatles are about to take America by storm, but Sam finds himself as a brilliant, blind concert pianist who must save a young woman from both her possessive mother and a killer stalking Central Park.
Michele Stevens Cynthia Bain
Agnes Stevens Jennifer Rhodes
Pete O'Shannon Kevin Skousen

Director: David G. Phinney

Good Morning, Peoria

w Chris Ruppenthal
9 September 1959: Sam leaps into the body of DJ Howlin' Chick Howell and helps a young woman save her radio station from a small-town's anti-rock 'n' roll campaign. (He also teaches Chubby Checker to do the Twist!)
Rachel Porter Patricia Richardson
Fred Beeman Richard McKenzie
Brian Todd Merrill
Himself Chubby Checker
Leland Steve Bean
Mayor Hal England
Sheriff Jake Foley E.R. Davies
Theora Barbara Perry

Director: Michael Zinberg

Thou Shalt Not . . .

w Tammy Ader
2 February 1974: Sam assumes the identity of a rabbi trying to prevent the break-up of a family unable to resolve their anger and guilt over the death of their son. (He also performs the Heimlich maneuver on a choking man—a Dr. Heimlich!)
Bert Glasserman Russ Tamblyn
Irene Basch Terri Hanauer
Karen Basch Lindsay Fisher
Joe Basch James Sutorius
Shirley Winnick Jill Jacobson
Hannah Twink Caplan

Director: Randy Roberts

Jimmy

w Paul M. Belous & Robert Wolterstorff
14 October 1964: Sam's eyes are opened to the prejudice facing the mentally handicapped when he leaps into the life of Down's Syndrome sufferer Jimmy La Matta.
Frank La Matta John DiAquino
Connie La Matta Laura Harrington
Corey La Matta Ryan McWhorter
Jimmy La Matta Brad Silverman
Blue Tamino Michael Madsen
Charlie Samuels Michael Alldredge

Director: James Whitmore Jr.

So Help Me God

w Deborah Pratt
29 July 1957: Sam becomes a lawyer in a bigoted Louisiana town, defending a young black woman accused of murdering the son of the most powerful man in town.
Delilah Barry Tyra Ferrell
Captain Cotter Byrne Piven
Bo Parsons John Shephard
Judge Haller William Schallert
Myrtle Ketty Lester
Sadie Cotter Kathleen Noone
Sugee Dancey Stacy Ray
Sheriff Dixon John Apicella

Director: Andy Cadiff

Catch a Falling Star

w Paul Brown
21 May 1979: Sam finds himself an understudy in an off-Broadway production of *Man of La Mancha* who must save the hard-drinking star from falling down on stage and ruining his life.
John O'Malley John Cullum
Nicole Michele Pawk
Michelle Janine Turner
Manny Ernie Sabella
Charlie Paul Sand
Dolores Myra Turley
Anita Maria Lauren

Director: Donald P. Bellisario

A Portrait for Troian

w Scott Shepherd & Donald P. Bellisario, story
by John Hill & Scott Shepherd
7 February 1971: Sam leaps into the world of the paranormal when he must save a young woman from being driven insane by her dead husband's spirit.

Troian Deborah Pratt
Jimmy Robert Torti
Miss Stoltz Carolyn Seymour

Director: Michael Zinberg

Animal Frat

w Chris Ruppenthal
19 October 1967: Sam becomes the craziest fraternity brother on campus, who must put aside beer and women to prevent a fellow student from making a fatal mistake by blowing up the chemistry lab.
Elizabeth Stacy Edwards
Duck Darren Dalton
Hags Stuart Fratkin
Guna Brian Haley
Will Raphael Sbarge
Scooter Robert Petkoff
Professor Davenport Edward Edwards

Director: Gilbert Shilton

Another Mother

w Deborah Pratt
30 September 1981: Sam leaps into a newly divorced mother of three and discovers the difficulties of coping with an adolescent son fated to run away from home and then vanish off the face of the Earth—plus a four-year-old who can see Sam as he really is, and Al, too.
Kevin Buckner Michael Stoyanov
Susan Buckner Olivia Burnette
Teresa Buckner Troian Bellisario
Jackie Arnett Allison Barron
Teddy Andrew Held
Ox Larron Tate
David Kevin Telles
Paul Eric Welch
Stick Terrence Evans
Lemule Michael Kemmerling

Director: Joseph L. Scanlan

All-Americans

w Paul Brown & Donald P. Bellisario
6 November 1962: This time, Sam's a star high-school quarterback whose goal is to stop his best friend and teammate from throwing a vital championship football game.
Chuey Martinez Richard Coca
Celia Martinez Ruth Britt
Manuel Vega Pepe Serna
Ruben de Guerra Fausto Bara
Coach Robert Benedetti

Director: John Cullum

Her Charm

w Deborah Pratt & Donald P. Bellisario, *story by*
Paul M. Belous, Robert Wolterstorff, Deborah Pratt & Donald P. Bellisario
26 September 1973: The Lone Ranger's latest leap lands him in the path of a hail of bullets as he becomes an FBI agent assigned to protect an abrasive young woman from a murderous mobster.
Dana Barrenger Teri Austin
Richardson Stanley Brock
Nick Kochifos John Snyder
Andry René Assa
Thomas John Shepherd
Prof. Sebastian LoNigro James Hardie

Director: Christopher T. Welch

Freedom

w Chris Ruppenthal
22 November 1970: Sam finds himself in the body of an American Indian who helped his grandfather escape from a nursing home, but must now find a way for him to die with dignity.
Joseph Washakie Frank Sotonoma Salsedo
Sheriff Taggart Leon Rippy
Suzanne Washakie Gloria Hayes
Deputy Hazlitt Tom Everett

Director: Alan J. Levi

Good Night, Dear Heart

w Paul Brown
9 November 1957: Sam becomes a mortician obsessed with the apparent suicide of a beautiful German girl.
Stephanie Heywood Marcia Cross
Roger Truesdale William Cain
Greg Truesdale Robert Duncan McNeill
Sheriff Lyle Roundtree W.K. Stratton
Aggie Deborah Strang
Hilla Danner Suzanne Tegman

Director: Christopher T. Welch

Pool Hall Blues

w Randy Holland
4 September 1954: Sam leaps into the body of Charlie "Black Magic" Walters, a pool player who is about to be challenged by an unscrupulous young pretender—and at stake is a young woman's future.
Violet Shari Headley

Eddie Davis J.W. Smith
Grady Teddy Wilson
"The Brush" Ken Foree
Mr. Griffin Robert Gossett

Director: Joe Napolitano

Leaping In without a Net

w Tommy Thompson
18 November 1958: Sam becomes a trapeze artist who must prevent his sister from suffering a fatal fall in a death-defying stunt. All Sam has to do is conquer his own fear of heights.
Eva Panzini Fabiana Udenio
Laszlo Panzini Jan Triska
Benny Skyler Jan Eddy
Big Moe Phil Fondacaro
Clifford Vargas Richard Riehle
Sybil Roya Megnot

Director: Christopher T. Welch

Maybe Baby

w Paul Brown & Julie Brown
11 March 1963: Sam leaps into the formidable body of a nightclub bouncer who is helping a stripper to kidnap a baby girl.
Bunny O'Hare Julie Brown
Sheriff Barnes Jimmie Ray Weeks
Reed Dalton Charles Frank
Deputy Sutton Travis McKenna
Margaret Cole Maggie Egan
Christy Cathy McAuley

Director: Michael Zinberg

Sea Bride

w Deborah Pratt
3 June 1954: Arriving on the *Queen Mary*, Sam finds he's a debonair adventurer who must try to prevent his ex-wife from going through with a disastrous remarriage.
Catherine Farlington Beverly Leech
Weathers Farlington John Hertzler
Jennifer Farlington Juliet Sorcey
Marian Farlington Patricia Harty
Vincent Loggia James Harper
Alfonso Louis Guss
Tony Tony Maggio
Captain Sheffield Kurt Knudson

Director: Joe Napolitano

M.I.A.

w Donald P. Bellisario
1 April 1969: Sam becomes an undercover detective and thinks he must be an April fool when Al tells him his task is merely to prevent a young woman, who believes her husband died in Vietnam, from falling for another man. What he doesn't know is the woman is Al's wife, Beth. (This was one loose end that was neatly tied up in the final episode.)
Beth Calavicci Susan Diol
Sgt. Robert Skaggs Jason Beghe
Dirk Simon Norman Large
Sgt. Riley Dan Ziskie
Tequila Pat Skipper
Boner William Shockley

Director: Michael Zinberg

Season Three

The Leap Home

w Donald P. Bellisario
25 November 1969: Sam leaps into his own body back in Elk Ridge, Indiana, at the age of 16, and gets a chance to alter his own family's destiny. His father is heading toward a fatal heart attack, sister Katey is to ruin her future by eloping with an abusive alcoholic, and Tom, the elder brother Sam never really got to know, has enlisted for Vietnam where he is fated to die. Can Sam save his family and rid himself of the guilt he has been carrying with him most of his adult life? (First of a two-part story.)
His father Scott Bakula
Thelma Beckett Caroline Kava
Tom Beckett David Newsom
Katey Beckett Olivia Burnette
Coach Donnelly Mik Scriba
Mary Lou Hannah Cutrona
Dr. Berger Miles Brewster
No Nose Pruitt John Tuell

Director: Joe Napolitano

The Leap Home, Part II—Vietnam

w Donald P. Bellisario
7 April 1970: Sam finds himself part of an elite marine squad headed by his brother Tom. Knowing his brother died on 8 April, Sam can't believe his mission is actually to save the life of a beautiful photojournalist, Maggie Dawson. He succeeds in saving Tom—but at the cost of Maggie's life. Later, when her last dramatic picture of a POW is developed, it's Al's face we see . . .
Tom Beckett David Newsom
Maggie Dawson Andrea Thompson
Col. Deke Grimwald Ernie Lively

Dempsey David Hayward
TiTi Tia Carrere
Preacher Adam Nelson
Blaster Patrick Warburton
Shamoo Ryan Reid
Doc Rich Whiteside

Director: Michael Zinberg

Leap of Faith

w Tommy Thompson, *story by* Nick Harding, Karen Hall & Tommy Thompson
19 August 1963: Sam leaps into the body of a priest and must prevent the death of a fellow priest who witnessed the murder of a 12-year-old boy.
Father McRoberts Sandy McPeak
Tony Pronti Danny Nucci
Joey Pronti Davey Roberts
Rose Montocelli Erica Yohn
Rita Montocelli Penny Santon
Father Pistano Bud Sabatino

Director: James Whitmore Jr.

One Strobe Over the Line

w Chris Ruppenthal
15 June 1965: Sam becomes a fashion photographer who has to babysit a glamorous model to prevent her from overdosing on pills and alcohol.
Helen Susan Anton
Edie Lansdale Marjorie Monaghan
Byron Kristoffer Tabori
Mike David Sheinkopf
Frank David Trumbull

Director: Michael Zinberg

The Boogieman

w Chris Ruppenthal
31 October 1964: Things go bump in the night as Sam becomes a second-rate horror novelist who witnesses a series of bizarre murders that lead him into a deadly dance with the devil who wants to put an end to Sam's "meddling." (This spooky tale also sees Sam give an aspiring young storyteller his horrific ideas.)
Mary Greeley Valerie Mahaffey
Sheriff Ben Masters Paul Linke
Dorothy Yeager Fran Ryan
Stevie King David Kriegel
Tully Maltin Donald Hotton
Nurse Jan Stratton
Joshua Rey Chris Ruppenthal

Director: Joe Napolitano

Miss Deep South

w Tommy Thompson
7 June 1958: Sam becomes a contestant in the Miss Deep South beauty pageant with the double task of ensuring he wins third prize, while keeping a beautiful fellow contestant from destroying her life by posing for nude photos.
Peg Myers Nancy Stafford
Connie Heather McAdam
Clint Beaumont David A. Brooks
Vicky Julie Ann Lowery
Judge Hugh Gillin
Arlene Monty Linda Hoy
Darlene Monty Theresa King

Director: Christopher T. Welch

Black on White on Fire

w Deborah Pratt
11 August 1965: On the eve of the Watts riots, Sam has become a promising black medical student involved with the white daughter of a police captain. With mayhem on the streets, Sam has to fight to keep the lovers together in an environment of racial hatred that threatens both their lives.
Susan Bond Corie Henninger
Captain Paul Bond Marc Alaimo
Lonnie Jordan Gregory Millar
Mama Harper C.C.H. Pounder
BB Sami Chester
Papa Dee Ron Taylor
Shari Hill Laverne Anderson

Director: Joe Napolitano

The Great Spontini

w Cristy Dawson & Beverly Bridges
9 May 1974: Oakland, California. Sam is Harry Spontini, a struggling magician whose 12-year-old daughter and assistant dreams of settling down with him. When her estranged mother walks back into their lives, Harry faces a custody battle.
Jamie Spontini Lauren Woodland
Maggie Amy F. Steel
Steve Slater Erich Anderson
Judge Mulhern Michael Fairman
Elaine Robin Greer

Director: James Whitmore Jr.

Rebel Without a Clue

w Randy Holland & Paul Brown
1 September 1958: Sam leaps into the body of Shane "Funny Bone" Thomas, a member of a rebellious bike gang, to stop the senseless death of a free-

spirited girl obsessed with experiencing the lifestyle of Jack Kerouac's novel *On the Road.*
Becky Josie Bissett
Dillon Dietrich Bader
Ernie Teddy Wilson
Jack Kerouac Michael Bryan
Mad Dog Mark Boone Junior
Ice Scott Kraft
Kraut Joshua Cadman

Director: James Whitmore Jr.

A Little Miracle

w Sandy Fries & Robert A. Wolterstorff, *story by* Sandy Fries
24 December 1962: On Christmas Eve, Sam re-enacts *A Christmas Carol* to remind millionaire financier Michael Blake that there is more to life than material wealth and, in doing so, prevents a Salvation Army hostel from being demolished.
Michael Blake Charles Rocket
Laura Downey Melinda McGraw
Calloway Robert Lesser
Jason Calloway Tom McTigue
Lt. Porterman Michael Dan Wagnet

Director: Michael Watkins

Runaway

w Paul Brown
4 July 1964: It's the eve of the feminist revolution and Sam has leaped into the body of 13-year-old Butchie Rickett, who must keep his mother from running out on her family.
Emma Rickett Sandy Faison
Alex Rickett Ami Foster
Hank Rickett Sherman Howard
Bill McCann Joseph Hacker
Beth McCann Amer Susa

Director: Michael Katleman

8½ months

w Deborah Pratt
15 November 1955: Having leaped into the body of 16-year-old Billie Jean of Claremore, Oklahoma, Sam finds himself in labor and on a mission to stop her losing her baby through adoption.
Dottie Lana Schwab
Bob James Whitmore Jr.
Keeter Hunter van Leer
Effy Tasha Scott
Mrs. Thailer Anne Haney
Dr. Rogers Parley Baer

Director: James Whitmore Jr.

Future Boy

w Tommy Thompson
6 October 1957: Sam becomes sidekick to Captain Galaxy, a popular fifties TV character, and must prevent the star, eccentric actor Moe Stein, from being committed to a mental institution due to his obsession with a time machine he has built that is curiously based on Sam's own "ball of string" theory . . .
Moe Stein Richard Herd
Irene Debra Stricklin
Ben George Wyner
Dr. Richard Sandler Alan Fudge
Judge David Sage

Director: Michael Switzer

Private Dancer

w Paul Brown
6 October 1979: Sam leaps into the body of an "exotic" male dancer who must steer a deaf girl toward a professional dancing career. (Guest star and director was *Fame*'s Debbie Allen.)
Dianna Perry Rhondee Beriault
Joanne Chapman Debbie Allen
Mario Louis Mustillo
Valerie Jackson Heidi Swedberg
Otto Robert Schuch

Director: Debbie Allen

Piano Man

w Ed Scharlach
10 November 1985: Tinkling the ivories in a crowded nightclub, Sam has leaped into the body of Chuck Danner whose ex-partner has found him again after a three-year search. But she is not the only one looking for Chuck, as an exploding car is soon to prove.
Lorraine Marietta DePrima
Carl Angelo Tiffe
Frank John Oldbach
Jenelle Denise Gentile

Director: James Whitmore Jr.

Southern Comforts

w Tommy Thompson
4 August 1961: Blowing out birthday candles in a New Orleans bordello may be Al's idea of heaven, but Sam has 24 hours to save one of the girls from a grisly death.
Marsha Rita Taggart
Gina Georgia Emelin
Sheriff Nolan David Graf
Jake Dan Butler
Sophie Lauren Tom

Director: Chris Ruppenthal

Glitter Rock

w Chris Ruppenthal
12 April 1974: English rock band King Thunder is performing in front of 80,000 screaming fans when Sam leaps into the body of their lead singer, Tonic. Is he there to enhance the sound of the seventies—or is his task a more noble one? (Featuring Peter Noone, former singer with pop band Herman's Hermits.)
Dwayne Peter Noone
Flash Jonathan Gries
Nick Robert Bauer
Phillip Christian Hoff
Sandy Liza Whitcraft
Whittler Jan Eddy
Cavin Michael Cerveris

Director: Andy Cadiff

A Hunting We Will Go

w Beverly Bridges
18 June 1976: Sam finds himself in the body of a professional bounty hunter handcuffed to a woman accused of a million-dollar embezzlement.
Diane Frost Jane Sibbett
Sheriff Michaels Cliff Bemis
Rodney Owens Ken Marshall
Jack Michael McCarty

Director: Andy Cadiff

Last Dance Before an Execution

w Deborah Pratt, *story by* Bill Bigelow, Donald P. Bellisario & Deborah Pratt
12 May 1971: Sam finds himself in the body of a convicted murderer, strapped into the electric chair. Given a last-minute reprieve, Sam has 48 hours to prove him innocent.
Theodore Moody James Sloyan
Tearsa Lorrea Jenny Gago
Raul Casta Julio Oscar Mechoso
Alan Ripley Christopher Allport

Director: Michael Watkins

Heart of a Champion

w Tommy Thompson
23 July 1955: Sam leaps into the body of wrestling tag team brother Terry Samis and must save his partner Ronnie from dying from heart failure during a title fight.
Ronnie Jerry Bossard
Lamar Don Hood
Sherry Deborah Wakeham
Lotty Angela Paton
Carl Terry Funk
Dr. Griggs Rance Howard

Director: Joe Napolitano

Nuclear Family

w Paul Brown
26 October 1962: Sam becomes a 19-year-old at the height of the Cuban missile crisis. With people expecting annihilation at any moment, he has to prevent a senseless murder caused by hysterical panic.
Mac Ellroy Timothy Carhart
Kate Ellroy Kim Flowers
Stevie Ellroy Robert Hy Gorman
Kimberly Ellroy Candy Hutson
Burt Rosecranes Kurt Fuller
Mrs. Klingman Delia Salvi

Director: James Whitmore Jr.

Shock Theater

w Deborah Pratt
3 October 1954: Sam leaps into the body of a manic depressive patient in a mental institution. His task is to assist another patient, but Sam is having trouble keeping his own mind clear in the face of a sadistic orderly who gives him unprescribed shock therapy.
Dr. Masters David Proval
Nurse Chatam Lee Garlington
Tibby Scott Lawrence
Butcher Bruce A. Young
Freddy Nick Brooks
Dr. Wickless Robert Symonds
Oswald Ralph Marrero
Dr. Beaks Candy Ann Brown
Jesse Tyler Howard Matthew Johnson
Samantha Stormer La Reine Chabut
Jimmy Brad Silverman

Director: Joe Napolitano

Season Four

The Leap Back

w Donald P. Bellisario
18 September 1999/15 June 1945: Sam and Al have leaped through time simultaneously—which means they have changed places. Now Sam's the hologram—but he is also reunited back at the project lab with Donna, the wife he had forgotten even existed. Meanwhile, back in 1945, Al must prevent the deaths of former POW Tom Jarret and his pre-war fiancée.
Suzanne Elsinga Amanda Wyss
Dr. Donna Elesee Mimi Kuzyk
Mike Douglas Roberts
Clifford Brown Robert Prescott
Kelly Jeanine Jackson
Dr. Beeks Candy Ann Brown
Gushie Dennis Wolfberg
Tina Gigi Rice
Navy admiral Susan Ann Connor

Director: Michael Zinberg

Play Ball

w Tommy Thompson
6 August 1961: Sam leaps into the life of Lester "Doc" Fuller, an ex-major-league baseball pitcher now ekeing out a living in a minor-league team, and helps him back to the big time, while also reuniting a young pitcher with his estranged father.
Chucky Neal McDonough
Margaret Twilly Maree Cheatham
Bunny Twilly Courtney Gebhart
Coach Harlan Don Stroud
Kilpatrick Peter Jason
Warren Monroe Casey Sanders
Radio reporter Royce D. Applegate

Director: Joe Napolitano

Hurricane

w Chris Ruppenthal
17 August 1969: Jackson Point, Mississippi: Sam becomes Sheriff Archie Necaise and must save girlfriend Cissy from getting killed by the approaching Hurricane Camille.
Cissy Davis Marilyn Jones
Lisa Tracy Kolis
Unabelle Marjorie Lovett
Mark Richard Grove
Joe James Morrison
Deever Bill Erwin
Sitter Stephanie Shroyer
Ma'maw Barbara Townsend

Director: Michael Watkins

Justice

w Toni Graphia
11 May 1965: Much to his disgust, Sam finds himself a member of the Ku Klux Klan. His mission, however, is to prevent the lynching of a black rights activist.
Gene/Grand Dragon Noble Willingham
Lilly Lisa Waltz
Nathaniel Simpson Michael Beach
Ada Simpson Fran Bennett
Tom Dirk Blocker
Cody Jacob Gelman
Grady Glenn Morshower
Herman Thompson Lee Weaver
Sheriff Otis Charlie Holliday
Leon Steve Blackwood
Jim Michael Craig Patterson

Director: Rob Bowman

Permanent Wave

w Beverly Bridges
2 June 1983: Sam becomes a hairstylist and must protect a mother and her young handicapped son after the boy witnesses a shooting.
Laura Doran Clark
Kyle Joseph Gordon-Levitt
Chloe Lela Ivey
Detective Arnie Ward Harry Groener
Ralph Stephen Kay
Mimi Christine Cattell

Director: Scott Bakula

Raped

w Beverly Bridges
20 June 1980: Sam experiences the pressures exerted on a date rape victim who is made to feel guiltier than the perpetrator.
Katie McBain Cheryl Pollak
Nancy Hudson Penny Peyser
Colleen McBain Nancy Lenehan
Jim McBain Arthur Rosenberg
Libby McBain Amy Ryan
Kevin Wentworth Matthew Sheehan
Officer Neil Shumway Eugene Lee
Paula Fletcher Liz Vassey
Dr. Samuel Markoff Michael Griswold

Director: Michael Zinberg

The Wrong Stuff

w Paul Brown
24 January 1961: In one of his most unusual leaps so far, Sam finds himself in the body of Bobo, a chimp in the space program destined to die instead in a cruel crash helmet research project.
Dr. Leslie Ashton Caroline Goodall
Dr. Frank Winger Gary Swanson
Dr. Max Tucker Albert Stratton
Kenny Kim Robillard
Roland Peter Murnik

Director: Joe Napolitano

Dreams

w Deborah Pratt
28 February 1979: Sam leaps into the body of Lt. Jack Stone, a police officer investigating a gruesome murder, and is strangely affected by something terrible that happened to Stone, which he must overcome to identify the killer and save his own life.
Pamela Roselli Jocelyn O'Brien
Mason Crane Alan Scarfe

Capt. Vincent Bill Marcus
Peter DeCaro Tim Ahern
Lea DeCaro Noely Thornton
P.J. DeCaro Michael Patrick Carter
Officer Talbot Anthony Pena

Director: Anita Addison

A Single Drop of Rain

w Richard C. Okie, *story by* Richard Stanley **&** Ralph Meyering Jr.
7 September 1953: Sam has leaped into the life of Billy Beaumont, a traveling rain-maker. His mission is to save Billy's brother's marriage.
Annie K. Beaumont Phyllis Lyons
Ralph Beaumont Patrick Massett
Clinton Levering Carl Anthony Payne II
Vern Coutis Britt Leach
Gid Davison R.G. Armstrong
Grace Beaumont Anne Haney
Norm Sanford Hal Landon Jr.
Velma Waters Lesly Kahn

Director: Virgil W. Vogel

Unchained

w Paris Qualles
2 November 1956: Sam leaps into the body of Chance Cole, a 40-year-old prisoner sentenced to nine months on a chain gang for passing dud checks, but must prove the innocence of a fellow inmate, wrongly convicted of armed robbery.
Jasper Boone Basil Wallace
Boss Cooley J.C. Quinn
Capt. Elias Claude Earl Jones
Jake Wiles Don Sparks
Monroe Jed Mills
Toot Robert V. Barron

Director: Michael Watkins

The Play's the Thing

w Beverly Bridges
9 September 1969: Sam awakes to find himself a struggling young actor and the boy toy of an older woman who wants to make it as a singer, but whose strait-laced son wants her to return to a life of dull domesticity.
Jane Lindhurst Penny Fuller
Neil Lindhurst Daniel Roebuck
Liz Lindhurst Anna Gunn
Ted Guest Robert Pine
Sheldon Craig Richard Nelson
Petra Eva Loseth
Rob Novack Paul Collins

Director: Eric Laneuville

Running for Honor

w Robert Harris Duncan
11 June 1964: Sam becomes a brilliant naval cadet whose roommate has been run off campus by a gay-bashing clique.
Admiral Spencer John Finn
Phillip Ashcroft Sean O'Bryan
Ronnie Chambers Anthony Palermo
Coach Capt. Randall Martz John Roselius
Karen Spencer Lisa Lawrence

Director: Bob Hulme

Temptation Eyes

w Paul Brown
1 February 1985: Sam leaps into the body of a television newsreader who becomes the unwitting confidant of a killer responsible for a series of gruesome murders in San Francisco's Chinatown. He also falls in love with a psychic who is able to see him as he really is.
Tamlyn Matsuda Tamlyn Tomita
Ross Tyler James Handy
Tony Beche Rob Labelle
Max Collins Kent Williams
Dylan Powell Harker Wade

Director: Christopher Hibler

The Last Gunfighter

w Sam Rolfe & Chris Ruppenthal, *story by* Sam Rolfe
28 November 1957: Sam becomes 82-year-old Tyler Means, the aging hero who cleaned up the town of Coffin, Arizona, by shooting the infamous Claggett brothers. But Tyler's claim to fame is challenged by a man from the past, seeking revenge.
Pat Knight John Anderson
Lucy Susan Isaacs
Stevie Sean Baca
Ben Steiner Kenneth Tigar
Sheriff Russ O'Neal Compton
Jerry Jerry Potter
Otis Joseph Burke
Cindy Bonnie Morgan

Director: Joe Napolitano

A Song for the Soul

w Deborah Pratt
7 April 1963: Sam becomes Cheree of the Lovettes singing group and must stop one of the girls from leaving school and running away from her disapproving father to try to make it as a singer.
Rev Walters Harrison Page

Bobby Lee Eric LaSalle
Lynell Tammy Townsend
Paula T'Keyah "Crystal" Keymah

Director: Michael Watkins

Ghost Ship

w Donald P. Bellisario, Paul Brown & Paris Qualles
13 August 1956: Sam finds himself flying a private plane through the Bermuda Triangle to reach Bermuda before one of his passengers dies of a burst appendix.
Grant Cutter Jr. Kurt Deutsch
Michelle Cutter Carla Cugino
Wendy Kimberly Foster
Capt. Dan Cooper Scott Hoxby

Director: Anita Addison

Roberto!

w Chris Ruppenthal
27 January 1982: Sam becomes Roberto, a TV talk show host with an abrasive attitude toward his colleagues. But as an investigative reporter, Roberto seeks to uncover the source of deadly gases being produced at a nearby pesticide plant.
Jani Eisenberg DeLane Matthews
Ed Saxton Jerry Hardin
Rick Marcus Giamatti
Earl Alan Oppenheimer
Tim Michael Heinzman
Red Norton Dennis Fimple
Gruel Don Gibb
Jeeters Charles Dougherty

Director: Scott Bakula

It's a Wonderful Leap

w Danielle Alexandra & Paul Brown, *story by* Danielle Alexandra
10 May 1958: Sam becomes a New York cabbie and accidentally runs over a woman who says she is a guardian angel sent to stop him from getting shot by robbers. What's more, she can see Al.
Angela Jiminez Liz Torres
Lenny Greenman Jerry Adler
Frank O'Connor Jr. Peter Iacangelo
Elizabeth Katz Robin Frates
Tony Jack R. Orand
Lucky Milt Kogan
Moe Douglas MacHugh

Director: Paul Brown

Moments to Live

w Tommy Thompson
4 May 1985: Sam finds himself in the body of a TV soap opera star kidnapped by an obsessed fan who wants to have his child.
Norma Jean Pilcher Kathleen Wilhoit
Hank Pilcher Pruitt Taylor Vince
Mama (Millie Reynolds) Frances Bay
Ben Ratcliff Brian George
TV husband Matthew Ashford
Roger Vickers James Gleason
Nurse Diane Kidman Krista Mione

Director: Joe Napolitano

The Curse of Ptah-Hotep

w Chris Ruppenthal
2 March 1957: Sam leaps into the body of Dale Conway, an archaeology professor exploring an Egyptian tomb where he is due to disappear, along with an attractive 32-year-old professor, Ginny Will.
Ginny Will Lisa Darr
Ali Chaim Jeraffi
Gamal Ali Dean
Dr. Mustafa John Kapelos

Director: Joe Napolitano

Stand Up

w Bill Richmond & Deborah Pratt
30 April 1959: Sam becomes a nightclub singer who must save his comedian partner, Mack, from being killed when a powerful club owner takes a liking to Mack's girlfriend, Frankie.
Mack MacKay Bob Saget
Frankie Amy Yasbeck
Joe the Heckler Tom LaGrua
Lou Mark Lonow
Carlo DeGorio Robert Miranda

Director: Michael Zinberg

A Leap for Lisa

w Donald P. Bellisario
22 June 1957: Sam leaps into the body of Al as a young naval pilot (with the nickname Bingo) and must prove he did not rape and murder the kinky wife of his commanding officer, Riker. But after Lisa, his alibi, dies in a car crash, the trial goes badly, and hologram Al disappears, even fading from Sam's mind, to be replaced by new man Edward St. John V. . . .
Lt. Lisa Sherman Terry Farrell
Cmdr. Hugh Dobbs Larry Brandenburg
Ensign Chip Ferguson Jeffrey Corbett
Cmdr. Dirk Riker Charles Rocket
Lt. Comdr. Kobliz Anthony Peck

Admiral Pollack Steve Carlisle
Edward St. John V. Roddy McDowall
Marci Riker Debbie L. James

Director: James Whitmore Jr.

Season Five

Lee Harvey Oswald

w Donald P. Bellisario
5 October 1957 to 22 November 1963: A feature-length special to tie in with the 30th anniversary of the shooting of John F. Kennedy. Sam leaps in and out of the body of Lee Harvey Oswald, taking on his personality and volatile emotions while affecting key events in his life—with the U.S. military in Japan and his meeting with the KGB—leading to 22 November 1963, the day Oswald shot the president.
Lee Harvey Oswald Willie Garson
Marina Oswald Natasha Pavlova
Major Yuri Kosenko Elya Baskin
Gushie Dennis Wolfberg
Bargirl Patty Toy
Lt. Obrigowitz Ward C. Boland
Mariska Donna Magnani
Sgt. Lopez Reni Santoni
PFC Briggs Philip McNiven
Corp. McBride Michael Rich
Lt. Anna Guri Erika Amato
Sgt. Bellisario Matthew Charles Nelson
Jackie Kennedy Karen Ingram

Director: James Whitmore Jr.

Leaping of the Shrew

w Richard C. Okie & Robin Jill Bernheim
27 September 1956: Sam leaps into the body of a Greek sailor shipwrecked with a beautiful, but spoiled, rich girl and teaches her to follow her heart.
Vanessa Foster Brooke Shields

Director: Alan J. Levi

Nowhere to Run

w Tommy Thompson
10 August 1968: Sam takes over the body of a legless Vietnam veteran undergoing therapy at a hospital where he is befriended by a young volunteer nurse. But he must overcome a brutal and unsympathetic orderly to stop another crippled young soldier from drowning himself in despair.
Sgt. Bill Johnson Michael Boatman
Kiki Wilson Jennifer Aniston
Commander James Hartig Norman Snow
Holt Gene Lythgow
Julie Miller Judith Hoag
Carol Simone Allen

Director: Alan J. Levi

Killin' Time

w Tommy Thompson
18 June 1958: Sam leaps into the life of mass murderer Leon Stiles who has escaped custody and taken a mother and her young daughter hostage in their home, which is surrounded by police. Meanwhile, in the Imaging Chamber, the confused but desperate Stiles steals a guard's gun and escapes onto the streets. Sam must reluctantly hold on to his hostages to keep himself alive while Al tries to recapture Stiles.
Carol Pruitt Connie Ray
Becky Pruitt Beverley Mitchell
Leon Stiles Cameron Dye
Sheriff Hoyt Jim Haynie
Deputy Grimes Joseph Malone
Gushie Dennis Wolfberg

Director: Michael Watkins

Star Light, Star Bright

w Richard C. Okie
21 May 1966: As 79-year-old Max Stoddard, Sam must prove he has seen a UFO so his family does not have him committed to a mental institution. He must also cope with the attentions of two government agents whose investigations into Max's claims could force Sam to reveal details of Project Quantum Leap. He also finds time to play Hendrix's version of *Star Spangled Banner* on his amazed teenage grandson's electric guitar and pass on a warning about the dangers of drug abuse!
Tim Stoddard Morgan Weisser
John Stoddard Guy Boyd
Eva Stoddard Anne Lockhart
Major Meadows Michael L. Maguire
Dr. Hardy H. Richard Greene
Officer Milardi Joshua Cox

Director: Christopher Hibler

Deliver Us from Evil (aka Evil Leaper I)

w Robin Jill Bernheim, Deborah Pratt & Tommy Thompson
19 March 1966: This time Sam leaps back into the body of the retarded Jimmy La Matta with a mission to save the marriage of Jimmy's brother, Frank, and his wife, Connie. But dark forces are at work in the guise of another leaper—the wicked Alia and her hologram observer, Zoey. Alia has leaped into Connie's body and her mission is to get Jimmy institutionalized. But when they come into contact, there is an immediate connection between Sam and Alia . . .
Frank La Matta John DiAquino
Connie La Matta Laura Harrington
Shirley Kristen Cloke
Alia Renée Coleman
Zoey Carolyn Seymour
Corey La Matta Ryan McWhorter

Director: Bob Hulme

Trilogy Part I (aka One Little Heart)

w Deborah Pratt
8 August 1955: As Louisiana sheriff Clayton Fuller, Sam takes the first leap in a trilogy concerning the loves and tribulations of Fuller's daughter, Abagail, who is accused of two murders. Fuller's wife, Laura, is in a mental asylum and Sam finds out that her mother killed all her children except Laura, then killed herself. The simple townsfolk believe the family is cursed, and a crazed widow is out for revenge . . .
Abagail Kimberley Cullum
Leta Aider Mary Gordon Murray
Laura Fuller Meg Foster
Doc Kinman Max Wright
Bo Loman Stephen Lee
Marie Fran Bennett
Will Kinman Travis Fine

Director: James Whitmore Jr.

Trilogy Part II (aka For Your Love)

w Deborah Pratt
14 June 1966: Sam now leaps into Will Kinman, the teenager from Part 1, who is now a deputy. He and Abagail are about to marry when the young boy she has been babysitting disappears and she is once again accused of murder by an angry lynch mob.
Abagail Melora Hardin
Laura Fuller Meg Foster
Leta Aider Mary Gordon Murray
Ms. Takins Wendy Robie
Mr. Takins Christopher Curry
Bo Loman Stephen Lee
Marie Fran Bennett
Will Kinman Travis Fine
Stanton W.K. Stratton

Director: James Whitmore Jr.

Trilogy Part III (aka The Last Door)

w Deborah Pratt
28 July 1978: In the final part of this trilogy, Sam leaps into the body of elderly attorney Lawrence Stanton who must prove Abagail's innocence when she's put on trial for the murder of Leta Aider. Sam also discovers that Abagail's daughter, Sammy Jo, is his child.
Laura Fuller Meg Foster
Abagail Melora Hardin
Doc Kinman Max Wright
Denton Waters James Greene
Judge Shiner Parley Baer
Bo Loman Stephen Lee
Marie Fran Bennett
Cherlyn Stanton Diana Bellamy
Sammy Jo Kimberly Cullum
Violet Heather Lauren Olsen

Director: James Whitmore Jr.

Promised Land

w Gillian Horvath & Tommy Thompson
22 December 1971: Sam returns to his hometown of Elk Ridge, Indiana, as Bill Walters who, with his two brothers, is holding up the town's bank for the exact amount of money owed by the Walters farm.
Neil Walters Dwier Brown
John Walters Chris Stacy
Sheriff Mundy Arlen Dean Snyder
Gus Vernon Jonathan Hogan
Beth Ryan Elizabeth Dennehy
Carrie Young Kellie Overbey
Mary Walters Lorinne Dills-Vozoff
Cindy Wilkens Elizabeth Rainey
Carl Wilkens James C. Victor
Stan Pierce Charles Dugan
Lila Pierce Marion Dugan

Director: Scott Bakula

A Tale of Two Sweeties

w Robin Jill Bernheim
25 February 1958: Sam leaps into the body of Marty Ellroy, married to two women with two children from each marriage. Sam believes he must make Marty select one wife over the other and must save Marty from his excessive gambling problem. Eventually, however, it is the wives who make the decision for him.
Ellen Mary Lou Childs
Rachael Jill Tracy
Jessica Ashley Peldon
Josh J.D. Daniels
Vic Larry Manetti
Mary Shay Astar
Martin Jr. Michael Bellisario
Gus Jack Yates

Director: Christopher Hibler

Liberation

w Chris Abbott & Deborah Pratt
16 October 1968: Sam leaps into the life of Margaret Sanders, a housewife who joins her daughter in the fight for equal rights for women. Sam must save Margaret's marriage to her old-fashioned husband George, and stop their daughter Suzi and her radical associate Diana from being killed at a sit-in.
George Sanders Max Gail
Diana St. Cloud Deborah Van Valkenburgh
Suzi Sanders Megyn Price
Chief Tipton Stephen Mills
Peter Tipton Bill Calvert
Flanners Bill Cort
George Sanders Jr. Elan Rothschild
Evy Brownfield Jordan Baker
Dora Tipton Mary Elizabeth Murphy

Director: Bob Hulme

Dr. Ruth

w Robin Jill Bernheim
25 April 1985: Sam becomes sex counselor Dr. Ruth Westheimer and helps a radio show caller fight sexual harassment while also playing matchmaker to a young sparring couple. Meanwhile, back in the Imaging Chamber, Dr. Ruth is helping Al sort out *his* love life.
Doug Reiser Peter Spears
Debbie Shaefer Anita Barone
Jonathan James McDonnell
Annie Robyn Lively
Dr. Ruth Westheimer Herself
Grandma Ellen Albertini Dow

Director: Stuart Margolin

Blood Moon

w Tommy Thompson
10 March 1975: A taste of horror as Sam leaps into the body of Nigel Covington, an eccentric London artist who is also a vampire and is planning to sacrifice a woman and drain her blood at the Blood Moon ritual.
Victor Ian Buchanan
Claudia Deborah Maria Moore
Alexandria Shae D'Lynn
Horst Rod Loomi
Detective Garth Wilton

Director: Alan J. Levi

Return of the Evil Leaper (aka Evil Leaper II)

w Richard C. Okie
8 October 1956: Sam leaps into the body of Arnold Watkins, a college freshman who has been disguising himself as the Midnight Marauder and protecting the innocent from danger. Sam must stop him from killing himself in a suicidal stunt. But "evil leaper" Alia has leaped into another student. When they meet, Sam convinces Alia that she can change her evil ways and devises a plan to enable them to leap out together.
Mike Neil Patrick Harris
Alia Renée Coleman
Zoey Carolyn Seymour
Frank Bojesse Christopher
Jerry Michael Manasseri
Jack Paul Scherrer
Arnold Tristan Tait
Dawn Raquel Krelle

Director: Harvey Laidman

Revenge of the Evil Leaper

w Deborah Pratt
16 September 1987: Sam and Alia both leap into the bodies of prisoners in a women's jail. But Alia's observer, Zoey, has become a leaper herself—as the prison's warden—and is determined to track them down with the help of her computer, Lothos.
Alia/Angel Jenson Renée Coleman
Zoey/Meyers Carolyn Seymour
Vivian Barbara Montgomery
Sophie Katherine Cortez
Thames Hinton Battle
Fiddler Rosana DeSoto
Warden Meyers Sam Scarber
Masterson Maggie Roswell

Director: Debbie Allen

Goodbye Norma Jean

w Richard C. Okie
4 April 1960: Sam leaps into the body of Dennis Boardman, Marilyn Monroe's chauffeur, and must save her from killing herself before she makes her last movie.
Marilyn Monroe Susan Griffiths
Barbara Whitmore Liz Vassey
Peter Lawford Joris Stuyck
John Huston Tony Young
Clark Gable Larry Pennell
John Tremaine Jr. Stephen Root

Director: Christopher Hibler

The Beast Within

w John D'Aquino
6 November 1972: Sam leaps into the body of Henry Akers, a homeless Vietnam veteran, to save the lives of Roy Brown, a high school buddy and troubled fellow veteran, and Daniel Burke, the teenage son of another school classmate. And he gets a discreet helping hand from Bigfoot!
Luke Pat Skipper
Karen Eileen Seeley
Roy Brown Sean Gregory Sullivan
Daniel Burke David Tom
Deputy Curtis David Denney
John Burke John Worful

Director: Gus Trikonis

The Leap between the States

w Richard C. Okie
20 September 1862: Sam is shocked to find he's landed right in the middle of the Civil War as a Union infantry officer—and he's even more shocked when he gets shot! Al tells him he's in 1862 Virginia, and has become his own great-grandfather, Captain John Beckett. His mission is to make sure his great granddaddy marries his great grandma, Olivia, a Southern aristocrat—and also to save the life of a slave called

Isaac who takes on the name King and is destined to have a very famous grandson!
Olivia Kate McNeil
Lt. Montgomery Geoffrey Lower
Isaac Michael D. Roberts
Private Ryder Neil Guintoli
Capt. Beckett Rob Hyland

Director: David Hemmings

Memphis Melody

w Robin Jill Bernheim
3 July 1954: Sam leaps into the body of Elvis Presley two days before he is signed by Sam Phillips of Sun records. He not only has to ensure Elvis gets his contract but also that a nervous girl singer, Sue Anne Winters, also gets the chance to follow her dream.
Sue Anne Winters Mary Elizabeth McGlynn
Frank John Scott Clough
Marion Lisa Jane Persky
Mr. Phillips Gregory Itzin
Red West John Boyd West
Beau Eric Bruskotter

Director: James Whitmore Jr.

Mirror Image

w Donald P. Bellisario
8 August 1953: An enigmatic "last" leap for Sam sees him land in a Pennsylvania tavern, as himself on the day of his birth. As Al and Gushie work frantically to locate him, Sam befriends a wise bartender (played by Bruce McGill who had appeared in the very first "leap") and a group of coal miners. As a host of familiar-looking faces pass through the bar, including Frank La Matta and Captain Galaxy, Sam ponders his life and leaping with Al the bartender, who tells him that he controls his own destiny. Pressed for more of an explanation for why things happen the way they do he simply shrugs and says: "Sometimes, 'that's the way it is' is the best explanation." Sam realizes that he must right at least one more wrong before he can go home and leaps back to hologram Al's wife Beth (from "M.I.A.") to tell her to wait for Al who *will* be coming home to her . . . In the closing credits, it is stated that Beth and Al have four daughters and will shortly celebrate their 39th wedding anniversary, but that Sam never returned home.
Al the Bartender Bruce McGill
Tonchi John DiAquino
Mutta Dan Butler
Bearded Gushie W. Morgan Sheppard
Stawpah Stephen McHattie
Gushie Dennis Wolfberg
Miner Ziggy Richard Herd
Beth Susan Diol
Mr. Collins Mike Genovese
Kruger Kevin McDermott
Ghee Ferdinand Carangelo
Pete Brad Silverman
Police captain James Whitmore Jr.

Director: James Whitmore Jr.

QUARK

A short-lived U.S. sci-fi spoof that was high on in-jokes and satire but low on broad appeal. It was praised by the critics but missed with the masses and never made it past the first eight episodes.

Set in the year A.D. 2222, it starred Richard Benjamin as Adam Quark, head of an interplanetary crew of garbagemen whose mission was to go where other men have gone before and clean up after them, his ship scooping up weightless sacks of rubbish with a set of mechanical hands called Waldoes. From his base, Perma One, a huge space station run by a disembodied head called The Head, Quark got his orders from The United Galaxy Sanitation Patrol's fussy, pedantic supervisor, Otto Bob Palindrome.

Making up Quark's crew were Gene/Jean, a transmute with a full set of male and female chromosomes and an unpredictable habit of switching from macho Gene to gentle Jean; science officer Ficus, a humanoid vegetable with a Spock-like line in unemotional logic; Betty I and Betty II, a pair of sexy, semi-clad girls—one was a clone of the other but each claimed she was the original; and an android, Andy the Robot, a walking junkpile built out of spare parts.

The plots were spoofs of specific sci-fi films and series—the opening episode was a *Star Wars* parody featuring a sappy cosmic power called the Source. Other targets included *Star Trek, 2001: A Space Odyssey* and *Flash Gordon*.

This strange mix of sex, intellectual gags and slapstick comedy was created by Buck Henry, the man behind the hugely successful spy spoof *Get Smart*. It has now entered that twilight zone of archive TV, held in the memories of those who saw it but doomed to remain a mystery to everyone else.

REGULAR CAST
Adam Quark Richard Benjamin *Gene/Jean* Tim Thomerson
Ficus Richard Kelton *Betty I/Betty II* Tricia & Cyb Barnstable
Andy the Robot Bobby Porter *Otto Palindrome* Conrad Janis
The Head Alan Caillou

Creator: Buck Henry

8 color episodes, one 60 minutes,
7 30 minutes

U.S. premiere: 24 February 1978
(NBC)

QUATERMASS

The grand-daddy of TV science fiction, the Quatermass sagas still stand as landmarks of British television drama. Few creations have been as evocative or influential, and few characters as enduring as Professor Bernard Quatermass—a dedicated and well-intentioned rocket scientist, but a humanistic and fallible man.

There have been four Quatermass serials, all of them self-contained—three for the BBC in the 1950s and a belated fourth for Thames Television in 1979. The BBC trio was also memorably filmed by Hammer but, more significantly, the third—and best—story, *Quatermass and the Pit* (1959), was released on video in 1988, setting its eerie tale before a new generation to whom the early serials were only legendary heirlooms.

The only logical order in which to take the Quatermass legacy is the chronological one, and the story begins in 1953 . . .

THE QUATERMASS EXPERIMENT (1953)

In the summer of 1953, the BBC's new head of drama, Michael Barry, spent his entire first year's budget for commissioning new scripts—some £250—on one author, youthful staff writer Nigel Kneale.

Kneale responded with an adventurous six-part thriller far removed from the theatrically oriented productions that were the staple of television drama. His story: An experimental spaceship with its three-man crew is knocked hundreds of thousands of miles off-course before finally returning to Earth. The sole survivor has been contaminated with an alien life-form that causes him to metamorphose into a hundred-foot-tall vegetable monster capable of infinite reproduction, which wreaks havoc on London before it is finally destroyed in time to save the world. The scientist who tracks him down is the scientist who sent him up—British rocket group chief Bernard Quatermass (a name plucked at random from a telephone book).

The Quatermass Experiment was the first of several collaborations between Kneale and producer/director Rudolph Cartier, and it took great faith and ingenuity to bring script to screen. TV drama at that time was played live and special effects were virtually unknown. Such horrific elements as were required had to be created within a series budget of just over £3500 and created on the night. Kneale himself "played" the monster in the climax, using his gloved hands, covered with bits of vegetation and leather, stuck through a blown-up still of Westminster Abbey.

Aware of the technical limitations, Kneale relied on timeless dramatic strengths—a coherent plot and well-drawn characters—to tell his story. Its impact was tremendous, particularly as it was the first serial of its kind. Moreover, it was aimed at an adult audience and it *was* adults who climbed the walls in horrified excitement.

Hammer released a film version in 1956 that starred Brian Donlevy as Quatermass and was known in America as *The Creeping Unknown*.

MAIN CAST

Professor Bernard Quatermass Reginald Tate
Judith Carroon (chief assistant) Isabel Dean   *John Paterson* Hugh Kelly
James Fullalove Paul Whitsun-Jones   *Victor Carroon* Duncan Lamont
Dr. Gordon Briscoe John Glen *(from Ep. 2)*
Chief Insp. Lomax Ian Colin *(from Ep. 2)*
Det. Sgt. Best Frank Hawkins *(from Ep. 2)*

Writer: Nigel Kneale
Producer/director: Rudolph Cartier
Settings: Richard R. Greenhough, Stewart Marshall

A BBC Production
6 black and white 30-minute episodes
18 July–22 August 1953

Contact Has Been Established

A British experimental rocket orbits the planet and crashes back to Earth in Wimbledon. When the ship is opened, only one member of the three-man crew emerges, Victor Carroon.
Peter Marsh Moray Watson *(plus Ep. 2)*
Blaker W. Thorp Devereux
Len Matthews Van Boolen
Mrs. Matthews Iris Ballard
Policeman Neil Wilson *(plus Ep. 2)*
Miss Wilde Katie Johnson *(plus Eps. 3–4)*
News Editor of Daily Gazette Oliver Johnston *(plus Eps. 2, 4)*
Fireman Colyn Davies
Journalists Patrick Westwood, Dominic Le Foe *(plus Ep. 2)*
Police Inspector Eugene Leahy *(plus Ep. 2)*
Reveller Denis Wyndham
BBC newsreader Nicholas Bruce
BBC reporter Pat McGrath
Sandwichman Macgregor Urquhart

Persons Reported Missing

Victor Carroon is subjected to various tests which indicate that he has taken on the identities of the other two men. Quatermass and Paterson find a gelatinous substance spread around the capsule's interior.
Dr. Ludwig Rechenheim Christopher Rhodes *(plus Ep. 3)*
Charles Greene Peter Bathurst *(plus Ep. 3)*
Louisa Greene Enid Lindsay
Hospital sister Stella Richman
Policeman (Scotland Yard) Maurice Durant

Very Special Knowledge

Carroon is taken back to the crash site and a recording of what happened during the orbit is played back to him, with disturbing results. A group of journalists tries to kidnap him, but he, in turn, attacks one of them as he begins to change . . .
American reporter Philip Vickers
Indian reporter Edward David

Believed to Be Suffering

Carroon takes refuge inside a cinema (where a spoof film, *Planet of the Dragons,* is on screen). He then goes to a chemist where he appears to be in pain and his hand is seen to be badly mutated.

Photographer Darrell Runey
Ramsay Jack Rodney
Boy Anthony Green *(plus Ep. 5)*
Chemist Richard Cuthbert *(plus Ep. 5)*
Cinema manager Lee Fox
Cinemagoer Janet Joyce
Usherette Bernadette Milnes *(plus Ep. 5)*
"Space lieutenant" Keith Herrington
"Space girl" Pauline Johnson

An Unidentified Species

Quatermass picks up Carroon's trail and believes that the mixture of chemicals he has taken will accelerate his metamorphosis. Meanwhile, the killing starts—and at Westminster Abbey a pulsating mass is revealed clinging to the building.

Janet Christie Humphrey
Ted John Stone
Park keeper Frank Atkinson
Police inspector Reginald Hearne
Drunk Wilfred Brambell
Sir Vernon Dodds John Kidd *(plus Ep. 6)*
OB producer Tony Van Bridge *(plus Ep. 6)*
OB commentator Neil Arden *(plus Ep. 6)*
Secretary Joseph Crombie

State of Emergency

A state of emergency is declared and the army is brought in. Quatermass plays the creature the rocket tape and appeals to the last vestiges of humanity left in Carroon to fight what he has become. The creature finally dies, just before it is due to spore . . .

Cabinet minister Keith Pyott

QUATERMASS II (1955)

Set some years after the first fateful mission, this second story was not a sequel, and only the central character of Quatermass himself was carried over from the first serial.

In the two years since *The Quatermass Experiment* space exploration had become an imminent fact, though the way ahead was dogged by frustration and failure. Such technical "doldrums" provided the background for Kneale's second tale, with Quatermass's own work on his ambitious new Mark II Moon rocket at a standstill.

With a track record behind them, a bigger budget (some £7500) before them and the BBC's new Visual Effects Department (run by Bernard Wilkie and John Kine) beside them, Kneale and Cartier were able to create a very different story, reversing the man into monster idea, in favour of a covert Martian invasion by infiltrating human minds and bodies.

The role of Quatermass was taken by a new actor, John Robinson, following the death of Reginald Tate just a few weeks earlier. Among now-familiar names lower down the cast were Rupert Davies, Roger Delgado and Wilfred Brambell, the latter already cornering the market in low-life roles following his "old drunk" in the first Quatermass serial and "old man" in *Nineteen Eighty-Four.*

The six 30-minute episodes (which inevitably overran slightly) were transmitted live on Saturday nights, and telerecorded for a repeat the following Monday. The serial polarized its audience—viewers either loved its "thrilling story and effects," or loathed its "horror comics" plot. A film version (aka *Enemy From Space*) was released by Hammer in 1957, again with Brian Donlevy in the star role.

MAIN CAST
Prof. Bernard Quatermass John Robinson
Paul Quatermass (his daughter) Monica Grey
Dr. Leo Pugh (his assistant) Hugh Griffiths
Capt. John Dillon John Stone *(Eps. 1–2, 5–6)*
Vincent Broadhead Rupert Davies *(Eps. 2–3 only)*

Writer: Nigel Kneale
Producer: Rudolph Cartier
Designer: Stephen Taylor
Film cameraman: Charles de Jaeger
Special effects: Bernard Wilkie, Jack Kine

Location filming at the Shellhaven refinery, Essex
A BBC Production
6 black and white 30-minute episodes
22 October–26 November 1955

The Bolts

Army captain John Dillon defies a clamp-down to take the remains of a crashed object to Quatermass's British Rocket Group. Quatermass returns with him to the crash site—a huge domed chemical plant. While they are there, another small object crashes, a gas seeps out and a small bubble appears on Dillon's cheek.

Sgt. Grice Brian Hayes
Private Tony Lyons
Fred Large Eric Lugg
Mrs. Large Hilda Barry
Robert Herbert Lomas
Landlord Richard Cuthbert
Technicians Kim Grant, Peter Macarté
Australian commentator Peter Carver

The Mark

Dillon has been affected and now has a scar on his cheek. He is taken away to the plant by some zombie-like guards and Quatermass is unable to find out what has happened to him. He later visits Vincent Broadhead, an MP who has been probing the plant's activities, and joins him at an official inquiry. But several of the commission also bear scars . . .

Fowler Austin Trevor *(plus Eps. 3–4)*
Stenning John Miller *(plus Ep. 3)*
Tramp Wilfred Brambell
Insp. Clifford Peter Carver
Dawson Michael Brennan
Child Sheila Martin
Mother Hilda Fenemore
Thompson Michael Collins
Secretary Diana Chesney
Head of commission O'Donovan Sheill *(plus Ep. 3)*

The Flood

Broadhead becomes the latest victim of the gas. Quatermass tricks his way inside the plant with Ward and Fowler. Ward gets separated and strays into one of the food domes—then emerges covered in a burning synthetic food, and dies. Back at the rocket base, Pugh has discovered the origin of the objects—an asteroid on the dark side of the Earth.

Ward Derek Aylward
Doctor John Cazabon
Waitress Margaret Flint
Mother Ilona Ference
Father Sydney Bromley
Frankie Melvyn Hayes
Analyst Trevor Reid
Supervisor Philip Levene*
Guard Stephen Scott

* Later a writer on *The Avengers*.

The Coming

Quatermass visits the community near the plant but encounters suspicion as he tries to stir up the workers—until a new falling of objects convinces them. They march on the plant and, inside, Quatermass sees a huge alien creature growing inside one of the food domes.

Conrad Roger Delgado
Paddy Michael Golden *(plus Ep. 5)*
McLeod John Rae *(plus Ep. 5)*
Mrs. McLeod Elsie Arnold
Ernie Ian Wilson *(plus Ep. 5)*
Young workman Desmond Jordan *(plus Ep. 5)*
Technician Martin Lane
Guard Tom Clegg

The Frenzy

The workers take over the plant and it is destroyed by an explosion. Quatermass gets back to the Rocket Group and prepares to launch his *Quatermass II* rocket—destination: the asteroid.

Technicians Denton de Gray *(plus Ep. 6)*, Martin Lane

The Destroyers

Quatermass succeeds in launching his rocket and he and Pugh head for the asteroid. But Pugh has been taken over and Quatermass must overcome his attack before he can defeat the evil force on the asteroid.

Doctor: Denis McCarthy
Control assistant: Cyril Shaps

QUATERMASS AND THE PIT (1958–59)

By the time *Quatermass and the Pit* came along, the world had embraced a real space age, and audience expectations had undoubtedly moved on from the pioneering rocket project of the first "experiment."

But the character of Professor Quatermass, with his pangs of conscience and loathing of bureaucracy, was far from obsolete and the timing of the first episode—just before Christmas 1958—was clear evidence that the BBC knew it had a ratings winner on its hands.

The Pit of the title sets the story firmly in its time, when the last of London's blitzed areas were being rebuilt. Real excavations had unearthed Roman or medieval remains, but Nigel Kneale's teasing premise had something far stranger being stirred up in the mud—evidence that Earth had been visited eons ago by Martians who had imbued man's simian ancestors with their own faculties.

Drawing on elements of demonology and the occult, Kneale's idea thus explained all manner of unexplained superstitions and phenomena, from poltergeists to second sight and race memories. Everything is drawn together in a chilling climax as the dormant Martian influence reasserts itself.

Though much of the drama was again told—live—through the characters and actions, *Quatermass and the Pit* made the greatest use yet of filmed inserts and refined special effects: the workman, Sladden, attempting to flee the demonic forces that have gripped him, the ground rippling beneath his hand; the animated "Wild Hunt" sequence; and the climactic appearance of the energy force rising up over London.

This was also the first major contribution by the BBC's newly formed Radiophonic Workshop producing an array of bizarre sound effects.

André Morell, who had been a chilling O'Brien in the Kneale/Cartier adaptation of *Nineteen Eighty-Four*, became the third (and definitive) TV incarnation of Quatermass, and Canadian Cec Linder played the palaeontologist Matthew Roney. Hammer filmed this story in 1967, in terrifying Technicolor, with Andrew Keir as the good professor, though in America it labored under the title *Five Million Years to Earth*.

MAIN CAST

Professor Quatermass André Morell *Barbara Judd* Christine Finn
Dr. Matthew Roney Cec Linder *Col. Breen* Anthony Bushell
Capt. Potter John Stratton *Sergeant* Michael Ripper
Corp. Gibson Harold Goodwin *Pvt. West* John Walker
Soldiers Clifford Cox, Brian Gilmar
James Fullalove Brian Worth *Sladden* Richard Shaw
Minister Robert Perceval *Private secretary* Richard Dare

Writer: Nigel Kneale
Producer: Rudolph Cartier
Film cameraman: A.A. Englander
Film editor: Ian Callaway
Designer: Clifford Hatts
Special effects: Jack Kine, Bernard Wilkie
Music: Trevor Duncan

A BBC Production
6 black and white 35-minute* episodes
22 December 1958–26 January 1959
Omnibus repeat: Two 90-minute episodes 2, 9 January 1960

* approx.

The Halfmen

Prof. Quatermass is resisting the planners of a grisly rocket project known as the Dead Man's Deterrent. But then comes an interruption . . . Excavation work at a building site in Hobbs Lane, London, unearths a human skull that Dr. Roney estimates to be five million years old. Then a strange projectile is dug up . . .
Truck driver Van Boolen
Old workman George Dudley
Foreman John Rae
Museum official Malcolm Watson
Baines Arthur Hewlett
Armitage Michael Bird
Interviewer Janet Burnell
Teddy boy Tony Lyon

Police inspector Ian Ainsley *(plus Eps. 4, 6)*
Stout woman Janet Joyce

The Ghosts

Col. Breen believes the projectile is a bomb—it's cold to the touch, slightly radioactive and made of an unknown substance. Roney's assistant Barbara Judd finds the area has a history of supernatural events, and a terrified Pvt. West claims to have seen an imp-like ghost: "It went through the wall!"
Mrs. Chilcot Hilda Barry *(plus Ep. 1)*
Mr. Chilcot Howell Davies *(plus Ep. 1)*
Young PC Kenneth Warren *(plus Ep. 1)*
PC Ellis Victor Platt *(plus Ep. 1)*
Miss Groome Madge Brindley

Imps and Demons

Journalist James Fullalove helps Quatermass research the history of Hobbs Lane, finding its name derives from Hob—the devil. A technician, Sladden, succeeds in opening a sealed compartment in the capsule, revealing three petrified alien insects.
News editor Tony Quinn *(plus Eps. 4, 6)*
Nuttall Keith Banks
George Frank Crane
Policeman Patrick Connor *(plus Ep. 4)*
Elderly librarian Donald McCollum
Abbey librarian Fletcher Lightfoot

The Enchanted

Roney and Quatermass develop their theory about the Martians' visit to Earth, instilling their essence into man's ancestors. Sladden, alone in the pit, flees in terror as strange forces are conjured up.
Dr. Klein Kenneth Seeger
News vendor Bernard Spear
Journalists Allan McClelland *(plus Ep. 6)*, Bill Shine *(plus Ep. 6)*, Ian Wilson
Vicar Noel Howlett *(plus Ep. 5)*

The Wild Hunt

A brain scanner reveals alien pictures in Barbara Judd's mind of "the Wild Hunt'—the frenetic purging of the Martian hives. A skeptical Breen dismisses it as a hoax. In the pit, a technician is killed as the capsule starts to glow . . .
Electrician Harold Siddons *(plus Ep. 6)*
Official Edward Burnham *(plus Ep. 6)*
Technician John Scott Martin
Woman journalist Anne Blake

Hob

Chaos reigns in the pit and the long-dormant Martian inheritance begins to assert itself in many people in the area—including Quatermass himself—driving them to a new racial purge. The capsule breaks open and an energy form rises up over London. Roney finds he is immune and strives to defeat it.
TV interviewer Anthony Pendrell
Newsvendor John Hamblin
Customer Bernard Spear
Blonde Louise Gainsborough
Man in blazer Arthur Brander
Tattered man Sydney Bromley
Newscaster Stuart Nichol
American pilot Budd Knapp

QUATERMASS (1979)

Twenty years later, Quatermass's last case is as much rooted in the anxieties of its age as the previous three had been. Kneale this time creates a fearful vision of a near-future in which civilization is tottering on its last legs. Petrol is running out, law and order has surrendered to lawlessness, with violent street gangs, the Badders, battling it out behind the barricades, while the superpowers squander resources on a useless space project.

An older, world-weary Quatermass has been living as a recluse in Scotland. Now, as he comes south to search for his missing granddaughter, Hettie, he teams up with a young Jewish astronomer, Joe Kapp, to defeat an alien force that is "harvesting" the young of the planet, sweeping them up in beams of light at ancient ritual sites, such as stone circles.

Like its predecessors, the series was intended to be "science fiction with a human face," but its vastly increased budget of £1,250,000 and the greater expectations of its audience in terms of effects and locations, meant a more lavish production, lacking the intimacy of the old live serials. Its makers, Euston Films, took the show on the road, using Wembley Stadium for one key scene where the Planet People—young, anarchistic hippies—mass to await the beam they believe will take them to another galaxy.

Highly respected actor Sir John Mills, whose only previous TV series had been *The Zoo Gang*, five years earlier, was a credible Quatermass, but after a promising start the series was a comparative disappointment. Expectations were perhaps inflated, as the first episode was the main offering of ITV's first night back on the air after a 75-day strike.

The final chapter in this Quatermass saga was produced in two versions—the four-part, four-hour story for home TV (repeated in May 1984 as two two-hour installments), and a shorter 105-minute TV movie, *The Quatermass Conclusion*, for the foreign market. Kneale also turned the tale into a novel that included slightly different material.

MAIN CAST
Prof. Quatermass John Mills Joe Kapp Simon MacCorkindale
Clare Kapp Barbara Kellerman (Eps. 1–2 only) Kickalong Ralph Arliss
Caraway Paul Rosebury Bee Jane Bertish Hettie Rebecca Saire (Eps. 1–2, 4)
Marshall Tony Sibbald (Eps. 1–3) Annie Morgan Margaret Tyzack (Eps. 2–3)
Sal Toyah Willcox (Eps. 2–4) Chisholm Donald Eccles (Eps. 3–4)
Gurov Brewster Mason (Eps. 2–4, plus voice-over Ep. 1)

Writer: Nigel Kneale
Script executive: Linda Agran
Executive in charge of production: Johnny Goodman
Executive producer: Verity Lambert
Producer: Ted Childs
Director: Piers Haggard
Designer: Arnold Chapkin
Music: Marc Wilkinson, Nic Rowley

A Euston Films Production
4 color 60-minute episodes
24 October–14 November 1979
Repeat: 9–16 May 1984
(ITV)

Ringstone Round

Professor Quatermass comes out of retirement to search for his missing granddaughter and finds a world on the verge of anarchy, and an American-Russian space station destroyed by unknown forces. He is befriended by astronomer Joe Kapp and they witness the obliteration of thousands of Planet People by a beam of light at the stone circle, Ringstone Round.
Roach Bruce Purchase (plus Ep. 2)
Chen David Yip (plus Ep. 2)
Alison Brenda Fricker (plus Ep. 2)
Toby Gough Neil Stacy (plus Ep. 3)
TV producer Joy Harrington
Make-up lady Barbara Keogh
First pay cop James Leith
Pay police captain Luke Hanson
Muggers Charles Bolton, Chris Driscoll
Taxi driver Stewart Harwood
Charm seller Rita Webb
Catskin man Trevor Lawrence
Medicine man Frederick Radley
Kapp children Joanna Joseph (plus Ep. 2), Sophie Kind (plus Ep. 2)

Lovely Lightning

Following the devastation at Ringstone Round, Quatermass hears of similar incidents worldwide and returns to London with district commissioner Annie Morgan and a Ringstone "survivor" Isabel. En route they become separated in a shootout between rival gangs. Meanwhile, the beam of light descends again—near to Joe Kapp's home.
Isabel Annabelle Lanyon (plus Ep. 3)

What Lies Beneath

Joe Kapp returns home to find no signs of life. Hiding out below the London streets, Quatermass meets an elderly scientist, Chisholm, who he believes could help solve the growing mystery. Then the beam strikes again—on a vast gathering of 70,000 young people at Wembley Stadium.
TV director Tudor Davies
Prime minister Kevin Stoney
Hatherley David Ashford
Russian astronaut Jan Murzynowski
Woman minister Elsie Randolph (plus Ep. 4)
Jack Larry Noble (plus Ep. 4)
Edna Gretchen Franklin (plus Ep. 4)
Arthur James Ottaway (plus Ep. 4)
Jane Clare Ruane (plus Ep. 4)
Winnie Kathleen St John
Susie Beatrice Shaw
Security guard Declan Mulholland
Torrance Ian Price
Soldier Chris Quinten

An Endangered Species

The sky has turned green from the "undigested particles" in the atmosphere. Quatermass, joined by the Russian, Gurov, recruits a team of old people to lay a trap for the alien force, using an artificial composite of the sound, smell and heat of a huge human crowd to bait a poison—a nuclear bomb. As the light descends, there is a final clash with the Planet People and Kapp is shot dead. But Quatermass's granddaughter suddenly appears and together they detonate the device.
Misru Ishaq Bux
Woman researcher Lennox Milne
Electronics expert John Dunbar
Lt. general John Richmond
Orderly Charles Lamb
Pay police lt. Brian Croucher

THE RAY BRADBURY THEATER

"I never know where the next story will take me. The
trip—exactly one half exhilaration, exactly one half
terror."

—Ray Bradbury

Introduced by: Ray Bradbury

The Bradbury Trilogy
3 color 30-minute episodes
6–20 October 1985
(Grampian)

Marionettes Inc.

w Ray Bradbury
Computer salesman John Braling has a good job,
an affectionate wife and a nice suburban home, but
is desperately seeking his freedom. One day, a
cryptic message "Marionettes Inc.: We Shadow
Forth" appears on his computer screen and continues to do so until Braling seeks out the sender. The
company's rep Fantocinni explains his motive—to
help an unhappy man. He reveals a life-size robot
of Braling and explains that he can be off enjoying
himself while the robot is at home with his wife.
The idea works well—until the robot makes a better job of being John Braling than the real one
does.
Braling James Coco
Fantocinni Leslie Nielsen

Director: Paul Lynch

The Playground

w Ray Bradbury
Charles Underhill is a man haunted by memories of
childhood bullying and vows that he will always
protect his own son from such cruelty. But while
watching his son and some friends in a playground,
Charles is suddenly, strangely summoned to fight
the last battle of his childhood against some very
bestial children.
Charles Underhill William Shatner
Steve Keith Dutson
Carol Kate Trotter
Ralph Mirko Malish
Charlie Steven Andrade
Peerless Barry Flatman

Director: William Fruet

The Crowd

w Ray Bradbury
One Christmas, Joe Spallner is returning home from
a party when his car spins out of control and throws
him on to the pavement. In great pain, Spallner
looks up to find a menacing crowd gathering around
him, the threat growing until he is taken to hospital.
A few days later, Spallner is visited by his friend
Morgan. As the two talk, Spallner hears a crash outside. He rushes out to find a crash victim surrounded
by the same crowd and sets out to find out more
about this mysterious group.
Spallner Nick Mancuso
Morgan R.H. Thomson

Director: Ralph Thomas

Other episodes

The Screaming Woman

w Ray Bradbury
Heather Leary has an active imagination and spends
much of her time reading stories about evil spirits.
One afternoon she hears a faint moan from nearby
woods. Investigating, she realizes it is coming from
underground. But when she tells her parents there is
a woman buried alive they dismiss it as just another
of her outlandish tales. So with her friend Dippy,
Heather sets out to discover who is buried—and
who buried her!
Heather Leary Drew Barrymore
Mrs. Leary Janet-Laine Green
Mr. Leary Roger Dunn
Dippy Ian Heath
Mr. Kelly Ken James
Mrs. Kelly Jacqueline McLeod
Mr. Nesbitt Alan Scarfe
Screaming woman Mary Anne Cotes

Director: Bruce Pittman

(11 May 1989, Thames)

The Town Where No One Got Off

w Ray Bradbury
On a boring train ride across Midwest America, a
cynical salesman challenges Sam Cogswell to back
up his belief that every town they pass is special.
Sam accepts and disembarks at the next small hamlet, called Erehwon. There he is drawn into a cat-
and-mouse game with an old man who has been
waiting 20 years for a stranger to arrive—so he
could kill him.
Sam Cogswell Jeff Goldblum
with Ed McNamara & Cec Linder

Director: Don McBrearty

(18 May 1979, Thames)

Banshee

w Ray Bradbury
Hollywood screenwriter Douglas Rogers visits
movie director John Hampton at his stately manor
in Ireland. Hampton, a lady-killer and devilish
scoundrel, is an incurable practical joker and when
a mournful cry emanates from the mist outside
Hampton tells Rogers that the noise occurs one hour
before someone dies. Rogers ventures forth and
meets a beautiful woman who tells him she is seeking a notorious womanizer—who once lived at the
mansion.
Douglas Rogers Charles Martin Smith
John Hampton Peter O'Toole
Banshee Jennifer Dale

Director: Doug Jackson
Producer: Seaton McLean

(25 May 1989, Thames)

*Produced by Atlantis Films Ltd. in association with
John Wilcox Productions Inc.*

(Author's note: the following stories were made in
Britain by Granada Television as part of an international package of *Ray Bradbury Theater* but over-
cautiously aired here in August 1988 under the
heading *Twist in the Tale* [no relation to the 1978
American anthology series].

Of the 12 shows, Granada produced four, with the
others being made in France and Canada. But though
they played successfully there, and in America, the
macabre mood of the tales didn't sit comfortably with
ITV's light entertainment schedules.

The first two of the Granada quartet—"The Coffin" and "Punishment without Crime"—were seen
in August 1988. The second duo, "Small Assassin"
and "There Was an Old Lady," were shown a year
later.)
Producer: Tom Cotter
Music: Bill Connor

Granada Television Production
4 color 30-minute episodes

The Coffin

w Ray Bradbury
Wealthy inventor Charles Brayling creates a coffin
that literally walks to its own funeral and digs its
own grave—with his avaricious ne'er-do-well
brother trapped helplessly inside.
Charles Brayling Dan O'Herlihy
Richard Brayling Denholm Elliott
St. John Court Clive Swift

Director: Tom Cotter
Designer: Margaret Coombes

(7 August 1988)

Punishment without Crime

w Ray Bradbury
George Hill's wife takes a lover and George has
murder in his heart. "Facsimiles Ltd." offers him a
way to commit the ultimate crime in such a way as
to avoid the penalty.
Governor Bill Croasdale
Priest Will Tacey
George Hill Donald Pleasence
Katherine Lynsey Baxter
Facsimile interviewer John McGlynn
Lover George Anton
Policeman William Ivory
Judge Peggy Mount
Prosecuting counsel Iain Cuthbertson
Defense counsel Frank Williams

Director: Bruce Macdonald
Designer: Alan Price

(28 August 1988)

Small Assassin

w Ray Bradbury
Alice Leiber gives birth to a baby and is strangely
frightened of it—not without reason, for the child
has a peculiarly advanced sense of awareness and is
out to kill both its parents.
Alice Leiber Susan Wooldridge
David Leiber Leigh Lawson
Dr. Jeffers Cyril Cusack

Director: Tom Cotter
Designer: Margaret Coombes

Producer: Tom Cotter

(13 August 1989)

There Was an Old Woman

w Ray Bradbury

Aunt Tildy receives a visit from a mysterious stranger—Death, who has come to claim her. But Aunt Tildy is a strong-willed old lady who doesn't want to go, and her spirit proceeds to reclaim her body.
Aunt Tildy Mary Morris

Mr. Death Ronald Lacey
Emily Sylvestra Le Touzel
Mortician Roy Kinnear

Director: Bruce Macdonald
Designer: Alan Price

(20 August 1989)

REALLY WEIRD TALES

Trio of fantasy stories from Canada unimaginatively screened in the U.K. as *Mystery Theater*. *Really Weird Tales* is a stablemate of Atlantis Films' *The Ray Bradbury Theater*—stories present an amiable balance of humor and fantasy with comic actors John Candy (*Planes, Trains and Automobiles*) and Martin Short (*The Three Amigos*) among the stars.

REGULAR CAST
Host: Joe Flaherty

Executive producers: Michael MacMillan, Joe Flaherty
Producers: Seaton McLean, Pat Whitley
Theme: Fred Mollin

An Atlantis Films Ltd. Production for Home Box Office
3 color 30-minute episodes
U.S. debut: 1986

I'll Die Loving

w Joe & David Flaherty, Catherine O'Hara
Raised in a convent, Theresa Sharpe always thought she was an orphan. Then she learns her father had left her with nuns because she was cursed with a love that kills: she has awesome powers of destruction, and her affection literally blew up her mother. Resigned to go through life hating the world, she gets a job in a complaints department. Then her boss falls in love with her . . .
Theresa Sharpe Catherine O'Hara
Todd Lamont David McIlwraith

Director: John Blanchard

Cursed with Charisma

w Joe & David Flaherty, John McAndrew
Fitchville's inhabitants have seen better days—they can't even repair the community's sole statue. At a town meeting, depression is rife until Howard Jensen, a huge, well-coiffed albino, appears. This stranger spouts the power of positive thinking and soon everyone in Fitchville is a real estate tycoon. But who—or what—is Howard Jensen?
Howard Jensen John Candy
with Sheila McCarthy, Don Lake

Director: Don McBrearty

All's Well That Ends Strange

w Joe & David Flaherty
Life for girlie magazine publisher Wade Jeffries is an unending party. One of his amusements is Shucky Forme, a second-rate lounge act with third-rate patter. While in Wade's Jacuzzi, Shucky falls for one of his mentor's buxom playmates. But before he can propose, he's confronted with a dead damsel and a workroom full of robots programmed to act like humans. What's going on in Wade's House of Ecstasy?
Wade Jeffries Don Harron
Shucky Forme Martin Short
Tippy Olivia d'Abo

Director: Paul Lynch

RED DWARF

Spaced-out British sci-fi comedy that boldly went where precious few sitcoms had gone before—and then kept on going.

This saga of a ragtag band of space travelers began modestly enough, as a novel variation on a time-honored "comedy-in-a-bottle" routine. But by Season Three it had gained a bigger budget, beefed up the sci-fi, and displayed vastly improved special effects—with ratings to match.

The early comedy, though, was rooted in tradition, but instead of a bed-sit in East Cheam or a junkyard in West London, we got a mining ship in outer space—the *Red Dwarf*, a five-mile-long, three-mile-wide hybrid of *Dark Star* and the *Nostromo*.

In the first episode all but one of the 169-strong crew are killed off in a radiation leak. Sole survivor is Dave Lister, technician third class, the lowest of lowly crewmen, who had been placed in suspended animation for keeping a pet cat, revived after three million years. Lister's only companions are a humanoid life-form that has evolved from his cat, and a hologram of his obnoxious, pompous supervisor, Arnold Rimmer. The other regular character is Holly, the ship's lugubrious computer. Megaslob Lister and zealous under-achiever Rimmer are as compatible as Steptoe and Son, and the sparks that fly from their bickering during the first two seasons give the humor a sharp, cutting edge.

Cat, though, was a real one-off creation. Played as a hopelessly narcissistic black dude in sharp suits, he got some of the best lines, plus terrific sight gags, including spraying cologne to mark his territory and "licking" his laundry clean.

Season Three saw a couple of personnel changes. Holly became a she and the crew were augmented by an android, the admirable Kryten, as their odyssey continued, with them eventually losing the mother ship and continuing in a claustrophic shuttle called *Starbug*.

BBC2's longest-running comedy (an eighth series was imminent as this volume went to press), *Red Dwarf* was created by Rob Grant and Doug Naylor, one-time head writers for the satirical puppet show *Spitting Image*. For executive producer Paul Jackson it represented continued success after such innovative comedy series as *The Young Ones* and *Happy Families*. Excellently cast, it gave first major TV roles to Liverpudlian poet/comedian Craig Charles and song and dance man Danny John-Jules. Chris Barrie, the voice behind many a *Spitting Image* puppet, went on to more mainstream success in *The Brittas Empire*.

What makes *Red Dwarf* special is that the series is not just a sci-fi spoof. It has fun with the genre, but however contrived the situations, it is, at its heart, a character-based comedy.

MAIN CAST

Arnold Rimmer, BSC, SSC Chris Barrie *Dave Lister* Craig Charles
Cat Danny John-Jules *Holly* Norman Lovett
Kryten Robert Llewellyn *Holly* Hattie Hayridge *(both from Season 3)*
Christine Kochanski Chloe Annett *(from Season Seven)*

Writers: Rob Grant, Doug Naylor
Designers: Paul Montague, Mel Bibby
Visual effects designer: Peter Wragg
Music: Howard Goodall
Executive producer: Paul Jackson, Rob Grant, Doug Naylor *(Seasons Five, Six)*
Producer/Director: Ed Bye
Directors: Juliet May, "Grant Naylor" *(both Season Five)*, Andy De Emmony *(Season Six)*
Producers: Hilary Bevan Jones *(Season Five)*, Justin Judd *(Season Six)*

A Paul Jackson Production for BBC North West (Seasons 1–3),
A Grant Naylor Production for BBC North (Seasons 4–6)
36 color 30-minute episodes

Season One: 15 February–21 March 1988
Season Two: 6 September–11 October 1988
Season Three: 14 November–19 December 1989
Season Four: 14 February–21 March 1991
Season Five: 20 February–26 March 1992
Season Six: 7 October–11 November 1993

The End

Lister is put in suspended animation for 18 months for having a pet cat; Rimmer's radiation leak kills the crew. Three million years later, the stage is set . . .

Todhunter Robert Bathurst

Chen Paul Bradley
Selby David Gillespie
Captain Hollister Mac McDonald
McIntyre Robert McCulley
Peterson Mark Williams
Kochanski C.P. Grogan

Future Echoes

Having accelerated constantly for three million years, *Red Dwarf* breaks the light barrier. Rimmer and Lister overtake themselves in time and witness images of the future.
Toaster John Lenahan
Dispensing machine Tony Hawks

Balance of Power

A bored Lister wants a date with dead console officer Christine Kochanski—but first he must persuade Rimmer to turn himself off so she can take his place for a few hours.
Kochanski C.P. Grogan
Chef/Trout à la Creme Rupert Bates
Chen Paul Bradley
Selby David Gillespie
Peterson Mark Williams

Waiting for God

Cat's holy book of smells reveals Lister in a divine light as the cat-god Cloister and leads to an encounter with a cat-priest.
Cat priest Noel Coleman
Toaster John Lenahan

Confidence & Paranoia

Lister develops a mutated form of pneumonia that causes his hallucinations to become solid. These include the two sides of his personality, the overbearing Confidence and the insecure Paranoia. Egged on by Confidence, Lister tries to revive Kochanski as a hologram but duplicates Rimmer instead.
Paranoia Lee Cornes
Confidence Craig Ferguson

Me²

The two Rimmer holograms move in together and all is tickety-boo until they begin to get on each other's nerves—and Lister's. One Rimmer will have to go.
Arnold Rimmer 2 Chris Barrie
Capt. Hollister Mac McDonald

Season Two

Kryten

A distress call from a marooned spaceship with "three woman survivors" has *all* the Red Dwarfers preparing for their first date in three million years. But all they find are skeletons, tended by a servile android, the very admirable Kryten.
Kryten David Ross
Esperanto woman Johanna Hargreaves
Android actor Tony Slattery

Better Than Life

A post pod brings a batch of computer games including the latest "total immersion video" Better Than Life which enables the players to experience their wildest dreams.
Rimmer's dad John Abineri
Marilyn Monroe Debbie Ash
Rathbone Jeremy Austin
Captain Nigel Carrivick
Guide Tony Hawks
McGruder Judy Hawkins
Newsreader Tina Jenkins
Taxman Ron Pember
Gordon Gordon Salkilld

Thanks for the Memory

The crew of the *Red Dwarf* awake one morning to discover that someone has erased their memory of the last four days, broken Lister and the Cat's legs and done Lister's jigsaw. Finding out why brings even more pain . . . for Rimmer.
Lise Yates Sabra Williams

Stasis Leak

A leak creates a doorway to the past. Lister tries his luck with Kochanski; Rimmer tries to warn himself about the future.
Lift hostess Morwenna Banks
Kochanski C.P. Grogan
Room mate Sophie Doherty
Medical orderly Richard Hainsworth
Suitcase Tony Hawks
Capt. Hollister Mac McDonald
Petersen Mark Williams

Queeg

Holly's increasingly erratic behavior prompts a takeover by the *Red Dwarf*'s back-up computer, a "black drill-sergeant" type called Queeg 500. The crew is driven to despair until Holly reveals it was him all along—his "wheeze of the week."
Queeg Charles Augins

Parallel Universe

Holly devises a faster-than-light drive that immediately goes wrong and propels *Red Dwarf* into a parallel universe, where Holly, Lister and Rimmer meet their female counterparts and the Cat is paired off with a dog.
Arlene Suzanne Bertish
Deb Angela Bruce
Pooch Matthew Devitt
Hilly Hattie Hayridge

Season Three

Backwards

Lister and Rimmer finally arrive back on Earth—
only to discover Time is behaving rather strangely.
Waitress Maria Friedman
Compere Tony Hawks
Customer in café Anna Palmer
Pub manager Arthur Smith

Marooned

As *Red Dwarf* heads on a collision course toward a
minefield of black holes, the crew are forced to
abandon ship. Lister and Rimmer find themselves
marooned on an arctic moon with only a pot noodle
and a tin of dogfood between them. And there's no
way Dave's eating the pot noodle.
(No guest cast)

Polymorph

A genetic mutant that salivates unspeakable slob-
ber gets loose aboard the *Red Dwarf* and subjects
the crew to a 24-hour ordeal of non-stop horror.
Genny Frances Barber
Rimmer's mother Kalli Greenwood
Young Rimmer Simon Gaffney

Bodyswap

Lister has been abusing his body, and Rimmer proposes a novel way for him to lose weight—he'll take
over Lister's body and look after it while Lister has
a spell as a hologram. But once he's "real" again,
Rimmer doesn't want to change back.
Carol Brown Lia Williams (*voice-over*)

Timeslides

Kryten discovers some amazing developing fluid
that makes old photos come to life and allows the
Dwarfers to actually step into the action and change
their destiny.
Gilbert Robert Addie
Bodyguards Rupert Bates, Richard Hainsworth
Young Lister Emile Charles
Young Rimmer Simon Gaffney
Thicky Holden Stephen McKintosh
Lady Sabrina Mulholland-Jones Koo Stark
Ski woman Louisa Ruthven
Ski man Mark Steel
American presenter Ruby Wax

The Last Day

All androids are supplied with an in-built expiry
date, and when Kryten discovers he has less than 24
hours to live, the rest of the crew are determined to
give him the best night of his life.
Girl android Julie Higginson
Hudzen Gordon Kennedy

Season Four

Camille

Kryten rescues a female droid from a crashed vessel. She, like him, is a 4000 series, but Camille is the
GTi model, with realistic toes and a slide-back sun-
roof head. Kryten finds himself falling in advanced
mutual compatibility on the basis of a primary
initial ident, only to find that the course of true
advanced mutual compatibility never runs in a non-
glitch bug-free way.
Mechanoid Camille Judy Pascoe
Hologram Camille Francesca Polan
Kochanski Camille Suzanne Rhatigan

D.N.A.

The crew lock on to an unidentified craft that contains the ultimate in genetic engineering technology—a machine that can transform any living thing
into any other living thing, by rewriting its DNA.
The Dwarfers are unsure whether this is a blessing
or a curse until Lister's curry finds its way into the
transmogrifier and assumes near-human form.
D.N.A. machine voice Richard Ridings

Justice

On Justice World, the consequences of a crime are
inflicted on its perpetrator. The innocent have nothing to fear, but Rimmer is in big trouble.
Justice computer voice James Smillie
Simulant Nicholas Ball

White Hole

Holly regains her genius-level IQ and for some reason, best known to herself, powers down the ship,
leaving the crew drifting helplessly toward a white
hole. Will Rimmer sacrifice his hologramatic life to
save the rest of the crew?
Talkie toaster David Ross

Dimension Jump

In another universe, almost identical to our own,
there is another Arnold Rimmer also almost identical, except that he's courageous, charming, an ace
pilot and a great chap to have around in a crisis . . .
Mrs. Rimmer Kalli Greenwood
Young Rimmer Simon Gaffney
Cockpit computer voice Hetty Baynes

Meltdown

A matter transporter whisks the crew to Wax-world—a giant theme park, where the waxdroids have broken their programming and are running amok. Hitler and Caligula lead an army of darkness against the forces of light, led by Elvis, Gandhi and Stan Laurel.
Elvis Clayton Mark
Hitler Kenneth Hadley
Einstein Martin Friend
Pythagoras Stephen Tiller
Abraham Lincoln Jack Klaff
Caligula Tony Hawks
Pope Gregory Michael Burrell
Stan Laurel Forbes Masson
Noel Coward Roger Blake
Marilyn Monroe Pauline Bailey

Season Five

Holoship

Lister is in a state. Kryten and Holly are on the blink. Rimmer escapes the chaos when he is transmitted to the advanced holoship, *Enlightenment*, crewed by an elite band of holograms. It's everything he's ever dreamed of. But can he pass the exams and earn a commission to join this fantastic vessel?
Nirvanah Crane Jane Horrocks
Captain Platine Matthew Marsh
Cmdr. Binks Don Warrington
Harrison Lucy Briers
Number Two Simon Day
Number One Jane Montgomery

Inquisitor

The Inquisitor roams through time weeding out life's wastrels and deleting the worthless—the *Red Dwarf* crew are in big, big trouble.
Inquisitor John Docherty
Second Lister Jake Abrahams
Thomas Allman James Cormack

Terrorform

Rimmer is taken prisoner inside his own mind on a planet where his fears take physical shape and threaten to overwhelm the crew who realize that the only way they can escape is by pretending to like him.
Handmaidens Sara Stockbridge, Francine Walker-Lee

Quarantine

After an encounter with a viral research center, Rimmer forces the crew into quarantine for 12 weeks but when a holo-virus is unleashed, he becomes its victim.
Dr. Hildegarde Lanstrom Maggie Steed

Demons and Angels

The *Red Dwarf* crew find out what evil lurks within the hearts of men (and holograms, androids and cats) when they encounter their dark sides—four evil doppelgängers hell bent on their destruction.
(No guest cast)

Back to Reality

The crew find an abandoned spaceship whose occupants have committed suicide. Then a gigantic "despair squid" monster attacks, so it's time to escape to Earth where . . . they find their space adventures have all been a total immersion game that they've been playing for four years. Rimmer is really an alky dropout called Billy Doyle. Lister is his half-brother Sebastian and head of a fascist ministry, Kryten is really a cybernautic detective, Jake Speed, and Cat is a sad figure, in anorak, plastic sandals and nylon shirt, called Dwayne Dibley. But . . . the Dwarfers are *really* hallucinating, an effect of the ink from the despair squid.
Andy Timothy Spall
Fascist cop Lenny Van Dohlen

Season Six

Psirens

In pursuit of the stolen *Red Dwarf*, Lister and Co. are attacked by Psirens, creatures who lure unwary space-farers to their doom with a lethal combination of telepathic manipulation and scanty clothing.
Dr. Mamet Jenny Agutter
Pete Tranter's sister Samantha Robson
Captain Tau Anita Dobson
Crazed Astro Richard Ridings
Kochanski C.P. Grogan
Temptress 1 Zoe Hilson
Temptress 2 Elizabeth Anson
with The hands of Phil Manzanera

Legion

Supplies are low. The water has been recycled so often, it's beginning to taste like Dutch lager. Then a malfunctioning guidance beam drags the Dwarfers to a deserted space station.
Legion Nigel Williams

Gunmen of the Apocalypse

Kryten contracts a deadly computer virus and Rimmer and Co. are forced to enter his electronic mindscape, where they find themselves in a Wild West town, facing a gunfight against metaphorical gunslingers.
Loretta Jennifer Calvert
Simulant captain/Death Denis Lill
Female simulant Liz Hickling
Lola Imogen Bain
Jimmy Steve Devereaux
War Robert Inch
Pestilence Jeremy Peter
Famine Dinny Powell
Bear Strangler McGee Stephen Marcus

Emohawk—Polymorph II

The Dwarfers need replacement engine parts from the fearsome and stomach-churningly ugly Kinatowi. But as a trade, Lister must marry the chief's daughter.
Computer Hugh Quarshie
Gelf Martin Sims
Gelf chief Ainsley Harriott
Gelf bride Steven Wickham

Rimmerworld

Trapped aboard a disintegrating ship, Rimmer abandons his crewmates, taking the only remaining escape pod. As he accelerates toward a nearby wormhole, he realizes the pod has no steering.
Rogue simulant Liz Hickling

Out of Time

The *Starbug* crew receives an SOS call from themselves—15 years into the future—and heads toward an explosive fate.
(No guest cast)

Season Seven

(Author's note: This is the first season not to be written exclusively by Rob Grant and Doug Naylor. A laugh track was added later by showing an audience the completed episode; it was not filmed live.)

Tikka to Ride

w Doug Naylor
The *Starbug* loses her Indian food supply, and Lister time-travels back to Earth for curry take-out, inadvertently destroying the future.
John F. Kennedy Michael J. Shannon
Lee Harvey Oswald Toby Aspin
FBI agent Peter Gaitens
Cop Robert Ashe

Stoke Me a Clipper

w Doug Naylor & Paul Alexander
Arnold "Ace" Rimmer, galactic hero, is mortally wounded and shows up to recruit "our" Rimmer as his replacement.
Ace Rimmer Chris Barrie
King Brian Cox
Captain Voorhese Ken Morley
Queen Sarah Alexander
Good Knight John Thompson
Princess Bonjella Alison Senior
Lieutenant Mark Carlisle
Gestapo officer Mark Lingwood
Soldier #1 Kai Maurer
Soldier #2 Stephan Grothgar
Soldier #3 Andy Gell

Ouroboros

w Doug Naylor
Lister discovers the secret to his birth and meets an alternate-dimension version of Christine Kochanski, who helps save the ship.
Baby Alexander John-Jules

Duct Soup

w Doug Naylor
The ship's systems fail abruptly, forcing everyone into a trek to the engine room through the ducts.
(No guest cast)

Blue

w Kim Fuller
Lister realizes he misses Rimmer and seeks medical help from Kryten.
(No guest cast)

Beyond a Joke

w Doug Naylor & Robert Llewellyn
Kochanski's simulation of Jane Austen World has Kryten blowing his top—literally.
Simulant Don Henderson
Mrs. Bennett Vicky Ogden
Jane Bennett Alina Proctor
Kitty Bennett Catherine Harvey
Lydia Bennett Sophia Thierens
Mary Bennett Rebecca Katz
Elizabeth Bennett Julia Lloyd

Epideme

w Doug Naylor & Paul Alexander
Lister is infected with the deadly Epideme virus in a darkly comic episode.
Caroline Carmen Nicky Leatherbarrow
Epideme Gary Martin *(voice-over)*

Nanarchy

w Doug Naylor, Paul Alexander & James Hendry
While searching for nanobots to replace Lister's arm, the crew discovers Holly and the remains of *Red Dwarf.*
Holly Norman Lovett

Red Dwarf (U.S. pilot)

w Linwood Boomer
A pilot for a U.S. version was made in 1992. It's a partial reworking of the first episode, "The End," but with Kryten introduced from the outset. There are also a few changes to the characters—Lister is less of a slob and more of a laid-back guy, Rimmer is more comical than vindictive and the whole thing is generally more toned down. Among the stars is Jane Leeves, now well-known as Daphne in the sit-

com *Frasier.* It was never shown, however, and unfortunately no one wanted to buy it.
Lister Craig Bierko
Rimmer Chris Eigeman
Holly Jane Leeves
Cat Hinton Battle
Kryten Robert Llewellyn

Director: Jeff Melman
Music: Todd Rundgren

Satin City Inc., in association with Universal Television

A second attempt to launch the series was made with a new title, *Red Dwarf USA*. Bierko and Leeves were retained, Anthony Fuscle replaced Chris Eigeman as Rimmer and the Cat was revamped into a fearless female warrior played by Terry Farrell (later Dax in *Star Trek: Deep Space Nine*). This didn't work either.

ROAR

Shaun Cassidy's follow-up to his nifty dark fantasy *American Gothic* and Ron Koslow's follow-up to *Beauty and the Beast* proved to be a confusing amalgam of Celtic history called *Roar.* Set in A.D. 400, this action-adventure drama chronicled the life of Conor (Heath Ledger), a reluctant hero who had to rise above personal tragedy to lead his people against the advancing Romans. Mixing magic, swordplay, gloomy sets, and historical illiteracy, this sometimes-engaging mish-mash earned a cult following—but not one big enough to keep it on network Fox.

REGULAR CAST
Conor Heath Ledger   *Diana* Lisa Zane
Longinus Sebastian Roche   *Catlin* Vera Farmiga
Fergus John Saint Ryan   *Tully* Alonzo Greer

Creators: Shaun Cassidy, Ron Koslow
Executive producers: Ron Koslow, Shaun Cassidy
Co-executive producer: Michael Nankin
Co-producers: Lawrence Meyers, Brian Chambers
Producers: Paul, Larry Barber
Produced by Howard Grigsby
Associate producer: Todd London
A Universal Roar Production in association with Universal Television
U.S. premiere: 14 July 1997

Episodes
Pilot
Projector
The Chosen
Banshee
Doyle's Solution
Red Boot Stolen
The Spear of Destiny
The Eternal

ROBOCOP

"Somewhere a crime is happening."

Small-screen spin-off from the movie blockbusters with Richard Eden taking over the role of the indestructible half-man, half-machine battling diabolical criminals in a nightmarish future.

Set in the year 2005, it begins with police officer Alex Murphy and his female partner called to a crime while on patrol in Old Detroit and Delta City. Murphy is seriously wounded and to save him, his body is melded with robot implants and parts by Omni Consumer Products (OCP) scientists. But the price is high—Alex's memory is erased. In his place stands the ultimate enforcer of justice—Robocop.

Gradually, however, glimpses of Murphy's past life seep back into his consciousness, inspiring and haunting him as he struggles to maintain his hold on humanity. Both victim and hero, he's a deadpan observer of a strident, twisted and deadly future, where the shiny new Delta City towers over the husk of Old Detroit.

Other recurring characters include OCP's chairman, who's something of a father figure to Murphy, his new partner, feisty young officer Lisa Madigan, his beat sergeant, Stan Parks, Parks' friend and soon-to-be adopted daughter Gadget, Murphy's scientist caretaker Charlie Lippencott, and secretary Diana Powers, who "lives on" in cyberspace as a ghost in the machine after being murdered in the series' premiere episode.

On the crooks' side are mad scientists Dr. Cray Z. Mallardo, OCP overachiever Chip Chaykin, and disfigured psychopath Pudface Morgan.

The series' two-hour premiere episode was written by Michael Miner and Ed Neumeier, writers of the original *Robocop* movie, which starred Peter Weller.

REGULAR CAST
Alex Murphy/Robocop Richard Eden *OCP Chairman* David Gardner
Sgt. Stan Parks Blu Mankuma *Officer Lisa Madigan* Yvette Nipar *Gadget* Sarah Campbell
Charlie Lippencott Ed Sahely *Diana Powers* Andrea Roth
Dr. Cray Z. Mallardo Cliff de Young *Chip Chaykin* John Rubinstein
Pudface Morgan James Kidnie

Based upon characters created by Edward Neumeier, Michael Miner
Writers: Various, including Edward Neumeier, Michael Miner *(pilot)*
Executive producers: Stephen Downing, Brian K. Ross, Kevin Gillis
Directors: Various, including Paul Lynch *(pilot)*

Sky Vision Entertainment Production
20 color 60-minute episodes (pilot 120 minutes)
U.S. premiere: March 1994
U.K. premiere: 15 March 1995
(Sky One)

SABRINA THE TEENAGE WITCH

One of the few fantasy-comedies to work since *Bewitched*, *Sabrina the Teenage Witch* chronicles the life of Sabrina, a 16-year-old girl (Melissa Joan Hart) who comes to live with her aunts, only to discover she is half mortal and half witch. Of course, her aunts begin teaching her how to use her magic—which comes with more rules and regulations than a teenage girl really wants to learn. When apprentice-level magic mixes with school, boyfriend, and growing up, chaos and comedy ensue.

The real scene-stealer, though, is Salem, a warlock who was turned into a cat for 100 years after he tried to take over the world. Voiced purrfectly by Nick Bakay, one of the writers on the series, Salem's animatronic body improves sharply in the second season—his scruffy stuffed body was the show's primary flaw until that point.

REGULAR CAST
Sabrina Melissa Joan Hart *Hilda* Carolina Rhea
Zelda Beth Broderick *Salem* Nick Bakay *(voice)*
Harvey Nate Richert *Valerie* Lindsay Sloane
Libby Jenna Leigh Green *Mr. Kraft* Martin Mull *(Season Two)*
Quizmaster Alimi Ballard *(Season Two)* *Jenny* Michelle Beaudoin *(Season Two only)*
Mr. Pool Paul Feig *(Season One)* *Cee Cee* Melissa Murray *(Season One)*,
CeeCee Harshaw *(Season Two)*
Jill Bridget Flannery *Mrs. Quick* Mary Gross *(Season Two)*

Creator: Nell Scovell
Based on characters appearing in Archie Comics
Developed by Jonathan Schmock
Executive producers: Nell Scovell *(Season One)*, Paula Hart *(Seasons One & Two)*, Miriam Trogdon *(Season Two)*
Co-executive producer: Norma Safford Vela *(Season One)*, Holly Hester *(Season Two)*
Co-producers: Jonathan Sherman, Rachel Lipman *(Season One)*
Produced by Kenneth R. Koch
Producer: Gary Halvorson *(Season Two)*

Supervising producers: Connie Honigblum, Renee Phillips
Associate producer: James Hilton
Coordinating producer: Ron Martinez
Story editors: Nick Bakay, Frank Conniff, Neal Baushell, Sam O'Neal *(Season One)*
Executive story editors: Nick Bakay, Frank Conniff *(Season Two)*
Executive consultants: Barney Cohen, Kathryn Wallack, Michael Silberkleit, Richard Goldwater
Finishing the Hat Productions/Hartbreak Films, Inc./Viacom

Season One
Pilot
Bundt Friday
The True Adventures of Rudy Kazootie
Terrible Things
A Halloween Story
Dream Date
Third Aunt from the Sun
Magic Joel
Geek Like Me
Sweet & Sour Victory
A Girl and Her Cat
Trial by Fury
Jenny's Non-Dream
Sabrina Through the Looking Glass
Hilda and Zelda: The Teenage Years
Mars Attracts!
First Kiss
Sweet Charity
Cat Showdown
Meeting Dad's Girlfriend
As Westbridge Turns
The Great Mistake
The Crucible
Troll Bride

Season Two
Sabrina Gets Her License (Part 1)
Sabrina Gets Her License (Part 2)
Dummy for Love
Dante's Inferno
A Doll's Story
Sabrina, the Teenage Boy
A River of Candy Corn Runs Through It
Inna-Gadda-Sabrina
Witch Trash
To Tell a Mortal
Oh, What a Tangled Spell She Weaves
Sabrina Claus
Little Big Kraft
Five Easy Pieces of Libby
Finger Lickin' Flu
Sabrina and the Beanstalk
The Equalizer
The Band Episode
When Teens Collide
My Nightmare, the Car
Quiz Show
Fear Strikes Up a Conversation
Rumor Mill
Mom vs. Magic

SALVAGE-1

"A one-hour adventure series that proves one man's trash is another man's treasure."

—Series publicity

The exploits of scrap dealer Harry Broderick and his "junkyard spaceship" resulted in an oddball series that at times came to resemble a live version of *Thunderbirds*!

Salvage expert Harry builds his rocket to fly to the Moon to pick up the multimillion-dollar pieces left behind there by the *Apollo* missions. He hires two ex-NASA engineers, Fred and Mack, recruits maverick astronaut Skip Carmichael and shapely rocket fuel expert Melanie Slozar and begins procuring vast amounts of NASA surplus stock—all of which arouses the suspicions of the FBI.

Salvage-1 takes off minutes before FBI agents storm the junkyard and, after navigating various dangers, the mission is a success, turning Harry and his cohorts into national heroes.

Therefore, *Salvage-1* (also known as the *Vulture*) becomes their own unique mode of transport enabling them to travel to the furthest corners of the world at a moment's notice. In future episodes they help an amnesiac robot ("Mermadon"), tow an iceberg to a drought-stricken island ("Hard Water"), stage a space rescue ("Golden Orbit"), depressurise a volcano ("Diamond Volcano"), help a stranded Andromedan visitor ("The Haunting of Manderly Mansion"), rescue a little girl trapped by an earthquake ("Shelter Five") and, in the series' opener, encounter a Robinson Crusoe scientist and a giant King-Kong-like apeman ("Dark Island"). All invariably under the glowering eye of FBI agent Jack Klinger.

The series, produced by Harve *"Six Million Dollar Man"* Bennett and Harris Katleman, was actually canceled in America after the opening two-parter of the second season, but *all* the episodes were shown in the U.K., between 1979 and 1981.

REGULAR CAST
Harry Broderick Andy Griffith *Melanie Slozar* Trish Stewart
Skip Carmichael Joe Higgins *Mack* J. Jay Saunders
Jack Klinger Richard Jaeckel
Lorene Jacqueline Scott *Heather McAdam* Michelle Ryan (*Season Two*)

Creator/Supervising producer: Mike Lloyd Ross
Executive producers: Harve Bennett, Harris Katleman
Producer: Ralph Sariego
Writers: Various, including Mike Lloyd Ross, Robert Swanson, Ruel Fischmann
Directors: Various, including Ray Austin, Ron Satloff

A Bennett/Katleman Production in association with Columbia Pictures Television
18 color 60-minute episodes (pilot 100 minutes)
U.S. premiere: 20 January 1974
U.K. premiere: 15 May 1979
(Thames)

U.S. Season One

Salvage (pilot movie)
Dark Island
Shangri-La Lil
Shelter Five
The Haunting of Manderly Mansion (aka Ghost Trap)
Bugatti Treasure (aka The Bugatti Map)
Golden Orbit *(a 2-part story)*
Operation Breakout
Mermadon

Up, Up and Away
Energy Solution
Confederate Gold

Season Two

Hard Water *(a 2-part story)*
Round Up
Harry's Doll
Dry Spell
Diamond Volcano

SAPPHIRE & STEEL

> "All irregularities will be handled by the forces controlling each dimension. Transuranic heavy elements may not be used where there is life. Medium atomic weights are available: Gold, Mercury, Copper, Jet, Diamond, Radium, Sapphire, Silver and Steel. Sapphire and Steel have been assigned!"

Thus spake . . . someone (it was never clear who), announcing the imminent arrival of two time detectives, elemental beings who assumed human form to deal with the aforementioned irregularities—threats to or from time.

Their twice-weekly series of adventures was created by P.J. Hammond, better known for scripting more routine police shows such as *Z-Cars* or *Hunter's Walk*. His premise was that instead of having people going from everyday life into time, he would have time breaking into everyday life.

Thus, Sapphire tells us, in the first episode, that "time is a corridor . . . Once in a while Time itself can try to enter into the Present—break in—burst through, to take things . . . to take people."

It was the job of the "timebusters" to confront whatever malevolent force had broken through and seal up the holes in the time corridor. As a drama, it relied almost wholly on the careful build-up of suspense rather than gadget-filled action. With intensely claustrophic and theatrical settings, the atmosphere of menace or unease was often conveyed by sound effects, lighting and moody music.

The principals in this paranormal crime squad were ex-*New Avenger* Joanna Lumley, dressed in blue as the psychic Sapphire (described by one critic as "the head girl of the universe"), and David McCallum as the gray-suited, broody Steel, a cool and logical character with enormous strength and the power to withstand the flow of time. A couple of other elements appeared from time to time—Silver, a slightly wimpish technical genius, and Lead, a huge, powerful character.

Sapphire & Steel polarized the viewing public and the critics—you were either baffled and bored or baffled and absorbed. None of the stories had titles and became known simply as Adventure One, Adventure Two, etc.

REGULAR CAST

Sapphire Joanna Lumley *Steel* David McCallum
Silver David Collings

Creator/Writer: P.J. Hammond
Producer: Shaun O'Riordan
Executive producer: David Reid
Designer: Stanley Mills (*except Adventure Five:* Su Chases)
Music: Cyril Ornadel

An ATV Network Production
34 color 30-minute episodes

Season One:
10 July–22 November 1979
Season Two:
6 January–5 February 1981
Season Three:
11–26 August 1981
Season Four:
19–31 August 1982

Season One
14 episodes

Adventure One

(a 6-part story)
In an isolated country house, young Rob is bent over his homework. Clocks tick and the muffled sounds of his parents reading to his younger sister, Helen, drift downstairs. Suddenly, a great rushing wind sweeps the house, then dies away, leaving an absolute silence in its wake—all the clocks in the house have stopped ticking. Rob dashes upstairs to find his sister alone—their parents have vanished. Minutes later, Sapphire and Steel arrive to challenge the "invader" who has spirited away the children's parents. It's a battle in which only the ground floor is safe and in which Sapphire enters a painting and is menaced by Roundhead soldiers. Steel calls on Lead's assistance and between them they finally defeat the enemy—depicted as patches of light—and reunite the children with their parents.
Rob Steven O'Shea
Helen Tamasin Bridge
Mother Felicity Harrison
Father John Golightly
Countryman Ronald Goodale
Lead Val Pringle
Policeman Charles Pemberton

Director: Shaun O'Riordan

Adventure Two

(an 8-part story)
Psychic expert George Tully is convinced his railway station is haunted. His ghost-hunting involves Sapphire and Steel in a clash with a sinister outside force that is feeding on the resentment of the dead and creating havoc with the balance of time. The specter appears as a figure dressed in the uniform of a World War One soldier. Tully succeeds in contacting the "dead man" only to unleash a frightening force that becomes a duplicate of Sapphire.
Tully Gerald James
Soldier (Pearce) Tom Kelly
Pilot David Cann
Submariner David Woodcock

Directors: Shaun O'Riordan (*Eps. 1–4, 7, 8*), David Foster (*Eps. 1–7*)

Season Two
10 episodes

Adventure Three

(a 6-part story)
Sapphire and Steel investigate an invisible penthouse atop a modern-day block of flats that is occupied by Eldred and Rothwyn, two time travelers from the future. But the couple, who are heard but not seen, have brought something with them—a strange "changeling" that seizes Sapphire. Joined by Silver, Steel tracks down the time source, which is endangering Earth and must be closed.
Silver David Collings
Eldred David Gant
Rothwyn Catherine Hall
Changeling Russell Wootton

Director: Shaun O'Riordan

Adventure Four

(a 4-part story)
Sapphire and Steel find the "in between" children who have been released from old photographs, and encounter the Shape, a being that can pass in and out of photographs, escaping to their time zones. Sapphire and Steel find themselves trapped in a photograph, where the Shape will kill them.
Liz Alyson Spiro
Shapes Philip Bird, Bob Hornery
Ruth Shelagh Stephenson
Parasol girl Natalie Hedges

Director: David Foster

Season Three
6 episodes

Adventure Five

(a 6-part story)
w Don Houghton *(Eps. 1, 3, 4)* & Anthony Read *(Eps. 2, 5, 6)*
A murder is rerun in a time warp at a party given by businessman Lord Mullrine, and Sapphire and Steel find themselves watching the events turn toward an inevitable conclusion.
Emma Mullrine Patience Collier
Lord Mullrine Davy Kaye
Felicity McDee Nan Munro
Felix Harborough Jeffry Wickham

Howard McDee Jeremy Child
Annabelle Harborough Jennie Stoller
Greville Peter Laird
George McDee Stephen Macdonald
Tony Purnell Christopher Bramwell
Anne Shaw Patricia Shakesby
Veronica Blamey Debbie Farrington
Radio commentator Valentine Dyall

Director: Shaun O'Riordan

Season Four
4 episodes

Adventure Six

(a 4-part story)
On what starts as a normal patrol, Sapphire and Steel discover a service station where the only travelers are from the past. A man is heard approaching, but only a shadow arrives. Silver joins them and suggests there must be a plan behind such trickery, and the time detectives duly discover that they are the central figures in a drama that ends with their being cast adrift in time and space in a window in the sky.
Silver David Collings
Man Edward de Souza
Woman Johanna Kirby
Old man John Boswall
Johnny Jack Chris Fairbank

Director: David Foster

SCIENCE FICTION THEATER

Based on flights of fact rather than fancy, *Science Fiction Theater* was hosted and narrated by newsman Truman Bradley who opened each show with a demonstration of the scientific concept at the heart of that week's story. These included suspended animation, telepathy, transplants, time and space travel and medical advancements. A series aimed at adults, it generally took a positive view of science and avoided twist-in-the tail endings.

One episode singled out for critical praise was "The Strange People at Pecos," in which the words "Martians Go Home!" are scrawled in childish letters on a pavement as a town—adults and children alike—turns against a family who appear to be alien. The story offered no definitive conclusion, but that week's "scientific concept" was teleportation . . .

Several familiar names, including Vincent Price and Vera Miles, appeared in the series. In one story, "The Strange Dr. Lorenz," Edmund Gwenn (Kris Kringle in *Miracle on 34th Street*) played a beekeeper whose honey had remarkable healing properties. In another, William Lundigan, moonbound star of the 1959 series *Men into Space*, played a test pilot driven frantic by high-level refusal to believe his story of *something* flying at three times the speed of sound that nearly collided with his plane. And "Bones" himself, DeForest Kelley, appeared in an episode, "Y.O.R.D.," about strange signals from space picked up by a weather station.

In America, the series ran for 78 episodes between 1955 and 1957, in both black and white and color.

Host/Narrator: Truman Bradley
Producer: Ivan Tors

ZIV Productions

U.S. premiere: April 1955
First U.K. transmission:
24 February–14 September 1956
(ATV Midlands)

SEAQUEST DSV

There's a line in *Jaws* when shark-hunting Roy Scheider realizes what he's up against. "We're gonna need a bigger boat," he says.

Well, Steven Spielberg finally found him one in this big-budget undersea adventure series. Spielberg, who directed Scheider in his 1975 film classic, gave his star a 1000 ft. long super-sub to play with—the *seaQuest* Deep Submergence Vehicle, a combination military and science research vessel.

Scheider plays Captain Nathan Bridger, designer, architect and driving force behind the *seaQuest*'s creation, who is lured out of island retirement to take command of the ship he never saw finished.

It's the year 2018, mankind is colonizing the oceans and exploiting their resources, establishing small undersea farming, mining and manufacturing communities. But with the new-found potential comes old-fashioned conflict and the United Earth/Oceans Organization (UEO) assigns the *seaQuest DSV* to keep the underwater peace and generally patrol the planet's final frontier.

It's a derivative show, with echoes of *Star Trek* and *Voyage to the Bottom of the Sea*, but its massive budget—some $2 million an episode—guarantees a high proportion of hi-tech toys and special effects.

The *seaQuest* set sail with a mixed crew that included Chief Science Officer Dr. Kristin Westphalen; second-in-command Jonathan Ford; a rather intense Chief Engineer, Commander Katherine Hitchcock; Chief of Security Manilow Crocker, a crusty, long-term Navy man who fondly remembers "the old days"; talented Communications Officer Lt. O'Neill; Sensor Chief Miguel Ortiz; and Supply Officer Benjamin Krieg.

There's also a 16-year-old computer whiz, Lucas Wolenczak, and Darwin, Bridger's "pet" dolphin, who roams the vessel via a series of access tubes spanning the craft, and who can understand human speech and reply in kind, thanks to the interpretive powers of the *seaQuest* computers—brainchild of the *wunderkind* Lucas. And there's The Professor, a holographic representation of the ship's computer, projected onto a wall of dry ice, who acts as a kind of Obi Wan Kenobi in times of moral conflict.

And during much of the pilot there's plenty of conflict—both on-board and off, as the ship tries to track down a renegade sub that's skippered by *seaQuest*'s disgraced former captain, Marilyn Stark (a very unangelic role for Shelley Hack), who's now roaming the seas in an Ahab-like quest for revenge.

That threat solved, the series settled into a pattern of science fact pushed on into the future—extrapolations of current technology and its potential rather than speculative science fiction, plus a large dose of political, military and environmental issues. Among the guest stars were William Shatner, as an exiled dictator, and Charlton Heston, as an outlaw scientist, while another episode, with overtones of *The Abyss*, saw the crew have a close encounter with a sunken alien spacecraft. And, as the first season's tour of duty ended, the *seaQuest* was sacrificed in a drastic but successful bid to halt an oceanic catastrophe that threatened to destroy the world.

That gave the show's producers a chance to reinvent the series—with a new, more intimate vessel and a fresh cast. Returning: Bridger, Ford, Lucas, Darwin and support crew O'Neill and Ortiz. New crew: Dr. Wendy Smith, a telepathic biophysicist and psychologist; Lt. James Brody, a cocky weapons and tactics expert; and naive young Ensign Henderson. Season Two also introduced acting brothers Michael and Peter DeLuise as Tony Piccolo, a misfit physically altered as the result of a scientific experiment, and ship's janitor Dagwood, a member of a genetically engineered race known as Daggers.

seaQuest DSV aired to a mixed reception in America—one critic dubbed it "seaQuest PMS" on account of its hostile female characters and another predicted it would be "Voyage to the Bottom of the Ratings." As the series surfaced for a second season it promised to take a more hardcore sci-fi tack.

For its third season, *seaQuest* dropped the *DSV* (and Roy Scheider, for a while, at least!) and added on ten years for a new title, *seaQuest 2032*, and a new skipper, former *V* star Michael Ironside as hardball Captain Oliver Hudson.

It tried to relaunch itself, but failed to impress, and after 12 episodes finally admitted defeat.

MAIN CAST

Captain Nathan Bridger Roy Scheider *Dr. Kristin Westphalen* Stephanie Beacham
Lt. Commander Katherine Hitchcock Stacy Haiduk
Commander Jonathan Ford Don Franklin *Lucas Wolenczak* Jonathan Brandis
Lt. Benjamin Krieg John D'Aquino *Chief Manilow Crocker* Royce D. Applegate
Lt. J.G. Tim O'Neill Ted Raimi *Sensor Chief Miguel Ortiz* Marco Sanchez
Semi-regulars: UEO Admiral William Noyce Richard Herd
The Professor W. Morgan Sheppard
From Season Two: Lonnie Ellen Henderson Kathy Evison
Dr. Wendy Smith Rosalind Allen *Lt. James Brody* Edward Kerr
Tony Piccolo Michael DeLuise *Dagwood* Peter DeLuise
From Season Three: Captain Oliver Hudson Michael Ironside
Lt. J.J. Fredericks Elise Neal

Creator: Rockne S. O'Bannon
Executive producers: Steven Spielberg, David J. Burke, Tommy Thompson, Rockne S. O'Bannon (*pilot only*), Patrick Hasburgh
Producers: Gregg D. Fienberg, Les Sheldon, David Kemper; Oscar L. Costo, Carleton Eastlake (*both Season Two*)
seaQuest 2032:
Executive producers: Patrick Hasburgh, Clifton Campbell, Carleton Eastlake

Amblin Television Production in association with Universal Television
Season One: 23 color 60-minute episodes (pilot 90 minutes)
U.S. premiere: 12 September 1993
U.K. premiere: 16 October 1993

Season One

To Be or Not to Be (pilot)

w Rockne S. O'Bannon & Tommy Thompson, *story by* Rockne S. O'Bannon
It's the year 2018, and Capt. Nathan Bridger is reluctantly coaxed back into naval service to command the massive deep-submergence vehicle *seaQuest*, which serves peacekeeping and scientific roles in the world's oceans. His first crisis is to track down a renegade sub whose captain, *seaQuest*'s own disgraced ex-commander, Marilyn Stark, is determined to blow her old ship out of the water.
Captain Marilyn Stark Shelley Hack
Admiral Noyce Richard Herd
George LeChein Michael Parks
Bobby Scott Coffey
Maxwell Eric DaRe
Old man W. Morgan Sheppard
Aunt Jenny Rebecca Stanley

Director: Irvin Kershner

The Devil's Window

w David J. Burke & Hans Tobeason
When the *seaQuest*'s dolphin, Darwin, becomes ill during the exploration of an underwater phenomenon—hot hydrothermal vents—Bridger is forced to choose between the mission at hand and the life of one of his "crew."
Dr. Raleigh Young Roscoe Lee Browne
Malcolm Lansdowne Robert Engels
Admiral Noyce Richard Herd

Director: Les Landau

Treasures of the Mind

w David Kemper
Bridger and his crew are caught up in an international incident after the *seaQuest* discovers an annex of the great library of Alexandria in the Mediterranean.
Dr. Rafik Hassan Topol
Dimitri Rossovich Turhan Bey
Savannah Rossovich Lindsay Frost
Louis Jacobi Gene Ross
Admiral Noyce Richard Herd

Director: Bryan Spicer

Games

w David Venable
A deranged scientist and mass murderer continues his killing spree aboard the *seaQuest*, holding the sub in a siege of terror as he demands that missiles are launched at Hawaii or he will release a deadly toxin into the ship.
Dr. Zellar Alan Scarfe
Williams Jean Barrett

Director: Joe Napolitano

Treasures of the Tonga Trench

w John J. Sakmar & Kerry Lenharr
Gold fever strikes the *seaQuest* when Lt. Krieg returns from a sea crab test drive with an exotic underwater gem. Meanwhile a very strict visiting captain puts the crew through a tough series of proficiency exams.
Captain Jack Clayton Yaphet Kotto
Murray Goldwater Stephen Kronish
Ensign Fillie Tom Provost

Director: Les Sheldon

Brothers and Sisters

w Art Monterastelli
The *seaQuest* discovers children living in an undersea munitions plant that was thought to be deserted and which must be entombed before structural weaknesses unleash a deadly explosion.
Cleo Kellie Martin
Zachary Christopher Pettiet
Matthew Jonathan Dohring
Brawley Robert Dohring

Director: Bill L. Norton

Give Me Liberte . . .

w John J. Sakmar & Kerry Lenharr
A chemical leak from a space station that crashed into the sea years before contaminates some of the *seaQuest* crew.
Guy Peche Udo Kier
Levin Tim Omundson

Director: Bill Norton

Knight of Shadows

w Melinda Snodgrass
While investigating the wreck of a 100-year-old sunken liner, Bridger and his crew undergo a strange paranormal experience.
Dr. Levin Tim Omundson
Professor Martinson W. Morgan Sheppard
Captain Wideman John St. Ryan

Director: Helaine Head

Bad Water

w David Kemper
The *seaQuest* crew battle a violent storm in a lifeboat when a rescue mission runs into trouble in the Bermuda Triangle.
(*No guest cast*)

Director: Bryan Spicer

The Regulator

w David J. Burke
When the sub's air conditioning breaks down, causing tempers to rise with the temperature, Bridger reluctantly calls in an eccentric broker called The Regulator who arrives on board with his pet orangutan, Verne.
Regulator John Bedford Lloyd
Professor W. Morgan Sheppard

Director: Les Sheldon

seaWest

w John J. Sakmar & Kerry Lenharr
Bridger finds gold and greed in an Old West–style undersea mining community off the Great Barrier Reef.
Cobb David McCallum
Gibby Ethan Glazer
Joan Sutter Bari Hochwald
Lenny Sutter David Morse

Director: Gabrielle Beaumont

Photon Bullet

w David Kemper
Lucas links up with a team of computer hackers at an undersea communications installation that acts as a central nervous system for all information sent via optic computer highways under the Pacific. But Bridger discovers the hackers' leader has a more sinister objective than playing innocent games.
Martin Clemons Tim Russ
Julianna Sarah Koskoff
Nick Seth Green

Director: Bryan Spicer

Better Than Martians

w David Kemper & Dan Brecher
The *seaQuest* is the only hope for the survival of a group of astronauts whose space capsule plummets into the Andaman Sea. But Bridger's personal motives are called into question when the sub experiences its own apparent difficulties in reaching the stricken capsule.
Keller Kent McCord
President Hoi Chi James Shigeta
U.S. President Steven Williams
Tran Aki Aleong
Sakata Una Damon
Admiral Noyce Richard Herd

Director: John T. Kretchmer

Nothing but the Truth

w David Kemper
The *seaQuest* is attacked and overrun by a maverick environmentalist and his team of commandos, and Bridger has to decide whether or not to destroy his own ship.
Col. Steven Philip Shraeder John Finn
Professor W. Morgan Sheppard
Bowman Tim Kelleher
Jackson Bradford Tatum

Director: Les Sheldon

Greed for a Pirate's Dream

w David J. Burke
A magna buoy, developed to prevent volcanic eruptions and earthquakes, ends up on an island that is about to be destroyed by a new eruption. Bridger discovers that it's fallen into the hands of treasure hunters and must persuade them to give it up before the volcano kills them all.
Bobby Anthony Denison
Jessie Rya Kihlstedt
Mack David Marciano
Grant Sandy Peak
Professor W. Morgan Sheppard
Admiral Noyce Richard Herd
Dr. Raleigh Young Roscoe Lee Browne

Director: James A. Contner

Whale Song

w Patrick Hasburgh
Captain Bridger is faced with the most difficult decision of his life—resigning his command of the *seaQuest* or using deadly force to stop a group of aqua-vigilantes who are sinking whaling ships.
Scully Jonathan Banks
Malcolm Lansdowne Robert Engels
Mike Lutz Jack McGee
Wiggins Peter DeLuise
Corbett Derek Webster
General Thomas Jesse Doran
Smith Leo V. Gordon
Jones Frank McCarthy
Bickle Denis Arndt
Secretary General Noyce Richard Herd

Director: Bryan Spicer

Stinger

w John J. Sakmar, David J. Burke & Patrick Hasburgh
The *seaQuest* gets caught up in the fierce competition to develop a prototype of a high-speed single seat sub.
Navy Quartermaster Bickle Denis Arndt
Martin Tucker Dennis Lipscomb
Edgar Gaye Jack Blessing

Enzo Dinato Matt Landers
Secretary General Noyce Richard Herd

Director: Jonathan Sanger

Hide and Seek

w Robert Engels
An exiled dictator wants Darwin to teach his autistic son to speak. When his terrorist enemies locate him, the *seaQuest* is threatened by a nuclear warhead.
Milos Tezlof William Shatner
Malcolm Lansdowne Robert Engels
Caesar Tezlof Christopher Miller
Secretary General Noyce Richard Herd

Director: Lindsley Parsons III

The Last Lap at Luxury

w Zora Quayton
The *seaQuest* becomes involved in a traitor's plot to take world leaders hostage. (This episode was shown out of sequence—in it Noyce is still only an admiral!)
Secretary General Andrea Dre Bonnie Bartlett
Hoi Chi James Shigeta
Maxwell Hank Stratton
Lamm Carl Lumbly
Admiral Noyce Richard Herd

Director: Bryan Spicer

Abalon

w Patrick Hasburgh
Ford is held captive in the underwater lair of an outlaw scientist who has been conducting experiments to allow humans to breathe underwater.
Abalon Charlton Heston
Mika Felicity Waterman
Julianna Sarah Koskoff
Kaman Rob Youngblood
Shapra Matt Sheehan
Chief William Shan Dustin Nguyen
Bartender Gary Eimiller

Director: Les Sheldon

Such Great Patience

w David Kemper
When an undersea earthquake exposes the entombed tail section of a huge alien spacecraft, Bridger and some of his crew have a close encounter with a strange extraterrestrial—but the dolphin Darwin is the only one who is able to communicate with it.
Commander Scott Keller Kent McCord
Professor W. Morgan Sheppard
General Frank Thomas Jesse Doran
Chief William Shan Dustin Nguyen
Ensign Shephard Thom Sherman
Alien Karyn Malchus

Director: Bryan Spicer

The Good Death

w Hans Tobeason & Douglas Burke
Bridger and the *seaQuest* are tricked into firing on a sub they are told is smuggling emeralds, only to find it contains a young couple—one of whom is Westphalen's daughter—who are trying to save poor children from an Amazonian general's death squads.
General Guzmano Luis Guzman
Cynthia Westphalen Marianne Hagan
Colonel Carlos Carrasco
Malique Garfield Bright
Chief William Shan Dustin Nguyen
Secretary General Noyce Richard Herd

Director: Hans Tobeason

Higher Power

w David J. Burke & Patrick Hasburgh
Lucas's father, Dr. Lawrence Wolenczack's, dream of bringing free electric power to the entire world by harnessing the natural energy of the Earth comes to a devastating end as the ocean floor is ripped apart by catastrophic forces. The only way to close the rent is to bury the *seaQuest* in the lava well and detonate her nuclear weapons.
Dr. Wolenczak Kristoffer Tabori
Calvin Shelley Charles Cyphers
Jordan Patricia Harty
Rosenthal Tom Henschel
Secretary General Noyce Richard Herd
Chief William Shan Dustin Nguyen

Director: John T. Kretchmer

Season Two
(21 episodes)

Daggers

(Two-hour episode)
w Jonathan Falls
The redesigned, rebuilt *seaQuest* is dispatched to deal with a revolt by Daggers, genetically engineered warriors who've been kept in a guarded colony all their lives. The Daggers have stolen a stealth submarine and are destroying the oxygen regenerators. If they destroy the four largest, the Earth will have less than 21 percent oxygen and all people will die except Daggers who only need eight percent.
Lonnie Ellen Henderson Kathy Evison (*intro*)
Dr. Wendy Smith Rosalind Allen (*intro*)
Lt. James Brody Edward Kerr (*intro*)
Tony Piccolo Michael DeLuise (*intro*)
Dagwood Peter DeLuise (*intro*)
Mariah Sam Jenkins
Joseph Spike Alexander
General Thomas Jesse Doran
David Philip Tanzini
Dinato Larry Brandenburg
Matthew William deVry
Sarah Kim Faze

Director: Bryan Spicer

The Fear That Follows

w Clifton Campbell
The aliens from Season One's "Such Great Patience" return and reveal an astonishing secret of the universe to Bridger and his crew.
Commander Keller Kent McCord
Lemus Karyn Malchus
Reinhardt Neil Giuntoli
General Thomas Jesse Doran
Anka Yan Chen
Booa Christina Chauncey

Director: Robert Weimer

Sympathy for the Deep

w Carleton Eastlake
Responding to a frantic plea, *seaQuest* finds a Utopian undersea colony stricken with a disease that is turning the colonists mad and violent.
Royce Shelton Robert Foxworth
Laura Huxley Mimi Kuzyk
Jim Huxley Bill Welter
Richard Huxley Matt Davison
Tyler Keith Hudson

Director: Bruce Seth Green

Vapors

w David J. Burke
Bridger and Dr. Smith rekindle a romance, while Lonnie Henderson and Tim O'Neill realize that beginning a relationship can be very difficult.
Marie Piccolo Leslie Hope
Nick Piccolo Dom DeLuise

Director: Les Sheldon

Playtime

w Lawrence Hertzog
A note from the past leads to the world of the future when Bridger receives an obsolete Morse code message, followed by a child's voice pleading for help.
Aaron Kelly Morgan
Iris Joanna Garcia

Director: Robert Wiemer

The Sincerest Form of Flattery

w Carleton Eastlake
A catastrophic error sends a computerised sub on a mission of worldwide destruction and *seaQuest* is ordered to stop it at all costs.
Angie Piccolo Amie Bluff
Admiral Noyce Richard Herd
Rose Piccolo Mimi Lieber
Prof. Martinson W. Morgan Sheppard

Director: Jésus Trevino

By Any Other Name

w Lawrence Hertzog
An urgent distress signal takes the crew to a deep sea botanical research lab where the plants have turned into vicious killers.
UEO Security General McGrath Michael Costello
Trigg Michael Deeg
Hansen Roger Ranney

Director: Burke Brinkerhoff

When We Dead Awaken

w Clifton Campbell
A mysterious woman is released from a cryogenics institute after 22 years and is targeted by an assassin. Brody tries to help her and is surprised to learn the woman is his mother!
General Thomas Jesse Doran
Jonathan Packard Sherman Howard
Allison Alison Moir
Dr. Dharavi Jack Swenson
Lee Colzi Michael Moss

Director: Annette H. Carter

Special Delivery

w Patrick Hasburgh
Dagwood maintains his innocence when he is found guilty of murdering his creator despite being caught in the act on video.
Dr. Wilhelm Brown Ian Sullivan
Prosecuting attorney Karen Fraction
Defense attorney David Silverthorn
Judge Leroy Mitchell

Director: Gus Trikonis

Dead End

w Carleton Eastlake
When their shuttle is pulled into a fierce whirlpool, Henderson, Lucas, Brody and O'Neill find themselves in a maze of ancient caverns inhabited by giant wormlike creatures.
Marcus Rawlings Gregory Martin

Director: Steven Robman

Meltdown

w Tom Szollosi
A terrifying 200 ft. prehistoric crocodile is thawed out from an ice block when undersea farming and mining cause the South Atlantic's temperature to rise. (First of several episodes directed by Anson Williams, better known as Potsie in *Happy Days*.)
Charles Ford J.A. Preston

Benjamin Ford T.E. Russell
Mike Ranier Parker Whitman
Paulie Tony Sago
Jenna Dorian Field
Rick Gary Bristow

Director: Anson Williams

Lostland

w Ted Raimi *&* David J. Burke
Ford discovers evidence—a gold helmet—that the lost continent of Atlantis actually existed. But the helmet carries a curse that puts the *seaQuest* crew's lives in danger.
Professor Obatu/Warrior Charles G. Maina
Ernst Barry Primus
UEO Secretary General McGrath Michael Costello

Director: Bruce Seth Green

And Everything Nice

w Lawrence Hertzog
Lucas falls in love with a beautiful woman who is abducted by terrorists bent on taking over *seaQuest*.
Sandra Leslie Bega
David Michael A. Nickles
Dr. Kirby Max Brown
Insp. Donnegan David Spielberg

Director: Burt Brinckerhoff

Dream Weaver

w Clifton Campbell
A blind astrophysicist and a NASA commander help the crew battle a hostile alien who emerges from a fallen comet.
Commander Scott Keller Kent McCord
Tobias LeConte Mark Hamill
Alien Karyn Malchus

Director: Oscar L. Costo

Alone

w Carleton Eastlake
Wendy uses her psychic abilities in a deadly battle against Avatar, a powerful paranormal who is putting world leaders into comas and causing meltdowns of nuclear reactors.
Avatar Raphael Sbarge
Professor Bingham Joe Seneca
UEO Security General McGrath Michael Costello
Colonel Manheim Marc Macaulay
Aide Michele T. Carter
General Reed Tom Celli

Director: David J. Burke

Watergate

w Patrick Hasburgh
The crew of *seaQuest* is transporting a pop star to an island military base but encounters an apparition of the sea god Neptune who believes the singer and Henderson are actually Minerva and Medusa.
Sarah/Minerva Dawn Robinson
Preacher Charles Noel

Director: Cassey Rohrs

Something in the Air

w Lawrence Hertzog
An ancient chest found buried in the Mediterranean is found to contain a vicious demon.
Kearny Lewis Arquette
Dr. William Crichton Nicolas Surovy
Mrs. Crichton Tricia Matthews
Dr. Kaufman Peggy O'Neal

Director: Steven Robman

Dagger Redux

w Patrick Hasburgh
A renegade nuclear physicist sets out to destroy *seaQuest* so he can illegally mine an underwater reef.
Maria Sam Jenkins
Marauder Luca Bercovici
UEO Secretary General McGrath Michael Costello
Dinah Dana Tyson

Director: Oscar L. Costo

The Siamese Dream

w Jonathan Brandis & David J. Burke
Intent on gaining control of *seaQuest*, a powerful psychic implants a common nightmare in the minds of Piccolo and Dagwood.
Laura Tamara Tunie
Clay Marshall Todd Allen
Dr. Roberts Robert Small

Director: Jesus Trevino

Blindsided

w Clifton Campbell
Piccolo is kidnapped and tortured by a ruthless South American dictator who has been secretly creating artificial lifeforms.
Dictator Juan Fernandez
Esteros Mario Ernest Sanchez
Eddie Leif Riddell
UEO Security General McGrath Michael Costello

Director: Anson Williams

Splashdown

w Carleton Eastlake
seaQuest is seized by an alien spacecraft and transported to a water planet, where the crew becomes embroiled in a civil war.
Commander Scott Keller Kent McCord
Tobias LeConte Mark Hamill
Ariel Kristy Eisenberg
Mitbor Tom Nowicki

Director: Anson Williams

Season Three
As seaQuest 2032

Brave New World

w Clifton Campbell
Ten years after mysteriously disappearing, the *seaQuest* is found back on Earth along with its dazed crew. Captain Hudson, a tough Navy careerist who's been obsessed with finding the sub, assumes control from Captain Bridger and confronts a right-wing organization bent on taking over the world's oceans.
Captain Oliver Hudson Michael Ironside *(intro)*
Lt. J.J. Fredericks Elise Neal *(intro)*
President Alexander Michael York
UEO Secretary General McGrath Michael Costello
General Armand Stassi Andrew Stahl
Lt. Marrs Damon Jones
Shepps Paul Kiernan
Janitor Phillip Martinez
Dr. Perry Karen Fraction
Catherine Kristy Eisenberg

Director: Anson Williams

In the Company of Ice and Profit

w Patrick Hasburgh
A mining company guilty of polluting the southern oceans causes a giant iceberg to break off the polar cap. Hudson is ordered to destroy it—but discovers it's occupied by refugees, led by a former *seaQuest* crewman.
Benjamin Krieg John D'Aquino
Deo Tim DeKay
Mason Freeman Ralph Wilcox
UEO Secretary General McGrath Michael Costello
Johnson Lou Bedford
Booth Vivienne Sendaydiego

Director: Jesus Trevino

Smoke on the Water

w Lee Goldberg *&* William Rabkin
seaQuest is engaged to provide a safe escort for underwater haulers of precious metals, which have been disappearing without trace. But Hudson has to share command of the operation with a long-lost love.
Elaine Morse Patricia Charbonneau

Director: Oscar L. Costo

Destination Terminal

w Javier Grillo-Marxuach
Lucas tries to prevent a disaster, when a new supersonic undersea train loaded with dignitaries is programmed to crash in Beijing.
Tim DeKay Lawrence Deon
Dumont Cameron Thor

Director: Bruce Seth Green

Chains of Command

w Lee Goldberg *&* William Rabkin
Hudson is captured by his former commanding officer, now a renegade who intends to ignite a war. (This episode sees the death of one of the crew, Lt. Brody.)

Director: Anson Williams

SpinDrift

w Carleton Eastlake
Lt. Henderson is captured when she tries to rescue two children from a badly damaged submarine.
Alexander Bourne Michael York
Martin Trevor St. John
Secretary General McGrath Michael Costello

Director: Oscar L. Costo

Equilibrium

w Naren Shankar *&* Javier Grillo-Marxuach
The crew of *seaQuest* is forced to go to war against former captain Nathan Bridger when he opposes Hudson's plans for stopping a plague.
Nathan Bridger Roy Scheider

Director: Anson Williams

Resurrection

w Lee Goldberg *&* William Rabkin
The *seaQuest* crew reluctantly escort a mass murderer to an undersea colony. (Features a guest appearance by Jonathan Banks reprising his first season

DSV role as Scully, now the president of an underwater utopia.)
Scully Jonathan Banks
Nathan Bridger Roy Scheider
with Patricia Charbonneau

Director: Oscar L. Costo

Good Soldiers

w Naren Shankar
seaQuest is sent to destroy a UEO base where horrific genetic research is being carried out—and which Bridger and Ford may have been involved in.
Nathan Bridger Roy Scheider

Director: Jesus Trevino

Second Chance

w Carleton Eastlake
The crew members travel through a "space-time sphere" that rockets them back to October 1962—in the middle of the Cuban missile crisis.

Director: Frederick K. Keller

Brainlock

w Carleton Eastlake
Hudson and the crew race to prevent the assassination of the UEO Secretary General. (This episode has played out of sequence, as Brody is still alive in it! Should go before *Spindrift*.)

Director: Jesus Trevino

Reunion

w Carleton Eastlake
Lt. Henderson is reunited with her first lover who is now a prisoner in a labor camp, and causes a breakout.

Director: Anson Williams

Weapons of War

w Javier Grillo-Marxuach
The *seaQuest* risks destruction—and one crew member is killed—when it grants asylum to Lt. O'Neill's secret Internet chat pal who turns out to be a hi-tech warrior fleeing a warlike society, and her fearsome comrades will keep attacking until she is returned.
Lt. Cmdr. Heinko Kimura Julia Nickson

Director: Steve Beers

THE SECRET SERVICE

This curious blend of live action and puppetry has become something of an enigmatic detour in the upwardly mobile career of Gerry Anderson.

The Andersons had already branched out into live action via the movie feature *Doppelgänger* (1969) and an earlier film called *Crossroads to Crime* (1961), but, in television terms, *The Secret Service* appears as a partially submerged stepping stone between the last of the pure Supermarionation puppet shows, *Joe 90*, and the first of Century 21's live action series, *UFO*.

Released in the autumn of 1969, *The Secret Service* blends the two forms of production by using a human star and his puppet double (or vice versa!)—appropriate casting for double-talk comedy actor Stanley Unwin whose gobbledygook was a feature of the shows. Essentially, puppets were used for close-ups and studio work, while actors stood in on long shots and location. In particular this enabled the characters to be seen walking and standing properly, overcoming a perennial puppet problem.

It's a series bereft of the futuristic hardware of *Thunderbirds* or *Captain Scarlet*, set instead in an England of the then present day (à la *Avengers*), and centering on the exploits of Father Stanley Unwin, an amiable 57-year-old country vicar who unexpectedly finds himself working for the Bishop—British Intelligence Service Headquarters Operation Priest. Father Unwin uses a device called a minimizer—a bequest from a late parishioner—concealed inside a book, to miniaturize his gardener Matthew Harding (a highly trained agent posing as a slow-witted country bumpkin) and carry him around in a briefcase equipped with a chair, periscope and miniature tool kit.

Totally unaware of their covert activities is kindly housekeeper Mrs. Appleby, voiced by Sylvia Anderson.

The series' other "star" was Gabriel—Father Unwin's vintage Model T Ford. The genuine article was used on location, with a radio-controlled replica used for the puppet Unwin.

Gerry Anderson has described *The Secret Service* as "one of the most charming series I've ever made." But the charm didn't work on ATV chief Lew Grade who had reservations about its commercial potential—and its cost. At £20,000 an episode, it was proving extremely expensive and with just six episodes filmed, Grade called time, setting a limit of unlucky 13 for Anderson.

REGULAR CAST
Father Unwin Stanley Unwin

WITH THE VOICES OF:

Stanley Unwin *(Father Unwin)*, Gary Files *(agent Matthew)*, Sylvia Anderson *(Mrs. Appleby)*, Jeremy Wilkin *(The Bishop)*, David Healy
Other voices: Keith Alexander, David Healy

Creators: Gerry *and* Sylvia Anderson
Producer: David Lane
Executive producer: Reg Hill
Production supervisor: Des Saunders
Script editor: Tony Barwick
Visual effects supervisor: Derek Meddings
Music: Barry Gray
Vocal title music: The Mike Sammes Singers

Century 21/ITC Production
13 color 30-minute episodes
21 September–14 December 1969
(ATV Midlands)

A Case for the Bishop

w Gerry & Sylvia Anderson
The Bishop discovers that a stolen computer—vital for future exports—is to be smuggled out of the country in a foreign ambassador's diplomatic bag. He calls in Father Unwin who sneaks a miniaturized Matthew on board the ambassador's plane to commit sabotage.

Director: Alan Perry

A Question of Miracles

w Donald James
Father Unwin and Matthew race against time as they probe into the possibility of sabotage at a series of water-purifying plants that have exploded after 250 hours of service.

Director: Leo Eaton

To Catch a Spy

w Pat Dunlop
When a top spy is sprung from jail in a daring night-time helicopter raid, a homing device in his uniform leads the security services to the home of influential Sir Humphrey Burton. A minimized Matthew infiltrates his house and discovers that the spy is to be smuggled away by submarine.

Director: Brian Heard

The Feathered Spies

w Tony Barwick
Father Unwin discovers that pigeons are being used to take aerial photos of a new fighter plane at an isolated airfield . . . but the next one will be carrying a bomb.

Director: Ian Spurrier

Last Train to Bufflers Halt

w Tony Barwick
After one successful robbery attempt, Father Unwin and Matthew are assigned to guard a trainload of used banknotes and when the train is hijacked and the crew captured, it's up to mini-Matthew to beat the crooks.

Director: Alan Perry

Hole in One

w Shane Rimmer
General Brompton is suspected of passing on information being used to tamper with a vital satellite's orbit. Father Unwin believes the general is unwittingly involved and finds the answer lies on the golf course—at the 15th hole.

Director: Brian Heard

Recall to Service

w Pat Dunlop
Father Unwin gets miniaturized Matthew hidden inside a new tank that has suffered a computer fault and finds it heading straight for a building containing top NATO officials.

Director: Peter Anderson

Errand of Mercy

w Tony Barwick
Confined to bed by illness, Father Unwin dreams that he and Matthew are flying to Africa in his Model T Ford, Gabriel, to deliver vital medical supplies and are forced to fight off a rocket attack.

Director: Leo Eaton

The Deadly Whisper

w Donald James
Matthew discovers that Father Unwin's friend Prof. Soames and his daughter are being held hostage by saboteurs who want to use the scientist's latest sonic invention to wreck a new aircraft.

Director: Leo Eaton

The Cure

w Pat Dunlop
Father Unwin trails an infamous agent, Sakov, to a health center and discovers that the man is planning to sabotage a car testing a revolutionary new fuel. But he is unable to warn Matthew, who is hidden inside the car.

Director: Leo Eaton

School for Spies

w Donald James
Father Unwin infiltrates a group of mercenaries who are posing as priests for a series of sabotage missions. His role: explosive expert.

Director: Ken Turner

May-day, May-day!

w Bob Kesten
Having survived four assassination bids, an Arab king arrives in London to sign an oil treaty. Father Unwin and Matthew are assigned to protect him and find themselves on a plane with a bomb on board. What's more: the crew has all been gassed!

Director: Alan Perry

More Haste Less Speed

w Tony Barwick
Father Unwin miniaturizes himself, Matthew and Gabriel to thwart an eccentric bunch of crooks all trying to get their hands on a counterfeiter's printing plates.

Director: Ken Turner

THE SECRET WORLD OF ALEX MACK

Better-than-average U.S. children's adventure series about a better-than-average Californian teenager.

Alex Mack is just a normal 14-year-old girl, until one day she's nearly hit by a truck carrying a secret diet chemical, GC-161. The truck smashes into a fire hydrant causing a geyser-like fountain of water that mixes with the chemical and drenches poor Alex. When she gets home she finds out she's glowing, can shoot electric currents from her fingers, emit magnetic fields to attract objects to her, and morph into a pool of liquid.

Only two other people are in on her secret—her mean, brilliant older sister, Annie, and her best friend, Ray. Even her parents don't know, and her dad happens to work at the plant where the chemical is made. Naturally the head of the plant, Danielle Atron, wants to find Alex and the efforts of her head security guard Vince and truck driver Dave to find the unknown kid form a running thread through the series.

The writing's cute, without being too clever; Larissa Oleynik makes a winsome heroine and the special effects are neat rather than fussy.

REGULAR CAST

Alex Mack Larissa Oleynik *Annie Mack* Meredith Bishop *Ray Alvarado* Darris Love *George Mack* Michael Blakley *Barbara Mack* Dorian LoPinto *Danielle Atron* Louan Gideon *Vince* John Marzilli *Dave* John Nielsen *Robyn Russo* Natanya Ross *Nicole Wilson* Alexis Fields *Louis Driscoll* Benjamin Smith *(from Season Two)*

Creators: Thomas W. Lynch, Ken Lipman
Executive producers: Thomas W. Lynch, John
  D. Lynch, Robert Halmi Jr.
Producers: Ken Lipman, Doug Yellin
Theme: John Coda
Lynch Entertainment Production in association with
Hallmark Entertainment and Nickelodeon

Season One:
13 color 30-minute episodes
Season Two:
13 color 30-minute episodes
U.K. premiere: 5 November 1994
(Nickelodeon)

SHADOW CHASERS

In the wake of the *Ghostbusters* craze came this short-lived 1985 series about a pair of supernatural investigators—one a sleazy reporter, the other a serious researcher—and the various supernatural forces they came up against . . . ranging from the usual haunted-house type ghosts to Egyptian spirits possessing teenage gang members.

Edgar "Benny" Benedek Dennis Dugan *Dr. Jonathan MacKensie* Trevor Eve
Dr. Juliana Moorhouse Nina Foch *Melody Lacey* Hermione Baddeley
Liz Corki Grazer

SHE-WOLF OF LONDON

Randi Wallace left Los Angeles to study mythology in London. Unfortunately, while camping on the moors, she is attacked by a werewolf, and so begins her quest for a cure. Aided by boyfriend Ian Matheson, she hunts down the Gypsy who infected her—only to see him die.

Filmed in London under the name *She-Wolf of London* (pilot through "Beyond the Beyond") and in Los Angeles under the name *Love and Curses* ("Curiosity Killed the Cravitz" through "Mystical Pizza"), the series never developed much of a following and only lasted one season.

REGULAR CAST

Randi Wallace Kate Hodge   *Ian Matheson* Neil Dickson
Mum Matheson Jean Challis   *Dad Matheson* Arthur Cox
Julian Scott Fults   *Aunt Elsa* Dorothea Phillips
Skip Seville Dan Gilvezan

Creators: Tom McLoughlin, Mick Garris
Executive producers: Sheldon Pinchuck, Pat Finnegan, Bill Finnegan
Executive producers: Patrick Dromgoole, Paul Sarony, David Roessell
Producer: Chuck Murray

Supervising producers: Lee Goldberg, William Rabkin, Tom Mcloughlin
Executive consultant: Mick Garris
Aired from October 1990 to March 1991 in syndication only.

Episodes

Pilot ("She-Wolf of London")
The Bogman of Letchmour Heath
The Juggler
Moonlight Becomes You
Nice Girls Don't
Little Book Shop of Horrors
The Wild Hunt
What's Got into Them
Can't Keep a Dead Man Down (Part 1)
Can't Keep a Dead Man Down (Part 2)

Big-Top She-Wolf
She-Devil
Voodoo Child
Beyond the Beyond
Curiosity Killed the Cravitz
Habeas Corpses
Bride of the Wolfman
Heart Attack
Eclipse
Mystical Pizza

SIERRA NINE

British children's adventure series about a trio of scientific trouble-shooters who were a sort of junior-league cross between *The Avengers* and *The Professionals.*

Sierra Nine was a watchdog organization set up to keep tabs on anything—or anyone—that threatened the scientific equilibrium of the age, be it a stolen missile, secret formula or deadly new weapon. S9 was led by Sir Willoughby Dodd, an eccentric aging scientist described by his creator, scriptwriter Peter Hayes, as "a nut case at first sight, but a genius underneath." Sir Willoughby directed two young assistants, Peter Chance and Anna Parsons, from an exotic office off Trafalgar Square.

The 1963 series was devised when John Rhodes, then ITV's head of Children's Television, asked Hayes and director Marc Miller to come up with a new slant on science fiction. The result was four assorted stories, spread over 13 weeks.

REGULAR CAST

Sir Willoughby Dodd Max Kirby   *Dr. Peter Chance* David Sumner
Anna Parsons Deborah Stanford   *The Baron* Harold Kasket *(Stories 1 and 4)*

Writer: Peter Hayes
Director: Marc Miller

Associated Rediffusion Network Production
13 black and white 30-minute episodes
7 May–30 July 1963

Story One

The Brain Machine

(a 4-part story)
Peter and Anna are rushed off to the oil kingdom of Mirzan in the Middle East to locate and destroy a device operated by a renegade scientist known as "The Baron." Using microwave radio, he is warping the minds of research workers all over the world by telepathic hypnosis.

Prof. Portman Ronald Ibbs
Jane Brightside Ann Rye
Beamish Robert Mill
Arab spy Robert Chapman
King Sharifa Henry Soskin
Col. Selim Julian Sherrier
Bernard Portman Raymond Mason
Arab guard Oswald Laurence
Paratroop major John Trenaman

Settings: Bernard Goodwin

Story Two

The Man Who Shook the World

(a 3-part story)
A minute atomic warhead, designed by eminent nuclear physicist Sir Hugo Petersham, is stolen on its way to be tested in America. When the detonator circuit is activated, Anna and Peter must track down the thieves before the device explodes.
Sir Hugo Petersham David Garth
Graham Lambert George Roubicek
Security guard Norman Mitchell
Ernie Timothy Bateson
Scowse Peter Thomas
U.S. Army colonel Gordon Tanner
Miguel Alvarez George Little

Settings: Duncan Cameron

Story Three

The Elixir of Life

(a 2-part story)
Chance and Anna go to a French monastery where monks claim to have a potion enabling people to live forever, to find out who is out to steal the secret.
Father Gabriel Jack May
Brother Theodore Brian Poiser
Brother Victor Blake Butler

Settings: Andrew Drummond

Story Four

The Q-Radiation

(a 4-part story)
The theft of a terrifying new weapon leads to another encounter with "The Baron" for Chance and Anna who find themselves facing annihilation by death ray.
Dr. John Quendon Peter Halliday
Tom Batley Rodney Bewes
Lord Cardington John Gabriel
Prof. Tudor Owen Ivor Salter
Foley Alan White
Galliver Robert Brown

Settings: Ken Jones

THE SIX MILLION DOLLAR MAN

Based on the novel *Cyborg* by Martin Caidin, *The Six Million Dollar Man* began with a strong science fiction premise that became less significant as the series wore on.

The bionic man, played by former *Big Valley* star Lee Majors, was introduced in a 1974 TV movie that told how astronaut and NASA test pilot Col. Steve Austin—"a man barely alive"—was literally rebuilt after a catastrophic plane crash which robbed him of both legs, an arm and an eye. At a cost of six million dollars, medical scientists, led by Dr. Rudy Wells, equipped him with nuclear-powered limbs and a bionic eye (vividly depicted in the series' opening graphics), enabling him to run and swim at 60 mph, bend metal, smash down walls, leap fences (and small buildings) at a single bound, and see vast distances.

Initially, Austin finds it hard to reconcile himself with being a "freak" and tries to commit suicide—a touching display of human emotion that went down well with critics and public. Once he came to terms with his lot, however, there was no stopping him. The man, like the series, ran and ran.

Austin starts work for a CIA-like government agency, the Office of Strategic Investigations (OSI), headed by the intransigent Oscar Goldman who assigns his high-priced agent all the high-risk missions. These ran the gamut of story possibilities, from political, crime or scientific thrillers and personal dramas, to a few more overtly sf adventures involving space and aliens.

In "Burning Bright," William Shatner guest-starred as an astronaut friend of Austin who is affected in space by an electrical field that gives him the power to communicate with dolphins and control people's minds. In "Straight on 'Til Morning" Austin befriends a radioactive extraterrestrial (Meg Foster) and helps her return to her mother spacecraft before the authorities get to her.

"The Pioneers" featured *M*A*S*H* star Mike Farrell as one half of a cryogenically frozen pair of astronauts who gains superhuman strength; and "Just a Matter of Time" had Steve Austin returning from an orbital flight to learn six years had elapsed.

Lee Majors' wife Farrah Fawcett-Majors guest-starred in three stories—twice as Major Kelly Wood, stranded in space in "The Rescue of Athena One" and accused of espionage in "Nightmare in the Sky," and once as a gambler, Trish Hollander, in "The Golden Pharoah."

Then, of course, there was *The Bionic Woman*, Jaime Sommers (Lindsay Wagner) (see separate entry) whose successful introduction in a couple of SMDM stories earned her a series of her own, and *The Bionic Boy* (Vince Van Patten). One episode, "The Seven Million Dollar Man," featured a new "state of the art" bionic man, but he cracked up under the strain.

Another of the series' more memorable characters was Bigfoot (played first by André the Giant, and later by *Addams Family* star Ted Cassidy). Sasquatch was first revealed in "The Secret of Bigfoot" as a creature created by aliens in their underground laboratory.

REGULAR CAST
Steve Austin Lee Majors   *Oscar Goldman* Richard Anderson
Dr. Rudy Wells Alan Oppenheimer (*later* Martin E. Brooks)

Executive producers: Glen A. Larson, Harve Bennett, Allan Balter
Producers: Michael Gleason, Lee Sigel, Joe L. Cramer, Fred Freiberger
Writers: Numerous
Directors: Various
Music: Oliver Nelson

A Universal Television Production
102 color episodes (60 minutes unless stated), plus pilot movie

U.S. premiere: 18 January 1974
U.K. premiere: 5 September 1974

(Author's note: ITV regionalization meant that the length and composition of the various U.K. runs varied considerably around the country. So, for ease of reference, I've listed the episodes in their original American seasons.)

Pilot Film

The Six Million Dollar Man (85 min.)

Season One

Wine, Women and War (90 min.)
The Solid Gold Kidnapping (90 min.)
Population Zero
Survival of the Fittest
Operation Firefly
Day of the Robot
Little Orphan Airplane
Doomsday and Counting
Eyewitness to Murder
The Rescue of Athena One
Dr. Wells is Missing
The Last of the Fourth of Julys
Burning Bright
The Coward
Run, Steve, Run

Season Two

Nuclear Alert
The Pioneers
Pilot Error
The Pal-Mir Escort
The Seven Million Dollar Man
Straight on 'Til Morning
The Midas Touch
The Deadly Replay
Act of Piracy

The Peeping Blonde
Cross Country Kidnap
Lost Love
Return of the Robot Maker
Taneha
Last Kamikaze
Look Alike
The E.S.P. Spy
The Bionic Woman *(a 2-part story)*
Stranger in Broken Fork
Outrage in Balinderry
Steve Austin, Fugitive

Season Three

The Return of the Bionic Woman *(a 2-part story)*
The Price of Liberty
The Song and Dance Spy
The Wolf Boy
The Deadly Test
Target in the Sky
One of Our Running Backs Is Missing
The Bionic Criminal
The Blue Flash
The White Lightning War
Divided Loyalty
Clark Templeton O'Flaherty
The Winning Smile
Welcome Home, Jaime (Part 1)
Hocus-Pocus
The Secret of Bigfoot *(a 2-part story)*
The Golden Pharaohs
Love Song for Tanya
The Bionic Badge
Big Brother

Season Four

The Return of Bigfoot (Part 1)
Nightmare in the Sky
Double Trouble
The Most Dangerous Enemy
H+2+0 = Death
Kill Oscar (Part 2)
The Bionic Boy *(2 hours in U.S,. shown as a 2-part story in U.K.)*
Vulture of the Andes
The Thunderbird Connection *(2 hours in U.S., shown as a 2-part story in U.K.)*
A Bionic Christmas Carol
Task Force
The Ultimate Impostor *(unsold pilot)*
Death Probe *(a 2-part story)*
Danny's Inferno
The Fires of Hell
The Infiltrators
Carnival of Spies
U-509
Privacy of the Mind

To Catch the Eagle
The Ghostly Teletype

Season Five

Sharks *(a 2-part story)*
Deadly Countdown *(a 2-part story)*
Bigfoot V
Killer Wind
Rollback
Dark Side of the Moon *(a 2-part story)*
Target: Steve Austin
The Cheshire Project
Walk a Deadly Wing
Just a Matter of Time
Return of Death Probe *(a 2-part story)*
The Lost Island *(2 hours)*
The Madonna Caper
Deadly Ringer
Date With Danger *(a 2-part story)*
The Moving Mountain

SKY

Back in the 1970s, when nearly every science fiction series British BBC competitor ITV mounted was touted as a rival to *Doctor Who*, all the best ideas emerged in the children's slots (*Timeslip, Ace of Wands, The Tomorrow People*).

Sky was another such contender. Written by onetime *Doctor Who* writers Bob Baker and Dave Martin, it told the story of a young time-traveling deity from another dimension who gets knocked off course by a black hole and becomes stranded on Earth. Though immature, Sky has the power to compel humans to do what he wants. Enter a trio of West Country teenagers, Arby and Jane Vennor and Roy Briggs, who become caught up in helping the blond, blue-eyed stranger to return to his own dimension, via the "Juganet." Neither outright hero nor villain, Sky is opposed on Earth by Goodchild, a sinister character who can materialize and dematerialize at will, representing "the natural opposition of Earth to anything out of place." Sky's presence has evoked a disturbing reaction from nature—one scene has tree roots trying to throttle him when he shelters below ground. Sky must find the "Juganet" before the opposing forces grow too strong.

Much of the series was filmed around Stonehenge, Glastonbury and Avebury, giving it an added mystical twist. Of the cast, Richard Speight, who played Roy, had done his own traveling through space and time as the young Time Guardian, Peter, in *The Tomorrow People*.

Sky, which appeared in 1976, was one of several strong fantasy and adventure series produced by HTV, whose output also included *Children of the Stones* (1977) and *King of the Castle* (1978), the latter also scripted by Baker and Martin.

CAST

Sky Mark Harrison *Roy Briggs* Richard Speight *Arby Vennor* Stuart Lock
Jane Vennor Cherrald Butterfield *Goodchild* Robert Eddison
Major Briggs Jack Watson *Mr. Vennor* Thomas Heathcote
Mrs. Vennor Frances Cuka
with: *Sgt. Simmons* David Jackson *Dr. Marshall* Rex Holdsworth
Nurses Ursula Barclay, Monica Lavers *Orderly* Geoff Serle
Dr. Saul Gerard Hely *Tom* Meredith Edwards *Receptionist* Barbara Baber
Michael Sean Lynch *Susannah* Prunella Ransome *Rex* Trevor Ray
Policeman John Curry *Haril* Bernard Archard *Revil* Peter Copley

Writers: Bob Baker, Dave Martin
Director: Derek Clark
Producer: Leonard White
Executive producer: Patrick Dromgoole
Designer: John Biggs

An HTV Production
7 color 30-minute episodes

Burning Bright
Juganet
Goodchild
What Dread Hand
Evalake
Life Force
Chariot of Fire
7 April–19 May 1976

SLEEPWALKERS

From the NBC press release: *"Sleepwalkers* travels to the worlds that exist only in your wildest, sometimes deadliest, dreams. The last hope for those plagued by their nocturnal world is a place called The Morpheus Institute. Founded by top neurophysiologist Nathan Bradford, the Institute allows members of its elite staff to enter other people's dream worlds—and help combat their demons. More often than not, the lines between reality and dream are dangerously blurred."

Canceled after only two episodes; one cannot help but wonder why NBC bothered to even put it on the air: clearly they had no interest in giving it a chance to find viewers. On the other hand, the first three episodes weren't terribly good, either. But by that measure, *Babylon 5* never should have made it beyond its first movie, and it evolved into one of the best science fiction series ever aired.

REGULAR CAST
Dr. Nathan Bradford Bruce Greenwood *Kate Russel* Naomi Watts
Ben Costigan Jeffrey D. Sams *Vincent Konefke* Abraham Benrubi
Gail Kathrin Nicholson

Creators: David S. Goyer, Stephen Kronish
Co-producers: Stephen Gaghan, Sara B. Charno
Consulting producer: David Nutter
Supervising producer: Tim Iacofano
Executive producers: Stephen Kronisk, David S. Goyer
Executive producers/writers: David S. Goyer, Stephen Kronish
NBC Studios in association with Columbia TriStar Television

Episodes
Pilot
Night Terrors
Eye of the Beholder
Counting Sheep
Passed Imperfect
Forlorn
A Matter of Fax
Cassandra
Sub-Conscious

SLIDERS

"What if you could travel to parallel worlds. The same year, the same Earth, only different dimensions. A world where the Russians rule America, or where your dreams of being a superstar come true. Or where San Francisco was a maximum security prison. My friends and I found the gateway. Now the problem is finding a way back home."
—Quinn Mallory, *Sliders'* opening narration

"What if . . .?" Two of the most tantalizing words in the sci-fi lexicon. A question that picks at reality like a loose seam, unraveling it to explore what our lives and our world might have been like if at some point in time history had taken a different turn.

"What if . . .?" is the provocative premise of this U.S. action adventure series that follows four characters who slide through a man-made wormhole into parallel dimensions of Earth, experiencing alternate versions of our world, or at least the bit of it we call San Francisco!

Sliders was created by award-winning *Star Trek: The Next Generation* writer Tracy Tormé, after he read a biography of George Washington and realized that if one British soldier had aimed a little better there wouldn't have been a United States.

He's peppered the series with intriguing scenarios such as a world where Einstein withheld the secret of nuclear energy and now there are no weapons capable of destroying an asteroid hurtling toward the planet; a world where antibiotics are unknown and an incurable epidemic is raging; a world where America lost the Cold War, or where women hold the upper hand (no change there, then). Even a world where Elvis is still alive.

Slip-sliding through these parallel dimensions are Quinn Mallory (former child actor Jerry O'Connell), a young physics genius who creates the wormhole in the basement of his San Francisco home; the arrogant Professor Maximillian Arturo (played by Welsh actor John Rhys-Davies) who is forced to acknowledge his student's brilliance; Mallory's computer technician friend and, initially at least, unrequited love Wade Wells (Sabrina Lloyd); and Rembrandt "Crying Man" Brown (Cleavant Derricks), a washed-up sixties soul singer from the Spinning Tops group, accidentally swept along for the ride when his car is engulfed by the portal while he's driving by Quinn's house.

Sliders is a fun, watchable show that certainly works in a few thought-provoking ideas about what might happen if you introduce ideas from one reality into another—e.g., a nuclear bomb, penicillin or even the American Constitution—or even meet your other selves. But too many storylines fail to live up to their teasing premise, as the plot too often falls back on the same formula—the Sliders arrive in a parallel world, get in trouble, get chased and escape in the nick of time. There's an echo, too, of *Quantum Leap* as, like Sam Beckett, the quartet can't return to their own reality at will and each time they leap into the vortex it's with the hope that the next slide will be "the slide home." They actually make it back once, but an "oiled" squeaky gate at Quinn's house fools them into believing it's not their reality.

One consequence of exploring different versions of the same place (aside from helping the series' budget!) is that the Sliders keep on bumping into some of the same people, which makes it enjoyable to watch out for recurring characters such as motel and Dominion hotel manager Gomez Calhoun, taxi driver Pavel Kurlienko and student Conrad Bennish.

Sliders premiered in the U.S. in March 1995 but though it never set the ratings alight, it did well enough to be renewed—even to a full third season of 22 episodes, for 1996–97. The Sci-Fi Channel picked it up for a new 1998 season.

REGULAR CAST:
Quinn Mallory Jerry O'Connell *Professor Maximillian Arturo* John Rhys-Davies
Wade Wells Sabrina Lloyd *Rembrandt "Crying Man" Brown* Cleavant Derricks

---

Creators: Tracy Tormé, Robert K. Weiss
Executive producers: Robert K. Weiss, Jacob Epstein, Tracy Tormé, Alan Barnette, Leslie Belzberg, John Landis
Producers: Steve Ecclesine, Jon Povill, Tony Blake, Paul Jackson
Music: Dennis McCarthy, Stephen Graziano, Mark Mothersbaugh

A St. Clare Entertainment Production
Season One:
9 color 60-minute episodes (pilot two hours)
Season Two:
13 color 60-minute episodes
U.S. premiere: 22 March 1995
U.K. premiere: 20 January 1996
(Sky One)

Season One

Pilot

w Tracy Tormé, *story by* Tracy Tormé & Robert K. Weiss

In his basement lab, 25-year-old physics student Quinn Mallory creates a wormhole portal through which he can travel to parallel dimensions of Earth. He persuades his professor Maximillian Arturo and friend Wade Wells to embark on the joy-ride of their lives. Setting the timer for four hours, Quinn turns up the power, so much so that the portal engulfs Rembrandt Brown, a washed-up soul singer on his way to sing the National Anthem at a local baseball game. The Sliders land in a San Francisco submerged by ice and when a tornado threatens to engulf them, Quinn ignores the timer and creates the portal to escape. This time they land in a San Francisco ruled by the Soviets. After becoming embroiled with revolutionary forces and narrowly escaping death (of course), the quartet jumps into the portal believing they'll return to their own dimension.

Mrs. Mallory Linda Henning
Commissar Wapner Joseph A. Wapner
Comrade Llewelyn Doug Llewelyn
Doc Garwin Sanford
Wilkins Roger R. Cross
Wing Yee Jee Tso
Crazy Kenny Frank C. Turner
Michael Hurley Gary Jones
Ross J. Kelly/Interrogator John Novak
Artie Field Don MacKay
Pavel Kurlienko Alex Bruhanski
KGB colonel Jay Brazeau
Vendor Andrew Kavadas
Pat Sook Yin Lee
PBS spokesman Wayne Cox
Sentry Raoul Ganee
Michael Mallory Tom Butler

Director: Andy Tennant

Fever

w Ann Powell & Rose Schacht

The Sliders arrive on a parallel Earth where antibiotics were never discovered and where a raging virus threatens to wipe out the population. Quinn is horrified to learn that in this dimension *he* is "patient zero." When Wade becomes ill, Arturo uses primitive ingredients to create penicillin that he is able to pass on to the diseased.

Dr. Morton Ken Pogue
Dr. Eileen Stanley Allison Hossack
Wing Yee Jee Tso
Pavel Kurlienko Alex Bruhanski
Waitress Marie Stillin

Gomez Calhoun William Sasso
Stock boy Dean Haglund
Tactical moonsuit David L. Gordon
Medical moonsuit William MacDonald
Trucker James Bell
Pharmacist James Timmins
Sick Man Gavin Cross

Director: Mario Azzopardi

Last Days

w Dan Lane

The group slides to a world that is about to be destroyed by an asteroid hurtling toward Earth. Only an atomic bomb can stop it, but in this dimension Einstein never allowed nuclear weapons to be created. With time running out, Arturo works feverishly with Bennish, an eccentric young scientist, to re-create Einstein's equation. Meanwhile Quinn and Wade face their feelings for each other.

Conrad Bennish Jr. Jason Gaffney
Dr. Lee Antonovich George Touliatos
Caroline Fontaine Jennifer Hetrick
Allan Fontaine Malcom Stewart
Mace Moon Gerry Nairn
Reverend Carlton Watson
Nurse Pamela Robyn Palmer
Jimmy Patrick Stevenson
Meter maid Jacqueline Dandenequ
News anchor Norma Wick

Director: Michael Keusch

Prince of Wails

w Lee Goldberg & William Rabkin

The group slides from a parallel world where San Francisco is about to go underwater to a world where the British won the Revolution. Arturo is horrified to discover his dimensional double is the wicked Sheriff of San Francisco who is plotting to kill the ruling monarch, Crown Prince Harold. (This episode was screened out of order, and should have been aired after "Summer of Love," which ends with the Sliders about to be engulfed in the tidal wave that starts this episode!)

Prince Harold Ben Bode
Hendrick Sherman Howard
Miss Miller Liz Sheridan
Captain Michael Hurley Gary Jones
Rebecca Kathleen Duborg
Dixon Vallely Tracey Olson
Raiders Chris Humphreys, Bernie Coulson
Driver Gerard Plunkett

Director: Felix Alcala

Summer of Love

w Tracy Tormé
The Sliders encounter a parallel world where Oliver North is President, the U.S. is involved in a bitter war in Australia and hippies still roam the streets of San Francisco. After stumbling on his own "funeral," Rembrandt discovers he would have lived in hen-pecked misery if he had married his childhood sweetheart.
Sharon Brown Deborah Lacey
Rembrandt Jr. Arthur Reggie III
Conrad Bennish Jr. Jason Gaffney
Mace Moon Gerry Nairn
Copeland Michele Goodger
Harold Yenn Robert Lee
Skid Barry Pepper
Fling Gabrielle Miller
Seeker Ajay Karan
Tremelo Richard Leacock
Cezanne Obba Babatunde
Mrs. Tweak Joy Coghill

Director: Mario Azzopardi

Eggheads

w Scott Smith Miller, *story by* Scott Smith Miller & Jacob Epstein
The Sliders travel to a dimension where academics, not athletes are the national heroes—and Quinn's double is the biggest hero of them all! Meanwhile Arturo tries to patch up his relationship with the love of his life . . . (Making a "blink and you'll miss it" appearance is William B. Davis, better known as *The X-Files'* Smoking Man.)
Coach Almquist Charles Cyphers
Jimmy Fountain Peter Spellos
Kristina Fox Arturo Gabrielle Rose
Lydia Karen Austin
Professor Myman William B. Davis
Wilson Andrew Guy
Victor Johnny Mah
Boyer Roman Danylo
Mrs. Bingham Sheelah Megill
Karen Rachel Hayward
Agent Cannon Anthony Harrison
Agent O'Malley Marc Baur

Director: Timothy Bond

The Weaker Sex

w Dawn Prestwich & Nicole Yorkin
In this parallel dimension, traditional male and female roles are reversed and Arturo decides to lead a "men's rights" movement by running for mayor.

Serena Braxton Jill Teed
Mayor Anita Ross Sara Botsford
Danny Eizenbach Robert Curtis-Brown
Lois Liza Huget
Bernie Joe Maffei
Pete Alf Humphreys
Ken Andrew Wheeler
Glenn Peter Kelamis
Ed Douglas Sills
Jeanie Moses Tamara Stanners
Hillary Clinton Teresa Barnwell

Director: Vern Gillum

The King Is Back

w Tracy Tormé
The Sliders arrive in a world where Rembrandt's double is as popular as Elvis—but he's been dead for eight years, so Rembrandt's "re-appearance" creates havoc.
Captain Jack Brim Chuck McCan
Alternate Rembrandt Clinton Derricks-Carroll
Maurice Fish Tom Pickett
Lawyer Janice Kent
Penny Jensen Michelle T. Carter
Secretary Sheri D. Wilson
Charmange Judith Maxie
Nick Nicholas Harrison
Gomez Calhoun William Sasso
Judge Richard Ihara
Del Rubio Sisters Milly, Eadie and Elena Del Rubio

Director: Vern Gillum

Luck of the Draw

w Jon Povill
This latest dimension seems like paradise—until Wade wins the lottery and the Sliders finds that as a means of controlling the population, lottery winners are treated like royalty and given anything they want in return for which they must agree to die. Naturally, they escape in the nick of time—but as they leap into the vortex, Quinn is shot . . .
Ryan Simms Nicholas Lea
Julianne Murphy Cynthia "Alex" Datcher
Ken Neisser Kevin Cooney
Agent Jones Tim Henry
Agent Wilson Mike Kopsa
Father Fergus Nathan Venering
Himself Geoff Edwards

Director: Les Landau

Season Two

Into the Mystic

w Tracy Tormé
With Quinn seriously injured from his gunshot wound, the Sliders search for a doctor on what seems to be a world in the grip of witchcraft. They learn of an all-powerful sorcerer said to know the secret of sliding, and embark on a *Wizard of Oz*–style quest to his castle beyond the Golden Gate bridge. There they discover that the sorcerer is Quinn's double who agrees to return them home. Arriving back at his house Quinn tests the squeaky gate that will tell them if they really are home. When it does not squeak, the Sliders slide on, believing this is not their Earth. As they depart we learn that Quinn's mom has just had the gate oiled . . .
Dr. Xang Christopher Neame
Bounty hunter Phil Fondacaro
Mr. Gale Hrothgar Mathews
Ryan Nicholas Lea
Nurse Mikal Dughi
Ross J. Kelly John Novak
Fortune teller Karin Konoval
Pavel Kurlienko Alex Bruhanski
Mrs. Mallory Deanne Henry
Sorcerer Rod Wilson

Director: Richard Compton

Love Gods

w Tony Blake & Paul Jackson
Arriving on a world where the male population has become almost extinct, due to a virus, the male Sliders find themselves elevated to the status of "love gods" by the society of women eager to repopulate the planet.
Det. L. Specateli Gwynyth Walsh
Diana Jennifer Nash
Billie Jean Georgia Emelin
David Jon Pennell
O'Grady Deb Podowski
Jane Kathryn Anderson
Trevor Grant Andrew Guy
Cara Kendall Cross
Aussie guard Kathleen Barr
Debra Ona Grauer

Director: John McPherson

Gillian of the Spirits

w Tony Blake & Paul Jackson
When the wormhole is hit by lightning during their slide, Quinn becomes separated from the others, trapped alone on the astral plane. With the timer damaged and the world they've arrived in opposed to any technology, the Sliders' only hope lies with Gillian, a troubled young girl with psychic powers, and the only one who can see and hear Quinn.
Gillian Deanna Milligan
Michael Mallory Tom Butler
Nicole Gillian Barber
Father Jerry Gerard Plunkett
Major Phillips Greg Rogers
Gomez Calhoun William Sasso
Mrs. Henry Sheelah Megill
Monica Nicole Parker
Traffic cop Peter Fleming

Director: Paris Barclay

The Good, the Bad, and the Wealthy

w Scott Miller
The Sliders land in a world that lives by the code of the Wild West and corporate takeovers are handled by gunfights. When Quinn interferes with a "business deal" and ends up shooting a man, his reputation makes him a much sought-after man . . .
Priscilla Karen Witter
Jamie Keegan MacIntosh
Jack Bullock Jamie Denton
Billy Rae Kent Faulcon
Sheriff Peter LaCroix
Cliff Sutter Stephen Fanning
Jed Dalton Barry Levy
Hank Arnette Greg Thirloway
Deputy Joe Bob Adrian Hughes
Lonnie Skayler Bart Anderson
Exchange official Roger Barnes
Poker player Jackson Cole
Billy the Kid Gates Lochlyn Munro

Director: Oscar L. Costo

El Sid

w Jon Povill
The Sliders are about to escape from a chaotic world ruled by violence when Quinn rescues a young woman from her homicidal boyfriend, El Sid. But he follows them into the vortex to the next dimension—where San Francisco is a maximum security prison and Quinn is held responsible for Sid's "good behavior."
Sid Jeffery Dean Morgan
Michele Rebecca Chambers
L.J. Claude Brooks
Leo Jed Dixon
Big Jake Raimund Stamm
Delores Maria Herrera
Blade Reese McBeth
Hostage Scott Swanson
Gladys Chappelle Jaffe
M.S.W. Sandra P. Grant

Director: Paris Barclay

Time Again and World

w Jacob Epstein
Wade witnesses a shooting seconds before a slide, and when they land on the next world they find the same murder about to be committed. Wade intervenes and the Sliders become embroiled in a bizarre plot involving a disgraced federal judge, an underground resistance movement and a country under martial law.
Natalie Rebecca Gayheart
Lt. Graves Garry Chalk
Michael Hurley Garry Jones
Judge John Nassau George Delhoyo
Alverez Garvin Cross
L.C. Ravinder Toor
Deitrich Barry Greene
O'Neill Lesley Ewen
Hipster Jed Rees
Gomez Calhoun William Sasso
Rummy Tom Heaton
Bartender Robert Metcalfe

Director: Vern Gillum

In Dino Veritas

w Steve Brown
The quartet lands in a San Francisco that's been developed as a game reserve—for dinosaurs! While his friends are trapped in a cave and menaced by a man-eating allosaurus, Quinn must go in search of the timer, which has been lost somewhere outside.
Ranger Alessandra Petlin
Poacher Jack Kehler
Wayne Davies Brent Sheppard
Angelica Marcy Mellish

Director: Oscar L. Costo

Post Traumatic Slide Syndrome

w Nan Hagen
The Sliders finally seem to have made it back to their own Earth, much to the delight of all but Quinn. When Rembrandt's musical career takes off, Wade wins a publishing deal, and Arturo becomes famous after taking credit for his invention, Quinn must prove that this is not really home (Big hint: the Golden Gate Bridge is blue!).
Dr. Whelan Kristoffer Tabori
Miss Vonbaeck Stacy Grant
Artie Field Don MacKay
Mrs. Mallory Deanne Henry
Sebastian Smith Carlton Watson

Leroy Hopkins Tom Picket
Barry King Brian Arnold
Tanika Linda Ko
Miss Jennings Tina Klassen
Guard Mike Mitchell

Director: Adam Nimoy

Obsession

w Jon Povill, *story by* Jon Povill & Steve Brown
When the Sliders land in a society dominated by psychics, Wade literally meets the man of her dreams. Not only is he obsessed with her, but he happens to be next in line for the post of Prime Oracle, the most powerful man in the world . . .
Derek Bond James Patrick Stuart
Dominique Heather Hanson
Prime Oracle Isaac Hayes
Regent Malcolm Stewart
Melanie Sandra P. Grant
First officer Paul McGillion
Henry Hiro Kanagawa
Young woman Gillian Carfra

Director: Paris Barclay

Greatfellas

w Scott Smith Miller, *story by* Sean Clark & Scott Smith Miller
In a San Francisco dominated by rival gangster families and where Prohibition was never repealed, the Sliders are thrust into a vicious struggle between rival families, corrupt government officials and the Feds—for whom this world's Rembrandt is the No. 1 crimebuster. (Features a guest appearance by Mel Tormé, creator Tracy Tormé's dad.)
Ben Greenfield Donnelly Rhodes
Leah Greenfield Sarah Strange
Tommy Greenfield Benjamin Ratner
June Venus Terzo
Rembrandt 2 Clinton Derricks-Carroll
John Byron Lucas
Gomez Calhoun William Sasso
Joseph Biacchi Jano Frandsen
Agent Reid Ted Cole
Dabelle Patriarch Joe Maffei
Bartender Russell Ferrier

Director: Allan Eastman

The Young and the Relentless

w T. Edward Anthony & Von Whisenhant, *story by* Michael X. Farrara, T. Edward Anthony & Von Whisenhant
In a world where only the young have any power or respect, and where Quinn and Wade's doubles were married—until he recently drowned—Quinn agrees to impersonate himself. Then he and Wade find their doubles were up to their necks in a shady computer-software deal.
Margo Laura Harris
Kenny Hatcher Russell Porter
Tiffany August Kristy Cohen
Kyle Beck Kyle Alisharan
Razor Gillette Paul Jarrett
Richard Richard Cox
Judge Gordon Michael Woolvett
Joanne Britt Lind
Melanie White Elisabeth Rosen
Bartender Trevor Roberts
Kromagg Paul Anderson

Director: Richard Compton

Invasion

w Tracy Tormé
Landing briefly in an eerily quiet and deserted San Francisco, the Sliders encounter a vicious and technologically advanced alien race, the Kromaggs, who can slide at will and intend to conquer Earth throughout every dimension!
Hilton Brown Lee W. Weaver
Mary Una Damon
Mr. Clarke Robert Lewis
Prisoner Jason Gaffney
Kromagg Gerry South

Director: Richard Compton

As Times Go By

w Steve Brown
The Sliders find themselves in a puzzling situation: each time they slide into a new world, they encounter the same people they did in the previous one. One of these is Quinn's long-lost love Daelin, who seems to be heading for a fate only Quinn can prevent.
Dennis McMillan Matthew Flint
Daelin Anna Maria Richards Brooke Langton
Kit Richards Charlie O'Connell
Judge Estevez Mina E. Mina
Gloria Sanchez Dennys Payamps
La Migra Eli Gabay
La Padrona Lori Triolo

Director: Richard Compton

Season Three

Rules of the Game

w Josef Anderson
The Sliders enter a world where human war games determine social status.
Nicky Laurie Fortier
Egghead Joshua Malina

Director: Oscar Costo

Doublecross

w Tony Blake & Paul Jackson
On an Earth with depleted natural resources, scientists are trying to develop sliding as a way to plunder other worlds.
Logan St. Clair Zoe McLellan
Monique Mari Morrow
Elston Diggs Lester Barrie
Adrian Fayne Michael Bryan French
Mrs. Arturo Diana Castle

Director: Richard Compton

Electric Twister Acid Test

w Scott Smith Miller
A desertlike world ravaged by electrical tornadoes has one small safe haven: a pocket of stability ruled by a technophobic zealot.
Reed Michener Corey Feldman
Jenny Julie Benz
Jacob Tim Griffin
Martin Joshua Cox
Caleb Jordan Blake Warkol
Franklin Michener Bill Bolender

Director: Oscar L. Costo

The Guardian

w Tracy Tormé
The Sliders find a world where time is moving slower than normal, and Quinn meets himself as a boy.
Young Quinn Phillip Van Dyke
Mrs. Mallory Linda Henning
Heather Hanley Leslie Horan
Ambrosia Meadow Sisto
Brady Oaks Marty York
Rex Crandell Timothy Wiley

Director: Adam Nimoy

The Dream Masters

w Melinda Snodgrass, *story by* Scott Miller & Melinda Snodgrass
A gang of thugs rules an Earth with their ability to kill while sleeping; unfortunately, their leader has eyes for Wade.
Gerald Thomas Zack Ward
Dr. Olivia Lujan Katherine LaNasa
Byron Rodney Eastman
Diggs Lester Barrie
Henry J. Steven Smith

Director: Jefery Levy

Desert Storm

w Matt Dearborn
On a water-poor Earth, the Sliders encounter Mad Max casting refugees and a woman who can psychically locate underground water.
Devin Gina Philips
Jeremy Kristofer Lindquist
Cutter Ken Steadman
Diggs Lester Barrie
Master healer Michael Lee Gogin

Director: Jim Johnston

Dragonslide

w Tony Blake & Paul Jackson
In a world where magic has developed instead of science, Quinn is mistaken for a wizard.
Melinda Michelle Rene Thomas
Gareth Gregory Martin
Skuldar Max Grodenchik
Sean Nuinn Francis Guinan
Elston Diggs Lester Barrie
Alesha Avo Francoise Robertson

Director: David Livingston

The Fire Within

w Josef Anderson
The Sliders carry a flame-creature with them to an oil-rich Los Angeles.
J.C. Ashton Anthony Tyler Quinn
Amanda Brigitta Dau
Diana Sylvius Lynn Clark
Flame Veronica Cartwright *(voice-over)*

Director: Jefery Levy

Prince of Slides

w Eleah Horwitz
In a world where men give birth, Rembrandt is mistaken as the father of the next heir to the American throne.

Lady Mary Hallie Foote
Duchess Danielle Victoria Mahoney
Rembrandt No. 2 Clinton Derricks-Carroll
George Stellos Dan Gauthier

Director: Richard Compton

Dead Man Sliding

w Nan Hagen
Quinn is arrested and sentenced to death for crimes his double committed in this world.
People's Proponent Lawrence Hilton-Jacobs
Contestant coordinator Perrey Reeves Taryn
Phil Fredric Lane
Deanne Bloch Lisa Rieffel

Director: Richard Compton

State of the Art

w Nan Hagen, *story by* Schuyler Kent
The Sliders land in a world ruled by androids, where humanity may be extinct.
D.E.R.I.C. Eddie Mills
E.R.I.C.A./Shauna Kathleen McClellan
Paul Jerry Rector
Scarface Paul Jeff Rector
James Aldohn Robert Englund
T.E.D. Ted Detwiler

Director: John Kretchmer

Season's Greedings

w Eleah Horwitz
The Sliders land in a giant shopping mall, where consumers spend their lives trying to pay off shopping bills.
Kelly Welles Chase Masterson
President Ted Bernsen Neil Roberts
Don Welles Allen Williams

Director: Richard Compton

Murder Most Foul

w David Peckinpah
In a world where fantasy role-playing relieves stress, Arturo is reprogrammed to be a 19th-century detective.
Inspector Reed Brian McNamara
Erin Brigid Brannagh
Dr. Bolivar David Purdham
Trevor Adam Wylie
Diggs Lester Barrie
Dr. Punch Suzanne Mara

Director: Jeff Woolnough

Slide Like an Egyptian

w Scott Miller Smith
The Sliders reach a world based on Egyptian religion, complete with pyramids and giant scarabs.
Kheri-Heb Shaun Toub
Sheilah Claudette Mink
Dr. Achtbit Rocco Vienhage
Mike Mallory Jim Turner
Seyn Jebid Armando Valdes-Kennedy
R.D.I. Agent Steven Meek
Dr. Deera Mubaric Apollonia

Director: Adam Nimoy

Paradise Lost

w Steven Stoliar
The Sliders enter a world of perpetual youth.
Lara Steinick Laurie Miller
Sheriff Burke Rob Youngblood
Parker Whitmore Will Schaub
Trudy Whitmore Pat Gebhard
Alice Kristi McDaniel

Director: Jim Johnston

The Exodus, Part 1

w Tony Blake & Paul Jackson, *story by* John Rhys-Davies
In a world about to be destroyed by pulsars, the last hope for humanity may be sliding to another, safer world. The only problem: Col. Rickman, who's in charge of the project, runs it like a dictator.
Captain Maggie Beckett Kari Wuhrer
Dr. Steven Jensen Mark Kiely
Malcolm Wes Charles Jr.
Mrs. Mallory Linda Henning
Street person Steve Larson
Colonel Angus Rickman Roger Daltrey

Director: Jim Charleston

The Exodus, Part 2

w Josef Anderson, Paul Jackson & Tony Blake
The exodus from a doomed world continues, at terrific cost for the four Sliders, as Col. Rickman begins killing to keep himself alive.
Captain Maggie Beckett Kari Wuhrer
Dr. Steven Jensen Mark Kiely
Malcolm Wes Charles Jr.
Colonel Angus Rickman Roger Daltrey

Director: Jefrey Levy

Sole Survivors

w Steven Kriozere
Maggie Beckett joins the Sliders as they hunt for Col. Rickman on a world plagued with zombies.

Debra Carbol Stephanie Niznik
Dr. Tassler Jay Acovone

Director: David Peckinpah

The Breeder

w Eleah Horwitz
On a world where the young and healthy can be forced to give up organs to older and more important people, Maggie discovers she's carrying a parasite that wants to breed.
Dr. Sylvius Dawn Lewis
Elston Diggs Lester Barrie
Tami Deborah Kellner
Roger Spencer Garbett

Director: Paris Barclay

The Last of Eden

w Josef Anderson
On a world plagued by violent earthquakes, civilization lies in towering apartment complexes.
Brock Ron Melendez
Keegan Don Jeffcoat

Director: Allan Eastman

The Other Slide of Darkness

w Nan Hagen & Scott Smith Miller
On a world of mysterious toxic fogs, Quinn finds Col. Rickman . . . and the human who gave the Cromaggs sliding technology.
Adra Oona Hart
Bunt La Croix Kevin Quigley
Col. Angus Rickman Neil Dickson
Billy T. Franc Ross

Director: Jeff Woolnough

Slither

w Tony Blake & Paul Jackson
Rembrandt and Quinn charter a plane for a vacation, only to come up agaisnt an intelligent snake who may prevent them from reaching the rest of the party in time to slide.
Kyra Julie St. Claire
Carlos Randy Vasquez
Don Marc Tissot
Angel Danny Mora
Randy Thomas G. Waites
Customs official David Correia

Director: Jim Johnston

Dinoslide

w David Peckinpah
The Sliders discover the world they brought refugees to in "Exodus" harbors carnivorous dinosaurs.
Gretchen Rainer Grant
Col. Angus Rickman Neil Dickson
Malcolm Eastman Wes Charles Jr.
Andrews Michael Woolson
Hinds Mike Terner

Director: Richard Compton

Stoker

w Josef Anderson
The hunt for Col. Rickman continues in a world plagued by vampires.
Morgan Ryan Alosio

Col. Angus Rickman Neil Dickson
Harker Duff McKagan
Renfield Danny Masterson
Van Elsinger Tommy Chong

Director: Jerry O'Connell

This Slide of Paradise

w Nan Hagen
In a world where human and animal DNA has been mixed, creating murderous creatures, the Sliders finally corner Col. Rickman.
Alisandra Melinda Clarke
Col. Angus Rickman Neil Dickson
Ceres Deron Michael McBee
Daniel Marc Riffon
Dr. Vargas Michael York

Director: Jim Johnston

SMALL WONDER

Amiable U.S. sitcom about a precocious ten-year-old girl called Vicki who is really a robot. Adopted by her inventor's family, the Lawsons, Vicky is actually VICI—Voice Input Child Indenticat—and gets up to the usual domestic hi-jinks, especially with the Lawsons' son, Jamie. Routine comedy with a dutiful moral tagged onto the end of each episode.

REGULAR CAST
Ted Dick Christie   *Joan* Marla Pennington
Jamie Jerry Supiran   *Vicki* Tiffany Brissette
Harriet Emily Schulman

Executive producer: Howard Leeds, *for* Metromedia Producers Corporation

U.K.: 18 color 30-minute episodes
U.K. premiere: 5 October 1985
(Anglia, and other ITV regions—not fully networked)
1985–1989

SOMETHING IS OUT THERE

Short-lived U.S. yarn about a beautiful mind-reading alien who teams up with a cynical, streetwise cop to fight crime and evil in an American city.

The series was based on a hugely successful 1988 four-hour mini-series in which the alien, Ta'ra, came to Earth in pursuit of a marauding monster that had terrorized her spaceship. She teamed up with detective Jack Breslin, and together they tracked down the beast, a shape-shifting creature called a Xenomorph that had been slashing its victims to death and removing internal organs.

The follow-up series saw the duo tackle an assortment of earthbound crooks, killers and oddballs plus a new extra-terrestrial threat. Poor ratings for the first three episodes prompted the producers to announce the impending return of the Xenomorph, but the series didn't even last that long.

MAIN CAST
Jack Breslin Joe Cortese   *Ta'ra* Maryam d'Abo
Lt. Victor Maldonado Gregory Sierra

Creator: Frank Lupo
Executive producers: Frank Lupo, John Ashley
Writers: Frank Lupo, Burt Pearl, Paul Bern-
baum, Christian Darren
Directors: Various, including Richard Colla,
Larry Shaw, Lyndon Chubbuck, James Dar-
ren, Don Medford
Special effects: John Dykstra

8 color 60-minute episodes
Gladiator
Don't Look Back

In His Own Image
Good Psychics Are Hard to Come By
Night of the Visitors
A Message from Mr. Cool
A Hearse of Another Color
The Keeper

U.S. premiere: mini-series May 1988
Series: 21 October 1988
U.K. run: from 2 October 1991
(Sky One)

SPACE: ABOVE AND BEYOND

"We thought we were alone. We believed the universe was
ours. Until one night in 2063, on an Earth colony 16 light-
years away, they struck. Now we're at war. We fight when
called, in space, on land, and at sea. To lose this war means
more than defeat; to surrender is to never go home. All of
us must rise to the call . . . above and beyond"
—Col. McQueen, opening narration

In space no one can hear you scream—unless it's the battle cry of the U.S. Marine Corps . . .
Semper Fi? Semper Sci-fi!

This futuristic action adventure series has the pedigree of being created by *X-Files* producers
Glen Morgan and James Wong—but the two shows are worlds apart.

Space: Above and Beyond focuses on five young Marine Corps space cadets, collectively known
as the Wildcards, who suddenly find themselves thrust into the front line of battle against a mysterious
alien enemy. While still trying to deal with the emotions that drove them to enlist, they must learn faith
in each other and find an answer to the question "What would you be willing to die for?"

It's been unfairly called "Melrose Space" and even *"Top Gun"* in space," but the look and feel is
closer to a World War Two movie, with Morgan and Wong drawing on such classic war films as
the Civil War drama *Red Badge of Courage, Guadalcanal Diary, Twelve O'Clock High* and *The
Naked and the Dead*, to create an intense, pressure cooker atmosphere. There's a lot of action, but
it's punctuated by long, introspective periods of character-rooted drama.

The only echo of *The X-Files* is a streak of paranoia about whether the world government has
prior knowledge of the aliens, known as Chigs.

The series comes with an impressively complex history that is gradually sketched in as it
progresses. But two key events that have shaped this future are the Artificial Intelligence (AI)
Wars and the creation of a race of In Vitro humans to fight the AIs.

The AIs, also known as Silicates, are human replicas, built as soldiers and servants. Physically
perfect, but with eerie white eyes and rifle crosshairs for pupils, they were restricted from original
thought until a disgruntled programmer infected them with a virus that gave them a risk-taking
perspective, and sparked a revolt.

High human casualties led to the creation of a race of humans called Tanks, conceived by *in
vitro* fertilization in artificial gestation chambers, and held in suspended animation until the age
of 18, before being awakened and sent into battle. Unfortunately, the In Vitros—distinguished by
a "navel" on their neck—proved poor soldiers. Born of unknown parents and denied a home life
or a childhood, they had no feelings of patriotism. The In Vitro platoons were dissolved and the
Tanks became a disenfranchised underclass.

SAAB opens in the year 2063. After many years of deep space exploration have found no
answering voice, mankind believes it is alone in the galaxy. Fledgling colonies are being
established some 16 light-years from home, when an unknown and unprovoked alien force
suddenly wipes them out, and Earth finds itself in a war in which it's seriously outgunned.

Our heroes, played by a largely unknown ensemble cast, are the wet-behind-the-ears recruits of
the 58th Squadron of the U.S. Marine Corps Space Aviator Cavalry.

The group is led by Shane Vansen, a beautiful but serious young woman with a tragic past. Her
Marine parents were brutally slain by AIs while Shane and her sisters hid in an attic.

Nathan West is a would-be space colonist who joined the Corps just before the war broke out, to try to find his lost love, Kylen. They were both due to be part of the Tellus colony mission until, just hours before launch, Nathan had to give up his place to an In Vitro. Kylen was with the colony when it was destroyed, but Nathan clings to the hope that she may be alive . . . somewhere.

Cooper Hawkes is a Tank, a rebellious In Vitro who was sentenced by a judge to join the Marines. Defiant and with a huge chip on both shoulders, Cooper is thrust into combat before he has had a chance to learn friendship and loyalty.

Vanessa Damphousse, nicknamed "Damn Fool" by her friends, enlisted to find "direction." She's the most objective of the group.

Completing the regular quintet is sports fan Paul Wang, a curious but unsure young man, and keeping a watchful eye over the recruits is their intense veteran squadron commander Tyrus Cassius McQueen, a Tank for whom the Marine Corps is the only family he has known.

SAAB is a series you warm to. At times too melodramatic, there are enough neat touches to keep you coming back, such as a blues-playing space carrier commander and a load of pancakes ejected into space as a tribute to a fallen comrade. And though it's a character-driven show, the special effects—nearly all computer-generated—are impressive, from the Marine "Hammerhead" space fighters to the darkly mysterious alien ships, especially the marauding super-fighter, nicknamed *Chiggy Von Richthofen*.

Launched into a difficult Sunday night slot in the U.S. in autumn 1995, the series never really caught fire the way Morgan & Wong's previous show had done, and despite a ratings-boosting late guest appearance from David Duchovny as a silicate pool shark, the 58th didn't live to fight a second year.

REGULAR CAST
Nathan West Morgan Weisser *Shane Vansen* Kristen Cloke
Cooper Hawkes Rodney Rowland *Vanessa Damphousse* Lanei Chapman
Paul Wang Joel De La Fuente *Colonel McQueen* James Morrison

SEMI-REGULAR:
Commodore Ross Tucker Smallwood

Creators/Executive producers: Glen Morgan, James Wong
Co-executive producer: Stephen Zito
Producers: Howard Grigsby, Tim McHugh, Michael Lake
Music: Shirley Walker
Pilot filmed on location in Queensland, Australia

A Hard Eight Pictures Inc. Production in association with Village Roadshow Pictures

22 color 60-minute episodes (pilot 120 minutes)
U.S. premiere: 24 September 1995
U.K. premiere: 13 March 1996
(Sky One)

Season One

Pilot

w Glen Morgan & James Wong
A.D. 2063: Having called out to the farthest reaches of space for some 150 years, mankind believes it is alone in the galaxy. Nathan West and his girlfriend, Kylen Celina, are preparing to join a group of colonists when they learn that, for political reasons, one of them must step down. Nathan reluctantly complies but when his attempt to stow away fails he realizes his only hope of seeing Kylen again is to join the Marine Corps Space Cavalry. There he finds himself commencing training with a motley band of fellow recruits. But when an advanced alien civilization suddenly launches an attack on the space colonies, the raw Marines find themselves thrust into the front line.
Secretary General Chartwell Bill Hunter
Lt. Colonel Fouts Colin Friels

Kylen Celina Amanda Douge
Sgt. Major Frank Bougus R. Lee Ermey
Mike "Pags" Pagodin Peter Kent
Michelle Low Theresa Wong
Bartley Anja Coleby
Carter Darrin Klimek
Stone Chris Kirby
Colonial Governor Jonathan Overmeyer Robert Coleby
Colonial Governor Borman Alan Dale
Maxwell Michael Edwards-Stevens
Nelson Charles Anthony
Richard West Bartholomew John
Anne West Gennie Nevinson
John West James Campbell
Young Shane Melissa Bullock
Slayton Ric Anderson
Neil West Angus Grant
Sergeant Vansen Colin Handley
Mrs. Vansen Rebecca Riggs

Director: David Nutter

The Farthest Man from Home

w Glen Morgan *&* James Wong

A crazed survivor from the Tellus colony is brought aboard the giant spacecraft U.S.S. *Saratoga*, and interrogated by the shadowy Aerotech chief, Sewell. After breaking into the room where the man is being held, West learns Kylen did not die in the alien attack and goes AWOL in an attempt to find and rescue her.

Survivor French Stewart
Howard Sewell Michael Mantell
Theresa Ashford Linda Carlson
Yuko Kayaguest Bok Yun Chon
Commodore Ross Tucker Smallwood *(intro)*
Captain Joyner Thomas Mills
Controller Robert Crow
Soldier Tedd Taskey
Squad Leader Leslie Pratt

Director: David Nutter

The Dark Side of the Sun

w Glen Morgan *&* James Wong

Tormented by recurring nightmares about her parents' death at the hands of Silicates, Shane leads the marines in a desperate battle to prevent vital raw materials from falling into the hands of the artificial intelligence rebels. In the process, she learns a shocking truth about her parents' murder.

Feliciti OH 519 Kimberly Patton
Lt. Nelson Susan Priver
Justin EB 774 Paul Keeley
Sabrine EW 177 Iva Franks

Director: Charles Martin Smith

Mutiny

w Stephen Zito

Cooper and McQueen find their loyalties divided when a crew of fellow Tanks threaten mutiny aboard a space cargo vessel after the captain orders the termination of his cargo of In Vitros.

Captain Lewelyn Tony Amendola
First Mate Potter Calvin Levels
CPO Keats Tom Everett
Sgt. Monk Robert Louis Kempf
Ashby Ping Wu
Sorrel Christopher Michael-Moore
Mercer William Forward
Harris Jeffrey Howard
Harkin Steven Hack
Chief mechanic Thom Barry
Triage nurse Lisa Dinkins

Director: Stephen Cragg

Ray Butts

w Glen Morgan *&* James Wong

A tough-as-nails war veteran arrives on the *Saratoga* to take command of the 58th for a mysterious mission behind enemy lines. Initially suspicious and resentful, the Marines find the truth about the mission and a reason to respect the maverick officer. (Two neat touches here: the black hole sequence and the flying pancakes!)

Raymond Butts Steve Rankin
Commodore Ross Tucker Smallwood
Bowman Lar Park-Lincoln
Sailor John Voldstad
Cochran David Prudhomme
Master of arms John L. Bennett

Director: Charles Martin Smith

Eyes

w Glen Morgan *&* James Wong

The 58th is assigned to protect a powerful ambassador after an assassin murders Earth's leader, and Nathan and Cooper both find themselves pawns in a further assassination plot.

Diane Hayden Harriet Sansom Harris
Cwirko John Verea
Chaput George DelHoyo
Commodore Ross Tucker Smallwood
Feliciti OH Kimberly Patton
Thompson Daniel Stewart
Lt. Pisarek Josie DiVincenzo
Lt. Stone James Lesure
Kurosowa Ken Takemoto
Man Mark Lentry
Questioner Michael Harney
Master of arms John L. Bennett

Director: Felix Alcala

The Enemy

w Marilyn Osborn

The Marines become their own worst enemies when they encounter a mind-altering alien weapon on the planet Tartarus—a nightmare world of swirling volcanic fog and darkness. (This episode was first broadcast in U.K. with a warning about its strobe effects.)

The Crazy Marine Bob Koherr
Sergeant Danny Goldring
Commodore Ross Tucker Smallwood

Director: Michael Katleman

Hostile Visit (aka A Good Day to Die)

w Peyton Webb
First of a two-part story. The *Saratoga* is attacked by Chig fighters, but the 58th succeed in crippling an alien bomber. Instead of destroying the craft, McQueen proposes it be used as a Trojan Horse, for a dangerous morale-boosting attack on the Chigs' home planet.
Sewell Michael Mantell
Lt. Stroud Melissa Bowen
Commodore Ross Tucker Smallwood
Crew chief Sharon Washington
Krantz Jim Anzide
Webb Billy Mayo
Connor Steven Jang
Gates Susan Vee
Klein David Gardner
Donne Randy Mulkey

Director: Thomas J. Wright

Choice or Chance (aka To Die For)

w Doc Johnson
Second of a two-part story. The Marines' life-pod crash-lands on a moon deep in enemy territory. Shane, Nathan, Damphousse and Wang are captured by silicates, but McQueen and Cooper manage to stay free. Wang is tortured, Shane and Damphousse are given a choice of death by execution or slave labor, and Nathan discovers that Kylen is a fellow prisoner . . . (Wang's torturer is better known as ol' yellow eyes, Eugene Tooms, from *The X-Files*.)
Torturer Doug Hutchison
Sewell Michael Mantell
Kylen Amanda Douge
Feliciti OH Kimberly Patton
Lt. Stroud Melissa Bowen
Commodore Ross Tucker Smallwood
Brandon Rob Farrior
Justin Paul Keeley
Sabrine Iva Franks
Crossland Chip Heller
Klein David Gardner
Webb Billy Mayo
Krantz Jim Anzide
Donne Randy Mulkey
Connor Steven Jang
Gates Susan Vee

Director: Felix Alcala

Stay With the Dead

w Matt Kiene & Joe Reinkemeyer
A badly wounded Nathan is transported aboard the *Saratoga*, where his insistence that his fellow Marines are still alive is dismissed by everyone—including McQueen.
Dr. Kanelos Steven Anderson
Shankowicz James Parks

Hatfield Scott MacDonald
Nurse Marnie McPhall
Mark Lindon Rich Willis
Chaplain Edmund Shaff
Lt. Clayton Leo Garcia
Delgado Sebastian Cetina

Director: Thomas J. Wright

The River of Stars

w Marilyn Osborn
The 58th are stranded in space when their ship is crippled by the enemy on Christmas Day. While the *Saratoga* searches for them, Wang intercepts a cryptic message of alien origin, which he interprets as instructions for hitching a ride on an oncoming comet . . .
Winslow Tasia Valenza
Lewis Leslie O'Neil
Commodore Ross Tucker Smallwood
Lt. Thomas J. August Richards
Kelcher Chris Kirby
Reynolds Robert Crow
Lieutenant Tyrone Batista
Communications officer Sharon Annett
Larkin Billy Maddox
Ensign Christopher Wiehl
Horn Robert Arevalo

Director: Tucker Gates

Who Monitors the Birds

w Glen Morgan & James Wong
Trapped deep in enemy territory on a top-secret mission that could be his ticket out of the Marines, Cooper recalls moments from his past while fighting desperately to stay alive as his pursuers close in.
Major Colquitt Dale Dye
Monitors Brian Cousins, David Botrell
In Vitro friend Denyn Pysz
Friendly alien Robert Thomas

Director: Winrich Kolbe

Level of Necessity

w Matt Kiene & Joe Reinkemeyer
Damphousse experiences psychic visions during combat, and becomes the subject of an official investigation. Anxious to monitor her, a Psi Corps colonel follows the 58th on their next mission—with fatal results.
Colonel Burke Richard Kind
Winslow Tasia Valenza
Lubin Kane Picoy
Captain Kremens Timothy Dale Agee

Director: Thomas J. Wright

Never No More

w James Wong *&* Glen Morgan
Shane fights alongside an old love as the Marines search for a powerful new "cloaked" alien ship capable of shielding itself from radar.
Captain John Oakes Michael Reilly Burke
Sullivan Xavier Montalvo
Admiral Broden David St James
Burnett Jonathan Williams
Paterno Will Schaub
Fenris Heinrich James
General Alcott David Jean Thomas
Spud Randy Stone
Mr. Saber Rob Elk
Hadden Jacquelyn Houston
Curran Ashley Smock
Jennifer Brandt Michelle Clunie
Ensign Julio Dolce Vita

Director: James Charleston

The Angriest Angel

w Glen Morgan *&* James Wong
McQueen insists that he be allowed to participate in a crucial mission to destroy the enemy's invisible-to-radar spacecraft, nicknamed *Chiggy Von Richthofen,* using a new missile. Initially denied, he has a surgeon remove the implant in his head, which is there to suppress his vertigo and nausea. When the first mission fails, resulting in Winslow's death, McQueen boards a Hammerhead fighter and goes after his quarry alone . . .
Elroy El Doug Hutchison
Winslow Tasia Valenza
Howard Sewell Michael Mantell
Captain Fischer Charmin Lee
Commodore Ross Tucker Smallwood
Admiral Broden David St James
Chaplain Edmund Shaff
General Alcott David Jean Thomas
Mr. Saber Rob Elk
Controller Robert Crow
Spud Randy Stone
Supervisor David Ramsey

Director: Henri Safran

Toy Soldiers

w Marilyn Osborn
Nathan is shocked when his sees his kid brother Neil arriving with a bunch of new Marine recruits, and his anger grows when he realizes the new squadron is led by an inexperienced but gung-ho lieutenant, Herrick. And on their first mission, Herrick's determination to get into the action has tragic consequences.
Neil West Marc Worden

Herrick David Barrera
Commodore Ross Tucker Smallwood
Miller Christian Hoff
Eichler P.J. Ochian
Donovan Al Garrett
Intelligence officer Steven Jang
Young Nathan Michael Malota
Young Neil Adam Sutton

Director: Stephen Posey

Dear Earth

w Richard Whitley
Mail call brings letters from Earth—and mixed news. Damphousse gets a "Dear John" letter from her boyfriend, Shane is notified that she's being promoted to captain, and hears that her sister is having a baby, and Nathan realizes the military never notified his parents of Neil's death. Meanwhile Cooper and McQueen are chosen as the focus of a TV documentary on In Vitros in the military.
Director Steve Hynter
Ensign Boasberg Charles Carpenter
Lt. John Hill Darren Gray Ward
Commodore Ross Tucker Smallwood
Mank Bob Clendenin
Supply sergeant John Battle
Ann Jennifer Burns
Armed guard Rock Reiser
Ophthalmologist Carl Gilliard
Crow Robert Crow
Ed Gibson Frazier
Mrs. West Loren Chase

Director: Winrich Kolbe

Sugar Dirt

w Matt Kiene *&* Joe Reinkemeyer
Earth forces launch a major offensive against a Chig planet—but the strategy means abandoning the 58th on an enemy stronghold where they struggle to survive for over two months with no ground or air support.
General Weirick Granville Van Dusen
Lt. Price Jennifer Balgobin
Admiral Broden David St. James
General Alcott David Jean Thomas
Commodore Ross Tucker Smallwood
Chaplain Edmund Shaff
General Ming James Kiriyama-Lem
Admiral Vetter Nancy Linehan Charles
General Siraj Iqbal Theba
Comm. Preising Bill Kalmenson
Lt. Smith Mark Adair Rios
Lt. Nelson Josh Abramson
Lt. Feeley David Cooley

Director: Thomas J. Wright

Pearly

w Richard Whitley

Pinned down during an enemy bombardment on a war-torn planet, the Marines take refuge aboard a huge armored personnel carrier tank and encounter a couple of eccentric soldiers—cavalry sergeant Louie Fox and British officer Major Cyril MacKendrick (a guest role for British TV actor Martin Jarvis).

Louie Fox Adam Goldberg
Elroy El Doug Hutchison
MacKendrick Martin Jarvis
Feliciti Kimberly Patton
Commodore Ross Tucker Smallwood
Marine Guy Garner

Director: Charles Martin Smith

R & R

w Jule Selbo

Fatigued and stressed from constant battles, the 58th are granted 48 hours leave aboard the *Bacchus,* a Vegas-like spaceship, lorded over by The Host, and where Shane wages a blue baize duel with a Silicate pool shark named "Handsome" Alvin. Back in action, the Marines struggle to readjust and, in the midst of battle, Wang and Damphousse share a desperate, passionate kiss. (Guest roles here for rap star Coolio and *The X-Files'* David Duchovny.)

"Handsome" Alvin El David Duchovny
Susie Janet Gunn
Host Coolio Vincent Guastaferro
Commodore Ross Tucker Smallwood
Nurse Larlee Jennifer Crystal
Bartender Julius Branca
Guy David Scott Gordon
with The Blazers

Director: Thomas J. Wright

Stardust

w Howard Grigsby

The Marines participate in Operation Naye'i, a top secret misinformation campaign designed to confuse the enemy and enable Earth Forces to launch Operation Roundhammer—a crucial attack against the Chigs.

General Oliver Radford Ronald G. Joseph
Colonel Klingman Gail O'Grady
Chaplain Edmund Shaff
James Dark Moon Pato Hoffman
Commodore Ross Tucker Smallwood
Officer Crow Robert Crow
Military officer Tim Hutchinson
Ensign Lewis David A.R. White
Commando Eric Whitmore
Technician Christopher Kirby
Colonel Onico Edain

Director: Jesus Trevino

"And If They Lay Us to Rest . . ."

w Glen Morgan & James Wong

First of a two-part story. During intelligence gathering on a moon of the Chigs' home planet, the 58th encounter an unidentified extraterrestrial creature—possibly the last of its kind. Cooper goes to kill it then changes his mind and manages to tell the creature to flee the area as it's about to be torn apart by a huge battle. Later, a lone enemy ship hails the *Saratoga* and is allowed to dock. The enemy soldier removes its helmet to reveal an alien much like the creature the 58th unwittingly informed about Operation Roundhammer.

Colonel Rabwin Don Pugsley
Chig Envoy Derek Mark Lochran
Commodore Ross Tucker Smallwood
Communications officer Robert Crow

Director: Vern Gillum

". . . Tell Our Moms We Done Our Best"

w Glen Morgan & James Wong

Second of a two-part story. Aboard the *Saratoga,* Earth's leaders prepare to negotitate peace with the Chig envoy who insists that Aerotech's Chief Executive Officer, E. Alan Wayne, attend the meetings. He then implicates Wayne and Aerotech in a conspiracy, accusing them of being aware that the aliens were out there. Angry words are exchanged and suddenly the envoy detonates an explosive device . . . Meanwhile, the 58th had been assigned to rescue a group of POWs released as a goodwill gesture—and Nathan finds Kylen is among them. But when the ceasefire unravels, the Marines are caught up in a furious battle in which three of the 58th are reported lost in action . . .

E. Alan Wayne Richard Fancy
Kylen Amanda Douge
Diane Hayden Harriet Samson Harris
Colonel Rabwin Don Pugsley
Frank Shaffner J. Patrick McCormack
Chig Envoy Derek Mark Lochran
Commodore Ross Tucker Smallwood
General Alcott David Jean Thomas
Lt. Pruitt Robert Crow
Weapons specialist Elliot Woods
Engineer Steve Monroe
Sentries Marlon Chopper Young, Amy Loubalu
Sgt. Parker Lisa Talerico
Wallace Reggie Hayes
German colonist Tom Ayers
Colonist Christopher Boyer
Sims Lawrence T. Wrentz
Reporter Nilla Westerlund

Director: Thomas J. Wright

SPACE ACADEMY

American adventure series about a new generation of space explorers being trained to push mankind's frontiers into deepest space.

15 color 25-minute episodes	*A Filmation Production*
(7-episode run on LWT)	*1977–1979*

SPACE CASES

It's not surprising this children's drama has been compared to *Lost in Space*—its co-creator is Bill Mumy, former child star of the sixties series.

These days, Mumy is better known as the Minbari attaché Lennier in *Babylon 5*—and the *B5* link is further forged by the fact that fellow co-creator Peter David has also written several *Babylon 5* episodes.

Space Cases follows the adventures of five Star Academy cadets who board an alien spaceship, the *Christa*, and then get swept through a spatial rip that sends them seven years from home.

Power Rangers fans will doubtless spot Walter Emmanuel Jones in the cast. Jones was Zack the Black Ranger, but better still are the guest stars—Bill Mumy himself, Mark Hamill and George Takei as a villainous warlord.

It's fairly juvenile stuff on the whole, but one neat in-joke in the first episode has the Andromedan, Radu, rescuing a teddy bear found floating in space. The bear was originally a gift from Peter David to *Babylon 5* creator Joe Michael Straczynski. JMS, it turned out, didn't care for it, and had it ejected into space in a *Babylon 5* episode!

REGULAR CAST
Harlan Band Walter Emmanuel Jones *Radu* Christian Ayre *Catalina* Jewel Staite
Rosie Ianni Paige Christina *Bova* Rahi Azizi *Thelma* Anik Mattern
T.J. Davenport Cary Lawrence *Commander Seth Goddard* Paul Boretski

Creators: Bill Mumy, Peter David
Writers: Various, including Peter David, Bill Mumy, Jerry Colker, Magda Liolis
Directors: Various, including John Bell Otta Hanus, Iain Patterson
Opening credits read by Harlan Ellison
Closing theme written by Bill Mumy, Paul Gordon; *sung by* Lisa La Shawn, Walter Emmanuel Jones

Cinar Productions

Season One
13 color 25-minute episodes
U.K. premiere: 2 September 1996
(Nickelodeon)

SPACE: 1999

Space: 1999 was the series that began with a bang and went out with a whimper.

Stylishly and extravagantly filmed, it devoured a fortune in special effects, took two years to plan, 15 months to make and should have been one of TV's most exhilarating adult space odysseys.

But though it spent two more years and 48 episodes roaming the outer reaches of the universe, *Space: 1999* never found the audience it was looking for. Its creator, Gerry Anderson, was the proverbial prince without honor in his own land. While the series was a worldwide success, with particularly big followings in America, Japan, France and Italy, Britain dithered, dallied and, by the end, virtually ignored it.

The format was simple enough: In the opening episode the Moon is devastated by a massive atomic explosion—the result of a 20-year build-up of nuclear waste from Earth. With the 300-strong colony of Moonbase Alpha aboard, it is hurled out of Earth orbit and off on an endless journey through space. Thereafter, as the Alphans search in vain for a new home, they have a string of bizarre encounters with invariably hostile aliens, cosmic phenomena and strange worlds.

American husband-and-wife stars Martin Landau and Barbara Bain teamed up for the first time since *Mission: Impossible*, as Moonbase commander John Koenig and chief medical officer Dr. Helena Russell. And *Fugitive*-chasing Barry Morse played the intellectual scientist father-figure, Victor Bergman.

Visually, *Space: 1999* was a treat—its spectacular sets and effects masterminded by Brian Johnson who brought much of the grace of his work on *2001: A Space Odyssey* to the aerial sequences with the insect-like spacecraft, the Eagles. But the show was marred by po-faced acting, wildly implausible plots, one-dimensional characters and an almost total lack of warmth or humor.

For the second season, American producer Fred Freiberger (of *Star Trek* fame) was brought in to try to "Americanize" the series, beefing up the romantic bond between Koenig and Dr. Russell and adding a few new regulars, notably Maya, an exotic alien with the power to transform herself into any living thing. But the stories became increasingly silly and the Alphans reached the end of the road without ever getting anywhere.

MAIN CAST
Cmdr. *John Koenig* Martin Landau   Dr. *Helena Russell* Barbara Bain
Prof. *Victor Bergman* Barry Morse*   *Alan Carter* Nick Tate
Sandra Benes/Sahn Zienia Merton   *Paul Morrow* Prentis Hancock*
Dr. *Bob Mathias* Anton Phillips   *David Kano* Clifton Jones*
Maya Catherine Schell†   *Tony Verdeschi* Tony Anholt†
Semi-regulars: *Yasko* Yasuko Nagazumi   Dr. *Ben Vincent* Jeffrey Kissoon
Bill Fraser John Hog   *Voice of Moonbase computer* Barbara Kelly
*Season One only   †Season Two only

Creators: Gerry & Sylvia Anderson
Executive producer: Gerry Anderson
Producers: Sylvia Anderson *(Season One)*, Fred Freiberger *(Season Two)*
Special effects: Brian Johnson
Music: Barry Gray *(Season One)*, Derek Wadsworth *(Season Two)*
Costumes: Rudi Gernreich *(Season One)*, Keith Wilson *(Season Two)*

An ITC RAI Co-Production produced by Group Three (Season One), *A Gerry Anderson Production ITC Television* (Season Two)
48 color 60-minute episodes
Season One:
4 September 1975–19 February 1976
Season Two:
4 September–23 December 1976
4 August–1 September 1977
plus 1 May 1978 and August Bank Holiday 1978 (ATV Midlands)
U.S.: September 1975

Season One
24 episodes

Director: Lee H. Katzin

Breakaway

w George Bellak
John Koenig arrives at Moonbase Alpha to oversee final plans for a deep space probe, and finds his crew stricken by a mysterious illness linked to the nuclear waste dumps on the dark side of the Moon. Within hours a massive nuclear explosion rips the heart out of the Moon, hurling it out of Earth orbit and into the depths of space.
Commissioner Simmonds Roy Dotrice
Commander Gorski Philip Madoc
Ouma Lon Satton
Collins Eric Carte

Force of Life

w Johnny Byrne
Technician Anton Zoref is possessed by an alien force with an all-consuming craving for heat. Everything he touches—including people—freezes instantly. To destroy him, Koenig must deny him any source of light and warmth.
Anton Zoref Ian McShane
Eva Zoref Gay Hamilton
Dominix John Hamill
Jane Eva Rueber-Staier

Director: David Tomblin

Collision Course

w Anthony Terpiloff

The Moon is on a collision course with the giant planet Atheria. Bergman suggests diverting their path with a series of mines in space, but Koenig meets the planet's aged queen, Arra, who says the "collision" is their destiny: "Our separate planets have met in the body of Time for the great purpose of mutation."

Arra Margaret Leighton

Director: Ray Austin

War Games

w Christopher Penfold

Moonbase Alpha finds itself seemingly under attack from an unnamed planet. With 129 dead and Moonbase no longer habitable, Koenig and Dr. Russell journey to the enemy planet to seek terms and a new life—but they are told the Alphans carry a "plague of fear" that would destroy the perfect world, and that they have nothing to fear but fear itself . . .

Alien man Anthony Valentine
Alien woman Isla Blair

Director: Charles Crichton

Death's Other Dominion

w Anthony Terpiloff & Elizabeth Barrows

The Alphans discover an ice planet, Ultima Thule, where they are invited to share an immortal life on "this paradise" with former inhabitants of Earth.

Dr. Cabot Rowland Brian Blessed
Captain Jack Turner John Shrapnel
Freda Mary Miller

Director: Charles Crichton

Voyager's Return

w Johnny Byrne

Moonbase encounters an old Voyager probe that has been polluting space with deadly "fast neutrons" from its Queller driver. Koenig wants to destroy the probe, but Bergman wishes to salvage its information and enlists the help of scientist Ernst Linden—unaware that he is really Queller, inventor of the deadly drive.

Dr. Ernst Linden Jeremy Kemp
Jim Haines Barry Stokes
Aarchon Alex Scott
Pilot Abrams Lawrence Trimble

Director: Bob Kellett

Alpha Child

w Christopher Penfold

The first birth on Alpha—and the astonishingly quick growth of the child—draws Moonbase into an alien attempt to save its own race from its pursuing enemies by inhabiting the bodies of others.

Cynthia Crawford/Rena Cyd Hayman
Jarak Julian Glover
Jackie Wayne Brooks

Director: Ray Austin

Dragon's Domain

w Christopher Penfold

Astronaut Tony Cellini—lone survivor of a deep space probe—has endured years of mental torment; his story of a spaceship graveyard and a terrifying, tentacled monster has never been believed. Now Moonbase has drifted into the same area, involving Koenig in a crescendo of horror.

Tony Cellini Gianni Garko
Commissioner Dixon Douglas Wilmer
Dr. Monique Bouchere Barbara Kellerman
Dr. Darwin King Michael Sheard
Dr. Juliet Mackie Susan Jameson

Director: Charles Crichton

Mission of the Darians

w Johnny Byrne

Moonbase responds to a distress call and finds a colossal spaceship, the S.S. *Dana*, which has been flying through space for some 900 years. But its survivors have kept alive through a form of cannibalism and the Alphans look like becoming human fodder.

Kara Joan Collins
High priest Aubrey Morris
Neman Dennis Burgess
Hadin Robert Russell
Lowry Paul Antrim

Director: Ray Austin

Black Sun

w David Weir

When Moonbase gets drawn into a "black sun," Koenig pins hopes of survival on Prof. Bergman's new forcefield. But they are in for a strange, bewildering experience . . .

Mike Ryan Paul Jones
Smitty Jon Laurimore

Director: Lee H. Katzin

Guardian of Piri

w Christopher Penfold
A beautiful woman offers the Alphans a blissful existence on the paradise planet Piri. Only Koenig has the will to resist and he fights to save his people from the "living death."
Servant of the Guardian Catherine Schell
Pete Irving Michael Culver
Davis John Lee-Barber
Johnson James Fagan

Director: Charles Crichton

End of Eternity

w Johnny Byrne
Koenig inadvertently frees a psychopathic killer with the power of immortality, and must put his own life on the line to defeat him.
Balor Peter Bowles
Baxter Jim Smilie

Director: Ray Austin

Matter of Life and Death

w Art Wallace & Johnny Byrne
Helena's husband, Lee, believed killed on a space mission years before, reappears with a grim warning for the Alphans—that Terra Nova, the planet they are preparing to land on, is anti-matter and will destroy them.
Lee Russell Richard Johnson
Parks Stuart Damon

Director: Charles Crichton

Earthbound

w Anthony Terpiloff
An alien spaceship lands on the Moon and its captain, Zantor, reveals that they are heading for Earth. Commissioner Simmonds, trapped on the Moon since it broke out of orbit, is determined to take this chance to return to Earth.
Simmonds Roy Dotrice
Captain Zantor Christopher Lee

Director: Charles Crichton

The Full Circle

w Jesse Lasky Jr. & Pat Silver
Eagle Six returns to Alpha from the planet Retha, but the crew are missing and the only occupant is a dead caveman, Koenig and Helena lead a rescue team, but they, too, go missing . . .
Spearman Oliver Cotton

Director: Bob Kellett

Another Time, Another Place

w Johnny Byrne
A strange phenomenon creates duplicates of the Moon and Moonbase personnel who are surprised to find themselves in Earth's orbit again. But it is a duplicate Earth and the Alphans find themselves face-to-face with other, future selves.
Regina Kesslann Judy Geeson

Director: David Tomblin

The Last Sunset

w Christopher Penfold
As the Moon approaches the planet Ariel, hundreds of alien devices land on the lunar surface, emitting oxygen and turning the Moon into an atmosphere-rich world.

Director: Charles Crichton

The Infernal Machine

w Anthony Terpiloff & Elizabeth Barrows
A living machine and its aged, sick "companion" arrive on Moonbase. When the companion dies, the machine demands that Koenig and Helena take his place—for the rest of their lives.
Companion Gwent Leo McKern
Winters Gary Waldhorn

Director: David Tomblin

Ring Around the Moon

w Edward di Lorenzo
Moonbase becomes a prisoner of a probe from the long-dead alien planet Triton—and Dr. Russell is turned into an involuntary informer. To save her—and Moonbase—Koenig must convince the Tritonians that their home planet no longer exists.
Ted Clifford Max Faulkner

Director: Ray Austin

Missing Link

w Edward di Lorenzo
Critically injured in an Eagle crash, Koenig finds himself "transported" in time and space to the planet Zenno where an anthropologist wants to study him. His daughter Vana falls in love with Koenig who is torn between staying with her or "returning" to his real life.
Raan Peter Cushing
Vana Joanna Dunham

Director: Ray Austin

Space Brain

w Christopher Penfold
Moonbase is heading for a strange gossamer-like space organism that destroys one investigating Eagle and takes over the mind of another crewman. The Alphans hope to destroy it by aiming an explosive-packed Eagle straight at it—but the plan threatens to backfire.
Kelly Shane Rimmer
Wayland Derek Anders
Melita Carla Romanelli

Director: Charles Crichton

The Troubled Spirit

w Johnny Byrne
Botanist Mateo, forbidden to continue his experiments in communicating with plants, is haunted by his own murderous ghost seeking to avenge a death that has not yet happened.
Dan Mateo Giancarlo Prete
Dr. James Warren Anthony Nicholls
Laura Adams Hilary Dwyer

Director: Ray Austin

The Testament of Arkadia

w Johnny Byrne
The Moon comes to an inexplicable halt—held by some strange influence from a nearby planet. Investigating the barren world, called Arkadia, Koenig's team find evidence that life on Earth originated here, its seeds carried there by Arkadians fleeing their dying world.
Luke Ferro Orso Maria Guerrini
Anna Davis Lisa Harrow

Director: David Tomblin

The Last Enemy

w Bob Kellett
The Moon drifts into the middle of an interplanetary war and Koenig must negotiate a ceasefire between the two planets before Moonbase is destroyed in the "crossfire."
Dione Caroline Mortimer
Talos Kevin Stoney
Theia Maxine Audley

Director: Bob Kellett

Season Two
24 episodes

The Metamorph

w Johnny Byrne
The Alphans are threatened by an evil-minded alien, Mentor, who wants to drain their minds to repair his planet's biological computer and restore its civilization. But Mentor's daughter Maya—who can transform herself into any living creature—discovers his plan and helps the Alphans to escape.
Maya Catherine Schell (*intro*)
Mentor Brian Blessed
Annette Fraser Anouska Hempel
Bill Fraser John Hug (*intro*)
Ray Torens Nick Brimble
Petrov Peter Porteous
Lew Picard Gerard Pacquis

Director: Charles Crichton

The Exiles

w Donald James
The Alphans revive two apparently harmless young aliens found inside mysterious cylinders circling the Moon. But the pair turn out to be rebel leaders and abduct Helena and Tony, transporting them to their home planet.
Cantar Peter Duncan
Zova Stacy Dorning
Mirella Margaret Inglis
Stal Anthony Blackett
Old lady Peggy Ledger

Director: Ray Austin

Journey to Where

w Donald James
Moonbase receives a message from 22nd-century Earth offering to bring the Alphans home via a transference device. But instead, Koenig, Helena and Alan Carter are transported back in time to Scotland in the year 1339 where they face execution as plague carriers.
Dr. Charles Logan Freddie Jones
Carla Isla Blair
Macdonald Roger Bizley
Dr. Ben Vincent Jeffrey Kissoon (*semi-regular*)
Jackson Laurence Harrington
First Operative Texas Norwich Duff
Old crone Peggy Paige

Director: Tom Clegg

One Moment of Humanity

w Tony Barwick
Helena and Tony are abducted by Zamara who wants to use them as emotional blueprints for her race of androids and so teach them how to kill.
Zamara Billie Whitelaw
Zarl Leigh Lawson
Number Eight Geoffrey Bayldon

Choreographer: Lionel Blair
Director: Charles Crichton

Brian and Brain

w Jack Ronder
A super-robot, built by an early Earth space mission, kidnaps Koenig and Helena, taking them to a small planet. Tony and Maya mount a rescue bid and, with Maya's powers of transformation, manage to trick Brian into defeat.
Capt. Michaels Bernard Cribbins
Brian robot Michael Sharvill-Martin
Fraser John Hug (*semi-regular*)
First operative Annie Lambert
Security lieutenant Marc Zuber

Director: Kevin Connor

New Adam New Eve

w Terence Feely
Magus, a saintly, impressive figure, appears before the Alphans, declaring himself to be "your creator" and offering them a new Eden—with Koenig and Maya, Helena and Tony as his chosen Adams and Eves.
Magus Guy Rolfe
Humanoid Bernard Kay
Beautiful girl Barbara Wise

Director: Charles Crichton

The Mark of Archanon

w Lew Schwartz
Two aliens, Pasc and his son Etrec, are discovered in suspended animation in a metal cabinet below the Moon's surface. But Pasc is affected by a strange virus and all Moonbase is at risk.
Pasc John Standing
Etrec Michael Gallagher
Lyra Maruna Veronica Lang
Dr. Raul Nunez Raul Newney
Carson Anthony Forrest
Johnson John Alkin

Director: Charles Crichton

The Rules of Luton

w Charles Woodgrove (*alias* Fred Freiberger)
After picking a flower and some berries on a planet rich in vegetation, Koenig and Maya are abruptly accused of murder by the "Judges of Luton" (trees!) and forced to fight for their lives against three terrifyingly powerful aliens.
Alien Strong David Jackson
Alien Transporter Godfrey James
Alien Invisible Roy Marsden

Director: Val Guest

All That Glisters

w Keith Miles
The Alphans are lured to an arid planet by a strange life form—living rocks that can communicate, move and kill. The rocks need water ... and the human body is mostly water.
Dave Reilly Patrick Mower

Director: Ray Austin

The Taybor

w Thom Keyes
A flamboyant, nautical-sounding space trader arrives on Alpha and offers to trade a jump-drive device that could take them back to Earth—but he wants Maya in exchange!
Taybor Willoughby Goddard
Karen Laraine Humphreys
Slatternly woman Rita Webb
Andrews Mel Taylor

Director: Bob Brooks

Seed of Destruction

w John Goldsmith
A jewel-like asteroid is draining power from Alpha. Koenig investigates and encounters a replica of himself that returns to Moonbase in his place, carrying a crystal seed that will use the Moon's store of energy to restore life to the asteroid.
Dr. Ben Vincent Jeffrey Kissoon
Female operative Martha Nairn
Creature Albin Pahernik

Director: Kevin Connor

The A B Chrysalis

w Tony Barwick
Alpha is rocked by powerful energy beams from an unidentified planet. One more could spell destruction. Koenig's team investigate and find that the planet's humanoid population are in a chrysalid stage of evolution, protected by a computer that automatically destroys any threat—and that includes Alpha.
A Ina Skriver
B Sarah Douglas
Sphere voice Robert Rietty

Director: Val Guest

Catacombs of the Moon

w Anthony Terpiloff
Dr. Russell fights to save the life of an Alphan woman whose engineer husband had visions of Moonbase being destroyed by fire—visions made more ominous when a fire storm heads toward them.
Patrick Osgood James Laurenson
Michelle Osgood Pamela Stephenson
First engineer Lloyd McGuire
Nurse Karen Ford

Director: Robert Lynn

Space Warp

w Charles Woodgrove (*alias* Fred Freiberger)
Moonbase Alpha disappears into a space warp, instantly moving five light-years away. Left behind in Eagle One, Koenig and Tony search desperately for the space "window," while on Moonbase Maya is afflicted by a mysterious fever and her transformation powers run wild.
Security guard Tony Osoba
Petrov Peter Porteous

Director: Peter Medak

A Matter of Balance

w Pip & Jane Baker
While exploring an apparently lifeless planet, Alphan botanist Shermeen comes under the influence of Vindrus, an anti-matter being who wants to replace all the Moonbase personnel with members of his own race.
Shermeen Williams Lynne Frederick
Vindrus Stuart Wilson
Eddie Collins Nicholas Campbell

Director: Charles Crichton

The Beta Cloud

w Charles Woodgrove (*alias* Fred Freiberger)
A mystery illness strikes the Alphans and a terrifying space creature runs amok in Moonbase, impervious to laser gun fire. All efforts to stop it fail until Maya realizes that it is a robot and finds a way to reach its control center.
Creature Dave Prowse
Space Kreno animal Albin Pahernik

Director: Robert Lynn

The Lambda Factor

w Terrance Dicks
The Moon passes close to an ion gas cloud that gives one of the Alphan women fearsome paranormal powers, which she uses to take control of Moonbase.
Carolyn Powell Deborah Fallender
Mark Sanders Jess Conrad
George Crato Antony Stamboulieh
Carl Renton Michael Walker
Peter Garforth Gregory de Polnay
Sally Martin Lydia Lisle

Director: Charles Crichton

(Season break)

The Bringers of Wonder

w Terence Feely (*a 2-part story*)
Everyone on Moonbase Alpha is celebrating the arrival of a spaceship from Earth whose crew promise to take the Alphans home. Everyone, that is, except Koenig. Where the others see old friends or relatives, he sees hideous aliens.
Guido Stuart Damon
Diana Morris Toby Robins
Jack Bartlett Jeremy Young
Joe Ehrlich Drewe Henley
Louisa Cher Cameron
Sandstrom Earl Robinson
Dr. Shaw Patrick Westwood
Peter Rockwell Nicholas Young
Lizard animal Albin Pahernik

Director: Tom Clegg

The Seance Spectre

w Donald James
A group of Alphans hold a seance that convinces them that a newly sighted planet is habitable. Koenig goes to investigate and finds nothing but a dust bowl. Worse, the planet is on a collision course with the Moon.
Sanderson Ken Hutchison
Eva Carolyn Seymour
Cernik Nigel Pegram
Stevens James Snell

Director: Peter Medak

Dorzak

w Christopher Penfold
A spaceship arrives on Moonbase carrying a prisoner, Dorzak, a survivor from Maya's home planet, Psychon. His ability to control minds threatens all on Alpha.
Dorzak Lee Montague
Sahala Jill Townsend
Yesta Kathryn Leigh Scott

Director: Val Guest

Devil's Planet

w Michael Winder
Answering a distress signal, Koenig is forced to crash-land his Eagle on a planet's penal colony where he is taken prisoner by the beautiful Elizia and her cat-suited prison guards.
Elizia Hildegard Neil
Crael Roy Marsden
Blake Maine Michael Dickinson
Sares/Controller Cassandra Harris
Interrogator Dora Reisser
Alibe Alibe Parsons

Director: Tom Clegg

The Immunity Syndrome

w Johnny Byrne
Exploring an Earth-type planet, Koenig's reconnaissance team comes across a "being" composed of blinding light and sound whose efforts to communicate drive unprotected people insane.
Zoran Nadim Sawalha
Joe Lustig Roy Boyd
Gerry Travers Karl Held
Voice Hal Galili
Alibe Alibe Parsons

Director: Bob Brooks

(1 May 1978)

The Dorcons

w Johnny Byrne
A huge Dorcon spaceship appears on the Moonbase screens and its leader, Varda, demands that the Alphans hand over Maya, who the Dorcons believe can give them immortality. Koenig refuses but Moonbase is attacked and invaded. Forced to hand over Maya, Koenig makes a desperate bid to save her.
Archon Patrick Troughton
Consul Varda Ann Firbank
Malic Gerry Sundquist
Alibe Alibe Parsons
Medical officer Hazel McBride

Director: Tom Clegg

(12 November 1977: LWT)

SPACE PATROL (U.K.)

"Gamma rays on . . . Yabba rays on!"

Space Patrol is one of the "lost brigade" of television fantasy, overshadowed by the federation of TV puppet shows created by Gerry Anderson.

It debuted in Britain in 1963, a few months after Anderson's *Fireball XL5,* and in some ITV regions the two overlapped. Invariably linked with and often confused with its more illustrious contemporary, *Space Patrol* did succeed, however, in its own right. In America it became the top-rated children's show within one month of its launch.

Its creator was Roberta Leigh, a former romantic novelist who had previously written the stories for Gerry Anderson's earliest series, *The Adventures of Twizzle* and *Torchy the Battery Boy* (who himself took off for the stars in a rocket fired by sparklers). Like *Fireball XL5, Space Patrol* charted the interplanetary adventures of one crew and one craft among a fleet of many. Set in the year 2100 its heroes were Earthman Captain Larry Dart, Slim the Venusian and Husky the Martian who patrolled the solar system in their melodious Galasphere 347, as part of the United Galactic Organization—a peace-keeping force set up by Earth, Mars and Venus.

Other main characters were the base commander Colonel Raeburn; his blonde Venusian secretary, Marla; a wacky genius inventor, Professor Aloysius O'Rourke O'Brien Haggerty and his daughter, Cassiopea; and a loquacious Martian parrot called the Gabblerdictum (a *tour de force* vocal performance from comedienne Libby Morris).

VOICE CAST
Capt. Larry Dart Dick Vosburgh   *Husky/Slim/Prof. Haggerty* Ronnie Stevens
Col. Raeburn Murray Kash   *Marla/Cassiopea/Gabblerdictum* Libby Morris

Creator/Writer: Roberta Leigh
Producers: Roberta Leigh, Arthur Provis
Director: Frank Goulding
Models: Derek Freeborn
Special effects/animation: Bill Palmer, Brian Stevens, Bert Walker
A *National Interest Picture Production/Wonderama Productions Ltd.*

39 black and white 30-minute episodes
Season One: 5 July 1963–30 January 1964
Season Two: 19 March–11 June 1964
(Dates as Associated Rediffusion, London)

(NB: The running order is taken from *TV Times'* London edition.)

Season One
26 episodes

The Wandering Asteroid

Larry Dart and his crew are assigned to destroy an asteroid that has been deflected from its orbit and is heading straight for the Martian capital.

The Dark Planet

Prof. Haggerty discovers that a new breed of plant brought from Uranus can walk and talk.

The Slaves of Neptune

Dart's crew investigate the strange disappearance of three spaceships and find themselves in the grip of mysterious forces. (Introducing the Gabblerdictum.)

Fires of Mercury

Haggerty develops a machine that can translate the language of ants and turn infra-red rays into radio waves. Col. Raeburn grows concerned that Pluto is becoming too cold to sustain life.

The Shrinking Spaceman

When a sonar beam transmitter on the asteroid Pallas stops working, Galasphere 347 is sent to check it out. Husky cuts his hand on a contaminated meteorite fragment and later begins to shrink.

The Robot Revolution

Slim goes home to Venus on leave, while Larry and Husky visit an Atlantic undersea farm where an explosion makes the 5000 robot workers run amok.

The Cloud of Death

The sky goes dark above Space Control due to a cloud created by alien invaders to cut the Earth off from the sun's rays and freeze the planet to death. Galasphere finds itself playing a deadly game of cat and mouse.

The Rings of Saturn

Dart encounters a Saturnian ship in space and is taken down to the planet where he is able to persuade its reptilian leader to join the United Galactic Organization.

Volcanoes of Venus

Col. Raeburn's secretary, Marla, is concerned about a mysterious virus that is paralyzing her home planet. Slim goes to investigate.

Mystery on the Moon

A powerful beam from the Moon is destroying buildings at Space Headquarters. The Space Patrol are sent to investigate and clash with a dangerous criminal who threatens to destroy the world.

The Miracle Tree of Saturn

A mystery fungus is wiping out food crops on Earth. Haggerty discovers that leaves from the Miracle Tree of Saturn can counteract it, but Dart's mission to collect some is jeopardized by a stowaway.

The Forgers

A glut of forged banknotes is flooding world currencies. Dart and Husky set off for the Dictum Forest to track down the forgers and encounter some strange insects called glooks.

The Swamps of Jupiter

Larry Dart and his crew are sent to investigate the unexplained fate of a team of scientists exploring Jupiter and discover they've been killed by two wicked Martians who are now skinning the Loomis birds. (This episode features a different Galasphere and was used as a pilot episode in some other regions.)

The Planet of Thought

Tyro, leader of the Neptunians, persuades Col. Raeburn's secretary Marla to go to Neptune with him, but Raeburn does not believe she has gone willingly and sends Dart to bring her back.

The Glowing Eggs of Titan

When Dart and Co. make an emergency landing on Titan to repair their Galasphere, they make a curious discovery that could prove the answer to Mars's electricity crisis.

Planet of Light

Dart and Slim visit Lumen, a planet with no oxygen in its atmosphere, as the gas means death to its inhabitants.

The Time Watch (aka Time Stands Still)

Haggerty's new invention, a time watch, enables Dart to defeat a renegade Martian, Zota, by speeding up his reactions 60 times, thus rendering himself invisible.

The Invisible Martian (aka Husky Becomes Invisible)

Prof. Zeffer of the Martian observatory invents a machine for measuring the distance between stars—but Husky finds it has *other* properties when he accidentally gets caught in its rays.

The Walking Lake of Jupiter

A strange moving lake is discovered on Jupiter that brings peril to the planet.

The New Planet

Galasphere 347 hurtles off course into deep space where the crew discover a new planet out beyond Pluto, populated by giants.

The Human Fish

Larry, Slim and Husky investigate reports that a breed of fish on Venus is developing human form and starting to attack fishermen.

The Invisible Invasion

Strange beings from Uranus plan to take over Earth by becoming invisible and entering the minds of other people.

The Talking Bell

On a hunting trip Col. Raeburn and Prof. Haggerty trap a strange bell-like creature that at first seems like a nuisance, but finally helps save Dart when he is buried in a cave without food or water.

The Buried Space Ship

The Galasphere 347 crew is assigned to take part in Operation Ice Cube—transporting ice blocks from the frozen planet Pluto to help alleviate a desperate drought on Mars—but their ship becomes trapped in an icy crevasse.

Message from a Star

Signals from Alpha Centauri herald a visit by a creature from another galaxy seeking Space Patrol's help.

Explosion on the Sun

Col. Raeburn is faced with a dangerous situation when a would-be dictator sets himself up on the satellite Ganymede and starts interfering with the Sun—causing a tremendous heatwave.

Season Two
13 episodes

The Unknown Asteroid

Col. Raeburn sends Larry Dart and his crew to track down some space pirates who have been plundering cargo ships.

The Evil Eye of Venus

Venusian scientist Borra invents a mechanical eye that will repel any alien metal that comes within three miles. But when Borra is accidentally killed, the Eye goes out of control threatening *all* metal. Dart's crew set out to destroy the Eye using ultrasonic beams. It's a mission that calls for precise maneuvering . . .

Secret Formula

Husky gets trapped in a Martian spider's web and looks like being there for good until Prof. Haggerty and Gabbler come up with a solution.

The Telepathic Robot

Prof. Haggerty's latest invention, a robot servant, is supposed to respond to the brain impulses of its controller. But it soon develops a will of its own.

The Deadly Whirlwind

The Galasphere 347 crew is ordered to spray a chemical poison over every inch of Martian vegetation to halt a dust virus.

The Jitter Waves

The Earth's surface is shaken by a strange force and Space Patrol is given the task of finding out who—or what—is behind it.

Sands of Death

The Martian president calls on Col. Raeburn for help in thwarting an opposition plot to seize power using a nerve gas.

The Hairy Men of Mars

Forced to land in unexplored jungle terrain, Captain Dart and his crew encounter the Martian equivalent of the missing link.

The Grass of Saturn

A new anti-UGO leader assumes power on Saturn and plots to conquer Earth by planting a Saturnian species of grass there, which absorbs oxygen and gives off CO_2, thus making the population drowsy and listless.

Force Field X

The Neptunians evolve a diabolical plan to enslave Earth by inflicting extreme heat on the planet. When Dart returns from an unsuccessful effort to counter the plan, things look grim . . .

The Water Bomb

Taking an urgent cargo of oxygen and hydrogen for an irrigation project on Mars, Dart and his Galasphere are captured by a sinister Martian renegade.

Destruction by Sound

Haggerty uses his daughter, Cassiopea, for a strange travel experiment that affects events in another galaxy.

The Shrinking Gas of Jupiter

Slim starts to shrink after an encounter with a strange gas in a Jupiter swamp.

SPACE PATROL (U.S.)

One of the earliest U.S. space operas, *Space Patrol* was one of a revered trio of "golden age" sci-fi pioneers that fired the imaginations of the post-war baby boom, America's first TV generation.

Some seven or more years before Russia sent the first man-made satellite into orbit, in 1957, Commander Buzz Corry and the crew of the *Terra V*, along with *Tom Corbett, Space Cadet* and *Captain Video,* were exploring the depths of the universe and planting the concept of space travel in millions of impressionable young minds.

Space Patrol began as a West Coast local show in early 1950 and was quickly picked up by the ABC network where it ran until 1955. Set in the 30th century, it made much play of time travel, visiting various historical periods. But while it was simplistic in execution, it also broached sophisticated sci-fi themes including suspended animation, cloning and the nature of UFOs. And one story, about an energy source devouring the universe, would have been right at home on *Star Trek.*

The Space Patrol kept law and order for the United Planets of the Universe, an Earth-based UN-style political set-up. From their base on Terra Station—an artificial planetoid with a core built out of the soils of all Earth's nations—Buzz and his crew patrolled the universe—and on live TV, too!

Buzz was a jut-jawed hero who never needed to kill anyone, instead immobilizing foes with his Paralyzer Ray Gun, before showing them the error of their ways with the Brainograph, a device that removed anti-social tendencies.

His youthful co-pilot, Cadet Happy, was a space teenager whose language was peppered with such exclamations as "smokin' rockets!" Other regular characters were UP Secretary General Mr. Karlyle and his pretty daughter, Carol, who, naturally, had a crush on Buzz; Tonga, a reformed villainess; and Major Robbie Robertson, Security Chief of the Universe.

Corry's archenemy was Prince Baccarratti, a power-hungry foe who also called himself the Black Falcon. He had a malevolent sidekick called Malengro. Also in the villains' ranks was Mr. Proteus, a master of disguise.

The U.K. never got to see *Space Patrol* back in its heyday (though satellite channel Sky did show some episodes during the 1980s). The British "golden age" of TV sci-fi was still to come . . .

MAIN CAST
Commander Buzz Corry Ed Kremmer   *Cadet Happy* Lyn Osborn
Carol Karlyle Virginia Hewitt   *Tonga* Nina Bara   *Mr. Karlyle* Norman Jolley
Major Robbie Robertson Ken Mayer   *Mr. Proteus* Marvin Miller
Prince Baccarratti Bella Kovacs

Created by Mike Moser

Made in black and white
U.S. premiere: early 1950

A KECA Production

SPACE PRECINCT

Gerry Anderson returned to television with his most spectacular series ever—a $36 million space cop show featuring live-action and movie-style alien effects.

This is the series Anderson spent ten years trying to make, an obsession that saw an abortive pilot in 1987, called *Space Police*, and that was hauled back from the brink of extinction by an Anglo-American partnership between New York–based Grove Television and London production company Mentorn Films.

Set in the mid-21st century, *Space Precinct* is the story of veteran New York police lieutenant Patrick Brogan who gets a transfer to Demeter City, the crime capital of the galaxy. Nothing, not even 20 years on the streets of New York, could prepare Brogan for fighting alien crooks millions of light-years from Earth.

Demeter City is a parable for all our large urban jungles. *Space Precinct* rejects the *Trek* philosophy that space travel has been the answer to all man's problems. The Demeter system—located along a spiral arm of the Milky Way—has all Earth's problems, but with an added twist—the bulk of the population is alien. Demeter City, on the planet Altor, is home to two species who have migrated here from their homeworlds, the Creons and the Tarns. The larger Creons are big on ritual and ceremony and are highly superstitious, while the Tarns have telepathic and kinetic powers.

Helping Brogan deal with the riff-raff is his sidekick, Officer Haldane, and the beautiful Officer Jane Castle. They are based in an orbiting Precinct House (Precinct 88) and get about in flying police cruisers: a kind of *Hill Street Blues* in space. Brogan's family—wife Sally, ten-year-old Liz and teenage son Matthew—are also trying to adjust to their new life in an orbiting Space Suburb.

Space Precinct is, inevitably, light-years from the Supermarionated puppet series with which Anderson made his name. The early pilot (which starred Anderson voice veteran Shane Rimmer) featured a mix of puppets and robotics, dubbed "Galactronics" by Anderson. *Space Precinct*, filmed at Pinewood and Shepperton Studios, at a cost of $1.5 million per episode, utilizes computer-generated animatronics, robotics, prosthetics and stop-motion, and stars Ted Shackelford (*Dallas*'s Gary Ewing) and Rob Youngblood.

REGULAR CAST
Lt. Patrick Brogan Ted Shackelford   *Officer Jack Haldane* Rob Youngblood
Officer Jane Castle Simone Bendix   *Sally Brogan* Nancy Paul
Matt Brogan Nic Klein   *Liz Brogan* Megan Olive   *Captain Rexton Podly* Jerome Willis
Officer Hubble Orrin Richard James   *Officer Aurelia Took* Mary Woodvine
Sgt. Thorald Fredo David Quilter   *Officer Silas Romek* Lou Hirsch
Voice of Slomo Gary Martin   *Officer Lionel Carson* Joe Mydell

Creator/producer: Gerry Anderson
Executive producer: Tom Gutteridge
Co-executive producers: John Needham, Roger Lefkon
Producers: J. Larry Carroll, David Bennett Carven
Story editor: Sam Graham
Director of photography: Alan Hume
Music: Crispin Merrell
Live action designer: Tony Curtis
Creature effects designer: Neill Gorton

Animatronic Makeup effects designer: Richard Gregory
Grove Television Enterprises/Mentorn Films in association with The Space Precinct LP and Gilman Securities Corporation
Season One: 24 color 60-minute episodes
U.S. premiere: October 1994
U.K. premiere: 18 March–26 August 1995
(Sky One)

Episode order is as broadcast on Sky.

Protect and Survive

w Paul Mayhew-Archer
Lt. Brogan and his sidekick, Jack Haldane, must protect a Melazoid murder witness from an evil criminal who has brought a deadly disease to Altor by smuggling in illegal immigrants.
Gershom Oliver Cotton
Slik Burt Kwouk
Beezle Tom Watt *(uncredited)*
Lawyer David Shaw-Parker
Loyster Rob Thirtle
Voice of Loyster David Healy
Medic Leigh Tinkler
Judge Andy Dawson

Director: John Glen

The Snake

w J. Larry Carroll & David Bennett Carren
An alien extortionist and explosives expert targets a huge tanker en route to Altor with 200 million gallons of liquified hydrogen.
Gray David Baxt
Kane Joseph Mydell
Azusa Ken Drury
Dallas Paul Humpoletz
Captain Tecopa Leigh Tinkler

Director: John Glen

Time to Kill

w Hans Beimler & Richard Manning
During a raid on a counterfeiting operation, an innocent participant is badly injured. Then an invulnerable cyborg mysteriously appears and starts slaughtering Brogan's fellow officers!
Tamsin Nigel Gregory
Ross Stephen Billington
Dr. Grant Alison Rose
Cyborg Glenn Marks
Zipload Rob Thirtle
Drako Will Barton

Director: Alan Birkinshaw

Body & Soul

w Marc Scott Zicree, *story by* Mark Harris
Brogan investigates a body found aboard a derelict spaceship that has been lost in space for 20 years.
Alden Humes Bob Sherman
Jomore Rob Thirtle
Underling Will Barton

Director: Sidney Hayers

Deadline

w David Bennett Carren & J. Larry Carroll
The chance discovery of a murder victim whose vital organs have been removed leads Brogan and Haldane to a transplant racket—and the crooks mark Brogan as the next donor.
Jorry Steven Berkoff
Speedy Truan Munro
Rik Ken Whitfield
Nurse Leigh Tinkler
Patrol Joanna Burns
Prosperous Creon Will Barton
Wirt Rob Thirtle

Director: John Glen

Enforcer

w Marc Scott Zicree
Brogan and Haldane tackle an alien vigilante who promises to end violence on the streets of Demeter City—but his price is high . . .
Vala Jade Punt
Andy Sturgeon Andrew Tiernan
Nick Tom Radcliffe
Beezle Tom Watt *(uncredited)*
Madam Kazia Pelka
Lurzan Leigh Tinkler
Trask Rob Thirtle
Skeevan Andy Dawson

Director: Sidney Hayers

Two Against the Rock

w Paul Robert Coyle
Haldane would rather be watching a baseball match and Jane has flu, but they have to escort a criminal to an asteroid prison, unaware that it's been taken over by armed gangsters.
Volker Stephen Greif
"Houdini" Danny Webb
Dr. Ellis Richard Huw
Con Ray Winstone
Sportscaster John Chancer
Bronkov Ken Whitfield
Tarn P.C. Leigh Tinkler

Director: Peter Duffell

Predator and Prey

w Nicholas Sagan
Following the death of an officer from the 79th Precinct in Demeter City's hottest nightspot, Brogan and Haldane are teamed with maverick Lt. Walker in a search for a serial killer.
Lt. Walker Rolf Saxon
Chloe Natalie Roles
Kmada Richard James
Bouncer Ken Whitfield
Mags Alexa Rosewood

Director: Sidney Hayers

Seek and Destroy

w J. Larry Carrol *&* David Bennett Carren
While investigating a series of murders, Brogan and Haldane are warned that an alien nomadic race, the Omera, are planning to invade Altor.
Vachel David Burke
Noah Ingram John Warnaby
Slan Nuri Paul Brennan
Mr. Douglas Sidney Livingstone

Director: Jim Goddard

Illegal

w Marc Scott Zicree
An illegal immigrant saves Brogan's life in a shooting incident, and Brogan learns that his rescuer's son is being held by a snuff fight promoter. The Precinct 88 officers go undercover but soon Brogan finds himself fighting for his life.
Tildon Tony Haygarth
Nillim Tim Matthews
Ogree Pat Roach
Guard Terry Richards

Director: John Glen

Double Duty

w J. Larry Carroll *&* David Bannett Carren
A scaly killer runs loose in the Space Precinct house. It's target is pretty alien Aleesha Amyas, sole survivor of an attack on a drug baron.
Nissim Nickolas Grace
Aleesha Lana Citron
Bag lady Matyelok Gibbs
Beezle Tom Watt *(uncredited)*
Delivery man Idris Elba
Inazy Nitzan Sharron

Director: Colin Bucksey

The Power

w Sam Graham, *story by* Mark Harris
Jane and Took are assigned to protect a shipment of a component in a new solar power system. Meanwhile, Brogan and Haldane investigate the death of a reformed jewel thief and discover a link that leads to a deadly struggle for control of Demeter City's energy franchise.
Zeller Tom Chadbon
Numar Sheila Ruskin
Sylvain Alison Fielding
Paramedic Mark Carey

Director: Sidney Hayers

Takeover

w J. Larry Carrol *&* David Bennett Carren
Brogan and Haldane are accused of cold-blooded murder and subjected to an Internal Affairs investigation.
Cambria Maryam D'Abo
Reseda Clive Merrison
Tev Rob Thirtle
Yorba Andy Dawson
Bailiff Ken Whitfield

Director: John Glen

Hate Street

w Steve Brown
Brogan and Haldane are assigned to find Burl Flak, a wanted murderer, and the mastermind behind a series of race and hate crimes. But their investigation is hampered by the arrival of a bounty hunter who wants to claim the reward for Flak, and who happens to be one of Brogan's old flames.
Erika Frances Barber
Flak Christopher Fairbank
Sandoff David Quilter
Dr. Eastman Jeff Harding
Tate Robert Hamilton
Maya Kate Harper
Skog Peter O'Farrell
Tanni Kiran Shah

Director: Piers Haggard

The Witness

w Eric Gethers
Small-time crooks are being murdered but as the search begins for the killer, Fredo's daughter is taken ill and Brogan realizes she is picking up the murderer's thoughts.
Datch Kate Harper
Morgan Todd Boyce
Estes Kiran Shah
Maharg Peter Hugo Daly
Ziploud Rob Thirtle

Director: Peter Duffell

Flash

w James Hendrie
A deadly new designer drug hits Demeter City, causing users to spontaneously combust!
Dr. Jansen Michael J. Shannon
Carmel Pippa Guard
Morgo Anthony Venditti
Beezle Tom Watt *(uncredited)*
Droon Rob Thirtle
Forensic Andy Dawson
Pola Leigh Tinkler

Director: Alan Birkinshaw

Friends

w Chris Hubbell, Philip Morrow *&* Carl Jahnsen, *story by* Carl Jahnsen
When a computer hacker is taken into custody, his friends kidnap Jane and demand his freedom or they'll kill her.
Reeve Pataki Ben Walden
Lynn/Sprite Jacqueline Defferary
Glen Christopher Thomas

Director: Peter Duffell

Smelter Skelter

w Arthur Sellers
Brogan's wife and daughter are violently threatened during an armed robbery and Brogan naturally takes a personal interest in finding the culprit. But the investigation takes a different turn when he finds that the robber is planning another raid, using a device that could punch a hole in the fabric of the universe!
Zann Bradley Lavelle
Bank assistant Leigh Tinkler
Dr. Rudd Alexa Rosewood

Director: Peter Duffell

The Fire Within

w Steve Brown *&* Burt Prelutsky
First of a two-part story. Teamed with Captain Podly's daughter, Samina, Haldane goes undercover at the fire-worshipping Pyrist Temple to find out the truth behind the mysterious death of a Pyrist priest during a sacred ritual.
Icar Vedra Jack Hedley
Brok Lisa Orgolini
Kalamondro David Quilter
Fama Kate Harper
Kyster Wayne Forester
Samina Alexa Rosewood

Director: John Glen

The Fire Within, Part 2

w Steve Brown *&* Burt Prelutsky
Conclusion. Samina disappears and Haldane resigns from the force to join the Pyrists. Then a witness accuses Haldane of murdering Samina, and Podly issue a warrant for his arrest, as the priests prepare for the Day of Immolation—the end of the world.
Icar Vedra Jack Hedley
Brok Lisa Orgolini
Kalamondro David Quilter
Fama Kate Harper
Kyster Wayne Forester
Samina Alexa Rosewood

Director: John Glen

The Forever Beetle

w Peter Dunne
Brogan and Haldane are assigned to investigate the theft of a rare beetle from a research lab. But Brogan is preoccupied with nailing the drug dealer he believes killed his best friend.
Wolf Constantine Gregory
Murphy Sam Douglas
Cole Glen McCrory
Sena M Kiran Shah
Dr. Long Andy Dawson
Nardo Wayne Forester

Director: Peter Duffell

Divided We Stand

w Arthur Sellers
A dishonest politician finds a way to win a vital election and in the process discredits Brogan and Haldane.
Regina Baylek/Mrs. Dodrek Suzanne Bertish
Reporter Kate Beckett
Vinny Artak David Quilter
Dr. Kyte Christopher Baines
Drak Rebecca Steele
Hospital administrator Dominic Letts

Director: Alan Birkinshaw

Deathwatch

w Michael Berlin *&* Eric Estrin
First of a two-part story. The discovery of a mysterious meteor fragment heralds the start of strange events at an apartment building, where residents are being terrorized into moving out. But when their investigations are blocked by the military, Brogan and Haldane realize that something very sinister is going on.
Weldon Cecilia Noble
Bertha Anne Kristen
Borden Ken Farrington
Skid Rob Thirtle
Gullis Wayne Forester
Shopper Leigh Tinkler

Director: Piers Haggard

Deathwatch, Part 2

w Arthur Sellers
Conclusion. Brogan must prevent the meteor fragment found at Butler's farm being brought together with the meteor buried beneath Poetern Towers, as the meteor is a parasitic alien seed and the fragment a spore to fertilize it. The result would be the destruction of all life on Altor.
Weldon Cecilia Noble
Commander Burnell Tucker
Duty officer Andy Dawson
Nox Wayne Forester
Relma Alexa Rosewood

Director: Piers Haggard

Also:

Space Police (1987 pilot)
Star Laws

w Gerry Anderson & Tony Barwick
Lt. Brogan, an old-style U.K. cop in charge of Space Police Precinct 44, fights the organized crime of V. Lann and his sidekick E. Vile, who attempt to assas-sinate the planet's president by sabotaging his monorail train. Brogan is aided by various aliens as well as Officer Cathy Costello who can turn her body into an indestructible black substance.
Lt. Brogan Shane Rimmer
Cathy Costello Catherine Chevalier

Director: Tony Bell
Music: Gerry Anderson & Christopher Burr
An Anderson Burr Picture

SPACE RANGERS

1993 saw the launch of three new science fiction series in the U.S.: *Star Trek: Deep Space 9*, *Babylon 5* (with its first movie, *Babylon 5: The Gathering*), and *Space Rangers*.

Set in the 22nd century, this half-hour series about intergalactic police on the frontiers of space tried hard to be quality fare, but created a muddled and confusing background and did little to develop characters beyond stereotype—although one could argue that its cancellation after only one episode had aired didn't give it sufficient time to develop or find its own voice. (Of the six filmed episodes, only four were broadcast in America, although they have turned up in foreign countries.) Also, showing the episodes out of their chronological order (fixed below) probably didn't help: "Fort Hope" is clearly meant to be the first episode, since it introduces the characters . . . Too bad it aired fourth!

REGULAR CAST
Commander Chennault Linda Hunt *Captain John Boon* Jeff Kaake
Doc Jack McGee *JoJo* Marjorie Monagham
Zylyn Cary-Hiroyuki Tagawa *Danny Kincaid* Danny Quinn
Mimmer Clint Howard *Erik Weiss* Gottfried John

Creator: Pen Densham

Aired 6 January 1993–27 January 1993
6 color 30-minute episodes

Episodes

Fort Hope

The Rangers mount a rescue mission to retrieve an old friend of Boon's, who has crashed on a planet that's also a sacred Graaka burial site.
Guest stars: Wings Hauser, Pat Morita, Salli Elise Richardson

Banshees

The Rangers must rescue a young boy and capture a deadly alien, both of whom are on an abandoned spaceship.
Guest stars: Rick Latini III, Dawn Jeffory, James Cooper, Gary Byron

The Replacements

The Rangers add an android to their team, little re-alizing Col. Weiss plans to replace all Rangers with androids if his test works out.

Death before Dishonor

When Boon offends a visiting dignitary, he is sen-tenced to death and aliens declare war on Fort Hope.
Guest stars: Claudia Christian, Sherman Howard, Dana Gladstone

The Trial

Zylyn is accused of the murder of another Graakan; when they fail to find council for him, the rest of the Rangers are forced to defend him in court them-selves. Convinced there is a conspiracy to bring dis-credit to the Graaka race, they hunt for a clue as to the real murderer is.
Never aired in the U.S.

The Entertainer

To get out of tedious duty, the Rangers launch a mis-sion to rescue a has-been comedian who crashed on a prison planet.
Guest star: Buddy Hackett
Never aired in the U.S.

SPACEVETS

British kids' sitcom about a creaky intergalactic mobile vets' surgery, plying the highways and byways of deep space to bring aid to ailing alien animals.

And in the tradition of kids' comedy there's a 13-year-old in charge of the ship, the *Dispensable*, albeit a 13-year-old with a computer-enhanced brain. But while Captain K. Pubble displayed experience, maturity and a hole in the head for his slot-in computer chip, his adult crew acted like they were the juveniles.

Pubble's right-hand man was No. 2, from a planet with numbers for names, who, after 800 years in the space service has only risen as far as second officer. He got all the "bitter and twisted" lines. Navigator and chocoholic Mona was played by comic actress and Philadelphia ad star Ann Bryson, while the ship's engineer is a dog—Dogsbody, a creation of puppeteer Robin Kingsland.

The series, which has clocked up three seasons, saw the crew deal with strange animals and their stranger owners, plus the usual run of life-threatening scrapes, feuds and jealousies. Season Three saw the Space Vets with a new ship and led by a new captain, played by comedian Mark Arden, star of the Carling Black Label ads.

REGULAR CAST

Captain K. Pubble Linden Kirk *No. 2* Bernard Wright *Mona* Ann Bryson
Dogsbody Robin Kingsland
Captain Skip Chip Mark Arden (*Season Three*)

Writer: Christopher Middleton, *idea by* Stephen Edmondson, Jerome Vincent
Producer: Greg Childs

BBC Production
39 color 15-minute episodes
(BBC1)

Series One

The Edge of the Abyss
A Game of Chance
The Government Inspector
The Eyes of Darkness
A Matter of Life and Death
The Love Ship
The Guilty Party
The Teeth of the Storm (*a 2-part story*)
Slaves of the Emperor
Dying for the Loo
The Jaws of Destruction
The Final Conflict

29 September–22 December 1992

Series Two

Law of the Jungle
A Race against Time
Riddle of the Sands
The Caves of Doom
The Scum of the Earth
Sunday Rotten Sunday
The Swamps of Corruption (Part 1)
The Swamps of Corruption (Part 2)
The Shrunken Brain
Menace of the Machines
A Matter of Honor

28 September–7 December 1993

Series Three (Spacevets III)

A Hero's Welcome
Baby on Board
Megastew
A Touch of Toothache
Too Close for Comfort
The Gizmo
Queen for a Day
Just Kidding
Pappy Days
That Shrinking Feeling
The Man with No Brain
Two the Rescue
Auto Pilot

27 September–6 December 1994

STAR COPS

When Nathan Spring and his posse of space deputies rode into the BBC schedules in 1987, they evoked echoes of the lawmen of the Old West.

Space was (as someone once said) the final frontier, and this nine-part series set in 2027 depicted an international frontier community of around 3000 strung out over five permanently manned space stations, a Moonbase and a colony on Mars—but with *no* aliens.

The International Space Police Force (nicknamed the Star Cops) were initially a handful of part-timers, volunteers who got the badge and had to keep law and order while holding down other jobs.

Nathan Spring is a dedicated, irascible, professional detective appointed to whip them into shape. An outsider, he is immensely suspicious of the computerized world in which he lives, believing that it discourages people from thinking for themselves. He starts to build an international team around himself, beginning with Theroux, a young black American flight engineer, Australian Pal Kenzy, and chauvinistic womanizer chubby Colin Devis, and later to include young Japanese scientist Anna Shoun.

The Star Cops investigate everything from murder, sabotage, and theft to hijacking, with Spring frequently clashing—somewhat half-heartedly—with Krivenko, the Russian coordinator of Moonbase where they establish their headquarters.

The series was devised by Chris Boucher, a veteran of *Doctor Who* and *Blake's 7*, who was keen to get away from space opera and back to what he considered the nuts and bolts of an intelligent, realistic detective series set in space. A contributor to such earthbound crime series as *Bergerac*, *Juliet Bravo* and *Shoestring*, Boucher intended the drama to come, not from the realms of the fantastic, but from the developing characters and the strength of the plots.

REGULAR CAST
Nathan Spring David Calder   *David Theroux* Erick Ray Evans
Pal Kenzy Linda Newton   *Colin Devis* Trevor Cooper *(from Ep. 2)*
Alexander Krivenko Jonathan Adams *(from Ep. 4)*
Anna Shoun Sayo Inaba *(from Ep. 6)*

Devised by Chris Boucher	*A BBC Production*
Producer: Evgeny Gridneff	9 color 55-minute episodes
Script editor: Joanna Willett	6 July–31 August 1987
Video effects: Robin Lobb	(BBC2)
Theme: Justin Haywood	

An Instinct for Murder

w Chris Boucher
The year: 2027. At the Charles de Gaulle space station, crew members die when their spacesuit backpacks malfunction. On Earth, Nathan Spring, an old-fashioned, instinctive policeman, proves a drowned man was murdered, but is far from pleased when he is told that he has been short-listed for the post of Head of the International Space Force—whose inefficiency has branded them with the nickname "Star Cops."
Commander Moray Watson
Controller Keith Varnier
Lee Jones Gennie Nevinson
Brian Lincoln Andrew Secombe
Hans Diter Frederik de Groot
Lars Hendvorrsen Luke Hanson
Marie Mueller Katja Kersten

Director: Christopher Baker
Designer: Dick Coles

Conversations with the Dead

w Chris Boucher
A freight ship on its way to the Martian colony suddenly develops computer failure and goes off course. The crew is still alive but, as any recovery mission might take years, technically the two men are dead. In Britain, Nathan's girlfriend, Lee Jones, is murdered in his flat.
Lee Jones Gennie Nevinson
Corman Siân Webber
Paton Alan Downer
Fox Sean Scanlan
Gina Carmen Gomez
John Smith Benny Young
Traffic controller Deborah Manship
Mike Richard Ireson
Lara Rosie Kerslake

Director: Christopher Baker
Designer: Dick Coles

Intelligent Listening for Beginners

w Chris Boucher
Nathan and Theroux visit an outpost on the Moon that is owned by millionaire Michael Chandri who appears to be involved in listening systems and bugging devices. He tells them that he has heard of a plot to hijack an Earth-Moon shuttle.
Michael Chandri David John Pope
Leo Trevor Butler
Ben Thomas Coulthard
Shuttle hostess Tara Ward
Shift foreman Peter Quince
Process operator Peter Glancy

Director: Christopher Baker
Designer: Dick Coles

Trivial Games and Paranoid Pursuits

w Chris Boucher
Dilly Goodman tries to contact her brother who has been working as a research scientist on the American space station, the *Ronald Reagan*. But they have no record of him. He does not seem to exist. Meanwhile, Moonbase gets a new Russian commander.
Cmdr. Griffin Daniel Benzali
Dilly Goodman Marlena Mackey
Pete Lennox Robert Jezek
Marty Russell Wootton
Lauter Angela Crow
Harvey Goodman Morgan Deare
Receptionist Shope Shodeinde

Director: Graeme Harper
Designer: Malcolm Thornton

This Case to Be Opened in a Million Years

w Philip Martin
A shuttle, used for dumping nuclear waste in space, crashes on launch, causing a nuclear alert on Moonbase. Nathan has to return to Earth where a killer is lying in wait for him in the catacombs of northern Italy. (Stewart Guidotti, who appears in this episode, was one of television's earliest men in space as young Geoffrey Wedgwood in ITV's pioneering *Pathfinders* series in 1960–61.)
Carlo Santanini Michael Chesden
Marla Condarini Susan Curnow
Insp. Canova Stewart Guidotti
Lina Margello Vikki Chambers
Personnel officer Flip Webster
Angelo Pordenone André Winterton
Tour guide Carl Forgione

Director: Graeme Harper
Designer: Malcolm Thornton

In Warm Blood

w John Collee
When the geological survey ship, *Pluto 5*, returns from an exploratory mission, the Star Cops are presented with a complicated problem: the whole crew has been dead for at least a year—and they all died at the same moment.
Anna Shoun Sayo Inaba *(intro)*
Richard Ho Richard Rees
Christina Janssen Dawn Keeler
Receptionist Susan Tan

Director: Graeme Harper
Designer: Malcolm Thornton

A Double Life

w John Collee
Three embryos are mysteriously stolen from the Moonbase hospital, and their mother, Chamsya Assadi, threatens to withdraw financial support. Anna identifies the kidnapper as concert pianist James Bannerman—but he was giving a concert on Earth at the time . . .
James Bannerman/Albi Brian Gwaspari
Chamsya Assadi Nitza Saul

Director: Christopher Baker
Designer: Dick Coles

Other People's Secrets

w John Collee
Psychiatrist Dr. Angela Parr visits Moonbase to conduct a study into the effects of living in space. And a series of small technical faults occur while Safety Controller Ernest Wolffhart is on Moonbase. Overworked maintenance engineer Hooper claims it's sabotage.
Ernest Wolffhart Geoffrey Bayldon
Dr. Angela Parr Maggie Ollerenshaw
Hooper Barrie Rutter
Beverley Anderson Leigh Funnell

Director: Christopher Baker
Designer: Dick Coles

Little Green Men and Other Martians

w Chris Boucher
The news that something outstanding has been discovered on Mars and is now on its way to the Moon results in Moonbase being invaded by nosy journalists. Meanwhile, Nathan also has to cope with a case of drug smuggling.
Daniel Larwood Roy Holder
Andrew Philpott Nigel Hughes
Susan Caxton Lachelle Carl
Operations manager Wendy Macadam
Co-pilot Bridget Lynch-Rose
Pilot Kenneth Lodge
Customs officer Peter Neathy
Outpost controller Phillip Rowlands
Surveyor David Janes

Director: Graeme Harper
Designer: Malcolm Thornton

STAR FLEET

Animated puppet series from Japan, set in the year 2999. Space War Three has ended and the solar system is being rebuilt, led by planet Earth. But hostile powers and aliens are out to sabotage their efforts.

At the heart of the story is Lamia, a young princess-like character whose destiny is bound up with the advent of the new millennium when she will emerge as the mysterious F-01, a benign force with the power to bring peace and order to the whole solar system.

The top bad guy, the Imperial Master, wants her dead before the year 3000; otherwise his evil power cannot rule the galaxy. He sends his forces, led by Commander Makara, a bizarre male/female Fu Manchu–type character, on a seek and destroy mission. Standing in their way is Earth's Star Fleet, under General Kyle. The fleet's principal craft is the X-bomber, designed by Prof. Hagen and crewed by his son, Shiro, Barry Hercules, John Lee, Doctor Benn and Lamia. Lurking protectively in the background is another mystery man, Capt. Halley, commander of a space galleon called *The Skull*. The tide of battle ebbs and flows until Lamia and the Star Fleet win a final victory.

Writer: Michael Sloan
Producer/Director: Louis Elman
Executive producer: Kevin Morrison
Music: Paul Bliss

A Leah International Jin Production
24 color 30-minute episodes
23 October 1982–4 September 1983
(LWT)

STAR MAIDENS

Question: in what TV series did Gareth Thomas play a rebel on the run, pursued by a powerful, dominant female? Yes, yes, *Blake's 7*, of course. But two years earlier he was fleeing a regiment of women in a quite different science fiction series, *Star Maidens*.

Touted as a tongue-in-cheek fantasy, this 13-part Anglo-German production depicted a role-reversed planet, Medusa, where women rule and men are the domestic drudges. Two male servants, Adam and Shem, escape to Earth in a stolen spacecraft in search of a better life. But they are pursued by Supreme Councillor Fulvia who wants to rechain them to the kitchen sink. When they are unable to recapture the runaways, Fulvia and her crew return with two Earth hostages. Thus the scene is set for a two-center culture clash.

The series, based on an original idea by a pair of German film-makers, Graf and Graefin Von Hardenberg, was made by a British independent company, Portman Productions, at Bray Studios. Its quartet of writers included three renowned exponents of British telefantasy—Eric Paice, Ian Stuart Black and John Lucarotti—and it boasted a starry international cast, including Judy Geeson, Dawn Addams and Lisa Harrow. Ronald Hines appeared as a dour police inspector bewildered by his encounter with the liberated ladies of Medusa, and Alfie Bass chipped in a cameo role as a castle gatekeeper captured by the Medusan runaways. The foreign stars included Christiane Kruger (daughter of Hardy) and Christian Quadflieg, from Germany, plus French-born Pierre Brice.

Produced at a cost of around £50,000 per episode, *Star Maidens* was sold to more than 40 countries as diverse—given the "liberated" theme—as America, Hungary, South Africa and the Arab states of the Middle East.

But the maidens won few admirers, something Portman executive Ian Warren attributed to the difficulty of doing comedy with the Germans. "It was meant to be fantasy but the Germans kept trying to make it more realistic."

Plans were laid to make a second series in Canada but they proved too expensive and were quietly shelved.

MAIN CAST
Fulvia Judy Geeson   *The President* Dawn Addams   *Adam* Pierre Brice
Shem Gareth Thomas   *Octavia* Christiane Kruger
Dr. Liz Becker Lisa Harrow   *Dr. Rudi Schmidt* Christian Quadflieg   *Prof. Evans* Derek Farr

Producer: James Gatward

A Portman Production (for Scottish and Global Television Enterprises in co-production with Jost Graf von Hardenberg & Co. and Werbung-in-Rundfunk, Frankfurt/Main)

13 color 30-minute episodes
U.K. premiere:
1 September–1 December 1976
(STV)

Escape to Paradise

w Eric Paice
Medusan servants Adam and Shem steal a space yacht belonging to Adam's mistress, Supreme Councillor Fulvia, and head for Earth. A distraught Fulvia decides to lead the pursuit herself.
Insp. Stanley Ronald Hines *(plus Ep. 2)*
Announcer Penelope Hunter

Director: James Gatward

Nemesis

w Eric Paice
Earth scientist Prof. Evans has monitored the arrival of the spacecraft. Adam and Shem, recoiling in horror from all contact with the female sex, seek police protection. Meanwhile, Fulvia and Octavia step up their pursuit.
Katy Moss Jenny Morgan
Sgt. Innes Wilfred Grove
Mrs. Moss Kristine Howarth
Desk Sgt. Norman Warwick *(plus Ep. 3)*

Director: Wolfgang Storch

The Nightmare Cannon

w Eric Paice
Adam and Shem capture a castle. Octavia and Fulvia, treating the Earth men as servants, demand the return of the runaways. Thwarted, they take Prof. Evans's assistants Rudi and Liz as hostages.
Gatekeeper Alfie Bass
Minister Graham Crowden *(plus Ep. 11)*

Director: Wolfgang Storch

The Proton Storm

w John Lucarotti
Fulvia returns to Earth and offers an exchange with the hostages, but the two Medusans refuse—unless they can return as equals. On Mendusa the Earth pair are separated—Rudi to the men's menial quarters, Liz to a life of luxury.
Andrea Uschi Mellin *(plus Ep. 5)*

Director: Wolfgang Storch

Kidnap

w John Lucarotti
Two foreign scientists get Fulvia drunk on champagne, then take her to a villa to link her with a computer brain to store her advanced scientific knowledge. Adam, experiencing the novel emotion of jealousy, stages a rescue.
Sforza Philip Stone
Gregori Terence Alexander
Carlo Stanley Lebor
Hotel manager Hedger Wallis

Director: Freddie Francis

The Trial

w Ian Stuart Black
On Medusa, the men stage a revolt against the "Petticoat Government." Liz is forced to treat Rudi as an inferior in order to obtain a spacecraft in which they can escape. Rudi is caught trying to learn the planet's security secrets and is sent for trial by computers.
Troy Roland Astor
Guard Susie Baker
Octavia's assistant Ann Maj-Britt *(plus Eps. 9–10)*
Clara's assistants Annette Lynton *(plus Eps. 7–8)* Clare Russell *(plus Ep. 7)*

Director: Wolfgang Storch

Test for Love

w Ian Stuart Black
Liz keeps up the pretense of treating Rudi as an inferior while secretly plotting with him to escape. To discredit her, Octavia puts Liz on a "sexometer"—but she causes it to blow up!
Nola Veronica Lang
Ercule John Wyman
Zita Belinda Mayne
Guard Diana Weston

Director: Freddie Francis

The Perfect Couple

w Ian Stuart Black
Two women's libbers try to use Fulvia as a propagandist for their cause, but Adam is succeeding in winning her over to domestic life on Earth. They decide to become a suburban couple—though reversing the normal roles—but Fulvia becomes jealous of Adam's tea-parties with the local housewives!
Col. Kipple Ronald Fraser
Garcia Dorothea Kaiser
Freda Marianne Nebel
Wife Jenny Till

Director: Hans Heinrich

What Have They Done to the Rain?

w Ian Stuart Black
Rudi discovers that there has been a chemical change on Medusa which is causing the planet's surface to dissolve—but only Liz will heed his warnings.
Announcer Anna Carteret
Guard Kirstie Pooley

Director: Freddie Francis

The End of Time

w Eric Paice
Octavia returns to Medusa with Prof. Evans to arrange an exchange of hostages. The streets are deserted, all the women have disappeared and the men look like zombies. They find the President, Clara, who appears to be dead.
Fidelia Ciaren Madden
Theda Barbara Trentham
Doctor Imogen Clare

Director: Wolfgang Storch

Hideout

w Otto Strang
Adam and Shem are on the run again—the Minister assures Fulvia that they will be recaptured. Shem is sheltered by a woman, Rose, and the two fall in love. But capture comes eventually.

Rose Corny Collins
Police sgt. Don McKillop
Desk sgt. George Hilsdon
Youth Adrian Shergold
Policeman David Ellison
TV announcer John Pennington

Director: Freddie Francis

Creatures of the Mind

w Ian Stuart Black
Asked to help search out old records of experiments in physical, biological and mental energy, Liz is terrified when she is trapped in a vault, sees strange shapes and hears voices.

Director: James Gatward

The Enemy

w Otto Strang
Arrangements are made for the exchange of hostages. Two spaceships, one taking Liz and Rudi back to Earth, the other taking Adam and Shem to Medusa, will pass each other midway. But as they cross, an enemy craft intercepts—and the Medusan code forbids them to fight.

Director: Freddie Francis

STAR TREK

"I realized that by creating a separate world, a new world with new rules, I could make statements about sex, religion, Vietnam, unions, politics and intercontinental missiles. Indeed, we did make them on *Star Trek*; we were sending messages, and fortunately they all got by the network."
—Gene Roddenberry, creator/producer

Today, boosted by a cartoon series and the fleet of feature films, and kept alive by the devotion of its fans, *Star Trek* remains a multimillion-dollar industry. And the series—now known simply as "Classic Trek"—with its unforgettable characters and catchphrases, has become an indelible part of Western culture. Watching it has become the TV equivalent of comfort eating; you know there are better things to do but you just can't help yourself . . .

Star Trek was created by Gene Roddenberry, a former World War Two aviator and Los Angeles cop, who conceived it as an adult science fiction series.

Its premise: in the 23rd century, Earth is part of the United Federation of Planets, a peaceful alliance of democratic worlds that runs a "Starfleet" of space vessels to patrol the "final frontier" of space.

These, then, were the voyages of the Starship *Enterprise*. Its mission, restated at the start of each episode; "to explore strange new worlds, to seek out new life and new civilizations, to boldly go where no man has gone before."

Its heroes: Captain James T. Kirk (the "T" stood for Tiberius), a courageous and unflinchingly noble commander; his first officer Mr. Spock, a half-human, half-Vulcan with pointed ears and arched eyebrows who lived by logic; Chief Medical Officer Leonard "Bones" McCoy, an intemperate Southerner who insisted he was "just a simple country doctor at heart"; and Chief Engineer Montgomery "Scotty" Scott, an old-fashioned nuts 'n' bolts man devoted to his engines.

The characters may have been corny (with the exception of Spock), but the chemistry was special, creating a unique sense of family—especially between Kirk, Spock and McCoy. You just knew that beneath that grumpy exterior, McCoy really cared for Spock. And the Vulcan's own inner turmoil as he strove to reconcile his logical self with the human side of his nature made him the most interesting character.

Yet Roddenberry had had to fight to keep Spock in the show in the face of a network initially unwilling to welcome him aboard, in the belief that nobody would relate to him.

Leonard Nimoy, too, was reluctant about the part. He believed the ears would wipe him out as an actor. Roddenberry promised him an "ear job" after the 13th episode if he was still unhappy. He wasn't.

Star Trek's special effects weren't elaborate, but they were memorable. The *Enterprise* itself consisted of several different models, ranging in size from three inches to 14 feet. The warp drive, phasers, photon torpedoes and communicators became an integral part of the show but the most famous trick was the transporter, the device used to "beam" the crew down to nearby planets. Aluminium dust was thrown into a beam of light to enhance the dematerialization effect.

But every assessment of *Star Trek*'s enduring appeal has always come down to two things—its humanity and its optimism. The crew's line-up reflected a united mankind, a society free of racial and sexual discrimination. Aside from the half-caste science officer, it had a black woman, Lt. Uhura, as head of communications, and the navigators were Japanese (Mr. Sulu) and Russian (Chekov was reputedly added to the crew when a *Pravda* critic acidly noted that the first nation into space was unrepresented on the *Enterprise*).

Each episode was a morality tale and the series constantly maintained an indomitable faith in man as an essentially noble animal. Flawed maybe, a little impulsive at times, but with his heart in the right place.

And so it was with *Star Trek*. For all its faults—and critics have always loved to pick holes—its heart was in the right place. As Roddenberry remarked: "We were probably the only show on American television that said there is a tomorrow, that all the excitement and adventures and discoveries were not behind us."

REGULAR CAST
Captain James T. Kirk William Shatner *Mr. Spock* Leonard Nimoy
"Bones" McCoy DeForest Kelley *Scotty* James Doohan
Mr. Sulu George Takei *Ensign Chekov* Walter Koenig *(from Season Two)*
Lt. Uhura Nichelle Nichols *Nurse Christine Chapel* Majel Barrett
Yeoman Janice Rand Grace Lee Whitney *(Season One only)*

Creator/Executive producer: Gene Roddenberry
Producers: Gene Roddenberry, Gene L. Coon
(late Season One, early Season Two), John
Meredyth Lucas *(late Season Two)*, Fred
Freiberger *(Season Three only)*
Story consultants: Steven Carabatsos, D.C.
Fontana, Arthur H. Singer
Theme: Alexander Courage
*A Desilu Production in association with Norway
Corporation (Season One, early Season Two), A
Paramount Production in association with Norway
Corporation (late Season Two, Season Three)*
79 color 50-minute episodes

U.S. premiere: 8 September 1966
U.K. premiere: 12 July 1969*
(BBC1)—color from 15 November 1969

(Author's note: The BBC running order for *Star Trek*
differed considerably from the U.S. original, with a
fair amount of season crossovers. And while the series
enjoyed regular repeats, three episodes—"Plato's
Stepchildren," "The Empath" and "Whom Gods Destroy"—only received their U.K. premieres on 22
December 1993, 5 January and 19 January 1994
respectively. For ease of reference, the episodes are
listed in their original American seasons.)

The Cage

w Gene Roddenberry
The original pilot episode, rejected by network chiefs as "too cerebral." Aliens on Talos IV trap Captain Christopher Pike in a glass-walled cage where illusions are taken for reality. Footage from this pilot showed up later in the two-part story "The Menagerie."
Captain Pike Jeffrey Hunter
Mr. Spock Leonard Nimoy
Vena Susan Oliver
The Keeper Meg Wylie
Number One Majel Barrett
Dr. Boyce John Hoyt
Tyler Peter Duryea
with Laurel Goodwin

Director: Robert Butler

A Desilu Production
(U.K. broadcast: 19 August 1992)

Season One
29 episodes

The Man Trap

w George Clayton Johnson
On a routine visit to the planet M113, McCoy meets an old flame, Nancy Crater, and refuses to believe that she is really a salt vampire capable of assuming human form.
Nancy Jeanne Bal/Francine Pyne
Prof. Crater Alfred Ryder
Green Bruce Watson
Darnell Michael Zaslow

Director: Marc Daniels

Charlie X

w D.C. Fontana, *story by* Gene Roddenberry
The petulance of a young passenger struggling to cope with human emotions develops into a trial of wills with Kirk which threatens the safety of the *Enterprise*.
Charlie Evans Robert Walker
Thasian Abraham Sofaer

Director: Lawrence Dobkin

Where No Man Has Gone Before

w Samuel A. Peeples
The *Enterprise* is ordered beyond the limits of explored space and after penetrating a strange force-field, two crew members become god-like beings.
Lt. Cmdr. Gary Mitchell Gary Lockwood
Dr. Elizabeth Dehner Sally Kellerman
Dr. Piper Paul Fix
Lt. Alden Lloyd Haynes

Lt. Lee Kelso Paul Carr
Yeoman Smith Andrea Dromm

Director: James Goldstone

The Naked Time

w John D.F. Black
The *Enterprise* is assigned to observe the disintegration of a doomed planet. But a mystery virus robs the crew of their emotional control and the ship hurtles toward the planet—and certain destruction.
Riley Bruce Hyde
Tormolen Stewart Moss
Dr. Harrison John Bellah
Lt. Brent Frank da Vinci
Singing crewman William Knight

Director: Marc Daniels

The Enemy Within

w Richard Matheson
The roles of good and evil are thrown into stark relief when a transporter malfunction splits Kirk into two people—one heroic and good, the other aggressive and negative.
Lt. John Farrell Jim Goodwin
Technician Fisher Edward Madden
Technician Wilson Garland Thompson

Director: Leo Penn

Mudd's Women

w Stephen Kandel, *story by* Gene Roddenberry
Kirk and his crew have to make room for Harry Mudd and his illicit human cargo of three gorgeous girls.
Mudd Roger C. Carmel
Magda Susan Denberg
Ruth Maggie Thrett
Eve Karen Steele
Ben Childress Gene Dynarski

Director: Harvey Hart

What Are Little Girls Made Of?

w Robert Bloch
Crazed Dr. Korby dreams of conquest with his race of androids, including a duplicate of Kirk.
Dr. Roger Korby Michael Strong
Andrea Sherry Jackson
Ruk Ted Cassidy
Dr. Brown Harry Basch

Director: James Goldstone

Miri

w Adrian Spies
The *Enterprise* crew beams down to a planet inhabited by a Peter Pan race who look like children but are 300 years old. (First screened in an "abridged" form in the U.K..)
Miri Kim Darby
Jahn Michael J. Pollard
Lt. Farrell Jim Goodwin
"Creatures" Ed McCready

Director: Vincent McEveety

Dagger of the Mind

w S. Bar-David (alias Shimon Wincelberg)
Pressed by nagging doubts over a crate received from the penal colony, Tantalus, Kirk probes further and uncovers a cruel and dangerous conspiracy.
Dr. Helen Noel Marianna Hill
Dr. Simon Van Gelder Morgan Woodward
Dr. Tristan Adams James Gregory
Lethe Susanne Wasson

Director: Vincent McEveety

The Corbomite Maneuver

w Jerry Sohl
Threatened by a horrifying alien's all-powerful space craft, Kirk plays a tactical bluff to save his ship from destruction—and then discovers his adversary is not what he seems . . .
Lt. Bailey Anthony Call
Balok Clint Howard

Director: Joseph Sargent

The Menagerie

w Gene Roddenberry *(a 2-part story)*
A mutinous Spock kidnaps his former commanding officer Capt. Pike and sets the *Enterprise* on a course for the forbidden planet Talos IV. In Part 2, Spock submits to a court martial and tells the bizarre story of Captain Pike's journey to Talos IV 13 years before. (This Hugo Award-winning story used footage from *Star Trek*'s original pilot, "The Cage.")
Capt. Pike Jeffrey Hunter/Sean Kenney
Commodore Mendez Malachi Throne
Vina Susan Oliver
The Keeper Meg Wyllie
Miss Piper Julie Parrish
Dr. Phillip Boyce John Hoyt
Number One M. Leigh Hudec *(Majel Barrett)*
Yeoman Colt Laurel Goodwin
Jose Tyler Peter Duryea
CPO Garrison Adam Roarke

Directors: Marc Daniels *(Part 1)*, Robert Butler *(Part 2)*

The Conscience of the King

w Barry Trivers
The arrival of a troupe of actors raises the curtain on the last scene of a drama that began 20 years before with the slaughter of innocents, by Kodos the Executioner.
Dr. Leighton William Sargent
Anton Karidian (Kodos) Arnold Moss
Lenore Barbara Anderson
Lt. Kevin Riley Bruce Hyde

Director: Gerd Oswald

Balance of Terror

w Paul Schneider
Kirk wages a battle of wits and courage with a Romulan ship's commander.
Lt. Andrew Stiles Paul Comi
Romulan commander Mark Lenard
Centurion John Warburton
Decius Lawrence Montaigne
Angela Martine Barbara Baldavin

Director: Vincent McEveety

Shore Leave

w Theodore Sturgeon
The crew look forward to a well-earned rest on a beautiful planet but pleasure turns to terror as they encounter people and images from their past—including a ferocious Samurai warrior and a large white rabbit!
Finnegan Bruce Mars
Lt. Rodriguez Perry Lopez
Tonia Barrows Emily Banks
Ruth Shirley Bonne
Caretaker Oliver McGowan

Director: Robert Sparr

The Galileo Seven

w Oliver Crawford & S. Bar David *(alias Shimon Wincelberg), story by* Oliver Crawford
Mr. Spock's first independent command looks like it may be his last when his shuttle becomes marooned on Taurus II where the crew comes under attack from its ape-like inhabitants.
High Commissioner Ferris John Crawford
Gaetano Peter Marko
Latimer Rees Vaughn
Lt. Boma Don Marshall
Lt. Commander Kelowitz Grant Woods

Director: Robert Gist

The Squire of Gothos

w Paul Schneider
Kirk is forced to play a deadly game with an urbane alien maniac with the fate of the *Enterprise* at stake. (The character of Trelane was the inspiration for *Next Generation*'s guest pest, Q.)
Yeoman Teresa Ross Venita Wolf
General Trelane William Campbell
Lt. DeSalle Michael Barrier
Lt. Jaeger Richard Carlyle
Mother's voice Barbara Babcock
Father's voice James Doohan

Director: Don McDougall

Arena

w Gene L. Coon, *story by* Fredric Brown
After the relentless pursuit of a treacherous alien vessel, Kirk must fight the rival commander—a godzilla-like creature called Gorn—in single combat.
Lt. O'Herlihy Jerry Ayres
Metron Carole Shelyne
DePaul Sean Kenny

Director: Joseph Pevney

Tomorrow Is Yesterday

w D.C. Fontana
A freak of gravity propels the *Enterprise* back into the past where it becomes a UFO of the 1960s, and beams aboard a fighter pilot.
Major Christopher Roger Perry
Col. Fellini Ed Peck
Crew woman Sherri Townsend
Air policeman Jim Spencer

Director: Michael O'Herlihy

Court Martial

w Don Mankiewicz & Steven Carabatsos, *story by* Steven Carabatsos
Charged with causing the death of a missing officer, Kirk is put on trial, but finds his version of the events is at odds with the computer record—and the computer doesn't lie.
Portmaster Stone Percy Rodriguez
Lt. Areel Shaw Joan Marshall
Samuel T. Cogley Elisha Cook
Lt. Cmdr. Finney Richard Webb
Jamie Finney Alice Rawlings

Director: Marc Daniels

The Return of the Archons

w Boris Sobelman, *story by* Gene Roddenberry
On the planet Beta 3000, Kirk encounters a pecu-
liarly placid community ruled by Landru—a baleful computer deity.
Landru Charles McAulay
Reger Harry Townes
Tula Brioni Farrell
Marplon Torin Thatcher
Tamar John Lormer
Hacom Morgan Farley

Director: Joseph Pevney

Space Speed

w Carey Wilbur & Gene L. Coon, *story by* Gene L. Coon
The *Enterprise* encounters a derelict spaceship carrying the survivors of a past civilization—a race of supermen, lead by the wrathful Kahn. (The character was revived again in the second Star Trek feature film *The Wrath of Kahn.*)
Kahn Ricardo Montalban
Lt. Marla McGivers Madlyn Rhue
Lt. Spinelli Blaisdell Makee
Joaquin Mark Tobin
Crew woman Kathy Ahart

Director: Marc Daniels

A Taste of Armageddon

w Robert Hamner & Gene L. Coon, *story by* Robert Hamner
Kirk and Spock take an Earth ambassador to a distant planet that has been engaged in a 500-year-long war, waged at long distance by computer.
Ambassador Fox Gene Lyons
Anan 7 David Opatoshu
Mea 3 Barbara Babcock
Star 6 Robert Sampson
Lt. DePaul Sean Kenny
Lt. Galloway David L. Ross

Director: Joseph Pevney

This Side of Paradise

w D.C. Fontana, *story by* Nathan Butler (*alias* Jerry Sohl) & D.C. Fontana
Seeking survivors on a planet exposed to deadly rays, Kirk is astounded to find the colonists alive and content, but he is enraged at the insidious effect their behavior has on his crew—even Spock.
Elias Sandaval Frank Overton
Leila Jill Ireland
Lt. Cmdr. Kelowitz Grant Woods
Lt. DeSalle Michael Barrier

Director: Ralph Senensky

The Devil in the Dark

w Gene L. Coon
Kirk confronts an unknown monster that has been hideously destroying workers on the mining colony of Janus. (Notable for Spock's mind-meld with the "monster," Horta.)
Chief Engineer Vanderberg Ken Lynch
Lt. Cmdr. Giotto Barry Russo
Horta Janos Prohaska
Ed Appel Brad Weston

Director: Joseph Pevney

Errand of Mercy

w Gene L. Coon
Kirk tries to warn the rulers of the planet Organia of the threat of Klingon invasion, but finds them curiously indifferent to his efforts.
Ayelborne Jon Abbott
Trefayne David Hillary Hughes
Claymore Peter Brocco
Cmdr. Kor John Colicos

Director: John Newland

The Alternative Factor

w Don Ingalls
An immense magnetic phenomenon fractures space from end to end and Kirk and crew are bound up in the struggle of a crazed time traveler.
Lazarus Robert Brown
Lt. Charlene Masters Janet MacLachlen
Commodore Barstow Richard Derr
Lt. Lesley Eddie Paskey
Assistant Engineer Arch Whiting

Director: Gerd Oswald

The City on the Edge of Forever

w Harlan Ellison
When a time vortex sweeps a deranged McCoy back to New York in the 1920s, Kirk and Spock follow him and Kirk finds himself faced with the agonizing choice of preserving something fine in the past and so changing history for the worse, or letting events take their natural course. (Hugo Award winner.)
Sister Edith Keeler Joan Collins
Lt. Galloway David L. Ross
Rodent John Harmon

Director: Joseph Pevney

Operation—Annihilate!

w Steven Carabatsos
A spaceship hurtling to the sun, her crew preferring the holocaust to the horror that befell them, warns Kirk of danger on the planet Deneva—a parasitic invader that drives its hosts insane, and that attacks Spock.
Aurelan Kirk Joan Swift
Peter Kirk Craig Hundley
Kartan Dave Armstrong
Yeoman Zahra Jamal Maurishka Taliferro
Denevans Fred Carson, Jerry Catron

Director: Herschel Daugherty

Season Two
26 episodes

Amok Time

w Theodore Sturgeon
When Spock is gripped by the mind-bending Vulcan mating drive, Kirk accompanies him to his home planet where he finds he must fight his friend in a contest to the death.
T'Pring Arlene Martel
T'Pau Celia Lovsky
Stonn Lawrence Montaigne
Admiral Komack Byron Morrow

Director: Joseph Pevney

Who Mourns for Adonais?

w Gene L. Coon & Gilbert Ralston
A huge hand reaches out from the heavens and seizes the *Enterprise*. Kirk reaches Olympian heights in his defiance of the god-like being who demands his homage.
Apollo Michael Forest
Carolyn Leslie Parrish
Lt. Kyle John Winston

Director: Marc Daniels

The Changeling

w John Meredyth Lucas
Nomad, an ancient man-made exterminator of imperfect life forms, comes aboard the *Enterprise* and the ship is threatened with destruction until Kirk succeeds in outwitting the robot probe.
Voice of Nomad Vic Perrin
Mr. Singh Blaisdell Makee
Astrochemist Barbara Gates
Security guard Arnold Lessing

Director: Marc Daniels

Mirror, Mirror

w Jerome Bixby
An ion storm during transportation hurls Kirk and three officers into a parallel universe, while their counterparts materialize aboard the *Enterprise*.
Marlena Barbara Luna
Tharn Vic Perrin
Lt. Kyle John Winston
Kirk's henchman Peter Kellett

Director: Marc Daniels

The Apple

w Max Erlichn *&* Gene L. Coon
Kirk discovers a Garden of Eden where life could not be more perfect—or less like living. Someone must play the snake to free the people of Paradise from innocence and their ruler Vaal.
Yeoman Martha Landon Celeste Yarnall
Akuta Keith Andes
Makora David Soul
Sayana Shari Nims

Director: Joseph Pevney

The Doomsday Machine

w Norman Spinrad
The *Enterprise* is nearly destroyed by a rampaging "doomsday machine" after rescuing Commodore Decker from the disabled starship, *Constellation*.
Commodore Decker William Windom
Elliot John Copage
Lt. Palmer Elizabeth Rogers
Washburn Richard Compton

Director: Marc Daniels

Catspaw

w Robert Block *&* D.C. Fontana
The *Enterprise* is trapped in a cosmic cauldron and the landing party of Pirus VI becomes the "guests" of Korob and Sylvia, weavers of sinister spells.
Korob Theo Marcuse
Sylvia Antoinette Bower
Lt. DeSalle Michael Barrier

Director: Joseph Pevney

I, Mudd

w Stephen Kandel *&* David Gerrold
Kirk and his crew are abducted to a planet where space scoundrel Harry Mudd seems to be living a life of ease with beautiful androids programmed to satisfy his every desire. But Harry wants his freedom . . .
Mudd Roger C. Carmel
Norman Richard Tatro
Stella Mudd Kay Elliot

Director: Marc Daniels

Metamorphosis

w Gene L. Coon
A shuttlecraft carrying Kirk, Spock and a critically ill Federation Commissioner is held by a mysterious force.
Cochrane Glenn Corbett
Commissioner Nancy Hedford Elinor Donahue
Voice of companion Majel Barrett

Director: Ralph Senensky

Journey to Babel

w D.C. Fontana
The *Enterprise* takes charge of a group of feuding Federation members and Spock meets again the father from whom he parted in bitterness 18 years before.
Sarek Mark Lenard
Amanda Jane Wyatt
Thelev William O'Connell
Shras Reggie Nalder

Director: Joseph Pevney

Friday's Child

w D.C. Fontana
Kirk inadvertently breaks a tribal taboo on the planet Capella and the crew has to flee—along with the chief's wife.
Eleen Julie Newmar
Kras Tige Andrews
Maab Michael Dante
Keel Cal Bolder

Director: Joseph Pevney

The Deadly Years

w David P. Harmon
On a visit to the planet Gamma Hydra IV, Kirk, Spock, Scott and McCoy pick up a strange infection that causes them to age rapidly.
Commodore Stocker Charles Drake
Janet Wallace Sarah Marshall
Lt. Arlene Galway Beverly Washburn
Robert Johnson Felix Locher

Director: Joseph Pevney

Obsession

w Art Wallace
For the second time in his career, Kirk encounters a deadly gaseous creature that kills two of his crew, and he disregards vital orders in a fanatical bid to destroy it and ease his conscience.
Ensign Rizzo Jeffrey Ayres
Ensign Garrovick Stephen Brooks

Director: Ralph Senensky

Wolf in the Fold

w Robert Bloch
All the evidence points to Scotty as having savagely slain three women, until Kirk isolates the real culprit—the evil spirit of Jack the Ripper.
Hengist John Fiedler
Jaris Charles Macaulay
Sybo Pilar Seurat
Tark Joseph Bernard
Morla Charles Dierkop

Director: Joseph Pevney

The Trouble with Tribbles

w David Gerrold
The *Enterprise* crew finds its troubles multiplying—in the cuddly, purring form of Cyrano Jones's tiny creatures, the tribbles.
Cyrano Jones Stanley Adams
Nilz Barris William Schallert
Koloth William Campbell
Mr. Lurry Whit Bissell

Director: Joseph Pevney

The Gamesters of Triskelion

w Margaret Armen
Kirk, Uhura and Chekov are spirited to a planet where they are trained to fight for the amusement of the planet's rulers.
Galt Joseph Ruskin
Shahna Angelique Pettyjohn
Lars Steven Sandor
Ensign Jana Haines Victoria George

Director: Gene Nelson

A Piece of the Action

w David Harmon & Gene L. Coon, *story by* David Harmon
Investigating the disappearance of a Federation starship 100 years earlier, the crew lands on a remote planet resembling Prohibition-era Chicago.
Bela Anthony Caruso
Krako Vic Tayback
Kalo Lee Delano
Zabo Steve Marlo
Tepo John Harmon

Director: James Komack

The Immunity Syndrome

w Robert Sabaroff
The *Enterprise* is confronted by a 1000-mile-wide amoeba-like creature and Spock embarks on a suicide mission.

Lt. Kyle John Winston

Director: Joseph Pevney

A Private Little War

w Gene Roddenberry, *story by* Jud Crucis
Starfleet orders specifically forbid intervention in the evolution of other races, but when the Klingons arm natives on a primitive planet, Kirk takes the grave risk of running guns to rival tribes to maintain the balance of power.
Nona Nancy Kovak
Tyree Michael Witney
Krell Ned Romero
Mugato Janos Prohaska

Director: Marc Daniels

Return to Tomorrow

w John Kingsbridge (*alias* Gene Roddenberry), *story by* John T. Dugan
The *Enterprise* is lured a thousand light-years beyond explored space by a strange distress call from a seemingly lifeless world and Kirk and Spock find themselves playing hosts to the minds of an advanced civilization.
Ann Mulhall Diana Muldaur

Director: Ralph Senensky

Patterns of Force

w John Meredyth Lucas
Kirk and Spock land on a backwood planet with a Nazi-type military regime.
Melakon Skip Homeier
Isak Richard Evans
Daras Valora Noland
Gill David Brian
Abrom William Wintersole
SS major Gilbert Green

Director: Vincent McEveety

By Any Other Name

w Jerome Bixby & D.C. Fontana, *story by* Jerome Bixby
Kirk and his crew are hijacked by Andromedan monsters intent on destroying all human existence. Masters of metabolism, the many-limbed monsters fortunately assume the frailty of human form to achieve their aims.
Rojan Warren Stevens
Kelinda Barbara Bouchet
Hanar Stewart Moss
Yeoman Leslie Thompson Julie Cobb
Lt. Shea Carl Byrd

Director: Marc Daniels

The Omega Glory

w Gene Roddenberry
"If you've come aboard, you're dead men—don't go back to your starship." After finding a sinister warning in a deserted, aimlessly orbiting starship, the U.S.S. *Exeter*, Kirk and his boarding party beam down to the planet Omega where they meet a strange man who believes he has found the secret of immortality.
Capt. Tracey Morgan Woodward
Cloud William Roy Jensen
Lt. Galloway David L. Ross
Dr. Carter Ed McCready
Sirah Irene Kelly

Director: Vincent McEveety

The Ultimate Computer

w D.C. Fontana, *story by* Lawrence N. Wolfe
M5, a huge computer, is installed in the *Enterprise* in place of the human crew. But it goes beserk and Starfleet Command orders its other starships to "Destroy the *Enterprise*!"
Dr. Richard Daystrom William Marshall
Commodore Wesley Barry Russo
Voice of M5 James Doohan

Director: John Meredyth Lucas

Bread and Circuses

w Gene L. Coon & Gene Roddenberry
Kirk is forced into furious combat to save his crew from being butchered on a planet whose society is just like that of ancient Rome with its gladiators and arena.
Merik William Smithers
Claudius Logan Ramsey
Septimus Ian Wolfe
Drusilla Lois Jewell
Flavius Rhodes Reason

Director: Ralph Senensky

Assignment: Earth

w Art Wallace, *story by* Gene Roddenberry & Art Wallace
Cosmic records say that the old world narrowly escaped disaster in 1968 and the *Enterprise* is assigned to discover what happened. But the mission assumes more than academic interest when the mysterious Gary Seven is beamed aboard. (Unsuccessful pilot for a new series.)
Gary Seven Robert Lansing
Roberta Lincoln Terri Garr

Director: Marc Daniels

Season Three
24 episodes

Spock's Brain

w Lee Cronin (*alias* Gene L. Coon)
A beautiful and mysterious woman renders Spock the victim of a critical brain-drain. Kirk and McCoy have just 24 hours to restore his brain to his body.
Kara Marj Dusay

Director: Marc Daniels

The Enterprise Incident

w D.C. Fontana
To the astonishment of his own crew—including Spock—Kirk orders his ship to invade the Romulan neutral zone where it is captured and threatened with confiscation.
Romulan commander Joanne Linville

Director: John Meredyth Lucas

The Paradise Syndrome

w Margaret Armen
Oblivious to his duties, Kirk takes a wife and idles time away while Spock tries to divert a huge asteroid hurtling on a collision course.
Miramanee Sabrina Scharf
Salish Rudy Solari

Director: Jud Taylor

And the Children Shall Lead

w Edward J. Lakso
Investigating a disaster call from the planet Triacus, Kirk is puzzled to find children playing beside the sprawled bodies of their dead parents. Under the influence of the alien Gorgan, the children play on the hidden fears of the crew.
Gorgan Melvin Belli
Tommy Starnes Craig Hundley
Professor Starnes James Wellman

Director: Marvin Chomsky

Is There in Truth No Beauty?

w Jean Lisette Aroeste
Special visors are issued to the *Enterprise* officers for the arrival of the Medusan ambassador, emissary of a gentle race but so hideous in appearance that one look can drive a man mad. Spock unfortunately gazes on the Medusan—and only a Vulcan mind-link can save him.
Dr. Miranda Jones Diana Muldaur
Lawrence Marvick David Frankham

Director: Ralph Senensky

Spectre of the Gun

w Lee Cronin (*alias* Gene L. Coon)
As a result of Kirk's persistence in exploring a forbidden planet, he, Chekov, Spock and McCoy are trapped in a reconstruction of the Gunfight at the OK Corral.
Sylvia Bonnie Beecher
Wyatt Earp Ron Soble
Morgan Earp Rex Holman
Doc Holliday Sam Gilman
Johnny Behan Bill Zuckert
Melkotian voice Abraham Sofaer

Director: Vincent McEveety

Day of the Dove

w Jerome Bixby
An intangible monster that feeds upon hatred insidiously invades the *Enterprise*, bringing the ship to the brink of destruction as crew and Klingons clash in blind fury, until Kirk finds a "peaceful" solution.
Kang Michael Ansara
Mara Susan Howard
Lt. Johnson David L. Ross

Director: Marvin Chomsky

For the World Is Hollow and I Have Touched the Sky

w Rik Vollaerts
A stricken McCoy, who learns he has only one year to live, submits to electronic enslavement by the alien queen of a mysterious asteroid speeding toward a populated planet and certain doom.
Natira Kate Woodville

Director: Tony Leader

The Tholian Web

w Judy Burns & Chet Richards
While Kirk finds himself a lonely passenger aboard the devastated hulk of the Starship *Defiant*, his own vessel lies floundering in another universe, slowly being strangled by a web of pure energy.
(No guest cast)

Director: Herb Wallerstein

Plato's Stepchildren

w Meyer Dolinsky
Responding to a distress call from the planet Platonius, *Enterprise* officers are enslaved by a creature with advanced telepathic powers. (This episode has become famous for featuring American television's first inter-racial kiss, between Kirk and Uhura.)
Alexander Michael Dunn

Parmen Liam Sullivan
Philana Barbara Babcock

Director: David Alexander

Wink of an Eye

w Arthur Heinemann, *story by* Lee Cronin (*alias* Gene L. Coon)
A strange high-pitched hum, noticed on the planet Scalos, pervades the *Enterprise*, intangible evidence of a takeover by the rapid-moving Scalosian Queen Deela—to whom every second is like an hour.
Deela Kathie Brown
Rael Jason Evers
Compton Geoffrey Binney
Ekor Erik Holland

Director: Jud Taylor

The Empath

w Joyce Muskat
On a doomed planet, Kirk, Spock and McCoy are tortured by powerful aliens who are testing the capacity for self-sacrifice and compassion of a frail, mute girl called Gem, to determine whether her empathic species should be saved.
Gem Kathryn Hays
Lal Alan Bergman
Thann Willard Sage

Director: John Erman

Elaan of Troyius

w John Meredyth Lucas
A clash with the Klingons is the least of Kirk's worries as he tries to cope with the peculiar potency of an alien woman's tears.
Elaan France Nuyen
Lord Petri Jay Robertson
Kryton Tony Young
Watson Victor Brandt
Evans Lee Duncan

Director: John Meredyth Lucas

Whom Gods Destroy

w Lee Erwin, *story by* Jerry Sohl & Lee Erwin
Journeying to an asylum planet with a new cure for mental illness, Kirk and Spock are threatened by Garth, a madman with the ability to change his form, who wants to conquer the universe, using an "ultimate" explosive.
Garth of Izar Steve Ihnat
Marta Yvonne Craig
Donald Cory Keye Luke
Andorian Richard Geary
Tellarite Gary Downey

Director: Herb Wallerstein

Let That Be Your Last Battlefield

w Oliver Crawford, *story by* Lee Cronin (*alias* Gene L. Coon)
Two warring aliens carry a 50,000-year conflict on to the *Enterprise* and Kirk orders the destruction of his own ship in an extreme bid to end it.
Lokai Lou Antonio
Bele Frank Gorshin

Director: Jud Taylor

The Mark of Gideon

w George F. Slavin & Stanley Adams
Kirk is lured on to a fake—and deserted—*Enterprise* where he feels the shattering experience of the tormented inhabitants of the planet Gideon.
Odona Sharon Acker
Hodin David Hurst
Krodak Gene Dynarski
Admiral Fitzgerald Richard Derr

Director: Jud Taylor

That Which Survives

w John Meredyth Lucas, *story by* D.C. Fontana
Stranded on a hostile planet after the *Enterprise* is flung a thousand light-years away, Kirk and McCoy face starvation and a deadly enemy. It hardly seems the time for childish games . . .
Lt. D'Amato Arthur Batanides
Lt. Rahda Naomi Pollack
Losira Lee Meriwether

Director: Herb Wallerstein

The Lights of Zetar

w Jeremy Tarcher & Shari Lewis
In the vicinity of Memory Alpha, Lt. Mira Romaine proves exceedingly attractive to Scotty—and to some very colorful bodysnatchers.
Lt. Mira Romaine Jan Shutan
Lt. Kyle John Winston
Technician Libby Erwin

Director: Herb Kenwith

Requiem for Methuselah

w Jerome Bixby
The *Enterprise* crew meets a powerful alien who claims to be immortal and to have lived his life as a series of famous Earth figures.
Flint James Daly
Reena Louise Sorel

Director: Murray Golden

The Way to Eden

w Arthur Heinemann, *story by* Michael Richards (*alias* D.C. Fontana) & Arthur Heinemann
A band of space hippies boards the *Enterprise* en route to the mythical planet of Eden. The normally "square" Spock finds a rapport with them, but Kirk is short on peace, love and understanding.
Dr. Sevrin Skip Homeier
Adam Charles Napier
Irina Mary-Linda Rapelye
Tongo Rad Victor Brandt
Lt. Palmer Elizabeth Rogers
Mavig Deborah Downey

Director: David Alexander

The Cloud Minders

w Margaret Armen, *story by* David Gerrold & Oliver Crawford
A mercy mission to Stratos City leads to Kirk's involvement in a slave rebellion, as he tries to make both sides see reason.
Plasus Jeff Corey
Vanna Charlene Polite
Droxine Diana Ewing

Director: Jud Taylor

The Savage Curtain

w Gene Roddenberry & Arthur Heinemann, *story by* Gene Roddenberry
Kirk and Spock are teamed with their historical heroes against the most wicked men in history in a bizarre test of good versus evil.
Abraham Lincoln Lee Bergere
Surak Barry Atwater
Col. Green Phillip Pine
Ghengis Khan Nathan Yung
Zora Carol Daniels DeMent
Kahless Robert Herron

Director: Herschel Daughtery

All Our Yesterdays

w Jean Lisette Aroeste
An extraordinary device in the library of a doomed planet sends Kirk, McCoy and Spock into different eras of Earth's past.
Atoz Ian Wolfe
Zarabeth Mariette Hartley
Woman Anna Karen

Director: Marvin Chomsky

Turnabout Intruder

w Arthur Singer, *story by* Gene Roddenberry
Kirk's mind is transferred to the body of Dr. Janice
Lester—while she takes over the *Enterprise* as the
Captain.
Dr. Janice Lester Sandra Smith
Dr. Coleman Harry Landers
Angela Barbara Baldavin

Director: Herb Wallerstein

The BBC first screened *Star Trek* in four seasons
(interspersed with repeats), which were as follows:

U.K. Series One
(12 July–27 December 1969)
Where No Man Has Gone Before
The Naked Time
The City on the Edge of Forever
A Taste of Armageddon
Mudd's Women
Tomorrow Is Yesterday
The Menagerie (a 2-part story)
The Devil in the Dark
Charlie X
Shore Leave
Space Seed
The Man Trap
Dagger of the Mind
The Corbomite Maneuver
Balance of Terror
The Squire of Gothos
What Are Little Girls Made Of?
Arena
The Return of the Archons
This Side of Paradise
The Doomsday Machine
Errand of Mercy
The Conscience of the King
The Galileo Seven

U.K. Series Two
(6 April–7 September 1970)
Court Martial
The Enemy Within
Catspaw
Who Mourns for Adonais?
The Apple
Metamorphosis
Wolf in the Fold

The Changeling
The Trouble with Tribbles
Bread and Circuses
Journey to Babel
The Deadly Years
A Private Little War
Obsession
By Any Other Name
I, Mudd
Patterns of Force
The Immunity Syndrome
Return to Tomorrow
The Omega Glory
A Piece of the Action

U.K. Series Three
(7 October 1970–10 February 1971)
The Ultimate Computer
Friday's Child
Assignment: Earth
Mirror, Mirror
The Gamesters of Triskelion
Amok Time
Miri
Operation—Annihilate
The Paradise Syndrome
Requiem for Methuselah
All Our Yesterdays
Day of the Dove
The Way to Eden
Let That Be Your Last Battlefield
Wink of an Eye
The Cloud Minders

U.K. Series Four
(15 September–15 December 1971)
Spectre of the Gun
Elaan of Troyius
The Enterprise Incident
And the Children Shall Lead
Spock's Brain
Is There in Truth No Beauty?
For the World Is Hollow and
I Have Touched the Sky
That Which Survives
The Mark of Gideon
The Lights of Zetar
The Savage Curtain
The Tholian Web
The Alternative Factor
Turnabout Intruder

STAR TREK:
THE NEXT GENERATION

"Let's see what's out there . . ."

However boldly you go about it, going where others have gone before does have its problems.
The history of film and TV is littered with failed re-makes, revivals and sequels that probably
seemed like good ideas at the time.

Star Trek: The Next Generation had to do more than just live up to the memory of its ancestor; it also had to confront the prejudices of entrenched Trekkies who brought some 20 years' faithful devotion with them. This new sci-fi show had to deal with the laws of physics and the lore of *Star Trek*—and it could not change either of them!

If the diehards had had their way, the new series might never have got off the ground. But Gene Roddenberry's *Next Generation* not only flew—it breathed new life into the *Star Trek* dynasty and, more significantly, revitalized the whole TV science fiction genre, which had become commercially tainted.

Consistently among the top ten hour-long syndicated series on U.S. television, and *the* number one show among men aged 18–49, it was an ad executive's demographic dream. And when the profits started to stack up alongside the plaudits, Hollywood took note.

Star Trek: The Next Generation achieved all of this by remaining true to Roddenberry's optimistic vision of the future. But while the philosophy endured, the style was vastly improved. With budgets of around $1.5 million an episode, this is TV with a feature film look. Its Emmy Award–winning effects are astonishingly good and the permanent sets that spanned two huge soundstages at Paramount were packed with intricate detail.

Next Generation is set some 78 years after the original mission. The new *Enterprise*, NCC 1701-D, is eight times the size of the old one, with a complement of 1012 crew and their families.

And with the new ship came a new cast and a new captain, the somewhat aloof Frenchman Jean-Luc Picard. Played by English Shakespearean actor Patrick Stewart, Picard is an older, balder man than Kirk, and less impulsive, less headstrong. Stewart, a Yorkshireman, was virtually unknown in America. In Britain he had played Sejanus in the BBC's *I, Claudius* and had starred as psychiatrist Eddie Roebuck in a 1981 series, *Maybury*. *Star Trek* has turned him into a TV icon.

Heading up a strong supporting cast is Jonathan Frakes as Picard's First Officer, Riker, the Kirk-style man of action. The Chief Medical Officer is a woman, Dr. Beverly Crusher (played by acting coach and choreographer Gates McFadden) and there's a healer of minds aboard, too—the telepathic, half-human, half-Betazoid ship's counselor Deanna Troi (played by Londoner Marina Sirtis who once actually auditioned for the part of Dayna in *Blake's 7*).

Denise Crosby lasted one season as security chief Tasha Yar (though she subsequently guested both as Tasha and her Romulan daughter Sela). Wil Wheaton literally grew into his role as Dr. Crusher's teenage prodigy of a son, Wesley, LeVar Burton pulled on a special VISOR (Visual, Instrument and Sight Organ Replacement) to play the blind navigator (later chief engineer) Geordi La Forge and Michael Dorn learned to love prosthetics as the ship's Klingon officer Lt. Worf, a character forever trying to reconcile his warrior heritage with Starfleet-imposed discipline.

And with no Spock aboard, the logical voice was an android Science Officer, Data, played by Broadway actor Brent Spiner. A pasty-faced 24th-century Pinocchio, Data is an android who dreams of becoming human and his efforts to grasp the nuances of human behavior provide some of the series' lightest and most poignant moments.

Also along for the ride were Diana Muldaur as Dr. Crusher's second season replacement, the slightly abrasive Dr. Kate Pulaski, and a couple of semi-regulars, Irish actor Colm Meaney as Transporter Chief Miles O'Brien who later jumped ship to join *Deep Space Nine*, and Whoopi Goldberg who dispensed cocktails and wisdom as the enigmatic Ten Forward barmaid Guinan. There was also a short-lived role for Michelle Forbes as a feisty Bajoran officer, Ensign Ro Laren.

It's very much an ensemble affair and this series was not troubled by the well-documented friction that existed among the original *Trek* cast.

With the Klingons and the Federation now allies, *The Next Generation* needed to find new villains. It immediately introduced us to Q, an omnipotent prankster who regularly returned to plague the crew in general and Picard in particular. Then there were the lascivious, avaricious Ferengi, the lizard-necked militaristic regime of the Cardassians and the Borg—a seemingly unstoppable cybernetic super-race who subjugated, then assimilated all other races into their insect-like hive culture. And, of course, those shoulder-padded galactic power-dressers, the Romulans, also returned.

Five star veterans of the original Trek have also left their imprint on the Next Generation. DeForest Kelley hobbled down a corridor in a pair of appalling bell-bottoms to give the new *Enterprise* the blessing of the venerable Dr. McCoy; Majel Barrett has been a recurring guest as Troi's amorous mother, Lwaxana, Mark Lenard twice reprised his role as Spock's father, Sarek, Leonard Nimoy returned as Spock in the two-part Season Five story "Unification," and James Doohan (Scotty) was found hidden in a transporter circuit in the sixth season's "Relics."

As the series has progressed, Jonathan Frakes, Patrick Stewart, LeVar Burton and Gates McFadden have all slipped behind the cameras to direct episodes, as has Leonard Nimoy's son Adam.

With the death of Gene Roddenberry in October 1991, custody of the *Star Trek* flame passed fully into the hands of the series' executive producers, Rick Berman and Michael Piller. Besides taking *Next Generation* to seven seasons before hitting the movie trail in November 1994 with *Star Trek: Generations* (linking classic *Trek* cast with the new crew, and killing off Captain Kirk!), they also expanded the *Trek* universe into *Star Trek: Deep Space Nine* and the new baby, *Star Trek: Voyager*.

In the tradition of its predecessor, *Next Generation* continued to be a vehicle for issues, from AIDS to terrorism, from single-parent families to the treatment of political prisoners.

Over the course of seven years, the series has shifted between comedy, drama, action and adventure, between epic conflict and character-driven installments. There have been a few stinkers, but in its finest hours, the series has produced some stunning television. My recommended viewing are "11001001" (Season One), "The Measure of a Man" and "Q Who" (Season Two), "Yesterday's Enterprise," "Sins of the Father" and "Best of Both Worlds" (Season Three), "First Contact" (Season Four)—just for Bebe Neuwirth!, "Darmok" (Season Five), "Relics," "Chain of Command" and "Tapestry" (Season Six), also "Schisms" (Season Six)—just for Data's "Ode to Spot"—and the epic finale "All Good Things."

Although the final episode neatly bookends the series, it's not the end of the story. *Star Trek: Generations*, the seventh *Trek* movie, but the first to feature the *TNG* crew, launched Picard's team into a continuing mission on the big screen. That one killed off Captain Kirk *and* wrote off Picard's *Enterprise* in a spectacular crash landing. The excellent eighth movie, 1996's *Star Trek: First Contact*, directed by Jonathan Frakes, introduced another new *Enterprise* and brought back the Borg, in a time-travel tale that elegantly played on the themes of the "Best of Both Worlds" episodes and tossed in a touch of Moby Dick. Here's to the next one.

REGULAR CAST
Captain Jean-Luc Picard Patrick Stewart
Commander William T. Riker Jonathan Frakes
Lt. Cmdr. Data Brent Spiner *Lt. Geordi La Forge* LeVar Burton
Lt. Worf Michael Dorn *Dr. Beverly Crusher* Gates McFadden (*except Season Two*)
Counsellor Deanna Troi Marina Sirtis
Lt. Tasha Yar Denise Crosby (*Season One only*)
Ensign Wesley Crusher Wil Wheaton (*to Season Four only*)
Dr. Kate Pulaski Diana Muldaur (*Season Two only*)
Recurring regulars: Guinan Whoopi Goldberg (*from Season Two*)
Chief Miles O'Brien Colm Meaney (*episodes as indicated*)
Also: Computer voice Majel Barrett

Creator/Executive producer: Gene Roddenberry
Executive producers: Rick Berman, Michael Piller, Jeri Taylor
Producers: Various, including Robert Justman, Maurice Hurley, Hans Beimler, Richard Manning, Ira Steven Behr, Herbert J. Wright, Peter Lauritson, David Livingston, Ronald D. Moore, Brannon Braga, Joe Menosky
Production designers: Herman Zimmerman, Richard James (*from Season Two*)
Music: Jerry Goldsmith, Alexander Courage (*main title theme*), Dennis McCarthy, Ron Jones, Jay Chattaway (*from Season Three*)

A Paramount Pictures Production
176 color episodes*, 50 minutes (except where stated)
U.S. premiere: 26 September 1987
U.K. premiere: 26 September 1990 (BBC2)
From Season Four, U.K. first runs have all been on Sky One
Last first-run episode: 29 January 1995 (Sky One)

*178 episodes if first story, "Encounter at Farpoint," and last, "All Good Things," are shown as two-parters.

Season One
25 episodes
(26 if Encounter at Farpoint *shown as two parts)*

Encounter at Farpoint
(90 minutes)

w D. C. Fontana *&* Gene Roddenberry
The new "Galaxy Class" Starship *Enterprise*, bigger
and better than ever before, sets out on her new jour-
ney "to boldly go where *no one* has gone before"
(with the blessing of an aged Bones McCoy). The
crew's first mission is to explore the mystery sur-
rounding the creation of the new Farpoint Station.
En route, they are threatened by the godlike Q who
places them on trial for all the crimes of mankind.
To prove their innocence, they must uncover the se-
cret of Farpoint.
Q John de Lancie
Groppler Zorn Michael Bell
Admiral Dr. Leonard H McCoy, ret. DeForest
  Kelley
Con Ensign Colm Meaney
Mandarin Bailiff Cary-Hiroyuki
Torres Jimmy Ortega

Director: Corey Allen

The Naked Now

w J. Michael Bingham, *story by* John D.F. Black
  & J. Michael Bingham
A familiar virus is unleashed aboard the *Enterprise*
that strips the crew of their inhibitions, including security chief Tasha Yar who seduces Data. (A reworking of "The Naked Time" from the original
series, an incident acknowledged when Riker pores
through old records.)
Sara McDougal Brooke Bundy
Jim Shimoda Benjamin W.S. Lum
Transporter chief Michael Rider

Director: Paul Lynch

Code of Honor

w Katharyn Powers *&* Michael Baron
When Tasha Yar is kidnapped to become his mate by
the leader of an alien culture, she must fight to the
death against his vengeful first wife.
Lutan Jessie Lawrence Ferguson
Yareena Karole Selmon
Hagon James Louis Watkins
Transporter chief Michael Rider

Director: Russ Mayberry

The Last Outpost

w Herbert Wright, *story by* Richard Krzemien
The *Enterprise* and a Ferengi starship are disabled
by Portal, the sentinel of a distant outpost of a long-
dead empire. Responding to Portal's challenge,
Riker earns the guardian's respect with his wisdom
and philosophies. (Notable as the series debut of the
Ferengi and of Armin Shimerman, better known
later as Quark in *Deep Space Nine*.)
Letek Armin Shimerman
Mordoc Jake Dengel
Kayron Tracey Walter
Portal Darryl Henriques
Daimon Tarr Mike Gomez

Director: Richard Colla

Where No One Has Gone Before

w Diane Duane *&* Michael Reaves
An accident during a warp experiment hurtles the
ship a billion light-years away to a surreal galaxy
where the crew's thoughts are tuned into alternate
realities. Young Wes Crusher and a mysterious
dying alien, The Traveler, are the crew's only hope
of returning to their system.
Kosinski Stanley Kamel
The Traveler Eric Menyuk
Maman Picard Herta Ware
Lt. Cmdr. Argyle Biff Yeager

Director: Rob Bowman

Lonely Among Us

w D.C. Fontana, *story by* Michael Halperin
The *Enterprise* inadvertently traps an alien lifeforce
that occupies the bodies of various crew members
searching for a host, before finally choosing Picard.
Chief Antican delegate John Durbin
Asst. chief engineer Singh Kavi Raz
First security guard Colm Meaney

Director: Cliff Bole

Justice

w Worley Thorne, *story by* Ralph Willis (*alias*
  John D.F. Black) *&* Worley Thorne
The *Enterprise* reaches a primitive world of scantily
clad love-makers. But Wesley is sentenced to death
for innocently violating a local custom and Picard
must choose between saving Wesley's life or adher-
ing to the Federation's prime directive.
Rivan Brenda Bakke
Liator Jay Louden
Conn Josh Clark

Director: James L. Conway

The Battle

w Herbert Wright, *story by* Larry Forrester
A revenge-seeking Ferengi captain uses a mind-control device to force Picard to relive the battle in which his son was killed. But this time the *Enterprise* is threatened unless Data can devise a defense for the famous "Picard Maneuver."
DaiMon Bok Frank Corsentino
First Officer Kazago Doug Warhit
Rata Robert Towers

Director: Rob Bowman

Hide and Q

w C.J. Holland & Gene Roddenberry, *story by* C.J. Holland (*alias* Maurice Hurley)
The teasing Q returns, offering Riker his god-like powers with which he can grant his friends' greatest desires including sight for Geordi and humanity for Data.
Q John de Lancie
Survivor Elaine Nalee
Wes at 25 William A. Wallace

Director: Cliff Bole

Haven

w Tracy Tormé, *story by* Tracy Tormé & Lan O'Kun
First appearance of Troi's Betazoid mother, Lwaxana, with Deanna caught between her feelings for Riker and her devotion to family customs as she faces a prearranged marriage with a man, Wyatt Miller, who is himself "haunted" by a vision of another woman, who later turns up on a Tarellian plague ship seeking refuge around the planet Haven. (Carel Struycken, who played Lwaxana's aide Mr. Homm, appeared as the enigmatic giant in *Twin Peaks*.)
Lwaxana Troi Majel Barrett
Wyatt Miller Rob Knepper
Victoria Miller Nan Martin
Steven Miller Robert Ellenstein
Mr. Homm Carel Struycken
Valeda Innis Anna Katarina
Wrenn Raye Birk
Ariana Danita Kingsley
Transporter chief Michael Rider

Director: Richard Compton

The Big Goodbye

w Tracy Tormé
A "film noir" homage as Picard takes on the persona of fictional gumshoe Dixon Hill for a little holodeck relaxation. But a malfunction traps Picard, Data and Crusher in the re-creation of 1941 San Francisco where they are held hostage by murderous gangsters.
Cyrus Redblock Lawrence Tierney
Felix Leach Harvey Jason
Lt. Dan Bell William Boyett
Whalen David Selburg
Lt. McNary Gary Armagnac
Desk sergeant Mike Genovese
News vendor Dick Miller
Jessica Bradley Carolyn Allport
Secretary Rhonda Aldrich

Director: Joseph Scanlan

Datalore

w Robert Lewin & Gene Roddenberry, *story by* Robert Lewin & Maurice Hurley
The away team discover the body parts of Data's duplicate, Lore, on the planet where he was built. Once assembled, Data's evil brother summons up the deadly crystalline space entity that destroyed the planet's original colonists.
Lore Brent Spiner
Lt. Cmdr. Argyle Biff Yeager

Director: Rob Bowman

Angel One

w Patrick Barry
While Riker struggles to save the lives of a group of male fugitives on a matriarchal planet, the *Enterprise* is ravaged by a deadly alien flu virus.
Beate Karen Montgomery
Ramsey Sam Hennings
Ariel Patricia McPherson
Trent Leonard John Crofoot

Director: Michael Rhodes

11001001

w Maurice Hurley & Robert Lewin
The *Enterprise* is hijacked by the Bynars, an alien race who communicate in binary language. Needing the ship's computer to regenerate one damaged on their home planet, they divert the attention of Riker and Picard with a holodeck creation, a sultry brunette called Minuet.
Minuet Carolyn McCormick
Cmdr. Quinteros Gene Dynarski
Zero One Katy Boyer
One Zero Alexandra Johnson
Zero Zero Iva Lane
One One Kelli Ann McNally

Director: Paul Lynch

Too Short a Season

w Michael Michaelian & D.C. Fontana, *story by* Michael Michaelian

The *Enterprise* escorts an aging Federation admiral to a planet to negotiate the release of hostages. It's just a ruse by the planet's governor to lure him back so he can gain revenge for an earlier crisis, but the admiral has his own secret—he's using a drug to make himself younger.

Admiral Mark Jameson Clayton Rohner
Anne Jameson Marsha Hunt
Karnas Michael Pataki

Director: Rob Bowman

When the Bough Breaks

w Hannah Louise Shearer

Wesley and several children from the *Enterprise* are kidnapped by a sterile civilization that wants to use them to start its own next generation.

Radue Jerry Hardin
Rashella Brenda Strong
Katie Jandi Swanson
Melian Paul Lambert
Duana Ivy Bethune
Dr. Bernard Derek Torsek
Leda Michele Marsh
Accolan Dan Mason
Harry Philip N. Waller
Toya Connie Danese

Director: Kim Manners

Home Soil

w Robert Sabaroff, *story by* Karl Guers, Ralph Sanchez & Robert Sabarof

A powerful microscopic life-form declares war on humans, takes over the *Enterprise*'s lab and computers and threatens to destroy the ship in retaliation for terraforming work on their planet, which is destroying them.

Kurt Mandl Walter Gotell
Louisa Kim Elizabeth Lindsey
Bjorn Benson Gerard Prendergast
Arthur Malencon Mario Roccuzzo

Director: Corey Allen

Coming of Age

w Sandy Fries

While Wesley endures the gruelling Starfleet Academy entrance exam, Picard faces an investigation into his competency as a commander. (This episode also hints at a conspiracy in the Federation, a theme developed in a later episode, "Conspiracy.")

Adm. Gregory Quinn Ward Costello
Lt. Cmdr. Dexter Remick Robert Schenkkan
Mordok John Putch
Lt. Chang Robert Ito
Jake Kurland Stephen Gregory
T'Shanik Tasia Valenza
Oliana Mirren Estee Chandler

Director: Michael Vejar

Heart of Glory

w Maurice Hurley, *story by* Maurice Hurley, Herbert Wright & D.C. Fontana

Worf must choose between his loyalty to Starfleet and his Klingon heritage when two Klingon fugitives attempt to take over the *Enterprise*.

Koras Vaughn Armstrong
Konmel Charles H. Hyman
Captain K'Nera David Froman
Kunivas Robert Bauer
Nurse Brad Zerbst
Ramos Dennis Madalone

Director: Rob Bowman

The Arsenal of Freedom

w Richard Manning & Hans Beimler, *story by* Maurice Hurley & Robert Lewin

Picard and the away team fight for their lives against energy spheres, sinkholes and invisible attackers on a planet run by a computerised weapons system.

The Peddler Vincent Schiavelli
Capt. Paul Rice Marco Rodriguez
Chief engineer Logan Vyto Ruginis
Ensign Lian T'Su Julia Nickson
Lt. Solis George de la Pena

Director: Les Landau

Symbiosis

w Robert Lewin, Richard Manning & Hans Beimler, *story by* Robert Lewin

The *Enterprise* is caught in the middle of a drug war between two alien races—one of them addicted to a narcotic. Only by violating the Prime Directive can Picard break the cycle of dependence.

Sobi Judson Scott
T'Jon Merritt Butrick
Romas Richard Lineback
Langor Kimberly Farr

Director: Win Phelps

reetings Earthlings! Sally (Kristen Johnston), Dick (John Lithgow), Harry (French Stewart) nd Tommy (Joseph Gordon-Levitt) in the spaced-out sitcom **3rd Rock from the Sun**.

liders rule: Wade (Sabrina Lloyd), Rembrandt (Cleavant Derricks), Arturo (John Rhys-Davies) nd Quinn (Jerry O'Connell) anticipate another inter-dimensional adventure.

Computer-animated effects enabled special effects producer Tim McHugh to create a glossy, metallic look for the spaceships in **Space: Above and Beyond**.

Devon (Debrah Farentino) and her band of settlers face a long journey after crash-landing in the pilot episode of **Earth 2**.

Kate Mulgrew made **Star Trek** history as the first female lead of a *Trek* series, playing Captain Kathryn Janeway in **Star Trek: Voyager**.

and of the Giants' Steve Burton (Gary Conway) and Valerie Scott (Deanna Lund) demonstrate one use for sticky-backed plastic the Gadget Guru never thought of.

Bruce Boxleitner as John Sheridan and Andreas Katsulas as G'Kar in the **Babylon 5** episode "Day of the Dead."

Zen Gesner as Sinbad and Mariah Shirley as Bryn watch each other's backs in a publicity shot from **The Adventures of Sinbad**. *Courtesy Atlantis Films/All American Television, Inc.*

Buck (Gil Gerard) helps a beautiful prisoner (guest star Jamie Lee Curtis) break out of jail in the **Buck Rogers in the 25th Century** episode "Unchained Woman."

A good vintage . . . The Doctor (William Hartnell) and Steven (Peter Purves) in the 1966 **Doctor Who** story "The Massacre of St. Batholomew's Eve."

Cook 'em Danno. Jack Lord guest starred in a first season episode of **The Invaders** as Vikor, an industrialist whose factory is infiltrated by aliens led by Nexus (Alfred Ryder).

Jessica (Heather Menzies) and Logan (Gregory Harrison) in a classic publicity shot from the futuristic 1970s adventure series **Logan's Run**.

Is this what photographers call a head shot? **The Incredible Hulk** duo Lou Ferrigno and Bill Bixby pose for the inevitable publicity pic.

Will Sharron (Alexandra Bastedo) realize guest star Donald Sutherland is the mastermind behind a devious plot in **The Champions** story "Shadow of the Panther"? What else are guest stars for...

Puppetmeister Gerry Anderson and his wife, Sylvia, meet young **Thunderbirds** fans in a rare shot used in **TVTimes** in 1966.

Above: The launch of *Thunderbird 3*, the under-used orange spaceship piloted by Alan Tracy in Gerry Anderson's evergreen **Thunderbirds**.

Above right: The witch-queen of Guk: Zelda, an android with a face like a pickled walnut who plotted the destruction of Earth in Gerry Anderson's 1980s series **Terrahawks**.

Jungle survival techniques help Joe 90 retrieve a hidden microfilm in the episode "The Fortress."

That cravat with that waistcoat? I don't think so . . . Sam (Tony Selby), Tarot (Michael Mackenzie) and Lulli (Judy Loe) starred in the otherwise excellent ITV children's adventure series **Ace of Wands**.

In the ITV series **Journey to the Unknown** villainous agent Sonny (Maurice Kaufmann) takes an early bath after goading young mutant Boy (Anthony Corlan) into using his telekinetic powers. Only the intervention of Paula (Janice Rule) saves him from drowning.

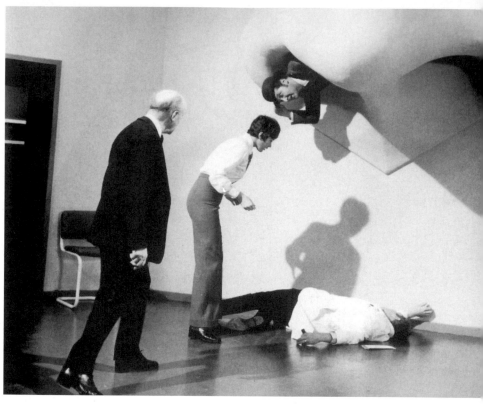

Bless you! Steed (Patrick Macnee) finds a novel way to nobble the villain Glover (Fulton Mackay) in **The Avengers** episode "You'll Catch Your Death."

Leni Parker as Da'an and Robert Leeshock as Liam Kincaid play a round of *foovlashaa* in **Gene Roddenberry's Earth: Final Conflict**. *Courtesy Atlantis Films/Tribune Entertainment.*

Skin of Evil

w Joseph Stefano & Hannah Louise Shearer,
  story by Joseph Stefano
Troi's shuttlecraft crashes on a planet inhabited by a sadistic goo-like entity called Armus that derives pleasure from human suffering. But a rescue mission turns to tragedy when Armus kills Tasha Yar.
Armus Mart McChesney, *voiced by* Ron Gans
Leland T. Lynch Walker Boone
Nurse Brad Zerbst
Ben Prieto Raymond Forchion

Director: Joseph L. Scanlan

We'll Always Have Paris

w Deborah Dean Davis & Hannah Louise Shearer
Picard is unexpectedly reunited with his first love in the midst of an investigation into lethal time warp experiments that threaten to rip open the interdimensional fabric of space! (The holodeck is at its most charming with a re-creation of Paris.)
Jenice Manheim Michelle Phillips
Dr. Paul Manheim Rod Loomis
Gabrielle Isabel Lorca
Lt. Dean Dan Kern
Edouard Jean-Paul Vignon
Francine Kelly Ashmore

Director: Robert Becker

Conspiracy

w Tracy Tormé, *story by* Robert Sabaroff
Picard and Riker travel to Earth to investigate a conspiracy in the highest ranks of Starfleet command. They find that alien parasites have taken over the minds of top-ranking officers. But though the threat is repelled, the aliens' source remains a mystery. (A graphically violent episode that was cut for its original U.K. transmission.)
Adm. Savar Henry Darrow
Adm. Quinn Ward Costello
Lt. Cmdr. Remmick Robert Schenkkan
Adm. Aaron Ray Reinhardt
Capt. Walker Keel Jonathan Farwell
Capt. Rixx Michael Berryman
Captain Tryla Scott Ursaline Bryant

Director: Cliff Bole

The Neutral Zone

w Maurice Hurley, *story by* Deborah McIntyre
  & Mona Glee
Three humans cryogenically frozen in the 20th century are revived when their capsule is taken aboard the *Enterprise*, and cause comic havoc aboard the ship—just what Picard doesn't want when facing a tense encounter with the Romulans over the unex-

plained disappearance of outposts along the Neutral Zone.
Commander Tebok Marc Alaimo
Sub-Commander Thei Anthony James
L.Q. "Sonny" Clemonds Leon Rippy
Clare Raymond Gracie Harrison
Ralph Peter Mark Richmond

Director: James L. Conway

Season Two
22 episodes

The Child

w Jaron Summers, Jon Povill & Maurice Hurley
A sleeping Troi is impregnated by an alien entity. Within days she has given birth to what appears to be a normal child, but one who ages rapidly, through toddler to ten-year-old and inadvertently affects a deadly organism that threatens to sweep the ship.
Dr. Pulaski (intro) Diana Muldaur
Guinan Whoopi Goldberg
Lt. Commander Hester Dealt Seymour Cassel
Ian R. J. William
Transporter chief Colm Meaney
Miss Gladstone Dawn Arnemann
Young Ian Zachary Benjamin
Crewman Dore Keller

Director: Rob Bowman

Where Silence Has Lease

w Jack B. Sowards
The *Enterprise* is trapped in a hole in space where a super-powerful alien conducts experiments of ship and crew until Picard threatens to self-destruct the vessel.
Nagillum Earl Boen
Haskell Charles Douglas
Transporter chief Colm Meaney

Director: Winrich Kolbe

Elementary, Dear Data

w Brian Alan Lane
Data and Geordi assume the roles of Holmes and Watson for a spot of holodeck relaxation, but when Geordi attempts to create a worthwhile opponent, the result is a Moriarty not only capable of defeating Data, but of taking over the *Enterprise*, too.
Professor James Moriarty Daniel Davis
Inspector Lestrade Alan Shearman
Ruffian Biff Manard
Prostitute Diz White
Assistant Engineer Clancy Anne Elizabeth Ramsey
Pie Man Richard Merson

Director: Rob Bowman

The Outrageous Okona

w Burton Armus, story by Les Menchen, Lance Dickson & David Landsburg

The *Enterprise* takes in tow a small craft whose sole occupant is the roguish Captain Okona. He is welcomed aboard until two ships from the local feuding planets appear, each threatening the *Enterprise* unless Okona is handed over to answer for his "crimes." Meanwhile, Guinan and a holodeck comedian try to teach Data about humor.
Guinan Whoopi Goldberg
Captain Okona William O. Campbell
Debin Douglas Rowe
Kushell Albert Stratton
Yanar Rosalind Ingledew
Benzan Kieran Mulroney
Comic Joe Piscopo

Director: Robert Becker

Loud As a Whisper

w Jacqueline Zambrano

Riva, a deaf-mute mediator who communicates telepathically through three interpreters is hoping to bring a centuries-old conflict to an end, when his companions are killed in an ambush. Forced to communicate in sign language, it takes all Troi's skills as a counselor to help him overcome his handicap.
Riva Howie Seago
Woman Marnie Mosiman
Scholar Thomas Oglesby
Warrior/Adonis Leo Damian
Transporter chief Colm Meaney
Warriors Chip Heller, Richard Lavin
Lieutenant John Garrett

Director: Larry Shaw

The Schizoid Man

w Tracy Tormé, story by Richard Manning & Hans Beimler

A egotistic, dying cyberneticist places his consciousness in Data's body, resulting in some strange new behavior from the android. (Suzie Plakson, who appears as the Vulcan doctor Selar, later played Worf's mate K'Ehleyr.)
Dr. Ira Graves W. Morgan Sheppard
Kareen Brianon Barbara Alyn Woods
Lt. Selar Suzie Plakson

Director: Les Landau

Unnatural Selection

w John Mason & Mike Gray

A mysterious ailment is rapidly aging the scientists on a research colony, but not their genetically engineered "children." Pulaski contracts the malady and literally works against time to find a cure.

Dr. Sara Kingsley Patricia Smith
Chief O'Brien Colm Meaney
Captain Taggert J. Patrick McNarama
Ensign Scott Trost

Director: Paul Lynch

A Matter of Honor

w Burton Armus, story by Wanda M. Haight, Gregory Amos & Burton Armus

As part of a Federation exchange program, Riker becomes the first human to serve aboard a Klingon vessel and swears an oath of allegiance to its commander. But his loyalty is severely tested when the Klingon commander believes the *Enterprise* responsible for a breach in his ship and orders Riker to support an attack on his former starship.
Ensign Mendon John Putch
Captain Kargan Christopher Collins
Lt. Klag Brian Thompson
Chief O'Brien Colm Meaney
Tactics officer Peter Parros
Vekma Laura Drake

Director: Rob Bowman

The Measure of a Man

w Melinda M. Snodgrass

One of the series' finest episodes. Picard and Riker compete in court to decide if Data is a sentient being when a Starfleet Commander arrives insisting the android be disassembled for research. Obliged to speak against his friend, Riker's demonstration of Data's "disposability" is breathtakingly brutal.
Captain Philipa Louvois Amanda McBroom
Commander Bruce Maddox Brian Brophy
Admiral Nakamura Clyde Kusatsu
Chief O'Brien Colm Meaney
Guinan Whoopi Goldberg

Director: Robert Scheerer

The Dauphin

w Scott Rubenstein & Leonard Mlodinow

The *Enterprise* collects a young woman called Salia to take her to become the Dauphin of her homeworld and end its civil war. When Wesley falls in love with Salia, her shape-shifting alien guardian warns him off.
Guinan Whoopi Goldberg
Anya Paddi Edwards
Salia Jamie Hubbard
Chief O'Brien Colm Meaney
Aron Peter Neptune
Teenage girl Madchen Amick
Furry animal Cindy Sorenson
Ensign Gibson Jennifer Barlow

Director: Rob Bowman

Contagion

w Steve Gerber *&* Beth Woods
The *Enterprise* crosses the Romulan Neutral Zone to go to the rescue of a Federation starship ravaged by a computer virus. Soon the *Enterprise* is also infected. To save the ship Picard and Data beam down to the legendary Iconia where they must unravel the secrets of its dormant computer network.
Captain Varley Thalmus Rasulala
Subcommander Toras Carolyn Seymour
Weapons officer Dana Sparks
Chief O'Brien Colm Meaney
Doctor Folkert Schmidt

Director: Joseph L. Scanlan

The Royale

w Keith Mills (*alias* Tracy Tormé)
Beaming down to a mysterious planet, the Away Team find themselves trapped along with the body of a long-dead 21st-century NASA astronaut inside a replica of a Las Vegas casino.
Chief O'Brien Colm Meaney
Mickey D Gregory Beecroft
with Sam Anderson, Jill Jacobson, Leo Garcia and Noble Willingham

Director: Cliff Bole

Time Squared

w Maurice Hurley, *story by* Kurt Michael Bensmiller
The *Enterprise* finds a shuttlecraft floating helplessly in space. Inside, the lone occupant is another Picard—sent back in time to warn them of the ship's impending demise.
Chief O'Brien Colm Meaney

Director: Joseph L. Scanlan

The Icarus Factor

w David Assael *&* Robert L. McCullough, *story by* David Assael
Riker must resolve his feelings toward his estranged father when he is offered his own captaincy. Meanwhile, Worf must undergo the Age of Ascension, a Klingon test of warriorhood.
Kyle Riker Mitchell Ryan
Chief O'Brien Colm Meaney
Ensign Herbert Lance Spellerberg

Director: Robert Iscove

Pen Pals

w Melinda M. Snodgrass, *story by* Hannah Louise Schearer
Data makes a pen pal of a little alien girl on a planet in the grips of geographic turmoil, and in doing so violates the Prime Directive. Meanwhile, Wesley gets his first taste of command, on an Away Team survey mission.
Davies Nicholas Cascone
Sarjenka Nikki Cox
Hildebrandt Ann H. Gillespie
Chief O'Brien Colm Meaney
Alans Whitney Rydbeck

Director: Winrich Kolbe

Q Who

w Maurice Hurley
A classic episode, eerily done. Q returns and throws the ship into deepest space where it encounters the Borg—an unstoppable, cybernetic super race with a remorseless insect-like hive mentality, and that is totally impervious to reason.
Q John de Lancie
Ensign Sonya Gomez Lycia Naff
Chief O'Brien Colm Meaney
Guinan Whoopi Goldberg

Director: Rob Bowman

Samaritan Snare

w Robert L. McCullough
The Pakleds, a seemingly dim-witted alien race, enlist Geordi's help to make some ship repairs but then hold him hostage to aid their technological development. Meanwhile, Picard, en route to Starbase 515 for medical treatment, shares some memories with Wesley.
Grebnedlog Christopher Collins
Reginald Leslie Morris
Surgeon Daniel Benzali
Sonya Gomez Lycia Naff
Biomolecular specialist Tzi Ma

Director: Les Landau

Up the Long Ladder

w Melinda M. Snodgrass
The *Enterprise* transports a primitive, rural farming colony away from its doomed planet along with an advanced race of clones who want to copy the DNA of Riker and Pulaski to save themselves from extinction.
Danilo O'Dell Barrie Ingham
Granger Jon de Vries
Brenna O'Dell Rosalyn Landor
Chief O'Brien Colm Meaney

Director: Winrich Kolbe

Manhunt

w Terry Devereaux (*alias* Tracy Tormé)
Against a backdrop of aliens conspiring to wreck a diplomatic conference, the predatory Lwaxana Troi sets her sights on Picard, who quickly retreats to the holodeck to take refuge in another Dixon Hill story. (Fleetwood Mac drummer Mick Fleetwood makes a heavily disguised cameo appearance.)
Lwaxana Troi Majel Barrett
Slade Bender Robert Costanzo
Antedian dignitary Mick Fleetwood
Mr. Homm Carel Struycken
Rex Rod Arrants
Chief O'Brien Colm Meaney
Madeline Rhonda Aldrich
Thug Robert O'Reilly
Transport Pilot Wren T. Brown

Director: Rob Bowman

The Emissary

w Richard Manning & Hans Beimler, *story by* Thomas H. Calder
Worf is reunited with his half-human, half-Klingon former lover K'Ehleyr, who is acting as an ambassador to a ship full of Klingons who are being released from cryogenic freezing, believing the Empire is still at war with the Federation.
K'Ehleyr Suzie Plakson
K'Temoc Lance LeGault
Admiral Gromek Georgann Johnson
Chief O'Brien Colm Meaney
Ensign Clancy Anne Elizabeth Ramsay
Tactical crewman Dietrich Bader

Director: Cliff Bole

Peak Performance

w David Kemper
Riker takes command of an old Starfleet ship, the *Hathaway*, for some war games with the *Enterprise*, but his ship comes under real attack from the Ferengi.
Sirna Kdrani Roy Brocksmith
Bractor Armin Shimerman
Tactician David L. Lander
Ensign Nagel Leslie Neale
Ensign Burke Glenn Morshower

Director: Robert Scheerer

Shades of Gray

w Maurice Hurley, Hans Beimler & Richard Manning, *story by* Maurice Hurley
A cheap way to end the season. During a planetary survey, Riker is wounded and his body infected by a lethal parasite. To fight its spread, Riker must relive memories of past missions. (Features flashbacks to episodes from the first two seasons, including a shot cut from the original U.K. transmission of "Conspiracy.")
Chief O'Brien Colm Meaney

Director: Rob Bowman

Season Three
26 episodes

Evolution

w Michael Piller, *story by* Michael Piller & Michael Wagner
Dr. Crusher returns to the *Enterprise*, where Wesley accidentally releases some intelligent micro-organisms called nannites, into the computer system, jeopardizing an important scientific mission.
Dr. Paul Stubbs Ken Jenkins
Guinan Whoopi Goldberg
Nurse Mary McCusker
Crewman Randal Patrick

Director: Winrich Kolbe

The Ensigns of Command

w Melinda M. Snodgrass
Data gets his first taste of command responsibility on a planet whose illegal human colonists are in danger from a violent alien race, the Sheliak. When the colonists refuse to leave, Data finds logic is not the answer as he tries to figure out how to persuade them to go.
Ard'rian MacKenzie Eileen Seeley
Haritath Mark L. Taylor
Kentor Richard Allen
Chief O'Brien Colm Meaney
Sheliak Mart McChesney
Gosheven Grainger Hines

Director: Cliff Bole

The Survivors

w Michael Wagner
When the *Enterprise* finds only two survivors of an alien attack that destroyed a planet's entire population, they are suspicious of the story told by Kevin Uxbridge and uncover a tale of galactic genocide.
Kevin Uxbridge John Anderson
Rishon Uxbridge Anne Haney

Director: Les Landau

Who Watches the Watchers

w Richard Manning *&* Hans Beimler
The crew face a dilemma when a primitive culture the Federation is secretly observing seizes Troi and prepares to sacrifice her to Picard, believing him to be a god.
Nuria Kathryn Leigh Scott
Liko Ray Wise
Dr. Barron James Greene
Fento John McLiam
Oji Pamela Segall
Hali James McIntire
Warren Lois Hall

Director: Robert Wiemer

The Bonding

w Ronald D. Moore
After leading an Away Team mission in which archaeologist Marla Aster is killed, Worf feels compelled to play surrogate father to the 12-year-old son she left behind and performs a mysterious Klingon "bonding" ceremony.
Lt. Marla Aster Susan Powell
Jeremy Aster Gabriel Damon
Chief O'Brien Colm Meaney

Director: Winrich Kolbe

Booby Trap

w Ron Roman, Michael Piller *&* Richard Danus,
     story by Michael Wagner *&* Ron Roman
The *Enterprise* becomes trapped in a minefield that converts the ship's energy into lethal radiation. Searching for a solution, Geordi creates a hologram of the ship's engine designer, Dr. Leah Brahms, to help him.
Dr. Leah Brahms Susan Gibney
Chief O'Brien Colm Meaney
Galek Dar Albert Hall
Christy Julie Warner
Guinan Whoopi Goldberg

Director: Gabrielle Beaumont

The Enemy

w David Kemper *&* Michael Piller
Geordi is stranded on a hostile planet with a wounded Romulan centurion while Picard maneuvers diplomatically with the captain of a Romulan warbird. Meanwhile, in sickbay, Worf refuses to donate his blood to help Dr. Crusher save a dying Romulan.
Centurion Bochra John Snyder
Commander Tomalak Andreas Katsulas
Chief O'Brien Colm Meaney
Patahk Steve Rankin

Director: David Carson

The Price

w Hannah Louise Shearer
The Federation vies with the Ferengi in negotiations with the planet Crystalia for control of a stable wormhole, and Troi becomes intimately involved with one of the planet's negotiators, the half-Betazoid Devinoni Ral.
Devinoni Ral Matt McCoy
Premier Bhavani Elizabeth Hoffman
Mendoza Castulo Guerra
DaiMon Goss Scott Thomson
Leyor Kevin Peter Hall
Dr. Arridor Dan Shor
Chief O'Brien Colm Meaney

Director: Robert Scheerer

The Vengeance Factor

w Sam Rolfe
Picard's attempts to mediate in a violent dispute between pirate clans are sabotaged by a mysterious assassin.
Yuta Lisa Wilcox
Brull Joey Aresco
Sovereign Marouk Nancy Parsons
Chorgon Stephen Lee
Volnath Marc Lawrence
Temarek Elkanah J. Burns

Director: Timothy Bond

The Defector

w Ronald D. Moore
A Romulan defector leads the *Enterprise* crew into a showdown that could erupt into full-scale war.
Admiral Jarok/Setal James Sloyan
Commander Tomalak Andreas Katsulas
Admiral Haden John Hancock
John Bates S.A. Templeman

Director: Robert Scheerer

The Hunted

w Robin Bernheim
Visiting the planet Angosia, which is seeking Federation membership, the *Enterprise* helps capture an escaped prisoner from the planet's penal colony, which is revealed as the "home" of exiled veterans of Angosia's war.
Roga Danar Jeff McCarthy
Prime Minister Nayrok James Cromwell
Chief O'Brien Colm Meaney
Zayner J. Michael Flynn
Wagnor Andrew Bicknell

Director: Cliff Bole

The High Ground

w Melinda M. Snodgrass
Dr. Crusher is kidnapped by terrorists demanding
independence and who believe the Federation has
ranged itself with their government. (This allegory
on Northern Ireland was dropped in Britain by the
BBC, though it was shown on Sky.)
Alexana Devos Kerrie Keane
Kyril Finn Richard Cox
Waiter Marc Buckland
Policeman Fred G. Smith
Boy Christopher Pettiet

Director: Gabrielle Beaumont

Deja Q

w Richard Danus
Q returns, but this time he's been stripped of his
powers by the Q continuum. When the *Enterprise* is
pursued by some of Q's past "victims," Data saves
him and he repays his debt by sacrificing himself to
save the *Enterprise*, whereupon his powers are re-
stored by Q2.
Q John de Lancie
Dr. Garin Richard Cansino
Guinan Whoopi Goldberg
Scientist Betty Muramoto
Q2 Corbin Bernsen

Director: Les Landau

A Matter of Perspective

w Ed Zuckerman
Riker is suspected of murdering a respected scientist
who had accused Riker of seducing his wife. Picard
orders a holodeck re-creation of events to determine
whether Riker should be extradited for the crime.
Investigator Krag Craig Richard Nelson
Manua Apgar Gina Hecht
Dr. Nel Apgar Mark Margolis
Tayna Juli Donald
Chief O'Brien Colm Meaney

Director: Cliff Bole

Yesterday's Enterprise

w Ira Stephen Behr, Richard Manning, Hans
Beimler, Ronald D. Moore & Michael Piller,
story by Trent Christopher Ganino & Eric A.
Stillwell
A time rift brings the *Enterprise 1701-C* from the
past into the present and our crew unknowingly
finds itself in an alternate universe in which Tasha
Yar is still alive, and where the Federation is still
fighting the Klingons—and losing. Only Guinan

senses something is awry and urges Picard to send
the ship back or risk forever changing history.
Tasha Yar Denise Crosby
Lt. Richard Castillo Christopher McDonald
Captain Rachel Garrett Tricia O'Neil
Guinan Whoopi Goldberg

Director: David Carson

The Offspring

w René Echevarria
Data uses his own neural programming to create an
android daughter. But when Starfleet wants to take
Lal away for research, Picard defends Data's right to
keep his daughter. (This episode marked Jonathan
Frakes's directorial debut.)
Lal Hallie Todd
Admiral Haftel Nicolas Coster
Lt. Ballard Judyann Elder
Ten Forward crew Diane Moser, Hayne Bayle,
Maria Leone, James G. Becker

Director: Jonathan Frakes

Sins of the Father

w Ronald D. Moore & W. Reed Moran, *story by*
Drew Deighan
Accompanied by Picard as his "chadich" (second),
Worf returns to the Klingon homeworld to defend
his late father against charges of treason and finds
his younger brother, Kurn, is still alive. But he be-
comes a victim of the political in-fighting and ac-
cepts excommunication for the sake of preserving
the council's stability.
Commander Kurn Tony Todd
K'mpec Charles Cooper
Duras Patrick Massett
Kahlest Thelma Lee
Transporter technician Teddy Davis

Director: Les Landau

Allegiance

w Richard Manning & Hans Beimler
Picard is abducted and imprisoned with three other
aliens as part of a bizarre experiment. His place
aboard the *Enterprise* is taken by a duplicate—who
acts in a very un-Picard-like manner, carousing in
Ten Forward and seducing Dr. Crusher.
Tholl Stephen Markle
Esoqq Reiner Schöne
Haro Joycelyn O'Brien
Aliens Jeff & Jerry Rector

Director: Winrich Kolbe

Captain's Holiday

w Ira Steven Behr
While reluctantly taking a holiday, Picard becomes involved with the unscrupulous but beautiful Vash, and her search for a legendary treasure, pursued by her former Ferengi ally and two time travelers from the 27th century.
Vash Jennifer Hetrick
Sovak Max Grodenchik
Ajur Karen Landry
Boratus Michael Champion
Joval Deirdre Imershein

Director: Chip Chalmers

Tin Man

w Dennis Bailey, Lisa Putnam & David Bischoff
The *Enterprise* is ordered to transport telepathic Betazoid Tam Elbrun, a specialist in contact with new life forms, to communicate with a living space vessel in orbit around a star that is about to explode. The interference of two Romulan vessels is an added complication.
Tam Elbrun Harry Groener
Captain DeSoto Michael Cavanaugh
Romulan commander Peter Vogt
Chief O'Brien Colm Meaney

Director: Robert Scheerer

Hollow Pursuits

w Sally Caves
A painfully shy crewman creates a holodeck fantasy world that threatens the entire crew. (First of several appearances for former *A-Team* star Dwight Schultz.)
Lt. Reg Barclay Dwight Schultz
Guinan Whoopi Goldberg
Duffy Charley Lang
Chief O'Brien Colm Meaney

Director: Cliff Bole

The Most Toys

w Shari Goodhartz
The *Enterprise* crew are deceived into believing Data has perished in a shuttle explosion by an alien who wants to add the android to his collection of rare and valuable exhibits.
Kivas Fajo Saul Rubinek
Varria Jane Daly
Toff Nehemiah Persoff

Director: Timothy Bond

Sarek

w Peter S. Beagle, *story by* Marc Cushman & Jake Jacobs
An aging Sarek boards the *Enterprise* for a delicate diplomatic conference. But his mind is deteriorating and Picard volunteers to mind-meld with the Vulcan to help him through the negotiations.
Sarek Mark Lenard
Perrin Joanna Miles
Ki Mendrossen William Denis
Sakkath Rocco Sisto
with John H. Francis

Director: Les Landau

Ménage à Troi

w Fred Bronson & Susan Sackett
Chaos ensues when Troi and her mother are kidnapped by a lovestruck Ferengi who wants the hand (and the Betazoid brain) of Lwaxana.
Lwaxana Troi Majel Barrett
DaiMon Tog Frank Corsentino
Reittan Grax Rudolph Willrich
Dr. Farek Ethan Phillips
Nibor Peter Slutsker
Mr. Homm Carel Struycken

Director: Robert Legato

Transfigurations

w René Echevarria
Dr. Crusher saves an amnesiac alien by hooking him up to Geordi's nervous system. During the process a wave of visible energy passes into Geordi, which does wonders for his self-confidence with women. Meanwhile the alien is undergoing an evolutionary process.
John Doe Mark La Mura
Sunad Charles Dennis
Christy Henshaw Julie Warner
Nurse Temple Patti Tippo

Director: Tom Benko

The Best of Both Worlds, Part 1

w Michael Piller
The Borg are back! Confronting the *Enterprise*, the cybernetic race kidnaps Picard and transforms him into the terrifying Locutus, a spokesman to announce their intention to conquer Earth. With the Borg on an invasion course, Riker pins his hopes on a desperate attempt to destroy their vessel.
Lt. Cmdr. Shelby Elizabeth Dennehy
Admiral Hanson George Murdock
Chief O'Brien Colm Meaney
Guinan Whoopi Goldberg

Director: Cliff Bole

Season Four
26 episodes

The Best of Both Worlds, Part 2

w Michael Piller
The tense conclusion to Season Three's cliffhanger. Picard is now mutilated into a half-Borg, half-human called Locutus, as the Borg use his knowledge against Starfleet. Riker must risk destroying his friend in order to save Earth from enslavement by the powerful alien race.
Guinan Whoopi Goldberg
Lt. Cmdr. Shelby Elizabeth Dennehy
Admiral Hanson George Murdock
Chief O'Brien Colm Meaney
Gleason Todd Merrill

Director: Cliff Bole

Family

w Ronald D. Moore, *based in part on a premise* by Susanne Lambdin *&* Bryan Stewart
While the *Enterprise* undergoes repairs, crew members find time for family reunions. Worf is visited by his adoptive human parents, Wesley views a holographic message from his dead father and Picard, still suffering from his ordeal with the Borg, returns home for the first time in 20 years to come face-to-face with his jealous older brother.
Guinan Whoopi Goldberg
Robert Picard Jeremy Kemp
Marie Picard Samantha Eggar
Louis Dennis Creaghan
Sergey Rozhenko Theodore Bikel
Helena Rozhenko Georgia Brown
Jack Crusher Doug Wert
Rene Picard David Tristan Birkin
Chief O'Brien Colm Meaney

Director: Les Landau

Brothers

w Rick Berman
Data's elderly creator, Dr. Noonian Soong, summons him home to be fitted with a computer chip that will give him emotion. But their reunion is disrupted by the unexpected arrival of Data's evil brother, Lore.
Dr. Noonian Soong/Lore Brent Spiner
Jake Potts Cory Danziger
Willie Potts Adam Ryen
Chief O'Brien Colm Meaney
Ensign Kopf James Lashly

Director: Rob Bowman

Suddenly Human

w John Whelpley & Jeri Taylor, *story by* Ralph Phillips
The *Enterprise* finds a stricken Talarian vessel manned by five teenagers—one of whom is human. When Dr. Crusher finds that the boy, Jono, has been abused, Picard is prepared to risk war rather than return him to the alien father who comes to claim him.
Jono Chad Allen
Endar Sherman Howard
Admiral Connaught Rossa Barbara Townsend

Director: Gabrielle Beaumont

Remember Me

w Lee Sheldon
When Wesley's warp field experiments go awry, Dr. Crusher is unknowingly catapulted into a universe created by her own mind. When people start disappearing from the ship she begins to doubt her own sanity, especially when only she believes they ever existed.
Traveler Eric Menyuk
Dr. Dalen Quaice Bill Erwin
Chief O'Brien Colm Meaney

Director: Cliff Bole

Legacy

w Joe Menosky
A rescue mission leads the crew to Turkana Four, the birthplace of their late colleague Tasha Yar. There, they encounter her sister—and Data learns a sad lesson about betrayal.
Ishara Yar Beth Toussaint
Hayne Don Mirault
Tan Tsu Vladimir Velasco
Chief O'Brien Colm Meaney
Man Christopher Michael

Director: Robert Scheerer

Reunion

w Thomas Perry, Jo Perry, Ronald D. Moore & Brannon Braga, *story by* Drew Deighan, Thomas Perry & Jo Perry
When Picard is chosen to mediate a power struggle between the potential successors to the Klingon Empire, Worf is reunited with his former mate, K'Ehleyr, and their son, Alexander. And Worf confronts Duras, the Klingon whose lies disgraced Worf's family.
K'Ehleyr Suzie Plakson
K'Mpec Charles Cooper
Gowron Robert O'Reilly
Duras Patrick Massett
Alexander Jon Steuer
Transporter technician April Grace
Klingon guards Basil Wallace, Mirron E. Willis
Security guard Michael Rider

Director: Jonathan Frakes

Future Imperfect

w J Larry Carroll & David Bennett Carren
After an Away Team mission goes awry, Riker
awakens in Sickbay to find that 16 years have
passed and that he is now Captain, a widower with a
young son, and is about to negotiate a treaty with the
Romulans. But while perusing his family records to
fill in the blanks, he realizes all is not as it seems
when he finds the image of his wife is actually Min-
uet, a woman he once created on the Holodeck.
Tomalak Andreas Katsulas
Jean-Luc/Ethan Chris Demetral
Transporter chief George O'Hanlon Jr.
Minuet Carolyn McCormick
Transporter Chief Hubbell April Grace
Nurse Patti Yusutake
Gleason Todd Merrill

Director: Les Landau

Final Mission

w Kacey Arnold-Ince & Jeri Taylor, *story by*
Kacey Arnold-Ince
After being accepted at Starfleet Academy, Wesley
accompanies Picard on a final, routine mission, only
to find himself struggling to keep his captain alive
when their shuttle crashes on a strange planet where
the only water is protected by a powerful force-
field.
Dirgo Nick Tate
Chairman Songi Kim Hamilton
Ensign Tess Allenby Mary Kohnert

Director: Corey Allen

The Loss

w Hilary J. Bader, Alan J. Adler & Vanessa
Greene, *story by* Hilary J. Bader
While the *Enterprise* struggles to contend with a
mysterious two-dimensional life-form, Troi loses
her empathic powers and resigns her post, unable to
cope with her disability.
Guinan Whoopi Goldberg
Ensign Janet Brooks Kim Braden
Ensign Tess Allenby Mary Kohnert

Director: Chip Chalmers

Data's Day

w Harold Apter & Ronald D. Moore, *story by*
Harold Apter
While the *Enterprise* carries a famous Vulcan diplo-
mat to a secret rendezvous inside the Neutral Zone,
the impending wedding of O'Brien and botanist
Keiko compounds Data's confusion about the nu-
ances of human feelings.
Keiko Rosalind Chao
Chief O'Brien Colm Meaney

T'Pel Sierra Pecheur
Mendak Alan Scarfe
Transporter Chief Hubbell April Grace
V'Sal Shelly Desai

Director: Robert Wiemer

The Wounded

w Jeri Taylor, *story by* Stuart Charno, Sara
Charno & Cy Chermak
Picard must stop a renegade Federation captain
whose starship is making apparently unprovoked at-
tacks on a former enemy's ships. (Debut of the vil-
lainous, lizard-necked Cardassians.)
Chief O'Brien Colm Meaney
Keiko Rosalind Chao
Captain Maxwell Bob Gunton
Gul Macet Marc Alaimo
Daro Time Winters
Admiral Haden John Hancock
Telle Marco Rodriguez

Director: Chip Chalmers

Devil's Due

w Philip Lazebnik, *story by* Philip Lazebnik &
William Douglas Lansford
Picard fights to save a terrorised planet from Ardra,
a powerful being who claims to be the Devil and
who has returned to fulfil a thousand-year-old con-
tract: an age of peace and prosperity in return for
enslavement.
Ardra Marta Dubois
Dr. Clarke Paul Lambert
Jared Marcelo Tubet
Klingon monster Tom Magee
Devil monster Thad Lamey
Marley William Glover

Director: Tom Benko

Clues

w Bruce D. Arthurs & Joe Menosky, *story by*
Bruce D. Arthurs
Data must lie to protect the crew when the *Enter-
prise* encounters an isolationist race while passing
through a "wormhole." The aliens wanted the ship
destroyed but agreed to erase the crew's short-term
memory instead. However, clues pointing to a "lost
day" arouse their curiosity.
Guinan Whoopi Goldberg
Chief O'Brien Colm Meaney
Ensign Pamela Winslow
Nurse Ogawa Patti Yasutake
Madeline Rhonda Aldrich
Gunman Thomas Knickerbocker

Director: Les Landau

First Contact

w David Bischoff, Dennis Russell Bailey, Joe Menosky, Ronald D. Moore & Michael Piller, story by Marc Scott Zicree

When Riker is stranded and critically wounded while on an undercover first contact mission, Picard must risk exposing their presence among an alien culture that may not be ready for them. (*Cheers* star Bebe Neuwirth guests as an amorous nurse with her own ideas about first contact!)

Durken George Coe
Lanel Bebe Neuwirth
Mirasta Carolyn Seymour
Krola Michael Ensign
Berel George Hearn
Nilrem Steven Anderson
Tava Sachi Parker

Director: Cliff Bole

Galaxy's Child

w Maurice Hurley, story by Thomas Kartozian

The *Enterprise* becomes surrogate mother to a huge alien creature after Picard is forced to destroy its real mother. Meanwhile Geordi finally gets to meet Dr. Leah Brahms whom he once "created" on the holodeck—but is disappointed to find her cold and humorless.

Guinan Whoopi Goldberg
Dr. Leah Brahms Susan Gibney
Ensign Estevez Lanei Chapman
Ensign Pavlik Jana Marie Hupp
Transporter Chief Hubbell April Grace

Director: Winrich Kolbe

Night Terrors

w Pamela Douglas & Jeri Taylor, story by Shari Goodhartz

Trapped in a rift in space, the crew are plagued by unexplained hallucinations and increasing paranoia that threaten to destroy them. The answer seems locked in the minds of Deanna Troi and a comatose Betazoid.

Chief O'Brien Colm Meaney
Keiko Rosalind Chao
Gillespie Duke Moosekian
Zaheva Deborah Taylor
Hagan John Vickery
Ensign Rager Lanei Chapman
Kenny Lin Brian Tochi
Peeples Craig Hurley
Guinan Whoopi Goldberg

Director: Les Landau

Identity Crisis

w Brannon Braga, story by Timothy De Haas

A five-year-old mystery returns to haunt Geordi, and Dr. Crusher finds herself fighting against time to combat a parasite that threatens to turn him into an alien creature.

Guinan Whoopi Goldberg
Susanna Leijten Maryann Plunkett
Nurse Ogawa Patti Yasutake
Hickman Amick Byram
Ensign Graham Mona Grudt
Transporter technician Dennis Madalone
Breville Paul Tompkins

Director: Winrich Kolbe

The Nth Degree

w Joe Menosky

Notoriously shy crewman Reg Barclay (who caused so much trouble in the Season Three holodeck story "Hollow Pursuits") is endowed with super-human intelligence by an alien probe. He connects up his brain to the ship's computer and refuses to relinquish control.

Lt. Barclay Dwight Schultz
Lt. Linda Larson Saxon Trainor
Ensign April Anaya Page Leong
Einstein Jim Norton
Ensign Brower David Coburn
Cytherian Kay E. Kuter

Director: Robert Legato

Qpid

w Ira Steven Behr, story by Randee Russell & Ira Steven Behr

Picard's reunion with old flame Vash is complicated when Q steps in to encourage the romance by transporting the bridge crew to Sherwood Forest where, as Robin Hood and his merry men, they must battle Sir Guy of Gisbourne to save the fair maid Marion who is, of course, Vash. (A silly episode though it does contain Worf's immortal refrain "I am *not* a merry man.")

Q John de Lancie
Vash Jennifer Hetrick
Sir Guy Clive Revill
Servant Joi Staton

Director: Cliff Bole

The Drumhead

w Jeri Taylor

A retired Starfleet admiral aids a search for a traitor aboard the *Enterprise* after a visiting Klingon officer admits to spying. But when her investigation turns into a witch-hunt, even Picard finds himself accused.

Admiral Satie Jean Simmons
Sabin Bruce French
Simon Tarses Spencer Garrett
J'Ddan Henry Woronicz
Nellen Ann Shea
Admiral Thomas Henry Earl Billings

Director: Jonathan Frakes

Half a Life

w Peter Allan Fields, *story by* Ted Roberts &
Peter Allan Fields
Troi's amorous mother becomes infatuated with
Timicin, a scientist searching for a way to save his
world, but a custom of his people requires his ritual
suicide at the age of 60—and Picard finds himself
risking war when he becomes embroiled in Lwax-
ana's fight to save her lover's life. (Michelle Forbes,
later Ensign Ro Laren, plays Timicin's daughter.)
Lwaxana Troi Majel Barrett
Dr. Timicin David Odgen Stiers
Dara Michelle Forbes
B'Tardat Terrence E. McNally
Chief O'Brien Colm Meaney
Mr. Homm Caryl Struycken

Director: Les Landau

The Host

w Michel Horvat
Dr. Crusher falls madly in love with a handsome
Trillian ambassador, but her love is put to the test
when he is badly injured and reveals that he is a
symbiont—a parasite being—who exists in differ-
ent host bodies to survive, and that his new body
will be that of a beautiful young woman.
Odan Franc Luz
Kalin Trose William Newman
Leka Barbara Tarbuck
Kareel Nicole Orth-Pallavicini
Nurse Ogawa Patti Yasutake
Lathal Robert Harper

Director: Marvin V. Rush

The Mind's Eye

w René Echevarria, *story by* Ken Schafer &
René Echevarria
Geordi is kidnapped by Romulan forces and sub-
jected to intense brainwashing to turn him into a
lethal assassin. (Around this time Majel Barrett
began to be credited as Computer Voice.)
Ambassador Kell Larry Dobkin
Vagh Edward Wiley
Taibak John Fleck
Chief O'Brien Colm Meaney

Director: David Livingston

In Theory

w Joe Menosky & Ronald D. Moore
Data finds himself the object of a young crew member's affection and decides to experiment with love
by pursuing a romantic relationship. He creates a
special program to guide him through the intricacies
of courtship.

Ensign Jenna D'Sora Michele Scarabelli
Chief O'Brien Colm Meaney
Keiko Rosalind Chao
Ensign Pamela Winslow
Guinan Whoopi Goldberg

Director: Patrick Stewart

Redemption, Part 1

w Ronald D. Moore
The *Enterprise* travels to the Klingon Empire where
Picard is to attend the installation of Gowron as new
leader of the High Council. En route they learn that
the family of Duras is amassing a rebel challenge.
As civil war threatens the Empire, Worf's loyalties
are torn between the Federation and his people and
he feels compelled to resign his post.
Gowron Robert O'Reilly
Kurn Tony Todd
Lursa Barbara March
B'Etor Gwynyth Walsh
K'Tal Ben Slack
Movar Nicholas Kepros
Toral J.D. Cullum
Klingon first officer Tom Ormeny
Helmsman Clifton Jones
Romulan commander Denise Crosby

Director: Cliff Bole

Season Five
26 episodes

Redemption, Part 2

w Ronald D. Moore
Conclusion to Season Four's cliffhanger. Picard dis-
covers the Romulans are secretly aiding the Duras
family's plot to take over the Klingon Empire, in the
hope of destroying the Klingon-Federation alliance.
Worf joins brother Kurn in trying to reinstate
Gowron, but the surprise package is the Romulan
commander Sela who claims to be the daughter of
Tasha Yar.
Guinan Whoopi Goldberg
Sela Denise Crosby
Kurn Tony Todd
Lursa Barbara March
B'Etor Gwynyth Walsh
Toral J.D. Cullum
Gowron Robert O'Reilly
Larg Michael G. Hagerty
Admiral Fran Bennett
Movar Nicholas Kepros
Chief O'Brien Colm Meaney
Hobson Timothy Carhart
Kulge Jordan Lund
Helmsman Stephen James Carver

Director: David Carson

Darmok

w Joe Menosky, *story by* Philip Lazebnik & Joe Menosky

Picard is abducted to an uninhabited planet by the captain of an alien starship who communicates solely through metaphors such as "Darmok and Jilad at Tanagra." Picard is confused until he comes to understand that the Tamarians communicate by example, using references to people and places in their history. He realizes that he is being asked to unite to fight a dangerous monster.

Captain Dathon Paul Winfield
Chief O'Brien Colm Meaney
Tamarian first officer Richard Allen
Ensign Robin Lefler Ashley Judd

Director: Winrich Kolbe

Ensign Ro

w Michael Piller, *story by* Rick Berman & Michael Piller

The *Enterprise* is sent to help negotiate a peace between the Cardassians and the militant leader of the Bajorans, a race fighting to regain its home planet. Aided by a new Bajoran officer, Ensign Ro, Picard uncovers a plot by a Starfleet admiral to destroy the Bajoran leaders.

Guinan Whoopi Goldberg
Ensign Ro Michelle Forbes
Barber Mott Ken Thorley
Admiral Kennelly Cliff Potts
Orta Jeffrey Hayenga
Dolak Frank Collison
Keeve Falor Scott Marlowe
Collins Harley Venton

Director: Les Landau

Silicon Avatar

w Jeri Taylor, *story by* Lawrence V. Conley

The Crystalline Entity (from the first season episode "Datalore") returns and destroys a Federation colony on Melona Four. Picard then struggles to communicate with the mysterious, destructive force before a vengeful visiting scientist can destroy it.

Dr. Marr Ellen Geer
Carmen Susan Diol

Director: Cliff Bole

Disaster

w Ronald D. Moore, *story by* Ron Jarvis & Philip A. Scorza

The *Enterprise* is disabled by a rare natural phenomenon, cutting off and trapping members of the crew throughout the ship—Picard in an elevator with three children, and Worf with Keiko who goes into labor. With the vessel in danger of exploding, Troi holds their lives in her hands when she is forced to assume command on the bridge.

Marissa Erika Flores
Jay Gordon John Christian Graas
Patterson Max Supera
Chief O'Brien Colm Meaney
Keiko Rosalind Chao
Ensign Ro Michelle Forbes
Ensign Mandel Cameron Arnett
Ensign Monroe Jana Marie Hupp

Director: Gabrielle Beaumont

The Game

w Brannon Braga, *story by* Susan Sackett, Fred Bronson & Brannon Braga

The fate of the Federation is in Wesley Crusher's hands when he returns to find the *Enterprise* crew addicted to a dangerous new electronic mind game that masks a subversive alien plot.

Wesley Crusher Wil Wheaton
Robin Lefler Ashley Judd
Chief O'Brien Colm Meaney
Etana Katherine Moffat
Nurse Alyssa Ogawa Patti Yasutake
Woman Diane M. Hurley

Director: Corey Allen

Unification I

w Jeri Taylor, *story by* Rick Berman & Michael Piller

Leonard Nimoy crosses the generation gap, returning as Spock in this two-part story. When the Federation learns that legendary Ambassador Spock has gone on an unauthorized mission to Romulus, Picard and Data are sent after him to find out what he's up to. (This episode also features the death of Spock's father, Sarek.)

Spock Leonard Nimoy
Dokachin Graham Jarvis
B'Ijik Erick Avari
Perrin Joanna Miles
Sarek Mark Lenard
K'Vada Stephen D. Root
Pardek Malachi Throne
Romulan Daniel Roebuck
Neral Norma Large
Soup woman Mimi Cozzens
Admiral Karen Hensel

Director: Les Landau

Unification II

w Michael Piller, *story by* Rick Berman &
Michael Piller

Picard learns that Spock is engaged in a bit of "cowboy diplomacy" involving a secret plan to reunify the Romulans with the Vulcans. But they find Spock is an unwitting pawn in Romulan plotter Sela's own scheme to invade and take over Vulcan.

Guest cast: See Part 1, plus:
Sela Denise Crosby
Omag William Bastiani
Romulan Susan Fallender
D'Tan Vidal Peterson
Amarie Harriet Leider

Director: Cliff Bole

A Matter of Time

w Rick Berman

A mysterious visitor, claiming to be a historian from the future, materializes on the *Enterprise*, as the crew are preparing a desperate plan to save an endangered planet. Picard, faced with a life or death decision, attempts to persuade him to reveal the outcome if the plan goes ahead.

Berlingoff Rasmussen Matt Frewer
Hail Moseley Stefan Gierasch
Ensign Sheila Franklin
Female scientist Shay Garner

Director: Paul Lynch

New Ground

w Grant Rosenberg, *story by* Sara Charno &
Stuart Charno

Worf learns some painful lessons about parenting when his son, Alexander, arrives to join his father on the *Enterprise*.

Alexander Brian Bonsall
Helena Rozhenko Georgia Brown
Dr. Ja'Dar Richard McGonagle
Lowry Jennifer Edwards
Ensign Sheila Franklin

Director: Robert Scheerer

Hero Worship

w Joe Menosky, *story by* Hilary J. Bader

A traumatized young boy, sole survivor of a devastated space vessel, becomes obsessed with emulating Data, even simulating some of his android mannerisms.

Timothy Joshua Harris
Teacher Steven Einspahr
Ensign Sheila Franklin
Transporter chief Harley Venton

Director: Patrick Stewart

Violations

w Pamela Gray & Jeri Taylor, *story by* Shari
Goodhartz, T. Michael & Pamela Gray

Troi, Riker and Dr. Crusher fall into unexplained comas while the *Enterprise* plays host to a delegation of Ullians, an alien race of telepathic historians who conduct research by probing their subjects' long-forgotten memories.

Tarmin David Sage
Jev Ben Lemon
Keiko Rosalind Chao
Inad Eve Brenner
Crewman Davis Craig Benton
Dr. Martin Rick Fitts
Jack Crusher Doug Wert

Director: Robert Wiemer

The Masterpiece Society

w Adam Belanoff & Michael Piller, *story by*
James Kahn & Adam Belanoff

A Utopian genetically engineered society living in a biosphere is threatened by a natural disaster. When the *Enterprise* offers assistance, the presence of the crew undermines the society's delicate balance, while Troi falls for the colony's leader, Aaron Conor.

Aaron Conor John Snyder
Hannah Bates Dey Young
Marcus Benbeck Ron Canada
Ensign Sheila Franklin

Director: Winrich Kolbe

Conundrum

w Barry M. Schkolnick, *story by* Paul Schiffer

While suffering an unexplained case of amnesia, the crew is manipulated into fighting a war they neither remember nor understand.

Ensign Ro Michelle Forbes
Kristin Liz Vassey
Executive Officer Keiran MacDuff Erich Anderson
Crewman Erick Weiss

Director: Les Landau

Power Play

w Rene Balcer, Herbert J. Wright & Brannon
Braga, *story by* Paul Ruben & Maurice Hurley

Troi, Data and O'Brien are possessed by alien spirits after responding to a distress signal. Back aboard the *Enterprise*, they stage a violent revolt and seize control of the ship.

Keiko Rosalind Chao
Chief O'Brien Colm Meaney
Ensign Ro Michelle Forbes
Transporter technician Ryan Reid

Director: David Livingston

Ethics

w Ronald D. Moore, *story by* Sara Charno & Stuart Charno

The crew is torn when Worf, paralyzed after an accident, opts to follow Klingon custom and commit ritual suicide rather than accepting his life as a cripple. Dr. Crusher clashes with a renowned neurogeneticist who wants to try a radical experimental technique on Worf.

Dr. Russell Caroline Kava
Nurse Ogawa Patti Yasutake
Alexander Brian Bonsall

Director: Chip Chalmers

The Outcast

w Jeri Taylor

An allegory for sexual tolerance. Riker falls in love with a member of an androgynous alien race, the J'-naii, whose species forbids inter-gender relationships.

Soren Melinda Culea
Krite Callan White
Noor Megan Cole

Director: Robert Scheerer

Cause and Effect

w Brannon Braga

The *Enterprise* becomes trapped in a time warp that forces the crew to endlessly repeat the same experiences, while the ship faces inevitable destruction after a collision with a starship from the past. (Kelsey Grammer has a cameo as the captain of the other starship, the *Bozman*.)

Ensign Ro Michelle Forbes
Nurse Ogawa Patti Yasutake
Captain Bateman Kelsey Grammer

Director: Jonathan Frakes

The First Duty

w Ronald D. Moore & Naren Shankar

Wesley becomes involved in a cover-up after a devastating accident at Starfleet Academy. Torn between loyalty to his friends and the need to tell the truth, he learns a bitter lesson in honesty. (Ray Walston guest stars as the academy's wise old gardener.)

Wes Crusher Wil Wheaton
Boothby Ray Walston
Nicholas Locarno Robert Duncan McNeill
Lt. Commander Albert Ed Lauter
Admiral Brand Jacqueline Brookes
Captain Satelk Richard Fancy

Hajar Walker Brandt
Sito Shannon Fill
Cadet Richard Rothenberg

Director: Paul Lynch

Cost of Living

w Peter Allan Fields

A story about living life on your own terms. Preparing for Troi's wedding aboard the *Enterprise*, her freewheeling mother Lwaxana upsets Deanna and Worf when she introduces his son Alexander to her somewhat hedonist lifestyle.

Lwaxana Troi Majel Barrett
Alexander Brian Bonsall
Campio Tony Jay
Mr. Homm Carel Struycken
Young man David Oliver
Juggler Albie Selznick
Erko Patrick Cronin
Young woman Tracey d'Arcy
Poet George Edie
First learner Christopher Halste

Director: Winrich Kolbe

The Perfect Mate

w Gary Perconte & Michael Piller, *story by* René Echevarria & Gary Perconte

Picard falls in love with a beautiful woman who is to be given as a peace offering to end a centuries-long war.

Kamala Famke Janssen
Briam Tim O'Connor
Par Lenor Max Grodenchik
Alrik Mickey Cottrell
Qol Michael Snyder
Transporter officer April Grace

Director: Cliff Bole

Imaginary Friend

w Edithe Swensen & Brannon Braga, *story by* Ronald Wilkerson, Jean Matthias & Richard Fliegel

A little girl's imaginary friend is "hijacked" by an alien energy source and becomes a frightening reality for the crew when she threatens to destroy the *Enterprise*.

Alexander Brian Bonsall
Clara Noley Thornton
Isabella Shay Astar
Daniel Sutter Jeff Allin
Nurse Ogawa Patti Yasutake
Guinan Whoopi Goldberg
Ensign Sheila Franklin

Director: Gabrielle Beaumont

I, Borg

w René Echevarria
Picard and the crew experience conflicting emotions when an Away Team rescues a critically-injured, but harmless, adolescent Borg. Picard wants the creature reprogrammed to destroy his race but Geordi finds himself befriending the Borg, who he names Hugh.
Guinan Whoopi Goldberg
Hugh Borg Jonathan Del Arco

Director: Robert Lederman

The Next Phase

w Ronald D. Moore
Geordi and Ro are pronounced dead after a transporting maneuver from a distressed Romulan ship goes awry. In fact they have been phased into another plane of existence by a Romulan cloaking experiment and end up using their own memorial service to attract their friends' attention.
Mirok Thomas Kopache
Varel Susanna Thompson
Ensign McDowell Kenneth Meseroll
Ensign Ro Michelle Forbes
Brossmer Shelby Leverington
Parem Brian Cousins

Director: David Carson

The Inner Light

w Morgan Gendel & Peter Allan Fields, *story by* Morgan Gendel
Picard is rendered unconscious by an alien space probe and experiences an entire lifetime on another world while only 25 minutes pass aboard the *Enterprise*. (Patrick Stewart's son Daniel has a guest role.)
Eline Margot Rose
Batal Richard Riehle
Administrator Scott Jaeck
Meribor Jennifer Nash
Nurse Ogawa Patti Yasutake
Young Batal Daniel Stewart

Director: Peter Lauritson

Time's Arrow, Part 1

w Joe Menosky & Michael Piller, *story by* Joe Menosky
When Data's head is unearthed in a cave on Earth, with artifacts dating back 500 years, the *Enterprise* goes in search of extra-terrestrials that may have visited the planet. But a freak accident propels Data back to 19th-century San Francisco where he is surprised to see a picture of Guinan in a newspaper. Meanwhile Picard leads an Away Team to follow him.
Guinan Whoopi Goldberg
Samuel Clemens Jerry Hardin
Doorman Barry Kivel
Jack the Bellboy Michael Aron
Seaman Ken Thorley
Indian Sheldon Peters Wolfchild
Beggar Jack Murdock
Gambler Marc Alaimo
Scientist Milt Tarver
Roughneck Michael Hungerford

Director: Les Landau

Season Six
26 episodes

Time's Arrow, Part 2

w Jeri Taylor, *story by* Joe Menosky
Conclusion to Season Five's cliffhanger. Data has become trapped in 19th-century San Francisco with a 19th-century Guinan and a very curious Samuel Clemens (better known as author Mark Twain). Following him, the *Enterprise* crew find that time-traveling aliens are slowly killing off the population, stealing their neural energy and sending it to the 24th century to feed their own people.
Guinan Whoopi Goldberg
Samuel Clemens Jerry Hardin
Young reporter Alexander Enberg
Jack the Bellboy Michael Aron
Morgue attendant Van Epperson
Mrs. Carmichael Pamela Kosh
Dr. Appollinaire James Gleason
Alien nurse Mary Stein
Policeman William Boyett
Male patient Billy Cho Lee

Director: Les Landau

Realm of Fear

w Brannon Braga
Nervous Reg Barclay is forced to confront his paralyzing fear of beaming on and off ship, to solve a mystery encounter with a sinister creature in the transporter while in molecular form.
Barclay Dwight Schultz
Chief O'Brien Colm Meaney
Admiral Hayes Renata Scott
Crew member Thomas Velgrey
Nurse Ogawa Patti Yasutake

Director: Cliff Bole

Man of the People

w Frank Abatemarco
Alkar, an ambitious Lumerian ambassador desperate to achieve his greatest diplomatic success, secretly "uses" Troi by channelling his dark thoughts into her, thus keeping his own mind free of unwanted emotions. But the psychic burden causes her to age rapidly into a white-haired, disheveled old woman.
Alkar Chip Lucia
Maylor Susan French
Liva Stephanie Erb
Jarth Rick Scarry
Ensign J.P. Hubbell
Ensign Janeway Lucy Boryer
Admiral George D. Wallace

Director: Winrich Kolbe

Relics

w Ronald D. Moore
Much-loved episode with James Doohan reprising his original *Trek* role. The *Enterprise* crew is astonished to discover Scotty hidden in a crashed starship's transporter system where he has survived for 75 years after literally beaming himself into limbo. But the veteran engineer finds it hard to adjust and seeks solace in maudlin boozing sessions and a holodeck version of the old *Enterprise* bridge. But it's just not the same without his old mates and poor old Scotty is left feeling old and useless—until a crisis occurs that, of course, only he can solve.
Captain Montgomery Scott James Doohan
Ensign Rager Lanei Chapman
Ensign Kane Erick Weiss
Engineer Bartel Stacie Foster
Waiter Ernie Mirich

Director: Alexander Singer

Schisms

w Brannon Braga, *story by* Jean Louise Matthias
& Ron Wilkerson
When various crew members start suffering strange symptoms including pain, anxiety, tiredness and "lost time" it is found that aliens from a parallel universe are abducting crewmen for drastic medical experiments. (This episode also features Data's attempt at poetry, "Ode to Spot.")
Ensign Rager Lanei Chapman
Mott Ken Thorley
Lt. Shipley Scott T. Trost
Crewman Angelo McCabe
Kaminer Angelina Fiordellisi
Medical technician John Nelson

Director: Robert Wiemer

True Q

w René Echevarria
Amanda, a gifted young intern, learns that she is a Q. She is initially reluctant to give up her life as a "lowly human"; it takes a global crisis on a dying planet, which she can use her powers to prevent, to make her realize her destiny lies with the Q Continuum.
Q John de Lancie
Amanda Olivia d'Abo
Lote John P. Connolly

Director: Robert Scheerer

Rascals

w Allison Hock, *story by* Ward Botsford, Diana
Dru Botsford & Michael Piller
A bizarre transporter mishap transforms Picard, Ro, Keiko and Guinan into children. But before the process can be reversed, the *Enterprise* is mysteriously disabled and Ferengis invade, claiming the vessel as salvage.
Guinan Whoopi Goldberg
Young Guinan Isis J. Jones
Alexander Brian Bonsall
Young Picard David Tristan Birkin
Keiko Rosalind Chao
Young Keiko Caroline Junko King
Ensign Ro Michelle Forbes
Young Ro Megan Parlen
Lurin Mike Gomez
Berik Tracey Walter
Morta Michael Snyder
Chief O'Brien Colm Meaney
Molly Hana Hatae
Kid Morgan Nagler

Director: Adam Nimoy

A Fistful of Datas

w Robert Hewitt Wolfe & Brannon Braga, *story by* Robert Hewitt Wolfe
A holodeck fantasy goes wrong, trapping Worf and his son into a Wild West showdown with a villain who's a dead ringer for Data.
Alexander Brian Bonsall
Eli Hollander John Pyper-Ferguson
Annie Joy Garrett
Bandito Jorge Cervera Jr.

Director: Patrick Stewart

The Quality of Life

w Naren Shankar
Data risks the lives of Picard and Geordi to protect a new "living machine," the exocomp, claiming he cannot sacrifice one form of life to save another.
Dr. Farallon Ellen Bry
Transporter Chief Kelso J. Downing

Director: Jonathan Frakes

Chain of Command, Part 1

w Ronald D. Moore, *story by* Frank Abatemarco

Tension is growing between the Federation and the Cardassians who are believed to be developing bacteriological weapons. Picard is ordered to resign his command to take part in a dangerous mission with Worf and Beverly to locate and destroy the weapons, but when they are ambushed Picard is taken prisoner by the Cardassians. Meanwhile, an insensitive new captain is assigned to the *Enterprise*.

Gul Madred David Warner
Captain Jellico Ronny Cox
Admiral Nechayev Natalija Nogulich
Gul Lemec John Durbin
Solok Lou Wagner

Director: Robert Scheerer

Chain of Command, Part 2

w Frank Abatemarco

Picard is brutalized and tortured by the sadistic Gul Madred, while the *Enterprise* attempts to unravel the truth about the Cardassian "weapons," discovering it was a ruse to lure Picard into Cardassian space so the enemy could learn about Federation strategy for resisting a Cardassian attack. Jellico—still at odds with his crew—engages in a touch of brinkmanship to ensure Picard's return.

Captain Jellico Ronny Cox
Gul Lemec John Durbin
Gul Madred David Warner
Jil Orra Heather Lauren Olson

Director: Les Landau

Ship in a Bottle

w René Echevarria

While enjoying a Sherlock Holmes mystery on the holodeck, Geordi and Data ask Barclay to check out some anomalies in the program. While he's doing so, Professor Moriarty appears, stating that the computer system has created him so well that he has come alive. He then takes control of the ship, demanding that the love of his life, the Countess Regina, be brought to life as well.

Moriarty Daniel Davis
Barclay Dwight Schultz
Countess Regina Stephanie Beacham
Gentleman Clement Von Franckenstein

Director: Alexander Singer

Aquiel

w Brannon Braga & Ronald D. Moore, *story by* Jeri Taylor

Geordi falls in love with an alien Starfleet lieutenant who is a suspect in a bizarre murder and fights to prove her innocence.

Aquiel Renée Jones
Governor Torak Wayne Grace
Morag Reg E. Cathey

Director: Cliff Bole

Face of the Enemy

w Naren Shankar, *story by* René Echevarria

Abducted and transformed to look like a Romulan, Troi is forced to impersonate a Romulan Intelligence agent as a pivotal part of an elaborate defection scheme.

N'Vek Scott MacDonald
Toreth Carolyn Seymour
DeSeve Barry Lynch
Pilot Robertson Dean
Alien captain Dennis Cockrum
Ensign McKnight Pamela Winslow

Director: Gabrielle Beaumont

Tapestry

w Ronald D. Moore

After Picard dies in a surprise attack, Q gives him the chance to change his destiny by reliving and avoiding the fight that led to him receiving an artificial heart as a young ensign. But he finds his career would have taken a different, more lowly path . . .

Q John de Lancie
Corey Ned Vaughn
Marta J.C. Brandy
Nausicaan Clint Carmichael
Penny Rae Norman
Maurice Picard Clive Church
Young Picard Marcus Nash

Director: Les Landau

Birthright, Part 1

w Brannon Braga

While the *Enterprise* is docked at Deep Space Nine, Worf learns that his father did not die at the infamous Khitomer massacre, but was taken prisoner to a remote Romulan prison planet. Worf is furious as the idea of a Klingon being held prisoner is so dishonorable in Klingon culture, but determines to set out to find the planet—and the truth. Meanwhile Data is having dreams of his own "father," Dr. Noonian Soong.

Dr. Julian Bashir Sidig El Fadil
Dr. Soong Brent Spiner
Shrek James Cromwell
Gi'ral Christine Rose
Ba'el Jennifer Gatti
L'Kor Richard Herd

Director: Winrich Kolbe

Birthright, Part 2

w René Echevarria

Captured and imprisoned in a society of Klingons and Romulans living together in peace, Worf has learned his father did die at Khitomer. Now he risks his life to show the younger Klingons their lost heritage and inspire them to reclaim their honor.

Gi'ral Christine Rose
Shrek James Cromwell
Toq Sterling Macer Jr.
Tokath Alan Scarfe
Ba'el Jennifer Gatti
L'Kor Richard Herd

Director: Dan Curry

Starship Mine

w Morgan Gendel

With the *Enterprise* undergoing a lethal baryon ray bombardment in a kind of galactic carwash, Picard finds himself trapped aboard the ship with a band of interstellar thieves and must work alone to prevent them stealing material for a deadly weapon. Meanwhile Data tries to get the hang of "small talk."

Hutchinson David Spielberg
Kelsey Marie Marshall
Devor Tim Russ
Orton Glenn Morshower
Neil Tom Nibley
Satler Tim deZarn
Kiros Patricia Tallman
Waiter Arlee Reed
Pomet Alan Altshuld

Director: Cliff Bole

Lessons

w Ronald Wilkerson & Jean Louise Matthias

Picard falls in love with a brilliant, beautiful new officer, cartographer Nella Daren, but is torn between love and duty when he is forced to send her on a potentially deadly mission.

Nella Daren Wendy Hughes

Director: Robert Wiemer

The Chase

w Joe Menosky, *story by* Joe Menosky & Ronald D. Moore

Following a mysterious visit from his old archaeology professor, Picard finds himself in a race with Cardassians, Klingons and Romulans to solve a billion-year-old genetic puzzle with staggering implications for all four races.

Professor Galen Norman Lloyd
Humanoid Salome Jens
Nu'Daq John Cothran Jr.
Romulan captain Maurice Roëves
Gul Ocett Linda Thorson

Director: Jonathan Frakes

Frame of Mind

w Brannon Braga

Trapped in an alien mental asylum, with little memory of the past, Riker is convinced he is going insane and struggles to retain his grip on reality.

Dr. Syrus David Selburg
Administrator Andrew Prine
Mavek Gary Werntz
Inmate Susanna Thompson
Wounded crew member Allan Dean Moore

Director: James L. Conway

Suspicions

w Joe Menosky & Naren Shankar

Beverly risks her career to prove that a pioneering Ferengi scientist was murdered by one of three rivals over his radical invention to protect a craft from the destructive forces of a star's corona.

Guinan Whoopi Goldberg
Dr. Reyga Peter Slutsker
Kurak Tricia O'Neil
Jo'Bril James Horan
Dr. Christopher John S. Ragin
T'Pan Joan Stuart Morris
Nurse Ogawa Patti Yasutake

Director: Cliff Bole

Rightful Heir

w Ronald D. Moore, *story by* James E. Brooks

Worf finds his faith sorely tested when it appears that Kahless, the greatest Klingon warrior of all time, has returned from the dead to reclaim the empire.

Koroth Alan Oppenheimer
Gowron Robert O'Reilly
Kahless Kevin Conway
Torin Norman Snow
Divok Charles Esten

Director: Winrich Kolbe

Second Chances

w René Echevarria, *story by* Michael A. Medlock

Returning to the site of an eight-year-old mission, Riker encounters an identical double of himself, created in a freak transporter incident. He finds it hard to accept his other self—particularly when the double tries to rekindle his relationship with Troi. (This episode features a cameo role for the only person on the show who has ever actually been in space: shuttle astronaut Mae Jemison.)

Ensign Palmer Dr. Mae Jemison

Director: LeVar Burton

Timescape

w Brannon Braga
Caught in a temporal disturbance, the *Enterprise* is frozen in time on the brink of total annihilation and Picard, Data, Troi and Geordi must figure out how to restore normal time without destroying the ship.
Romulan/Alien Michael Bofshever

Director: Adam Nimoy

Descent, Part 1

w Ronald D. Moore, *story by* Jeri Taylor
The Borg return to do battle with the Federation but this time they boast a new individuality and lure Data away after helping him feel his first emotion. Going in pursuit, Picard leads a heavily armed Away Team to search a remote planet, but he, Troi and Geordi are ambushed and captured. (This episode also features, early on, a cameo appearance, in a holodeck poker game, by scientist Stephen Hawking.)
Isaac Newton John Neville
Albert Einstein Jim Norton
Admiral Nechayev Natalija Nogulich
Crosis Brian J. Cousins
Professor Stephen Hawking Himself
Bosus Richard Gilbert-Hill

Director: Alexander Singer

Season Seven

25 episodes
(26 if last episode, All Good Things, *is shown in two parts)*

Descent, Part 2

w René Echevarria
Picard, Troi and Geordi are held captive by Data and his evil brother, Lore, who has assumed control of the Borg. They learn that when Hugh, the young Borg they once rescued, returned to his ship, his acquired individuality infected the collective, disrupting their sense of shared identity, until Lore gave them leadership and a new purpose. Picard and Geordi are able to break Lore's hold over Data, and with Hugh's help, succeed in overpowering him. As the *Enterprise* party prepares to leave, Hugh hopes the reformed Borg will one day learn to function effectively as individuals. (But what a shame! An awesome enemy goes out with a whimper. Little did we know . . .)
Hugh Jonathan Del Arco
Taitt Alex Datcher
Barnaby James Horan
Crosis Brian Cousins

Salazar Benito Martinez
Goral Michael Reilly Burke

Director: Alexander Singer

Liaisons

w Jeanne Carrigan Fauci & Lisa Rich, *story by* Roger Eschbacher & Jaq Greenspon
While the *Enterprise* crew plays host to two unpredictable alien ambassadors, Loquel and Byleth, as part of a cultural exchange, Picard is stranded on a barren planet with a woman who falls desperately in love with him.
Anna Barbara Williams
Voval Eric Pierpoint
Loquel Paul Eiding
Byleth Michael Harris
Boy Rickey D'Shon Collins

Director: Cliff Bole

Interface

w Joe Menosky
Geordi's VISOR is connected to an interface unit that enables him to establish direct mental communication with a mechanical probe, allowing him to work in dangerous situations as if he were actually present. But while on a mission "aboard" a trapped science vessel, he defies Picard's orders and risks his life in what seems a futile attempt to rescue his missing mother.
Captain Silva La Forge Madge Sinclair
Doctor La Forge Ben Vereen
Admiral Holt Warren Munson

Director: Robert Wiemer

Gambit, Part 1

w Naren Shankar, *story by* Christopher Hatton & Naren Shankar
Riker is captured by aliens he believes to have killed Picard, who has been presumed dead after disappearing during an archaeological trip, but is shocked to find his captain posing as a mercenary on the alien ship, which has been looting ancient artifacts.
Baran Richard Lynch
Tallera Robin Curtis
Vekor Caitlin Brown
Narik Cameron Thor
Yranac Alan Altshuld
Admiral Chekote Bruce Gray
Ensign Giusti Sabrina LeBeauf
Bartender Stephen Lee
Lt. Sanders Derek Webster

Director: Peter Lauritson

Gambit, Part 2

w Ronald D. Moore, *story by* Naren Shankar
While Data is left in command of the *Enterprise* (with an impatient Worf as his First Officer), Riker poses as a rogue Starfleet officer alongside the "mercenary" Picard in an attempt to retrieve the looted artifacts, which are actually fragments of a potentially lethal Vulcan weapon. (The 6' 9" American football star James Worthy of the L.A. Lakers became *Star Trek*'s tallest ever Klingon in his guest role.)
Baran Richard Lynch
Tallera Robin Curtis
Vekor Caitlin Brown
Narik Cameron Thor
Koral James Worthy
Ensign Giusti Sabrina LeBeauf
Setok Martin Goslins

Director: Alexander Singer

Phantasms

w Brannon Braga
Data is disturbed by his first bad dreams, but as he attempts to get to the bottom of his nightmares—even trying a holodeck session of psychoanalysis with Sigmund Freud—the problem turns into a real-life nightmare for the rest of the *Enterprise* crew.
Ensign Tyler Gina Ravarra
Dr. Sigmund Freud Bernard Kates
Admiral Nakamura Clyde Kusatsu
Workman David L. Crowley

Director: Patrick Stewart

Dark Page

w Hilary J. Bader
Troi must probe her mother's psyche when a traumatic secret causes a psychic breakdown that threatens Lwaxana's life—and uncovers a family tragedy hidden in the past.
Lwaxana Troi Majel Barrett
Maques Norman Large
Hedril Kirsten Dunst
Mr. Troi Amick Byram
Kestra Andreana Weiner

Director: Les Landau

Attached

w Nicholas Sagan
Imprisoned and telepathically joined by an insular and hostile alien society, Picard and Beverly are able to read each other's thoughts—whether they want to or not—and realize the deep feelings they have always had for each other could be love!
Mauric Robin Gammell
Lorin Lenore Kasdorf
Kes aide J.C. Stevens

Director: Jonathan Frakes

Force of Nature

w Naren Shankar
An alien brother and sister resort to desperate measures to prove their theory that warp drive is destroying the universe, disabling offending ships to force Starfleet to investigate. When the *Enterprise* becomes trapped while trying to rescue a disabled vessel from a rift in space, Geordi finds the way out is to take the ship surfing!
Rabal Michael Corbett
Serova Margaret Reed
Daimon Prak Lee Arenberg

Director: Robert Lederman

Inheritance

w Dan Koeppel & René Echevarria, *story by* Dan Koeppel
A routine mission to save an endangered planet brings Data face-to-face with Juliana Tainer, a woman who claims she was once married to his "father," Dr. Soong, and is, in effect, his mother. Data is encouraged by Geordi and Toi to get to know Juliana but, as he does, he begins to sense something strange about her.
Juliana Fionnula Flanagan
Pran William Lithgow

Director: Robert Scheerer

Parallels

w Brannon Braga
Returning to the *Enterprise* after a Klingon competition, Worf finds reality constantly shifting and is troubled that no one else seems to notice. His shock grows when he finds Troi is his wife!
Wesley Wil Wheaton
Nurse Ogawa Patti Yasutake
Gul Nador Mark Bramhall

Director: Robert Wiemer

The Pegasus

w Ronald D. Moore
The *Enterprise* is joined by Admiral Pressman, who was Riker's first commanding officer, for a secret assignment to find some lost equipment from their old ship, the *Pegasus*, before it falls into Romulan hands. But Riker is torn when Pressman orders him to hide from Picard the real purpose of the mission—to re-create the forbidden cloaking experiment that had destroyed the vessel 12 years earlier.
Admiral Pressman Terry O'Quinn
Admiral Blackwell Nancy Vawter
Sirol Michael Mack

Director: LeVar Burton

Homeward

w Naren Shankar, *television story by* Spike Steingasser
Worf clashes with his foster brother, Nikolai Rozhenko, who proposes to violate the Prime Directive in an unorthodox effort to save a doomed alien race.
Nikolai Paul Sorvino
Dobara Penny Jonson
Vorin Brian Markinson
Kateras Edward Penn
Tarrana Susan Christy

Director: Alexander Singer

Sub Rosa

w Brannon Braga, *story by* Jeri Taylor
Shortly after her grandmother's death, Beverly falls under the spell of a ghost lover who has been in her family for 800 years! Meanwhile, the *Enterprise* crew grapples with some inclement weather.
Ronin Duncan Regehr
Maturin Michael Keenan
Ned Quint Shay Duffin

Director: Jonathan Frakes

Lower Decks

w René Echevarria, *story by* Ronald Wilkerson & Jean Louise Matthias
While enduring the *Enterprise*'s tough promotion evaluation program, four junior officers, Ogawa, Lavelle, Sito and Taurik, find themselves involved in a top-secret mission to return a Federation agent to Cardassia. (Sito was one of Wesley's "co-conspirators" in the fifth-season episode "The First Duty.")
Lavelle Dan Gauthier
Sito Shannon Fill
Taurik Alexander Enberg
Ben Bruce Beatty
Ogawa Patti Yasutake
Joret Don Reilly

Director: Gabrielle Beaumont

Thine Own Self

w Ronald D. Moore, *story by* Christopher Hatton
Having completely lost his memory while on a routine mission to retrieve some radioactive material from a crashed probe, Data is stranded on a primitive planet where the inhabitants fear he is carrying a deadly plague. Meanwhile, back on the *Enterprise*, Deanna goes for her commander's badge, and has to make a difficult decision.
Talur Ronnie Claire Edwards
Garvin Michael Rothhaar
Gia Kimberly Cullum
Skoran Michael G. Hagerty
Apprentice Andy Kossin
Rainer Richard Ortega-Miro

Director: Winrich Kolbe

Masks

w Joe Menosky
While an alien archive transforms the *Enterprise* into its ancient society—including a tropical jungle in Ten Forward—Data is taken over by a string of different personalities from the extinct civilization. *(No guest cast)*

Director: Robert Wiemer

Eye of the Beholder

w René Echevarria, *story by* Brannon Braga
While experiencing empathic visions after an officer's mysterious suicide, Troi becomes romantically involved with Worf as they succumb to their growing feelings for each other.
Lt. Walter Pierce Mark Rolston
Lt. Nara Nancy Harewood
Lt. Kwan Tim Lounibos
Ensign Calloway Johanna McCloy
Woman Nora Leonhardt
Man Dugan Savoye

Director: Cliff Bole

Genesis

w Brannon Braga
Picard and Data return to the *Enterprise* after a routine mission to find the entire crew has been infected with a virus that is causing them to de-evolve into prehistoric beings. Worf become a huge, terrifying monster, Riker a stone age man and Troi a strange amphibian.
Ogawa Patti Yasutake
Lt. Reg Barclay Dwight Schultz
Ensign Dern Carlos Ferro

Director: Gates McFadden

Journey's End

w Ronald D. Moore
Picard is forced to relocate a group of American Indians from a planet they have colonized, which has now become Cardassian territory in a treaty with the Federation. But while Picard struggles with echoes from the Indians' past, a brooding Wesley Crusher re-assesses his future—outside Starfleet—with the Traveler as his "spirit guide."
Wesley Crusher Wil Wheaton
Lakanta Tom Jackson
Admiral Necheyev Natalija Nogulich
Anthwara Ned Romero
Wakasa George Aguilar
Gul Evek Richard Poe
Traveler Eric Menyuk
Jack Crusher Doug Wert

Director: Corey Allen

Firstborn

w René Echevarria, *story by* Mark Kalbfeld
Worf is excited that his son, Alexander, has reached the age for the First Rite of Ascension at which he should declare his intention to become a warrior. But he is disappointed when Alexander says he has no such intention. Then a mysterious family friend arrives to help train the reluctant young Klingon.
K'mtar James Sloyan
Alexander Brian Bonsall
B'Etor Gwynyth Walsh
Lursa Barbara March
Quark Armin Shimerman
Yog Joel Swetow
Gorta Colin Mitchell
Singer Michael Danek
Molor John Kenton Shull
Eric Rickey D'Shon Collins

Director: Jonathan West

Bloodlines

w Nicholas Sagan
Picard is surprised to learn that he has a son, and that the young man, Jason Vigo, has been targeted for murder by an old Ferengi enemy, Daimon Bok, who wants revenge for the death of his own son, killed in battle by Picard years before.
Jason Vigo Ken Olandt
Daimon Bok Lee Arenberg
Birta Peter Slutsker
Lt. Rhodes Amy Pietz
Tol Michelan Sisti

Director: Les Landau

Emergence

w Joe Menosky, *story by* Brannon Braga
The lives of the *Enterprise* crew are endangered when the ship suddenly develops its own intelligence, defending itself against anyone who tries to regain control. The focal point is on holodeck—aboard a runaway train.
Conductor David Huddleston
Hitman Vinny Argiro

Engineer Thomas Kopache
Hayseed Arlee Reed

Director: Cliff Bole

Preemptive Strike

w René Echevarria, *story by* Naren Shankar
Ro Laren (now a lieutenant) is forced to choose between her loyalty to Picard and her hatred of the Cardassians when she accepts an assignment to infiltrate the Maquis, a renegade Federation group dedicated to harassing the Cardassians. (The Maquis are also active in *Deep Space Nine*.)
Ro Laren Michelle Forbes
Macias John Franklyn-Robbins
Admiral Necheyev Natalija Nogulich
Santos William Thomas Jr.
Kalita Shannon Cochrany
Gul Evek Richard Poe

Director: Patrick Stewart

All Good Things

w Ronald D. Moore & Brannon Braga
The final episode, a double-length story that features guest appearances by old *Enterprise* favorites Tasha Yar and Chief O'Brien—and with Q in tow, too—helps to bookend the series, harking back to the premiere episode, "Encounter at Farpoint." Picard finds himself shifting back and forth in time as he attempts to prevent the destruction of humanity by a spatial anomaly of "anti-time," created by his own actions. The solution lies in a dangerous maneuver that must be carried out by the *Enterprises* of the past, present and future—and which could destroy all three ships.
Q John de Lancie
Commander Tomalak Andreas Katsulas
Admiral Nakamura Clyde Kusatsu
Ogawa Patti Yasutake
Androna Martha Hackett
Tasha Yar Denise Crosby
Chief O'Brien Colm Meaney
Jessel Pamela Kosh
Lt. Gaynes Tim Kelleher

Director: Winrich Kolbe

STAR TREK: DEEP SPACE NINE

*S*tar *Trek*'s enduring appeal has been its sense of wonder and adventure, with two generations of enterprising explorers boldly going in search of whatever lay "out there."

As a mission statement, "to boldly go" struck an immediate and lasting chord. But when *Star Trek: Deep Space Nine* dumped a new bunch of Starfleet officers on a remote, ramshackle space station that was going nowhere, the crew found themselves facing their deadliest enemy yet—bored Trekkies.

"To boldly sit" didn't have quite the same ring to it—and no amount of grit or personal conflict could make up for that sense of something being missing. It was hardly surprising then, that by the third season the *DS9* ers had been given a ship of their own, the *Defiant*, to go off exploring in, while the Trek dynasty had expanded still further with a fourth series, *Star Trek: Voyager*, that promised to take fans into new, uncharted territory.

At the outset, however, the *Deep Space Nine* mission is a singular one: set on a space station orbiting Bajor—a planet recently freed from 60 years of Cardassian occupation—the Starfleet team, led by Commander Benjamin Sisko, is here to help the Bajorans reunite and rebuild their world.

It's not a comfortable place. When the lizard-necked Cardassians abandoned Bajor, they effectively trashed the place, ravaging the planet and stripping DS9 of much of its advanced technology and defense systems, as well as looting the shops along its 360 degree high street called the Promenade.

As an assignment, it seems like a hiding to nothing, until the discovery of a stable "wormhole"—a crack in space—through which travelers can leap 70,000 light-years at a single bound, to reach the Gamma Quadrant, an unexplored region of the galaxy. Suddenly, DS9 is of strategic importance—as the only service station on this new intergalactic superhighway, they find new life and new civilizations coming to them.

Star Trek creator Gene Roddenberry's vision of the future had always maintained a keen sense of optimism, based on mutual respect and cooperation. *Next Generation* executive producers and *Deep Space Nine* creators Rick Berman and Michael Piller set about bringing a little conflict into that pristine universe. Doubts and fears, suspicion and danger, lust and envy, frustration and depression, were all present in one or other of the characters.

Sisko—played by Avery Brooks who had been Robert Urich's shadowy friend Hawk in *Spenser: For Hire*—should have been a chip off the heroic block. But, at the series' outset, he's a man eaten up with bitterness against *Enterprise* captain Jean-Luc Picard whom he blames for the death of his wife three years earlier when, as Locutus, Picard had led a Borg attack on the starship they were serving on. Their personal conflict is played out in the pilot story, "Emissary."

Sisko's First Officer is a Bajoran woman, Major Kira Nerys, a prickly ex-freedom fighter who suffers the Federation presence as a means of keeping the Cardassians at bay.

The outpost's Security Officer is Odo, a grumpy, shape-shifting alien whose natural form is a pool of gelatinous liquid.

Science Officer is Lt. Jadzia Dax. One of the "joined species" known as the Trill, she's a 300-year-old parasitic lifeform (symbiont) in the body of a beautiful woman (the host).

DS9's Medical Officer is Dr. Julian Bashir, a wet-behind-the-ears medic fresh out of Starfleet Academy with lofty ideas about heroic adventures in the wilderness.

Bashir regularly gets on the nerves of Chief Operations Officer Miles O'Brien, the down-to-earth ex-Transporter Chief from the *Enterprise*, and the only really familiar face in the new series. That is, unless you count the jug-eared visage of Quark, the typically lascivious and greedy Ferengi owner of DS9's sleazy bar and casino, which comes complete with the ultimate in safe sex, a computer-simulated brothel known as the holosuites. Quark rubs along with Sisko, but is a thorn in the side of Odo.

Sisko also has to contend with his 14-year-old son, Jake, a troubled adolescent still wounded by his mother's death. O'Brien, too, has family troubles as his wife, Keiko, and their daughter Molly have, of course, transferred to DS9 with him. But Keiko would rather be back on the *Enterprise*.

Regular *Next Generation* guests, Q, Vash and Lwaxana Troi all made cross-over appearances in the new show.

For Armin Shimerman, who stars as Quark, this was not his first time in Ferengi makeup. He had played one of the first Ferengis encountered in the *Next Generation* series. Rene Auberjonois who plays Odo was best known previously as the snooty Clayton Endicott III in the sitcom *Benson*.

By the end of the Season Two, *Deep Space Nine* was looking in better shape to carry the *Trek* torch toward the millennium. Teasing hints of a powerful alien force beyond the wormhole had climaxed in the introduction of an evil enemy known as the Jem'Hadar, soldiers of the Dominion who rule the Gamma Quadrant. With the arrival of the *Defiant*—a powerful, fully weaponed ship three times the size of a DS9 runabout, Season Three begins with a two-part story, "The Search," in which Sisko and Co set off to search out the Founders of the Dominion and confront the Jem'Hadar in a fierce battle. Part 2 of the story is directed by Jonathan Frakes, thus further cementing the ties between *Deep Space Nine* and *Next Generation*.

Season Three played out that story with the Founders of the Dominion revealed as Odo's race of shape-shifters—though Odo himself resisted their repeated attempts to lure him back to the fold.

Jonathan Frakes also made a guest appearance in the third season, as his maverick "twin," as *DS9* showed marked signs of improvement. But in the U.S. ratings were still declining, and it took the return of another *Next Generation* regular to bring the series back up to warp speed. Michael Dorn was persuaded to pull on the prosthetics once again as everyone's favorite Klingon, Worf, who was pressed back into service as Sisko's new diplomatic liaison when executive producer Rick Berman decided to unravel the shaky peace treaty between the Federation and the Klingon Empire.

However, Dorn's name wasn't the only new one added to *DS9*'s credits for Season Four. The Sudanese-born artist formerly known as Siddig El Fadil sent merchandisers into a spin by changing his oft-mispronounced name to Alexander Siddig.

Season Five opened with the DS9 crew infiltrating the Klingon Empire to expose Gowron as an imposter Changeling and, to celebrate *Trek*'s 30th birthday, there was a *Forrest Gump*–like fusion of the *DS9* cast with Kirk and Spock as they were in classic *Trek*'s "The Trouble with Tribbles." Plus: Kira gives birth to the child she's carrying for Keiko. Also returning: Quark's mom and his Klingon "wife," Grilka. However, you won't see so much of Sisko's precious *Defiant*—it was all but destroyed in the eighth *Trek* movie, *First Contact*.

MAIN CAST

Commander Benjamin Sisko Avery Brooks   *Odo* Rene Auberjonois
Major Kira Nerys Nana Visitor   *Lt. Jadzia Dax* Terry Farrell
Chief Operations Officer Miles O'Brien Colm Meaney
Dr. Julian Bashir Siddig El Fadil   *Quark* Armin Shimerman
Jake Sisko Cirroc Lofton
Lt. Commander Worf Michael Dorn *(from Season 4)*

Creators: Rick Berman, Michael Piller
Executive producers: Rick Berman, Michael Piller, Ira Steven Behr *(from Season Four)*
Story editor: Peter Allan Fields
Producer: Ronald D. Moore, Peter Allan Fields *(Season Two)*, Peter Lauritson *(from Season Two)*, René Echevarria *(from Season Three)*, Hans Beimler, Steve Oster *(both from Season Four)*

Creative consultant: Michael Piller *(from Season Three)*
A Paramount Production
U.S. Premiere: January 1993
U.K. Premiere: 15 August 1993
(Sky One)

Season One
19 episodes, including two-hour pilot, shown in U.K. in two parts

Emissary

w Michael Piller, *story by* Michael Piller & Rick Berman
A reluctant Benjamin Sisko arrives on Deep Space Nine to oversee the repair of the space station and help the Bajorans to rebuild their world and to join the Federation. Still tortured by his wife's death at the hands of the Borg, he has a frosty meeting with the *Enterprise*'s Captain Picard whom he blames for her death. The Bajorans' spiritual leader, Kai Opaka, reveals that Sisko's arrival has a deep spiritual purpose linked to the recovery of eight mystical orbs stolen by the Cardassians. The discovery of a stable wormhole brings Sisko to an encounter with the strange alien force behind the orbs and a chance to exorcise his personal demons by reliving the circumstances leading up to his wife's death.
Captain Picard/Locutus Patrick Stewart
Kai Opaka Camille Saviolla
Jennifer Felecia Bell

Gul Dukat Marc Alaimo

Director: David Carson

A Man Alone

w Gerald Sanford & Michael Piller
The adjustment period aboard DS9 continues as the new residents try to come to terms with their new life and each other. Keiko O'Brien attempts to start a school and Jake Sisko befriends a rowdy Ferengi boy, Nog. Meanwhile, Security Chief Odo's character is questioned when he is implicated in the murder of a shady Bajoran and Bashir works to prove his innocence.
Keiko Rosalind Chao
Zayra Edward Laurance Albert
Rom Max Grodenchik
Nog Aron Eisenberg
Ibudan Stephen James Carver
Bajoran man Peter Vogt
Old man/Ibudan Yom Klunis

Director: Paul Lynch

Past Prologue

w Peter Allan Fields, *story by* Kathryn Powers
A reunion with a member of the Bajoran underground who wants to close off the wormhole to diminish Bajor's strategic importance, forces Kira to choose between her people and her duty as a Federation officer.
Tahna Los Jeffrey Nordling
Garak Andrew Robinson
Lursa Barbara March
B'Etor Gwynyth Walsh
Gul Dunar Vaughn Armstrong
Bajoran deputy Richard Ryder
Admiral Susan Bay

Director: Winrich Kolbe

Babel

w Ira Steven Behr
A mysterious epidemic sweeps through Deep Space Nine, and it falls to Kira to find an antidote.
Jaheel Jack Kehler
Surmak Ren Matthew Faison
Nurse Jabara Ann Gillespie
Galis Blin Geraldine Farrell
Asoth Bo Zenga
Bajoran deputy Richard Ryder

Director: Paul Lynch

Captive Pursuit

w Tim Burns *&* Michael Piller
O'Brien befriends the "prey" in an alien hunting game whose contestants play by strange and violent rules, and helps him elude his pursuers.
Tosk Scott MacDonald
The Hunter Gerrit Graham
Miss Sarda Kelly Curtis

Director: Corey Allen

Q-Less

w Robert Hewitt Wolfe, *story by* Hannah Louise Shearer
After the irrepressible Q and the adventuress Vash arrive on DS9, the station begins to experience mysterious power drains. At first the crew suspects Q is behind the power losses. But with the station in danger of being sucked into the wormhole, they struggle to find the real cause.
Vash Jennifer Hetrick
Q John de Lancie
Bajoran Clerk Van Epperson
Kolos Tom McCleister
Bajoran woman Laura Cameron

Director: Paul Lynch

Dax

w Dorothy C. Fontana *&* Peter Allan Fields, *story by* Peter Allan Fields
Curzon Dax, Jadzia's former Trill identity, is accused of murder. Although Jadzia remains strangely tight-lipped, Sisko directs Kira, Bashir and Odo to find evidence to prove Dax's innocence.
Ilon Tandro Gregory Itzin
Judge Renora Anne Haney
Selin Peers Richard Lineback
Enina Fionnula Flanagan

Director: David Carson

The Passenger

w Morgan Gendel, Robert Hewitt Wolfe *&* Michael Piller, *story by* Morgan Gendel
The crew's efforts to thwart a hijack are complicated when a sinister alien criminal hides his consciousness in the brain of someone aboard Deep Space Nine.
Ty Kajada Caitlin Brown
Lt. George Primmin James Lashly
Durg Christopher Collins
Rao Vantika James Harper

Director: Paul Lynch

Move Along Home

w Frederick Rappaport, Lisa Rich *&* Jeanne Carrigan-Fauci, *story by* Michael Piller
Quark's attempt to cheat a delegation from a newly discovered species from the Gamma Quadrant, called the Wadi, places DS9's senior officers in a labyrinth of danger, where they are forced to play out a bizarre and deadly alien game.
Falow Joel Brooks
Lt. George Primmin James Lashly
Chandra Clara Bryant

Director: David Carson

The Nagus

w Ira Steven Behr, *story by* David Livingston
Quark is astonished when he is suddenly named leader of the Ferengi financial empire—but not so thrilled when he becomes a target for assassins.
Rom Max Grodenhik
Nog Aron Eisenberg
Grand Nagus Zek Wallace Shawn
Maihar'du Tiny Ron
Gral Lee Arenberg
Krax Lou Wagner
Nava Barry Gordon

Director: David Livingston

Vortex

w Sam Rolfe
An alien fugitive from the Gamma Quadrant tempts Odo into helping him escape by telling the shapeshifter he encountered a Changeling colony on an uncharted asteroid.
Croden Cliff DeYoung
Ah-Kel/Ro-Kel Randy Oglesby
Rom Max Grodenchik
Hadan Gordon Clapp
Yareth Leslie Engelberg
Vulcan captain Kathleen Garrett

Director: Winrich Kolbe

Battle Lines

w Richard Danus & Evan Carlos Somers, *story by* Hilary Bader
On a trip into the Gamma Quadrant, Sisko, Kira, Bashir and the Bajoran spiritual leader Kai Opaka are stranded on a war-torn world where the warriors can never die and are doomed to fight for eternity.
Kai Opaka Camille Saviola
Shel-la Jonathan Banks
Zlangco Paul Collins

Director: Paul Lynch

The Storyteller

w Kurt Michael Bensmiller & Ira Steven Behr, *story by* Kurt Michael Bensmiller
Much against his will, O'Brien becomes spiritual leader of a Bajoran village whose people believe he is the only one who can save them from a destructive energy force called the Dal'Rok.
Hovath Lawrence Monoson
Sirah Kay E. Kuter
Varis Gina Philips
Faren Jim Jansen
Nog Aron Eisenberg
Woban Jordan Lund

Director: David Livingston

Progress

w Peter Allan Fields
A stubborn old Bajoran farmer who won't leave his home on a moon that is about to be cracked open for an energy project, forces Kira to take a good look at how much she has been changed by her alliance with the Federation.
Mullibok Brian Keith
Baltrim Terrence Evans
Keena Annie O'Donnell
Nog Aron Eisenberg
Alien captain Nicholas Worth
Toran Michael Bofshever

Director: Les Landau

If Wishes Were Horses

w Nell McCue Crawford, William L. Crawford & Michael Piller, *story by* Nell McCue Crawford & William L. Crawford
Personnel on the space station find their fantasies coming to life as a prelude to a dangerous rupture in space that threatens to engulf them.
Keiko Rosalind Chao
Buck Bokai Keone Young
Rumpelstiltskin Michael John Anderson
Molly Hana Hatae

Director: Robert Legato

The Forsaken

w Don Carlos Dunaway & Michael Piller, *story by* Jim Trombetta
While an alien entity wreaks havoc with the station's computer, Odo finds himself trapped in a turbolift with the irrepressible Lwaxana Troi who has set her sights on a romance with him. (With her appearance in this episode, Majel Barrett became the only performer to have spanned three *Trek* incarnations.)
Lwaxana Troi Majel Barrett
Ambassador Taxco Constance Towers
Ambassador Lojal Michael Ensign
Ambassador Vadosia Jack Shearer
Anara Benita Andre

Director: Les Landau

Dramatis Personae

w Joe Menosky
Odo is caught in the middle when an alien influence forces Kira and Sisko to wage a deadly power struggle.
Klingon Tom Towles
Valerian Stephen Parr
Guard Randy Pflug
Ensign Jeff Pruitt

Director: Cliff Bole

Duet

w Peter Allan Fields, *story by* Lisa Rich & Jeanne Carrigan Fauci
Kira discovers that a visiting Cardassian could actually be a notorious war criminal known as the "Butcher of Gallitepp," responsible for countless atrocities at a Bajoran labor camp.
Marritza Harris Yulin
Gul Dukat Marc Alaimo
Kaval Red Sorel
Kainon Tony Rizzoli
Captain Norman Large
Neela Robin Christopher

Director: James L. Conway

In the Hands of the Prophets

w Robert Hewitt Wolfe
When a Bajoran spiritual leader objects to Keiko's secular teachings about the wormhole, she stirs up unrest on DS9 and threatens to destroy the alliance between Bajor and the Federation.
Vedek Winn Louise Fletcher
Keiko O'Brien Rosalind Chao
Vedek Bareil Philip Anglim
Neela Robin Christopher
Vendor Michael Eugene Fairman

Director: David Livingston

Season Two
26 episodes

The Homecoming

w Ira Steven Behr, *story by* Jeri Taylor & Ira Steven Behr
Kira risks her life and war with the Cardassians to rescue Li Nalas, a mythical Bajoran hero from a distant prison colony. (First of a trilogy of stories that gets Season Two off to a strong start.)
Li Nalas Richard Beymer
Minister Jaro Frank Langella
Rom Max Grodenchik
Borum Michael Bell
Gul Dukat Marc Alaimo

Director: Winrich Kolbe

The Circle

w Peter Allan Fields
Relieved of her post on DS9 in favor of Li Nalas, and sent back to Bajor, Kira helps to reveal the secret force behind "The Circle," an extremist Bajoran group that is plotting a revolution.
Li Nalas Richard Beymer
Minister Jaro Frank Langella
Vedek Winn Louise Fletcher
Krim Stephen Macht
Admiral Chekote Bruce Gray
Zef'no Mike Genovese
Vedel Bareil Philip Anglim

Director: Corey Allen

The Siege

w Michael Piller
Sisko evacuates Deep Space Nine but stays behind to lead a daring last stand against the Bajoran takeover forces. Meanwhile Kira and Dax embark on a desperate mission to reveal the truth about the coup—that the Cardassians are secretly behind it.

Vedek Winn Louise Fletcher
Minister Jaro Frank Langella
Keiko Rosalind Chao
Colonel Day Steven Weber
Over-General Krim Stephen Macht
Li Nalas Richard Beymer
Vedek Bareil Philip Anglim
Rom Max Grodenchik
Nog Aron Eisenberg

Director: Winrich Kolbe

Invasive Procedures

w John Whelpley & Robert Hewitt Wolfe, *story by* Robert Hewitt Wolfe
The crew must fight for Jadzia's life when a desperate Trill takes the group hostage and steals the Dax symbiont, leaving Jadzia's host body to die.
Verad John Glover
Mareel Megan Gallagher
T'Kar Tim Russ
Yeto Steve Rankin

Director: Les Landau

Cardassians

w James Croker, *story by* Gene Wolande & John Wright
A young Cardassian, orphaned in the war and raised by Bajorans, becomes a pawn in a sinister political game when his people attempt to reclaim him.
Keiko Rosalind Chao
Garak Andrew Robinson
Kotan Pa'Dar Robert Mandan
Proka Terrence Evans
Rugal Vidal Peterson
Zolan Dion Anderson
Gul Dukat Marc Alaimo

Director: Cliff Bole

Melora

w Evan Carlos Somers, Steven Baum, Michael Piller & James Crocker, *story by* Evan Carlos Somers
After falling in love with an Elaysian woman whose species is unable to walk in "normal" gravity, Bashir develops a technology that could free her from her wheelchair forever. Meanwhile Quark welcomes an old acquaintance who says he has come to the station to kill him.
Ensign Melora Pazlar Daphne Ashbrook
Fallit Kot Peter Crombie
Ashrock Don Stark

Director: Winrich Kolbe

Rules of Acquisition

w Ira Steven Behr, *story by* Hilary J. Bader
A Ferengi female who has defied the law and disguised herself as a male risks it all when she falls in love with Quark.
Pel Helene Udy
Grand Nagus Zek Wallace Shawn
Inglatu Brian Thompson
Rom Max Grodenchik
Zyree Emilia Crow
Maihar'du Tiny Ron

Director: David Livingston

Necessary Evil

w Peter Allan Fields
An attack on Quark's life revives Odo's memories of a five-year-old unsolved murder—for which Kira was a prime suspect—and threatens to break the bond of trust that has grown between them.
Pallra Katherine Moffat
Rom Max Grodenchik
Gul Dukat Marc Alaimo

Director: James L. Conway

Second Sight

w Mark Gehred-O'Connell, Ira Steven Behr & Robert Hewitt Wolfe, *story by* Mark Gehred-O'Connell
Sisko falls in love for the first time since his wife's death, but the beautiful stranger hides a mysterious secret—she is just an image created by a dying "psychoprojective" telepath.
Fenna/Nidell Salli Elise Richardson
Professor Seyetik Richard Kiley

Director: Alexander Singer

Sanctuary

w Frederick Rappaport, *story by* Gabe Essoe & Kelley Miles
Kira's desire to help a displaced alien race, the Skrreeans, who arrive on Deep Space Nine from the Gamma Quadrant, is rocked when they claim Bajor as their people's legendary homeland.
Haneek Deborah May
Varani William Schallert
Tumak Andrew Koenig
Nog Aron Eisenberg
General Hazar Michael Durrell
Vayna Betty McGuire
Vedek Sorad Robert Curtis-Brown
Rozahn Kitty Swink

Director: Les Landau

Rivals

w Joe Menosky, *story by* Jim Trombeta & Michael Piller
Quark feels threatened when a charming swindler arrives on the station and opens a competing bar, but more than his profits are affected by his rival's strange gambling device, which is upsetting the natural laws of probability.
Keiko Rosalind Chao
Roana Barbara Bosson
Alsia K. Callan
Martus Chris Sarandon
Rom Max Grodenchik
Cos Albert Henderson

Director: David Livingston

The Alternate

w Bill Dial, *story by* Jim Trombetta & Bill Dial
Odo's Bajoran mentor arrives on *DS9* intent on resuming his search for Odo's true origin. But when their quest leads them to a planet in the Gamma Quadrant, it results in havoc aboard the station.
Dr. Mora Pol James Sloyan

Director: David Carson

Armageddon Game

w Morgan Gendel
Bashir and O'Brien work to rid two alien races of a deadly bio-mechanical weapon called Harvesters, unaware that their hosts plan to eliminate them as part of the peace process. While their DS9 comrades are informed they are dead, the pair struggles to stay alive and send out a distress signal to the station.
Keiko Rosalind Chao
E'Tyshra Darleen Carr
Sharat Peter White
Nydrom Larry Cedar

Director: Winrich Kolbe

Whispers

w Paul Robert Coyle & Michael Piller, *story by* Paul Robert Coyle
O'Brien returns from a security mission to the Paradas system to notice that everyone on DS9 has seemingly turned against him.
Keiko Rosalind Chao
Ensign DeCurtis Todd Waring
Admiral Rollman Susan Bay
Coutu Philip LeStrange

Director: Les Landau

Paradise

w Jeff King, Richard Manning *&* Hans Beimler,
   story by Jim Trombetta *&* James Crocker

Sisko and O'Brien are stranded on a planet inhabited by a colony of humans who have rejected any form of technology. Here Sisko gets firsthand experience of the leader's harsh methods of discipline.

Alixus Gail Strickland
Cassandra Julia Nickson
Joseph Steve Vinovich
Vinod Michael Buchman Silver
Stephan Erick Weiss

Director: Corey Allen

Shadowplay

w Robert Hewitt Wolfe

In the Gamma Quadrant, Odo and Dax try to solve the mystery of an alien planet whose inhabitants are disappearing without explanation.

Colyus Kenneth Mars
Rurigan Kenneth Tobey
Taya Noley Thornton
Vedek Bareil Philip Anglim

Director: Robert Scheerer

Playing God

w Jim Trombetta *&* Michael Piller, *story by* Jim
   Trombetta

While training her first Trill initiate, Arjin, Dax discoves a tiny, developing universe, which, as it grows, is displacing their universe and will engulf the station. Reluctant to destroy it after finding signs of life within, she and Arjin set off to return it to where they found it.

Arjin Geoffrey Blake
Klingon host Ron Taylor
Cardassian Richard Poe

Director: David Livingston

Profit and Loss

w Flip Kobler *&* Cindy Marcus

Quark is reunited with the love of his life, Natima Lang, a Cardassian who is now a fugitive with leaders of the Cardassian underground movement, and finds himself caught up in her struggle as he tries to win back her affections.

Prof. Natima Lang Mary Crosby
Garak Andrew Robinson
Hogue Michael Reilly Burke
Rekelen Heidi Swedberg
Gul Toran Edward Wiley

Director: Robert Wiemer

Blood Oath

w Peter Allan Fields, *based on material by*
   Andrea Moore Alton

Dax risks her life and her future with Starfleet to fulfill a blood oath made with three aged Klingons when she was Curzon Dax, to kill a vicious enemy called the Albino.

Kor John Colicos
Kang Michael Ansara
Koloth William Campbell
Albino Bill Bolender
Assistant Christopher Collins

Director: Winrich Kolbe

The Maquis, Part 1

w James Crocker, *story by* Rick Berman,
   Michael Piller, Jeri Taylor *&* James Crocker

After the destruction of a Cardassian freighter leaving DS9, Sisko uncovers a Federation terrorist group who feel betrayed by the recent Federation/Cardassia treaty, and whose actions could provoke a new war with the Cardassians.

Gul Dukat Marc Alaimo
Lt. Commander Cal Hudson Bernie Casey
Amaros Tony Plana
Sakonna Bertila Damas
Gul Evek Richard Poe
Samuels Michael A. Krawic
Kobb Amanda Carlin

Director: David Livingston

The Maquis, Part 2

w Ira Steven Behr, *story by* Rick Berman,
   Michael Piller, Jeri Taylor *&* Ira Steven Behr

Sisko and Gul Dukat join forces in an effort to avert a war between the Cardassians and a group of Federation colonists led by Sisko's old friend, Cal Hudson.

Cal Hudson Bernie Casey
Gul Dukat Marc Alaimo
Amaros Tony Plana
Legate Parn John Schuck
Admiral Necheyev Natalija Nogulich
Sakonna Bertila Damas
Xepolite Michael Bell
Kobb Amanda Carlin

Director: Corey Allen

The Wire

w Robert Hewitt Wolfe
Bashir fights to save his Cardassian friend Garak, who is slowly being killed by a brain implant to which he is addicted, and discovers details about Garak's past as a member of the Obsidian Order—the eyes and ears of the Cardassian Empire.
Garak Andrew Robinson
Glinn Boheeka Jimmie F. Skaggs
Jabara Ann Gillespie
Enabran Tain Paul Dooley

Director: Kim Friedman

Crossover

w Peter Allan Fields & Michael Piller, *story by* Peter Allan Fields
A mishap in the wormhole sends Kira and Bashir into an alternate universe where Bajor is a tyrannical power and humans are slaves, and where the space station is run by Kira's ruthless counterpart, Kira II.
Garak Andrew Robinson
Telok John Cothran Jr.

Director: David Livingston

The Collaborator

w Gary Holland, Ira Steven Behr & Robert Hewitt Wolfe, *story by* Gary Holland
On the eve of elections for Bajor's new spiritual leader, Kira must investigate the leading candidate—and the man she loves—Vedek Bareil, when she learns he may be the Cardassian collaborator responsible for the massacre of 43 Bajoran freedom fighters.
Vedek Bareil Philip Anglim
Vedek Winn Louise Fletcher
Kubus Bert Remsen
Kai Opaka Camille Saviola

Director: Cliff Bole

Tribunal

w Bill Dial
While en route with Keiko for a vacation, O'Brien is arrested by the Cardassians and put on trial for a crime he insists he did not commit. (Avery Brooks makes his directorial debut on the series with this episode.)
Keiko Rosalind Chao
Makbar Caroline Lagerfelt
Boone John Beck
Gul Evek Richard Poe
Cardassian voice Julian Christopher
Kovat Fritz Weaver

Director: Avery Brooks

The Jem'Hadar

w Ira Steven Behr
During a camping trip to the Gamma Quadrant with Jake and Nog, Sisko and Quark are captured and imprisoned by the Jem'Hadar, soldiers of a mysterious power known as the Dominion.
Eris Molly Hagan
Nog Aron Eisenberg
Talak'talan Cress Williams
Captain Keogh Alan Oppenheimer

Director: Kim Friedman

Season Three
26 episodes

The Search, Part 1

w Ronald D. Moore, *story by* Ira Steven Behr & Robert Hewitt Wolfe
Hoping to avert an invasion, Sisko and his officers board a new Starfleet warship, the *Defiant*—equipped with a Romulan cloaking device—for a mission into the Gamma Quadrant in search the "Founders," the mysterious leaders of the Dominion. Along for the ride, Odo finds himself compelled to follow his own agenda . . .
T'Rul Martha Hackett
Ornithar John Fleck
Lt. Cmdr. Eddington Kenneth Marshall
Female Alien Salome Jens

Director: Kim Friedman

The Search, Part 2

w Ira Steven Behr, *story by* Ira Steven Behr & Robert Hewitt Wolfe
In the wake of the Jem'Hadar attack on the *Defiant*, Odo struggles to learn the ways of his people, while Sisko discovers that the price of peace with the Dominion may be too high and embarks on a desperate suicide mission to seal the wormhole.
Female shapeshifter Salome Jens
Garak Andrew Robinson
Admiral Necheyev Natalija Nogulich
T'Rul Martha Hackett
Eddington Kenneth Marshall
Male shapeshifter William Frankfather
Borath Dennis Christopher
Jem'Hadar officer Christopher Doyle

Director: Jonathan Frakes

The House of Quark

w Ronald D. Moore, *story by* Tom Benko
In order to boost his business and gain respect, Quark lies about killing a Klingon, then winds up forced to marry the dead man's widow, Grilka.
Keiko Rosalind Chao
Grilka Mary Kay Adams
D'Ghor Carlos Carrasco
Rom Max Grodenchik
Gowron Robert O'Reilly
Tumek Joseph Ruskin
Kozak John Lendale Bennett

Director: Les Landau

Equilibrium

w René Echevarria, *story by* Christopher Teague
Sisko and Bashir journey to the Trill homeworld where a deadly secret from Dax's past could mean the end of Jadzia's life.
Dr. Renhol Lisa Banes
Joran Belar Jeff Magnus McBride
Timor Nicholas Cascone
Yolad Harvey Vernon

Director: Cliff Bole

Second Skin

w Robert Hewitt Wolfe
Kira is kidnapped by the Cardassians, who try to prove to her that she is really one of their people—Iliana Ghemor—an agent of the Obsidian Order who had volunteered for an undercover operation on Bajor a decade before.
Garak Andrew Robinson
Ghemor Lawrence Pressman
Entek Gregory Sierra
Yeln Tony Papenfuss
Yteppa Cindy Katz
Gul Benil Christopher Carroll
Alenis Grem Freyda Thomas
Ari Billy Burke

Director: Les Landau

The Abandoned

w D. Thomas Maio & Steve Warnek
Odo tries to convince a young, violent Jem'Hadar that there is more to life than fighting and killing. Meanwhile Sisko learns some new things about his own son, Jake, who has started dating a 20-year-old Dabo girl, Marta.
Marta Jill Sayre
Teenage Jem'Hadar Bumper Robinson
Boslic captain Leslie Bevis
Alien high roller Matthew Kimbrough
Jem'Hadar boy Hassan Nicholas

Director: Avery Brooks

Civil Defense

w Mike Krohn
A series of force-fields trap the DS9 crew in various parts of the station when an automated Cardassian security program is accidentally activated. Gul Dukat transports onto the station to taunt the officers, then finds himself unable to leave and powerless to halt the self-destruction sequence.
Garak Andrew Robinson
Gul Dukat Marc Alaimo
Legate Kell Danny Goldring

Director: Reza Badiyi

Meridian

w Mark Gehred-O'Connell, *story by* Hilary Bader & Evan Carlos Somers
Dax falls in love with a man who will soon disappear with his planet, Meridian, into another dimension for 60 years.
Deral Brett Cullen
Deltin Christine Healy
Tiron Jeffrey Combs

Director: Jonathan Frakes

Defiant

w Ronald D. Moore
Will Riker's renegade duplicate, Thomas Riker (TNG: "Second Chances"), now a Maquis terrorist, steals the *Defiant*—with Kira aboard—and attacks Cardassian territory. Worried the Cardassians will believe Starfleet wanted the Maquis to have the warship, Sisko feels obliged to assist Gul Dukat in going after Riker.
Riker Jonathan Frakes
Gul Dukat Marc Alaimo
Korinas Tricia O'Neil
Kalita Shannon Cochran
Tamal Michael Canavan
Cardassian soldier Robert Kerbeck

Director: Cliff Bole

Fascination

w Philip LaZebnik, *story by* Ira Steven Behr & James Crocker
A somewhat embarrassing episode in which a Bajoran celebration on the station is the backdrop for an epidemic of inexplicable romantic attractions among the crew . . . starting with Jake mooning over Kira, and ending with Quark proclaiming his undying love for Keiko!
Lwaxana Troi Majel Barrett
Vedek Bareil Philip Anglim
Keiko Rosalind Chao
Molly Hana Hatae

Director: Avery Brooks

Past Tense, Part 1

w Robert Hewitt Wolfe, *story by* Ira Steven
 Behr & Robert Hewitt Wolfe
One of the better two-parters. A transporter accident
sends Sisko, Bashir and Dax 300 years back in time
to a crucial point in Earth's history—the Bell
Riots—in which hundreds died, but which led to
sweeping social reforms.
Chris Brynner Jim Metzler
B.C. Frank Military
Vin Dick Miller
Bernardo Al Rodrigo
Lee Tina Lifford
Webb Bill Smitrovich
Gabriel Bell John Lendale Bennett

Director: Reza Badiyi

Past Tense, Part 2

w Ira Steven Behr & René Echevarria, *story by*
 Ira Steven Behr & Robert Hewitt Wolfe
With the real Gabriel Bell dead after a scuffle, Sisko
must pose as the rioters' leader in order to restore the
future, even though Bashir reminds him that Bell is
destined to die . . .
Guest cast as previous episode, plus:
Det. Preston Deborah Van Valkenburgh
Grady Clint Howard
Danny Richard Lee Jackson
Swat leader Mitch David Carter
Henry Garcia Daniel Zacapa

Director: Jonathan Frakes

Life Support

w Ronald D. Moore, *story by* Christian Ford &
 Roger Soffer
When Vedek Bareil is critically injured in an acci-
dent, Bashir must use experimental drugs and artifi-
cial brain implants to keep him alive long enough to
help bring about a peace treaty with the Cardassians.
Vedek Bareil Philip Anglim
Kai Winn Louise Fletcher
Nog Aron Eisenberg
Leanne Lark Voorhies
Nurse Ann Gillespie
Legate Turrel Andrew Prine
Riska Eva Loseth

Director: Reza Badiyi

Heart of Stone

w Ira Steven Behr & Robert Hewitt Wolfe
On a deserted moon, Kira is trapped by a strange
crystal formation that starts to grow around her
body, threatening to kill her and forcing Odo to face
the depth of his feelings for his Bajoran friend.
Rom Max Grodenchik
Nog Aron Eisenberg
Female changeling Salome Jens

Director: Alexander Singer

Destiny

w David S. Cohen & Martin A. Winer
Sisko ignores an ancient Bajoran prophecy of doom
in order to undertake a joint scientific venture with
the Cardassians that would allow communication
through the wormhole for the first time.
Gilora Tracy Scoggins
Ulani Wendy Robie
Vedek Yarka Erick Avari
Dejar Jessica Hendra

Director: Les Landau

Prophet Motive

w Ira Steven Behr & Robert Hewitt Wolfe
More comic relief. When the Grand Nagus inexplic-
ably decides to abolish his race's greedy ways by
rewriting the Rules of Acquisition—"If they want
their money back . . . give it to them!"—Quark is
determined to find out what lies behind his actions.
Rom Max Grodenchik
Emi Juliana Donald
Grand Nagus Zek Wallace Shawn
Maihar'du Tiny Ron
Medical big shot Bennet Guillory

Director: Rene Auberjonois

Visionary

w John Shirley, *story by* Ethan H. Calk
An accident causes O'Brien inadvertently to jump
briefly into the near future, where he witnesses his
own death and worse—the destruction of DS9 and
the collapse of the wormhole!
Ruwon Jack Shearer
Karina Annette Helde
Morka Ray Young
Bo'rak Bob Minor
Atul Dennis Madalone

Director: Reza Badiyi

Distant Voices

w Ira Steven Behr & Robert Hewitt Wolfe, *story*
 by Joe Menosky
After an encounter with a dubious acquaintance of
Quark's, Bashir finds himself trapped in a strange
dream world where other DS9 crew assume differ-
ent facets of his personality. He begins to age
rapidly and realizes he must solve the puzzle before
he dies of old age.
Garak Andrew Robinson
Altovar Victor Rivers
Nurse Ann Gillespie
Dabo girl Nicole Forester

Director: Alexander Singer

Through the Looking Glass

w Ira Steven Behr & Robert Hewitt Wolfe
Sequel to Season Two's "Crossover." Sisko is
snatched into the parallel universe where he must as-
sume the identity of his dead counterpart to rescue the
alternate version of his late wife before she hands over
a detection device capable of locating the rebels. Only
problem . . . in this dimension, Jennifer hates him!
Garak Andrew Robinson
Jennifer Felecia M. Bell
Rom Max Grodenchik
Tuvok Tim Russ
Cardassian overseer John Patrick Hayden
Marauder Dennis Madalone

Director: Winrich Kolbe

Improbable Cause

w René Echevarria, *story by* Robert Lederman
& David R. Long
First of a two-part story. When Garak's tailor's shop
is blown up, Odo launches an investigation to find
out who is trying to kill the Cardassian exile—and
why—and unravels a sinister and dangerous plot in-
volving the Romulans.
Garak Andrew Robinson
Retaya Carlos LaCamara
Informant Joseph Ruskin
Romulan Darwyn Carson
Mila Julianna McCarthy
Enabran Tain Paul Dooley

Director: Avery Brooks

The Die Is Cast

w Ronald D. Moore
Part 2 of a two-part story. On the eve of a joint
Romulan/Cardassian attack against the Dominion,
Garak faces having to prove his loyalty to his former
mentor by eliminating Odo.
Garak Andrew Robinson
Enabran Tain Paul Dooley
Lovok Leland Orser
Lt. Commander Eddington Kenneth Marshall
Toddman Leon Russom
Romulan pilot Wendy Schenker

Director: David Livingston

Explorers

w René Echevarria, *story by* Hilary J. Bader
Sisko builds a new version of an elegant ancient Ba-
joran space vessel and Jake joins him on an adven-
ture to prove an 800-year-old legend that Bajorans
once traveled to Cardassia.
Gul Dukat Marc Alaimo
Dr. Elizabeth Lense Bari Hochwald
Leeta Chase Masterson

Director: Cliff Bole

Family Business

w Ira Steven Behr & Robert Hewitt Wolfe
When his bar is shut down because of his mother's il-
licit activities, Quark returns to the Ferengi Home-
world to confront her and discovers she has broken the
Ferengi law prohibiting females from earning a profit.
Meanwhile Sisko embarks on a new relationship.
Kasidy Yates Penny Johnson
Rom Max Grodenchik
Liquidator Brunt Jeffrey Combs
Ishka Andrea Martin
Secretary Mel Green

Director: Rene Auberjonois

Shakaar

w Gordon Dawson
Sent to Bajor on a mission against her former leader
in the resistance movement, Kira ends up joining
him as a fugitive when Kai Wynn sends in troops to
arrest him.
Shakaar Duncan Regehr
Lupaza Diana Salinger
Furel William Lucking
Syvar Sherman Howard
Lenaris John Doman
Kai Wynn Louise Fletcher

Director: Jonathan West

Facets

w René Echevarria
Jadzia "meets" her former personas through a Trill
ceremony, the zhian'tara, the rite of closure, where
their personalities take over another person as tem-
porary hosts. But problems start when one of the
past hosts refuses to give up its newfound body.
Guardian Jeffrey Alan Chandler
Rom Max Grodenchik
Nog Aron Eisenberg
Leeta Chase Masterson

Director: Cliff Bole

The Adversary

w Ira Steven Behr & Robert Hewitt Wolfe
A visiting ambassador briefs the DS9 command personnel on a *coup d'état* within one of the Federation's newer allies and recommends the *Defiant* be
dispatched as a show of strength. But as the crew
nears its destination they realize they've been
tricked and that the ship is under the control of a
Founder who is determined to provoke a war.
Krajensky Lawrence Pressman
Eddington Kenneth Marshall
Bolian Jeff Austin

Director: Alexander Singer

Season Four
25 episodes

The Way of the Warrior

w Ira Steven Behr & Robert Hewitt Wolfe
A fleet of Klingon ships uncloaks around DS9, and their leader, General Martok, tells Sisko they've come to help the Federation fight the Dominion—though no request has been made. To try to understand the Klingon motives, Sisko aks for a new diplomatic liaison—Worf. When the Klingons then invade Cardassia, the Federation condemns the attack and, as the 20-year-old peace treaty with the Klingons unravels, the station becomes a battleground. (Cracking feature-length episode to bring Worf into the series.)
Gul Dukat Marc Alaimo
Garak Andrew Robinson
Martok J.G. Hertzler
Kaybok Christopher Darga
Gowron Robert O'Reilly
Kasidy Yates Penny Johnson
Huraga William Dennis Hunt
Drex Obi Ndefo
Weapons officer Patricia Tallman

Director: James L. Conway

The Visitor

w Michael Taylor
When a tragic accident aboard the *Defiant* causes Sisko to vanish before his son's eyes, Jake begins a lifelong obsession to bring him back. (An especially poignant episode.)
Adult Jake Tony Todd
Korena Galyn Gorg
Nog Aron Eisenberg
Melanie Rachel Robinson

Director: David Livingston

Hippocratic Oath

w Lisa Klink, *story by* Nick Corea & Lisa Klink
O'Brien and Bashir are captured by a group of rebel Jem'Hadar who force Julian to find a cure for their forced addiction to Ketracel-whirte, the drug that ensures their loyalty to the Founders.
Goran'Agar Scott MacDonald
Arak'Taral Stephen Davies
Meso'Clan Jeremy Roberts
Temo'Zuma Marshall Teague
Shady alien Roderick Garr

Director: Rene Auberjonois

Indiscretion

w Nick Corea, *story by* Toni Marberry & Jack Trevino
When Kira investigates the six-year-old disappearance of a Cardassian ship containing Bajoran prisoners, she is dismayed when Gul Dukat accompanies her. And she's even more dismayed when she learns the real reason he's come along—to find and kill his daughter by his Bajoran mistress.
Kassidy Yates Penny Johnson
Gul Dukat Marc Alaimo
Razka Roy Brocksmith
Ziyal Cyia Batten
Heler Thomas Prisco

Director: LeVar Burton

Rejoined

w Ronald D. Moore & René Echevarria, *story by* René Echevarria
Jadzia Dax must choose between her feelings and the taboos of Trill society when she is reunited with the wife of one of Dax's previous hosts. (Hyped-up episode containing Dax's controversial lesbian kiss.)
Lenara Susanna Thompson
Bejal Tim Ryan
Pren James Noah
Eddington Kenneth Marshall

Director: Avery Brooks

LittleGreen Men

w Ira Steven Behr & Robert Hewitt Wolfe, *story by* Toni Marberry & Jack Trevino
A shuttle malfunction while en route to Starfleet Academy sends Quark, Rom and Nog back to Roswell, New Mexico, in 1947. While the military suspect them of being invaders, Quark senses a business opportunity . . . (Surprisingly funny dig at the Roswell hype.)
Rom Max Grodenchik
Nog Aron Eisenberg
Nurse Garland Megan Gallagher
Denning Charles Napier
Carlson Conor O'Farrell
Wainwright James G. MacDonald

Director: James L. Conway

Starship Down

w David Mack & John J. Ordover
A trade mission goes wrong and a fierce battle with the Jem'Hadar leaves the *Defiant* trapped in a planet's volatile atmosphere. Dax and Bashir are trapped in a turbolift with the air running out, and Quark must help defuse a torpedo embedded in the hull.
Hanok James Cromwell
Muniz F.J. Rio
Stevens Jay Baker
Carson Sara Mornell

Director: Alexander Singer

The Sword of Kahless

w Hans Beimler, *story by* Richard Danus
Worf, Dax and the ancient Klingon warrior Kor set out to find a mythical sword that they believe has the power to unite the Klingon Empire. But there's precious little unity between the two bickering Klingons . . .
Kor John Colicos
Toral Rick Pasqualone
Soto Tom Morga

Director: LeVar Burton

Our Man Bashir

w Ronald D. Moore, *story by* Robert Gillan
Posing as a 1960s secret agent in a malfunctioning holosuite program, Bashir is all that stands between his trapped fellow officers and certain death.
Garak Andrew Robinson
Rom Max Grodenchik
Eddington Kenneth Marshall
In the holosuite:
Anastasia Nana Visitor
Falcon Colm Meaney
Professor Honey Terry Farrell
Duchamps Michael Dorn
Dr. Noah Avery Brooks
Caprice Melissa Young
Mona Luvsitt Marci Brickhouse

Director: Winrich Kolbe

Homefront

w Ira Steven Behr & Robert Hewitt Wolfe
First of a two-part story. Evidence that Changelings are targetting Earth sends Sisko back to his home planet, where he and Odo must prevent—or prepare for—war with the Dominion.
Admiral Leyton Robert Foxworth
President Jaresh-Inyo Herschel Sparber
Commander Benteen Susan Gibney
Cadet Nog Aron Eisenberg
Joseph Sisko Brock Peters
Head officer Dylan Chalfy

Director: David Livingston

Paradise Lost

w Ira Steven Behr & Robert Hewitt Wolfe, *story by* Ronald D. Moore
Part 2 of a two-part story. While preparing Earth for a possible war with the Dominion, Sisko and Odo discover evidence of a Starfleet plot to overthrow the Federation government and replace it with military rule.
Admiral Leyton Robert Foxworth
President Jaresh-Inyo Herschel Sparber
Commander Benteen Susan Gibney
Cadet Nog Aron Eisenberg

Joseph Sisko Brock Peters
Riley Shepard David Drew Gallagher
Security officer Mina Badie
Academy commandant Rudolph Willrich

Director: Reza Badiyi

Crossfire

w René Echevaerria
Odo's hidden feelings for Kira interfere with his duty to protect the Bajoran First Minister, Shakaar—who also happens to be attracted to her. As he watches the relationship between the pair deepen, Odo must choose between his duties and his own love.
Shakaar Duncan Regehr
Sarish Bruce Wright
Jimenez Charles Tentindo

Director: Les Landau

Return to Grace

w Hans Beimler, *story by* Tom Benko
A demoted Dukat enlists Kira's help in hunting down a ship of murderous Klingons, in a bid to regain his former status in the Cardassian Empire.
Dukat Marc Alaimo
Ziyal Cyia Batten
Damar Casey Biggs
K'Temang John K. Shull

Director: Jonathan West

Sons of Mogh

w Ronald D. Moore
Cast out of Klingon society because of Worf's dishonor, his outcast brother, Kurn, asks Worf to help him regain his honor by killing him in the Mauk-to'Vor death ritual.
Kurn Tony Todd
Noggra Robert Doqui
Tilikia Dell Yount
Klingon officer Elliot Woods

Director: David Livingston

Bar Association

w Robert Hewitt Wolfe & Ira Steven Behr, *story by* Barbara J. Lee & Jennifer A. Lee
Fed up with being pushed around by his brother, Rom organizes Quark's employees into a union and calls a strike.
Rom Max Grodenchik
Leeta Chase Masterson
Grimp Jason Marsden
Frool Emilio Borelli
Liquidator Brunt Jeffrey Combs

Director: LeVar Burton

Accession

w Jane Espenson
A legendary Bajoran appears mysteriously after more than 200 years and challenges Sisko's claim to be the Emissary. Sisko is happy to step aside at first, but grows unhappy with the consequences of his act and the two men head off into the wormhole to ask the Prophets *who* is the real Emissary? And Keiko and Molly return to DS9.
Akorem Laan Richard Libertini
Vedek Porta Robert Symonds
Kai Opaka Camille Saviola
Keiko Rosalind Chao
Molly Hana Hatae
Onara David Carpenter
Latara Grace Zandarski
Gia Laura Jane Salvato

Director: Les Landau

Rules of Engagement

w Ronald D. Moore, *story by* Bradley Thompson & David Weddle
Worf faces a hearing to determine whether he should be extradited to the Klingon homeworld for destroying a civilian ship.
Ch'Pok Ron Canada
Admiral T'Lara Deborah Strange
Helm officer Christopher Michael

Director: LeVar Burton

Hard Time

w Robert Hewitt Wolfe, *story by* Daniel Keys Moran & Lynn Barker
After an alien race implants false memories of a 20-year prison sentence into O'Brien's mind, he has trouble readjusting to station life.
Keiko Rosalind Chao
Rinn Margot Rose
Molly Hana Hatae
Muniz F.J. Rio
Ee'char Craig Wasson

Director: Alexander Singer

Shattered Mirror

w Ira Steven Behr & Hans Beimler
Sisko follows his son into the war-torn mirror universe after Jake is lured there by the living counterpart of his late mother. But after helping the rebels take on the tyrannical Alliance, father and son must face losing Jennifer a second, painful time.
Jennifer Sisko Felicia Bell
Nog Aron Eisenberg
Garak Andrew Robinson
Klingon officer Carlos Carrasco
Helmsman James Black

Director: James L. Conway

The Muse

w René Echevarria, *story by* René Echevarria & Majel Barrett Roddenberry
Odo provides shelter for a pregnant Lwaxana Troi and even prepares to marry her so she can keep her baby. Jake falls under the spell of a mysterious woman who helps inspire his writing.
Lwaxana Troi Majel Barrett
Jeyal Michael Ansara
Onaya Meg Foster
Nurse Tagano Patricia Tallman

Director: David Livingston

For the Cause

w Ronald D. Moore, *story by* Mark Gehred-O'Connell
Sisko is shocked to learn that his girlfriend, Kasidy Yates, may be a Maquis smuggler. But the investigation reveals that another DS9 officer is a Maquis spy.
Kasidy Yates Penny Johnson
Eddington Kenneth Marshall
Tora Ziyal Tracy Middendorf
Brathaw John Prosky
Lt. Reese Steven Vincent Leigh
Garak Andrew Robinson

Director: James L. Conway

To the Death

w Ira Steven Behr & Robert Hewitt Wolfe
Attempting to stop a group of Jem'Hadar renegades from gaining power, Sisko and the *Defiant* crew must join forces with other Jem'Hadar soldiers.
Toman'torax Brian Thompson
Virak'kara Scott Haven
Omet'iklan Clarence Williams III
Weyoun Jeffrey Combs

Director: LeVar Burton

The Quickening

w Naren Shankar
Bashir tries to save a Gamma Quadrant society afflicted with an incurable, terminal disease by the Jem'Hadar, 200 years previously.
Ekoria Ellen Wheeler
Epran Dylan Haggerty
Trevean Michael Sarrazin
Norva Heide Margolis
Attendant Loren Lester
Patient Alan Echevarria
Latia Lisa Moncure

Director: Rene Auberjonois

Body Parts

w Hans Beimler, *story by* Louis P. DeSantis &
  Robert J. Bolivar
Misdiagnosed with a terminal disease, Quark sells
his body parts on the Ferengi market to pay off his
debts, then finds himself unable to break the con-
tract when he learns the truth.
Rom/Gint Max Grodenchik
Keiko Rosalind Chao
Molly Hana Hatae
Liquidator Brunt Jeffrey Combs
Garak Andrew Robinson

Director: Avery Brooks

Broken Link

w Robert Hewitt Wolfe & Ira Steven Behr, *story*
  by George A. Brozak
Struggling to maintain his solid form, Odo is forced
to return to his race's homeworld—where he must
face judgment for killing one of his own.
Female shapeshifter Salome Jens
Gowron Robert O'Reilly
Chalon Aroya Jill Jacobson
Boslic freighter captain Leslie Bevis
Garak Andrew Robinson
Amat'igan Andrew Hawkes

Director: Les Landau

Season Five
(26 episodes)

Apocalypse Rising

w Ira Steven Behr & Robert Hewitt Wolfe
Sisko, Worf, O'Brien and Odo infiltrate a Klingon
ceremony to try to expose Gowron as a Changeling.
Gowron Robert O'Reilly
General Martok J.G. Hertzler
Gul Dukat Marc Alaimo
Damar Casey Biggs

Director: James L. Conway

The Ship

w Hans Beimler, *story by* Pam Wiggington &
  Rick Cason
Sisko finds a crashed Jem'Hadar warship and tries
to take it back to the Federation; a Vorta arrives with
other plans in mind.
Kilana Kaitlin Hopkins
Enrique Muniz F.J. Rio

Director: Kim Friedman

Looking for Par'Mach in All the Wrong Places

w Ronald D. Moore
Quark's former wife, a Klingon named Grilka,

shows up in need of money, so Worf helps Quark
woo her back.
Keiko O'Brien Rosalind Chao
Grilka Mary Kay Adams
Tumek Joseph Ruskin
Thopok Phil Morris

Director: Andrew J. Robinson

Nor the Battle to the Strong

w René Echevarria, *story by* Brice R. Parker
Returning from a conference, Bashir and Jake lend
aid to a Federation colony and end up in a battle
zone.
Kirby Andrew Kavovit
Dr. Kalandra Karen Austin
Bolian nurse Mark Holton
Human nurse Lisa Lord
Ensign Jeb Brown

Director: Kim Friedman

The Assignment

w David Weddle & Bradley Thompson, *story by*
  David R. Long & Robert Lederman
Keiko returns from the Bajoran Fire Caverns pos-
sessed by an alien creature, who wants to use
O'Brien for revenge.
Keiko O'Brien Rosalind Chao
Molly O'Brien Hana Hatae

Director: Allan Kroeker

Trials and Tribble-ations

w Ronald D. Moore & René Echevarria, *story*
  by Ira Steven Behr, Hans Beimler & Robert
  Hewitt Wolfe
In one of the greatest DS9 episodes ever, the crew
travels back in time to stop a Klingon from killing
James T. Kirk and end up interacting with the old
crew in the classic "The Trouble with Tribbles"
episode.
Dulmur Jack Blessing
Lucsly James W. Jansen
Arne Darvin Charlie Brill

Director: Jonathan West

Let He Who Is without Sin

w Robert Hewitt Wolfe & Ira Steven Behr
Worf and Dax vacation at Risa to work out their dif-
ferences, accompanied by Bashir and Leeta, who
have formal separation in mind.
Pascal Fullerton Monte Markham
Bolian Aide Frank Kopyc

Director: Rene Auberjonois

Things Past

w Michael Taylor
Sisko, Odo, Garak and Dax live through a shared vision, linked to Odo's memories of Deep Space Nine under Cardassian rule.
Thrax Kurtwood Smith

Director: LeVar Burton

The Ascent

w Ira Steven Behr & Robert Hewitt Wolfe
On their way to testify at a trial, Odo and Quark crash on a barren mountain and must learn to cooperate or die.
Rom Max Grodenchik
Nog Aron Eisenberg

Director: Allan Kroeker

Rapture

w Hans Beimler, *story by* L.J. Strom
Sisko seeks a legendary lost city on Bajor on the eve of Bajor's acceptance into the Federation . . . and on the eve of war with the Dominion.

Director: Jonathan West

The Darkness and the Light

w Ronald D. Moore, *story by* Bryan Fuller
Members of Kira's former resistance cell are being murdered one by one, so Kira tracks down the true culprit.

Director: Michael Vejar

The Begotten

w Rene Echevarria
Quark sells Odo an injured baby Changeling, and Odo tries to correct the mistakes the Cardassians made while raising him.

Director: Jesus Salvador Trevino

For the Uniform

w Peter Allan Fields
Sisko goes after Michael Eddington, the Starfleet officer who betrayed him and joined the Maquis.
Michael Eddington Kenneth Marshall
Captain Sanders Eric Pierpoint
Cadet Nog Aron Eisenberg

Director: Victor Lobl

In Purgatory's Shadow

w Robert Hewitt Wofe & Ira Steven Behr
When Garak receives a message from his old boss, who is being held captive in a Dominion prison camp, he mounts a rescue mission with Worf.
Enabran Tain Paul Dooley

Director: Gabrielle Beaumont

By Inferno's Light

w Ira Steven Behr & Robert Hewitt Wolfe
The long-anticipated Domion assault finally arrives—but instead of attacking, they head for Cardassian space . . . and Dukat joins them in a great betrayal.

Director: Les Landau

Doctor Bashir, I Presume

w Ronald D. Moore, *story by* Jimmy Diggs
Dr. Lewis Zimmerman—who created the holographic doctor aboard *Voyager*—arrives on DS9 to work on a new holographic doctor based on Bashir.
Dr. Zimmerman Robert Picardo

Director: David Livingston

A Simple Investigation

w René Echevarria
Odo aides a mysterious woman named Arissa, who is fleeing the Orion Syndicate hit men.
Arissa Dey Young
Traidy John Durbin
Serm Nicholas Worth

Director: John Kretchmer

Business as Usual

w Bradley Thompson & David Weddle
Quark's money problems lead him to investigate employment in the arms trade, much to Sisko's displeasure.
Hagath Steven Berkoff

Director: Siddig el Fadil

Ties of Blood and Water

w Robert Hewitt Wolfe, *story by* Edmund Newton & Robbin L. Slocum
Ghemor, a Cardassian who once believed Kira to be his daughter (see "Second Skin"), arrives at DS9 to die and pass his secrets on to Kira.
Taban Thomas Kopache
Ghemor Lawrence Pressman
Furel William Lucking

Director: Avery Brooks

Ferengi Love Songs

w Ira Steven Behr *&* Hans Beimler
Quark is shocked to learn his mother is having an affair with the Grand Nagus and plots to break them up.
Zek Wallace Shawn
Ishka Cecily Adams

Director: Rene Auberjonois

Soldiers of the Empire

w Ronald D. Moore
General Martok, along with Worf and Dax, searches for the missing battlecruiser. Unfortunately, Martok has developed a fear of fighting from his years in a Dominion prison camp.
Tavana Sandra Nelson

Director: LeVar Burton

Children of Time

w René Echevarria, *story by* Gary Holland *&* Ethan H. Calk
The *Defiant* breaks through a time/energy barrier in the Gamma Quadrant, and the crew meet their own descendants—marooned there for generations.
Yedrin Dax Gary Frank
Miranda O'Brien Jennifer S. Parsons

Director: Allan Kroeker

Blaze of Glory

w Robert Hewitt Wolfe *&* Ira Steven Behr
When the Federation intercepts a secret Maquis message about missiles being launched at Cardassia, Sisko appeals to Eddington to help stop them.
Rebecca Eddington Gretchen German

Director: Kim Friedman

Empok Nor

w Hans Beimler, *story by* Bryan Fuller
O'Brien leads a salvage team to an abandoned Cardassian space station in search of spare parts, but runs into boobytraps, including psychotic Cardassian experimental subjects left cryogenically frozen on board.
Pechetti Tom Hodges
Boq'ta Andy Milder
Stolzoff Marjean Holden
Armaco Jeffrey King

Director: Michael Vejar

In the Cards

w Ronald D. Moore, *story by* Truly Barr Clark *&* Scott J. Neal
War approaches, casting a pall over the station, and a Vorta visits to negotiate with Kai Winn. To cheer up his father, Jake tries to bid for a rare baseball card with Nog's help.
Dr. Elias Giger Brian Markinson

Director: Michael Dorn

Call to Arms

w Ira Steven Behr *&* Robert Hewitt Wolfe
Sisko mines the wormhole's exit, preventing Dominion ships from passing through, as war is declared and DS9 is abandoned to the Dominion and Dukat.
General Martok J.G. Hertzler

Director: Allan Kroeker

STAR TREK: VOYAGER

The universe was looking like a crowded place as the *Star Trek* franchise prepared its fourth TV model for launch in 1995.

With more than 250 hours of classic *Trek* and *Next Generation* already on the road, *Deep Space Nine* in its third season, and *Star Trek: Generations* to add to the six previous *Trek* feature films, *Voyager* needed to make a quick impact. It did so.

The highly publicized departure of actress Genevieve Bujold, who jumped ship after just three days in the captain's chair, nearly left the newest starship stalled in the interstellar driveway, and gave the "woman driver" wags a field day. But it got the show noticed.

Bujold reportedly found the rigors of the infamous 18-hour *Trek* days too much of a captain's slog, but with cast and crew locked into a tight schedule, executive producer Rick Berman continued filming on the two-hour, $23 million pilot while scrambling to find a new captain.

Kate Mulgrew—who once starred as Mrs. Columbo in the mystery series about the shabby sleuth's wife—was cast as *Star Trek*'s newest captain, Kathryn Janeway. While not the first woman to command a Starfleet ship (*Next Generation* featured several, including Geordi's mother!), Janeway has certainly raised the female profile from the *Enterprise*'s doctor and counselor.

In the pilot episode, Janeway's ship, the *Voyager*, is dispatched to search for a Maquis vessel that has disappeared in the Badlands, a stretch of space along the demilitarized zone between Federation territory and the Cardassian Empire. The Maquis, introduced in an eponymous *Deep Space Nine* two-parter, is a group of outlaw Federation resistance fighters opposed to the Cardassian/Federation treaty.

The *Voyager* finds the Maquis ship, but both vessels are swept up in a strange phenomenon that sends them into the far reaches of the galaxy—so far that, even at warp speeds, it would take nearly 70 years to return. The two diverse crews band together aboard the *Voyager* to explore this distant part of space and try to find a short-cut home.

Janeway's First Officer is Chakotay, formerly captain of the Maquis ship. A Native American who attended Starfleet Academy and became a lieutenant commander, Chakotay resigned his position to join the Maquis.

Lieutenant Tom Paris comes from a proud family steeped in Starfleet traditions. When the pressures of living up to the family name resulted in tragedy, Paris was given a second chance by Janeway and is determined to prove his worth.

Tuvok, a Vulcan male, is the Starfleet Tactical Officer. A skillful fighter, but with a calm manner, he's the *Voyager*'s peace-keeper. Harry Kim, a youthful Academy graduate, is the Ops/Communication Officer, nervous about living up to his own expectations but looking forward to the challenge, while Chief Engineer is B'Elanna Torres, a half-Klingon, half-human woman who quit the Academy to join the Maquis.

There are a couple of new aliens aboard—Neelix, the guide and all-around handyman, who comes from an unexplored galaxy, and his young lover, Kes, a member of the Ocampa species, another new race to add to *Star Trek*'s alien almanac. Although she appears as a 20-year-old in human years, in the Ocampa's time-scale she's just one year old!

Completing the cast of regulars is Doc Zimmerman, a hologram programmed with up-to-date medical knowledge and capable of treating any disease or injury.

The series quickly introduced a new enemy alien, too—the Kazon, a volatile race split into warring tribes, each of which wants to capture the Federation's superior technology so it can obliterate the others.

With *DS9* locked in its orbit around Bajor and its wormhole, *Star Trek: Voyager* is seen as filling the void left by the departing *Enterprise* for a series that can continue the *Trek* mission in the outgoing style to which we have become accustomed.

Its main problem, however, is that it's just too boring ever to fill that void. Given that the primary aim is for the ship to get home, there's so little progress. *Voyager* just trundles around its corner of the universe (Kazon space seems pretty big) with neither the plots nor the charismatic characters to convince us that it's better to travel hopefully than to arrive.

The series' third season included the first appearance of classic *Trek* stars in *Voyager*, with guest roles for George Takei as Sulu and Grace Lee Whitney as Janice Rand in an episode called "Flashback," which also has references back to the sixth *Trek* movie, *The Undiscovered Country*.

MAIN CAST

Captain Kathryn Janeway Kate Mulgrew *Chakotay* Robert Beltran
Lieutenant Tom Paris Robert Duncan McNeill *Tuvok* Tim Russ
Harry Kim Garrett Wang *B'Elanna Torres* Roxann Biggs-Dawson
Neelix Ethan Phillips *Kes* Jennifer Lien *The Doctor* Robert Picardo

Creators/Executive producers: Rick Berman, Michael Piller, Jeri Taylor
Producers: Merri Howard, Peter Lauritson, Brannon Braga
Theme: Jerry Goldsmith

A Paramount Network Production
U.S. premiere: 16 January 1995
U.K. premiere: 22 October 1995
(Sky 1)

Season One
15 episodes

Caretaker

(90-minute pilot)
w Michael Piller & Jeri Taylor, *story by* Rick Berman, Michael Piller & Jeri Taylor
The USS Starship *Voyager*, captained by renowned commander Captain Kathryn Janeway, is sent on a mission to retrieve a renegade Maquis ship from a dangerous region of space known as the Badlands. But an inexplicable force catapults both vessels 70,000 light-years away to a previously uncharted area. Now the two crews must work together to escape the clutches of an alien life-form known as The Caretaker, and find their way back home.
Banjo man Basil Langton
Jabin Gavan O'Herlihy
Aunt Adah Angela Paton
Quark Armin Shimerman
Lt. Stadi Alicia Coppola
Ocampa doctor Bruce French
Ocampa nurse Jennifer Parsons
Toscat David Selburg
Human doctor Jeff McCarthy
Mark Stan Ivar
Rollins Scott MacDonald
Carey Josh Clark
Gul Evek Richard Poe
Farmer's daughter Keely Sims
Daggin Eric David Johnson
Computer voice Majel Barrett

Director: Winrich Kolbe

Parallax

w Brannon Braga, *story by* Jim Trombetta
The ship encounters a quantum singularity—a star that has collapsed in upon itself, thereby creating a powerful energy field around it—and what it believes to be another ship in jeopardy. But the crew soon realizes it's a mirror image of *Voyager* and the race begins to free the ship before it is destroyed. B'Elanna is promoted to Chief Engineer.
Seska Martha Hackett
Carey Josh Clark
Jarvin Justin Williams

Director: Kim Friedman

Time and Again

w David Klemper & Michael Piller, *story by* David Klemper
Janeway and Paris must defy the Federation's Prime Directive to warn a group of dissenters on a planet that their actions will obliterate all life on their world.
Makull Nicolas Surovy
Teria Joel Polis

Latika Brady Bluhm
Shopkeeper Ryan MacDonald

Director: Les Landau

Phage

w Skye Dent & Brannon Braga, *story by* Timothy De Haas
During an Away Team expedition to a planet to find dilithium crystals, Neelix is attacked and his lungs surgically removed by aliens fighting a disease that eats away at their own bodies and organs.
Seska Martha Hackett
Aliens Cully Fredrickson, Stephen B. Rappaport

Director: Winrich Kolbe

The Cloud

w Tom Szollosi & Michael Piller, *story by* Brannon Braga
While investigating what they believe to be a nebula in search of fuel, the crew realizes they have in fact entered and injured a new life-form that they must help heal as they try to escape.
Ricky Angela Dohrmann
Sandrine Judy Geeson
Gaunt Gary Larry A. Hankin
The Gigolo Luigi Amodeo

Director: David Livingston

Eye of the Needle

w Bill Dial & Jeri Taylor, *story by* Hilary J. Bader
The crew encounters a small wormhole through which they communicate with a cargo vessel on the other side—in the Alpha Quadrant. But it's a Romulan ship and first Janeway must convince its suspicious captain that their story is true.
Telek Vaughn Armstrong
Baxter Tom Virtue

Director: Winrich Kolbe

Ex Post Facto

w Evan Carlos Somers & Michael Piller, *story by* Evan Carlos Somers
Visiting a world at war with a neighboring planet, Paris finds himself accused of a murder he didn't commit. His sentence—to relive the crime from the victim's point of view every 14 hours for the rest of his life. It's up to Tuvok to prove his innocence with a Vulcan mind-meld.
Lidell Robin McKee
Minister Kray Francis Guinan
Doctor Aaron Lustig
Tolen Ren Ray Reinhardt
Numiri captain Henry Brown

Director: LeVar Burton

Emanations

w Brannon Braga
Harry is accidentally transported to an alien culture's world where his presence causes many to doubt their traditional belief in the afterlife. And "dying" may be his only way back . . .
Dr. Neria Jerry Hardin
Hatil Jefrey Alan Chandler
Ptera Cecile Callan
Seska Martha Hackett
Hatil's wife Robin Groves

Director: David Livingston

Prime Factors

w Michael Perricone *&* Greg Elliot, *story by* David R. George III *&* Eric A. Stillwell
Voyager encounters an alien race, the Sikarians, renowned for their hospitality, and with the technology to fold space and travel more than 40,000 light-years in an instant. It sounds like the answer the crew have been looking for, but the Sikarians' hospitality is not all it seems to be . . .
Gath Ronald Guttman
Eudana Yvonne Suhor
Jaret Andrew Hill Newman
Seska Martha Hackett
Carey Josh Clark

Director: Les Landau

State of Flux

w Chris Abbott, *story by* Paul Robert Coyle
Voyager responds to a Kazon distress call and finds a ship crippled by an accident caused by Federation technology—a clear sign that *Voyager* is carrying a traitor.
Seska Martha Hackett
Carey Josh Clark
Kazon dude Anthony DeLongis

Director: Robert Scheerer

Heroes and Demons

w Naren Shankar
The Doctor must overcome his computer-programmed limitations and operate outside sickbay when an alien life-form takes over the ship's holodecks and transforms the living crew members into pure energy. But can he save himself from an amorous female Viking!
Freya Marjorie Monaghan
Unferth Christopher Neame
Hrothgar Michael Keenan

Director: Les Landau

Cathexis

w Brannon Braga, *story by* Brannon Braga *&* Joe Menosky
Chakotay is rendered brain-dead by an attack on his and Tuvok's shuttle. Then Tuvok is possessed by an alien presence that forces the ship into a black nebula and only the spirit of Chakotay can save the crew.
Durst Brian Markinson
Lord Burleigh Michael Cumpsty
Mrs. Templeton Carolyn Seymour

Director: Kim Friedman

Faces

w Kenneth Biller, *story by* Jonathan Glassner *&* Adam Grossman
B'Elanna is captured by the Phage aliens and literally split into two separate beings—one Klingon, the other human. Can both work together to escape the alien laboratory?
Sulan/Durst Brian Markinson
Talaxian prisoner Rob LaBelle
Guard Barton Tinapp

Director: Winrich Kolbe

Jetrel

w Jack Klein, Karen Klein *&* Kenneth Biller, *story by* Scott Nimerfro *&* Jim Thornton
Neelix is confronted by the man responsible for the annihilation of much of the Talaxian race—including his own family.
Ma'bor Jetrel James Sloyan
Gaunt Gary Larry Hankin

Director: Kim Friedman

Learning Curve

w Ronald Wilkerson *&* Jean Louise Matthias
When several former Maquis crew members break Federation rules, it is up to Tuvok to train them in the finer points of Star Fleet protocol and discipline—which are put to the test when a strange virus invades *Voyager*'s bio-neural circuitry, destablizing the ship.
Dalby Armand Schultz
Chell Derek McGrath
Geron Kenny Morrison
Henley Catherine MacNeal
Henry Thomas Dekker
Beatrice Lindsey Haun

Director: David Livingston

Season Two
26 episodes

The 37s

w Jeri Taylor & Brannon Braga
The discovery of an ancient Earth artifact—an old Ford car—floating in space leads the *Voyager* crew to a mysterious planet where they find a cryogenic chamber containing eight humans—one of whom is aviator Amelia Earhart. They learn that the eight are the last surviving members of the 37s, 300 people abducted from Earth in 1937, whose descendants now live contentedly on the planet. Janeway gives each of her crew the chance to choose whether to stay or continue with *Voyager*'s search for a way home. (This episode features the first successful landing of a starship on a planet in any *Trek* series.)
Amelia Earhart Sharon Lawrence
Noonan David Graf
Japanese soldier James Saito
Jack Hayes Mel Winkler
John Evansville John Rubinstein

Director: James L. Conway

Initiations

w Kenneth Biller
When Chakotay borrows a shuttlecraft to perform a solitary Indian ritual, he inadvertently drifts into Kazon-Ogla territory and becomes the target of a Kazon youth attempting to earn his Ogla warrior name by killing the Federation enemy.
Kar Aron Eisenberg
Razik Patrick Kilpatrick
Haliz Tim de Zarn

Director: Winrich Kolbe

Projections

w Brannon Braga
Believing the ship has suffered a massive attack, the Doctor ventures from sickbay via a remote holo-projection system, but then has a problem distinguishing what is real and what isn't. Discovering he has a wife is one thing, but being told he must destroy *Voyager* is quite another!
Lt. Reg Barclay Dwight Schultz

Director: Jonathan Frakes

Elogium

w Kenneth Biller & Jeri Taylor, *story by* Jimmy Diggs & Steve J. Kay
When alien life-forms cause Kes's reproductive process to accelerate, she prematurely enters the elogium, the time of life when Ocampa bodies become fertile. However, this only happens once, so it's Kes's one and only chance to have a child—much to the bewilderment of Neelix.
Ensign Clarke Nancy Hower
Crew members Gary O'Brien, Terry Correll

Director: Winrich Kolbe

Non Sequitur

w Brannon Braga
Ensign Kim is confused when he awakens to find himself back on Earth, working as a design specialist at Starfleet Engineering and engaged to be married. When he accesses his service records they indicate he was never aboard *Voyager* . . .
Cosimo Louis Giambalvo
Libby Jennifer Gatti
Admiral Strickler Jack Shearer
Lt. Lasco Mark Kiely

Director: David Livingston

Twisted

w Kenneth Biller, *story by* Arnold Rudnick & Rich Hosek
A spatial distortion changes *Voyager*'s structural layout and disables the ship. The crew must work quickly to halt the effects—but just finding their way around the ship has become a problem.
Sandrine Judy Geeson
Gaunt Gary Larry Hankin
Baxter Tom Virtue
Crewman Terry Correll

Director: Kim Friedman

Parturition

w Tom Szollosi
As tensions rise between Neelix and Paris over Kes, their shuttle crash-lands on a planet where they find an embryonic pod that hatches an alien baby. The two rivals must work together to sustain the newborn—and keep each other alive when its angry mother approaches.
(No guest cast)

Director: Jonathan Frakes

Persistence of Vision

w Jeri Taylor

A strange force causes the crew to become delusional, and brings their deepest thoughts to the surface. Janeway's holonovel characters become real, Paris confronts his father, Tuvok talks to his wife and Chakotay seduces Torres. It's up to an unaffected Kes and the Doctor to find a solution.

Lord Burleigh Michael Cumpsty
Mrs. Templeton Carolyn Seymour
Mark Stan Ivar
Admiral Paris Warren Munson
Beatrice Lindsay Haun
Henry Thomas Alexander Dekker
Bothan Patrick Kerr
T'Pel Marva Hicks
Crew member MTV's VJ Kennedy

Director: James L. Conway

Tattoo

w Michael Piller, *story by* Larry Brody

When an Away Team encounters hostile natives, Chakotay has flashbacks of himself as a defiant young boy who disappointed his father by not embracing the cultural traditions of his tribe. Left alone on the planet, Chakotay discovers he has more in common with the aliens than he first realized . . . Back on the ship, the Doctor programs himself with a flu virus so he can better understand his patients' discomfort.

Kolopak Henry Darrow
Alien Richard Fancy
Young Chakotay Douglas Spain
Ensign Wildman Nancy Hower
Chief Richard Chaves
Antonio Joseph Palmas

Director: Alexander Singer

Cold Fire

w Brannon Braga, *story by* Anthony Williams

The crew get their hopes up of returning home when they are hailed by Ocampa colonists who agree to lead them to a female mate of The Caretaker—but she has revenge in mind. And as Tuvok trains Kes in using her emerging mental abilities, it becomes clear her powers have been seriously underestimated—a factor noted by the sinister Ocampa leader Tanis who does his evil best to lure her away from the ship.

Tanis Gary Graham
Suspira/Girl Lindsay Ridgeway
Ocampa man Norman Large

Director: Cliff Bole

Maneuvers

w Kenneth Biller

Chakotay feels compelled to defy orders and head off on his own when he learns that Seska is the mastermind behind a Kazon scheme to persuade rival sects to join together to conquer *Voyager*.

Seska Martha Hackett
Culluh Anthony De Longis
Haron Terry Lester
Kelat John Gegenhuber

Director: David Livingston

Resistance

w Lisa Klink, *story by* Kevin Ryan & Michael J. Friedman

When Tuvok and Torres are captured by an oppressive race called the Mokra, Janeway must go undercover to rescue them—accompanied by an eccentric old man who believes she is his long-lost daughter.

Caylem Joel Grey
Augris Alan Scarfe
Darod Tom Todoroff
Guard Glenn Morshower

Director: Winrich Kolbe

Prototype

w Nicholas Corea & Kenneth Biller

B'Elanna Torres reactivates a damaged robot found floating in space—but when it abducts her and orders her to build a prototype for more of its kind, *Voyager* finds itself caught in a robot war.

3947 Rick Worthy
6263 Hugh Hodgin

Director: Jonathan Frakes

Alliances

w Jeri Taylor

After the latest in a series of Kazon attacks, Janeway reluctantly decides to forge an alliance with one or more of the Kazon sects. She's also befriended by the Trabe, an exiled sect and enemies of the Kazon. Thinking their goals are compatible, Janeway forms an alliance with them—with treacherous results.

Mabus Charles Lucia
Culloh Anthony De Longis
Seska Martha Hackett
Michael Jonas Raphael Sbarge
Tersa Larry Cedar
Kelat John Gegenhuber
Hogan Simon Billig
Rettik Mirron E. Willis

Director: Les Landau

Threshold

w Brannon Braga, *story by* Michael DeLuca
Paris's test-flight attempt to reach Warp Ten (Transwarp velocity) goes horribly wrong. First he "dies," then begins to mutate into a bizarre amphibian-like creature. (Woeful episode, little more than an excuse for the five stages of makeup needed to transform McNeill.)
Michael Jonas Raphael Sbarge
Rettik Mirron E. Willis

Director: Alexander Singer

Meld

w Michael Piller, *story by* Michael Sussman
When a crew member is murdered, Tuvok's obsession with understanding the violent impulses of a criminal lead him to mind-meld with the killer, Ensign Suder—with dangerous results.
Ensign Suder Brad Dourif
Ricky Angela Dohrman
Hogan Simon Billig

Director: Cliff Bole

Dreadnought

w Gary Holland
A race-against-time episode. Torres must reprogram a Cardassian-designed rogue missile before it destroys a planet. But the warhead's on-board computer tries to destroy her first . . .
Jonas Raphael Sbarge
Ensign Wildman Nancy Hower
Lorrum Michael Spound
Kellan Dan Kern

Director: LeVar Burton

Death Wish

w Michael Piller, *story by* Shawn Piller
Voyager's crew accidentally frees a renegade Q who demands asylum aboard the ship and the right to commit suicide. When the familiar Q (from *TNG* and *DS9*) arrives to collect him, Janeway holds a hearing to consider the renegade's asylum request, and "our" Q calls a number of witnesses in defense of the Continuum . . . (A father/son collaboration in the writing of this episode.)
Q John de Lancie
Rebel Q Gerrit Graham
William T. Riker Jonathan Frakes

Director: James L. Conway

Lifesigns

w Kenneth Biller
Voyager comes across a Vidiian woman dying from the Phage, and the doctor's attempts to cure her leads him to experience love and romance. Meanwhile Paris continues to be insubordinate, and Seska orders Jonas to plan an accident to damage *Voyager*.
Dr. Denara Pel Susan Diol
Michael Jonas Raphael Sbarge
Seska Martha Hackett
Lorrum Michael Spound
Gigolo Rick Gianasi

Director: Cliff Bole

Investigations

w Jeri Taylor, *story by* Jeff Schnaufer & Ed Bond
A disenchanted Paris leaves *Voyager* to become a pilot with a Talaxian colony. Almost immediately he is abducted by the Kazon-Nistim. Meanwhile, Neelix suspects someone aboard *Voyager* has been spying for the Kazon, and his sleuthing leads him to conclude it was Paris.
Michael Jonas Raphael Sbarge
Laxeth Jerry Sroka
Hogan Simon Billig

Director: Les Landau

Deadlock

w Brannon Braga
Attempting to evade pursuing Vidiian vessels, *Voyager* enters a plasma cloud where a freak subspace accident creates a duplicate ship and crew. Unfortunately, there's not enough anti-matter to sustain both vessels and Janeway meets her other self to find a solution . . .
Wildman Nancy Hower
Hogan Simon Billig
Vidiian surgeon Bob Clendenin
Vidiian commander Ray Proscia
Vidiians Keythe Farley, Christopher Johnston

Director: David Livingston

Innocence

w Lisa Klink, *story by* Anthony Williams
Tuvok tries to help three alien children abandoned by her own people—and discovers a bizarre truth about their race.
Alicia Marnie McPhail
Tressa Tiffany Taubman
Elani Sarah Rayne
Corin Tahj D. Mowry
Bennet Richard Garon

Director: James L. Conway

The Thaw

w Joe Menosky, *story by* Richard Gadas & Michael Piller

An attempt to save some humanoids trapped in deep stasis leads to a strange virtual-reality confrontation with a malevolent clown who is the embodiment of fear.

Clown Michael McKean
Viorsa Thomas Kopache
Specter Carel Struycken
Little Woman Patty Maloney
Physician Tony Carlin
Programmer Shannon O'Hurley

Director: Marvin Rush

Tuvix

w Kenneth Biller, *story by* Andrew Price & Mark Gaberman

A bizarre transporter accident causes Tuvok and Neelix to become one entity—Tuvix—who possesses the memories of both and does not wish to be separated again.

Tuvix Tom Wright
Hogan Simon Billig
Swinn Bahni Turpin

Director: Cliff Bole

Resolutions

w Jeri Taylor

Janeway and Chakotay both contract a deadly virus and are left behind on a planet that can protect them from the disease's effects. While the *Voyager* crew must decide whether to defy their captain's orders and contact the Vidiians who may be able to cure their comrades, Janeway and Chakotay begin to explore another side of their relationship.

Dr. Denara Pel Susan Diol
Hogan Simon Billig
Swinn Bahni Turpin

Director: Alexander Singer

Basics, Part 1

w Michael Piller

Cliffhanger episode. A rescue mission goes horribly wrong when Janeway is forced to surrender *Voyager* to the Kazon, who abandon the crew on a hostile, primitive planet. However, two crew members are still on board . . .

Culluh Anthony De Longis
Teirna John Gegenhuber
Suder Brad Dourif
Seska Martha Hackett
Kolopak Henry Darrow

Director: Winrich Kolbe

Season Three

Basics, Part 2

w Michael Piller

Marooned on a desert-like planet, Janeway and most of the crew face monsters and hostile natives on a primitive planet; meanwhile, Paris tries to save the ship.

Maje Culluh Anthony De Longis
Seska Martha Hackett
Ensign Samantha Wildman Nancy Hower
Ensign Hogan Simon Billig

Director: Winrich Kolbe

Flashback

w Brannon Braga

When Tuvok suffers mental problems, Janeway asks him to mind-meld with her. Together they revisit Ruvok's tour of duty with Captain Sulu.

Captain Sulu George Takei
Cmdr. Janice Rand Grace Lee Whitney
Lt. Dmitri Valtane Jeremy Roberts
Helmsman Lojur Boris Krutonog
Kang Michael Ansara

Director: David Livingston

The Chute

w Kenneth Biller, *story by* Clayvon C. Harris

Paris and Kim face a death sentence when they are accused of terrorism while visiting a planet.

Zio Don McManus
Ambassador Liria Robert Pine
Vel James Parks
Pit Ed Trotta
Rib Beans Morocco

Director: Les Landau

The Swarm

w Mike Sussman

A space-going swarm of aliens attack the ship, penetrating all defenses; the Doctor's program is erased.

The Diva Carole Davi

Director: Alexander Singer

False Profits

w Joe Menosky, *story by* George A. Brozak

Chakotay and Paris thwart two Ferengi who are passing themselves off as demigods to the inhabitants of an impoverished planet.

Dr. Arridor Dan Shor
Kol Leslie Jordan
Bard Michael Ensign
Kafar Rob LaBelle
Sandalmaker Alan Altshuld

Director: Cliff Bole

Remember

w Lisa Klink, *story by* Brannon Braga & Joe Menosky
While *Voyager* transports a small party of aliens, Torres shares the dreams of one—revealing a terrible act of genocide.
Jor Brel Eugene Roche
Dathan Alaris Charles Esten
Jessen Athena Massey
Jora Mirell Eve H. Brenner
Jareth Bruce Davison

Director: Winrich Kolbe

Sacred Ground

w Lisa Klink, *story by* Geo Cameron
When Kes trespasses in a sacred shrine, Janeway must undergo a series of spiritual tests to spare her from death.

Director: Robert Duncan McNeill

Future's End, Part 1

w Brannon Braga & Joe Menosky
Voyager time-travels to 1996 to stop a power-mad industrialist who has found a time-traveling spaceship from the future and is mining it for technology.
Henry Starling Ed Begley Jr.
Rain Robinson Sarah Silverman
Captain Braxton Allan G. Royal

Director: David Livingston

Future's End, Part 2

w Brannon Braga & Joe Menosky
Starling takes the Doctor hostage and prepares to launch his unstable timeship, which will destroy Earth.
Henry Starling Ed Begley Jr.
Rain Robinson Sarah Silverman
Captain Braxton Allan G. Royal
Militiaman #1 Brent Hinkley
Militiaman #2 Clayton Murray

Director: Cliff Bole

Warlord

w Lisa Klink, *story by* Andrew Shepard Price & Mark Gaberman
A dying alien warlord transfers his soul into Kes, igniting a battle of wills.
Adin Anthony Crivello
Demmas Brad Greenquist
Nori Galyn Go"rg
Resh Charles Emmett
Ameron Karl Wiedergott
Tieran Leigh J. McCloskey

Director: David Livingston

The Q and the Gray

w Kenneth Biller, *story by* Shawn Piller
Q returns to *Voyager* in search of a mate, in the belief that his child can save the Q continuum, which is in the middle of civil war.
Q Suzie Plakson
Q Harve Presnell
Q John de Lancie

Director: Cliff Bole

Macrocosm

w Brannon Braga
A life-form evolved from a virus attacks the ship, and the Doctor takes his first Away Mission in an attempt to find the source of the infection.
Tak Tak Albie Selznick

Director: Alexander Singer

Fair Trade

w Andre Bormanis, *story by* Ronald Wilkerson & Jean Louise Mathias
On a remote space station, Neelix meets an old friend, who tricks him into helping smuggle drugs.

Director: Jesus Trevino

Alter Ego

w Joe Menosky
When Ensign Kim falls for an attractive holodeck character, he asks Tuvok to teach him how to suppress his emotions.

Director: Robert Picardo

Coda

w Jeri Taylor
After being severely injured in a shuttle crash, Captain Janeway has a vision of her dead father, Admiral Janeway.
Admiral Edward Janeway Len Cariou

Director: Nancy Malone

Blood Fever

w Lisa Klink
A Vulcan crewman begins to go into Pon Farr, triggering Torres's own mating instincts.
Ensign Torik Alexander Enberg
Ishan Bruce Bohne

Director: Andrew Robinson

Unity

w Kenneth Biller
Voyager encounters a dead-in-space Borg cube and a colony of former Borg drones, who are forming a new collective.

Director: Robert Duncan McNeill

The Darkling

w Alex Singer
When the Doctor tries to tweak his personality using traits from historical figures, he creates a Hyde-like alter ego.

Director: Alex Singer

Rise

w Brannon Braga, *story by* Jimmy Diggs
Tuvok and Nelix visit a planet bombarded by asteroids, trying to help, but find a traitor in their midst.

Director: Robert Sheerer

Favorite Son

w Lisa Klink
Kim becomes convinced he's originally from the Delta Quadrant when a planet of beautiful women want him to stay for reproductive purposes.

Director: Marvin Rush

Before and After

w Kenneth Biller
The Doctor's life-extension treatments knock Kes out of temporal sync, allowing her to visit the past and the future.

Director: Allan Kroeker

Real Life

w Jeri Taylor, *story by* Harry Kloor
The Doctor creates a holographic family to improve his ability to interact with people, but Torres modifies it to make it horrifyingly (to the Doctor) realistic.

Director: Anson Williams

Distant Origin

w Brannon Braga & Joe Menosky
Alien scientists descended from terrestrial dinosaurs find prejudice among their own people when they uncover genetic similarities between humans and their own people.

Director: David Livingston

Displaced

w Lisa Klink
One by one, Janeway's crew is disappearing as aliens launch a subtle attack to seize control of *Voyager*.
Dammar Kenneth Tigar
Jarlath Mark L. Taylor
Rislan James Noah
Taleen Nancy Youngblut

Director: Allan Kroeker

Worst Case Scenario

w Kenneth Biller
Paris discovers a secret holodeck program showing Seska and Chakotay leading a Maquis mutiny.

Director: Alex Singer

Scorpion, Part 1

w Brannon Braga & Joe Menosky
It seems the Borg have met their match in an alien life-form from another dimension, and only Janeway has the key to their survival. But can she trade that information to form an alliance with the Borg that will get *Voyager* home?
Leonardo da Vinci John Rhys-Davies

Director: David Livingston

STARGATE SG-1

Based on the film hit *Stargate,* the original-to-cable series *Stargate SG-1* is shown on pay network Showtime, then a year later episodes enter the syndicaiton market, following the same marketing formula as the original-to-Showtime programs *The Outer Limits*, and *Poltergeist: The Legacy.*

Stargate SG-1 began well, with the discovery of other stargates in the galaxy and the organization of a team of explorers to boldly go where no heavily armed technologically advanced humans have gone before. Various peoples—Vikings, Greeks, Arabs—kidnapped from Earth by alien races over the last few thousand years occupy many of the worlds. Of course, they all speak contemporary English . . . and there is the heart of the problem with this series. Plenty of attention is paid to giving its special effects a slick professional look, but little is being spent on scripts. Stupidity abounds, which is too bad, since there is a really good series hiding in here somewhere.

REGULAR CAST

Col. Jack O'Neill Richard Dean Anderson *Capt. Samantha Carter* Amanda Tapping
Dr. Daniel Jackson Michael Shanks *Teal'c* D. Christopher Judge
Gen. Hammond Don S. Davis *Dr. Frasier* Teryl Rothery

Executive producers: Jonathan Glassner, Brad Wright	Co-executive producer: Michael Greenburg
U.S. premiere: 27 July 1997

Theatrical Movie
Stargate (1994)
James Spader Daniel Jackson
Colonel Jack O'Neill Kurt Russell
Ra Jaye Davidson
Sha'uri Mili Avital

Season One
Children of the Gods *(2-hour premiere)*
The Enemy Within
Emancipation
The Broca Divide
First Commandment
Cold Lazarus

The Nox
Brief Candle
Thor's Hammer
The Torment of Tantulas
Bloodlines
Fire & Water
Hathor
Singularity
Enigma
Solitudes
Tin Man
There but for the Grace of God
Politics
Within the Serpent's Grasp

STARK

A cautionary tale about pollution based on comedian Ben Elton's best-selling 1989 satirical novel. Elton not only wrote the book, he adapted it for TV and starred in it as well, so if it had turned out a disaster we'd know who to blame.

Set mainly in Australia, it tells of a dastardly plot being hatched by a powerful group of international financiers and power brokers. The plan—known as the Stark Conspiracy—is simple: to destroy the already ravaged world but save themselves, by building a space ark to carry them off to a bright new future.

The only ones standing in their way are a very motley crew of eco-activist hippies, roused by the rebellious Rachel. Tagging along, and providing the comic sub-plot, is Elton himself, as would-be writer Colin "CD" Dobson, who's more concerned about bedding the lovely Rachel than saving the planet.

Veteran actor John Neville heads the supporting cast as the chief conspirator De Quincey, and Derrick O'Connor, well-known for his "menacing heavy" roles, played a wacked-out eco-crusader.

MAIN CAST
Colin "CD" Dobson Ben Elton *Rachel* Jacqueline McKenzie
Sly Morgan Colin Friels *Zimmerman* Derrick O'Connor *Walter* Bill Wallis
Chrissie Debora-Lee Furness *De Quincey* John Neville *Karen* Fiona Press
Ocker Tyron Bill Hunter *Dixie* Colette Mann *Mrs. Tyron* Gwen Plumb

Adapted by Ben Elton, *from his own novel*
Producers: Michael Wearing, David Parker, Timothy White
Director: Nadia Tass
Music: Colin Towns	*A BBC and Cascade Ash Productions Presentation in association with the Australian Broadcasting Corporation*
3 color 55-minute episodes
8–22 December 1993
(BBC1)

THE STARLOST

This was the voyage of the Earthship *Ark*—an enormous organic cluster of environmental domes called biospheres, looped together by tubular corridors.

Launched in 2785, it was designed to carry the brightest and best from our dying planet to a new world. But, 500 years and countless generations later, Earth and the reason for the journey are long forgotten. Indeed, the *Ark*'s population, living isolated lives in the separate domes, are unaware they are even on a spaceship.

That is, until a young trio—farm boy Devon, the beautiful Rachel and her ex-fiancé Garth—stumble on the truth and set out on an episodic odyssey through its corridors and communities to find out more.

This noble-sounding Canadian project was begun with noted writer Harlan Ellison as its guiding hand. But he became disillusioned with the direction it was taking, and quit. When it did appear, in 1973, as a syndicated series, it met with almost universal derision, for its dull plots, cardboard characters, static dialogue and distractingly cheap visual tricks. *Star Trek*'s William Koenig appeared in a couple of episodes as an alien called Oro.

Only 16 of the planned 24 episodes were shown.

REGULAR CAST
Devon Keir Dullea   *Rachel* Gay Rowan   *Garth* Robin Ward
Computer voice William Osler

A Glen-Warren Production
16 color 60-minute episodes

Voyage of Discovery
Lazarus from the Mist
The Goddess Calabra
The Pisces
Children of Methuselah
Only Man Is Vile
The Alien Oro

Circuit of Death
Gallery of Fear
Mr. Smith from Manchester
Astro Medics
The Implant People
The Return of Oro
Farthing's Comet
The Beehive
Space Precinct

STARMAN

TV spin-off from the 1984 movie that had starred Jeff Bridges as an alien stranded on Earth.

In this sequel, Robert Hays, star of the *Airplane* films, takes on the role of the alien, Starman, who, having fathered a child by an Earth woman 14 years before, returns to find his lost love and help raise his son.

Assuming the body of a freelance photographer killed in a wilderness plane crash, he finds his son, Scott, living in an orphanage. Scott is skeptical about his alien origins until convinced by the Starman's strange powers and his own emerging paranormal abilities, including telekinesis, which are triggered by his dad's "magic marbles," a set of small glowing spheres.

Together they embark on a quest to find Scott's mother, Jenny (played by *Buck Rogers*'s Erin Gray), pursued by a government agent, Fox, who has learned of Starman's secret and is determined to bring him in for experimentation. The series had an almost happy ending, with the family reunited before they are again forced back on the run.

REGULAR CAST
Paul Forrester/Starman Robert Hays   *Scott Hayden* C.B. Barnes
George Fox Michael Cavanaugh

Creators: Bruce A. Evans, Raynold Gideon
Executive producers: James Henerson, James
Hirsch, Michael Douglas
Writers: Various, including James Henerson,
James Hirsch, Geoffrey Fischer, Tom Lazarus,
Michael Marks
Directors: Various, including Charles S. Dubin,
Claudio Guzman, Mike Gray, Bill Duke,
Robert Chenault, Robert Hays

22 color 60-minute episodes

The Return
Like Father, Like Son
Fatal Flaw
Blue Lights
Best Buddies
One for the Road
Peregrine
Society's Pet
Fever
The Gift
The System
Appearances
The Probe
Dusty
Barriers
Grifters
The Wedding
Fathers and Sons
Starscape (Part 1)
Starscape (Part 2)
The Test

U.S. premiere: 19 September 1986

STEPHEN KING'S GOLDEN YEARS

Always be suspicious of anything with the author or director's name in the title—sure, it's a selling point in a crowded TV universe, but it can also be an admission that the show is so weak it needs a boost from a big name.

And that could be said of this six-part series written specially for TV by Stephen King. Take away King's name and you've an OK mini-series memorable mostly for David Bowie's eponymous song that closes each episode.

As with much of King's work, there's an intriguing premise, but an overlong execution. Harlan Williams is the elderly janitor of Falco Plains, a secret government lab. An explosion that kills two researchers leaves Harlan exposed to an unknown chemical cocktail. At first he exhibits no adverse effects—then his wife begins to notice changes in his behavior and appearance. Harlan is getting younger—the aging process is in reverse. Naturally the government wants to study him and will stop at nothing to get hold of him, putting a ruthless agent, Jude Andrews, on his tail.

With the help of a sympathetic former colleague of Andrews, Terry Spann, Harlan and his wife, Gina, become fugitives and a cross-country chase ensues, before the inevitable dramatic climax.

MAIN CAST
Harlan Williams Keith Szarabajka   *Gina Williams* Frances Sternhagen
Terry Spann Felicity Huffman   *Gen. Louis Crewes* Ed Lauter   *Jude Andrews* R.D. Call
Dr. Richard Todhunter Bill Raymond   *Dr. Ackerman* John Rothman   *Redding* Matt Malloy
Jackson Adam Redfield   *Lt. Vester* Jeff Williams   *Lt. McGiver* Peter McRobbie
Dr. Eakins J.R. Horne   *Francie* Harriet Sansom Harris

Writer/Executive producer: Stephen King
Director: Kenneth Fink
Producers: Mitchell Galin, Peter R. McIntosh

U.K. premiere: 2 January–6 February 1993
(Channel Four)

STEVEN SPIELBERG'S AMAZING STORIES

On the face of it, this collection of fantastic tales of the bizarre and the unusual had everything going for it—a remarkable line-up of acting and directorial talent, movie-style budgets and the Midas touch of Spielberg himself.

Shame it wasn't more successful. *Amazing Stories* was largely ignored by U.S. audiences, endorsed with reservations by U.S. critics and has aired in the U.K. in such piecemeal fashion as to dissipate its potential impact. It doesn't quite deserve the tag of TV's *Heaven's Gate*, but at around $1 million per half-hour episode, this most expensive of TV shows of its day certainly didn't live up to its price tag.

Amazing Stories's greatest strength is its visual appeal. With such resources at his disposal, Spielberg could extend the visual frontiers of television beyond what was normal for the mid-eighties. Each tale had the look of a feature film, with special effects ranging from charming to lavish.

In the series premiere, "Ghost Train" (shown second in the U.K.), which Spielberg directed, a huge locomotive ploughs through a house, while in the double-length episode, "The Mission," again directed by Spielberg and including Kevin Costner and Kiefer Sutherland among its stars, a crippled World War Two bomber suddenly develops cartoon wheels, enabling it to land safely.

Spielberg called *Amazing Stories* a "director's series" and certainly enticed some of Hollywood's finest to support his venture. Martin Scorsese, Robert Zemeckis, Clint Eastwood, Joe Dante, Irving Kershner, Burt Reynolds, Peter Hyams, Danny DeVito and Tobe Hooper were among big-name directors lured aboard. As well as directing some episodes himself, Spielberg also contributed many of the story ideas.

His privileged status also enabled him to give big-budget breaks to many little-known directors, such as Phil Joanou whose later career included a segment of *Wild Palms*. As such, *Amazing Stories* was an expensive experiment, a rare event in a usually conservative medium.

Such worthy motives couldn't counter the series' shortcomings. All too often, the segments were built around an over-simplified premise and one-dimensional characters that never really amounted to much. There's plenty of charm but not enough wonder, much sentiment but little pathos, a few laughs but insufficient irony. Surface without substance.

It's not all bad, though. Scorsese's "Mirror, Mirror," about a horror novelist terrorized by a black-caped phantom, is a really creepy little chiller, and "The Amazing Falsworth," about a psychic nightclub performer who encounters a serial killer in his audience, has its unsettling moments. Eastwood's segment, "Vanessa in the Garden," is unexpectedly poignant, while "You Gotta Believe Me," in which Charles Durning plays a man with a premonition of disaster, recalls the paranoia of a *Twilight Zone*.

Amazing Stories marked Spielberg's return to television—the medium that gave him his first break as a director on an episode of *Rod Serling's Night Gallery*, and led to success for his supervising producers, Joshua Brand and John Falsey, who went on to create the drama *St. Elsewhere* and one of television's best cult series, *Northern Exposure*.

In the face of audiences used to seeing recurring characters and familiar settings, short story anthologies will always have a hard time sustaining their place in ratings-led schedules. Spielberg had enough clout to secure a two-year prime-time deal. A lesser man wouldn't have got nearly so far.

Developed by Steven Spielberg, Joshua Brand & John Falsey
Executive producer: Steven Spielberg
Supervising producers: Joshua Brand, John Falsey
Story editor: Mick Garris
Theme: John Williams

An Amblin Entertainment and Universal Production
45 color episodes (30 minutes unless stated)
U.S. premiere: 29 September 1985
U.K. premiere: 19 April 1992
(BBC1)

Season One
24 episodes

Ghost Train

w Frank Deese, *story by* Steven Spielberg
An old man is convinced it's his destiny to board the Highball Express, a train he caused to crash 75 years before, and tells his nine-year-old grandson it will careen through their house, which was built on the site of the wreck.

Cast includes:
Old Pa Roberts Blossom
Brian Globe Lukas Haas
Joleen Globe Gail Edwards
Fenton Globe Scott Paulin
Conductor Hugh Gillin
Engineer Sandy Ward
Passengers Amy Irving, Priscilla Pointer, Drew Barrymore

Director: Steven Spielberg

The Main Attraction

w Brad Bird & Mick Garris, *story by* Steven
Spielberg
A meteor shower has a startling effect on conceited
high school hunk Brad Bender, turning him into a
human magnet, with a strong attraction to the
school's most unattractive girl.
Cast includes:
Brad Bender John Scott Clough
Shirley Lisa Jane Persky
Cliff Bill Allen
Mrs. Bender Barbara Sharma
Mr. Hiller Richard Bull
Wylie Tom Napier
Darcy Cook Piper Cochrane

Director: Matthew Robbins

Alamo Jobe

w Joshua Brand & John Falsey, *story by* Steven
Spielberg
A buckskin-clad teenager fighting at the Alamo is
tossed through time, stumbling through the fort's
front gates into 20th-century San Antonio.
Cast includes:
Jobe Farnum Kelly Reno
Gen Travis William Boyett
Davey Crockett Richard Young
Col. John Lefferts Michael Cavanaugh
Jim Bowie Jon Van Ness
Harriet Wendse Lurene Tuttle

Director: Mickey Moore

Mummy, Daddy

w Earl Pomerantz, *story by* Steven Spielberg
A father-to-be, bandaged from head to toe for his
role in a horror film, causes havoc in a small South-
ern town steeped in the eerie legend of an Egyptian
mummy, as he tries to reach his wife's bedside.
Cast includes:
Harold Tom Harrison
Harold's wife Susan Dear
Ra Amin Ka Michael Zand
with Billy Beck, Oliver Dear, Len Lesser, Lucy
Lee Flippen, Arnold Johnson, Joann Willette,
William Frankfather, Larry Hankin, Brion
James, Bronson Pinchot, Tracey Walter

Director: William Dear

The Mission

(60 minutes)
w Menno Meyies, *story by* Steven Spielberg
A courageous young World War Two gunner—and
aspiring cartoonist—trapped in the belly of a crippled B17 bomber, faces certain death—and calls on
his imagination to save him.
Cast includes:
Captain Kevin Costner

Jake Jeffrey Jay Cohen
Bullseye John Philbin
Jonathan Casey Siemaszko
Lamar Ken Stovitz
Static Kiefer Sutherland
Liz Karen Kopins
Sam Gary Mauro
Dave Glen Mauro

Director: Steven Spielberg

The Amazing Falsworth

w Mick Garris, *story by* Steven Spielberg
A nightclub audience gasps at the Amazing
Falsworth's psychic powers, but the blindfolded
performer is plunged into a living nightmare when
he picks up the vibes of a serial killer in the room.
Cast includes:
Falsworth Gregory Hines
Trent/Tinker Richard Masur
Jimmy Joe Medalis
Showgirl Nori Morgan
Gail Suzanne Bateman
Messenger Don Calfa
Young man Robert Lesser

Director: Peter Hyams

Fine Tuning

w Earl Pomerantz, *story by* Steven Spielberg
Three school pals build a revolutionary TV antenna
that picks up broadcasts from another planet, where
a news item reveals the aliens are landing in Holly-
wood tonight.
Cast includes:
George Jimmy Gatherum
Andy Matthew Laborteaux
Jimmy Gary Riley
Milton Berle Himself
Aliens Debbie Carrington, Daniel Frishman,
Patty Maloney, Kevin Thompson

Director: Bob Balaban

Mr. Magic

w Joshua Brand & John Falsey
An old-time conjurer, now fumbling every trick, is
desperate to regain his prowess for one last perfor-
mance and gets his chance when he buys an amaz-
ing old deck of cards at a small magic shop.
Cast includes:
Lou Bundles Sid Caesar
Murray Tropicana Leo Rossi
Boo Boo Campos Jane West
Joe Julius Harris
Johnny Hugh Warden
Jack Tim Herbert
Danny Larry Cedar

Director: Donald Petrie

Guilt Trip

w Gail Parent & Kevin Parent
Overworked and exhausted, Guilt takes a relaxing cruise and falls for Lovely, unaware of her real identity.
Cast includes:
Guilt Dom DeLuise
Lovely Loni Anderson
Asst. to boss Charles Durning
Enchantress Abbe Lane
Father McClintley Charles Nelson Reilly
Maître d' Fritz Feld

Director: Burt Reynolds

Remote Control Man

w Douglas Lloyd McIntosh, story by Steven Spielberg
An unhappy husband with a nagging wife and an incorrigible son, finally finds solace in his new TV set, which comes alive with a magic remote control.
Cast includes:
Walter Poindexter Sydney Lassick
Mr. Beasley Philip Bruns
Ralph Jeff B. Cohen
Salesman Charlie Dell
Cameo appearances include Dirk Benedict, Gary Coleman & Ed McMahon

Director: Bob Clark

Santa '85

w Joshua Brand & John Falsey
Kris Kringle's Christmas is rudely interrupted when he lands in jail with a bunch of bogus Santas after tripping a home burglar alarm while delivering gifts.
Cast includes:
Real Santa Claus Douglas Seale
Bobby Gabriel Damon
Sheriff Smivey Pat Hingle
Wetherby Marvin J. McIntyre

Director: Phil Joanou

Vanessa in the Garden

w Steven Spielberg
1895: When his beloved wife dies in a carriage wreck, grief-stricken young artist Byron is possessed with an incredible plan to bring her back through his paintings.
Byron Harvey Keitel
Vanessa Sondra Locke

Teddy Beau Bridges
Eve Margaret Howell
Dr. Northrup Thomas Randall Oglesby
Mrs. Northrup Jamie Rose
Waiter Milton Murrill

Director: Clint Eastwood

The Sitter

w Mick Garris, story by Joshua Brand & John Falsey
Jamaican babysitter Jennifer Mowbray uses voodoo to tame a pair of mischievous, prank-playing boys.
Jennifer Mabel King
Lance Seth Green
Gloria Wendy Phillips
Dennis Joshua Rudoy
Mrs. Abbott Fran Ryan
Patti Suzanne Snyder
Indian Michael Horse

Director: Joan Darling

No Day at the Beach

w Mick Garris, story by Steven Spielberg
Scorned by his poker-playing troop, Arnold Skamp becomes a war hero when he miraculously saves the lives of the GIs who shunned him.
Cast includes:
Arnold Larry Spinak
Irish Ray "Boom Boom" Mancini
Casey Charlie Sheen
Tiny Tom Hodges
Ira Ralph Seymour
Stick Philip McKeon
Evergreen Leo Geter
Granville Luca Bercovici

Director: Lesli Linka Glatter

One for the Road

w James D. Bissell
A couple of barflies try to kill a drunk for his insurance money and find they're tangling with more than they bargained for.
Cast includes:
Mike Malloy Douglas Seale
Francis James Cromwell
Dan Geoffrey Lewis
Joe Joe Pantoliano
Tony Maroni Al Ruscio

Director: Thomas Carter

Gather Ye Acorns

w Stu Krieger, *story by* Steven Spielberg
Jonathan Quick, the bane of his practical parents'
existence, takes an ancient tree troll's advice to pack
up his treasured comic book collection, follow his
heart and so become rich.
Cast includes:
Jonathan Quick Mark Hamill
Alma Quick Lois de Banzie
Elmer Quick Royal Dano
Troll David Rappaport
Jonathan (aged 12) David Friedman
Francine Mary Deschanel
David Bill Dear
Jerry Forest Whitaker

Director: Norman Reynolds

Boo!

w Lowell Ganz & Babaloo Mandel
Sweet, old-fashioned ghosts Nelson and Evelyn
Chumsky are shocked when a porn queen and her
sleazy husband move into their home, and try to
scare off the raunchy residents.
Nelson Chumsky Eddie Bracken
Evelyn Chumsky Evelyn Keyes
Barbara Tucker Andrea Marcovicci
Richard Tucker Bruce Davison
Tony Sepulveda Robert Picardo
Sheena Sepulveda Wendy Schaal
Scott Tucker Taliesin Jaffe
Deena Tucker Heidi Zeigler

Director: Thomas Carter

Dorothy and Ben

w Michael De Guzman, *story by* Steven Spiel-
berg
It is shocking enough when old Ben Dumfy emerges
from a 40-year coma like Rip Van Winkle, but his
special mental communication with Dorothy, a co-
matose seven-year-old, leads to an even greater
miracle.
Cast includes:
Ben Dumfy Joe Seneca
Dorothy Natalie Gregory
Samantha Kathleen Lloyd
Merle Joe Regalbuto
Dr. Caruso Lane Smith
Dr. Templeton Louis Giambalvo

Director: Thomas Carter

Mirror, Mirror

w Joseph Minion, *story by* Steven Spielberg
Horror novelist Jordan Manmouth is terrorized by a
black-caped phantom he sees stalking him every
time he looks in a mirror.
Cast includes:
Jordan Manmouth Sam Waterston
Karen Helen Shaver
Jeffrey Gelb Glenn Scarpelli
Himself Dick Cavett
Jordan's Phantom Tim Robbins

Director: Martin Scorsese

Deathrace 2000 (aka Secret Cinema)

w Paul Bartel
Jane thinks she has lost her mind when she finds her
daily life is being treated as a serialized film by
everyone around her—with herself as the star.
Cast includes:
Jane Penny Peyser
Dick Griffin Dunne
Dr. Shreck Paul Bartel
Jane's mother Eve Arden
Mr. Krupp Richard Paul

Director: Paul Bartel

Hell Toupee

w Gail Parent & Kevin Parent
Mild-mannered accountant Murray Bernstein buys
a toupee with strange hidden powers that compel
him to murder the first lawyer he sees.
Cast includes:
Harry Ballentine Tony Kienitz
Murray Bernstein E. Hampton Beagle
Beth Hollander Cindy Morgan
Clifford Monroe Ken Olsson
Mitchell Stanley Brock
Floyd King Mitch Krindel

Director: Irvin Kershner

The Doll

w Richard Matheson
A shy bachelor's lonely life takes an astounding turn
when he buys a very special doll made by a myste-
rious German toymaker.
John Waters John Lithgow
Mr. Liebemacher Albert Hague
Mary Dickinson Annie Helm
Doris Rasmussen Rainbow Phoenix
Sally Rasmussen Sharon Spelman
Vin Rasmussen John Christopher Jones

Director: Phil Joanou

One for the Books

w Richard Matheson
An elderly college janitor amazes himself, his wife and scientists when fluent French and complex mathematical theories tumble from his lips.
Cast includes:
Fred Elderman Leo Penn
Eva Elderman Joyce Van Patten
Dr. Fetlock Nicholas Pryor
Prof. Rand John Alvin
Prof. Gilbert Gary Bergher
Prof. Smith Ben Kronen

Director: Lesli Linka Glatter

Grandpa's Ghost

w Michael de Guzman, *story by* Timothy Hutton
Edwin's grandpa died last night, so why is the old man still hanging round the apartment, playing the piano and swapping stories with his unsuspecting wife?
Edwin Andrew McCarthy
Grandpa Charlie Ian Wolfe
Grandma Helen Herta Ware

Director: Timothy Hutton

Season Two
21 episodes

The Wedding Ring

w Stu Krieger, *story by* Steven Spielberg
Herbert steals a wax museum statue's gold ring as a special anniversary gift for his weary waitress wife, Lois. Instantly, it transforms her into a sexy seductress—as it did to the Black Widow who wore it when she murdered three husbands.
Herbert Danny DeVito
Lois Rhea Perlman
Haggerty Louis Giambalvo
Tina Bernadette Birkett
Blaze Tracey Walter
Eines David Byrd

Director: Danny DeVito

Miscalculation

w Michael McDowell
A nerdy college kid vainly tries every trick in the book to meet girls, until he discovers a potion that makes gorgeous magazine pin-ups spring to life.
Phil Jon Cryer
Angela Joann Willette
Bert Jeffrey Jay Cohen
Ms. Laura Liz de Turenne
Ms. Eyeful Galyn Gorg

Ms. Awesome Catherine Gilmour
Miss Crowningshield Rebecca Schaeffer
Ms. Allure Lana Clarkson

Director: Todd Holland

Magic Saturday

w Richard Matheson
Marky adores his seemingly indefatigable Grampa, and when the old man takes ill, the boy invokes a magic spell from China to switch bodies and allow his Grampa to play one last game of baseball.
Marky Taliesin Jaffe
Grampa Norman M. Emmet Walsh
Dorothy Caren Kaye
Ken Carter Gibson
Umpire David Arnott
Eddie Jeff B. Cohen

Director: Robert Markowitz

Welcome to My Nightmare

w Todd Holland
Sci-fi and horror movies are Harry's life, but when the obsessed teenager suddenly steps into a blood-curdling scene from *Psycho*, the real world looks a whole lot better.
Cast includes:
Harry David Hollander
Bud Steve Antin
Kate Robyn Lively
Holly Christina Applegate
Mom Sharon Spelman
Dad Robert L. Gibson
Larry Parker Jacobs

Director: Todd Holland

You Gotta Believe Me

w Stu Krieger & Kevin Reynolds, *story by* Steven Spielberg
Convinced the vivid nightmare of a Jumbo Jet crashing into his house is more than just a dream, Earl Sweet speeds to the airport where he desperately tries to alter fate.
Cast includes:
Earl Sweet Charles Durning
Nancy Mary Betten
Red bag lady Cassandra Gava
Pilot Joel Lawrence
Airline reps Wade Meyer, Jennie Sadler
Controllers Todd Allen, Richard Burns
Drunk pilot Wil Shriner

Director: Kevin Reynolds

The Greibble

w Mick Garris
A houseproud mom's cleaning spree is turned up-side down when a giant, floppy, furry, pink and purple creature with a huge appetite for inanimate objects appears out of the storm outside to wreak havoc in her home.
Joan Hayley Mills
Bobby Justine Mooney
Greibble Don McLeod
Fred Dick Miller
Gloria Ivy Bethune
Man in commercial Jim Jansen

Director: Joe Dante

Life on Death Row

w Rockne S. O'Bannon, *story by* Mick Garris
Hours before his scheduled execution, a murderer on death row is infused with an incredible power to heal by touch, and a desperate race against the clock begins to save his life.
Cast includes:
Peterson Patrick Swayze
Meadows Hector Elizondo
Erhardt James T. Callahan
Casey T.J. Worzalla
Johnny Arnold Johnson
Fowler Hawthorne James

Director: Mick Garris

Go to the Head of the Class

(60 minutes)
w Mick Garris & Tom McLoughlin
A teenage horror buff is so smitten with his seductive classmate that he helps her use black magic on their loathsome English teacher.
Peter Brand Scott Coffey
Mr. Beane Christopher Lloyd
Cynthia Mary Stuart Masterson
Caretaker Billy Beck
Cusimano Tom Bresnahan

Director: Robert Zemeckis

Thanksgiving

w Robert C. Fox & Pierre Debs, *story by* Harold Rolseth
Eighteen-year-old Dora is miserable living in an isolated desert town with her dour stepfather, Calvin, but their communication with a dried-up well's mysterious "hole people" changes each of their fates.
Dora Kyra Sedgwick
Calvin David Carradine

Director: Todd Holland

The Pumpkin Competition

w Peter Orton
Livid at losing her local pumpkin-growing contest for the 22nd year, rich but miserly Elma Dinnock gets help from a mysterious botanist, with incredible results. But there's a surprise in store for the selfish woman.
Elma Dinnock Polly Holliday
Mildred June Lockhart
Prof. Carver J.A. Preston
Mayor Barnsworth Ritch Brinkley
Billy Joshua Rudoy
Ma Ann Walker
Ernie Britt Leach

Director: Norman Reynolds

What If?

w Anne Spielberg
Ignored by his self-absorbed parents, a five-year-old boy is touched by magic that gives his life a new dimension.
Jonah Kelley Jake Hart
Pamela Kelley Clare Kirkconnell
Raymond Kelley Tom McConnell
Pregnant woman Ann Bell
Crosswalk man Ric Kane

Director: Joan Darling

The Eternal Mind

w Julie R. Moskowitz & Gary Stephens
A dying scientist transfers his mind into a computer, but his unique survival after physical death brings unexpected heartaches.
Cast includes:
John Baldwin Jeffrey Jones
Katherine Baldwin Kathryn Borowitz
Ben Oltman Gregory Wagrowski
Frank Robert Axelrod

Director: Michael Riva

Lane Change

w Ali Marie Matheson
One stormy night on a deserted highway, a distressed Charlene Benton glimpses her past through the windshield after picking up a mysterious woman.
Charlene Benton Kathy Baker
Woman Priscilla Pointer
Father Cletus Young
Little girl Misty Forrest

Director: Ken Kwapis

Blue Man Down

w Jacob Epstein, Daniel Lindley & Cynthia Darnell, *story by* Steven Spielberg
A disillusioned cop who blames himself for his partner's death gets a new partner, a pretty policewoman who restores his spirit and stamina, before he learns that she died 12 years earlier . . .
Duncan Moore Max Gail
Patty O'Neil Kate O'Neil
DeSoto Chris Nash
Beckloff Frank Doubleday

Director: Paul Michael Glaser

The 21-Inch Sun

w Bruce Kirschbaum
A struggling sitcom writer becomes the toast of television, thanks to the typing tendrils of his scriptwriting spider plant, nurtured by the rays of a black and white TV set.
Billy Robert Townsend
Dick Castel Craig Richard Nelson
Mrs. Luthaker Anne Seymour
Marvin Michael Lerner
Barry Robert Starr
Mr. Shimmerman Peter Fitzsimmons

Director: Nick Castle

Family Dog

w Brad Bird
A trilogy of animated tales of middle-class, suburban family life, as seen through the eyes of their put-upon pooch.
With the voices of Stan Freberg, Annie Potts, Mercedes McCambridge

Director: Brad Bird

Gershwin's Trunk

w John Meyer & Paul Bartel
Frantic to deliver a hit musical, conniving Broadway composer Jo-Jo Gillespie contacts the spirit of George Gershwin through psychic Sister Teresa.
Cast includes:
Jo-Jo Bob Balaban
Jerry John McCook
Laurie Carrie Fisher
Sister Teresa Lainie Kazan
Det Watts Paul Bartel
Carmen Irene Olga Lopez

Director: Paul Bartel

Such Interesting Neighbours

w Mick Garris, Tom McLaughlin & Michael McDowell
Sudden quakes and time warps unsettle the Lewis family in their new house—and the answer seems linked to the bizarre next-door neighbors, the Hellenbecks.
Ted Hellenbeck Adam Ant
Ann Hellenbeck Victoria Catlin
Al Lewis Frederick Coffin
Nell Lewis Marcia Strassman
Randy Lewis Ian Fried
Brad Hellenbeck Ryan McWhorter

Director: Graham Baker

Without Diana

w Mick Garris
A little girl whose disappearance devastated her parents 40 years before mystically reappears at their door and teaches her father a spiritual lesson as he struggles to cope with the impending loss of his wife.
George Billy Green Bush
Kathryn Diana Hull
Diana Gennie James
Policeman Rick Andosca
Dr. Wittenberg Fredric Cook

Director: Lesli Linka Glatter

Moving Day

w Frank Kerr
When Alan Webster's parents tell him they have to move, the 17-year-old is understandably upset—but not as much as when he hears his folks are aliens and their destination is a planet 85 billion miles away.
Alan Webster Stephen Geoffreys
Mara Webster Mary Ellen Trainor
Val Webster Dennis Lipscomb
Karen Kristen Vigard
Big boy Bill Wesley

Director: Bob Stevens

Miss Stardust

w Thomas Szollosi & Richard Matheson, *story by* Richard Matheson
A beauty contest promoter is visited by Cabbage Man, a representative from outer space demanding that contestants from other planets be allowed to compete.
Joe Willoughby Dick Shawn
Cabbage Man Weird Al Yankovic
Miss Schroedinger Laraine Newman
Mike the bartender Rick Overton
Grassblood Angel Tompkins
Ms. Colorado Wendy Sherwood

Director: Tobe Hooper

STINGRAY

Gerry and Sylvia Anderson's third venture in the Supermarionation series, after *Supercar* (1961) and *Fireball XL5* (1962). Though outstripped later, this was their costliest yet, running up a £1 million bill for the 39 half-hour adventures. It introduced the men and women of WASP—the World Aquanaut Security Patrol—dedicated to making the undersea world of the year 2065 a safer place.

Stingray, an atomic-powered sub equipped with 16 Sting missiles and possessing dolphin-like agility, was captained by Troy Tempest, a handsome, fearless 22-inch chip off the Mike Mercury/Steve Zodiac block. Alongside him were loyal hydrophones operator Lt. George "Phones" Sheridan, and the enchanting, green-haired Marina, mute daughter of Aphony, emperor of the peaceful undersea kingdom of Pacifica. Pulling their strings at WASP headquarters, Marineville, was the organization's founder, Commander Sam Shore, a crippled sub veteran who controlled operations from his hover-chair.

The series' bad guys were the tyrannical Titan, ruler of Titanica, and his aquaphibians, a monstrous underwater race who waged war in their mechanical Terror Fish, which fired missiles from their gaping mouths. Other regular characters were Commander Shore's daughter, Atlanta, Sub-Lieutenant Fisher and agent X20, a hapless Titan spy whose subversive efforts invariably ended in failure and a ticking off from his boss.

A running subplot, highlighted by the closing credit sequence, was the unrequited eternal triangle—Atlanta doted on Troy who mooned over Marina.

Though produced for the traditional children's teatime slot, *Stingray* has enjoyed enduring success with a wider audience. Its visual invention, imaginative flair, characterization and continuity of detail endeared it to the discerning Supermarionation fans. The first Gerry Anderson series to be shot in color, it was originally screened here in black and white, but has been seen in color since 1969.

VOICE CAST
Troy Tempest Don Mason *Phones/Agent X20* Robert Easton
Commander Shore/Titan/Sub-Lt. Fisher Ray Barrett
Atlanta Lois Maxwell
With: Admiral Denver David Graham *(three episodes only)*
Other voices David Graham

Creators: Gerry & Sylvia Anderson
Producer: Gerry Anderson
Associate producer: Reg Hill
Special effects director: Derek Meddings
Music: Barry Gray
Title song sung by Gary Miller

An AP Films Production in association with ATV for ITC Worldwide Distribution
39 color 30-minute episodes
4 October 1964–27 June 1965
(Dates as ATV, London region)

Stingray

w Gerry & Sylvia Anderson
Investigating strange explosions at sea, Troy and Phones are captured by Titan and condemned to die. They are saved by Titan's slave girl, Marina, who helps them to escape and joins the WASP crew.

Director: Alan Pattillo

Emergency Marineville

w Alan Fennell
While investigating a missile threat to Marineville, the *Stingray* crew are captured. Troy is forced to give the correct course for the missile but manages to remove the explosive warhead so that it lands with a harmless thud—and a message that brings rescue.

Director: John Kelly

The Ghost Ship

w Alan Fennell
Checking out a mysterious fog-shrouded galleon, Commander Shore and Phones find themselves in the clutches of a strange creature called Idotee who orders Troy to join them. But wily Troy fills his air cylinders with laughing gas and when he releases it Idotee collapses with laughter.

Director: Desmond Saunders

Subterranean Sea

w Alan Fennell

The *Stingray* crew's holiday in the sun is interrupted by a mission to investigate the depth of the Subterrain—but they end up discovering a beautiful tropical island in the Pacific. It's the perfect place for a holiday.

Director: Desmond Saunders

Loch Ness Monster

w Dennis Spooner

Stingray is sent to Scotland to investigate the legend of the Loch Ness monster. But the ferocious-looking dragon that "attacks" them turns out to be a fake, rigged up by two brothers to attract the tourist trade.

Director: Alan Pattillo

Set Sail for Adventure

w Dennis Spooner

Phones and Lt. Fisher find themselves before the mast on an ancient sailing ship when Commander Shore takes up an old friend's challenge to test the mettle of his men. But when a storm blows up and mishaps mount, it's a good job *Stingray* is close behind.

Director: David Elliott

The Man from the Navy

w Alan Fennell

A feud flares between Troy and a boastful naval captain. When the navy man becomes the innocent pawn in another of X20's plots to destroy *Stingray*, it is Troy who clears his adversary's name, though he gets little thanks!

Director: John Kelly

An Echo of Danger

w Dennis Spooner

Agent X20's decoy signal and psychiatrist disguise succeed in discrediting Phones. X20 turns his attention to Troy, but Lt. Fisher helps thwart his plot and Phones is cleared.

Director: Alan Pattillo

Raptures of the Deep

w Alan Fennell

Going to the rescue of two illicit treasure hunters, Troy runs short of air and deliriously dreams that he is in a fabulous palace with Marina, Atlanta and Phones at his beck and call. But he is glad to

reawaken when the dream turns nasty. (Sylvia Anderson voices Marina, and Gary Miller is Troy's singing voice.)

Director: Desmond Saunders

Titan Goes Pop

w Alan Fennell

Titan is totally baffled by the strange VIP that Agent X20 has kidnapped from Marineville. It turns out to be pop star Duke Dexter, but such is Duke's power to throw the terrans into a tizzy, that Titan is convinced the singer is on their side!

Director: Alan Pattillo

In Search of the Tajmanon

w Dennis Spooner

How can a submerged palace just disappear? That's the riddle facing the *Stingray* crew who are joined by Atlanta on a perilous quest to Africa where the mystery is finally solved.

Director: Desmond Saunders

A Christmas to Remember

w Dennis Spooner

It's definitely a memorable experience for the young orphaned son of an ex-WASP aquanaut who comes to stay at Marineville where he joins Troy on *Stingray* patrol with unexpectedly dangerous results.

Director: Alan Pattillo

Tune of Danger

w Alan Fennell

Troy discovers that a bomb has been planted inside one of the instruments of a jazz group that is due to perform for Marina's father, Aphony, in his underwater city. Troy starts a desperate race against time to avert a disaster.

Director: John Kelly

The Ghost of the Sea

w Alan Fennell

The story behind Commander Shore's injury, which has left him a cripple, is revealed in a series of nightmare "flashbacks." But the mysterious stranger who once saved his life is now suspected of destroying an oil rig. Troy and the Commander investigate and Troy saves the stranger's life, so repaying Commander Shore's debt—and bringing peace.

Director: David Elliott

Rescue from the Skies

w Dennis Spooner
Lt. Fisher's training exercise in *Stingray* runs into danger when X20 cripples the vessel and places a sticker bomb on the hull to finish it off. Troy must jet to the scene in time to remove the bomb and save his friends.

Director: Desmond Saunders

The Lighthouse Dwellers

w Alan Fennell
When a pilot crashes after mistaking the flashing beacon of a supposedly disused lighthouse for his airstrip, *Stingray* is sent to investigate. Troy and Phones discover that a race of underwater people has been harnessing the lighthouse's power for their own city.

Director: David Elliott

The Big Gun

w Alan Fennell
Troy and his crew investigate the mysterious destruction of three Pacific islands and must face enemies from an ocean *below* the Pacific itself. Only Marina can withstand the intense water pressure and destroy the underwater city.

Director: David Elliott

The Cool Cave Man

w Alan Fennell
Troy is stuck for a costume for Atlanta's fancy dress party, until a dream that he and Phones clash with a band of underwater cavemen gives him a novel idea—or so he thinks . . .

Director: Alan Pattillo

Deep Heat

w Alan Fennell
Two underwater beings lure *Stingray* to their stronghold beneath the Earth's crust and beg to be rescued from destruction by a volcanic eruption. But the crew's kindness is repaid by treachery!

Director: John Kelly

Star of the East

w Alan Fennell
Would-be WASP member El Hudat is enraged when a revolution in his home state robs him of WASP eligi-

bility. He kidnaps Marina, and Troy needs all his aquanaut's skills to bring the renegade to book.

Director: Desmond Saunders

Invisible Enemy

w Alan Fennell
Troy and his crew rescue a mysterious stranger and resume patrol, unaware that the man has been hypnotized by an alien underwater race to put the whole of Marineville into a trance, leaving the city vulnerable to attack. Luckily they return in time to revive everyone!

Director: David Elliott

Tom Thumb Tempest

w Alan Fennell
Danger and adventure as *Stingray* shrinks to miniature size and the crew find themselves midgets in a bewildering giant world, threatened by Titan's forces and trapped in a fish tank. All seems lost . . . until Troy awakens from his vivid dream.

Director: Alan Pattillo

Eastern Eclipse

w Alan Fennell
Which brother is which? That's the poser for Commander Shore after Agent X20 frees Eastern dictator El Hudat from Marineville by substituting his deposed twin brother, Ali Khali. The only answer is to lock them both up!

Director: Desmond Saunders

Treasure Down Below

w Dennis Spooner
An old treasure map leads *Stingray* into a rocky cavern where the crew are taken prisoner by two fish-people who have lived comfortably for 300 years on the proceeds of underwater piracy. Troy's bravery saves his friends and foils the fishy felons.

Director: Alan Pattillo

Stand By for Action

w Dennis Spooner
Troy is put out when a film unit makes a movie at Marineville—with a handsome screen star playing his part! But it's really just another of Agent X20's fiendish schemes to dispose of the superhero, and when the plot thickens it's the real Troy who saves the day—and gets the girl!

Director: Alan Pattillo

Pink Ice

w Alan Fennell

Investigating a strange pink liquid that is freezing over the world's oceans, *Stingray* becomes trapped as the water around it turns to pink ice. Only a missile bombardment from Marineville can free them—but one stray shot could scupper them!

Director: David Elliott

The Disappearing Ships

w Alan Fennell

Probing the disappearance of three disused freighters that were due to be blown up, Troy and Phones discover them in a Shipwreck City inhabited by a Nomad tribe who are unaware that their new homes are time-bombs—until, one by one, the ships explode.

Director: David Elliott

Secret of the Giant Oyster

w Alan Fennell

Marina is worried when Troy is sent to help two conniving divers retrieve a huge, priceless pearl from a giant oyster, protected by thousands of satellite oysters; bad luck is said to befall whoever removes it. Troy does indeed run into danger but both he and the giant oyster are saved by the protective satellites.

Director: John Kelly

The Invaders

w Dennis Spooner

Captured by an underwater race, Troy, Phones and Marina little realize their thoughts have been read—and vital secrets revealed. The invaders burrow into Marineville but Troy is able to sound the alarm and foil the takeover bid.

Director: David Elliott

A Nut for Marineville

w Gerry *&* Sylvia Anderson

Egghead boffin Professor Burgoyne is called in to design a new super missile after *Stingray*'s old ones fail to destroy a powerful alien craft heading for Marineville.

Director: David Elliott

Trapped in the Depths

w Alan Fennell

Atlanta is staying on a remote fish farm when she stumbles on a crazy professor's plan to hijack *Stingray* by luring Troy and Phones into a mock-up, while his forces use the real one to attack Marineville.

Director: John Kelly

Count Down

w Dennis Spooner

Claiming to be able to teach mute people to speak, Agent X20 lures Marina into his underwater craft and leaves her trapped aboard it in *Stingray*'s pen with a bomb primed to explode. Troy and Phones thwart his master-plan with just seconds to spare.

Director: Alan Pattillo

Sea of Oil

w Dennis Spooner

Atlanta is captured by an undersea race who believe Troy is trying to destroy their city. She is told a bomb has been placed on *Stingray* that will explode when the craft submerges . . .

Director: John Kelly

Plant of Doom

w Alan Fennell

Marina is used by Agent X20 as the unsuspecting dupe in a deadly scheme that has her suspected of trying to kill Atlanta—until Troy proves her innocence.

Director: David Elliott

The Master Plan

w Alan Fennell

Poisoned in an aquaphibian attack, Troy lies dying. Only Titan has the antidote but he wants his ex-slave girl, Marina, in exchange.

Director: John Kelly

The Golden Sea

w Dennis Spooner

Titan tries to use a giant swordfish's electrical energy to destroy *Stingray*, which has been assigned to assist scientists who have found a way to mine gold from the sea—but Troy turns the tables on the old tyrant.

Director: John Kelly

Hostages of the Deep

w Alan Fennell

Stingray responds to a distress call that includes a coded warning of a trap, and the crew encounters Gadus, a dastardly underwater inhabitant. Marina is captured and looks set to meet a nasty end at the point of a swordfish's razor-sharp sword until Troy and Phones effect a last-minute rescue.

Director: Desmond Saunders

Marineville Traitor

w Alan Fennell

Commander Shore a traitor? Surely not! But when a vital piece of equipment is stolen, it certainly looks that way. However, it's all a trap to lure the *real* traitor into the open and the Commander finds himself in deadly danger.

Director: Desmond Saunders

Aquanaut of the Year

w Gerry *&* Sylvia Anderson

After a party to celebrate his Aquanaut of the Year award, Troy finds himself the subject of *This Is Your Life* and relives moments from his most exciting adventures. But just as the host is asking whether he and Atlanta are more than just good friends, the alert is sounded, leaving Atlanta to remark that "there just isn't time for romance in the World Aquanaut Security Patrol."

Director: Alan Pattillo

THE STRANGE WORLD OF PLANET X

". . . we must go on, they cry, and hurtle to destruction, and they don't care who they take with them." Its producer, Arthur Lane, called it "adult science fiction" and paralleled it with *Gun Law*, "the adult Western."

The *Observer* TV critic Maurice Richardson voted it British network ITV's "worst serial of the year," and called it "a poor man's *Quatermass*."

Those viewers who opted to make the trip were transported to *The Strange World of Planet X* over the space of seven autumn weeks in 1956. The story, penned by actress, novelist and scriptwriter Rene Ray, followed the experiences of two scientists, David Graham and Gavin Laird, whose discovery of the "devastating" Formula MFX—Magnetic Field X (where X equals the unknown!)—gave them the freedom of Time—the Fourth Dimension. Two others who came under the influence of Formula MFX were Laird's wife, Fenella (played by Trevor Howard's actress wife, Helen Cherry), and another woman, Pollie Boulter (played by comedienne Maudie Edwards). As the episodes unfolded, the characters were transported to the strange, eerie world of Planet X—depicted as an abstract, moon-like landscape.

The serial was directed by Quentin Lawrence who, just a couple of months later, unleashed *The Trollenberg Terror* on ITV.

(The quote at the beginning is from the *TVTimes* billing for Episode Four. The previous week's asked: "Was it just a dream? Or have you been to *The Strange World of Planet X*?")

CAST

Fenella Laird Helen Cherry   *David Graham* William Lucas
Gavin Laird David Garth   *Prof. Kollheim* Paul Hardtmuth
Pollie Boulter Maudie Edwards

Writer: Rene Ray
Producer: Arthur Lane
Directors: Quentin Lawrence *(Eps. 2, 4, 5–7)*
   Arthur Lane *(Eps. 1, 3)*

An ATV Network Production
7 black and white 30-minute episodes

The Formula
The Terrible Cabinet
The Unholy Threshold
The Dimension Discovered
(Eps. 5–7 no titles available)

15 September–27 October 1956

THE STRANGER

Science fiction tale from Australia about three teenagers who become involved in an alien's mission to Earth to find a new home for his people.

The story was told in two six-part serials, screened by the BBC in 1965 and 1966. In the first series, the stranger, Adam Suisse, arrives in Australia to seek help for the people of his planet, Soshuniss, who want to migrate to Earth. He is befriended by Bernie and Jean Walsh, whose father is the headmaster of the local school, and their pal Peter. Intrigued by the stranger's lengthy expeditions to the Blue Mountains, the trio follow him, learning his real identity and meeting a co-emissary, Varossa, as well as taking a trip of their own to Soshuniss.

As the sequel opens, the people of Soshuniss are no nearer a solution, and are unhappy about the way the world—and particularly the Press—have reacted to the visit of their emissaries. As a result they hold Peter hostage on Soshuniss.

Happily, a peaceful solution is eventually found—thanks in large part to the Australian Prime Minister.

REGULAR CAST
Mr. Walsh John Fraser *Mrs. Walsh* Jessica Noad
Bernard Walsh Bill Levis *Jean Walsh* Janice Dinnen
Peter Cannon Michael Thomas
Adam Suisse (The Stranger) Ron Haddrich
Varossa Reginald Livermore *Prof. Mayer* Owen Weingott

Writer: G.K. Saunders
An Australian Broadcasting Corporation Production
12 black and white 30-minute episodes

25 February–1 April 1965
11 January–15 February 1966
(BBC1)

STRANGER FROM SPACE

Britain's very first science fiction cliffhanger serial was a fortnightly offering broadcast as part of *Whirligig*—the children's corner of the box back in the innocent early 1950s.

First shown in 1951, with viewers encouraged to write in with their suggestions for what should happen next, the tale of young Ian Spencer and his adventures with a Martian boy, Bilaphodorus, whose "Space Boat" crashes on Earth, gained enough response to justify a second serial the following autumn. That one also featured Valentine Dyall (the Black Guardian in *Doctor Who*) as a Martian, Gorgol.

Stranger From Space was a departure for the BBC whose previous ventures into science fiction had been one-off plays—Karel Capek's *R.U.R.* (1937) and H.G. Wells's *The Time Machine* (1949). In its modest way it opened the door for a succession of interplanetary adventures for the corporation's various Children's Television slots.

CAST
Ian Spencer Brian Smith *Bilaphodorous* Michael Newell
John Armitage John Gabriel *Mrs. Spencer* Betty Woolfe*
Professor Watkins Richard Pearson*
Pamela Vernon Isabel George* *Delpho* Bruce Beeby*
Gorgol Valentine Dyall† *Petrio* Peter Hawkins†
*Series One only   †Series Two only

Writers: Hazel Adair, Ronald Marriott
Devised and produced by Michael Westmore
Introduced by Humphrey Lestocq

A BBC Production
17 black and white (short) episodes

Series One:
Crash Landing
On the Run
Come to the Fair
The Trap
The House on Reigate Downs
The Intruders
Lost Energy
The New Power
Journey Through Space
Journey Through Space (cont.)
The Prisoner

20 October 1951–22 March 1952

Series Two:
Message From Mars
Return Journey
The Cage
Trouble in the Air
Total Eclipse
The Battle of Power

11 October–20 December 1952

SUPERBOY

From the team that brought the *Superman* legend to the big screen in 1978, came . . . *Superboy*—the Series.

Superboy focuses on a hitherto neglected chapter in the life of the Man of Steel—his college years, between Smallville High and Metropolis. Clark Kent is a journalism student at Shuster University where his best friends are Lana Lang and T.J. White, aspiring photographer son of the *Daily Planet* editor. Occasional glimpses of villainy are provided by another Shuster student—Lex Luthor.

The name Shuster was a nod to one of Superman's original creators, Joe Shuster. Co-creator Jerry Siegel wasn't forgotten—they named the student union building after him.

The series set out out portray a time of transition—both psychological and physical—for Clark who, for the first time, unveils the famous costume to an incredulous world while reciting the immortal creed of "truth, justice and the American way."

And it's set firmly in the 1980s/90s—allowing the boy of steel to tackle contemporary ills such as drug abuse, environmental issues, big-city gangs and the homeless.

There was no problem about making a TV audience believe a boy could fly. Besides the involvement of Alexander and Ilya Salkind, other *Superman* "old boys" made the transition to the small screen, including producer Bob Simmonds, directors Colin Chilvers and Jackie Cooper (who played the movies' Perry White) and Bob Harmon who supervised the flying effects. A wry twist in the first episode had Superboy catch Lana Lang in a fall from a helicopter—as Christopher Reeve had done with Lois Lane in his first *Superman* film.

Clark/Superboy was played by an unknown actor, John Haymes Newton, a 22-year-old former bodyguard.

In Britain *Superboy* was dropped abruptly by ITV, after just 11 episodes of the first season—poor ratings and disquiet over a torture sequence were blamed. Episodes have since aired on Sky. In America, however, *Superboy* flew on for three more seasons with a new actor, Gerard Christopher, in the lead role.

T.J. had gone to work for the *Daily Planet*, leaving Clark with a new, trouble-prone roommate, Andy McAlister, and Lex Luthor had undergone plastic surgery to age himself 15 years and hide his identity.

Superboy's other enemies also became more outlandish than the everyday crooks he had faced during the first season, and included aliens, vampires and witches, as well as a couple of foes from the old comic strips—the tragic monster figure of Bizarro, an attempted Superboy duplicate gone wrong, and Mr. Mxyzptlk, the imp from the fifth dimension, who could be returned by tricking him into saying his name backward.

For the third season, the title was changed to *The Adventures of Superboy*, and Clark and Lana were now working at the Bureau of Extranormal Matters in Capital City.

MAIN CAST

Superboy/Clark Kent John Haymes Newton *(Season One)*, Gerard Christopher *(from Season Two)* Lana Lang Stacy Haiduk
T.J. White Jim Calvert *(Season One only)* Lex Luthor Scott Wells *(Season One)*,
Sherman Howard *(from Season Two)*
Andy McAlister Ilan Mitchell-Smith *(Season Two)*

Creators: Alexander & Ilya Salkind
Executive producer: Ilya Salkind
Producer: Bob Simmonds
Executive story consultant: Fred Freiberger
Director of photography: Orson Ochoa
Theme: Kevin Kiner

An Alexander and Ilya Salkind Production
U.S. premiere: October 1988
Seasons 1–4: 100 color 30-minute episodes
U.K. first run: 11 episodes
7 January–18 March 1989

Season One
26 episodes

Countdown to Nowhere

w Fred Freiberger
Superboy makes his presence known for the very first time when Lana unwittingly gets caught up in a plot to steal an experimental laser gun.
Roscoe Williams Doug Barr
Theodore Duriell Harris

Director: Colin Chilvers

The Jewel of Techacal

w Fred Freiberger
Prof. Lang visits his daughter, Lana, at the university with his latest archaeological find: the Jewel of Techacal.
Prof. Thomas Lang Peter White
Leo Michael Manno

Director: Reza Badiyi

A Kind of Princess

w Michael Morris & Howard Dimsdale
Superboy fights organized crime as he rescues Sarah Danner, one of "Clark's" classmates and the daughter of mob boss Matt Danner, from the clutches of a rival mobster.
Sarah Julie McCullough
Matt Danner Ed Winter
Casey Harry Cup

Director: Reza Badiyi

Back to Oblivion (aka The Hiding Place)

w Fred Freiberger
Superboy must overcome some maniacal machines built out of scrap metal to rescue Lana from the clutches of an old man who has mistaken her for his

daughter, killed by the Nazis in World War Two.
Wagner Abe Vigoda
Henry Dennis Michael

Director: Colin Chilvers

The Russian Exchange Student

w Sarah V. Finney & Vida Spears
T.J. falls in love with a Russian exchange student who is suspected of sabotaging secret energy experiments at Shuster University. (Guest star Ray Walston played Uncle Martin in the 1960s series *My Favorite Martian*.)
Natasha Pokrovsky Heather Haase
Prof. Abel Gordon Ray Walston
Jeff Hilford Courtney Gaines
Elena Tania Hartley
Det. Zeke Harris Roger Pretto

Director: Reza Badiyi

Bringing Down the House

w Michael Morris
Superboy probes a strange and deadly link between bizarre threats at a baseball game and amusement park and the return of rock star Judd Faust.
Judd Faust Leif Garrett
Andy Don Sheldon
Henry Dennis Michael

Director: Colin Chilvers

The Beast and Beauty

w Bernard M. Kahn
Superboy confronts a crazed imposter who wants to steal a million dollars to "buy" the hand of a beauty queen.
Hugo Stone David Marciano
Jennifer Jenkins Lonnie Shaw
Det. Zeke Harris Roger Pretto

Director: Jackie Cooper

The Fixer

w Aiden Schwimmer
The boy of steel foils a plot to fix a university basketball game masterminded by Lex Luthor.
Lex Luthor Scott Wells
Stretch Michael Landon Jr.

Director: Colin Chilvers

The Alien Solution

w Michael Carlin *&* Andrew Helfer
A strange gaseous alien kidnaps Lana as a ploy to lure Superboy into battle, so he can take over his body and add it to his collection of warriors.
Alien warrior Jeff Moldovan
Henry Dennis Michael
Dr. Howard Christine Page

Director: Colin Chilvers

Troubled Waters

w Dick Robbins
Superboy returns to his parents' home in Smallville and uncovers a sinister plot to sell all the water from an underground river in the town.
Jonathan Kent Stuart Whitman
Martha Kent Salome Jens
Ellen Jensen Juli Donald
Carl Kenderson Peter Palmer

Director: Reza Badiyi

Kryptonite Kills

w Michael Carlin *&* Andrew Helfer
Lex steals a sample of Kryptonite sent to a geology professor and plans to use it to overload the city's power plant, plunging the city into darkness as a cover for a crime spree.
Professor Peterson George Chakiris
Veronica Lawlor Pamela Bach
Oswald Paul Cohn
Agnes Cyndi Vance
Felix Larry Francer

Director: Jackie Cooper

Revenge of the Alien

(a 2-part story)
w Michael Carlin *and* Andrew Helfer
The gaseous alien from "The Alien Solution" escapes from the canister he was imprisoned in and seeks his revenge on Superboy, taking over his father's body and again using Lana as bait to trap the boy of steel.
Pa Kent Stuart Whitman
Johnson Glenn Scherer
Lt. Zeke Harris Roger Pretto
Henry Dennis Michael
Dean Lockhardt Dana Mark

Director: Peter Kiwitt

Stand Up and Get Knocked Down

w David Patrick Columbia *&* Toby Martin
T.J. gets into danger when he signs up to perform at a comedy club he believes to be involved in the death of a friend.
Dexter Linton Gary Lockwood
Michael Hayden Logston
Angel Cindy Hamsey
Emcee Lester Bibbs

Director: David Grossman

Meet Mr. Mxyzptlk

w Dennis O'Neill
Superboy removes an Indian totem and inadvertently releases a mysterious imp from the fifth dimension.
Mr. Mxyzptlk Michael J. Pollard
Prof. Royer Russ Wheeler

Director: Peter Kiwitt

Birdwoman of the Swamps

w Bernard M. Kahn
The construction of new housing for the poor is endangering the local wildlife, and a mysterious old woman, claiming to use ancient Indian magic, is sabotaging it for the sake of the environment.
Birdwoman Marlene Cameron
Mr. Hogan James MacArthur
Woody Mike Walter

Director: Reza Badiyi

Terror from the Blue

w George Kirgo
Lana finds herself running for her life after she witnesses a bent cop shooting an honest one.
Lt. Zeke Harris Roger Pretto
Det. Jed Slade Cary-Haroyuki Tagawa
Oscar Chase Randolph
Stone Michael Stark

Director: David Grossman

War of the Species

w Steven L. Sears
T.J. and Lana find a scientist's dead body in his lab which leads Superboy to find androids from outer space who are trying to develop a super-robot to do their killing for them.
Dr. Stuart Kevyn Major Howard
Android John Matuzak

Director: Peter Kiwitt

The Invisible People

w Mark Evanier
Superboy goes to the assistance of some homeless people whose "tent city" has been savagely fire-bombed.
Gerold Manfred Sonny Shroyer
Damon Greg Morris
Alice Cynthia Ann Roses

Director: Jackie Cooper

Little Hercules

w Wayne A. Rice
A precocious young teenager tries to impress an older girl by sending a romantic poem by computer, but accidentally sets off a missile code that may trigger World War Three.
Billy Hercules Leaf Phoenix
Lt. Redman Allen Hall
Commander Mal Jones
Amanda Elizabeth Marion

Director: David Grossman

Mutant

w Michael Morris
Time-traveling mutants kidnap a scientist and demand that he helps them build a nuclear weapon.
Professor Lipcott Jack Swanson
Val Skye Aubrey
Hol Bill Christie

Director: Joe Ravitz

Black Flamingo

w Cary Bates
Superboy goes undercover in a punk nightclub where a terrorist called Snake-Man is hypnotizing teenagers to turn them into killers.
Snake-Man Fernando Allende
Natasha Ada Maris
Agar Herbert Hopper
Senator Ron Knight

Director: Chuck Martinez

The Phantom of the Third Division

w Bernard M. Kahn
Clark returns to Smallville to visit his parents and finds that Pa Kent is being stalked by a fellow Korean War veteran out for revenge on Pa who he blames for his capture during the war.
Phantom Joseph Campanella

Director: David Nutter

Hollywood

w Fred Freiberger
An inventor tricks Superboy into powering his time machine, which whisks them back to 1939 Hollywood, where Superboy falls for a beautiful movie star.
Professor Zugo Doug McClure
Victoria Letour Gail O'Grady
Stoddard Fred Buch
Willis Nick Stannard
Gus Stephen Geng

Director: David Nutter

Succubus

w Cary Bates
A beautiful vampire-like creature seeks to drain Superboy of his life force and seduces T.J. as part of her plot.
Pamela Dare (Succubus) Sybil Danning
Professor Myers Rita Rehn

Director: David Nutter

Luthor Unleashed

w Stephen Lord
Superboy saves Lex Luthor's life when a chemical weapon he's been working on explodes. But the incident causes all Luthor's hair to fall out and he vows to get even with Superboy.
Leo Michael Manno
Lt. Harris Roger Pretto
Colonel Rance Howard
Oswald Paul Cohn
Felix Larry Francer

Director: David Nutter

Season Two
26 episodes
With This Ring I Thee Kill
Lex Luthor: Sentenced to Die!
Metallo
Young Dracula
Nightmare Island
Bizarro . . . The Thing of Steel
The Battle with Bizarro
Mr. and Mrs. Superboy
Programmed for Death
Superboy's Deadly Touch
The Power of Evil
Superboy . . . Rest in Peace
Super Menace!
Yellow Peri's Spell of Doom
Microboy
Run, Dracula, Run
Brimstone
Abandon Earth
Escape to Earth
Superstar

Nick Knack
The Haunting of Andy McAlister
Revenge from the Deep
The Secrets of Superboy
Johnny Casanova and the Case of Secret Serum
The Woman Called Tiger Eye

Season Three
26 episodes
Bride of Bizarro *(2-part story)*
The Lair
Neila
Roads Not Taken *(2-part story)*
Sons of Icarus
Carnival
Test of Time
Mindscape
Superboy . . . Lost
Special Effects
Neila and the Beast
The Golem
A Day in the Double Life
Bodyswap
Rebirth *(2-part story)*
Werewolf
People vs Metallo

Jackson and Hyde
Mind Games
Wish for Armageddon
Standoff
The Road to Hell *(2-part story)*

Season Four
22 episodes
A Change of Heart *(2-part story)*
The Kryptonite Kid
The Basement
Darla Goes Ballistic
Paranoia
Know Thine Enemy *(2-part story)*
Hell Breaks Loose
Into the Mystery
To Be Human *(2-part story)*
West of Alpha Centauri
Threesome *(2-part story)*
Out of Luck
Who Is Superboy?
Cat and Mouse
Obituary for a Super-Hero
Metamorphosis
Rites of Passage *(2-part story)*

SUPERCAR

*S*upercar started the run of Supermarionation sci-fi series in 1961, but the Gerry Anderson puppet story was already five years old by then.

It all began, as they say, in 1956, in a converted mansion in Maidenhead, Berkshire, where the 27-year-old, near-penniless former film cutting-room assistant launched his own company AP Films into its maiden venture, a low-budget puppet project about a character who could stretch his limbs. *The Adventures of Twizzle* ran for 52 15-minute episodes, closely followed by 52 tales of *Torchy The Battery Boy*, dazzling the first generation of ITV toddlers. (Both of these were scripted by Roberta Leigh who later created *Space Patrol*.) Then came a full-scale puppet production, the Western series *Four Feather Falls*, with Nicholas Parsons and Kenneth Connor among the actors voicing the characters.

Anderson's technique was improving—incorporating moving eyes and electronically controlled mouth movements—and he and his associates, Reg Hill, John Read, and wife, Sylvia, were realizing the potential of this type of filmmaking. A new word was coined to set the puppets as a race apart—Supermarionation—and *Supercar* swept it across the screens.

A wonderfully versatile craft, Supercar could travel over land, in the sea and through the air—anywhere in the world. It had folding wings for flights and a periscope for submarine work. The regular cast included Supercar's fatherly inventor, Professor Rudolph Popkiss, a sort of mid-European scientist; his assistant Dr. Horatio Beaker, a British boffin with a balding head and a stammer; fearless test pilot Mike Mercury; 10-year-old Jimmy Gibson who was the first person to be rescued by Supercar, after a plane crash; and his pal Mitch, a mischievous talking monkey. They were the good guys. Out to steal Supercar were Masterspy, a devious deep-voiced mercenary, and his weedy, worm-like accomplice Zarin; and their British counterparts Harper and Judd.

Supercar itself, a seven-foot craft made mostly of lightweight balsa wood, was designed by Reg Hill and cost £1000 to build—a small fortune for a company so short of cash that it used 1500 empty egg cartons stuck on the walls to soundproof its new studio in a disused factory in Slough.

Supercar was dreamed up in 1959, but with Anderson's previous backer, Granada Television, shying away from the new project, production was saved when Lew Grade's ITC put up the money.

The series was a soaraway success. Its 39 episodes turned the tide for Anderson, selling into more than 100 U.S. markets and more than 40 countries. Indeed, Lew Grade liked the results so much he subsequently bought the company!

VOICE CAST

Mike Mercury Graydon Gould *Jimmy Gibson* Sylvia Anderson (Sylvia Thamm)
Prof. Rudolph Popkiss/Masterspy George Murcell *(Season One)*, Cyril Shaps
(Season Two) *Mitch/Zarin/Dr. Horatio Beaker* David Graham

From an original idea by Gerry Anderson, Reg Hill	*An AP Films Production for ATV/ITC*
Producer: Gerry Anderson	39 black and white 30-minute episodes
Music: Barry Gray	Season One:
Special effects: Derek Meddings *(Season Two)*	28 January–6 April 1961
Title song sung by Gary Miller *(Season One)/*	Season Two:
The Mike Sammes Singers *(Season Two)*	4 February–29 April 1962
	(Dates as London, ATV)

Season One
26 episodes

Rescue

w Martin & Hugh Woodhouse
On his maiden rescue flight Mike Mercury uses Supercar's Clearvu device to navigate through dense fog to save brothers Bill and Jimmy Gibson who are drifting on a life-raft after their plane crashed into the sea.

Director: David Elliott

False Alarm

w Martin & Hugh Woodhouse
Masterspy and Zarin send out a phony SOS so they can steal Supercar when it comes to the rescue. Their plan nearly works until Prof. Popkiss switches Supercar to remote and hands the controls over to Mitch who gives the dastardly duo a hair-raising ride.

Director: Alan Pattillo

The Talisman of Sargon

w Martin & Hugh Woodhouse
Masterspy, disguised as a geologist, tricks Dr. Beaker into deciphering the secret of the Tomb of Sargon, which contains a priceless jewel said to bestow magic powers on its owner. Mike and his team race to stop him using it.

Director: David Elliott

What Goes Up

w Martin & Hugh Woodhouse
When a test balloon carrying a new USAF rocket fuel drifts out of control, Mike risks his life to take Supercar close enough to detonate it before it can fall back to Earth and returns with only scorched paintwork to show for his adventure.

Director: David Elliott

Amazonian Adventure

w Martin & Hugh Woodhouse
Mitch goes down with sleeping sickness and Mike and Dr. Beaker take off to the Amazon jungle to find a cure—the rare t'logi plant. Captured by headhunters, Mike uses Supercar to impress the natives while Beaker conjures up some magic of his own.

Director: Alan Pattillo

Grounded

w Martin & Hugh Woodhouse
Crooks Harper and Judd steal some printed circuits designed by Beaker and sabotage Supercar, causing it to crash as it takes off in pursuit. Down but not out, Supercar takes its first journey by road to intercept the unsuspecting thieves before they can leave the country.

Director: David Elliott

Keep It Cool

w Martin & Hugh Woodhouse
Masterspy and Zarin ambush Bill Gibson and Dr. Beaker in the desert, stealing the highly volatile new fuel they are carrying. Knowing the fuel will explode when the temperature rises above freezing point, Mike sets out in Supercar to find them.

Director: Alan Pattillo

Jungle Hazard

w Martin *&* Hugh Woodhouse
Masterspy and Zarin plot to take over a dilapidated Malayan plantation from its new owner, Felicity Farnsworth. Unknown to them, however, Felicity is Beaker's cousin and the Supercar team is quickly on the scene.

Director: Alan Pattillo

High Tension

w Martin *&* Hugh Woodhouse
Masterspy kidnaps Dr. Beaker and demands Supercar in exchange for his release. But when Masterspy and Zarin try to take possession they get a nasty shock—the hull has been secretly charged with electricity "to scare away inquisitive creatures."

Director: David Elliott

Island Incident

w Martin *&* Hugh Woodhouse
The deposed president of the island of Pelota seeks Supercar's help in exposing his brother who has usurped his rule. Mike takes Supercar underwater to breach the island's defenses.

Director: David Elliott

Ice-Fall

w Martin *&* Hugh Woodhouse
Exploring an ice-fall in an underground cavern, Beaker becomes trapped when more ice collapses around him. Mike fires Supercar's jets at the wall of ice to free his friend.

Director: Desmond Saunders

Phantom Piper

w Martin *&* Hugh Woodhouse
Mike and the Supercar team fly to Scotland to help Beaker's cousin Felicity and their great-uncle Angus solve the mystery of the phantom piper. They uncover a cunning scheme to steal a priceless topaz.

Director: Alan Pattillo

Pirate Plunder

w Martin *&* Hugh Woodhouse
The Supercar team decides to rid the seas of the pirate Black Morgan, using a millionaire's yacht as bait. But their plan nearly ends in disaster when Morgan fires a torpedo at them. Luckily Beaker is able to jam the missile and Mike finally sinks the pirate ship.

Director: David Elliott

A Little Art

w Martin *&* Hugh Woodhouse
Beaker buys a painting from a shady art dealer who later discovers it contains a clue to the location of a forger's counterfeit plates and steals it back. But Beaker has photographed it and Supercar joins the hunt.

Director: Alan Pattillo

Flight of Fancy

w Gerry *&* Sylvia Anderson
Jimmy dreams that he and Mitch fly off in Supercar to rescue a princess from the clutches of the wicked politicians Hertz and Marzak—who look more than a little like Masterspy and Zarin.

Director: Alan Pattillo

Deep Seven

w Martin *&* Hugh Woodhouse
Supercar undergoes a rigorous underwater test, diving 400 feet to the sea bed. Then the cockpit starts leaking and the craft becomes entangled in a mine cable. Bill Gibson dons his diving gear and swims to the rescue.

Director: Desmond Saunders

Hostage

w Martin *&* Hugh Woodhouse
On holiday in Ireland, Dr. Beaker calls up Mike and Supercar to help foil a kidnap plot staged by crooked duo Judd and Harper. The villains nearly succeed in blowing up Supercar but the tables are turned on them by an irate Mitch armed with a baseball bat.

Director: Desmond Saunders

The Sunken Temple

w Martin *&* Hugh Woodhouse
A harmless underwater expedition in the Med turns into a dangerous encounter with the ruthless bandit Spyros when Mike and Dr. Beaker discover his stolen loot in a safe on the sea bed.

Director: David Elliott

The Lost City

w Gerry *&* Sylvia Anderson
Mike and Dr. Beaker stumble on the secret hideout of a mad English scientist, Professor Watkins, who plans to launch a missile upon Washington. It takes all their courage and ingenuity to foil this plot.

Director: Alan Pattillo

Trapped in the Depths

w Martin & Hugh Woodhouse
When contact is lost with the crew of a new bathyscape in the Pacific, Supercar dives to the rescue and finds it has been attacked by a giant fish. Using Supercar's ultrasonic gun to drive away the monster, Mike succeeds in saving the trapped divers.

Director: Alan Pattillo

Dragon of Ho Meng

w Martin & Hugh Woodhouse
Grounded by a typhoon near China, Mike, Jimmy and Mitch meet Ho Meng and his daughter Lotus Blossom, guardians of an ancient temple. Ho Meng regards Supercar as a dragon, a harbinger of disaster, but is soon glad it's around when he is seized by the villainous Mr. Fang who wants to blow up the temple.

Director: David Elliott

Magic Carpet

w Martin & Hugh Woodhouse
On a mercy mission to deliver medicines to Prince Hassan, the Supercar team are thrown into jail by the dastardly Alif Bey who wants the prince to die so that he can assume power. But with the aid of a pocket remote control Mike and Co. manage to save the day.

Director: Desmond Saunders

Supercar Take One

w Gerry & Sylvia Anderson
Dr. Beaker makes a movie of Supercar with his new cine camera but when his processed film gets mixed up with one taken by some spies, Mike and the team fly to New York to challenge the foreign agents.

Director: Desmond Saunders

Crash Landing

w Gerry & Sylvia Anderson
Engine trouble forces Supercar down in the jungle. Then Mitch goes missing and after an anxious search is found in the company of an adoring female monkey. Mitch is mortified to leave her—but delighted when they find she has stowed away in Supercar!

Director: Desmond Saunders

The Tracking of Masterspy

w Martin & Hugh Woodhouse
Masterspy steals the plans to Supercar plus what he thinks is a new secret project. But it's really a tracking device, enabling Mike to trail him back to his lair.

Director: David Elliott

The White Line

w Martin & Hugh Woodhouse
The Supercar team is called in by Scotland Yard to solve a series of bank and armored car raids by a pair of Chicago gangsters—the Hoyle Brothers. When Dr. Beaker takes out the next armored car, Supercar must move fast to stop him driving into the brothers' deadly detour trap.

Director: Alan Pattillo

Season Two
13 episodes

The Runaway Train

w Gerry & Sylvia Anderson
Dr. Beaker's latest invention, a magnet capable of lifting 100 tons, helps save the lives of Beaker and Prof. Popkiss when the atomic train they're traveling on is sabotaged by Masterspy and Zarin.

Director: David Elliott

Precious Cargo

w Gerry & Sylvia Anderson
Servant girl Zizi, badly treated by her wine merchant employer, hits upon an idea to escape when a special order arrives from the Supercar lab.

Director: Alan Pattillo

Operation Superstork

w Gerry & Sylvia Anderson
Beaker, Jimmy and Mike are cast adrift in a new air balloon when Mitch unties a guy rope, so Mike has to parachute to the ground before he can rescue the others in Supercar.

Director: Desmond Saunders

Hi-Jack

w Gerry & Sylvia Anderson
Jimmy's brother Bill takes Beaker and Jimmy with him on his first flight to train airline pilots. Unknown to him, his first pupil is an imposter—part of a plan by Masterspy and Zarin to hijack an airliner.

Director: Bill Harris

Calling Charlie Queen

w Gerry *&* Sylvia Anderson
Mike and Dr. Beaker answer a ham radio message for help and find themselves involved in a plot by Prof. Karloff to take over America by "miniaturizing" its citizens.

Director: Alan Pattillo

Space for Mitch

w Gerry *&* Sylvia Anderson
Supercar sets off to rescue Mitch after the mischievous monkey has shot himself into space in a rocket.

Director: Desmond Saunders

Atomic Witch Hunt

w Gerry *&* Sylvia Anderson
The Supercar team tries to find out who planted atomic bombs all over America, set to explode simultaneously, and find themselves in the clutches of a villainous sheriff.

Director: Desmond Saunders

70-B-Low

w Gerry *&* Sylvia Anderson
Prof. Popkiss needs an urgent blood transfusion. But his is a rare blood group and the nearest donor is a scientist stranded in the Arctic.

Director: Alan Pattillo

The Sky's the Limit

w Gerry *&* Sylvia Anderson
Masterspy and Zarin try to buy Supercar, using counterfeit money. When this doesn't work they hire two villains to steal it—but all four get a surprise.

Director: Bill Harris

Jail Break

w Gerry *&* Sylvia Anderson
Dr. Beaker's latest invention—an ejector seat—helps to recapture an escaped criminal, Joe Anna, who forces Mike to fly him across the Mexican border in Supercar.

Director: Bill Harris

The Day That Time Stood Still

w Gerry *&* Sylvia Anderson
Mike's birthday is interrupted when time is frozen and a stranger from space presents him with a flying belt . . . but Mike awakes to find it was just another flight of fancy . . .

Director: Alan Pattillo

Transatlantic Cable

w Gerry *&* Sylvia Anderson
Answering a call from the Tele-Cable Corporation, the Supercar team finds Masterspy has been tapping into a transatlantic cable from his undersea hideout. So Mike decides to tap into Masterspy's lair!

Director: Desmond Saunders

King Kool

w Gerry *&* Sylvia Anderson
Mitch resents Jimmy's interest in King Kool, a gorilla jazz-drummer, but when he visits the star he is tricked into a cage.

Director: Bill Harris

SURVIVORS

*S*urvivors saw the end of civilization as we knew it—the world going down not with a nuclear bang but with a global whimper that wiped out 95 percent of the human race.

A virus accidentally released into the atmosphere (the credit sequence showed an Asian scientist dropping a test-tube) spreads rapidly around the world, killing all but the five percent who either don't catch it or recover.

The BBC series took up the story from there, following a central group of British characters as they struggle, initially to come to terms with their situation, then to adapt and, finally, to try and rebuild something of the world they've lost.

Survivors was created by Terry Nation who saw disaster round the corner and worried about mankind's ability to cope. What if, he queried, the rug was pulled from beneath our complex society based (as it still is) on mutual cooperation and increased dependence on technology. Could impractical modern man adapt to the rigors of survival?

As a notion it was ripe for the 1970s advocates of "alternative lifestyles," and it was also something everyone could relate to—every viewer could wonder "what would *I* do? How would *I* cope?"

But this wasn't a *Good Life* vision of suburban self-sufficiency. *Survivors* depicted a grim, relentless struggle in which even mundane items such as soap or matches became precious.

Contemporary critics carped that the heroes were almost exclusively middle class, and took perverse delight in their discomfiture. Certainly, the lead roles of Abby Grant (suburban housewife), Greg Preston (engineer), Charles Vaughan (architect) and Jenny Richards (secretary/young mum) represented the acceptable face of survival, ranged against the bolshie regional and working classes. But the series was, nevertheless, an uncompromising portrait of civilization in reverse.

Survivors ran for three seasons, each with a distinct theme. Initially there was the aftermath and the "quest"—Abby's search for her son, Peter, the survivors' search for trust, friendship, order from chaos, the need to regroup on the smallest of scales.

Season Two saw more settled and established communities, forming in rural areas away from the towns, which were depicted as plague-pits, rife with pollution and vermin. The challenge they now faced was to acquire—and acquire fast—the skills to replace their diminishing supplies of things they had once taken for granted.

Season Three again took to the road, as the survivors began to explore further afield, to establish links with other settlements and seek out people with the special skills to build a future, through trade, a railway and, ultimately, hydro-electricity. The series, which began on an overwhelmingly gloomy note, ended on an optimistic one.

REGULAR CAST

SEASON ONE
Abby Grant Carolyn Seymour   *Jenny Richards* Lucy Fleming
Greg Preston Ian McCulloch   *Tom Price* Talfryn Thomas *(Eps. 1–3, 7–10)*
John Stephen Dudley *(from Ep. 5)   Lizzie* Tanya Ronder *(from Ep. 5)*
Vic Thatcher Terry Scully *(Eps. 2, 8–10),* Hugh Walters *(Eps. 11, 13)*
Paul Pitman Christopher Tranchell *(from Ep. 8)*
Mrs. Emma Cohen Hana-Maria Pravda *(from Ep. 7)*
Charmian Wentworth Eileen Helsby *(from Ep. 8)*
Arthur Russell Michael Gover *(from Ep. 8)*

SEASON TWO
Ian McCulloch *(Eps. 1–8, 10–13),* Lucy Fleming *(Eps. 1–3, 5, 7–8, 11–13)*
Stephen Dudley *and* Tanya Ronder *(Eps. 1–2, 5–8, 10–13)*
Michael Gover *(Eps. 1–2, 5, 7–8, 11),* Chris Tranchell *(Eps. 1 & 2 only)*

PLUS
Charles Vaughan Denis Lill   *Pet Simpson* Lorna Lewis *(Eps. 1–2, 5–13)*
Ruth Anderson Celia Gregory *(Eps. 1–6, 8, 10–13)*
Hubert John Abineri *(Eps. 1, 5–8, 11–13)*
Jack Gordon Salkild *(Eps. 2, 5–6, 8, 11, 13)*

SEASON THREE
Denis Lill *(Eps. 1, 3–9, 11–12),* Lucy Fleming *(Eps. 1–3, 5–9, 11–12)*
John Abineri *(Eps. 1, 3, 5–9, 11–12),* Lorna Lewis *(Eps. 1, 6–7, 10)*
Stephen Dudley *(Eps. 1, 6, 10),* Ian McCulloch *(Eps. 2, 10)*
Gordon Salkild *(Eps. 1, 6, 10)*

PLUS
Lizzie Angie Stevens *(Eps. 1, 6, 10) Agnes* Anna Pitt *(Eps. 2–3, 5, 10–11)*

Creator: Terry Nation
Producer: Terence Dudley
Music: Anthony Isaac

A BBC Production
38 color 50-minute episodes

Season One:
16 April–16 July 1975
Season Two:
31 March–23 June 1976
Season Three:
16 March–8 June 1977

Season One
13 episodes

The Fourth Horseman

w Terry Nation
A deadly virus is accidentally released and spreads rapidly around the world. A decimated civilization begins to break down: the trains stop running, traffic piles up, a radio station goes off the air, hospitals can't cope. In a Home Counties stockbroker belt, Abby Grant goes into a coma. When she recovers she finds her husband dead and the village strewn with corpses. Meanwhile, in London, secretary Jenny Richards has set out on foot to find other survivors.
Mrs. Transon Margaret Anderson
Dr. Gordon Callum Mill
Mr. Pollard Blake Butler
Patricia Elizabeth Sinclair
David Grant Peter Bowles
Andrew Tyler Christopher Reich
First youth Len Jones
Tom Price Talfryn Thomas *(intro)*
Kevin Lloyd Giles Melville
Dr. Bronson Peter Copley

Director: Pennant Roberts
Designer: Austin Ruddy

Genesis

w Terry Nation
Engineer Greg Preston arrives back in England by helicopter. After discovering his wife is dead, he drives aimlessly across country, encountering "spoilt bitch" Anne Tranter and Vic Thatcher. Vic is injured in a tractor accident, but Anne callously tells Greg he is dead. Abby encounters ex-union leader Arthur Wormley who is bent on imposing his own brand of martial law.
Greg Preston Ian McCulloch *(intro)*
Anne Tranter Myra Frances
Vic Thatcher Terry Scully *(intro)*
Arthur Wormley George Baker
Dave Long Brian Peck
First man Peter Jolley
Colonel Edward Brooks

Director: Gerald Blake
Designer: Ray London

Gone Away

w Terry Nation
Abby, Jenny and Greg's camp is broken into by Welsh laborer Tim Price. Needing to replenish their supplies, they visit a food warehouse. Inside is the hanged body of a looter. Abby insists that they start to load their cars, but they are interrupted by the arrival of three of Wormley's men.
Boy Graham Fletcher
Phillipson Robert Fyfe
Dave Long Brian Peck

Reg Gunnel Barry Stanton
John Milner Robert Gillespie

Director: Terence Williams
Designer: Richard Morris

Corn Dolly

w Jack Ronder
"We must make sure there is a next generation . . . we're being helped . . . I've found that with the scarcity of people, the problems we face, everyone loves everyone." Abby and her friends come across former architect Charles who has his own ideas about how to ensure the survival of the human race.
Charles Denis Lill *(intro)*
Isla Yvonne Bonnamy
Loraine Annie Hayes
Mick Keith Jayne
Tessa June Bolton
Woman Maureen Nelson

Director: Pennant Roberts
Designer: Austin Ruddy

Gone to the Angels

w Jack Ronder
"Abby, you're truthful and you're searching. Please don't be afraid." Abby gets a clue that her son may have gone to a religious community in the Peak District. She sets off with Jenny and Greg, but circumstances force her to continue alone.
John Stephen Dudley *(intro)*
Lizzie Tanya Ronder *(intro)*
Lincoln Peter Miles
Jack Frederick Hall
Matthew Nickolas Grace
Robert Kenneth Caswell

Director: Gerald Blake
Designer: Ray London

Garland's War

w Terry Nation
Abby gets drawn into the struggle between young landowner Jimmy Garland and a group of men, led by the ruthless Knox, who have taken over his house to set up a self-appointed "shotgun and pickaxe" government.
Peter Steve Fletcher
Garland Richard Heffer
John Carroll Dennis Chinnery
Bates David G. Marsh
Knox Peter Jeffrey
Harris Robert Oates
Sentry Roger Elliott
Ken Michael Jamieson
Betty Susanna East

Director: Terence Williams
Designer: Richard Morris

Starvation

w Jack Ronder
Abby and her friends, still on their travels, encounter a teenage girl, Wendy, and an old Jewish lady, Mrs. Cohen, who are living in an area ravaged by wild dogs, and rescue them from the clutches of Price.
Wendy Julie Neubert *(intro)*
Mrs. Cohen Hana-Maria Pravda *(intro)*
Barney John Hallet *(intro)*

Director: Pennant Roberts
Designer: Robert Berk

Spoil of War

w M.K. Jeeves *(alias* Clive Exton)
"You left me! You left me to die like a pig in my own filth! You left me in agony . . . just took what you wanted and left me." The community is swelled by agricultural student Paul Pitman, ex-financier Arthur Russell and his secretary Charmian. Returning to the quarry, Greg meets a man he thought was dead . . .
Paul Pitman Christopher Tranchell *(intro)*
Barney John Hallet
Wendy Julie Neubert
Charmian Wentworth Eileen Helsby *(intro)*
Arthur Russell Michael Gover *(intro)*
Vic Thatcher Terry Scully *(re-intro)*

Director: Gerald Blake
Designer: Richard Morris

Law and Order

w M.K. Jeeves *(alias* Clive Exton)
To raise morale, Abby suggests holding a party. But during the festivities Wendy is killed and the finger of blame points at the simple-minded Barney. He is "tried," convicted and executed, before Greg discovers Tom Price was the real murderer.
Barney John Hallet *(exit)*
Wendy Julie Neubert *(exit)*

Director: Pennant Roberts
Designer: Richard Morris

The Future Hour

w Terry Nation
A young pregnant widow seeks shelter with Abby's community because her own group has ruled that her child must be abandoned at birth.
Laura Foster Caroline Burt
Norman Denis Lawson
Bernard Huxley Glyn Owen
Phil James Hayes

Director: Terence Williams
Designer: Richard Morris

Revenge

w Jack Ronder
Vic Thatcher has now become accepted as the tutor of the two children, John and Lizzie. Confined to a wheelchair, he finds his incapacity irksome, but is comforted by the children's need for him. Then Anne Tranter, who had abandoned him badly injured in the quarry, wanders into the community.
Anne Tranter Myra Frances
Donny Robert Tayman

Director: Gerald Blake
Designer: Richard Morris

Something of Value

w Terry Nation
A storm floods the cellar that houses the community's precious provisions. Everything is ruined and Greg starts out with the tanker to a neighboring settlement where he hopes to trade petrol for supplies. While he is away, the community is raided.
Robert Lawson Matthew Long
Jim Buckmaster Murray Hayne
Thorpe Paul Chapman

Director: Terence Williams
Designer: Richard Morris

A Beginning

w Terry Nation
A sick girl, Ruth, is left at the community where the weight of leadership has taken its toll on Abby. At the end of her tether, she leaves and makes for Waterhouse, the home of Jimmy Garland, while Greg and Arthur try to get the communities in the area to join together.
Burton Harry Markham
Ruth Annie Irving
Jimmy Garland Richard Heffer

Director: Pennant Roberts
Designer: Richard Morris

Season Two
13 episodes

Birth of a Hope

w Jack Ronder
Decimated by a fire that kills several of their number, Greg's community joins the Whitecross settlement led by Charles Vaughan. Jenny's baby is due and Greg anxiously awaits the return of Ruth, their doctor.
Pet Simpson Lorna Lewis *(intro)*
Hubert John Abineri *(intro)*
Ruth Anderson Celia Gregory *(intro)*

Director: Eric Hills
Designer: Ian Watson

Greater Love

w Don Shaw
Jenny falls ill and Ruth needs to operate to save her life. But that means getting equipment from a hospital and it's courting death to enter the urban area. Paul volunteers to try . . .
Jack Gordon Salkild *(intro)*

Director: Pennant Roberts
Designer: Ian Watson

Lights of London, Part 1

w Jack Ronder
Ruth is tricked into going to London by the leaders of the 500 survivors there. The Londoners, led by an exhausted former health officer and an ambitious ex-street trader, have gone to ground. Once there, Ruth cannot escape, for the metropolis is in the grip of disease and menaced by rats.
Doctor Patrick Holt
Nessie Lennox Milne
Stan David Troughton
Amul Nadim Sawalha
Penny Coral Atkins
Wally Roger Lloyd Pack
George Lloyd McGuire
Maisie Paula Williams
Manny Sydney Tafler
Barbara Wendy Williams

Director: Terence Williams
Designers: Ian Watson, Peter Kindred

Lights of London, Part 2

w Jack Ronder
Greg and Charles finally reach Ruth, only to find she is unwilling to return with them. Reluctantly, they decide to stay on and help the Londoners in their big move.
Guest cast as Part 1, except David Troughton, Paula Williams

Director: Pennant Roberts
Designers: Paul Allen, Ian Watson

Face of the Tiger

w Don Shaw
Greg welcomes a stranger, Alistair McFadden, who says he has lived alone for a year. He seems a gentle man, but the community is chilled to discover the truth, in an old newspaper, that he is a child murderer.
Alistair McFadden John Line

Director: Terence Williams
Designer: Ian Watson

The Witch

w Jack Ronder
Mina, an eccentric who lives apart from the community with her baby son, spurns Hubert's amorous advances. He then stirs up the children, John and Lizzie, into believing that she is a witch. When their fear spreads to Peggy, a superstitious Irish woman, the whole group is affected and Mina's life is threatened.
Mina Delia Paton
Peggy Catherine Finn

Director: Terence Williams
Designer: Ian Watson

A Friend in Need

w Ian McCulloch
The community hunt for a sniper who is killing attractive young women and are startled to discover the killer is also a woman.
Boult William Wilde
Mrs. McGregor Vivienne Burgess
Roberts Emrys Leyshon
Morris Paul Grist
Daniella Gigi Gatti

Director: Eric Hills
Designer: Ian Watson

By Bread Alone

w Martin Worth
The community, which has forgotten spiritual needs in the struggle for survival, is unsettled by the revelation that Lewis Fearn was formerly a curate.
July Julie Peasgood
Lewis Fearn Roy Herrick
Alan Stephen Tate
Philip Martin Neil
Daniella Gigi Gatti

Director: Pennant Roberts
Designer: Ian Watson

The Chosen

w Roger Parkes
Charles and Pet, returning from a trip to the Cheshire brine pits, stumble upon a Spartan-like community run by Max Kershaw. Charles is curious about the settlement, but his interest is misinterpreted by Kershaw who decides to eliminate the "intruders."
Max Kershaw Philip Madoc
Kim David Sibley
Nancy Vanessa Millard
Lenny Carter James Cosmo
Joy Clare Kelly
Sammy Waters David Goodland
Mike David Neilson
Susan Elizabeth Cassidy

Director: Eric Hills
Designer: Ian Watson

Parasites

w Roger Marshall
A traveling man, John Millen, is in love with Mina, but ultimately falls foul of two ex-Dartmoor prisoners who menace the Whitecross community and hold John and Lizzie hostage.
John Millen Patrick Troughton
Mina Delia Paton
Lewis Roy Herrick
Kane Kevin McNally
Grice Brian Grellis

Director: Terence Williams
Designer: Ian Watson

New Arrivals

w Roger Parkes
Ruth brings to Whitecross the remaining members of a community ravaged by a flu epidemic. Among them is Mark Carter, who has a degree in agriculture but whose manner quickly alienates everyone in the settlement.
Carter Ian Hastings
Alan Stephen Tate
Melanie Heather Wright
Sally June Page
Dave Peter Duncan
Pete Roger Monk

Director: Pennant Roberts
Designer: Ian Watson

Over the Hills

w Martin Worth
The Whitecross women are in open revolt over Charles's latest attempt to spark a "baby boom." When it's learned that Sally is expecting Alan's child, Charles is delighted. But she will only have the baby if she can live with Alan as his wife—and he prefers Melanie . . .
Guest cast as previous episode, except Ian Hastings, *plus:*
Daniella Gigi Gatti

Director: Eric Hills
Designer: Ian Watson

New World

w Martin Worth
The settlers sight a balloon passing over Whitecross and give chase. When they track it down they find the balloonists are a Norwegian engineer and his daughter, Agnes, offering hope of contacts with mainland Europe. Greg is determined to make the most of this unexpected windfall and plans to go to Norway.
Guest cast as previous episode, except Gigi Gatti, *plus:*
Seth Dan Meaden
Agnes Sally Osborn

Director: Terence Williams
Designer: Ian Watson

Season Three
12 episodes

Manhunt

w Terence Dudley
Jack, who had ballooned off with Greg, is back with a sorry tale about Greg being in danger. Charles and Jenny ride off to find him. It's a search that will invariably see them one step behind the always felt but rarely seen Greg who is trying to make contact with as many settlements as possible in the quest for a unified federation.
Seth Dan Meaden
Susan June Brown
Roberts David Freedman
Summers John Rolfe
Clifford Michael Hawkins
Miedel Anthony Jacobs

Director: Peter Jefferies
Designer: Geoff Powell *(all Season Three)*

A Little Learning

w Ian McCulloch
Greg and Agnes meet an elderly woman, Mrs. Butterworth, who asks them to protect her from "raiding Indians." However the marauders turn out to be a gang of children who are found to be dying after eating contaminated rye.
Agnes Anna Pitt *(intro)*
Millar Sean Caffrey
McIntosh Prentis Hancock
Mrs. Butterworth Sylvia Coleridge
Eagle Joseph McKenna
Mr. Oliver John Harrard
Philip Christopher Huxtable
Libbie Johanna Sheffield
Cliff Richard Beaumont
Bernie Keith Collins
Annie Nicola Glickman

Director: George Spenton-Foster

Law of the Jungle

w Martin Worth
Brod, an ex-butcher, believes that man must revert to hunting to survive. His community hunts with crossbows, on horseback, and lives in three abandoned railway carriages. When Charles and Jenny arrive in the area, Brod sees them as a threat.
Brod Brian Blessed
Edith Barbara Lott
Steve Eric Deacon
Owen Keith Varnier
Mavis Cheryl Hall

Director: Peter Jefferies

Mad Dog

w Don Shaw
Charles meets Fenton, a former lecturer, who reveals that he has rabies. Charles is later forced to run for his life from men who believe he is also infected.
Fenton Morris Perry
Sanders Bernard Kay
Jim Ralph Arliss
Phil Max Faulkner
Ron Stephen Bill
Ellen Heather Canning
Engine driver Eric Francis
Fireman Robert Pugh
Young girl Jane Shaw

Director: Tristan de Vere Cole

Bridgehead

w Martin Worth
Charles decides that the survivors need a market—not just for the exchange of goods, but as a place where people can meet and make contacts, and exchange ideas and skills.
Edith Barbara Lott
Steve Eric Deacon
Owen Keith Varnier
Mavis Cheryl Hall
Bill Sheridan John Ronane
Alice Hazel McBride
Elphick Harry Jones
Bagley John Ruddock
Susan Rosalind Elliot

Director: George Spenton-Foster

Reunion

w Don Shaw
Jenny and Hubert, continuing their search for Greg, come across a young widow called Janet Milton. Going through a family album, Jenny realizes Janet is young John's mother, and the two are reunited.
Walter George Waring
Philip Hurst John Lee
Janet Milton Jean Gilpin

Director: Terence Dudley

The Peacemaker

w Roger Parkes
Charles, Jenny and Hubert discover a community which survives by milling grain for other settlements. Frank Garner claims to be its leader, but Charles begins to suspect that he is really a prisoner.
Frank Garner Edward Underdown *(plus Eps. 8–9)*
Bentley Norman Robbins
Michael Brian Conly
Henry Alan Halley

Grant Paul Seed
Blossom Nicolette Roeg
Rutna Heather Emmanuel
McLain John Grieve
Cyril Derek Martin

Director: George Spenton-Foster

Sparks

w Roger Parkes
Alec Campbell, an electrical engineer, lives alone in squalor, refusing all invitations to join Charles's group. Campbell is racked with guilt for abandoning his wife and children when plague overtook them, but the community badly needs an electrician and resorts to shock treatment to bring him round.
Alec William Dysart *(plus Eps. 9, 11–12)*
Letty Gabrielle Hamilton
Jim John Bennett
Vic John White
Bet Linda Polan

Director: Tristan de Vere Cole

The Enemy

w Roger Parkes
Leonard Woollen, the leader of a mining community, clashes with Sam Mead, a latter-day Luddite, who tries to persuade the survivors to abandon their quest for hydro-electricity.
Sam Robert Gillespie *(plus Eps. 11–12)*
Grant Martyn Whitby
Leonard Woollen Bryan Pringle
Harper Terence Davies
Mrs. Jay Peggy Ann Wood
Mary-Jean Frances Tomelty

Director: Peter Jefferies

The Last Laugh

w Ian McCulloch
Hunting for a doctor he believes is being held prisoner, Greg is attacked by an apocalyptic quartet of horsemen, and his list of settlements is stolen. Recovering, he finds Dr. Adams, only to discover he has smallpox, Greg also contracts the disease but, before his inevitable death, is able to use it to exact "revenge" on his earlier attackers.
Mason George Mallaby
Chris Richard Cornish
Tilley Roy Boyd
Dave Jon Glover
Irvine David Cook
Powell Paul Humpoletz
Dr. Adams Clifton Jones

Director: Peter Jefferies

Long Live the King

w Martin Worth
Heading north, Charles finds a message from Greg seeking a meeting at a disued army camp. There he learns about Greg's work in bringing people together from Agnes who is determined to see him "live on" as the symbolic king of the new emerging nation. But a villainous character, the Captain, also wants to take over.
Captain Roy Marsden
Mitch Frank Vincent
Mrs. Hicks Gabrielle Day
Les Norton John Comer
Mike Sean Mathias
Joe Briggs Ray Mort
Tom Walter Barry Stokes
Albert Banks Denis Holmes

Director: Tristan de Vere Cole

Power

w Martin Worth
Charles and his companions arrive in the Scottish Highlands where they find Scottish nationalism alive and well in the form of McAlister, a local laird who resents their attempts to tap his hydroelectricity to revive English industry.
McAlister Iain Cuthbertson
Davey William Armour
Mrs. Crombie Dorothy Dean
Hamish Brian Carey
Rob Ray Jefferies

Director: George Spenton-Foster

SWAMP THING

DC Comics' comic character Swamp Thing came to life for three years in this made-for-cable series. The talent behind the scenes—led by Joseph Stefano, who worked on the original *Outer Limits* TV show—made the series as human as possible, blending humor, more than adequate special effects, and strong acting to create a series on par with anything on the big three networks.

REGULAR CAST
Swamp Thing Dick Durock   *Dr. Anton Arcane* Mark Lindsay Chapman
Graham Kevin Quigley   *Will Kipp* Scott Garrison
Dr. Alex Holland Patrick Neill Quinn   *Tressa Kipp* Carrel Myers
Sheriff Andrews Marc Macaulay   *Jim Kipp* Jesse Ziegler
Abigail Kari Wuhrer   *Dr. Hollister* William Whitehead
Dr. Ann Fisk Janet Julian   *General Sutherland* Jacob Witkin
Oboe Anthony Galde

Creators: Len Wein, Berni Wrightson
Based on the DC comic book character
Developed for TV by Joseph Stefano
Executive producers: Benjamin Melniker, Michael E. Uslan
Executive producer: Andy Heyward, Tom Blomquist *(Season Two)*
Executive producer: Tom Greene *(Eps. 14–22)*

Produced by Boris Malden
Co-producers: Jeff Myrow, Steven Sears
Music: Christopher L. Stone

72 color 30-minute episodes
U.S. premiere: 27 July 1990
Shown in the U.S. on USA Network

Episodes
The Emerald Heart
The Living Image
The Death of Dr. Arcane
Legend of the Swamp Maiden
Spirit of the Swamp
Blood Wind
Grotesquery
Natural Enemy
Treasure
New Acquaintance
Falco

From Beyond the Grave
The Shipment
Birthmarks
Dark Side of the Mirror
Silent Screams
Walk a Mile in My Shoots
The Watchers
The Hunt
Touch of Death
Tremors of the Heart
The Prometheus Parabola
Night of the Dying

Love Lost
Mist Demeanor
Nightmare on Jackson Street
Better Angels
Children of the Fool
A Jury of His Fears
Poisonous
Smoke and Mirrors
This Old House of Mayan
Sonata
Dead and Married
Powers of Darkness
Special Request
What Goes Around, Comes Around
Lesser of Two Evils
Future Tense
A Most Bitter Pill
Fear Itself
Changes
Destiny
Tatania
Mirador's Brain
Vendetta
Easy Prey
The Handyman

Revelations
Hide in the Night
Pay-Day
Return of La Roche
Rites of Passage
Never Alone
The Curse
Judgement Day
Eye of the Storm
The Hurting
The Burning Times
Spectre of Death
Cross-Fired
Patient Zero
The Chains of Forever
In the Beginning
Brotherly Love
An Eye for an Eye
Yo Ho Ho
Heart of Stone
Romancing Arcane
Swamp of Dreams
Heart of the Mantis
That's a Wrap

TALES OF MYSTERY

Early-sixties British anthology series of uncanny and supernatural tales by renowned ghost storyteller Algernon Blackwood. These forays into an at times bizarre imagination were hosted by Scottish actor John Laurie whose wide, staring eyes and quietly sinister delivery set the tone for an eerie series.

Though early tales stuck closely to the "ghost story" theme, the second season saw the series' scope branch out to include some broader-based fantasies. "The Man Who Found Out" starred Charles Lloyd Pack as a man seeking for the secret of the universe. He discovers a set of engraved tablets buried in the Middle East, deciphers them and finds that they tell the story of the whole future of humanity. But the secret is too terrible to bear and he dies after reading the message. Another story, "Nephele," concerns an archaeologist who finds the shoes of a slave dancer of ancient Rome and is possessed by their strange power, which compels him to "witness" a tragic drama played out 17 centuries before. "The Telephone" explored the teasing idea of inanimate objects apparently developing lives of their own. In "The Pikestaffe Case" an enigmatic lodger offers his landlady the chance to change the whole pattern of her life. And in a Season Three tale, "The Insanity of Jones," a man who can see back through time avenges a 400-year-old crime.

Among familiar names appearing in the series were Dinsdale Landen, Harry H. Corbett, Peter Barkworth, Patrick Cargill, Francesca Annis, John Barron and Tenniel Evans.

REGULAR CAST
Narrator/Algernon Blackwood John Laurie

All stories by Algernon Blackwood
Adapted by Giles Cooper, Owen Holder, Philip Broadley, Barbara S. Harper, John Richmond, Bill MacIlwraith, Kenneth Hyde, Denis Butler
Directors: John Frankau (Stories 2, 4, 6, 8–13, 15–16, 18–22, 24, 28–29), Geoffrey Hughes, Peter Graham Scott, Jonathan Alwyn, Peter Moffatt, Raymond Menmuir, Mark Lawton, Wilfred Eades, James Omerod
Producer: Peter Graham Scott
Executive producer: John Frankau (Season Three)

An Associated-Redifusion Network Production
29 black and white 30-minute stories

Season One
The Terror of the Twins
The Promise
The Man Who Was Milligan
The Tradition
The Empty Sleeve
Accessory before the Fact
The Woman's Ghost Story
The Decoy

29 March–17 May 1961

Season Two
Confession
Chinese Magia
Max Hensig
The Man Who Found Out
Nephele
Ancient Sorceries
Deferred Appointment

The Pikestaffe Case
The Telephone
The Call
Wolves of God

4 July–12 September 1962

Season Three
Old Clothes
The Doll
Egyptian Sorcery
The Damned
The Second Generation
A Case of Eavesdropping
Petershin and Mr. Snide
The Lodger
The Insanity of Jones
Dream Cottage

10 January–14 March 1963

TATTOOED TEENAGE ALIEN FIGHTERS FROM BEVERLY HILLS

What a title! And, yes, what a load of rubbish this *Power Rangers* pastiche is, however much of a send-up it's intended to be.

Evil Emperor Gorganus has vowed to use his army of alien monsters to conquer Earth, the focal point of a system of power portals he needs to rule the universe. Nimbar, head protector of the power portals, is a glowing alien blob whose mission it is to stop Gorganus, and he chooses four teenagers from Beverly Hills to help him, summoning them by flashing their tattoos. They then transform into galactic sentinels, Scorpio, Taurus, Centaur, and Apollo. The fate of Earth is in their hands . . .

REGULAR CAST
Lori/Scorpio Lesley Danon *Gordon/Taurus* Richard Nasor *Drew/Centauri* K. Jill Sorgen
Swinton/Apollo Rugg Williams *Voice of Nimbar* Glenn Shadix
Voice of Gorganus Ed Gilbert

Creators: Jim Fisher, Jim Staahl
DIC Productions

U.K. premiere: July 1996
(Sky One)

TEEN ANGEL

From the Emmy award–winning executive producers of *The Simpsons* and *The Critic* comes an irreverent look at high school life and teen friendship. When fifteen-year-old Marty eats a six-month-old hamburger he finds under his best friend's bed, "What's the worst thing that could happen?" he asks.

He wakes up dead and in heaven.

Marty and Steve are quickly reunited, however, when Marty is sent back to Earth to act as Steve's guardian angel. However, Marty's less-than-heavenly guidance constantly gets Steve into hot water. It takes more than wings to make an angel.

REGULAR CAST

Marty Mike Damus *Steve* Corbin Allred
Judy Maureen McCormick *Jordan* Jordan Brewer
The Head John Amos *Pam* Conchata Ferrell
Katie Katie Volding

Episodes

Marty Buys the Farm
Date with an Angel
Sings Like an Angel
Wrestling with an Angel
Honest Abe and Popular Steve
I Love Nitzke
One Dog Night
Jeremiah Was a Bullfrog
Feather's Day

Steve & Marty & Jordan & Uncle Lou
Living Doll
Grumpy Young Men
Who's the Boss
The Play's the Thing
The Un-Natural
Back to DePolo
The Un-Natural
Look Ma, No Face

TEKWAR

Even before he was done trekkin', William Shatner had begun tekkin'. The man who capered around the cosmos as Captain James T. Kirk started working on his series of Tek novels to kill time during a strike on the set of the fifth *Star Trek* movie.

Ten novels, *TekWar, TekLords, TekLab, TekJustice, Tek Vengeance, Tek Secret, Tek Power, Tek Money, Tek Kill,* and *Tek Net,* were the result, and four TV movies led to a short-lived weekly series.

As in the books, the hero is tough ex-cop turned private eye Jake Cardigan, and Shatner's 2045 world is fitted out with cyberpunk flourishes such as *Blade Runner*–style androids called simulacrums, hi-tech talking houses and, of course, Tek, a computer chip that works like an addictive virtual reality drug, allowing the user to live out the fantasy of his choice.

Shatner is executive producer, directs and has a cameo role as Walt Bascom, Cardigan's boss at the Cosmos Detective Agency. The anti-Tek hero himself is played by Greg Evigan from the sitcom *My Two Dads.* The series started in the U.S. in January 1995 and came to Sky 2 in September 1996, though the movies aired earlier that year

MAIN CAST

Jake Cardigan Greg Evigan *Walt Bascom* William Shatner
Sid Gomez Eugene Clark *Beth Kettridge* Torri Higginson
Nika Natalie Radford *Warbride* Sheena Easton

Creators/Executive producers:
William Shatner, Peter Sussman

Producer: John Calvert
An Atlantis Films/Universal Production

18 color 60-minute episodes
Unknown Soldier
Tek Posse
Sellout
Promises to Keep
Stay of Execution
Alter Ego
Killer Instinct
Chill Factor
Deadline
Carlotta's Room
Deep Cover
Cyberhunt
Zero Tolerance

Forget Me Knot
The Gate
Skin Deep
Redemption
Betrayal

Also: 4 color 120-minute TV movies
TekWar
TekWar: Teklords
TekWar: Teklab
TekWar: Tek Justice

U.K. series premiere: 4 September 1996
(Sky 2)

TERRAHAWKS

Terrahawks was Gerry Anderson's return to puppetry after his forays into live-action TV. And, 14 years on from 1969's *The Secret Service*, Anderson coined a new word for a new sophisticated technique—Supermacromation.

These puppets had no strings attached. Deployed at a cost of £5 million for the first 26 episodes, the Terrahawks were packed with advanced electronics and operated by hand—in some cases, more than one pair.

The format was familiar enough. In the year 2020, a crack fighting force, the Terrahawks, are dedicated to saving Earth from attack by an evil intergalactic adversary—in this case Zelda, the witch-queen of Guk. An android with a face like a pickled chestnut and a horrible harridan's cackle, Zelda was assisted by her equally ugly cronies, inept son Yung-Star and bitchy sister Cy-Star.

Heading the Terrahawks was Dr. Tiger Ninestein, one of nine clones created from an American-Austrian professor called Gerhard Stein. On his team were daredevil pilot Mary Falconer, pop-singer/pilot Kate Kestrel, Japanese computer genius Lt. Hiro, and Lt. Hawkeye, an American athlete with computer-assisted eyesight. They were aided by a battalion of silver spherical robots called Zeroids, commanded by Sgt. Major Zero.

From their secret base, Hawknest, in South America, the Terrahawks foiled every dastardly plot and fiendish monster that Zelda could throw at them. And these being the "sophisticated" 1980s, it was all done with plenty of tongue-in-cheek humor. Sgt. Major Zero was played by Windsor Davies in his fruitest *It Ain't Half Hot, Mum* voice and there was a nod to the pink star of *Thunderbirds* with Hudson, a posh-talking Rolls-Royce, which drove itself and changed color with its moods.

Despite its impressive array of hardware and some imaginative baddies, *Terrahawks* relied too much on elements from series past, but without ever coming close to re-creating their charm.

VOICE CAST

Zelda/Mary Falconer Denise Bryer *Sgt. Major Zero* Windsor Davies
Dr. Ninestein/Hiro/Johnson/It-Star (Boy) Jeremy Hitchin
Kate Kestrel/Cy-Star/It-Star (Girl) Anne Ridler
Hudson/Space Sgt. 101/Yung-Star/Hawkeye/Stew Dapples/Dix-Huit/TIM Ben Stevens
Kate's singing voice Moya Griffiths

Creator: Gerry Anderson
Producers: Gerry Anderson, Christopher Burr
Asociate producer: Bob Bell
Writer: Tony Barwick (*except where stated*)*
Music: Richard Harvey
Special effects director: Stephen Begg

* Nearly all episodes written under an assortment of feline pseudonyms, such as Cubby Dreistein, Kit Tenstein, Koo Garstein, T. I. Gerstein, Effie Linestein, Claude Backstein and other puns, including Sheik Spearstein, Manny Pheak-stein and Sue Donymstein.

Produced by Anderson Burr Pictures in association with London Weekend Television

39 color 30-minute episodes
Season One:
9 October–31 December 1983
Season Two:
23 September–30 December 1984
Season Three:
3 May–26 July 1986

Season One
13 episodes

Expect the Unexpected

w Gerry Anderson (*a 2-part story*)
The year is 2020. The evil android Zelda has invaded Mars from where she plans to strike against Earth. The Terrahawks mobilize to counter the attack, but using her incredible powers and aided by her robot Cubes, Zelda traps Ninestein and Mary in a force field. Will Zero come to the rescue in time?

Director: Alan Pattillo

Thunder-Roar

Zelda releases a hideous ally, Sram, from suspended animation and unleashes him on Earth. Sram has a thunderous voice so powerful that it can destroy a mountain.

Director: Alan Pattillo

Happy Madeday

Moid, a faceless alien who is a master of disguise, assumes the form of Hiro and takes his place as Spacehawk's commander. With the Terrahawks' first line of defense neutralized, Zelda launches a massive attack.

Director: Tony Lenny

The Ugliest Monster of All

Zelda releases Yuri, a cuddly space bear from cyrogenic storage. It's picked up by the unsuspecting Terrahawks and Mary and Kate take it to their hearts—but the bear has strange and terrible powers.

Director: Tony Lenny

Close Call

In an effort to trace the secret location of Hawknest, Zelda places unscrupulous journalist Mark Darrol aboard the Overlander, a futuristic land train that takes vital supplies to the Terrahawks' base.

Director: Desmond Saunders

The Gun

An unmanned space transporter carrying a rare titanium ore returns to Earth but with a deadly surprise aboard—Zelda's robot cubes, ready to transform themselves into a giant space gun.

Director: Tony Bell

Gunfight at Oaky's Corral

After a gunfight between Zelda's cubes and Sgt. Major Zero out in the Arizona desert, one of the cubes escapes. Ninestein leads the chase and finds himself in a final shoot-out at high noon.

Director: Tony Bell

Thunder Path

The Overlander is hijacked by the fearsome Lord Sram who drives it straight at an oil refinery. The Terrahawks race against time to stop him.

Director: Tony Lenny

From Here to Infinity

Spacehawk sights the battered remains of Space Probe Alpha, first launched in 1999. The Terrahawks set to work examining it, unaware that Zelda has placed one of her cube robots on it, with a gravity bomb.

Director: Alan Pattillo

Mind Monster

The Terrahawks discover a capsule which, when opened, is apparently empty. But they have released a mind monster and each find themselves facing a deadly foe.

Director: Tony Bell

A Christmas Miracle

As all at Hawknest prepare to celebrate Christmas, Zelda realizes their guard will be down and decides to launch an all-out attack—on Christmas Day.

Director: Tony Lenny

To Catch a Tiger

Zelda takes the two-man crew of a space transporter hostage on Mars and demands Ninestein in exchange for their release.

Director: Tony Lenny

Season Two
13 episodes

Operation S.A.S

When Yung-Star seizes the chance to fly to Earth, Zelda makes him take Yuri the Space Bear with him. Then Kate is captured and only an SAS-style operation, led by Zero, can rescue her.

Director: Tony Lenny

Ten Top Pop

As determined as ever, Zelda takes control of Stew Dapples and uses him as a dupe in another assault.

Director: Tony Bell

Play It Again, Sram

After Kate Kestrel wins the World Song Contest, Zelda issues an unexpected challenge—and the mighty Sram lurks ready to destroy the Terrahawks.

Director: Tony Bell

The Ultimate Menace

The Terrahawks are baffled when Ninestein orders the whole team to fly to Mars—Zelda's base—but team up with Zelda to battle the Zyclon which threatens them all.

Director: Tony Lenny

Midnight Blue

Spacehawk fires at a Zeaf but it gets through. Now Hawkwing takes up the pursuit, until Ninestein realizes the Zeaf has been miniaturized. But Hawkwing has chased too far and is trapped in orbit.

Director: Tony Lenny

My Kingdom for a Zeaf

What is Richard III doing with Yung-Star in the 21st century? The answer threatens death for one of the Terrahawks team.

Director: Tony Lenny

Zero's Finest Hour

Zelda delivers some flowers to the Terrahawks via the Overlander and the pollen puts Ninestein and the rest of his team into a coma. It's left to Zero to save the day.

Director: Tony Bell

Cold Finger

Zelda and her new ally Cold Finger plan to attack Earth by bombarding it with millions of tons of ice. Can the Terrahawks save the world?

Director: Tony Bell

Unseen Menace

Moid (Master Of Infinite Disguise) perfects his most awesome impersonation to date, traveling to earth as the Invisible Man to wreak havoc among the Terrahawks.

Director: Tony Bell

Space Giant

When two space miners capture a small Sporilla, they decide to smuggle it back to Earth. But it's just another fiendish plan devised by Zelda and a terrifying monster is unleashed.

Director: Tony Lenny

Cry UFO

When Stew Dapples sees a UFO, no one will believe him. But the ship is part of Zelda's latest plan—and the Terrahawks must find and destroy it.

Director: Tony Bell

The Midas Touch

w Trevor Lansdown & Tony Barwick
The world's gold reserves are locked in a space Fort Knox. Zelda realizes that to wipe it out would cause economic havoc on Earth and despatches the monstrous Krell to do the job.

Director: Alan Pattillo

Ma's Monsters

So far, the best efforts of Zelda's worst monsters have failed to defeat the Terrahawks. But she has a powerful surprise in store.

Directors: Tony Bell & Tony Lenny

Season Three
13 episodes

Two for the Price of One

The Terrahawks plan an attack on Zelda's Martian base and find out that Cy-Star is about to produce a baby.

Director: Tony Lenny

First Strike

Against Ninestein's better judgement, the military sends a giant space carrier on a first-strike raid against Zelda's base. The Terrahawks just manage to avert a major disaster.

Director: Tony Lenny

Terratomb

A Zeaf crash-lands on Earth, and Battle Tank is sent out to investigate and destroy it. Then Zelda announces that there is a bomb in Hawknest. But how did it get there? And can the Terrahawks find it in time?

Director: Tony Bell

Space Cyclops

An alien meteorite crashes into the Moon and a terrifying Cyclops begins to form from the wreckage. The Zeroids attack, but the Cyclops can absorb metal.

Director: Tony Lenny

Doppelganger

The Terrahawks investigate the mysterious appearance of two statues in a museum—one of Yung-Star, and the other of Cy-Star. Then one of the statues begins to move . . .

Director: Tony Lenny

Child's Play

Birlgoy produces a super explosive and Zelda plants a giant bomb under the trans-American pipeline. Mary has to try to defuse it—but it could be a trap.

Director: Tony Bell

Jolly Roger One

A space pirate joins forces with Zelda and her family to confront the Terrahawks, and the pirate spaceship and Spacehawk fight out a terrifying battle.

Director: Tony Lenny

Runaway

All looks hopeless for the Terrahawks when it seems that Zelda has at last discovered the location of Hawknest and sends her missiles to destroy it.

Director: Tony Bell

Space Samurai

Tamura, space samurai and the commander of a powerful space cruiser, insists that Zelda and Ninestein meet to work out their differences. Ninestein reluctantly agrees, but can Zelda be trusted?

Director: Desmond Saunders

Timewarp

Zelda, using Lord Tempo's powers, tries to introduce a time warp into Hawknest. Mary's mind is too strong and rejects the attempt, but Sgt. Major Zero is more receptive.

Director: Tony Bell

Operation Zero

Sgt. Major Zero is admitted to the Zeroid hospital for an operation. When he recovers, he finds to his horror that Zelda has infiltrated Hawknest and Ninestein speaks with Yung-Star's voice.

Director: Tony Lenny

The Sporilla

The Terrahawks travel to the distant moon Callisto, where an unarmed remote tracker station has gone off the air. When they arrive they are faced by one of Zelda's most terrifying monsters, the Sporilla.

Director: Tony Bell

Gold

When the Zeroids explore the crater of a meteorite they think they have found a nugget of gold. Secretly, they bring it back to Hawknest, but it's really a golden bomb planted by Zelda.

Director: Desmond Saunders

3RD ROCK FROM THE SUN

If you want to make some wry observations about the human condition, and throw in a few laughs along the way, just make an "alien on Earth" sitcom.

Every decade should have at least one—in the sixties it was the homespun philosophies of *My Favorite Martian*, in the seventies the frenetic ad-libbing of Robin Williams in *Mork and Mindy*, while the eighties saw fit to leave the wisecracks to a furry puppet in *Alf*.

Now, for the nineties, we have *3rd Rock from the Sun*, described by its creators, *Saturday Night Live*'s Bonnie and Terry Turner, as "Carl Sagan meets the Marx Brothers." That sounds thoroughly pretentious, but really *3rd Rock is* fun, in a predictably dumb sort of way, with some smart one-liners and good performances, particularly from John Lithgow. He stars as the high commander of a quartet of extra-terrestrial explorers who assume the guise of an "ordinary" American family.

Lithgow poses as Dick Solomon, a middle-aged physics professor; Kristen Johnston is a tough male lieutenant obliged to assume the mysterious form of a statuesque blonde woman, supposedly his sister (played in the style of Kirstie Alley as Rebecca in *Cheers*). French Stewart plays the misfit brother Harry and Joseph Gordon-Levitt is Tommy—a seasoned intelligence officer in the body of an adolescent boy, he's actually older than his commander.

Their mission is to find out what makes us tick, so nearly all the jokes revolve around them trying to understand our funny little ways. This makes for some great visual gags—in one episode, when Dick has the flu, he marvels at the way tissues keep popping up as he pulls them from a box.

Kate & Allie star Jane Curtin shares top billing as the straight woman—she's Dick's office mate and love interest. Completing the regulars are Elmarie Wendel as the Solomons' eccentric landlady and Simbi Khali as Dick's secretary.

REGULAR CAST
Dick Solomon John Lithgow *Sally Solomon* Kristen Johnston
Harry Solomon French Stewart *Tommy Solomon* Joseph Gordon-Levitt
Dr. Mary Albright Jane Curtin *Nina* Simbi Khali *Mrs. Dupeczech* Elmarie Wendel

Creators: Bonnie Turner, Terry Turner
Executive producers: Bonnie Turner, Terry Turner, Caryn Mandabach, Marcy Carsey, Tom Werner, Linwood Boomer, Joe Fisch
Music: Ben Vaughn
Writers: Various, including Bonnie Turner, Terry Turner, Bill Martin & Mike Schiff
Directors: Various, including Robert Berlinger

A Carsey-Werner/Fremantle Production

U.S. premiere: 9 January 1996
U.K. premiere: 19 April 1996
(Sky One)

Season One
Brains and Eggs (pilot)
Post Nasal Dick
Dick's First Birthday
Dick Is from Mars, Sally Is from Venus
Dick, Smoker
Green-Eyed Dick
Lonely Dick
Body & Soul & Dick
Ab-Dick-Ted
Truth or Dick
The Art of Dick
Frozen Dick
Angry Dick
The Dicks They Are A-Changin'
I Enjoy Being a Dick
Dick Like Me
Assault with a Deadly Dick
Father Knows Dick
Selfish Dick
See Dick Run

Season Two
See Dick Continue to Run
See Dick Continue to Run, Continued
Hotel Dick
Big Angry Virgin from Outer Space
Much Ado About Dick
Dick The Vote
Fourth and Dick
World's Greatest Dick
My Mother Is an Alien
Gobble, Gobble, Dick, Dick
Dick Jokes
Jolly Old St. Dick
Proud Dick
Romeo & Juliet & Dick

Guilty As Dick
A Dick on One Knee
Same Old Song and Dick
I Break for Dick
Dick Behaving Badly
Dickmalion
Sensitive Dick
15 Minutes of Dick
Will Work for Dick
Dick and the Single Girl
Nightmare on Dick Street

Season Three
Fun with Dick and Janet
Tricky Dick
Dick-in-Law
Scaredy Dick
Moby Dick
Eleven Angry Men & One Dick
A Friend in Dick
Tom, Dick and Mary
Jailhouse Dick
Pickles and Ice Cream
Auto Eurodicka
Portrait of Tommy as an Old Man
Dick on a Roll
The Great Dickdater
36! 24! 36! Dick! (1 hour)
Stuck with Dick
My Daddy's Little Girl
The Physics of Being Dick
Just Your Average Dick
Dick and the Other Guy
Sally and Don's First Kiss
When Aliens Camp
The Tooth Harry
Eat, Drink, Dick, Mary

THUNDERBIRDS

One of the most popular TV series ever, *Thunderbirds* has become engrained in the popular culture of more than one generation.

Gerry Anderson's seventh puppet series and the fourth in the Supermarionation saga, it was television's first one-hour puppet series, with the big wide world of family prime time as its prize. Anderson had originally intended it to continue the half-hour format established by *Supercar*, *Fireball XL5* and *Stingray*, but his British network backer Lew Grade—who was paying the piper to the tune of some £38,000 an episode—insisted on hour-long stories. It meant adding new footage to ten episodes but gave unprecedented scope for plot development, characterization and technological invention.

Boasting an unusually large regular cast—both of characters and creations—the series centered on the exploits of a secret organization called International Rescue, run from a hidden base on a remote Pacific island by former astronaut and multi-millionaire Jeff Tracy and his five sons, named after the first American astronauts. Using a remarkable range of five supercraft, they performed heroic feats of rescue against the odds anywhere in the world—and sometimes out of it, too.

The protagonists—mechanical and marionette—were:

Thunderbird 1—a silver-gray scout craft whose 7000 mph top speed enabled it to be first at the scene of a crisis. Piloted by Scott Tracy, eldest son and decisive rescue organizer.

Thunderbird 2—a giant green freighter designed to carry heavy rescue equipment to the danger zone in a range of integral pods. Piloted by Virgil, a reliable and steady character who worked closely with Scott.

Thunderbird 3—an orange spaceship piloted by Alan, the impetuous youngest brother, also an expert motor racing driver and "romantic lead."

Thunderbird 4—a yellow, underwater craft, carried to rescues in one of *Thunderbird 2*'s pods. Controlled by Gordon, enthusiastic and a bit of a joker.

These four craft were based at International Rescue's island HQ, but completing the quintet was the space satellite *Thunderbird 5*, the organization's eyes and ears in outer space where it monitored every frequency on Earth, automatically translating any SOS into English and transmitting the alerts back to Earth. On duty in *Thunderbird 5* was the patient and solitary figure of John Tracy.

The other "star" of the show was a shocking-pink, six-wheeled Rolls Royce, FAB 1, equipped with a formidable battery of gadgets including TV and radio transmitters, retro-rocket brakes, hydrofoils, oil slick ejector and a machine gun housed behind the radiator grille. It was owned by Lady Penelope, International Rescue's chic blonde London agent, and driven by Parker, Lady P's chauffeur/manservant, a droll Cockney ex-con with a talent for safe-blowing.

Other regular characters were Brains, the bespectacled, hesitantly spoken scientific genius; the Hood, principal villain and master of disguise, dedicated to getting his hands on the secrets of the Thunderbirds; Kyrano, the Hood's half-brother but loyal servant to the Tracys; Tin-Tin, Kyrano's daughter and romantically linked to Alan. Last, there was Grandma Tracy who looked after Jeff and the boys.

Although the Tracy "airwalk" became the butt of countless affectionate jokes, *Thunderbirds* did continue AP Films's progressive ingenuity in the puppet world—each character had a variety of heads to reflect its different moods—and in 1966 the series won a Television Society Silver Medal as "work of outstanding artistic merit."

First screened on ITV from October 1965, the series enjoyed repeat ITV runs during the 1970s and 1980s, before being picked up by the BBC for a network run in 1991. Two feature films were made for United Artists—*Thunderbirds Are Go* (1966) and *Thunderbird 6* (1968)—and in 1986, a Japanese-made cartoon series, *Thunderbirds 2086*, cashed in on the name,

Thunderbirds continued to push up AP Films's production costs, swallowing around £1 million. But it also made a fortune, notching up advance world sales of £350,000 even before it was screened here. The 32 episodes have been seen in 66 countries, and, indeed, are still being seen somewhere.

VOICE CAST

The Hood/John Tracy Ray Barrett Jeff Tracy Peter Dyneley
Brains/Kyrano/Parker/Gordon Tracy David Graham
Lady Penelope Sylvia Anderson Tin-Tin/Grandma Christine Finn
Virgil Tracy (Season One) David Holliday Scott Tracy Shane Rimmer
Alan Tracy Matt Zimmerman Virgil (Season Two) Jeremy Wilkin
Other voices: Paul Maxwell, John Tate, Charles Tingwell

Creators: Gerry & Sylvia Anderson
Producers: Gerry Anderson (Season One), Reg Hill (Season Two)
Associate producer: Reg Hill (Season One), John Read (Season Two)
Director of photography: John Read (Season One)
Supervising special effects director: Derek Meddings
Art director: Bob Bell

Music: Barry Gray

An AP Films Production for ATV/ITC
32 color 60-minute episodes
Season One:
2 October 1965–2 April 1966
Season Two:
2–30 October 1966, plus 25 December 1966
(dates as ATV, London)

Season One

Trapped in the Sky

w Gerry & Sylvia Anderson
Mysterious villain the Hood plants a bomb aboard atomic-powered new airliner, the *Fireflash*, thus drawing International Rescue into its first mission so that he can take photographs of the fabulous *Thunderbirds*. The organization must help the stricken airliner to land safely, using three remote-controlled landing vehicles, while Lady Penelope goes after the snap-happy Hood in her remarkable Rolls.

Director: Alan Pattillo

Pit of Peril

w Alan Fennell
A revolutionary new army vehicle, the *Sidewinder*, runs into trouble on a jungle test-run, disappearing beneath the ground into a disused rubbish dump that has become a raging inferno. International Rescue faces one of its trickiest operations to reach the trapped men.

Director: Desmond Saunders

The Perils of Penelope

w Alan Pattillo
Lady Penelope winds up tied to a railway track in the path of an oncoming express by the opportunistic Dr. Godber who's trying to extort a secret fuel formula from her traveling companion, Sir Jeremy Hodge.

Directors: Alan Pattillo & Desmond Saunders

Terror in New York City

w Alan Fennell
While filming the moving of the Empire State Building to another part of New York, TV reporter Ned Cook and his cameraman are trapped in the icy waters of an underground river when the ground gives way and the building collapses above them. Only *Thunderbird 4* can get to them, but *Thunderbird 2* is out of action following an earlier run-in with Cook!

Directors: David Lane & David Elliott

Edge of Impact

w Donald Robertson
The Hood sabotages a Red Arrow aircraft, causing it to crash into a tall tele-relay station manned by two controllers. When a storm blows up, the weakened structure is in danger of imminent collapse. Conventional rescue is impossible and the Thunderbirds move in.

Director: Desmond Saunders

Day of Disaster

w Dennis Spooner
A giant Martian Probe rocket is being transported across a bridge when the structure collapses beneath its weight, sending the rocket toppling into the water below. Two horrified technicians in the nose cone realize the fall has triggered the countdown. Working in *Thunderbird 4*, Gordon tries to clear the debris piled around the capsule. But it's a painfully slow job . . .

Director: David Elliott

30 Minutes after Noon

w Alan Fennell
A complex underworld plot to destroy a nuclear store misfires, trapping a British security service agent in a vault with explosives that could cause the biggest blast the world has seen. In a delicate laser operation, Scott, Virgil and Alan must reach the man before the bombs go off.

Director: David Elliott

Desperate Intruder

w Donald Robertson
Brains and Tin-Tin go in search of treasure believed to be hidden in a submerged temple in Lake Anasta. But the Hood learns of their plans and overpowers them in an attempt to get to the treasure first. Worried when Brains fails to phone home, Jeff Tracy sends his Thunderbirds team to the scene where they clash with the Hood.

Director: David Lane

End of the Road

w Dennis Spooner
International Rescue faces a dilemma when they are called in to save a man who knows them, construction boss Eddie Houseman whose bid to avert a mountain sliding into his new road has left him on a precarious perch on a high ledge. Pulling off the rescue without showing their faces proves a tricky test for the Tracys.

Director: David Lane

The Uninvited

w Alan Fennell
Scott flies to the Sahara to help two stranded archaeologists who had earlier helped *him* after unknown attackers had forced *Thunderbird 1* to crash-land in the desert. He arrives just as the two men stumble on the lost pyramid of Khamandides—secret base of a subterranean race, the Zombites, who capture them.

Director: Desmond Saunders

Sun Probe

w Alan Fennell
A super spaceship on a mission to collect particles of matter from the Sun loses control and is heading straight for the great ball of fire. Alan and Scott set off in *Thunderbird 3* and succeed in steering the Sun Probe clear—only to find themselves on a collision course instead . . .

Director: Alan Pattillo

Operation Crash-Dive

w Martin Crump
International Rescue agrees to help solve a series of mysterious crashes that are plaguing the giant *Fireflash* airliners, and Gordon catches a saboteur in the act. But can he undo the damage in time to avert yet another crash?

Director: Desmond Saunders

Vault of Death

w Dennis Spooner
A Bank of England employee is trapped in an impregnable new vault that automatically pumps all the air out. As Virgil and Alan try to find a way in via the tunnels of the London Underground, Lady Penelope arrives with bank boss Lord Sefton. But he has forgotten the key and, with time running out, it's left to Parker—and a hairpin—to save the day.

Director: David Elliott

The Mighty Atom

w Dennis Spooner
The best-laid plans of mice and men go awry for the Hood when he steals a robot rodent equipped with a camera device to take secret snaps of the Thunderbirds. Setting an atomic plant ablaze to lure the craft to the scene, he is doubly thwarted when the IR boys' quick work averts disaster while his pet paparazzo returns with nothing more revealing than shots of Lady Penelope screaming her lovely head off.

Director: David Lane

City of Fire

w Alan Fennell
Fire, set off when a woman driver crashes in an underground car park, is raging through the basement of a vast new shopping complex. A family is trapped in a sealed-off corridor. To reach them, Scott and Virgil must use Brains's new cutting gas—gas that has already caused them to pass out during trials.

Director: David Elliott

The Impostors

w Dennis Spooner
Two mystery men posing as members of International Rescue steal some top secret papers—prompting a worldwide search for the organization's base. Jeff Tracy dares not launch the Thunderbirds until their name is cleared, but a scanning satellite needs their help . . .

Director: Desmond Saunders

The Man from MI.5

w Alan Fennell
Lady Penelope is kidnapped in the South of France while trying to track down saboteurs who have stolen vital nuclear plans. Tied up aboard a boat with a bomb at her feet, she manages to summon International Rescue who must find the gang before they detonate the bomb.

Director: David Lane

Cry Wolf

w Dennis Spooner
Two young Australian boys playing International Rescue on their two-way radios inadvertently draw *Thunderbird 1* to the scene. Accepting the boys' apology over the false alarm, the Tracys show them the IR base. Later, a second SOS is received from the boys, but this time it's for real.

Director: David Elliott

Danger at Ocean Deep

w Donald Robertson
John joins Virgil in *Thunderbird 2* as the International Rescue team races to save the crew of a tanker, *Ocean Pioneer II*, before the vessel is blasted sky high by a chemical reaction between its cargo of liquid fuel and a substance called OD 60 in the sea.

Director: Desmond Saunders

Move—and You're Dead

w Alan Pattillo
Victims of a plot by a vanquished motor-racing rival, Alan and Grandma are trapped on a high bridge girder with a fiendish bomb that will explode if they move. Unable to get near in the Thunderbirds, Brains must disarm the bomb, using a long-distance neutralizer.

Director: Alan Pattillo

The Duchess Assignment

w Martin Crump
Lady Penelope's old friend the Duchess of Royston is kidnapped by art thieves and imprisoned in the basement of an old house. Rescue is hampered when, in trying to escape, the Duchess sets the house ablaze. With the building collapsing, Virgil brings on the Mole!

Director: David Elliott

Brink of Disaster

w Alan Fennell
Posing as an investor in a dubious monorail scheme, Jeff Tracy, Tin-Tin and Brains face deadly peril in a monotrain that's heading toward a broken section of track. Their only chance of survival lies with the resourceful Thunderbirds.

Director: David Lane

Attack of the Alligators!

w Alan Pattillo
Scott and four other men are besieged in an isolated house up the Amazon by three giant alligators that have grown to four times their normal size after drinking water polluted with a startling new growth drug. Armed with tranquilizing guns, Virgil, Alan and Gordon try to lure the monsters away.

Director: David Lane

Martian Invasion

w Alan Fennell
International Rescue are called in to free two actors trapped in a cave while filming a sci-fi movie. Also on location is the Hood who uses one of the movie cameras to record the Thunderbirds in action. When his treachery is discovered, the chase is on to recover the film.

Director: David Elliott

The Cham-Cham

w Alan Pattillo
American air transporters flights are mysteriously crashing and, astonishingly, the finger of suspicion points to chart-topping pop group, the Cass Carnaby Five. Each time the rockets crashed the band were performing live. Penelope and Tin-Tin go undercover in the music biz.

Director: Alan Pattillo

Security Hazard

w Alan Pattillo
A small boy stows away in *Thunderbird 2* during a rescue and reaches the Tracy's hideout. As Scott, Alan, Gordon and Virgil happily chatter to their young security hazard, Jeff wonders how to get him home without blowing their cover.

Director: Desmond Saunders

Season Two

Atlantic Inferno

w Alan Fennell

A vacationing Jeff leaves Scott in charge, then chides him for getting involved after an underwater blast starts a fire near the Seascape oil rig. When a second SOS comes from the rig, Scott delays until the situation becomes critical . . .

Director: Desmond Saunders

Path of Destruction

w Donald Robertson

An atomic-powered logging machine called the Crablogger goes out of control after its drivers pass out from heat and food poisoning, and rips through a town as it heads toward a huge dam. To avert certain catastrophe, Scott, Virgil and Brains must shut down the machine's reactor.

Director: David Elliott

Alias Mr. Hackenbacker

w Alan Pattillo

Lady Penelope organizes a charity fashion show aboard the maiden flight of a new safety device invented by Brains, alias Hiram K. Hackenbacker. When the plane is hijacked, Brain's new invention is put to an early test.

Director: Desmond Saunders

Lord Parker's 'Oliday

w Tony Barwick

The Mediterranean resort of Monte Bianco is threatened when a storm dislodges a giant solar reflector, pointing it straight at the town. As *Thunderbird 2* struggles to right the reflector before the Sun's rays strike, Parker avoids panic among hotel guests by getting them to play bingo.

Director: Brian Burgess

Ricochet

w Tony Barwick

The destruction of a space rocket damages pop pirate Rick O'Shea's orbiting TV station. Alan is launched in *Thunderbird 3* to evacuate the two-man crew while Brains and Virgil wait to destroy the space station before it crashes back to Earth on a large oil refinery.

Director: Brian Burgess

Give or Take a Million

w Alan Pattillo

A robbery is foiled when two crooks take an unexpected ride in a rocket full of toys destined for a children's hospital, and one lucky child gets to spend a fairytale Christmas with International Rescue on Tracy Island.

Director: Desmond Saunders

TIME TRAX

"You are Darien Lambert, the best police officer on Earth. You have pledged your sacred honor to rid this place of those who came to plunder, a task you began well this day—two down, many to go. What else is of consequence?"

—Selma (at end of pilot)

Lighthearted adventure series from *The Six Million Dollar Man* creator, Harve Bennett.

Its hero isn't bionic and he can't run as fast—a sluggish 8.6 seconds for 100 meters—but he does have a 208 IQ and a life expectancy of 120 years. He's Captain Darien Lambert, a dedicated marshal from the year 2193, who discovers that the world's worst crooks and terrorists are secretly being sent back in time to 1993. He decides to go back himself to track them down.

Lambert is armed with a zappy pulse weapon disguised as a car alarm and he does have a sidekick—a computer called SELMA (Specified Encapsulated Limitless Memory Archive) which is also disguised, as a credit card, but which also appears "in visual mode" as a kind of holographic Mary Poppins, with a sharp nanny's tongue to match her prim appearance. "You're not the wasteful type," she tells Lambert early on. "Your profile is too anally retentive."

Dale Midkiff stars as the brave—but stiff—Captain Lambert, and Peter Donat has a regular guest role as the scientific mastermind behind the time bandits, now organizing the fugitives from the future to establish a power base in the past.

The TRAX of the title is an acronym for Trans-Time Research And Experimentation. There's some attempt in the pilot to depict a hi-tech 23rd century landscape, and with it a racially turbulent age when Lambert, as part of a white minority, is abused as a "blanco." But from there on the effects are mostly 20th century.

REGULAR CAST

Darien Lambert Dale Midkiff *Selma* Elizabeth Alexander
Mordicai Sahmbi Peter Donat

Creators: Harve Bennett, Jeffrey Hayes, Grant Rosenberg
Executive producers: Harve Bennett, Gary Nardino, Jeffrey Hayes, Grant Rosenberg
Line producer: Darryl Sheen

A Gary Nardino Production in association with Lorimar Television

Season One
21 color episodes, 60 minutes unless stated
U.S. premiere: January 1993
(syndicated)
U.K. premiere: 16 July 1994
(ITV)

A Stranger in Time (pilot)
(95 mins)

w Harve Bennett
2193: After graduating top of his class at the International Police Academy, police marshal Darien Lambert is coming to doubt his abilities, as crooks just seem to keep disappearing. When he learns of a plot by brilliant scientist Dr. Mordicai Sahmbi to send crooks back in time he persuades Sahmbi's assistant Dr. Elissa Knox to help trap him. But Sahmbi kills her and escapes back in time himself. Lambert follows but in 1993 finds himself suspected of being an assassin out to kill the U.S. president and must convince secret service agent Annie Knox (who just happens to be Elissa's double) of his innocence.
Elissa Knox/Annie Knox Mia Sara
Frank Motumba Michael Warren
The Chief Henry Darrow
Duke Monroe Reimers
Dietrich Henk Johannes
Wahlgren Peter Whittle
Fredric David Franklin
Wilson Rob Steele

Director: Lewis Teague

To Kill a Billionaire

w Harold Gast
Sahmbi starts a business getting rid of nuclear waste, but Darien and Selma realize he is merely transporting it into the future and set out to close down his operation, aided by a judge who is himself a fugitive from the 22nd century.
Annie Knox Mia Sara
The Chief Henry Darrow
Judge Benedict Choate Jerry Hardin
Agent Hayes Chad Tyler
Davenport Alan Fletcher
Stern Malcolm Cork

Director: Colin Budds

Fire and Ice

w Garner Simmons
Darien teams up with a beautiful Houston police officer, Nicole Nolan, to try to capture two 22nd-century thieves who are stealing the world's most precious gems. But Sahmbi is also interested in their activities.
Kristen Conrad Gail O'Grady
Jorge Santiago Andrew McFarlane
Nicole Nolan Natalie McCurry
Dag Van Meer Mark Fairall
Captain Corvo Peter Hosking

Director: Brian Trenchard-Smith

Showdown

w David Loughery
Darien's friendship and respect for 20th-century lawman Tom Kane puts him in a difficult dilemma when he learns that Kane is actually Edward T. Kanigher, a 22nd-century fugitive he has been searching for.
Tom Kane Stuart Whitman
Stacy Galt Brian Vriends
Sunny Tyler Jennifer Congram

Director: Colin Budds

The Prodigy

w Tracy Friedman
Darien encounters William, a young boy with a remarkable athletic talent, who he suspects was kidnapped from the future by a fugitive wanted for murder and armed robbery, and is able to reunite the youngster with his mother—back in the future.
William Peterman Rider Strong
Jason Peterman Eric Pierpoint
Bob Meyers Tiriel Mora
Lenny Duckworth Steve Jones

Director: Donald Crombie

Death Takes a Holiday

w Ronald Cohen
Darien tries to infiltrate a casino operated by fugitive Clinton Sayjack, and becomes involved with a beautiful girl who has become addicted to "clinks," a powerful narcotic invented in the 21st century.
Sydney Elizabeth Gracen
Clinton Sayjack Matt Roe
Oscar Marshall Napier
Manfred Michael Muntz
Anthony De Martini Luciano Martucci
Carla De Martini Dominique Miller
Gina De Martini Yvonne Troedson

Director: Rob Stewart

The Contender

w Grant Rosenberg
A TRAX janitor arrives in the past to ask a favor of Darien—to send his fugitive boxer son, Mikk, back to 2193 where he belongs, before he kills someone in a title fight. But before he can convince Mikk to go, Darien must fight him himself.
Mikk Davis Victor Love
Ernest Cooper Bernie Casey
Vince LaBarbara Gianni Russo
Sal Madriano James Condon

Director: Rob Stewart

Night of the Savage

w Mark Rodgers
Darien suspects that a London serial killer, the "Soho Savage" who drains his victims' bodies of blood like a vampire, is a fugitive from the future.
Sgt. Leeds Peter O'Brien
Claudia Baker Elaine Smith
Sgt. Callander Steven Grives
Dr. Roland John Dicks

Director: Colin Budds

Treasure of the Ages

w Jeffrey Hayes
A newspaper ad leads Darien to the Florida Keys to apprehend Haskell, a 22nd-century marine archaeologist, wanted for looting. But he must arrest his man during the worst hurricane to hit the Keys this century. On top of that he finds himself having to deliver a baby.
Noah Eddie Albert
Haskell Edward Laurence Albert
Mary Haskell Lise Hilboldt

Director: Donald Crombie

The Price of Honor

w Maryanne Kasica & Michael Scheff
Darien uncovers a fugitive's plot to blackmail John Shaw, a man destined to become one of America's greatest presidents.
John Shaw Dorian Harewood
Alice Shaw Margaaret Avery
Janice Pippa Grandison
Nigel Jerome Ehlers

Director: Colin Budds

Face of Death

w Garner Simmons
The death of a plastic surgeon puts Darien on the trail of a 22nd-century killer and master thief who is out to steal ancient treasures from an Inca temple in Peru.
Korda/Cordan Fuller Patrick Kilpatrick
Reed Luca Bercovici
Lofgren Matt Battaglia
Manheim Jeffrey Nordling

Director: Rob Stewart

Revenge

w Ruel Fischmann
Sepp Dietrich returns, leading a gang of white supremacist terrorists. Darien sets out to stop him, but Dietrich eludes him once again.
Sepp Dietrich Henk Johannes
Charley Kalanee Ray Bumatai
Al Don Halbert
Hank Cranston Brect

Director: Rob Stewart

Darien Comes Home

w Grant Rosenberg
Darien goes to Chicago (his hometown) to infiltrate a computer company founded by two criminals from the future who plan to steal millions from the U.S. Treasury.
Josh Elliott Christopher Daniel Barnes
Zach Elliott Robert Mammone
Megan Edwards Tiffany Lamb
Andrew Edwards Tamblyn Lord

Director: Brian Trenchard-Smith

Two Beans in a Wheel

w George Yanok
Eve Thorn, another future cop, lures Darien into a trap to help Sahmbi in his quest to find the Holy Grail.
Eve Chelsea Field
Delacroix Dennis Price
Brother Pio Basil Clarke
Mallory Joss McWilliam

Director: Donald Crombie

Little Boy Lost

w Harve Bennett

George Castas, Darien's former teacher who is now a fugitive and dying, needs Darien's 22nd-century technology to find his deaf, adopted son, who is lost in the woods.

George Castas George Henare
Robbie Castas Borhan Borhani
Sheriff Dobbs Peter Curtin
Carolina Helen Dobbs
Dr. Keneally Peter Hardy

Director: Donald Crombie

A Mysterious Stranger

w George Yanok *&* Harve Bennett

Darien's efforts to find a 22nd-century doctor who developed a deadly narcotic are complicated by his encounter with a 22nd-century unemployed actor who has traveled back to the 1990s in the hope of finding a job and revenge—on the real doctor, whose drug killed his wife.

Dr. Alwyn/Kyle Fernando David Dukes
Hector Silvio Ofria

Director: Colin Budds

Framed

w Bill Froelich

Darien forms an alliance with pretty computer operator Tulsa Giles, to foil the plans of a fugitive who works for a powerful international security agency.

Tulsa Giles Mary-Margaret Humes
C.L. Burke Lewis Fitz-Gerald
Wahlgren Peter Whittle
Andrew Michaels Peter Webb
Jennings Simon Burville-Holmes
Aubrey Faulkner Steven Tandy

Director: Chris Thomson

Beautiful Songbird

w Tracy Friedman

Darien meets Kaitlin Carlyle, a woman who he knows will go on to become a country music legend. But a psychotic criminal from the future is determined to control her.

Kaitlin Carlyle Kassie Wesley
Elvin Travers Gary Grubbs
Gandolf Reicher John de Lancie
Rosa Tabitha Neeson
J.T. Robert Smith

Director: Colin Budds

Photo Finish

w Garner Simmons

Darien and Selma go to Australia to investigate a fugitive, Rufio Jans, who is using a dangerous, futuristic laser device to boost the performances of racehorses.

Rufio Jans Mark Hembrow
Randall Quinn Bryan Marshall
Kate Vickers Nikki Coghill
Des Miller Roy Billings
Gus Brown Andrew Buchanan

Director: Chris Thomson

Darrow for the Defense

w Ruel Fischmann

After an escaped convict is teleported to the past, his attorney, Laura Darrow, follows him to tell him that his conviction has been overturned. But the man is now working for Sahmbi, and helps trap her and Darien.

Laura Darrow Amy Steele Pulitzer
Dr. Lawrence Carpenter Bruce Jarchow
Fredric David Franklin
Karl Von Rittersdorf Colin Handy

Director: Colin Budds

One to One

w Harold Gast

Sahmbi invents a way to control men's minds, which he intends to sell to unscrupulous businessmen, and plans to use it on his biggest enemy, Darien, as proof that it works.

Primo Sears Joseph Bugner
Michaels John Noble
Ostrander Eric Oldfield
Nevins Jerry Lowley

Director: Colin Budds

THE TIME TUNNEL

"Two American scientists are lost in the swirling maze of past and future ages during the first experiments on America's greatest and most secret project—The Time Tunnel. Tony Newman and Doug Phillips now tumble helplessly toward a new fantastic adventure somewhere along the infinite corridors of time."

For anyone growing up with television from the mid-1960s, Irwin Allen's contribution to the cultural shock has been virtually inescapable. For around a decade, hardly a week passed when one of his science fiction series wasn't playing . . . somewhere.

The Time Tunnel was his third offering (after *Voyage to the Bottom of the Sea* and *Lost in Space*) and followed the time-traveling adventures of two scientists, Doug Phillips and Tony Newman, into the past and, occasionally, the future, while back in the lab their colleagues watched and waited to pull them back in the nick of time.

The series began with a scientific premise—the invention of a machine that can transport people back and forth through time. Pressed by fears of losing their government grant and over-anxious to test it out, Newman steps into the tunnel and is thrown back into the past, landing on the deck of the *Titanic*. While he tries—unsuccessfully—to persuade the captain to change course (and history), his scientist colleagues send Phillips to help him while they figure out a way to bring both men back. A last-minute rescue is achieved.

Thereafter, the series became virtually a guide to the hot-spots of history, from the Alamo and Pearl Harbor to Krakatoa and the Little Big Horn.

The tunnel itself was the most impressive effect in the series, a striking two-tone vortex that seemed to stretch into the back of the TV set. But commercial success didn't come and only 30 trips were made.

REGULAR CAST
Dr. Tony Newman James Darren *Dr. Doug Phillips* Robert Colbert
Dr. Ann MacGregor Lee Meriwether *Dr. Raymond Swain* John Zaremba
Lt. Gen. Heywood Kirk Whit Bissell

Creator: Irwin Allen
Executive producer: Irwin Allen
Director of photography: Winton Hoch
Special effects: L.B. Abbott
Theme: Johnny Williams

Irwin Allen Productions/Kent Productions Inc/20th Century Fox Television Inc
30 color 50-minute episodes
U.S. premiere: 9 September 1966
U.K. premiere: 9 July 1968
(BBC)

Rendezvous with Yesterday

w Harold Jack Bloom & Shimon Wincelberg, *story by* Irwin Allen, Harold Jack Bloom & Shimon Wincelberg
Dr. Tony Newman takes his first trip in the Time Tunnel and tries to change the course of history when he lands on the deck of the *Titanic*.
Capt. Malcolm Smith Michael Rennie
Althea Hall Susan Hampshire
Senator Clark Gary Merrill
Grainger Don Knight
Marcel Gerald Michenand

Director: Irwin Allen

One Way to the Moon

w William Welch
When the time travelers land in a Mars-bound spaceship, their added weight endangers the trip.
Sgt. Jiggs Wesley Lau
Beard James T. Callahan
Harlow Warren Stevens

Kane Larry Ward
Admiral Killian Barry Kelley
Dr. Brandon Ross Elliott
Nazarro Ben Cooper

Director: Harry Harris

End of the World

w William Welch, *story by* Peter Germano & William Welch
Tony and Doug land in a small American town at the time of an appearance by Halley's Comet and have to convince a panicking population that the world is not coming to an end.
Henderson Paul Fix
Blaine Paul Carr
Prof. Ainsley Gregory Morton
Preacher Nelson Leigh
Jerry Sam Groom
Sheriff James Westerfield

Director: Sobey Martin

The Day the Sky Fell In

w Ellis St. Joseph
The time tunnelers are trapped in Pearl Harbor just before the Japanese attack—and Tony meets both his own father and himself as a child.
Jerry Sam Groom
Cmdr. Newman Linden Chiles
Lt. Anderson Lew Gallo
Tasaka Bob Okazaki
Louise Susan Flannery
Little Tony Sheldon Golomb
Okuno Jerry Fujikawa

Director: William Hale

The Last Patrol

w Bob & Wanda Duncan
The time tunnelers are nearly executed as British spies when they land in the last battle of the war of 1812.
General Southall/Col. Southall Carroll O'Connor
Capt. Hotchkiss Michael Pate
Lt. Rynerson David Watson
Capt. Jenkins John Napier

Director: Sobey Martin

Crack of Doom

w William Welch
Doug and Tony choose the wrong day in 1883 to visit Krakatoa—it's the day the island blew up.
Dr. Holland Torin Thatcher
Karnosu Vic Lundin
Eve Holland Ellen McRae
Young native George Matsui

Director: William Hale

Revenge of the Gods

w William Read Woodfield & Allan Balter
Arriving in the Mediterranean in about 1200 B.C., Doug and Tony become involved in the Greeks' war against the Trojans.
Sgt. Jiggs Wesley Lau
Ulysses John Doucette
Helen of Troy Dee Hartford
Epeios Abraham Sofaer
Greek sword leader Kevin Hagen
Sardis Joseph Ruskin
Paris Paul Carr

Director: Sobey Martin

Massacre

w Carey Wilber
Doug and Tony land on the site of Custer's last stand and try to save themselves from the massacre.
Crazy Horse Christopher Dark
Yellow Elk Lawrence Montaigne
Gen. Custer Joe Maross
Sitting Bull George Mitchell
Major Reno John Pickard
Tom Custer Bruce Mars
Tim Tim Halferty
Captain Benteen Paul Comi

Director: Murray Golden

Devil's Island

w Bob & Wanda Duncan
Tony and Doug are mistaken for escaped prisoners when they land on Devil's Island.
Boudaire Marcel Hillaire
Commandant Oscar Beregi
Lescaux Theo Marcuse
Perrault Steven Geray
Claude Alan Patrice
Capt. Dreyfuss Ted Roter

Director: Jerry Hopper

Reign of Terror

w William Welch
Materializing in 1793 at the time of the French Revolution, Doug and Tony plot to save the life of Marie Antoinette's son, the Dauphin.
Shopkeeper David Opatoshu
Simon Louis Mercier
Dauphin Patrick Michenau
Querque Whit Bissell
Bonaparte Joey Tata
Marie-Antoinette Monique Lemaire

Director: Sobey Martin

Secret Weapon

w Theodore Apstein
When an enemy scientist, Dr. Biraki, arrives claiming to have defected to the West, Tony and Doug go back in time to check him out and discover a primitive version of the Time Tunnel.
Jerry Sam Groom
Dr. Biraki Nehemiah Persoff
Hruda Michael Ansara
Alexis Gregory Gay
McDonnell Kevin Hagen
Gen. Parker Russell Conway

Director: Sobey Martin

The Death Trap

w Leonard Stadd
The famous detective Pinkerton thinks Tony and Doug are part of a plot to assassinate Lincoln when they arrive before the Civil War.
Jeremiah Scott Marlowe
Pinkerton R.G. Armstrong
Matthew Tom Skerritt
David Christopher Harris
Lincoln Ford Rainey

Director: William Hale

The Alamo

w Bob & Wanda Duncan
The untimely travelers arrive at the Alamo—just nine hours before it's due to fall to Santa Ana's Mexican army.
Dr. Armandez Edward Colmans
Capt. Reynerson John Lupton
Mrs. Reynerson Elizabeth Rogers
Col. Bowie Jim Davis
Col. Travis Rhodes Reason
Capt. Rodriguez Rodolfo Hoyos

Director: Sobey Martin

Night of the Long Knives

w William Welch
1886: Tony and Doug materalize in the Indian desert during a critical battle between British forces and a border chieftain.
Jerry Sam Groom
Kipling David Watson
Ali George Keymas
Gladstone Dayton Lummis
Cabinet minister Ben Wright
Singh Malachi Throne
Major Kabir Perry Lopez
Col. Fettretch Brendan Dillon

Director: Paul Stanley

Invasion

w Bob & Wanda Duncan
The time travelers land in Cherbourg two days before D-Day and Doug falls into the hands of a German scientist experimenting with brainwashing techniques.
Major Hoffman Lyle Bettger
Mirabeau Robert Carricart
Dr. Kleinemann John Wengraf
Duchamps Michael St. Clair
Verlaine Joey Tata

Director: Sobey Martin

The Revenge of Robin Hood

w Leonard Stadd
The time travelers are dropped into the conflict between Robin Hood and King John.
Little John John Alderson
Baroness Erin O'Brien Moore
Dubois James Lanphier
Friar Tuck Ronald Long
Huntingdon Donald Harron
King John John Crawford

Director: William Hale

Kill Two by Two

w Bob & Wanda Duncan
Dropped onto a Pacific Island in 1945, Tony and Doug engage in a deadly game with a despairing Japanese flyer.
Lt. Nakamura Mako Iwamatsu
Sgt. Itsugi Kam Tong
Dr. Nakamura Philip Ahn

Director: Herschel Daugherty

Visitors from Beyond the Stars

w Bob & Wanda Duncan
The time travelers fall into the hands of silver-skinned aliens ruthlessly scouring the universe for food.
Williams Byron Foulger
Crawford Tris Coffin
Centauri Jan Merlin
Taureg Fred Beir
Alien leader John Hoyt
Deputy Gary Haynes
Sheriff Ross Elliott

Director: Sobey Martin

The Ghost of Nero

w Leonard Stadd
Doug and Tony wrestle with the avenging ghost of Nero during an Italian-German battle in World War One.
Galba Eduardo Ciannelli
Neistadt Gunnar Helstrom
Dr. Steinholtz John Hoyt
Mussolini Nino Candido
Mueller Richard Jaeckel

Director: Sobey Martin

The Walls of Jericho

w Ellis St. Joseph
Landing outside the biblical city of Jericho, Tony and Doug become the spies who, the Bible says, entered the city.
Captain Michael Pate
Father Abraham Sofaer
Malek Arnold Moss
Joshua Rhodes Reason
Rahab Myrna Fahey
Ahza Lisa Gaye

Director: Nathan Juran

Idol of Death

w Bob & Wanda Duncan
Tony and Doug are once again mistaken for spies—this time in Mexico at the time of Cortés as they try to stop the Spaniards butchering the Aztec Indians.
Alvarado Lawrence Montaigne
Cortez Anthony Caruso
Young chief Teno Pollick
Castillano Rodolfo Hoyos
Retainer Peter Brocco
Bowman Abel Fernandez

Director: Sobey Martin

Billy the Kid

w William Welch
Doug and Tony have a near-fatal run-in with Wild West outlaw William Bonney—alias Billy the Kid.
Billy the Kid Robert Walker
Pat Garrett Allen Case
Marshal Phil Chambers
Wilson Harry Lauter
Tom McKinney Pitt Herbert
John Poe John Crawford

Director: Nathan Juran

Pirates of Deadman's Island

w Barney Slater
Doug and Tony fall into the hands of Barbary Coast pirates in the year 1805.
Dr. Berkhart Regis Toomey
Capt. Beal Victor Jory
Mr. Hampton James Anderson
Stephen Decatur Charles Bateman
Armando Pepito Gallindo

Director: Sobey Martin

Chase through Time

w Carey Wilber
When a technician turned spy plants a bomb in the Time Tunnel complex and then escapes into time, Tony and Doug pursue him into the far future and to the distant past.
Nimon Robert Duvall
Vokar Lew Gallo
Zee Vitina Marcus
Jiggs Wesley Lau
Magister Joe Ryan

Director: Sobey Martin

The Death Merchant

w Bob & Wanda Duncan
Tony and Doug land at Gettysburg and find themselves on opposite sides of the Civil War.
Major John Crawford
Sgt. Maddox Kevin Hagen
Michaels Malachi Throne
Corporal Kevin O'Neal

Director: Nathan Juran

Attack of the Barbarians

w Robert Hamner
Tony and Doug are caught between the forces of Kubla Khan and the Mongol hordes.
Marco Polo John Saxon
Ambahai Paul Mantee
Batu Arthur Batanides
Sarit Vitina Marcus

Director: Sobey Martin

Merlin the Magician

w William Welch
In sixth-century England, Merlin forces Tony and Doug to help Arthur, the future king, defeat the Vikings.
Merlin Christopher Cary
Guinevere Lisa Jak
King Arthur Jim McMullan
Wogan Vincent Beck

Director: Harry Harris

The Kidnappers

w William Welch
Tony and Doug are sent to rescue their colleague, Ann MacGregor, who has been kidnapped by an aluminum-colored man from the distant future.
Otto Del Monroe
Curator Michael Ansara
Hitler Bob May

Director: Sobey Martin

Raiders from Outer Space

w Bob & Wanda Duncan
At the battle of Khartoum, the time travelers encounter an alien who has come to destroy the world.
Henderson John Crawford
Planet leader Kevin Hagen

Director: Nathan Juran

Town of Terror

w Carey Wilber
Landing in a New England town, in 1978, Tony and Doug find it has been taken over by aliens who want to drain the oxygen from Earth's atmosphere.
Sarah Mabel Albertson
Alien Sarah Kelly Thordsen
Pete Gary Hughes
Joan Heather Young
Alien leader Vincent Beck

Director: Herschel Daugherty

TIMESLIP

Few series, let alone a British children's drama, can claim to have started with a lesson in scientific theory. Yet that was how *Timeslip* began in 1970, with ITN's science correspondent Peter Fairley demonstrating the program's concept of time travel.

Sitting in a transparent sphere intended to represent the Universe, Fairley bounced a balloon back and forth to convey the idea of a bubble of information moving around in time and in which someone could be carried into the past and the future.

It was a measure of how seriously this intelligent 26-part series took both itself and its audience, though it was never po-faced about it. Devised by Ruth Boswell (later to produce another time-travel drama, *The Tomorrow People*) and her husband, James, *Timeslip* took its two young heroes, Liz Skinner and Simon Randall, through four exciting adventures in time.

Also heavily involved were Liz's parents, Frank and Jean, and the sinister figure of Commander Traynor—seen in no fewer than five different incarnations, including a clone. Liz and Simon also met a younger version of Liz's father and an older version of her mother, plus older versions of themselves. And Liz's mother had a telepathic link with her daughter enabling her to "see" Liz's experiences in the past.

The time travel itself was painless. Encountering an invisible barrier in a Midlands village, Liz and Simon simply fell through a "hole" into another time and sometimes another location. It made for some imaginative paradoxes. At one point Liz and Simon, in 1940, can see, beyond the barrier, Frank and Traynor in 1970, while, in their time, Frank and Traynor *cannot* see the children. Later, Liz is shot but though she feels pain and sees blood, there is no wound as she does not really exist in that time.

The effect of the barrier itself was achieved using a split-screen process whereby the same film was used twice, each time with a different half masked, thus allowing a character apparently to vanish into thin air.

Among the regular cast, Spencer Banks, who played Simon, went on to star in two further ITV series—a spy drama, *Tightrope* (1972) and another time adventure, *The Georgian House* (1976). He also appeared in *Crossroads* . . .

Derek Benfield, who played Frank Skinner, became a familiar face to adult TV audiences in the BBC saga *The Brothers* while Iris Russell had been "Father" in one episode of *The Avengers*.

REGULAR CAST
Simon Randall Spencer Banks *Liz Skinner* Cheryl Burfield
Frank Skinner Derek Benfield *Jean Skinner* Iris Russell
Commander Traynor Denis Quilley

Script editor: Ruth Boswell
Producer: John Cooper
Scientific adviser: Geoffrey Hoyle
An ATV Network Production

26 half-hour episodes, color (except Eps. 22 and 23—made in black and white)
28 September–22 March 1971
(ATV, Midlands)

Story One

The Wrong End of Time

w Bruce Stewart *(Eps. 1–6)*
In the Midlands village of St. Oswald, a young girl, Sarah, feels her way along an apparently invisible barrier near the site of a disused wartime naval base. Suddenly, she vanishes into thin air, her disappearance witnessed only by a local drunk.

Also in St. Oswald are Simon Randall and Liz Skinner, on holiday with Liz's parents, Jean and Frank, who was stationed at the base during the war. Out for a walk, they meet Commander Traynor, Frank's old CO, who has come to investigate the disappearance of the girl, Sarah. The children's walk takes them to the base and they, too, find the hole in the invisible barrier.

Liz and Simon emerge in 1940, where—or rather, when—they find the base fully operational and the scene of secret laser experiments. They encounter younger versions of Liz's father and Traynor, and Simon's belief that they have somehow traveled back in time is borne out by an invasion by a party of Germans, led by scientist Gottfried, bent on learning the secrets of the base's work. They also meet the now distraught Sarah, and Liz manages to escape with her back through the barrier to 1970 where their story confirms Traynor's theory of an energy bubble by which certain sensitive people can move back and forward in time.

Liz learns that her father was supposed to have dismantled the laser equipment before the Nazis got to it, but due to an accident cannot remember if he succeeded. Liz returns to 1940 when she and Simon help the younger Frank to complete his task. They leave the base as Gottfried also decides to make an "honorable" withdrawal. But as one story ends, another begins. Crawling through the barrier, Liz and Simon emerge, not in familiar 1970, but in an icy wasteland where, overcome by the cold, they quickly collapse.

Frank (1940) John Alkin
Gottfried Sandor El's
Graz Paul Humpoletz
Arthur Griffiths John Garrie
George Bradley Royston Tickner
Ferris Peter Sproule
Phipps John Abbott
Dr. Fordyce Kenneth Watson
Alice Fortune Virginia Balfour
Sarah Sally Templer
Fritz Hilary Minster

Director: John Cooper
Designer: Gerry Roberts
Introduced by Peter Fairley *(Ep. 1)*

Story Two

The Time of the Ice Box

w Bruce Stewart *(Eps. 7–12)*
After collapsing from the severe cold, Liz and Simon awake to find themselves in the year 1990, in the Ice Box, an Antarctic research base, where a series of experiments are being carried out on humans, including trials of a longevity drug HA57. Liz hates the place, particularly a rude woman called Beth. As they depart, Liz suddenly sees her mother there . . .

Arriving back in 1970, Simon is persuaded by Traynor to return to the future to try to learn more about the Ice Box and HA57. Liz follows, curious to find out why her mother should be there, and discovers that Beth is an elder version of herself!

The most horrific discovery though, is of the body of New Zealander, Dr. Edith Joynton, who took a faulty dose of HA57 and aged dramatically to 100 years old. Errors begin to mount, linked to the base director Morgan C. Devereaux, who, Simon learns, is actually the world's first clone. Liz finds her father preserved in an ice block—result of an earlier failed experiment. Finally, unable to live with his own imperfection, Devereaux runs out on to the icecap and freezes to death. Appalled by the callous experiments, Liz and Simon return to the time barrier, determined to prevent what they know to be a projection of a possible future.

Devereaux John Barron
Beth Skinner Mary Preston
Dr. Edith Joynton Peggy Thorpe-Bates
Dr. Bukov John Barcroft
Larry Robert Oates

Director: Peter Jefferies
Designer: Michael Eve
Introduced by Peter Fairley *(Ep. 7)*

Story Three

The Year of the Burn-Up

w Bruce Stewart *(Eps. 13–19)* & Victor Pemberton *(Ep. 20)*
Simon is manipulated by Traynor into going into the future once again. A reluctant Liz follows. This time the barrier opens out onto a jungle. In a small straw hut community, the children meet a different, friendly Beth and also Simon's future self, a man known only as 2957. He is leading a group of clones, ranked from high-grade Alphas to lower Deltas, on a project to change world climates (hence a tropical England in 1990). But Simon discovers that an aging Traynor is sabotaging the project.

As things go disastrously wrong, the world's atmosphere thins, the heat level soars, the water level fails and wildlife withers. Saddened by the prospect of such a grim future, Liz and Simon manage to halt the project, before returning to the barrier, leaving at least some vestige of hope.

Beth Mary Preston
2957 David Graham
Miss Stebbins Teresa Scoble
Vera Merdel Jordine
Alpha 4 Ian Fairbairn
Alpha 16 Teresa Scoble
Alpha 17 Lesley Scoble
Paul Brian Pettifer
Delta 22 Patrick Durkin
Technician Stuart Henry

Directors: Ron Francis *(Eps. 13, 20)* Peter Jeffries *(Eps. 14–19)*
Designers: Gerry Roberts *(Eps. 13, 20)* Michael Eve *(Eps. 14–19)*

Story Four

The Day of the Clone

w Victor Pemberton *(Eps. 21–26)*
Simon sets out to rescue Liz who is being held by Traynor in a research station, R1, near St. Oswald. Aided by Dr. Frazer, he finds and frees her. Pursued by Traynor's men, the children head for the barrier, passing through it into Simon's living room in 1965. Heading back to St. Oswald, and R1, they witness strange experiments and discover Devereaux in charge of a cloning project. Escaping *back* to 1971, they are recaptured by Traynor and taken again to R1.

Meanwhile, Liz's mother has had visions of her daughter's various plights and she and Frank follow the trail to R1, where Traynor has now discovered that *he himself* is a clone, created in the sixties by Devereaux. The knowledge has unhinged him, but Dr. Frazer is on hand to reunite them with the children. They then come across the *real* Traynor who has been imprisoned since 1965. As the story—and the series—ends they *all* pursue the Traynor clone to the barrier and the closing sequence has him/it being dragged screaming through the hole to . . . who knows where—or when.

Dr. Frazer Ian Fairbairn
Pitman John Swindells
Miss Stebbins Teresa Scoble
Maria Mary Larkin
Desk attendant Bruce Beeby
Commissionaire Harry Davis
Driver Dennis Balcombe
Devereaux John Barron
De Sarem Derek Sydney
Mr. Randall John Cazabon
News vendor John Herrington
Ward sister Hilary Liddell
Dr. Ferguson Keith Grenville
George Pointer Richard Thorp

Directors: Dave Foster *(Eps. 21–24)*, Ron Francis *(Eps. 25–26)*
Designer: Gerry Roberts

TOM CORBETT, SPACE CADET

Tom Corbett differed from the heroes of the other pioneering American space operas in that he was just a cadet, a 24th-century teenager doing the best he could.

Loosely adapted from Robert Heinlein's 1948 novel, *Space Cadet*, the series aired in America from 1950 to 1955, appearing on all four U.S. networks of the day. Ace pilot Tom Corbett and his fellow cadets went on missions from the Space Academy USA, where they were training to join the Solar Guards, a peacekeeping force of the Solar Alliance, a Federation of Earth and its colonies on Venus, Mars and the Saturn moon Titan.

Tom and his crew—smart-alec gunner Roger Manning and navigator Astro—rarely took on super-villains. Their adventures, in their spaceship *Polaris*, were more of exploration and discovery. The show even employed a scientific consultant, rocket expert Willy Ley, to keep the technology plausible, if not probable.

MAIN CAST
Tom Corbett Frankie Thomas *Roger Manning* Jan Merlin
Cadet Astro Al Markin
Dr. Joan Dale (Tom's girlfriend) Margaret Garland
Commander Arkwright (head of the academy) Carter Blake

Made in black and white   U.S. premiere: 2 October 1950

THE TOMORROW PEOPLE

This 1970s British children's adventure series introduced a new breed of youngster—Homo Superior. Described by creator/writer/director Roger Price as the next stage in human evolution, *The Tomorrow People* were completely telepathic, possessed telekinetic powers and had the ability to teleport themselves instantaneously from place to place—a process catchily known as "jaunting," a term swiped from Alfred Bester's classic novel, *The Stars My Destination*.

From their secret base—called The Lab—off a disused tunnel of the London Underground, *The Tomorrow People* looked out for one another's emergence and dedicated their amazing powers to saving mankind and the world from diverse alien threats. In this they were aided by TIM, their talking biotronic computer, and various friends, including Ginge and Lefty, a pair of leather-jacketed motorcyclists.

As the opening story revealed, *The Tomorrow People* weren't always Homo Superior. They all began as plain Homo Sapiens (affectionately referred to as "Saps") and the evolution into a Tomorrow Person was called "breaking out." You, too, the theory went, could be a latent Homo Superior.

Over the series' first eight seasons, Tomorrow People came and went, with departing stars explained away as representing Earth on the Galactic Trig, a kind of huge space complex, staffed by super-intelligent beings from all over the Universe.

The group's leader, John, was the only member to last the series' distance, though Elizabeth (played by black actress Elizabeth Adare) joined in Season Two and stayed to the end. The other longest-serving recruits were Stephen (four seasons) and Mike (five seasons), the latter being played by actor/singer Mike Holoway of the Flintlock pop group.

The Tomorrow People was revived for the nineties in 1992, with former *Neighbours* star Kristian Schmid in the lead role of Adam.

REGULAR CAST

THE TOMORROW PEOPLE

John (Seasons 1–8) Nicholas Young *Stephen (Seasons 1–4)* Peter Vaughan-Clarke
Carol (Season 1) Sammie Winmill *Kenny (Season 1)* Stephen Salmon
Elizabeth (Seasons 2–8) Elizabeth Adare *Tyso (Seasons 3–4)* Dean Lawrence
Mike Bell (Seasons 4–8) Mike Holoway *Hsui Tai (Seasons 6–8)* Misako Koba
Andrew Forbes (Seasons 7–8) Nigel Rhodes

OTHERS

Voice of TIM Philip Gilbert *Ginge (Season 1)* Michael Standing
Lefty (Season 1) Derek Crewe *Prof. Cawston (Seasons 2–3)* Brian Stanion
Chris (Seasons 2 and 3) Christopher Chittell

Created by Roger Price
Producers: Ruth Boswell *(Seasons 1–3)*, Roger Price *(Seasons 1 and 4)*, Vic Hughes *(Seasons 5–8)*
Script editor (Season 4): Ruth Boswell
Title: Dudley Simpson

Thames Television Production
68 color 30-minute episodes
Season One:
30 April–30 July 1973
Season Two:
4 February–6 May 1974
Season Three:
26 February–21 May 1975
Season Four:
28 January–10 March 1976
Season Five:
28 February–4 April 1977

Season Six:
15 May–26 June 1978
Season Seven:
9 October–13 November 1978
Season Eight:
29 January–19 February 1979

(NB: From Season Two onward each episode has its own title, but the stories are known collectively by the title given here.)

Also: The Revival
Season Nine:
18 November–16 December 1992
Season Ten:
4 January–8 March 1994
Season Eleven:
4 January–8 March 1995

Season One

The Slaves of Jedikiah

w Brian Finch *&* Roger Price *(a 5-part story)*
Introductions all round . . . as Stephen, an ordinary 14-year-old schoolboy haunted by strange voices in his head, learns that he's not going mad, but is "breaking out"—changing into a Tomorrow Person. He meets the other Tomorrow People, Carol, John

and Kenny, and they face the threat of Jedikiah, a fierce, shape-changing alien robot.
Jedikiah Francis de Wolff
Cyclops Robert Bridges
Mrs. Jameson Patricia Denys
Dr. Stuart Neville Barber
Policeman Peter Weston
Staff nurse Christine Shaw

Director: Paul Bernard
Designer: Harry Clark

The Medusa Strain

w Brian Finch & Roger Price *(a 4-part story)*
The Tomorrow People combat a revenge-seeking Jedikiah who has teamed up with a space pirate, Rabowski, to capture Peter, a young guardian of time, and succeeded in immobilizing the world with the aim of stealing the Crown Jewels.
Jedikiah Roger Bizley
Rabowski Roger Booth
Peter Richard Speight
Android David Prowse
Medusa Norman McGlen

Director: Roger Price
Designer: Harry Clark

The Vanishing Earth

w Brian Finch & Roger Price *(a 4-part story)*
The Tomorrow People face the awesome challenge of the Spidron, an alien with the power to inflict earthquakes and hurricanes and cause volcanoes to erupt. As the full force of his fury is unleashed, the jaunters stand by helplessly, unable to warn the Saps that the world may be coming to an end.
Steen Kevin Stoney
Smithers Kenneth Farrington
Joy Nora Llewellyn
Spidron John Woodnutt

Director: Paul Bernard
Designer: Harry Clark

Season Two

The Blue and the Green

w Roger Price *(a 5-part story)*
With Carol and Kenny departed (to represent Earth on the Galactic Federation Council), Stephen and John are joined by a new Tomorrow Person, a student teacher called Elizabeth. Together they solve the mystery surrounding a series of riots spreading through schools all over England, and the strange changing paintings that cast an evil spell on those around them.
Robert Jason Kemp
Johnson Ray Burdis
Grandfather Nigel Pegram
Police inspector Simon Merrick

Director: Roger Price
Director: Michael Minas

A Rift in Time

w Roger Price *(a 4-part story)*
Stephen and John share a dream in which Peter, the young Time Guardian (from "The Medusa Strain"), calls for their help in stopping a time meddler who is tampering with the past by giving Roman tech-nology the steam engine. Using a time disc, the Tomorrow People must correct the time warp to save civilization as they know it.
Peter Richard Speight
Prof. Freda Garner Sylvia Coleridge
Prof. Cawston (intro) Bryan Stanion
Gaius Stanley Lebor
Zenon Stephen Jack
Guthrun Mike Lee Lane
Lothar Leonardo Pieroni
Cotus Peter Duncan
Trystan Leonard Gregory
Carol Sammie Winmill

Director: Roger Price
Designer: Michael Minas

The Doomsday Men

w Roger Price *(a 4-part story)*
The Tomorrow People clash with a secret society dedicated to preserving war who take over the space station Damocles and threaten to devastate the world with its nuclear power. Striving to halt the catastrophe, Stephen and his friends jaunt up to Damocles where they come face-to-face with General "Iron Mac" McLelland, leader of the Doomsday Men.
Paul Simon Gipps-Kent
Douglas McLelland William Relton
Lt. Gen. McLelland Lindsay Campbell
Dr. Laird Arnold Peters
Lee Wan Eric Young
Major Longford Derek Murcott
Traffic warden Nigel Pegram

Director: Roger Price
Designer: Michael Minas

Season Three

Secret Weapon

w Roger Price *(a 4-part story)*
John, Elizabeth and Stephen hear a new Tommorow Person, Tyso, breaking out, asking for help. Their search for him leads them to Col. Masters and a secret Research Establishment where the colonel's assistant, Miss Conway, is trying to use her mind-reading ability to learn the secrets of Homo Superior.
Tyso (intro) Dean Lawrence
Col. Masters Trevor Bannister
Tricia Conway Ann Curthoys
Mrs. Boswell Joanna Tope
Evergreen Denise Cook
Father O'Connor Frank Gatliff
Professor Cawston Brian Stanion
Chris Christopher Chittell
Prime minister Hugh Morton

Director: Stan Woodward
Designer: Philip Blowers

Worlds Away

w Roger Price *(a 3-part story)*
Timus Irnok Mosta, ambassador from the Galactic Federation, begs the Tomorrow People to try to free the enslaved inhabitants of the planet Peerie, who are being terrorized by a strange creature, the dreaded Khultan. They find the Vesh, the Tomorrow People of Peerie, are being hunted and burned by the Veshtakers.
Timus/Tikno Philip Gilbert
Lenda Lydia Lisle
Veshtaker Barry Linehan
Arkron Keith Chegwin
Vanyon Reg Lye
Mrs. Boswell Joanna Tope
Evergreen Denise Cook

Directors: Dennis Kirkland & Vic Hughes
Designer: Philip Blowers

A Man for Emily

w Roger Price *(a 3-part story)*
John and Elizabeth jaunt into space to investigate an alien spaceship and meet The Momma, her spoiled daughter Emily and Emily's servant/companion Elmer. When Elmer escapes to Earth, where he causes chaos, lands up in jail and refuses to return to the ship, John finds himself on the Momma's "wanted" list as Elmer's replacement.
Momma Margaret Burton
Emily Sandra Dickinson
Elmer Peter Davison
Publican Robin Parkinson
Mr. Greenhead Bill Dean

Director: Stan Woodward
Designer: Philip Blowers

The Revenge of Jedikiah

w Roger Price *(a 3-part story)*
A vengeful Jedikiah assumes Stephen's form (appearing on *Opportunity Knocks!*) to shoot Col. Masters at his research establishment. Then, as Miss Conway, he sets a deadly trap for John and Elizabeth. A desperate TIM seeks the aid of Tikno. Though this is against the galactic code, Tikno agrees—but pays with his life. The stage is set for a final confrontation in the Lab.
Jedikiah Francis de Wolff
Tricia Conway Ann Curthoys
Prof. Cawston Bryan Stanion
Mustaf Ali Bongo
Evergreen Denise Cook
TIM/Timus/Tikno Philip Gilbert
Prof. Johnston Anne Ridler
Sgt. Evans John Lyons

Director: Vic Hughes
Designer: Philip Blowers

Season Four

One Law

w Roger Price *(a 3-part story)*
Young Mike Bell has discovered that he can open locks with his mind. Unaware that he is really "breaking out," he decides to use his power to "break in" and rob banks, but falls into the unscrupulous clutches of Lord Dunning who is out to steal a fortune in gold. The Tomorrow People must convince Mike that his true destiny lies elsewhere.
Mr. O'Reilly Patrick McAlinney
Two Tone John Hollis
Slow Norman Hitchell
Insp. Burke Tim Barrett
Lord Dunning Harold Kasket
Thwaites Arnold Diamond
Mike's mother Anne Gabrielle
Mike's sister Debbie Thau

Director: Leon Thau
Designer: Peter Elliott

Into the Unknown

w Jon Watkins *(a 4-part story)*
Mike is composing a pop song in the Lab when an SOS comes in from Outer Space, taking the Tomorrow People on a journey to the Pluto Five region of the solar system to help a stricken spaceship which is being slowly drawn into a black hole. But treachery is afoot and they find themselves helplessly trapped.
Kwaan Stephen Garlick
Tiriayaan Geoffrey Bayldon
Vaktaan Brian Coburn
Ralaa Raymond Boyd
Timus Philip Gilbert

Director: Roger Price
Designer: Peter Elliott

Season Five

The Dirtiest Business

w Roger Price *(a 2-part story)*
Mike, John and Elizabeth race against time to free Pavla, a young girl agent, from the clutches of the SIS and the KGB. Can they rescue her from Major Turner's sinister brainwashing machine and prevent the Russians triggering off their mysterious X-delta device?
Pavla Anulka Dubinska
Major Ann Turner Vivien Heilbron
KGB man Jan Murzynowski
Radio producer Beth Ellis
SIS sgt. Steve Ismay
KGB driver Freddie Clemson
Policeman Ian Barritt
Hippie girl Gaynor Ward
Doctor Taylor Royce Mills
Senior KGB man Gabor Vernon

Director: Vic Hughes
Designer: David Richens

A Much Needed Holiday

w Roger Price *(a 2-part story)*
A trip to the planet Gallia to carry out an archaeological survey involves the Tomorrow People in a daring attempt to rescue the Gallian boy slaves from the clutches of their tyrannical masters, the Kleptons.
Gremlon Anthony Garner
Trig Guy Humphries
Trop David Corti
Timus Philip Gilbert

Director: Richard Mervyn
Designer: David Richens

The Heart of Sogguth

w Roger Price *(a 2-part story)*
Jake, a university head of Ethnic Studies and leader of a religious sect, offers to manage Mike's pop group and the Tomorrow Person finds that playing an African tribal drum on television could raise the forces of hell to bring about the destruction of the Universe.
Jake Roddy Maude-Roxby
Mike Harding James Smilie
Susan Gill Rosalyn Elvin
Derek Derek Pascoe
Bill Bill Rice
Group members Jamie Stone, John Summerton

Director: Vic Hughes
Designer: David Richens

Season Six

The Lost Gods

w Roger Price *(a 2-part story)*
A telepathic message from an oriental "goddess" takes the Tomorrow People to the Far East where they meet a new Homo Superior, Hsui Tai, and find themselves lined up to become sacrifices in a religious cult's ceremony of fire.
Matsu Tan Burt Kwouk
Sage Robert Lee

Director: Peter Webb
Designer: David Richens

Hitler's Last Secret

w Roger Price *(a 2-part story)*
Why do a group of young British soldiers turn against their commanding officer when they hear the sound of Hitler's voice? The answer brings the Tomorrow People face-to-face with the evils of the Third Reich.
Hitler Michael Sheard
Prof. Friedl Richard Warner
Major Hughes Leon Eagles

Karl Brandt Nicholas Lyndhurst
Willi Frisch Earl Rhodes
Blitz Ray Burdis
Wolfgang Grass Charles Skinner
Corporal Francis Mortimer

Director: Leon Thau
Designer: David Richens

The Thargon Menace

w Roger Price *(a 2-part story)*
A terrifying Ripper Ray weapon, powerful enough to destroy a planet, falls into the hands of a mad despot, General Papa Minn. From space he broadcasts his ultimatum to the governments of the world—surrender all power within one hour or perish. It's up to the Tomorrow People to save the world.
General Papa Minn Olu Jacobs
Major Marcos Eric Roberts
Sula Jackie Cowper
Flyn Michael Audreson
Captain Graham Lines
Puppet voices David Graham

Director: Peter Yolland
Designer: Martyn Hebert

Season Seven

Castle of Fear

w Roger Price *(a 2-part story)*
A fifth member joins the team—Scots lad Andrew Forbes—in an adventure in which the Tomorrow People dream of a headless highlander, go in search of the Loch Ness Monster and meet Frankenstein's creation.
Bruce Forbes Dominic Allan
Dr. Gail Mayer Jennifer Watts
Angus MacDuff Bill Gavin
Prof. Young Brian Jackson

Director: Vic Hughes
Designer: Gordon Toms

Achilles Heel

w Roger Price *(a 2-part story)*
With their special powers stripped by two mysterious alien visitors, the Tomorrow People have just ten minutes to prevent a disaster that will instantaneously affect every corner of the galaxy. Directed by Gabrielle Beaumont, later a *Next Generation* regular.
Bruce Forbes Dominic Allan
Yagon Hilary Minster
Cantor Christian Rodska
Glip Stanley Bates
Timus Philip Gilbert

Director: Gabrielle Beaumont
Designer: Gordon Toms

The Living Skins

w Roger Price *(a 2-part story)*
The Tomorrow People investigate the link between sinister goings-on in the cellar of a fashionable boutique and disturbances in deep space. John gives a priceless gift to the world that costs him nothing, but saves all life on Earth from becoming extinct.
Wilton Ralph Lawford
Girl Judith Fielding
Guard David Carter

Director: Stan Woodward
Designer: Gordon Toms

Season Eight

War of the Empires

w Roger Price *(a 4-part story)*
When Earth becomes drawn into an inter-galactic conflict between two warring races, the Thargons and the Sorsons, the Tomorrow People appeal in vain for help from the Galactic Federation. Then the Sorson leader makes a pact with the American president. Finally, the young heroes find themselves facing the might of the Thargon space fleet, armed only with their "imagination."
American president John F. Parker
American general Hal Galili
Morgan Evans David Baxt
Dave Ricardo Weston Gavin
Sorson general Richard Bartlett
Sorson captain Terence Woodfield
Thargon commander Percy Herbert
Thargon officer Anthony Stafford
American lady Mary Law
Chaircreature David Cann
Thargon general Oliver Maguire
Timus Philip Gilbert

Director: Vic Hughes
Designer: John Plant

Season Nine

The Tomorrow People (1992)

w Roger Damon Price *(a 5-part story)*
Adam, Lisa and Kevin are the Tomorrow People in this nineties revival. Mysteriously marooned on a faraway island, they're a long way from home—Australia, America and Britain. And they're not sure how they got there, or why. The answer lies waiting for them underground—inside the buried wreck of an alien spaceship. But others have discovered their secret, too, and will stop at nothing to steal their powers of telepathy and teleportation.
Adam Kristian Schmid
Lisa Kristen Ariza
Kevin Adam Pearce
Megabyte Christian Tessier
Colonel Masters Manning Redwood
Professor Galt Hugh Quarshie
General Damon Jeff Harding
Mrs. Davies Shezwae Powell
Jones Lou Hirsch
Gloria Romilly Nolan

Director: Ron Oliver
Producer: Roger Damon Price
Executive producer: Alan Horrox
Designer: Mark Tildesley

A Tetra Films Production in association with Reeves Entertainment for Thames Television and Nickelodeon

Season Ten

The Culex Experiment

w Lee Pressman & Grant Cathro *(a 5-part story)*
Witnessing a bizarre kidnap, Kevin is attacked by a form of mosquito and is himself abducted by the strange Dr. Culex whose next target is the organic matter duplicator created by Dr. Connor.
Adam Kristian Schmid
Megabyte Christian Tessier
Kevin Adam Pearce
Ami Naomi Harris
Dr. Culex Jean Marsh
Dr. Connor Connie Booth
Insp. Platt Roger Sloman
Aunt Ruth Denise Coffey
General Damon Jeff Harding

Directors: Alex Horrox & Vivianne Albertine
Designer: Mark Tildesley

Monsoon Man

w Lee Pressman & Grant Cathro *(a 5-part story)*
The Tomorrow People must halt an American cereal producer who plans to sabotage a space shuttle so he can use a rain-making machine to ruin his competitors' crops, so that everyone will be forced to eat his own foul-tasting products.
Colonel Cobb William Hootkins
Wilkie Kerry Shale
Middlemass Christopher Benjamin
Lucy Laurence Bouvard
Les Bishop John Judd

Director: Niall Leonard
Designer: Jon Henson

Season Eleven

The Rameses Connection

w Grant Cathro *(a 5-part story)*
The Tomorrow People receive a bizarre SOS across 4000 years when a priceless Egyptian artifact is stolen from a London museum by the shadowy Sam Rees, a figure who has evil plans for cosmic domination.
Adam Kristian Schmid
Megabyte Christian Tessier
Ami Naomie Harris
Sam Rees Christopher Lee
Millicent Rutherford Elizabeth Spriggs
Hubert Tate Robert Lang
Scully Andrew Powell
Red Rainwear Anthony O'Donnell

Director: Roger Gartland

The Living Stones

w Lee Pressman *(a 5-Part story)*
A shower of mysterious objects rains down on a sleepy corner of rural England, turning the villagers—and infamous rock star Byron Lucifer—into zombies with glowing green eyes.
Byron Lucifer Danny John-Jules
with Rosemary Leach, Patricia Hayes, George Raistrick *&* Sharon Duce

Director: Crispin Reece

A Tetra Films Production in association with Thames Television and Nickelodeon

TOUCHED BY AN ANGEL

Touched by an Angel, the highest-rated drama series on CBS as of 1998, continues to offer inspirational episodes, as angels visit Earth to help or inspire people at a crossroads in their lives—whether they know it or not. Three continuing characters—Monica, an angel who still needs some assistance with her earthly assignment; Tess, her supervisor; and Andrew, the Angel of Death, who sometimes helps Tess on various assignments—offer continuity, since the problem, setting, and guest cast change every week.

REGULAR CAST
Monica Roma Downey   *Tess* Della Reese
Andrew John Dye

Executive producer: Martha Williamson
CBS Productions, in association with Moon Water Productions, Inc.

U.S. premiere: 21 September 1994

THE TRIPODS

It was supposed to be the adventure story to cap all adventure stories—a £1 million BBC family science fiction serial spread over three seasons, a saga to woo the Saturday teatime audience for years to come.

In the end, BBC1 controller Michael Grade pulled the plug two-thirds of the way through, as poor reviews and lousy ratings persuaded the corporation to cut and run. And unlike with the 1985 axe Grade dangled over *Doctor Who*, there was no reprieve. The TV story of *The Tripods* remains unfinished.

Adapted by Alick Rowe and Christopher Penfold from John Christopher's trilogy of the same name, *The Tripods* is set in the 21st century and follows the adventures of two teenage cousins, Will and Henry Parker, and their friends, as they get caught up in a struggle to free Earth from alien control. The Tripods themselves are towering three-legged alien machines that dominate mankind, stifling rebellion by a mind-control technique called "capping." Under their 100-year rule society has reverted to a medieval pattern.

The young protagonists, Will and Henry, are due to be capped in a special ceremony at their village in England, which will mark their transition to adulthood. But the pair wishes to remain free and decide to head off in search of the "Free Men" in the White Mountains of Switzerland.

The series was generally well acted and its special effects scenes with the Tripods well realized. Extensive location filming made appealing use of the settings (including Portmeirion). Its downfall lay in the relative brevity of the original work and an overall lack of incident, especially in the crucial first season, when the metal monsters themselves were seen all too infrequently, their presence felt more off-stage than on.

REGULAR CAST
William Parker John Shackley *Beanpole* Ceri Seel
Henry Parker Jim Baker *(Season One; Season Two, Eps. 1–2)*
Fritz Robin Hayter *(Season Two only)*

Adapted by Alick Rowe, *(Season One)*, Christopher Penfold *(Season Two)* from the trilogy by John Christopher
Producer: Richard Bates
Music: Ken Freeman
Video effects designers: Robin Lobb, Jon Mitchell
Visual effects designers: Steven Drewett, Kevin Molloy *(Season One)* Steve Bowman, Simon Tayler, Michael Kelt *(Season Two)*

A BBC Production in association with Fremantle International Inc (Season One) and The Seven Network, Australia (Seasons One & Two)
25 color 30-minute episodes
Season One:
15 September–8 December 1984
Season Two:
7 September–23 November 1985
(BBC1)
Repeat: U.K. Gold 1994–95

Season One

(a 13-part story)
The year: 2089. The place: rural England. The Tripods have ruled for more than 100 years and, by "capping" each child at 16, control men's minds and ensure total submission. But cousins Will and Henry Parker are determined to stay free and, encouraged by a vagrant, Ozymandias, run away.

Setting out to join the Free Men in the Swiss mountains, Will and Henry cross to France where they gain a new companion Jean-Paul (Beanpole), and visit the abandoned city of Paris. When Will gets a fever, the trio are given refuge at Château Ricordeau where Will falls in love with the beautiful Eloise. He is torn between her and his friends who go on without him. But the jealous Duc de Sarlat chooses the already capped Eloise to serve the Tripods and a broken-hearted Will leaves to rejoin his friends.

However, he is captured by a Tripod and freed with a homing device inserted in his armpit to lead it to the others. Though the device is found and cut away, Will loses much blood and needs help. The trio finds brief sanctuary at the Vichot family's vineyard before pressing on toward the White Mountains.

Tired and hungry, they are caught stealing a loaf of bread and again face the prospect of capping, but manage to escape—destroying a Tripod.

Then, with their goal in sight, they are caught by "black guards." Only after an interrogation do they find that they are really safe in the hands of the Free Men.
Ozymandias Roderick Horn
Mrs. Parker Lucinda Curtis
Jack Michael Gilmour
Mr. Parker Peter Dolphin
Schoolmster John Scott Martin
Captain Curtis Harry Meacher
Duc de Sarlat Robin Langford
Count Jeremy Young
Countess Pamela Salem
Eloise Charlotte Long
Trouillon Terry Forrestal
Mme. Vichot Anni Lee Taylor
Monsieur Vichot Stephen Marlowe
Daniel Julian Jones
Chief black guard Peter Halliday
Julius Richard Wordsworth

Directors: Graham Theakston *(Eps. 1–8)*, Christopher Barry *(Eps. 9–13)*
Designers: Victor Meredith *(Eps. 1–8)*, Martin Collins *(Eps. 9–13)*

Season Two

(a 12-part story)
At their hideout in the Swiss Alps the Free Men must devise a plan to overthrow the Tripods and free mankind. Will, Beanpole and a German boy, Fritz, are among those chosen to compete at the Tripods' Annual Games in the hope that may provide a means to get inside the Tripods' city and learn some of their secrets.

During a hazardous journey they fall foul of the villainous Kommandant Goetz, but are helped by a couple of girls, Zerlina and Papagena.

After success in the Games, Will and Fritz are transported to the City of Gold, leaving Beanpole to wait for their return. Will is chosen to serve one of the "Masters"—the alien creatures who created the Tripods—and Fritz winds up working with the slave gangs in underground caverns, but both learn much about the Masters' plans for the future of Earth. Will also finds Eloise—in suspended animation in a hall of beauty—and dances with her in a dream.

When their intentions are found out, Fritz elects to stay in the city, while Will escapes via an under-ground river. Meeting up with Beanpole, they join Ali Pasha's traveling circus disguised as clowns, in the hope of getting their vital information back to the White Mountains.

Julius Richard Wordsworth
Goetz Godfrey James
Zerlina Lisa Maxwell
Papagena Eizabeth Morton
Master 468 John Woodvine
Speyer Alfred Hoffman
Power Master Bernard Holley
Borman James Coyle
Boll Edward Highmore
Eloise Cindy Shelley
Coggy Christopher Guard
Dorfen Alex Leppard
Slave master Garfield Morgan
Ali Pasha Bruce Purchase

Directors: Christopher Barry *(Eps. 1–4, 11–12)*,
  Bob Blagden *(Eps. 5–10)*
Designers: Martin Collins *(Eps. 1–4, 11–12)*,
  Philip Lindley *(Eps. 5–10)*

THE TWILIGHT ZONE (1959–64)

"There is a fifth dimension beyond those known to man. It is a dimension vast as space and timeless as infinity. It is the middle ground between light and shadow, between the pit of his fears and the summit of his knowledge. This is the dimension of imagination. It is an area we call . . . *The Twilight Zone*."

One of the most revered fantasy series ever made, *The Twilight Zone* still stands as the role model for the anthology genre. Its trenchant parables on humanity draw the viewer in by quietly tugging at the sleeve of his imagination and, through fantasy, explore human hopes and despairs, prides and prejudices, strengths and weaknesses, in ways conventional drama never can.

The Zone was created by Rod Serling, a butcher's son from Binghamton, New York, whose writing talent had flourished in the early days of TV drama, winning him three Emmy awards. A relentless, prolific writer, Serling himself wrote the majority of the show's 156 scripts. Said to have suffered from insomnia, he kept a tape recorder by his bed to dictate ideas that came to him as he tried to sleep.

The series' other major contributors were Richard Matheson and Charles Beaumont and each had his own distinctive style. Where Serling's tales tended to be more whimsical and sentimental, Beaumont's were darker and more disturbing, while Matheson wrung every nuance of suspense out of his carefully structured stories. But *all* the episodes were topped and tailed by Serling's memorable, measured narration.

On the acting side, *The Twilight Zone* featured many young, now established stars, from *Star Trek*'s William Shatner, Leonard Nimoy and George Takei, to film giants such as Charles Bronson, Lee Marvin, James Coburn, Burt Reynolds, Telly Savalas, Roddy McDowell, Robert Redford, Burgess Meredith, Mickey Rooney and Dennis Hopper, plus Jack "*Quincy*" Klugman and Peter "*Columbo*" Falk.

The Twilight Zone premiered in America on 2 October 1959 and its original five-season run lasted until 1964.

REGULAR CAST
Host/Narrator Rod Serling

Created by Rod Serling
Executive producer: Rod Serling
Producers: Buck Houghton, Herbert Hirschman, Bert Granet, William Froug
Special effects: Virgil Beck, Bob Waugh
Theme: Bernard Herrmann, Marius Constant, Jerry Goldsmith

A Cayuga Production (filmed at MGM)
156 black and white episodes (138 half-hour, 18 one-hour)
U.S. premiere: 2 October 1959
U.K. premiere: 27 January 1963
(Border)

Season One
36 30-minute episodes

Where Is Everybody?

w Rod Serling
Greeted by empty streets, a man searches a small town to find that he is completely alone—and inexplicably terrified.
Cast: Earl Holliman, James Gregory

Director: Robert Stevens

One for the Angels

w Rod Serling
Informed that his time on Earth is about up, a gentle-natured sidewalk salesman talks Mr. Death into letting him make one really big pitch. When he tries to welsh on the deal, Mr. Death picks a little girl to die in his place, forcing him to keep his side of the bargain.
Cast: Ed Wynn, Murray Hamilton, Dana Dillaway, Jay Overholts, Merritt Bohn, Mickey Maga

Director: Robert Parrish

Mr. Denton on Doomsday

w Rod Serling
A broken-down gunslinger finds a magic potion that restores his shooting skill, but brings an end to his fast-draw career.
Cast: Dan Duryea, Malcolm Atterbury, Martin Landau, Ken Lynch, Doug McClure, Jeanne Cooper, Arthur Batanides, Robert Burton

Director: Allen Reisner

The Sixteen-Millimeter Shrine

w Rod Serling
A forgotten star of the thirties uses films of her old movies to re-create the spirit of her heyday.
Cast: Ida Lupino, Martin Balsam, Alice Frost, Ted de Corsia, John Clarke, Jerome Cowan

Director: Mitch Leisen

Walking Distance

w Rod Serling
A man's need to escape the pressure of his work is so great that he slips back 30 years into his own childhood.
Cast: Gig Young, Michael Montgomery, Byron Foulger, Joseph Corey, Frank Overton, Irene Tedrow, Buzz Martin

Director: Robert Stevens

Escape Clause

w Rod Serling
A man makes a pact with the devil for immortality then finds he doesn't get a kick out of living anymore.
Cast: David Wayne, Wendell Holmes, Raymond Bailey, Dick Wilson, Paul E. Burns, Allan Lurie, Virginia Christine, Thomas Gomez, Nesdon Booth, Joe Flynn, George Baxter

Director: Mitch Leisen

The Lonely

w Rod Serling
Convicted of murder and sent to a deserted asteroid for 40 years, a man is given a robot woman for company.
Cast: Jack Warden, John Dehner, Jim Turley, Jean Marsh, Ted Knight

Director: Jack Smight

Time Enough at Last

w Rod Serling, *story by* Lynn Venable
Near-sighted, meek bank clerk Henry Bemis is the sole survivor of an H-bomb attack. At last he has the time to engulf himself in his passion for books.
Cast: Burgess Meredith, Vaughn Taylor, Jacqueline de Wit, Lela Bliss

Director: John Brahm

Perchance to Dream

w Charles Beaumont
A terrified man stumbles into a psychiatrist's office, afraid that if he falls asleep a woman in his dream will murder him.
Cast: Richard Conte, John Larch, Suzanne Lloyd, Eddie Marr, Ted Stanhope, Russell Trent

Director: Robert Florey

Judgment Night

w Rod Serling
A passenger on board a wartime freighter has a premonition that the ship will be sunk by a Nazi submarine at 1:15 A.M.—but no one believes him.
Cast: Nehemiah Persoff, Patrick Macnee, Leslie Bradley, Kendrick Huxham, Ben Wright, Hugh Sanders, Deirdre Owen, James Franciscus

Director: John Brahm

And When the Sky Was Opened

w Rod Serling, *short story by* Richard Matheson
Three astronauts, returning from man's first space flight, cannot remember the events of their trip. Then each disappears without trace.
Cast: Rod Taylor, James Hutton, Charles Aidman, Sue Randall, Gloria Pall, Maxine Cooper, Paul Bryar

Director: Douglas Heyes

What You Need

w Rod Serling, *story by* Lewis Padgett *(alias Henry Kuttner & C.L. Moore)*
A down-and-out man tries to turn another man's ability to tell the future into a money-making scheme.
Cast: Steve Cochran, Read Morgan, Arline Sax, Frank Alloca, Ernest Truex, William Edmonson, Norman Sturgis, Mark Sunday

Director: Alvin Ganzer

The Four of Us Are Dying

w Rod Serling, *story by* George Clayton Johnson
Arch Hammer can change his face to look exactly like someone else, a talent that he depends on for a living—but that could prove fatal.
Cast: Harry Townes *(Arch)*, Philip Pine, Don Gordon, Bernard Fein, Beverly Garland, Ross Martin, Peter Brocco, Milton Frome

Director: John Brahm

Third from the Sun

w Rod Serling, *story by* Richard Matheson
Two families steal a rocket ship and flee to another world before atomic war devastates their own. Destination . . . Earth.
Cast: Fritz Weaver, Edward Andrews, Lori March, Will J. White, Joe Maross, Denise Alexander, Jeanne Evans

Director: Richard Bare

I Shot an Arrow Into the Air

w Rod Serling, *idea by* Madelon Champion
A panicky space traveler, believing his ship has crashed on a deserted asteroid, kills his two companions to save water, then discovers a highway and the sign "Las Vegas—15 miles."
Cast: Dewey Martin, Edward Binns, Ted Otis

Director: Stuart Rosenberg

The Hitch-Hiker

w Rod Serling, *radio play by* Lucille Fletcher
Driving cross-country, a girl keeps seeing the same hitch-hiker on the road ahead, beckoning her toward a fatal accident.
Cast: Inger Stevens, Leonard Strong, Adam Williams, Dwight Townsend, Mitzi McCall, Eleanor Audley, Lew Gallo, Russ Bender, George Mitchell

Director: Alvin Ganzer

The Fever

w Rod Serling
A man fanatically opposed to gambling battles a Las Vegas one-armed bandit with a malevolent will of its own
Cast: Everett Sloane, William Kendis, Art Lewis, Carole Kent, Vivi Janiss, Lee Millar

Director: Robert Florey

The Last Flight

w Richard Matheson
Fleeing from a World War One dogfight, a cowardly British pilot lands his 1917 biplane at a modern jet air base in France . . . in 1959. There he learns that a fellow pilot he had moments before left to the mercy of German planes is now a high-ranking officer.
Cast: Kenneth Haigh, Alexander Scourby, Simon Scott, Robert Warwick, Harry Raybould

Director: William Claxton

The Purple Testament

w Rod Serling
A soldier unexpectedly acquires the power to recognize death in the faces of men about to die in battle.
Cast: William Reynolds, Dick York, Barney Phillips, Warren Oates, Ron Masak, William Phipps, Marc Cavell, Paul Mazursky

Director: Richard Bare

Elegy

w Charles Beaumont
Earth-like scenes from many historical periods greet three space travelers who land on a strange planet.
Cast: Cecil Kellaway, Kevin Hagen, Jeff Morrow, Don Dubbins

Director: Douglas Heyes

Mirror Image

w Rod Serling
A young woman grows panicky when she is haunted by a strange double who keeps appearing in a bus depot.
Cast: Vera Miles, Martin Milner, Joe Hamilton

Director: John Brahm

The Monsters Are Due on Maple Street

w Rod Serling
A mysterious power failure causes paranoid suburban residents to suspect one another of being disguised creatures from outer space.
Cast: Claude Akins, Jack Weston, Barry Atwater, Jan Handzlik, Burt Metcalfe, Mary Gregory, Anne Barton, Lea Waggner, Ben Erway, Lyn Guild, Sheldon Allman, William Walsh

Director: Ron Winston

A World of Difference

w Richard Matheson
A businessman inexplicably finds his office has become a set for a movie in which he is a character.
Cast: Howard Duff, Gail Kobe, Peter Walker, Eileen Ryan, Frank Maxwell

Director: Ted Post

Long Live Walter Jameson

w Charles Beaumont
A college professor is startled to learn that his young colleague and prospective son-in-law was born 2000 years ago with the gift of eternal life.

Cast: Kevin McCarthy (Walter), Edgar Stehli, Dody Heath, Estelle Winwood

Director: Anton Leader

People Are Alike All Over

w Rod Serling, story by Paul Fairman
Sam Conrad, the first Earthman to visit Mars, is relieved to find that Martians resemble humans and treat him kindly, even building him a house like his home on Earth, until he realizes he is an exhibit in a Martian zoo.
Cast: Roddy McDowall (Conrad), Paul Comi, Vic Perrin, Susan Oliver, Byron Morrow, Vernon Gray

Director: Mitchell Leisen

Execution

w Rod Serling, story by George Clayton Johnson
An outlaw in the Wild West of the 1880s is snatched from the hangman's noose by a modern scientist's time machine.
Cast: Albert Salmi, Russell Johnson, Than Wyenn, George Mitchell, Jon Lormer, Fay Roope, Richard Karlan, Joe Howarth

Director: David Orrick McDearmon

The Big Tall Wish

w Rod Serling
A ten-year-old boy tells a prize fighter that he will make a wish for him to win his comeback fight.
Cast: Steven Perry, Ivan Dixon, Kim Hamilton

Director: Ron Winston

A Nice Place to Visit

w Charles Beaumont
A small-time hoodlum gets killed by the police during a robbery and finds an afterlife where anything he wants he can have.
Cast: Larry Blyden, Sebastian Cabot, Sandra Warner

Director: John Brahm

Nightmare as a Child

w Rod Serling
A schoolteacher's encounter with herself as a child unlocks her memory of witnessing her mother's murder.
Cast: Janice Rule, Terry Burnham, Shepperd Strudwick

Director: Alvin Ganzer

A Stop at Willoughby

w Rod Serling
A harassed executive escapes into the peaceful town of Willoughby—July 1880.
Cast: James Daly, Howard Smith, Patricia Donahue, James Maloney

Director: Robert Parrish

The Chaser

w Robert Presnell Jr., *story by* John Collier
A lovesick man buys a potion from a stranger to help woo the woman he desires—with unexpected results.
Cast: George Grizzard, John McIntire, Patricia Barry, J. Pat O'Malley

Director: Doug Heyes

A Passage for Trumpet

w Rod Serling
A down-on-his-luck trumpet player is given a second crack at life—after being struck down by a truck.
Cast: Jack Klugman, Mary Webster, John Anderson, Frank Wolff

Director: Don Medford

Mr. Bevis

w Rod Serling
A happy-go-lucky man loses his job, his car and his home in one morning, then meets his "guardian angel" who tells him they will start the day anew.
Cast: Orson Bean, Henry Jones, Charles Lane, William Schallert, Horace McMahon

Director: William Asher

The After Hours

w Rod Serling
A woman buys a gold thimble on the ninth floor of a department store, then later discovers that the floor doesn't exist and that the salesgirl was really a mannequin.
Cast: Anne Francis, Elizabeth Allen, James Millhollin, John Conwell, Nancy Rennick

Director: Douglas Heyes

The Mighty Casey

w Rod Serling
The manager of a baseball team on a losing streak hires a robot pitcher called Casey.

Cast: Robert Sorrells, Jack Warden, Don O'Kelly, Abraham Sofaer

Directors: Robert Parrish & Alvi Ganzer

A World of His Own

w Richard Matheson
A playwright describes characters into his tape recorder and they materialize in front of his eyes.
Cast: Keenan Wynn, Phyllis Kirk, Mary La Roche

Director: Ralph Nelson

Season Two
29 30-minute episodes

King Nine Will Not Return

w Rod Serling
A downed bomber pilot crash-lands in the desert. When he regains consciousness he cannot find any of his crew members.
Cast: Bob Cummings, Gene Lyons, Seymour Green, Richard Lupino, Paul Lambert, Jenna McMahon

Director: Buzz Kulik

The Man in the Bottle

w Rod Serling
An impoverished pawnbroker is granted four wishes by a genie in a bottle and inadvertently finds himself transformed into Hitler in the last days of the war.
Cast: Luther Alder, Joseph Ruskin, Vivi Janiss, Lisa Golm, Olan Soule, Peter Coe, Albert Szabo

Director: Don Medford

Nervous Man in a Four-Dollar Room

w Rod Serling
A small-time hood assigned to kill an old man finds himself confronted by his conscience in the shape of his own living reflection.
Cast: Joe Mantell, William D. Gordon

Director: Douglas Heyes

A Thing About Machines

w Rod Serling
A bad-tempered writer is convinced the machines in his home are conspiring to destroy him.
Cast: Richard Haydn, Barbara Stuart, Barney Phillips

Director: David Orrick McDearmon

The Howling Man

w Charles Beaumont
Taking refuge in a European monastery run by a "Truth" order, a man hears someone howling and is told it's the devil who is being held prisoner. But he doesn't believe it . . .
Cast: H.M. Wynant, John Carradine, Robin Hughes, Ezelle Poule

Director: Douglas Heyes

The Eye of the Beholder

w Rod Serling
In a future state, a beautiful girl longs to be like her peers—ugly, pig-like humanoids. (This episode was also billed under the title "The Private World of Darkness.")
Cast: Joanna Hayes, Jennifer Howard, William D. Gordon, Maxine Stuart, Donna Douglas

Director: Douglas Heyes

Nick of Time

w Richard Matheson
A superstitious newlywed husband finds a penny fortune-telling machine that makes uncannily accurate predictions about his life.
Cast: William Shatner, Patricia Breslin

Director: Richard L. Bare

The Lateness of the Hour

w Rod Serling
A young woman, bored with the precise, faultless routine of her family's life, persuades her father to dismantle their robot servants.
Cast: Inger Stevens, John Hoyt, Irene Tedrow, Mary Gregory

Director: Jack Smight

The Trouble with Templeton

w E. Jack Neuman
A distinguished, aging actor who reflects on the happier days of his youth gets a sobering glimpse of the past.
Cast: Brian Aherne, Pippa Scott, Charles S. Carlson, Sydney Pollack

Director: Buzz Kulik

A Most Unusual Camera

w Rod Serling
A pair of petty thieves find that a camera they have just stolen can predict the future by the pictures it takes.
Cast: Jean Carson, Fred Clark, Adam Williams

Director: John Rich

Night of the Meek

w Rod Serling
Henry Corwin, a down-at-the-heels department store Santa, dispenses Christmas cheer to a mission house with the help of a sack that will produce whatever one asks for.
Cast: Art Carney (Corwin), John Fiedler, Meg Wylie, Robert Lieb

Director: Jack Smight

Dust

w Rod Serling
An unscrupulous traveling salesman sells some "magic dust" he claims will save a man due to hang for killing a little girl during a drunken spree.
Cast: Thomas Gomez, Vladimir Sokoloff, John Alonso, John Larch

Director: Douglas Heyes

Back There

w Rod Serling
A man tries to prevent the assassination of Abraham Lincoln when he finds himself thrust back in time.
Cast: Russell Johnson, Paul Hartman, Bartlett Robinson, John Lasell

Director: David Orrick McDearmon

The Whole Truth

w Rod Serling
The disreputable patter of a used-car dealer changes when he buys a haunted car from an old man and finds he is suddenly unable to lie to his customers.
Cast: Jack Carson, Jack Ging, Arte Johnson, Nan Peterson, George Chandler, Loring Smith

Director: James Sheldon

The Invaders

w Richard Matheson
A lone woman battles two miniature spacemen whose craft crashes into her isolated farmhouse, finally destroying the tiny invaders who come from . . . Earth.
Cast: Agnes Moorehead

Director: Douglas Heyes

A Penny for Your Thoughts

w George Clayton Johnson
Timid bank clerk Victor Pool discovers that a coin that lands on its edge as he pays for a paper leaves him with the power to read minds.
Cast: Dick York *(Pool)*, Dan Tobin, Hayden Rorke, June Dayton, Cyril Delevanti

Director: James Sheldon

Twenty-Two

w Rod Serling, *based on an anecdote in* Famous Ghost Stories
A young woman complains of a recurring nightmare in which she always ends up in Room 22—the hospital morgue. Discharged from hospital she goes to catch a plane to Miami and finds she's on—Flight 22.
Cast: Barbara Nichols, Jonathan Harris, Fredd Wayne

Director: Jack Smight

The Odyssey of Flight 33

w Rod Serling
A commercial airliner, en route to New York, breaks through the time barrier into the prehistoric past.
Cast: John Anderson, Paul Comi, Sandy Kenyon, Harp McGuire, Wayne Heffley, Nancy Rennick, Beverly Brown, Jay Overholt, Betty Garde

Director: Justus Addiss

Mr. Dingle, the Strong

w Rod Serling
A timid little man is experimentally endowed with superhuman strength by a visiting Martian scientist.
Cast: Burgess Meredith, Don Rickles, James Westerfield, Edward Ryder, James Millhollin

Director: John Brahm

Static

w Charles Beaumont, *story by* O. Cee Ritch
An old radio picks up signals from the past that unexpectedly rejuvenate a pair of elderly lovers.
Cast: Dean Jagger, Carmen Matthews, Robert Emhardt

Director: Buzz Kulik

The Prime Mover

w Charles Beaumont, *story by* George Clayton Johnson
Two men try to make their fortune at Las Vegas from the power one of them has to move inanimate objects.

Cast: Dane Clark, Buddy Ebsen, Christine White, Nesdon Booth, Jane Burgess

Director: Richard L. Bare

Long Distance Call

w Charles Beaumont & William Idelson
A young boy keeps in touch with his dead grandmother via the toy telephone she once gave him.
Cast: Bill Mumy, Philip Abbott, Patricia Smith, Lili Darvas

Director: James Sheldon

A Hundred Yards Over the Rim

w Rod Serling
A 19th-century Western settler, desperate for medicine for his sick son, takes an inexplicable journey into the future where he obtains life-saving penicillin.
Cast: Cliff Robertson, Miranda Jones, John Crawford, Evan Evans

Director: Buzz Kulik

The Rip Van Winkle Caper

w Rod Serling
Four thieves plot to hide out with their loot for 100 years in a state of suspended animation.
Cast: Oscar Beregi, Simon Oakland, John Mitchum, Lew Gallo

Director: Justus Addiss

The Silence

w Rod Serling
A garrulous man, bet half a million dollars that he can't keep silent for one year, goes to bizarre lengths to win the wager.
Cast: Franchot Tone, Liam Sullivan, Jonathan Harris

Director: Boris Segal

Shadow Play

w Charles Beaumont
A condemned man tries to convince the people around him that everything—and everyone—is merely part of a recurring nightmare that always ends in his execution.
Cast: Dennis Weaver, Harry Townes, Wright King

Director: John Brahm

The Mind and the Matter

w Rod Serling
A book about thought gives a clerk the power to accomplish anything just by willing it, leaving him free to create an ideal world.
Cast: Shelley Berman, Jack Grinnage, Jeane Wood, Chet Stratton

Director: Buzz Kulik

Will the Real Martian Please Stand Up

w Rod Serling
Seven people at a diner claim to be authentic Earthmen—but one of them is really a Martian.
Cast: Morgan Jones, John Archer, Bill Kendis, John Hoyt, Jack Elam, Jean Wiles, Barney Phillips

Director: Montgomery Pittman

The Obsolete Man

w Rod Serling
A librarian in a future society is declared obsolete and told he must die.
Cast: Burgess Meredith, Fritz Weaver

Director: Elliot Silverstein

Season Three
37 30-minute episodes

Two

w Montgomery Pittman
A man and a woman, sole survivors of a nuclear holocaust, try to overcome their distrust and start the world anew.
Cast: Charles Bronson, Elizabeth Montgomery

The Arrival

w Rod Serling
An airline official tests his theory that a newly arrived but totally empty plane is imaginary—with startling results.
Cast: Harold J. Stone, Robert Karnes, Jim Boles, Fredd Wayne, Bing Russell, Noah Keen, Robert Brubaker

Director: Boris Segal

The Shelter

w Rod Serling
A group of neighbors turns into a hostile mob when they try to invade one family's bomb shelter, believing a nuclear attack is imminent.

Cast: Larry Gates, Peggy Stewart, Michael Burns, Jack Albertson, John McLiam, Jo Helton, Joseph Bernard, Moira Turner, Sandy Kenyon, Mary Gregory

Director: Lamont Johnson

The Passersby

w Rod Serling
A crippled Civil War soldier comes to realize that he and the people around him are not walking away from battle—they are dead.
Cast: James Gregory, Joanne Linville, Austin Green, Rex Holman, David Garcia, Warren Kemmerling

Director: Elliot Silverstein

A Game of Pool

w George Clayton Johnson
A pool master returns from the dead to play one last game with an eager young hustler for the highest stakes of all—the young man's life.
Cast: Jack Klugman, Jonathan Winters

Director: A. E. Houghton

The Mirror

w Rod Serling
A victorious revolutionary is shown a mirror in the presidential office that is reputed to show the watcher his own assassins.
Cast: Peter Falk, Richard Karlan, Tony Carbone, Val Ruffino, Arthur Batanides, Rodolfo Hoyos, Will Kuluva, Vladimir Sokoloff

Director: Don Medford

The Grave

w Montgomery Pittman
A hired gunman defies a Western outlaw's warning that if he ever came near his grave he'd reach up and snatch away his life.
Cast: Lee Marvin, Strother Martin, Lee Van Cleef, Stafford Repp, Richard Geary, James Best, Ellen Willrad, William Challee, Larry Johns

Director: Montgomery Pittman

It's a Good Life

w Rod Serling, *story by* Jerome Bixby
A six-year-old boy holds a town in terror with his powers to change or destroy anyone or anything at will.
Cast: Billy Mumy, Cloris Leachman, Alice Frost, Jeanne Bates, Casey Adams, John Larch, Tom Batcher, Don Keefer, Lenore Kingston

Director: James Sheldon

Deaths-Head Revisited

w Rod Serling
A former Nazi is tried and sentenced to insanity by a phantom jury of his tortured victims, when he revisits Dachau concentration camp.
Cast: Oscar Beregi, Joseph Schildkraut, Ben Wright, Karen Verne, Chuck Fox, Robert Boone

Director: Don Medford

The Midnight Sun

w Rod Serling
The Earth has fallen out of its orbit and is drawing closer to the Sun—inflicting ever increasing heat on its citizens.
Cast: Lois Nettleton, Betty Garde, Jason Wingreen, Ned Glass, June Ellis, John McLiam, William Keene, Robert J. Stevenson, Tom Reese

Director: Anton Leader

Still Valley

w Rod Serling, *story by* Manly Wade Wellman
A troop of Confederate soldiers declines to use a magical book that could guarantee their victory, because it would mean making a pact with the devil.
Cast: Gary Merrill, Jack Mann, Addison Myers, Ben Cooper, Vaughn Taylor, Mark Tapscott

Director: James Sheldon

The Jungle

w Charles Beaumont
A prospector, threatened with death by a native conjuror for violating African land, feels himself stalked in the deserted streets of Manhattan by some giant jungle beast.
Cast: John Dehner, Emily McLaughlin, Walter Brooke, Jay Adler, Hugh Sanders, Howard Wright, Donald Foster, Jay Overholts

Director: William Claxton

Once Upon a Time

w Richard Matheson
Nineteenth-century janitor Woodrow Mulligan tries on a time "helmet" invented by his boss and is catapulted 72 years into the future. (Featured two of comedian Buster Keaton's most memorable routines—the lock step and putting on a pair of trousers while walking.)
Cast: Buster Keaton *(Mulligan)*, Gil Lamb, James Flavin, Milton Parsons, Stanley Adams, Warren Parker, George E. Stone

Directors: Norman Z. McLeod *&* Les Goodwins *(uncredited)*

Five Characters in Search of an Exit

w Rod Serling, *story by* Marvin Petal
Five people—a ballet dancer, a major, a clown, a tramp and a bagpipe player—trapped in a deep enclosure, are revealed to be dolls due to be distributed to orphans at Christmas.
Cast: Bill Windom, Susan Harrison, Clark Allen, Murray Matheson, Kelton Garwood, Mona Houghton, Carol Hill

Director: Lamont Johnson

A Quality of Mercy

w Rod Serling, *idea by* Sam Rolfe
A fanatical soldier sees the futility of his militaristic thinking when he mysteriously experiences the situation through the eyes of his Japanese counterpart.
Cast: Dean Stockwell, Albert Salmi, Rayford Barnes, Leonard Nimoy, Michael Pataki, Ralph Votrian, Dale Ishimoto, Jerry Fujikawa

Director: Buzz Kulik

Nothing in the Dark

w George Clayton Johnson
An aged recluse barricades herself in an abandoned building to avoid meeting "Mr. Death."
Cast: Gladys Cooper, Robert Redford, R.G. Armstrong

Director: Lamont Johnson

One More Pallbearer

w Rod Serling
A wealthy man devises an elaborate hoax to force three people to apologize for humiliating him earlier in his life.
Cast: Joseph Wiseman, Gage Clark, Trevor Bardette, Katherine Squire, Josip Elic, Ray Galvin, Robert Snyder

Director: Lamont Johnson

Dead Man's Shoes

w Charles Beaumont *&* O. Cee Ritch *(uncredited)*
A down-and-out man steals the fancy shoes from the body of a murdered gangster and finds himself living in the dead man's footsteps.
Cast: Warren Stevens, Ben Wright, Harry Swoger, Joan Marshall, Eugene Borden, Richard Devon, Florence Marly, Ron Hagerthy, Joe Mell

Director: Montgomery Pittman

The Hunt

w Earl Hamner Jr.

A hunter and his faithful dog are drowned while chasing a raccoon, and confront a gatekeeper who implies that he is St. Peter and that Heaven lies inside. But when the dog declines to enter, the hunter wisely decides to stay with his trusty companion.

Cast: Arthur Hunnicutt, Titus Moede, Charles Seel, Dexter Dupont, Jeanette Nolan, Orville Sherman, Robert Foulk

Director: Harold Schuster

Showdown with Rance McGrew

w Rod Serling, *idea by* Frederic Louis Fox

The ghost of Jesse James takes revenge on an insufferable cowboy star for his shabby film treatment of all the bad guys.

Cast: Larry Blyden, Troy Melton, Robert J. Stevenson, Arch Johnson *(Jesse)*, Hal K. Dawson, William McLean, Jay Overholts, Robert Cornthwaite, Robert Kline

Director: Christian Nyby

Kick the Can

w George Clayton Johnson

The magic of a children's game enables a group of old people to recapture their youth.

Cast: Ernest Truex, Hank Patterson, Russell Collins, Earle Hodgins, Burt Mustin, Gregory McCabe, Marjorie Bennett, Lenore Shanewise, Anne O'Neal, John Marley, Barry Truex, Eve McVeagh, Marc Stevens

Director: Lamont Johnson

A Piano in the House

w Earl Hamner Jr.

A strange piano allows the listener's hidden character to be suddenly revealed.

Cast: Barry Morse, Joan Hackett, Muriel Landers, Don Durant, Phil Coolidge, Cyril Delevanti

Director: David Greene

The Last Rites of Jeff Myrtlebank

w Montgomery Pittman

When a young man steps out of his coffin at his own funeral the townsfolk grow to suspect that the devil has assumed the man's body.

Cast: James Best, Ralph Moody, Ezelle Poule, Vickie Barnes, Sherry Jackson, Helen Wallace, Lance Fuller, Bill Fawcett, Edgar Buchanan, Mabel Forrest, Dub Taylor, Jon Lormer, Pat Hector

Director: Montgomery Pittman

To Serve Man

w Rod Serling, *story by* Damon Knight

Apparently benign alien emissaries show mankind how to end the misery of war, plague and famine. But the aliens' master manual for Earth turns out to be a cookbook.

Cast: Richard Kiel, Hardie Albright, Robert Tafur, Lloyd Bochner, Lomax Study, Theodore Marcuse, Susan Cummings, Nelson Olmstead

Director: Richard L. Bare

The Fugitive

w Charles Beaumont

A magical old man whose power to change his appearance delights the local children is really the revered king of another planet.

Cast: J. Pat O'Malley, Nancy Kulp, Susan Gordon, Russ Bender, Wesley Lau, Paul Tripp, Stephen Talbot, Johnny Eiman

Director: Richard L. Bare

Little Girl Lost

w Richard Matheson

A couple is awakened in the middle of the night by the cries of their six-year-old daughter who has fallen through a mysterious door into another dimension.

Cast: Sarah Marshall, Robert Sampson, Tracy Stratford, Charles Aidman

Director: Paul Stewart

Person or Persons Unknown

w Charles Beaumont

A man awakens one morning to find that no one recognizes him—not even his mother!

Cast: Richard Long, Frank Silvera, Shirley Ballard, Julie Van Zandt, Betty Harford, Ed Glover, Michael Kelp, Joe Higgins, John Newton

Director: John Brahm

The Little People

w Rod Serling

A space traveler terrorizes the tiny inhabitants of a space station into accepting him as their God, but when another space ship arrives the tyrannical man discovers everything is relative . . .

Cast: Joe Maross, Claude Akins, Michael Ford, Robert Eaton

Director: William Claxton

Four O'Clock

w Rod Serling, *story by* Price Day
To combat all that he considers evil, a cranky man decides to make every evil person two feet tall at exactly 4:00 P.M.
Cast: Theodore Bikel, Linden Chiles, Moyna MacGill, Phyllis Love

Director: Lamont Johnson

Hocus Pocus and Frisby

w Rod Serling, *story by* Frederic Louis Fox
A celebrated yarn-spinner finds no one will believe his latest tale—that he was kidnapped by aliens.
Cast: Andy Devine, Howard McNear, Clem Bevans, Milton Selzer, Dabbs Greer, Larry Breitman, Peter Brocco

Director: Lamont Johnson

The Trade-Ins

w Rod Serling
Unable to afford a personality transplant for both himself and his wife, a pain-wracked old man has his mind placed in a new youthful body only to find he cannot face life without the companionship of his beloved wife.
Cast: Joseph Schildkraut, Alma Platt, Noah Keen, Theodore Marcuse, Terence de Marney, Billy Vincent, Mary McMahon, David Armstrong, Edson Stroll

Director: Elliot Silverstein

The Gift

w Rod Serling
A crashed space traveler is hounded to death by mistrustful villagers who discover, too late, that the gift he bore was a formula to cure all types of cancer.
Cast: Geoffrey Horne, Nico Minardos, Cliff Osmond, Edmund Vargas, Carmen D'Antonio, Paul Mazursky, Vladimir Sokoloff, Vito Scotti, Henry Corden

Director: Allen H. Miner

The Dummy

w Rod Serling, *story by* Lee Polk
A ventriloquist becomes convinced that his dummy has a will and a life of its own.
Cast: Cliff Robertson, Frank Sutton, George Murdock, Bethelynn Grey, John Harmon, Sandra Warner, Rudy Dolan, Ralph Manza

Director: Abner Biberman

Young Man's Fancy

w Richard Matheson
A man's intense longing for the happy days of his boyhood succeeds in actually making the past reappear—to the chagrin of his new bride.
Cast: Alex Nicol, Phyllis Thaxter, Wallace Rooney, Rickey Kelman, Helen Brown

Director: John Brahm

I Sing the Body Electric

w Ray Bradbury
A widowed father buys his three young children an electronic grandmother to the delight of all but one of them—until she comes to realize that electric grandmas have feelings, too.
Cast: Josephine Hutchinson, David White, June Vincent, Vaughn Taylor, Judy Morton, Dana Dillaway, Paul Nesbitt, Charles Herbert, Veronica Cartwright, Susan Crane

Directors: James Sheldon & William Claxton

Cavender Is Coming

w Rod Serling
A hapless apprentice angel is given one last chance to win his wings—by helping awkward, inept Agnes Grep. (Pilot for an unmade series—with laugh track.)
Cast: Carol Burnett *(Agnes)*, Jesse White, Howard Smith, William O'Connell, Pitt Herbert, John Fiedler, G. Stanley Jones, Frank Behrens, Albert Carrier, Roy Sickner, Norma Shattuc, Rory O'Brien, Sandra Gould, Adrienne Marden, Jack Younger, Danny Kulick, Donna Douglas, Maurice Dallimore, Barbara Morrison

Director: Chris Nyby

The Changing of the Guard

w Rod Serling
A well-loved teacher feels his useful life is over when he is asked to retire.
Cast: Donald Pleasence, Liam Sullivan, Philippa Bevans, Kevin O'Neal, Jimmy Baird, Kevin Jones, Bob Biheller, Tom Lowell, Russell Horton, Buddy Hart, Darryl Richard, James Browning, Pat Close, Dennis Kerlee

Director: Robert Ellis Miller

Season Four

18 One-hour episodes
Series now became known simply as *Twilight Zone.*

In His Image

w Charles Beaumont
A scientific genius creates an almost-perfect mechanical man, combining all the qualities he feels are missing in his own imperfect, human self.
Cast: George Grizzard, Gail Kobe, Katherine Squire, Wallace Rooney, George Petrie, James Seay, Jamie Forster, Sherry Granato

Director: Perry Lafferty

The Thirty-Fathom Grave

w Rod Serling
Sounds heard from a submarine sunk 20 years before cause the death of the man who believes himself responsible for the sinking.
Cast: Mike Kellin, Simon Oakland, David Sheiner, John Considine, Bill Bixby, Conlan Carter, Forrest Compton

Director: Perry Lafferty

Valley of the Shadow

w Charles Beaumont
A reporter comes upon a peaceful village that guards the secret of creating and obliterating matter. Once he learns the secret, it takes another miracle to release him from the responsibility of the knowledge.
Cast: David Opatoshu, Ed Nelson, Natalie Trundy, Jacques Aubuchon, Dabbs Greer, Suzanne Cupito, James Doohan

Director: Perry Lafferty

He's Alive

w Rod Serling
The ghost of Adolf Hitler inspires a young American hate-monger to achieve a short-lived success.
Cast: Dennis Hopper, Ludwig Donath, Paul Mazursky, Howard Cain, Barnaby Hale, Curt Conway, Jay Adler, Wolfe Barzell, Bernard Fein

Director: Stuart Rosenberg

Mute

w Richard Matheson
Experimenting with the powers of telepathy, a couple raise their daughter in a world free of verbal communication. But when they die she faces a world with which she cannot communicate.
Cast: Barbara Baxley, Frank Overton, Irene Dailey, Ann Jillian, Eva Soreny, Oscar Beregi, Claudia Bryar, Percy Helton

Director: Stuart Rosenberg

Death Ship

w Richard Matheson
A man's refusal to admit to his own death keeps him and his two companions alive in a world that has accepted their passing.
Cast: Jack Klugman, Ross Martin, Frederick Beir, Mary Webster, Ross Elliot, Sara Taft

Director: Don Medford

Jess-Belle

w Earl Hamner Jr.
A girl strikes a deadly bargain with a witch to assure the attention of a young man.
Cast: Anne Francis, James Best, Laura Devon, Jeanette Nolan, Virginia Gregg, George Mitchell, Helen Kleeb, Jim Boles, Jon Lormer

Director: Buzz Kulik

Miniature

w Charles Beaumont
Charley Parkes, a shy bachelor, falls in love with a tiny, beautiful museum doll who he believes is alive. (Parts of this episode have since been "colorized.")
Cast: Robert Duvall *(Parkes)*, Pert Kelton, Barbara Barrie, Len Weinrib, William Windom, John McLiam, Claire Griswold, Nina Roman, Richard Angarola, Barney Phillips, Joan Chambers, Chet Stratlon

Director: Walter E. Grauman

Printer's Devil

w Charles Beaumont
A newspaper editor who is facing bankruptcy hires the Devil as his chief reporter.
Cast: Robert Sterling, Patricia Crowley, Burgess Meredith, Ray Teal, Charles Thompson, Doris Kemper, Camille Franklin

Director: Ralph Senensky

No Time Like the Past

w Rod Serling
A time traveler attempts to alter history by vainly trying to warn the people of Hiroshima, assassinate Hitler, and persuade the captain of the *Lusitania* to change course.
Cast: Dana Andrews, Patricia Breslin, Malcolm Atterbury, Robert Cornthwaite, John Zaremba, Robert F. Simon, Lindsay Workman, Marjorie Bennett, Tudor Owen, James Yagi

Director: Justus Addis

The Parallel

w Rod Serling
An orbiting astronaut passes into a strange parallel world.
Cast: Steve Forrest, Jacqueline Scott, Frank Aletter, Philip Abbott, Shari Lee Bernath, Paul Comi, Morgan Jones, William Sargent

Director: Alan Crosland

I Dream of Genie

w John Furia Jr.
A mild-mannered clerk finds Aladdin's lamp but decides that using his one wish for wealth, power or the girl of his dreams would be a waste of the lamp's power.
Cast: Howard Morris, Patricia Barry, Loring Smith, Mark Miller, Jack Albertson, Joyce Jameson, James Milhollin, Bob Hastings, Robert Ball

Director: Robert Gist

The New Exhibit

w Charles Beaumont & Jerry Sohl *(uncredited)*
Discarded by a wax museum, the effigies of famous murderers kill people who would part them from their custodian, and when the custodian spurns them they murder him as well.
Cast: Martin Balsam, Will Kuluva, Maggie Mahoney, William Mims, Milton Parsons

Director: John Brahm

Of Late I Think of Cliffordville

w Rod Serling, *story by* Malcolm Jameson
A ruthless captain of industry strikes a deal with the Devil and goes back in time to the life he remembers as a young man.
Cast: Albert Salmi, John Anderson, Julie Newmar, Wright King, Guy Raymond, Christine Burke

Director: David Rich

The Incredible World of Horace Ford

w Reginald Rose
A toy manufacturer recalls his youth with such longing that he becomes a boy again.
Cast: Pat Hingle, Nan Martin, Ruth White, Philip Pine, Vaughn Taylor, Mary Carver

Director: Abner Biberman

On Thursday We Leave for Home

w Rod Serling
The leader of an expedition to a remote asteroid cannot bring himself to face the dissipation of his authority that returning to Earth would bring.
Cast: James Whitmore, Tim O'Connor, James Broderick, Paul Langton, Jo Helton, Mercedes Shirley, Russ Bender

Director: Buzz Kulik

Passage on the *Lady Anne*

w Charles Beaumont
An unhappily married old couple finds love when they sail the Atlantic aboard an old ship that was originally designed for honeymooners.
Cast: Gladys Cooper, Wilfrid Hyde-White, Cecil Kellaway, Lee Philips, Joyce Van Patten

Director: Lamont Johnson

The Bard

w Rod Serling
A hack TV writer conjures up William Shakespeare to act as his collaborator but his network bosses throw out the final script.
Cast: Jack Weston, John McGiver, Diro Merande, John Williams, Burt Reynolds, Henry Lascoe, William Lanteau, Howard McNear, Marge Redmond, Clegg Hoyt, Judy Strangis

Director: David Butler

Season Five
36 half-hour episodes

In Praise of Pip

w Rod Serling
Bookie Max Phillips learn that his, son Pip, has been critically wounded in Vietnam. Remorseful over the way he raised him, Max pleads with God to take his life in place of his son's.
Cast: Jack Klugman *(Max)*, Billy Mumy *(young Pip)*, Kreg Martin, Ross Elliott, Stuart Nisbet, Russell Horton, Connie Gilchrist, Bob Diamond, John Launer, Gerald Gordon

Director: Joseph M. Newman

Steel

w Richard Matheson
A small-time promoter, desperate for his purse from a robot prize fight, takes the place of his robot when it gets damaged.
Cast: Lee Marvin, Joe Mantell, Merritt Bohn, Frank London, Tipp McClure, Chuck Hicks, Larry Barton

Director: Don Weis

Nightmare at 20,000 Feet

w Richard Matheson
A newly released mental patient is the only one able to see a gremlin ripping up the wing of his airliner.
Cast: William Shatner, Edward Kemmer, Christine White, Asa Maynor, Nick Cravat

Director: Richard Donner

A Kind of Stopwatch

w Rod Serling, story by Michael D. Rosenthal
A talkative man acquires a stopwatch with the power to halt all other action in the world.
Cast: Richard Erdman, Leon Balasco, Herbie Faye, Roy Roberts, Doris Singleton, Richard Wessel, Ken Drake, Ray Kellogg, Sam Balter

Director: John Rich

The Last Night of a Jockey

w Rod Serling
A down-and-out jockey yearns to be a giant of a man so that everyone would look up at him.
Cast: Mickey Rooney

Director: Joseph M. Newman

Living Doll

w Charles Beaumont & Jerry Sohl (uncredited)
A man is threatened with revenge by the expensive talking doll he is planning to dispose of.
Cast: Telly Savalas, Tracy Stratford, Mary LaRoche

Director: Richard C. Sarafian

The Old Man in the Cave

w Rod Serling, story by Henry Slesar
A small community has survived the aftermath of a nuclear holocaust by accepting the advice of The Old Man in the Cave.
Cast: James Coburn, John Anderson, Josie Lloyd, John Craven, Natalie Masters, John Marley, Frank Watkins, Don Wilbanks, Lenny Geer

Director: Alan Crosland Jr.

Uncle Simon

w Rod Serling
A woman learns that she has inherited the estate of the uncle she left to die provided she looks after his latest invention—a robot that mysteriously takes on the nature of her dead uncle.
Cast: Sir Cedric Hardwicke, Constance Ford, John McLiam, Ian Wolfe

Director: Don Siegel

Night Call

w Richard Matheson
A bedridden spinster receives mysterious phone calls from her long-dead fiancé.
Cast: Gladys Cooper, Nora Marlowe, Martine Bartlett

Director: Jacques Tourneau

Probe 7—Over and Out

w Rod Serling
The lone survivors of two devastated planets meet on a new world, Earth, and introduce themselves—as Adam Cook and Eve Norda.
Cast: Richard Basehart, Antoinette Bower, Barton Heyman, Harold Gould

Director: Ted Post

The 7th Is Made Up of Phantoms

w Rod Serling
During maneuvers near the site of Custer's Last Stand, three national guardsmen find themselves plunged into the battle of the Little Big Horn.
Cast: Ron Foster, Warren Oates, Randy Boone, Robert Bray, Wayne Mallory, Greg Morris, Jeffrey Morris, Jacque Shelton, Lew Brown

Director: Alan Crosland Jr.

A Short Drink from a Certain Fountain

w Rod Serling, idea by Lou Holtz
A wealthy man begs his doctor-brother to inject him with an experimental youth serum—but ends up regressing into an infant.
Cast: Patrick O'Neal, Ruta Lee, Walter Brooks

Director: Bernard Girard

Ninety Years without Slumbering

w Richard DeRoy, story by George Clayton Johnson
An old man believes that his life will end the moment his grandfather clock stops ticking.
Cast: Ed Wynn, Carolyn Kearney, James Callahan, William Sargent, Carol Byron, John Pickard, Dick Wilson, Chuck Hicks

Director: Roger Kay

Ring-a-Ding Girl

w Earl Hamner Jr.
A movie star receives a gift from her hometown fan club that shows her images of the future.
Cast: Maggie McNamara, Mary Munday, David Macklin, George Mitchell, Bing Russell, Betty Lou Gerson, Hank Patterson, Bill Hickman, Vic Perrin

Director: Alan Crosland Jr.

You Drive

w Earl Hamner Jr.
A motorist's car won't let him forget his guilt over killing a young cyclist and fleeing from the scene.
Cast: Edward Andrews, Kevin Hagen, Hellena Westcott, Totty Ames, John Hanek

Director: John Brahm

The Long Morrow

w Rod Serling
A deep-space probe astronaut smashes the suspended animation device that will keep him young, so that he can age at the same rate as the woman he loves.
Cast: Robert Lansing, Mariette Hartley, George MacReady, Edward Binns, William Swan

Director: Robert Florey

The Self-Improvement of Salvadore Ross

w Jerry McNeeley, story by Henry Slesar
A man finds he has the power to trade character traits, infirmities, even his lifespan, with others.
Cast: Don Gordon, Gail Kobe, Vaughn Taylor, Douglas Dumbrille, Doug Lambert, J. Pat O'Malley, Ted Jacques, Kathleen O'Malley, Seymour Cassel

Director: Don Siegel

Number Twelve Looks Just Like You

w Charles Beaumont & John Tomerlin (uncredited)
A young woman resists pressure to be transformed into a state-controlled image of flawless beauty.
Cast: Suzy Parker, Collin Wilcox, Richard Long, Pam Austin

Director: Abner Biberman

Black Leather Jackets

w Earl Hamner Jr.
An advance party of an alien invasion force arrive in a quiet residential neighborhood disguised as leather-jacketed youths.

Cast: Lee Kinsolving, Shelly Fabares, Michael Forest, Wayne Heffley, Tom Gilleran, Denver Pyle, Irene Hervey, Michael Conrad

Director: Joseph Newman

From Agnes—With Love

w Bernard C. Shoenfeld
A computer programmer grows to realize that under the stainless steel exterior of the world's most advanced computer is the complex soul of a jealous woman who has fallen in love with him.
Cast: Wally Cox, Ralph Taeger, Sue Randall, Raymond Bailey, Don Keefer, Byron Kane, Nan Peterson

Director: Richard Donner

Spur of the Moment

w Richard Matheson
A young woman out riding fails to understand the significance of an encounter with her future, older self—until it is too late.
Cast: Diana Hyland, Marsha Hunt, Philip Ober, Roger Davis, Robert Hogan, Jack Raine

Director: Elliot Silverstein

An Occurrence at Owl Creek Bridge

w Robert Enrico, story by Ambrose Bierce
A Confederate spy is to hang in the civil war but appears to make a miraculous escape. (This was an award-winning French film recut for the series.)
Cast: Roger Jacquet, Anne Cornaly

Director: Robert Enrico

Queen of the Nile

w Charles Beaumont & Jerry Sohl (uncredited)
A magazine writer is determined to discover the secret of an ageless movie star's everlasting youth.
Cast: Ann Blyth, Lee Philips, James Tyler, Celia Lovsky, Ruth Phillips, Frank Ferguson

Director: John Brahm

What's in the Box

w Martin M. Goldsmith
A cab driver turns on the television and sees a portent of his wife's death after an argument. When he tries to tell his wife she won't listen and an argument starts . . .
Cast: Joan Blondell, William Demarest, Sterling Holloway, Herbert Lytton, Howard Wright, Ron Stokes, John L. Sullivan, Sandra Gould, Ted Christy, Douglas Bank, Tony Miller

Director: Richard L. Baer

The Masks

w Rod Serling

A wealthy old man compels his hateful family to wear masks they think are the opposite of their personalities. When they remove the masks a frightening change has taken place.

Cast: Robert Keith, Milton Selzer, Brooke Hayward, Virginia Gregg, Alan Sues, Bill Walker, Willis Bouchey

Director: Ida Lupino

I Am the Night—Color Me Black

w Rod Serling

The sun fails to rise on the morning that a town's "idealist" is due to be executed for killing one of his bigoted neighbors, and the community finds itself locked in the darkness of hate.

Cast: Michael Constantine, Paul Fix, George Lindsey, Terry Becker, Douglas Bank, Ward Wood, Eve McVeagh, Elizabeth Harrower, Ivan Dixon

Director: Abner Biberman

Sounds and Silences

w Rod Serling

A man who has lived his life joyously surrounded by loud noise suddenly finds that trivial sounds, such as dripping water, begin to drive him insane.

Cast: John McGiver, Penny Singleton, Michael Fox, Francis Defales, Renee Aubrey, William Benedict

Director: Richard Donner

Caesar and Me

w A. T. Strassfield

An impoverished ventriloquist accedes to his dummy's demands that he turn to crime to make some money.

Cast: Jackie Cooper, Susanne Cupito, Stafford Repp, Olan Soule, Sarah Selby, Don Gazzaniga, Sidney Marion, Ken Konopka

Director: Robert Butler

The Jeopardy Room

w Rod Serling

A KGB agent sent to kill a Russian defector plants a bomb in the man's hotel room and gives him three hours to find and disarm it and so win his freedom, or fail and die.

Cast: Martin Landau, John van Dreelen, Robert Kelljan

Director: Richard Donner

Stopover in a Quiet Town

w Earl Hamner Jr.

A young married couple awakes to find themselves in an unfamiliar artificial environment. As a giant hand starts reaching for them out of the sky, they hear the sound of a child's laughter.

Cast: Barry Nelson, Karen Norris, Nancy Malone, Denise Lyon

Director: Ron Winston

The Encounter

w Martin M. Goldsmith

A Japanese gardener finds that a samurai sword has vowed to avenge the murder of its master.

Cast: Neville Brand, George Takei

Director: Robert Butler

Mr. Garrity and the Graves

w Rod Serling, story by Mila Korologos

A con man convinces the inhabitants of a Western town that he can raise the dead from the local cemetery.

Cast: John Dehner, Stanley Adams, J. Pat O'Malley, Norman Leavitt, Percy Helton, John Mitchum, Patrick O'Moore, Kate Murtagh, John Cliff

Director: Ted Post

The Brain Center at Whipple's

w Rod Serling

A heartless industrialist fires his entire factory staff and replaces them with machines. Then the machines start acting mischievously.

Cast: Richard Deacon, Paul Newlan, Shawn Michaels, Ted de Corsia, Burt Conroy, Jack Crowder

Director: Richard Donner

Come Wander with Me

w Anton Wilson

A bogus folk singer persuades a backwoods girl to sing an authentic ballad into his tape recorder—and finds the song coming tragically true.

Cast: Gary Crosby, Bonnie Beecher, John Bolt, Hank Patterson

Director: Richard Donner

The Fear

w Rod Serling
A state trooper and an unstable woman both think they have found traces of a giant visitor from outer space.
Cast: Mark Richman, Hazel Court

Director: Ted Post

The Bewitchin' Pool

w Earl Hamner Jr.
Two unloved children escape from their squabbling parents to a world that offers them a chance of happiness with a strange, kindly woman.
Cast: Mary Badham, Tim Stafford, Kim Hector, Tod Andrews, Dee Hartford, Georgia Simmons, Harold Gould

Director: Joseph Newman

THE TWILIGHT ZONE (1985–86)

What's in a name? Everything, as far as this 1980s revival of a television icon is concerned.

It's not been a runaway commercial success and has never achieved the heights of critical acclaim reached by Rod Serling's original, but while it lacks his cohesive presence it's not at all bad. Some stories are excellent and many are a sight more entertaining then much of today's prime-time TV.

Many of the industry's top names have brought their talents to bear—casts have included Bruce Willis, Danny Kaye, Elliot Gould, Tom Skerritt, Ralph Bellamy, Richard Mulligan, Martin Landau and M. Emmet Walsh, while Joe Dante, John Milius and William Friedkin are among the directors.

Besides many original scripts, the series culled short stories from leading sf writers as well as indulging in a few remakes of tales from the old Zone.

Creator: Rod Serling
Narrator: Charles Aidman
Executive producer: Philip DeGuere
Supervising producer: James Crocker
Producer: Harvey Frand
Executive story consultant: Alan Brennert
Story editor: Rockne S. O'Bannon
Creative consultant: Harlan Ellison
Special effects coordinator: M. Kam Cooney

New main title theme: Grateful Dead *and* Merl Saunders
CBS Broadcast International Production
Series One (U.S.): 24 color 60-minute episodes (autumn 1985)
Series Two: 19 color 30-minute episodes
(A third series of 30 episodes followed.)
U.K. premiere: 17 October 1987
(STV)

Series One
(one-hour episodes)

Shatterday

w Alan Brennert, *story by* Harlan Ellison
Jay Nolan absent-mindedly dials his home number from a bar and is jolted when the phone is picked up by . . . Jay Novins.
Cast: Bruce Willis

Director: Wes Craven

A Little Peace and Quiet

w James Crocker
A harried wife and mother yearns for silence—a wish that comes horrifyingly true when she chances upon a way to "freeze" time and motion.
Cast: Melinda Dillon

Director: Wes Craven

Word Play

w Rockne S. O'Bannon
An overburdened salesman thinks he's losing his sanity when everyone's speech gradually becomes gibberish to him.
Cast: Robert Klein, Annie Potts

Director: Wes Craven

Dreams for Sale

w Joe Gannon
A young woman goes on a picnic with her husband and twin daughters, where everything is so nearly perfect it seems too good to be true.
Cast: Meg Foster, David Hayward

Director: Tommy Lee Wallace

Chameleon

w James Crocker
A space shuttle returns from a mission with something on board that wasn't there when it was launched.
Cast: John Ashton, Ben Piazza, Terrence O'Quinn

Director: Wes Craven

Healer

w Alan Brennert
A young drifter becomes an overnight sensation as a hands-on healer after he steals an ancient Mayan stone that holds magic powers.
Cast: Eric Bogosian, Vincent Gardenia

Director: Sig Neufeld

Children's Zoo

w Chris Hubbell & Gerrit Graham
A withdrawn little girl, caught between combative parents, receives an invitation to a most unusual zoo.
Cast: Steven Keats, Lorna Luft

Director: Robert Downey

Kentucky Rye

w Richard Krzemien & Chip Duncan
A salesman with a drink problem who takes refuge in a bar after getting involved in a car crash is offered the deal of a lifetime.
Cast: Jeffrey Demunn

Director: John Hancock

Little Boy Lost

w Lynn Barker
A professional photographer on the verge of a major career move finds she has been taking pictures of her own alternative future.
Cast: Season Hubley, Nicholas Surovy

Director: Tommy Lee Wallace

Wish Bank

w Michael Cassut
A bargain hunter finds an Aladdin's lamp at a jumble sale, rubs it and is amazed to discover she will be granted three wishes. However, certain restrictions apply . . .
Cast: Dee Wallace

Director: Rick Friedberg

Night Crawlers

w Philip DeGuere
A Vietnam veteran haunted by his memories of war is terrified of falling asleep in case his nightmares come true.
Cast: Scott Paulin

Director: William Friedkin

If She Dies

w David Bennet Carren
A distraught father whose young daughter lies in a coma is drawn to a strange apparition in an abandoned orphanage.
Cast: Tony Lo Bianco

Director: John Hancock

Ye Gods

w Anne Collins
An up-and-coming executive suffering the pangs of unrequited love discovers that Cupid and the other gods of Olympus are alive—but with hang-ups of their own.
Cast: David Dukes, Robert Morse

Director: Peter Medak

Examination Day

w Philip DeGuere, *story by* Henry Slesar
Tale set in the future. A 12-year-old boy's birthday wish, to get a good mark in a government exam, makes his parents uneasy.
Cast: Christopher Allpost, Elizabeth Normant, David Mendenhall

Director: Paul Lynch

A Message From Charity

w Alan Brennert, *story by* William M. Lee
Peter, a boy living in present-day Massachusetts, makes telepathic contact with Charity, a Puritan girl from the past, and each experiences the world through the other's eyes.
Cast: Robert Duncan McNeill, Kerry Noonan

Director: Paul Lynch

Teacher's Aide

w Steven Barnes
An English teacher at a school terrorized by a teenage gang falls under the spell of a gargoyle-like demon.
Cast: Adrienne Barbeau

Director: Bill Norton

Paladin of the Lost Hour

w Harlan Ellison
An old man who holds the last hour of the world in a magical timepiece finds an unlikely keeper to assume the awesome responsibility.
Cast: Danny Kaye, Glynn Turman

Director: Gilbert Cates

Act Break

w Haskell Barkin
A mediocre playwright, given a magic amulet by his dying partner, makes the one wish that will grant him dramatic immortality.
Cast: James Coco, Bob Dishy

Director: Ted Flicker

The Burning Man

w J. D. Feigelson, *story by* Ray Bradbury
An aunt and her nephew, picnicking in the country on a scorching hot day, meets a crazed raggedy man who talks of "genetic evil."
Cast: Piper Laurie, Roberts Blossom

Director: J.D. Feigelson

Dealer's Choice

w Don Todd
The Devil sits in on a friendly poker game in New Jersey.
Cast: Garret Morris, Dan Hedaya, M. Emmet Walsh, Morgan Freeman

Director: Wes Craven

Dead Woman's Shoes

w Lyn Barker, *story by* Charles Beaumont
Reworking of a 1961 *Zone* story, "Dead Man's Shoes," in which a derelict inherited a gangster's life along with his shoes. This time a timid clerk slips on a pair of shoes once owned by a woman who was murdered, and becomes possessed by the victim's vengeful spirit.
Cast: Helen Mirren, Theresa Saldana, Jeffrey Tambor

Director: Peter Medak

Wong's Lost and Found Emporium

w Alan Brennert, *story by* William F. Wu
A young man seeking answers to his bitter questions stumbles upon a warehouse in another dimension, where everything that's ever been lost is stored.
Cast: Brian Tochi, Anna Maria Poon

Director: Paul Lynch

The Shadow Man

w Rochne S. O'Bannon
A timid 13-year-old boy, desperate to impress a beautiful classmate, finds a macabre ally in the Shadow Man, a ghoulish figure who emerges nightly from beneath his bed. But he gets *too* cocky.
Cast: Jonathan Ward, Heather Haase, Jeff Calhoun

Director: Joe Dante

The Uncle Devil Show

w Don Todd
A boy's parents have no idea what devilish tricks their young son will learn from the video of *Tim Ferret and Friends* they've rented for him.
Cast: Murphy Dunne

Director: David Steinberg

Opening Day

w Chris Hubbell & Gerrit Graham
Joe Farrell murders his lover's husband and then finds that he has somehow replaced him in a new loop of time.
Cast: Jeffrey Jones, Martin Kove

Director: John Milius

The Beacon

w Martin Pasko & Rebecca Parr
A doctor whose car breaks down on a deserted ocean road comes across the village of Bellwether, which has an eerie lighthouse that only shines inland.
Cast: Martin Landau, Cheryl Anderson, Charles Martin Smith

Director: Gerd Oswald

One Life, Furnished in Early Poverty

w Alan Brennert, *story by* Harlan Ellison
A writer who returns to his childhood home in search of the emblem of youth is transported back in time to when he was a boy.
Cast: Peter Reigert, Jack Kehoe, Chris Hebert

Director: Don Dunway

Her Pilgrim Soul

w Alan Brennert
A scientist experimenting with computer holography somehow captures the image of an infant, which takes on a life of its own.
Cast: Kristofer Tabori, Gary Cole, Anne Twomey

Director: Wes Craven

I of Newton

w Alan Brennert
A mathematician, obsessed with a complex equation, accidentally invokes a hellish curse and a very "hip" demon materializes to claim his soul.
Cast: Sherman Hemsley, Ron Glass

Director: Ken Gilbert

Night of the Meek

w Rockne S. O'Bannon
Remake of Rod Serling's original 1960 festive fantasy in which a down-at-the-heels department store Santa magically brings the true spirit of Christmas to his humble neighborhood.
Cast: Richard Mulligan, William Atherton, Teddy Wilson, Bill Henderson

Director: Martha Coolidge

But Can She Type

w Martin Pasko & Rebecca Parr
On Christmas Eve, the overworked secretary of a tyrannical boss discovers the heaven-on-earth for all secretaries.
Cast: Pam Dawber, Charles Levin

Director: Shelley Levinson

The Star

w Alan Brennert, story by Arthur C. Clarke
Space explorers from Earth discover the remains of an ancient civilization on a burned-out planet.
Cast: Fritz Weaver, Donald Moffat

Director: Gerd Oswald

Still Life

w Gerrit Graham & Chris Hubbell
A photographer finds an antique camera used on an Amazon expedition 70 years earlier that still has exposed film on it—photos of fierce warriors who believed that to take their picture was to steal their souls.
Cast: John Carradine, Robert Carradine, Marilyn Jones

Director: Peter Medak

The Little People

w J.D. Feigelson
The regulars at Kelly's Pub are skeptical when Liam O'Shaughnessy comes in and swears he's seen the little people . . .
Cast: Hamilton Camp, Anthony Palmer, Michael Aldridge

Director: J.D. Feigelson

The Misfortune Cookie

w Rockne S. O'Bannon, story by Charles. E. Fritch
An arrogant food critic gets his just desserts at a Chinese restaurant he has panned without even dining there.
Cast: Elliot Gould

Director: Allan Arkush

Monsters

w Robert Crais
A ten-year-old horror fan moves into a new neighborhood where he meets a nice old man who informs him that he is a vampire.
Cast: Ralph Bellamy, Oliver Robins, Kathleen Lloyd, Bruce Solomon

Director: B. W. L. Norton

A Small Talent for War

w Charlie Scholtz & Allan Brennert
An emissary of aliens who engineered Earth's evolution declares his race displeased with the planet's petty squabbles and gives world leaders 24 hours to get their act together or face total annihilation.
Cast: John Glover, Peter Michael Goetz, Stefan Gierasch, Fran Bennett

Director: Claudia Weill

A Matter of Minutes

w Rockne S. O'Bannon, story by Theodore Sturgeon
A couple awakes to find themselves four hours ahead of "real" time—in the minute 11:37, which is literally being built around them by a strange blue-clad workforce.
Cast: Adam Arkin, Karen Austin, Adolph Caesar

Director: Sheldon Larry

The Elevator

w Ray Bradbury
Two brothers search an abandoned factory for their scientist father who's been experimenting on the formula for perfect food.
Cast: Stephen Geoffreys, Robert Prescott

Director: R. L. Thomas

To See the Invisible Man

w Steven Barnes, *story by* Robert Silverberg
In an alternative future, the state finds a man guilty of the crime of coldness and condemns him to a year of ostracism.
Cast: Cotter Smith, Karlene Crockett, Mary-Robin Redd, Peter Hobbs

Director: Noel Black

Tooth and Consequences

w Haskell Barkin
A despondent dentist, near the end of his tether because all his patients hate to see him, is saved when the Tooth Fairy appears.
Cast: David Birney, Kenneth Mars, Oliver Clark, Theresa Ganzel

Director: Robert Downey

Welcome to Winfield

w Les Enloe
Griffin St. George, an agent of Death who's trying to get the hang of his new job, tracks his quarry to a dusty desert town that's not even on his map.
Cast: Gerrit Graham, Henry Gibson, Alan Fudge, Elish Cook

Director: Bruce Bilson

Quarantine

w Alan Brennert, *story by* Philip DeGuere & Steve Bochco
A space weapons engineer, cyrogenically frozen at near-death in the 21st century, is revived 300 years later by a biologically perfect but technologically backward community that needs his specialized skills to destroy a threat from space.
Cast: Scott Wilson, Tess Harper, Larry Riley, D. W. Brown, Jeanne Mori

Director: Martha Coolidge

Gramma

w Harlan Ellison, *story by* Stephen King
A young boy, left alone by his mother, is scared to death to go near his huge, grotesque grandmother in the shuttered room at the end of the hall.
Cast: Barret Oliver, Darlanne Fluegel, Frederick Long

Director: Bradford May

Cold Reading

w Martin Pasko & Rebecca Parr
A flamboyant young radio prodigy, broadcasting in 1943, inadvertently invokes the powers of the air for authentic sound effects—bringing the *real* sights and sounds of Africa into his studio.
Cast: Dick Shawn, Janet Carroll, Joel Brooks, Lawrence Poindexter, Annette McCarthy, Ralph Manza

Director: Gus Trikonis

Personal Demon

w Rockne S. O'Bannon
"Rockne O'Bannon," a hack screenwriter up against the biggest writer's block of his whole mediocre career, is confronted by his own personal demons.
Cast: Martin Balsam, Clive Revill, Joshua Shelley

Director: Peter Medak

Three Irish Wishes

w Tommy Lee Wallace, *story by* James Crocker
Shaun McGool, a Hawaiian-shirted leprechaun peeved at being caught by three boys while on his holidays, grants them their three entitled wishes—to the letter!
Cast: Cork Hubbert, Bradley Gregg, Joey Green, Danny Nucci

Director: Tommy Lee Wallace

Dead Run

w Alan Brennert, *story by* Greg Bear
An unemployed truck driver gets a job driving in unfamiliar territory and learns to his horror that he's delivering a cargo of condemned souls to hell.
Cast: Steve Railsback, John de Lancie, Barry Corbin, Ebbe Roe Smith

Director: Paul Tucker

Button, Button

w Logan Swanson
A hard-up young couple is presented with a wooden box with a button on it and told that if they push it, two things will happen: Someone they don't know will die and they will immediately receive $200,000.
Cast: Mare Winningham, Brad David, Basil Hoffman

Director: Peter Medak

Profile in Silver

w J. Neil Schulman
A historian from the future returns to 1963 to study President John F. Kennedy but unwittingly prevents his assassination, thereby initiating a disastrous chain of events.
Cast: Andrew Robinson, Lane Smith, Louis Gimbalvo, Barbara Baxley

Director: John Hancock

Red Snow

w Michael Cassutt
A Russian KGB officer is sent to a Siberian gulag to investigate the mysterious murders of party officials.
Cast: George Dzundza, Barry Miller, Vladimir Skomarovsky

Director: Jeannot Szwarc

Need to Know

w Mary & Sydney Sheldon
In a small town, a government investigator finds insanity spreading from person to person. But the cause is not a virus—it's knowledge, a "Chinese whisper" that completely overwhelms . . .
Cast: William L. Peterson, Robin Gammell, Frances McDormand, Harold Ayer, Eldon Quick

Director: Paul Lynch

Take My Life . . . Please

w Gordon Mitchell
A callous stand-up comic, killed in a car crash, awakens onstage at the Club Limbo where he's told he has to audition for his place in eternity.
Cast: Ray Buktenica, Tim Thomerson, Xander Berkeley, Jim Mackrell

Director: Gus Trikonis

Devil's Alphabet

w Robert Hunter
In 1876, a group of cynical Cambridge men who call themselves the Devil's Alphabet Society sign a solemn oath in blood to meet annually on All Soul's Day—forever.
Cast: Ben Cross, Hywel Bennett, Robert Schenkkan, Osmund Bullock

Director: Ben Bolt

The Library

w Anne Collins
A woman goes to work in a bizarre library containing a book on every living person, and innocently decides to make a minor change in one of them.
Cast: Frances Conroy, Lori Petty, Joe Santos

Director: John Hancock

Shadow Play

w James Crocker, *story and teleplay by* Charles Beaumont
Reworking of Beaumont's 1961 story. A man who waits on Death Row to be hanged is haunted by an obsession that everyone around him is a figment of his recurring nightmare.
Cast: Peter Coyote, Guy Boyd, Janet Elber, Deborah May

Director: (not known)

Grace Note

w Patrice Messina
A gifted young singer who dreams of performing grand opera but is held back by family responsibilities is given a poignant glimpse into the future through her dying sister's last wish.
Cast: Julia Migenes Johnson, Sydney Penny, Rhoda Gemignani, Kay E. Kuter

Director: Peter Medak

A Day in Beaumont

w David Gerrold
An earnest young scientist and his fiancée see a flying saucer land and bug-eyed aliens emerge carrying ray guns and large green pods. But oddly enough, they can find no one who will believe them.
Cast: Victor Garber, Stacy Neilkin, Jeff Morrow, John Agar, Kenneth Tobey

Director: Philip DeGeure

The Last Defender of Camelot

w George R. R. Martin, *story by* Roger Zelazny
A world-weary Lancelot, all but immortal and now living in London, is summoned by his ancient nemesis, the enchantress Morgan Le Fey, to meet again with Merlin who has resurrected a grand scheme to restore Camelot.
Cast: Richard Kiley, Jenny Agutter, Norman Lloyd, John Cameron Mitchell

Director: Jeannot Szwarc

Series Two
30-minute episodes

The Once and Future King

w George R.R. Martin & Bryce Maritano
An Elvis Presley impersonator is transported back to 1954 where he meets his idol preparing for an historic audition. In a fight over the music the *real* Elvis is accidentally killed, so the impersonator assumes the mantle of the king.
Cast: Jeff Yagher, Lisa Jane Persky, Red West, Banks Harper

Director: Jim McBride

Lost and Found

w George R.R. Martin, *story by* Phyllis Esenstein
A college student destined to become a famous anthropologist finds "souvenir hunters" from the future have been taking items from her flat as mementos.
Cast: Akosua Busia, Cindy Harrell, Leslie Ackerman, Raye Birk

Director: Gus Trikonis

The After Hours

w Rockne S. O'Bannon
Reworking of Rod Serling's 1960 tale. A young woman entering a shopping center just as it closes finds herself trapped in a strange after-hours world of shop mannequins and learns that she, too, is really a mannequin.
Cast: Terry Farrell, Ned Bellamy, Ann Wedgeworth, Chip Heller

Director: Bruce Malmouth

A Saucer of Loneliness

w David Gerrold, *story by* Theodore Sturgeon
A young woman refuses to disclose the "personal" message given to her by a flying saucer. Driven to the brink of suicide, she finally meets a man who claims he knows what it was.
Cast: Shelley Duvall, Richard Libertini, Nan Martin, Edith Diaz, Andrew Massett

Director: John Hancock

The World Next Door

w Jeffrey Tambor
Saddled with a boring job and the antithesis of an understanding wife, a basement inventor discovers a "doorway" into a parallel world where he and his creations are truly appreciated. (George Wendt—Norm in *Cheers*—co-starred with his real-life wife, Bernadette Birkette.)
Cast: George Wendt, Bernadette Birkette, Tom Finnegan, Jeffrey Tambor

Director: Paul Lynch

Voices in the Earth

w Alan Brennert
A mining ship in the distant future returns to find Earth a completely dead planet. As they prepare to destroy the planet for its internal minerals, the ship's historian becomes possessed by the ethereal souls of Earth's past inhabitants.
Cast: Martin Balsam, Jenny Agutter, Wortham Krimmer, Tim Russ

Director: Curtis Harrington

What Are Friends For

w J. Michael Straczynski
A man returns to his old vacation cabin with his eight-year-old son and discovers that his imaginary childhood friend is *real* and has been waiting for him all these years. (Writer Straczynski went on to create *Babylon 5*.)
Cast: Tom Skerritt, Fred Savage, Luke Haas, Joy Claussen

Director: Gus Trikonis

The Storyteller

w Rockne S. O'Bannon
An elderly schoolteacher encounters a former pupil with an amazing gift. As a young man he kept his 131-year-old great-great-grandfather alive by reading stories to him.
Cast: Glynnis O'Connor, David Faustino, Parley Baer, Nike Doukas

Director: Paul Lynch

Aqua Vita

w Jeremy Betrand Finch *&* Paul Chitlik
A 40-year-old TV celebrity discovers a special brand of water that acts like a fountain of youth. But there is a hidden cost.
Cast: Mimi Kennedy, Joseph Hacker, Barbra Horan, Christopher McDonald

Director: Paul Tucker

Time and Teresa Golowitz

w Alan Brennert, *story by* Parke Godwin
A middle-aged man suffers a fatal heart attack, then finds he can relive any moment of his life he chooses.
Cast: Gene Barry, Grant Heslov, Paul Sand, Kriski Lynes, Wally Ward, Gina Gershon

Director: Shelley Levinson

Song of the Younger World

w Anthony *&* Nancy Lawrence
A pair of young lovers, forbidden to meet, seeks happiness through a book of mystic teachings that allows them to leave their physical bodies and escape into the souls of wild wolves.
Cast: Peter Kowanko, Paul Benedict, Jennifer Rubin

Director: Corey Allen

Nightsong

w Michael Reaves
When a lady disc jockey plays an obscure album made by a former lover, the musician magically appears in her life again, ten years after he suddenly "disappeared."
Cast: Lisa Eilbacher, Anthony Hamilton, Kenneth David Gilman

Director: Bradford May

The Convict's Piano

w Patricia Messina, *story by* James Crocker
A prisoner wrongly convicted of murder plays a battered old piano in the prison chapel and finds himself transported back in time to 1920s New Orleans.
Cast: Joe Penny, Norman Fell, Tom O'Brien, John Hancock

Director: (not known)

The Card

w Michael Cassutt
A special credit card gives a wife unlimited spending power but when she forgets to settle the account she finds the penalties have unusually severe implications for her family.
Cast: Susan Blakeley, William Atherton, Ken Lerner

Director: Bradford May

The Road Less Traveled

w George R.R. Martin
A middle-aged family man confronts a bearded, wheelchair-bound "intruder" and learns he is himself living on a parallel plane. Each man gains a poignant insight into what might have been.
Cast: Cliff De Young, Margaret Klenck, Jaclyn-Rose Lester, Clare Nono

Director: Wes Craven

The Girl I Married

w J.M. DeMatteis
A married couple's mutual desire for the partner they knew years earlier is so strong that younger versions of themselves are conjured up—giving each the basis for a unique affair.
Cast: Linda Kelsey, James Whitmore Jr.

Director: Philip DeGuere

Shelter, Skelter

w Ron Cobb *&* Robin Love
A survivalist takes to his bunker when a nuclear bomb goes off and settles down for a 30-year wait, convinced that the rest of the world has been destroyed.
Cast: Joe Montegna, Joan Allen, Johnathan Gries

Director: Martha Coolidge

The Toys of Calisan

w George R.R. Martin, *story by* Terry Matz
A 16-year-old retarded boy possesses the amazing gift of being able to conjure up anything after seeing its picture.
Cast: Richard Mulligan, Anne Haney, David Greenlee, Alexandra Borrie

Director: Tom Wright

Joy Ride

w Cal Willingham
Two teenage brothers and their girlfriends "hotwire" a classic old car, then find themselves reliving a 30-year-old murder.
Cast: Rob Knepper, Brooke McCarter, Heidi Kozak, Tamara Mark, Burr Middleton, Danny Spear

Director: Gil Bettman

Private Channel

w Edward Redlich, *story by* Edward Redlich &
John Bellucci
A freak lightning strike on an airliner causes a
teenager's Walkman to malfunction, enabling him
to tune in on the thoughts of other passengers, one of
whom is planning to blow up the plane.
Cast: Scott Coffey, Andrew Robinson, Claudia
Cron, Louise Fitch

Director: Peter Medak

The Junction

w Virginia Aldridge
Two coal miners—one from 1986, the other from
1912—find themselves trapped in the same cave-in.
When the 1912 man is rescued he writes a letter to
be opened 74 years in the future.
Cast: William Allen Young, Chris Mulkey, John
Dennis Johnston

Director: Bill Duke

TWIST IN THE TALE
(A.K.A. TALES OF THE UNEXPECTED)

Short-lived American anthology series from 1978. A cousin of *Tales of the Unexpected* (its U.S.
title); several of the stories had science fiction themes.

"No Way Out" starred Bill Bixby as a naval officer "too busy" to pay much attention to his
young son. He sails his boat through a time warp, emerging 25 years in the future when he
discovers his grown-up son making the same mistake he did.

In "The Nomads," a Vietnam veteran (David Birney) with a history of mental breakdown
discovers that space-roving vampires are about to take over Earth. But no one will believe him.

"The Mask of Adonis" featured *Falcon Crest* star Robert Foxworth as a film producer offered
eternal rejuvenation at an isolated clinic run by a sinister doctor.

And in "A Hand for Sonny Blue," a baseball pitcher receives a new hand in a transplant, only to
discover it came from a vicious young hoodlum, killed in a shoot-out, and is taking on a life of its own.

REGULAR CAST
Narrator William Conrad

Producer: John Wilder
Quinn Martin Productions
9 color 55-minute episodes
The Final Chapter
The Mask of Adonis
Devil Pack
The Nomads
A Hand for Sonny Blue
Force of Evil *(a 2-part story)*
No Way Out
You Are Not Alone

U.K. premiere: 14 October 1978
(London)

(N.B.: This series is not to be confused with two
1988 dramas from Granada that went out under the
same title, but that were really part of that company's contribution to an international package of
The Ray Bradbury Theater—see separate entry.)

UFO

With *UFO* Gerry Anderson finally cut the strings that tied him to his Supermarionated puppets.
He'd flirted with live action in *The Secret Service* and made the jump with his 1969 feature film
Doppelgänger, but *UFO* was his first fully flesh-and-blood TV series.

It was a natural development, and one that offered the chance to dust off many of the props, vehicles
and costumes lying around after *Doppelgänger* (aka *Journey to the Far Side of the Sun*). All the same,
production costs were high—around £100,000 for each of the 26 hour-long episodes.

UFO's format was similar to *Captain Scarlet and the Mysterons*, that of an alien force attacking an Earth defended by a powerful secret organization. But this one was set in the "near-future," 1980. The premise: For ten years a dying, sterile race has been raiding Earth in search of human organs to keep itself alive. All that stops our planet from becoming one giant body bank is SHADO—Supreme Headquarters Alien Defense Organization—operating from a secret base beneath the Harlington-Straker film studios (actually MGM in Borehamwood, where the series was made) which act as a cover for SHADO personnel led by ex-USAF colonel Ed Straker. SHADO also has a center on the Moon—base for its interceptor craft and the first line of defense against marauding pyramid-shaped UFOs. Its hi-tech resources include SID—Space Intruder Detector—a sophisticated computer satellite, submarine/aircraft called Skydivers and a range of tank-like SHADOmobiles to pursue UFOs that reach Earth.

The aliens themselves were rarely seen—and nothing was revealed of their possible origins. But they were shown to have a liquid environment inside their space helmets for interstellar travel— a womb principle that Anderson told *TV Times* he devised after hearing of genuine scientific experiments involving keeping a dog alive under water for an hour by filling its lungs with a special combination of water and gases.

The series had one of the biggest semi-resident casts for any TV show, though not all the regulars appeared in every episode. In fact, only one had a 100 percent record. That was Commander Straker, played by Canadian actor Ed Bishop—the voice of Captain Blue in *Captain Scarlet and the Mysterons*. His right-hand men were Col. Alec Freeman and Col. Paul Foster, the former played by *Special Branch* star George Sewell who had also appeared with Ed Bishop in *Doppelgänger*.

UFO also boasted one of television's shapeliest regiments of women, dressed to kill in tight-fitting catsuits and mauve wigs. The glamorous commander of Moonbase, Lt. Gay Ellis, was played by Gabrielle Drake who later went on to head a very down-to-earth ITV outpost—the *Crossroads* motel.

Although many of Century 21's regular writers were used on *UFO*, script editor Tony Barwick was responsible for 12 of the 26 scripts. There were notable contributions, too, from David Tomblin and Terence Feely.

This was a more adult science fiction show than the Supermarionation adventures, often edgy and downbeat in its plots and characterization. Straker, for example, was shown as having a broken marriage behind him. ITV, though, didn't know how to take it. First screened in September 1970, it didn't get a network launch and was buried by many regions.

A planned second series, with the emphasis switched to Moonbase, turned into *Space: 1999*— but that's another story.

Main Cast

Cmdr. Edward Straker Ed Bishop *Col. Alec Freeman* George Sewell
Col. Paul Foster Michael Billington *Lt. Gay Ellis* Gabrielle Drake
Lt. Nina Barry Dolores Mantez *Dr. Doug Jackson* Vladek Sheybal
Col. Virginia Lake Wanda Ventham *Capt. Peter Carlin* Peter Gordeno

With:

Capt. Lew Waterman Gary Myers *Miss Ealand* Norma Ronald
Lt. Keith Ford (SHADO Radio Operator) Keith Alexander
SHADO operative Ayshea Brough *Skydiver navigator* Jeremy Wilkin
Skydiver engineer Jon Kelley *Skydiver operative* Georgina Moon
General Henderson Grant Taylor
Lt. Mark Bradley Harry Baird *Joan Harrington* Antonia Ellis

Format: Gerry & Sylvia Anderson
  with Reg Hill
Executive producer: Gerry Anderson
Producers: Reg Hill, Gerry Anderson
Script editor: Tony Barwick
Special effects: Derek Meddings
Music: Barry Gray

*A Century 21 Pictures Ltd. Production for
ITC Worldwide Distribution*
26 color 60-minute episodes
16 September 1970–15 March 1973
(ATV, Midlands)
U.S. release: autumn 1972

Identified

w Gerry & Sylvia Anderson & Tony Barwick

Cmdr. Straker discovers the grim secret behind the long-standing UFO attacks on Earth in which people have been mutilated or abducted, when an alien craft is forced down and its pilot captured. (Ed Bishop was "rejuvenated" ten years for early flashback scenes, while two actors were used for the role of the alien who ages dramatically in a matter of moments.)

Minister Basil Dignam
Seagull X-Ray co-pilot Shane Rimmer
Ken Matthews Michael Mundell
Kurt Mahler Paul Gillard
Phil Wade Gary Files
Dr. Harris Matthew Robertson
Dr. Shroeder Maxwell Shaw
Alien Gito Santana/Stanley Bray

Director: Gerry Anderson

Exposed

w Tony Barwick

Civilian test pilot Paul Foster sees and photographs a UFO, and his quest to uncover its secret leads him to the heart of SHADO—and a new career.

Kofax Robin Bailey
Janna Jean Marsh
Co-pilot Matt Zimmerman
Dr. Frazer Basil Moss
Nurse Sue Gerrard
Tsi Paula Li Schiu
Louis Arthur Cox

Director: David Lane

The Cat with Ten Lives

w David Tomblin

An innocent-looking Siamese cat turns out to be an alien being sent to take over the mind of SHADO pilot Jim Regan. (This was Alexis Kanner's first TV role since *The Prisoner*, and a reunion for him and David Tomblin.)

Jim Regan Alexis Kanner
Morgan Windsor Davies
Jean Regan Geraldine Moffatt
Muriel Eleanor Summerfield
Miss Holland Lois Maxwell
Albert Colin Gordon

Director: David Tomblin

Conflict

w Ruric Powell

An alien satellite uses space debris as a cover for its attacks—but Straker has a hard time convincing General Henderson to clear away the junk—until SHADO HQ itself is threatened.

Pilot Gerard Norman
Navigator Alan Tucker

Maddox Drewe Henley
Crewman David Courtland
Steiner Michael Kilgarriff

Director: Ken Turner

A Question of Priorities

w Tony Barwick

Straker faces an agonizing dilemma when a rare chance to rescue an alien defector who could hold the key to saving the world means risking the life of his critically injured son.

John Rutland Barnaby Shaw
Mary Rutland Suzanne Neve
Rutland Philip Madoc
Dr. Segal Peter Halliday
Mrs. O'Connor Mary Merrall
Dr. Green Russell Napier
Alien Richard Aylen

Director: David Lane

E.S.P.

w Alan Fennell

Straker and Freeman are threatened by an alien agent whose ESP powers are so pronounced he can predict their every thought and movement.

Croxley John Stratton
Stella Croxley Deborah Stanford
Dr. Ward Douglas Wilmer
Dr. Shroeder Maxwell Shaw
Gateman Donald Tandy
Security man Stanley McGeogh

Director: Ken Turner

Kill Straker!

w Donald James

A close encounter with a UFO turns loyal SHADO officers Foster and Craig into ferocious adversaries and Straker faces a grim challenge to his command—and his life.

Craig David Sumner
Moonbase guard Steve Cory
Nurse Louise Pajo

Director: Alan Perry

Sub-smash

w Alan Fennell

Straker and Nina Barry become trapped on the ocean bed in Skydiver after a search for an alien craft. As hopes of rescue fade, a tender bond develops between them.

Lt. Chin Anthony Chinn
Lt. Lewis Paul Maxwell
Pilot Burnell Tucker
SHADO divers John Golightly, Alan Haywood

Director: David Lane

Destruction

w Dennis Spooner
A beautiful Admiralty secretary is the innocent dupe in an alien plot to steal and release nerve gas that would destroy all life on Earth.
Sarah Bosanquet Stephanie Beacham
Naval captain Philip Madoc
Admiral Sheringham Edwin Richfield
Skydiver captain David Warbeck
Skydiver engineer Barry Stokes
Astronaut Steven Berkoff

Director: Ken Turner

The Square Triangle

w Alan Pattillo
Lovers Liz Newton and Cass Fowler are horrified when an alien pilot becomes the unexpected victim of their plot to murder her husband.
Liz Newton Adrienne Corri
Cass Fowler Patrick Mower
Jack Newton Allan Cuthbertson
Alien Anthony Chinn
Gamekeeper Godfrey James
SHADO Mobile navigator Hugo Panczak

Director: David Lane

Close Up

w Tony Barwick
A powerful new telescope could help SHADO track the origins of the UFOs. But one scientist, Dr. Kelly, resorts to unusual methods to convince Straker that inner space is just as important as outer space!
Dr. Kelly Neil Hallett
Dr. Young James Beckett
Launch controller Frank Mann
Interceptor pilot Mark Hawkins

Director: Alan Perry

The Psychobombs

w Tony Barwick
Three average people—Linda, a secretary; Mason, a motorway construction boss; and Clark, a bank clerk—become super-humans when they are taken over by the aliens who plan to use them in a powerful plan to wreck SHADO.
Linda Deborah Grant
Clark David Collings
Mason Mike Pratt
Capt. Lauritzen Tom Adams
Executive Alex Davion
Skydiver navigator Christopher Timothy
Police motorcyclist Gavin Campbell

Director: Jeremy Summers

Survival

w Tony Barwick
Joining the search for a UFO that has attacked Moonbase, Col. Foster comes face-to-face with its alien pilot after their craft "collide." In the fight to survive on the Moon's inhospitable surface a surprising bond of friendship is forged.
Grant Robert Swann
Alien Gito Santana
Tina Duval Suzan Farmer
Rescuers Ray Armstrong, David Weston

Director: Alan Perry

Mindbender

w Tony Barwick
A deadly Moon-rock causes two members of an interceptor crew to go berserk and attack their colleagues in the belief that they are seeing their enemies.
Conroy Al Mancini
Dale Craig Hunter
Beaver James Charles Tingwell
Howard Byrne Stuart Damon
Radio operator Anouska Hempel

Director: Ken Turner

Flight Path

w Ian Scott Stewart
Threats to his wife force Moonbase officer Paul Roper to turn traitor, revealing vital information that will bring in a major UFO attack. But once the truth is uncovered, Roper gets the chance to even the score.
Paul Roper George Cole
Carol Roper Sonia Fox
Dawson Keith Grenville
Dr. Shroeder Maxwell Shaw

Director: Ken Turner

The Man Who Came Back

w Terence Feely
Spaceship pilot Craig Collins is found alive and well two months after he disappeared and was presumed dead. But he's a changed man—now programmed by the aliens to kill Straker.
Craig Collins Derren Nesbitt
Miss Holland Lois Maxwell
Col. Grey Gary Raymond
Sir Esmond Roland Culver
Radio operator Anouska Hempel

Director: David Lane

The Dalotek Affair

w Ruric Powell
When all radio and video equipment on Moonbase breaks down, Col. Foster suspects that a lunar survey team may be responsible. But the breakdowns continue until the surveyors report seeing something strange at the bottom of a deep new crater.
Jane Carson Tracey Reed
Tanner Clinton Greyn
Mitchell David Weston
Blake Philip Latham
Reed John Breslin
Doctor Basil Moss

Director: Alan Perry

Timelash

w Terence Feely
Straker runs amok and when a dead body is found he is suspected of being a killer. But under the influence of a powerful truth drug he pieces together the startling mystery of an alien-controlled man with the power to cheat time.
Turner Patrick Allen
Casting agent Ron Pember
Actor Jean Vladon
Actress Kirsten Lindholm

Director: Cyril Frankel

Ordeal

w Tony Barwick
Abducted by an alien! That's the apparent fate of Col. Foster when he passes out in a sauna the morning after a very indulgent night before. What a nightmare!
Sylvia Graham Quinn O'Hara
Joe Franklin David Healy
Astronaut Mark Hawkins
Dr. Harris Basil Moss
Perry Peter Burton

Director: Ken Turner

Court Martial

w Tony Barwick
Soon after interviewing a young starlet and her agent in his "cover" capacity as a movie executive, Foster is accused of espionage and convicted at a court martial. With the death sentence hanging over his colleague's head, Straker decides to dig deeper.
Webb Jack Hedley
Carl Mason Neil McCallum
Diane Pippa Steel
Artist's agent Noel Davis
Miss Scott Louise Pajo
Miss Grant Georgina Cookson

Director: Ron Appleton

Reflections in the Water

w David Tomblin
Investigating strange reports of a "flying fish," Straker and Foster find themselves in a bewildering underwater replica of SHADO control, manned by doubles of all the staff—including themselves!
Skipper Conrad Phillips
Lt. Anderson James Cosmo
Film producer Richard Caldicott
Skydiver capt. David Warbeck
Skydiver operative Anouska Hempel
Skydiver navigator Barry Stokes

Director: David Tomblin

Computer Affair

w Tony Barwick
The death of an astronaut in a UFO attack has strange implications for Gay Ellis of Moonbase Control and interceptor pilot Mark Bradley when a computer assessment shows they are in love.
Ken Matthews Michael Mundell
Dr. Shroeder Maxwell Shaw
Dr. Murray Peter Burton
Moonbase operative Nigel Lambert

Director: David Lane

Confetti Check A-O.K.

w Tony Barwick
Flashback episode in which Straker recalls the origins of SHADO and the call of duty that doomed his marriage—right from the start of his honeymoon!
Mary Straker Suzanne Neve
Lt. Grey Julian Grant
CIA man Shane Rimmer
Mary's father Michael Nightingale
Hotel clerk Geoffrey Hinsliff
Porter Frank Tregear

Director: David Lane

The Sound of Silence

w David Lane & Bob Bell
A top showjumper mysteriously disappears after a UFO is reported to have landed near his family's farm.
Russ Michael Jayston
Anne Susan Jameson
Culley Nigel Gregory
Alien Gito Santana
Stone Richard Vernon
Doctor Basil Moss

Director: David Lane

The Responsibility Seat

w Tony Barwick
Col. Freeman finds it can be tough at the top when he takes over from Cmdr. Straker who himself learns that a pretty girl can be as lethal as a UFO when he becomes entangled with reporter Jo Fraser.
Jo Fraser Jane Merrow
Film director Ralph Ball
Stuntman Royston Rowe
Astronaut Mark Hawkins
Russian base commander Patrick Jordan

Director: Alan Perry

The Long Sleep

w David Tomblin
The file on a longstanding UFO case is reopened when a girl regains consciousness after a ten-year coma. Straker pieces together a traumatic mystery that leads to a race against time to prevent a deadly alien bomb from being detonated. (A controversial episode with sepia-tinted black and white flash-backs, a drugs trip and an implied rape attempt, "The Long Sleep" was originally kept back by cautious ITV companies.)
Catherine Tessa Wyatt
Tim Christian Roberts
Van driver Jon Garrie
Bomb disposal expert Christopher Robbie
SHADO Radio operator Anouska Hempel

Director: Jeremy Summers

UNDERMIND

"These people have been brainwashed to wage a silent war. They're part of a pattern—a pattern of evil. We've got to find the other pieces before they undermine the whole country."

Highly unusual 1960s British thriller about alien subversion—with not a rocket, flying saucer or extra-terrestrial in sight.

Its premise: An alien force, identified neither by name nor by location, seeks to establish a foothold in Britain by undermining society and morale. It has sent high frequency signals from space that are picked up by people who become brainwashed into subversive acts, to create a climate of unrest.

The series' villains are ordinary people from all walks of life—teachers, businessmen, politicians, clergymen, doctors and policemen—who have undergone a dramatic personality change. All have one thing in common—an acute susceptibility to high frequency signals, akin to dogs and dog whistles.

Undermind begins with personnel officer Drew Heriot returning from Australia to find his policeman brother Frank behaving strangely. In the course of the 11 more-or-less self-contained episodes, Drew and his sister-in-law Anne Heriot foil a string of brainwashed people plotting to undermine the nation in different ways, some violent, some subtle.

REGULAR CAST
Drew Heriot Jeremy Wilkin   *Anne Heriot* Rosemary Nicols
Prof. Val Randolph (Eps. 2–5) Denis Quilley

Devised and evolved by Robert Banks Stewart
Producer: Michael Chapman
An ABC Television Production

11 black and white 60-minute episodes
8 May–17 July 1965
(ITV—Midlands)

Instance 1, aka Onset of Fear

w Robert Banks Stewart
Drew Heriot returns from Australia to find his policeman brother Frank has provoked a scandal involving a top politician. Appalled by this uncharacteristic behavior, Drew and his brother's estranged wife Anne search for a cause behind Frank's strange actions. With the help of a psychologist, they discover that Frank has become "emotionless" and uncover a web of similar cases—the victims all being susceptible to high frequency signals. Frank, meanwhile, kills Polson and tries to have Drew and Anne eliminated. But it is *he* who ends up being shot. As he dies, he tells Drew: "There are more of us . . ."
Frank Heriot Jeremy Kemp
Hugh Bishop Tony Steedman
Dr. Polson Paul Maxwell
Macridos David Swift
Paget Hugh Latimer
Inspector Frank Mills

Director: Bill Bain

Flowers of Havoc

w Robert Banks Stewart, *story by* Jon Manchip White
Drew Heriot's search for clues about why his brother was brainwashed, takes him and Anne to a south coast resort where they find that the local vicar is the surprising ringleader behind an invasion by hundreds of rioting teenagers.
Prof. Val Randolph Denis Quilley *(intro)*
Wilma Strickland Pauline Jameson
Charles Ogilvie Glynn Edwards
Rev. Austen Anderson Michael Gough
Dave Finn Gil Sutherland
Verger Edwin Finn

Director: Peter Potter

The New Dimensions

w David Whitaker
Drew finds himself the victim of an elaborate plot to frame him for the murder of a call-girl, involved with an MP and a welfare worker. Anne goes undercover to get at the truth.
Smith Garfield Morgan
Fenway Patrick Allen
Beymer Derek Francis
Ellerway John Collin
Marion Gordon July Parfitt
Dorothy Vivienne Martin

Director: Bill Bain

Death in England

w Hugh Leonard
Drew and Anne uncover a plot to kill an old IRA revolutionary in London, and so spark off violence around Britain.

General Riordon Paul Curran
Sir Geoffrey Savage Robert James
Kennefick David Kelly
Pat Neary Patrick Bedford
Capt. Morrell Mark Burns
Rumbold Terence Lodge

Director: Peter Potter

Too Many Enemies

w Robert Banks Stewart
The trail of a mystery "emotionless" man called Gill leads Drew and Anne to Prof. Randolph's radio telescope at Kimberley Vale and the shocking revelation that he, too, is one of the "Undermind" and is out to brainwash them as well.
Gill Aubrey Richards
Dr. Hepworth Tenniel Evans
Dr. Burath Lesley Nunnerley
Alice Gill Margaret Whiting
Tubby Chalmers Dave King

Director: Peter Dews

Intent to Destroy

w John Kruse
A strange astrologer is the link between the poisoning of a thousand acres of Kent orchard, unsettling stock market tips, and a bomb plot to kill a famous TV celebrity on a live television show.
Stanley Shaw Ewan Hooper
Victor Liberton Peter Barkworth
Ursula Smythe Jan Holden
Mr. Banbridge John Garvin
Mrs. Banbridge Margaret Gordon
Effie Lally Bowers
Himself Eamonn Andrews

Director: Bill Bain

Song of Death

w Bill Strutton
Drew and Anne discover that a large number of doctors in London have committed suicide—each shortly after having a birthday on which they received a birthday greetings record. Clues lead them to a recording studio and they uncover a plot to hypnotize the doctors by "doping" the records.
Dr. John Rossleigh Jeremy Burnham
Donald Ames William Wilde
Sam Freed Ralph Nossek
Dr. Hugh Christian David Bauer
Dr. Spring John Wentworth
Jesse Spring Joan Heath

Director: Laurence Bourne

Puppets of Evil

w Max Sterling
When children start behaving badly—influenced by a fictional child character—Drew and Anne suspect that the author, Kate Orkney, has been brainwashed. Unraveling a complex web of involvement, they find the true culprit behind the unsettling stories is a school headmaster, Edmonds.
Cyrus Benton Norman Tyrell
Homer Benton Derek Nimmo
Kate Orkney Katharine Blake
Morgan Fay Stanley Meadows
Edmonds Philip Latham
Nancy Long Delena Kidd

Director: Patrick Dromgoole

Test for the Future

w David Whittaker
With Anne held hostage by hired thugs, Drew is forced into cooperating with a brainwashed accountant's scheme to send government exam papers to potential failures, thus creating future havoc when inferior men achieve important posts.
Kennedy Barrie Ingham
Davies Maurie Taylor
Jeffreys Godfrey Quigley
Lodge Dudley Jones
Col. Matherson Charles Carson

Director: Laurence Bourne

Waves of Sound

w Robert Holmes
Investigating a pirate radio station, Drew and Anne find the trail leads to a cold cure clinic in Tunbridge Wells where the physician, Dr. Whittaker, plans to spread a new flu virus that causes a middle ear infection, making victims receptive to a new brainwashing signal from space. Drew is able to substitute ordinary cold pills and obtains a list of brainwashed people.
Dr. Whittaker Ruth Dunning
Sir Geoffrey Tillinger John Barron
Ensign James George Moon
Ian Jenner John Barcroft
Billy Jarvis George Betton
Caper David Phethean

Director: Raymond Menmuir

End Signal

w Robert Holmes
Using Drew's list, security forces round up brainwashed people, and communications chief Tillinger prepares to jam the expected signal from space. Drew and Anne relax—until someone tries to kill them and they realize it's not yet over. As jamming is about to start, Tillinger reveals himself as the main Undermind and tries to stop the jamming. But in a struggle he is killed. Thus Britain is saved!
Thallon George Baker
Reynolds Richard Owens
Veronica Beryl Baxter
Killick Barry Warren
Raison Michael Lees
Prof. Emmett Alex McCrindle
Sir Geoffrey Tillinger John Barron

Director: Peter Potter

THE UNFORESEEN

A prototype *Tales of the Unexpected*, this early fantasy anthology series appeared on Britain's Granada Television in 1960 (initially twice weekly) as a late-night series of short plays covering the inexplicable, the supernatural, the occult and science fiction.

All these "Tales of" *The Unforeseen* featured an element of intrigue to hook the viewer and a surprise ending to pull him up with a start. The series ran for 18 weeks in the Granada region, but was never picked up by the network.

Executive producer: Peter Francis

A Granada Television Production
24 (out of 37) 30-minute episodes, black and white
28 June–8 November 1960

The Voice

w Hillary Waugh
A young woman, terrorized by a phone caller, agrees to act as a police decoy.
With: Susan Douglas, George Robertson

Director: Robert Christie

The Tintype

w Peter Francis & Vincent McConnor
A strange early form of photograph seems to confirm a young Victorian woman's belief that her former lover has returned from the dead.
With: Aileen Seaton, Patrick Macnee, Sean Mulcahy
Director: John Ashby

When Greek Meets Greek

w Graham Greene
A crooked professor running a phony correspondence course meets his match in a new student.
With: Barry Morse, Paddy Croft, Adrian Waller
Director: Eric Till

The Freedom Fighters

w Edith Pargeter
The commander of an occupying force must take strong measures to stamp out a youthful Resistance movement.
With: Claude Rae, Barry Lavender
Director: Peter Francis

The Late Departed

(writer not known)
An unhappily married wife disappears. Has her errant husband murdered her?
With: Joseph Shaw, Norma Renault
Director: Eric Till

The New Member

(writer not known)
A hungover visitor to a country club is alarmed by the odd activities of the other members.
With: Peter Mews
Director: Melwyn Breen

The Mask

w Vincent McConnor
An executed murderer's sinister influence lives on in the form of his death mask.
With: Barry Morse, Henry Comor
Director: Charles Jarrott

The Monsters

w Bob Foshko
Two young scientists pilot their rocket into space—in defiance of their own government.

With: John Vernon, John Sullivan
Director: Leo Orenstein

Master Used-to-Be

w Hal Hackaday
An eight-year-old boy moves into an old house and starts talking about people and events from 200 years ago.
With: Hayward Morse
Director: Basil Coleman

Time Exposure

w Ralph Rose
A news photographer buys an old camera that takes pictures of non-existent scenes.
With: Dave Broadfoot, Pegi Loder
Director: Robert Christie

Rendezvous

w Gil Braun
An American airman is at a busy railway station—but no one seems able to see him or answer him.
With: Jill Foster, Frank Perry, Walter Massey
Director: Eric Till

Torgut

w Ralph Rose & Charles Smith
A scientist disappears, leaving just two clues—an unusual rock-like object and the strange word "torgut."
With: Frank Perry, Trudi Wiggins, Uriel Luft
Director: Robert Christie

The Three Marked Pennies

w Jack Paritz
Three marked coins hold a prize for their holder on a given date—two will bestow fabulous prizes, the third sudden death. Which is which?
With: Ed McNamara, Kay Livingston, George Luscombe, Alex McKee
Director: Melwyn Breen

Desire

w James Stephens & Cecil Bennett
A young man saves the life of a blind man who, in return, invites him to express a wish.
With: Barry Morse, Frances Hyland, Ted Borrows
Director: Peter Francis

Checkmate

w Michael Dyne
The owner of an amazing robot chess player invites all comers to play against his machine, for very high stakes . . .
With: John Colicos, Marcia Morris, Chris Wiggins

Director: Norman Campbell

The Proposal

w Morris Hersham, Norah Perez
A man tries to stop his sister's marriage to a middle-aged suitor.
With: Anna Reiser, George Sperdakos, Alexander Dixon, Peg Dixon

Director: Ted Pope

The Brooch

w F. Britten Austin, *adapted by* Joseph de Courcey
An antique brooch has a sinister history—one that leads to murder.
With: Gillie Fenwick, Kathleen Kidd, Hedley Mattingley

Director: David Gardner

The Haunted

w Gill Paust
A young couple shipwrecked on an island beach seeks refuge in a ruined house said to be haunted.
With: Frank Matthias, Rosemary Palin

Director: Leo Orenstein

The Metronome

w August Derleth
A woman is kept awake by a constant ticking sound. Has her small stepson returned from the dead to drive her crazy?
With: Norma Renault, Frank Perry

Director: Rex Hagan

Shelter for the Night

w Robert Arthur
A honeymoon couple lose their way at night and seek shelter at a derelict house where they accidentally uncover the owner's terrible secret.
With: William Bell, Sharan Acker, Larry Mann

Director: David Gardner

The Doomdorf Mystery

w M.D. Post, *adapted by* Lester Powell
Everything points to a supernatural death when a brutal farmer is found shot in a room no human being could have entered.
With: Charles Palmer, Ron Hartman

Director: Peter Francis

Man Running

w Timothy Warriner
A gangster gets his revenge on a man who double crosses him—in a strange way.
With: Don Francis, Larry Mann, Laddy Denis

Director: Peter Francis

V

V was one of the great science fiction "events" to hit television in the 1980s. The ten-hour American blockbuster cost around £25 million to make.

A thriller about aliens conquering the Earth and encountering a stubborn Resistance, *V* was a clearly stated allegory about the evils of totalitarianism, and it pulled out all the stops to make sure its message got home. These aliens were intergalactic Nazis down to their jackboots, semi-swastikas and insidious propaganda. They rounded up Earth's scientists and herded them off to concentration camps, started a brown-shirted Visitor Youth corps and took over the media. Just in case you still hadn't guessed, up popped an elderly Jew to compare it to the rise of Nazi Germany.

Subtlety wasn't *V*'s strongpoint, but then when you aim for the mainstream you go for the jugular. That meant easy-to-identify heroes and villains, lots of action and lavish special effects. *V*'s makeup and hardware were well up to scratch, but it was something soft and furry that gave the series its most vivid and memorable image. Underneath their reassuring human exteriors the alien "Visitors" were really a race of hideous reptiles with a taste for live meat, and one scene called for Diana, the alien leader, to "eat" a live rat. To achieve the startling effect, actress Jane Badler dangled the rat in front of her mouth, but it was actually "swallowed" by a mechanical head. The camera cut back to the real actress who was fitted with a false throat with built-in air sacs that inflated and deflated to give the illusion of the rodent sliding down her throat. Yuk!

If that wasn't enough, *V* tossed in sex between a lounging lizard called Brian and an Earth girl, Robin, producing two babies—one a lizard creature that dies, the other a "human" girl with forked tongue, Elizabeth, who eventually provides the key to defeating the aliens.

Heroes of the Resistance were TV cameraman Mike Donovan—capable of dodging umpteen laser blasts at a single bound—scientists Julie Parris and Robert Maxwell, and gruff mercenary Ham Tyler. They were aided by a handful of alien sympathisers, notably Fifth Columnist Martin and the soft-hearted Willie.

Given the mini-series' phenomenal success, a sequel was inevitable. But *V* (The Series) never made the same impact. Most of the main characters returned, but the political overtones were largely discarded in favor of formula action-adventures, with the metamorphosis of the alien/human "starchild" Elizabeth the only real sign of progress.

V (THE MINI-SERIES)
Main Cast
Diana Jane Badler   *Mike Donovan* Marc Singer   *Julie* Faye Grant
Robert Maxwell Michael Durrell   *Brian* Peter Nelson
Robin Blair Tefkin   *Daniel* David Packer   *Elias* Michael Wright
Eleanor Dupres (Donovan's mother) Neva Patterson
Abraham Bernstein Leonardo Cimino   *Steven* Andrew Prine
Supreme Commander John Richard Herd
Willie Robert Englund   *Martin* Frank Ashmore
Kristine Walsh Jenny Sullivan
Ham Tyler Michael Ironside

Created by Kenneth Johnson
Writer/Director/Executive producer:
  Kenneth Johnson
Producer: Chuck Bowman
Makeup: Leo Lotito

A Kenneth Johnson Production in association with Warner Bros. Television
5 color 110-minute episodes
U.S. premiere: 1 May 1983
U.K. premiere: 30 July–3 August 1984

V/The Final Battle

Earth, present day: Out of the blue, gigantic UFOs hover above 31 cities around the world. Their humanoid occupants announce that they have come in peace, offering friendship and advanced technology in return for a few minerals. Earth agrees and the "benevolent invasion" begins with the Visitors manipulating the hearts and minds of people in a propaganda campaign reminiscent of Nazi Germany. Then thousands of scientists start to disappear and communities split into collaborators and resisters. Suspicious TV cameraman Mike Donovan sneaks aboard the Mother Ship and discovers that the Visitors are really revolting lizards who devour live mice and rats for lunch. He learns, too, that their mission is to drain all of Earth's water and cart off as many people as they can—for food! Back on Earth he teams up with fugitive scientist Julie Parris and the Resistance move-

ment grows, adopting the letter "V" as its symbol of victory. Aided by a Fifth Column of sympathizers, they fight back, finally defeating the invaders by manufacturing a "red dust" poison from the cells of "starchild" Elizabeth, and sprinkling it into Earth's atmosphere from thousands of balloons around the world.

Kathleen Maxwell Penelope Windust
Stanley Bernstein George Morfogen
Ben Taylor Richard Lawson
Arthur Dupres Hansford Rowe
Tony Wah Chong Evan Kim
Josh Brooks Tommy Peterson
Lynn Bonnie Bartlett
Caleb Taylor Jason Bernard
Ruby Camila Ashlend
Sancho Rafael Campos
Brad William Russ
Sean Eric Johnson

V (THE SERIES)
REGULAR CAST
Diana Jane Badler *Donovan* Marc Singer *Julie* Faye Grant
Lydia June Chadwick *Willie* Robert Englund
Elizabeth Jenny Beck *(Eps. 1–2)*/Jennifer Cooke *(from Ep. 2)*
Ham Michael Ironside *(Eps. 1–12)* *Nathan Bates* Lane Smith *(Eps. 1–12)*
Robin Blair Tefkin *(Eps. 1–12)* *Elias* Michael Wright *(Eps. 1–11)*
Kyle Jeff Yagher *(Ep. 3)* *Chaing* Aki Aleong *(Eps. 5–12)*
Charles Duncan Regehr *(Eps. 10–14)* Lt. *James Judson Scott (from Ep. 11)*
Philip Frank Ashmore *(from Ep. 14)*

Creator: Kenneth Johnson
Executive producers: Daniel H. Blatt, Robert Singer
Producers: Steven E. de Souza, Dean O'Brien, Garner Simmons, David Latt, Skip Ward, Don Boyle, Ralph R. Riskin
Makeup: Leo Lotito

A Daniel H. Blatt and Robert Singer Production in association with Warner Bros Television
19 color 60-minute episodes
U.S.: 26 October 1984–5 July 1985
U.K.: 3 June–23 September 1985
(Includes two double-length episodes; 1/2, 18/19)
(Thames Television).

Liberation Day (aka The Pursuit of Diana)

w Paul Monash
One year after "The Final Battle," the world celebrates the anniversary of Liberation Day. The evil Diana is due to stand trial for crimes against the human race, but is kidnapped by corrupt magnate Nathan Bates who wants to gain her knowledge. However, Diana escapes and rejoins the Visitors' armada on the dark side of the Moon. Meanwhile, "star-child" Elizabeth begins a startling metamorphosis.
Robert Maxwell Michael Durrell
Martin Frank Ashmore
Steve Roller Burt Marshall

Director: Paul Krasny

Dreadnought (aka The Visitors Strike Back)

w Steven E. de Souza
Reunited with her troops, Diana vows to take Earth by force and, under the guise of agreeing to make Los Angeles an "open city," activates her Triax super-weapon to reduce the city to rubble. Donovan organizes the Resistance to take over the Mother Ship; Elizabeth emerges from her metamorphosis as a fully grown teenager; Robert sacrifices himself to halt the deadly Triax.
Robert Maxwell Michael Durrell
Air Force general Linden Chiles
Roller Burt Marshall

Director: Paul Krasny

Breakout

w David Braff
Donovan and Ham are captured and imprisoned in a Visitor work camp guarded by a terrifying sand monster called a crivit. Bates mounts a desperate search for Elizabeth to exchange for his son Kyle who is in Diana's custody. At the camp, Donovan and Ham organize a mass escape.
Annie Pamela Ludwig
Billy Christian Jacobs
Vanik Herman Pope
Roller Burt Marshall

Director: Ray Austin

The Deception

w Garner Simmons
While the Resistance works to help Elizabeth escape to safety in New York, Diana launches another scheme to capture the star-child by first seizing Donovan and drugging him into disclosing her whereabouts.
Sean Donovan Nick Katt
Alien captain Sandy Lang

Director: Victor Lobl

The Sanction (aka Klaus—The Exterminator)

w Brian Taggert
Desperate to free his son Sean from the Visitors' influence, Donovan clashes with a powerful alien killer, Klaus. Meanwhile the relationship intensifies between Kyle and Elizabeth, who is finally reunited with her mother Robin.
Klaus Thomas Callaway
Sean Nick Katt

Director: Bruce Seth-Green

Visitor's Choice

w David Braff

Nathan Bates resolves to crush the Resistance, starting with a showdown with his son Kyle. Donovan, Julie and Ham stage a daring sabotage at a convention of Visitor commanders where Diana plans to show off an "encapsulator"—the ultimate device in processing humans for food.

Barry Boddicker Jonathan Caliri
Dean Boddicker Chad McQueen
Gen. Maxwell Larson Robert Ellenstein
Mary Kruger Sybil Danning

Director: Gilbert Shilton

The Overlord (aka Showdown at Rawlinsville)

w David Abramowitz

The Resistance runs into a double-cross when they go to help a mining community rid itself of alien-backed thugs. Back at Science Frontiers, Bates's Asian henchman Chaing finds evidence that could expose Julie's true allegiance.

Glenna Sheryl Lee Raph
Garrison Michael Champion
Daniel Robert Thaler

Director: Bruce Seth Green

The Dissident (aka Force Field of Doom)

w Paul F. Edwards

Diana tests a powerful new force field which she intends using to seal off Los Angeles. Donovan and Ham must kidnap the alien genius responsible for the invention, and find a way to destroy it.

Jacob John McLiam
Galen Anthony DeLongis

Director: Walter Grauman

Reflection in Terror (aka A Christmas Miracle)

w Chris Manheim

Using a blood sample from Elizabeth, Diana creates a deadly clone which seeks out and ultimately *saves* the star-child. Bates sets a trap to test Julie's loyalty, once and for all.

Chris Mickey Jones
Elizabeth clone (aged 8) Jenny Beck
Dennis James Daughton
Laird Anthony James
Rev. Turney William Wellman Jr.

Director: Kevin Hooks

The Conversion

w Brian Taggert

Ham and Kyle are captured by the Visitors. Aboard the Mother Ship, Charles, the Leader's special envoy, arrives to assume command of the alien forces, with Lydia as his second in command. Charles brainwashes Ham, programming him to kill Donovan, but his plan is thwarted by Elizabeth's uncanny powers.

Chris Mickey Jones
Lin Catherine Nguyen

Director: Gilbert Shilton

The Hero

w Carleton Eastlake

Aliens posing as rebels stage a terrorist raid on Science Frontiers hoping to turn public opinion against the Resistance. Chaing and Charles round up rebel sympathizers and announce that they will kill one hostage a day until the leaders surrender. Robin falls for an apparently heroic comrade; Elias dies in a rescue bid.

John Langley Bruce Davison
George Caniff Robert Hooks
Carol Caniff Judyann Elder

Director: Kevin Hooks

The Betrayal

w Mark Rosner

When Willie is critically injured, Donovan and Ham kidnap a Visitor doctor who is sympathetic to the rebels' cause and reveals that Charles is smuggling arms into the city. Kyle has a poignant reconciliation with his father before Nathan is killed by his old henchman, Chaing. Robin is seduced by Langley and learns to her horror that he is a Visitor.

Langley Bruce Davison
Howie Richard Minchenberg

Director: Gilbert Shilton

The Rescue

w Garner Simmons

The scattered rebels struggle for survival in the war-torn city. Julie delivers a friend's baby in the midst of a battle. Charles forces Diana to marry him—but their wedding night ends in murder.

Alan Davis Terence Knox
Jo Ann Davis Darleen Carr
John Davis Ian Fried

Director: Kevin Hooks

The Champion

w Paul F. Edwards
Arriving to investigate Charles' death, Visitor General Philip allows Lydia and Diana to fight a laser duel. Donovan helps a beautiful widow organize the Resistance in her apathetic town.
Sheriff Roland Hugh Gillin
Kathy Deborah Wakeham
Jesse Sherri Sconer

Director: Cliff Bole

The Wildcats

w David Braff
Needing medicine to treat a deadly diphtheria epidemic, Julie and Kyle recruit a youth gang, one of whom may be a Visitor spy, to help steal the serum. Lydia and Diana conspire to frame a scapegoat for Charles's murder.
Tony Jeffrey Jay Cohen
Ellen Rhonda Aldrich
Andy Adam Silbar
Marta Gela Jacobson

Director: John Florea

The Little Dragon

w David Abramowitz
Philip, convinced that Donovan killed his brother, Martin, hunts down the rebel leader. But in the heat of their personal battle Philip learns that it was Diana who killed him, and he and Donovan forge a friendship and new understanding.
Robert Brett Cullen
Glenda Wendy Fulton
Angela Leslie Bevis

Director: Cliff Bole

War of Illusions

w John Simmons
When the Visitors install a hi-tech computer, Battlesphere, to launch a final assault on Earth, the Resistance pin their hopes of thwarting the plans on a teenage computer hacker.
Dr. David Atkins Conrad Janis
Henry Atkins Josh Richman
Oswald Peter Eibling

Director: Earl Bellamy

Secret Underground

w David Braff & Colley Cibber
Alerted by Philip, Donovan and Julie sneak aboard the Mother Ship to look for a hidden list naming all the rebel leaders. Diana schemes to have Lydia's brother slain during a ritual celebration. Julie discovers a former lover seemingly helping the Visitors to develop a virus that would prove deadly to humans.
Dr. Steven Maitland John Calvin
Oswald Peter Eibling
Nigel Ken Olandt
Judith Debbie Gates
Jonathan Derek Barton

Director: Cliff Bole

The Return

w David Abramowitz & Donald R. Boyle
The leader stuns the Visitors by ordering a truce and traveling to Earth to negotiate peace, but Diana plots to disrupt the peace and it takes the combined powers of Elizabeth and the Leader to prevent an appalling holocaust.
Thelma Marilyn Jones

Director: John Florea

THE VISITOR

Pilot Adam MacArthur disappeared into the Bermuda Triangle 50 years ago. Now he's back, sent by aliens to help steer Earth away from a path of destruction. Pursued by government agents, he travels the U.S. helping the right people put their lives on track . . . all for the benefit of humanity. Yet another series in the vein of *The Fugitive* (see also *Nowhere Man, The Pretender, Logan's Run,* etc.), *The Visitor* suffered quickly from the already-seen-it syndrome: not enough new or interesting to keep an audience's lasting attention.

REGULAR CAST
Adam MacArthur John Corbett *Agent Douglas Wilcox* Grand L. Bush
Agent Nicholas LaRue Leon Rippy *Agent Craig Van Patten* John Storey
Colonel James Vice Steve Railsback

12 color 60-minute episodes
Aired in the U.S. 19 September 1997–16 January
1998

Episodes
Pilot
Fear of Flying
The Devil's Rainbow
Dreams

Remember
The Black Box
Teufelsnacht
Reunion
Caged
Going Home
The Chain
The Trial

VOYAGE TO THE BOTTOM OF THE SEA

Submarine adventures were in vogue in 1964—Britain gave America *Stingray* and got *Voyage to the Bottom of the Sea* . . .

These were the voyages of the supersub *Seaview*, a TV spin-off from Irwin Allen's 1961 film epic of the same name, and the first of his lucrative quartet of television sci-fi sagas.

Seaview was a 600-foot-long atomic submarine capable of diving farther and faster than any craft in history and equipped with minisub, diving bell, a "flying" sub and atomic torpedoes. As if to underline the view that there were no half measures about the *Seaview*, even its creator and skipper was an admiral—Admiral Harriman Nelson, sailor-scientist head of the Nelson Institute of Marine Research. The crew's mission, though ostensibly scientific research, was to combat threats to world peace from anyone who felt a bit restless—be they foreign power, alien invader or one of many multi-tentacled monsters lurking in the gloomy depths.

Nelson was played by Richard Basehart, and his principal sidekick among the crew was Capt. Lee Crane (played by David Hedison, star of the 1959 movie original of *The Fly*).

The sub itself was a hand-me-down from the film *Voyage*, as were the sets, costumes, props and reel upon reel of underwater footage (Allen admitted that this saving in production costs was crucial to the TV series' birth). Special effects were masterminded by 20th Century Fox's William Abbott who picked up a brace of Emmys for his work on the show. And with the services of Oscar-winning cinematographer Winton Hoch, the series achieved a distinctive visual style.

But eventually that look became one of *déjà vu*, with the increasingly ludicrous plots and pictures being recycled more times than the crew's drinking water. In America, critics grew to loathe it, but *Seaview* kept on coming, for 110 episodes in four years.

REGULAR CAST
Admiral Harriman Nelson Richard Basehart *Capt. Lee Crane* David Hedison
Lt. Commander Chip Morton Robert Dowdell
Chief Sharkey Terry Becker (*from Season Two*)
Kowalski Del Monroe *CPO Curley Jones* Henry Kulky
Patterson Paul Trinka *Sparks* Arch Whiting *Sonar* Nigel McKeand

Creator/Producer: Irwin Allen
Special effects: William Abbott
Makeup: Ben Nye

An Irwin Allen Production for 20th Century Fox Television
110 60-minute episodes
black and white (Season One)
color (from Season Two)

U.S. premiere: 14 September 1964
U.K. premieres:

Season One:
10 October 1964–29 May 1965
(ABC Weekend Television)
Season Two (incomplete run):
8 January–10 April 1966
(ABC Weekend Television)
(Author's note: After an initial Season Two run of 13 episodes, subsequent U.K. runs were made up of episodes from more than one American season. For ease of reference, all episodes are grouped in their original American seasons.)

Season One
32 episodes

Eleven Days to Zero

w Irwin Allen
The *Seaview* is sent to avert worldwide tidal waves by detonating a polar nuclear device—but finds its mission threatened by enemy agents.
Malone Mark Slade
Chairman Booth Colman
O'Brien Gordon Gilbert
Army general Barney Biro
Dr. Fred Wilson Eddie Albert
Dr. Gamma Theodore Marcuse
Dr. Selby John Zaremba
Capt. Phillips Bill Hudson

Director: Irwin Allen

The City Beneath the Sea

w Richard Landau
While investigating the disappearance of two research vessels in the Aegean, Crane and a girl diver, Melina, are kidnapped and taken to a hostile underwater city.
Melina Linda Cristal
Zeraff Hurd Hatfield
Round Face John Anderson

Director: John Brahm

The Fear Makers

w Anthony Wilson
Enemy agents pump "feargas" into two atomic subs to slow down undersea research work.
Dr. Kenner Edgar Dergen
Dr. Davis Lloyd Bochner
Malone Mark Slade

Director: Leonard Horn

The Mist of Silence

w John McGreevey
Seaview is ordered to rescue a Latin American president who is the unwilling front man for a military junta and its new gas weapon.
Detta Rita Gam
Ricardo Alejandro Rey
Gen. D'Alvarez Mike Kellin
Capt. Serra Henry Delgado
President Fuentes Edward Colmans
Williams Doug Lambert
Chairman Booth Colman

Director: Leonard Horn

The Sky Is Falling

w Don Brinkley
Rays from a mysterious spacecraft knock out all *Seaview*'s power systems.
Rear Adm. Tobin Charles McGraw
Spaceman Joseph di Reda
Air Force general Frank Ferguson

Director: Leonard Horn

Turn Back the Clock

w Sheldon Stark
Investigating the story of a man who turns up tanned and healthy after being lost for nine months in Antarctica, Nelson, Crane and the man's fiancée, Carol, are led to a strange prehistoric world. (Features footage from Allen's film *Lost World*, and guest stars Yvonne "Batgirl" Craig.)
Jason Kemp Nick Adams
Carol Yvonne Craig
Dr. Denning Les Tremayne
Native girl Vitina Marcus
Zeigler Robert Cornthwaite
Crewman Mark Slade

Director: Alan Crosland Jr.

Hot Line

w Berne Giler
One of two Russian scientists being taken by *Seaview* to disarm a defective Soviet atomic satellite is an impostor.
Gronski Everett Sloan
Gregory Malinoff Michael Ansara

Director: John Brahm

The Price of Doom

w Harlan Ellison
The *Seaview* is infiltrated by mysteriously expanding plankton.
Julie Lyle Jill Ireland
Dr. Karl Reisner David Opatoshu
Phillip Wesley John Milford
Pennell Steve Ihnat
Mrs. Pennell Pat Priest
General Dan Seymour
Crewcut man Ivan Triesault

Director: James Goldstone

Submarine Sunk Here

w William Tunberg
The *Seaview* blunders into a minefield, where an explosion cripples the sub and sends it to the bottom of the sea.
Evans Carl Reindel
Harker Eddie Ryder
Blake Robert Doyle
Dr. Baines Wright King

Director: Leonard Horn

The Magnus Beam

w Alan Caillou
Aided by a beautiful female spy and an offbeat team of Resistance men, Crane and Harriman attempt to destroy a fantastic new weapon that could start World War Three.
Luana Monique Lemaire
Gen. Gamal Malachi Throne
Abdul Azziz Jacques Aubuchon
Amadi Mario Alcalde
Inspector Falazin Joseph Ruskin

Director: Leonard Horn

The Village of Guilt

w Berne Giler
Seaview investigates the activities of a beautiful girl, a mad scientist and his terrifying creation—a sea monster that has a whole village frozen into silence.
Mattson Richard Carlson
Sigrid Anna-Lisa
Dalgren Steven Geray
Hassler Frank Richards
Anderson G. Stanley Jones

Director: Irwin Allen

No Way Out

w Robert Hamner
Smuggling a defecting Red agent to the U.S. involves *Seaview* in a web of spies and counterspies.
Koslow Than Wyenn
Anna Ravec Danielle de Metz
Col. Lascoe Oscar Beregi
Victor Vail Jan Merlin
Wilson Don Wilbanks
Parker Richard Webb

Director: Felix Feist

The Blizzard Makers

w William Welch
A top scientist has been turned into a killer—programmed to eliminate Nelson before he discovers the truth behind a blizzard in Florida.

Dr. Melton Milton Selzer
Cregar Werner Klemperer

Director: Joseph Leytes

The Ghost of Moby Dick

w Robert Hamner
A marine biologist becomes a modern-day Ahab when he enlists *Seaview*'s aid in pursuing a 200-ton whale that crippled him. (Also features *Lost in Space* "mom" June Lockhart.)
Dr. Walter Bryce Edward Binns
Ellen Bryce June Lockhart
Jimmy Bryce Bob Beekman

Director: Sobey Martin

Hail to the Chief

w Don Brinkley
Enemy agents plot to prevent the recovery of the U.S. president aboard *Seaview* following an accident. (This episode features *Star Trek*'s James Doohan.)
Laura Rettig Viveca Lindfors
General Beeker John Hoyt
Commander Jamison Malcolm Atterbury
Morgan Edward C. Platt
Dr. Taylor Tom Palmer
Tobin James Doohan
Monique Nancy Kovack
Oberhansly Lorence Kerr

Director: Gerd Oswald

The Last Battle

w Robert Hamner
Nelson is kidnapped by a group of diehard Nazis who plan to use *Seaview* to destroy the world and build a Fourth Reich.
Schroder John Van Dreelen
Reinhardt Dayton Lummis
Miklos Joe de Santis
Brewster Ben Wright
Tomas Rudy Solari
Deiner Eric Feldary
Stewardess Sandra Williams

Director: Felix Feist

Doomsday

w William Read Woodfield
The nation goes on war alert following a sudden mass missile launching by a foreign power.
Corbett Donald Harron
Corporal Sy Prescott
Clark Paul Carr
Gen. Ashton Paul Genge
President Ford Rainey
Doctor Richard Bull

Director: James Goldstone

Mutiny

w William Read Woodfield
While investigating the loss of an experimental sub, Nelson shows sign of a mental breakdown.
Admiral Starke Harold J. Stone
Doctor Richard Bull
Captain Jay Lanin

Director: James Goldstone

Long Live the King

w Raphael Hayes
Racing to get young Prince Ang back to assume his throne before the Reds take over, the *Seaview* encounters an enigmatic stranger, Old John, floating on a rowboat in mid-ocean.
Old John Carroll O'Connor
Prince Ang Michel Petit
Col. Meger Michael Pate
Countess Sara Shane
Georges Jan Arvan

Director: Laslo Benedek

The Invaders

w William Read Woodfield
A man-like creature preserved in suspended animation for 20 million years is found on the ocean floor and taken aboard *Seaview*.
Zar Robert Duvall
Foster Michael McDonald

Director: Sobey Martin

The Indestructible Man

w Richard Landau
Scientists aboard *Seaview* discover that a robot recovered from a fallen space capsule has been converted into a destructive monster.
Dr. Brand Michael Constantine

Director: Felix Feist

The Buccaneer

w William Welch & Albert Gail
A mad art collector takes over *Seaview* in a plot to steal the *Mona Lisa* from a French ship.
Logan Barry Atwater
Igor George Keymas
French captain Emile Genest

Director: Laslo Benedek

The Human Computer

w Robert Hamner
The *Seaview* sails on an automated mission with Captain Crane supposedly the only human on board . . .
Man Harry Millard
Reston Simon Scott
Admirals Herbert Lytton, Walter Sande
Foreign general Ted De Corsia

Director: James Goldstone

The Saboteur

w William Read Woodfield & George Read (*alias* Allan Balter)
Capt. Crane is brainwashed by enemy agents into sabotaging the *Seaview*'s latest mission.
Forester Warren Stevens
Dr. Ullman Bert Freed

Director: Felix Feist

Cradle of the Deep

w Robert Hamner
A microscopic particle of matter, taken aboard *Seaview* from the ocean floor, grows into an enormous protoplasm that threatens all aboard.
Dr. Janus John Anderson
Dr. Benton Howard Wendell
O'Brien Derrick Lew
Helmsman Robert Pane

Director: Sobey Martin

The Amphibians

w Rik Vollaerts
Scientists in an undersea lab convert themselves into amphibious creatures.
Doc Richard Bull
Dr. Jenkins Skip Homeier
Dr. Winslow Curt Conway
Angie Zale Parry

Director: Felix Feist

The Exile

w William Read Woodfield
Nelson is stranded on a life-raft with Brynov, ex-premier of a hostile foreign power.
Brynov Edward Asner
Josip David Sheiner
Konstantin Harry Davis
Semenev James Frawley
Mikhil Jason Wingreen

Director: James Goldstone

The Creature

w Rik Vollaerts
Capt. Wayne Adams, sole survivor of a missile disaster, joins *Seaview* to search the ocean floor for the mysterious force which foiled the missile launch.
Adams Leslie Nielsen
Crewman Pat Culliton
Radar man William Stevens

Director: Sobey Martin

The Secret of the Loch

w Charles Bennett
The *Seaview* follows a natural underwater conduit leading to Loch Ness where a scientist claims to have seen a monster kill several men.
Prof. MacDougall Torin Thatcher
Insp. Lester Hedley Mattingly
Angus George Mitchell
Andrews John McLiam

Director: Sobey Martin

The Enemies

w William Read Woodfield
Nelson and Crane are captured by foreign scientists who use them in an experiment aimed at turning friends into bitter enemies.
Gen. Tau Henry Silva
Dr. Shinera Malachi Throne
Captain Williams Robert Sampson
Richardson Tom Skerritt

Director: Felix Feist

The Condemned

w William Read Woodfield
Nelson and Crane are ordered to turn the *Seaview* over to a publicity-seeking scientist who plans to break the "crush barrier."
Admiral Falk J.D. Cannon
Archer Arthur Franz
Hoff Alvy Moore

Director: Leonard Horn

The Traitor

w William Welch & Al Gail
Enemy agents in France capture Nelson's young sister hoping to force him to reveal the location of underwater missile silos.
Major Gen. Fenton George Sanders
Hamid Michael Pate
Sister Susan Flannery

Director: Sobey Martin

Season Two
26 episodes

Jonah and the Whale

w Simon Wincelberg
Trying to salvage information about an underwater laboratory, Nelson and Russian scientist Katya Markhova are swallowed by a whale.
Katya Markhova Gia Scala
Helmsman Robert Pane
Crewman Pat Culliton

Director: Sobey Martin

. . . And Five of Us Are Left

w Robert Vincent Wright
Admiral Nelson heads an expedition to find the survivors of a sunken submarine trapped for 28 years in an undersea cave.
Wilson James Anderson
Werden Robert Doyle
Hill Ed McCready
Ryan Phillip Pine
Brenda Francoise Ruggieri
Nakamura Teru Shimada
Johnson Kent Taylor

Director: Harry Harris

The Cyborg

w William Read Woodfield & Allan Balter
A deranged scientist creates a robot duplicate of Nelson and orders it to target *Seaview*'s nuclear warheads at Washington, Peking and Moscow in a plot to rule the world.
Tabor Ulrich Victor Buono
Gundi Brooke Bundy
Tish Sweetly Nancy Hsueh
Cyborg voices Fred Crane
Technician Tom Curtis
Sailor Stanley Schneider
Reporter Nicholas Colasanto

Director: Leo Penn

Escape from Venice

w Charles Bennett
Nelson engineers a daring rescue of Capt. Crane from the clutches of enemy agents in Venice.
Count Staglione Renzo Cesana
Lola Hale Danica D'Hondt
Bellini Vincent Gardenia
Julietta Delphi Lawrence

Director: Alex March

Time Bomb

w William Read Woodfield *&* Allan Balter
An oriental secret agent's bid to turn Nelson into a human time bomb almost starts a war between Russia and America.
Katie Susan Flannery
Litchka Ina Balin
Adm. Johnson John Zaremba
Li Tung Richard Loo

Director: Sobey Martin

The Left-Handed Man

w William Welch
Nelson faces death several times as he strives to foil a subversive plot to infiltrate the Defense Department.
George Penfield Regis Toomey
Noah Grafton Cyril Delevanti
Left-handed man Charles Dierkop
Tippy Penfield Barbara Bouchet
Angie Judy Lang
Cabrillo Michael Barrier

Director: Jerry Hopper

The X Factor

w William Welch
Admiral Nelson and the *Seaview* crew battle enemy agents in a toy factory to save a kidnapped U.S. scientist who has been coated in wax and transformed into a life-size mannequin.
Henderson Jan Merlin
Liscomb George Tyne
Alexander Corby John McGiver
Capt. Shire Bill Hudson
Technician Anthony Brand

Director: Leonard Horn

Leviathan

w William Welch
Leaking radiation from a strange underwater fissure in the Earth's crust turns an old scientist colleague of Nelson's into a giant monster bent on destroying *Seaview*.
Cara Karen Steele
Dr. Sterling Liam Sullivan

Director: Harry Harris

The Peacemaker

w William Read Woodfield *&* Allan Balter
A fanatical scientist, Everett Lang, threatens to destroy the world with his new super-bomb.

Everett Lang John Cassavetes
Su Yin Irene Tsu
Policeman Lloyd Kino
Connors Whit Bissell
Premier Dale Ishimoto
Hansen Walter Woolf King

Director: Sobey Martin

The Silent Saboteurs

w Sidney Marshall *story by* Max Ehrlich
Crane takes the flying sub on a daring mission to destroy a secret computer being used to intercept manned Venus space flights. (Features *Star Trek*'s George Takei.)
Moana Pilar Seurat
Li Cheng George Takei
Halden Bert Freed
Lago Alex D'Arcy
Stevens Phil Posner
Astronauts Robert Chadwick, Ted Jordon

Director: Sobey Martin

The Deadliest Game

w Rik Vollaerts
Nelson foils a plot by a U.S. general to kill the President and trigger a nuclear war.
Gen. Hobson Lloyd Bochner
President Robert F. Simon
Lydia Parrish Audrey Dalton
Gen. Reed Michaels Robert Cornthwaite

Director: Sobey Martin

The Monsters from Outer Space

w William Read Woodfield *&* Allan Balter
A Saturn space probe reenters Earth's atmosphere with a strange tentacled monster attached to it.
Seaview doctor Wayne Heffley
Space Center technician Lee Delano
Flight director Preston Hanson
Naval commander Hal Torey

Director: James Clark

The Machines Strike Back

w John *&* Ward Hawkins
Unmanned submarines inexplicably turn their devastating missiles toward America.
Adm. Halder Roger Carmel
Capt. Verna Trober Francoise Ruggieri
Adm. Johnson John Gallaudet
Senator Kimberly Bert Ramsden

Director: Nathan Juran

The Death Ship

w William Read Woodfield & Allan Balter
Nelson averts an enemy plot to blow up a seven-nation peace conference.
Stroller Lew Gallo
Tracy Elizabeth Perry
Ava June Vincent
Klaus Ivan Triesault
Chandler David Sheiner
Templeton Harry Davis

Director: Abner Biberman

Killers of the Deep

w William Read Woodfield & Allan Balter
Aboard a U.S. destroyer, Nelson wages a harrowing battle with an enemy sub trying to steal undersea defense missiles.
Fraser Patrick Wayne
Capt. Tomas Ruiz Michael Ansara
Manolo James Frawley
Capt. Lawrence John Newton
Sonar men Dallas Mitchell, Gus Trikonis

Director: Harry Harris

Terror on Dinosaur Island

w William Welch
Nelson and Chief Sharkey parachute from the flying sub onto a volcanic island inhabited by prehistoric monsters (further footage culled from Allen's film *The Lost World*).
Benson Paul Carr

Director: Leonard Horn

Deadly Creature Below!

w William Read Woodfield & Allan Balter
Two escaped convicts try to hijack the flying sub while a sea monster menaces the *Seaview*.
Dobbs Nehemiah Persoff
Hawkins Paul Comi
Seaview doctor Wayne Heffley

Director: Sobey Martin

The Phantom Strikes

w William Welch
The *Seaview* is nearly destroyed by a phantom sub and its ghostly captain who tries to reincarnate himself via Crane.
Gerhardt Krueger Alfred Ryder

Director: Sutton Roley

The Sky's On Fire

w William Welch, *screenplay by* Irwin Allen & Charles Bennett
While the Van Allen radiation belt burns, a fanatical UN official tries to sabotage Nelson's plan to explode the burning gases from the atmosphere.
Weber David J. Stewart
Carleton Robert H. Harris
McHenry Frank Martin

Director: Sobey Martin

Graveyard of Fear

w Robert Vincent Wright
The *Seaview* is menaced by a giant jellyfish.
Dr. Ames Robert Loggia
Karyl Marian Moses

Director: Justus Addis

The Shape of Doom

w William Welch
In a race to protect a ship carrying the President, Nelson and Crane battle a giant whale that has swallowed an atomic bomb.
Dr. Alex Holden Kevin Hagen

Director: Nathan Juran

Dead Man's Doubloons

w Sidney Marshall
The flying sub is attacked by a ghostly underwater pirate ship.
Capt. Brent Albert Salmi
Sebastian Allen Jaffe
Adm. Howard Robert Brubaker

Director: Sutton Roley

The Monster's Web

w Al Gail & Peter Packer, *story by* Peter Packer
The *Seaview* battles a giant spider while retrieving high-explosive fuel from a wrecked nuclear sub.
Capt. Gantt Mark Richman
Baltar Barry Coe
Sonar man Sea Morgan

Director: Justus Addis

The Menfish

w William Read Woodfield *&* Allan Balter
The *Seaview* tangles with yet another monster—a half-man, half-fish creature created by a mad scientist.
Admiral Park Gary Merrill
Johnson Roy Jenson
Hansjurg Victor Lundin
Dr. Borgman John Dehner

Director: Tom Gries

The Mechanical Man

w John *&* Ward Hawkins
A life-like robot uses the *Seaview* to seek control of the world.
Omir James Darren
Paul Arthur O'Connell
Jensen Seymour Cassel
Van Druten Cec Linder

Director: Sobey Martin

The Return of the Phantom

w William Welch
The Phantom returns from the dead in a renewed attempt to capture Crane's body.
Gerhardt Krueger Alfred Ryder
Lani Vitina Marcus
Doctor Richard Bull

Director: Sutton Roley

Season Three
26 episodes

Monster from the Inferno

w Rik Vollaerts
A scientist-diver animates a brain-shaped mass that tries to take over the *Seaview*.
Lindsay Arthur Hill
Doctor Richard Bull

Director: Harry Harris

Werewolf

w Donn Mullally
Nelson and the *Seaview* crewmen are transformed into werewolves.
Hollis Charles Aidman
Witt Douglas Bank

Director: Justus Addiss

The Day the World Ended

w William Welch
The *Seaview* loses contact with the world as a fanatical power-crazed senator hypnotizes the entire crew.
Senator Dennis Skip Homeier

Director: Jerry Hopper

Night of Terror

w Robert Bloomfield
Shipwrecked on a mysterious island, Nelson, Sharkey and a geologist are terrorized by a giant lizard and hallucinations.
Sprague Henry Jones
Buccaneer Jerry Catron

Director: Justus Addiss

The Terrible Toys

w Robert Vincent Wright
Aliens aboard a UFO rig six wind-up toys to destroy the *Seaview*.
Sam Burke Paul Fix
Old man Francis X. Bushman
Voice Jim Mills

Director: Justus Addiss

Day of Evil

w William Welch
An alien stranger tries to force Nelson to destroy the Pacific fleet with a nuclear missile.
Doctor Richard Bull

Director: Jerry Hopper

Deadly Waters

w Robert Vincent Wright
Kowalski's injured, unreasonable brother, Stan, saves the *Seaview* crew from a deep-sea death.
Kruger Lew Gallo
Stan Kowalski Don Gordon
Commander Finch Harry Lauter

Director: Gerald Mayer

Thing from Inner Space

w William Welch
An adventurer leads the *Seaview* crew in search of a monster that killed his camera crew.
Bainbridge Wells Hugh Marlowe
Monster Dawson Palmer

Director: Alex March

The Death Watch

w William Welch
Nelson and Crane are the subjects of an experiment in which they are ordered to kill each other.
(No guest cast)

Director: Leonard Horn

Deadly Invasion

w John *&* Ward Hawkins
Faceless aliens invade Earth and try to take over an underwater atomic base.
Sam Garrity Warren Stevens
Gen. Haine Michael Fox
Kelly Ashley Gilbert
Peters Brent Davis

Director: Nathan Juran

The Haunted Submarine

w William Welch
Nelson is plagued by a ghostly slave trader ancestor who has come to take him away.
Captain Seamus O'Hara Nelson Richard Basehart

Director: Harry Harris

The Plant Man

w Donn Mullally
The *Seaview* battles multiplying plant monsters and the twin scientists who created them.
John/Ben Wilson William Smithers

Director: Harry Harris

The Lost Bomb

w Oliver Crawford
An enemy sub vies with the *Seaview* for an activated super bomb that threatens to explode.
Dr. Bradley John Lupton
Vadim Gerald Mohr
Zane George Keymas

Director: Gerald Mayer

The Brand of the Beast

w William Welch
Radiation exposure causes Nelson to suffer a recurrence of the Werewolf virus. (You can't keep a good plot down!)
Doctor Richard Bull

Director: Justus Addiss

The Creature

w John *&* Ward Hawkins
Nelson attempts to destroy a creature that threatens to grow large enough to demolish whole cities.
Dr. King Lyle Bettger

Director: Justus Addiss

Death from the Past

w Sidney Marshall *&* Charles Bennett, *story by* Charles Bennett
The *Seaview* battles two Nazi officers left over from World War Two who attempt to launch missiles at the Allied capitals.
Adm. Von Neuberg John Van Dreelen
Lt. Froelich Jan Merlin

Director: Justus Addiss

The Heat Monster

w Charles Bennett
The *Seaview* battles an invasion of alien heat monsters on the Arctic ice cap.
Sven Larsen Don Knight
Dr. Bergstrom Alfred Ryder

Director: Gerald Mayer

The Fossil Men

w James Whiton
The *Seaview* battles hostile fossil men who want to take over the world.
Capt. Wren Brendan Dillon
Richards Jerry Catron

Director: Justus Addiss

The Mermaid

w William Welch
Crane captures a mermaid who eventually leads the sub to an undersea nuclear bomb about to explode.
Mermaid Diane Webber

Director: Jerry Hopper

The Mummy

w William Welch
A 3000-year-old mummy puts a spell on Crane and terrorizes the *Seaview*.
Doctor Richard Bull

Director: Harry Harris

Shadowman

w Rik Vollaerts
The *Seaview* is taken over by a hostile energy mass from a distant galaxy.
(No guest cast)

Director: Justus Addiss

No Escape from Death

w William Welch
While trying to surface after a crippling collision, the *Seaview* is threatened by a gigantic Portuguese man-o-war.
(No guest cast)

Director: Harry Harris

Doomsday Island

w Peter Germano
The sub encounters terrifying alien creatures who want to use *Seaview*'s power to take over the Earth.
Lars Jock Gaynor

Director: Jerry Hopper

The Wax Man

w William Welch
Hostile wax replicas of the crew take over *Seaview*.
Clown Michael Dunn

Director: Harmon Jones

Deadly Cloud

w Rik Vollaerts
The *Seaview* is sent to check out a mysterious cloud that has caused widespread destruction around the world.
Jurgenson Robert Carson

Director: Jerry Hopper

Destroy Seaview!

w Donn Mullally
Nelson is brainwashed into trying to destroy the *Seaview*—and nearly succeeds.
Leader Jerry Catron
Dr. Land Arthur Space

Director: Justus Addiss

Season Four
26 episodes

Man of Many Faces

w William Welch
A mad scientist imperils the Earth by drawing the Moon toward it.
Dr. Mason Jock Gaynor
Page Bradd Arnold
Reporter Howard Culver

Director: Harry Harris

Time Lock

w William Welch
A man of the future tries to add Nelson to his collection of zombie-like military officers.
Alpha John Crawford

Director: Jerry Hopper

The Deadly Dolls

w Charles Bennett
Nelson and Crane battle a puppet master, the tool of a machine-ruled civilization.
Prof. Multiple Vincent Price
Puppeteer Ronald P. Martin

Director: Harry Harris

Fires of Death

w Arthur Weiss
The crew battle to stop an aged alchemist who's endangering the entire southern hemisphere to obtain an elixir of youth from an exploding volcano.
Dr. Turner Victor Jory

Director: Jerry Hopper

Cave of the Dead

w William Welch
Nelson is the target of a seaman from the past, trying to transfer the curse of the Flying Dutchman onto him.
Doctor Richard Bull
Van Wyck Warren Stevens

Director: Harry Harris

Sealed Orders

w William Welch
Mass hallucinations grip the *Seaview* crew when a secret missile they are carrying begins to emit strange fumes.
(No guest cast)

Director: Jerry Hopper

Journey with Fear

w Arthur Weiss
Nelson, Crane and Morton are captured by aliens and transported in a flash to their planet.
Maj. Wilson Eric Matthews
Centaur I Gene Dynarski
Centaur II Jim Gosa

Director: Harry Harris

Terror

w Sidney Ellis
Alien plant creatures arrive to take over the Earth, possessing Nelson and some of the *Seaview* crew.
Dr. Thompson Damian O'Flynn
Dunlap Pat Culliton
Crewmen Brent Davis, Thom Brann

Director: Jerry Hopper

Fatal Cargo

w William Welch
Nelson's decision to carry on with the animal experiments of a friend who has mysteriously died almost proves fatal to him, too.
Brock Woodrow Parfrey
Dr. Blanchard Jon Lormer

Director: Jerry Hopper

Rescue

w William Welch
Nelson battles a saboteur and a mystery sub that threatens to destroy them.
CPO Beach Don Dubbins

Director: Justus Addiss

The Death Clock

w Sidney Marshall
The *Seaview* crew survives a fourth-dimensional nightmare of death and destruction.
Mallory Chris Robinson

Director: Charles Rondeau

Secret of the Deep

w William Welch
A traitor nearly undermines *Seaview*'s mission to destroy a group of men threatening the world.
John Hendrix Mark Richman

Director: Charles Rondeau

Blow Up

w William Welch
A gas gives Nelson temporary paranoia and he tries to torpedo Navy subs.
Doctor Richard Bull

Director: Justus Addiss

Deadly Amphibians

w Arthur Weiss
An amphibian race tries to take over the *Seaview* and use its nuclear power for its own ends.
Proto Don Matheson
Corpsman Joey Tata
Guard Pat Culliton

Director: Jerry Hopper

The Abominable Snowman

w Robert Hamner
In Antarctica, the *Seaview* is menaced by a creature created by weather experiments.
Corpsman Frank Babich
Guard Bruce Mars
Rayburn Dusty Cadis

Director: Robert Sparr

The Return of Blackbeard

w Al Gail
Blackbeard the pirate appears and tries to take over the *Seaview*.
Blackbeard Malachi Throne

Director: Justus Addiss

A Time to Die

w William Welch
The super-sub is menaced by an odd little man capable of moving people about through time.
Mr. Pem Henry Jones

Director: Robert Sparr

The Edge of Doom

w William Welch
An enemy agent impersonates a crewman to sabotage a mission.
Helmsman Scott McFadden

Director: Justus Addiss

Nightmare

w Sidney Marshall
Crane finds the entire crew against him as he tries to stop Nelson from launching a missile attack on Washington . . . but it's all an alien trick!
Bentley Paul Mantee

Director: Charles Rondeau

The Lobster Man

w Al Gail
A lobster-like alien plots to destroy Earth. (Now that's what I call a plot!)
Alien Victor Lundin

Director: Justus Addiss

Terrible Leprechaun

w Charles Bennett
The *Seaview* crew match wits with an unusual elfin enemy to prevent a nuclear explosion.
Leprechaun Mickey/Leprechaun Patrick Walter Burke
Somers Ralph Garrett
Corpsman Pat Culliton
Crewman John Bellah

Director: Jerry Hopper

Savage Jungle

w Arthur Weiss
A jungle growth planted by aliens threatens to over-run the Earth.
Alien Pat Culliton
Keeler Perry Lopez

Director: Robert Sparr

Man-Beast

w William Welch
Crane turns into a beast-like creature and menaces all on board the *Seaview*.
Dr. Kermit Braddock Lawrence Montaigne

Director: Jerry Hopper

Flaming Ice

w Arthur Browne Jr.
The super-sub is sent to the polar ice cap to find the cause of destructive worldwide floods.
Gelid Michael Pate
Frost men Frank Babich, George Robotham

Director: Robert Sparr

Attack!

w William Welch
With the help of a peace-loving alien, Nelson and Crane prevent an invasion of Earth.
Robek Skip Homeier
Komal Kevin Hagen

Director: Jerry Hopper

No Way Back

w William Welch
The mysterious Mr. Pem returns to try to use the *Seaview* to go back in time and change the course of history.
Mr. Pem Henry Jones
Benedict Arnold Barry Atwater
Maj. John Andre William Beckley

Director: Robert Sparr

VOYAGERS

History's a tenuous thing—it doesn't just happen, it needs a little nudge here and there to make sure everything falls into place. That's the premise behind this U.S. children's time-travel adventure series of the early eighties.

Phineas Bogg is a member of a group of specialist time travelers called Voyagers, who nip back and forth in time, via a device called the Omni, putting history to rights. That could mean anything from making sure the Wright Brothers get off the ground, to keeping George Washington on the right side, from helping Spartacus get out of jail to organize the slaves' revolt to making sure the baby Moses is found by the right people.

By mistake, however, Bogg lands in the Manhattan bedroom of young Jeffrey Jones, where, unfortunately, Bogg's all-important travel guide is eaten by Jeffrey's pet dog. Without it, Bogg doesn't have a clue how history's great events are supposed to turn out, but luckily Jeffrey knows his dates and agrees to accompany Bogg on his travels. The format usually saw them visit two or three historical hot spots each episode, at the end of which Meeno Peluce, who played Jeffrey, would urge his young viewers to seek out more information.

REGULAR CAST
Phineas Bogg Jon-Erik Hexum *Jeffrey Jones* Meeno Peluce

Creator: James D. Parriott
Producer: Jill Sherman
Co-producer: Robert Steinhauer
Writers: Various, including James D. Parriott, Jill Sherman, Don Shelly, Robert Janes, Nick Thiel
Directors: Various, including James D. Parriott, Virgil Vogel, Alan J. Levi, Ron Satlof, Bernard McEveety, Sigmund Neufeld, Winrich Kolbe, Paul Stanley

21 color 60-minute episodes
Voyagers (pilot)
Created Equal
Bully and Billy
Agents of Satan
Worlds Apart
Cleo and the Babe

The Day the Rebs Took Lincoln
Old Hickory and the Pirate
The World of Marco Polo
An Arrow Pointing East
Merry Christmas, Bogg
Buffalo Bill and Annie Oakley Play the Palace
Princess Victoria and Albert Schweitzer
The Trial of Phineas Bogg
Sneak Attack
Voyagers of the Titanic
Pursuit
Destiny's Choice
All Fall Down
Barriers of Sound
Arthur Conan Doyle and Nellie Bly

U.S. premiere: 3 October 1982

VR5

TV's flirted with virtual reality before—remember *Wild Palms?*—but this is the first time anyone's made an entire series out of it, creating what you might call Cyberspace: Above and Beyond.

Virtual reality, as any game-playing kid knows, is a computer-generated, interactive, three-dimensional environment in which a person is immersed, usually through wearing a special helmet or goggles. VR5 stands for the fifth level of virtual reality, a previously unattainable state in which the user is taken into the virtual world and "accessed" directly via the subconscious mind. To all intents and purposes what is then experienced is real.

VR5 is a thriller series about beautiful but shy Sydney Bloom who repairs phone lines by day and after hours tinkers with virtual reality technology. One day she inadvertently taps into an open phone line and hooks it up to her computer modem, bringing the person on the other end of the line—a cranky neighbor played by maverick magician Penn Jillette—into her computer world of virtual reality.

Sydney is subsequently shanghaied by a shadowy government agency called The Committee to carry out assignments that require something more than conventional investigative methods. Pre-selecting an environment, her forays into the VR dimension begin with a simple phone call to her subject who then joins her in her computer-generated world.

Sounds a straightforward enough premise for an adventure series, but our Sydney's a girl with hang-ups. Her father, Dr. Joseph Bloom (played by guest star David McCallum), was a neurobiologist pioneering work in virtual reality research and technology. When Sydney was a little girl, both Dad and her twin sister, Samantha, were apparently killed in a car crash that she survived and that left her mother severely traumatized. VR provides a way for Sydney to explore her family relationships and memories and she discovers that her past may not be what she thought it was . . . She is eventually reunited with her sister and learns that her father is still alive and being hunted by a faction of the Committee.

VR5 is such a technically smart series that it's a shame that in crucial areas of plot, dialogue and character, it's so dry. Lori Singer, the cello-playing kid from *Fame*, stars as Sydney and looks terrific in some way-out costumes and tumbling blond hair. But it's hard to love her. So much of the series is played for visual thrills that the viewer is kept at an emotional distance.

In fact, at times watching *VR5* is almost literally like watching paint dry. One of the most advanced film colorization techniques is used to create the virtual reality sequences, whereby the scenes are filmed in black and white, then put through a computerized coloring process that spans a palette of more than 16 million colors, creating some bizarre and otherworldly landscapes. *VR5*'s style is completed by some minimalistic, airy sets for Sydney's home and all-involving surround sound.

One nice touch: Sydney has a couple of goldfish—called Steed and Mrs. Peel. The series ran for one season in the U.S., but failed to set the ratings alight. Sky One gave it a run in 1995, repeated on Sky Two in 1996.

REGULAR CAST

Sydney Bloom Lori Singer   *Duncan* Michael Easton
Dr. Frank Morgan Will Patton   *(Eps. 1–4)*
Oliver Sampson Anthony Head   *(Eps. 4–10)*
Dr. Joseph Bloom David McCallum   *Nora Bloom* Louise Fletcher
Samantha Bloom Tracey Needham

Creators: Thania St. John, Michael Katleman, Geoffrey Hemwall, Jeannine Renshaw, Adam Cherry
Executive producer: John Sacret Young
Co-executive producer: Thania St. John
Supervising producer: Michael Katleman
Writers: Various, including Thania St. John, Eric Blakeney, Jeannine Renshaw
Directors: Various, including Michael Katleman, John Sacret Young, Lorraine Senna Ferrara, Steve Dubin
Samoset Productions, in association with Rysher Entertainment

13 color 60-minute episodes
Pilot
Dr. Strangechild

Love and Death
5D
Escape
Facing the Fire
Simon's Choice
Control Freak
The Many Faces of Alex
Reunion
Send Me an Angel
Sisters
Parallel Lives

U.S. premiere: 10 March 1995
U.K. Premiere: 21 October 1995
(Sky One)

WAR OF THE WORLDS

"They're back, they're back!"

Somewhat under-rated "sequel" to the 1953 movie in which marauding Martian invaders were stopped at the 11th hour by a common bacteria.

Now, 35 years later, the stored remains of alien invaders (no longer referred to as Martians) are reactivated by irradiated toxins during a terrorist attack on a nuclear waste dump. Coming alive, the creatures kill the terrorists and "absorb" their bodies. In this way, the aliens can carry out their mission undetected, although the rapid effects of radiation poisoning are soon noticeable to the naked eye, making it necessary for the aliens to constantly take over new human bodies, as they resume their plan to conquer the Earth.

A combination of *The Invaders* and *Invasion of the Body Snatchers*, this U.S. series blended often gruesome shocks—when killed, the bodies dissolved into a slimy mess—with some elegantly subtle touches.

In one early episode, a small boy whose parents and grandmother have been "taken over" realizes he is traveling with aliens and holds up a sign to passing vehicles that reads "help me." Later on, a busload of tourists taken over by aliens crosses the Canadian/U.S. border. Aboard is the same young boy, waving a new sign that reads "save me."

Another episode, "Eye for an Eye," takes as its premise that the notorious 1938 Orson Welles radio broadcast of H.G. Wells's original story was in fact a government cover-up for a *real* invasion.

These aliens are totally ruthless, as they strive to strengthen their foothold on Earth, seeking out their old spaceships. Led by a trinity of leaders known as the Advocacy, these aliens also have a disturbing knack of beating the good guys to the punch. It's an invasion by stealth, but it seems unstoppable. As many episodes end on a downbeat note as on an optimistic one.

Leading the Earth fightback is renowned astrophysicist Dr. Harrison Blackwood, whose parents died in the 1953 invasion. He's helped by his paraplegic friend and computer whiz Norton Drake and microbiologist Suzanne McCullough who constantly strives to find a strain of bacteria that could defeat the aliens. Military muscle and combat strategy are provided by tough soldier and Cherokee Indian Lt. Colonel Paul Ironhorse. Other semi-regular characters include Suzanne's teenage daughter Debi, and a kindly housekeeper, Mrs. Pennyworth.

The first season's final episode also introduced an apparent new ally—an android from another world also threatened by the aliens, who arrives on Earth and begins systematically eliminating groups of invaders. She vows to return with reinforcements from her planet, thus setting up the continuation of the struggle into its second season.

In the event, ratings were not good enough to justify a second season. What emerged instead was a whole new show built around several of the original characters, battling a new wave of alien enemies, the Morthren.

War of the Worlds, Mark 2, subtitled *The Second Invasion*, began with the virtual destruction of The Blackwood Project and the deaths of two team members, Ironhorse and Norton Drake. With the aid of a maverick ex-soldier, Kincaid (played by *Highlander*'s Adrian Paul), the remaining trio of Harrison, Suzanne and Debi take to the road, eventually setting up a new base in an old military command bunker.

Meanwhile, newly arrived humanoid aliens are destroying the old Advocacy for its failure to prepare our planet for colonization, and leadership is assumed by the powerful military commander Maltzor and chief scientist Mana. These chilling new invaders can also create clones of humans to take the place of real people and do their bidding. The usual sparring continues until the final episode when Maltzor's personal ambitions are exposed by his own people. He dies in a climactic shootout and the invasion is finally called off.

Jared Martin, who plays Harrison, had starred as a 23rd-century traveler in the seventies series *The Fantastic Journey*.

REGULAR CAST

Dr. Harrison Blackwood Jared Martin **Suzanne McCullough** Lynda Mason Green
Lt. Col. Paul Ironhorse Richard Chaves **Norton Drake** Philip Akin
Debi McCullough Rachel Blanchard
Semi-regular: **Mrs. Pennyworth** Corrine Conley
The Second Invasion: **John Kincaid** Adrian Paul **Maltzor** Denis Forest
Mana Catherine Disher

Creator: Greg Strangis
Executive producers: Greg Strangis, Sam Strangis, Frank Mancuso Jr. (*The Second Invasion*)
Producer: Jonathan Hackett
Executive story consultant: Tom Lazarus
Creative consultant: Herb Wright
Music: Billy Thorpe, Larry Brown

Triumph Entertainment Corporation in association with Universal
A Ten Four Production
43 color episodes, 60 minutes unless stated
U.S. premiere: October 1988
U.K. premiere: 1991/1992
(ITV)

Season One
23 episodes

The Resurrection
(120 mins)

w Greg Strangis

A toxic spill during a terrorist attack on a nuclear waste site reactivates the 35-year-old remains of alien invaders who resume their plan to take over the world. Picking up their transmissions, astrophysicist Harrison Blackwood, his friend Norton Drake and assistant Suzanne McCullough become aware of the aliens' presence and join with Pentagon forces led by Lt. Col Ironhorse in trying to stop the aliens from

reaching their spaceships, stored in a top secret hangar.

General Wilson John Vernon
Finney Martin Neufeld
Teal Ric Sarabia
Orel Desmond Ellis
Doc Jack Mather
Sheriff Harry Booker
Chambers/Advocate One Richard Comar
Urick/Advocate Two Ilse von Glatz
Tom Kensington Larry Reynolds
Advocate Three Michael Rudder
General Arquette Ted Fellows

Director: Colin Chilvers

The Walls of Jericho

w Forrest T. Van Buren *(pen-name)*
While Harrison tries to convince skeptical officials that the alien invasion is moving forward, the aliens discover a new way to acclimatize to Earth—by stealing vast quantities of liquid nitrogen to cool their radiation-ravaged human bodies and thus slow their deterioration.
General Wilson John Vernon
Advocate One Richard Comar
Advocate Two Ilse von Glatz
Sheriff Dale Wilson

Director: Colin Chilvers

Thy Kingdom Come

w Herb Wright
While aliens transmit messages to their leaders in space, Harrison's stepmother Sylvia Van Buren, a survivor of the 1953 invasion, has a psychic vision that leads the team to the newest alien stronghold. (Ann Robinson reprises her role from the 1953 movie.)
Sylvia Van Buren Ann Robinson
Bobby Stuart Stone
Advocate One Richard Comar
Advocate Two Ilse von Glatz
Advocate Three Michael Rudder
Alien hunter Alar Aedma
Mom Joy Thompson
Dad John Blackwood
Granny Helen Carscallen

Director: Winrich Kolbe

A Multitude of Idols

w Tom Lazarus
While investigating a story on radioactive waste, a reporter stumbles upon the aliens' plot to colonize the planet by "rebirthing" their brethren in the bodies of a group of kidnapped church-goers.
Alise Conway Michele Scarabelli
FBI leader Ray James
Alex Von Flores
Blanche Jackie Richardson
Simons Garfield Andrews

Director: Neill Fearnley

Eye for an Eye

w Tom Lazarus
On the 50th anniversary of Orson Welles's notorious radio broadcast, the town of Grover's Mill, New Jersey, celebrates the "Martian" invasion, unaware that the aliens are back in town in the guise of a gang of leather-clad bikers.
Francis Flannery Jeff Corey
Sam Jack Ammon
Bill Jack Jessop
Harv John Ireland

Red Mark Holmes
Dog Kevin Rushto

Director: Mark Sobel

The Second Seal

w Patrick Barry
Harrison, Suzanne and Ironhorse gain clearance to an army base to examine top secret files giving the location of the burial sites of 10,000 hibernating aliens—only to discover the invaders have got there first.
General Masters Greg Morris
Amanda Burke Lynne Griffin
Lt. Hamill Michael McKeever
Captain Murphy James Kidnie

Director: Neill Fearnley

Goliath is My Name

w Tom Lazarus
In their latest plan to eliminate the human race, alien guerillas invade a Midwestern campus to steal a deadly virus from the college's research lab.
Jefferson Eric Bruskotter
Pete Jason Blicker
Debra Carolyn Dunn
Kim Kelly Rowan
Robert Parkins James Kee
Advocate Ilse von Glatz

Director: George Bloomfield

To Heal the Leper

w David Tynan
When one of the alien leaders is incapacitated by chickenpox, the invaders steal dozens of human brains to create a cure.
Sylvia Van Buren Ann Robinson
Leo Paul Boretski
Scott Kim Coates
Beth Guylaine St. Onge
Advocate One Richard Comar
Advocate Two Ilse von Glatz

Director: William Fruet

The Good Samaritan

w Sylvia Clayton
The aliens plan to wipe out a large part of the world's population by tainting a massive grain shipment with a deadly poison.
Terri Lori Hallier
Franklin Warren Davies
Marcus Mason Alex Cord
Advocate One Richard Comar
Advocate Two Ilse von Glatz
Advocate Three Michael Rudder

Director: Paul Tucker

Epiphany

w Sylvia Van Buren *(pen-name)*
Harrison meets an old flame, Katya, a visiting Soviet scientist who wants to defect. Meanwhile, the aliens plan to build and detonate a nuclear bomb that would trigger off a worldwide nuclear war.
Dr. Katia Roadna Deborah Wakeman
Valery Kedrov Patrick Macnee
Cop David Ferry
Advocate One Richard Comar
Advocate Two Ilse von Glatz
Advocate Three Michael Rudder

Director: Neill Fearnley

Among the Philistines

w Patrick Barry
The aliens move one step closer to their goal when one of them infiltrates the defense team's headquarters and gains access to its top secret computer files. In an ensuing clash, the stuffy but kindly groundsman Kensington is murdered—the team's first casualty in their war . . .
Dr. Adrian Bushard Cedric Smith
Mr. Kensington Larry Reynolds
Advocate One David Calderisi
Advocate Two Ilse von Glatz

Director: William Fruet

Choirs of Angels

w Herb Wright
Using subliminal audio messages on a rock star's new record, the aliens trick a famous scientist into working on a vaccine to protect them from Earth's deadly bacteria—and Harrison, too, becomes a victim of the brainwashing techniques!
Dr. Eric von Deer Jan Rubes
Billy Carlos Billy Thorpe
Advocate One David Calderisi
Advocate Two Ilse von Glatz
Alien soldiers John Novak, Alex Carter, Heidi Von Palleske

Director: Herb Wright

Dust to Dust

w Richard Krzemien
The aliens invade an Indian reservation, where they hope to retrieve a warship left behind in a previous invasion.
Joseph Lonefree Ivan Naranjo
Darrow Eric Schweig
Grace Robin Sewell
Kirk Elias Zarou
Pat Joseph Zeigler

Connie Linda Goranson
Mark Newport R.D. Reid
Advocate Two Ilse von Glatz
Advocate Three Michael Rudder

Director: George Bloomfield

He Feedeth Among the Lilies

w Tom Lazarus
Harrison falls in love with a beautiful woman who is haunted by nightmares of a terrifying alien encounter. Desperate to learn the secrets of man's immune system, the aliens begin operating on terrified human victims.
Karen McKinney Cynthia Belliveau
Estelle Maria Del Mar
Pat Thistle Carole Galloway
Arnold Thistle Graham Batchelor
Advocate One David Calderisi
Advocate Two Ilse von Glatz
Advocate Three Michael Rudder

Director: George Bloomfield

The Prodigal Son

w Herb Wright, *story by* Patrick Barry
Harrison is kidnapped by a half-human, half-alien mutant, called Quinn, who wants his help in his own scheme to take over the world.
Quinn John Colicos
McGinnis James Purcell
Hwang Jim Yip
Margo Randall Carpenter
Advocate One David Calderisi
Advocate Two Ilse von Glatz
Advocate Three Michael Rudder

Director: George McCowan

The Meek Shall Inherit

w Dorothy C. Fontana
A desperate Harrison searches for his stepmother who has escaped from the sanitarium to look for the aliens whose latest plan is to destroy global phone links.
Sylvia van Buren Ann Robinson
Molly Stone Diana Reis
Pollito Sam Malkin
Dayton Michael Copeman
Sensky John Gilbert
Bull Gene Mack
Advocate One David Calderisi
Advocate Two Michael Kramer
Advocate Three Martin Neufeld

Director: William Fruet

Unto Us a Child is Born

w David Braff
A pregnant woman whose body has been absorbed by an alien gives birth to a half-human, half-alien baby who grows at a startling rate.
First alien Brent Carver
Nancy Salvo Amber Lea Weston
Colin Geoffrey Bowes
Young Clark Johnson

Director: George Bloomfield

The Last Supper

w Tom Lazarus
Harrison calls a top secret meeting of alien experts, unaware that one of them is an invader in disguise, with a mission to massacre the scientists.
Gabriel Morales Efrain Figueroa
Dr. Sunethra Menathong Suzanne Coy
Leonid Argochev Colm Feore
Soo Tak James Hong
Jerry Raymond Barry Kennedy
Morris Burnobi Abbot Jones Anderson

Director: George McCowan

Vengeance Is Mine

w Arnold Margolin
While aliens attempt to perfect a deadly laser weapon, a fatal error pits Ironhorse against a man seeking revenge for the accidental murder of his wife.
Martin Cole Denis Forest
Sarah Cole Carolyn Dunn
Milton Don Allison
Henchman Roger Montgomery
Samantha Alannah Myles
Stavrakos Vito Rezza
Advocate One Ilse von Glatz
Advocate Two Ric Sarabia
Advocate Three Michael Copeman

Director: George Bloomfield

My Soul to Keep

w John Kubichan
The aliens set up an incubation site in an industrial ice house. But the team's efforts to combat this threat in secret are threatened when Suzanne's ex-husband, an investigative reporter, comes to town.
Cash McCullough Michael Parks
Old Clerk Handy Atmadja

Quinn John Colicos
Stavrakos Vito Rezza
Advocate One Ilse von Glatz
Advocate Two Ric Sarabia
Advocate Three Michael Copeman

Director: William Fruet

So Shall Ye Reap

w Michael McCormack
The aliens go into the drug business, with a highly addictive serum which turns humans into deadly killers.
Envoy Jill Jacobson
Lt. Novack Dixie Seatle
Jack Sawyer Jonathan Welsh
Alien scientist Angelo Rizacos
Sherry Isabelle Mejias
Advocate One Ilse von Glatz
Advocate Two Ric Sarabia
Advocate Three Frank Pellegrino

Director: George Bloomfield

The Raising of Lazarus

w Durnford King
An ambitious scientist with bizarre ideas about communing with the aliens endangers the team's lives when he begins injecting himself with alien blood.
Col. Frederick Alexander Nicholas Coster
Col. Manning Thomas Hauff
Perry Janet Bailey
Sgt. Tex Dale Wilson

Director: Neill Fearnley

The Angel of Death

w Herb Wright
The aliens face an enemy far deadlier than humans when an android from the planet Qar'To arrives and begins to unceremoniously terminate them. Linking up with this new ally gives the Earth team hope that they can ultimately defeat the invaders.
Qar'To Synth Elaine Giftos
Alien Jake John Evans
Stavrakos Vito Rezza
Max David McKnight
Advocate One Ilse von Glatz
Advocate Two Ric Sarabia
Advocate Three Frank Pellegrino

Director: Herb Wright

The Second Invasion
20 color 60-minute episodes

The Second Wave
No Direction Home
Doomsday
Terminal Rock
Breeding Ground
Seft of Emun
Loving the Alien
Night Moves
Synthetic Love

The Defector
Time to Reap
The Pied Piper
The Deadly Disease
Path of Lies
Candle in the Night
Video Messiah
Totally Real
Max
The True Believer
The Obelisk

WATT ON EARTH

Comedy sits awkwardly with sci-fi—there are more unintentional laughs in bad series than real jokes in good ones—but this nineties children's comedy thriller did enough to warrant two 12-part series.

Written by Pip and Jane Baker, graduates of *Doctor Who*, it was a familiar enough tale of earthling meets alien, with alien causing chaos. Watt is a 300-year-old extra-terrestrial who looks like a man in his twenties, but thinks and acts like a child of seven, and is capable of turning himself into inanimate objects, such as a teapot or a loaf of bread, a knack he calls "transanimateobjectification." It's a raw talent—when he changes back, his ears are back to front. He's also on the run from another alien, Jemadah, who has been sent from their home planet by Watt's uncle to track him down. Jemadah always appears in human form—the question is, which one, as he, too, is able to alter his looks.

Watt's escapades bring color and chaos into the lives of 12-year-old schoolboy Sean Ruddock, his irritating big sister, Zoe, and hard-pressed parents who run a family newspaper business, the *Haxton Weekly*.

The second series repeated the formula, with Sean again doing his utmost to keep Watt's secret, while his evasive friend managed to turn into a helicopter and ended up taking part in a production of *The Mikado*.

MAIN CAST
Sean Tom Brodie *Watt* Garth Napier-Jones *Zoe* Jessica Simpson
Jemadah John Grillo *Councillor Carrington* Edward Peel
Brigadier Jones Michael Godley *Val Ruddock* Heather Wright
Tom Ruddock Simon Cook
Voice of Watt's Uncle Michael Kilgarriff

Series Two only: *Oliver* Jotham Annan *Isobel Harrison* Anna Wing
Eve Carter Angela Bruce *Raymond Drabble* Christopher Blake
J.J. Jefferson Davyd Harries *Jennifer Tate* Francesca Ryan

Writers: Pip & Jane Baker
Producer: Angela Beeching
Director: Roger Singleton-Turner

BBC Production
24 color 15-minute episodes (twice weekly)

Series One:
11 November–17 December 1991
Series Two:
16 November–23 December 1992
(BBC1)

WEIRD SCIENCE

A pair of high school geeks create the perfect girl on their computer; of course, as so often happens, she magically comes to life and gives them important lessons. Allegedly a comedy, based on the 1985 movie of the same title, it went on too long and zapped the teens into too many TV shows, video games, and historical periods.

REGULAR CAST
Lisa Vanessa Angel   *Wyatt Donnelly* Michael Manasseri
Gary Wallace John Mallory Asher   *Chett Donnelly* Lee Tergesen
Marcia Donnelly Melendy Britt   *Wayne Donnelly* Richard Fancy/Andrew Prine
Al Wallace Jeff Doucette   *Emily Wallace* Joyce Bulifant
Principal Scampi Bruce Jarchow

Based on the 1985 movie
Developed for TV by Alan Cross and Tom Spezialy

84 color 30-minute episodes
U.S. premiere: 5 March 1994
Shown in the U.S. on USA Network

Season One
She's Alive
Universal Remote
Cyrano De Brainiac
Magnifico Dad
The Feminine Mistake
Airball Kings
Party High, U.S.A.
One Size Fits All
Keeps On Tickin'
Mr. President
Fatal Lisa
Killer Party
Sex Ed

Season Two
Lisa's Virus
The Bazooka Boys
The Most Dangerous Wish
Wyatt Erectus
A Tale of Two Lisas
Nightmare on Chett Street
Magic for Beginners
Copper Top Girl
Switched at Birth
Camp Wannabe
Circuit Courtship
Chett Reborn
Unplugged

Season Three
Earth Boys Are Easy
Horseradish
Grampira
Rock Hard Chett
Lucky Suit
Gary Wallace, Boy Reporter
Hot Wheels
Bikini Camp Slasher
What Genie?
Sci-Fi Zoned
Wyatt Brief
Free Gary
Quantum Wyatt
Fly Boy
Teen Lisa

Dead Can Dance
Legend of Red Brick Wallace
Spys-R-Us

Season Four
Searching for Boris Karloff
Men in Tights
Puppet Love
Chet-A-Nator
Phantom Scampi
Grumpy Old Genie
Funhouse of Death
It Takes a Geek
Slow Times at Farber High
Chett World
By the Time We Got to Woodstock . . .
You'll Never Eat Brains in This Town Again
Demon Lisa
Cyborg Sam I Am
It's a Wonderful Life Without You
Lisa's Childhood Memories
Lisarella
Family Affair
Gary & Wyatt's Bloodsucking Adventure
It's A Mob, Mob, Mob, Mob World
Strange Daze
Community Property
Master Chett
Pirates!
Swallow 13
Strangers In Paradise

Season Five
Forbidden Janet
Man's Best Friend
Show Chett
Bee in There
Future Bride
Stalag 16
I, Chettus
The Genie Detective
Genie Junior
Wicked Wish
School Spirits
Magic Comet Ride
Night of the Swingin' Steves
WS4

THE WILD, WILD WEST

On the face of it, *The Wild, Wild West* sounds like just another Western adventure series, set as it is in post-Civil War America.

The good guys are a debonair government undercover agent, James T. West, and his aide, master of disguise and inventor Artemus Gordon, who have been chosen by President Ulysses S. Grant to spearhead the government's efforts to enforce law and order on the frontier. They operate from a mobile base on a plush private train with weapons and gadgets strategically hidden throughout.

But the bad guys aren't your average rustler or gun-toting outlaw. They're often criminal geniuses threatening the newly united American nation with all manner of scientific devices from robots to atomic bombs, wave-makers to time machines, cyborgs to a volcano-creating device.

Thus, the elements of Western and tongue-in-cheek spy drama combined to produce one of the purest and most outrageously bizarre fantasies ever made for television.

The series' most charismatic "super" villain, Miguelito Loveless, is a dwarf with a fanatical hatred of everyone taller than himself! A brilliant scientist, he invents robots, LSD and time travel devices. He also devised the means to shrink people and to escape by passing into another dimension and hiding in old paintings!

One episode even brought on the aliens—a trio of Venusians who land on Earth in their "flying pie plate" in search of fuel. Another, "The Night of the Burning Diamond," featured a thief who melted down diamonds to create an elixir with which he could travel faster than light.

REGULAR CAST
Major James T. West Robert Conrad *Artemus Gordon* Ross Martin
Tennyson (a butler) Charles Davis *(Season One only)*
Dr. Miguelito Loveless Michael Dunn *(semi-regular)*
Jeremy Pike Charles Aidman*

* Stood in for several Season Four episodes while Ross Martin was recovering from a heart attack.

Creator: Michael Garrison
Producers: Michael Garrison, Fred Freiberger,
 Gene L. Coon, Collier Young, John Mantley,
 Bruce Lansbury
Writers: Various, including John Kneubuhl,
 Stephen Kandel, Oliver Crawford, Gene L.
 Coon, Paul Playdon, Edward J. Lakso
Directors: Various, including Irving Moore, Paul
 Wendkos, Richard Sarafian

A Michael Garrison Production in association with
CBS
104 60-minute episodes
black and white (Season One)
color (from Season Two)
U.S. premiere: 17 September 1965
U.K. premiere run: 5 May–28 July 1968
(ABC Weekend Television)

Season One
(28 black and white episodes)
The Night of the Inferno
The Night of the Deadly Bed
The Night the Wizard Shook the Earth
The Night of the Sudden Death
The Night of the Casual Killer
The Night of a Thousand Eyes
The Night of the Glowing Corpse
The Night of the Dancing Death
The Night of the Double-Edged Knife
The Night the Terror Stalked Town
The Night of the Red-Eyed Madman
The Night of the Human Trigger
The Night of the Torture Chamber

The Night of the Howling Light
The Night of the Fatal Trap
The Night of the Steel Assassin
The Night the Dragon Screamed
The Night of the Grand Emir
The Night of the Flaming Ghost
The Night of the Whirring Death
The Night of the Puppeteer
The Night of the Bars of Hell
The Night of the Two-Legged Buffalo
The Night of the Druid's Blood
The Night of the Freebooters
The Night of the Burning Diamond
The Night of the Murderous Spring
The Night of the Sudden Plague

Season Two
(28 color episodes)
The Night of the Eccentrics
The Night of the Golden Cobra
The Night of the Raven
The Night of the Big Blast
The Night of the Returning Dead
The Night of the Flying Pie Plate
The Night of the Poisonous Posy
The Night of the Bottomless Pit
The Night of the Watery Death
The Night of the Green Terror
The Night of the Ready-Made Corpse
The Night of the Man-Eating House
The Night of the Skulls
The Night of the Infernal Machine
The Night of the Lord of Limbo
The Night of the Tottering Tontine
The Night of the Feathered Fury
The Night of the Gypsy Peril
The Night of the Tartar
The Night of the Vicious Valentine
The Night of the Brain
The Night of the Deadly Bubble
The Night of the Surreal McCoy
The Night of the Colonel's Ghost
The Night of the Deadly Blossom
The Night of the Cadre
The Night of the Wolf
The Night of the Bogus Bandits

Season Three
(24 color episodes)
The Night of the Bubbling Death
The Night of the Firebrand
The Night of the Assassin
The Night Dr. Loveless Died
The Night of the Jack o'Diamonds
The Night of the Samurai
The Night of the Hangman
The Night of Montezuma's Hordes
The Night of the Circus of Death
The Night of the Falcon

The Night of the Cut-Throat
The Night of the Legion of Death
The Night of the Turncoat
The Night of the Iron Fist
The Night of the Running Death
The Night of the Arrow
The Night of the Headless Woman
The Night of the Vipers
The Night of the Underground Terror
The Night of the Death Masks
The Night of the Undead
The Night of the Amnesiac
The Night of the Simian Terror
The Night of the Death-Maker

Season Four
(24 color episodes)
The Night of the Big Blackmail
The Night of the Doomsday Formula
The Night of the Juggernaut
The Night of the Sedgewick Curse
The Night of the Gruesome Games
The Night of the Kraken
The Night of the Fugitive
The Night of the Egyptian Queen
The Night of the Fire and Brimstone
The Night of the Camera
The Night of the Avaricious Actuary
The Night of Miguelito's Revenge
The Night of the Pelican
The Night of the Spanish Curse
The Night of the Winged Terror *(a 2-part story)*
The Night of Sabatini's Death
The Night of the Janus
The Night of the Pistoleros
The Night of the Diva
The Night of the Bleak Island
The Night of the Cossacks
The Night of the Tycoons
The Night of the Plague

There are also two TV movie revivals:
The Wild, Wild West Revisited (1979)
More Wild, Wild West (1980)

WONDER WOMAN

It took a number of attempts to liberate America's favorite comic strip heroine from the printed page.

She was first seen in a 1974 pilot, starring Cathy Lee Crosby, then in a 1975 effort, with former Miss World and 1973 Miss USA Lynda Carter amply filling out the star-spangled costume and flexing her bullet-proof bracelets. A short run of specials followed, under the banner *The New Original Wonder Woman*, before *Wonder Woman* finally became a weekly series in December 1976.

It was set in the 1940s, and saw the Amazon Princess, alias Diana Prince, leave her idyllic home on Paradise Island to help World War Two flying ace, Major Steve Trevor, battle the Nazis—and a few aliens from outer space for good measure. During this time the Nazis even occupied Paradise Island and created their own version of Wonder Woman, Fausta. Occasionally around to help Diana was her kid sister, Wonder Girl, played by Debra Winger.

The second series, more properly known as *The New Adventures of Wonder Woman*, updated the scenario to the 1970s, with the ageless, leggy heroine now being recruited to Steve Trevor Jr.'s undercover organization, the International Agency Defense Command (IADC), initially headed by Joe Atkinson. Wonder Woman again found herself championing good and fighting evil—this time in the shape of mad scientists, spies, would-be dictators, supercrooks and aliens. The series tried hard to avoid the camp elements of *Batman*, but didn't always succeed.

Adversaries included: a rock musician hypnotizing young women into stealing for him ("The Pied Piper"); Roddy McDowall as a crazy scientist who uses a laser weapon to create volcanic eruptions across the globe ("The Man Who Made Volcanoes"); the Skrill—alien mind-thieves out to take over the world's top brains ("The Mind Stealers from Outer Space"); an occult magician ("Diana's Disappearing Act"); Henry Gibson as an athlete-kidnapping megalomaniac ("Screaming Javelins"); Frank Gorshin as a mad toymaker using human androids to steal top-secret plans ("The Deadly Toys"); a group of Nazis plotting to clone Hitler ("Anschluss '77"); Wolfman Jack as a psychic vampire ("Disco Devil"); Joan Van Ark as a greedy 22nd-century scientist ("Time Bomb"); a billionaire's disembodied brain ("Gault's Brain"); and an alien criminal able to assume any shape ("The Boy Who Knew Her Secrets").

REGULAR CAST

Wonder Woman/Diana Prince Lynda Carter *Major Steve Trevor* Lyle Waggoner

THE NEW ORIGINAL WONDER WOMAN

Gen Phillip Blankenship Richard Eastman *Queen Mother* Carolyn Jones
Corp Etta Candy Beatrice Colen *Drusilla (Wonder Girl)* Debra Winger

THE NEW ADVENTURES:

Joe Atkinson Norman Burton

Based on characters created by Charles Moulton
Developed for television by Stanley Ralph Ross
Producers: Wilfred Baumes, John G. Stevens, Bruce Lansbury (TNOWW), Charles B. Fitzsimons (TNAOWW), Mark Rodgers (TNAOWW)

Writers: Various, including Stephen Kandel, Anne Collins, Alan Brennert, Bruce Shelley
Directors: Various, including Alan Crosland, Michael Caffey, Seymour Robbie

---

The New Original Wonder Woman:

14 color episodes (60 minutes unless stated)
U.S. premiere: 12 March 1974 (1st pilot)
7 November 1975 (2nd pilot)
December 1976 (1st series)
The New Original Wonder Woman *(two hours)*
Wonder Woman Meets Baroness Von Gunther
Fausta: The Nazi Wonder Woman
Beauty on Parade
The Feminum Mystery *(a 2-part story)*
Wonder Woman vs. Gargantua
The Pluto File
Last of the $2 Bills
Judgement from Outer Space *(a 2-part story)*
Formula 407
The Bushwackers
Wonder Woman in Hollywood

The New Adventures of Wonder Woman:

A Warner Brothers Television Production
45 color 45-minute episodes (+ one × 80 mins)
U.S. release: September 1977
U.K.: 1 July–26 August 1978

23 December 1978–4 May 1979
12 January–17 June 1980
(BBC1)
(Author's note: The BBC running order differed considerably at times from the U.S. original but got there in the end. In America the series was shown in one "strung out" season over two years.)
The Return of Wonder Woman (80 mins)*
Anschluss '77
The Man Who Could Move the World
The Bermuda Triangle Crisis
Knockout
The Pied Piper
The Queen and the Thief
I Do, I Do
The Man Who Made Volcanoes
The Mind Stealers from Outer Space *(a 2-part story)*
The Deadly Toys
Light-Fingered Lady
Screaming Javelin
Diana's Disappearing Act
Death in Disguise
IRAC Is Missing
Flight to Oblivion
Seance of Terror
The Man Who Wouldn't Tell

The Girl from Ilandia
The Murderous Missile
One of Our Teen Idols Is Missing
Hot Wheels
The Deadly Sting
The Fine Art of Crime
Disco Devil
Formicida
Time Bomb
Skateboard Whiz
The Deadly Dolphin
Stolen Faces
Pot O'Gold
Gault's Brain

Going, Going, Gone
Spaced Out
The Starships Are Coming
Amazon Hot Wax
The Richest Man in the World
A Date With Doomsday
The Girl With the Gift for Disaster
The Boy Who Knew Her Secret
  (a 2-part story)†
The Man Who Could Not Die
Phantom of the Roller Coaster (a 2-part story)

† Shown in U.K. as one 90-minute episode: 17 June 1980

XENA: WARRIOR PRINCESS

A spin-off from *Hercules: The Legendary Journeys*, this equally campy series takes former *Hercules* villainess Xena and turns her into a wandering heroine, giving her a complete about-face and a more open mind. Set in a mythic world, Xena wanders from place to place (and seemingly from time period to time period as she ends up in medieval sets, Greek sets and generic fantasy world sets) . . . the only constants her sword, her friend Gabrielle (who really needs to learn to ride a horse) and her wisecracks.

The series is filmed on location in and around Auckland, New Zealand, and airs in syndication in the U.S.

REGULAR CAST
Xena Lucy Lawless   *Gabrielle* Reneé O'Connor
Joxer Theodore Raimi

Executive producers: Rob Tapert, Sam Raimi
Co-executive producer: R.J. Stewart
Supervising producer: Steven L. Sears
Producer: Eric Gruendemann
Co-producer: Liz Friedman
Coordinating producer: Bernadette Joyce

Line producer: Chloe Smith
Music: Joseph LoDuca

Produced by Renaissance Pictures in association with MCA TV
U.S. premiere: the week of 4 September 1995

Movies
The Battle for Mt. Olympus
  (animated, 1998)

Season One
24 color 60-minute episodes

Sins of the Past
Chariots of War
Dreamworker
Cradle of Hope
The Path Not Taken
The Reckoning
The Titans
Prometheus
Death in Chains

Hooves and Harlots
The Black Wolf
Beware of Greeks Bearing Gifts
Athens City Academy of the Performing Bards
A Fistful of Dinars
Warrior . . . Princess
Mortal Beloved
The Royal Couple of Thieves
The Prodigal
Altared States
Ties That Bind
The Greater Good
Callisto
Death Mask
Is There a Doctor in the House?

Season Two
24 color 60-minute episodes

Orphan of War
Remember Nothing
Giant Killer
Girls Just Wanna Have Fun
Return of Callisto
Warrior . . . Princess . . . Tramp
Intimate Stranger
Ten Little Warlords
A Solstice Carol
The Xena Scrolls
Here She Comes . . . Miss Amphipolis
Destiny
The Quest
A Necessary Evil
A Day in the Life
For Him the Bell Tolls
The Execution
Blind Faith
Ulysses
The Price
The Lost Mariner
Comedy of Eros

Season Three
22 color 60-minute episodes

The Furies
Been There, Done That
The Dirty Half Dozen
The Deliverer
Gabrielle's Hope
The Debt (Part I) (Betrayal)
The Debt (Part II)
King of Assassins
Warrior . . . Priestess . . . Tramp
The Quill Is Mightier
Maternal Instincts
The Bitter Suite
One Against an Army
Forgiven
King Con
When in Rome . . .
Forget Me Not
Fins, Femmes and Gems
Tsunami
Vanishing Act
Sacrifice (Part I)
Sacrifice (Part II)

THE X-FILES

"The Truth is out there."

America's *TV Guide* called it "the most genuinely unsettling television since the heyday of *The Twilight Zone*." They were right.

A series about two FBI agents who investigate the paranormal and unexplainable phenomena, *The X-Files* is intelligent, thought-provoking and wonderfully creepy. It takes newspaper or magazine stories, even documented accounts of such incidents, and extrapolates them into taut mysteries, blending elements of crime drama and thriller to produce a tug-of-war between intuition and logic, seen and unseen forces.

The FBI team assigned to crack these bizarre cases are special agents Fox Mulder and Dana Scully, played by David Duchovny and Gillian Anderson, a chalk-and-cheese combo, professionally devoted to each other, with just a hint of something more.

Mulder is the "believer," a wry-witted maverick, haunted by an incident in his own childhood when his sister was apparently a victim of alien abduction. Frankly, Mulder's an embarrassment to the bureau. Condescendingly nicknamed "Spooky" by his colleagues, he calls himself "the FBI's Most Unwanted" and sees working on the X-Files as a quest for truth. When plausible explanations for a crime don't fit, Mulder explores his theories, such as UFO visitations, mind over matter and genetic mutation. Government cover-ups is another favorite theme. He's single-minded to the point of obsession.

And that's where Scully comes in. Dressing and acting like Clarice Starling in *The Silence of the Lambs*, Scully is a by-the-book medical expert who is so determined to find rational explanations that she won't accept the irrational—even when it leaps on her and tries to rip out her liver! Her loyalty to Mulder, however, is as unyielding as her skepticism. She's fiercely protective in the face of bureau bosses who'd love to close down the X-Files and ship Mulder out to the funny farm.

And she's not alone. Mulder has a "friend" in high places, a shadowy government contact called "Deep Throat," who is not averse to sending him on the odd wild goose chase. But he covers Mulder's back, and frequently confirms the otherwise unconfirmable. It's an ambivalent ploy that works on the theory that it's better to have Mulder working to expose the truth from the inside than making waves on the outside. When "Deep Throat" is murdered in the first season's final episode his last words to Scully are "Trust no one."

The X-Files was created by Chris Carter, a writer for an American surfing magazine before Hollywood beckoned. He saw the show as a kind of *Kolchak* for the nineties, a scary, yet sophisticated drama telling tales that lie within the realm of extreme scientific possibility.

The role of Mulder was not Duchovny's first federal agent. He'd played the transvestite FBI man in *Twin Peaks*.

In America, fans—or X-philes—made the show a real cult hit, with a growing following on the Internet, the interactive worldwide computer network. In the U.K., it made a compelling reason for getting hooked up to Sky, before the BBC aired it on BBC2.

No series since *Star Trek* has made a bigger impact on popular culture. While remaining true to Carter's promise to keep it "the same subversive little show it's always been," *The X-Files* has way outstripped its cult origins.

One of the many delights of *The X-Files* is the variety of cases and characters encountered. Everyone loves the alien conspiracy stories—but these are paced out through each season so as not to dominate, while a ghoulish gallery of psychos, freaks and monsters is also built up—from the yellow-eyed Tooms to the Internet killer, from the mutant fluke worm to the alien cockroaches.

And while the tantalizingly tender-yet-platonic relationship between Mulder and Scully remains at the heart of *The X-Files*'s human appeal, the series has also developed a wonderful supporting cast of enigmatic heroes and villains including the duo's put-upon boss, Skinner— (Mulder: "Where do you stand?"; Skinner: "Right on the line you keep crossing!")—the oddball trio of conspiracy theorists, The Lone Gunmen; Mulder's shadowy contact, X; the doomed Krycek, and, of course, The Cigarette Smoking Man, one of TV's most arrogant bad guys.

And, finally, you don't need tons of hardware to play *X-Files* games. Just a torch and a darkened room will do nicely . . .

REGULAR CAST

Fox Mulder David Duchovny   *Dana Scully* Gillian Anderson
Semi-regulars: Deep Throat Jerry Hardin *(Season One)*
Walter Skinner: Mitch Pileggi   *Smoking Man* William B. Davis
X Steven Williams   *Byers* Bruce Harwood   *Langly* Dean Haglund
Frohike Tom Braidwood

Creator/Executive producer: Chris Carter
Co-executive producers: James Wong, Glen Morgan, R.W. Goodwin
Executive story consultant: Chris Ruppenthal
Supervising producers: Howard Gordon, Alex Gansa

Ten Thirteen Productions, in association with 20th Century Television
Season One: 24 color 50-minute episodes
U.S. premiere: 10 September 1993
U.K. premiere: 19 January–11 July 1994
(Sky One)

Pilot

w Chris Carter
Agent Dana Scully is assigned to investigate—and debunk—an FBI project dubbed the X-Files, a burial ground for unsolved cases linked to the paranormal. Her contact is agent Fox Mulder, a maverick and a loner obsessed with UFOs and other strange phenomena. Together they investigate a series of mysterious deaths linked by one common clue: two strange red marks on the victims' skin. Scully is convinced there is a rational explanation, but her views are challenged by strange events in the dark forests of Oregon.

Chief Scott Blevins Charles Cioffi
Dr. Jay Nemman Cliff DeYoung
Teresa Nemman Sarah Loskoff
Detective Miles Leon Russom
Billy Miles Zachary Ansley
Coroner Truitt Stephen E. Miller
Dr. Heitz Werber Jim Jansen
Peggy O'Dell Katya Gardener
Smoking Man William B. Davis

Director: Robert Mandel

Deep Throat

w Chris Carter

Mulder and Scully investigate the mysterious case of a military test pilot who disappeared after experiencing strange psychotic behavior. Their inquiries lead them to a secret air base where Mulder believes the military are flying planes built using technology from a crashed UFO. And in a cryptic meeting with a shadowy contact "Deep Throat," Mulder is told "they've been here for years . . ."

Deep Throat Jerry Hardin *(intro)*
Paul Mossinger Michael Bryan French
Mrs. Budahas Gabrielle Rose
Lt. Colonel Budahas Andrew Johnston
Verla McLennen Sheila Moore
Emil Seth Green
Zoe Lalainia Lindbjerg
Ladonna Monica Parker

Director: Daniel Sackheim

Squeeze

w Glen Morgan & James Wong

Mulder and Scully search for a "mutant" serial killer whose savage murder spree recurs every 30 years. The victims were all murdered inside locked or secured rooms. Each had their liver ripped out.

Eugene Tooms Doug Hutchison
Tom Colton Donal Logue
Sheriff Briggs Henry Beckman
Fuller Kevin McNulty
Usher Terence Kelly
Detective Johnson James Bell

Director: Harry Longstreet

Conduit

w Alex Gansa & Howard Gordon

Mulder becomes obsessed with solving a case that closely parallels an "encounter" he experienced as a child, in which he believes his sister was abducted by aliens.

Darlene Morris Carrie Snodgrass
Jack Withers Michael Cavanaugh
Kip Don Gibb
Kevin Morris Joel Palmer
Tessa Sears Shelley Owens
NSA Agent Holtzman Don Thompson
Ruby Morris Taunya Dee
Chief Scott Blevins Charles Cioffi

Director: Daniel Sackheim

The Jersey Devil

w Chris Carter

Scully and Mulder track a legendary creature that has roamed the New Jersey countryside for over 40 years. And they clash with local police determined to keep its existence under wraps.

Creature Claire Stansfield
Detective Thomson Wayne Tippit
Dr. Roger Diamond Gregory Sierra
Ranger Brouillet Michael MacRae
Glenna Jill Teed
Jack Hrothgar Matthews

Director: Joe Napolitano

Shadows

w Glen Morgan & James Wong

Investigating the deaths of two men believed to have been killed by a powerful psychokinetic force leads Mulder and Scully to a woman who is being "guarded" by the ghost of her dead boss.

Robert Dorlund Barry Primus
Lauren Kyte Lisa Waltz
Ellen Bledsoe Lorena Gale
Ms. Saunders Veena Sood
Webster Deryl Hayes

Director: Michael Katleman

Ghost in the Machine

w Alex Gansa & Howard Gordon

Mulder and Scully look into the death of a corporate executive who may have been murdered by a thinking computer trying to protect itself from being shut down.

Deep Throat Jerry Hardin
Steven Wilczek Rob LaBelle
Agent Jerry Lamana Wayne Duvall
Clyde Petersen Blu Mankuma
Drake Tom Butler
Jane Spiller Gillian Barber

Director: Jerrold Freedman

Ice

w Glen Morgan & James Wong

Mulder and Scully find danger and paranoia when they investigate the deaths of a team of geophysicists at a remote Alaskan outpost. They discover a parasitic alien life-form that feeds on a chemical controlling aggressive behavior.

Dr. Lawrence Hodge Xander Berkeley
Dr. Nancy DaSilva Felicity Huffman
Dr. Denny Murphy Steve Hytner
Bear Jeff Kober
Richter Ken Kirzinger
Campbell Sonny Surowiec

Director: David Butler

Space

w Chris Carter

When a space shuttle mission is sabotaged, Mulder suspects it may be the work of an evil extraterrestrial spirit that has inhabited the body of a former Gemini astronaut.

Lt. Colonel Marcus Aurelius Belt Ed Lauter
Michelle Generoo Susanna Thompson
Scientist Tom McBeath
Mission controller Terry David Mulligan
Preacher French Tickner

Director: William Graham

Fallen Angel

w Howard Gordon *&* Alex Gansa

The future of the X-Files project is jeopardized after Mulder secretly infiltrates the site of a government cover-up of a UFO crash, desperate to find hard evidence to prove his theories.

McGrath Frederick Coffin
Colonel Calvin Henderson Marshall Bell
Deep Throat Jerry Hardin
Max Fenig Scott Bellis
Corporal Taylor Brent Stait
Deputy Sheriff Jason Wright Alvin Sanders
Gina Watkins Sheila Paterson
Lt. Fraser Tony Pantages
Mrs. Wright Freda Parry
Lt. Griffin Michael Rogers

Director: Larry Shaw

Eve

w Kenneth Biller *&* Chris Brancato

Mulder and Scully's search for two girls who disappeared after their fathers were murdered in identical fashion uncovers the existence of a top secret government program to raise a group of genetically controlled children.

Deep Throat Jerry Hardin
Dr. Sally Kendrick/Eve Six/Hughes Harriet Harris
Teena Simmons Sabrina Krievins
Cindy Reardon Erika Krievins
Ellen Reardon Tasha Simms
Dr. Marvin Katz George Touliatos
Ms. Wells Christine Upright-Letain
Ted Watkins David Kirby
Donna Watkins Tina Gilbertson

Director: Fred Gerber

Fire

w Chris Carter

Mulder's ex-classmate and former lover Phoebe Greene, now a Scotland Yard inspector, seeks his help to find a man with alarming pyrokinetic powers who is stalking and killing members of the British aristocracy.

Phoebe Greene Amanda Pays
Bob the caretaker Mark Sheppard
Sir Malcom Marsden Dan Lett
Lady Marsden Laurie Paton
Melvin Beatty Duncan Fraser
Driver Phil Hayes
Michael Keegan Macintosh

Director: Larry Shaw

Beyond the Sea

w Glen Morgan *&* James Wong

Swayed by his knowledge of the burial of her dead father, Scully believes that the psychic predictions of death row inmate Luther Boggs are the only hope in apprehending a vicious murderer. Mulder, on the other hand, believes Boggs is a fraud.

Luther Boggs Brad Dourif
Captain Jonathan Scully Don David
Margaret Scully Sheila Larken
Lucas Henry Lawrence King
Agent Thomas Fred Henderson
Warden Cash Don Mackay
Liz Hawley Lisa Vultaggio
Jim Summers Chad Willett

Director: David Nutter

Genderbender

w Larry Barber *&* Paul Barber

Mulder and Scully investigate an isolationist religious sect called The Kindred, when a sect member capable of changing sex becomes the prime suspect in a murder case.

Brother Andrew Brent Hinkley
Sister Abby Michele Goodger
Marty (Male) Peter Stebbings
Marty (Female) Kate Twa
Michel Nicholas Lea
Brother Wilton Paul Batten

Director: Rob Bowman

Lazarus

w Alex Gansa *&* Howard Gordon

The consciousness of a dangerous criminal possesses FBI agent Willis, an ex-boyfriend of Scully who finds her life in danger when she is taken hostage by him.

Agent Willis Christopher Allport
Lula Velasquez Cec Verrell
Agent Bruskin Jackson Davies
Warren Dupre Jason Schombing
Tommy Callum Keith Rennie
Prof. Varnes Jay Brazeau

Director: David Nutter

Young at Heart

w Scott Kaufer *&* Chris Carter
An armed robber, John Barnett, believed to have died in prison years earlier, wages a vendetta against Mulder who has still not forgiven himself for not killing him at the time of his capture—an error that caused two deaths.
Special Agent Reggie Purdue Dick Anthony Williams
John Barnett Alan Boyce
Heather Henderson Christine Estabrook
Dr. Austin Graham Jarvis
Dr. Ridley Robin Mossley
Joe Crandall Gordon Tipple
CIA agent William B. Davis
Deep Throat Jerry Hardin

Director: Michael Lange

E.B.E.

w Glen Morgan *&* James Wong
Mulder and Scully become the focus of a misinformation campaign—including lies from the previously reliable Deep Throat—when they attempt to trace the government's secret transport of an Extraterrestrial Biological Entity.
Deep Throat Jerry Hardin
Chief Cash Allan Lysell
Ranheim Peter Lacroix
Byers Bruce Harwood
Langly Dean Haglund
Frohike Tom Braidwood

Director: William Graham

Miracle Man

w Howard Gordon *&* Chris Carter
Mulder's curiosity is aroused by a ministry led by a man whose adopted son possesses the power to heal with the touch of his hand, but whose ability has now apparently become the "touch of death."
Sheriff Daniels R.D. Call
Samuel Scott Bairstow
Reverend Hartley George Gerdes
Leonard Vance Dennis Lipscomb
Judge Walter Marsh
Hohman's father Campbell Lane
Deputy Tyson Roger Haskett

Director: Michael Lange

Shapes

w Marylin Osborn
In a remote area of Montana, Mulder and Scully track a wolf-like creature linked to the Native American legend of the Manitou, an evil spirit capable of changing a man into a beast.
Lyle Parker Ty Miller
Charlie Tskany Michael Horse

Jim Parker Donnelly Rhodes
Ish Jimmy Herman
Gwen Goodensnake Renae Morriseau
David Gates Dwight McFee
Dr. Josephs Paul McLean

Director: David Nutter

Darkness Falls

w Chris Carter
A group of loggers working in a remote forest unearths thousands of deadly insect-like creatures that swarm at night to paralyze—and then cocoon—their victims. Investigating their disappearance, Mulder and Scully become trapped in the remote camp—with a failing supply of petrol to power the generator that provides light.
Larry Moore Jason Beghe
Steve Humphreys Tom O'Rourke
Spinney Titus Welliver
Clean suited man David Hay
Perkins Barry Greene
Dyer Ken Tremblett

Director: Joe Napolitano

Tooms

w Glen Morgan *&* James Wong
Eugene Tooms, the supernatural killer Mulder helped to put away, is released on parole. Mulder believes he will kill again before finding somewhere to hibernate for another 30 years and hounds him, determined to keep him under constant surveillance.
Eugene Tooms Doug Hutchison
Dr. Aaron Monte Paul Ben Victor
Skinner Mitch Pileggi
Frank Briggs Henry Beckman
Detective Talbot Timothy Webber
Judge Kann Jan D'Arcy
Christine Ranford Teryl Rothery
Frank Ranford Pat Bermel
Smoking Man William B. Davis

Director: David Nutter

Born Again

w Glen Morgan *&* James Wong
An eight-year-old girl is the prime suspect in a series of bizarre, seemingly unrelated deaths. Mulder concludes that she is the reincarnation of a policeman who is avenging his own murder nine years previously.
Tony Fiore Brian Markinso
Anita Fiore Mimi Lieber
Sharon Lazard Maggie Wheeler
Judy Bishop Dey Young
Michelle Bishop Andrea Libman
Dr. Sheila Braun P. Lynn Johnson
Detective Barbala Dwight Koss

Director: Jerrold Freedman

Roland

w Chris Ruppenthal
When top scientists at an aeronautics research lab die under mysterious circumstances, the agents suspect Roland, the mentally challenged janitor, may somehow be the culprit.
Dr. Nollette James Sloyan
Roland Fuller Zeljko Ivanek
Mrs. Stodie Micole Mercurio
Tracy Kerry Sandomirsky
Keats Garry Davey
Surnow Matthew Walker
Barrington Dave Hurtubise
Lisa Dole Sue Mathew

Director: David Nutter

The Erlenmeyer Flask

w Chris Carter
Deep Throat tips off Mulder about a critically important case involving the cloning of extraterrestrial viruses in a secret government experiment. But it's a secret government agents are determined to preserve, and when Mulder finds himself taken hostage, Deep Throat helps Scully to steal an alien foetus to exchange for his return. But during the exchange Deep Throat is shot by government agents. Later, Scully is woken by a phone call from Mulder with the news: "They're closing us down."
Deep Throat Jerry Hardin
Crew-cut man Lindsey Ginter
Dr. Simon Anne DeSalvo
Fugitive (Dr. Secare) Simon Webb
Captain Lacerio Jim Leard
Dr. Berube Ken Kramer
Smoking Man William B. Davis

Director: R.W. Goodwin

Season Two
22 color 45-minute episodes

Little Green Men

w Glen Morgan & James Wong
With the X-Files project officially disbanded, Mulder and Scully return to everyday duties. Mulder is growing increasingly depressed until he's summoned by Senator Richard Matheson, an X-Files patron, who reveals that an abandoned radio telescope in Puerto Rico was the site of a UFO encounter. Mulder immediately flies out, ahead of a Blue Beret UFO Retrieval Team out to destroy all evidence, and has a bizarre, frightening "encounter."
Skinner Mitch Pileggi
Senator Richard Matheson Raymond J. Berry
Jorge Mike Gomez
Smoking Man William B. Davis
Dr. Troisky Les Carlson
Young Mulder Marcus Turner

Samantha Vanessa Morley
Aide Fulvio Cecere
Agent Morris Derly Hayes
Commander Dwight McFee
Student Lisa Anne Beley
Lewin Gary Hetherington
Rand Bob Wilde

Director: David Nutter

The Host

w Chris Carter
Mulder pursues a humanoid, parasitic organism living in a sewage system, while receiving mysterious messages that reinstatement of the X-Files depends on his success. (Wonderfully ghoulish episode with a truly freakish fluke monster—watch for the scene where an infected workman tries to get the taste of bile from his mouth by brushing his teeth, before the creature forces its way from his body in the shower.)
Skinner Mitch Pileggi
Flukeman Darin Morgan
Workman Matthew Bennett
Detective Norman Freddy Andreiucci
Charlie Don Mackay
Agent Brisentine Marc Bauer
Man on phone Hrothgar Mathews
Dr. Zenzola Gabrielle Rose
Foreman Ron Sauve
Russian engineer Dmitri Boudrine
Dmitri Raoul Ganee
Federal marshall William MacDonald

Director: Daniel Sackheim

Blood

w Glen Morgan & James Wong, *story by* Darin Morgan
Mulder and Scully investigate a series of violent killings in a small town, committed by seemingly normal residents. They discover an LSD-like chemical being sprayed on local orchards is triggering an extreme reaction to phobias. Is the town being used for some kind of controlled experiment? And if so, by whom?
Ed Funsch William Sanderson
Sheriff Spenser John Cygan
Mrs. McRoberts Kimberly Ashlyn Gere
Larry Winter George Touliatos
Byers Bruce Harwood
Langly Dean Haglund
Frohike Tom Braidwood
Mechanic Gerry Rouseau
Harry McNally Andre Daniels
Bus driver William MacKenzie
Mrs. Adams Diana Stevan
Security guard Kathleen Duborg
Taber John Harris
Clerk B.J. Harrison

Director: David Nutter

Sleepless

w Howard Gordon

Mulder searches for a Vietnam vet who can project his consciousness into other people's minds. Augustus Cole, a survivor of a sleep-deprivation experiment to create aggressive, fearless soldiers, has not slept in 24 years and is seeking revenge. Mulder is teamed with another agent, Alex Krycek, unaware that he is reporting back to a mysterious tribunal bent on eliminating Mulder and Scully . . .

Skinner Mitch Pileggi
X Steven Williams
Alex Krycek Nicholas Lea
Augustus Cole Tony Todd
Salvatore Matola Jonathan Gries
Henry Willig Don Thompson
Dr. Giradi David Adams
Dr. Pilsson Michael Puttonen
Dr. Charyn Anna Hagan
Smoking Man William B. Davis
Detective Morton Mitch Kosterman
Team leader Paul Bittante
Dr. Grissom Claude De Martino

Director: Rob Bowman

Duane Barry

w Chris Carter

First of a two-part story. Mulder and Krycek are assigned to a hostage negotiation at a travel agency. Duane Barry, a former FBI agent who claims he was abducted and tortured by aliens, has taken his psychologist, Dr. Hakkie, and three other people hostage and is demanding safe passage to an alien abduction site.

Duane Barry Steve Railsback
Alex Krycek Nicholas Lea
Agent Lucy Kazden C.C.H. Pounder
Tactical commander Stephen E. Miller
Dr. Hakkie Frank C. Turner
Agent Rich Fred Henderson
Gwen Barbara Pollard
Kimberly Sarah Strange
Officer Robert Lewis
Marksmen John Sampson, Michael Dobson
Clerk Tosca Baggoo
Bob Tim Dixon
Agent Janus Prince Maryland

Director: Chris Carter

Ascension

w Paul Brown

Part 2 of a two-part story. Scully is kidnapped by Duane Barry and Mulder finds himself in a race not only against time, but also against Krycek who is out to stop him rescuing his partner. Mulder finally catches Barry at the summit of Skyland Mountain in Virginia, but Scully is nowhere to be seen. Mulder is convinced she's the victim of a covert military operation, and Skinner officially reopens the X-Files. (Trivia point: Scully's abduction was necessary to allow mum-to-be Gillian Anderson some maternity leave. Trivia point 2: The song used in Duane Barry's drive is "Red Right Hand" by Nick Cave and the Bad Seeds!)

Duane Barry Steve Railsback
Skinner Mitch Pileggi
Alex Krycek Nicholas Lea
X Steven Williams
Margaret Scully Sheila Larken
Dr. Ruth Slaughter Meredith Bain Woodward
Dwight Peter Lacroix
Patrolman Steve Makaj
Smoking Man William B. Davis
Deputy Bobby L. Stewart

Director: Michael Lange

3

w Glen Morgan & James Wong, *original script by* Chris Ruppenthal

With Scully still missing, Mulder works alone on a series of grisly deaths linked to a group of modern-day vampires, called the Trinity Killers. His inquiries lead him to a bar called Club Tepes, and an erotic encounter with a mysterious woman called Kristen (played by David Duchovny's then-girlfriend Perrey Reeves).

Unholy Spirit Justina Vail
Kristen Perrey Reeves
Son Frank Military
Det. Munson Tom McBeath
Commander Carver Malcolm Stewart
Det Nettles Frank Ferrucci
Dr. Browning Ken Kramer
Garrett Lore Roger Allford
David Yung Richard Yee
Fireman Brad Loree
Father Gustovo Moreno
Dr. Jacobs John Tierney
Guard David Livingstone
Officer Guyle Fraizer

Director: David Nutter

One Breath

w Glen Morgan & James Wong
When Scully's comatose body suddenly turns up at a local hospital, Mulder suspects the government was behind her disappearance. While his partner hovers between life and death, a furious Mulder pursues his vendetta against the Smoking Man.
Margaret Scully Sheila Larken
Melissa Scully Melinda McGraw
Skinner Mitch Pileggi
X Steven Williams
Smoking Man William B. Davis
William Scully Don Davis
Nurse Owens Nicola Cavendish
Nurse Wilkins Lorena Gale
Byers Bruce Harwood
Langly Dean Haglund
Frohike Tom Braidwood
Dr. Daly Jay Brazeau
Overcoat man Ryan Michael
Young Dana Tegan Moss

Director: R.W. Goodwin

Firewalker

w Howard Gordon
A team of scientists researching a volcano becomes victim to a parasitic silicon-based life form that grows inside the body before violently exploding out ready to infect a new host. (Shades of *Alien* here!)
Dr. Daniel Trepkos Bradley Whitford
Jason Ludwig Leland Orser
Eric Parker David Kaye
Jesse O'Neal Shawnee Smith
Dr. Pierce Tuck Milligan
Tanaka Hiro Kanagawa
Vosberg David Lewis
Technician Torben Rolfsen

Director: David Nutter

Red Museum

w Chris Carter
Cattle ranchers in a remote Wisconsin town blame a religious cult when local teenagers are drugged and abducted. When Scully recognizes the Crewcut Man who killed Deep Throat, she believes they're being injected with alien DNA, but their investigation throws up no real answers . . .
Jerry Thomas Paul Sand
Sheriff Bill Mazeroski Steve Eastin
Richard Odin Mark Rolston
Crewcut Man Lindsey Ginter
Beth Kane Gillian Barber
Gary Kane Bob Frazer
Old man Robert Clothier
Katie Elisabeth Rosen
Rick Cameron Labine
Brad Tony Sampson

Director: Win Phelps

Excelsius Dei

w Paul Brown
Mulder and Scully investigate a series of violent attacks at a convalescent home linked to angry spirits from beyond the grave.
Michelle Charters Teryl Rothery
Gung Sab Shimono
Dorothy Frances Bay
Stan Phillips Eric Christmas
Hal Arden David Fresco
Mrs. Dawson Sheila Moore
Dr. Grago Jerry Wasserman
Laura Tasha Simms
Tiernan Jon Cuthbert
Upshaw Paul Jarrett
Leo Ernie Prentice

Director: Stephen Surjik

Aubrey

w Sara B. Charno
In the town of Aubrey, Missouri, B.J. Morrow, a pregnant woman detective, experiences visions of serial killings that span half a century. Investigating, Mulder and Scully unravel B.J.'s past and find that she is the "granddaughter" of the original rapist, known as the Slash Killer.
Lt. Brian Tillman Terry O'Quinn
Det. B.J. Morrow Deborah Sprang
Old Cokely Morgan Woodward
Linda Thibedeaux Joy Coghill
Det. Joe Darnell Robyn Driscoll
Officer Peter Fleming
Young mom Sarah Jane Redmond
Young Cokely Emanuel Hajek

Director: Rob Rowman

Irresistible

w Chris Carter
Scully and Mulder track down a corpse-mutilating fetishist who is the incarnation of pure evil. Meanwhile, an anxious Scully is plagued by nightmares about a demon and fears she may become one of the killer's victims.
Agent Bocks Bruce Weitz
Donnie Pfaster Nick Chinlund
Satin Deanna Milligan
Toews Robert Thurston
Ellen Glynis Davies
Agent Karen E. Kosseff Christine Willes
Mr. Fiebling Tim Progosh
Suspect Dwight McFee
Marilyn Denalda Williams
Young woman Maggie O'Hara
Prostitute Kathleen Duborg
Agent Busch Mark Saunders
Coed Ciara Hunter

Director: David Nutter

Die Hand Die Verletzt

w Glen Morgan **&** James Wong
The agents investigate an apparent black magic murder in a small New Hampshire town. Mulder's sense that a powerful force is at work is confirmed when toads start dropping from the sky and when he notices that water drains in a counterclockwise direction—against the laws of gravity. They find that the town school's parents are devil worshippers, but someone—or something—doesn't want the secret to come out . . . (Not an episode for anyone with a phobia about giant snakes!)
Jim Ausbury Dan Butler
Phyllis Paddock Susan Blommaert
Shannon Ausbury Heather McComb
Deborah Brown P. Lynn Johnson
Pete Calcagni Shawn Johnston
Dave Duran Travis MacDonald
Barbara Ausbury Michelle Goodger
Sheriff John Oakes Larry Musser
Jerry Thomas Franky Czinege
Andrea Laura Harris
Paul Vitaris Doug Abrahams

Director: Kim Manners

Fresh Bones

w Howard Gordon
Mulder suspects that the alleged suicides of two Marines stationed at a Haitian refugee camp are caused by a voodoo curse. (Daniel Benzali, who plays the camp's commander, became better known as *Murder One*'s charismatic lawyer Teddy Hoffman.)
Pierre Beauvais Bruce Young
Col. Wharton Daniel Benzali
Chester Bonaparte Jamil Walker Smith
X Steven Williams
Private Dunham Matt Hill
Groundskeeper Callum Keith Rennie
Private McAlpin Kevin Conway
Robin McAlpin Katya Gardner
Private Kittel Roger Cross
Lt. Foyle Peter Kelamis

Director: Rob Bowman

Colony

w Chris Carter, *story by* David Duchovny **&** Chris Carter
First of a two-part story, told in flashback. As the agents search for a killer capable of morphing into different identities, Mulder's long-lost sister Samantha suddenly reappears and reveals that the killer is an alien bounty hunter . . .
Mulder's father Peter Donat
CIA agent Ambrose Chapel Tom Butler

Skinner Mitch Pileggi
Gregor Dana Gladstone
Samantha Mulder Megan Leitch
Federal marshal Tim Henry
Agent Weiss Andrew Johnston
Mrs. Mulder Rebecca Toolan
Motel proprietor Ken Roberts
Field doctor Bonnie Hay
Pilot Brian Thompson
Sgt. Al Dixon James Leard
Rev. Sistrunk Linden Banks
FBI agent David L. Gordon
Military policeman Michael McDonald

Director: Nick Marck

End Game

w Frank Spotnitz
Part 2 of a two-part story. Samantha tells Mulder that the bounty hunter (who has now kidnapped Scully) has been sent to terminate a colony of aliens who have been experimenting with cloning and that it's her he's now after. When she's apparently killed during a hostage exchange with Scully, Mulder follows the trail first to a clinic where he finds more alien clones who look like his sister, and then to Alaska for a potentially fatal encounter with the killer . . .
Skinner Mitch Pileggi
X Steven Williams
Mulder's father Peter Donat
Samantha Megan Leitch
Lt. Wilson Colin Cunningham
Captain Garry Davey
Able Gardner Allan Lysell
Sharpshooter J. B. Bivens
Pilot Barry Thompson
Field doctor Bonnie Hay
Paramedic Beatrice Zeilinger

Director: Rob Bowman

Fearful Symmetry

w Steve De Jarnett
A powerful invisible force is behind a series of deaths linked to an Idaho zoo and Mulder suspects that aliens have been impregnating the animals for some unknown purpose.
Willa Ambrose Jayne Atkinson
Kyle Lang Lance Guest
Ed Meecham Jack Rader
Byers Bruce Harwood
Langly Dean Haglund
Frohike Tom Braidwood
Ray Floyd Charles Andre
Sophie Jody St. Michael

Director: James Whitmore Jr.

Dod Kalm

w Howard Gordon & Alex Gansa, *story by* Howard Gordon
An American destroyer, the U.S.S. *Ardent* disappears in the Norwegian equivalent of the Bermuda Triangle. When a boatload of survivors is found all have aged dramatically. Traveling to Norway in search of answers, Mulder and Scully become stranded aboard the *Ardent* where they, too, fall victim to the rapid aging process . . .
Lt. Harper Dmitry Chepovetsky
Halverson Mar Anderson
Henry Trondheim John Savage
Capt. Barclay David Cubitt
Olafsson Vladimir Kulich
Ionesco Stephen Dimopoulos
Dr. Laskos Claire Riley

Director: Rob Bowman

Humbug

w Darin Morgan
Mulder and Scully search for a killer in a Florida town inhabited by side-show freaks. (An oddball episode even by this series' standards, with a lot of humor mixed with some real eccentric acts, including The Conundrum, a tattooed man who eats anything, and Blockhead who hammers nails up his nose! Also contains Scully's famous locust-eating sequence, though Gillian Anderson later denied she actually ate the insect.)
Dr. Blockhead Jim Rose
Sheriff Hamilton Wayne Grace
Mr. Nutt Michael Anderson
Lanny Vincent Schiavelli
Conundrum "The Enigma"
Curator Alex Diakun
Jerald Glazebrook John Payne
Hepcat Helm Gordon Tipple

Director: Kim Manners

The Calusari

w Sam Charno
The agents investigate the death of a two-year-old child who was run over by a miniature train in an amusement park, and uncover a supernatural link involving the boy's brother, Charley. When the boy's father is also killed, his Romanian grandmother calls in the Calusari, a group of ritualists, to perform an exorcism.
Charlie/Michael Holvey Joel Palmer
Golda Lilyan Chauvin
Maggie Holvey Helena Clarkson
Steve Holvey Ric Reid
Teddy Holvey Oliver & Jeremy Isaac Wildsmith
Dr. Charles Burk Bill Dow
Agent Karen Kosseff Christine Willes
Head Calusari Kay E. Kuter

Director: Michael Vejar

F. Emasculata

w Chris Carter & Howard Gordon
Confused by their involvement in the retrieval of two escaped convicts, Scully and Mulder dig a little deeper and discover that a highly contagious and deadly disease has infected many inmates—including the two escapees—as part of a drugs company's experiments using human guinea pigs. (The victims all develop horrific pustules that burst without warning—and the climactic "boil on the bus" sequence is as stomach-tightening as anything on TV. N.B.: The *F. Emasculata* stands for Faciphaga Emasculata, a parasitic insect—the original cause of the disease.)
Paul John Pyper-Ferguson
Steve John Tench
U.S. Marshal Tapia Dean Norris
Skinner Mitch Pileggi
Smoking Man William B. Davis
Dr. Simon Auerbach Morris Manych
Dr. Osbourne Charles Martin Smith
Angelo Garza Angelo Vacca

Director: Michael Bowman

Soft Light

w Vince Gilligan
Detective Kelly Ryan, an ex-student of Scully's, asks the agents to help her with her first case, concerning a number of mysterious disappearances, and the duo find themselves hunting down a scientist who is literally afraid of his own shadow.
Dr. Chester Ray Banton Tony Shalhoub
Det Kelly Ryan Kate Twa
X Steven Williams
Det. Barron Nathaniel Deveaux
Barney Guyle Frazier
Dr. Christopher Davey Kevin McNulty
Government scientist Forbes Angus
Night nurse Donna Yamamoto
Doctor Robert Rozen

Director: James Contner

Our Town

w Frank Spotnitz
A meat processing plant is the scene of a grisly missing persons investigation and Mulder suspects that a cult of cannibals is systematically killing people and eating their flesh to stay young.
Sheriff Tom Arens Gary Grubbs
Doris Kearns Caroline Kava
George Kearns John McLaren
Creighton Jones Hrothgar Matthews
Walter Chaco John Milford
Paula Gray Gabrielle Miller
Dr. Vance Randolph Robin Mossley
Jess Harold Timothy Webber

Director: Rob Bowman

Anasazi

w Chris Carter, *story by* David Duchovny & Chris Carter

First of a three-part story concluded at the start of Season Three. The Lone Gunmen put Mulder in touch with a hacker who has managed to download the Defense Department's top secret files on extraterrestrial life—but they are encrypted into Navajo. Scully's faith in her partner is sorely tested when his behavior becomes increasingly abnormal—even punching Skinner in a fight. Meanwhile, as the Smoking Man takes swift action of his own, Scully enlists the help of a Navajo translator and Mulder follows the trail to a boxcar buried in the New Mexico desert.

The Thinker (aka Kenneth Soona) Bernie Coulson
Frohike Tom Braidwood
Langly Dean Haglund
Byers Bruce Harwood
Skinner Mitch Pileggi
Smoking Man William B. Davis
Bill Mulder Peter Donat
Alex Krycek Nicholas Lea
Agent Kautz Paul McLean
Albert Hosteen Floyd "Red Crow" Westerman
Antonio Aurelio Dinunzio
Father Byron Chief Moon
Senior agent Michael David Simms
Josephine Doane Renae Morriseau

Director: R.W. Goodwin

Season Three
24 color 45-minute episodes

The Blessing Way

w Chris Carter

Part 2 of the three-part story. Scully faces possible dismissal from the bureau, and a manhunt is mounted for the missing Mulder who's found in the desert by Albert and his family. He's taken to a Navajo hogan, where Albert performs a mystic healing ritual called The Blessing Way, during which Mulder encounters visions of Deep Throat and his father. Meanwhile, at Mulder's father's funeral, Scully is approached by a Well-Manicured Man who warns her that a hit squad is out to kill her . . .

Skinner Mitch Pileggi
Mulder's father Peter Donat
Albert Floyd Red Crow Westerman
Melissa Scully Melinda McGraw
Margaret Scully Sheila Larken
Alex Krycek Nicholas Lea
Smoking Man William B. Davis
Deep Throat Jerry Hardin
Well-Manicured Man John Neville
Frohike Tom Braidwood
Dr. Pomerantz Alf Humphreys
Eric Dakota House
Senior FBI agent Michael David Simms

Mrs. Mulder Rebecca Toolan
Elder Don S. Williams
M.D. Forbes Angus
Camouflage Man Mitch Davies
Tour guide Benita Ha
Minister Ian Victor
Security guard Ernie Foort
Hispanic man Lenno Britos

Director: R.W. Goodwin

Paperclip

w Chris Carter

Part 3 of a three-part story. Mulder breaks up the stand-off between Skinner and Scully (that ended the previous episode), and Skinner comes down off his fence to side with the two agents in staving off the government hit squad, using the computer disk as leverage. Mulder searches for clues about his father's involvement in a secret project and his quest leads him and Scully to a ramshackle mine in West Virginia that hides a vast underground vault containing files and tissue samples on hundreds of millions of U.S. citizens—a huge DNA database . . .

Albert Floyd "Red Crow" Westerman
Victor Klemper Walter Gotell
Melissa Scully Melinda McGraw
Margaret Scully Sheila Larken
Alex Krycek Nicholas Lea
Smoking Man William B. Davis
Well-Manicured Man John Neville
Frohike Tom Braidwood
Langly Dean Haglund
Byers Bruce Harwood
Mrs. Mulder Rebecca Toolan
Elder Don S. Williams
ER doctor Robert Lewis
Hispanic man Lenno Britos

Director: Rob Bowman

D.P.O.

w Howard Gordon

Mulder and Scully investigate the deaths of several young people who were apparently struck by lightning in the same small town, and their inquiries lead them to a teenager, Darin Peter Oswald, with the freakish power to generate bolts of lightning.

Darin Oswald Giovanni Ribisi
Zero Jack Black
Sheriff Teller Ernie Lively
Sharon Kiveat Karen Witter
Frank Kiveat Steve Makaj
Stan Buxton Peter Anderson
Mrs. Oswald Kate Robbins
Jack Hammond Mar Andersons
Traffic cop Brent Chapman
Paramedic Jason Anthony Griffith

Director: Kim Manners

Clyde Bruckman's Final Repose

w Darin Morgan

Clyde Bruckman, an insurance salesman with psychic powers, assists Mulder and Scully in their hunt for The Puppet, a serial killer who is murdering fortune tellers. Bruckman also predicts in detail that Mulder will also be one of the killer's victims. (This episode won five Emmys, including one for guest star Peter Boyle, and for writer Darin Morgan. Story editor Morgan quit at the end of the season due to exhaustion.)

Clyde Bruckman Peter Boyle
Puppet Stu Charno
Det. Cline Frank Cassini
Det. Havez Dwight McFee
Tarot dealer Alex Diakun
Madame Zelma Karin Konoval
Clerk Ken Roberts
Yappi Jaap Broeker
Young husband David Mackay
Photographer Greg Anderson

Director: David Nutter

The List

w Darin Morgan

Death row inmate Napoleon "Neech" Manley goes to the electric chair vowing to return from the grave to take revenge on five men who mistreated him. Several days later his enemies begin dying one by one.

Roque Bokeem Woodbine
Neech Badja Djola
Warden J.T. Walsh
Speranza John Toles-Bey
Parmelly Ken Foree
Danielle April Grace
Daniel Charez Greg Rogers
Fornier Mitchell Kosterman
Oates Don MacCay
Ullrich Paul Raskin
Key guard Denny Arnold
Guard Craig Brunanski
Chaplain J.P. Finn

Director: David Nutter

2 Shy

w Jeffrey Vlaming

Mulder and Scully hunt for a grisly killer who uses the Internet to attract his victims whose bodies he leaves covered in a mucus-like slime after he drains them of fat, which he needs to replenish a chemical deficiency.

Det. Alan Cross James Handy
Virgil Incanto Timothy Carhart
Ellen Catherine Paolone
Joanne Kerry Sandomirsky
Jesse Aloka McLean
Jennifer Suzy Joachim
Monica Glynis Davies
Lauren Randi Lynne
Agent Dan Kazanjian William MacDonald

Director: David Nutter

The Walk

w John Shiban

A quadruple amputee becomes the prime suspect in a series of bizarre deaths at an army base—Mulder suspects the man, Rappo, is committing the murders via astral projection.

General Callahan Thomas Kopache
Roach Willie Garson
Lt. Colonel Victor Stans Don Thompson
Captain Janet Draper Nancy Sorel
Leonard "Rappo" Trimble Ian Tracey
Trevor Callahan Brennan Kotowich
Mrs. Callahan Andrea Barclay
Ward nurse Paula Shaw

Director: Rob Bowman

Oubliette

w Charles Grant Craig

A woman experiences an uncanny psychic link with a teenager held captive by a deranged man. Mulder discovers that the woman had been kidnapped by the same man when she was a child—and is now "sharing" the new victim's ordeal.

Lucy Householder Tracey Ellis
Carl Wade Michael Chieffo
Amy Jacobs Jewel Staite
Special Agent Walt Eubanks Ken Ryan
Tow truck driver Dean Wray
Henry Jacques LaLonde
Larsen David Fredericks
Myra Jacobs Sidonie Boll
Paramedic Robert Underwood

Director: Kim Manners

Nisei

w Chris Carter, Howard Gordon & Frank Spotnitz

First of a two-part story. An alien autopsy videotape and a Japanese diplomat's murder spark Mulder's search for a strange creature aboard a secret train. And Scully has a close encounter with a group of people who recognize her as a fellow abductee!

Skinner Mitch Pileggi
Red-Haired Man Stephen McHattie
Senator Richard Matheson Raymond J. Barry
Dr. Zama/Dr. Ishimaru Robert Ito
Frohike Tom Braidwood
Langly Dean Haglund
Byers Bruce Harwood
X Steven Williams
Penny Gillian Barber
Agent Pendrell Brendan Beiser
Lottie Holloway Corrine Koslo
Diane Lori Triolo
Coastguard officer Paul McLean
Kazuo Sakurai Yasuo Sakurai

Director: David Nutter

731

w Frank Spotnitz
Part 2 of a two-part story. Mulder becomes trapped along with the assassin, the Red-Haired Man, aboard a train rigged with explosives. And Scully searches for the truth behind her implant and the government's involvement with a Japanese scientist's secret experiments.
X Steven Williams
Red-Haired Man Stephen McHattie
Smoking Man William B. Davis
Dr. Zama/Dr. Ishimaru Robert Ito
Escalante Colin Cunningham
Syndicate elder Don S. Williams
Agent Pendrell Brendan Beiser
Conductor Michael Puttonen

Director: Rob Bowman

Revelations

w Kim Newton
Scully is at odds with Mulder when she believes she is the one "chosen" by God to protect a stigmatic boy whose death at the hands of a killer called the Millennium Man could trigger the coming of Armageddon.
Rev. Finley R. Lee Ermey
Kevin Kryder Kevin Zegers
Millennium Man/Simon Gates Kenneth Welsh
Michael Kryder Sam Bottoms
Susan Kryder Hayley Tyson
Owen Jarvis Michael Berryman
Carina Maywald Lesley Ewen
Mrs. Tynes Nicole Robert
Priest Fulvio Cecere

Director: David Nutter

War of the Coprophages

w Darin Morgan
Mulder stumbles upon a town seemingly under attack by killer cockroaches and meets Dr. Bambi Berenbaum, a voluptuous entomologist . . . (This episode contains some wonderfully playful dialogue—just listen for Scully's remark to Bambi as she prepares to rush inside a crazed scientist's lab.)

Sheriff Frass Dion Anderson
Dr. Eckerle Raye Birk
Dr. Bambi Berenbaum Bobbie Phillips
Dr. Newton Bill Dow
Dr. Bugger Alex Bruhanski
Dr. Ivanov Ken Kramer
Dude Alan Buckley
Chick Nicole Parker
Stoner Tyler Labine

Director: Kim Manners

Syzygy

w Chris Carter
A rare alignment of the planets causes tempers to rise in a small town and gives two teenage girls deadly telekinetic powers. Scully and Mulder find they, too, are affected as they become unusually short with each other.
Det. Angela White Dana Wheeler-Nicholson
Margi Kleinjan Wendy Benson
Terri Roberts Lisa Robin Kelly
Bob Spitz Garry Davey
Madame Zirinka Denalda Williams
Brenda Summerfield Gabrielle Miller
Jay "Boom" DeBoom Ryan Reynolds
Dr. Richard W. Godfrey Tim Dixon
Minister Ryk Brown
Eric Bauer Jeremy Radick
Scott Simmons Russell Porter

Director: Rob Bowman

Grotesque

w Howard Gordon
Mulder clashes with his old bureau teacher and becomes dangerously obsessed with the agent's three-year-old case involving an incarcerated serial killer who claims he was possessed by a gargoyle.
Skinner Mitch Pileggi
Agent Bill Patterson Kurtwood Smith
Mostow Levani Outchaneichvili
Agent Nemhauser Greg Thirloway
Agent Sheherlis Susan Bain
Young agent Kasper Michaels
Model Zoran Vukelic

Director: Kim Manners

Piper Maru

w Frank Spotnitz & Chris Carter
First of a complicated two-part story. Acute radiation burns kill all except one of the crew of a French salvage ship investigating a sunken World War Two plane at the same location visited by the *Talapus* (a ship Mulder became interested in in the episode "Nisei"). The lone survivor has become possessed by a strange entity he encountered on the sea bed, but this entity has the power to transfer from one person to another . . . While Scully visits an old neighbor and World War Two vet to find out what he might know, Mulder follows a trail to Hong Kong where he is surprised to find Alex Krycek. Meanwhile, back in Washington, Skinner is shot by the Hispanic Man who killed Scully's sister (in "The Blessing Way").
Skinner Mitch Pileggi
Bernard Gauthier Ari Solomon
Joan Gauthier Kimberly Unger
Jeraldine Kallenchuk Jo Bates
Commander Johansen Robert Clothier
Gray-Haired Man Morris Panych
Wayne Morgan Stephen E. Miller
Dr. Seizer Paul Batten
Alex Krycek Nicholas Lea
Hispanic Man (aka Luis Cardinal) Lenno Britos
Young Dana Tegan Moss
World War Two pilot Robert F. Maier
Medic Russell Ferrier
Waitress Rochelle Greenwood
Young Johansen Tom Scholte

Director: Rob Bowman

Apocrypha

w Frank Spotnitz & Chris Carter
Part 2 of a two-part story. With Krycek now the alien entity's latest host, Mulder uncovers more clues about a government cover-up involving the entity and meets the Well-Manicured Man who tells him a UFO was shot down by U.S. pilots during World War Two. As Skinner recovers in the hospital, a vengeful Scully pursues his—and her sister's—assailant who tells her Krycek is heading for an abandoned missile site in North Dakota . . .
Skinner Mitch Pileggi
Well-Manicured Man John Neville
Smoking Man William B. Davis
Frohike Tom Braidwood
Langly Dean Haglund
Byers Bruce Harwood
Alex Krycek Nicholas Lea
Agent Pendrell Brendan Beiser
Hispanic Man Lenno Britos
Elder Don S. Williams
Agent Fuller Kevin McNulty
Government man Dmitry Chepovetsky
Navy doctor Barry Levy
Agent Caleca Sue Matthew
Nurse Frances Flanagan

Sick crewman Peter Scoular
Armed man Jeff Chivers

Director: Kim Manners

Pusher

w Vince Gilligan
A dying killer who can control people's minds plays a deadly game of cat-and-mouse with Mulder and Scully.
Skinner Mitch Pileggi
Pusher/Robert Modell Robert Wisden
Agent Frank Burst Vic Polizos
SWAT Lieutenant Roger Cross
Agent Collins Steve Bacic
Judge Don Mackay
Prosecutor Brent Sheppard
Deputy Scott Kerber D. Neil Mark
Defense attorney Meredith Bain Woodward
Holly Julia Arkos
Lobby guard Ernie Foort
Lead SWAT cop Darren Lucas

Director: Rob Bowman

Teso Dos Bichos

w John Shiban
A curse befalls members of an archaeological team after a sacred urn is excavated in Ecuador and transported to a Boston museum. (Not an episode for anyone afraid of cats . . .)
Bilac Vic Trevino
Mona Wustner Janne Mortil
Shaman Gordon Tootoosis
Dr. Lewton Tom McBeath
Mr. Decker Ron Sauve
Roosevelt Alan Robertson
Dr. Winters Garrison Chrisjohn

Director: Kim Manners

Hell Money

w Jeff Vlaming
With the aid of a Chinese detective, Glen Chao, the agents investigate a deadly game in San Francisco's Chinatown district in which the losers are killed and their bodies harvested for their organs.
Det. Glen Chao B.D. Wong
Kim Lucy Alexis Liu
Hsin Michael Yama
Hard-Faced Man James Hong
Det. Neary Doug Abrahams
OPO Staffer Ellie Harvie
Johnny Lo Derek Lowe
Vase Man Donald Fong
Dr. Wu Diana Ha
Large man Stephen M.D. Change
Wiry man Paul Wong

Director: Tucker Gates

Jose Chung's *From Outer Space*

w Darin Morgan
Scully relates the story of an investigation of an alleged UFO abduction for a famous author researching his latest novel.
Jose Chung Charles Nelson Reilly
Roky William Lucking
Lt. Jack Shaeffer Daniel Quinn
Man in Black Jesse Ventura
Chrissy Sarah Sawatsky
Harold Jason Gaffney
Dr. Fingers Alex Diakun
Det. Manners Marry Musser
Blaine Faulkner Allan Zinyk
Sgt. Hynek Michael Dobson
Dr. Hand Mina E. Mina
Yappi Jaap Broeker
Himself Alex Trebek

Director: Rob Bowman

Avatar

w Howard Gordon, *story by* Howard Gordon & David Duchovny
Skinner becomes the prime suspect in the murder of a prostitute, but Mulder suspects he is being set up by someone within the government (having failed to kill him in a previous episode, "Piper Maru"). However, Skinner also admits that he is being troubled by a recurring dream in which he is confronted by an old woman—a vision he first encountered during a near-death experience in Vietnam.
Skinner Mitch Pileggi
Jay Cassal Tasha Simms
Carina Sayles Amanda Tapping
Det. Waltos Tom Mason
Lorraine Kelleher Jennifer Hetrick
Smoking Man William B. Davis
Agent Bonnecaze Malcolm Stewart
Gray-Haired Man Morris Panych
Judy Fairly Stacy Grant
Sharon Skinner Janie Woods-Morris
Agent Pendrell Brendan Beiser
Senior agent Michael David Simms

Director: James Charleston

Quagmire

w Kim Newton
Mulder suspects that Big Blue, a legendary beast similar to the Loch Ness monster, is responsible for several deaths at a lake in Georgia. (Good episode let down by a woefully sentimental ending.)
Sheriff Lance Hindt Chris Ellis
Dr. Paul Farraday Timothy Webber

Ansel Bray R. Nelson Brown
Ted Bertram Mark Acheson
Dr. William Bailey Peter Hanlon
Stoner Tyler Labine
Chick Nicole Parker
Snorkel dude Terrance Leigh

Director: Kim Manners

Wetwired

w Mat Beck
Acting on a tip from a mysterious Plain-Clothed Man, Mulder and Scully investigate a series of murders linked to a device that alters television signals and acts as a mind control, inducing violent behavior. And when Scully becomes affected, Mulder finds his own life is in danger . . .
Skinner Mitch Pileggi
Smoking Man William B. Davis
X Steven Williams
Mrs. Scully Sheila Larken
Frohike Tom Braidwood
Langly Dean Haglund
Byers Bruce Harwood
Dr. Stroman Colin Cunningham
Plain-Clothed Man Tim Henry
Joseph Patnik Linden Banks
Dr. Lorenz Crystal Verge
County coroner Andre Danyliu
Motel manager Joe Maffei

Director: Rob Bowman

Talitha Cumi

w Chris Carter
First of a two-part story. After his mother suffers a stroke following a heated argument with the Smoking Man, Mulder searches for a strange alien being who possesses miraculous healing powers.
Skinner Mitch Pileggi
Smoking Man William B. Davis
X Steven Williams
Mulder's father Peter Donat
Deep Throat Jerry Hardin
Melissa Scully Melinda McGraw
Jeremiah Smith Roy Thinnes
Bounty hunter Brian Thompson, Angelo Vacco
Galen Muntz Hrothgar Mathews
Mrs. Mulder Rebecca Toolan
Detective Stephen Dimopoulos
Doctor John McLaren
Paramedic Cam Cronin
Night nurse Bonnie Hay

Director: R.W. Goodwin

Season Four
24 color 60-minute episodes

Herrenvolk

w Chris Carter
Mulder and Scully try to protect Jeremiah Smith, the man with a strange healing touch, from an unstoppable alien killer.
Jeremiah Smith Roy Thinnes
Skinner Mitch Pileggi
Cigarette-Smoking Man William B. Davis
X Steven Williams
Bounty hunter Brian Thompson
Repairman Garvin Cross
Elder Don Williams
Gray-Haired Man Morris Panych
Mrs. Mulder Rebecca Toolan
Agent Pendrell Brendan Beiser

Director: R.W. Goodwin

Unruhe

w Vince Gilligan
A killer's mind leaves impressions on undeveloped film wherever he goes, and the psychotic images in the photographs may be the only clue to tracking him down.
Gerry Schnauz Pruitt Vince
Mary LeFante Sharon Alexander
Officer Trott William Macdonald
Inspector Puett Ron Chartier

Director: Rob Bowman

Home

w Glen Morgan *&* James Wong
Sheriff Andy Taylor calls the FBI when a deformed infant turns up dead in a shallow grave, leading to a clan of in-bred monsters.
Sheriff Andy Taylor Tucker Smallwood
Deputy Barney Paster Sebastian Spence
Mrs. Barbara Taylor Judith Maxie
Edmund Peacock Chris Norris
George Peacock John Trottier
Sherman Peacock Adrian Hughes
Peacock Mother Karin Konoval

Director: Kim Manners

Teliko

w Howard Gordon
African-American men are disappearing in Philadelphia, and the only lead is the body of one victim, whose pigmentation is gone—and whose pituitary gland has been destroyed. Clues lead to a Teliko, an African evil spirit of the air who emerges at night to suck the life and color out of victims.
Skinner Mitch Pileggi
Dr. Simon Bruin Bob Morrisey
Marcus Duff Carl Lumbly
Agent Pendrell Brendan Beiser
Alfred Kittel Dexter Bell
Marita Covarrubias Laurie Holden
Diabria Zakes Mokae
Lt. Madsen Sean Campbell

Director: James Charleston

The Field Where I Died

w Glen Morgan *&* James Wong
While defusing the threat of a religious cult, Mulder discovers a cult member who may be the reincarnation of a past lover.
Skinner Mitch Pileggi
Melissa Riedal-Ephesian Kristen Cloke
Vernon Ephesian Michael Massee
Harbaugh Doug Abrahams
Agent Riggins Anthony Harrison

Director: Rob Bowman

Sanguinarium

w Vivian Mayhew *&* Valerie Mayhew
When a doctor who murdered a patient claims demonic possession, Mulder and Scully investigate his claims, uncovering a nurse who is a practicing witch . . . but when she is murdered by magic, Mulder must look elsewhere for the true cause.
Nurse Rebecca Waite O-Lan Jones
Dr. Harrison Lloyd John Juliani
Dr. Theresa Shannon Arlene Mazerolle
Dr. Jack Franklin Richard Beymer
Dr. Prabu Amanpour Paul Raskin
Dr. Mitchell Kaplan Gregory Thirloway
Jill Holwagerm Nina Roman
Dr. Hartman Martin Evans
Dr. Sally Sanford Marie Stillin

Director: Kim Manners

Musings of a Cigarette-Smoking Man

w Glen Morgan
Frohike pieces together the life story of the Cigarette-Smoking Man as the Cigarette-Smoking Man eavesdrops with a sniper's rifle trained on him.
Cigarette-Smoking Man William B. Davis
Young Cigarette-Smoking Man Chris Owens
Young Bill Mulder Dean Aylesworth
Lee Harvey Oswald Morgan Weisser
Corporal Anthony Ashbee
General Francis Donnelly Rhodes
Mob Man Peter Mele
Agent Man Dan Zukovic
Cuban Man Gonzalo Canton
Supervisor Steve Oatway
Director David Fredericks
Aide Peter Hanlon
Major general Michael St. John Smith
James Earl Ray Paul Jarrett
Lydon Laurie Murdoch
Matlock Marc Baur
Jones Jude Zachary
Deep Throat Jerry Hardin
Frohike Tom Braidwood
Byers Bruce Harwood

Director: James Wong

Paper Hearts

w Vince Gilligan
Mulder discovers the skeleton of a murdered child and recognizes the work of serial killer John Lee Roche, who confessed to killing 13 girls between 1979 and 1990. When Mulder locates Roche's trophies, he finds 16 hearts cut from the dead girls' clothing and realizes there are two more unknown victims. When he interviews Roche, he begins to suspect Roche—and not aliens—may be responsible for his sister's abduction.
Skinner Mitch Pileggi
John Lee Roche Tom Noonan
Mrs. Mulder Rebecca Toolan
Robert Sparks Byrne Piven
Samantha Mulder Vanessa Morely
Caitlin Ross Carly Mckillip

Director: Rob Bowman

Tunguska

w Frank Spotnitz & Chris Carter
Krycek promises to help Mulder expose the Cigarette-Smoking Man and the whole shadowy conspiracy, then leads him to a Russian courier transporting four billion-year-old rocks filled with an alien substance called the "black cancer," which seems to have a life of its own. Using his UN contact, Mulder and Krycek go to Siberia to investigate—and Mulder ends up in a secret gulag where the patients are experimental subjects.

Skinner Mitch Pileggi
Cigarette-Smoking Man William B. Davis
Alex Krycek Nicholas Lea
Committee chairman Campbell Lane
Senator Sorenson Fritz Weaver
Vassily Peskow Jan Rubes
Dr. Kingsley Looker Robin Mossley
Agent Pendrell Brendan Beiser
Well-Manicured Man John Neville
Dr. Sacks Malcolm Stewart
Dr. Bonita Sayre Jessica Schreier
Terry Edward Mayhew Brent Stait
Angie Eileen Pedde
Marita Covarrubias Laurie Holden

Director: Rob Bowman

Terma

w Frank Spotnitz & Chris Carter
Mulder escapes the gulag, only to return home to face a skeptical Senate committee investigating matters and a Russian assassin carefully erasing all evidence of the "black cancer."
Skinner Mitch Pileggi
Cigarette-Smoking Man William B. Davis
Alex Krycek Nicholas Lea
Committee chairman Campbell Lane
Senator Sorenson Fritz Weaver
Vassily Peskow Jan Rubes
Dr. Kingsley Looker Robin Mossley
Agent Pendrell Brendan Beiser
Well-Manicured Man John Neville
Dr. Sacks Malcolm Stewart
Dr. Bonita Sayre Jessica Schreier
Terry Edward Mayhew Brent Stait
Angie Eileen Pedde

Director: Rob Bowman

El Mundo Gira

w John Shiban
Mulder and Scully investigate mutilation deaths in California at a shantytown populated with migrant workers, many of them illegal Mexicans. Fortean events, alien fungi and the Puerto Rican myth of El Chupacabra—"the goatsucker," a monster—combine to make an exciting episode.
Skinner Mitch Pileggi
Conrad Lozano Ruben Blades
Eladio Buente Raymond Cruz
Maria Dorantes Pamela Diaz
Soledad Buente Jose Yenque
Flakita Lillian Hurst
Dr. Larry Steen Robert Thurston
Gabrielle Buente Simi
Rick Culver Mike Kopsa

Director: Tucker Gates

Kaddish

w Howard Gordon

When the fingerprints of a dead man turn up at a murder scene, Mulder suspects a golem, a man-made monster described in Jewish folklore, may be taking revenge for the death of a Jewish man who was murdered out of racial hate.

Ariel Luria Justine Miceli
Jacob Weiss David Groh
Issac Luria Harrison Coe
Derek Banks Channon Roe
Clinton Bascombe Jabin Litwiniec
Tony Timur Karabilgin
Curt Brunjes Jonathan Whittaker
Kenneth Ungar David Wohl
Detective George Gordon
1st Hasidic Man Murrey Rabinovitch
Rabbi David Freedman

Director: Kim Manners

Never Again

w Glen Morgan & James Wong

Scully solos while Mulder is on vacation, but the handsome man she's dating has a tattoo of Betty Page, and the tattoo doesn't like strange women cutting in on her man.

Ed Jerse Rodney Rowland
Judge Carla Stewart
Bartender Barry "Bear" Hortin
Vsevlod Pudovkin Igor Morozov
Ms. Hadden Jan Bailey Mattia
Ms. Vansen Rita Bozi
Mrs. Shima-Tsuno Marilyn Chin
Kaye Schilling Jillian Fargey
Hannah B.J. Harrison
Detective Gouveia Jay Donahue
Detective Smith Ian Robison

Director: Rob Bowman

Leonard Betts

w Frank Spotnitz, John Shiban & Vince Gilligan

When a decapitated corpse strolls out of a morgue, Mulder launches a search for a man with incredible regenerative powers . . . who may be stealing organs and other body parts to survive.

Michele Wilkes Jennifer Clement
Leonard Betts Paul McCrane
EMT Lucia Walters
Elaine Tanner Marjorie Lovett
Dr. Charles Burks Bill Dow

Director: Kim Manners

Memento Mori

w Chris Carter, Frank Spotnitz, John Shiban & Vince Gilligan

Scully learns she has an inoperable cancer, and she and Mulder track down a group of women who had similar situations—abductees who removed their implants and also came down with the disease. As Scully undergoes cancer treatments, Mulder investigates further and encounters clones, a fake fertility clinic and new layers of conspiracy.

Kurt Crawford David Lovgren
Penny Northern Gillian Barber
Mrs. Scully Shiela Larken
Frohike Tom Braidwood
Langly Dean Haglund
Byers Bruce Harwood
Cigarette-Smoking Man William B. Davis
Skinner Mitch Pileggi
Woman Julie Bond
Gray-Haired Man Morris Panych
Dr. Kevin Scanlon Sean Allen

Director: Rob Bowman

Unrequited

w Howard Gordon & Chris Carter

The FBI is protecting top military men from an assassin who has the ability to seemingly disappear at will. As Mulder investigates, he uncovers a conspiracy going back to the Vietnam War.

Skinner Mitch Pileggi
Gen. Benjamin Bloch Scott Hylands
Nathaniel Teager Peter Lacroix
Agent Cameron Hill Ryan Michael
P.F.C. Gus Burkholder Don McWilliams
Lt. General Peter MacDougal Bill Agnew
Agent Eugene Chandler Mark Holden
Denny Markham Larry Musser
Renee Davenport Lesley Ewen
Dr. Ben Keyser Allan Franz
Gen. Jon Steffan William Nunn
Gen. Leitch William Taylor

Director: Michael Lange

Tempus Fugit

w Chris Carter & Frank Spotnitz

When a commercial airplane crashes, Mulder investigates reports that a UFO caused the accident. When he investigates at the crash site, he realizes there is a nine-minute discrepancy between the official time of the crash and the time indicated on passengers' wristwatches. And the lone survivor was exposed to high levels of radiation . . .

Skinner Mitch Pileggi
Mike Millar Joe Spano
Corporal Frish Tom O'Brien
Max Fenig Scott Bellis
Sharon Graffia Chilton Crane
Agent Pendrell Brendan Beiser
Scott Garrett Greg Michaels
Bruce Bearfeld Robert Moloney
Sgt. Armondo Gonzales Rick Dobran
Larold Rebhun Jerry Schram

Director: Rob Bowman

Max

w Chris Carter *&* Frank Spotnitz
Mulder continues his investigation into the plane crash and uncovers what may be a second crash site—this one for a UFO. But the military arrests Mulder and puts the site off limits. After his release, Mulder continues his search and comes to believe an air force jet shot down both the UFO and the commercial plane to keep proof of extraterrestrial life from being made public.
Skinner Mitch Pileggi
Mike Millar Joe Spano
Corporal Frish Tom O'Brien
Max Fenig Scott Bellis
Sharon Graffia Chilton Crane
Agent Pendrell Brendan Beiser
Scott Garrett Greg Michaels
Bruce Bearfeld Robert Moloney
Motel Manager Felicia Shulman
Sgt. Armondo Gonzales Rick Dobran
Larold Rebhun Jerry Schram
Dark Man David Palffy
Pilot Mark Wilson

Director: Kim Manners

Synchrony

w Howard Gordon *&* David Greenwalt
A man from the future tries to change the present by killing researchers with a chemical freezing compound.
Lucas Menand Jed Rees
Jason Nichols Joseph Fuqua
Lisa Ianelli Michael Fairman
Dr. Yonechi Hiro Kanagwa
Chuck Lukerman Jonathan Walker

Director: Jim Charleston

Small Potatoes

w Vince Gilligan
A mini epidemic of babies born with tails leads Mulder and Scully to Eddie Van Blundht, who suddenly exhibits the ability to change his appearance at will.
Skinner Mitch Pileggi
Amanda Nelligan Christine Cavanaugh
Eddie Van Blundht Darin Morgan

Director: Clifford Bole

Zero Sum

w Howard Gordon *&* Frank Spotnitz
Skinner gets sucked into a conspiracy to hide killer bees genetically engineered to spread disease, and ends up framed for murder.

Skinner Mitch Pileggi
Cigarette-Smoking Man William B. Davis
1st Elder Don S. Williams
Gray-Haired Man Morris Panych
Jane Brody Lisa Stewart
Misty Nicolle Nattrass
Detective Hugel Fred Keating
Dr. Peter Valedespino Allan Gray
Mrs. Kemper Theresa Puskar
Dr. Emile Linzer Barry Creene
Special Agent Kautz Paul Mclean
Marita Covarrubias Laurie Holden

Director: Kim Manners

Elegy

w John Shiban
Mulder and Scully trace the murders of several girls to a psychiatric institution—but is their suspect the murderer or merely a psychic picking up messages from the dead girls' spirits?
Harold Spuller Steven M. Porter
Angelo Pintero Alex Bruhanski
Chuck Forsch Sydney Lassick
Nurse Innes Nancy Fish
Detective Hudak Daniel Kamin
Attorney Lorena Gale
Martin Alpert Mike Puttonen
Karen Kosseff Christine Willes
Sgt. Conneff Gerry Naim

Director: Jim Charleston

Demons

w R.W. Goodwin
Mulder suffers a mental blackout and wakes up covered with blood in a motel room, leading to the possibility that he is a murderer. But the case has quite a few twists, including a psychiatrist using experimental techniques to awaken dormant memories.
Detective Joe Curtis Jay Acovone
Dr. Charles Goldstein Mike Nussbaum
Young Cigarette-Smoking Man Chris Owens
Mrs. Mulder Rebecca Toolan
Medical Examiner Andrew Johnston
Imhof Terry Jang Barclay
Young Samantha Vanessa Morley
Admitting Officer Eric Breker
Housekeeper Rebecca Harker
Young Mrs. Mulder Shelley Adam
Young Bill Mulder Dean Aylesworth
Young Mulder Alex Haythorne

Director: Kim Manners

Gethsemane

w Chris Carter
Mulder investigates the discovery of a frozen alien found in 200-year-old ice in Canada and finds thieves and assassins out to prevent the body from reaching civilization.
Michael Kritschgau John Finn
Arlinsky Matthew Walker
Babcock James Sutorius
Mrs. Scully Sheila Larken
Bill Scully Jr. Pat Skipper
Rolston John Oliver
Scott Blevins Charles Cioffi
Ostelhoff Steve Makha
Agent Hedin Nancy Kerr
Vitagliano Barry W. Levy
Father McCue Arnie Walters
Detective Rempulski Rob Freeman
Saw Operator Craig Burnanski

Director: R. W. Goodwin

Season Five
24 60-minute episodes

Unusual Suspects

w Vince Gilligan
It's the story of the Lone Gunmen as they meet for the first time in 1989 and try to help a woman who claims the government is using people as guinea pigs in secret experiments.
Skinner Mitch Pileggi
Detective Munch Richard Belzer
Byers Bruce Harwood
Langly Dean Haglund
Frohike Tom Braidwood
Hacker dude Eric Knight
Susanne Modeski Signy Coleman
Ken Hawryliw Ken Hawryliw
Mr. X Steven Williams
SWAT Lieutenant Chris Nelson Norris
1st SWAT Cop Stuart O'connell

Director: Kim Manners

Redux

w Chris Carter
Picking up from last season's cliffhanger, Mulder infiltrates a government agency using a dead man's ID to try to find the cure for Scully's cancer. Meanwhile, Scully continues her analysis of cells from the frozen ice core sample . . . and discovers a match to her own DNA.
Cigarette-Smoking Man William B. Davis
Scott Kritschgau John Finn
Ostelhoff Steve Makaj
Senior agent Ken Camroux
Blevins Charles Cioffi
Dr. Vitagliano Barry W. Levy
Byers Bruce Harwood
Elder Don S. Williams
Langly Dean Haglund
Frohike Tom Briadwood
Holly Julie Arkos

Director: Kim Manners

Redux II

w Chris Carter
Mulder continues to try to find a cure for Scully's cancer as she's dying, but the one man holding out hope is his greatest enemy—the Cigarette-Smoking Man. Meanwhile, hearings continue on Mulder and the agency, and Skinner has been framed as a mole working for conspirators.
Cigarette-Smoking Man William B. Davis
Senior agent Ken Camroux
Blevins Charles Cioffi
Doctor Brent Sheppard
Byers Bruce Harwood
Elder Don S. Williams
Langly Dean Haglund
Frohike Tom Braidwood
Mrs. Scully Sheila Larken
Bill Scully Jr. Pat Skipper
Dr. Zuckerman Robert Wright
Kritschgau John Finn
Samantha Mulder Megan Leitch
Father McCue Arnie Walters

Director: Kim Manners

Detour

w Frank Spotnitz
When several people disappear in the Florida woods, Mulder and Scully go hunting for a reported red-eyed monster . . . and find what may be the Fountain of Youth.
Michael Sloan Tom Scholte
Marty Fox Simon Longmore
Father Alf Humphreys
Louis Asekoff Tyler Thompson
Agent Kinsley Scott Burkholder
Agent Stonecypher J.C. Wendel
Mrs. Asekoff Merrilyn Gann
Michele Fazekas Colleen Flynn
Jeff Glaser Anthony Rapp

Director: Brett Dowler

Christmas Carol

w Vince Gilligan, John Shiban & Frank Spotnitz
While visiting her family, Scully gets a mysterious phone call from a little girl in need of help . . . a girl who Scully comes to believe is her dead sister's daughter.
Tara Scully Karri Turner
Mrs. Scully Sheila Larken
Bill Scully Jr. Pat Skipper
Detective Kresge John Pyper-Ferguson
Marshall Sim Rob Freeman
Emily Sim Lauren Diewold
Susan Chambliss Patricia Dahlquist

Director: Peter Markle

Post-Modern Prometheus

w Chris Carter
The Frankenstein myth plays out (in glorious black and white) in rural Indiana, with Mulder and Scully on hand to investigate.
Shaineh Pattie Tierce
Izzie Stewart Gale
Booger Chris Giacoletti
Mutato Chris Owens
Dr. Pollidori John O'Hurley
Elizabeth Pollidori Miriam Smith
J. J. Vitaliy Kravchenko

Director: Chris Carter

Emily

w Frank Spotnitz, Vince Gilligan & John Shiban
Scully's hearing regarding the custody of her biological daughter doesn't go well, as Dark Forces conspire to keep her from the medical experiment that is Emily. Meanwhile, Emily continues to undergo treatment for her strange ailments, and when treatment is interrupted, weird things start to happen to her, including a snakelike creature stirring beneath her skin.
Tara Scully Karri Turner
Mrs. Scully Sheila Larken
Bill Scully Jr. Pat Skipper
Detective Kresge John Pyper-Ferguson
Emily Sim Lauren Diewold
Susan Chambliss Patricia Dahlquist
Judge Maibaum David Abbott
Dr. Vinet Bob Morrisey
Dr. Calderon Gerard Plunkett
Anna Fugazzi Sheila Paterson
Frohike Tom Braidwood

Director: Kim Manners

Kitsunegari

w Vince Gilligan & Tim Minear
Robert Modell—the Pusher from Season Three episode "Pusher," who is able to force his will on other people—escapes and begins stalking Fox Mulder. But he is in terrible shape and soon Mulder begins to suspect there may be a second person out there capable of controlling the minds of others.
Skinner Mitch Pileggi
Linda Bowman Diana Scarwid
Pusher/Robert Modell Robert Wisden
Therapist Colleen Winton
Old orderly Scott Oughterson
Female agent Donna Yamamoto

Director: Daniel Sackheim

Schizogeny

w Jessica Scott & Mike Wollaeger
When a man is killed by mud, his stepson becomes the prime suspect. But a strange force may be at work when a second strange death occurs, linked only by a therapist.
Bobby Rich Chad Lindberg
Phil Rich Bob Dawson
Patti Rich Cynde Harmon
John Ramirez George Josef
Lisa Baiocchi Katharine Isabelle
Joey Agostino Myles Ferguson
Mr. Baiocchi Gardiner Millar
Karin Matthews Sarah-Jane Redmond
Lisa's Aunt Kate Robbins
Mr. Baiocchi Gardinar Millar

Director: Ralph Hemecker

Chinga

w Stephen King & Chris Carter
When a doll is dredged up from the ocean, a Maine fisherman gives it to his daughter, unaware that it will use the girl to terrorize the town.
Melissa Turner Susannah Hoffman
Polly Turner Jenny-Lynn Hutcheson
Jane Froelich Carolyn Tweedle
Assistant manager Gordan Tipple
Dave the Fishmonger Harrison Coe
Jack Bonsaint Larry Musser
Buddy Riggs William Macdonald
Rich Turner Dean Wray

Director: Kim Manners

Kill Switch

w William Gibson & Tom Maddox
An intelligent computer program seeks to protect its existence, and it will stop at nothing—not even murder—to carry out its goals. When Mulder and Scully stumble onto its existence, it makes them its next target.
Byers Bruce Harwood
Langly Dean Haglund
Frohike Tom Braidwood
Donald Gelman Patrick Keating
Jackson Peter Williams
Bunny Rob Daprocida
Boyce Jerry Schram
Figgis Dan Weber
Esther Nairn Kristin Lehman

Director: Rob Bowman

Bad Blood

w Vince Gilligan
When Mulder kills a teenager he believes is a vampire, the boy's parents sue the FBI, and Mulder must recount the story step-by-step to clear himself . . . or prove his guilt.
Skinner Mitch Pileggi
Ronnie Strickland Patrick Renna
Sheriff Hartwell Luke Wilson
Funeral Director Forbes Angus
Coroner Brent Bunt
Detective Marion Killinger

Director: Cliff Bole

Patient X

w Chris Carter & Frank Spotnitz
UFO nuts are gathering—and being incinerated alive in an attempt to cover up one phase of the great conspiracy. When Scully finds herself drawn to join the next gathering, Mulder must protect her and try to uncover the truth.
Alex Krycek Nicholas Lea
Cassandra Veronica Cartwright
Maria Covarrubias Laurie Holden
Special Agent Spender Chris Owens
Dr. Heitz Werber Jim Jansen
Well-Manicured Man John Neville
Bounty Hunter Brian Thompson
Dmitri Alex Shostak Jr.
Elder Don S. Williams
Dr. Floyd Fazio Ron Halder
Ranger Kurt Max Runte
2nd Elder John Moore
Guard Raoul Ganeen
Commandant Anatol Rezmeritsa
Dr. Per Lagerqvist Max Wyman
Dr. Dominique Alepin Barbara Dyke
Quiet Willy Willy Ross

Director: Kim Manners

The Red and the Black

w Chris Carter & Frank Spotnitz
The alien conspiracy takes new turns, as good aliens and bad aliens appear to be battling each other for the right to colonize Earth. Scully undergoes hypnosis and recovers a memory of another UFO incident, and Mulder fights to save an alien from incineration.
Skinner Mitch Pileggi
Cigarette-Smoking Man William B. Davis
Alex Krycek Nicholas Lea
Cassandra Veronica Cartwright
Well-Manicured Man John Neville
3rd Elder George Murdock
Special Agent Spender Chris Owens
Maria Covarrubias Laurie Holden
Bounty hunter Brian Thompson
Elder Don S. Williams
Dr. Heitz Werber Jim Jansen
Dmitri Alex Shostak Jr.
Dr. Patou Chapelle Jaffe
2nd Elder John Moore
Young Jeffrey Spender Michal Suchanek

Director: Chris Carter

Travelers

w John Shiban & Frank Spotnitz
In a flashback episode set in 1990 and 1952, Mulder uncovers some of his father's past, including involvement in the McCarthy hearings—and a serial killer who removes people's internal organs.
Agent Arthur Dales Darren McGavin
Sheriff Mitchell Kosterman
Landlord J. Douglas Stewart
Edward Skur Garret Dillahunt
Hayes Michel Brian Leckner
Young Arthur Dales Fredric Lane
Mrs. Skur Eileen Pedde
Roy Cohn David Moreland
Dorothy Bahnsen Jane Perry
Young Bill Mulder Dean Aylesworth
Old Edward Skur Eric W. Gilder
Cohn's Assistant Dean Barrett
Coroner Roger Haskett
Director David Fredericks
Bartender Cory Dagg

Director: Bill Graham

Mind's Eye

w Tim Minnear
When a blind woman suffers visions of a murderer and tries to help the victim, she is accused of the crime. Mulder must prove her innocent and find the real killer.
Marty Glenn Lili Taylor
Detective Pennock Blu Mankuma
Gotts Richard Fitzpatrick
Dr. Wilkenson Henri Lubatti
Ada Costa Peter Kelamis

Director: Kim Manners

All Souls

w Frank Spotnitz *&* John Shiban, *story by* Billy
   Brown *&* Dan Angel
When a handicapped girl who can't walk gets out of
her wheelchair in the middle of the night, walks into
the street and dies with her eyes burned out, a priest
asks for Scully's help. Then the handicapped girl's
sister—still in an orphanage—dies in the same way
and Scully calls in Mulder.
Father McCue Arnie Walters
Mrs. Kernoff Patti Allan
Lance Kernof Eric Keenleyside
Dara/Paula Emily Perkins
Gregory Jody Racicot
Pathologist Vicki Belon Lorraine Landry
Aaron Starkey Glenn Morshower
Emily Lauren Diewold
George Vincent Dyer Bob Wilde
Sergeant Tim O'Halloran
Four-Faced Man Tracy Elofson

Director: Rob Bowman

The Pine Bluff Variant

w Frank Spotnitz *&* John Shiban
Skinner, Scully and Mulder help in an undercover
operation to catch a terrorist armed with a powerful
biological weapon.
Haley Daniel Von Bargen
Field Agent J.B. Bivens
Goatee Man Armin Moattar
Leamus Sam Anderson
August Bremer Michael Macrae
Usherette Kate Braidwood
Manager Ralph Alderman
Martin Trevor Roald
Brit Kett Turton
Skin-Head Man Douglas Arthurs
Dr. Leavitt John B. Lowe
CIA Operative Michael St. John Smith

Director: Rob Bowman

Folie a Deux

w Vince Gilligan
Workplace shootings get the X-Files treatment, as a
man who claims his boss is a monster takes his co-
workers hostage. Mulder digs a little deeper and
soon realizes that something about the man's boss
bugs him too . . . a pattern of crazy behavior that
may prove the gunman right.
Skinner Mitch Pileggi
Gary Lambert Brian Markinson
Supervisor Dmitry Chepovetsky
Nancy Aaronson Cynthia Preston
Mrs. Loach Brenda Mcdonald
Grag Pincus John Apicella

Director: Rob Bowman

The End

w Chris Carter
A boy with the ability to read minds becomes a
pawn in a power struggle, and Mulder and Scully
are almost powerless to protect him.
Skinner Mitch Pileggi
Agent Diana Fowley Mimi Rogers
Cigarette-Smoking Man William B. Davis
Agent Spender Chris Owens
Well-Manicured Man John Neville
Byers Bruce Harwood
Frohike Tom Braidwood
Langly Dean Haglund
Agent Krycek Nick Lea
Gibson Jeff Gulka
Shooter Martin Ferraro
1st Elder Don S. Williams
2nd Elder George Murdock
3rd Elder John Moore

Director: R.W. Goodwin

SERIES DATABANK:
41 Obscure Shows You'll Probably Never Hear of Again

THE BIG PULL

A six-part 1962 BBC serial of the "something is out there and it ain't friendly" variety, as aliens invade by stealth instead of military conflict. Starred William Dexter, June Tobin, Susan Purdie, Ray Robert, and a cast of more than 90 others—one of the biggest casts ever assembled for such a serial.

BLISS

Dr. Sam Bliss, scientist and part-time radio show personality, investigates such phenomena as a cure for aging, precognition, the paranormal, memory transference, and telepathy. After a 90-minute pilot in 1995, a four-episode series aired in 1997. Bliss: Simon Shepherd.

THE CHANGES

The ten-part 1975 BBS children's series, based on a trilogy of books by Peter Dickinson, chronicled the end of the technological world, as a strange phenomenon made people destroy all trappings of civilization: televisions, phones, cars, etc. After fleeing the cities, they took up subsistence living in the countryside. Ultimately, a few children who were immune to the effect discovered its cause and set the world right again. Starred Vicky Williams, Keith Ashton and David Garfield.

CENTURY FALLS

Six-part 1993 BBC serial, in which the inhabitants of a small town conjured up a demon 40 years previously, with disastrous results. Now they are preparing to conjure Century again, and they are making all the same mistakes, as teenage Tess Hunter discovers. Starred Catherine Sanderson, Simon Fenton, Bernard Kay, Tatiana Straus and Alex Mollo.

CHILDREN OF THE DOG STAR

Filmed entirely in South Auckland, New Zealand, this 1984 six-part science fiction series follows three children who locate various pieces of a prehistoric space probe and reassemble it. The adventures of the children are contrasted nicely with the lives of the adults, who are involved with developing sacred Maori land.

CHILDREN OF THE STONES

Six-part 1977 British series about a small village whose people are held in mental slavery by a power in a Neolithic circle of stones. When a scientist and his son arrive to study the stones, they stumble onto the problem and work to save everyone . . . before they themselves are enslaved, too. Starred Iain Cuthbertson, Gareth Thomas and Freddie Jones.

CHIMERA

A four-part horror story concerning a man-ape created by genetic engineering, who murders his captors and escapes into the Yorkshire moors. Adapted by Stephen Gallagher from his novel of the same title. Starred John Lynch, David Calder, Gillian Barge and Emer Gillespie.

CITY BENEATH THE SEA

Sequel series to *Plateau of Fear* sends science reporter Mark Bannerman and his assistant aboard an atomic submarine to observe a new transmitter. But a pirate sub captures them and takes them to Aegira, the underwater kingdom of a fanatical professor who dreams of conquering the world. See also *Secret Beneath the Sea*. Starred Gerald Flood, Stewart Guidotti, Caroline Blakiston, Haydn Jones and Aubrey Morris.

COME BACK MRS. NOAH

1977 Britcom, from the creators of *'Allo, 'Allo* and *Are You Being Served,* focusing on a 21st-century housewife who wins a trip to Britain's new space station and gets accidentally launched into orbit. Jokes centered on Mrs. Noah regarding the spaceship as no more complicated than a vacuum cleaner as she and the others adjusted to live in the 35,000 mph fast lane and awaited rescue. Starred Molly Sugden, Ian Lavender, Donald Hewlett and Michael Knowles.

DARK SEASON

Six-part BBC series, in which three spunky teenagers save the world. In the first of two stories, the teens discover a plot to use computers to enslave mankind. In the second, an archaeological dig uncovers Behemoth, a mechanical war machine that plans to destroy the world. Starred Victoria Lambert, Kate Winslet and Ben Chandler.

DIMENSION OF FEAR

Four-part British series set in a peaceful English village. Mysterious deaths linked to a nearby research center studying the problems of feeding astronauts in space raises the specter of a threat to the world by powers from a fourth-dimensional world. Starred Katharine Blake, Peter Copley, Robin Bailey and Richard Coleman.

DRAMARAMA

A series of plays for children, which features the supernatural frequently and science fiction occasionally. Some of the science fiction plays include: "Mr. Stabs," "The Universe Downstairs," "The Come-Uppance of Captain Katt," "Flashback" and "Now You See Them."

EDGE OF DARKNESS

Apocalyptic six-part eco-thriller from the BBC, as a detective investigates the death of his daughter and uncovers political conspiracies, ecological terrorism, stolen plutonium. And then his daughter appears to him as a specter. Starred Bob Peck, Joe Don Baker, Joanne Whalley, Jack Watson, Kenneth Nelson and Hugh Fraser.

THE ESCAPE OF R.D. 7

Five-part BBC series from 1961, as a researcher develops a virus to wipe out rats. When her assistant is accidentally infected, the disease escape the lab and may be the cause of a nationwide plague. Starred Barbara Murray, Roger Croucher, Eddie Malin, Derek Waring, Ellen Pollock and Joan Newell.

FIRST BORN

Three-part 1988 BBC saga about the birth, life, and violent death of a man/gorilla hybrid, based on the futuristic novel *Gorgosa* by Maureen Duffy. Starred Charles Dance, Julie Peasgood, Philip Madoc and Peter Tilbury.

THE GEORGIAN HOUSE

Two children are sucked back in time to the 18th century to help save a young slave boy from a return to plantation life in this seven-part 1975 HTV drama. Starred Spencer Banks, Adrienne Byrne and Brinsley Forde.

KING OF THE CASTLE

Shy, sensitive Roland Wright's mind snaps under the strain of living at the top of an apartment building. He clashes with his parents, teachers, and local bullies, then retreats into a fantasy world in which all the people he knows are transformed into nightmarish doubles. The story is similar to *The Odyssey,* but dates from 1977. Seven episodes were produced.

KINVIG

Seven-episode sitcom from London Weekend Television, focusing on an ineffectual dreamer who imagines he meets a beautiful Venusian and that the world is about to be invaded by ant-like creatures called the Xux, who are plotting to replace people with humanoid robots and indiscrimately hand out the power to bend cutlery. Starred Tony Haygarth, Patsy Rowlands, Colin Jeavons, Prunella Gee, Patrick Newell and Simon Williams.

THE LOST PLANET

1954 saw the adaptation of this BBC 1952 children's radio show as a six-part series. The story charted the voyage of an assorted group of travelers to the lost panet of Hesikos. Besides the perils of space travel (meteorites!), the crew had to deal with the villainous Hermanoff before reaching their goal. Starred John Stuart, Geoffrey Lumsden, John Springett, Mary Law, Joan Allen, Peter Kerr, Van Boolen and Wolfe Morris.

See also: *Return to the Lost Planet.*

LEGEND OF DEATH

Five-part 1965 BBC reworking of the Theseus/Minotaur myth given a science fiction twist and a modern setting. Starred David Anders, John Phillips, Sarah Lawson, Victor Brooks, James Cossins, Gerald Sim, Andrew Sachs and John Hollis.

MAN DOG

Little-known BBC drama series from 1972, about a trio of present-day children who become involved in a conflict between a band of renegades and secret police from the 26th century. Starred Carol Hazell, Jane Anthony, Adrian Shergold, Christopher Owen, Jonathan Hardy, Mollie Sugden, John Rapley and Roy Boyd.

THE MASTER

Not a spin-off series featuring the popular villain from *Doctor Who,* but an entirely different series about a 150-year-old Shakespeare-quoting telepathic madman out to take over the world. This six-part 1966 drama beat *Doctor Who* in the ratings and features one of the creepiest villains ever on television. Starred Olaf Pooley, Terence Soall, Paul Guess, Adrienne Posta, George Baker, John Laurie, Thomas Baptiste, John Woodnutt, Richard Vernon and Anthony Eady.

MISSION EUREKA

Seven-episode Euro-drama series from 1991, centering around the efforts to rescue the European satellite Palladio, which has become lost in space. Starred Peter Bongartz, Delia Boccardo, Patrick Fierry, Agnes Dunneisen, Michael Degen, James Aubrey, Sergio Fantoni and Elisabeth Rath.

THE MONSTERS

Four-part 1962 BBC production, in which a honeymooning zoologist in search of a fabled "Loch Ness"–style monster ends up uncovering an even greater mystery involving the existence of such monsters and the survival of mankind. Starred William Greene, Elizabeth Weaver, Mark Dignam, Clifford Cox, Alan Gifford, Robert Harris, Gordon Wing, Helen Lindsay, Norman Mitchell, Howard Douglas, Philip Madoc, George Pravda, Kenneth Mackintosh, Clive Morton, Stuart Hoyle and Arthur Skinner.

MOONBASE 3

Six-part BBC series from 1973, set 30 years in the future when the moon has been colonized. Unfortunately, the moonbases are a tenuous foothold in a hostile environment, operating on shoestring budgets. Psychological problems rank alongside the technological ones. This series set out to provide intelligent, realistic drama rather than science fantasy—a change of pace for creators Barry Letts and Terrance Dicks, who were then steering Doctor Who through some of his most testing adventures. Starred Donald Houston, Barry Lowe, Ralph Bates and Fiona Gaunt.

THE NIGHTMARE MAN

Atmospheric four-part BBC thriller from 1981, which combined brutal murder, Russian agents, and a secret experiment gone horribly wrong that ripped half a man's brain away and turned him into the title creature. Starred James Warwick, Celia Imrie, Maurice Roëves, Tom Watson, Jonathan Newth, James Cosmo, Fraser Wilson, Tony Sibbald, Elaine Wells, Jon Crost, Ronald Forfar, Jeffrey Stewart, Robert Vowles and Pat Gorman.

PLATEAU OF FEAR

Six-episode British children's series from 1961 features a journalist investigating mysterious attacks at a nuclear power station in the Andes, complete with reports of a strange giant beast being responsible. Starred Gerald Flood, John Barron, Jan Miller, Stewart Guidotti, Peter Allenby, Maureen Lindholm, Ferdy Mayne, Richard Coleman and Cognac the dog.

PLAY FOR TOMORROW

In 1982, the BBC aired six specially commissioned plays about the near future—providing six chastening visions of almost unrelieved gloom. The plays were: "Crimes," "Bright Eyes," "Cricket," "The Nuclear Family," "Shades" and "Easter 2016."

RETURN TO THE LOST PLANET

This 1955 sequel to *The Lost Planet* featured much of the same cast and featured the Hesikosians—a gentle race of aliens—and the return of villain Hermanoff. Starred Peter Kerr, John Stuart, Joan Allen, Wolfe Morris, Greta Watson, Derek Benfield, Van Boolen, Michael Alexander, Peter Alexander, Julie Webb and Michael Segal.

SECRET BENEATH THE SEA

1963 six-part sequel to *City Beneath the Sea* sends journliast Mark Bannerman to the ocean floor in search of Phenicium, a rare metal vital for space research. Of course, the bad guys want it, too. Starred Gerald Flood, Stewart Guidotti, Peter Williams, Richard Coleman, Ingrid Sylvester, Delena Kidd, Robert James, David Spenser, Michael Darlow, Derek Smee, Murray Hayne, Reginald Smith, Anthony Woodruff and Denis Goacher.

SECRET WORLD OF POLLY FLINT

Enchanting 1987 British six-part series, following the adventures of a girl who must live with her aunt as she encounters the strange world of a village lost in time. Starred Michael Hordern, Katie Reynolds, Emily Richard, Malcolm Storry, Susan Jameson, Don Henderson, Dylan Champion, Daniel Pope, Brenda Bruce, Jeremy Coote and Daphne Neville.

SPACE SCHOOL

Four-part BBC serial from 1956, following the adventures of four siblings in a small house on the inside rim of Earth Satellite One. The series was notable as much as anything for the efforts taken to improve the quality of the hardware and sets, including an artificial satellite turning slowly in space and space tankers darting from planet to planet. Starred John Stuart, Matthew Lane, Donald McCorkindale, Julie Webb, Meurig Jones, David Drummond, Anthony Toller, Alanna Boyce, Maud Long, Neil McCallum, Michael Maguire and Anne Cooke.

TARGET LUNA

In this six-part 1960 British series, the young son of a brilliant professor secretly substitutes for astronaut and is launched into space by his father. First of four related series (*Pathfinders*). Starred David Markham, Michael Hammond, Sylvia Davies, Michael Craze, Annette Kerr, Frank Finlay, John Cairney, Deborah Stanford, Robert Stuart, Michael Verney, Phyllis Kenny and William Ingram.

THEY CAME FROM SOMEWHERE ELSE

Six-part science fiction comedy series written and performed by a British theater group who adapted it from their own stage show. It wasn't quite a sitcom, but neither was it sketch comedy; it plundered soap opera, SF adventure and other genres. Starred Rebecca Stevens, Peter McCarthy, Tony Haase, Robin Driscoll and Paddy Fletcher.

TIME EXPRESS

Four-episode BBC series with Vincent Price and wife Carol Browne as host and hostess aboard a mysterious train that transports passengers back into the past to relive crucial moments, alter previous decisions, and hopefully create a new and better future. Aired in 1979.

TIME IS THE ENEMY

Seven-part 1958 British series about a man who steps through an attic door in his new London home and finds himself in the year 1808—150 years in the past—when he is accused of being a French spy. Starred Clifford Elkin, Nigel Arkwright, Betty Huntley-Wright, David Lander, Edward Rhodes, Anne Reid, Derek Waring, Edward Higgins, Ross Hutchinson, Lilian Grasson and Laurence Taylor.

TIME RIDERS

British TV's short-lived answer to *Back to the Future* —with a fraction of the budget and even less of the style. This four-part 1991 children's adventure featured a time-traveling scientist (with a Yamaha motorbike instead of a De Loran) and her sidekick, a Victorian-era street urchin. Starred Haydn Gynne, Clive Merrison and Kerry Swale.

TORCH

Six-part 1992 BBC production set in a Europe of the future, when society has collapsed and reverted to pre-industrial conditions on island communities. Five teenagers honor a dying man's request to take the Olympic torch from its hiding place and "find the games." Starred Judi Dench, Michael Williams, Altay Lawrence, Graham McGrath, Finty Williams, Lyndon Davies, Kate McGrath, Taylor Scipio and John Carney.

A TRAVELLER IN TIME

Five-part 1978 BBC production in which a young girl goes to stay with her uncle and aunt in their Derbyshire farmhouse and finds heself slipping back into the past, where she becomes involved with an Elizabethan family and an attempt to save Mary, Queen of Scots. Starred Sophie Thompson, Gerald James, Elizabeth Bradley, Mary Maude, Sarah Benfield, Simon and Gipps-Kent.

THE TROLLENBERG TERROR

British 1956 six-part series combining suspense and horror, focusing on malevolent aliens at work around the Trollenberg mountain in the Swiss Alps. Much of the action centered around a small Alpine hotel. Starred Sarah Lawson, Rosemary Miller, Michael Anthony, Laurence Payne, Roland O'Casey, Stuart Saunders, Glyn Owen, Frederick Schrecker and Raf de la Torre.

VOODOO FACTOR

British six-part serial from 1959, focusing on Dr. David Whittaker, who comes in conflict with a legendary Polynesian goddess who died 2000 years earlier and now seems to be reaching out across the centuries to make her power felt. Starred Maurice Kaufmann, Maxine Audley, Eric Young, Philip Bond, Jill Hyem, Richard Bennett, Tony Church and Charles Carson.

ABOUT THE AUTHORS

A journalist for longer than he cares to remember, ROGER FULTON is deputy editor of England's *TVTimes,* which he says is as good an excuse to watch TV as any. He lives with his family in Hertfordshire and in his spare time runs half marathons and other races.

Bestselling novelist JOHN BETANCOURT has more than a million copies of his books in print. He has worked extensively in the media fiction field, writing novels and short stories set in the *Star Trek, Star Wars*, and Marvel and DC Comics universes. With his wife, Kim, he runs Wildside Press, a book publishing and packaging company. They live in New Jersey.